W9-BAP-433

Security in Computing

THIRD EDITION

ISBN 0-13-035548-8

Security in Computing

THIRD EDITION

Charles P. Pfleeger
Cable & Wireless

Shari Lawrence Pfleeger
RAND

PRENTICE HALL
Professional Technical Reference
Upper Saddle River, NJ 07458
www.phptr.com

Library of Congress Cataloging-in-Publication Data

Pfleeger, Charles P.
Security in computing / Charles P. Pfleeger, Shari Lawrence Pfleeger.—3rd ed.
p. cm.
Includes bibliographical references and index.
ISBN 0-13-035548-8
1. Computer security. 2. Data protection. 3. Privacy, Right of. I. Pfleeger, Shari Lawrence. II. Title.

QA76.9.A25 P45 2003
005.8—dc21

2002034368

Editorial/production supervision: *Jane Bonnell*
Copy editor: *Mary Lou Nohr*
Composition: *Pine Tree Composition*
Cover design director: *Jerry Votta*
Cover design: *Anthony Gemmellaro*
Interior design: *Meg Van Arsdale*
Manufacturing manager: *Alexis R. Heydt-Long*
Executive editor: *Paul Petralia*
Editorial assistant: *Richard Winkler*
Marketing manager: *Debby vanDijk*

Publishing as Prentice Hall Professional Technical Reference
Upper Saddle River, New Jersey 07458

Printed in the United States of America

10 9 8 7

ISBN: 0-13-035548-8

Pearson Education LTD.
Pearson Education Australia PTY, Limited
Pearson Education Singapore, Pte. Ltd.
Pearson Education North Asia Ltd.
Pearson Education Canada, Ltd.
Pearson Educación de Mexico, S.A. de C.V.
Pearson Education—Japan
Pearson Education Malaysia, Pte. Ltd.

About Prentice Hall Professional Technical Reference

With origins reaching back to the industry's first computer science publishing program in the 1960s, Prentice Hall Professional Technical Reference (PH PTR) has developed into the leading provider of technical books in the world today. Formally launched as its own imprint in 1986, our editors now publish over 200 books annually, authored by leaders in the fields of computing, engineering, and business.

Our roots are firmly planted in the soil that gave rise to the technological revolution. Our bookshelf contains many of the industry's computing and engineering classics: Kernighan and Ritchie's *C Programming Language*, Nemeth's *UNIX System Administration Handbook*, Horstmann's *Core Java*, and Johnson's *High-Speed Digital Design*.

PRENTICE HALL PTR

PH PTR acknowledges its auspicious beginnings while it looks to the future for inspiration. We continue to evolve and break new ground in publishing by providing today's professionals with tomorrow's solutions.

Contents

Foreword

In the 1950s and 1960s, the prominent conference gathering places for practitioners and users of computer technology were the twice yearly Joint Computer Conferences (JCCs)—initially called the Eastern and Western JCCs, but later renamed the Spring and Fall JCCs and even later, the annual National (AFIPS) Computer Conference. From this milieu, the topic of computer security—later to be called information system security and currently also referred to as "protection of the national information infrastructure"—moved from the world of classified defense interests into public view.

A few people—Robert L. Patrick, John P. Haverty, and myself among others—all then at The RAND Corporation (as its name was then known) had been talking about the growing dependence of the country and its institutions on computer technology. It concerned us that the installed systems might not be able to protect themselves and their data against intrusive and destructive attacks. We decided that it was time to bring the security aspect of computer systems to the attention of the technology and user communities.

The enabling event was the development within the National Security Agency (NSA) of a remote-access time-sharing system with a full set of security access controls, running on a Univac 494 machine, and serving terminals and users not only within the headquarters building at Fort George G. Meade, Maryland, but also worldwide. Fortuitously, I knew details of the system.

Persuading two others from RAND to help—Dr. Harold Peterson and Dr. Rein Turn—plus Bernard Peters of NSA, I organized a group of papers and presented it to the SJCC conference management as a ready-made additional paper session to be chaired by me. [1] The conference accepted the offer, and the session was presented at the Atlantic City (NJ) Convention Hall in 1967.

Soon thereafter and driven by a request from a defense contractor to include both defense classified and business applications concurrently in a single mainframe machine functioning in a remote-access mode, the Department of Defense, acting through the Advanced Research Projects Agency (ARPA) and later the Defense Science Board (DSB), organized a committee, which I chaired, to study the issue of security controls for computer systems. The intent was to produce a document that could be the basis for formulating a DoD policy position on the matter.

The report of the committee was initially published as a classified document and was formally presented to the sponsor (the DSB) in January 1970. It was later declassified and republished (by The RAND Corporation) in October 1979. [2] It was widely circulated and became nicknamed "the Ware report." The report and a historical introduction are available on the RAND web site. [3]

Subsequently, the United States Air Force (USAF) sponsored another committee chaired by James P. Anderson. [4] Its report, published in 1972, recommended a 6-year R&D security program totaling some $8M. [5] The USAF responded and funded several projects, three of which were to design and implement an operating system with security controls for a specific computer.

Eventually these activities led to the "Criteria and Evaluation" program sponsored by the NSA. It culminated in the "Orange Book" [6] in 1983 and subsequently its supporting array of documents, which were nicknamed "the rainbow series." [7] Later, in the 1980s and on into the 1990s, the subject became an international one leading to the ISO standard known as the "Common Criteria." [8]

It is important to understand the context in which system security was studied in the early decades. The defense establishment had a long history of protecting classified information in document form. It had evolved a very elaborate scheme for compartmenting material into groups, sub-groups and super-groups, each requiring a specific personnel clearance and need-to-know as the basis for access. [9] It also had a centuries-long legacy of encryption technology and experience for protecting classified information in transit. Finally, it understood the personnel problem and the need to establish the trustworthiness of its people. And it certainly understood the physical security matter.

Thus, "the" computer security issue, as it was understood in the 1960s and even later, was how to create in a computer system a group of access controls that would implement or emulate the processes of the prior paper world, plus the associated issues of protecting such software against unauthorized change, subversion and illicit use, and of embedding the entire system in a secure physical environment with appropriate management oversights and operational doctrine and procedures. The poorly understood aspect of security was primarily the software issue with, however, a collateral hardware aspect; namely, the risk that it might malfunction—or be penetrated—and subvert the proper behavior of software. For the related aspects of communications, personnel, and physical security, there was a plethora of rules, regulations, doctrine and experience to cover them. It was largely a matter of merging all of it with the hardware/software aspects to yield an overall secure system and operating environment.

However, the world has now changed and in essential ways. The desk-top computer and workstation have appeared and proliferated widely. The Internet is flourishing and the reality of a World Wide Web is in place. Networking has exploded and communication among computer systems is the rule, not the exception. Many commercial transactions are now web-based; many commercial communities—the financial one in particular—have moved into a web posture. The "user" of any computer system can literally be anyone in the world. Networking among computer systems is ubiquitous; information-system outreach is the goal.

The net effect of all of this has been to expose the computer-based information system—its hardware, its software, its software processes, its databases, its communications—to an environment over which no one—not end-user, not network administrator or system owner, not even government—has control. What must be done is to provide appropriate technical, procedural, operational and environmental safeguards against threats as they might appear or be imagined, embedded in a societally acceptable legal framework.

And appear threats did—from individuals and organizations, national and international. The motivations to penetrate systems for evil purpose or to create malicious software—generally with an offensive or damaging consequence—vary from personal intellectual satisfaction to espionage, to financial reward, to revenge, to civil disobedience, and to other reasons. Information-system security has moved from a largely self-contained bounded environment interacting with a generally known and disciplined user community to one of worldwide scope with a body of users that may not be known and are not necessarily trusted. Importantly, security controls now must deal with circumstances over which there is largely no control or expectation of avoiding their impact. Computer security, as it has evolved, shares a similarity with liability insurance; they each face a threat environment that is known in a very general way and can generate attacks over a broad spectrum of possibilities; but the exact details or even time or certainty of an attack is unknown until an event has occurred.

On the other hand, the modern world thrives on information and its flows; the contemporary world, society and institutions cannot function without their computer-communication-based information systems. Hence, these systems must be protected in all dimensions—technical, procedural, operational, environmental. The system owner and its staff have become responsible for protecting the organization's information assets.

Progress has been slow, in large part because the threat has not been perceived as real or as damaging enough; but also in part because the perceived cost of comprehensive information system security is seen as too high compared to the risks—especially the financial consequences—of not doing it. Managements, whose support with appropriate funding is essential, have been slow to be convinced.

This book addresses the broad sweep of issues above: the nature of the threat and system vulnerabilities (Chapter 1); cryptography (Chapters 2 and 10); the Common Criteria (Chapter 5); the World Wide Web and Internet (Chapter 7); managing risk (Chapter 8); software vulnerabilities (Chapter 3); and legal, ethical and privacy issues (Chapter 9). The book also describes security controls that are currently available such as encryption protocols, software development practices, firewalls, and intrusion-detection systems. Overall, this book provides a broad and sound foundation for the information-system specialist who is charged with planning and/or organizing and/or managing and/or implementing a comprehensive information-system security program.

Yet to be solved are many technical aspects of information security—R&D for hardware, software, systems, and architecture; and the corresponding products. Notwithstanding, technology per se is not the long pole in the tent of progress. Organizational and management motivation and commitment to get the security job done is. Today, the collective information infrastructure of the country and of the world is slowly moving up the learning curve; every mischievous or malicious event helps to push it along. The terrorism-based events of recent times are helping to drive it. Is it far enough up the curve to have reached an appropriate balance between system safety and threat? Almost certainly, the answer is "no, not yet; there is a long way to go." [10]

Willis H. Ware
RAND
Santa Monica, California
September 2002

Citations

1. "Security and Privacy in Computer Systems," Willis H. Ware; RAND, Santa Monica, CA; P-3544, April 1967. Also published in Proceedings of the 1967 Spring Joint Computer Conference (later renamed to AFIPS Conference Proceedings), pp 279 seq, Vol. 30, 1967.

   "Security Considerations in a Multi-Programmed Computer System," Bernard Peters; Proceedings of the 1967 Spring Joint Computer Conference (later renamed to AFIPS Conference Proceedings), pp 283 seq, vol 30, 1967.

   "Practical Solutions to the Privacy Problem," Willis H. Ware; RAND, Santa Monica, CA; P-3544, April 1967. Also published in Proceedings of the 1967 Spring Joint Computer Conference (later renamed to AFIPS Conference Proceedings), pp 301 seq, Vol. 30, 1967.

   "System Implications of Information Privacy," Harold E. Peterson and Rein Turn; RAND, Santa Monica, CA; P-3504, April 1967. Also published in Proceedings of the 1967 Spring Joint Computer Conference (later renamed to AFIPS Conference Proceedings), pp 305 seq, vol. 30, 1967.

2. "Security Controls for Computer Systems," (Report of the Defense Science Board Task Force on Computer Security), RAND, R-609-1-PR. Initially published in January 1970 as a classified document. Subsequently, declassified and republished October 1979.

3. http://rand.org/publications/R/R609.1/R609.1.html

   "Security Controls for Computer Systems"; R-609.1, RAND, 1979

   http://rand.org/publications/R/R609.1/intro.html

   Historical setting for R-609.1

4. "Computer Security Technology Planning Study," James P. Anderson; ESD-TR-73-51, ESD/AFSC, Hanscom AFB, Bedford, MA; October 1972.

5. All of these documents are cited in the bibliography with this book. For images of these historical papers on a CDROM, see the "History of Computer Security Project, Early Papers Part 1," Professor Matt Bishop; Department of Computer Science, University of California at Davis. http://seclab.cs.ucdavis.edu/projects/history

6. "DoD Trusted Computer System Evaluation Criteria," DoD Computer Security Center, National Security Agency, Ft George G. Meade, Maryland; CSC-STD-001-83; Aug 15, 1983.

7. So named because the cover of each document in the series had a unique and distinctively colored cover page. For example, the "Red Book" is "Trusted Network Interpretation," National Computer Security Center, National Security Agency, Ft. George G. Meade, Maryland; NCSC-TG-005, July 31, 1987. USGPO Stock number 008-000-00486-2.

8. "A Retrospective on the Criteria Movement," Willis H. Ware; RAND, Santa Monica, CA; P-7949, 1995.

9. This scheme is nowhere, to my knowledge, documented explicitly. However, its complexity can be inferred by a study of Appendices A and B of R-609.1 (item [2] above).

10. "The Cyberposture of the National Information Infrastructure," Willis H. Ware; RAND, Santa Monica, CA; MR-976-OSTP, 1998. Available online at: http://www.rand.org/publications/MR/MR976/mr976.html. Also available as http://rand.org/publications/MR/MR976/mr976.pdf.

Preface to the Third Edition

Every day, the news media give more and more visibility to the effects of computer security on our daily lives. For example, on a single day in June 2002, the *Washington Post* included three important articles about security. On the front page, one article described the possibility that a terrorist group was plotting to—and actually could—invade computer systems and destroy huge dams, disable the power grid, or wreak havoc with the air traffic control system. A second article, also on the front page, considered the potential loss of personal privacy as governments and commercial establishments begin to combine and correlate data in computer-maintained databases. Further back, a third article discussed yet another software flaw that could have widespread effect. Thus, computer security is no longer relegated to esoteric discussions of what might happen; it is instead a hot news topic, prominently featured in newspapers, magazines, radio talk shows, and documentary television programs. The audience is no longer just the technical community; it is ordinary people, who feel the effects of pervasive computing.

In just a few years the world's public has learned the terms "virus," "worm," and "Trojan horse" and now appreciates the concepts of "unauthorized access," "sabotage," and "denial of service." During this same time, the number of computer users has increased dramatically; with those new users have come new uses: electronic stock trading, sharing of medical records, and remote control of sensitive equipment, to name just three. It should be no surprise that threats to security in computing have increased along with the users and uses.

WHY READ THIS BOOK?

Are your data or programs at risk? If you answer "yes" to any of the following questions, you have a potential security risk.

- Do you connect to the Internet?
- Do you read e-mail?

- Have you gotten any new programs—or any new versions of old programs—within, say, the last year?
- Is there any important program or data item of which you do not have a second copy stored somewhere other than on your computer?

Almost every computer user today meets at least one of these conditions, and so you, and almost every other computer user, are at risk of some harmful computer security event. Risk does not mean you should stop using computers. You are at risk of being hit by a falling meteorite or of being robbed by a thief on the street, but you do not hide in a fortified underground bunker all day. You learn what puts you at risk and how to control it. Controlling a risk is not the same as eliminating it; you simply want to bring it to a tolerable level.

How do you control the risk of computer security?

- Learn about the threats to computer security.
- Understand what causes these threats by studying how vulnerabilities arise in the development and use of computer systems.
- Survey the controls that can reduce or block these threats.
- Develop a computing style—as a user, developer, manager, consumer, and voter—that balances security and risk.

USERS AND USES OF THIS BOOK

This book is intended for the study of computer security. Many of you want to study this topic: college and university students, computing professionals, managers, and users of all kinds of computer-based systems. All want to know the same thing: how to control the risk of computer security. But you may differ in how much information you need about particular topics: Some want a broad survey, whereas others want to focus on particular topics, such as networks or program development.

This book should provide the breadth and depth that most readers want. The book is organized by general area of computing, so that readers with particular interests can find information easily. The chapters of this book progress in an orderly manner, from general security concerns to the particular needs of specialized applications, and finally to overarching management and legal issues. Thus, the book covers five key areas of interest:

- *Introduction:* threats, vulnerabilities, and controls
- *Encryption:* the "Swiss army knife" of security controls
- *Code:* security in programs, including applications, operating systems, database management systems, and networks
- *Management:* implementing and maintaining a computing style
- *Law, privacy, ethics:* nontechnical approaches by which society controls computer security risks

These areas are not equal in size; for example, more than half the book is devoted to code because so much of the risk is at least partly caused by program code that executes on computers.

The first chapter introduces the concepts and basic vocabulary of computer security. The second chapter provides an understanding of what encryption is and how it can be used or misused. Just as a driver's manual does not address how to design or build a car, Chapter 2 is for users of encryption, not designers of new encryption schemes. Chapters 3 through 7 cover successively larger pieces of software: individual programs, operating systems, complex applications like database management systems, and finally networks, which are distributed complex systems. Chapter 8 discusses managing and administering security, and finding an acceptable balance between threats and controls. Chapter 9 covers the way society at large addresses computer security, through its laws and ethical systems and through its concern for privacy. Finally, Chapter 10 returns to cryptography, this time to look at the details of the encryption algorithms themselves.

Within that organization, you can move about, picking and choosing topics of particular interest. Everyone should read Chapter 1 to build a vocabulary and a foundation. It is wise to read Chapter 2 because cryptography appears in so many different control techniques. Although there is a general progression from small programs to large and complex networks, you can in fact read Chapters 3 through 7 out of sequence or pick topics of greatest interest. Chapters 8 and 9 may be just right for the professional looking for nontechnical controls to complement the technical ones of the earlier chapters. These chapters may also be important for the computer science student who wants to look beyond a narrow view of bytes and protocols. Chapter 10 is for people who want to understand some of the underlying mathematics and logic of cryptography.

What background should you have to appreciate this book? The only assumption is an understanding of programming and computer systems. Someone who is an advanced undergraduate or graduate student in computer science certainly has that background, as does a professional designer or developer of computer systems. A user who wants to understand more about how programs work can learn from this book, too; we provide the necessary background on concepts of operating systems or networks, for example, before we address the related security concerns.

This book can be used as a textbook in a one- or two-semester course in computer security. The book functions equally well as a reference for a computer professional or as a supplement to an intensive training course. And the index and extensive bibliography make it useful as a handbook to explain significant topics and point to key articles in the literature. The book has been used in classes throughout the world; instructors often design one-semester courses that focus on topics of particular interest to students or that relate well to the rest of a curriculum.

WHAT IS NEW IN THIS BOOK?

This is the third edition of *Security in Computing*, first published in 1989. Since then, the specific threats, vulnerabilities, and controls have changed, even though many of the basic notions have remained the same.

The two changes most obvious to people familiar with the previous editions are networks and encryption. Networking has evolved even since the second edition was published, and there are many new concepts to master, such as distributed denial-of-service attacks or scripted vulnerability probing. As a consequence, the networks chapter is almost entirely new. Previous editions of this book presented encryption details in the same chapter as encryption uses. Although encryption is a fundamental tool in computer security, in this edition the *what* is presented straightforwardly in Chapter 2, while the *how* is reserved for the later Chapter 10. This structure lets readers get to the technical uses of encryption in programs and networks more quickly.

There are numerous other additions, of which these are the most significant ones:

- the Advanced Encryption System (AES), the replacement for the Data Encryption System (DES) from the 1970s
- programming flaws leading to security failures, highlighting buffer overflows, incomplete mediation, and time-of-check to time-of-use errors
- recent malicious code attacks, such as Code Red
- software engineering practices to improve program quality
- assurance of code quality
- authentication techniques such as biometrics and password generators
- privacy issues in database management system security
- mobile code, agents, and assurance of security in them
- denial-of-service and distributed denial-of-service attacks
- flaws in network protocols
- security issues in wireless computing
- honeypots and intrusion detection
- copyright controls for digital media
- threats to and controls for personal privacy
- software quality, vulnerability reporting, and vendors' responsibilities
- the ethics of hacking

In addition to these major changes, there are numerous small corrective and clarifying ones, ranging from wording changes to subtle notational changes for pedagogic reasons to replacement, deletion, rearrangement, and expansion of sections.

ACKNOWLEDGMENTS

It is increasingly difficult to acknowledge all the people who have influenced this book. Colleagues and friends have contributed their knowledge and insight, often without knowing their impact. By arguing a point or sharing explanations of concepts, our associates have forced us to question or rethink what we know.

We thank our associates in at least two ways. First, we have tried to include references to their written works as they have influenced this book. References in the text cite specific papers relating to particular thoughts or concepts, but the bibliography also includes broader works that have played a more subtle role in shaping our approach to security. So, to all the cited authors, many of whom are friends and colleagues, we happily acknowledge your positive influence on this book. In particular, we are grateful to RAND for permission to present material about its Vulnerability, Assessment and Mitigation method and to use its government e-mail analysis as a case study in Chapter 8. Second, rather than name individuals, we thank the organizations where we have interacted with creative, stimulating, and challenging people from whom we learned a lot. These places include the University of Tennessee, Trusted Information Systems, the Institute for Defense Analyses, the Contel Technology Center, the Centre for Software Reliability of the City University of London, Arca Systems, Exodus Communications, RAND, and Cable & Wireless. If you worked with us at any of these locations, chances are high that you had some impact on this book. And for all the side conversations, debates, arguments, and light moments, we are grateful.

Authors are the products of their environments. We write to educate because we had good educations ourselves and because we think the best response to a good education is to pass it along to others. Our parents, Paul and Emma Pfleeger and Emanuel and Beatrice Lawrence, were critical in supporting us and encouraging us to get the best educations we could. Along the way, certain teachers gave us gifts through their teaching. Robert L. Wilson taught Chuck how to learn about computers, and Libuse L. Reed taught him how to write about them. Florence Rogart, Nicholas Sterling, and Mildred Nadler taught Shari how to analyze and probe.

To all these people, we express our sincere thanks.

Charles P. Pfleeger
Shari Lawrence Pfleeger
Washington D.C.

1

Is There a Security Problem in Computing?

In this chapter:

- The risks involved in computing
- The goals of secure computing: confidentiality, integrity, availability
- The threats to security in computing: interception, interruption, modification, fabrication
- Controls available to address these threats: encryption, programming controls, operating systems, network controls, administrative controls, law, and ethics

1.1 WHAT DOES "SECURE" MEAN?

How do we protect our most valuable assets? One option is to place them in a safe place, like a bank. We seldom hear of a bank robbery these days, even though it was once a fairly lucrative undertaking. In the American Wild West, banks kept large amounts of cash on hand, as well as gold and silver, which could not be traced easily. In those days, cash was much more commonly used than checks. Communications and transportation were primitive enough that it might have been hours before the legal authorities were informed of a robbery and days before they could actually arrive at the scene of the crime, by which time the robbers were long gone. To control the situation, a single guard for the night was only marginally effective. Should you have wanted to commit a robbery, you might have needed only a little common sense and perhaps several days to analyze the situation; you certainly did not require much sophisticated training. Indeed, you usually learned on the job, assisting other robbers in a form of apprenticeship. On balance, all these factors tipped very much in the favor of the criminal, so that bank robbery was, for a time, considered to be a profitable business. Protecting assets was difficult and not always effective.

Today, however, asset protection is easier, with many factors working against the potential criminal. Very sophisticated alarm systems silently protect secure places like banks whether people are around or not. The techniques of criminal investigation have become very effective, so that a person can be identified by genetic material (DNA), fingerprints, retinal patterns, voice, a composite sketch, ballistics evidence, or other hard-to-mask characteristics. The assets are stored in a safer form. For instance, many bank branches now contain less cash than some large retail stores because much of a bank's business is conducted with checks, electronic transfers, credit cards, or debit cards. Sites that must store large amounts of cash or currency are protected with many levels of security: several layers of physical systems, complex locks, multiple-party systems requiring the agreement of several people to allow access, and other schemes. Significant improvements in transportation and communication mean that police can be at the scene of a crime in minutes; dispatchers can alert other officers in seconds about the suspects to watch for. From the criminal's point of view, the risk and required sophistication are so high that there are usually easier ways than bank robbery to make money.

Protecting Valuables

This book is about protecting our computer-related assets, not about protecting our money and gold bullion. That is, we plan to discuss security for computing systems, not banks. But we can learn from our analysis of banks because they tell us some general principles about protection. In other words, when we think about protecting valuable information, we can learn a lot from the way we have protected other valuables in the past. For example, Table 1-1 presents the differences between how people protect computing systems and how banks protect money. The table reinforces the notion that we have many challenges to address when protecting computers and data, but the nature of the challenges may mean that we need different and more effective approaches than we have used in the past.

Protecting our valuables, whether they are expressed as information or in some other way, ranges from quite unsophisticated to very sophisticated. We can think of the Wild West days as an example of the "unsophisticated" end of the security spectrum.

TABLE 1-1 Protecting Money vs. Protecting Information.

Characteristic	Bank Protecting Money	People Protecting Information
Size and portability	Sites storing money are large, unwieldy, not at all portable. Buildings require guards, vaults, many levels of physical security to protect money.	Items storing valuable assets are very small and portable. The physical devices in computing can be so small that thousands of dollars' worth of computing gear can fit comfortably in a briefcase.
Ability to avoid physical contact	Difficult. When banks deal with physical currency, a criminal must physically demand the money and carry it away from the bank's premises.	Simple. When information is handled electronically, no physical contact is necessary. Indeed, when banks handle money electronically, almost all transactions can be done without any physical contact. Money can be transferred through computers, mail, or telephone.
Value of assets	Very high.	Variable, from very high to very low. Some information, such as medical history, tax payments, investments, or educational background, is confidential. Other information, about troop movements, sales strategies, buying patterns, can be very sensitive. Still other information, such as address and phone number, may be of no consequence and easily accessible by other means.

And even today, when we have more sophisticated means of protection than ever before, we still see a wide range in how people and businesses actually use the protections available to them.

In fact, we can find far too many examples of computer security that seem to be back in the Wild West days. Although some organizations recognize computers and their data as valuable and vulnerable resources and have applied appropriate protection, others are dangerously deficient in their security measures. In some cases, the situation is even worse than that in the Wild West; as Sidebar 1-1 illustrates, some enterprises do not even

Sidebar 1-1 Protecting Software in Automobile Control Systems

The amount of software installed in an automobile grows larger from year to year. Most cars, especially more expensive ones, use dozens of microcontrollers to provide a variety of features to entice buyers. There is enough variation in microcontroller range and function that the Society of Automotive Engineers (Warrendale, Pennsylvania) has set standards for the U.S. automotive industry's software. Software in the microcontrollers ranges through three classes:

- low speed (class A—less than 10 kb per second) for convenience features, such as radios.
- medium speed (class B—10 to 125 kb per second) for the general transfer of information, such as that related to emissions, speed, or instrumentation.
- high speed (class C—more than 125 kb per second) for real-time control, such as the power train or a brake-by-wire system.

These digital cars use software to control individual subsystems, and then more software to connect the systems in a network. [WHI01]

However, the engineers designing and implementing this software see no reason to protect it from hackers. Whitehorn-Umphres reports that, from the engineers' point of view, the software is too complicated to be understood by a hacker. "And even if they could [understand it], they wouldn't want to."

Whitehorn-Umphres points out a major difference in thinking between hardware designers and software designers. "As hardware engineers, they assumed that, perhaps aside from bolt-on aftermarket parts, everything else is and should be a black box." But software folks have a different take: "As a software designer, I assume that all digital technologies are fair game for being played with.... it takes a special kind of personality to look at a software-enabled device and see the potential for manipulation and change—a hacker personality."

He points out that hot-rodders and auto enthusiasts have a long history of tinkering and tailoring to make specialized changes to mass-produced cars. And the unprotected software beckons them to continue the tradition. For instance, there are reports of recalibrating the speedometer of two types of Japanese motorcycles, to fool the bike about how fast it is really going (and thereby enable faster-than-legal speeds). Whitehorn-Umphres speculates that soon you will be able to "download new ignition mappings from your PC. The next step will be to port the PC software to handheld computers so as to make on-the-road modifications that much easier."

recognize that their resources should be controlled and protected. And as software consumers, we find the lack of protection is all the more dangerous when we are not even aware that we are susceptible to software piracy or corruption.

The possibility of crime is bad enough. But worse yet, in the event of a crime, some organizations neither investigate nor prosecute for fear that the revelation will damage their public image. For example, would you feel safe depositing your money in a bank that had just suffered a several million-dollar loss through computer-related embezzlement? In fact, the breach of security makes that bank painfully aware of all its security weaknesses. Once bitten, twice shy; after the loss, the bank will probably enhance its security substantially, quickly becoming safer than a bank that had not been recently victimized.

Even when organizations want to take action against criminal activity, criminal investigation and prosecution can be hindered by statutes that do not recognize electromagnetic signals as property. The news media sometimes portray computer intrusion by teenagers as a prank no more serious than tipping over an outhouse. But, as we shall see in later chapters, computer intrusion can hurt businesses and even take lives. The legal systems around the world are coming to grips with the nature of electronic property as intellectual property critical to organizational or mission success; laws are being implemented and court decisions declared that acknowledge the value of information stored or transmitted via computers. But this area is still new to many courts, and few precedents have been established.

Throughout this book, we look at examples of how computer security affects our lives—directly and indirectly. And we examine techniques to prevent security breaches or at least to mitigate their effects. We address the security concerns of software practitioners as well as those professionals, managers, and users whose products, services, and well being depend on the proper functioning of computer systems. By studying this book, you will develop an understanding of the basic problems underlying computer security and the methods available to deal with them.

In particular, we do the following:

- Examine the *risks* of security in computing
- Consider available *countermeasures* or *controls*
- Stimulate thought about *uncovered vulnerabilities*
- Identify areas where *more work* is needed

In this chapter, we begin by examining *what* kinds of vulnerabilities computing systems are prone to. We then consider *why* these vulnerabilities are exploited: the different kinds of attacks that are possible. This chapter's third focus is on *who* is involved: the kinds of people who contribute to the security problem. Finally, we introduce *how* to prevent possible attacks on systems.

Characteristics of Computer Intrusion

Any part of a computing system can be the target of a crime. When we refer to a **computing system**,[1] we mean a collection of hardware, software, storage media, data, and

[1] In this book, **boldface** identifies new terms being introduced.

people that an organization uses to perform computing tasks. Sometimes, we assume that parts of a computing system are not valuable to an outsider, but often we are mistaken. For instance, we tend to think that the most valuable property in a bank is the cash, gold, or silver in the vault. But in fact the customer information in the bank's computer may be far more valuable. Stored on paper, recorded on a storage medium, resident in memory, or transmitted over telephone lines or satellite links, this information can be used in myriad ways to make money illicitly. A competing bank can use this information to steal clients or even to disrupt service and discredit the bank. An unscrupulous individual could move money from one account to another without the owner's permission. A group of con artists could contact large depositors and convince them to invest in fraudulent schemes. The variety of targets and attacks makes computer security very difficult.

Any system is most vulnerable at its *weakest point.* A robber intent on stealing something from your house will not attempt to penetrate a two-inch-thick metal door if a window gives easier access. Similarly, a sophisticated perimeter physical security system does not compensate for unguarded access by means of a simple telephone line and a modem. We can codify this idea as one of the principles of computer security:

> **Principle of Easiest Penetration:** An intruder must be expected to use any available means of penetration. The penetration may not necessarily be by the most obvious means, nor is it necessarily the one against which the most solid defense has been installed.

This principle implies that computer security specialists must consider all possible means of penetration. Moreover, the penetration analysis must be done repeatedly, and especially whenever the system and its security change. Strengthening one aspect of a system may simply make another means of penetration more appealing to intruders. For this reason, let us look at the various ways that a system can be breached.

1.2 ATTACKS

When you test any computer system, one of your jobs is to imagine how the system could malfunction. Then, you improve the system's design so that the system can withstand any of the problems you have identified. In the same way, we analyze a system from a security perspective, thinking about ways in which the system's security can malfunction and diminish the value of its assets.

Threats, Vulnerabilities, and Controls

A computer-based system has three separate but valuable components: **hardware, software,** and **data.** Each of these assets offers value to different members of the community affected by the system. To analyze security, we can brainstorm about the ways in which the system or its information can experience some kind of loss or harm. For example, we can identify data whose format or contents should be protected in some way. We want our security system to make sure that no data are disclosed to unauthorized parties. Neither do we want the data to be modified in illegitimate ways. At the same time, we want to ensure that legitimate users have access to the data. In this way, we can identify weaknesses in the system. A **vulnerability** is a weakness in the security system, for example, in procedures, design, or implementation, that might be exploited to cause loss or harm. For instance, a particular system may be vulnerable to unauthorized data manipulation because the system does not verify a user's identity before allowing data access.

A **threat** to a computing system is a set of circumstances that has the potential to cause loss or harm. To see the difference between a threat and a vulnerability, consider the illustration in Figure 1-1. Here, a wall is holding water back. The water to the left of the wall is a threat to the man on the right of the wall: the water could rise, overflowing onto the man, or it could stay beneath the height of the wall, causing it to collapse. So the threat of harm is the potential for the man to get wet, get hurt, or drown. For now, the wall is intact, so the threat to the man is unrealized.

However, we can see a small crack in the wall—a vulnerability that threatens the man's security. If the water rises to or beyond the level of the crack, it will exploit the vulnerability and harm the man.

There are many threats to a computer system, including human-initiated and computer-initiated ones. We have all experienced the results of inadvertent human errors, hardware design flaws, and software failures. But natural disasters are threats, too; they can bring a system down when the computer room is flooded or the data center collapses from an earthquake, for example.

A human who exploits a vulnerability perpetrates an **attack** on the system. An attack can also be launched by another system, as when one system sends an overwhelming set of messages to another, virtually shutting down the second system's ability to function. Unfortunately, we have seen this type of attack frequently, as denial-of-service attacks flood servers with more messages than they can handle. (We take a closer look at denial of service in Chapter 7.)

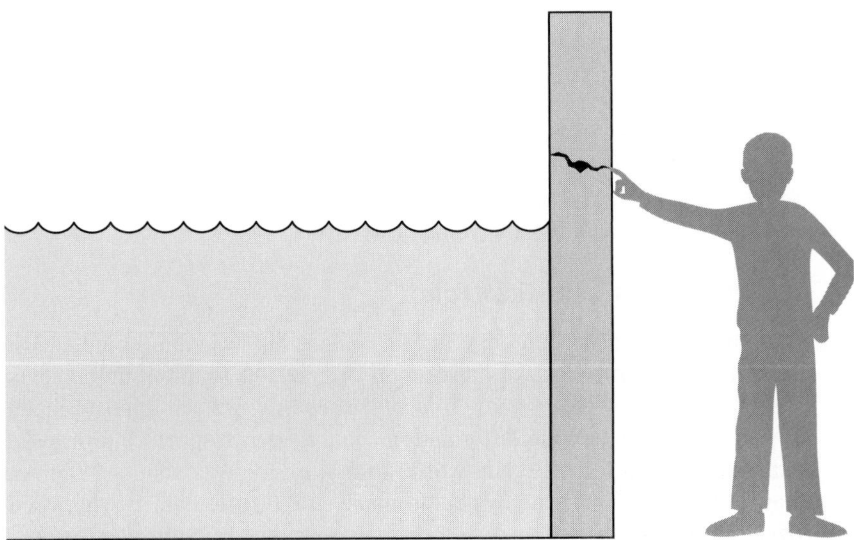

FIGURE 1-1 Threats, Controls, and Vulnerabilities.

How do we address these problems? We use a **control** as a protective measure. That is, a control is an action, device, procedure, or technique that removes or reduces a vulnerability. In Figure 1-1, the man is placing his finger in the hole, controlling the threat of water leaks until he finds a more permanent solution to the problem. In general, we can describe the relationship among threats, controls, and vulnerabilities in this way:

A *threat* is blocked by *control of* a *vulnerability*.

Much of the rest of this book is devoted to describing a variety of controls and understanding the degree to which they enhance a system's security.

To devise controls, we must know as much about threats as possible. We can view any threat as being one of four kinds: interception, interruption, modification, and fabrication. Each threat exploits vulnerabilities of the assets in computing systems; the threats are illustrated in Figure 1-2.

- An **interception** means that some unauthorized party has gained access to an asset. The outside party can be a person, a program, or a computing system. Examples of this type of failure are illicit copying of program or data files, or wiretapping to obtain data in a network. Although a loss may be discovered fairly quickly, a silent interceptor may leave no traces by which the interception can be readily detected.
- In an **interruption**, an asset of the system becomes lost, unavailable, or unusable. An example is malicious destruction of a hardware device, erasure of a

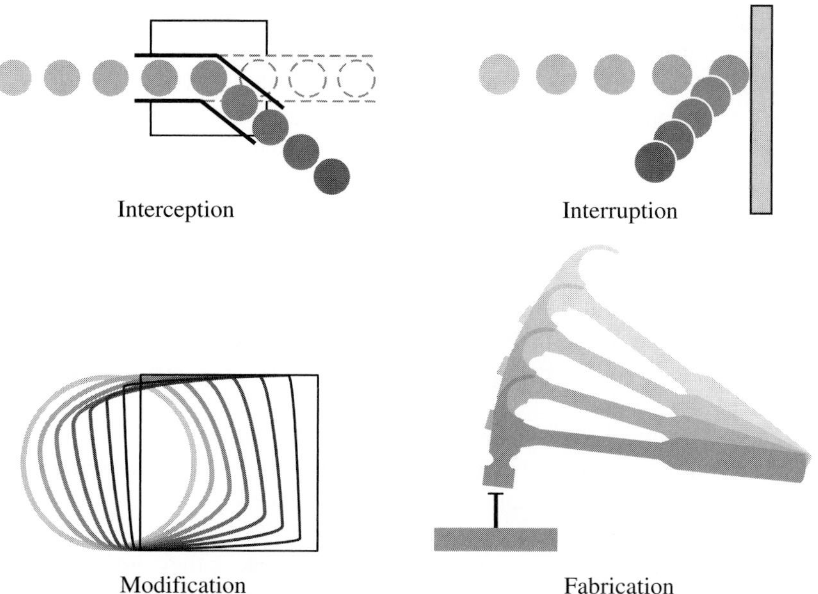

FIGURE 1-2 System Security Threats.

program or data file, or malfunction of an operating system file manager so that it cannot find a particular disk file.

- If an unauthorized party not only accesses but tampers with an asset, the threat is a **modification**. For example, someone might change the values in a database, alter a program so that it performs an additional computation, or modify data being transmitted electronically. It is even possible to modify hardware. Some cases of modification can be detected with simple measures, but other, more subtle, changes may be almost impossible to detect.
- Finally, an unauthorized party might create a **fabrication** of counterfeit objects on a computing system. The intruder may insert spurious transactions to a network communication system or add records to an existing database. Sometimes these additions can be detected as forgeries, but if skillfully done, they are virtually indistinguishable from the real thing.

These four classes of threats—interception, interruption, modification, and fabrication—describe the kinds of problems we might encounter. In the next section, we look more closely at a system's vulnerabilities and how we can use them to set security goals.

Method, Opportunity, and Motive

A malicious attacker must have three things:

- *Method:* the skills, knowledge, tools, and other things with which to be able to pull off the attack
- *Opportunity:* the time and access to accomplish the attack
- *Motive:* a reason to want to perform this attack against this system

(Think of the acronym "MOM.") Deny any of those three things and the attack will not occur. However, it is not easy to cut these off.

Knowledge of systems is widely available. Mass market systems (such as the Microsoft or Apple or Unix operating systems) are readily available, as are common products, such as word processors or database management systems. Sometimes the manufacturers release detailed specifications on how the system was designed or operates, as guides for users and integrators who want to implement other complementary products. But even without documentation, attackers can purchase and experiment with many systems. Often, only time and inclination limit an attacker.

Many systems are readily available. Systems available to the public are, by definition, accessible; often their owners take special care to make them fully available, so that if one hardware component fails, the owner has spares instantly ready to be pressed into service.

Finally, it is difficult to determine motive for an attack. Some places are what are called "attractive targets," meaning they are very appealing to attackers. Popular targets include law enforcement and defense department computers, perhaps because they are presumed to be well protected against attack (so that a successful attack shows the attacker's prowess). Other systems are attacked because they are easy. (See Sidebar 1-2 on universities as targets.) And other systems are attacked simply because they are there: random, unassuming victims.

Sidebar 1-2 Why Universities Are Prime Targets

Universities make very good targets for attack, according to an Associated Press story from June 2001 [HOP01]. Richard Power, editorial director for the Computer Security Institute has reported that universities often run systems with vulnerabilities and little monitoring or management. Consider that the typical university research or teaching lab is managed by a faculty member who has many other responsibilities or by a student manager who may have had little training. Universities are havens for free exchange of ideas. Thus, their access controls typically are configured to promote sharing and wide access to a population that changes significantly every semester.

A worse problem is that universities are really loose federations of departments and research groups. The administrator for one group's computers may not even know other administrators, let alone share intelligence or tools. Often, computers are bought for a teaching or research project, but there is not funding for ongoing maintenance, either buying upgrades or installing patches. Steve Hare, managing director of the computer security research group at Purdue University, noted that groups are usually strapped for resources.

David Dittrich, a security engineer at the University of Washington, said he is certain that cracker(s) who attacked the eBay and CNN.com web sites in 2000 first practiced on university computers. The large and frequently changing university student body gives the attacker great opportunity to maintain anonymity while developing an attack.

Protecting against attacks can be difficult. Anyone can be a victim of an attack perpetrated by an unhurried, knowledgeable attacker. In the remainder of this book we discuss the nature of attacks and how to protect against them.

1.3 THE MEANING OF COMPUTER SECURITY

We have seen that any computer-related system has both theoretical and real weaknesses. The purpose of computer security is to devise ways to prevent the weaknesses from being exploited. To understand what preventive measures make the most sense, we consider what we mean when we say that a system is "secure."

Security Goals

We use the term "security" in many ways in our daily lives. A "security system" protects our house, warning the neighbors or the police if an unauthorized intruder tries to get in. "Financial security" involves a set of investments that are adequately funded; we hope the investments will grow in value over time, so that we have enough money to survive later in life. And we speak of a child's "physical security," hoping he or she is safe from any potential harm. Just as each of these terms has a very specific meaning in the context of its use, so too does the phrase "computer security."

When we talk about "computer security," we mean that we are addressing three very important aspects of any computer-related system: **confidentiality, integrity,** and **availability.**

- *Confidentiality* ensures that computer-related assets are accessed only by authorized parties. That is, only those who should have access to something will actually get that access. By "access," we mean not only reading but also viewing, printing, or simply knowing that a particular asset exists. Confidentiality is sometimes called **secrecy** or **privacy**.
- *Integrity* means that assets can be modified only by authorized parties or only in authorized ways. In this context, modification includes writing, changing, changing status, deleting, and creating.
- *Availability* means that assets are accessible to authorized parties at appropriate times. In other words, if some person or system has legitimate access to a particular set of objects, that access should not be prevented. For this reason, availability is sometimes known by its opposite, **denial of service**.

Security in computing addresses these three goals. One of the challenges in building a secure system is finding the right balance among the goals, which often conflict. For example, it is easy to preserve a particular object's confidentiality in a secure system simply by preventing everyone from reading that object. However, this system is not secure, because it does not meet the requirement of availability for proper access. That is, there must be a balance between confidentiality and availability.

But balance is not all. In fact, these three characteristics can be independent, can overlap (as shown in Figure 1-3), and can even be mutually exclusive. For example, we have seen that strong protection of confidentiality can severely restrict availability. Let us examine each of the three qualities in depth.

Confidentiality

You may find the notion of confidentiality to be straightforward: only authorized people or systems can access protected data. However, as we see in later chapters, ensuring confidentiality can be difficult. For example, who determines which people or systems are authorized to access the current system? By "accessing" data, do we mean that an authorized party can access a single bit? pieces of data out of context? Can someone who is authorized disclose those data to other parties?

Confidentiality is the security property we understand best because its meaning is narrower than the other two. We also understand confidentiality well because we can relate computing examples to those of preserving confidentiality in the real world.

Integrity

Integrity is much harder to pin down. As Welke and Mayfield [WEL90, MAY91, NCS91b] point out, *integrity* means different things in different contexts. When we survey the way some people use the term, we find several different meanings. For example, if we say that we have preserved the integrity of an item, we may mean that the item is:

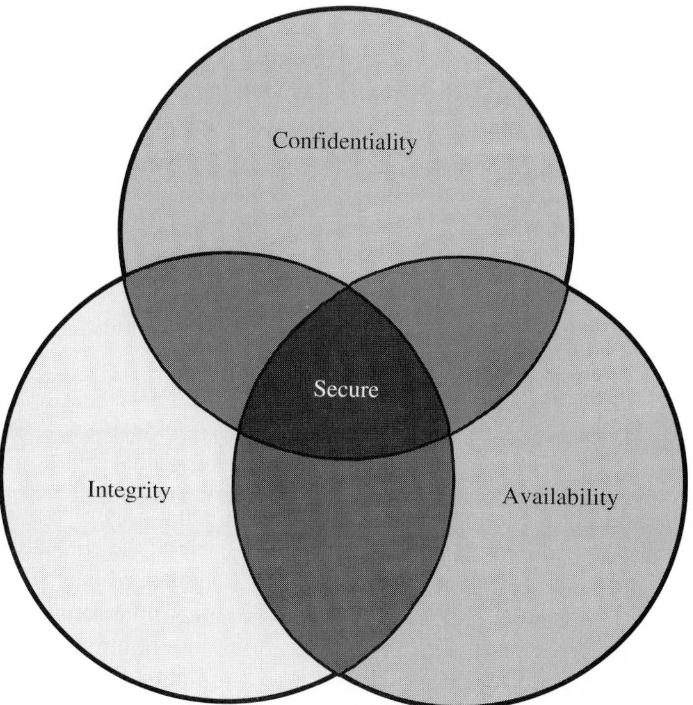

FIGURE 1-3 Relationship Between Confidentiality, Integrity, and Availability.

- precise
- accurate
- unmodified
- modified only in acceptable ways
- modified only by authorized people
- modified only by authorized processes
- consistent
- internally consistent
- meaningful and usable

The Trusted Network Interpretation [NCS87] clarifies by saying that integrity ensures that computerized data are the same as those in source documents; they have not been exposed to accidental or malicious alteration or destruction. Welke and Mayfield recognize three particular aspects of integrity—authorized actions, separation and protection of resources, and error detection and correction. Integrity can be enforced in much the same way as can confidentiality: by rigorous control of who or what can access which resources in what ways. Some forms of integrity are well represented in the real world, and those precise representations can be implemented in a computerized environment. But not all interpretations of integrity are well reflected by computer implementations.

Availability

Availability applies both to data and to services (that is, to information and to information processing), and it is similarly complex. As with the notion of confidentiality, different people expect *availability* to mean different things. For example, an object or service is thought to be available if

- It is present in a usable form.
- It has capacity enough to meet the service's needs.
- It is making clear progress, and, if in wait mode, it has a bounded waiting time.
- The service is completed in an acceptable period of time.

We can construct an overall description of availability by combining these goals. We say a data item, service, or system is available if

- There is a timely response to our request.
- There is a fair allocation of resources, so that some requesters are not favored over others.
- The service or system involved follows a philosophy of fault tolerance, whereby hardware or software faults lead to graceful cessation of service or to work-arounds rather than to crashes and abrupt loss of information.
- The service or system can be used easily and in the way it was intended to be used.
- There is controlled concurrency; that is, there is support for simultaneous access, deadlock management, and exclusive access, as required.

As you can see, expectations of availability are far-reaching. Indeed, the security community is just beginning to understand what availability implies and how to ensure it. A small, centralized control of access is fundamental to preserving confidentiality and integrity, but it is not clear that a single access control point can enforce availability. Much of computer security's past success has focused on confidentiality and integrity; full implementation of availability is security's next great challenge.

Vulnerabilities

When we prepare to test a system, we usually try to imagine how the system can fail; then, we look for ways in which the requirements, design, or code can enable such failures. In the same way, when we prepare to specify, design, code, or test a secure system, we try to imagine the vulnerabilities that would prevent us from reaching one or more of our three security goals.

It is sometimes easier to consider vulnerabilities as they apply to all three broad categories of system resources (hardware, software, and data), rather than to start with the security goals themselves. Figure 1-4 shows the types of vulnerabilities we might find as they apply to the assets of hardware, software, and data. These three assets and the connections among them are all potential security weak points. Let us look in turn at the vulnerabilities of each asset.

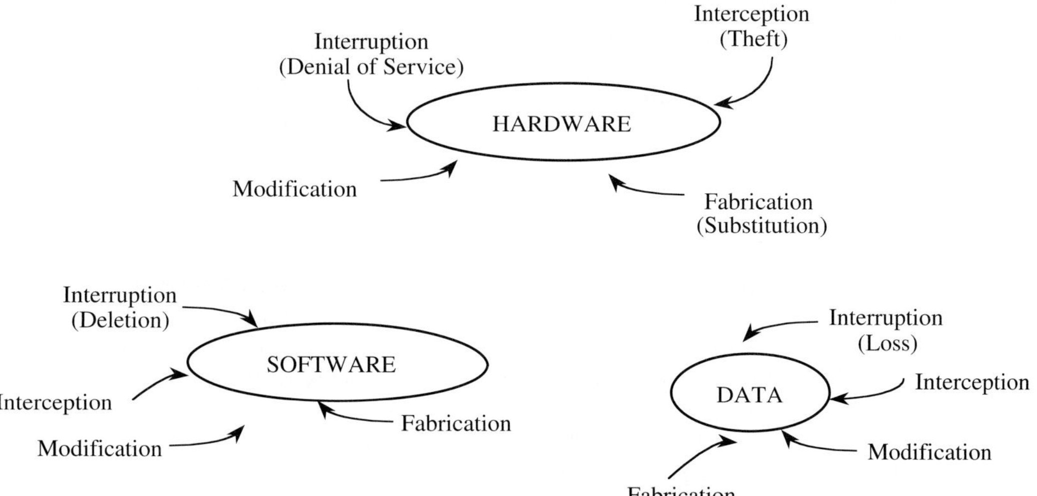

FIGURE 1-4 Vulnerabilities of Computing Systems.

Hardware Vulnerabilities

Hardware is more visible than software, largely because it is composed of physical objects. Because we can see what devices are hooked to the system, it is rather simple to attack by adding devices, changing them, removing them, intercepting the traffic to them, or flooding them with traffic until they can no longer function. However, designers can usually put safeguards in place.

But there are other ways that computer hardware can be attacked physically. Computers have been drenched with water, burned, frozen, gassed, and electrocuted with power surges. People have spilled soft drinks, corn chips, ketchup, beer, and many other kinds of food on computing devices. Mice have chewed through cables. Particles of dust, and especially ash from cigarette smoke, have threatened precisely engineered moving parts. Computers have been kicked, slapped, bumped, jarred, and punched. Although such attacks might be intentional, most are not; this abuse might be considered "involuntary machine slaughter": accidental acts not intended to do serious damage to the hardware involved.

A more serious attack, "voluntary machine slaughter" or "machinicide," usually involves someone who actually wishes to harm the computer hardware or software. Machines have been shot with guns and stabbed with knives. Bombs, fires, and collisions have destroyed computer rooms. Ordinary keys, pens, and screwdrivers have been used to short-out circuit boards and other components. Devices and whole systems have been carried off by thieves. The list of kinds of human attacks perpetrated on computers is almost endless.

In particular, deliberate attacks on equipment, intending to limit availability, usually involve theft or destruction. Managers of major computing centers long ago recognized these vulnerabilities and installed physical security systems to protect their machines.

However, the proliferation of microcomputers in office equipment has resulted in several thousands of dollars' worth of equipment sitting unattended on desks outside the carefully protected computer room. (Curiously, the supply cabinet, containing only a few hundred dollars' worth of pens, stationery, and paper clips, is often locked.) Sometimes the security of hardware components can be enhanced greatly by simple physical measures such as locks and guards.

Software Vulnerabilities

Computing equipment is of little use without the software (operating system, controllers, utility programs, and application programs) that users expect. Software can be replaced, changed, or destroyed maliciously, or it can be modified, deleted, or misplaced accidentally. Whether intentional or not, these attacks exploit the software's vulnerabilities.

Sometimes, the attacks are obvious, as when the software no longer runs. More subtle are attacks in which the software has been altered but seems to run normally. Whereas physical equipment usually shows some mark of inflicted injury when its boundary has been breached, the loss of a line of source or object code may not leave an obvious mark in a program. Furthermore, it is possible to change a program so that it does all it did before, and then some. That is, a malicious intruder can "enhance" the software to enable it to perform functions you may not find desirable. In this case, it may be very hard to detect that the software has been changed, let alone to determine the extent of the change.

A classic example of exploiting software vulnerability is the case in which a bank worker realized that software truncates the fractional interest on each account. In other words, if the monthly interest on an account is calculated to be $14.5467, the software credits only $14.54 and ignores the $.0067. He amended the software so that the throw-away interest (the $.0067) was placed into his own account. Since the accounting practices ensured only that all accounts balanced, he built up a large amount of money from the thousands of account throw-aways, without detection. It was only when he bragged to a colleague of his cleverness that the scheme was discovered.

Software Deletion

Software is surprisingly easy to delete. Each of us has, at some point in our careers, accidentally erased a file or saved a bad copy of a program, destroying a good previous copy. Because of software's high value to a commercial computing center, access to software is usually carefully controlled through a process called **configuration management** so that software is not deleted, destroyed, or replaced accidentally. Configuration management uses several techniques to ensure that each version or release retains its integrity. When configuration management is used, an old version or release can be replaced with a newer version only when it has been thoroughly tested to verify that the improvements work correctly without degrading the functionality and performance of other functions and services.

Software Modification

Software is vulnerable to modifications that either cause it to fail or cause it to perform an unintended task. Indeed, because software is so susceptible to "off by one" errors, it is quite easy to modify. Changing a bit or two can convert a working program into a failing one. Depending on which bit was changed, the program may crash when it begins, or it may execute for some time before it falters.

With a little more work, the change can be much more subtle, so that the program works well most of the time but fails in specialized circumstances. For instance, the program may be maliciously modified to fail when certain conditions are met or when a certain date or time is reached. Because of this delayed effect, such a program is known as a **logic bomb.** For example, a disgruntled employee may modify a crucial program so that it accesses the system date and halts abruptly after July 1. The employee might quit on May l and plan to be at a new job miles away by July.

Another type of change can extend the functioning of a program so that an innocuous program has a hidden side effect. For example, a program that ostensibly structures a listing of files belonging to a user may also modify the protection of all those files to permit access by another user.

Other categories of software modification include

- a **Trojan horse:** a program that overtly does one thing while covertly doing another
- a **virus:** a specific type of Trojan horse that can be used to spread its "infection" from one computer to another
- a **trapdoor:** a program that has a secret entry point
- **information leaks** in a program: code that makes information accessible to unauthorized people or programs

More details on these and other software modifications are provided in Chapter 3.

Of course, it is possible to invent a completely new program and install it on a computing system. Inadequate control over the programs that are installed and run on a computing system permits this kind of software security breach.

Software Theft

This attack includes unauthorized copying of software. Software authors and distributors are entitled to fair compensation for use of their product, as are musicians and book authors. Unauthorized copying of software has not been stopped satisfactorily. As we see in Chapter 9, the legal system is still grappling with the difficulties of interpreting paper-based copyright laws for electronic media.

Data Vulnerabilities

Hardware security is usually the concern of a relatively small staff of computing center professionals. Software security is a larger problem, extending to all programmers and analysts who create or modify programs. Computer programs are written in a dialect intelligible primarily to computer professionals, so a "leaked" source listing of a program might very well be meaningless to the general public.

Printed data, however, can be readily interpreted by the general public. Because of its visible nature, a data attack is a more widespread and serious problem than either a hardware or software attack. Thus, data items have greater public value than hardware and software, because more people know how to use or interpret data.

By themselves, out of context, pieces of data have essentially no intrinsic value. For example, if you are shown the value "42," it has no meaning for you unless you know what the number represents. Likewise, "326 Old Norwalk Road" is of little use unless you know the city, state, and country for the address. For this reason, it is hard to measure the value of a given data item.

On the other hand, data items in context do relate to cost, perhaps measurable by the cost to reconstruct or redevelop damaged or lost data. For example, confidential data leaked to a competitor may narrow a competitive edge. Data incorrectly modified can cost human lives. To see how, consider the flight coordinate data used by an airplane that is guided partly or fully by software, as many now are. Finally, inadequate security may lead to financial liability if certain personal data are made public. Thus, data have a definite value, even though that value is often difficult to measure.

Typically, both hardware and software have a relatively long life. No matter how they are valued initially, their value usually declines gradually over time. By contrast, the value of data over time is far less predictable or consistent. Initially, data may be valued highly. However, some data items are of interest for only a short period of time, after which their value declines precipitously.

To see why, consider the following example. In many countries, government analysts periodically generate data to describe the state of the national economy. The results are scheduled to be released to the public at a predetermined time and date. Before that time, access to the data could allow someone to profit from advance knowledge of the probable effect of the data on the stock market. For instance, suppose an analyst develops the data 24 hours before their release and then wishes to communicate the results to other analysts for independent verification before release. The data vulnerability here is clear, and, to the right people, the data are worth more before the scheduled release than afterward. However, there are simple ways to protect the data and control the threat. For example, we could devise a scheme that would take an outsider more than 24 hours to break; even though the scheme may be eminently breakable (that is, an intruder could eventually reveal the data), it is adequate for those data because there is no need for confidentiality beyond the 24-hour period.

Data security suggests the second principle of computer security:

> **Principle of Adequate Protection:** Computer items must be protected only until they lose their value. They must be protected to a degree consistent with their value.

This principle says that things with a short life can be protected by security measures that are effective only for that short time. The notion of a small protection window applies primarily to data, but it can in some cases be relevant for software and hardware, too.

Sidebar 1-3 confirms that intruders take advantage of vulnerabilities to break in by whatever means they can.

Figure 1-5 illustrates how the three goals of security apply to data. In particular, **confidentiality** prevents unauthorized disclosure of a data item, **integrity** prevents unauthorized modification, and **availability** prevents denial of authorized access.

Sidebar 1-3 Top Methods of Attack

In 2001, *Information Week* magazine commissioned a global information survey of 4,500 security professionals. As part of the survey, the respondents were asked to name the primary methods of attack used by intruders against their organizations. (Multiple responses were allowed.)

The top method was exploiting known operating system vulnerabilities; almost one-third of the respondents had experienced this kind of attack. The next most popular method was exploiting an unknown application (27 percent). Other commonly used attacks were guessing passwords (22 percent), abusing valid user accounts or permissions (17 percent), and using an internal denial of service (12 percent).

Common wisdom had always been that four out of five attacks on corporate networks or computers were perpetrated by malevolent insiders who could take advantage of their understanding of the system. The survey sought to determine if this "rule of thumb" were true. In fact, with the growing use of Internet applications, outsiders are now considered the greater threat. Hulme [HUL01b] points out that "Many companies suspect hackers and terrorists (46 percent) and even customers (14 percent) of trying to breach their systems." This suspicion is supported by another survey, conducted by the Computer Security Institute and the U.S. Federal Bureau of Investigation [CSI02]. The second survey notes that almost three in four businesses cite the Internet as a point of attack, whereas only one in three cites internal systems.

Data Confidentiality

Data can be gathered by many means, such as tapping wires, planting bugs in output devices, sifting through trash receptacles, monitoring electromagnetic radiation, bribing key employees, inferring one data point from other values, or simply requesting the data. Because data are often available in a form people can read, the confidentiality of data is a major concern in computer security.

Data Integrity

Stealing, buying, finding, or hearing data requires no computer sophistication, whereas modifying or making new data requires some understanding of the technology by which the data are transmitted or stored, as well as the format in which the data are maintained. Thus, a higher level of sophistication is needed to modify existing data or to fabricate new data than to intercept existing data. The most common sources of this kind of problem are malicious programs, errant file system utilities, and flawed communication facilities.

Data are especially vulnerable to modification. Small and skillfully done modifications may not be detected in ordinary ways. For instance, we saw in our truncated interest example that a criminal can perform what is known as a **salami attack:** the crook shaves a little from many accounts and puts these shavings together to form a valuable result, like the meat scraps joined together in a salami.

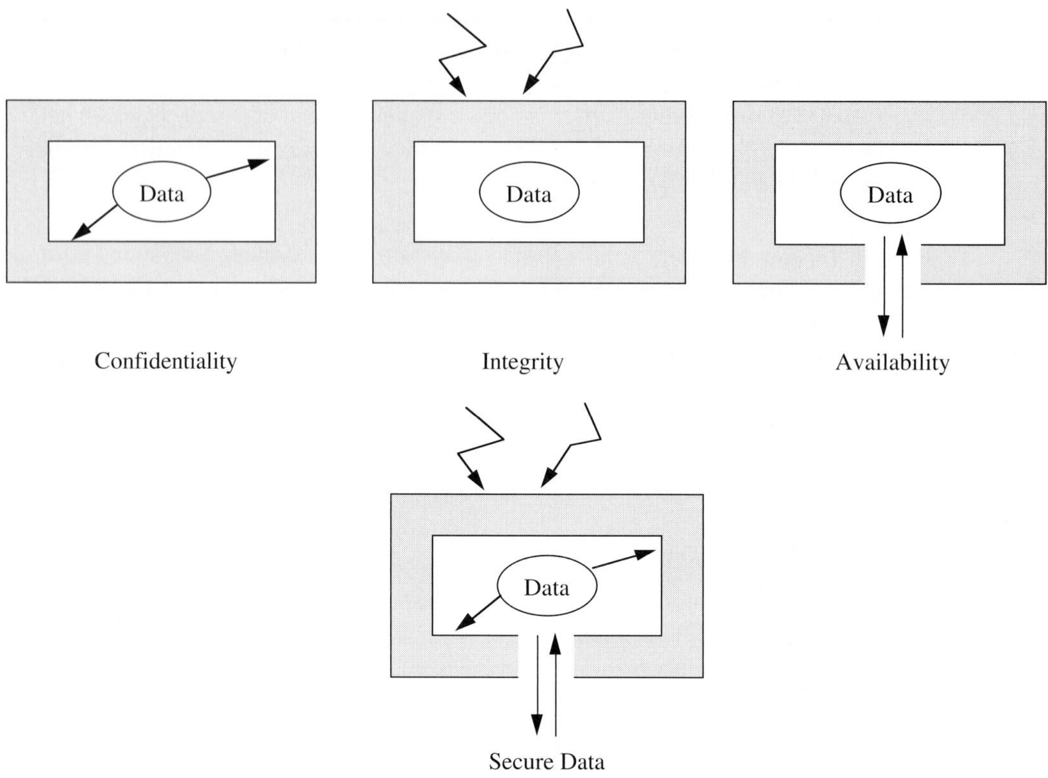

FIGURE 1-5 Security of Data.

A more complicated process is trying to reprocess used data items. With the proliferation of telecommunications among banks, a fabricator might intercept a message ordering one bank to credit a given amount to a certain person's account. The fabricator might try to **replay** that message, causing the receiving bank to credit the same account again. The fabricator might also try to modify the message slightly, changing the account to be credited or the amount, and then transmit this revised message.

Other Exposed Assets

We have noted that the major points of weakness in a computing system are hardware, software, and data. However, other components of the system may also be possible targets. In this section, we identify some of these other points of attack.

Networks

Networks are specialized collections of hardware, software, and data. Each network node is itself a computing system; as such, it experiences all the normal security problems. In addition, a network must confront communication problems that involve the interaction of system components and outside resources. The problems may be introduced by a very exposed storage medium or access from distant and potentially untrustworthy computing systems.

Thus, networks can easily multiply the problems of computer security. The challenges are rooted in a network's lack of physical proximity, use of insecure, shared media, and the inability of a network to identify remote users positively.

Access

Access to computing equipment leads to three types of vulnerabilities. In the first, an intruder may steal computer time to do general-purpose computing that does not attack the integrity of the system itself. This theft of computer services is analogous to the stealing of electricity, gas, or water. However, the value of the stolen computing services may be substantially higher than the value of the stolen utility products or services. Moreover, the unpaid computing access spreads the true costs of maintaining the computing system to other legitimate users. In fact, the unauthorized access risks affecting legitimate computing, perhaps by changing data or programs. A second vulnerability involves malicious access to a computing system, whereby an intruding person or system actually destroys software or data. Finally, unauthorized access may deny service to a legitimate user. For example, a user who has a time-critical task to perform may depend on the availability of the computing system. For all three of these reasons, unauthorized access to a computing system must be prevented.

Key People

People can be crucial weak points in security. If only one person knows how to use or maintain a particular program, trouble can arise if that person is ill, suffers an accident, or leaves the organization (taking her knowledge with her). In particular, a disgruntled employee can cause serious damage by using inside knowledge of the system and the data that are manipulated. For this reason, trusted individuals, such as operators and systems programmers, are usually selected carefully because of their potential ability to affect all computer users.

We have described common assets at risk. In fact, there are valuable assets in almost any computer system. (See Sidebar 1-4 for an example of exposed assets in ordinary business dealings.)

Next, we turn to the people who design, build, and interact with computer systems, to see who can breach the systems' confidentiality, integrity, and availability.

1.4 COMPUTER CRIMINALS

In television and film westerns, the bad guys always wore shabby clothes, had mean and sinister looks, and lived in gangs somewhere out of town. By contrast, the sheriff dressed well, stood proud and tall, was known and respected by everyone in town, and struck fear in the hearts of most criminals.

To be sure, some computer criminals are mean and sinister types. But many more wear business suits, have university degrees, and appear to be pillars of their communities. Some are high school or university students. Others are middle-aged business executives. Some are mentally deranged, overtly hostile, or extremely committed to a

Sidebar 1-4 Hollywood at Risk

Do you think only banks, government sites, and universities are targets? Consider Hollywood.

In 2001 Hollywood—specifically the motion picture industry—was hit with a series of attacks. Crackers entered computers and were able to obtain access to scripts for new projects, and digital versions of films in production, including *Ocean's 11* at Warner Brothers and *The One* at Columbia Pictures. The attackers also retrieved and made public executives' e-mail messages.

But, as is true of many computer security incidents, at least one attacker was an insider. Global Network Security Services, a security consulting firm hired by several Hollywood companies to test the security of their networks, found that an employee was copying the day's (digital) film, taking it home, and allowing his roommate to post it to an Internet site.

cause, and they attack computers as a symbol. Others are ordinary people tempted by personal profit, revenge, challenge, advancement, or job security. No single profile captures the characteristics of a "typical" computer criminal, and many who fit the profile are not criminals at all.

Whatever their characteristics and motivations, computer criminals have access to enormous amounts of hardware, software, and data; they have the potential to cripple much of effective business and government throughout the world. In a sense, then, the purpose of computer security is to prevent these criminals from doing damage.

For the purposes of studying computer security, we say **computer crime** is any crime involving a computer or aided by the use of one. Although this definition is admittedly pretty broad, it allows us to consider ways to protect ourselves, our businesses, and our communities against those who use computers maliciously.

The U.S. Federal Bureau of Investigation regularly reports uniform crime statistics. The data do not separate computer crime from crime of other sorts. Moreover, many companies do not report computer crime at all, perhaps because they fear damage to their reputation, they are ashamed to have allowed their systems to be compromised, or they have agreed not to prosecute if the criminal will "go away." These conditions make it difficult for us to estimate the economic losses we suffer as a result of computer crime; our dollar estimates are really only vague suspicions. Still, the estimates, ranging from $300 million to $500 billion per year, tell us that it is important for us to pay attention to computer crime and to try to prevent it or at least to moderate its effects.

One approach to prevention or moderation is to understand who commits these crimes and why. Many studies have attempted to determine the characteristics of computer criminals. By studying those who have already used computers to commit crimes, we may be able in future to spot likely criminals and prevent the crimes from occurring. In this section, we examine some of these characteristics.

Amateurs

Amateurs have committed most of the computer crimes reported to date. Most embezzlers are not career criminals but rather are normal people who observe a weakness in a security system that allows them to access cash or other valuables. In the same sense, most computer criminals are ordinary computer professionals or users doing their jobs, when they discover they have access to something valuable.

When no one objects, the amateur may start using the computer at work to write letters, maintain soccer league team standings, or do accounting. This apparently innocent time-stealing may expand until the employee is pursuing a business in accounting, stock portfolio management, or desktop publishing on the side, using the employer's computing facilities. Alternatively, amateurs may become disgruntled over some negative work situation (such as a reprimand or denial of promotion) and vow to "get even" with management by wreaking havoc on a computing installation.

Crackers

System **crackers**,[2] often high school or university students, attempt to access computing facilities for which they have not been authorized. Cracking a computer's defenses is seen as the ultimate victimless crime. The perception is that nobody is hurt or even endangered by a little stolen machine time. Crackers enjoy the simple challenge of trying to log in, just to see whether it can be done. Most crackers can do their harm without confronting anybody, not even making a sound. In the absence of explicit warnings not to trespass in a system, crackers infer that access is permitted. An underground network of hackers helps pass along secrets of success; as with a jigsaw puzzle, a few isolated pieces joined together may produce a large effect. Others attack for curiosity, personal gain, or self-satisfaction. And still others enjoy causing chaos, loss, or harm. There is no common profile or motivation for these attackers.

Career Criminals

By contrast, the career computer criminal understands the targets of computer crime. Criminals seldom change fields from arson, murder, or auto theft to computing; more often, criminals begin as computer professionals who engage in computer crime, finding the prospects and payoff good. There is some evidence that organized crime and international groups are engaging in computer crime. Recently, electronic spies and information brokers have begun to recognize that trading in companies' or individuals' secrets can be lucrative.

As mentioned earlier, some companies are reticent to prosecute computer criminals. In fact, after having discovered a computer crime, the companies are often thankful if the criminal quietly resigns. In other cases, the company is (understandably) more concerned about protecting its assets and so it closes down an attacked

[2] The security community distinguishes between a "hacker," someone who (nonmaliciously) programs, manages, or uses computing systems, and a "cracker," someone who attempts access to computing systems for malicious purposes. Crackers are the "evildoers." Now, hacker has come to be used outside security to mean both benign and malicious users.

system rather than gathering evidence that could lead to identification and conviction of the criminal. The criminal is then free to continue the same illegal pattern with another company.

1.5 METHODS OF DEFENSE

In Chapter 9, we investigate the legal and ethical restrictions on computer-based crime. But unfortunately computer crime is certain to continue for the foreseeable future. For this reason, we must look carefully at controls for preserving confidentiality, integrity, and availability. Sometimes these controls can prevent or mitigate attacks; other, less powerful methods can only inform us that security has been compromised, by detecting a breach as it happens or after it occurs.

Harm occurs when a threat is realized against a vulnerability. To protect against harm, then, we can neutralize the threat, close the vulnerability, or both. The possibility for harm to occur is called **risk**. We can deal with harm in several ways. We can seek to

- *prevent it,* by blocking the attack or closing the vulnerability
- *deter it,* by making the attack harder, but not impossible
- *deflect it,* by making another target more attractive (or this one less so)
- *detect it,* either as it happens or some time after the fact
- *recover* from its effects

Of course, more than one of these can be done at once. So, for example, we might try to prevent intrusions. But in case we do not prevent them all, we might install a detection device to warn of an imminent attack. And we should have in place incident response procedures to help in the recovery in case an intrusion does succeed.

Controls

To consider the controls or countermeasures that attempt to prevent exploiting a computing system's vulnerabilities, we begin by thinking about traditional ways to enhance physical security. In the Middle Ages, castles and fortresses were built to protect the valuable people and property inside. The fortress might have had one or more security characteristics, including

- a strong gate or door to repel invaders
- heavy walls to withstand objects thrown or projected against them
- a surrounding moat, to control access
- arrow slits, to let archers shoot at approaching enemies
- crenellations to allow inhabitants to lean out from the roof and pour hot or vile liquids on attackers
- a drawbridge to limit access to authorized people
- gatekeepers to verify that only authorized people and goods could enter

Similarly, today we use a multipronged approach to protect our homes and offices. We may combine strong locks on the doors with a burglar alarm, reinforced windows, and even a nosy neighbor to keep an eye on our valuables. In each case, we select one or more ways to deter an intruder or attacker, and we base our selection not only on the value of what we protect but also on the effort we think an attacker or intruder will expend to get inside.

Computer security has the same characteristics. We have many controls at our disposal. Some are easier than others to use or implement. Some are cheaper than others to use or implement. And some are more difficult than others for intruders to override. Figure 1-6 illustrates how we use a combination of controls to secure our valuable resources. We use one or more controls, according to what we are protecting, how the cost of protection compares with the risk of loss, and how hard we think intruders will work to get what they want.

In this section, we present an overview of the controls available to us. In later chapters, we examine each control in much more detail.

Encryption

We noted earlier that we seek to protect hardware, software, and data. We can make it particularly hard for an intruder to find data useful if we somehow scramble the data so that interpretation is meaningless without the intruder's knowing how the scrambling was done. Indeed, the most powerful tool in providing computer security is this scrambling or encoding.

Encryption is the formal name for the scrambling process. We take data in their normal, unscrambled state, called **cleartext**, and transform them so that they are unintelligible to the outside observer; the transformed data are called **enciphered text**. Using encryption, security professionals can virtually nullify the value of an intercep-

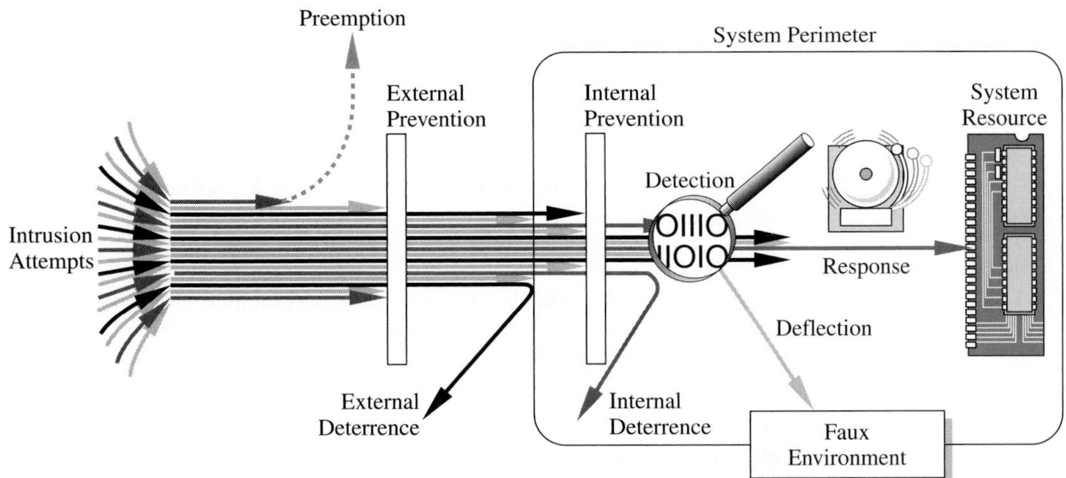

FIGURE 1-6 Multiple Controls.

tion and the possibility of effective modification or fabrication. In Chapters 2 and 10 we study many ways of devising and applying these transformations.

Encryption clearly addresses the need for confidentiality of data. Additionally, it can be used to ensure integrity; data that cannot be read generally also cannot easily be changed in a meaningful manner. Furthermore, as we will see throughout this book, encryption is the basis of **protocols** that enable us to provide security while accomplishing an important system or network task. A protocol is an agreed-upon sequence of actions that leads to a desired result. For example, some operating system protocols ensure availability of resources as different tasks and users request them. Thus, encryption can also be thought of as supporting availability. That is, encryption is at the heart of methods for ensuring all aspects of computer security.

Although encryption is an important tool in any computer security tool kit, we should not overrate its importance. Encryption does not solve all computer security problems, and other tools must complement its use. Furthermore, if encryption is not used properly, it may have no effect on security or could even degrade the performance of the entire system. Weak encryption can actually be worse than no encryption at all, because it gives users an unwarranted sense of protection. Therefore, we must understand those situations in which encryption is most useful, as well as ways to use it effectively.

Software Controls

If encryption is the primary way of protecting valuables, programs themselves are the second facet of computer security. Programs must be secure enough to prevent outside attack. They must also be developed and maintained so that we can be confident of the programs' dependability.

Program controls include the following:

- *internal program controls:* parts of the program that enforce security restrictions, such as access limitations in a database management program
- *operating system and network system controls:* limitations enforced by the operating system or network to protect each user from all other users
- *independent control programs:* application programs, such as password checkers, intrusion detection utilities, or virus scanners, that protect against certain types of vulnerabilities
- *development controls:* quality standards under which a program is designed, coded, tested, and maintained, to prevent software faults from becoming exploitable vulnerabilities

We can implement software controls by using tools and techniques such as hardware components, encryption, or information gathering. Software controls frequently affect users directly, such as when the user is interrupted and asked for a password before being given access to a program or data. For this reason, we often think of software controls when we think of how systems have been made secure in the past. Because they influence the way users interact with a computing system, software controls must be carefully designed. Ease of use and potency are often competing goals in the design of a collection of software controls.

Hardware Controls

Numerous hardware devices have been created to assist in providing computer security. These devices include a variety of means, such as

- hardware or smart card implementations of encryption
- locks or cables limiting access or deterring theft
- devices to verify users' identities
- firewalls
- intrusion detection systems
- circuit boards that control access to storage media.

Policies and Procedures

Sometimes, we can rely on agreed-upon procedures or policies among users, rather than enforcing security through hardware or software means. In fact, some of the simplest controls, such as frequent changes of passwords, can be achieved at essentially no cost but with tremendous effect. Training and administration follow immediately after establishment of policies, to reinforce the importance of security policy and to ensure their proper use.

We must not forget the value of community standards and expectations when we consider how to enforce security. There are many acts that most thoughtful people would consider harmful, and we can leverage this commonality of belief in our policies. For this reason, legal and ethical controls are an important part of computer security. However, the law is slow to evolve, and the technology involving computers has emerged relatively suddenly. Although legal protection is necessary and desirable, it may not be as dependable in this area as it would be when applied to more well understood and long-standing crimes.

Society in general and the computing community have not adopted formal standards of ethical behavior. As we see in Chapter 9, some organizations have devised codes of ethics for computer professionals. However, before codes of ethics can become widely accepted and effective, the computing community and the general public must discuss and make clear what kinds of behavior are inappropriate and why.

Physical Controls

Some of the easiest, most effective, and least expensive controls are physical controls. Physical controls include locks on doors, guards at entry points, backup copies of important software and data, and physical site planning that reduces the risk of natural disasters. Often the simple physical controls are overlooked while we seek more sophisticated approaches.

Effectiveness of Controls

Merely having controls does no good unless they are used properly. Let us consider several aspects that can enhance the effectiveness of controls.

Awareness of Problem

People using controls must be convinced of the need for security. That is, people will willingly cooperate with security requirements only if they understand why security is appropriate in a given situation. However, many users are unaware of the need for security, especially in situations in which a group has recently undertaken a computing task that was previously performed with lax or no apparent security.

Likelihood of Use

Of course, no control is effective unless it is used. The lock on a computer room door does no good if people block the door open. As Sidebar 1-5 tells, some computer systems are seriously uncontrolled.

> **Principle of Effectiveness:** Controls must be used—and used properly—to be effective. They must be efficient, easy to use, and appropriate.

This principle implies that computer security controls must be efficient enough, in terms of time, memory space, human activity, or other resources used, that using the control does not seriously affect the task being protected. Controls should be selective so that they do not exclude legitimate accesses.

Overlapping Controls

As we have seen with fortress or home security, several different controls may apply to address a single vulnerability. For example, we may choose to implement security for a

Sidebar 1-5 Barn Door Wide Open

In 2001, Wilshire Associates, Inc., a Santa Monica, California-based investment company that manages about $10 billion of other people's money, found that its e-mail system had been operating for months with little security. Outsiders potentially had access to internal messages containing confidential information about clients and their investments, as well as sensitive company information.

According to a *Washington Post* article [OHA01], Wilshire had hired an outside security investigator in 1999 to review the security of its system. Thomas Stevens, a senior managing director of Wilshire said "We had a report back that said our firewall is like Swiss cheese. We plugged the holes. We didn't plug all of them." Company officials were "not overly concerned" about that report because they are "not in the defense business." In 2001, security analyst George Imburgia checked the system's security on his own, from the outside (with the same limited knowledge an attacker would have) and found it was "configured to be available to everyone; all you need to do is ask."

Wilshire's system enabled employees to access their e-mail remotely. A senior Wilshire director suggested that the e-mail messages in the system should have been encrypted.

Sidebar 1-6 U.S. Government's Computer Security Report Card

The U.S. Congress requires government agencies to supply annual reports to the Office of Management and Budget (OMB) on the state of computer security in the agencies. In November 2001, two-thirds of the government agencies received a grade of F (the lowest possible) on the computer security report card based on the OMB data.

The agencies must report efforts to protect their computer networks against crackers, terrorists, and other attackers.

Among the failing agencies were Defense, Justice, and Treasury. The State Department received a D+. The highest grade was a B+ to the National Science Foundation. (*Washington Post*, 10 November 2001.)

microcomputer application by using a combination of controls on program access to the data, on physical access to the microcomputer and storage media, and even by file locking to control access to the processing programs.

Periodic Review

Few controls are permanently effective. Just when the security specialist finds a way to secure assets against certain kinds of attacks, the opposition doubles its efforts in an attempt to defeat the security mechanisms. Thus, judging the effectiveness of a control is an ongoing task. (Sidebar 1-6 reports on periodic reviews of computer security.)

Seldom, if ever, are controls perfectly effective. Controls fail, controls are incomplete, or people circumvent or misuse controls, for example. For that reason, we use **overlapping controls,** sometimes called a **layered defense,** in the expectation that one control will compensate for a failure of another. In some cases, controls do nicely complement each other. But two controls are not always better than one and, in some cases, two can even be worse than one. This brings us to another security principle.

> **Principle of Weakest Link:** Security can be no stronger than its weakest link. Whether it is the power supply that powers the firewall or the operating system under the security application or the human who plans, implements, and administers controls, a failure of any control can lead to a security failure.

1.6 WHAT'S NEXT

This book describes all aspects of security in computing. By studying it, you will become acquainted with computer security's major problem areas, the controls that are effective against them, and how current research is addressing the open problems.

To present security in a comprehensive way, this book is organized in four parts. The first part introduces encryption, an important tool on which many controls are based. That introduction presents encryption's goals, terminology, and use. You will be able to understand the role of encryption in addressing security needs without having to learn the intricate details of particular encryption methods. Then, the second part contains material on the hardware and software components of computing systems. We describe the types of problems to which each is subject and the kinds of protection that can be implemented for each component. The third part of the book discusses factors outside the system's hardware, software, and data that can influence the system's security. In particular, this part contains a study of physical factors in security, as well as characteristics of the people who use the system. The book's final section is a more detailed study of encryption, for those readers who are interested in understanding the intricacies of encryption techniques and evaluating their effectiveness.

The remainder of this section presents the contents of these parts in more depth.

Encryption Overview

Chapter 2 presents the goals and terminology of encryption so that you will understand not only why data are scrambled but also the role of the scrambling in the larger context of protecting assets. This chapter provides you with knowledge of encryption sufficient for us to study its use as part of other security tools and techniques.

Hardware and Software Security

Chapters 3 through 7 address the role of security in general programs, operating systems, database management systems, and networks. In particular, the security problems and features of programs are introduced in Chapter 3. Here, we look at viruses and other malicious code and ways to devise controls against them.

Operating systems are considered separately, in Chapter 4, because they play a major role in security and are fundamental to proper computer usage. While providing security features to protect one user from another, operating systems can at the same time introduce security vulnerabilities themselves. Chapter 5 focuses on a special type of operating system, called a trusted operating system, to study how to make certain data and functions accessible only to those who have need or permission to view or handle them. This chapter is especially important for those developers who plan to design their own operating systems or modify functions in an existing operating system.

Database management systems are also specialized programs; they permit many users to share access to one common set of data. Because these systems are partially responsible for the confidentiality, integrity, and availability of the shared data, we look at database security in Chapter 6.

Chapter 7 contains material on security problems and solutions particular to computer networks and the communications media by which networked computers are connected. Network security has become very significant because of the rapid growth in use of networks, especially the Internet.

Human Controls in Security

The first two parts of this book form a progression from simple security applications and tools to complex security technology in multiuser, multicomputer systems. These technology-based security methods are rather sophisticated, and researchers continue to look to technology to assist in security assurance. However, most computer-based security breaches are caused by either human or environmental factors. Thus, Chapters 8 and 9 suggest an alternative or supplemental approach to computer security: treat the causes (people and the environment) rather than the symptoms (attacks and vulnerabilities). We examine procedures that can be implemented in spite of, or in addition to, any controls built into hardware and software.

Chapter 8 addresses the administration of security. It begins with security planning and the particularly important role played by risk analysis. The chapter also explains physical security mechanisms that can be used to protect computing systems against human attacks or natural disasters. It explains why security policy is essential to security planning, illustrating the concepts with several examples from actual organizational policy documents. The chapter concludes with a discussion of disaster recovery: how to deal with the failure of other controls.

Chapter 9 considers the use of law and ethics to control malicious behavior. Although computer law is a relatively new field, it is evolving rapidly and is an important tool in the defense of computing systems. We look at how ethical systems may address some situations where the law is ineffective, inappropriate, or inadequately defined. Chapter 9 also addresses privacy, a computer security issue that has both technical and ethical aspects.

Encryption In-Depth

Chapter 10 builds on the simple encryption methods and terminology presented in Chapter 2. It progresses from theoretical encryption algorithms to current standard practices in the field. We study what makes a cryptosystem secure enough for commercial use, for protecting government data, or for securing your own private, personal information.

Throughout the book, we raise issues related to the important problems in computer security today. When the solution is known, we describe it or at least give you pointers to a fuller description of the solution. At the same time, we discuss work in progress so that you can watch the media and the literature for significant achievements in improving computer security.

It is important to remember that computer security is a relatively new field that is gaining prominence as computing itself becomes pervasive. The speed of new development in computing far outpaces capabilities in computer security. It sometimes seems as if each advance in computing brings with it new security problems. In a sense, this is true. However, there is reason to be optimistic. The fundamental work in security provides tools (such as encryption and operating system features) that form the basis of controls for these new problems as the problems arise. Part of the excitement of computer security is that there are always new challenges to address.

1.7 SUMMARY

Computer security attempts to ensure the confidentiality, integrity, and availability of computing systems' components. Three principal pieces of a computing system are subject to attacks: hardware, software, and data. These three, and the communications among them, constitute the basis of computer security vulnerabilities. In turn, those people and systems interested in compromising a system can devise attacks that exploit the vulnerabilities. This chapter has identified four kinds of attacks on computing systems: interception, interruption, modification, and fabrication.

Four principles affect the direction of work in computer security. By the principle of easiest penetration, a computing system penetrator will use whatever means of attack is the easiest; therefore, all aspects of computing system security must be considered at once. By the principle of timeliness, a system must be protected against penetration only so long as the penetration has value to the penetrator. The principle of effectiveness states that controls must be usable and used in order to serve their purpose. And the weakest link principle states that security is no stronger than its weakest point.

Controls can be applied at the levels of the data, the programs, the system, the physical devices, the communications links, the environment, and the personnel. Sometimes several controls are needed to cover a single vulnerability, and sometimes one control addresses many problems at once.

1.8 TERMS AND CONCEPTS

Virus, Trojan horse, worm, rabbit, salami, firewall, spray paint, mental poker, orange book, war dialer. The vocabulary of computer security is rich with terms that capture your attention. Also, the field is filled with acronyms: DES, AES, RSA, TCSEC, CTCPEC, ITSEC, PEM, PGP, and SSE CMM, to list a few. All of these are explained in this book. Each chapter ends with a list of terms and concepts, in order of their occurrence, as a way to review and see whether you have learned the important points of the chapter.

The list for this chapter includes some terms that may be new, as well as the major concepts introduced in this chapter. Although these terms are elaborated in future chapters, it is good to begin now to learn the terms and the underlying concepts.

computing system, 4
principle of easiest penetration, 5
hardware, 5
software, 5
data, 5
vulnerability, 6
attack, 6
threat, 6
control, 7
interruption, 7
interception, 7
modification, 8
fabrication, 8
method, 8
opportunity, 8
motive, 8
security, secure, 9
confidentiality, 10
integrity, 10
availability, 10
secrecy, 10
privacy, 10
configuration management, 14
logic bomb, 15
Trojan horse, 15
virus, 15
trapdoor, 15
information leak, 15
principle of adequate protection, 16
salami attack, 17
replay, 18
cracker, 21

prevention, 22
deterrence, 22
deflection, 22
detection, 22
recovery, 22
encryption, 23
protocol, 24
administrative control, 25
policy, 25
procedure, 25
physical control, 25
principle of effectiveness, 26
overlapping control, 26
layered defense, 27
principle of weakest link, 27

1.9 WHERE THE FIELD IS HEADED

We conclude most chapters with a paragraph or two highlighting some interesting work being done. For students interested in pursuing a career in security, these sections may identify an area of interest.

The number of computer security professionals is growing rapidly but so, too, is the number of attackers. The U.S. CERT and its counterpart organizations around the world do an exceptional job of tracking serious system vulnerabilities and countermeasures. Several efforts are underway to categorize and catalog computer security incidents and vulnerabilities (for example, Landwehr et al. [LAN94]). Being able to sort and correlate incident information is critical to successful forensic analysis of large incidents.

The severity of the computer security problem is causing many companies, schools and universities, government bodies, and individuals to address their security needs. Looking at these groups separately can be daunting and also risks your missing the ones who do it really well. Several groups have promulgated codes of security best practices. The Information Security Forum [ISF00] and the Internet Security Alliance [ISA02] have published codes of best security practices, which are recommendations for secure computing. Governments and regulatory bodies are beginning to enforce standards.

Obviously, the popular attack point today is computer networks, and specifically the Internet. Do not be misled, however, into thinking that all computer security is network security. As you will see throughout the remainder of this book, network security problems are often just the latest instantiation of computer security problems that predate the rise of the Internet—problems such as identification and authentication, limited privilege, and designing for security. So, although the problems of networks are pressing, they are long-standing, open problems.

1.10 TO LEARN MORE

Today's bookshelves are full of books about computer security: its meaning, its impact, and the people involved in preventing malicious behavior. However, two key works form the foundation for much of subsequent work in computer security: the exploration of vulnerabilities and controls by Ware [WAR79] and the security technology planning study by Anderson [AND72]. The concepts and ideas put forth are still relevant, even though the papers are several decades old.

Two very good surveys of the field of computer security are Denning's classic textbook [DEN82], much of which is still valid, and Gollmann's textbook [GOL99]. Also, Schneier's book [SCH00] is an enjoyable overview.

Some books focus on a particular aspect of security. Confidentiality is explored by the Dennings [DEN79a], and integrity is studied carefully by Welke and Mayfield [WEL90, MAY91, NCS91b]. Availability considerations are documented by Pfleeger and Mayfield [PFL92] and by Millen [MIL92].

Since 1991, the National Research Council of the National Academy of Science has published seven reports on the state of aspects of computer security. The first volume [NRC91] lays out the significant risk of the then current state of computing. Frighteningly, the latest report [NRC02] concludes: "not much has changed with respect to security as it is practiced." These volumes are worth reading for their realistic assessment of today's threats and preparedness.

For further study of threats affecting computer systems, see [DEN99]. For examples of how computer system vulnerabilities are exploited, you may want to read [STO89, SHI96].

1.11 EXERCISES

1. Distinguish among vulnerability, threat, and control.
2. Theft usually results in some kind of harm. For example, if someone steals your car, you may suffer financial loss, inconvenience (by losing your mode of transportation), and emotional upset (because of invasion of your personal property and space). List three kinds of harm a company might experience from theft of computer equipment.
3. List at least three kinds of harm a company could experience from electronic espionage or unauthorized viewing of confidential company materials.
4. List at least three kinds of damage a company could suffer when the integrity of a program or company data is compromised.
5. Describe two examples of vulnerabilities in automobiles for which auto manufacturers have instituted controls. Tell whether you think these controls are effective, somewhat effective, or ineffective.
6. One control against accidental software deletion is to save all old versions of a program. Of course, this control is prohibitively expensive in terms of cost of storage. Suggest a less costly control against accidental software deletion. Is your control effective against all possible causes of software deletion? If not, what threats does it not cover?
7. On a typical multiuser computing system (such as a shared Unix system at a university or an industry), who *can* modify the code (software) of the operating system? Of a major application program such as a payroll program or a statistical analysis package? Of a program developed and run by a single user? Who *should be* permitted to modify each of these examples of code?
8. Suppose a program to print paychecks secretly leaks a list of names of employees earning more than a certain amount each month. What controls could be instituted to limit the vulnerability of this leakage?
9. Some terms have been introduced intentionally without definition in this chapter. You should be able to deduce their meanings. What is an electronic spy? What is an information broker?
10. Preserving confidentiality, integrity, and availability of data is a restatement of the concern over interruption, interception, modification, and fabrication. How do the first three con-

cepts relate to the last four? That is, is any of the four equivalent to one or more of the three? Is one of the three encompassed by one or more of the four?

11. Do you think attempting to break in to (that is, obtain access to or use of) a computing system without authorization should be illegal? Why or why not?

12. Describe an example (other than the one mentioned in this chapter) of data whose confidentiality has a short timeliness, say, a day or less. Describe an example of data whose confidentiality has a timeliness of more than a year.

13. Do you currently use any computer security control measures? If so, what? Against what attacks are you trying to protect?

14. Describe an example in which absolute denial of service to a user (that is, the user gets no response from the computer) is a serious problem to that user. Describe another example where 10 percent denial of service to a user (that is, the user's computation progresses, but at a rate 10 percent slower than normal) is a serious problem to that user. Could access by unauthorized people to a computing system result in a 10 percent denial of service to the legitimate users? How?

15. When you say that software is of high quality, what do you mean? How does security fit in your definition of quality? For example, can an application be insecure and still be "good"?

16. Developers often think of software quality in terms of faults and failures. Faults are problems, such as loops that never terminate or misplaced commas in statements, that developers can see by looking at the code. Failures are problems, such as a system crash or the invocation of the wrong function, that are visible to the user. Thus, faults can exist in programs but never become failures, because the conditions under which a fault becomes a failure are never reached. How do software vulnerabilities fit into this scheme of faults and failures? Is every fault a vulnerability? Is every vulnerability a fault?

17. Consider a program to display on your web site your city's current time and temperature. Who might want to attack your program? What types of harm might they want to cause? What kinds of vulnerabilities might they exploit to cause harm?

18. Consider a program that allows consumers to order products from the web. Who might want to attack the program? What types of harm might they want to cause? What kinds of vulnerabilities might they exploit to cause harm?

19. Consider a program to accept and tabulate votes in an election. Who might want to attack the program? What types of harm might they want to cause? What kinds of vulnerabilities might they exploit to cause harm?

20. Consider a program that allows a surgeon in one city to assist in an operation on a patient in another city via an Internet connection. Who might want to attack the program? What types of harm might they want to cause? What kinds of vulnerabilities might they exploit to cause harm?

21. Computer security failures appear frequently in the daily news. Cite a reported failure that exemplifies one (or more) of the principles listed in this chapter: easiest penetration, adequate protection, effectiveness, weakest link.

2

Elementary Cryptography

In this chapter:

- Concepts of encryption
- Cryptanalysis: how encryption systems are "broken"
- Symmetric (secret key) encryption and the DES and AES algorithms
- Asymmetric (public key) encryption and the RSA algorithm
- Key exchange protocols and certificates
- Digital signatures
- Cryptographic hash functions

Cryptography—secret writing—is the strongest tool for controlling against many kinds of security threats. Well-disguised data cannot be read, modified, or fabricated easily. Cryptography is rooted in higher mathematics: group and field theory, computational complexity, and even real analysis, not to mention probability and statistics. Fortunately, it is not necessary to understand the underlying mathematics to be able to use cryptography.

We begin this chapter by examining what encryption does and how it works. We introduce the basic principles of encryption with two simple encryption methods: substitution and transposition. Next, we explore how they can be expanded and improved to create stronger, more sophisticated protection. Because weak or flawed encryption provides only the illusion of protection, we also look at how encryption can fail. We analyze techniques used to break through the protective scheme and reveal the original text. Three very popular algorithms are in use today: DES, AES, and RSA. We look at them in some detail to see how these and other algorithms can be used as building blocks with protocols and structures to perform other computing tasks, such as signing documents, detecting modification, and exchanging sensitive data.

Chapter 10 offers a deeper analysis of encryption techniques and algorithms, including their mathematical bases, the mechanisms that make them work, and their limitations. Most users of cryptography will never invent their own algorithms, just as most users of electricity do not build their own power generators. Still, deeper knowledge of how cryptography works can help you use it effectively, just as deeper knowledge of energy issues helps you understand the environmental and cost trade-offs among different energy sources. This chapter offers you a rudimentary understanding of what cryptography is; but we encourage you to study the details in Chapter 10 to help you understand the implications of each choice of cryptographic algorithm.

2.1 TERMINOLOGY AND BACKGROUND

Consider the steps involved in sending messages from a sender, *S*, to a recipient, *R*. If *S* entrusts the message to *T*, who then delivers it to *R*, *T* then becomes the **transmission medium.** If an outsider, *O*, wants to access the message (to read, change, or even destroy it), we call *O* an **interceptor** or **intruder.** Any time after *S* transmits it via *T*, the message is vulnerable to exploitation, and *O* might try to access the message in any of the following ways:

- *block* it, by preventing its reaching *R*, thereby affecting the availability of the message
- *intercept* it, by reading or listening to the message, thereby affecting the confidentiality of the message
- *modify* it, by seizing the message and changing it in some way, affecting the message's integrity
- *fabricate* an authentic-looking message, arranging for it to be delivered as if it came from *S*, thereby also affecting the integrity of the message

As you can see, a message's vulnerabilities reflect the four possible security failures we identified in Chapter 1. Fortunately, encryption is a technique that can address all these problems. Encryption, probably the most fundamental building block of secure computing, is a means of maintaining secure data in an insecure environment. (It is not the *only* building block, however.) In this book, we study encryption as a security technique, and we see how it is used in protecting programs, databases, networks, and electronic communications.

Terminology

Encryption is the process of encoding a message so that its meaning is not obvious; **decryption** is the reverse process, transforming an encrypted message back into its normal, original form. Alternatively, the terms **encode** and **decode** or **encipher** and **decipher** are used instead of encrypt and decrypt.[1] That is, we say that we encode, encrypt, or encipher the original message to hide its meaning. Then, we decode, decrypt, or decipher it to reveal the original message. A system for encryption and decryption is called a **cryptosystem.**

The original form of a message is known as **plaintext,** and the encrypted form is called **ciphertext.** This relationship is shown in Figure 2-1. For convenience in expla-

[1] There are slight differences in the meanings of these three pairs of words, although they are not significant in this context. Strictly speaking, **encoding** is the process of translating entire words or phrases to other words or phrases, whereas **enciphering** is translating letters or symbols individually; **encryption** is the group term that covers both encoding and enciphering.

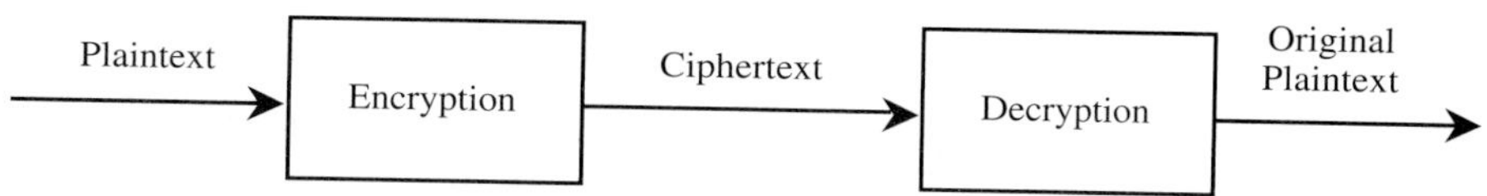

FIGURE 2-1 Encryption.

nation, we denote a plaintext message P as a sequence of individual characters $P = \langle p_1, p_2, \ldots, p_n \rangle$. Similarly, ciphertext is written as $C = \langle c_1, c_2, \ldots, c_m \rangle$. For instance, the plaintext message "I want cookies" can be thought of as the message string $\langle I, \ , w,a,n,t, \ ,c,o,o,k,i,e,s \rangle$. It may be transformed into ciphertext $\langle c_1, c_2, \ldots, c_{14} \rangle$, and the encryption algorithm tells us how the transformation is done.

We use this formal notation to describe the transformations between plaintext and ciphertext. For example, we write $C = E(P)$ and $P = D(C)$, where C represents the ciphertext, E is the encryption rule, P is the plaintext, and D is the decryption rule. What we seek is a cryptosystem for which $P = D(E(P))$. In other words, we want to be able to convert the message to protect it from an intruder, but we also want to be able to get the original message back so that the receiver can read it properly.

Encryption Algorithms

The cryptosystem involves a set of rules for how to encrypt the plaintext and how to decrypt the ciphertext. The encryption and decryption rules, called **algorithms,** often use a device called a **key,** denoted by K, so that the resulting ciphertext depends on the original plaintext message, the algorithm, and the key value. We write this dependence as $C = E(K, P)$. Essentially, E is a *set* of encryption algorithms, and the key K selects one specific algorithm from the set. We see later in this chapter that a cryptosystem such as the Caesar cipher is keyless but that keyed encryptions are more difficult to break.

This process is similar to using mass-produced locks in houses. As a homeowner, it would be very expensive for you to contract with someone to invent and make a lock just for your house. In addition, you would not know whether a particular inventor's lock was really solid or how it compared with those of other inventors. A better solution is to have a few well-known, well-respected companies producing standard locks that differ according to the (physical) key. Then, you and your neighbor might have the same model of lock, but your key will open only your lock. In the same way, it is useful to have a few well-examined encryption algorithms that everyone could use, but the differing keys would prevent someone from breaking into what you are trying to protect.

Sometimes the encryption and decryption keys are the same, so $P = D(K, E(K,P))$. This form is called **symmetric** encryption because D and E are mirror-image processes. At other times, encryption and decryption keys come in pairs. Then, a decryption key, K_D, inverts the encryption of key K_E, so that $P = D(K_D, E(K_E,P))$. Encryption algorithms of this form are called **asymmetric** because converting C back to P involves a series of steps and a key that are different from the steps and key of E. The difference between symmetric and asymmetric encryption is shown in Figure 2-2.

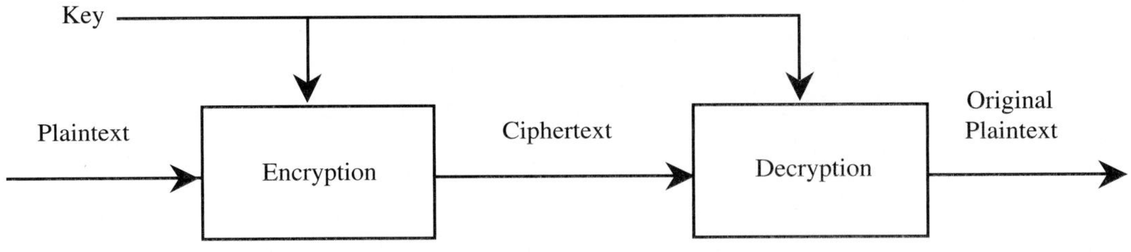

(a) Symmetric Cryptosystem

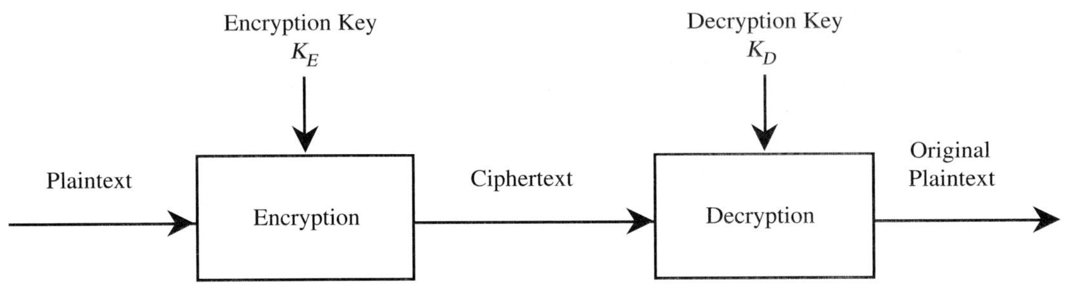

(b) Asymmetric Cryptosystem

FIGURE 2-2 Encryption with Keys.

A key gives us flexibility in using an encryption scheme. We can create different encryptions of one plaintext message just by changing the key. Moreover, using a key provides additional security. If the encryption algorithm should fall into the interceptor's hands, future messages can still be kept secret because the interceptor will not know the key value. An encryption scheme that does not require the use of a key is called a **keyless cipher.**

The history of encryption is fascinating; it is well documented in Kahn's book, [KAH96]. Encryption has been used for centuries to protect diplomatic and military communications, sometimes without full success. The word **cryptography** means hidden writing, and it refers to the practice of using encryption to conceal text. A **cryptanalyst** studies encryption and encrypted messages, hoping to find the hidden meanings. Sidebar 2-1 shows how the hidden meanings can be extracted even without knowledge of all of the encoding, reinforcing the principle of easiest penetration we introduced in Chapter 1!

Both a **cryptographer** and a cryptanalyst attempt to translate coded material back to its original form. Normally, a cryptographer works on behalf of a legitimate sender or receiver, whereas a cryptanalyst works on behalf of an unauthorized interceptor. Finally, **cryptology** is the research into and study of encryption and decryption; it includes both cryptography and cryptanalysis.

Sidebar 2-1 Hidden Meanings Change the Course of World War II

In the spring of 1942, the United States was fighting Japan in the Pacific. American cryptanalysts had cracked some of the Japanese naval codes, but they didn't understand the extra encoding the Japanese used to describe particular sites. A message intercepted by the United States told the Allies' officers that "AF" was to be the target of a major assault. The U.S. Navy suspected that the assault would be on Midway island, but it needed to be sure.

Commander Joseph Rochefort, head of the U.S. Navy's cryptography center at Pearl Harbor, devised a clever plan to unearth the meaning of "AF." He directed the naval group at Midway to send a message, requesting fresh water because the water distillery had been damaged. Soon, the United States intercepted a Japanese message indicating that "AF" was short of water—verifying that "AF" indeed meant Midway! [SEI01]

Cryptanalysis

A cryptanalyst's chore is to **break** an encryption. That is, the cryptanalyst attempts to deduce the original meaning of a ciphertext message. Better yet, he or she hopes to determine which decrypting algorithm matches the encrypting algorithm, so that other messages encoded in the same way can be broken. For instance, suppose two countries are at war and the first country is intercepting the encrypted messages of the second. It is important for the cryptanalysts of the first country to decipher a given message so that the first country can anticipate the movements and resources of the second. But it is even better to discover the actual decryption algorithm; then the first country can easily break the encryption of all messages sent by the second country.

Thus, a cryptanalyst can do any or all of six different things:

- attempt to break a single message
- attempt to recognize patterns in encrypted messages, to be able to break subsequent ones by applying a straightforward decryption algorithm
- attempt to infer some meaning without even breaking the encryption, such as noticing an unusual frequency of communication or determining something by whether the communication was short or long
- attempt to deduce the key, in order to break subsequent messages easily
- attempt to find weaknesses in the implementation or environment of use of encryption
- attempt to find general weaknesses in an encryption algorithm, without necessarily having intercepted any messages

In this book, we see examples of each type of activity.

An analyst works with a variety of pieces of information: encrypted messages, known encryption algorithms, intercepted plaintext, data items known or suspected to be in a ciphertext message, mathematical or statistical tools and techniques, properties of languages, computers, and plenty of ingenuity and luck. Each piece of evidence can provide a clue, and the analyst puts the clues together to try to form a larger picture of a message's meaning in the context of how the encryption is done. Remember that there are no rules. An interceptor can use any means available to tease out the meaning of the message.

Breakable Encryption

An encryption algorithm is called **breakable** when, given enough time and data, an analyst can determine the algorithm. However, an algorithm that is theoretically breakable may in fact be impractical to try to break. To see why, consider a 25-character message that is expressed in just uppercase letters. For a given cipher scheme, there may be 26^{25} (approximately 10^{35}) possible decipherments, so the task is to select the right one out of the 26^{25}. If your computer could perform on the order of 10^{10} operations per second, finding this decipherment would require on the order of 10^{16} seconds, or roughly 10^{11} years. In this case, although we know that theoretically we could generate the solution, determining the deciphering algorithm by examining all possibilities can be ignored as infeasible with current technology.

Two other important issues must be addressed when considering the breakability of encryption algorithms. First, the cryptanalyst cannot be expected to try only the hard, long way. In the example just presented, the obvious decryption might require 26^{25} machine operations, but a more ingenious approach might require only 10^{15} operations. At the speed of 10^{10} operations per second, 10^{15} operations take slightly more than one day. The ingenious approach is certainly feasible. As we see later in this chapter, some of the algorithms we study in this book are based on known "hard" problems that take an unreasonably long time to solve. But the cryptanalyst does not necessarily have to solve the underlying problem to break the encryption of a single message. As we noted in Sidebar 2-1, sloppy use of controls can reveal likely words or phrases, and an analyst can use educated guesses combined with careful analysis to generate all or most of an important message.

Second, estimates of breakability are based on current technology. An enormous advance in computing technology has occurred since 1950. Things that were infeasible in 1940 became possible by the 1950s, and every succeeding decade has brought greater improvements. A conjecture known as "Moore's Law" asserts that the speed of processors doubles every 1.5 years, and this conjecture has been true for over two decades. It is risky to pronounce an algorithm secure just because it cannot be broken with *current* technology, or worse, that it has not been broken yet.

Representing Characters

We want to study ways of encrypting any computer material, whether it is written as ASCII or EBCDIC characters, binary data, object code, or a control stream. However, to simplify the explanations, we begin with the encryption of messages written in the standard 26-letter English[2] alphabet, A through Z.

[2] Because this book is written in English, the explanations refer to English. However, with slight variations, the techniques are applicable to most other written languages as well.

Throughout the book, we use the convention that plaintext is written in UPPERCASE letters, and ciphertext is in lowercase letters. Because most encryption algorithms are based on mathematical transformations, they can be explained or studied more easily in mathematical form. Therefore, in this book, we switch back and forth between letters and the numeric encoding of each letter as shown here.

Letter	A	B	C	D	E	F	G	H	I	J	K	L	M
Code	0	1	2	3	4	5	6	7	8	9	10	11	12
Letter	N	O	P	Q	R	S	T	U	V	W	X	Y	Z
Code	13	14	15	16	17	18	19	20	21	22	23	24	25

Thus, the letter A is represented by a zero, B by a one, and so on. This representation allows us to consider performing arithmetic on the "letters" of a message. That is, we can perform addition and subtraction on letters by adding and subtracting the corresponding code numbers. Expressions such as A + 3 = D or K – 1 = J have their natural interpretation. Arithmetic is performed as if the alphabetic table were circular.[3] In other words, addition wraps around from one end of the table to the other, so that Y + 3 = B. Thus, every result of an arithmetic operation is between 0 and 25.

There are many types of encryption. In the next two sections we look at two simple forms of encryption: **substitutions,** in which one letter is exchanged for another, and **transpositions,** in which the order of the letters is rearranged. The goal of studying these two forms is to become familiar with the concept of encryption and decryption, to learn some of the terminology and methods of cryptanalysis, and to study some of the weaknesses to which encryption is prone. Once we have mastered the simple encryption algorithms, we explore "commercial grade" algorithms used in modern computer applications.

2.2 SUBSTITUTION CIPHERS

Children sometimes devise "secret codes" that use a correspondence table with which to substitute a character or symbol for each character of the original message. This technique is called a **monoalphabetic cipher** or **simple substitution.** A substitution is an acceptable way of encrypting text. In this section, we study several kinds of substitution ciphers.

The Caesar Cipher

The **Caesar cipher** has an important place in history. Julius Caesar is said to have been the first to use this scheme, in which each letter is translated to a letter a fixed number

[3] This form of arithmetic is called **modular arithmetic,** written mod n, which means that any result greater than n is reduced by n as many times as necessary to bring it back into the range $0 \le result < n$. Another way to reduce a result is to use the remainder after dividing the number by n. For example, the value of 95 mod 26 is the remainder of 95/26, which is 17, while 95 – 26 – 26 – 26 = 17; alternatively, starting at position 0 (A) and counting ahead 95 positions (and returning to position 0 each time after passing position 25) also brings us to position 17.

of places after it in the alphabet. Caesar used a shift of 3, so that plaintext letter p_i was enciphered as ciphertext letter c_i by the rule

$$c_i = E(p_i) = p_i + 3$$

A full translation chart of the Caesar cipher is shown here.

Plaintext	A	B	C	D	E	F	G	H	I	J	K	L	M	N	O	P	Q	R	S	T	U	V	W	X	Y	Z
Ciphertext	d	e	f	g	h	i	j	k	l	m	n	o	p	q	r	s	t	u	v	w	x	y	z	a	b	c

Using this encryption, the message

```
TREATY IMPOSSIBLE
```

would be encoded as

```
T R E A T Y   I M P O S S I B L E
w u h d w b   l p s r v v l e o h
```

Advantages and Disadvantages of the Caesar Cipher

Most ciphers, and especially the early ones, had to be easy to perform in the field. In particular, it was dangerous to have the cryptosystem algorithms written down for the soldiers or spies to follow. Any cipher that was so complicated that its algorithm had to be written out was at risk of being revealed if the interceptor caught a sender with the written instructions. Then, the interceptor could readily decode any ciphertext messages intercepted (until the encryption algorithm could be changed). Sidebar 2-2 describes how the British dealt with written codes in World War II.

The Caesar cipher is quite simple. During Caesar's lifetime, the simplicity did not dramatically compromise the safety of the encryption, because anything written, even

Sidebar 2-2 Silken Codes

Marks [MAR98] describes the life of a code-maker in Britain during World War II. That is, the British hired Marks and others to devise codes that could be used by spies and soldiers in the field. In the early days, the encryption scheme depended on poems that were written for each spy and relied on the spy's ability to memorize and recall them correctly.

Marks reduced the risk of error by introducing a coding scheme that was printed on pieces of silk. Silk hidden under clothing could not be felt when the spy was patted down and searched. And, unlike paper, silk burns quickly and completely, so that the spy could destroy the incriminating evidence, also ensuring that the enemy could not get even fragments of the valuable code. When pressed by superiors as to why the British should use valuable silk (which was already needed for war-time necessities like parachutes) for codes, Marks said that it was a choice "between silk and cyanide."

in plaintext, was rather well protected; few people knew how to read! The pattern $p_i + 3$ was easy to memorize and implement. A sender in the field could write out a plaintext and a ciphertext alphabet, encode a message to be sent, and then destroy the paper containing the alphabets.

Its obvious pattern is also the major weakness of the Caesar cipher. A secure encryption should not allow an interceptor to use a small piece of the ciphertext to predict the entire pattern of the encryption.

Cryptanalysis of the Caesar Cipher

Let us take a closer look at the result of applying Caesar's encryption technique to "TREATY IMPOSSIBLE." If we did not know the plaintext and were trying to guess it, we would have many clues from the ciphertext. For example, the break between the two words is preserved in the ciphertext, and double letters are preserved: The SS is translated to vv. We might also notice that when a letter is repeated, it maps again to the same ciphertext as it did previously. So the letters T, I, and E always translate to w, l, and h. These clues make this cipher easy to break.

Suppose you are given the following ciphertext message, and you want to try to determine the original plaintext.

```
wklv phvvdjh lv qrw wrr kdug wr euhdn
```

The message has actually been enciphered with a 27-symbol alphabet: A through Z plus the "blank" character or separator between words.[4] As a start, assume that the coder was lazy and has allowed the blank to be translated to itself. If your assumption is true, it is an exceptional piece of information; knowing where the spaces are allows us to see which are the small words. English has relatively few small words, such as *am*, *is*, *to*, *be*, *he*, *we*, *and*, *are*, *you*, *she*, and so on. Therefore, one way to attack this problem and break the encryption is to substitute known short words at appropriate places in the ciphertext until you have something that seems to be meaningful. Once the small words fall into place, you can try substituting for matching characters at other places in the ciphertext.

Look again at the ciphertext you are decrypting. There is a strong clue in the repeated r of the word wrr. You might use this text to guess at three-letter words that you know. For instance, two very common three-letter words having the pattern *xyy* are *see* and *too*; other less common possibilities are *add*, *odd*, and *off*. (Of course, there are also obscure possibilities like *woo* or *gee*, but it makes more sense to try the common cases first.) Moreover, the combination wr appears in the ciphertext, too, so you can determine whether the first two letters of the three-letter word also form a two-letter word.

[4] In fact, in most encryption schemes, spaces between words often are deleted, under the assumption that a legitimate receiver can breakmostmessagesintowordsfairlyeasily. For ease of writing and decoding, messages are then arbitrarily broken into blocks of a uniform size, such as every five characters, so that there is no significance to the places where the message is broken.

For instance, if `wrr` is `SEE`, `wr` would have to be `SE`, which is unlikely. However, if `wrr` is `TOO`, `wr` would be `TO`, which is quite reasonable. Substituting `T` for `w` and `O` for `r`, the message becomes

```
wklv phvvdjh lv qrw wrr kdug wr euhdn
T--- ------- -- -OT TOO ---- TO -----
```

The `-OT` could be *cot, dot, got, hot, lot, not, pot, rot,* or *tot;* a likely choice is *not.* Unfortunately, `q` = `N` does not give any more clues because `q` appears only once in this sample.

The word `lv` is also the end of the word `wklv`, which probably starts with `T`. Likely two-letter words that can also end a longer word include *so, is, in,* etc. However, *so* is unlikely because the form `T-SO` is not recognizable; `IN` is ruled out because of the previous assumption that `q` is `N`. A more promising alternative is to substitute `IS` for `lv` throughout, and continue to analyze the message in that way.

By now, you might notice that the ciphertext letters uncovered are just three positions away from their plaintext counterparts. You (and any experienced cryptanalyst) might try that same pattern on all the unmatched ciphertext. The completion of this decryption is left as an exercise.

The cryptanalysis described here is ad hoc, using deduction based on guesses instead of solid principles. But you can take a more methodical approach, considering which letters commonly start words, which letters commonly end words, and which prefixes and suffixes are common. Cryptanalysts have compiled lists of common prefixes, common suffixes, and words having particular patterns. (For example, *sleeps* is a word that follows the pattern *abccda.*) In the next section, we look at a different analysis technique.

Other Substitutions

In substitutions, the alphabet is scrambled, and each plaintext letter maps to a unique ciphertext letter. We can describe this technique in a more mathematical way. Formally, we say that a **permutation** is a reordering of the elements of a sequence. For instance, we can permute the numbers l to 10 in many ways, including the permutations π_1 = 1, 3, 5, 7, 9, 10, 8, 6, 4, 2; and π_2 = 10, 9, 8, 7, 6, 5, 4, 3, 2, 1. A permutation is a function, so we can write expressions such as $\pi_1(3) = 5$ meaning that the letter in position 3 is to be replaced by the fifth letter. If the set is the first ten letters of the alphabet, $\pi_1(3) = 5$ means that `c` is transformed into `E`.

One way to scramble an alphabet is to use a **key,** a word that controls the permutation. For instance, if the key is `word`, the sender or receiver first writes the alphabet and then writes the key under the first few letters of the alphabet.

```
ABCDEFGHIJKLMNOPQRSTUVWXYZ
word
```

The sender or receiver then fills in the remaining letters of the alphabet, in some easy-to-remember order, after the keyword.

```
ABCDEFGHIJKLMNOPQRSTUVWXYZ
wordabcefghijklmnpqstuvxyz
```

In this example, the key is short, so most plaintext letters are only one or two positions off from their ciphertext equivalents. With a longer keyword, the distance is greater and less predictable, as shown below. Because π must map one plaintext letter to exactly one ciphertext letter, duplicate letters in a keyword, such as the second `s` and `o` in `professional`, are dropped.

```
ABCDEFGHIJKLMNOPQRSTUVWXYZ
profesinalbcdghjkmqtuvwxyz
```

Notice that near the end of the alphabet replacements are rather close, and the last seven characters map to themselves. Conveniently, the last characters of the alphabet are among the least frequently used, so this vulnerability would give little help to an interceptor.

Still, since regularity helps an interceptor, it is more desirable to have a less regular rearrangement of the letters. One possibility is to count by threes (or fives or sevens or nines) and rearrange the letters in that order. For example, one encryption uses a table that starts with

```
ABCDEFGHIJKLMNOPQRSTUVWXYZ
adgj
```

using every third letter. At the end of the alphabet, the pattern continues mod 26, as shown below.

```
ABCDEFGHIJKLMNOPQRSTUVWXYZ
adgjmpsvybehknqtwzcfilorux
```

There are many other examples of substitution ciphers. For instance, Sidebar 2-3 describes a substitution cipher called a poem code, used in the early days of World War II by British spies to keep the Germans from reading their messages.

Sidebar 2-3 Poem Codes

During World War II, the British Special Operations Executive (SOE) produced codes to be used by spies in hostile territory. The SOE devised poem codes for use in encrypting and decrypting messages. For security reasons, each message had to be at least 200 letters long.

To encode a message, an agent chose five words at random from his or her poem, and then assigned a number to each letter of these words. The numbers were the basis for the encryption. To let the Home Station know which five words were chosen, the words were inserted at the beginning of the message. However, using familiar poems created a huge vulnerability. For example, if the German agents knew the British national anthem, then they might guess the poem from fewer than five words. As Marks explains, if the words included "'our,' 'gracious,' 'him,' 'victorious,' 'send,' then God save the agent." [MAR98]

For this reason, Leo Marks' job at SOE was to devise original poems, so that "no reference books would be of the slightest help" in tracing the poems and the messages.

Complexity of Substitution Encryption and Decryption

An important issue in using any cryptosystem is the time it takes to turn plaintext into ciphertext, and vice versa. Especially in the field (when encryption is used by spies or decryption is attempted by soldiers), it is essential that the scrambling and unscrambling do not deter the authorized parties from completing their missions. The timing is directly related to the complexity of the encryption algorithm. For example, encryption and decryption with substitution ciphers can be performed by direct lookup in a table illustrating the correspondence, like the ones shown in our examples. Transforming a single character can be done in a constant amount of time, so we express the complexity of the algorithm by saying that the time to encrypt a message of n characters is proportional to n. One way of thinking of this expression is that if one message is twice as long as another, it will take twice as long to encrypt.

Cryptanalysis of Substitution Ciphers

The techniques described for breaking the Caesar cipher can also be used on other substitution ciphers. Short words, words with repeated patterns, and common initial and final letters all give clues for guessing the permutation.

Of course, breaking the code is a lot like working a crossword puzzle: You try a guess and continue to work to substantiate that guess until you have all the words in place or until you reach a contradiction. For a long message, this process can be extremely tedious. Fortunately, there are other approaches to breaking an encryption. In fact, analysts apply every technique at their disposal, using a combination of guess, strategy, and mathematical skill.

Cryptanalysts may attempt to decipher a particular message at hand, or they may try to determine the encryption algorithm that generated the ciphertext in the first place (so that future messages can be broken easily). One approach is to try to reverse the difficulty introduced by the encryption.

To see why, consider the difficulty of breaking a substitution cipher. At face value, such encryption techniques seem secure because there are 26! possible different encipherments. We know this because we have 26 choices of letter to substitute for the `a`, then 25 (all but the one chosen for `a`) for `b`, 24 (all but the ones chosen for `a` and `b`) for `c`, and so on, to yield $26 * 25 * 24 * \ldots * 2 * 1 = 26!$ possibilities. By using a brute force attack, the cryptanalyst could try all 26! permutations of a particular ciphertext message. Working at one permutation per microsecond (assuming the cryptanalyst had the patience to review the probable-looking plaintexts produced by some of the permutations), it would still take over a thousand years to test all 26! possibilities.

We can use our knowledge of language to simplify this problem. For example, in English, some letters are used more often than others. The letters *E, T, O,* and *A* occur far more often than *J, Q, X,* and *Z,* for example. Thus, the frequency with which certain letters are used can help us to break the code more quickly. We can also recognize that the nature and context of the text being analyzed affect the distribution. For instance, in a medical article in which the term *x-ray* was used often, the letter *x* would have an uncommonly high frequency.

When messages are long enough, the frequency distribution analysis quickly betrays many of the letters of the plaintext. In this and other ways, a good cryptanalyst finds approaches for bypassing hard problems. An encryption based on a hard problem is not secure just because of the difficulty of the problem.

How difficult is it to break substitutions? With a little help from frequency distributions and letter patterns, you can probably break a substitution cipher by hand. It follows that, with the aid of computer programs and with an adequate amount of ciphertext, a good cryptanalyst can break such a cipher in an hour. Even an untrained but diligent interceptor could probably determine the plaintext in a day or so. Nevertheless, in some applications, the prospect of one day's effort, or even the appearance of a sheet full of text that makes no sense, may be enough to protect the message. Encryption, even in a simple form, will deter the casual observer.

The Cryptographer's Dilemma

As with many analysis techniques, having very little ciphertext inhibits the effectiveness of a technique being used to break an encryption. A cryptanalyst works by finding patterns. Short messages give the cryptanalyst little to work with, so short messages are fairly secure with even simple encryption.

Substitutions highlight the cryptologist's dilemma: An encryption algorithm must be regular for it to be algorithmic and for cryptographers to be able to remember it. Unfortunately, the regularity gives clues to the cryptanalyst.

There is no solution to this dilemma. In fact, cryptography and cryptanalysis at times seem together like a dog chasing its tail. First, the cryptographer invents a new encryption algorithm to protect a message. Then, the cryptanalyst studies the algorithm, finding its patterns and weaknesses. The cryptographer then sets out to try to secure messages by inventing a new algorithm, and then the cryptanalyst has a go at it. It is here that the principle of timeliness from Chapter 1 applies; a security measure must be strong enough to keep out the attacker only for the life of the data. Data with a short time value can be protected with simple measures.

One-Time Pads

A **one-time pad** is sometimes considered the perfect cipher. The name comes from an encryption method in which a large, nonrepeating set of keys is written on sheets of paper, glued together into a pad. For example, if the keys are 20 characters long and a sender must transmit a message 300 characters in length, the sender would tear off the next 15 pages of keys. The sender would write the keys one at a time above the letters of the plaintext and encipher the plaintext with a prearranged chart (called a **Vigenère tableau**) that has all 26 letters in each column, in some scrambled order. The sender would then destroy the used keys.

For the encryption to work, the receiver needs a pad identical to that of the sender. Upon receiving a message, the receiver takes the appropriate number of keys and deciphers the message as if it were a plain substitution with a long key. Essentially, this algorithm gives the effect of a key as long as the number of characters in the pad.

The one-time pad method has two problems: the need for absolute synchronization between sender and receiver, and the need for an unlimited number of keys. Although generating a large number of random keys is no problem, printing, distributing, storing, and accounting for such keys are problems.

Long Random Number Sequences

A close approximation of a one-time pad for use on computers is a random number generator. In fact, computer random numbers are not random; they really form a sequence with a very long period (that is, they go for a long time before repeating the sequence). In practice, a generator with a long period can be acceptable for a limited amount of time or plaintext.

To use a random number generator, the sender with a 300-character message would interrogate the computer for the next 300 random numbers, scale them to lie between 0 and 25, and use one number to encipher each character of the plaintext message.

The Vernam Cipher

The **Vernam Cipher** is a type of one-time pad devised by Gilbert Vernam for AT&T. The Vernam cipher is immune to most cryptanalytic attacks. The basic encryption involves an arbitrarily long nonrepeating sequence of numbers that are combined with the plaintext. Vernam's invention used an arbitrarily long punched paper tape that fed into a teletype machine. The tape contained random numbers that were combined with characters typed into the teletype. The sequence of random numbers had no repeats, and each tape was used only once. As long as the key tape does not repeat or is not reused, this type of cipher is immune to cryptanalytic attack because the available ciphertext does not display the pattern of the key. A model of this process is shown in Figure 2-3.

To see how this method works, we perform a simple Vernam encryption. Assume that the alphabetic letters correspond to their counterparts in arithmetic notation mod 26. That is, the letters are represented with numbers 0 through 25. To use the Vernam cipher, we sum this numerical representation with a stream of random two-digit numbers. For instance, if the message is

```
VERNAM CIPHER
```

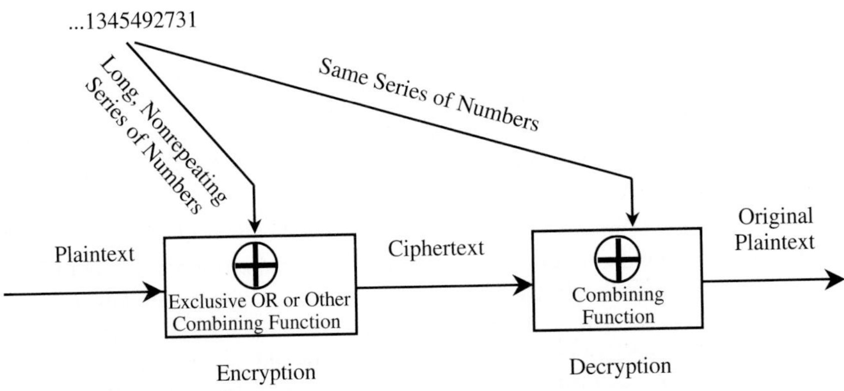

FIGURE 2-3 Vernam Cipher.

the letters would first be converted to their numeric equivalents, as shown here.

```
V   E   R   N   A   M   C   I   P   H   E   R
21  4   17  13  0   12  2   8   15  7   4   17
```

Next, we must generate random numbers to combine with the letter codes. Suppose the following series of random two-digit numbers is generated.

```
76 48 16 82 44 03 58 11 60 05 48 88
```

The encoded form of the message is the sum mod 26 of each coded letter with the corresponding random number. The result is then encoded in the usual base-26 alphabet representation.

Plaintext	V	E	R	N	A	M	C	I	P	H	E	R
Numeric Equivalent	21	4	17	13	0	12	2	8	15	7	4	17
+ Random Number	76	48	16	82	44	3	58	11	60	5	48	88
= Sum	97	52	33	95	44	15	60	19	75	12	52	105
= mod 26	19	0	7	17	18	15	8	19	23	12	0	1
Ciphertext	t	a	h	r	s	p	i	t	x	m	a	b

Thus, the message

```
VERNAM CIPHER
```

is encoded as

```
tahrsp itxmab
```

In this example, the repeated random number 48 happened to fall at the places of repeated letters, accounting for the repeated ciphertext letter a; such a repetition is highly unlikely. The repeated letter t comes from different plaintext letters, a much more likely occurrence. Duplicate ciphertext letters are generally unrelated when this encryption algorithm is used.

Book Ciphers

Another source of supposedly "random" numbers is any book, piece of music, or other object with which the structure can be analyzed. Both the sender and receiver need access to identical objects. For example, a possible one-time pad can be based on a telephone book. The sender and receiver might agree to start at page 35 and use two middle digits (*ddd-DDdd*) of each seven-digit phone number, mod 26, as a key letter for a substitution cipher. They use an already agree-on table (a Vigenère tableau) that has all 26 letters in each column, in some scrambled order.

Any book can provide a key. The key is formed from the letters of the text, in order. This type of encryption was the basis for Ken Follett's novel, *The Key to Rebecca*, in which Daphne du Maurier's famous thriller acted as the source of keys for spies in World War II. Were the sender and receiver known to be using a popular book, such as

The Key to Rebecca, the bible, or *Security in Computing*, it would be easier for the cryptanalyst to try books against the ciphertext, rather than look for patterns and use sophisticated tools.

As an example of a book cipher, you might select a passage from Descarte's meditation: *What of thinking? I am, I exist, that is certain.* The meditation goes on for great length, certainly long enough to encipher many very long messages. To encipher the message *MACHINES CANNOT THINK* by using the Descartes key, you would write the message under enough of the key and encode the message by selecting the substitution in row p_i, column k_i.

```
iamie xistt hatis cert
MACHI NESCA NNOTT HINK
```

If we use the substitution table shown as Table 2-1, this message would be encrypted as `uaopm kmkvt unhbl jmed` because row **M** column ***i*** is `u`, row **A** column ***a*** is `a`, and so on.

It would seem as though this cipher, too, would be impossible to break. Unfortunately, that is not true. The flaw lies in the fact that neither the message nor the key text is evenly distributed; in fact, the distributions of both cluster around high-frequency letters. For example, the four letters *A, E, O,* and *T* account for approximately 40 percent of all letters used in standard English text. Each ciphertext letter is really the intersection of a plaintext letter and a key letter. But if the probability of the plaintext or the key letter's being *A, E, O,* or *T* is 0.4, the probability of *both* being one of the four is $0.4 * 0.4 = 0.16$, or nearly one in six. Using the top six letters (adding *N* and *I*) increases the sum of the frequencies to 50 percent and thus increases the probability for a pair to 0.25, or one in four.

We look for frequent letter pairs that could have generated each ciphertext letter. The encrypted version of the message *MACHINES CANNOT THINK* is

```
uaopm kmkvt unhbl jmed
```

To break the cipher, assume that each letter of the ciphertext comes from a situation in which the plaintext letter (row selector) and the key letter (column selector) are both one of the six most frequent letters. (As we calculated above, this guess will be correct approximately 25 percent of the time.) The trick is to work the cipher inside out. For a ciphertext letter, look in the body of the table for the letter to appear at the intersection of one of the six rows with one of the six columns. Find combinations in the Vigenère tableau that could yield each ciphertext letter as the result of two high-frequency letters.

Searching through this table for possibilities, we transform the cryptogram.

```
Ciphertext   u a o p m   k m k v t   u n h b l   j m e d
Possible     ? A A ? E   ? E ? ? A   ? A N N ?   ? E A ?
plaintexts       O   I     I     T     N T T       I E
                     T     T                       T
```

This technique does not reveal the entire message, or even enough of it to make the message `MACHI NESCA NNOTT HINK` easy to identify. The technique did, how-

TABLE 2-1 Vigenère Tableau.

	0					5					10					15					20					25	
	a	*b*	*c*	*d*	*e*	*f*	*g*	*h*	*i*	*j*	*k*	*l*	*m*	*n*	*o*	*p*	*q*	*r*	*s*	*t*	*u*	*v*	*w*	*x*	*y*	*z*	*π*
A	a	b	c	d	e	f	g	h	i	j	k	l	m	n	o	p	q	r	s	t	u	v	w	x	y	z	0
B	b	c	d	e	f	g	h	i	j	k	l	m	n	o	p	q	r	s	t	u	v	w	x	y	z	a	1
C	c	d	e	f	g	h	i	j	k	l	m	n	o	p	q	r	s	t	u	v	w	x	y	z	a	b	2
D	d	e	f	g	h	i	j	k	l	m	n	o	p	q	r	s	t	u	v	w	x	y	z	a	b	c	3
E	e	f	g	h	i	j	k	l	m	n	o	p	q	r	s	t	u	v	w	x	y	z	a	b	c	d	4
F	f	g	h	i	j	k	l	m	n	o	p	q	r	s	t	u	v	w	x	y	z	a	b	c	d	e	5
G	g	h	i	j	k	l	m	n	o	p	q	r	s	t	u	v	w	x	y	z	a	b	c	d	e	f	6
H	h	i	j	k	l	m	n	o	p	q	r	s	t	u	v	w	x	y	z	a	b	c	d	e	f	g	7
I	i	j	k	l	m	n	o	p	q	r	s	t	u	v	w	x	y	z	a	b	c	d	e	f	g	h	8
J	j	k	l	m	n	o	p	q	r	s	t	u	v	w	x	y	z	a	b	c	d	e	f	g	h	i	9
K	k	l	m	n	o	p	q	r	s	t	u	v	w	x	y	z	a	b	c	d	e	f	g	h	i	j	10
L	l	m	n	o	p	q	r	s	t	u	v	w	x	y	z	a	b	c	d	e	f	g	h	i	j	k	11
M	m	n	o	p	q	r	s	t	u	v	w	x	y	z	a	b	c	d	e	f	g	h	i	j	k	l	12
N	n	o	p	q	r	s	t	u	v	w	x	y	z	a	b	c	d	e	f	g	h	i	j	k	l	m	13
O	o	p	q	r	s	t	u	v	w	x	y	z	a	b	c	d	e	f	g	h	i	j	k	l	m	n	14
P	p	q	r	s	t	u	v	w	x	y	z	a	b	c	d	e	f	g	h	i	j	k	l	m	n	o	15
Q	q	r	s	t	u	v	w	x	y	z	a	b	c	d	e	f	g	h	i	j	k	l	m	n	o	p	16
R	r	s	t	u	v	w	x	y	z	a	b	c	d	e	f	g	h	i	j	k	l	m	n	o	p	q	17
S	s	t	u	v	w	x	y	z	a	b	c	d	e	f	g	h	i	j	k	l	m	n	o	p	q	r	18
T	t	u	v	w	x	y	z	a	b	c	d	e	f	g	h	i	j	k	l	m	n	o	p	q	r	s	19
U	u	v	w	x	y	z	a	b	c	d	e	f	g	h	i	j	k	l	m	n	o	p	q	r	s	t	20
V	v	w	x	y	z	a	b	c	d	e	f	g	h	i	j	k	l	m	n	o	p	q	r	s	t	u	21
W	w	x	y	z	a	b	c	d	e	f	g	h	i	j	k	l	m	n	o	p	q	r	s	t	u	v	22
X	x	y	z	a	b	c	d	e	f	g	h	i	j	k	l	m	n	o	p	q	r	s	t	u	v	w	23
Y	y	z	a	b	c	d	e	f	g	h	i	j	k	l	m	n	o	p	q	r	s	t	u	v	w	x	24
Z	z	a	b	c	d	e	f	g	h	i	j	k	l	m	n	o	p	q	r	s	t	u	v	w	x	y	25

ever, make predictions in ten letter positions, and there was a correct prediction in seven of those ten positions. (The correct predictions are shown in **bold** type.) The algorithm made 20 assertions about probable letters, and seven of those 20 were correct. (A score of 7 out of 20 is 35 percent, even better than the 25 percent expected.) The algorithm does not come close to solving the cryptogram, but it substantially reduces the 26^{19} possibilities for the analyst to consider. Giving this much help to the cryptanalyst is significant. A similar technique can be used even if the order of the rows is permuted.

Summary of Substitutions

Substitutions are effective cryptographic devices. In fact, they were the basis of many cryptographic algorithms used for diplomatic communication through the first half of the twentieth century. Because they are interesting and intriguing, they show up in mysteries by Arthur Conan Doyle, Edgar Allan Poe, Agatha Christie, Ken Follett, and others.

But substitution is not the only kind of encryption technique. In the next section, we introduce the other basic cryptographic invention: the transposition (permutation). Substitutions and permutations together form a basis for some widely used commercial-grade encryption algorithms that we discuss later in this chapter.

2.3 TRANSPOSITIONS (PERMUTATIONS)

The goal of substitution is *confusion*; the encryption method is an attempt to make it difficult for a cryptanalyst or intruder to determine how a message and key were transformed into ciphertext. In this section, we look at a different kind of scrambling with the similar goal. A **transposition** is an encryption in which the letters of the message are rearranged. With transposition, the cryptography aims for *diffusion*, widely spreading the information from the message or the key across the ciphertext. Transpositions try to break established patterns. Because a transposition is a rearrangement of the symbols of a message, it is also known as a **permutation.**

Columnar Transpositions

As with substitutions, we begin this study of transpositions by examining a simple example. The **columnar transposition** is a rearrangement of the characters of the plaintext into columns.

The following set of characters is a five-column transposition. The plaintext characters are written in rows of five and arranged one row after another, as shown here.

$$
\begin{array}{lllll}
c_1 & c_2 & c_3 & c_4 & c_5 \\
c_6 & c_7 & c_8 & c_9 & c_{10} \\
c_{11} & c_{12} & \text{etc.} & &
\end{array}
$$

You form the resulting ciphertext by reading down the columns, as shown in Figure 2-4.

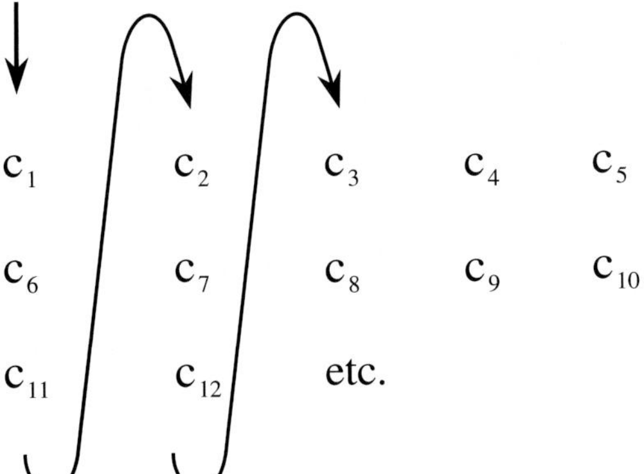

FIGURE 2-4 Columnar Transposition.

For instance, suppose you want to write the plaintext message `THIS IS A MESSAGE TO SHOW HOW A COLUMNAR TRANSPOSITION WORKS`. We arrange the letters in five columns as

```
T H I S I
S A M E S
S A G E T
O S H O W
H O W A C
O L U M N
A R T R A
N S P O S
I T I O N
W O R K S
```

The resulting ciphertext would then be read down the columns as

```
tssoh oaniw haaso lrsto imghw
utpir seeoa mrook istwc nasns
```

In this example, the length of this message happens to be a multiple of five, so all columns are the same length. However, if the message length is not a multiple of the length of a row, the last columns will be one or more letters short. When this happens, we sometimes use an infrequent letter such as `X` to fill in any short columns.

Encipherment/Decipherment Complexity

This cipher involves no additional work beyond arranging the letters and reading them off again. Therefore, the algorithm requires a constant amount of work per character, and the time needed to apply the algorithm is proportional to the length of the message.

However, we must also consider the amount of space needed to record or store the ciphertext. So far, the other ciphers we have seen require only a constant amount of space (admittedly up to 26^2 locations). But the columnar transposition algorithm requires storage for all characters of the message, so the space required is not constant; it depends directly on the length of the message.

Furthermore, we cannot produce output characters until all the message's characters have been read. This restriction occurs because all characters must be entered in the first column before output of the second column can begin, but the first column is not complete until all characters have been read. Thus, the delay associated with this algorithm also depends on the length of the message, as opposed to the constant delay we have seen in previous algorithms.

Because of the storage space needed and the delay involved in decrypting the ciphertext, this algorithm is not especially appropriate for long messages when time is of the essence.

Digrams, Trigrams, and Other Patterns

Just as there are characteristic letter frequencies, there are also characteristic patterns of pairs of adjacent letters, called **digrams.** Letter pairs such as *-re-*, *-th-*, *-en-*, and *-ed-* appear very frequently. Table 2-2 lists the ten most common digrams and **trigrams** (groups of three letters) in English. (They are shown with the most frequent ones first.)

It is also useful to know which pairs and triples do not occur often in English, because that information helps us eliminate possibilities when decrypting a message. For instance, digram combinations such as *-vk-* and *-qp-* occur very infrequently. (The infrequent combinations can occur in acronyms, in foreign words or names, or across word boundaries.) The frequency of appearance of letter groups can be used to match up plaintext letters that have been separated in a ciphertext.

Cryptanalysis by Digram Analysis

Suppose we want to decrypt a message that has used a columnar transposition for its encryption algorithm. The basic attack on columnar transpositions is not as precise as the attack on substitution ciphers. Even though transpositions look less secure than

TABLE 2-2 Most Common English Digrams and Trigrams.

Digrams	Trigrams
EN	ENT
RE	ION
ER	AND
NT	ING
TH	IVE
ON	TIO
IN	FOR
TF	OUR
AN	THI
OR	ONE

substitutions, they can in fact be more secure. Transpositions leave the plaintext letters intact, so the work for the cryptanalyst is more exhausting; more relies on a human's judgment of what "looks right."

The first step in analyzing the transposition is computing the letter frequencies. If we find that in fact all letters appear with their normal frequencies, we can infer that a transposition has been performed. Given a string of text, the trick then is to break it into columns.

Two different strings of letters from a transposition ciphertext can represent pairs of adjacent letters from the plaintext. The problem is to find where in the ciphertext a pair of adjacent columns lies and where the ends of the columns are.

We must do an exhaustive comparison of strings of ciphertext. The process compares a block of ciphertext characters against characters successively farther away in the ciphertext. To see how this works, imagine a moving window that locates a block of characters for checking. Assume the block being compared is seven characters. The first comparison is c_1 to c_8, c_2 to c_9, ..., c_7 to c_{14}. Then, we try a distance of eight characters, and so the window of comparison shifts, and c_1 is compared to c_9, c_2 to c_{10}, and continuing. For a block of nine characters, the window shifts again to c_1 against c_{10} and so forth. This process is shown in Figure 2-5.

For each window position, we ask two questions. First, do common digrams appear, and second, do most of the digrams look reasonable? When digrams indicate a possible match for a fragment of ciphertext, the next step is to try to extend the match. The distance between c_1 and c_{k+1} implies that another column might begin k positions later (because the distance is k). If c_i and c_{i+k} match, so also should c_{i+k} and c_{i+2k}, etc. To test that theory, c_k is checked against c_{2k}, and so on.

Combinations of Approaches

Substitution and transposition can be considered as building blocks for encryption. Other techniques can be based on each of them, both of them, or a combination with yet another approach. For instance, Sidebar 2-4 describes how substitution can be combined with a one-time pad. Keep in mind as you read about encryption that each technique is only one piece of the larger puzzle. Just as you may have a locked car inside a locked garage, you may also combine various approaches to encryption to strengthen the overall security of your system.

A combination of two ciphers is called a **product cipher**. Product ciphers are typically performed one after another, as in $E_2(E_1(P,k_1), k_2)$. Just because you apply two ciphers does not necessarily mean the result is any stronger than, or even as strong as, either individual cipher.

2.4 MAKING "GOOD" ENCRYPTION ALGORITHMS

So far, the encryption algorithms we have seen have been trivial, intended primarily to demonstrate the concepts of substitution and permutation. At the same time, we have examined several approaches cryptanalysts use to attack encryption algorithms. Now

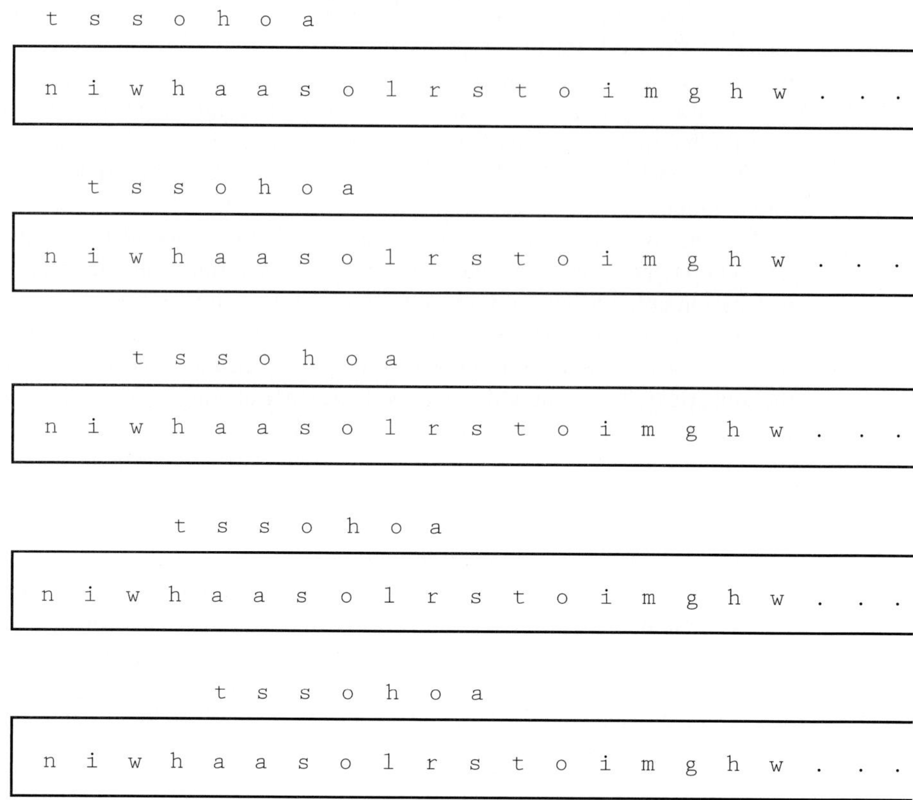

FIGURE 2-5 Moving Comparisons.

we examine algorithms that are widely used in the commercial world. Unlike the previous sections, this section does not delve deeply into the details either of the inner workings of an algorithm or its cryptanalysis. (We save that investigation for Chapter 10.)

What Makes a "Secure" Encryption Algorithm?

There are many kinds of encryption, including many techniques beyond those we discuss in this book. Suppose you have text to encrypt. How do you choose an encryption algorithm for a particular application? To answer this question, reconsider what we have learned so far about encryption. We looked at two broad classes of algorithms: substitutions and transpositions. Substitutions "hide" the letters of the plaintext, and multiple substitutions dissipate high letter frequencies to make it harder to determine how the substitution is done. By contrast, transpositions scramble text so that adjacent-character analysis fails.

Sidebar 2-4 Soviet Encryption During World War II

Kahn [KAH96] describes a system that the Soviet Union thought unbreakable during World War II. It combined substitution with a one-time pad. The basic idea was to diffuse high-frequency letters by mapping them to single digits. This approach kept the length of cryptograms small and thus reduced the on-air time as the message was transmitted.

To see how the encryption worked, consider the eight most common letters of the English language: ASINTOER, arranged as in "a sin to er(r)" to make them easy to remember. These letters were assigned to single digits, 0 to 7. To encode a message, an analyst would begin by selecting a keyword that became the first row of a matrix. Then, the remaining letters of the alphabet were listed in rows underneath, as shown below. Moving vertically through the matrix, the digits 0 to 7 were assigned to the eight common letters, and then the two-digit groups from 80 to 99 were mapped to the remaining letters of the alphabet plus any symbols. In our example, the keyword is SUNDAY:

```
S   U   N   D   A   Y
0   83  2   90  6   97
B   C   E   F   G   H
80  84  3   91  94  98
I   J   K   L   M   O
1   85  88  92  95  7
P   Q   R   T   V   W
81  86  4   5   96  99
X   Z   .   /
82  87  89  93
```

Then the message "whereis/456/airborne" would be encoded as

```
w  h  e r e i s /  4  5  6  /  a i
99 98 3 4 3 1 0 93 44 55 66 93 6 1

r b  o r n e
4 80 7 4 2 3
```

or 99983431 09344556 69361480 7423. (Digits of plaintext numbers were repeated.) Finally, the numerical message was encrypted with a one-time pad from a common reference book with numerical tables—one that would not arouse suspicion, such as a navigator's book of tables.

For each type of encryption we considered, we described the advantages and disadvantages. But there is a broader question: What does it mean for a cipher to be "good"? The meaning of *good* depends on the intended use of the cipher. A cipher to be used by military personnel in the field has different requirements from one to be used in a secure installation with substantial computer support. In this section, we look more closely at the different characteristics of ciphers.

Shannon's Characteristics of "Good" Ciphers

In 1949, Claude Shannon [SHA49] proposed several characteristics that identify a good cipher.

1. The amount of secrecy needed should determine the amount of labor appropriate for the encryption and decryption.

Principle 1 is a reiteration of the principle of timeliness from Chapter 1 and of the earlier observation that even a simple cipher may be strong enough to deter the casual interceptor or to hold off any interceptor for a short time.

2. The set of keys and the enciphering algorithm should be free from complexity.

This principle implies that we should restrict neither the choice of keys nor the types of plaintext on which the algorithm can work. For instance, an algorithm that works only on plaintext having an equal number of As and Es is useless. Similarly, it would be difficult to select keys such that the sum of the values of the letters of the key is a prime number. Restrictions such as these make the use of the encipherment prohibitively complex. If the process is too complex, it will not be used. Furthermore, the key must be transmitted, stored, and remembered, so it must be short.

3. The implementation of the process should be as simple as possible.

Principle 3 was formulated with hand implementation in mind: A complicated algorithm is prone to error or likely to be forgotten. With the development and popularity of digital computers, algorithms far too complex for hand implementation became feasible. Still, the issue of complexity is important. People will avoid an encryption algorithm whose implementation process severely hinders message transmission, thereby undermining security. And a complex algorithm is more likely to be programmed incorrectly.

4. Errors in ciphering should not propagate and cause corruption of further information in the message.

Principle 4 acknowledges that humans make errors in their use of enciphering algorithms. One error early in the process should not throw off the entire remaining ciphertext. For example, dropping one letter in a columnar transposition throws off the entire remaining encipherment. Unless the receiver can guess where the letter was dropped, the remainder of the message will be unintelligible. By contrast, reading the wrong row or column for a polyalphabetic substitution affects only one character—remaining characters are unaffected.

5. The size of the enciphered text should be no larger than the text of the original message.

The idea behind principle 5 is that a ciphertext that expands dramatically in size cannot possibly carry more information than the plaintext, yet it gives the cryptanalyst more data from which to infer a pattern. Furthermore, a longer ciphertext implies more space for storage and more time to communicate.

These principles were developed before the ready availability of digital computers, even though Shannon was aware of computers and the computational power they represented. Thus, some of the concerns he expressed about hand implementation are not really limitations on computer-based implementation. For example, a cipher's implementation on a computer need not be simple, as long as the time complexity of the implementation is tolerable.

Properties of "Trustworthy" Encryption Systems

Commercial users have several requirements that must be satisfied when they select an encryption algorithm. Thus, when we say that encryption is "commercial grade," we mean that it meets these constraints:

- *It is based on sound mathematics.* Good cryptographic algorithms are not just invented; they are derived from solid principles.
- *It has been analyzed by competent experts and found to be sound.* Even the best cryptographic experts can think of only so many possible attacks, and the developers may become too convinced of the strength of their own algorithm. Thus, a review by critical outside experts is essential.
- *It has stood the "test of time."* As a new algorithm gains popularity, people continue to review both its mathematical foundations and the way it builds upon those foundations. Although a long period of successful use and analysis is not a guarantee of a good algorithm, the flaws in many algorithms are discovered relatively soon after their release.

Three algorithms are popular in the commercial world: DES (data encryption standard), RSA (Rivest–Shamir–Adelman, named after the inventors), and AES (advanced encryption standard). The DES and RSA algorithms (as well as others) meet our criteria for commercial-grade encryption; AES, which is quite new, meets the first two and is starting to achieve widespread adoption.

Symmetric and Asymmetric Encryption Systems

Recall that the two basic kinds of encryptions are symmetric (also called "secret key") and asymmetric (also called "public key"). Symmetric algorithms use one key, which works for both encryption and decryption. Usually, the decryption algorithm is closely related to the encryption one. (For example, the Caesar cipher with a shift of 3 uses the encryption algorithm "substitute the character three letters later in the alphabet" with the decryption "substitute the character three letters earlier in the alphabet.")

The symmetric systems provide a two-way channel to their users: A and B share a secret key, and they can both encrypt information to send to the other as well as decrypt information from the other. As long as the key remains secret, the system also provides **authentication,** proof that a message received was not fabricated by someone other than the declared sender. Authenticity is ensured because only the legitimate sender can produce a message that will decrypt properly with the shared key.

The symmetry of this situation is a major advantage of this type of encryption, but it also leads to a problem: key distribution. How do A and B obtain their shared secret key? And only A and B can use that key for their encrypted communications. If A wants to share encrypted communication with another user C, A and C need a different shared key. Key distribution is the major difficulty in using symmetric encryption. In general, n users who want to communicate in pairs need $n * (n - 1)/2$ keys. In other words, the number of keys needed increases at a rate proportional to the *square* of the number of users! So a property of symmetric encryption systems is that they require a means of **key distribution**.

Public key systems, on the other hand, excel at key management. By the nature of the public key approach, you can send a public key in an e-mail message or post it in a public directory. Only the corresponding private key, which presumably is kept private, can decrypt what has been encrypted with the public key.

But for both kinds of encryption, a key must be kept well secured. Once the symmetric or private key is known by an outsider, all messages written previously or in the future can be decrypted (and hence read or modified) by the outsider. So, for all encryption algorithms, **key management** is a major issue. It involves storing, safeguarding, and activating keys.

Stream and Block Ciphers

Most of the ciphers studied in this chapter are **stream ciphers**; that is, they convert one symbol of plaintext immediately into a symbol of ciphertext. (The exception is the columnar transposition cipher.) The transformation depends only on the symbol, the key, and the control information of the encipherment algorithm. A model of stream enciphering is shown in Figure 2-6.

Some kinds of errors, such as skipping a character in the key during encryption, affect the encryption of all future characters. However, such errors can sometimes be recognized during decryption because the plaintext will be properly recovered up to a point, and then all following characters will be wrong. If that is the case, the receiver may be able to recover from the error by dropping a character of the key on the receiving end. Once the receiver has successfully recalibrated the key with the ciphertext, there will be no further effects from this error.

To address this problem and make it harder for a cryptanalyst to break the code, we can use block ciphers. A **block cipher** encrypts a *group* of plaintext symbols as *one* block. The columnar transposition and other transpositions are examples of block ci-

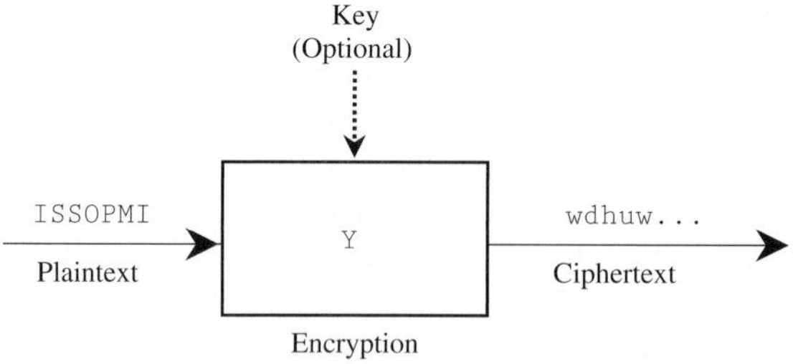

FIGURE 2-6 Stream Encryption.

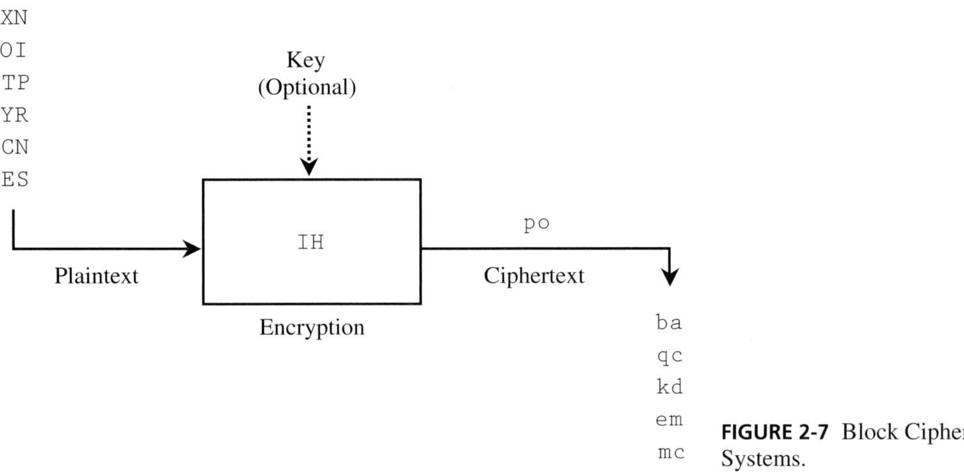

FIGURE 2-7 Block Cipher Systems.

phers. In the columnar transposition, the entire message is translated as one block. The block size need not have any particular relationship to the size of a character. Block ciphers work on blocks of plaintext and produce blocks of ciphertext, as shown Figure 2-7. In the figure, the central box represents an encryption machine: The previous plaintext pair is converted to `po`, the current one being converted is `IH`, and the machine is soon to convert `ES`.

Table 2-3 compares the advantages and disadvantages of stream and block encryption algorithms.

TABLE 2-3 Comparing Stream and Block Algorithms.

	Stream Encryption Algorithms	Block Encryption Algorithms
Advantages	• *Speed of transformation.* Because each symbol is encrypted without regard for any other plaintext symbols, each symbol can be encrypted as soon as it is read. Thus, the time to encrypt a symbol depends only on the encryption algorithm itself, not on the time it takes to receive more plaintext. • *Low error propagation.* Because each symbol is separately encoded, an error in the encryption process affects only that character.	• *High diffusion.* Information from the plaintext is diffused into several ciphertext symbols. One ciphertext block may depend on several plaintext letters. • *Immunity to insertion of symbols.* Because blocks of symbols are enciphered, it is impossible to insert a single symbol into one block. The length of the block would then be incorrect, and the decipherment would quickly reveal the insertion.
Disadvantages	• *Low diffusion.* Each symbol is separately enciphered. Therefore, all the information of that symbol is contained in one symbol of the ciphertext. • *Susceptibility to malicious insertions and modifications.* Because each symbol is separately enciphered, an active interceptor who has broken the code can splice together pieces of previous messages and transmit a spurious new message that may look authentic.	• *Slowness of encryption.* The person or machine using a block cipher must wait until an entire block of plaintext symbols has been received before starting the encryption process. • *Error propagation.* An error will affect the transformation of all other characters in the same block.

Confusion and Diffusion

Two additional important concepts are related to the amount of work required to perform an encryption. An encrypting algorithm should take the information from the plaintext and transform it so that the interceptor cannot readily recognize the message. The interceptor should not be able to predict what will happen to the ciphertext by changing one character in the plaintext. We call this characteristic **confusion.** An algorithm providing good confusion has a complex functional relationship between the plaintext/key pair and the ciphertext. In this way, it will take an interceptor a long time to determine the relationship between plaintext, key, and ciphertext; therefore, it will take the interceptor a long time to break the code.

As an example, consider the Caesar cipher. This algorithm is not good for providing confusion, because an analyst who deduces the transformation of a few letters can also predict the transformation of the remaining letters, with no additional information. By contrast, a one-time pad (with a key effectively as long as the message length) provides good confusion, because one plaintext letter can be transformed to any ciphertext letter at different places in the output. There is no apparent pattern to transforming a single plaintext letter.

The cipher should also spread the information from the plaintext over the entire ciphertext so that changes in the plaintext affect many parts of the ciphertext. This principle is called **diffusion,** the characteristic of distributing the information from single plaintext letters over the entire output. Good diffusion means that the interceptor needs access to much of the ciphertext to be able to infer the algorithm.

Before becoming too convinced of the strength of any algorithm, you should remember that there are people very interested in nullifying the effects of encryption. As we noted earlier in this chapter, the opponent can work to weaken the apparent strength of the algorithm, to decrypt a single piece encrypted text, or to derive a key with which to break subsequent encryptions. Commercial-grade cryptographers need to keep in mind the possibility of commercial-grade cryptanalysts as well.

Cryptanalysis—Breaking Encryption Schemes

So far we have looked at a few particular techniques a cryptanalyst could use to break the encryptions we have studied. Studying these techniques helps you appreciate the simplicity of the encryptions we have presented so far. We introduced these algorithms primarily to illustrate several encryption concepts as well as the analysis a cryptographer performs. But these techniques have been more instructional than practical; no one would use these cryptosystems to protect data of any significant value because the cryptosystems are relatively easy to break.

A different reason to consider cryptanalysis is to judge the difficulty of breaking an encryption or algorithm. After all, encrypting data does no good if the attacker can find some way of decrypting it.

Therefore, we look at cryptanalysis in general: What does a cryptanalyst do when confronted with an unknown, and possibly very strong, encryption scheme? Four possible situations confront the cryptanalyst, depending on what information is available.

- ciphertext
- full plaintext
- partial plaintext
- algorithm

In turn, these four cases suggest five different approaches the analyst can use to address them. As we describe each case, keep in mind that the cryptanalyst can also use any other collateral information that can be obtained.

Ciphertext Only

In most of the discussions so far, we assumed that the analyst had only the ciphertext with which to work. The decryption had to be based on probabilities, distributions, and characteristics of the available ciphertext, plus publicly available knowledge. This method of attack is called a **ciphertext-only attack.**

Full or Partial Plaintext

The analyst may be fortunate enough to have a sample message and its decipherment. For example, a diplomatic service may have intercepted an encrypted message, suspected to be the text of an official statement. If the official statement (in plaintext) is subsequently released, the interceptor has both C and P and needs only to deduce the E for which $C = E(P)$ to find D. In this case the analyst is attempting to find E (or D) by using a **known plaintext** attack.

The analyst may have additional information, too. For example, the analyst may know that the message was intercepted from a diplomatic exchange between Germany and Austria. From that information, the analyst may guess that the words Bonn, Vienna, and Chancellor appear in the message. Alternatively, the message may be a memorandum to the sales force from a corporate president, and the memo would have a particular form (To: Sales Force, From: The President, Subject: Weekly Sales Update, Date: nn/nn/nn).

In these cases, the analyst can use what is called a **probable plaintext** analysis. After doing part of the decryption, the analyst may find places where the known message fits with the deciphered parts, thereby giving more clues about the total translation.

After cryptanalysis has provided possible partial decipherments, a probable plaintext attack may permit a cryptanalyst to fill in some blanks. For example, letter frequencies may suggest a substitution for the most popular letters, but leave gaps such as *SA_ES _OR_E*. With a probable plaintext, the cryptanalyst could guess that *SALES FORCE* appears somewhere in the memo and could easily fill in these blanks.

Ciphertext of Any Plaintext

The analyst may have infiltrated the sender's transmission process so as to be able to cause messages to be encrypted and sent at will. This attack is called a **chosen plaintext** attack. For instance, the analyst may be able to insert records into a database and observe the change in statistics after the insertions. Linear programming sometimes enables such an analyst to infer data that should be kept confidential in the database.

Alternatively, an analyst may tap wires in a network and be able to notice the effect of sending a particular message to a particular network user. The cryptanalyst may be an insider or have an inside colleague and thus be able to cause certain transactions to be reflected in ciphertext; for example, the insider may forward messages resulting from a receipt of a large order. A chosen plaintext attack is very favorable to the analyst.

Algorithm and Ciphertext

The analyst may have available both the encryption algorithm and the ciphertext. In a **chosen ciphertext** attack, the analyst can run the algorithm on massive amounts of plaintext to find one plaintext message that encrypts as the ciphertext. The purpose of a chosen ciphertext attack is to deduce the sender's encryption key so as to be able to decrypt future messages by simply applying the sender's decryption key to intercepted ciphertext. This approach fails if two or more distinct keys can produce the same ciphertext as the result of encrypting (different) meaningful plaintext.

Ciphertext and Plaintext

The cryptanalyst may be lucky enough to have some pairs of plaintext and matching ciphertext. Then, the game is to deduce the key by which those pairs were encrypted so that the same key can be used in cases in which the analyst has only the ciphertext. Although it might seem uncommon to be able to obtain matching plain- and ciphertext, in fact it happens sometimes. For example, during World War II, cryptanalysts intercepted text from major diplomatic announcements sent in advance to embassies (encrypted) and then released to the public. Having a few such pieces allowed the cryptanalysts to determine current keys and decrypt other messages.

Weaknesses

A cryptanalyst works against humans, who can be hurried, lazy, careless, naïve, or uninformed. Humans sometimes fail to change cryptographic keys when needed, broadcast cryptographic keys in the clear, or choose keys in a predictable manner. That is, the algorithm may be strong and the implementation effective, but the people using it fail in some way and open up the encryption to detection. People have been known to be careless, discarding sensitive material that could give a spy access to plaintext by matching known ciphertext. And humans can sometimes be bribed or coerced. Sidebar 2-5 describes some examples of this behavior during World War II.

Not only are people fallible, but so are hardware and software implementations. Sometimes hardware fails in predictable ways, such as when disk reading heads lose their track alignment, so that sensitive data thought to be erased are still on the disk. At other times, seemingly small things can weaken an otherwise strong approach. For example, in one attack, the analyst accurately measured the electricity being used by a computer performing an encryption and deduced the key from the difference in power used to compute a 1 versus a 0.

These problems are separate from issues of the algorithm itself, but they offer ways that a cryptanalyst can approach the task of breaking the code. Remember that the only rule that applies to the attacker is that there are no rules.

Sidebar 2-5 Human Fallibility Led to Cracked Codes

Kahn [KAH96] describes the history of the Enigma machine, a mechanical tool used by the Germans in World War II to scramble messages and prevent the enemy from understanding them. Enigma was based on revolving wheels, or rotors, that were wired together and connected to a typewriter keyboard. There were so many ways to encrypt a message that even if 1,000 analysts tried four different ways each minute, all day, every day, it would have taken the team 1.8 billion years to test them all.

So how did the Allies break the encryption? First, they made use of the likely chatter over the wires about each day's events. By guessing that the Germans would be discussing certain places or issues, the Allies found sections of scrambled text that they could relate to the original messages, or cleartext. Next, they concentrated on Luftwaffe messages. Counting on the likelihood that the Luftwaffe signalmen were not as well trained as those in the Army or Navy, the Allies watched for slip-ups that increased the odds of understanding the encrypted messages. For instance, Luftwaffe signalmen often used "a girlfriend's name for a key setting or beginning a second message with the same setting as that left at the ending of the first." Such knowledge enabled the Allies to determine some of the Luftwaffe's plans during the Battle of Britain. Thus, sophisticated technology can be trumped when control protocols are not followed carefully and completely.

This background information has readied you to study the three most widely used encryption schemes today: DES, AES, and RSA. Using these schemes is fairly easy, even though the detailed construction of the algorithms can be quite complex. As you study the three algorithms, keep in mind the possibility that cryptanalysts are also working to defeat these encryptions.

2.5 THE DATA ENCRYPTION STANDARD (DES)

The Data Encryption Standard (DES) [NBS77], a system developed for the U.S. government, was intended for use by the general public. It has been officially accepted as a cryptographic standard both in the United States and abroad. Moreover, many hardware and software systems have been designed with the DES. However, recently its adequacy has been questioned.

Background and History

In the early 1970s, the U.S. National Bureau of Standards (NBS) recognized that the general public needed a secure encryption technique for protecting sensitive information. Historically, the U.S. Department of Defense and the Department of State had had continuing interest in encryption systems; it was thought that these departments were home to the greatest expertise in cryptology. However, precisely because of the sensitive nature of the information they were encrypting, the departments could not release any of their work. Thus, the responsibility for a more public encryption technique was delegated to the NBS.

At the same time, several private vendors had developed encryption devices, using either mechanical means or programs that individuals or firms could buy to protect their sensitive communications. The difficulty with this commercial proliferation of encryption techniques was exchange: Two users with different devices could not exchange encrypted information. Furthermore, there was no independent body capable of testing the devices extensively to verify that they properly implemented their algorithms.

It soon became clear that encryption was ripe for assessment and standardization, to promote the ability of unrelated parties to exchange encrypted information and to provide a single encryption system that could be rigorously tested and publicly certified. As a result, in 1972 the NBS issued a call for proposals for producing a public encryption algorithm. The call specified desirable criteria for such an algorithm:

- able to provide a high level of security
- specified and easy to understand
- publishable, so that security does not depend on the secrecy of the algorithm
- available to all users
- adaptable for use in diverse applications
- economical to implement in electronic devices
- efficient to use
- able to be validated
- exportable

The NBS envisioned providing the encryption as a separate hardware device. To allow the algorithm to be public, NBS hoped to reveal the algorithm itself, basing the security of the system on the keys (which would be under the control of the users).

Few organizations responded to the call, so the NBS issued a second announcement in August 1974. The most promising suggestion was the **Lucifer** algorithm on which IBM had been working for several years. This idea had been published earlier, so the basic algorithm was already public and had been open to scrutiny and validation. Although lengthy, the algorithm was straightforward, a natural candidate for iterative implementation in a computer program. Furthermore, unlike the Merkle–Hellman (which we study in Chapter 10) and RSA algorithms, which use arithmetic on 500- or 1,000-digit binary numbers (far larger than most machine instructions would handle as a single quantity), Lucifer used only simple logical operations on relatively small quantities. Thus, the algorithm could be implemented fairly efficiently in either hardware or software on conventional computers.

The data encryption algorithm developed by IBM for NBS was based on Lucifer, and it became known as the Data Encryption Standard (DES), although its proper name is DEA (Data Encryption Algorithm) in the United States and DEA1 (Data Encryption Algorithm-1) in other countries. Then, NBS called on the Department of Defense through its National Security Agency (NSA) to analyze the strength of the encryption algorithm. Finally, the NBS released the algorithm for public scrutiny and discussion.

The DES was officially adopted as a U.S. federal standard in November 1976, authorized by NBS for use on all public and private sector unclassified communication. Eventually, DES was accepted as an international standard by the International Standards Organization.

Overview of the DES Algorithm

The DES algorithm is a careful and complex combination of two fundamental building blocks of encryption: substitution and transposition. The algorithm derives its strength from repeated application of these two techniques, one on top of the other, for a total of 16 cycles. The sheer complexity of tracing a single bit through 16 iterations of substitutions and transpositions has so far stopped researchers in the public from identifying more than a handful of general properties of the algorithm.

The algorithm begins by encrypting the plaintext as blocks of 64 bits. The key is 64 bits long, but in fact it can be any 56-bit number. (The extra 8 bits are often used as check digits and do not affect encryption in normal implementations.) The user can change the key at will any time there is uncertainty about the security of the old key.

The algorithm, described in substantial detail in Chapter 10, leverages the two techniques Shannon identified to conceal information: confusion and diffusion. That is, the algorithm accomplishes two things: ensuring that the output bits have no obvious relationship to the input bits and spreading the effect of one plaintext bit to other bits in the ciphertext. Substitution provides the confusion, and transposition provides the diffusion. In general, plaintext is affected by a series of cycles of a substitution then a permutation. The iterative substitutions and permutations are performed as outlined in Figure 2-8.

DES uses only standard arithmetic and logical operations on numbers up to 64 bits long, so it is suitable for implementation in software on most current computers. Although complex, the algorithm is repetitive, making it suitable for implementation on a single-purpose chip. In fact, several such chips are available on the market for use as basic components in devices that use DES encryption in an application.

Double and Triple DES

As you know, computing power has increased rapidly over the last few decades, and it promises to continue to do so. For this reason, the DES 56-bit key length is not long enough for some people to feel comfortable. Since the 1970s, researchers and practitioners have been interested in a longer-key version of DES. But we have a problem: The DES algorithm is fixed for a 56-bit key.

Double DES

To address the discomfort, some researchers suggest using a double encryption for greater secrecy. The double encryption works in the following way. Take two keys, k_1 and k_2, and perform two encryptions, one on top of the other: $E(k_2, E(k_1,m))$. In theory, this approach should multiply the difficulty of breaking the encryption, just as two locks are harder to pick than one.

Unfortunately, that assumption is false. Merkle and Hellman [MER81] showed that two encryptions are no better than one. The basis of their argument is that the

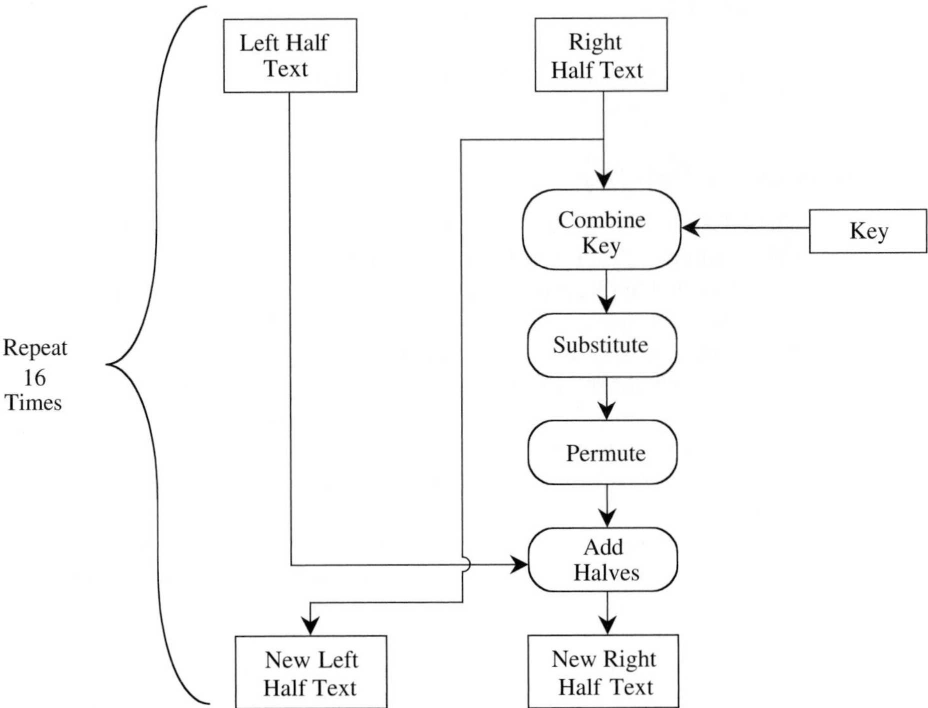

FIGURE 2-8 Cycles of Substitution and Permutation.

cryptanalyst works plaintext and ciphertext toward each other. The analyst needs two pairs of plaintext (call them P_1 and P_2) and corresponding ciphertext, C_1 and C_2, but not the keys used to encrypt them. The analyst computes and saves P_1 encrypted under each possible key. The analyst then tries decrypting C_1 with a single key and looking for a match in the saved *P*s. A match is a possible pair of double keys, so the analyst checks the match with P_2 and C_2. Computing all the *P*s takes 2^{56} steps, but working backward from C_1 takes only the same amount of time, for a total of $2 * 2^{56}$ or 2^{57}, equivalent to a 57-bit key. Thus, the double encryption only doubles the work for the attacker.

Triple DES

However, a simple trick does indeed enhance the security of DES. Using two keys and applying them in *three* operations adds apparent strength.

The so-called **triple DES** procedure is $C = E(k_1, D(k_2, E(k_1,m)))$. That is, you encrypt with one key, decrypt with the second, and encrypt with the first again. (The second decrypt step also makes this process work for single encryptions with one key: The decryption cancels the first encryption, so the net result is one encryption.)

Although this process is called triple DES, because of the three applications of the DES algorithm, it only doubles the effective key length. But a 112-bit effective key length is quite strong, and it is effective against all feasible known attacks.

Security of the DES

Since its was first announced, DES has been controversial. Many researchers have questioned the security it provides. Much of this controversy has appeared in the open literature, but certain DES features have neither been revealed by the designers nor inferred by outside analysts.

In 1990, Biham and Shamir [BIH90] invented a technique, **differential cryptanalysis,** that investigates the change in algorithmic strength when an encryption algorithm is changed in some way. In 1991 they applied their technique to DES, showing that almost any change to the algorithm weakens it. Their changes included cutting the number of iterations from 16 to 15, changing the expansion or substitution rule, or altering the order of an iteration. In each case, when they weakened the algorithm, Biham and Shamir could break the modified version. Thus, it seems as if the design of DES is optimal.

However, Diffie and Hellman [DIF77] argued in 1977 that a 56-bit key is too short. In 1977, it was prohibitive to test all 2^{56} (approximately 10^{15}) keys on then-current computers. But they argued that over time, computers would become more powerful and the DES algorithm would remain unchanged; eventually, the speed of computers would exceed the strength of DES. Exactly that has happened. In 1997 researchers using over 3,500 machines in parallel were able to infer a DES key in four months' work. And in 1998 researchers built a special "DES cracker" machine for approximately $100,000 that could find a DES key in approximately four days.

Does this mean the DES is insecure? No, not yet. No one has yet shown serious flaws in the DES. The 1997 attack required a great deal of cooperation, and the 1998 machine is still rather expensive. Triple DES is still well beyond the power of these attacks. Nevertheless, to anticipate the increasing power of computers, it was clear a new, stronger algorithm was needed. In 1995, the U.S. National Institute of Standards and Technology (NIST, the renamed NBS) began the search for a new, strong encryption algorithm. The response to that search has become the **Advanced Encryption Standard,** or **AES.**

2.6 THE AES ENCRYPTION ALGORITHM

The AES is likely to be the commercial-grade symmetric algorithm of choice for years, if not decades. Let us look at it more closely.

The AES Contest

In January 1997, NIST called for cryptographers to develop a new encryption system. As with the call for candidates from which DES was selected, NIST made several important restrictions. The algorithms had to be

- unclassified
- publicly disclosed
- available royalty-free for use worldwide
- symmetric block cipher algorithms, for blocks of 128 bits
- usable with key sizes of 128, 192, and 256 bits

In August 1998, fifteen algorithms were chosen from among those submitted; in August 1999, the field of candidates was narrowed to five finalists. The five then underwent extensive public and private scrutiny. The final selection was made on the basis not only security but also of cost or efficiency of operation and ease of implementation in software. The winning algorithm, submitted by two Dutch cryptographers, was Rijndael (pronounced RINE dahl or, to hear the inventors pronounce it themselves, visit *http://rijndael.com/audio/rijndael_pronunciation.wav*); the algorithm's name is derived from the creators' names, Vincent Rijmen and Joan Daemen. (NIST described the four not chosen as also having adequate security for the AES—no cryptographic flaws were identified in any of the five. Thus, the selection was based on efficiency and implementation characteristics.)

The AES was adopted for use by the U.S. government in December 2001 and became Federal Information Processing Standard 197 [NIS01].

Overview of Rijndael

Rijndael is a fast algorithm that can be implemented easily on simple processors. Although it has a strong mathematical foundation, it primarily uses substitution, transposition, and the shift, exclusive OR, and addition operations. Like DES, AES uses repeat cycles. There are 9, 11, or 13 cycles for keys of 128, 192, and 256 bits, respectively. In Rijndael, the cycles are called "rounds."

Each cycle consists of four steps.

- *Byte substitution:* This step uses a substitution box structure similar to the DES, substituting each byte of a 128-bit block according to a substitution table. This is a straight confusion operation.
- *Shift row:* A transposition step. For 128- and 192-bit block sizes, row n is shifted left circular $(n - 1)$ bytes; for 256-bit blocks, row 2 is shifted 1 byte and rows 3 and 4 are shifted 3 and 4 bytes, respectively. This is a straight confusion operation.
- *Mix column:* This step involves shifting left and exclusive-ORing bits with themselves. These operations provide both confusion and diffusion.
- *Add subkey:* Here, a portion of the key unique to this cycle is exclusive-ORed with the cycle result. This operation provides confusion and incorporates the key.

These four steps are described in more detail in Chapter 10. Note that the steps perform both diffusion and confusion on the input data. Bits from the key are combined with intermediate result bits frequently, so key bits are also well diffused throughout the result. Furthermore, these four steps are extremely fast. The AES algorithm is depicted in Figure 2-9.

Strength of the Algorithm

The Rijndael algorithm is quite new, so there are few reports of extensive experience with its use. However, between its submission as a candidate for AES in 1997 and its selection in 2001, it underwent extensive cryptanalysis by both government and inde-

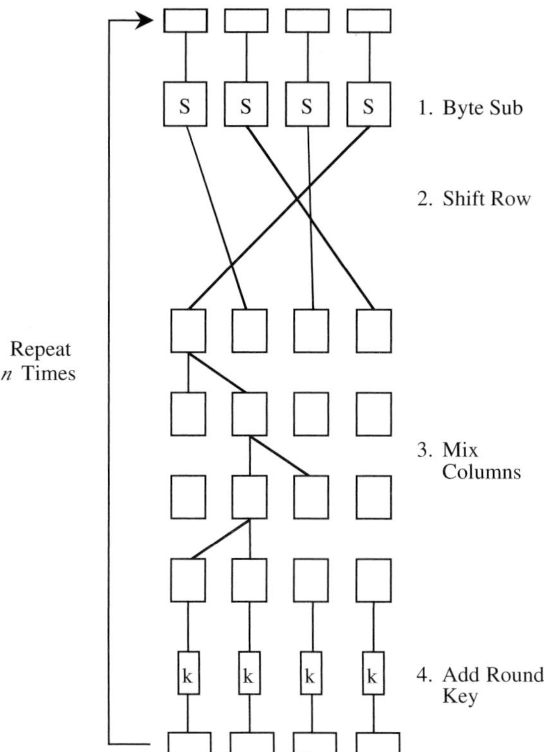

FIGURE 2-9 AES Algorithm.

pendent cryptographers. Its Dutch inventors have no relationship to the NSA or any other part of the U.S. government, so there is no suspicion that the government somehow weakened the algorithm or added a trapdoor. Although the steps of a cycle are simple to describe and seem to be rather random transformations of bits, in fact (as described in some detail in Chapter 10), these transformations have a sound mathematical origin.

Comparison of DES and AES

The characteristics of DES and AES are compared in Table 2-4.

When Rijndael's predecessor, DES, was adopted, two questions arose quickly:

1. How strong is it, and in particular, are there any backdoors?
2. How long would it be until the encrypted code could be routinely cracked?

With over 20 years of use, suspicions of weakness (intentional or not) and backdoors have pretty much been quashed. Not only have analysts failed to find any significant flaws, but in fact research has shown that seemingly insignificant changes weaken the strength of the algorithm—that is, the algorithm is the best it can be. The second question, about how long DES would last, went unanswered for a long time but then

TABLE 2-4 Comparison of DES and AES.

	DES	AES
Date	1976	1999
Block size	64 bits	128 bits
Key length	56 bits (effective length)	128, 192, 256 (and possibly more) bits
Encryption primitives	Substitution, permutation	Substitution, shift, bit mixing
Cryptographic primitives	Confusion, diffusion	Confusion, diffusion
Design	Open	Open
Design rationale	Closed	Open
Selection process	Secret	Secret, but accepted open public comment
Source	IBM, enhanced by NSA	Independent Dutch cryptographers

was answered very quickly by two experiments in which DES was cracked in days. Thus, after 20 years, the power of individual specialized processors and of massive parallel searches has overtaken the fixed DES key size.

We must ask the same questions about AES: Does it have flaws, and for how long will it remain sound? We cannot address the question of flaws yet, other than to say that teams of cryptanalysts pored over the design of Rijndael during the two-year review period without finding any problems. But the longevity question is more difficult to answer for AES than for DES. The AES algorithm as defined can use 128-, 192-, or 256-bit keys. This characteristic means that AES starts with a key more than double the size of a DES key and can extend to double it yet again. (Remember that doubling the key length *squares* the number of possible keys that need to be tested in attempts to break the encryption.) But because there is an evident underlying structure, it is also possible to use the same general approach on a slightly different underlying problem and accommodate keys of even larger size. (Even a key size of 256 is prodigious, however.) Thus, unlike DES, AES can move to a longer key length any time technology seems to allow an analyst to overtake the current key size.

Moreover, the number of cycles can be extended in a natural way. With DES the algorithm was defined for precisely 16 cycles; to extend that number would require substantial redefinition of the algorithm. The internal structure of AES has no a priori limitation on the number of cycles. If a cryptanalyst ever concluded that 9 or 11 or 13 rounds were too low, the only change needed to improve the algorithm would be to change the limit on a repeat loop.

However, we cannot rest on our laurels. It is impossible to predict now what limitations cryptanalysts might identify in the future. At present, AES seems to be a significant improvement over DES, and it can be improved in a natural way if necessary.

2.7 PUBLIC KEY ENCRYPTION

So far, we have looked at encryption algorithms from the point of view of making the scrambling easy to do (so that the sender can easily encrypt a message) and the decryption easy for the receiver but not for an intruder. But this functional view of transforming plaintext to ciphertext is only part of the picture. We can also examine the role of keys in encryption. We have noted how useful keys can be in deterring an intruder, but we have assumed that the key must remain secret for it to be effective. In this section, we look at ways to allow the key to be public but still protect the message. We also focus on the RSA algorithm, a public key system that is a popular commercial-grade encryption technique.

In 1976, Diffie and Hellman [DIF76] proposed a new kind of encryption system. With a public key[5] encryption system, each user has a key that does not have to be kept secret. Although counterintuitive, in fact the public nature of the key does not compromise the secrecy of the system. Instead, the basis for public key encryption is to allow the key to be divulged but to keep the decryption technique secret. Public key cryptosystems accomplish this goal by using two keys: one to encrypt and the other to decrypt.

Motivation

Why should making the key public be desirable? With a conventional symmetric key system, each pair of users needs a separate key. But with public key systems, anyone using a single public key can send a secret message to a user, and the message remains adequately protected from being read by an interceptor. Let us investigate why this is so.

Recall that in general, an n-user system requires $n * (n - 1)/2$ keys, and each user must track and remember a key for each other user with which he or she wants to communicate. As the number of users grows, the number of keys increases very rapidly, as shown in Figure 2-10. Determining and distributing these keys is a problem. More serious is maintaining security for the keys already distributed, because we cannot expect users to memorize so many keys.

Characteristics

We can reduce the problem of key proliferation by using a public key approach. In a **public key** or **asymmetric encryption system,** each user has two keys: a public key and a private key. The user may publish the public key freely because each key does only half of the encryption and decryption process. The keys operate as inverses, meaning that one key undoes the encryption provided by the other key.

To see how, let k_{PRIV} be a user's private key, and let k_{PUB} be the corresponding public key. Then, encrypted plaintext using the public key is decrypted by application of the private key; we write the relationship as

$$P = D(k_{PRIV}, E(k_{PUB}, P))$$

[5] Asymmetric or public key encryption systems use two keys, a **public key** and a **private key.** Unfortunately, a few people call a symmetric or secret key system a "private key" system. This terminology is confusing. We do not use it in this book, but you should be aware that you might encounter the terminology in other readings.

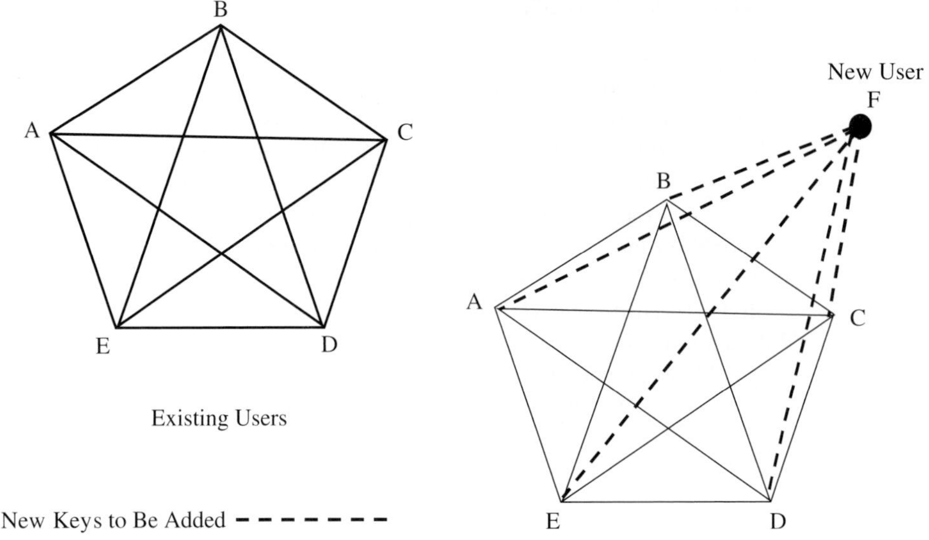

FIGURE 2-10 Key Proliferation.

That is, a user can decode with a private key what someone else has encrypted with the corresponding public key. Furthermore, with some public key encryption algorithms, including RSA, we have this relationship:

$$P = D(k_{PUB}, E(k_{PRIV}, P))$$

In other words, a user can encrypt a message with a private key, and the message can be revealed only with the corresponding public key. These two properties tell us that public and private keys can be applied in either order. In particular, the decryption function D can be applied to any argument so that we can decrypt before we encrypt. With conventional encryption, we seldom think of decrypting *before* encrypting. But the concept makes sense with public keys, where it simply means applying the private transformation first and then the public one.

We have noted that a major problem with symmetric encryption is the sheer number of keys a single user has to store and track. With public keys, only two keys are needed per user: one public and one private. Let us see what difference this makes in the number of keys needed. Suppose we have three users, B, C, and D, who must pass protected messages to user A as well as to each other. Since each distinct pair of users needs a key, each user would need three different keys; for instance, A would need a key for B, a key for C, and a key for D. But using public key encryption, each of B, C, and D can encrypt messages for A by using A's public key. If B has encrypted a message using A's public key, C *cannot* decrypt it, even if C knew it was encrypted with A's public key. Applying A's public key twice, for example, would not decrypt the message. (We assume, of course, that A's private key remains secret.) Thus, the number of keys needed in the public key system is relatively small.

TABLE 2-5 Comparing Secret Key and Public Key Encryption.

	Secret Key (Symmetric)	Public Key (Asymmetric)
Number of keys	1	2
Protection of key	Must be kept secret	One key must be kept secret; the other can be freely exposed
Best uses	Cryptographic workhorse; secrecy and integrity of data—single characters to blocks of data, messages, files	Key exchange, authentication
Key distribution	Must be out-of-band	Public key can be used to distribute other keys
Speed	Fast	Slow; typically, 10,000 times slower than secret key

The characteristics of secret key and public key algorithms are compared in Table 2-5.

Rivest–Shamir–Adelman (RSA) Encryption

The **Rivest–Shamir–Adelman (RSA) cryptosystem** is a public key system. Based on an underlying hard problem and named after its three inventors, this algorithm was introduced in 1978 and to date remains secure. RSA has been the subject of extensive cryptanalysis, and no serious flaws have yet been found. Although the amount of analysis is no guarantee of a method's security, our confidence in the method grows as time passes without discovery of a flaw.

Let us look at how the RSA encryption scheme works; we investigate it in greater detail in Chapter 10. RSA is similar to other methods, such as Merkle–Hellman (also studied in Chapter 10), in that solving the encryption amounts to finding terms that add to a particular sum or multiply to a particular product. It relies on an area of mathematics known as number theory, in which mathematicians study properties of numbers such as their prime factors. The RSA encryption algorithm combines results from number theory with the degree of difficulty in determining the prime factors of a given number. As do some of the other algorithms we have studied, the RSA algorithm also operates with arithmetic mod n.

The two keys used in RSA, d and e, are used for decryption and encryption. They are actually interchangeable: Either can be chosen as the public key but, having chosen one, you must keep the other one private. For simplicity, we call the encryption key e and the decryption key d. Also, because of the nature of the RSA algorithm, the keys can be applied in either order:

$$P = E(D(P)) = D(E(P))$$

(You can think of E and D as two complementary functions, each of which "undoes" the other.)

Any plaintext block P is encrypted as P^e mod n. Because the exponentiation is performed mod n, factoring P^e to uncover the encrypted plaintext is difficult. However, the decrypting key d is carefully chosen so that $(P^e)^d \bmod n = P$. Thus, the legitimate receiver who knows d simply computes $(P^e)^d \bmod n = P$ and recovers P without having to factor P^e.

The encryption algorithm is based on the underlying problem of factoring large numbers. So far, nobody has found a shortcut or easy way to factor large numbers in a finite set called a field. Because the problem has been open for many years, most cryptographers consider this problem a solid basis for a secure cryptosystem.

2.8 THE USES OF ENCRYPTION

Encryption algorithms alone are not the answer to everyone's encryption needs. Although encryption implements protected communications channels, it can also be used for other duties. In fact, combining symmetric and asymmetric encryption often capitalizes on the best features of each.

Public key algorithms are useful only for specialized tasks because they are very slow. A public key encryption can take 10,000 times as long to perform as a symmetric encryption because the underlying modular exponentiation depends on multiplication and division, which are inherently slower than the bit operations (addition, exclusive OR, substitution, and shifting) on which symmetric algorithms are based. For this reason, symmetric encryption is the cryptographers' "work horse," and public key encryption is reserved for specialized, infrequent uses, where slow operation is not a continuing problem.

Let us look more closely at four applications of encryption: cryptographic hash functions, key exchange, digital signatures, and certificates.

Cryptographic Hash Functions

Encryption is most commonly used for secrecy; we usually encrypt something so that its contents—or even its existence—are unknown to all but a privileged audience. In some cases, however, integrity is a more important concern than secrecy. For example, in a document retrieval system containing legal records, it may be important to know that the copy retrieved is exactly what was stored. Likewise, in a secure communications system, the need for the correct transmission of messages may override secrecy concerns. Let us look at how encryption provides integrity.

In most files, the elements or components of the file are not bound together in any way. That is, each byte or bit or character is independent of every other one in the file. This lack of binding means that changing one value affects the integrity of the file, but that one change can easily go undetected.

What we would like to do is somehow put a seal or shield around the file so that we can detect when the seal has been broken and thus know that something has been changed. This notion is similar to the use of wax seals on letters in medieval days; if the wax was broken, the recipient would know that someone had broken the seal and read the message inside. In the same way, cryptography can be used to **seal** a file, encasing it so that any change becomes apparent. One technique for providing the seal is to compute a cryptographic function, sometimes called a **hash** or **checksum** or **message digest** of the file.

The hash function has special characteristics. For instance, some encryptions depend on a function that is easy to understand but difficult to compute. For a simple example, consider the cube function, $y = x^3$. It is relatively easy to compute x^3 by hand, with pencil and paper, or with a calculator. But the inverse function, $\sqrt[3]{y}$ is much more difficult to compute. And the function $y = x^2$ has no inverse function, since there are two possibilities for $\sqrt[2]{y}$: $+x$ and $-x$. Functions like these, which are much easier to compute than their inverses, are called **one-way functions.**

A one-way function can be useful in an encryption algorithm. The function must depend on all bits of the file being sealed, so any change to even a single bit will alter the checksum result. The checksum value is stored with the file. Then, each time the file is accessed or used, the checksum is recomputed. If the computed checksum matches the stored value, it is likely that the file has not been changed.

A cryptographic function, such as the DES or AES, is especially appropriate for sealing values, since an outsider will not know the key and thus will not be able to modify the stored value to match with data being modified. For low-threat applications, algorithms even simpler than DES or AES can be used. In block encryption schemes, **chaining** means linking each block to the previous block's value (and therefore to all previous blocks), for example, by using an exclusive OR to combine the encrypted previous block with the encryption of the current one. A file's cryptographic checksum could be the last block of the chained encryption of a file since that block will depend on all other blocks.

As we see later in this chapter, these techniques address the nonalterability and nonreusability required in a digital signature. A change or reuse will be flagged by the checksum, so the recipient can tell that something is amiss.

The most widely used cryptographic hash functions are MD4, MD5 (where MD stands for Message Digest), and SHA/SHS (Secure Hash Algorithm or Standard). The MD4/5 algorithms were invented by Ron Rivest and RSA Laboratories. MD5 is an improved version of MD4. Both condense a message of any size to a 128-bit digest. SHA/SHS is similar to both MD4 and MD5; it produces a 160-bit digest.

Key Exchange

Suppose you need to send a protected message to someone you do not know and who does not know you. This situation is more common than you may think. For instance, you may want to send your income tax return to the government. You want the information to be protected, but you do not necessarily know the person who is receiving the information. Similarly, you may want to use your web browser to connect with a shopping web site, exchange private (encrypted) e-mail, or arrange for two hosts to establish a protected channel. Each of these situations depends on being able to exchange an encryption key in such a way that nobody else can intercept it. The problem of two previously unknown parties exchanging cryptographic keys is both hard and important. Indeed, the problem is almost circular: To establish an encrypted session, you need an encrypted means to exchange keys.

Public key cryptography can help. Since asymmetric keys come in pairs, one half of the pair can be exposed without compromising the other half. To see how, suppose *S* and R (our well-known sender and receiver) want to derive a shared symmetric key. Suppose also that S and R both have public keys for a common encryption algorithm; call these $k_{PRIV\text{-}S}$, $k_{PUB\text{-}S}$, $k_{PRIV\text{-}R}$, and $k_{PUB\text{-}R}$, for the private and public keys for S and R, respectively. The simplest solution is for S to choose any symmetric key K, and send $E(k_{PRIV\text{-}S},K)$ to R. Then, R takes S's public key, removes the encryption, and obtains K. Alas, any eavesdropper who can get S's public key can also obtain K.

Instead, let S send $E(k_{PUB\text{-}R},K)$ to R. Then, only R can decrypt K. Unfortunately, R has no assurance that K came from S.

But there is a useful alternative. The solution is for S to send to R:

$$E(k_{\text{PUB-}R}, E(k_{\text{PRIV-}S}, K))$$

We can think of this exchange in terms of lockboxes and keys. If S wants to send something protected to R (such as a credit card number or a set of medical records), then the exchange works something like this. S puts the protected information in a lockbox that can be opened only with S's public key. Then, that lockbox is put inside a second lockbox that can be opened only with R's private key. R can then use his private key to open the outer box (something only he can do) and use S's public key to open the inner box (proving that the package came from S). In other words, the protocol wraps the protected information in two packages: the first unwrapped only with S's public key, and the second unwrapped only with R's private key. This approach is illustrated in Figure 2-11.

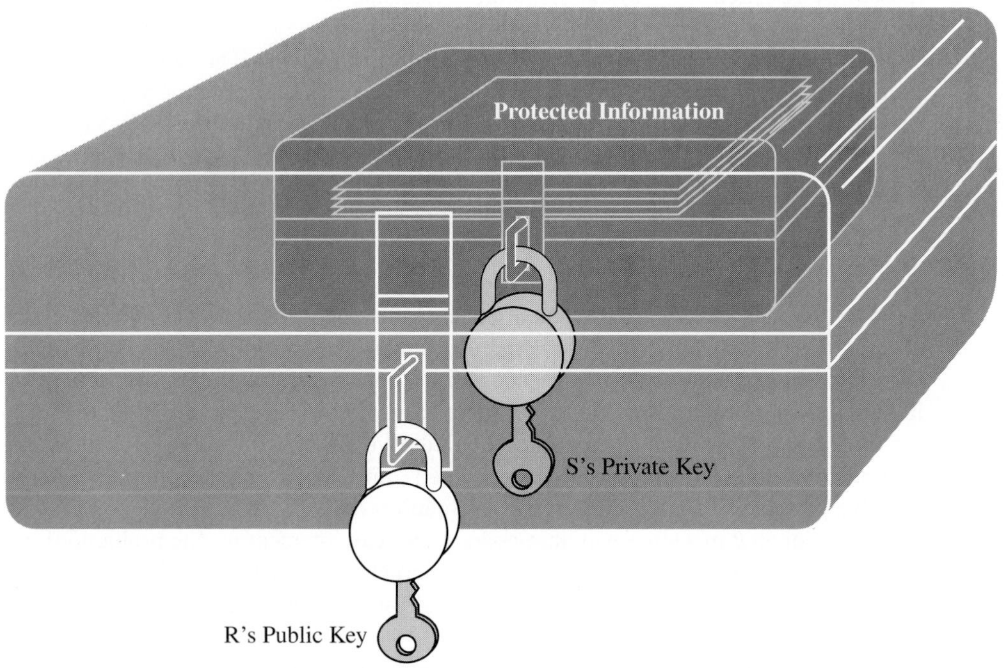

FIGURE 2-11 The Idea Behind Key Exchange.

Digital Signatures

Another typical situation parallels a common human need: an order to transfer funds from one person to another. In other words, we want to be able to send electronically the equivalent of a computerized check. We understand how this transaction is handled in the conventional, paper mode:

- A check is a *tangible object* authorizing a financial transaction.
- The signature on the check *confirms authenticity* since (presumably) only the legitimate signer can produce that signature.
- In the case of an alleged forgery, a third party can be called in to *judge authenticity.*
- Once a check is cashed, it is canceled so that it *cannot be reused.*
- The paper check is *not alterable*. Or, most forms of alteration are easily detected.

Transacting business by check depends on *tangible objects* in a *prescribed form.* But tangible objects do not exist for transactions on computers. Therefore, authorizing payments by computer requires a different model. Let us consider the requirements of such a situation, both from the standpoint of a bank and from the standpoint of a user.

Suppose Sandy sends her bank a message authorizing it to transfer $100 to Tim. Sandy's bank must be able to verify and prove that the message really came from Sandy if she should later disavow sending the message. The bank also wants to know that the message is entirely Sandy's, that it has not been altered along the way. On her part, Sandy wants to be certain that her bank cannot forge such messages. Both parties want to be sure that the message is new, not a reuse of a previous message, and that it has not been altered during transmission. Using electronic signals instead of paper complicates this process.

But we have ways to make the process work. A **digital signature** is a protocol that produces the same effect as a real signature: It is a mark that only the sender can make, but other people can easily recognize as belonging to the sender. Just like a real signature, a digital signature is used to confirm agreement to a message.

Properties

A digital signature must meet two primary conditions:

- *It must be unforgeable*. If person P signs message M with signature $S(P,M)$, it is impossible for anyone else to produce the pair $[M, S(P,M)]$.
- *It must be authentic*. If a person R receives the pair $[M, S(P,M)]$ purportedly from P, R can check that the signature is really from P. Only P could have created this signature, and the signature is firmly attached to M.

These two requirements, shown in Figure 2-12, are the major hurdles in computer transactions. Two more properties, also drawn from parallels with the paper-based environment, are desirable for transactions completed with the aid of digital signatures:

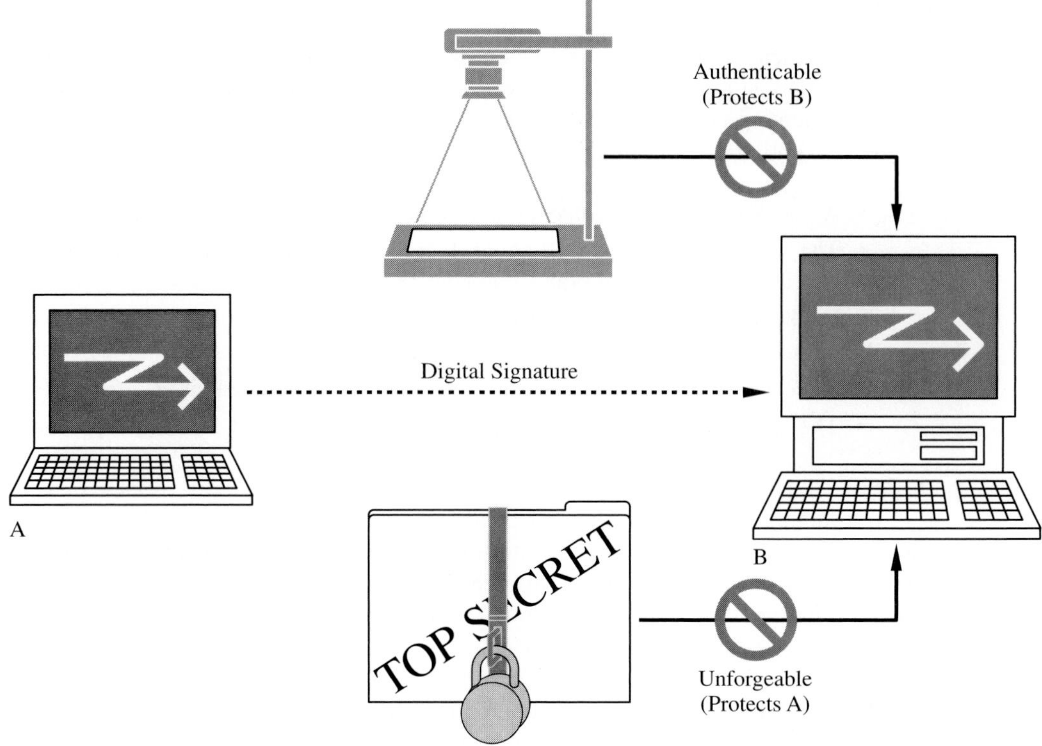

FIGURE 2-12 Requirements for a Digital Signature.

- *It is not alterable.* After being transmitted, *M* cannot be changed by *S*, *R*, or an interceptor.
- *It is not reusable.* A previous message presented again will be instantly detected by *R*.

To see how digital signatures work, we first present a mechanism that meets the first two requirements. Then, we add to that solution to satisfy the other requirements.

Public Key Protocol

Public key encryption systems are ideally suited to digital signatures. For simple notation, let us assume that the public key encryption for user *U* is accessed through $E(M, K_U)$ and that the private key transformation for *U* is written as $D(M,K_U)$. We can think of *E* as the *privacy* transformation (since only *U* can decrypt it) and *D* as the *authenticity* transformation (since only *U* can produce it). Remember, however, that under some asymmetric algorithms such as RSA, *D* and *E* are commutative, and either one can be applied to any message. Thus,

$$D(\ E(M,-),\ -)\ =\ M\ =\ E(\ D(M,-),\ -)$$

If S wishes to send M to R, S uses the authenticity transformation to produce $D(M, K_S)$. S then sends $D(M, K_S)$ to R. R decodes the message with the public key transformation of S, computing $E(D(M,K_S), K_S) = M$. Since only S can create a message that makes sense under $E(-,K_S)$, the message must genuinely have come from S. This test satisfies the authenticity requirement.

R will save $D(M,K_S)$. If S should later allege that the message is a forgery (not really from S), R can simply show M and $D(M,K_S)$. Anyone can verify that since $D(M,K_S)$ is transformed to M with the public key transformation of S—but only S could have produced $D(M,K_S)$—then $D(M,K_S)$ must be from S. This test satisfies the unforgeable requirement.

There are other approaches to implementing digital signature; some using symmetric encryption, others using asymmetric. The approach shown here illustrates how the protocol can address the requirements for unforgeability and authenticity. To add secrecy, S applies $E(M, K_R)$ as shown in Figure 2-13.

Next, we learn about cryptographic certificates, so that we can see how they are used to address authenticity.

Certificates

As humans we establish trust all the time in our daily interactions with people. We identify people we know by recognizing their voices, faces, or handwriting. At other times, we use an affiliation to convey trust. For instance, if a stranger telephones us and we hear, "I represent the local government..." or "I am calling on behalf of this charity..." or "I am calling from the school/hospital/police about your mother/father/son/daughter/brother/sister...," we may decide to trust the caller even if we do not know him or her. Depending on the nature of the call, we may decide to believe the caller's affiliation or to seek independent verification. For example, we may obtain the affiliation's number from the telephone directory and call the party back. Or we may seek additional information from the caller, such as "What color jacket was she wearing?" or "Who is the president of your organization?" If we have a low degree of trust, we may

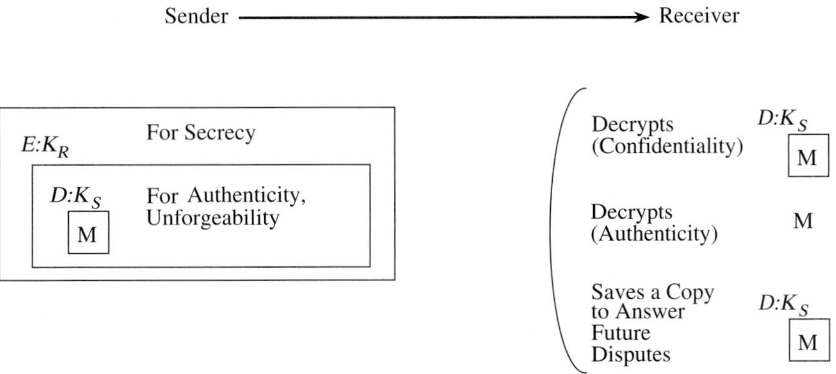

FIGURE 2-13 Use of Two Keys in Asymmetric Digital Signature.

even act to exclude an outsider, as in "I will mail a check directly to your charity rather than give you my credit card number."

For each of these interactions, we have what we might call a "trust threshold," a degree to which we are willing to believe an unidentified individual. This threshold exists in commercial interactions, too. When Acorn Manufacturing Company sends Big Steel Company an order for 10,000 sheets of steel, to be shipped within a week and paid for within ten days, trust abounds. The order is printed on an Acorn form, signed by someone identified as Helene Smudge, Purchasing Agent. Big Steel may begin preparing the steel even before receiving money from Acorn. Big Steel may check Acorn's credit rating to decide whether to ship the order without payment first. If suspicious, Big Steel might telephone Acorn and ask to speak to Ms. Smudge in the purchasing department. But more likely Big Steel will actually ship the goods without knowing who Ms. Smudge is, whether she is actually the purchasing agent, whether she is authorized to commit to an order of that size, or even whether the signature is actually hers. Sometimes a transaction like this occurs by fax, so that Big does not even have an original signature on file. In cases like this one, which occur daily, trust is based on appearance of authenticity (such as a printed, signed form), outside information (such as a credit report), and urgency (Acorn requested that the steel be shipped quickly).

For electronic communication to succeed, we must develop similar ways for two parties to establish trust without having met. A common thread in our personal and business interactions is the ability to have someone or something vouch for the existence and integrity of one or both parties. The police, the Chamber of Commerce, or the Better Business Bureau vouches for the authenticity of a caller. Acorn indirectly vouches for the fact that Ms. Smudge is its purchasing agent by transferring the call to her in the purchasing department. In a sense, the telephone company vouches for the authenticity of a party by listing it in the directory. This concept of "vouching for" by a third party can be a basis for trust in commercial settings where two parties do not know each other.

Trust Through a Common Respected Individual

A large company may have several divisions, each division may have several departments, each department may have several projects, and each project may have several task groups (with variations in the names, the number of levels, and the degree of completeness of the hierarchy). The top executive may not know by name or sight every employee in the company, but a task group leader knows all members of the task group, the project leader knows all task group leaders, and so on. This hierarchy can become the basis for trust throughout the organization.

To see how, suppose two people meet: Ann and Andrew. Andrew says he works for the same company as Ann. Ann wants independent verification that he does. She finds out that Bill and Betty are two task group leaders for the same project (led by Camilla); Ann works for Bill and Andrew for Betty. (The organizational relationships are shown in Figure 2-14.) These facts give Ann and Andrew a basis for trusting each other's identity. The chain of verification might be something like this:

- Ann asks Bill who Andrew is.
- Bill either asks Betty, if he knows her directly, or Camilla, if not.

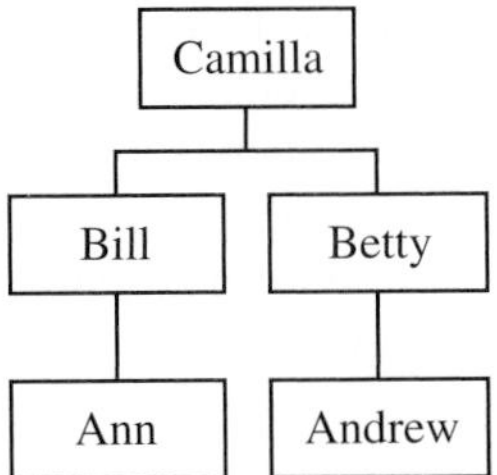

FIGURE 2-14 Organization in Hypothetical Company.

- Camilla asks Betty.
- Betty replies that Andrew works for her.
- Camilla tells Bill.
- Bill tells Ann.

If Andrew is in a different task group, it may be necessary to go higher in the organizational tree before a common point is found.

We can use a similar process for cryptographic key exchange, as shown in Figure 2-15. If Andrew and Ann want to communicate, Andrew can give his public key to Betty, who passes it to Camilla or directly to Bill, who gives it to Ann. But this sequence is not exactly the way it would work in real life. The key would probably be accompanied by a note saying it is from Andrew, ranging from a bit of yellow paper to a form 947 Statement of Identity. And if a form 947 is used, then Betty would also have to attach a form 632a Transmittal of Identity, Camilla would attach another 632a, and Bill would attach a final one, as shown in Figure 2-14. This chain of forms 632a would say, in essence, "I am Betty and I received this key and the attached statement of identity personally from a person I know to be Andrew," "I am Camilla and I received this key and the attached statement of identity and the attached transmittal of identity per-

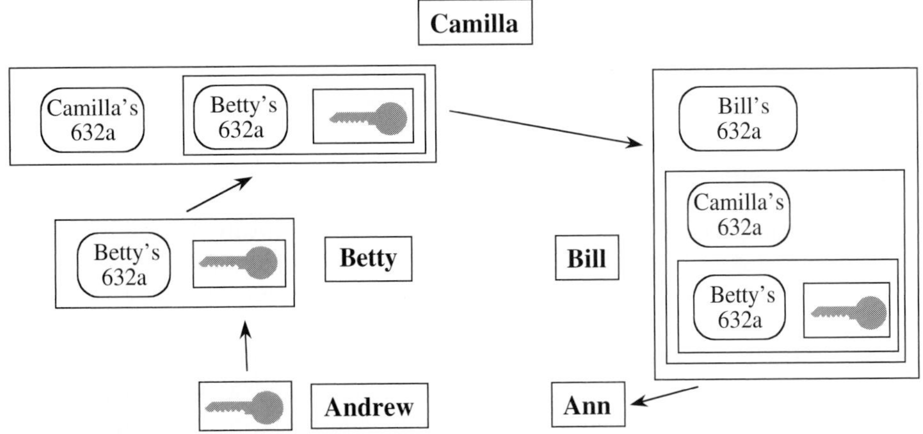

FIGURE 2-15 Andrew Passes a Key to Ann.

sonally from a person I know to be Betty," and so forth. When Ann receives the key, she can review the chain of evidence and conclude with reasonable assurance that the key really did come from Andrew. This protocol is a way of obtaining authenticated public keys, a binding of a key and a reliable identity.

This model works well within a company because there is always someone common to any two employees, even if the two employees are in different divisions so that the common person is the president. The process bogs down, however, if Ann, Bill, Camilla, Betty, and Andrew all have to be available whenever Ann and Andrew want to communicate. If Betty is away on a business trip or Bill is off sick, the protocol falters. It also does not work well if the president cannot get any meaningful work done because every day is occupied with handling forms 632a.

To address the first of these problems, Andrew can ask for his complete chain of forms 632a from the president down to him. Andrew can then give a copy of this full set to anyone in the company who wants his key. Instead of working from the bottom up to a common point, Andrew starts at the top and derives his full chain. He gets these signatures any time his superiors are available, so they do not need to be available when he wants to give away his authenticated public key.

The second problem is resolved by reversing the process. Instead of starting at the bottom (with task members) and working to the top of the tree (the president), we start at the top. Andrew thus has a preauthenticated public key for unlimited use in the future. Suppose the expanded structure of our hypothetical company, showing the president and other levels, is as illustrated in Figure 2-16.

The president creates a letter for each division manager saying "I am the Edward, the president, I attest to the identity of division manager Diana, whom I know personally, and I trust Diana to attest to the identities of her subordinates." Each division manager does similarly, copying the president's letter with each letter the manager creates, and so on. Andrew receives a packet of letters, from the president down through his task group leader, each letter linked by name to the next. If every employee in the company receives such a packet, any two employees who want to exchange authenticated keys need only compare each other's packets; both packets will have at least Edward in common, perhaps some other high managers, and at some point will deviate. Andrew and Ann, for example, could compare their chains, determine that they were the same through Camilla, and trace the bottom parts. Andrew knows Alice's chain is authentic through Camilla because it is identical to his chain, and Ann knows the same. Each knows the rest of the chain is accurate because it follows an unbroken line of names and signatures.

Certificates to Authenticate an Identity

This protocol is represented more easily electronically than on paper. With paper, it is necessary to guard against forgeries, to prevent part of one chain from being replaced and to ensure that the public key at the bottom is bound to the chain. Electronically the whole thing can be done with digital signatures and hash functions. Kohnfelder [KOH78] seems to be the originator of the concept of using an electronic certificate with a chain of authenticators, which is expanded in Merkle's paper [MER80].

A public key and user's identity are bound together in a **certificate,** which is then signed by someone called a **certificate authority,** certifying the accuracy of the bind-

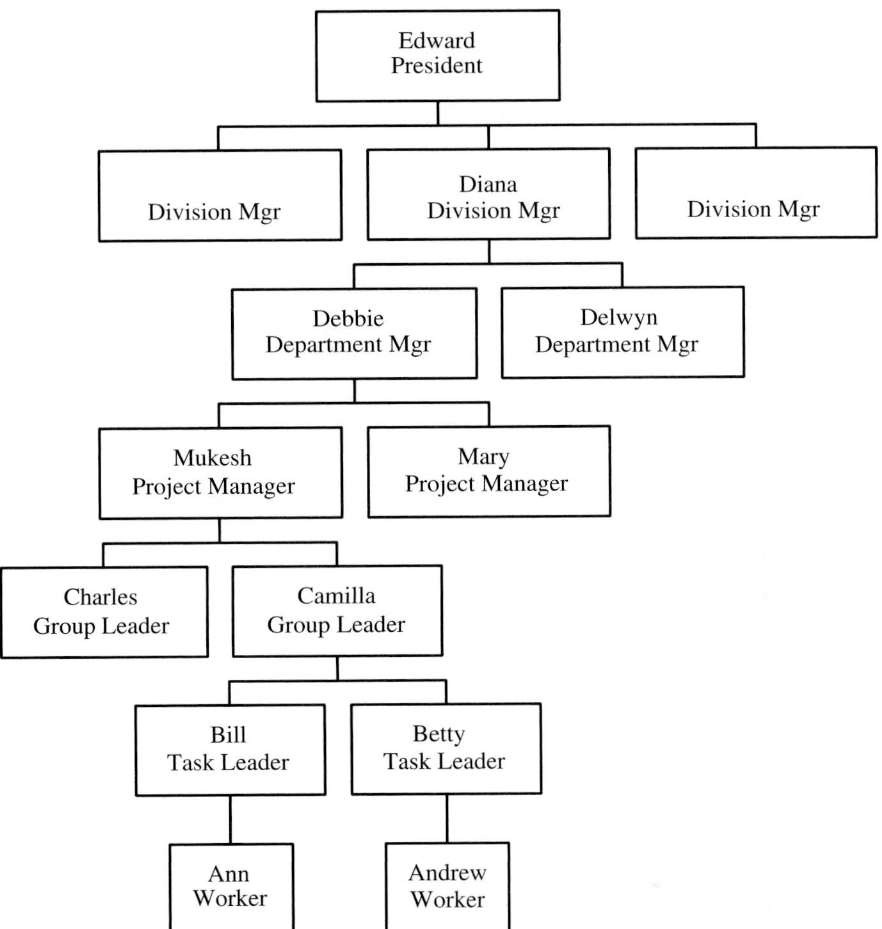

FIGURE 2-16 Expanded Corporate Structure.

ing. In our example, the company might set up a certificate scheme in the following way. First, Edward selects a public key pair, posts the public part where everyone in the company can retrieve it, and retains the private part. Then, each division manager, such as Diana, creates her public key pair, puts the public key in a message together with her identity, and passes the message securely to Edward. Edward signs it by creating a hash value of the message and then encrypting the message and the hash with his private key. By signing the message, Edward affirms that the public key (Diana's) and the identity (also Diana's) in the message are for the same person. This message is called Diana's **certificate.**

All of Diana's department managers create messages with their public keys, Diana signs and hashes each, and returns them. She also appends to each a copy of the certificate she received from Edward. In this way, anyone can verify a manager's certificate by starting with Edward's well-known public key, decrypting Diana's certificate to retrieve her public key (and identity), and using Diana's public key to decrypt the manager's certificate. Figure 2-17 shows how certificates are created for Diana and one of her managers, Delwyn. This process continues down the hierarchy to Ann and Andrew. As shown in Figure 2-18, Andrew's certificate is really his individual certificate combined with all certificates for those above him in the line to the president.

Trust Without a Single Hierarchy

In our examples, certificates were issued on the basis of the managerial structure. But it is not necessary to have such a structure or to follow it to use certificate signing for authentication. Anyone who is considered acceptable as an authority can sign a certificate. For example, if you want to determine whether a person received a degree from a university, you would not contact the president or chancellor but would instead go to the office of records or the registrar. To verify someone's employment, you might ask the personnel office or the director of human resources. And to check if someone lives at a particular address, you might consult the office of public records.

Sometimes, a particular person is designated to attest to the authenticity or validity of a document or person. For example, a notary public attests to the validity of a (written) signature on a document. Some companies have a security officer to verify that an

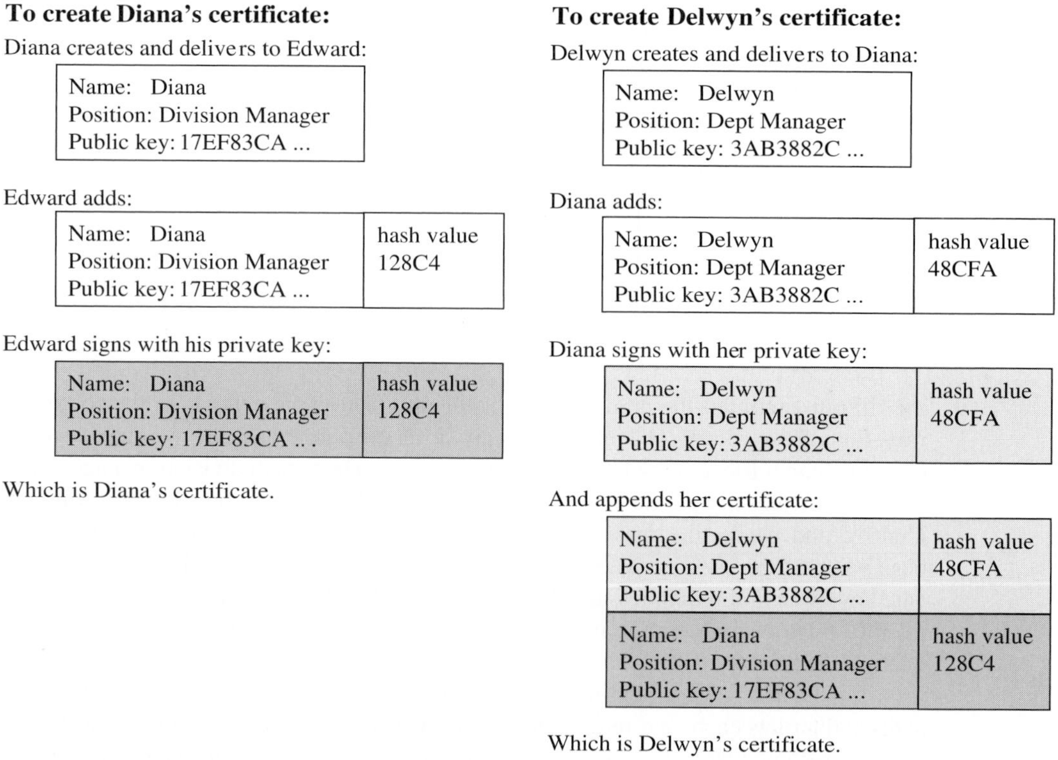

To create Diana's certificate:

Diana creates and delivers to Edward:

Name: Diana Position: Division Manager Public key: 17EF83CA ...

Edward adds:

Name: Diana Position: Division Manager Public key: 17EF83CA ...	hash value 128C4

Edward signs with his private key:

Name: Diana Position: Division Manager Public key: 17EF83CA	hash value 128C4

Which is Diana's certificate.

To create Delwyn's certificate:

Delwyn creates and delivers to Diana:

Name: Delwyn Position: Dept Manager Public key: 3AB3882C ...

Diana adds:

Name: Delwyn Position: Dept Manager Public key: 3AB3882C ...	hash value 48CFA

Diana signs with her private key:

Name: Delwyn Position: Dept Manager Public key: 3AB3882C ...	hash value 48CFA

And appends her certificate:

Name: Delwyn Position: Dept Manager Public key: 3AB3882C ...	hash value 48CFA
Name: Diana Position: Division Manager Public key: 17EF83CA ...	hash value 128C4

Which is Delwyn's certificate.

FIGURE 2-17 Signed Certificates.

Name: Andrew Position: Worker Public key: 7013F82A ...	hash value 60206
Name: Betty Position: Task Leader Public key: 2468ACE0 ...	hash value 00002
Name: Camilla Position: Group Leader Public key: 44082CCA ...	hash value 12346
Name: Mukesh Position: Project Manager Public key: 47F0F008 ...	hash value 16802
Name: Delwyn Position: Dept Manager Public key: 3AB3882C ...	hash value 48CFA
Name: Diana Position: Division Manager Public key:17EF83CA ...	hash value 128C4

Key to encryptions

- Encrypted under Betty's private key
- Encrypted under Camilla's private key
- Encrypted under Mukesh's private key
- Encrypted under Delwyn's private key
- Encrypted under Diana's private key
- Encrypted under Edward's private key

FIGURE 2-18 Chain of Certificates.

employee has appropriate security clearances to read a document or attend a meeting. Many companies have a separate personnel office for each site or each plant location; the personnel officer vouches for the employment status of the employees at that site. Any of these officers or heads of offices could credibly sign certificates for people under their purview. Natural hierarchies exist in society, and these same hierarchies can be used to validate certificates.

The only problem with a hierarchy is the need for trust at the top level. The entire chain of authenticity is secure because each certificate contains the key that decrypts the next certificate, except for the top. Within a company, it is reasonable to trust the person at the top. But if certificates are to become widely used in electronic commerce, people must be able to exchange certificates securely across companies, organizations, and countries.

The Internet is a large federation of networks for intercompany, interorganizational, and international (as well was intracompany, intraorganizational, and intranational) communication. It is not a part of any government, nor is it a privately owned company. It is governed by a board called the Internet Society. The Internet Society has power only because its members, the governments and companies that together make up the Internet, agree to work together. But there really is no "top" for the Internet. Different companies, such as C&W HKT, SecureNet, Verisign, Baltimore Technologies, Deutsche Telecom, Societá Interbancaria per l'Automatzione di Milano, Entrust, and Certiposte are root certification authority, which means each is a highest authority that signs certificates. So, instead of one root and one top, there are many roots, largely structured around national boundaries.

In this chapter, we introduced several approaches to key distribution, ranging from direct exchange to distribution through a central distribution facility to certified advance distribution. We explore the notions of certificates and certificate authorities in more depth in Chapter 7, in which we discuss Public Key Infrastructures. But no matter what approach is taken to key distribution, each has its advantages and disadvantages. Points to keep in mind about any key distribution protocol include the following:

- What *operational restrictions* are there? For example, does the protocol require a continuously available facility, such as the key distribution center?
- What *trust* requirements are there? Who and what entities must be trusted to act properly?
- What is the protection against *failure?* Can an outsider impersonate any of the entities in the protocol and subvert security? Can any party of the protocol cheat without detection?
- How *efficient* is the protocol? A protocol requiring several steps to establish an encryption key that will be used many times is one thing; it is quite another to go through several time-consuming steps for a one-time use.
- How easy is the protocol to *implement*? Notice that complexity in computer implementation may be different from manual use.

The descriptions of the protocols have raised some of these issues; others are brought out in the exercises at the end of this chapter.

2.9 SUMMARY OF ENCRYPTION

This chapter has examined the basic processes of encryption and cryptanalysis. We began by describing what might be called "toy cryptosystems" because they illustrate principles of encryption but are not suitable for real use. These cryptosystems allowed us to introduce the two basic methods of encipherment—substitution and transposition or permutation—as well as techniques of cryptanalysis.

Then, we examined three "real" cryptosystems: DES, AES, and RSA, two symmetric and one asymmetric, which are used daily in millions of applications. We presented the characteristics of these cryptosystems, focusing on where they come from and how they are used, but not necessarily how they work. We save the internal details for Chapter 10.

Finally, we introduced several very important and widely used applications of cryptography: hash functions, key exchange protocols, digital signatures, and certificates. Key exchange, especially with public key cryptography, is used by almost everyone. For example, any time a user enters "secure" (HTTPS) mode on a browser, a key exchange protocol is involved. Digital signatures give us a reliable means to prove the origin of data or code. To support digital signatures, cryptographic hash codes offer a fast, fairly reliable way of determining whether a piece of data has been modified between sender and receiver. Finally, certificates and their distribution allow us to trust information from someone or someplace else, even if we do not have direct interaction.

With these tools—symmetric encryption, public key encryption, key exchange protocols, digital signatures, cryptographic hash codes, and certificates—we are ready to study how threats in major application areas (such as program code, operating systems, database management systems, and networks) can be countered with controls, some of which depend on cryptography. Although cryptography is not the only control for the computer security specialist, it is certainly a very important one.

2.10 TERMS AND CONCEPTS

sender, 36
receiver, 36
transmission medium, 36
interceptor, 36
intruder, 36
encryption, 36
decryption, 36
encode, 36
decode, 36
encipher, 36
decipher, 36
cryptosystem, 36
cipher, 36
plaintext, 36
ciphertext, 36
key, 37
keyless cipher, 37
symmetric, 37
asymmetric, 37
cryptography, 38
cryptanalyst, 38
cryptology, 38
break an encryption, 39
breakable encryption, 40
substitution, 41
transposition, 41
substitution cipher, 41
monoalphabetic substitution, 41
simple substitution, 41
Caesar cipher, 41
permutation, 44
one-time pad, 47
Vigenère tableau, 48
Vernam cipher, 48
book cipher, 49
transposition, 52
columnar transposition, 52
digram, 54
trigram, 54
product cipher, 55
secure cryptographic system, 58
amount of secrecy, 58
error propagation, 58
authentication, 59
key distribution, 60
key management, 60
stream cipher, 60
block cipher, 60
confusion, 62
diffusion, 62
ciphertext-only attack, 63
known plaintext attack, 63
probable plaintext attack, 63
chosen plaintext attack, 63
chosen ciphertext attack, 64
Data Encryption Standard (DES), 65
Data Encryption Algorithm-1, 66
double DES, 67
triple DES, 68
Advanced Encryption Standard (AES), 69
Rijndael, 70
cycle or round, 70
public key, 73

private key, 73
secret key, 73
Rivest–Shamir–Adelman (RSA) algorithm, 75
cryptographic hash function, 77
message digest, 77
hash, 77
checksum, 77
MD4, MD5, 77
SHA/SHS, 77
one-way function, 77
chaining, 77
key exchange, 77
digital signature, 79
certificate, 81
certificate authority, 84

2.11 WHERE THE FIELD IS HEADED

Throughout history, cryptography has attracted a select few to perform basic research. The world always needs new and better algorithms, while at the same time, governments and others are continually looking for ways to break those algorithms.

Cryptography is not a field for amateurs. One word processor manufacturer found much to its chagrin that the encryption feature it had built into its product could be broken with a ciphertext-only attack in minutes with pencil and paper. Another browser manufacturer found that its means of generating cryptographic keys was predictable. Both of these companies had employed ordinarily smart developers but had not taken the step of involving an expert in cryptography. So while your homemade cipher may be adequate to protect e-mail messages to your friends, for serious use you should rely on the knowledge of professional cryptographers. Typically, professional cryptographers have done significant advanced study, often obtaining doctorates in advanced mathematics.

One interesting problem cryptographers are currently exploring is called "watermarking." The root of the problem is a need to protect digital data from unauthorized copying. How can someone tell by looking at a digital image picture file whether you took a similar photograph yourself or whether you have an unauthorized copy of a copyrighted publication? By embedding a cryptographic string, or watermark, a legitimate author can demonstrate the origin of the file. This research is the subject of papers at cryptographic forums such as the Crypto and EuroCrypt conferences.

Another major research and development topic, certificate and public key infrastructures, was addressed briefly in this chapter and is covered in Chapter 7.

2.12 TO LEARN MORE

This chapter does not present much of the history of encryption. Because encryption has been used for military and diplomatic communications, many of the stories are fascinating. David Kahn's thorough study of encryption [KAH67, KAH96] still stands as the masterpiece. Other interesting sources are the works by Friedman [FRI76a], [FRI76b], and [FRI76c]; [DEA85]; [BAM82]; and [YAR31].

The highly readable presentation of elementary cryptography by Sinkov [SIN66] is well worth study. A more precise and mathematical analysis is done by Konheim

[KON80] and Meyer and Matyas [MEY82]. Many more simple encryption algorithms are presented in [FOS82]. Singh [SIN99] presents an overview of the history of cryptography from primitive days to modern commercial uses. Schneier's book [SCH96] gives up-to-date and detailed description of practically all encryption systems.

2.13 EXERCISES

The first several exercises ask you to decrypt a piece of ciphertext. Each of these is an English prose quotation. More important than the precise quotation is the *process* you use to analyze the encryption. Justify your answer by describing the various tests you performed and the results you obtained for those tests.

1. Decrypt the following encrypted quotation.

```
fqjcb rwjwj vnjax bnkhj whxcq nawjv
nfxdu mbvnu ujbbf nnc
```

2. Decrypt the following encrypted quotation.

```
oczmz vmzor jocdi bnojv dhvod igdaz
admno ojbzo rcvot jprvi oviyv aozmo
cvooj ziejt dojig toczr dnzno jahvi
fdiyv xcdzq zoczn zxjiy
```

3. Decrypt the following encrypted quotation.

```
pbegu uymiq icuuf guuyi qguuy qcuiv
fiqgu uyqcu qbeme vp
```

4. Decrypt the following encrypted quotation.

```
jrgdg idxgq anngz gtgtt sitgj ranmn
oeddi omnwj rajvk sexjm dxkmn wjrgm
ttgdt gognj ajmzg ovgki nlaqg tjamn
xmsmj jrgko jtgnw jrgnj rgvat tmgta
wamno jjrgw izgtn sgnji babgu
```

5. Decrypt the following encrypted quotation.

```
ejitp spawa qleji taiul rtwll rflrl
laoat wsqqj atgac kthls iraoa twlpl
qjatw jufrh lhuts qataq itats aittk
stqfj cae
```

6. Decrypt the following encrypted quotation.

```
auqrq rkrzd dmhxk ageho kfalu hkmog
rlagm hznhf fhglm hkrlh mvzmr znvir
klhgl vhodw krnra przgr jozdl vzkra
gmvrw almka xomah gmvrf zbhka mtqho
dwxre dzwmh mzcro imvra khqgz gwwri
zkm
```

7. Decrypt the following encrypted quotation.

```
jmjmj gsmsg lrjgu csqyj quflr mfajq
erdmc cmqlv lqyhg gawgq arpgq sblce
jrlrj lnemc cyjqu flrmf ajqer d
```

8. Decrypt the following encrypted quotation.

```
vcwpc kwblm smljy glbgu gbtwj jyats
lwsgm lwjjy vcrfc rikwl qjwte fscpw
lbgqm jwscb ktpbc pqats vfwsm dvwpw
lbsfc ktrfu wtlsc brpgk cmdqj wtefs
cpgle vfmjc ncmnj cq
```

9. Decrypt the following encrypted quotation.

```
ptgpz ggprf bdkrg pequt tngtf ggpzf
zfqgp tukrw wkzfg kquyd qxwzu ltuet
zfrfl ptgpz ggprf bdkrg pequt dhmgw
tgokr wwdtt bxqug tuedq xequt fraty
rdaur erfzg rqfot gjzfr gorfa wrftd
hdgqx rfyxz hwgdz fokpt utuzg ptugp
zfrfq hudtw jtdpt gpzgu tzydz fyluq
kdfqk rdtud hdcta gdfqg prdqk fytxr
artfa omhga qecwz rfdqx pzuyk quydz
fyqmd ahutd tfgtf atdzf yzdbd kpomq
qbdzu tkurg gtfkp rapaz ffqgm thfyt
udgqq y
```

10. Decrypt the following encrypted quotation.

```
mszkx ijddj nzatm lrkdj mlwmc qrktj
tnwir zatnj bxdrj amlrs zxrzd dbjbk
wsrir mlrxc icnic qrkza tmlrb cbriz
mlkco mnizx r
```

11. Decrypt the following encrypted quotation.

```
gahzh zgaff irfcc fqgmx eefsp xmgab
bxscy gadgb afqbf dsfzh rvhqm xsgnq
fxmgf qgafz nsmfh gxmxn sxbqk faduh
xnsbf jdvft nhcgp xmxns yhzdz gfszg
afznq gafjx xqdqy gafzg dszdz hmbfb
fsfuh ccdhq zkpqf rfzzh gpmxx czkpa
fdufq cprxj enczh xq
```

12. Decrypt the following encrypted quotation.

```
gasaz afxfk hqbzp zbqnq hfkqf zdfgr
gsaaf afdfz fzujz fhhxh irxxg rvnqp
fhsdm cqbqx cmfyx fxjgc qsdaz ggvfk
mnfzp xqtga efndf exhsd fmczu sggdf
pfpzq xqxhc mgmmp gaxbr afnfx bzsbj
bnyfe xshsn smzfc cfduz yhzhh gggcx
axfcq dmsdi
```

13. What characteristics would make an encryption absolutely unbreakable? What characteristics would make an encryption impractical to break?

14. Does a substitution need to be a permutation of the plaintext symbols? Why or why not?

15. Explain why the product of two relatively simple ciphers, such as a substitution and a transposition, can achieve a high degree of security.

16. How would you test a piece of ciphertext to determine quickly if it was likely the result of a simple substitution?

17. How would you test a piece of ciphertext to determine quickly if it was likely the result of a transposition?

18. Suggest a source of a very long sequence of unpredictable numbers. Your source must be something that both the sender and receiver can readily access but that is not obvious to outsiders and is not transmitted directly from sender to receiver.

19. Given the speed of a current ordinary computer (for home or light office use), estimate the amount of time necessary to crack a DES encryption by testing all 2^{56} possible keys. Make a similar estimate for a 128-bit AES key.

20. List three kinds of data whose lifetime (amount of time for which confidentiality protection is needed) is approximately one day. List three whose lifetime is closer to one year. List three whose lifetime is closer to one century.

21. Obtain manufacturers' specifications on two current cryptographic products for the same algorithm, such as AES, DES, a proprietary algorithm from the manufacturer, or some other algorithm. The products should have different implementations, such as one in hardware and the other software, or one on a smart card and one in software. Determine the amount of time it would take to encrypt a block of characters of some modest size (for example, 3,000 characters) with each.

22. List three applications in which a stream cipher would be desirable. Are applications for block ciphers more prevalent? Why or why not? Why do you think this is true?

23. Are DES and AES stream or block ciphers?

24. What are the risks in the U.S. government's selecting a cryptosystem for widespread commercial use (both inside and outside the United States)? How could users from outside the United States overcome some or all of these risks?

25. DES and AES are both "turn the handle" algorithms in that they use repetition of some number of very similar cycles. What are the advantages (to implementer, users, cryptanalysts, etc.) of this approach?

26. Why should exportability be a criterion for selection of a cryptographic standard?

27. How do the NIST criteria for selection of DES and AES relate to Shannon's original standards of a good cryptographic system? What are the significant differences? How do these standards reflect a changed environment many years after Shannon wrote his standards?

28. Obtain the manufacturer's specifications for a commercial product that performs symmetric encryption (e.g., a DES, AES, or proprietary encryption module). Obtain specifications for an asymmetric algorithm (from the same or a different manufacturer). What is the expected time for each to encrypt a short (e.g., 1,500-character) piece of plaintext?

29. If the useful life of DES was about 20 years (1977–1999), how long do you predict the useful life of AES to be? Justify your answer.

30. Assume you are in charge of product development for a company that makes cryptographic equipment. At its simplest, a cryptographic implementation is a black box: insert key, insert plaintext, press "start," retrieve ciphertext. And for the same algorithm, these so-called black boxes from different manufacturers will be very similar. What other features or capabilities would differentiate your cryptographic product from the competition. Be specific. Do not simply say "user interface," for example, but list specific features of capabilities you think users would like to have.

31. Should a cryptographic product manufacturer try to develop an "all in one" product that could perform, for example, DES, AES, and RSA cryptography? Why or why not?

3

Program Security

In this chapter:

- Programming errors with security implications—buffer overflows, incomplete access control
- Malicious code—viruses, worms, Trojan horses
- Program development controls against malicious code and vulnerabilities—software engineering principles and practices
- Controls to protect against program flaws in execution—operating system support and administrative controls

In the first two chapters, we learned about the need for computer security and we studied encryption, a fundamental tool in implementing many kinds of security controls. In this chapter, we begin to study how to apply security in computing. We start with *why* we need security at the program level and *how* we can achieve it.

In one form or another, protecting programs is at the heart of computer security. So we need to ask two important questions:

- How do we keep programs free from flaws?
- How do we protect computing resources against programs that contain flaws?

In later chapters, we will examine particular types of programs—including operating systems, database management systems, and network implementations—and the specific kinds of security issues that are raised by the nature of their design and functionality. In this chapter, we address more general themes, most of which carry forward to these special-purpose systems. Thus, this chapter not only lays the groundwork for future chapters but also is significant on its own.

This chapter deals with the writing of programs. It defers to a later chapter what may be a much larger issue in program security: trust. The trust problem can be framed as follows: Presented with a finished program, for example, a commercial software package, how can you tell how secure it is or how to use it in its most secure way? In part the answer to these questions is independent, third-party evaluations, presented for operating systems (but applicable to other programs, as well) in Chapter 5. The reporting and fixing of discovered flaws is discussed in Chapter 9, as are liability and software warranties. For now, however, the unfortunate state of commercial software development is largely a case of trust your source, and buyer beware.

3.1 SECURE PROGRAMS

Consider what we mean when we say that a program is "secure." We saw in Chapter 1 that security implies some degree of trust that the program enforces expected confidentiality, integrity, and availability. From the point of view of a program or a programmer, how can we look at a software component or code fragment and assess its security? This question is, of course, similar to the problem of assessing software quality in general. One way to assess security or quality is to ask people to name the characteristics of software that contribute to its overall security. However, we are likely to get different answers from different people. This difference occurs because the importance of the characteristics depends on who is analyzing the software. For example, one person may decide that code is secure because it takes too long to break through its security controls. And someone else may decide code is secure if it has run for a period of time with no apparent failures. But a third person may decide that *any* potential fault in meeting security requirements makes code insecure.

An assessment of security can also be influenced by someone's general perspective on software quality. For example, if your manager's idea of quality is conformance to specifications, then she might consider the code secure if it meets security requirements, whether or not the requirements are complete or correct. This security view played a role when a major computer manufacturer delivered all its machines with keyed locks, since a keyed lock was written in the requirements. But the machines were not secure, because all locks were configured to use the same key! Thus, another view of security is fitness for purpose; in this view, the manufacturer clearly had room for improvement.

In general, practitioners often look at quantity and types of faults for evidence of a product's quality (or lack of it). For example, developers track the number of faults found in requirements, design, and code inspections and use them as indicators of the likely quality of the final product. Sidebar 3-1 explains the importance of separating the faults—the causes of problems—from the failures—the effects of the faults.

Fixing Faults

One approach to judging quality in security has been fixing faults. You might argue that a module in which 100 faults were discovered and fixed is better than another in which only 20 faults were discovered and fixed, suggesting that more rigorous analysis and testing had led to the finding of the larger number of faults. *Au contraire,* challenges your friend: a piece of software with 100 discovered faults is inherently full of problems and could clearly have hundreds more waiting to appear. Your friend's opinion is confirmed by the software testing literature; software that has many faults early on is likely to have many others still waiting to be found.

Early work in computer security was based on the paradigm of "**penetrate and patch**," in which analysts searched for and repaired faults. Often, a top-quality "tiger team" would be convened to test a system's security by attempting to cause it to fail.

The test was considered to be a "proof" of security; if the system withstood the attacks, it was considered secure. Unfortunately, far too often the proof became a counterexample, in which not just one but several serious security problems were uncovered. The problem discovery in turn led to a rapid effort to "patch" the system to repair or restore the security. (See Schell's analysis in [SCH79].) However, the patch efforts were largely useless, making the system less secure rather than more secure because they frequently introduced *new* faults. There are three reasons why.

- The pressure to repair a specific problem encouraged a narrow focus on the fault itself and not on its context. In particular, the analysts paid attention to the immediate cause of the failure and not to the underlying design or requirements faults.
- The fault often had nonobvious side effects in places other than the immediate area of the fault.
- The fault could not be fixed properly because system functionality or performance would suffer as a consequence.

Unexpected Behavior

The inadequacies of penetrate-and-patch led researchers to seek a better way to be confident that code meets its security requirements. One way to do that is to compare the requirements with the behavior. That is, to understand program security, we can examine programs to see whether they behave as their designers intended or users expected. We call such unexpected behavior a **program security flaw**; it is inappropriate program behavior caused by a program vulnerability. Unfortunately, the terminology in the computer security field is not consistent with the IEEE standard described in Sidebar 3-1; there is no direct mapping of the terms "vulnerability" and "flaw" into the characterization of faults and failures. A flaw can be either a fault or failure, and a vulnerability usually describes a class of flaws, such as a buffer overflow. In spite of the inconsistency, it is important for us to remember that we must view vulnerabilities and flaws from two perspectives, cause and effect, so that we see what fault caused the problem and what failure (if any) is visible to the user. For example, a Trojan horse may have been injected in a piece of code—a flaw exploiting a vulnerability—but the user may not yet have seen the Trojan horse's malicious behavior. Thus, we must address program security flaws from inside and outside, to find causes not only of existing failures but also of incipient ones. Moreover, it is not enough to identify these problems. We must also determine how to prevent harm caused by possible flaws.

Program security flaws can derive from any kind of software fault. That is, they cover everything from a misunderstanding of program requirements to a one-character error in coding or even typing. The flaws can result from problems in a single code component or from the failure of several programs or program pieces to interact compatibly through a shared interface. The security flaws can reflect code that was intentionally designed or coded to be malicious, or code that was simply developed in a sloppy or misguided way. Thus, it makes sense to divide program flaws into two separate logical categories: inadvertent human errors versus malicious, intentionally induced flaws.

Sidebar 3-1 IEEE Terminology for Quality

Frequently, we talk about "bugs" in software, a term that can mean many different things, depending on context. A "bug" can be a mistake in interpreting a requirement, a syntax error in a piece of code, or the (as-yet-unknown) cause of a system crash. The IEEE has suggested a standard terminology (in IEEE Standard 729) for describing "bugs" in our software products [IEEE83].

When a human makes a mistake, called an **error**, in performing some software activity, the error may lead to a **fault**, or an incorrect step, command, process, or data definition in a computer program. For example, a designer may misunderstand a requirement and create a design that does not match the actual intent of the requirements analyst and the user. This design fault is an encoding of the error, and it can lead to other faults, such as incorrect code and an incorrect description in a user manual. Thus, a single error can generate many faults, and a fault can reside in any development or maintenance product.

A **failure** is a departure from the system's required behavior. It can be discovered before or after system delivery, during testing, or during operation and maintenance. Since the requirements documents can contain faults, a failure indicates that the system is not performing as required, even though it may be performing as specified.

Thus, a fault is an inside view of the system, as seen by the eyes of the developers, whereas a failure is an outside view: a problem that the user sees. Not every fault corresponds to a failure; for example, if faulty code is never executed or a particular state is never entered, then the fault will never cause the code to fail.

These categories help us understand some ways to prevent the inadvertent and intentional insertion of flaws into future code, but we still have to address their effects, regardless of intention. That is, in the words of Sancho Panza in *Man of La Mancha*, "it doesn't matter whether the stone hits the pitcher or the pitcher hits the stone, it's going to be bad for the pitcher." An inadvertent error can cause just as much harm to users and their organizations as can an intentionally induced flaw. Furthermore, a system attack often exploits an unintentional security flaw to perform intentional damage. From reading the popular press (see Sidebar 3-2), you might conclude that intentional security incidents (called **cyber attacks**) are the biggest security threat today. In fact, plain, unintentional, human errors cause much more damage.

Regrettably, we do not have techniques to eliminate or address all program security flaws. There are two reasons for this distressing situation.

1. Program controls apply at the level of the individual program and programmer. When we test a system, we try to make sure that the functionality prescribed in the requirements is implemented in the code. That is, we take a "should do" checklist and verify that the code does what it is supposed to do. However, security is also about *preventing* certain actions: a "shouldn't do" list. It is almost impossible to ensure that a program does precisely what its designer or user in-

Sidebar 3-2 Dramatic Increase in Cyber Attacks

Carnegie Mellon University's Computer Emergency Response Team (CERT) tracks the number and kinds of vulnerabilities and cyber attacks reported worldwide. Part of CERT's mission is to warn users and developers of new problems and also to provide information on ways to fix them. According to the CERT coordination center, fewer than 200 known vulnerabilities were reported in 1995, and that number ranged between 200 and 400 from 1996 to 1999. But the number increased dramatically in 2000, with over 1,000 known vulnerabilities in 2000, almost 2,420 in 2001, and an expectation of at least 3,750 in 2002 (over 1,000 in the first quarter of 2002).

How does that translate into cyber attacks? The CERT reported 3,734 security incidents in 1998, 9,859 in 1999, 21,756 in 2000, and 52,658 in 2001. But in the first quarter of 2002 there were already 26,829 incidents, so it seems as if the exponential growth rate will continue [HOU02]. Moreover, as of June 2002, Symantec's Norton antivirus software checked for 61,181 known virus patterns, and McAfee's product could detect over 50,000 [BER01]. The Computer Security Institute and the FBI cooperate to take an annual survey of approximately 500 large institutions: companies, government organizations, and educational institutions [CSI02]. Of the respondents, 90 percent detected security breaches, 25 percent identified between two and five events, and 37 percent reported more than ten. By a different count, the Internet security firm Riptech reported that the number of successful Internet attacks was 28 percent higher for January–June 2002 compared with the previous six-month period [RIP02].

A survey of 167 network security personnel revealed that more than 75 percent of government respondents experienced attacks to their networks; more than half said the attacks were frequent. However, 60 percent of respondents admitted that they could do more to make their systems more secure; the respondents claimed that they simply lacked time and staff to address the security issues [BUS01]. In the CSI/FBI survey, 223, or 44 percent of respondents, could and did quantify their loss from incidents; their losses totaled over $455,000,000.

It is clearly time to take security seriously, both as users and developers.

---

tended, and nothing more. Regardless of designer or programmer intent, in a large and complex system, the number of pieces that have to fit together properly interact in an unmanageably large number of ways. We are forced to examine and test the code for typical or likely cases; we cannot exhaustively test every state and data combination to verify a system's behavior. So sheer size and complexity preclude total flaw prevention or mediation. Programmers intending to implant malicious code can take advantage of this incompleteness and hide some flaws successfully, despite our best efforts.

2. Programming and software engineering techniques change and evolve far more rapidly than do computer security techniques. So we often find ourselves trying to secure last year's technology while software developers are rapidly adopting today's—and next year's—technology.

Still, the situation is far from bleak. Computer security has much to offer to program security. By understanding what can go wrong and how to protect against it, we can devise techniques and tools to secure most computer applications.

Types of Flaws

To aid our understanding of the problems and their prevention or correction, we can define categories that distinguish one kind of problem from another. For example, Landwehr et al. [LAN94] present a taxonomy of program flaws, dividing them first into intentional and inadvertent flaws. They further divide intentional flaws into malicious and nonmalicious ones. In the taxonomy, the inadvertent flaws fall into six categories:

- validation error (incomplete or inconsistent)
- domain error
- serialization and aliasing
- inadequate identification and authentication
- boundary condition violation
- other exploitable logic errors

This list gives us a useful overview of the ways programs can fail to meet their security requirements. We leave our discussion of the pitfalls of identification and authentication for Chapter 4, in which we also investigate separation into execution domains. In this chapter, we address the other categories, each of which has interesting examples.

3.2 NONMALICIOUS PROGRAM ERRORS

Being human, programmers and other developers make many mistakes, most of which are unintentional and nonmalicious. Many such errors cause program malfunctions but do not lead to more serious security vulnerabilities. However, a few classes of errors have plagued programmers and security professionals for decades, and there is no reason to believe they will disappear. In this section we consider three classic error types that have enabled many recent security breaches. We explain each type, why it is relevant to security, and how it can be prevented or mitigated.

Buffer Overflows

A buffer overflow is the computing equivalent of trying to pour two liters of water into a one-liter pitcher: Some water is going to spill out and make a mess. And in computing, what a mess these errors have made!

Definition

A buffer (or array or string) is a space in which data can be held. A buffer resides in memory. Because memory is finite, a buffer's capacity is finite. For this reason, in many programming languages the programmer must declare the buffer's maximum size so that the compiler can set aside that amount of space.

Let us look at an example to see how buffer overflows can happen. Suppose a C language program contains the declaration:

```
char sample[10];
```

The compiler sets aside 10 bytes to store this buffer, one byte for each of the ten elements of the array, `sample[0]` through `sample[9]`. Now we execute the statement:

```
sample[10] = 'A';
```

The subscript is out of bounds (that is, it does not fall between 0 and 9), so we have a problem. The nicest outcome (from a security perspective) is for the compiler to detect the problem and mark the error during compilation. However, if the statement were

```
sample[i] = 'A';
```

we could not identify the problem until `i` was set during execution to a too-big subscript. It would be useful if, during execution, the system produced an error message warning of a subscript out of bounds. Unfortunately, in some languages, buffer sizes do not have to be predefined, so there is no way to detect an out-of-bounds error. More importantly, the code needed to check each subscript against its potential maximum value takes time and space during execution, and the resources are applied to catch a problem that occurs relatively infrequently. Even if the compiler were careful in analyzing the buffer declaration and use, this same problem can be caused with pointers, for which there is no reasonable way to define a proper limit. Thus, some compilers do not generate the code to check for exceeding bounds.

Let us examine this problem more closely. It is important to recognize that the potential overflow causes a serious problem only in some instances. The problem's occurrence depends on what is adjacent to the array `sample`. For example, suppose each of the ten elements of the array `sample` is filled with the letter A and the erroneous reference uses the letter B, as follows:

```
for (i=0; i<=9; i++)
       sample[i] = 'A';
sample[10] = 'B'
```

All program and data elements are in memory during execution, sharing space with the operating system, other code, and resident routines. So there are four cases to consider in deciding where the 'B' goes, as shown in Figure 3-1. If the extra character overflows into the user's data space, it simply overwrites an existing variable value (or it may be written into an as-yet unused location), perhaps affecting the program's result, but affecting no other program or data.

In the second case, the 'B' goes into the user's program area. If it overlays an already executed instruction (which will not be executed again), the user should perceive no effect. If it overlays an instruction that is not yet executed, the machine will try to execute an instruction with operation code 0x42, the internal code for the character 'B'. If there is no instruction with operation code 0x42, the system will halt on an illegal instruction exception. Otherwise, the machine will use subsequent bytes as if they

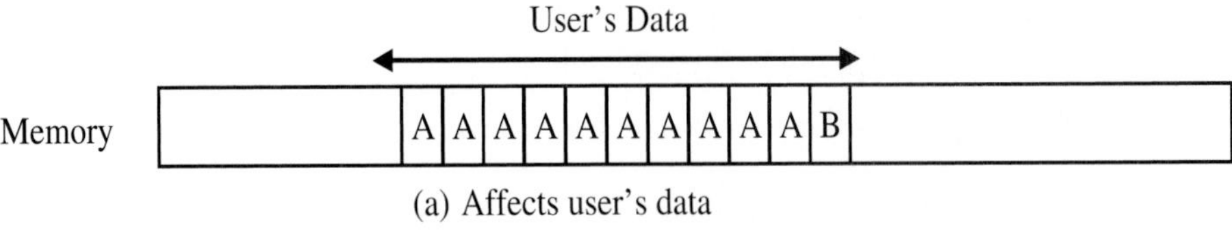

(a) Affects user's data

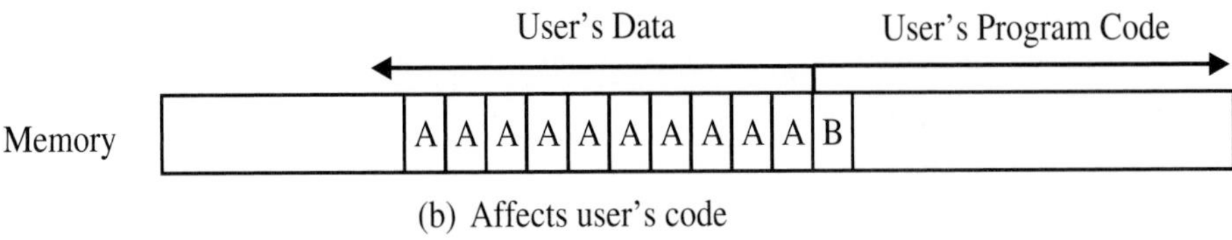

(b) Affects user's code

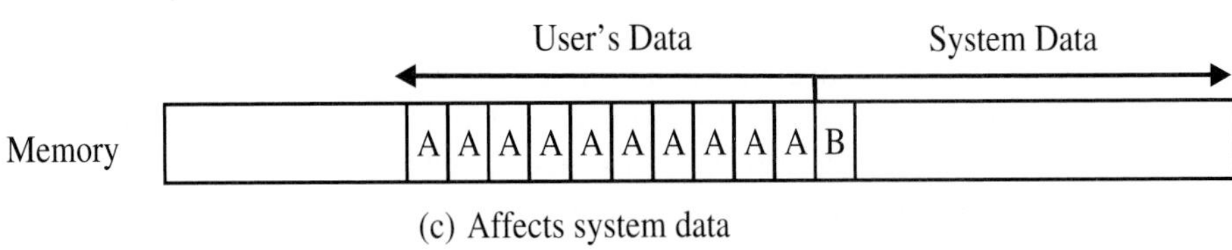

(c) Affects system data

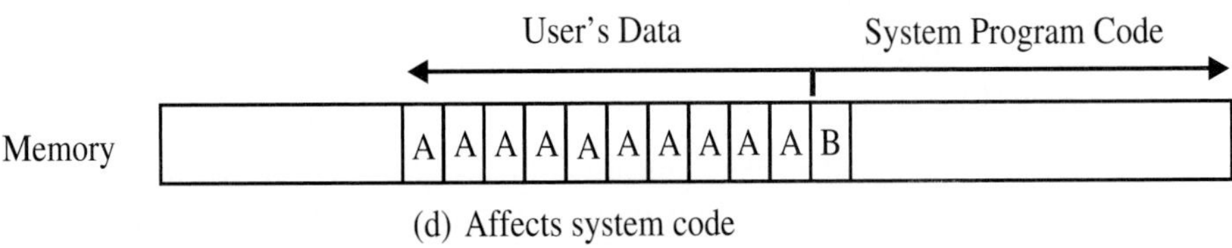

(d) Affects system code

FIGURE 3-1 Places Where a Buffer Can Overflow.

were the rest of the instruction, with success or failure depending on the meaning of the contents. Again, only the user is likely to experience an effect.

The most interesting cases occur when the system owns the space immediately after the array that overflows. Spilling over into system data or code areas produces similar results to those for the user's space: computing with a faulty value or trying to execute an improper operation.

Security Implication

Let us suppose that a malicious person understands the damage that can be done by a buffer overflow; that is, we are dealing with more than simply a normal, errant programmer. The malicious programmer looks at the four cases illustrated in Figure 3-1 and thinks deviously about the last two: What data values could the attacker insert just after the buffer so as to cause mischief or damage, and what planned instruction codes could the system be forced to execute? There are many possible answers, some of which are more malevolent than others. Here, we present two buffer overflow attacks that are used frequently. (See [ALE96] for more details.)

First, the attacker may replace code in the system space. Remember that every program is invoked by the operating system and that the operating system may run with higher privileges than those of a regular program. Thus, if the attacker can gain control by masquerading as the operating system, the attacker can execute many commands in a powerful role. Therefore, by replacing a few instructions right after returning from his or her own procedure, the attacker can get control back from the operating system, possibly with raised privileges. If the buffer overflows into system code space, the attacker merely inserts overflow data that correspond to the machine code for instructions.

On the other hand, the attacker may make use of the stack pointer or the return register. Subprocedures calls are handled with a stack, a data structure in which the most recent item inserted is the next one removed (last arrived, first served). This structure works well because procedure calls can be nested, with each return causing control to transfer back to the immediately preceding routine at its point of execution. Each time a procedure is called, its parameters, the return address (the address immediately after its call), and other local values are pushed onto a stack. An old stack pointer is also pushed onto the stack, and a stack pointer register is reloaded with the address of these new values. Then, control is transferred to the subprocedure.

As the subprocedure executes, it fetches parameters that it finds by using the address pointed to by the stack pointer. Typically, the stack pointer is a register in the processor. Therefore, by causing an overflow into the stack, the attacker can change either the old stack pointer (changing the context for the calling procedure) or the return address (causing control to transfer where the attacker wants when the subprocedure returns). Changing the context or return address allows the attacker to redirect execution to a block of code the attacker wants.

In both these cases, a little experimentation is needed to determine where the overflow is and how to control it. But the work to be done is relatively small—probably a day or two for a competent analyst. These buffer overflows are carefully explained in a paper by Mudge [MUD95] of the famed l0pht computer security group.

An alternative style of buffer overflow occurs when parameter values are passed into a routine, especially when the parameters are passed to a web server on the Internet. Parameters are passed in the URL line, with a syntax similar to

```
http://www.somesite.com/subpage/userinput
&parm1=(808)555-1212&parm2=2004Jan01
```

In this example, the page `userinput` receives two parameters, `parm1` with value `(808)555-1212` (perhaps a U.S. telephone number) and `parm2` with value

`2004Jan01` (perhaps a date). The web browser on the caller's machine will accept values from a user who probably completes fields on a form. The browser encodes those values and transmits them back to the server's web site.

The attacker might question what the server would do with a really long telephone number, say, one with 500 or 1000 digits. But, you say, no telephone in the world has such a telephone number; that is probably exactly what the developer thought, so the developer may have allocated 15 or 20 bytes for an expected maximum length telephone number. Will the program crash with 500 digits? And if it crashes, can it be made to crash in a predictable and usable way? (For the answer to this question, see Litchfield's investigation of the Microsoft *dialer* program [LIT99].) Passing a very long string to a web server is a slight variation on the classic buffer overflow, but no less effective.

As noted above, buffer overflows have existed almost as long as higher-level programming languages with arrays. For a long time they were simply a minor annoyance to programmers and users, a cause of errors and sometimes even system crashes. Rather recently, attackers have used them as vehicles to cause first a system crash and then a controlled failure with a serious security implication. The large number of security vulnerabilities based on buffer overflows shows that developers must pay more attention now to what had previously been thought to be just a minor annoyance.

Incomplete Mediation

Incomplete mediation is another security problem that has been with us for decades. Attackers are exploiting it to cause security problems.

Definition

Consider the example of the previous section:

```
http://www.somesite.com/subpage/userinput
&parm1=(808)555-1212&parm2=2004Jan01
```

The two parameters look like a telephone number and a date. Probably the client's (user's) web browser enters those two values in their specified format for easy processing on the server's side. What would happen if `parm2` were submitted as 1800Jan01? Or 1800Feb30? Or 2048Min32? Or 1Aardvark2Many?

Something would likely fail. As with buffer overflows, one possibility is that the system would fail catastrophically, with a routine's failing on a data type error as it tried to handle a month named "Min" or even a year (like 1800) which was out of range. Another possibility is that the receiving program would continue to execute but would generate a very wrong result. (For example, imagine the amount of interest due today on a billing error with a start date of 1 Jan 1800.) Then again, the processing server might have a default condition, deciding to treat 1Aardvark2Many as 3 July 1947. The possibilities are endless.

One way to address the potential problems is to try to anticipate them. For instance, the programmer in the examples above may have written code to check for correctness on the *client*'s side (that is, the user's browser). The client program can search for and screen out errors. Or, to prevent the use of nonsense data, the program can restrict choices only to valid ones. For example, the program supplying the parameters might have solicited them by using a drop-down box or choice list from which only the twelve conventional months would have been possible choices. Similarly, the year could have been tested to ensure that the value was between 1995 and 2005, and date numbers would have to have been appropriate for the months in which they occur (no 30th of February, for example). Using these verification techniques, the programmer may have felt well insulated from the possible problems a careless or malicious user could cause.

However, the program is still vulnerable. By packing the result into the return URL, the programmer left these data fields in a place accessible to (and changeable by) the user. In particular, the user could edit the URL line, change any parameter values, and resend the line. On the server side, there is no way for the server to tell if the response line came from the client's browser or as a result of the user's editing the URL directly. We say in this case that the data values are not completely mediated: The sensitive data (namely, the parameter values) are in an exposed, uncontrolled condition.

Security Implication

Incomplete mediation is easy to exploit, but it has been exercised less often than buffer overflows. Nevertheless, unchecked data values represent a serious potential vulnerability.

To demonstrate this flaw's security implications, we use a real example; only the name of the vendor has been changed to protect the guilty. Things, Inc., was a very large, international vendor of consumer products, called Objects. The company was ready to sell its Objects through a web site, using what appeared to be a standard e-commerce application. The management at Things decided to let some of its in-house developers produce the web site so that its customers could order Objects directly from the web.

To accompany the web site, Things developed a complete price list of its Objects, including pictures, descriptions, and drop-down menus for size, shape, color, scent, and any other properties. For example, a customer on the web could choose to buy 20 of part number 555A Objects. If the price of one such part were $10, the web server would correctly compute the price of the 20 parts to be $200. Then the customer could decide whether to have the Objects shipped by boat, by ground transportation, or sent electronically. If the customer were to choose boat delivery, the customer's web browser would complete a form with parameters like these:

```
http://www.things.com/order/final&custID=101&part=555A
&qy=20&price=10&ship=boat&shipcost=5&total=205
```

So far, so good; everything in the parameter passage looks correct. But this procedure leaves the parameter statement open for malicious tampering. Things should not need to pass the price of the items back to itself as an input parameter; presumably Things knows how much its Objects cost, and they are unlikely to change dramatically since the time the price was quoted a few screens earlier.

A malicious attacker may decide to exploit this peculiarity by supplying instead the following URL, where the price has been reduced from $205 to $25:

```
http://www.things.com/order/final&custID=101&part=555A
&qy=20&price=1&ship=boat&shipcost=5&total=25
```

Surprise! It worked. The attacker could have ordered Objects from Things in any quantity at any price. And yes, this code was running on the web site for a while before the problem was detected. From a security perspective, the most serious concern about this flaw was the length of time that it could have run undetected. Had the whole world suddenly made a rush to Things's web site and bought Objects at a fraction of their price, Things probably would have noticed. But Things is large enough that it would never have detected a few customers a day choosing prices that were similar to (but smaller than) the real price, say 30 percent off. The e-commerce division would have shown a slightly smaller profit than other divisions, but the difference probably would not have been enough to raise anyone's eyebrows; the vulnerability could have gone unnoticed for years. Fortunately Things hired a consultant to do a routine review of its code, and the consultant found the error quickly.

This web program design flaw is easy to imagine in other web settings. Those of us interested in security must ask ourselves how many similar problems are there in running code today? And how will those vulnerabilities ever be found?

Time-of-Check to Time-of-Use Errors

The third programming flaw we investigate involves synchronization. To improve efficiency, modern processors and operating systems usually change the order in which instructions and procedures are executed. In particular, instructions that appear to be adjacent may not actually be executed immediately after each other, either because of intentionally changed order or because of the effects of other processes in concurrent execution.

Definition

Access control is a fundamental part of computer security; we want to make sure that only those who should access an object are allowed that access. (We explore the access control mechanisms in operating systems in greater detail in Chapter 4.) Every requested access must be governed by an access policy stating who is allowed access to what; then the request must be mediated by an access policy enforcement agent. But an incomplete mediation problem occurs when access is not checked universally. The **time-of-check to time-of-use** (TOCTTOU) flaw concerns mediation that is performed with a "bait and switch" in the middle. It is also known as a serialization or synchronization flaw.

To understand the nature of this flaw, consider a person's buying a sculpture that costs $100. The buyer removes five $20 bills from a wallet, carefully counts them in front of the seller, and lays them on the table. Then the seller turns around to write a receipt. While the seller's back is turned, the buyer takes back one $20 bill. When the seller turns around, the buyer hands over the stack of bills, takes the receipt, and leaves with the sculpture. Between the time when the security was checked (counting the bills) and the access (exchanging the sculpture for the bills), a condition changed: what was checked is no longer valid when the object (that is, the sculpture) is accessed.

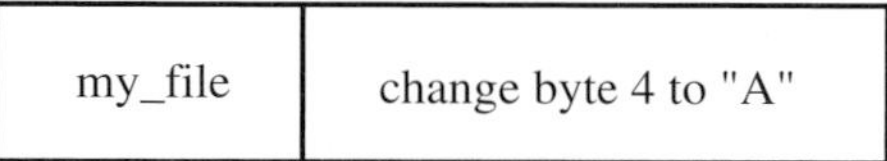

FIGURE 3-2 Data Structure for File Access.

A similar situation can occur with computing systems. Suppose a request to access a file were presented as a data structure, with the name of the file and the mode of access presented in the structure. An example of such a structure is shown in Figure 3-2.

The data structure is essentially a "work ticket," requiring a stamp of authorization; once authorized, it will be put on a queue of things to be done. Normally the access control mediator receives the data structure, determines whether the access should be allowed, and either rejects the access and stops or allows the access and forwards the data structure to the file handler for processing.

To carry out this authorization sequence, the access control mediator would have to look up the file name (and the user identity and any other relevant parameters) in tables. The mediator could compare the names in the table to the file name in the data structure to determine whether access is appropriate. More likely, the mediator would copy the file name into its own local storage area and compare from there. Comparing from the copy leaves the data structure in the user's area, under the user's control.

It is at this point that the incomplete mediation flaw can be exploited. While the mediator is checking access rights for the file my_file, the user could change the file name descriptor to your_file, the value shown in Figure 3-3. Having read the work ticket once, the mediator would not be expected to reread the ticket before approving it; the mediator would approve the access and send the now-modified descriptor to the file handler.

The problem is called a time-of-check to time-of-use flaw because it exploits the delay between the two times. That is, between the time the access was checked and the time the result of the check was used, a change occurred, invalidating the result of the check.

Security Implication

The security implication here is pretty clear: Checking one action and performing another is an example of ineffective access control. We must be wary whenever there is a time lag, making sure that there is no way to corrupt the check's results during that interval.

Fortunately, there are ways to prevent exploitation of the time lag. One way to do so is to use digital signatures and certificates. As described in Chapter 2, a digital signature is a sequence of bits applied with public key cryptography, so that many people—using a public key—can verify the authenticity of the bits, but only one person—using the corresponding private key—could have created them. In this case, the time of check is when the person signs, and the time of use is when anyone verifies the signature.

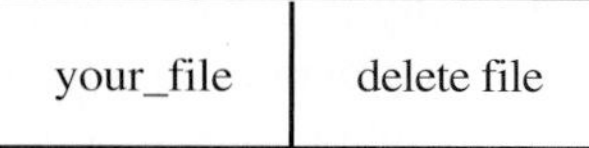

FIGURE 3-3 Modified Data.

Suppose the signer's private key is disclosed some time before its time of use. In that case, we do not know for sure that the signer did indeed "sign" the digital signature; it might have been a malicious attacker acting with the private key of the signer. To counter this vulnerability, a public key cryptographic infrastructure includes a mechanism called a key revocation list, for reporting a revoked public key—one that had been disclosed, was feared disclosed or lost, became inoperative, or for any other reason should no longer be taken as valid. The recipient must check the key revocation list before accepting a digital signature as valid.

Combinations of Nonmalicious Program Flaws

These three vulnerabilities are bad enough when each is considered on its own. But perhaps the worst aspect of all three flaws is that they can be used together, as one step in a multistep attack. An attacker may not be content with causing a buffer overflow. Instead the attacker may begin a three-pronged attack by using a buffer overflow to disrupt all execution of arbitrary code on a machine. At the same time, the attacker may exploit a time-of-check to time-of-use flaw to add a new user ID to the system. The attacker then logs in as the new user and exploits an incomplete mediation flaw to obtain privileged status, and so forth. The clever attacker uses flaws as common building blocks to build a complex attack. For this reason, we must know about and protect against even simple flaws. (See Sidebar 3-3 for other examples of the effects of unintentional errors.) Unfortunately, these kinds of flaws are widespread and dangerous. As we will see in the next section, innocuous-seeming program flaws can be exploited by malicious attackers to plant intentionally harmful code.

3.3 VIRUSES AND OTHER MALICIOUS CODE

By themselves, programs are seldom security threats. The programs operate on data, taking action only when data and state changes trigger it. Much of the work done by a program is invisible to users, so they are not likely to be aware of any malicious activity. For instance, when was the last time you saw a bit? Do you know in what form a document file is stored? If you know a document resides somewhere on a disk, can you find it? Can you tell if a game program does anything in addition to its expected interaction with you? Which files are modified by a word processor when you create a document? Most users cannot answer these questions. However, since computer data are not usually seen directly by users, malicious people can make programs serve as vehicles to access and change data and other programs. Let us look at the possible effects of malicious code and then examine in detail several kinds of programs that can be used for interception or modification of data.

Why Worry About Malicious Code?

None of us likes the unexpected, especially in our programs. Malicious code behaves in unexpected ways, thanks to a malicious programmer's intention. We think of the malicious code as lurking inside our system: all or some of a program that we are running

Sidebar 3-3 Nonmalicious Flaws Cause Failures

In 1989 Crocker and Bernstein [CRO89] studied the root causes of the known catastrophic failures of what was then called the ARPANET, the predecessor of today's Internet. From its initial deployment in 1969 to 1989, the authors found 17 flaws that either did cause or could have caused catastrophic failure of the network. They use "catastrophic failure" to mean a situation that causes the entire network or a significant portion of it to fail to deliver network service.

The ARPANET was the first network of its sort, in which data are communicated as independent blocks (called "packets") that can be sent along different network routes and are reassembled at the destination. As might be expected, faults in the novel algorithms for delivery and reassembly were the source of several failures. Hardware failures were also significant. But as the network grew from its initial three nodes to dozens and hundreds, these problems were identified and fixed.

More than ten years after the network was born, three interesting nonmalicious flaws appeared. The initial implementation had fixed sizes and positions of the code and data. In 1986, a piece of code was loaded into memory in a way that overlapped a piece of security code. Only one critical node had that code configuration, and so only that one node would fail, which made it difficult to determine the cause of the failure.

In 1987, new code caused Sun computers connected to the network to fail to communicate. The first explanation was that the developers of the new Sun code had written the system to function as other manufacturers' code did, not necessarily as the specification dictated. It was later found that the developers had optimized the code incorrectly, leaving out some states the system could reach. But the first explanation—designing to practice, not to specification—is a common failing.

The last reported failure occurred in 1988. When the system was designed in 1969, developers specified that the number of connections to a subnetwork, and consequently the number of entries in a table of connections, was limited to 347, based on analysis of the expected topology. After 20 years, people had forgotten the (undocumented) limit, and a 348th connection was added, which caused the table to overflow and the system to fail. But the system derived this table gradually by communicating with neighboring nodes. So when any node's table reached 348 entries, it crashed, and when restarted it started building its table anew. Thus, nodes throughout the system would crash seemingly randomly after running perfectly well for a while (with unfull tables).

None of these flaws were malicious nor could they have been exploited by a malicious attacker to cause a failure. But they show the importance of the analysis, design, documentation, and maintenance steps in development of a large, long-lived system.

or even a nasty part of a separate program that somehow attaches itself to another (good) program.

How can such a situation arise? When you last installed a major software package, such as a word processor, a statistical package, or a plug-in from the Internet, you ran one command, typically called INSTALL or SETUP. From there, the installation program took control, creating some files, writing in other files, deleting data and files, and perhaps renaming a few that it would change. A few minutes and a quite a few disk accesses later, you had plenty of new code and data, all set up for you with a minimum of human intervention. Other than the general descriptions on the box, in the documentation files, or on the web pages, you had absolutely no idea exactly what "gifts" you had received. You hoped all you received was good, and it probably was. The same uncertainty exists when you unknowingly download an application, such as a Java applet or an ActiveX control, while viewing a web site. Thousands or even millions of bytes of programs and data are transferred, and hundreds of modifications may be made to your existing files, all occurring without your explicit consent or knowledge.

Malicious Code Can Do Much (Harm)

Malicious code can do anything any other program can, such as writing a message on a computer screen, stopping a running program, generating a sound, or erasing a stored file. Or malicious code can do nothing at all right now; it can be planted to lie dormant, undetected, until some event triggers the code to act. The trigger can be a time or date, an interval (for example, after 30 minutes), an event (for example, when a particular program is executed), a condition (for example, when communication occurs on a modem), a count (for example, the fifth time something happens), some combination of these, or a random situation. In fact, malicious code can do different things each time, or nothing most of the time with something dramatic on occasion. In general, malicious code can act with all the predictability of a two-year-old child: We know in general what two-year-olds do, we may even know what a specific two-year-old often does in certain situations, but two-year-olds have an amazing capacity to do the unexpected.

Malicious code runs under the user's authority. Thus, malicious code can touch everything the user can touch, and in the same ways. Users typically have complete control over their own program code and data files; they can read, write, modify, append, and even delete them. And well they should. But malicious code can do the same, without the user's permission or even knowledge.

Malicious Code Has Been Around a Long Time

The popular literature and press continue to highlight the effects of malicious code as if it were a relatively recent phenomenon. It is not. Cohen [COH84] is sometimes credited with the discovery of viruses, but in fact Cohen gave a name to a phenomenon known long before. For example, Thompson, in his 1984 Turing Award lecture, "Reflections on Trusting Trust" [THO84], described code that can be passed by a compiler. In that lecture, he refers to an earlier Air Force document, the Multics security evaluation [KAR74, KAR02]. In fact, references to virus behavior go back at least to 1970. Ware's 1970 study (publicly released in 1979 [WAR79]) and Anderson's planning study for the U.S. Air Force [AND72] (to which Schell also refers) *still* accurately describe threats, vulnerabilities, and program security flaws, especially intentional ones. What *is* new about malicious code is the number of distinct instances and copies that have appeared.

So malicious code is still around, and its effects are more pervasive. It is important for us to learn what it looks like and how it works, so that we can take steps to prevent it from doing damage or at least mediate its effects. How can malicious code take control of a system? How can it lodge in a system? How does malicious code spread? How can it be recognized? How can it be detected? How can it be stopped? How can it be prevented? We address these questions in the following sections.

Kinds of Malicious Code

Malicious code or a **rogue program** is the general name for unanticipated or undesired effects in programs or program parts, caused by an agent intent on damage. This definition eliminates unintentional errors, although they can also have a serious negative effect. This definition also excludes coincidence, in which two benign programs combine for a negative effect. The **agent** is the writer of the program or the person who causes its distribution. By this definition, most faults found in software inspections, reviews, and testing do not qualify as malicious code, because we think of them as unintentional. However, keep in mind as you read this chapter that unintentional faults can in fact invoke the same responses as intentional malevolence; a benign cause can still lead to a disastrous effect.

You are likely to have been affected by a virus at one time or another, either because your computer was infected by one or because you could not access an infected system while its administrators were cleaning up the mess one made. In fact, your virus might actually have been a worm: The terminology of malicious code is sometimes used imprecisely. A **virus** is a program that can pass on malicious code to other nonmalicious programs by modifying them. The term "virus" was coined because the affected program acts like a biological virus: It infects other healthy subjects by attaching itself to the program and either destroying it or coexisting with it. Because viruses are insidious, we cannot assume that a clean program yesterday is still clean today. Moreover, a good program can be modified to include a copy of the virus program, so the infected good program itself begins to act as a virus, infecting other programs. The infection usually spreads at a geometric rate, eventually overtaking an entire computing system and spreading to all other connected systems.

A virus can be either transient or resident. A **transient** virus has a life that depends on the life of its host; the virus runs when its attached program executes and terminates when its attached program ends. (During its execution, the transient virus may have spread its infection to other programs.) A **resident** virus locates itself in memory; then it can remain active or be activated as a stand-alone program, even after its attached program ends.

A **Trojan horse** is malicious code that, in addition to its primary effect, has a second, nonobvious malicious effect.[1] As an example of a computer Trojan horse,

[1] The name is a reference to the Greek legends of the Trojan war, which tell how the Greeks tricked the Trojans into breaking their defense wall to take a wooden horse, filled with the bravest of Greek soldiers, into their citadel. In the night, the soldiers descended and signalled their troops that the way in was now clear, and Troy was captured.

consider a login script that solicits a user's identification and password, passes the identification information on to the rest of the system for login processing, but also retains a copy of the information for later, malicious use. In this example, the user sees only the login occurring as expected, so there is no evident reason to suspect that any other action took place.

A **logic bomb** is a class of malicious code that "detonates" or goes off when a specified condition occurs. A **time bomb** is a logic bomb whose trigger is a time or date.

A **trapdoor** or **backdoor** is a feature in a program by which someone can access the program other than by the obvious, direct call, perhaps with special privileges. For instance, an automated bank teller program might allow anyone entering the number 990099 on the keypad to process the log of everyone's transactions at that machine. In this example, the trapdoor could be intentional, for maintenance purposes, or it could be an illicit way for the implementer to wipe out any record of a crime.

A **worm** is a program that spreads copies of itself through a network. The primary difference between a worm and a virus is that a worm operates through networks, and a virus can spread through any medium (but usually uses copied program or data files). Additionally, the worm spreads copies of itself as a stand-alone program, whereas the virus spreads copies of itself as a program that attaches to or embeds in other programs.

White et al. [WHI89] also define a **rabbit** as a virus or worm that self-replicates without bound, with the intention of exhausting some computing resource. A rabbit might create copies of itself and store them on disk, in an effort to completely fill the disk, for example.

These definitions match current careful usage. The distinctions among these terms are small, and often the terms are confused, especially in the popular press. The term "virus" is often used to refer to any piece of malicious code. Furthermore, two or more forms of malicious code can be combined to produce a third kind of problem. For instance, a virus can be a time bomb if the viral code that is spreading will trigger an event after a period of time has passed. The kinds of malicious code are summarized in Table 3-1.

TABLE 3-1 Types of Malicious Code.

Code Type	Characteristics
Virus	Attaches itself to program and propagates copies of itself to other programs
Trojan horse	Contains unexpected, additional functionality
Logic bomb	Triggers action when condition occurs
Time bomb	Triggers action when specified time occurs
Trapdoor	Allows unauthorized access to functionality
Worm	Propagates copies of itself through a network
Rabbit	Replicates itself without limit to exhaust resource

Because "virus" is the popular name given to all forms of malicious code and because fuzzy lines exist between different kinds of malicious code, we will not be too restrictive in the following discussion. We want to look at how malicious code spreads, how it is activated, and what effect it can have. A virus is a convenient term for mobile malicious code, and so in the following sections we use the term "virus" almost exclusively. The points made apply also to other forms of malicious code.

How Viruses Attach

A printed copy of a virus does nothing and threatens no one. Even executable virus code sitting on a disk does nothing. What triggers a virus to start replicating? For a virus to do its malicious work and spread itself, it must be activated by being executed. Fortunately for virus writers, but unfortunately for the rest of us, there are many ways to ensure that programs will be executed on a running computer.

For example, recall the SETUP program that you initiate on your computer. It may call dozens or hundreds of other programs, some on the distribution medium, some already residing on the computer, some in memory. If any one of these programs contains a virus, the virus code could be activated. Let us see how. Suppose the virus code were in a program on the distribution medium, such as a CD; when executed, the virus could install itself on a permanent storage medium (typically, a hard disk), and also in any and all executing programs in memory. Human intervention is necessary to start the process; a human being puts the virus on the distribution medium, and perhaps another initiates the execution of the program to which the virus is attached. (It is possible for execution to occur without human intervention, though, such as when execution is triggered by a date or the passage of a certain amount of time.) After that, no human intervention is needed; the virus can spread by itself.

A more common means of virus activation is as an attachment to an e-mail message. In this attack, the virus writer tries to convince the victim (the recipient of an e-mail message) to open the attachment. Once the viral attachment is opened, the activated virus can do its work. Some modern e-mail handlers, in a drive to "help" the receiver (victim), will automatically open attachments as soon as the receiver opens the body of the e-mail message. The virus can be executable code embedded in an executable attachment, but other types of files are equally dangerous. For example, objects such as graphics or photo images can contain code to be executed by an editor, so they can be transmission agents for viruses. In general, it is safer to force users to open files on their own rather than automatically; it is a bad idea for programs to perform potentially security-relevant actions without a user's consent.

Appended Viruses

A program virus attaches itself to a program; then, whenever the program is run, the virus is activated. This kind of attachment is usually easy to program.

In the simplest case, a virus inserts a copy of itself into the executable program file before the first executable instruction. Then, all the virus instructions execute first; after the last virus instruction, control flows naturally to what used to be the first program instruction. Such a situation is shown in Figure 3-4.

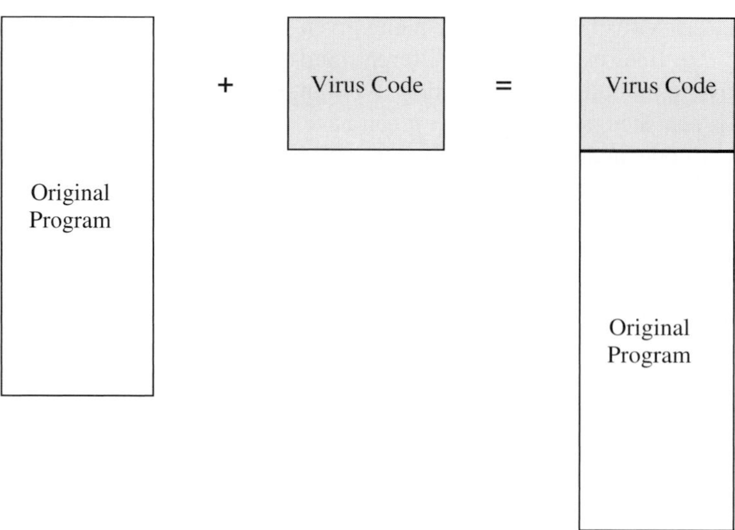

FIGURE 3-4 Virus Appended to a Program.

This kind of attachment is simple and usually effective. The virus writer does not need to know anything about the program to which the virus will attach, and often the attached program simply serves as a carrier for the virus. The virus performs its task and then transfers to the original program. Typically, the user is unaware of the effect of the virus if the original program still does all that it used to. Most viruses attach in this manner.

Viruses That Surround a Program

An alternative to the attachment is a virus that runs the original program but has control before and after its execution. For example, a virus writer might want to prevent the virus from being detected. If the virus is stored on disk, its presence will be given away by its file name, or its size will affect the amount of space used on the disk. The virus writer might arrange for the virus to attach itself to the program that constructs the listing of files on the disk. If the virus regains control after the listing program has generated the listing but before the listing is displayed or printed, the virus could eliminate its entry from the listing and falsify space counts so that it appears not to exist. A surrounding virus is shown in Figure 3-5.

Integrated Viruses and Replacements

A third situation occurs when the virus replaces some of its target, integrating itself into the original code of the target. Such a situation is shown in Figure 3-6. Clearly, the virus writer has to know the exact structure of the original program to know where to insert which pieces of the virus.

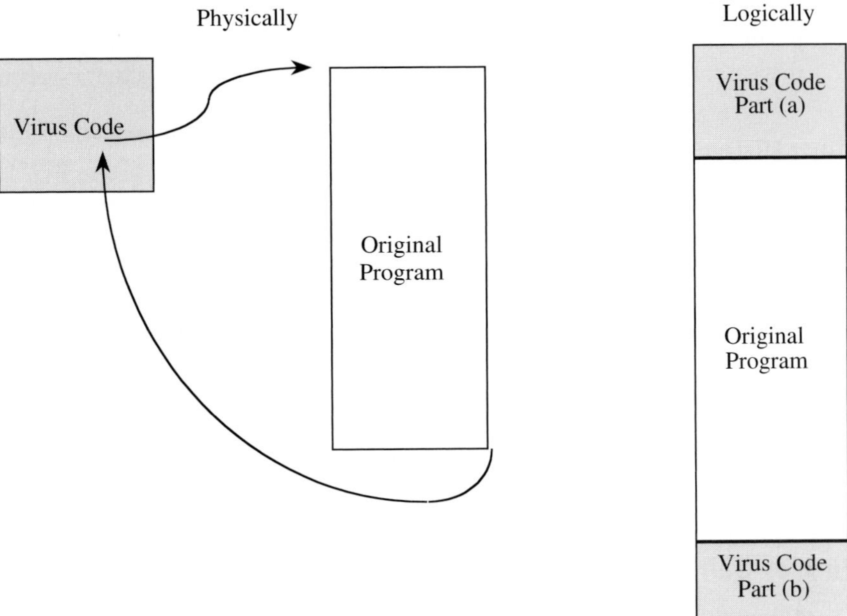

FIGURE 3-5 Virus Surrounding a Program.

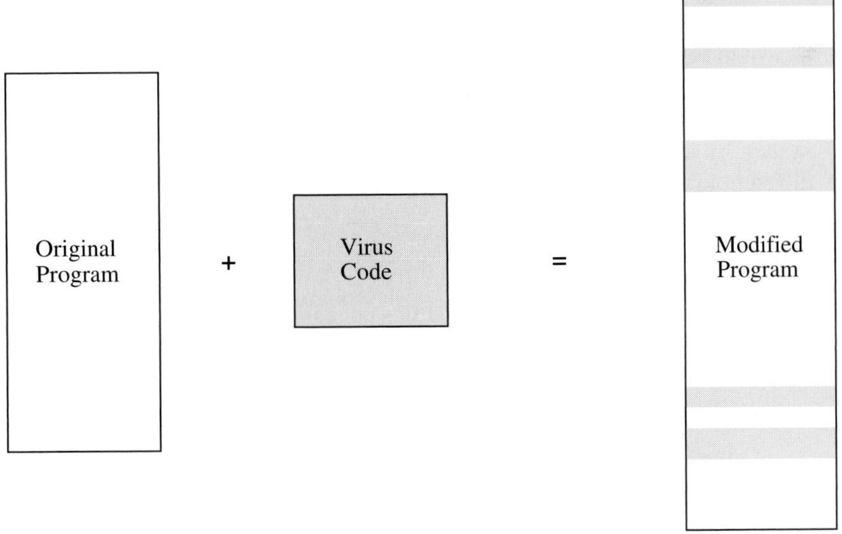

FIGURE 3-6 Virus Integrated into a Program.

Finally, the virus can replace the entire target, either mimicking the effect of the target or ignoring the expected effect of the target and performing only the virus effect. In this case, the user is most likely to perceive the loss of the original program.

Document Viruses

Currently, the most popular virus type is what we call the **document virus**, which is implemented within a formatted document, such as a written document, a database, a slide presentation, or a spreadsheet. These documents are highly structured files that contain both data (words or numbers) and commands (such as formulas, formatting controls, links). The commands are part of a rich programming language, including macros, variables and procedures, file accesses, and even system calls. The writer of a document virus uses any of the features of the programming language to perform malicious actions.

The ordinary user usually sees only the content of the document (its text or data), so the virus writer simply includes the virus in the commands part of the document, as in the integrated program virus.

How Viruses Gain Control

The virus (V) has to be invoked instead of the target (T). Essentially, the virus either has to seem to be T, saying effectively "I am T" (like some rock stars, where the target is the artiste formerly known as T) or the virus has to push T out of the way and become a substitute for T, saying effectively "Call me instead of T." A more blatant virus can simply say "invoke me [you fool]."

The virus can assume T's name by replacing (or joining to) T's code in a file structure; this invocation technique is most appropriate for ordinary programs. The virus can overwrite T in storage (simply replacing the copy of T in storage, for example). Alternatively, the virus can change the pointers in the file table so that the virus is located instead of T whenever T is accessed through the file system. These two cases are shown in Figure 3-7.

The virus can supplant T by altering the sequence that would have invoked T to now invoke the virus V; this invocation can be used to replace parts of the resident operating system by modifying pointers to those resident parts, such as the table of handlers for different kinds of interrupts.

Homes for Viruses

The virus writer may find these qualities appealing in a virus:

- It is hard to detect.
- It is not easily destroyed or deactivated.
- It spreads infection widely.
- It can reinfect its home program or other programs.
- It is easy to create.
- It is machine independent and operating system independent.

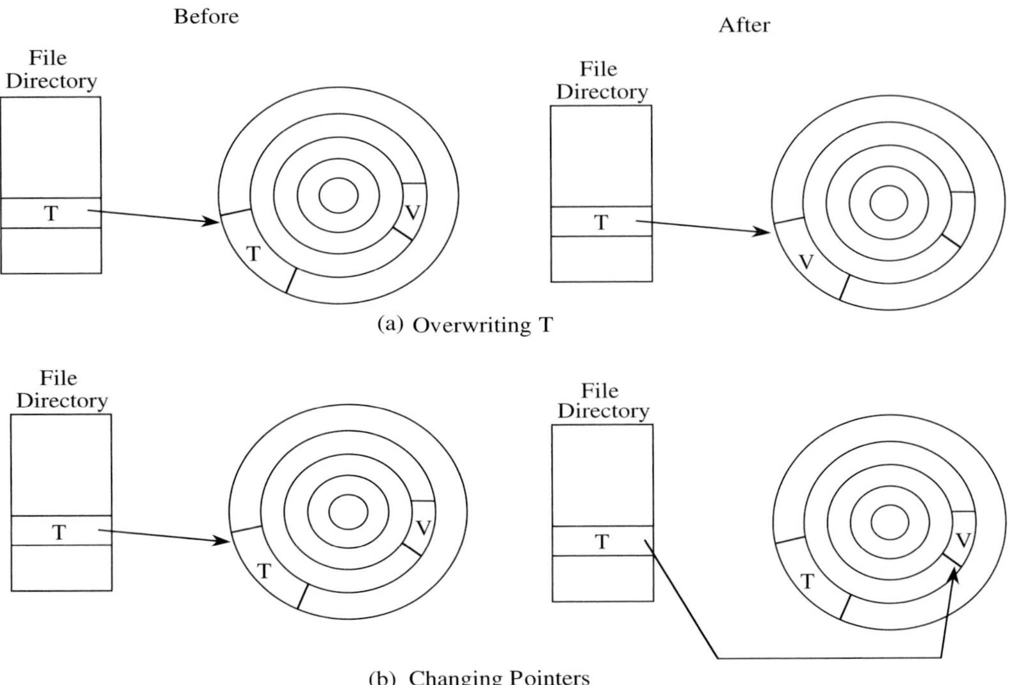

FIGURE 3-7 Virus Completely Replacing a Program.

Few viruses meet all these criteria. The virus writer chooses from these objectives when deciding what the virus will do and where it will reside.

Just a few years ago, the challenge for the virus writer was to write code that would be executed repeatedly so that the virus could multiply. Now, however, one execution is enough to ensure widespread distribution. Many viruses are transmitted by e-mail, using either of two routes. In the first case, some virus writers generate a new e-mail message to all addresses in the victim's address book. These new messages contain a copy of the virus so that it propagates widely. Often the message is a brief, chatty, non-specific message that would encourage the new recipient to open the attachment from a friend (the first recipient). For example, the subject line or message body may read "I thought you might enjoy this picture from our vacation." In the second case, the virus writer can leave the infected file for the victim to forward unknowingly. If the virus's effect is not immediately obvious, the victim may pass the infected file unwittingly to other victims.

Let us look more closely at the issue of viral residence.

One-Time Execution

The majority of viruses today execute only once, spreading their infection and causing their effect in that one execution. A virus often arrives as an e-mail attachment of a document virus. It is executed just by being opened.

Boot Sector Viruses

A special case of virus attachment, but formerly a fairly popular one, is the so-called **boot sector virus.** When a computer is started, control begins with firmware that determines which hardware components are present, tests them, and transfers control to an operating system. A given hardware platform can run many different operating systems, so the operating system is not coded in firmware but is instead invoked dynamically, perhaps even by a user's choice, after the hardware test.

The operating system is software stored on disk. Code copies the operating system from disk to memory and transfers control to it; this copying is called the **bootstrap** (often **boot**) load because the operating system figuratively pulls itself into memory by its bootstraps. The firmware does its control transfer by reading a fixed number of bytes from a fixed location on the disk (called the **boot sector**) to a fixed address in memory and then jumping to that address (which will turn out to contain the first instruction of the bootstrap loader). The bootstrap loader then reads into memory the rest of the operating system from disk. To run a different operating system, the user just inserts a disk with the new operating system and a bootstrap loader. When the user reboots from this new disk, the loader there brings in and runs another operating system. This same scheme is used for personal computers, workstations, and large mainframes.

To allow for change, expansion, and uncertainty, hardware designers reserve a large amount of space for the bootstrap load. The boot sector on a PC is slightly less than 512 bytes, but since the loader will be larger than that, the hardware designers support "chaining," in which each block of the bootstrap is chained to (contains the disk location of) the next block. This chaining allows big bootstraps but also simplifies the installation of a virus. The virus writer simply breaks the chain at any point, inserts a pointer to the virus code to be executed, and reconnects the chain after the virus has been installed. This situation is shown in Figure 3-8.

The boot sector is an especially appealing place to house a virus. The virus gains control very early in the boot process, before most detection tools are active, so that it can avoid, or at least complicate, detection. The files in the boot area are crucial parts of the operating system. Consequently, to keep users from accidentally modifying or deleting them with disastrous results, the operating system makes them "invisible" by not showing them as part of a normal listing of stored files, preventing their deletion. Thus, the virus code is not readily noticed by users.

Memory-Resident Viruses

Some parts of the operating system and most user programs execute, terminate, and disappear, with their space in memory being available for anything executed later. For very frequently used parts of the operating system and for a few specialized user programs, it would take too long to reload the program each time it was needed. Such code remains in memory and is called "resident" code. Examples of resident code are the routine that interprets keys pressed on the keyboard, the code that handles error conditions that arise during a program's execution, or a program that acts like an alarm clock, sounding a signal at a time the user determines. Resident routines are sometimes called TSRs or "terminate and stay resident" routines.

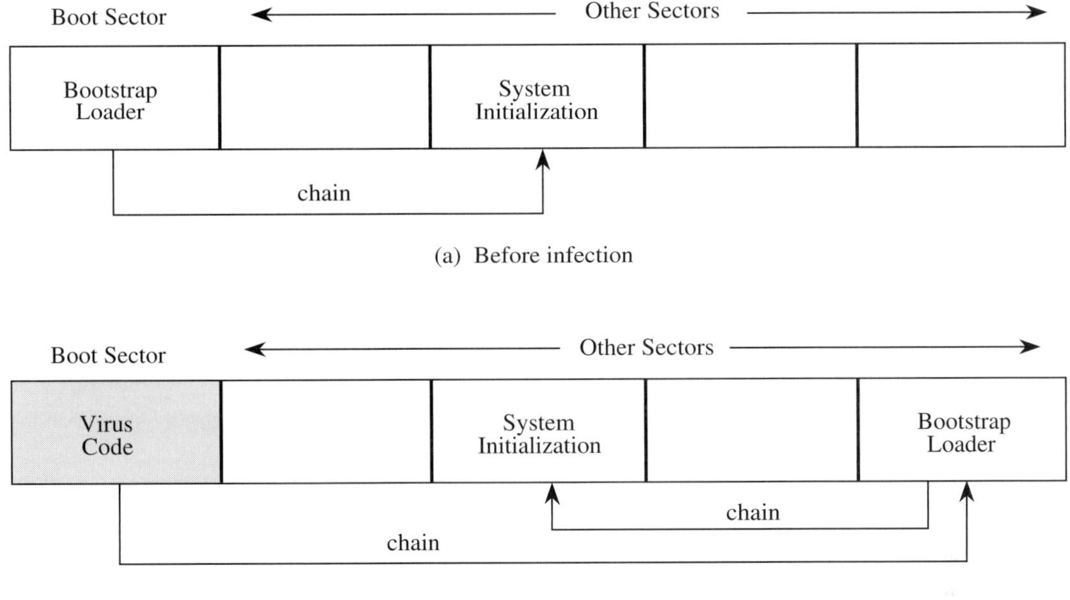

FIGURE 3-8 Boot Sector Virus Relocating Code.

Virus writers also like to attach viruses to resident code because the resident code is activated many times while the machine is running. Each time the resident code runs, the virus does too. Once activated, the virus can look for and infect uninfected carriers. For example, after activation, a boot sector virus might attach itself to a piece of resident code. Then, each time the virus was activated it might check whether any removable disk in a disk drive was infected and, if not, infect it. In this way the virus could spread its infection to all removable disks used during the computing session.

Other Homes for Viruses

A virus that does not take up residence in one of these cozy establishments has to fend more for itself. But that is not to say that the virus will go homeless.

One popular home for a virus is an application program. Many applications, such as word processors and spreadsheets, have a "macro" feature, by which a user can record a series of commands and repeat them with one invocation. Such programs also provide a "startup macro" that is executed every time the application is executed. A virus writer can create a virus macro that adds itself to the startup directives for the application. It also then embeds a copy of itself in data files so that the infection spreads to anyone receiving one or more of those files.

Libraries are also excellent places for malicious code to reside. Because libraries are used by many programs, the code in them will have a broad effect. Additionally, libraries are often shared among users and transmitted from one user to another, a practice that spreads the infection. Finally, executing code in a library can pass on the viral infection to other transmission media. Compilers, loaders, linkers, runtime monitors, runtime debuggers, and even virus control programs are good candidates for hosting viruses because they are widely shared.

Virus Signatures

A virus cannot be completely invisible. Code must be stored somewhere, and the code must be in memory to execute. Moreover, the virus executes in a particular way, using certain methods to spread. Each of these characteristics yields a telltale pattern, called a **signature**, that can be found by a program that knows to look for it. The virus's signature is important for creating a program, called a **virus scanner**, that can automatically detect and, in some cases, remove viruses. The scanner searches memory and long-term storage, monitoring execution and watching for the telltale signatures of viruses. For example, a scanner looking for signs of the Code Red worm can look for a pattern containing the following characters:

```
/default.ida?NNNNNNNNNNNNNNNNNNNNNNNNNNNNNNNNNNNN
NNNNNNNNNNNNNNNNNNNNNNNNNNNNNNNNNNNNNNNNNNNNN
NNNNNNNNNNNNNNNNNNNNNNNNNNNNNNNNNNNNNNNNNNNNN
NNNNNNNNNNNNNNNNNNNNNNNNNNNNNNNNNNNNNNNNNNNNN
NNNNNNNNNNNNNNNNNNNNNNNNNNNNNNNNNNNNNNNNNNNNN
%u9090%u6858%ucbd3
%u7801%u9090%u6858%ucdb3%u7801%u9090%u6858
%ucbd3%u7801%u9090
%u9090%u8190%u00c3%u0003%ub00%u531b%u53ff
%u0078%u0000%u00=a
HTTP/1.0
```

When the scanner recognizes a known virus's pattern, it can then block the virus, inform the user, and deactivate or remove the virus. However, a virus scanner is effective only if it has been kept up-to-date with the latest information on current viruses. Sidebar 3-4 describes how viruses were the primary security breach among companies surveyed in 2001.

Sidebar 3-4 The Viral Threat

Information Week magazine reports that viruses, worms, and Trojan horses represented the primary method for breaching security among the 4,500 security professionals surveyed in 2001 [HUL01c]. Almost 70 percent of the respondents noted that virus, worm, and Trojan horse attacks occurred in the 12 months before April 2001. Second were the 15 percent of attacks using denial of service; telecommunications or unauthorized entry was responsible for 12 percent of the attacks. (Multiple responses were allowed.) These figures represent establishments in 42 countries throughout North America, South America, Europe, and Asia.

Storage Patterns

Most viruses attach to programs that are stored on media such as disks. The attached virus piece is invariant, so that the start of the virus code becomes a detectable signature. The attached piece is always located at the same position relative to its attached file. For example, the virus might always be at the beginning, 400 bytes from the top, or at the bottom of the infected file. Most likely, the virus will be at the beginning of the file, because the virus writer wants to obtain control of execution before the bona fide code of the infected program is in charge. In the simplest case, the virus code sits at the top of the program, and the entire virus does its malicious duty before the normal code is invoked. In other cases, the virus infection consists of only a handful of instructions that point or jump to other, more detailed instructions elsewhere. For example, the infected code may consist of condition testing and a jump or call to a separate virus module. In either case, the code to which control is transferred will also have a recognizable pattern. Both of these situations are shown in Figure 3-9.

A virus may attach itself to a file, in which case the file's size grows. Or the virus may obliterate all or part of the underlying program, in which case the program's size does not change but the program's functioning will be impaired. The virus writer has to choose one of these detectable effects.

The virus scanner can use a code or checksum to detect changes to a file. It can also look for suspicious patterns, such as a JUMP instruction as the first instruction of a system program (in case the virus has positioned itself at the bottom of the file but wants to be executed first, as in Figure 3-9).

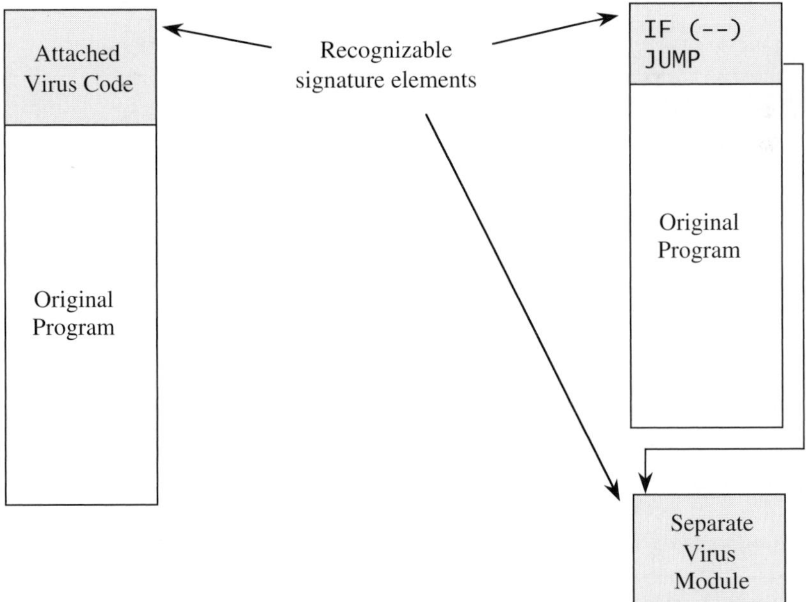

FIGURE 3-9 Recognizable Patterns in Viruses.

Execution Patterns

A virus writer may want a virus to do several things at the same time, namely, spread infection, avoid detection, and cause harm. These goals are shown in Table 3-2, along with ways each goal can be addressed. Unfortunately, many of these behaviors are perfectly normal and might otherwise go undetected. For instance, one goal is modifying the file directory; many normal programs create files, delete files, and write to storage media. Thus, there are no key signals that point to the presence of a virus.

Most virus writers seek to avoid detection for themselves and their creations. Because a disk's boot sector is not visible to normal operations (for example, the contents of the boot sector do not show on a directory listing), many virus writers hide their code there. A resident virus can monitor disk accesses and fake the result of a disk operation that would show the virus hidden in a boot sector by showing the data that *should* have been in the boot sector (which the virus has moved elsewhere).

There are no limits to the harm a virus can cause. On the modest end, the virus might do nothing; some writers create viruses just to show they can do it. Or the virus can be relatively benign, displaying a message on the screen, sounding the buzzer, or playing music. From there, the problems can escalate. One virus can erase files, another an entire disk; one virus can prevent a computer from booting, and another can prevent writing to disk. The damage is bounded only by the creativity of the virus's author.

TABLE 3-2 Virus Effects and Causes.

Virus Effect	How It Is Caused
Attach to executable program	• Modify file directory • Write to executable program file
Attach to data or control file	• Modify directory • Rewrite data • Append to data • Append data to self
Remain in memory	• Intercept interrupt by modifying interrupt handler address table • Load self in nontransient memory area
Infect disks	• Intercept interrupt • Intercept operating system call (to format disk, for example) • Modify system file • Modify ordinary executable program
Conceal self	• Intercept system calls that would reveal self and falsify result • Classify self as "hidden" file
Spread infection	• Infect boot sector • Infect systems program • Infect ordinary program • Infect data ordinary program reads to control its execution
Prevent deactivation	• Activate before deactivating program and block deactivation • Store copy to reinfect after deactivation

Transmission Patterns

A virus is effective only if it has some means of transmission from one location to another. As we have already seen, viruses can travel during the boot process, by attaching to an executable file or traveling within data files. The travel itself occurs during execution of an already infected program. Since a virus can execute any instructions a program can, virus travel is not confined to any single medium or execution pattern. For example, a virus can arrive on a diskette or from a network connection, travel during its host's execution to a hard disk boot sector, reemerge next time the host computer is booted, and remain in memory to infect other diskettes as they are accessed.

Polymorphic Viruses

The virus signature may be the most reliable way for a virus scanner to identify a virus. If a particular virus always begins with the string 47F0F00E08 (in hexadecimal) and has string 00113FFF located at word 12, it is unlikely that other programs or data files will have these exact characteristics. For longer signatures, the probability of a correct match increases.

If the virus scanner will always look for those strings, then the clever virus writer can cause something other than those strings to be in those positions. For example, the virus could have two alternative but equivalent beginning words; after being installed, the virus will choose one of the two words for its initial word. Then, a virus scanner would have to look for both patterns. A virus that can change its appearance is called a **polymorphic virus.** (*Poly* means "many" and *morph* means "form".)

A two-form polymorphic virus can be handled easily as two independent viruses. Therefore, the virus writer intent on preventing detection of the virus will want either a large or an unlimited number of forms so that the number of possible forms is too large for a virus scanner to search for. Simply embedding a random number or string at a fixed place in the executable version of a virus is not sufficient, because the signature of the virus is just the constant code excluding the random part. A polymorphic virus has to randomly reposition all parts of itself and randomly change all fixed data. Thus, instead of containing the fixed (and therefore searchable) string "HA! INFECTED BY A VIRUS," a polymorphic virus has to change even that pattern sometimes.

Trivially, assume a virus writer has 100 bytes of code and 50 bytes of data. To make two virus instances different, the writer might distribute the first version as 100 bytes of code followed by all 50 bytes of data. A second version could be 99 bytes of code, a jump instruction, 50 bytes of data, and the last byte of code. Other versions are 98 code bytes jumping to the last two, 97 and three, and so forth. Just by moving pieces around the virus writer can create enough different appearances to fool simple virus scanners. Once the scanner writers became aware of these kinds of tricks, however, they refined their signature definitions.

A more sophisticated polymorphic virus randomly intersperses harmless instructions throughout its code. Examples of harmless instructions include addition of zero to a number, movement of a data value to its own location, or a jump to the next instruction. These "extra" instructions make it more difficult to locate an invariant signature.

A simple variety of polymorphic virus uses encryption under various keys to make the stored form of the virus different. These are sometimes called **encrypting** viruses. This type of virus must contain three distinct parts: a decryption key, the (encrypted) object code of the virus, and the (unencrypted) object code of the decryption routine. For these viruses, the decryption routine itself or a call to a decryption library routine must be in the clear, and so that becomes the signature.

To avoid detection, not every copy of a polymorphic virus has to differ from every other copy. If the virus changes occasionally, not every copy will match a signature of every other copy.

The Source of Viruses

Since a virus can be rather small, its code can be "hidden" inside other larger and more complicated programs. Two hundred lines of a virus could be separated into one hundred packets of two lines of code and a jump each; these one hundred packets could be easily hidden inside a compiler, a database manager, a file manager, or some other large utility.

Virus discovery could be aided by a procedure to determine if two programs are equivalent. However, theoretical results in computing are very discouraging when it comes to the complexity of the equivalence problem. The general question, "are these two programs equivalent?" is undecidable (although that question *can* be answered for many specific pairs of programs). Even ignoring the general undecidability problem, two modules may produce subtly different results that may—or may not—be security relevant. One may run faster, or the first may use a temporary file for work space whereas the second performs all its computations in memory. These differences could be benign, or they could be a marker of an infection. Therefore, we are unlikely to develop a screening program that can separate infected modules from uninfected ones.

Although the general is dismaying, the particular is not. If we know that a particular virus may infect a computing system, we can check for it and detect it if it is there. Having found the virus, however, we are left with the task of cleansing the system of it. Removing the virus in a running system requires being able to detect and eliminate its instances faster than it can spread.

Prevention of Virus Infection

The only way to prevent the infection of a virus is not to share executable code with an infected source. This philosophy used to be easy to follow because it was easy to tell if a file was executable or not. For example, on PCs, a *.exe* extension was a clear sign that the file was executable. However, as we have noted, today's files are more complex, and a seemingly nonexecutable file may have some executable code buried deep within it. For example, a word processor may have commands within the document file; as we noted earlier, these commands, called macros, make it easy for the user to do complex or repetitive things. But they are really executable code embedded in the context of the document. Similarly, spreadsheets, presentation slides, and other office- or business-related files can contain code or scripts that can be executed in various ways—and thereby harbor viruses. And, as we have seen, the applications that run or use these files may try to be helpful by automatically invoking the executable code, whether you want it run or not! Against the principles of good security, e-mail handlers can be set to automatically open (without performing access control) attachments or embedded code for the recipient, so your e-mail message can have animated bears dancing across the top.

Another approach virus writers have used is a little-known feature in the Microsoft file design. Although a file with a *.doc* extension is expected to be a Word document, in fact, the true document type is hidden in a field at the start of the file. This convenience ostensibly helps a user who inadvertently names a Word document with a *.ppt* (PowerPoint) or any other extension. In some cases, the operating system will try to open the associated application but, if that fails, the system will switch to the application of the hidden file type. So, the virus writer creates an executable file, names it with an inappropriate extension, and sends it to the victim, describing it is as a picture or a necessary code add-in or something else desirable. The unwitting recipient opens the file and, without intending to, executes the malicious code.

More recently, executable code has been hidden in files containing large data sets, such as pictures or read-only documents. These bits of viral code are not easily detected by virus scanners and certainly not by the human eye. For example, a file containing a photograph may be highly granular; if every sixteenth bit is part of a command string that can be executed, then the virus is very difficult to detect.

Since you cannot always know which sources are infected, you should assume that any outside source is infected. Fortunately, you know when you are receiving code from an outside source; unfortunately, it is not feasible to cut off all contact with the outside world.

In their interesting paper comparing computer virus transmission with human disease transmission, Kephart et al. [KEP93] observe that individuals' efforts to keep their computers free from viruses lead to communities that are generally free from viruses because members of the community have little (electronic) contact with the outside world. In this case, transmission is contained not because of limited contact but because of limited contact outside the community. Governments, for military or diplomatic secrets, often run disconnected network communities. The trick seems to be in choosing one's community prudently. However, as use of the Internet and the World Wide Web increases, such separation is almost impossible to maintain.

Nevertheless, there are several techniques for building a reasonably safe community for electronic contact, including the following:

- *Use only commercial software acquired from reliable, well-established vendors*. There is always a chance that you might receive a virus from a large manufacturer with a name everyone would recognize. However, such enterprises have significant reputations that could be seriously damaged by even one bad incident, so they go to some degree of trouble to keep their products virus-free and to patch any problem-causing code right away. Similarly, software distribution companies will be careful about products they handle.
- *Test all new software on an isolated computer.* If you must use software from a questionable source, test the software first on a computer with no hard disk, not connected to a network, and with the boot disk removed. Run the software and look for unexpected behavior, even simple behavior such as unexplained figures on the screen. Test the computer with a copy of an up-to-date virus scan-

ner, created before running the suspect program. Only if the program passes these tests should it be installed on a less isolated machine.

- *Open attachments only when you know them to be safe.* What constitutes "safe" is up to you, as you have probably already learned in this chapter. Certainly, an attachment from an unknown source is of questionable safety. You might also distrust an attachment from a known source but with a peculiar message.
- *Make a recoverable system image and store it safely.* If your system does become infected, this clean version will let you reboot securely because it overwrites the corrupted system files with clean copies. For this reason, you must keep the image write-protected during reboot. Prepare this image now, before infection; after infection it is too late. For safety, prepare an extra copy of the safe boot image.
- *Make and retain backup copies of executable system files.* This way, in the event of a virus infection, you can remove infected files and reinstall from the clean backup copies (stored in a secure, offline location, of course).
- *Use virus detectors (often called virus scanners) regularly and update them daily.* Many of the virus detectors available can both detect and eliminate infection from viruses. Several scanners are better than one, because one may detect the viruses that others miss. Because scanners search for virus signatures, they are constantly being revised as new viruses are discovered. New virus signature files, or new versions of scanners, are distributed frequently; often, you can request automatic downloads from the vendor's web site. Keep your detector's signature file up-to-date.

Truths and Misconceptions About Viruses

Because viruses often have a dramatic impact on the computer-using community, they are often highlighted in the press, particularly in the business section. However, there is much misinformation in circulation about viruses. Let us examine some of the popular claims about them.

- *Viruses can infect only Microsoft Windows systems.* ***False***. Among students and office workers, PCs are popular computers, and there may be more people writing software (and viruses) for them than for any other kind of processor. Thus, the PC is most frequently the target when someone decides to write a virus. However, the principles of virus attachment and infection apply equally to other processors, including Macintosh computers, Unix workstations, and mainframe computers. In fact, no writeable stored-program computer is immune to possible virus attack. As we noted in Chapter 1, this situation means that *all* devices containing computer code, including automobiles, airplanes, microwave ovens, radios, televisions, and radiation therapy machines have the potential for being infected by a virus.
- *Viruses can modify "hidden" or "read only" files.* ***True***. We may try to protect files by using two operating system mechanisms. First, we can make a file a hidden file so that a user or program listing all files on a storage device will not see the file's name. Second, we can apply a read-only protection to the file so

that the user cannot change the file's contents. However, each of these protections is applied by software, and virus software can override the native software's protection. Moreover, software protection is layered, with the operating system providing the most elementary protection. If a secure operating system obtains control *before* a virus contaminator has executed, the operating system can prevent contamination as long as it blocks the attacks the virus will make.

- *Viruses can appear only in data files, or only in Word documents, or only in programs.* ***False***. What are data? What is an executable file? The distinction between these two concepts is not always clear, because a data file can control how a program executes and even cause a program to execute. Sometimes a data file lists steps to be taken by the program that reads the data, and these steps can include executing a program. For example, some applications contain a configuration file whose data are exactly such steps. Similarly, word processing document files may contain startup commands to execute when the document is opened; these startup commands can contain malicious code. Although, strictly speaking, a virus can activate and spread only when a program executes, in fact, data files are acted upon by programs. Clever virus writers have been able to make data control files that cause programs to do many things, including pass along copies of the virus to other data files.
- *Viruses spread only on disks or only in e-mail.* ***False***. File-sharing is often done as one user provides a copy of a file to another user by writing the file on a transportable disk. However, any means of electronic file transfer will work. A file can be placed in a network's library or posted on a bulletin board. It can be attached to an electronic mail message or made available for download from a web site. Any mechanism for sharing files—of programs, data, documents, and so forth—can be used to transfer a virus.
- *Viruses cannot remain in memory after a complete power off/power on reboot.* ***True***. If a virus is resident in memory, the virus is lost when the memory loses power. That is, computer memory (RAM) is volatile, so that all contents are deleted when power is lost.[2] However, viruses written to disk certainly can remain through a reboot cycle and reappear after the reboot. Thus, you can receive a virus infection, the virus can be written to disk (or to network storage), you can turn the machine off and back on, and the virus can be reactivated during the reboot. Boot sector viruses gain control when a machine reboots (whether it is a hardware or software reboot), so a boot sector virus may remain through a reboot cycle because it activates immediately when a reboot has completed.
- *Viruses cannot infect hardware.* ***True***. Viruses can infect only things they can modify; memory, executable files, and data are the primary targets. If hardware contains writeable storage (so-called firmware) that can be accessed under program control, that storage *is* subject to virus attack. There have been a few

[2] Some very low level hardware settings (for example, the size of disk installed) are retained in memory called "nonvolatile RAM," but these locations are not directly accessible by programs and are written only by programs run from read-only memory (ROM) during hardware initialization. Thus, they are highly immune to virus attack.

instances of firmware viruses. Because a virus can control hardware that is subject to program control, it may seem as if a hardware device has been infected by a virus, but it is really the software driving the hardware that has been infected. Viruses can also exercise hardware in any way a program can. Thus, for example, a virus could cause a disk to loop incessantly, moving to the innermost track then the outermost and back again to the innermost.

- *Viruses can be malevolent, benign, or benevolent.* ***True.*** Not all viruses are bad. For example, a virus might locate uninfected programs, compress them so that they occupy less memory, and insert a copy of a routine that decompresses the program when its execution begins. At the same time, the virus is spreading the compression function to other programs. This virus could substantially reduce the amount of storage required for stored programs, possibly by up to 50 percent. However, the compression would be done at the request of the virus, not at the request, or even knowledge, of the program owner.

To see how viruses and other types of malicious code operate, we examine four types of malicious code that affected many users worldwide: the Brain, the Internet worm, the Code Red worm, and web bugs.

First Example of Malicious Code: The Brain Virus

One of the earliest viruses is also one of the most intensively studied. The so-called Brain virus was given its name because it changes the label of any disk it attacks to the word "BRAIN." This particular virus, believed to have originated in Pakistan, attacks PCs running a Microsoft operating system. Numerous variants have been produced; because of the number of variants, people believe that the source code of the virus was released to the underground virus community.

What It Does

The Brain, like all viruses, seeks to pass on its infection. This virus first locates itself in upper memory and then executes a system call to reset the upper memory bound below itself, so that it is not disturbed as it works. It traps interrupt number 19 (disk read) by resetting the interrupt address table to point to it and then sets the address for interrupt number 6 (unused) to the former address of the interrupt 19. In this way, the virus screens disk read calls, handling any that would read the boot sector (passing back the original boot contents that were moved to one of the bad sectors); other disk calls go to the normal disk read handler, through interrupt 6.

The Brain virus appears to have no effect other than passing its infection, as if it were an experiment or a proof of concept. However, variants of the virus erase disks or destroy the file allocation table (the table that shows which files are where on a storage medium).

How It Spreads

The Brain virus positions itself in the boot sector and in six other sectors of the disk. One of the six sectors will contain the original boot code, moved there from the original boot sector, while two others contain the remaining code of the virus. The remaining three sectors contain a duplicate of the others. The virus marks these six sectors "faulty" so that the operating system will not try to use them. (With low-level calls, you can force the disk drive to read from what the operating system has marked as bad sectors.) The virus allows the boot process to continue.

Once established in memory, the virus intercepts disk read requests for the disk drive under attack. With each read, the virus reads the disk boot sector and inspects the fifth and sixth bytes for the hexadecimal value 1234 (its signature). If it finds that value, it concludes the disk is infected; if not, it infects the disk as described in the previous paragraph.

What Was Learned

This virus uses some of the standard tricks of viruses, such as hiding in the boot sector, and intercepting and screening interrupts. The virus is almost a prototype for later efforts. In fact, many other virus writers seem to have patterned their work on this basic virus. Thus, one could say it was a useful learning tool for the virus writer community.

Sadly, its infection did not raise public consciousness of viruses, other than a certain amount of fear and misunderstanding. Subsequent viruses, such as the Lehigh virus that swept through the computers of Lehigh University, the nVIR viruses that sprang from prototype code posted on bulletin boards, and the Scores virus that was first found at NASA in Washington D.C. circulated more widely and with greater effect. Fortunately, most viruses seen to date have a modest effect, such as displaying a message or emitting a sound. That is, however, a matter of luck, since the writers who could put together the simpler viruses obviously had all the talent and knowledge to make much more malevolent viruses.

There is no general cure for viruses. Virus scanners are effective against today's known viruses and general patterns of infection, but they cannot counter tomorrow's variant. The only sure prevention is complete isolation from outside contamination, which is not feasible; in fact, you may even get a virus from the software applications you buy from reputable vendors.

Another Example: The Internet Worm

On the evening of 2 November 1988, a worm was released to the Internet,[3] causing serious damage to the network. Not only were many systems infected, but when word of the problem spread, many more uninfected systems severed their network connections to prevent themselves from getting infected. Gene Spafford and his team at Purdue University [SPA89] and Mark Eichen and Jon Rochlis at M.I.T [EIC89] studied the worm extensively.

The perpetrator was Robert T. Morris, Jr., a graduate student at Cornell University who created and released the worm. He was convicted in 1990 of violating the 1986 Computer Fraud and Abuse Act, section 1030 of U.S. Code Title 18. He received a fine

[3] Note: this incident is normally called a "worm," although it shares most of the characteristics of viruses.

of $10,000, a three-year suspended jail sentence, and was required to perform 400 hours of community service.

What It Did

Judging from its code, Morris programmed the Internet worm to accomplish three main objectives:

1. determine to where it could spread
2. spread its infection
3. remain undiscovered and undiscoverable

What Effect It Had

The worm's primary effect was resource exhaustion. Its source code indicated that the worm was supposed to check whether a target host was already infected; if so, the worm would negotiate so that either the existing infection or the new infector would terminate. However, because of a supposed flaw in the code, many new copies did not terminate. As a result, an infected machine soon became burdened with many copies of the worm, all busily attempting to spread the infection. Thus, the primary observable effect was serious degradation in performance of affected machines.

A second-order effect was the disconnection of many systems from the Internet. System administrators tried to sever their connection with the Internet, either because their machines were already infected and the system administrators wanted to keep the worm's processes from looking for sites to which to spread or because their machines were not yet infected and the staff wanted to avoid having them become so.

The disconnection led to a third-order effect: isolation and inability to perform necessary work. Disconnected systems could not communicate with other systems to carry on the normal research, collaboration, business, or information exchange users expected. System administrators on disconnected systems could not use the network to exchange information with their counterparts at other installations, so status and containment or recovery information was unavailable.

The worm caused an estimated 6,000 installations to shut down or disconnect from the Internet. In total, several thousand systems were disconnected for several days, and several hundred of these systems were closed to users for a day or more while they were disconnected. Estimates of the cost of damage range from $100,000 to $97 million.

How It Worked

The worm exploited several known flaws and configuration failures of Berkeley version 4 of the Unix operating system. It accomplished—or had code that appeared to try to accomplish—its three objectives.

Where to spread. The worm had three techniques for locating potential machines to victimize. It first tried to find user accounts to invade on the target machine. In parallel, the worm tried to exploit a bug in the *finger* program and then to use a trapdoor in the *sendmail* mail handler. *All three of these security flaws were well known in the general Unix community.*

The first security flaw was a joint user and system error, in which the worm tried guessing passwords and succeeded when it found one. The Unix password file is stored in encrypted form, but the ciphertext in the file is readable by anyone. (This visibility is the system error.) The worm encrypted various popular passwords and compared their ciphertext against the ciphertext of the stored password file. The worm tried the account name, the owner's name, and a short list of 432 common passwords (such as "guest," "password," "help," "coffee," "coke," "aaa"). If none of these succeeded, the worm used the dictionary file stored on the system for use by application spelling checkers. (Choosing a recognizable password is the user error.) When it got a match, the worm could log in to the corresponding account by presenting the plaintext password. Then, as a user, the worm could look for other machines to which the user could obtain access. (See the article by Robert T. Morris, Sr. and Ken Thompson [MOR79] on selection of good passwords, published a decade before the worm.)

The second flaw concerned *fingerd*, the program that runs continuously to respond to other computers' requests for information about system users. The security flaw involved causing the input buffer to overflow, spilling into the return address stack. Thus, when the *finger* call terminated, *fingerd* executed instructions that had been pushed there as another part of the buffer overflow, causing the worm to be connected to a remote shell.

The third flaw involved a trapdoor in the *sendmail* program. Ordinarily, this program runs in the background, awaiting signals from others wanting to send mail to the system. When it receives such a signal, *sendmail* gets a destination address, which it verifies, and then begins a dialog to receive the message. However, when running in debugging mode, the worm caused *sendmail* to receive and execute a command string instead of the destination address.

Spread infection. Having found a suitable target machine, the worm would use one of these three methods to send a bootstrap loader to the target machine. This loader consisted of 99 lines of C code to be compiled and executed on the target machine. The bootstrap loader would then fetch the rest of the worm from the sending host machine. There was an element of good computer security—or stealth—built into the exchange between the host and the target. When the target's bootstrap requested the rest of the worm, the worm supplied a one-time password back to the host. Without this password, the host would immediately break the connection to the target, presumably in an effort to ensure against "rogue" bootstraps (ones that a real administrator might develop to try to obtain a copy of the rest of the worm for subsequent analysis).

Remain undiscovered and undiscoverable. The worm went to considerable lengths to prevent its discovery once established on a host. For instance, if a transmission error occurred while the rest of the worm was being fetched, the loader zeroed and then deleted all code already transferred and exited.

As soon as the worm received its full code, it brought the code into memory, encrypted it, and deleted the original copies from disk. Thus, no traces were left on disk, and even a memory dump would not readily expose the worm's code. The worm periodically changed its name and process identifier so that no single name would run up a large amount of computing time.

What Was Learned

The Internet worm sent a shock wave through the Internet community, which at that time was largely populated by academics and researchers. The affected sites closed some of the loopholes exploited by the worm and generally tightened security. Some users changed passwords. COPS, an automated security-checking program, was developed to check for some of the same flaws the worm exploited. However, as time passes and many new installations continue to join the Internet, security analysts checking for site vulnerabilities find that many of the same security flaws still exist. A new attack on the Internet would not succeed on the same scale as the Internet worm, but it could still cause significant inconvenience to many.

The Internet worm was benign in that it only spread to other systems but did not destroy any part of them. It collected sensitive data, such as account passwords, but it did not retain them. While acting as a user, the worm could have deleted or overwritten files, distributed them elsewhere, or encrypted them and held them for ransom. The next worm may not be so benign.

The worm's effects stirred several people to action. One positive outcome from this experience was development in the United States of an infrastructure for reporting and correcting malicious and nonmalicious code flaws. The Internet worm occurred at about the same time that Cliff Stoll [STO89] reported his problems in tracking an electronic intruder (and his subsequent difficulty in finding anyone to deal with the case). The computer community realized it needed to organize. The resulting Computer Emergency Response Team (CERT) at Carnegie Mellon University was formed; it and similar response centers around the world have done an excellent job of collecting and disseminating information on malicious code attacks and their countermeasures. System administrators now exchange information on problems and solutions. Security comes from informed protection and action, not from ignorance and inaction.

More Malicious Code: Code Red

Code Red appeared in the middle of 2001, to devastating effect. On July 29, the U.S. Federal Bureau of Investigation proclaimed in a news release that "on July 19, the Code Red worm infected more than 250,000 systems in just nine hours ... This spread has the potential to disrupt business and personal use of the Internet for applications such as e-commerce, e-mail and entertainment." [BER01] Indeed, "the Code Red worm struck faster than any other worm in Internet history," according to a research director for a security software and services vendor. The first attack occurred on July 12; overall, 750,000 servers were affected, including 400,000 just in the period from August 1 to 10. [HUL01] Thus, of the 6 million web servers running code subject to infection by Code Red, about one in eight were infected. Michael Erbschloe, vice president of Computer Economics, Inc., estimates that Code Red's damage will exceed $2 billion. [ERB01]

Code Red was more than a worm; it included several kinds of malicious code, and it mutated from one version to another. Let us take a closer look at how Code Red worked.

What It Did

There are several versions of Code Red, malicious software that propagates itself on web servers running Microsoft's Internet Information Server (IIS) software. Code Red takes two steps: infection and propagation. To infect a server, the worm takes advantage of a vulnerability in Microsoft's IIS. It overflows the buffer in the dynamic link library *idq.dll* to reside in the server's memory. Then, to propagate, Code Red checks IP addresses on port 80 of the PC to see if that web server is vulnerable.

What Effect It Had

The first version of Code Red was easy to spot, because it defaced web sites with the following text:

```
HELLO!
Welcome to
http://www.worm.com !
Hacked by Chinese!
```

The rest of the original Code Red's activities were determined by the date. From day 1 to 19 of the month, the worm spawned 99 threads that scanned for other vulnerable computers, starting at the same IP address. Then, on days 20 to 27, the worm launched a distributed denial-of-service attack at the U.S. web site, *www. whitehouse.gov*. A denial-of-service attack floods the site with large numbers of messages in an attempt to slow down or stop the site because the site is overwhelmed and cannot handle the messages. Finally, from day 28 to the end of the month, the worm did nothing.

However, there were several variants. The second variant was discovered near the end of July 2001. It did not deface the web site, but its propagation was randomized and optimized to infect servers more quickly. A third variant, discovered in early August, seemed to be a substantial rewrite of the second. This version injected a Trojan horse in the target and modified software to ensure that a remote attacker could execute any command on the server. The worm also checked the year and month, so that it would automatically stop propagating in October 2002. Finally, the worm rebooted the server after 24 or 48 hours, wiping itself from memory but leaving the Trojan horse in place.

How It Worked

The Code Red worm looked for vulnerable personal computers running Microsoft IIS software. Exploiting the unchecked buffer overflow, the worm crashed Windows NT-based servers but executed code on Windows 2000 systems. The later versions of the worm created a trapdoor on an infected server; then, the system was open to attack by other programs or malicious users. To create the trapdoor, Code Red copied *%windir%\cmd.exe* to four locations:

```
c:\inetpub\scripts\root.ext
c:\progra~1\common~1\system\MSADC\root.exe
d:\inetpub\scripts\root.ext
d:\progra~1\common~1\system\MSADC\root.exe
```

Code Red also included its own copy of the file *explorer.exe*, placing it on the c: and d: drives so that Windows would run the malicious copy, not the original copy. This Trojan horse first ran the original, untainted version of *explorer.exe*, but it modified the system registry to disable certain kinds of file protection and to ensure that some directories have read, write, and execute permission. As a result, the Trojan horse had a virtual path that could be followed even when *explorer.exe* was not running. The Trojan horse continues to run in background, resetting the registry every 10 minutes; thus, even if a system administrator notices the changes and undoes them, the changes are applied again by the malicious code.

To propagate, the worm created 300 or 600 threads (depending on the variant) and tried for 24 or 48 hours to spread to other machines. After that, the system was forcibly rebooted, flushing the worm in memory but leaving the backdoor and Trojan horse in place.

To find a target to infect, the worm's threads worked in parallel. Although the early version of Code Red targeted *www.whitehouse.gov*, later versions chose a random IP address close to the host computer's own address. To speed its performance, the worm used a nonblocking socket so that a slow connection would not slow down the rest of the threads as they scanned for a connection.

What Was Learned

As of this writing, more than 6 million servers use Microsoft's IIS software. The Code Red variant that allowed unlimited root access made Code Red a virulent and dangerous piece of malicious code. Microsoft offered a patch to fix the overflow problem and prevent infection by Code Red, but many administrators neglected to apply the patch. (See Sidebar 3-5.)

Some security analysts suggested that Code Red might be "a beta test for information warfare," meaning that its powerful combination of attacks could be a prelude to a large-scale, intentional effort targeted at particular countries or groups. [HUL01a] For this reason, users and developers should pay more and careful attention to the security of their systems. Forno [FOR01] warns that such security threats as Code Red stem from our general willingness to buy and install code that does not meet minimal quality standards and from our reluctance to devote resources to the large and continuing stream of patches and corrections that flows from the vendors. As we will see in Chapter 9, this problem is coupled with a lack of legal standing for users who experience seriously faulty code.

Malicious Code on the Web: Web Bugs

With the web pervading the lives of average citizens everywhere, malicious code in web pages has become a very serious problem. But sometimes the malice is not always clear; code can be used to good or bad ends, depending on your perspective. In this section, we look at a generic type of code called a **web bug**, to see how it can affect the code in which it is embedded.

What They Do

A **web bug**, sometimes called a **pixel tag**, **clear gif**, **one-by-one gif**, **invisible gif,** or **beacon gif**, is a hidden image on any document that can display HTML tags, such as a

Sidebar 3-5 Is the Cure Worse Than the Disease?

These days, a typical application program such as a word processor or spreadsheet package is sold to its user with no guarantee of quality. As problems are discovered by users or developers, patches are made available to be downloaded from the web and applied to the faulty system. This style of "quality control" relies on the users and system administrators to keep up with the history of releases and patches and to apply the patches in a timely manner. Moreover, each patch usually assumes that earlier patches can be applied; ignore a patch at your peril.

For example, Forno [FOR01] points out that an organization hoping to secure a web server running Windows NT 4.0's IIS had to apply over 47 patches as part of a service pack or available as a download from Microsoft. Such stories suggest that it may cost more to maintain an application or system than it cost to buy the application or system in the first place! Many organizations, especially small businesses, lack the resources for such an effort. As a consequence, they neglect to fix known system problems, which can then be exploited by hackers writing malicious code.

Blair [BLA01] describes a situation shortly after the end of the Cold War when the United States discovered that Russia was tracking its nuclear weapons materials by using a paper-based system. That is, the materials tracking system consisted of boxes of paper filled with paper receipts. In a gesture of friendship, the Los Alamos National Lab donated to Russia the Microsoft software it uses to track its own nuclear weapons materials. However, experts at the renowned Kurchatov Institute soon discovered that over time some files become invisible and inaccessible! In early 2000, they warned the United States. To solve the problem, the United States told Russia to upgrade to the next version of the Microsoft software. But the upgrade had the same problem, plus a security flaw that would allow easy access to the database by hackers or unauthorized parties.

Sometimes patches themselves create new problems as they are fixing old ones. It is well known in the software reliability community that testing and fixing sometimes reduce reliability, rather than improve it. And with the complex interactions between software packages, many computer system managers prefer to follow the adage "if it ain't broke, don't fix it," meaning that if there is no apparent failure, they would rather not risk causing one from what seems like an unnecessary patch. So there are several ways that the continual bug-patching approach to security may actually lead to a less secure product than you started with.

---

web page, an HTML e-mail message, or even a spreadsheet. Its creator intends the bug to be invisible, unseen by users but very useful nevertheless because it can track the activities of a web user.

For example, if you visit the Blue Nile home page, *www.bluenile.com*, the following web bug code is automatically downloaded as a one-by-one pixel image from Avenue A, a marketing agency:

```
<img height=1 width=1
src="http://switch.avenuea.com/action/bluenile_homepage/v2/a/
AD7029944">
```

What Effect They Have

Suppose you are surfing the web and load the home page for *Commercial.com*, a commercial establishment selling all kinds of housewares on the web. If this site contains a web bug for *Market.com*, a marketing and advertising firm, then the bug places a file called a **cookie** on your system's hard drive. This cookie, usually containing a numeric identifier unique to you, can be used to track your surfing habits and build a demographic profile. In turn, that profile can be used to direct you to retailers in whom you may be interested. For example, *Commercial.com* may create a link to other sites, display a banner advertisement to attract you to its partner sites, or offer you content customized for your needs.

How They Work

On the surface, web bugs do not seem to be malicious. They plant numeric data but do not track personal information, such as your name and address. However, if you purchase an item at *Commercial.com*, you may be asked to supply such information. Thus, the web server can capture such things as

- your computer's IP address
- the kind of web browser you use
- your monitor's resolution
- other browser settings, such as whether you have enabled Java technology
- connection time
- previous cookie values

and more.

This information can be used to track where and when you read a document, what your buying habits are, or what your personal information may be. More maliciously, the web bug can be cleverly used to review the web server's log files and determine your IP address—opening your system to hacking via the target IP address.

What Was Learned

Web bugs raise questions about privacy, and some countries are considering legislation to protect specifically from probes by web bugs. In the meantime, the Privacy Foundation has made available a tool called Bugnosis to locate web bugs and bring them to a user's attention.

In addition, users can invoke commands from their web browsers to block cookies or at least make the users aware that a cookie is about to be placed on a system. Each option offers some inconvenience. Cookies can be useful in recording information that is used repeatedly, such as name and address. Requesting a warning message can mean almost continual interruption as web bugs attempt to place cookies on your system. Another alternative is to allow cookies but to clean them off your system periodically, either by hand or by using a commercial product.

3.4 TARGETED MALICIOUS CODE

So far, we have looked at anonymous code written to affect users and machines indiscriminately. Another class of malicious code is written for a particular system, for a particular application, and for a particular purpose. Many of the virus writers' techniques apply, but there are also some new ones.

Trapdoors

A **trapdoor** is an undocumented entry point to a module. The trapdoor is inserted during code development, perhaps to test the module, to provide "hooks" by which to connect future modifications or enhancements or to allow access if the module should fail in the future. In addition to these legitimate uses, trapdoors can allow a programmer access to a program once it is placed in production.

Examples of Trapdoors

Because computing systems are complex structures, programmers usually develop and test systems in a methodical, organized, modular manner, taking advantage of the way the system is composed of modules or components. Often, each small component of the system is tested first, separate from the other components, in a step called **unit testing**, to ensure that the component works correctly by itself. Then, components are tested together during **integration testing**, to see how they function as they send messages and data from one to the other. Rather than paste all the components together in a "big bang" approach, the testers group logical clusters of a few components, and each cluster is tested in a way that allows testers to control and understand what might make a component or its interface fail. (For a more detailed look at testing, see Pfleeger [PFL01].)

To test a component on its own, the developer or tester cannot use the surrounding routines that prepare input or work with output. Instead, it is usually necessary to write "stubs" and "drivers," simple routines to inject data in and extract results from the component being tested. As testing continues, these stubs and drivers are discarded because they are replaced by the actual components whose functions they mimic. For example, the two modules MODA and MODB in Figure 3-10 are being tested with the driver MAIN and the stubs SORT, OUTPUT, and NEWLINE.

During both unit and integration testing, faults are usually discovered in components. Sometimes, when the source of a problem is not obvious, the developers insert debugging code in suspicious modules; the debugging code makes visible what is going on as the components execute and interact. Thus, the extra code may force components to display the intermediate results of a computation, to print out the number of each step as it is executed, or to perform extra computations to check the validity of previous components.

To control stubs or invoke debugging code, the programmer embeds special control sequences in the component's design, specifically to support testing. For example, a component in a text formatting system might be designed to recognize commands such as .PAGE, .TITLE, and .SKIP. During testing, the programmer may have invoked the debugging code, using a command with a series of parameters of the form *var* = *value*.

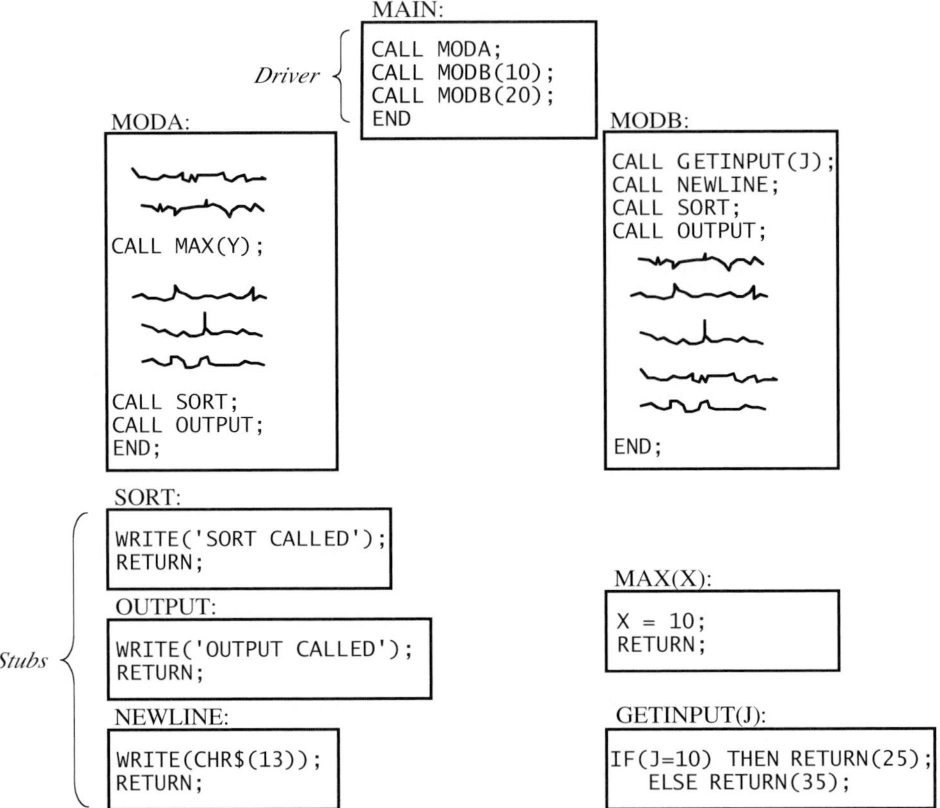

FIGURE 3-10 Stubs and Drivers.

This command allows the programmer to modify the values of internal program variables during execution, either to test corrections to this component or to supply values passed to components this one calls.

Command insertion is a recognized testing practice. However, if left in place after testing, the extra commands can become a problem. They are undocumented control sequences that produce side effects and can be used as trapdoors. In fact, the Internet worm spread its infection using just such a debugging trapdoor in an electronic mail program.

Poor **error checking** is another source of trapdoors. A good developer will design a system so that any data value is checked before it is used; the checking involves making sure the data type is correct as well as ensuring that the value is within acceptable bounds. But in some poorly designed systems, unacceptable input may not be caught and can be passed on for use in unanticipated ways. For example, a component's code may check for one of three expected sequences; finding none of the three, it should recognize an error. Suppose the developer uses a CASE statement to look for each of the three possibilities. A careless programmer may allow a failure simply to fall through the CASE without being flagged as an error. The *fingerd* flaw exploited by the Morris worm occurs exactly that way: A C library I/O routine fails to check whether characters are left in the input buffer before returning a pointer to a supposed next character.

Hardware processor design provides another common example of this kind of security flaw. Here, it often happens that not all possible binary opcode values have matching machine instructions. The **undefined opcodes** sometimes implement peculiar instructions, either because of an intent to test the processor design or because of an oversight by the processor designer. Undefined opcodes are the hardware counterpart of poor error checking for software.

As with viruses, trapdoors are not always bad. They can be very useful in finding security flaws. Auditors sometimes request trapdoors in production programs to insert fictitious but identifiable transactions into the system. Then, the auditors trace the flow of these transactions through the system. However, trapdoors must be documented, access to them should be strongly controlled, and they must be designed and used with full understanding of the potential consequences.

Causes of Trapdoors

Developers usually remove trapdoors during program development, once their intended usefulness is spent. However, trapdoors can persist in production programs because the developers

- *forget* to remove them
- intentionally leave them in the program for *testing*
- intentionally leave them in the program for *maintenance* of the finished program, or
- intentionally leave them in the program as a *covert means of access* to the component after it becomes an accepted part of a production system

The first case is an unintentional security blunder, the next two are serious exposures of the system's security, and the fourth is the first step of an outright attack. It is important to remember that the fault is not with the trapdoor itself, which can be a very useful technique for program testing, correction, and maintenance. Rather, the fault is with the system development process, which does not ensure that the trapdoor is "closed" when it is no longer needed. That is, the trapdoor becomes a vulnerability if no one notices it or acts to prevent or control its use in vulnerable situations.

In general, trapdoors are a vulnerability when they expose the system to modification during execution. They can be exploited by the original developers or used by anyone who discovers the trapdoor by accident or through exhaustive trials. A system is not secure when someone believes that no one else would find the hole.

Salami Attack

We noted in Chapter 1 an attack known as a **salami attack**. This approach gets its name from the way odd bits of meat and fat are fused together in a sausage or salami. In the same way, a salami attack merges bits of seemingly inconsequential data to yield powerful results. For example, programs often disregard small amounts of money in their computations, as when there are fractional pennies as interest or tax is calculated.

Such programs may be subject to a salami attack, because the small amounts are shaved from each computation and accumulated elsewhere—such as the programmer's bank account! The shaved amount is so small that an individual case is unlikely to be noticed, and the accumulation can be done so that the books still balance overall. However, accumulated amounts can add up to a tidy sum, supporting a programmer's early retirement or new car. It is often the resulting expenditure, not the shaved amounts, that gets the attention of the authorities.

Examples of Salami Attacks

The classic tale of a salami attack involves interest computation. Suppose your bank pays 6.5 percent interest on your account. The interest is declared on an annual basis but is calculated monthly. If, after the first month, your bank balance is $102.87, the bank can calculate the interest in the following way. For a month with 31 days, we divide the interest rate by 365 to get the daily rate, and then multiply it by 31 to get the interest for the month. Thus, the total interest for 31 days is $31/365*0.065*102.87 =$ $0.5495726. Since banks deal only in full cents, a typical practice is to round down if a residue is less than half a cent, and round up if a residue is half a cent or more. However, few people check their interest computation closely, and fewer still would complain about having the amount $0.5495 rounded down to $0.54, instead of up to $0.55. Most programs that perform computations on currency recognize that because of rounding, a sum of individual computations may be a few cents different from the computation applied to the sum of the balances.

What happens to these fractional cents? The computer security folk legend is told of a programmer who collected the fractional cents and credited them to a single account: hers! The interest program merely had to balance total interest paid to interest due on the total of the balances of the individual accounts. Auditors will probably not notice the activity in one specific account. In a situation with many accounts, the roundoff error can be substantial, and the programmer's account pockets this roundoff.

But salami attacks can net more and be far more interesting. For example, instead of shaving fractional cents, the programmer may take a few cents from each account, again assuming that no individual has the desire or understanding to recompute the amount the bank reports. Most people finding a result a few cents different from that of the bank would accept the bank's figure, attributing the difference to an error in arithmetic or a misunderstanding of the conditions under which interest is credited. Or a program might record a $20 fee for a particular service, while the company standard is $15. If unchecked, the extra $5 could be credited to an account of the programmer's choice. One attacker was able to make withdrawals of $10,000 or more against accounts that had shown little recent activity; presumably the attacker hoped the owners were ignoring their accounts.

Why Salami Attacks Persist

Computer computations are notoriously subject to small errors involving rounding and truncation, especially when large numbers are to be combined with small ones. Rather than document the exact errors, it is easier for programmers and users to accept a small amount of error as natural and unavoidable. To reconcile accounts, the programmer includes an error correction in computations. Inadequate auditing of these corrections is one reason why the salami attack may be overlooked.

Usually the source code of a system is too large or complex to be audited for salami attacks, unless there is reason to suspect one. Size and time are definitely on the side of the malicious programmer.

Covert Channels: Programs That Leak Information

So far, we have looked at malicious code that performs unwelcome actions. Next, we turn to programs that communicate information to people who should not receive it. The communication travels unnoticed, accompanying other, perfectly proper, communications. The general name for these extraordinary paths of communication is **covert channels**. The concept of a covert channel comes from a paper by Lampson [LAM73]; Millen [MIL88] presents a good taxonomy of covert channels.

Suppose a group of students is preparing for an exam for which each question has four choices (a, b, c, d); one student in the group, Sophie, understands the material perfectly and she agrees to help the others. She says she will reveal the answers to the questions, in order, by coughing once for answer "a," sighing for answer "b," and so forth. Sophie uses a communications channel that outsiders may not notice; her communications are hidden in an open channel. This communication is a human example of a covert channel.

We begin by describing how a programmer can create covert channels. The attack is more complex than one by a lone programmer accessing a data source. A programmer who has direct access to data can usually just read the data and write it to another file or print it out. If, however, the programmer is one step removed from the data—for example, outside the organization owning the data—the programmer must figure how to get at the data. One way is to supply a bona fide program with a built-in Trojan horse; once the horse is enabled, it finds and transmits the data. However, it would be too bold to generate a report labeled "Send this report to Jane Smith in Camden, Maine"; the programmer has to arrange to extract the data more surreptitiously. Covert channels are a means of extracting data clandestinely.

Figure 3-11 shows a "service program" containing a Trojan horse that tries to copy information from a legitimate user (who is allowed access to the information) to a "spy" (who ought not be allowed to access the information). The user may not know that a Trojan horse is running and may not be in collusion to leak information to the spy.

Covert Channel Overview

A programmer should not have access to sensitive data that a program processes after the program has been put into operation. For example, a programmer for a bank has no need to access the names or balances in depositors' accounts. Programmers for a securities firm have no need to know what buy and sell orders exist for the clients. During program testing, access to the real data may be justifiable, but not after the program has been accepted for regular use.

Still, a programmer might be able to profit from knowledge that a customer is about to sell a large amount of a particular stock or that a large new account has just been opened. Sometimes a programmer may want to develop a program that secretly commu-

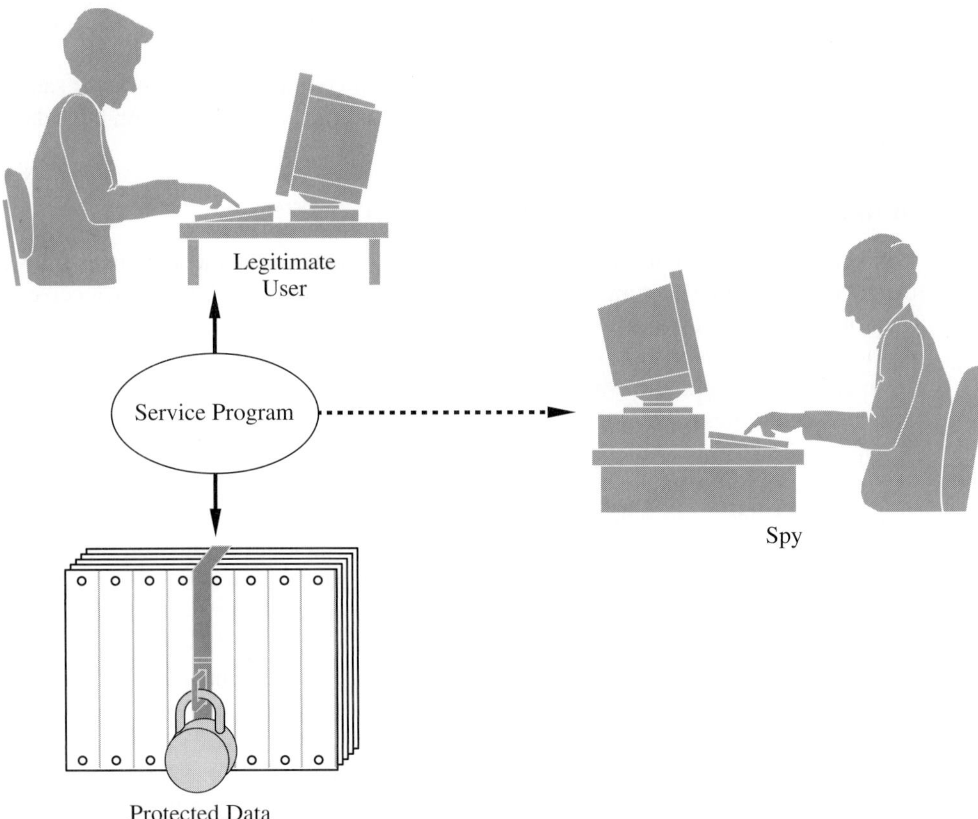

FIGURE 3-11 Covert Channel Leaking Information.

nicates some of the data on which it operates. In this case, the programmer is the "spy," and the "user" is whoever ultimately runs the program written by the programmer.

How to Create Covert Channels

A programmer can always find ways to communicate data values covertly. Running a program that produces a specific output report or displays a value may be too obvious. For example, in some installations, a printed report might occasionally be scanned by security staff before it is delivered to its intended recipient.

If printing the data values themselves is too obvious, the programmer can encode the data values in another innocuous report by varying the format of the output, changing the lengths of lines, or printing or not printing certain values. For example, changing the word "TOTAL" to "TOTALS" in a heading would not be noticed, but this creates a 1-bit covert channel. The absence or presence of the S conveys one bit of information. Numeric values can be inserted in insignificant positions of output fields, and the number of lines per page can be changed. Examples of these subtle channels are shown in Figure 3-12.

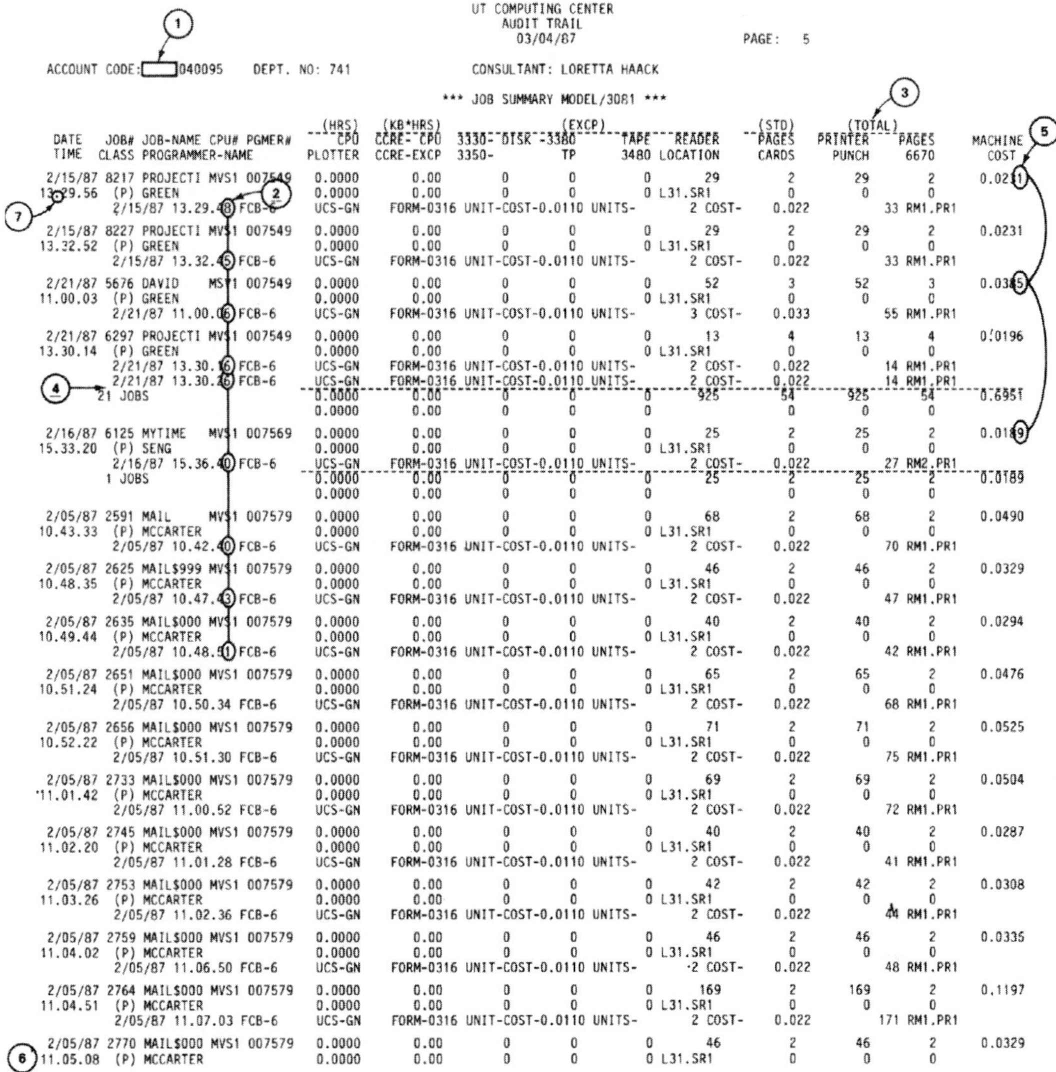

```
                                                UT COMPUTING CENTER
                                                    AUDIT TRAIL
                                                     03/04/87                          PAGE:   5

ACCOUNT CODE:     040095     DEPT. NO: 741            CONSULTANT: LORETTA HAACK

                                            *** JOB SUMMARY MODEL/3081 ***

                                      (HRS)   (KB*HRS)             (EXCP)                       (STD)     (TOTAL)
  DATE    JOB# JOB-NAME CPU# PGMER#      CPU  CCRE- CPU  3330- DISK -3380      TAPE    READER     PAGES  PRINTER    PAGES    MACHINE
  TIME  CLASS PROGRAMMER-NAME        PLOTTER  CCRE-EXCP  3350-          TP     3480 LOCATION     CARDS    PUNCH     6670       COST

  2/15/87 8217 PROJECTI MVS1 007549   0.0000       0.00      0        0         0       29        2        29        2     0.0231
13.29.56  (P) GREEN                   0.0000       0.00      0        0         0 L31.SR1         0         0        0
      2/15/87 13.29.48 FCB-6          UCS-GN  FORM-0316 UNIT-COST-0.0110 UNITS-         2 COST-   0.022         33 RM1.PR1

  2/15/87 8227 PROJECTI MVS1 007549   0.0000       0.00      0        0         0       29        2        29        2     0.0231
13.32.52  (P) GREEN                   0.0000       0.00      0        0         0 L31.SR1         0         0        0
      2/15/87 13.32.45 FCB-6          UCS-GN  FORM-0316 UNIT-COST-0.0110 UNITS-         2 COST-   0.022         33 RM1.PR1

  2/21/87 5676 DAVID    MST1 007549   0.0000       0.00      0        0         0       52        3        52        3     0.0385
11.00.03  (P) GREEN                   0.0000       0.00      0        0         0 L31.SR1         0         0        0
      2/21/87 11.00.06 FCB-6          UCS-GN  FORM-0316 UNIT-COST-0.0110 UNITS-         3 COST-   0.033         55 RM1.PR1

  2/21/87 6297 PROJECTI MVS1 007549   0.0000       0.00      0        0         0       13        4        13        4     0.0196
13.30.14  (P) GREEN                   0.0000       0.00      0        0         0 L31.SR1         0         0        0
      2/21/87 13.30.16 FCB-6          UCS-GN  FORM-0316 UNIT-COST-0.0110 UNITS-         2 COST-   0.022         14 RM1.PR1
      2/21/87 13.30.26 FCB-6          UCS-GN  FORM-0316 UNIT-COST-0.0110 UNITS-         2 COST-   0.022         14 RM1.PR1
    21 JOBS                        ---0.0000-------0.00------0--------0---------0------925-------54-------925-------54-----0.6951
                                      0.0000       0.00      0        0         0                 0         0        0

  2/16/87 6125 MYTIME   MVS1 007569   0.0000       0.00      0        0         0       25        2        25        2     0.0189
15.33.20  (P) SENG                    0.0000       0.00      0        0         0 L31.SR1         0         0        0
      2/16/87 15.36.40 FCB-6          UCS-GN  FORM-0316 UNIT-COST-0.0110 UNITS-         2 COST-   0.022         27 RM2.PR1
    1 JOBS                         ---0.0000-------0.00------0--------0---------0-------25--------2--------25--------2-----0.0189
                                      0.0000       0.00      0        0         0                 0         0        0

  2/05/87 2591 MAIL     MVS1 007579   0.0000       0.00      0        0         0       68        2        68        2     0.0490
10.43.33  (P) MCCARTER                0.0000       0.00      0        0         0 L31.SR1         0         0        0
      2/05/87 10.42.40 FCB-6          UCS-GN  FORM-0316 UNIT-COST-0.0110 UNITS-         2 COST-   0.022         70 RM1.PR1

  2/05/87 2625 MAIL$999 MVS1 007579   0.0000       0.00      0        0         0       46        2        46        2     0.0329
10.48.35  (P) MCCARTER                0.0000       0.00      0        0         0 L31.SR1         0         0        0
      2/05/87 10.47.43 FCB-6          UCS-GN  FORM-0316 UNIT-COST-0.0110 UNITS-         2 COST-   0.022         47 RM1.PR1

  2/05/87 2635 MAIL$000 MVS1 007579   0.0000       0.00      0        0         0       40        2        40        2     0.0294
10.49.44  (P) MCCARTER                0.0000       0.00      0        0         0 L31.SR1         0         0        0
      2/05/87 10.48.51 FCB-6          UCS-GN  FORM-0316 UNIT-COST-0.0110 UNITS-         2 COST-   0.022         42 RM1.PR1

  2/05/87 2651 MAIL$000 MVS1 007579   0.0000       0.00      0        0         0       65        2        65        2     0.0476
10.51.24  (P) MCCARTER                0.0000       0.00      0        0         0 L31.SR1         0         0        0
      2/05/87 10.50.34 FCB-6          UCS-GN  FORM-0316 UNIT-COST-0.0110 UNITS-         2 COST-   0.022         68 RM1.PR1

  2/05/87 2656 MAIL$000 MVS1 007579   0.0000       0.00      0        0         0       71        2        71        2     0.0525
10.52.22  (P) MCCARTER                0.0000       0.00      0        0         0 L31.SR1         0         0        0
      2/05/87 10.51.30 FCB-6          UCS-GN  FORM-0316 UNIT-COST-0.0110 UNITS-         2 COST-   0.022         75 RM1.PR1

  2/05/87 2733 MAIL$000 MVS1 007579   0.0000       0.00      0        0         0       69        2        69        2     0.0504
11.01.42  (P) MCCARTER                0.0000       0.00      0        0         0 L31.SR1         0         0        0
      2/05/87 11.00.52 FCB-6          UCS-GN  FORM-0316 UNIT-COST-0.0110 UNITS-         2 COST-   0.022         72 RM1.PR1

  2/05/87 2745 MAIL$000 MVS1 007579   0.0000       0.00      0        0         0       40        2        40        2     0.0287
11.02.20  (P) MCCARTER                0.0000       0.00      0        0         0 L31.SR1         0         0        0
      2/05/87 11.01.28 FCB-6          UCS-GN  FORM-0316 UNIT-COST-0.0110 UNITS-         2 COST-   0.022         41 RM1.PR1

  2/05/87 2753 MAIL$000 MVS1 007579   0.0000       0.00      0        0         0       42        2        42        2     0.0308
11.03.26  (P) MCCARTER                0.0000       0.00      0        0         0 L31.SR1         0         0        0
      2/05/87 11.02.36 FCB-6          UCS-GN  FORM-0316 UNIT-COST-0.0110 UNITS-         2 COST-   0.022         44 RM1.PR1

  2/05/87 2759 MAIL$000 MVS1 007579   0.0000       0.00      0        0         0       46        2        46        2     0.0335
11.04.02  (P) MCCARTER                0.0000       0.00      0        0         0 L31.SR1         0         0        0
      2/05/87 11.06.50 FCB-6          UCS-GN  FORM-0316 UNIT-COST-0.0110 UNITS-         2 COST-   0.022         48 RM1.PR1

  2/05/87 2764 MAIL$000 MVS1 007579   0.0000       0.00      0        0         0      169        2       169        2     0.1197
11.04.51  (P) MCCARTER                0.0000       0.00      0        0         0 L31.SR1         0         0        0
      2/05/87 11.07.03 FCB-6          UCS-GN  FORM-0316 UNIT-COST-0.0110 UNITS-         2 COST-   0.022        171 RM1.PR1

  2/05/87 2770 MAIL$000 MVS1 007579   0.0000       0.00      0        0         0       46        2        46        2     0.0329
11.05.08  (P) MCCARTER                0.0000       0.00      0        0         0 L31.SR1         0         0        0
```

① Number of spaces after :

② Last digit in field that would not be checked

③ Presence or absence of word (TOTAL) in header line

④ No space after last line of subtotal

⑤ Last digit in insignificant field

⑥ Number of lines per page

⑦ Use of . instead of :

FIGURE 3-12 Covert Channels.

Storage Channels

Some covert channels are called **storage channels** because they pass information by using the presence or absence of objects in storage.

A simple example of a covert channel is the **file lock** channel. In multiuser systems, files can be "locked" to prevent two people from writing to the same file at the same time (which could corrupt the file, if one person writes over some of what the other wrote). The operating system or database management system allows only one program to write to a file at a time, by blocking, delaying, or rejecting write requests from other programs. A covert channel can signal one bit of information by whether or not a file is locked.

Remember that the service program contains a Trojan horse written by the spy but run by the unsuspecting user. As shown in Figure 3-13, the service program reads confidential data (to which the spy should not have access) and signals the data one bit at a time by locking or not locking some file (any file, the contents of which are arbitrary and not even modified). The service program and the spy need a common timing source, broken into intervals. To signal a 1, the service program locks the file for the interval; for a 0, it does not lock. Later in the interval the spy tries to lock the file itself. If the spy program cannot lock the file, it knows the service program must have, and thus it concludes the service program is signaling a 1; if the spy program can lock the file, it knows the service program is signaling a 0.

This same approach can be used with disk storage quotas or other resources. With disk storage, the service program signals a 1 by creating an enormous file, so large that

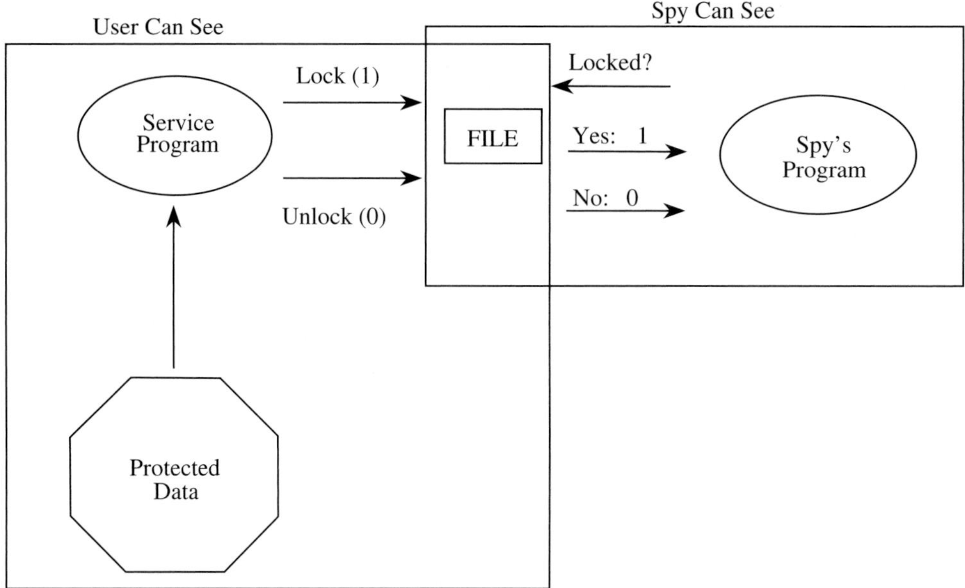

FIGURE 3-13 File Lock Covert Channel.

it consumes most of the available disk space. The spy program later tries to create a large file. If it succeeds, the spy program infers that the service program did not create a large file, and so the service program is signaling a 0; otherwise, the spy program infers a 1. Similarly the existence of a file or other resource of a particular name can be used to signal. Notice that the spy does not need access to a file itself; the mere existence of the file is adequate to signal. The spy can determine the existence of a file it cannot read by trying to create a file of the same name; if the request to create is rejected, the spy determines that the service program has such a file.

To signal more than one bit, the service program and the spy program signal one bit in each time interval. Figure 3-14 shows a service program signaling the string 100 by toggling the existence of a file.

In our final example, a storage channel uses a server of unique identifiers. Recall that some bakeries, banks, and other commercial establishments have a machine to distribute numbered tickets so that customers can be served in the order in which they arrived. Some computing systems provide a similar server of unique identifiers, usually numbers, used to name temporary files, to tag and track messages, or to record auditable events. Different processes can request the next unique identifier from the server. But two cooperating processes can use the server to send a signal: The spy

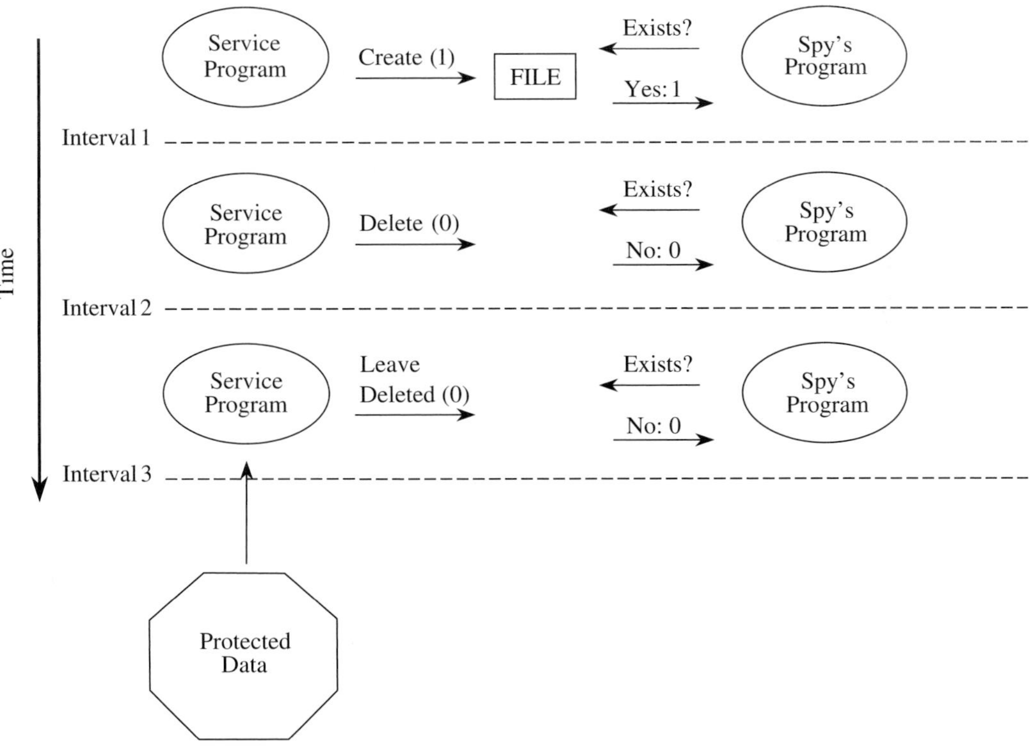

FIGURE 3-14 File Existence Channel Used to Signal 100.

process observes whether the numbers it receives are sequential or whether a number is missing. A missing number implies that the service program also requested a number, thereby signaling 1.

In all of these examples, the service program and the spy need access to a shared resource (such as a file, or even knowledge of the existence of a file) and a shared sense of time. As shown, shared resources are common in multiuser environments, where the resource may be as seemingly innocuous as whether a file exists, a device is free, or space remains on disk. A source of shared time is also typically available, since many programs need access to the current system time to set timers, to record the time at which events occur, or to synchronize activities.

Transferring data one bit at a time must seem awfully slow. But computers operate at such speeds that even the minuscule rate of 1 bit per millisecond (1/1000 second) would never be noticed but could easily be handled by two processes. At that rate of 1000 bits per second (which is unrealistically conservative), this entire book could be leaked in about two days. Increasing the rate by an order of magnitude or two, which is still quite conservative, reduces the transfer time to minutes.

Timing Channels

Other covert channels, called **timing channels**, pass information by using the speed at which things happen. Actually, timing channels are shared resource channels in which the shared resource is time.

A service program uses a timing channel to communicate by using or not using an assigned amount of computing time. In the simple case, a multiprogrammed system with two user processes divides time into blocks and allocates blocks of processing alternately to one process and the other. A process is offered processing time, but if the process is waiting for another event to occur and has no processing to do, it rejects the offer. The service process either uses its block (to signal a 1) or rejects its block (to signal a 0). Such a situation is shown in Figure 3-15, first with the service process and the spy's process alternating, and then with the service process communicating the string 101 to the spy's process. In the second part of the example, the service program wants to signal 0 in the third time block. It will do this by using just enough time to determine that it wants to send a 0 and then pause. The spy process then receives control for the remainder of the time block.

So far, all examples have involved just the service process and the spy's process. But in fact, multiuser computing systems typically have more than just two active processes. The only complications added by more processes are that the two cooperating processes must adjust their timings and deal with the possible interference from others. For example, with the unique identifier channel, other processes will also request identifiers. If on average n other processes will request m identifiers each, then the service program will request more than $n*m$ identifiers for a 1 and no identifiers for a 0. The gap dominates the effect of all other processes. Also, the service process and the spy's process can use sophisticated coding techniques to compress their communication and detect and correct transmission errors caused by the effects of other unrelated processes.

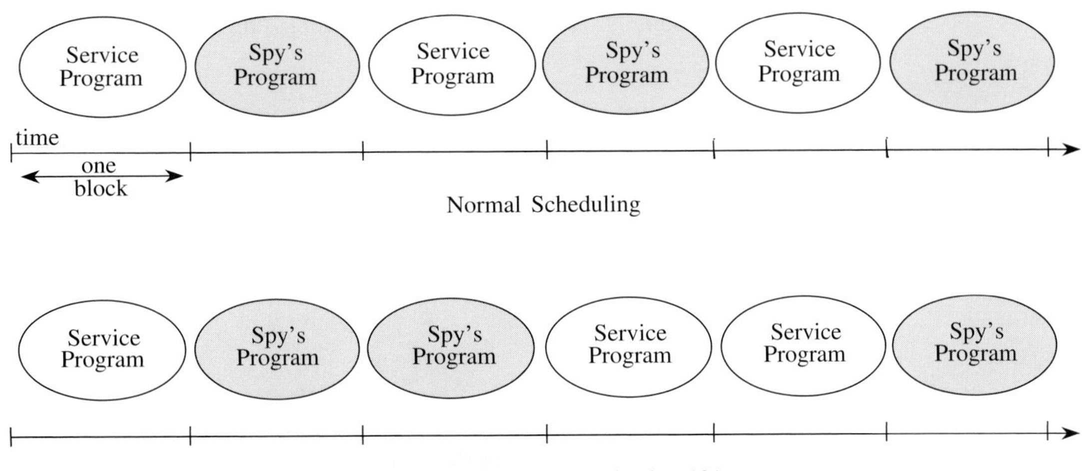

FIGURE 3-15 Covert Timing Channel.

Identifying Potential Covert Channels

In this description of covert channels, ordinary things, such as the existence of a file or time used for a computation, have been the medium through which a covert channel communicates. Covert channels are not easy to find because these media are so numerous and frequently used. Two relatively old techniques remain the standards for locating potential covert channels. One works by analyzing the resources of a system, and the other works at the source code level.

Shared Resource Matrix

Since the basis of a covert channel is a shared resource, the search for potential covert channels involves finding all shared resources and determining which processes can write to and read from the resources. The technique was introduced by Kemmerer [KEM83]. Although laborious, the technique can be automated.

To use this technique, you construct a matrix of resources (rows) and processes that can access them (columns). The matrix entries are R for "can read (or observe) the resource" and M for "can set (or modify, create, delete) the resource." For example, the file lock channel has the matrix shown in Table 3-3.

TABLE 3-3 Shared Resource Matrix.

	Service Process	Spy's Process
Locked	R, M	R, M
Confidential data	R	

You then look for two columns and two rows having the following pattern:

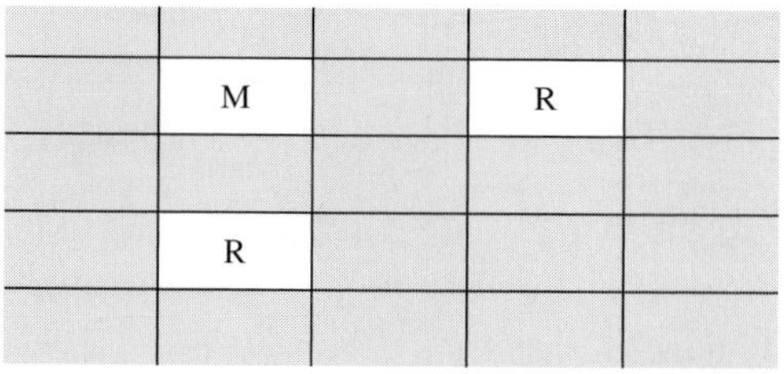

	M		R	
	R			

This pattern identifies two resources and two processes such that the second process is not allowed to read from the second resource. However, the first process can pass the information to the second by reading from the second resource and signaling the data through the first resource. Thus, this pattern implies the potential information flow as shown here.

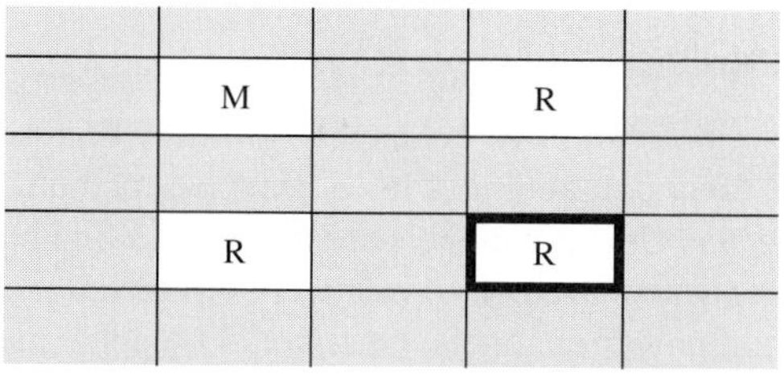

	M		R	
	R		**R**	

Next, you complete the shared resource matrix by adding these implied information flows, and analyze it for undesirable flows. Thus, you can tell that the spy's process can read the confidential data by using a covert channel through the file lock, as shown in Table 3-4.

Information Flow Method

Denning [DEN76a] derived a technique for flow analysis from a program's syntax. Conveniently, this analysis can be automated within a compiler so that information flow potentials can be detected as a program is under development.

Using this method, we can recognize that there are nonobvious flows of information between statements in a program. For example, we know that the statement B:=A,

TABLE 3-4 Complete Information Flow Matrix.

	Service Process	Spy's Process
Locked	R, M	R, M
Confidential data	R	R

which assigns the value of A to the variable B, obviously supports an information flow from A to B. This type of flow is called an "explicit flow." Similarly, the pair of statements B:=A; C:=B indicates an information flow from A to C (by way of B). The conditional statement IF D=1 THEN B:=A has two flows: from A to B because of the assignment, but also from D to B, because the value of B can change if and only if the value of D is 1. This second flow is called an "implicit flow."

The statement B:=*fcn*(*args*) supports an information flow from the function *fcn* to B. At a superficial level, we can say that there is a potential flow from the arguments *args* to B. However, we could more closely analyze the function to determine whether the function's value depended on all of its arguments and whether any global values, not part of the argument list, affected the function's value. These information flows can be traced from the bottom up: At the bottom there must be functions that call no other functions, and we can analyze them and then use those results to analyze the functions that call them. By looking at the elementary functions first, we could say definitively whether there is a potential information flow from each argument to the function's result and whether there are any flows from global variables. Table 3-5 lists several examples of syntactic information flows.

Finally, we put all the pieces together to show which outputs are affected by which inputs. Although this analysis sounds frightfully complicated, it can be automated during the syntax analysis portion of compilation. This analysis can also be performed on the higher-level design specification.

Covert Channel Conclusions

Covert channels represent a real threat to secrecy in information systems. A covert channel attack is fairly sophisticated, but the basic concept is not beyond the capabilities of even an average programmer. Since the subverted program can be practically

TABLE 3-5 Syntactic Information Flows.

Statement	Flow
B:=A	from A to B
IF C=1 THEN B:=A	from A to B; from C to B
FOR K:=1 to N DO *stmts* END	from K to *stmts*
WHILE K>0 DO *stmts* END	from K to *stmts*
CASE (*exp*) *val1*: *stmts*	from *exp* to *stmts*
B:=*fcn*(*args*)	from *fcn* to B
OPEN FILE *f*	none
READ (*f*, X)	from file *f* to X
WRITE (*f*, X)	from X to file *f*

any user service, such as a printer utility, planting the compromise can be as easy as planting a virus or any other kind of Trojan horse. And recent experience has shown how readily viruses can be planted.

Capacity and speed are not problems; our estimate of 1000 bits per second is unrealistically low, but even at that rate much information leaks swiftly. With modern hardware architectures, certain covert channels inherent in the hardware design have capacities of millions of bits per second. And the attack does not require significant finance. Thus, the attack could be very effective in certain situations involving highly sensitive data.

For these reasons, security researchers have worked diligently to develop techniques for closing covert channels. The closure results have been bothersome; in ordinarily open environments, there is essentially no control over the subversion of a service program, nor is there an effective way of screening such programs for covert channels. And other than in a few very high security systems, operating systems cannot control the flow of information from a covert channel. The hardware-based channels cannot be closed, given the underlying hardware architecture.

For variety (or sobriety), Kurak and McHugh [KUR92] present a very interesting analysis of covert signaling through graphic images.[4] In their work they demonstrate that two different images can be combined by some rather simple arithmetic on the bit patterns of digitized pictures. The second image in a printed copy is undetectable to the human eye, but it can easily be separated and reconstructed by the spy receiving the digital version of the image.

Although covert channel demonstrations are highly speculative—reports of actual covert channel attacks just do not exist—the analysis is sound. The mere possibility of their existence calls for more rigorous attention to other aspects of security, such as program development analysis, system architecture analysis, and review of output.

3.5 CONTROLS AGAINST PROGRAM THREATS

The picture we have just described is not pretty. There are many ways a program can fail and many ways to turn the underlying faults into security failures. It is of course better to focus on prevention than cure; how do we use controls during **software development**—the specifying, designing, writing, and testing of the program—to find and eliminate the sorts of exposures we have discussed? The discipline of software engineering addresses this question more globally, devising approaches to ensure the quality of software. In this book, we provide an overview of several techniques that can prove useful in finding and fixing security flaws. For more depth, we refer you to texts such as Pfleeger's [PFL01] and [PFL01a].

In this section we look at three types of controls: developmental, operating system, and administrative. We discuss each in turn.

[4] This form of data communication is called steganography, which means the art of concealing data in clear sight.

Developmental Controls

Many controls can be applied during software development to ferret out and fix problems. So let us begin by looking at the nature of development itself, to see what tasks are involved in specifying, designing, building, and testing software.

The Nature of Software Development

Software development is often considered a solitary effort; a programmer sits with a specification or design and grinds out line after line of code. But in fact, software development is a collaborative effort, involving people with different skill sets who combine their expertise to produce a working product. Development requires people who can

- *specify* the system, by capturing the requirements and building a model of how the system should work from the users' point of view
- *design* the system, by proposing a solution to the problem described by the requirements and building a model of the solution
- *implement* the system, by using the design as a blueprint for building a working solution
- *test* the system, to ensure that it meets the requirements and implements the solution as called for in the design
- *review* the system at various stages, to make sure that the end products are consistent with the specification and design models
- *document* the system, so that users can be trained and supported
- *manage* the system, to estimate what resources will be needed for development and to track when the system will be done
- *maintain* the system, tracking problems found, changes needed, and changes made, and evaluating their effects on overall quality and functionality

One person could do all these things. But more often than not, a team of developers works together to perform these tasks. Sometimes a team member does more than one activity; a tester can take part in a requirements review, for example, or an implementer can write documentation. Each team is different, and team dynamics play a large role in the team's success.

We can examine both product and process to see how each contributes to quality and in particular to security as an aspect of quality. Let us begin with the product, to get a sense of how we recognize high-quality secure software.

Modularity, Encapsulation, and Information Hiding

Code usually has a long shelf-life, and it is enhanced over time as needs change and faults are found and fixed. For this reason, a key principle of software engineering is to create a design or code in small, self-contained units, called **components** or **modules**; when a system is written this way, we say that it is **modular**. Modularity offers advantages for program development in general and security in particular.

If a component is isolated from the effects of other components, then it is easier to trace a problem to the fault that caused it and to limit the damage the fault causes. It is also easier to maintain the system, since changes to an isolated component do not affect other components. And it is easier to see where vulnerabilities may lie if the component is isolated. We call this isolation **encapsulation**.

Information hiding is another characteristic of modular software. When information is hidden, each component hides its precise implementation or some other design decision from the others. Thus, when a change is needed, the overall design can remain intact while only the necessary changes are made to particular components.

Let us look at these characteristics in more detail.

Modularity

Modularization is the process of dividing a task into subtasks. This division is done on a logical or functional basis. Each component performs a separate, independent part of the task. **Modularity** is depicted in Figure 3-16. The goal is to have each component meet four conditions:

- *single-purpose*: performs one function
- *small*: consists of an amount of information for which a human can readily grasp both structure and content
- *simple*: is of a low degree of complexity so that a human can readily understand the purpose and structure of the module
- *independent*: performs a task isolated from other modules

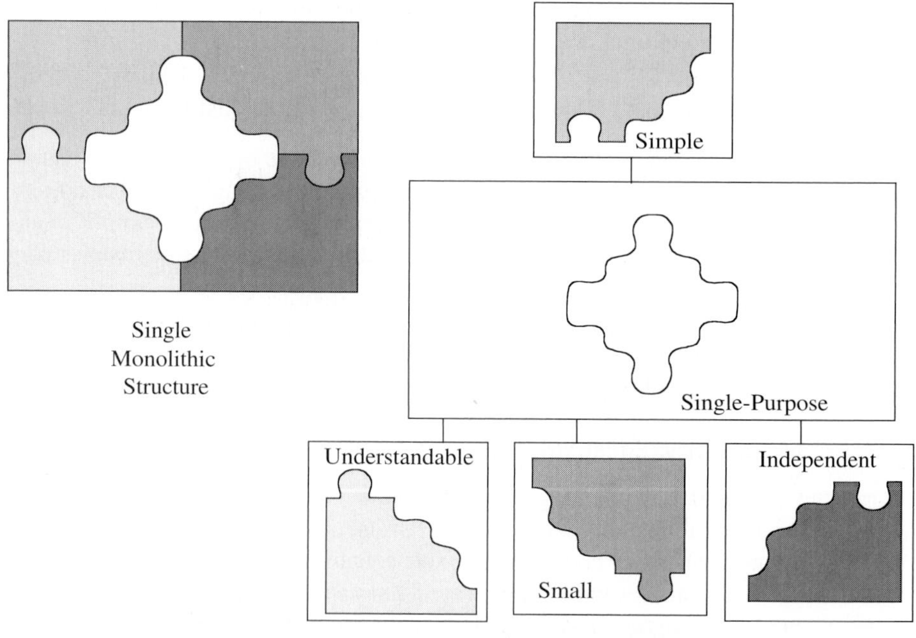

FIGURE 3-16 Modularity.

Often, other characteristics, such as having a single input and single output or using a limited set of programming constructs, help a component be modular. From a security standpoint, modularity should improve the likelihood that an implementation is correct.

In particular, smallness is an important quality that can help security analysts understand what each component does. That is, in good software, design and program units should be only as large as needed to perform their required functions. There are several advantages to having small, independent components.

- *Maintenance.* If a component implements a single function, it can be replaced easily with a revised one if necessary. The new component may be needed because of a change in requirements, hardware, or environment. Sometimes the replacement is an enhancement, using a smaller, faster, more correct, or otherwise better module. The interfaces between this component and the remainder of the design or code are few and well described, so the effects of the replacement are evident.
- *Understandability.* A system composed of many small components is usually easier to comprehend than one large, unstructured block of code.
- *Reuse.* Components developed for one purpose can often be reused in other systems. Reuse of correct, existing design or code components can significantly reduce the difficulty of implementation and testing.
- *Correctness.* A failure can be quickly traced to its cause if the components perform only one task each.
- *Testing.* A single component with well-defined inputs, output, and function can be tested exhaustively by itself, without concern for its effects on other modules (other than the expected function and output, of course).

Security analysts must be able to understand each component as an independent unit and be assured of its limited effect on other components.

A modular component usually has high cohesion and low coupling. By **cohesion**, we mean that all the elements of a component have a logical and functional reason for being there; every aspect of the component is tied to the component's single purpose. A highly cohesive component has a high degree of focus on the purpose; a low degree of cohesion means that the component's contents are an unrelated jumble of actions, often put together because of time-dependencies or convenience.

Coupling refers to the degree with which a component depends on other components in the system. Thus, low or loose coupling is better than high or tight coupling, because the loosely coupled components are free from unwitting interference from other components. This difference in coupling is shown in Figure 3-17.

Encapsulation

Encapsulation hides a component's implementation details, but it does not necessarily mean complete isolation. Many components must share information with other components, usually with good reason. However, this sharing is carefully documented so that a component is affected only in known ways by others in the system. Sharing is mini-

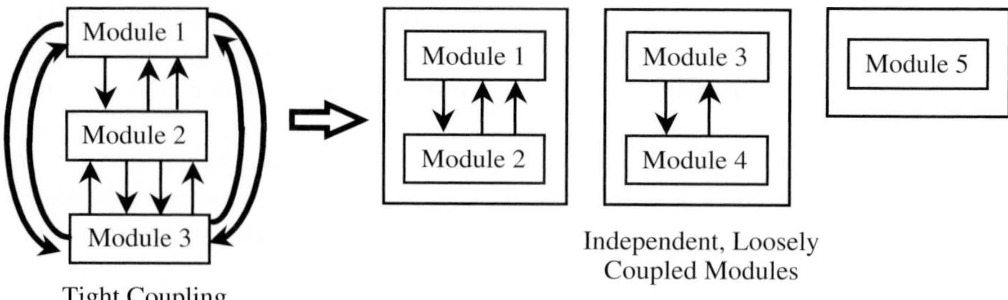

FIGURE 3-17 Coupling.

mized so that the fewest interfaces possible are used. Limited interfaces reduce the number of covert channels that can be constructed.

An encapsulated component's protective boundary can be translucent or transparent, as needed. Berard [BER00] notes that encapsulation is the "technique for packaging the information [inside a component] in such a way as to hide what should be hidden and make visible what is intended to be visible."

Information Hiding

Developers who work where modularization is stressed can be sure that other components will have limited effect on the ones they write. Thus, we can think of a component as a kind of black box, with certain well-defined inputs and outputs and a well-defined function. Other components' designers do not need to know *how* the module completes its function; it is enough to be assured that the component performs its task in some correct manner.

This concealment is the information hiding, depicted in Figure 3-18. Information hiding is desirable, because developers cannot easily and maliciously alter the components of others if they do not know how the components work.

These three characteristics—modularity, encapsulation, and information hiding—are fundamental principles of software engineering. They are also good security practices because they lead to modules that can be understood, analyzed, and trusted.

Peer Reviews

We turn next to the process of developing software. Certain practices and techniques can assist us in finding real and potential security flaws (as well as other faults) and fixing them before the system is turned over to the users. Of the many practices avail-

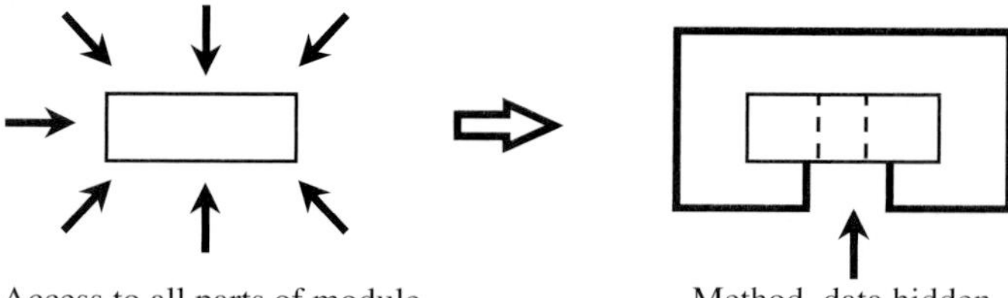

FIGURE 3-18 Information Hiding.

able for building what they call "solid software," Pfleeger et al. recommend several key techniques: [PFL01a]

- peer reviews
- hazard analysis
- testing
- good design
- prediction
- static analysis
- configuration management
- analysis of mistakes

Here, we look at each practice briefly, and we describe its relevance to security controls. We begin with peer reviews.

You have probably been doing some form of review for as many years as you have been writing code: desk-checking your work or asking a colleague to look over a routine to ferret out any problems. Today, a software review is associated with several formal process steps to make it more effective, and we review any artifact of the development process, not just code. But the essence of a review remains the same: sharing a product with colleagues able to comment about its correctness. There are careful distinctions among three types of peer reviews:

- *Review:* The artifact is presented informally to a team of reviewers; the goal is consensus and buy-in before development proceeds further.
- *Walk-through:* The artifact is presented to the team by its creator, who leads and controls the discussion. Here, education is the goal, and the focus is on learning about a single document.
- *Inspection:* This more formal process is a detailed analysis in which the artifact is checked against a prepared list of concerns. The creator does not lead the discussion, and the fault identification and correction are often controlled by statistical measurements.

A wise engineer who finds a fault can deal with it in at least three ways:

1. by learning how, when and why errors occur,
2. by taking action to prevent mistakes, and
3. by scrutinizing products to find the instances and effects of errors that were missed.

Peer reviews address this problem directly. Unfortunately, many organizations give only lip service to peer review, and reviews are still not part of mainstream software engineering activities.

But there are compelling reasons to do reviews. An overwhelming amount of evidence suggests that various types of peer review in software engineering can be extraordinarily effective. For example, early studies at Hewlett-Packard in the 1980s revealed that those developers performing peer review on their projects enjoyed a very significant advantage over those relying only on traditional dynamic testing tech-

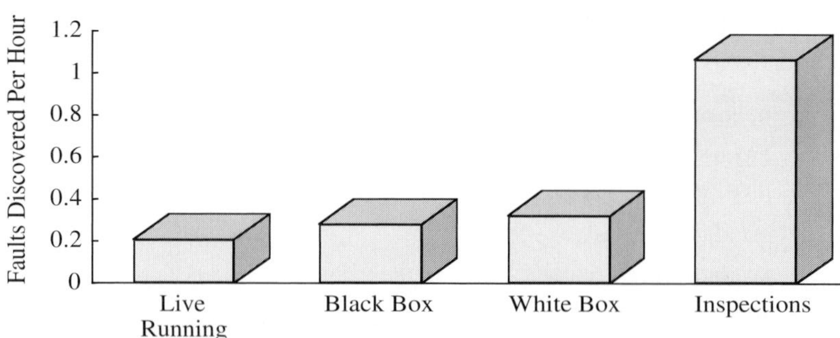

FIGURE 3-19 Fault Discovery Rate Reported at Hewlett-Packard.

niques, whether black-box or white-box. Figure 3-19 compares the fault discovery rate (that is, faults discovered per hour) among white-box testing, black-box testing, inspections, and software execution. It is clear that inspections discovered far more faults in the same period of time than other alternatives. [GRA87] This result is particularly compelling for large, secure systems, where live running for fault discovery may not be an option.

The effectiveness of reviews is reported repeatedly by researchers and practitioners. For instance, Jones [JON91] summarized the data in his large repository of project information to paint a picture of how reviews and inspections find faults relative to other discovery activities. Because products vary so wildly by size, Table 3-6 presents the fault discovery rates relative to the number of thousands of lines of code in the delivered product.

The inspection process involves several important steps: planning, individual preparation, a logging meeting, rework, and reinspection. Details about how to perform reviews and inspections can be found in software engineering books such as [PFL01] and [PFL01a].

During the review process, it is important to keep careful track of what each reviewer discovers and how quickly he or she discovers it. This log suggests not only whether particular reviewers need training but also whether certain kinds of faults are harder to find than others. Additionally, a root cause analysis for each fault found may reveal that the fault could have been discovered earlier in the process. For example, a requirements fault that surfaces during a code review should probably have been found during a requirements review. If there are no requirements reviews, you can start performing them. If there are requirements reviews, you can examine why this fault was missed and then improve the requirements review process.

The fault log can also be used to build a checklist of items to be sought in future reviews. The review team can use the checklist as a basis for questioning what can go wrong and where. In particular, the checklist can remind the team of security breaches, such as unchecked buffer overflows, that should be caught and fixed before the system is placed in the field. A rigorous design or code review can locate trapdoors, Trojan horses, salami attacks, worms, viruses, and other program flaws. A crafty programmer can conceal some of these flaws, but the chance of discovery rises when competent programmers review the design and code, especially when the components are small

TABLE 3-6 Faults Found During Discovery Activities.

Discovery Activity	Faults Found (Per Thousand Lines of Code)
Requirements review	2.5
Design review	5.0
Code inspection	10.0
Integration test	3.0
Acceptance test	2.0

and encapsulated. Management should use demanding reviews throughout development to ensure the ultimate security of the programs.

Hazard Analysis

Hazard analysis is a set of systematic techniques intended to expose potentially hazardous system states. In particular, it can help us expose security concerns and then identify prevention or mitigation strategies to address them. That is, hazard analysis ferrets out likely causes of problems so that we can then apply an appropriate technique for preventing the problem or softening its likely consequences. Thus, it usually involves developing hazard lists, as well as procedures for exploring "what if" scenarios to trigger consideration of nonobvious hazards. The sources of problems can be lurking in any artifacts of the development or maintenance process, not just in the code, so a hazard analysis must be broad in its domain of investigation; in other words, hazard analysis is a system issue, not just a code issue. Similarly, there are many kinds of problems, ranging from incorrect code to unclear consequences of a particular action. A good hazard analysis takes all of them into account.

Although hazard analysis is generally good practice on any project, it is required in some regulated and critical application domains, and it can be invaluable for finding security flaws. It is never too early to be thinking about the sources of hazards; the analysis should begin when you first start thinking about building a new system or when someone proposes a significant upgrade to an existing system. Hazard analysis should continue throughout the system life cycle; you must identify potential hazards that can be introduced during system design, installation, operation, and maintenance.

A variety of techniques support the identification and management of potential hazards. Among the most effective are **hazard and operability studies (HAZOP)**, **failure modes and effects analysis (FMEA)**, and **fault tree analysis (FTA)**. HAZOP is a structured analysis technique originally developed for the process control and chemical plant industries. Over the last few years it has been adapted to discover potential hazards in safety-critical software systems. FMEA is a bottom-up technique applied at the system component level. A team identifies each component's possible faults or fault modes; then, it determines what could trigger the fault and what systemwide effects each fault might have. By keeping system consequences in mind, the team often finds possible system failures that are not made visible by other analytical means. FTA complements FMEA. It is a top-down technique that begins with a postulated hazardous system malfunction. Then, the FTA team works backwards to identify the possible pre-

TABLE 3-7 Perspectives for Hazard Analysis (adapted from [PFL01]).

	Known Cause	Unknown Cause
Known effect	Description of system behavior	Deductive analysis, including fault tree analysis
Unknown effect	Inductive analysis, including failure modes and effects analysis	Exploratory analysis, including hazard and operability studies

cursors to the mishap. By tracing back from a specific hazardous malfunction, we can locate unexpected contributors to mishaps, and we then look for opportunities to mitigate the risks.

Each of these techniques is clearly useful for finding and preventing security breaches. We decide which technique is most appropriate by understanding how much we know about causes and effects. For example, Table 3-7 suggests that when we know the cause and effect of a given problem, we can strengthen the description of how the system should behave. This clearer picture will help requirements analysts understand how a potential problem is linked to other requirements. It also helps designers understand exactly what the system should do and helps testers know how to test to verify that the system is behaving properly. If we can describe a known effect with unknown cause, we use deductive techniques such as fault tree analysis to help us understand the likely causes of the unwelcome behavior. Conversely, we may know the cause of a problem but not understand all the effects; here, we use inductive techniques such as failure modes and effects analysis to help us trace from cause to all possible effects. For example, suppose we know that a subsystem is unprotected and might lead to a security failure, but we do not know how that failure will affect the rest of the system. We can use FMEA to generate a list of possible effects and then evaluate the trade-offs between extra protection and possible problems. Finally, to find problems about which we may not yet be aware, we can perform an exploratory analysis such as a hazard and operability study.

We see in Chapter 8 that hazard analysis is also useful for determining vulnerabilities and mapping them to suitable controls.

Testing

Testing is a process activity that homes in on product quality: making the product failure free or failure tolerant. Each software problem (especially when it relates to security) has the potential not only for making software fail but also for adversely affecting a business or a life. Thomas Young, head of NASA's investigation of the Mars lander failure, noted that "One of the things we kept in mind during the course of our review is that in the conduct of space missions, you get only one strike, not three. Even if thousands of functions are carried out flawlessly, just one mistake can be catastrophic to a mission." [NAS00] This same sentiment is true for security: The failure of one control exposes a vulnerability that is not ameliorated by any number of functioning controls. Testers improve software quality by finding as many faults as possible and by writing up their findings carefully so that developers can locate the causes and repair the problems if possible.

Testing usually involves several stages. First, each program component is tested on its own, isolated from the other components in the system. Such testing, known as *module testing, component testing,* or *unit testing*, verifies that the component functions properly with the types of input expected from a study of the component's design. **Unit testing** is done in a controlled environment whenever possible so that the test team can feed a predetermined set of data to the component being tested and observe what output actions and data are produced. In addition, the test team checks the internal data structures, logic, and boundary conditions for the input and output data.

When collections of components have been subjected to unit testing, the next step is ensuring that the interfaces among the components are defined and handled properly. Indeed, interface mismatch can be a significant security vulnerability. **Integration testing** is the process of verifying that the system components work together as described in the system and program design specifications.

Once we are sure that information is passed among components in accordance with the design, we test the system to ensure that it has the desired functionality. A **function test** evaluates the system to determine whether the functions described by the requirements specification are actually performed by the integrated system. The result is a functioning system.

The function test compares the system being built with the functions described in the developers' requirements specification. Then, a **performance test** compares the system with the remainder of these software and hardware requirements. It is during the function and performance tests that security requirements are examined, and the testers confirm that the system is as secure as it is required to be.

When the performance test is complete, developers are certain that the system functions according to their understanding of the system description. The next step is conferring with the customer to make certain that the system works according to customer expectations. Developers join the customer to perform an **acceptance test**, in which the system is checked against the customer's requirements description. Upon completion of acceptance testing, the accepted system is installed in the environment in which it will be used. A final **installation test** is run to make sure that the system still functions as it should. However, security requirements often state that a system should not do something. As Sidebar 3-6 demonstrates, it is difficult to demonstrate absence rather than presence.

The objective of unit and integration testing is to ensure that the code implemented the design properly; that is, that the programmers have written code to do what the designers intended. System testing has a very different objective: to ensure that the system does what the customer wants it to do. Regression testing, an aspect of system testing, is particularly important for security purposes. After a change is made to enhance the system or fix a problem, **regression testing** ensures that all remaining functions are still working and performance has not been degraded by the change.

Each of the types of tests listed here can be performed from two perspectives: black box and clear box (sometimes called white box). **Black-box testing** treats a system or its components as black boxes; testers cannot "see inside" the system, so they apply particular inputs and verify that they get the expected output. **Clear-box testing** allows visibility. Here, testers can examine the design and code directly, generating test cases based on the code's actual construction. Thus, clear-box testing knows that component

Sidebar 3-6 Absence vs. Presence

Pfleeger [PFL97] points out that security requirements resemble those for any other computing task, with one seemingly insignificant difference. Whereas most requirements say "the system will do this," security requirements add the phrase "and nothing more." As we pointed out in Chapter 1, security awareness calls for more than a little caution when a creative developer takes liberties with the system's specification. Ordinarily, we do not worry if a programmer or designer adds a little something extra. For instance, if the requirement calls for generating a file list on a disk, the "something more" might be sorting the list into alphabetical order or displaying the date it was created. But we would never expect someone to meet the requirement by displaying the list and then erasing all the files on the disk!

If we could determine easily whether an addition was harmful, we could just disallow harmful additions. But unfortunately we cannot. For security reasons, we must state explicitly the phrase "and nothing more" and leave room for negotiation in requirements definition on any proposed extensions.

It is natural for programmers to want to exercise their creativity in extending and expanding the requirements. But apparently benign choices, such as storing a value in a global variable or writing to a temporary file, can have serious security implications. And sometimes the best design approach for security is counterintuitive. For example, one cryptosystem attack depends on measuring the time to perform an encryption. That is, an efficient implementation can undermine the system's security. The solution, oddly enough, is to artificially pad the encryption process with unnecessary computation so that short computations complete as slowly as long ones.

In another instance, an enthusiastic programmer added parity checking to a cryptographic procedure. Because the keys were generated randomly, the result was that 255 of the 256 encryptions failed the parity check, leading to the substitution of a fixed key—so that 255 of every 256 encryptions were being performed under the same key!

No technology can automatically distinguish between malicious and benign code. For this reason, we have to rely on a combination of approaches, including human-intensive ones, to help us detect when we are going beyond the scope of the requirements and threatening the system's security.

X uses CASE statements and can look for instances in which the input causes control to drop through to an unexpected line. Black-box testing must rely more on the required inputs and outputs because the actual code is not available for scrutiny.

The mix of techniques appropriate for testing a given system depends on the system's size, application domain, amount of risk, and many other factors. But understanding the effectiveness of each technique helps us know what is right for each particular system. For example, Olsen [OLS93] describes the development at Contel IPC of a system containing 184,000 lines of code. He tracked faults discovered during various activities, and found differences:

- 17.3 percent of the faults were found during inspections of the system design
- 19.1 percent during component design inspection
- 15.1 percent during code inspection
- 29.4 percent during integration testing
- 16.6 percent during system and regression testing

Only 0.1 percent of the faults were revealed after the system was placed in the field. Thus, Olsen's work shows the importance of using different techniques to uncover different kinds of faults during development; it is not enough to rely on a single method for catching all problems.

Who does the testing? From a security standpoint, independent testing is highly desirable; it may prevent a developer from attempting to hide something in a routine, or keep a subsystem from controlling the tests that will be applied to it. Thus, independent testing increases the likelihood that a test will expose the effect of a hidden feature.

Good Design

We saw earlier in this chapter that modularity, information hiding, and encapsulation are characteristics of good design. Several design-related process activities are particularly helpful in building secure software:

- using a philosophy of *fault tolerance*
- having a consistent *policy* for handling failures
- capturing the *design rationale* and history
- using design patterns

We describe each of these activities in turn.

Designs should try to anticipate faults and handle them in ways that minimize disruption and maximize safety and security. Ideally, we want our system to be fault free. But in reality, we must assume that the system will fail, and we make sure that unexpected failure does not bring the system down, destroy data, or destroy life. For example, rather than waiting for the system to fail (called **passive fault detection**), we might construct the system so that it reacts in an acceptable way to a failure's occurrence. **Active fault detection** could be practiced by, for instance, adopting a philosophy of mutual suspicion. Instead of assuming that data passed from other systems or components are correct, we can always check that the data are within bounds and of the right type or format. We can also use **redundancy**, comparing the results of two or more processes to see that they agree before using their result in a task.

If correcting a fault is too risky, inconvenient, or expensive, we can choose instead to practice **fault tolerance**: isolating the damage caused by the fault and minimizing disruption to users. Although fault tolerance is not always thought of as a security technique, it supports the idea, discussed in Chapter 8, that our security policy allows us to choose to mitigate the effects of a security problem instead of preventing it. For example, rather than install expensive security controls, we may choose to accept the risk that important data may be corrupted. If in fact a security fault destroys important data, we may decide to isolate the damaged data set and automatically revert to a backup data set so that users can continue to perform system functions.

More generally, we can design or code defensively, just as we drive defensively, by constructing a consistent policy for handling failures. Typically, failures include

- failing to provide a service
- providing the wrong service or data
- corrupting data

We can build into the design a particular way of handling each problem, selecting from one of three ways:

1. *Retrying*: restoring the system to its previous state and performing the service again, using a different strategy
2. *Correcting*: restoring the system to its previous state, correcting some system characteristic, and performing the service again, using the same strategy
3. *Reporting*: restoring the system to its previous state, reporting the problem to an error-handling component, and not providing the service again

This consistency of design helps us check for security vulnerabilities; we look for instances that are different from the standard approach.

Design rationales and history tell us the reasons the system is built one way instead of another. Such information helps us as the system evolves, so we can integrate the design of our security functions without compromising the integrity of the system's overall design.

Moreover, the design history enables us to look for patterns, noting what designs work best in which situations. For example, we can reuse patterns that have been successful in preventing buffer overflows, in ensuring data integrity, or in implementing user password checks.

Prediction

Among the many kinds of prediction we do during software development, we try to predict the risks involved in building and using the system. As we see in depth in Chapter 8, we must postulate which unwelcome events might occur and then make plans to avoid them or at least mitigate their effects. Risk prediction and management are especially important for security, where we are always dealing with unwanted events that have negative consequences. Our predictions help us decide which controls to use and how many. For example, if we think the risk of a particular security breach is small, we may not want to invest a large amount of money, time, or effort in installing sophisticated controls. Or we may use the likely risk impact to justify using several controls at once, a technique called "defense in depth."

Static Analysis

Before a system is up and running, we can examine its design and code to locate and repair security flaws. We noted earlier that the peer review process involves this kind of scrutiny. But static analysis is more than peer review, and it is usually performed before peer review. We can use tools and techniques to examine the characteristics of design and code to see if the characteristics warn us of possible faults lurking within. For example, a large number of levels of nesting may indicate that the design or code is hard to read and understand, making it easy for a malicious developer to bury dangerous code deep within the system.

To this end, we can examine several aspects of the design and code:

- control flow structure
- data flow structure
- data structure

The control flow is the sequence in which instructions are executed, including iterations and loops. This aspect of design or code can also tell us how often a particular instruction or routine is executed.

Data flow follows the trail of a data item as it is accessed and modified by the system. Many times, transactions applied to data are complex, and we use data flow measures to show us how and when each data item is written, read, and changed.

The data structure is the way in which the data are organized, independent of the system itself. For instance, if the data are arranged as lists, stacks, or queues, the algorithms for manipulating them are likely to be well understood and well defined.

There are many approaches to static analysis, especially because there are so many ways to create and document a design or program. Automated tools are available to generate not only numbers (such as depth of nesting or cyclomatic number) but also graphical depictions of control flow, data relationships, and the number of paths from one line of code to another. These aids can help us see how a flaw in one part of a system can affect other parts.

Configuration Management

When we develop software, it is important to know who is making which changes to what and when:

- *corrective changes*: maintaining control of the system's day-to-day functions
- *adaptive changes*: maintaining control over system modifications
- *perfective changes*: perfecting existing acceptable functions
- *preventive changes*: preventing system performance from degrading to unacceptable levels

We want some degree of control over the software changes so that one change does not inadvertently undo the effect of a previous change. And we want to control what is often a proliferation of different versions and releases. For instance, a product might run on several different platforms or in several different environments, necessitating different code to support the same functionality. **Configuration management** is the process by which we control changes during development and maintenance, and it offers several advantages in security. In particular, configuration management scrutinizes new and changed code to ensure, among other things, that security flaws have not been inserted, intentionally or accidentally.

Four activities are involved in configuration management:

1. configuration identification
2. configuration control and change management
3. configuration auditing
4. status accounting

Configuration identification sets up baselines to which all other code will be compared after changes are made. That is, we build and document an inventory of all components that comprise the system. The inventory includes not only the code you and your colleagues may have created, but also database management systems, third-party software, libraries, test cases, documents, and more. Then, we "freeze" the baseline and carefully control what happens to it. When a change is proposed and made, it is described in terms of how the baseline changes.

Configuration control and **configuration management** ensure we can coordinate separate, related versions. For example, there may be closely related versions of a system to execute on 16-bit and 32-bit processors. Three ways to control the changes are separate files, deltas, and conditional compilation. If we use separate files, we have different files for each release or version. For example, we might build an encryption system in two configurations: one that uses a short key length, to comply with the law in certain countries, and another that uses a long key. Then, version 1 may be composed of components A_1 through A_k and B_1, while version 2 is A_1 through A_k and B_2, where B_1 and B_2 do key length. That is, the versions are the same except for the separate key processing files.

Alternatively, we can designate a particular version as the main version of a system, and then define other versions in terms of what is different. The difference file, called a **delta**, contains editing commands to describe the ways to transform the main version into the variation.

Finally, we can do **conditional compilation**, whereby a single code component addresses all versions, relying on the compiler to determine which statements to apply to which versions. This approach seems appealing for security applications because all the code appears in one place. However, if the variations are very complex, the code may be very difficult to read and understand.

Once a configuration management technique is chosen and applied, the system should be audited regularly. A **configuration audit** confirms that the baseline is complete and accurate, that changes are recorded, that recorded changes are made, and that the actual software (that is, the software as used in the field) is reflected accurately in the documents. Audits are usually done by independent parties taking one of two approaches: reviewing every entry in the baseline and comparing it with the software in use or sampling from a larger set just to confirm compliance. For systems with strict security constraints, the first approach is preferable, but the second approach may be more practical.

Finally, **status accounting** records information about the components: where they came from (for instance, purchased, reused, or written from scratch), the current version, the change history, and pending change requests.

All four sets of activities are performed by a **configuration and change control board**, or CCB. The CCB contains representatives from all organizations with a vested interest in the system, perhaps including customers, users, and developers. The board reviews all proposed changes and approves changes based on need, design integrity, future plans for the software, cost, and more. The developers implementing and testing the change work with a program librarian to control and update relevant documents and components; they also write detailed documentation about the changes and test results.

Configuration management offers two advantages to those of us with security concerns: protecting against unintentional threats and guarding against malicious ones. Both goals are addressed when the configuration management processes protect the integrity of programs and documentation. Because changes occur only after explicit approval from a configuration management authority, all changes are also carefully evaluated for side effects. With configuration management, previous versions of programs are archived, so a developer can retract a faulty change when necessary.

Malicious modification is made quite difficult with a strong review and configuration management process in place. In fact, as presented in Sidebar 3-7, poor configuration control has resulted in at least one system failure; that sidebar also confirms the principle of easiest penetration from Chapter 1. Once a reviewed program is accepted for inclusion in a system, the developer cannot sneak in to make small, subtle changes, such as inserting trapdoors. The developer has access to the running production program only through the CCB, whose members are alert to such security breaches.

Sidebar 3-7 There's More Than One Way to Crack a System

In the 1970s the primary security assurance strategy was "penetration" or "tiger team" testing. A team of computer security experts would be hired to test the security of a system prior to its being pronounced ready to use. Often these teams worked for months to plan their tests.

The U.S. Department of Defense was testing the Multics system, which had been designed and built under extremely high security quality standards. Multics was being studied as a base operating system for the WWMCCS command and control system. The developers from M.I.T. were justifiably proud of the strength of the security of their system, and the sponsoring agency invoked the penetration team with a note of haughtiness. But the developers underestimated the security testing team.

Led by Roger Schell and Paul Karger, the team analyzed the code and performed their tests without finding major flaws. Then one team member thought like an attacker. He wrote a slight modification to the code to embed a trapdoor by which he could perform privileged operations as an unprivileged user. He then made a tape of this modified system, wrote a cover letter saying that a new release of the system was enclosed, and mailed the tape and letter to the site where the system was installed.

When it came time to demonstrate their work, the penetration team congratulated the Multics developers on generally solid security, but said they had found this one apparent failure, which the team member went on to show. The developers were aghast because they knew they had scrutinized the affected code carefully. Even when told the nature of the trapdoor that had been added, the developers could not find it. [KAR74, KAR02]

Lessons from Mistakes

One of the easiest things we can do to enhance security is learn from our mistakes. As we design and build systems, we can document our decisions—not only what we decided to do and why, but also what we decided *not* to do and why. Then, after the system is up and running, we can use information about the failures (and how we found and fixed the underlying faults) to give us a better understanding of what leads to vulnerabilities and their exploitation.

From this information, we can build checklists and codify guidelines to help ourselves and others. That is, we do not have to make the same mistake twice, and we can assist other developers in staying away from the mistakes we made. The checklists and guidelines can be invaluable, especially during reviews and inspections, in helping reviewers look for typical or common mistakes that can lead to security flaws. For instance, a checklist can remind a designer or programmer to make sure that the system checks for buffer overflows. Similarly, the guidelines can tell a developer when data require password protection or some other type of restricted access.

Proofs of Program Correctness

A security specialist wants to be certain that a given program computes a particular result, computes it correctly, and does nothing beyond what it is supposed to do. Unfortunately, results in computer science theory (see [PFL85] for a description) indicate that we cannot know with certainty that two programs do exactly the same thing. That is, there can be no general decision procedure which, given any two programs, determines if the two are equivalent. This difficulty results from the "halting problem," which states that there is no general technique to determine whether an arbitrary program will halt when processing an arbitrary input.

In spite of this disappointing general result, a technique called **program verification** can demonstrate formally the "correctness" of certain specific programs. Program verification involves making initial assertions about the inputs and then checking to see if the desired output is generated. Each program statement is translated into a logical description about its contribution to the logical flow of the program. Finally, the terminal statement of the program is associated with the desired output. By applying a logic analyzer, we can prove that the initial assumptions, through the implications of the program statements, produce the terminal condition. In this way, we can show that a particular program achieves its goal. Sidebar 3-8 presents the case for appropriate use of formal proof techniques. We study an example of program verification in Chapter 5.

Proving program correctness, although desirable and useful, is hindered by several factors.

- Correctness proofs depend on a programmer or logician to translate a program's statements into logical implications. Just as programming is prone to errors, so also is this translation.
- Deriving the correctness proof from the initial assertions and the implications of statements is difficult, and the logical engine to generate proofs runs slowly. The speed of the engine degrades as the size of the program increases, so proofs of correctness are even less appropriate for large programs.

Sidebar 3-8 Formal Methods Can Catch Difficult-to-See Problems

Formal methods are sometimes used to check various aspects of secure systems. The notion "formal methods" means many things to many people, and many types of formal methods are proffered for use in software development. Each formal technique involves the use of mathematically precise specification and design notations. In its purest form, formal development is based on refinement and proof of correctness at each stage in the life cycle. But all formal methods are not created equal.

Pfleeger and Hatton [PFL97a] point out that, for some organizations, the changes in software development practices needed to support such techniques can be revolutionary. That is, there is not always a simple migration path from current practice to inclusion of formal methods, because the effective use of formal methods can require a radical change right at the beginning of the traditional software life cycle: how we capture and record customer requirements. Thus, the stakes in this area can be particularly high. For this reason, compelling evidence of the effectiveness of formal methods is highly desirable.

Gerhart, Craigen and Ralston [GER94] point out that

"There is no simple answer to the question: *do formal methods pay off*? Our cases provide a wealth of data but only scratch the surface of information available to address these questions. All cases involve so many interwoven factors that it is impossible to allocate payoff from formal methods versus other factors, such as quality of people or effects of other methodologies. Even where data was collected, it was difficult to interpret the results across the background of the organization and the various factors surrounding the application."

Naur [NAU93] reports that the use of formal notations does not lead inevitably to improving the quality of specifications, even when used by the most mathematically sophisticated minds. In his experiment, the use of a formal notation often led to a greater number of defects, rather than fewer. Thus, we need careful analyses of the effects of formal methods to understand what contextual and methodological characteristics affect the end results.

However, anecdotal support for formal methods has grown, and practitioners have been more willing to use formal methods on projects where the software is safety-critical. For example, McDermid [MCD93] asserts that "these mathematical approaches provide us with the best available approach to the development of high-integrity safety-critical systems." Formal methods are becoming used routinely to evaluate communication protocols and proposed security policies. Evidence from Heitmeyer's work [HEI01] at the U.S. Naval Research Laboratory suggests that formal methods are becoming easier to use and more effective. Dill and Rushby [DIL96] report that use of formal methods to analyze correctness of hardware design "has become attractive because it has focused on reducing the cost and time required for validation . . . [T]here are some lessons and principles from hardware verification that can be transferred to the software world." And Pfleeger and Hatton report that an air traffic control system built with several types of formal methods resulted in software of very high quality. For these reasons, formal methods are being incorporated into standards and imposed on developers. For

Sidebar 3-8 Formal Methods Can Catch Difficult-to-See Problems (Continued)

instance, the interim UK defense standard for such systems, DefStd 00-55, makes mandatory the use of formal methods.

However, more evaluation must be done. We must understand how formal methods contribute to quality. And we must decide how to choose among the many competing formal methods, which may not be equally effective in a given situation.

- The current state of program verification is less well developed than code production. As a result, correctness proofs have not been consistently and successfully applied to large production systems.

Program verification systems are being improved constantly. Larger programs are being verified in less time than before. As program verification continues to mature, it may become a more important control to ensure the security of programs.

Programming Practice Conclusions

None of the development controls described here can guarantee the security or quality of a system. As Brooks often points out [BRO87], the software development community seeks, but is not likely to find, a "silver bullet": a tool, technique, or method that will dramatically improve the quality of software developed. "There is no single development in either technology or management technique that by itself promises even one order-of-magnitude improvement in productivity, in reliability, in simplicity." He bases this conjecture on the fact that software is complex, it must conform to the infinite variety of human requirements, and it is abstract or invisible, leading to its being hard to draw or envision. While software development technologies—design tools, process improvement models, development methodologies—help the process, software development is inherently complicated and, therefore, prone to errors. This uncertainty does not mean that we should not seek ways to improve; we should. However, we should be realistic and accept that no technique is sure to prevent erroneous software. We should incorporate in our development practices those techniques that reduce uncertainty and reduce risk. At the same time, we should be skeptical of new technology, making sure each one can be shown to be reliable and effective.

In the early 1970s Paul Karger and Roger Schell led a team to evaluate the security of the Multics system for the U.S. Air Force. They republished their original report [KAR74] thirty years later with a thoughtful analysis of how the security of Multics compares to the security of current systems [KAR02]. Among their observations were that buffer overflows were almost impossible in Multics because of support from the programming language, and security was easier to ensure because of the simplicity and structure of the Multics design. Karger and Schell argue that we can and have designed and implemented systems with both functionality and security.

Operating System Controls on Use of Programs

Development controls are usually applied to large development projects in a variety of software production environments. However, not every system is developed in the ways we described above; sometimes projects are too small or too resource constrained to justify the extra resources needed for reviews and configuration control boards, for example. Although not the most desirable situation, the lack of proper controls is often a reality of development life. Even when development controls are incorporated in an organization's standard development process, it is difficult to ensure that each developer or user has followed official guidelines or standards. For these reasons, some of the software security enforcement is implemented by the operating system.

We examine operating systems in some detail in Chapters 4 and 5, in which we see what security features they provide for their users. In this chapter, we outline how an operating system can protect against some of the design and implementation flaws we have discussed here.

Trusted Software

We say that software is **trusted software** if we know that the code has been rigorously developed and analyzed, giving us reason to trust that the code does what it is expected to do and nothing more. Typically, trusted code can be a foundation on which other, untrusted, code runs. That is, the untrusted system's quality depends, in part, on the trusted code; the trusted code establishes the baseline for security of the overall system. In particular, an operating system can be trusted software when there is a basis for trusting that it correctly controls the accesses of components or systems run from it. For example, the operating system might be expected to limit users' accesses to certain files. We look at trusted operating systems in more detail in Chapter 5.

To trust any program, we base our trust on rigorous analysis and testing, looking for certain key characteristics:

- *Functional correctness:* The program does what it is supposed to, and it works correctly.
- *Enforcement of integrity:* Even if presented erroneous commands or commands from unauthorized users, the program maintains the correctness of the data with which it has contact.
- *Limited privilege:* The program is allowed to access secure data, but the access is minimized and neither the access rights nor the data are passed along to other untrusted programs or back to an untrusted caller.
- *Appropriate confidence level:* The program has been examined and rated at a degree of trust appropriate for the kind of data and environment in which it is to be used.

Trusted software is often used as a safe way for general users to access sensitive data. Trusted programs are used to perform limited (safe) operations for users without allowing the users to have direct access to sensitive data.

Mutual Suspicion

Programs are not always trustworthy. Even with an operating system to enforce access limitations, it may be impossible or infeasible to bound the access privileges of an untested program effectively. In this case, the user U is legitimately suspicious of a new program P. However, program P may be invoked by another program, Q. There is no way for Q to know that P is correct or proper, any more than a user knows that of P.

Therefore, we use the concept of **mutual suspicion** to describe the relationship between two programs. Mutually suspicious programs operate as if other routines in the system were malicious or incorrect. A calling program cannot trust its called subprocedures to be correct, and a called subprocedure cannot trust its calling program to be correct. Each protects its interface data so that the other has only limited access. For example, a procedure to sort the entries in a list cannot be trusted not to modify those elements, while that procedure cannot trust its caller to provide any list at all or to supply the number of elements predicted.

Confinement

Confinement is a technique used by an operating system on a suspected program. A **confined** program is strictly limited in what system resources it can access. If a program is not trustworthy, the data it can access are strictly limited. Strong confinement would be helpful in limiting the spread of viruses. Since a virus spreads by means of transitivity and shared data, all the data and programs within a single compartment of a confined program can affect only the data and programs in the same compartment. Therefore, the virus can spread only to things in that compartment; it cannot get outside the compartment.

Access Log

An **access** or **audit log** is a listing of who accessed which computer objects, when, and for what amount of time. Commonly applied to files and programs, this technique is less a means of protection than an after-the-fact means of tracking down what has been done.

Typically, an access log is a protected file or a dedicated output device (such as a printer) to which a log of activities is written. The logged activities can be such things as logins and logouts, accesses or attempted accesses to files or directories, execution of programs, and uses of other devices.

Failures are also logged. It may be less important to record that a particular user listed the contents of a permitted directory than that the same user tried to but was prevented from listing the contents of a protected directory. One failed login may result from a typing error, but a series of failures in a short time from the same device may result from the attempt of an intruder to break into the system.

Unusual events in the audit log should be scrutinized. For example, a new program might be tested in a dedicated, controlled environment. After the program has been tested, an audit log of all files accessed should be scanned to determine if there are any unexpected file accesses, the presence of which could point to a Trojan horse in the new program. We examine these two important aspects of operating system control in more detail in the next two chapters.

Administrative Controls

Not all controls can be imposed automatically by the computing system. Sometimes controls are applied instead by the declaration that certain practices will be followed. These controls, encouraged by managers and administrators, are called administrative controls. We look at them briefly here and in more depth in Chapter 8.

Standards of Program Development

No software development organization worth its salt allows its developers to produce code at any time in any manner. The good software development practices described earlier in this chapter have all been validated by many years of practice. Although none is Brooks's mythical "silver bullet" that guarantees program correctness, quality, or security, they all add demonstrably to the strength of programs. Thus, organizations prudently establish standards on how programs are developed. Even advocates of agile methods, which give developers an unusual degree of flexibility and autonomy, encourage goal-directed behavior based on past experience and past success. Standards and guidelines can capture wisdom from previous projects and increase the likelihood that the resulting system will be correct. In addition, we want to ensure that the systems we build are reasonably easy to maintain and are compatible with the systems with which they interact.

We can exercise some degree of administrative control over software development by considering several kinds of standards or guidelines.

- standards of *design,* including using specified design tools, languages, or methodologies, using design diversity, and devising strategies for error handling and fault tolerance
- standards of *documentation, language,* and *coding style*, including layout of code on the page, choices of names of variables, and use of recognized program structures
- standards of *programming,* including mandatory peer reviews, periodic code audits for correctness, and compliance with standards
- standards of *testing*, such as using program verification techniques, archiving test results for future reference, using independent testers, evaluating test thoroughness, and encouraging test diversity
- standards of *configuration management,* to control access to and changes of stable or completed program units

Standardization improves the conditions under which all developers work by establishing a common framework so that no one developer is indispensable. It also allows carryover from one project to another; lessons learned on previous projects become available for use by all on the next project. Standards also assist in maintenance, since the maintenance team can find required information in a well-organized program. However, we must take care so that the standards do not unnecessarily constrain the developers.

Firms concerned about security and committed to following software development standards often perform **security audits**. In a security audit, an independent security evaluation team arrives unannounced to check each project's compliance with standards and guidelines. The team reviews requirements, designs, documentation, test data and plans, and code. Knowing that documents are routinely scrutinized, a developer is unlikely to put suspicious code in a component in the first place.

Separation of Duties

Banks often break tasks into two or more pieces to be performed by separate employees. Employees are less tempted to do wrong if they need the cooperation of another employee to do so. We can use the same approach during software development. Modular design and implementation force developers to cooperate in order to achieve illicit results. Independent test teams test a component or subsystem more rigorously if they are not the authors or designers. These forms of separation lead to a higher degree of security in programs.

Program Controls in General

This section has explored how to control for faults during the program development process. Some controls apply to how a program is developed, and others establish restrictions on the program's use. The best is a combination, the classic layered defense.

Is one control essential? Can one control be skipped if another is used? Although these are valid questions, the security community does not have answers. Software development is both an art and science. As a creative activity, it is subject to the variety of human minds, but also to the fallibility of humans. We cannot rigidly control the process and get the same results time after time, as we can with a machine.

But creative humans can learn from their mistakes and shape their creations to account for fundamental principles. Just as a great painter will achieve harmony and balance in a painting, a good software developer who truly understands security will incorporate security into all phases of development. Thus, even if you never become a security professional, this exposure to the needs and shortcomings of security will influence many of your future actions. Unfortunately, many developers do not have the opportunity to become sensitive to security issues, which probably accounts for many of the unintentional security faults in today's programs.

3.6 SUMMARY OF PROGRAM THREATS AND CONTROLS

This chapter has covered development issues in computer security: the kinds and effects of security flaws, both unintentional and in malicious code, and the techniques that can help to control threats. Malicious code receives a great deal of attention in the media; the colorful terminology certainly draws people to stories about it, and the large numbers of affected systems ensure that major malicious code attacks get very wide visibility. But it is important for us to realize that the seriousness of the threat and the degree of vulnerability should also cause people to pay attention. The total amount of damage already done is not measurable, but it is certainly large. Many successful attacks go undetected—for now, at least. With the explosive growth in connectivity to massive public networks such as the Internet, the exposure to threats is increasing dramatically. Yet the public continues to increase its reliance on computers and networks, ignoring the obvious danger.

In this chapter, we considered two general classes of security flaws: those that compromise or change data and those that affect computer service. There are essentially three controls on such activities: development controls, operating system controls, and administrative controls. Development controls limit software development activities, making it harder for a developer to create malicious programs. These same controls are effective against inadvertent mistakes made by developers. The operating system provides some degree of control by limiting access to computing system objects. Finally, administrative controls limit the kinds of actions people can take.

These controls are important for more than simply the actions they prohibit. They have significant positive effects that contribute to the overall quality of a system, from the points of view of developer, maintainer, and user. Program controls help produce better software. Operating systems limit access as a way of promoting the safe sharing of information among programs. And administrative controls and standards improve system usability, reusability, and maintainability. For all of them, the security features are a secondary but important aspect of the controls' goals.

Program controls are part of the more general problem of limiting the effect of one user on another. In the next chapter, we consider the role of the operating system in regulating user interaction.

3.7 TERMS AND CONCEPTS

program, 95
user, 95
secure program, 95
penetrate and patch, 96
fault, 96
program security flaw, 97
bug, 98
error, 98
failure, 98
buffer overflow, 100
incomplete mediation, 104
time-of-check to time-of-use, 106
malicious code, 108
rogue program, 111
virus, 111
agent, 111
transient virus, 111
resident virus, 111
Trojan horse, 111
logic bomb, 112
time bomb, 112
backdoor, 112
trapdoor, 112
worm, 112
rabbit, 112
appended virus, 113
document virus, 116
macro virus, 116
boot sector virus, 118
virus signature, 120
polymorphic virus, 123
encrypting virus, 124
Brain virus, 128
The Internet worm, 129
Code Red, 132
web bug, 134
stub, 137
driver, 137
side effect, 138
error checking, 138
undefined operation, 139
salami attack, 139
information leakage, 141
covert channel, 141

timing channel, 146
software engineering, 150
encapsulation, 152
information hiding, 152
modularity, 152
maintainability, 153
understandability, 153
reusability, 153
correctability, 153
testability, 153
coupling, 153
cohesion, 153
peer review, 154
program design, 155
inspection, 155
walk-through, 155
review, 155
egoless programming, 155
hazard analysis, 157
failure modes and effects analysis, 157
fault tree analysis, 157
regression test, 159
black-box test, 159
clear-box test, 159
independent test team, 159
configuration management, 163
conditional compilation, 164
proof of program correctness, 166
program verification, 166
trusted software, 169
functional correctness, 169
enforcement of integrity, 169
limited privilege, 169
appropriate security level, 169
mutual suspicion, 170
confinement, 170
access log, 170
development standards, 171
configuration management standards, 171

3.8 WHERE THE FIELD IS HEADED

Software is increasingly used in systems which, should the software malfunction, may threaten life, health, national security, the environment, or the economy. This situation means that developers, regulators, and users place an increasing priority on **high-confidence software**: software for which compelling evidence is required that it delivers a specified set of services in a manner that satisfies specified critical properties. For this reason, we look to software engineering research to help us build software that is not only more secure but also is of generally higher quality than the software we build and use today. Thus, the security field can leverage work being done in other domains on high-confidence software development.

The software engineering practices that offer us the most benefit can involve processes, products, or resources. When software has tight quality constraints, we do not want to wait until the system is developed to see if they are met. Rather, we want to see some evidence during development that the completed system is likely to meet the quality requirements we have imposed. We want to have confidence, based on compelling and objective evidence, that the risk associated with using a system conforms with our willingness to tolerate that risk.

An **assurance argument** lays out the evidence, not only in terms of software properties but also in terms of steps taken, resources used, and any other relevant issue that may have bearing on our confidence in the software's quality. The Common Criteria (studied in Chapter 5) require such an assurance case for security-critical systems. A framework for assurance arguments includes a description of what assurance is required for the system, how the case will be made that the required confidence is justified, what evidence is to be gathered, and how the evidence will be combined and evaluated. Some such frameworks exist and are being used. However, assurance argument frameworks suffer from several deficiencies:

- They are strong on organization and layout but weak on process.
- They emphasize repeated but narrow measurements instead of offering a broad perspective.
- They offer no guidance on assurance for evolving systems.

Researchers at RAND and MITRE are addressing these issues. MITRE is mapping existing assurance arguments to a common, machine-processable form, using two kinds of notations: *Toulmin structures,* developed as a general framework for presenting and analyzing arguments in legal and regulatory contexts, and *Goal Structuring Notation*, developed in the U.K.'s safety-critical software community for structuring safety arguments. RAND researchers are examining questions of confidence and assurance, particularly about how bodies of evidence and constructions of arguments support confidence in the assurance case. In particular, RAND is determining how assurance activities and techniques, such as reliability modeling and design-by-contract, fit into the larger picture of providing an assurance argument.

At the same time, researchers are examining ways to make code **self-stabilizing** or **self-healing**. Such systems can sense when they reach an illegitimate state—that is, an insecure one—and can automatically return to a legitimate, secure state. The self-healing process is not so simple as realizing a failure and correcting it in one step. Imagine, instead, that you awaken one morning and discover that you are in poor physical shape, overweight, and bored. A program of exercise, nutrition, and mental stimulation can gradually bring you back, but there may be some missteps along the way. Similarly a program may realize that it has allowed many program extensions—some perhaps malicious—to become integrated into the system and wants to return gradually to a secure configuration. Dijkstra [DIJ74] introduced this concept, and Lamport [LAM84] publicized it; it is closely related to the Byzantine generals problem [LAM82] that has been studied in many similar contexts.

In looking to the future it is important not to forget the past. Every student of computer security should know the foundational literature of computer security, including the works of Saltzer and Schroeder [SAL75] and Lampson [LAM71]. Other historical papers of interest are listed in the "To Learn More" section.

3.9 TO LEARN MORE

Some of the earliest examples of security vulnerabilities are programs that compromise data. To read about them, start with the reports written by Anderson [AND72] and Ware [WAR79], both of which contain observations that are still valid today. Then read the papers of Thompson [THO84] and Schell [SCH79], and ask yourself why people act as if malicious code is a new phenomenon.

Various examples of program flaws are described by Parker [PAR83] and Denning [DEN82]. The volumes edited by Hoffman [HOF90] and Denning [DEN90a] are excellent collections on malicious code. A good summary of current malicious code techniques and examples is presented by Denning [DEN99].

Stoll's accounts of finding and dealing with intrusions are worth reading, both for their lighthearted tone and for the serious situation they describe [STO88, STO89].

Software engineering principles are discussed by numerous authors. The books by Pfleeger [PFL01] and Pfleeger et al. [PFL01a] are good places to get an overview of the issues and approaches. Corbató [COR91] reflects on why building complex systems is hard and how we can improve our ability to build them.

The books by DeMarco and Lister [DEM87] and DeMarco [DEM95] are filled with sensible, creative ways to address software development. More recent books about agile development and extreme programming can give you a different perspective on software development; these techniques try to address the need to develop products quickly in a constrained business environment.

3.10 EXERCISES

1. Suppose you are a customs inspector. You are responsible for checking suitcases for secret compartments in which bulky items such as jewelry might be hidden. Describe the procedure you would follow to check for these compartments.
2. Your boss hands you a microprocessor and its technical reference manual. You are asked to check for undocumented features of the processor. Because of the number of possibilities, you cannot test every operation code with every combination of operands. Outline the strategy you would use to identify and characterize unpublicized operations.
3. Your boss hands you a computer program and its technical reference manual. You are asked to check for undocumented features of the program. How is this activity similar to the task of the previous exercises? How does it differ? Which is the most feasible? Why?
4. Could a computer program be used to automate testing for trapdoors? That is, could you design a computer program that, given the source or object version of another program and a suitable description, would reply *Yes* or *No* to show whether the program had any trapdoors? Explain your answer.
5. A program is written to compute the sum of the integers from 1 to 10. The programmer, well trained in reusability and maintainability, writes the program so that it computes the sum of the numbers from k to n. However, a team of security specialists scrutinizes the code. The team certifies that this program properly sets k to 1 and n to 10; therefore, the program is certified as being properly restricted in that it always operates on precisely the range 1 to 10. List different ways that this program can be sabotaged so that during execution it computes a different sum, such as 3 to 20.
6. One means of limiting the effect of an untrusted program is confinement: controlling what processes have access to the untrusted program and what access the program has to other processes and data. Explain how confinement would apply to the earlier example of the program that computes the sum of the integers 1 to 10.
7. List three controls that could be applied to detect or prevent salami attacks.

8. The distinction between a covert *storage* channel and a covert *timing* channel is not clear-cut. Every timing channel can be transformed into an equivalent storage channel. Explain how this transformation could be done.

9. List the limitations on the amount of information leaked per second through a covert channel in a multiaccess computing system.

10. An electronic mail system could be used to leak information. First, explain how the leakage could occur. Then, identify controls that could be applied to detect or prevent the leakage.

11. Modularity can have a negative as well as a positive effect. A program that is overmodularized performs its operations in very small modules, so a reader has trouble acquiring an overall perspective on what the system is trying to do. That is, although it may be easy to determine what individual modules do and what small groups of modules do, it is not easy to understand what they do in their entirety as a system. Suggest an approach that can be used during program development to provide this perspective.

12. You are given a program that purportedly manages a list of items through hash coding. The program is supposed to return the location of an item if the item is present, or return the location where the item should be inserted if the item is not in the list. Accompanying the program is a manual describing parameters such as the expected format of items in the table, the table size, and the specific calling sequence. You have only the object code of this program, not the source code. List the cases you would apply to test the correctness of the program's function.

13. You are writing a procedure to add a node to a doubly linked list. The system on which this procedure is to be run is subject to periodic hardware failures. The list your program is to maintain is of very high importance. Your program must ensure the integrity of the list, even if the machine fails in the middle of executing your procedure. Supply the individual statements you would use in your procedure to update the list. (Your list should be fewer than a dozen statements long.) Explain the effect of a machine failure after each instruction. Describe how you would revise this procedure so that it would restore the integrity of the basic list after a machine failure.

14. Explain how information in an access log could be used to identify the true identity of an impostor who has acquired unauthorized access to a computing system. Describe several different pieces of information in the log that could be combined to identify the impostor.

15. Several proposals have been made for a processor that could decrypt encrypted data and machine instructions and then execute the instructions on the data. The processor would then encrypt the results. How would such a processor be useful? What are the design requirements for such a processor?

4

Protection in General-Purpose Operating Systems

In this chapter:

- Protection features provided by general-purpose operating systems—protecting memory, files, and the execution environment
- Controlled access to objects
- User authentication

In the previous chapter, we looked at several types of security problems that can occur in programs. The problems may be unintentional, as with buffer overflows, or intentional, as when a virus or worm is inserted in code. In addition to these general problems, certain kinds of programs may be vulnerable to certain kinds of security problems simply because of the nature of the program itself. For example, operating systems and databases offer security challenges beyond those in more general programs; these programs offer different access to different items by different kinds of users, so the program designers must pay careful attention to defining access, granting access, and controlling intentional and unintentional corruption of data and relationships. For this reason, we devote three chapters to these specialized programs and their particular security concerns. In this chapter and the next, we study operating systems and their role in computer security; we look at databases in Chapter 6.

We begin by studying the contributions that operating systems have made to user security. An operating system supports multiprogramming (that is, the concurrent use of a system by more than one user), so operating system designers have developed ways to protect one user's computation from inadvertent or malicious interference by another user. Among those facilities provided for this purpose are memory protection, file protection, general control of access to objects, and user authentication. This chapter surveys the controls that provide these four features. We have oriented this discussion to the user: How do the controls protect users, and how do users apply those controls? In the next chapter, we see how operating system design is affected by the need to separate levels of security considerations for particular users.

4.1 PROTECTED OBJECTS AND METHODS OF PROTECTION

We begin by considering the history of protection in operating systems. This background helps us understand what kinds of things operating systems can protect and what methods are available for protecting them.

A Bit of History

Once upon a time, there were no operating systems: Users entered their programs directly into the machine in binary by means of switches. In many cases, program entry was done by physical manipulation of a toggle switch; in other cases, the entry was performed with a more complex electronic method, by means of an input device such as a keyboard. Because each user had exclusive use of the computing system, users were required to schedule blocks of time for running the machine. These users were responsible for loading their own libraries of support routines—assemblers, compilers, shared subprograms—and "cleaning up" after use by removing any sensitive code or data.

The first operating systems were simple utilities, called **executives**, designed to assist individual programmers and to smooth the transition from one user to another. The early executives provided linkers and loaders for relocation, easy access to compilers and assemblers, and automatic loading of subprograms from libraries. The executives handled the tedious aspects of programmer support, focusing on a single programmer during execution.

Operating systems took on a much broader role (and a different name) as the notion of multiprogramming was implemented. Realizing that two users could interleave access to the resources of a single computing system, researchers developed concepts such as scheduling, sharing, and parallel use. Multiprogrammed operating systems, also known as **monitors**, oversaw each program's execution. Monitors took an active role, whereas executives were passive. That is, an executive stayed in the background, waiting to be called into service by a requesting user. But a monitor actively asserted control of the computing system and gave resources to the user only when the request was consistent with general good use of the system. Similarly, the executive waited for a request and provided service on demand; the monitor maintained control over all resources, permitting or denying all computing and loaning resources to users as they needed them.

Multiprogramming brought another important change to computing. When a single person was using a system, the only force to be protected against was the user himself or herself. A user making an error may have felt foolish, but one user could not adversely affect the computation of any other user. However, multiple users introduced more complexity and risk. User A might rightly be angry if User B's programs or data had a negative effect on A's program's execution. Thus, protecting one user's programs and data from other users' programs became an important issue in multiprogrammed operating systems.

Protected Objects

In fact, the rise of multiprogramming meant that several aspects of a computing system required protection.

- memory
- sharable I/O devices, such as disks
- serially reusable I/O devices, such as printers and tape drives
- sharable programs and subprocedures
- networks
- sharable data

As it assumed responsibility for controlled sharing, the operating system had to protect these objects. In the following sections, we look at some of the mechanisms with which operating systems have enforced these objects' protection. Many operating system protection mechanisms have been supported by hardware. But, as noted in Sidebar 4-1, that approach is not always possible.

Security Methods of Operating Systems

The basis of protection is **separation:** keeping one user's objects separate from other users. Rushby and Randell [RUS83] note that separation in an operating system can occur in several ways.

- *Physical separation*, in which different processes use different physical objects, such as separate printers for output requiring different levels of security
- *Temporal separation*, in which processes having different security requirements are executed at different times
- *Logical separation*, in which users operate under the illusion that no other processes exist, as when an operating system constrains a program's accesses so that the program cannot access objects outside its permitted domain
- *Cryptographic separation*, in which processes conceal their data and computations in such a way that they are unintelligible to outside processes

Of course, combinations of two or more of these forms of separation are also possible.

The categories of separation are listed roughly in increasing order of complexity to implement, and, for the first three, in decreasing order of the security provided. However, the first two approaches are very stringent and can lead to poor resource utilization. Therefore, we would like to shift the burden of protection to the operating system to allow concurrent execution of processes having different security needs.

But separation is only half the answer. We want to separate users and their objects, but we also want to be able to provide sharing for some of those objects. For example, two users with different security levels may want to invoke the same search algorithm or function call. We would like the users to be able to share the algorithms and functions without compromising their individual security needs. There are several ways an operating system can assist, offering protection at any of several levels.

- *Do not protect.* Operating systems with no protection are appropriate when sensitive procedures are being run at separate times.
- *Isolate.* When an operating system provides isolation, different processes running concurrently are unaware of the presence of each other. Each process has its own address space, files, and other objects. The operating system must

Sidebar 4-1 Hardware-Enforced Protection

From the 1960s to the 1980s, vendors produced both hardware and the software to run on it. The major mainframe operating systems—such as IBM's MVS, Digital Equipment's VAX, and Burroughs's and GE's operating systems, as well as research systems such as KSOS, PSOS, KVM, Multics, and SCOMP—were designed to run on one family of hardware. The VAX family, for example, used a hardware design that implemented four distinct protection levels: Two were reserved for the operating system, a third for system utilities, and the last went to users' applications. This structure put essentially three distinct walls around the most critical functions, including those that implemented security. Anything that allowed the user to compromise the wall between user state and utility state still did not give the user access to the most sensitive protection features. A BiiN operating system from the late 1980s offered an amazing 64,000 different levels of protection (or separation) enforced by the hardware.

Two factors changed this situation. First, the U.S. government sued IBM in 1969, claiming that IBM had exercised unlawful monopolistic practices. As a consequence, during the 1970s IBM made its hardware available to run with other vendors' operating systems (thereby opening its specifications to competitors). This relaxation encouraged more openness in operating system selection: Users were finally able to buy hardware from one manufacturer and go elsewhere for some or all of the operating system. Second, the Unix operating system, begun in the early 1970s, was designed to be largely independent of the hardware on which it ran. A small kernel had to be recoded for each different kind of hardware platform, but the bulk of the operating system, running on top of that kernel, could be ported without change.

These two situations together meant that the operating system could no longer depend on hardware support for all its critical functionality. So, although an operating system might still be structured to reach several states, the underlying hardware might enforce separation between only two of those states, with the remainder being enforced in software.

Today three of the most prevalent families of operating systems—the Windows NT/2000/XP series, Unix, and Linux—run on many different kinds of hardware. (Only Apple's Mac OS is strongly integrated with its hardware base.) The default expectation is one level of hardware-enforced separation (two states). This situation means that an attacker is only one step away from complete system compromise through a "get_root" exploit. (See the note at the end of this chapter, in the section "Where the Field Is Headed," to read of a recent Microsoft initiative to reintroduce hardware-enforced separation for security-critical code and data.)

confine each process somehow, so that the objects of the other processes are completely concealed.

- *Share all or share nothing*. With this form of protection, the owner of an object declares it to be public or private. A public object is available to all users, whereas a private object is available only to its owner.
- *Share via access limitation*. With protection by access limitation, the operating system checks the allowability of each user's potential access to an object. That

is, access control is implemented for a specific user and a specific object. Lists of acceptable actions guide the operating system in determining whether a particular user should have access to a particular object. In some sense, the operating system acts as a guard between users and objects, ensuring that only authorized accesses occur.

- *Share by capabilities*. An extension of limited access sharing, this form of protection allows dynamic creation of sharing rights for objects. The degree of sharing can depend on the owner or the subject, on the context of the computation, or on the object itself.
- *Limit use of an object*. This form of protection limits not just the access to an object but the use made of that object after it has been accessed. For example, a user may be allowed to view a sensitive document, but not to print a copy of it. More powerfully, a user may be allowed access to data in a database to derive statistical summaries (such as average salary at a particular grade level), but not to determine specific data values (salaries of individuals).

Again, these modes of sharing are arranged in increasing order of difficulty to implement, but also in increasing order of fineness of protection they provide. A given operating system may provide different levels of protection for different objects, users, or situations.

When we think about data, we realize that access can be controlled at various levels: the bit, the byte, the element or word, the field, the record, the file or the volume. Thus, the **granularity** of control concerns us. The larger the level of object controlled, the easier it is to implement access control. However, sometimes the operating system must allow access to more than the user needs. For example, with large objects, a user needing access only to part of an object (such as a single record in a file) must be given access to the entire object (the whole file).

Let us examine in more detail several different kinds of objects and their specific kinds of protection.

4.2 MEMORY AND ADDRESS PROTECTION

The most obvious problem of multiprogramming is preventing one program from affecting the memory of other programs. Fortunately, protection can be built into the hardware mechanisms that control efficient use of memory, so that solid protection can be provided at essentially no additional cost.

Fence

The simplest form of memory protection was introduced in single-user operating systems, to prevent a faulty user program from destroying part of the resident portion of the operating system. As its name implies, a **fence** is a method to confine users to one side of a boundary.

In one implementation, the fence was a predefined memory address, enabling the operating system to reside on one side and the user to stay on the other. An example of this situation is shown in Figure 4-1. Unfortunately, this kind of implementation was

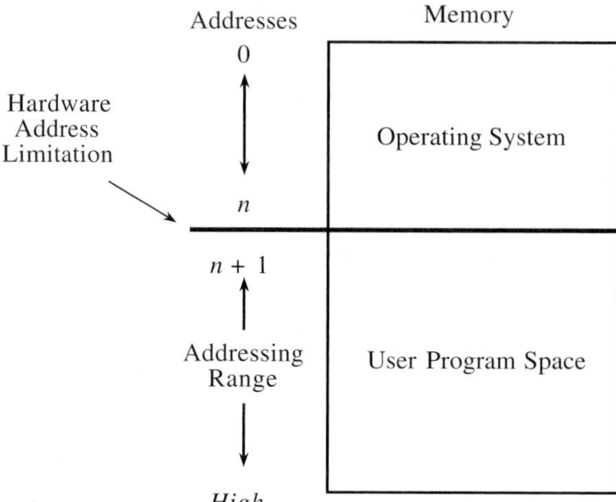

FIGURE 4-1 Fixed Fence.

very restrictive because a predefined amount of space was always reserved for the operating system, whether it was needed or not. If less than the predefined space was required, the excess space was wasted. Conversely, if the operating system needed more space, it could not grow beyond the fence boundary.

Another implementation used a hardware register, often called a **fence register**, containing the address of the end of the operating system. In contrast to a fixed fence, in this scheme the location of the fence could be changed. Each time a user program generated an address for data modification, the address was automatically compared with the fence address. If the address was greater than the fence address (that is, in the user area), the instruction was executed; if it was less than the fence address (that is, in the operating system area), an error condition was raised. The use of fence registers is shown in Figure 4-2.

A fence register protects only in one direction. In other words, an operating system can be protected from a single user, but the fence cannot protect one user from another user. Similarly, a user cannot identify certain areas of the program as inviolable (such as the code of the program itself or a read-only data area).

Relocation

If the operating system can be assumed to be of a fixed size, programmers can write their code assuming that the program begins at a constant address. This feature of the operating system makes it easy to determine the address of any object in the program. However, it also makes it essentially impossible to change the starting address if, for example, a new version of the operating system is larger or smaller than the old. If the size of the operating system is allowed to change, then programs must be written in a way that does not depend on placement at a specific location in memory.

Relocation is the process of taking a program written as if it began at address 0 and changing all addresses to reflect the actual address at which the program is located in memory. In many instances, this effort merely entails adding a constant **relocation**

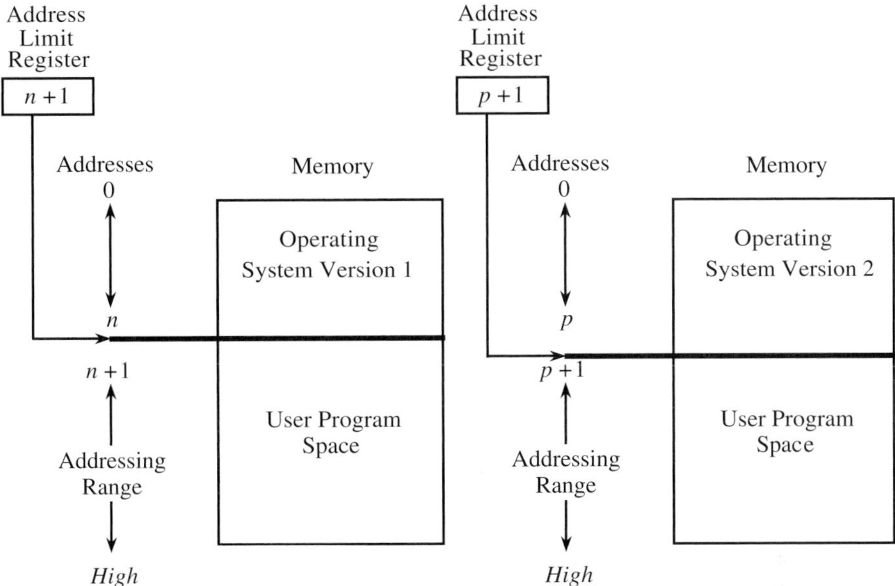

FIGURE 4-2 Variable Fence Register.

factor to each address of the program. That is, the relocation factor is the starting address of the memory assigned for the program.

Conveniently, the fence register can be used in this situation to provide an important extra benefit: The fence register can be a hardware relocation device. The contents of the fence register are added to each program address. This action both relocates the address and guarantees that no one can access a location lower than the fence address. (Addresses are treated as unsigned integers, so adding the value in the fence register to any number is guaranteed to produce a result at or above the fence address.) Special instructions can be added for the few times when a program legitimately intends to access a location of the operating system.

Base/Bounds Registers

A major advantage of an operating system with fence registers is the ability to relocate; this characteristic is especially important in a multiuser environment. With two or more users, none can know in advance where a program will be loaded for execution. The relocation register solves the problem by providing a base or starting address. All addresses inside a program are offsets from that base address. A variable fence register is generally known as a **base register**.

Fence registers provide a lower bound (a starting address) but not an upper one. An upper bound can be useful in knowing how much space is allotted and in checking for overflows into "forbidden" areas. To overcome this difficulty, a second register is often added, as shown in Figure 4-3. The second register, called a **bounds register**, is an upper address limit, in the same way that a base or fence register is a lower address

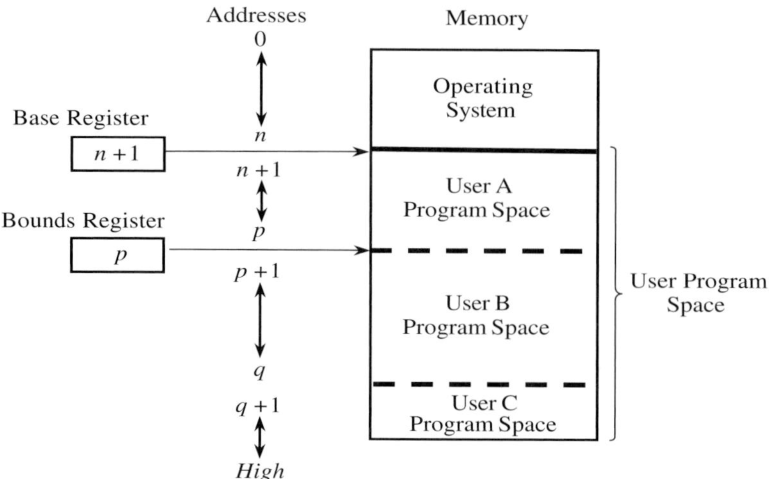

FIGURE 4-3 Pair of Base/Bounds Registers.

limit. Each program address is forced to be above the base address because the contents of the base register are added to the address; each address is also checked to ensure that it is below the bounds address. In this way, a program's addresses are neatly confined to the space between the base and the bounds registers.

This technique protects a program's addresses from modification by another user. When execution changes from one user's program to another's, the operating system must change the contents of the base and bounds registers to reflect the true address space for that user. This change is part of the general preparation, called a **context switch**, that the operating system must perform when transferring control from one user to another.

With a pair of base/bounds registers, a user is perfectly protected from outside users, or, more correctly, outside users are protected from errors in any other user's program. Erroneous addresses *inside* a user's address space can still affect that program because the base/bounds checking guarantees only that each address is inside the user's address space. For example, a user error might occur when a subscript is out of range or an undefined variable generates an address reference within the user's space but, unfortunately, inside the executable instructions of the user's program. In this manner, a user can accidentally store data on top of instructions. Such an error can let a user inadvertently destroy a program, but (fortunately) only the user's own program.

We can solve this overwriting problem by using another pair of base/bounds registers, one for the instructions (code) of the program and a second for the data space. Then, only instruction fetches (instructions to be executed) are relocated and checked with the first register pair, and only data accesses (operands of instructions) are relocated and checked with the second register pair. The use of two pairs of base/bounds registers is shown in Figure 4-4. Although two pairs of registers do not prevent all program errors, they limit the effect of data-manipulating instructions to the data space. The pairs of registers offer another more important advantage: the ability to split a program into two pieces that can be relocated separately.

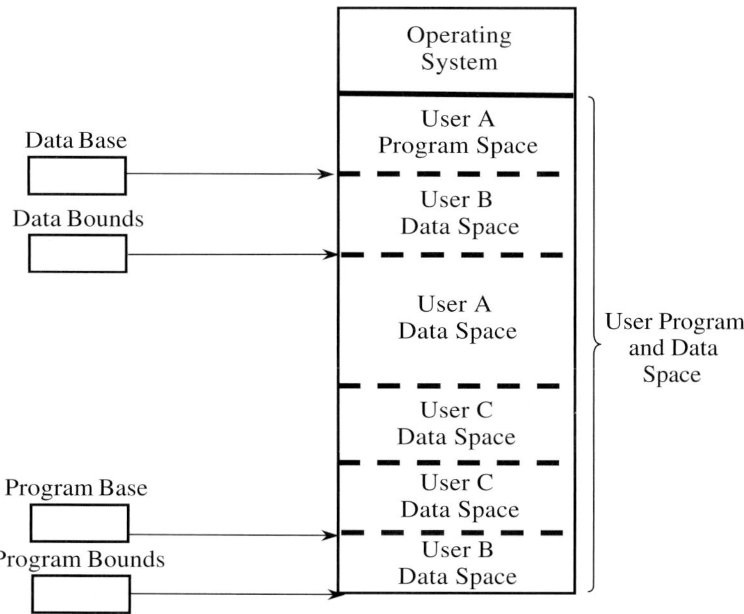

FIGURE 4-4 Two Pairs of Base/Bounds Registers.

These two features seem to call for the use of three or more pairs of registers: one for code, one for read-only data, and one for modifiable data values. Although in theory this concept can be extended, two pairs of registers are the limit for practical computer design. For each additional pair of registers (beyond two), something in the machine code of each instruction must indicate which relocation pair is to be used to address the instruction's operands. That is, with more than two pairs, each instruction specifies one of two or more data spaces. But with only two pairs, the decision can be automatic: instructions with one pair, data with the other.

Tagged Architecture

Another problem with using base/bounds registers for protection or relocation is their contiguous nature. Each pair of registers confines accesses to a consecutive range of addresses. A compiler or loader can easily rearrange a program so that all code sections are adjacent and all data sections are adjacent.

However, in some cases you may want to protect *some* data values but not *all*. For example, a personnel record may require protecting the field for salary but not office location and phone number. Moreover, a programmer may want to ensure the integrity of certain data values by allowing them to be written when the program is initialized but prohibiting the program from modifying them later. This scheme protects against errors in the programmer's own code. A programmer may also want to invoke a shared subprogram from a common library. We can address some of these issues by using good design, both in the operating system and in the other programs being run. Recall that in Chapter 3 we studied good design characteristics such as information hiding and modularity in program design. These characteristics dictate that one program module must share with another module only the *minimum* amount of data necessary for both of them to do their work.

Additional, operating-system-specific design features can help, too. Base/bounds registers create an all-or-nothing situation for sharing: Either a program makes all its data available to be accessed and modified or it prohibits access to all. Even if there were a third set of registers for shared data, all data would need to be located together. A procedure could not effectively share data items *A, B,* and *C* with one module, *A, C,* and *D* with a second, and *A, B,* and *D* with a third. The only way to accomplish the kind of sharing we want would be to move each appropriate set of data values to some contiguous space. However, this solution would not be acceptable if the data items were large records, arrays, or structures.

An alternative is **tagged architecture**, in which every word of machine memory has one or more extra bits to identify the access rights to that word. These access bits can be set only by privileged (operating system) instructions. The bits are tested every time an instruction accesses that location.

For example, as shown in Figure 4-5, one memory location may be protected as execute-only (e.g., the object code of instructions), whereas another is protected for fetch-only (e.g., read) data access, and another accessible for modification (e.g., write). In this way, two adjacent locations can have different access rights. Furthermore, with a few extra tag bits, different classes of data (numeric, character, address or pointer, and undefined) can be separated, and data fields can be protected for privileged (operating system) access only.

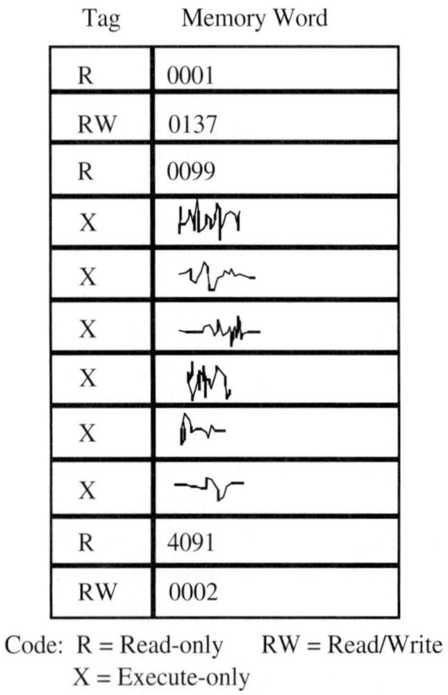

Tag	Memory Word
R	0001
RW	0137
R	0099
X	[illegible]
X	[illegible]
X	[illegible]
X	[illegible]
X	[illegible]
X	[illegible]
R	4091
RW	0002

Code: R = Read-only RW = Read/Write
X = Execute-only

FIGURE 4-5 Example of Tagged Architecture.

This protection technique has been used on a few systems, although the number of tag bits has been rather small. The Burroughs B6500-7500 system used three tag bits to separate data words (three types), descriptors (pointers), and control words (stack pointers and addressing control words). The IBM System/38 used a tag to control both integrity and access.

A variation used one tag that applied to a group of consecutive locations, such as 128 or 256 bytes. With one tag for a block of addresses, the added cost for implementing tags was not as high as with one tag per location. The Intel I960 extended architecture processor used a tagged architecture with a bit on each memory word that marked the word as a "capability," not as an ordinary location for data or instructions. A capability controlled access to a variable-sized memory block or segment. This large number of possible tag values supported memory segments that ranged in size from 64 to 4 billion bytes, with a potential 2^{256} different protection domains.

Compatibility of code presented a problem with the acceptance of a tagged architecture. A tagged architecture may not be as useful as more modern approaches, as we will see shortly. Some of the major computer vendors are still working with operating systems that were designed and implemented many years ago for architectures of that era. Indeed, most manufacturers are locked into a more conventional memory architecture because of the wide availability of components and a desire to maintain compatibility among operating systems and machine families. A tagged architecture would require fundamental changes to substantially all of the operating system code, a requirement that can be prohibitively expensive. But as the price of memory continues to fall, the implementation of a tagged architecture becomes more feasible.

Segmentation

We present two more approaches to protection, each of which can be implemented on top of a conventional machine structure, suggesting a better chance of acceptance. Although these approaches are ancient by computing's standards—they were designed between 1965 and 1975—they have been implemented on many machines since then. Furthermore, they offer important advantages in addressing, with memory protection being a delightful bonus.

The first of these two approaches, **segmentation**, involves the simple notion of dividing a program into separate pieces. Each piece has a logical unity, exhibiting a relationship among all of its code or data values. For example, a segment may be the code of a single procedure, the data of an array, or the collection of all local data values used by a particular module. Segmentation was developed as a feasible means to produce the effect of the equivalent of an unbounded number of base/bounds registers. In other words, segmentation allows a program to be divided into many pieces having different access rights.

Each segment has a unique name. A code or data item within a segment is addressed as the pair ⟨*name*, *offset*⟩, where *name* is the name of the segment containing the data item and *offset* is its location within the segment (that is, its distance from the start of the segment).

Logically, the programmer pictures a program as a long collection of segments. Segments can be separately relocated, allowing any segment to be placed in any available memory locations. The relationship between a logical segment and its true memory position is shown in Figure 4-6.

The operating system must maintain a table of segment names and their true addresses in memory. When a program generates an address of the form ⟨*name*, *offset*⟩, the operating system looks up *name* in the segment directory and determines its real beginning memory address. To that address the operating system adds *offset*, giving the true memory address of the code or data item. This translation is shown in Figure 4-7. For efficiency there is usually one operating system segment address table for each process in execution. Two processes that want to share access to a single segment would have the same segment name and address in their segment tables.

Thus, a user's program does not know what true memory addresses it uses. It has no way—and no need—to determine the actual address associated with a particular ⟨*name*, *offset*⟩. The ⟨*name*, *offset*⟩ pair is adequate to access any data or instruction to which a program should have access.

This hiding of addresses has three advantages for the operating system.

- The operating system can place any segment at any location or move any segment to any location, even after the program begins to execute. Because the operating system translates all address references by a segment address table, the operating system needs only to update the address in that one table when a segment is moved.

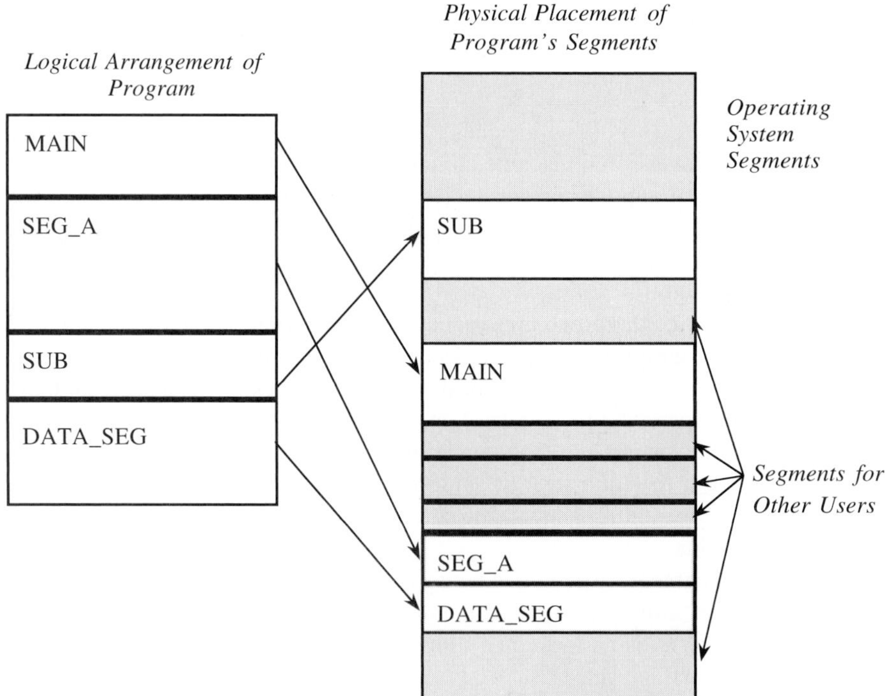

FIGURE 4-6 Logical and Physical Representation of Segments.

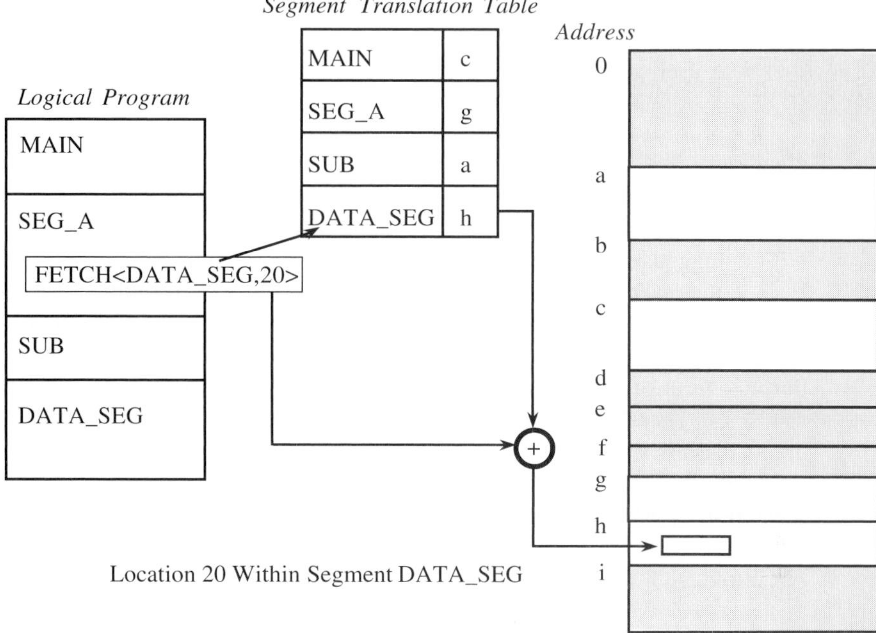

FIGURE 4-7 Translation of Segment Address.

- A segment can be removed from main memory (and stored on an auxiliary device) if it is not being used currently.
- Every address reference passes through the operating system, so there is an opportunity to check each one for protection.

Because of this last characteristic, a process can access a segment only if that segment appears in that process's segment-translation table. The operating system controls which programs have entries for a particular segment in their segment address tables. This control provides strong protection of segments from access by unpermitted processes. For example, program *A* might have access to segments *BLUE* and *GREEN* of user *X* but not to other segments of that user or of any other user.

We often want a user to have different protection classes for different segments of a program. To do this, the segmentation process uses both hardware and software. The overall system can associate certain levels of protection with certain segments, and it uses both the operating system and hardware to check that protection on each access to the segment. For example, one segment might be read-only data, a second might be execute-only code, and a third might be writeable data. In a situation like this one, segmentation can approximate the goal of separate protection of different pieces of a program, as outlined in the previous section on tagged architecture.

Segmentation offers these protective benefits.

- Each address reference is checked for protection.
- Many different classes of data items can be assigned different levels of protection.

- Two or more users can share access to a segment, with potentially different access rights.
- A user cannot generate an address or access to an unpermitted segment.

One protection difficulty inherent in segmentation concerns segment size. Each segment has a particular size. However, a program can generate a reference to a valid segment *name*, but with an *offset* beyond the end of the segment. For example, reference ⟨*A*,9999⟩ looks perfectly valid, but in reality segment *A* may be only 200 bytes long. If left unplugged, this security hole could allow a program to access any memory address beyond the end of a segment just by using large values of *offset* in an address.

This problem cannot be stopped during compilation, or even when a program is loaded, because effective use of segments requires that they be allowed to grow in size during execution. For example, a segment might contain a dynamic data structure such as a stack. Therefore, secure implementation of segmentation requires checking a generated address to verify that it is not beyond the current end of the segment referenced. Although this checking results in extra expense (in terms of time and resources), segmentation systems must perform this check; the segmentation process must maintain the current segment length in the translation table and compare every address generated.

Thus, we need to balance protection with efficiency, finding ways to keep segmentation as efficient as possible. However, efficient implementation of segmentation presents two problems: Segment names are inconvenient to encode in instructions, and the operating system's lookup of the name in a table can be slow. To overcome these difficulties, segment names are often converted to numbers by the compiler when a program is translated; the compiler also appends a linkage table matching numbers to true segment names. Unfortunately, this scheme presents an implementation difficulty when two procedures need to share the same segment, because the assigned segment numbers of data accessed by that segment must be the same.

Segmentation can also present a third problem: Segments cause fragmentation of main memory because they are of varying sizes. After time, unused fragments of space can lead to poor memory utilization. A solution to fragmentation is the periodic compacting of memory; however, compacting and updating appropriate tables takes time.

Paging

One alternative to segmentation is **paging**. The program is divided into equal-sized pieces called **pages**, and memory is divided into equal-sized units, called **page frames**. (For implementation reasons, the page size is usually chosen to be a power of two between 512 and 4096 bytes.) As with segmentation, each address in a paging scheme is a two-part object, this time consisting of ⟨*page*, *offset*⟩.

Each address is again translated by a process similar to that of segmentation: The operating system maintains a table of user page numbers and their true addresses in memory. The *page* portion of every ⟨*page*, *offset*⟩ reference is converted to a page frame address by a table lookup; the *offset* portion is added to the page frame address to produce the real memory address of the object referred to as ⟨*page*, *offset*⟩. This process is illustrated in Figure 4-8.

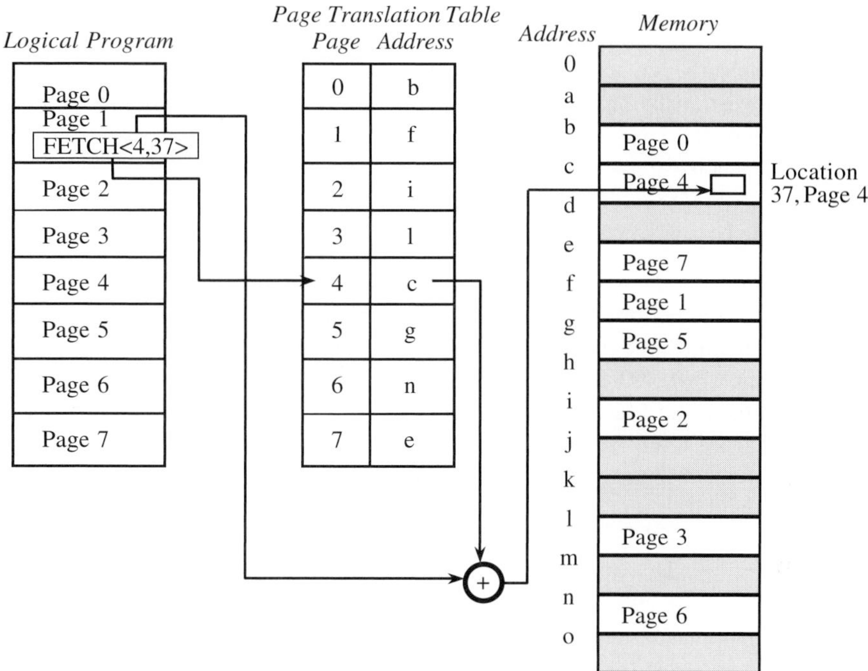

FIGURE 4-8 Page Address Translation.

Unlike segmentation, all pages in the paging approach are of the same fixed size, so fragmentation is not a problem; each page can fit in any available page in memory. Thus, there is no problem of addressing beyond the end of a page. The binary form of a ⟨*page*, *offset*⟩ address is designed so that the *offset* values fill a range of bits in the address. Therefore, an *offset* beyond the end of a particular page results in a carry into the *page* portion of the address, which changes the address.

To see how this idea works, consider a page size of 1024 bytes ($1024 = 2^{10}$), where 10 bits are allocated for the *offset* portion of each address. A program cannot generate an *offset* value larger than 1023 in 10 bits. Moving to the next location after $\langle x,1023\rangle$ causes a carry into the *page* portion, thereby moving translation to the next page. During the translation, the paging process checks to verify that a ⟨*page*, *offset*⟩ reference does not exceed the maximum number of pages the process has defined.

With a segmentation approach, a programmer must be conscious of segments. However, a programmer is oblivious to page boundaries when using a paging-based operating system. Moreover, with paging there is no logical unity to a page; a page is simply the next 2^n bytes of the program. Thus, a change to a program, such as the addition of one instruction, will push all subsequent instructions to lower addresses and move a few bytes from the end of each page to the start of the next. This shift is not something about which the programmer need be concerned, because the entire mechanism of paging and address translation is hidden from the programmer.

However, when we consider protection, this shift is a serious problem. Because segments are logical units, we can associate different segments with individual protection rights, such as read-only or execute-only. The shifting can be handled efficiently during address translation. But with paging there is no necessary unity to the items on a page, so there is no way to establish that all values on a page should be protected at the same level, such as read-only or execute-only.

Combined Paging with Segmentation

We have seen how paging offers implementation efficiency, while segmentation offers logical protection characteristics. Since each approach has drawbacks as well as desirable features, the two approaches have been combined.

The IBM 390 family of mainframe systems used a form of paged segmentation. Similarly, the Multics operating system (implemented on a GE-645 machine) applied paging on top of segmentation. In both cases, the programmer could divide a program into logical segments. Each segment was then broken into fixed-size pages. In Multics, the segment *name* portion of an address was an 18-bit number with a 16-bit *offset*. The addresses were then broken into 1024-byte pages. The translation process is shown in Figure 4-9. This approach retained the logical unity of a segment and permitted differentiated protection for the segments, but it added an additional layer of translation for each address. Additional hardware improved the efficiency of the implementation.

4.3 CONTROL OF ACCESS TO GENERAL OBJECTS

Protecting memory is a specific case of the more general problem of protecting *objects*. As multiprogramming has developed, the numbers and kinds of objects shared have also increased. Here are some examples of the kinds of objects for which protection is desirable:

- memory
- a file or data set on an auxiliary storage device
- an executing program in memory
- a directory of files
- a hardware device
- a data structure, such as a stack
- a table of the operating system
- instructions, especially privileged instructions
- passwords and the user authentication mechanism
- the protection mechanism itself

The memory protection mechanism can be fairly simple because every memory access is guaranteed to go through certain points in the hardware. With more general objects, the number of points of access may be larger, a central authority through which all accesses pass may be lacking, and the kind of access may not simply be limited to read, write, or execute.

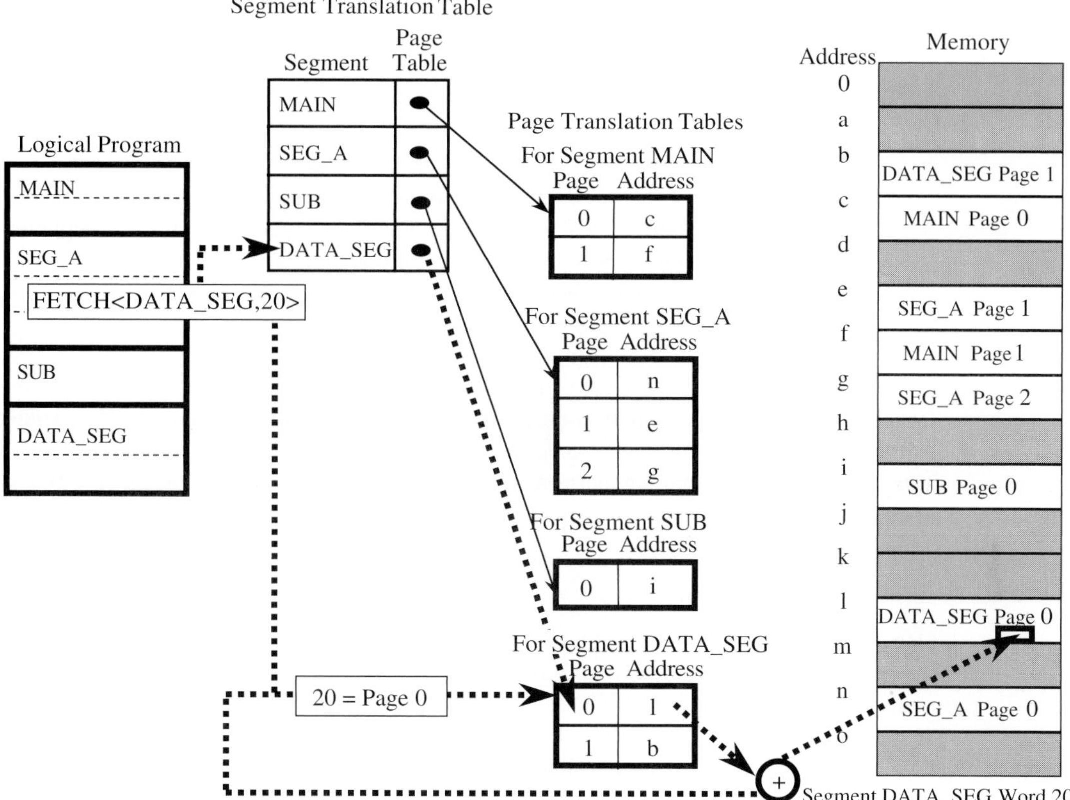

FIGURE 4-9 Paged Segmentation.

Furthermore, all accesses to memory occur through a program, so we can refer to the program or the programmer as the accessing agent. In this book, we use terms like *the user* or *the subject* in describing an access to a general object. This user or subject could be a person who uses a computing system, a programmer, a program, another object, or something else that seeks to use an object.

There are several complementary goals in protecting objects.

- *Check every access.* We may want to revoke a user's privilege to access an object. If we have previously authorized the user to access the object, we do not necessarily intend that the user should retain indefinite access to the object. In fact, in some situations, we may want to prevent further access immediately after we revoke authorization. For this reason, every access by a user to an object should be checked.
- *Enforce least privilege.* The principle of least privilege states that a subject should have access to the smallest number of objects necessary to perform some task. Even if extra information would be useless or harmless if the subject were to have access, the subject should not have that additional access. For

example, a program should not have access to the absolute memory address to which a page number reference translates, even though the program could not use that address in any effective way. Not allowing access to unnecessary objects guards against security weaknesses if a part of the protection mechanism should fail.

- *Verify acceptable usage.* Ability to access is a yes-or-no decision. But it is equally important to check that the activity to be performed on an object is appropriate. For example, a data structure such as a stack has certain acceptable operations, including *push*, *pop*, *clear*, and so on. We may want not only to control who or what has access to a stack but also to be assured that the accesses performed are legitimate stack accesses.

In the next section we consider protection mechanisms appropriate for general objects of unspecified types, such as the kinds of objects listed above. To make the explanations easier to understand, we sometimes use an example of a specific object, such as a file. Note, however, that a general mechanism can be used to protect any of the types of objects listed.

Directory

One simple way to protect an object is to use a mechanism that works like a file directory. Imagine that we are trying to protect files (the set of objects) from users of a computing system (the set of subjects). Every file has a unique owner who possesses "control" access rights (including the rights to declare who has what access) and to revoke access to any person at any time. Each user has a file directory, which lists all the files to which that user has access.

Clearly, no user can be allowed to write in the file directory because that would be a way to forge access to a file. Therefore, the operating system must maintain all file directories, under commands from the owners of files. The obvious rights to files are the common *read*, *write*, and *execute* familiar on many shared systems. Furthermore, another right, *owner*, is possessed by the owner, permitting that user to grant and revoke access rights. Figure 4-10 shows an example of a file directory.

This approach is easy to implement because it uses one list per user, naming all the objects that user is allowed to access. However, several difficulties can arise. First, the list becomes too large if many shared objects, such as libraries of subprograms or a common table of users, are accessible to all users. The directory of each user must have one entry for each such shared object, even if the user has no intention of accessing the object. Deletion must be reflected in all directories. (See Sidebar 4-2 for a different issue concerning deletion of objects.)

A second difficulty is revocation of access. If owner A has passed to user B the right to read file F, an entry for F is made in the directory for B. This granting of access implies a level of *trust* between A and B. If A later questions that trust, A may want to revoke the access right of B. The operating system can respond easily to the single request to delete the right of B to access F, because that action involves deleting one entry from a specific directory. But if A wants to remove the rights of *everyone* to access F, the operating system must search each individual directory for the entry F, an

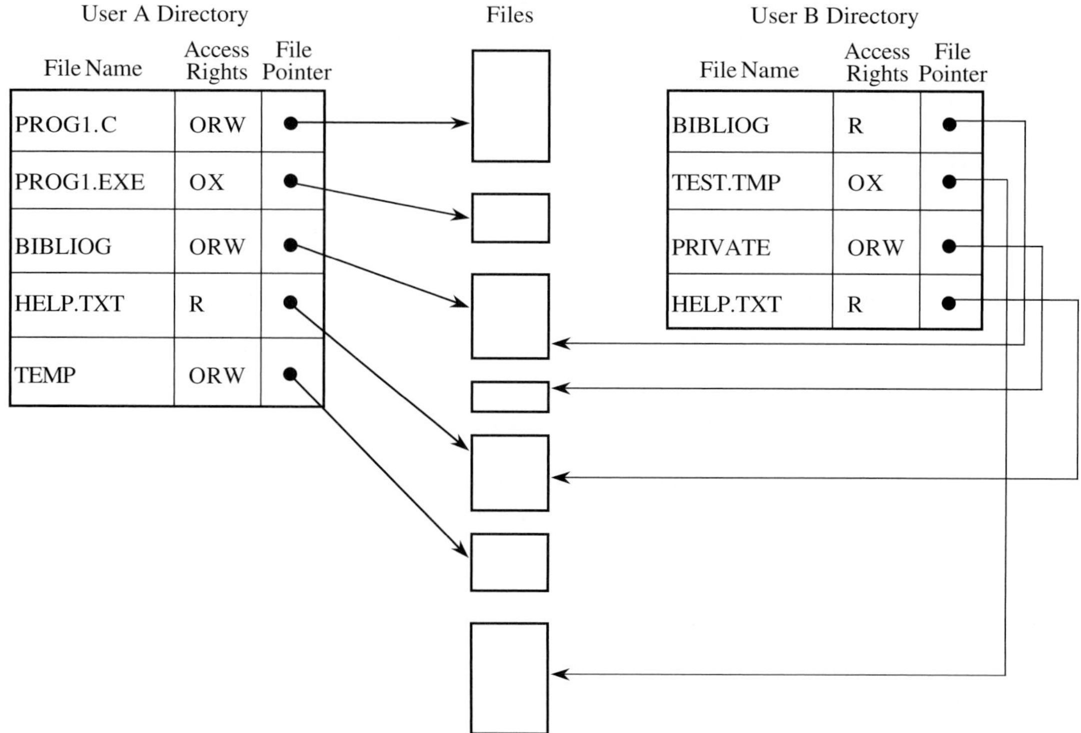

FIGURE 4-10 Directory Access.

activity that can be time consuming on a large system. For example, large timesharing systems or networks of smaller systems can easily have 5,000 to 10,000 active accounts. Moreover, *B* may have passed the access right for *F* to another user, so *A* may not know that *F*'s access exists and should be revoked. This problem is particularly serious in a network.

A third difficulty involves pseudonyms. Owners *A* and *B* may have two different files named *F*, and they may both want to allow access by *S*. Clearly, the directory for *S* cannot contain two entries under the same name for different files. Therefore, *S* has to be able to uniquely identify the *F* for *A* (or *B*). One approach is to include the original owner's designation as if it were part of the file name, with a notation such as *A*:*F* (or *B*:*F*).

Suppose, however, that *S* has trouble remembering file contents from the name *F*. Another approach is to allow *S* to name *F* with any name unique to the directory of *S*. Then, *F* from *A* could be called *Q* to *S*. As shown in Figure 4-11, *S* may have forgotten that *Q* is *F* from *A*, and so *S* requests access again from *A* for *F*. But by now *A* may have more trust in *S*, so *A* transfers *F* with greater rights than before. This action opens up the possibility that one subject, *S*, may have two distinct sets of access rights to *F*, one under the name *Q* and one under the name *F*. In this way, allowing pseudonyms leads to multiple permissions that are not necessarily consistent. Thus, the directory approach is probably too simple for most object protection situations.

Sidebar 4-2 "Out, Damned Spot! Out, I Say!"

Shakespeare's Lady Macbeth symbolically and obsessively sought to remove from her hands the blood of the man her husband had murdered at her instigation. As others have found (less dramatically), removing bits can be real, critical, and challenging.

Early Microsoft operating systems didn't actually erase a deleted file; they simply flagged its directory entry to show the file had been deleted. A user who accidentally deleted a file could recover the file by resetting the flag in the directory. Now Microsoft implements a recycle bin (originally an idea from Apple).

What happens to the bits of deleted files? In early multiuser operating systems, it was possible to retrieve someone else's data by looking through the trash. The technique was to create a large file. Before writing to the file, reading from it would give you the contents previously written in that memory or storage space. Although an attacker had to restructure the data (blocks might not be stored contiguously, and a large space might include scraps of data from several other users), sensitive data could be found with some luck and some work. This flaw led to an operating system's enforcing "object reuse." The operating system had to ensure that no residue from a previous user was accessible by another. The operating system could erase (for example, overwrite with all 0s) all storage being assigned to a new user, or it could enforce a policy that a user could read from a space only after having written into it.

Magnetic devices retain some memory of what was written in an area. As President Nixon's secretary discovered with her 17-minute gap, with specialized equipment engineers can sometimes bring back something previously written and then written over. This property, called "magnetic remanence," causes organizations with sensitive data to require a seven- or more pass erasure, rewriting first with 0s, then with 1s, and then with a random pattern of 0s and 1s. And agencies with the most sensitive data opt to destroy the medium rather than risk inadvertent disclosure.

Access Control List

An alternative representation is the **access control list**. There is one such list for each object, and the list shows all subjects who should have access to the object and what their access is. This approach differs from the directory list because there is one access control list per *object*; a directory is created for each *subject*. Although this difference seems small, there are some significant advantages.

To see how, consider subjects *A* and *S*, both of whom have access to object *F*. The operating system will maintain just one access list for *F*, showing the access rights for *A* and *S*, as shown in Figure 4-12. The access control list can include general default entries for any users. In this way, specific users can have explicit rights, and all other users can have a default set of rights. With this organization, a public file or program can be shared by all possible users of the system without the need for an entry for the object in the individual directory of each user.

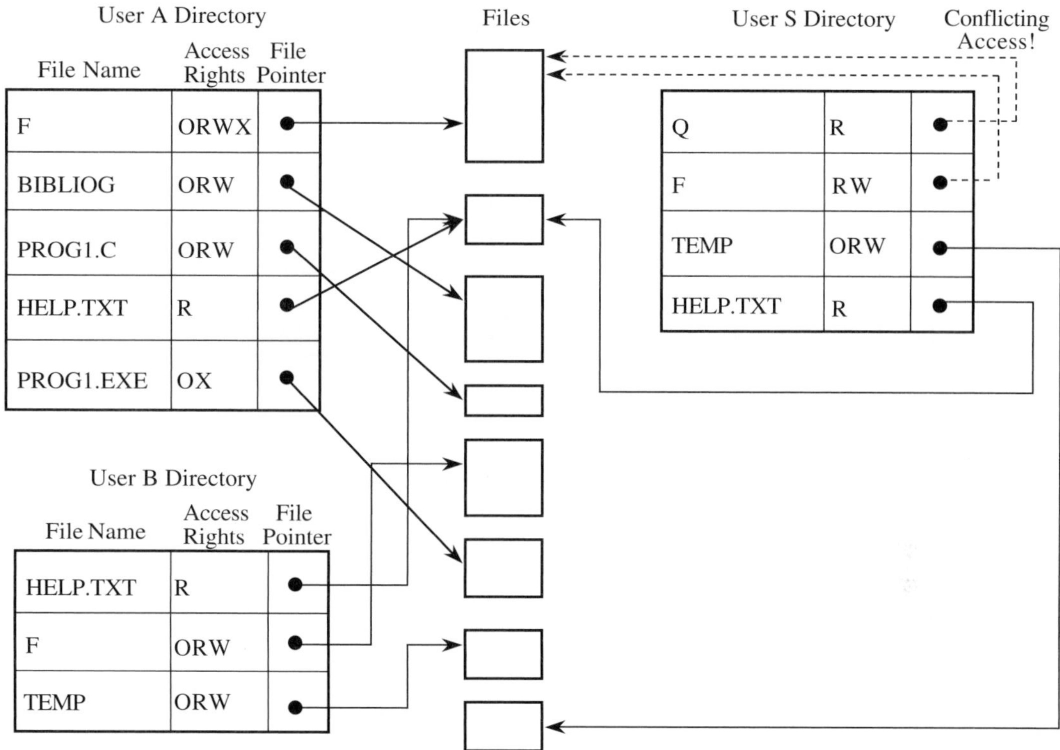

FIGURE 4-11 Alternative Access Paths.

The Multics operating system used a form of access control list in which each user belonged to three protection classes: a *user*, a *group*, and a *compartment*. The user designation identified a specific subject, and the group designation brought together subjects who had a common interest, such as coworkers on a project. The compartment confined an untrusted object; a program executing in one compartment could not access objects in another compartment without specific permission. The compartment was also a way to collect objects that were related, such as all files for a single project.

To see how this type of protection might work, suppose every user who initiates access to the system identifies a group and a compartment with which to work. If Adams logs in as user *Adams* in group *Decl* and compartment *Art2*, only objects having *Adams-Decl-Art2* in the access control list are accessible in the session.

By itself, this kind of mechanism would be too restrictive to be usable. Adams cannot create general files to be used in any session. Worse yet, shared objects would have not only to list Adams as a legitimate subject but also to list Adams under all acceptable groups and all acceptable compartments for each group.

The solution is the use of **wild cards**, meaning placeholders that designate "any user" (or "any group" or "any compartment"). An access control list might specify access by *Adams-Decl-Art1*, giving specific rights to Adams if working in group *Decl* on

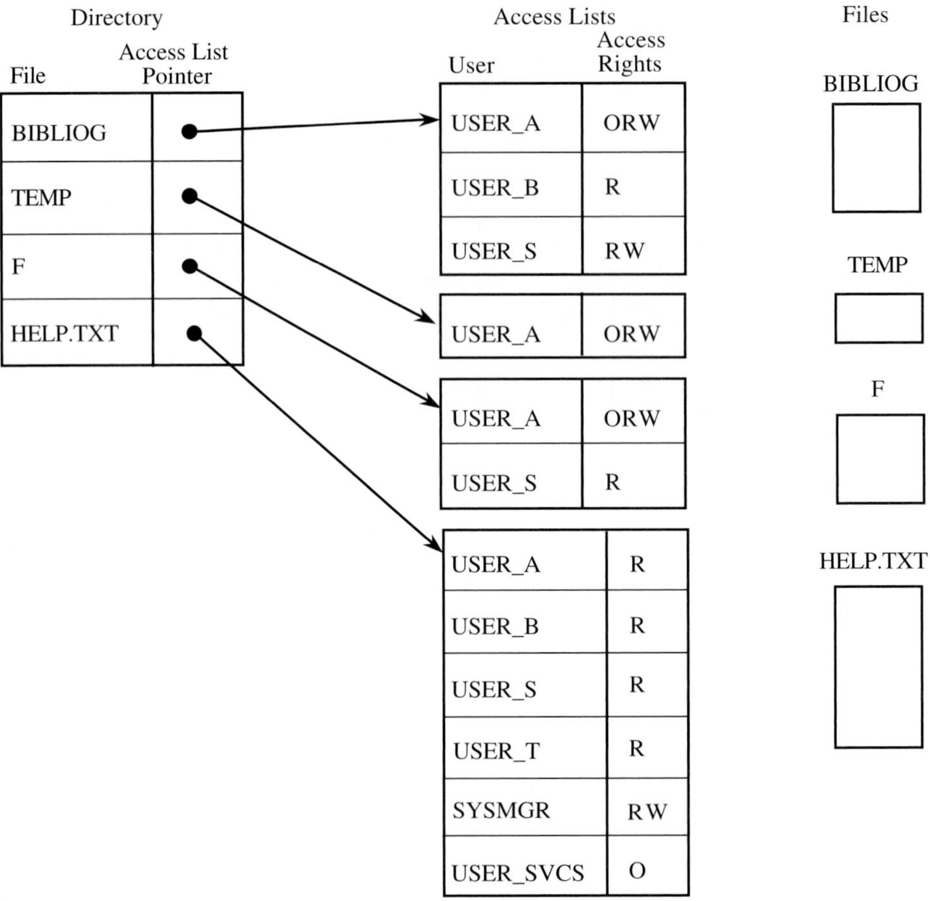

FIGURE 4-12 Access Control List.

compartment *Art1*. The list might also specify *Adams-∗-Art1*, meaning that Adams can access the object from any group in compartment *Art1*. Likewise, a notation of *∗-Decl-∗* would mean "any user in group *Decl* in any compartment." Different placements of the wildcard notation ∗ have the obvious interpretations.

The access control list can be maintained in sorted order, with ∗ sorted as coming after all specific names. For example, *Adams-Decl-∗* would come after all specific compartment designations for Adams. The search for access permission continues just until the first match. In the protocol, all explicit designations will be checked before wild cards in any position, so a specific access right would take precedence over a wildcard right. The last entry on an access list could be ∗-∗-∗, specifying rights allowable to any user not explicitly on the access list. By using this wildcard device, a shared public object can have a very short access list, explicitly naming the few subjects that should have access rights different from the default.

Access Control Matrix

We can think of the directory as a listing of objects accessible by a single subject, and the access list as a table, identifying subjects that can access a single object. The data in these two representations are equivalent, the distinction being the ease of use in given situations.

As an alternative, we can use an **access control matrix**, a table in which each row represents a subject, each column represents an object, and each entry is the set of access rights for that subject to that object. An example representation of an access control matrix is shown in Table 4-1. In general, the access control matrix is sparse (meaning that most cells are empty): Most subjects do not have access rights to most objects. The access matrix can be represented as a list of triples, having the form ⟨*subject, object, rights*⟩. Searching a large number of these triples is inefficient enough that this implementation is seldom used.

Capability

So far, we have examined protection schemes in which the operating system must keep track of all the protection objects and rights. But there are other approaches that put some of the burden on the user. For example, a user may be required to have a ticket or pass that enables access, much like a ticket or identification card that cannot be duplicated. More formally, we say that a **capability** is an unforgeable token that gives the possessor certain rights to an object. The Multics [SAL74], CAL [LAM76], and Hydra [WUL74] systems used capabilities for access control. These fundamental research efforts laid the groundwork for subsequent production use in systems such as Kerberos [STE88] (studied in greater detail in Chapter 7). In theory, a subject can create new objects and can specify the operations allowed on those objects. For example, users can create objects such as files, data segments, or subprocesses and can also specify the acceptable kinds of operations, such as *read*, *write*, and *execute*. But a user can also create completely new objects, such as new data structures, and define types of accesses previously unknown to the system.

TABLE 4-1 Access Control Matrix.

	BIBLIOG	TEMP	F	HELP.TXT	C_COMP	LINKER	SYS_CLOCK	PRINTER
USER A	ORW	ORW	ORW	R	X	X	R	W
USER B	R	-	-	R	X	X	R	W
USER S	RW	-	R	R	X	X	R	W
USER T	-	-	-	R	X	X	R	W
SYS_MGR	-	-	-	RW	OX	OX	ORW	O
USER_SVCS	-	-	-	O	X	X	R	W

A capability is a ticket giving permission to a subject to have a certain type of access to an object. For the capability to offer solid protection, the ticket must be unforgeable. One way to make it unforgeable is to not give the ticket directly to the user. Instead, the operating system holds all tickets on behalf of the users. The operating system returns to the user a pointer to an operating system data structure, which also links to the user. A capability can be created only by a specific request from a user to the operating system. Each capability also identifies the allowable accesses.

Alternatively, capabilities can be encrypted under a key available only to the access control mechanism. If the encrypted capability contains the identity of its rightful owner, user A cannot copy the capability and give it to user B.

One possible access right to an object is *transfer* or *propagate*. A subject having this right can pass copies of capabilities to other subjects. In turn, each of these capabilities also has a list of permitted types of accesses, one of which might also be *transfer*. In this instance, process *A* can pass a copy of a capability to *B,* who can then pass a copy to *C*. *B* can prevent further distribution of the capability (and therefore prevent further dissemination of the access right) by omitting the *transfer* right from the rights passed in the capability to *C*. *B* might still pass certain access rights to *C*, but not the right to propagate access rights to other subjects.

As a process executes, it operates in a **domain** or **local name space**. The domain is the collection of objects to which the process has access. A domain for a user at a given time might include some programs, files, data segments, and I/O devices such as a printer and a terminal. An example of a domain is shown in Figure 4-13.

As execution continues, the process may call a subprocedure, passing some of the objects to which it has access as arguments to the subprocedure. The domain of the subprocedure is not necessarily the same as that of its calling procedure; in fact, a calling procedure may pass only some of its objects to the subprocedure, and the subproce-

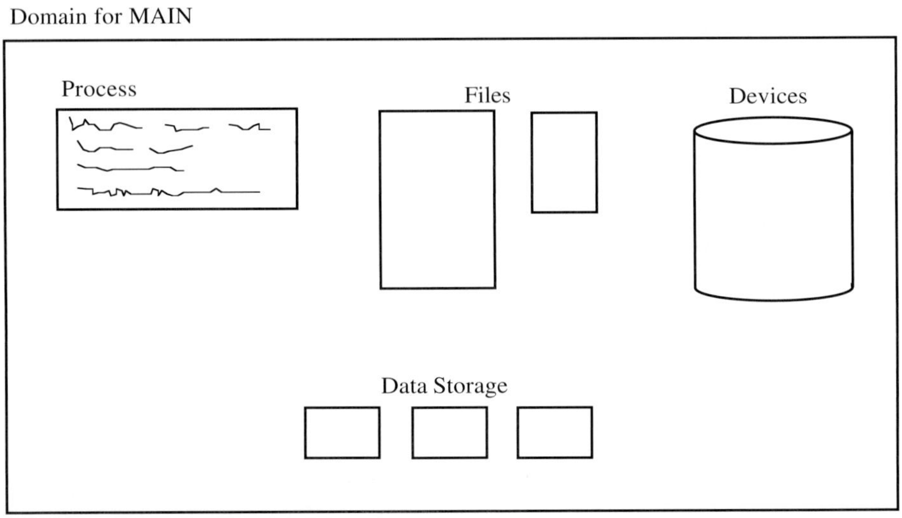

FIGURE 4-13 Process Execution Domain.

dure may have access rights to other objects not accessible to the calling procedure. The caller may also pass only some of its access rights for the objects it passes to the subprocedure. For example, a procedure might pass to a subprocedure the right to read but not modify a particular data value.

Because each capability identifies a single object in a domain, the collection of capabilities defines the domain. When a process calls a subprocedure and passes certain objects to the subprocedure, the operating system forms a stack of all the capabilities of the current procedure. The operating system then creates new capabilities for the subprocedure, as shown in Figure 4-14.

Operationally, capabilities are a straightforward way to keep track of the access rights of subjects to objects during execution. The capabilities are backed up by a more comprehensive table, such as an access control matrix or an access control list. Each time a process seeks to use a new object, the operating system examines the master list of objects and subjects to determine whether the object is accessible. If so, the operating system creates a capability for that object.

Capabilities must be stored in memory inaccessible to normal users. One way of accomplishing this is to store capabilities in segments not pointed at by the user's segment table or to enclose them in protected memory as from a pair of base/bounds registers. Another approach is to use a tagged architecture machine to identify capabilities as structures requiring protection.

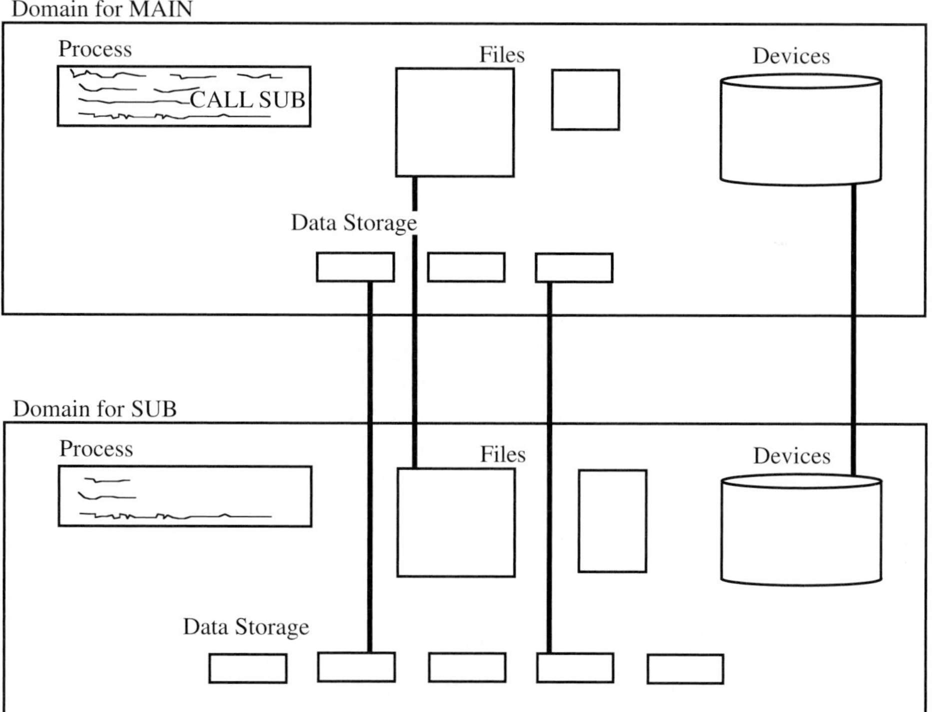

FIGURE 4-14 Passing Objects to a Subject.

During execution, only the capabilities of objects that have been accessed by the current process are kept readily available. This restriction improves the speed with which access to an object can be checked. This approach is essentially the one used in Multics, as described in [FAB74].

Capabilities can be revoked. When an issuing subject revokes a capability, no further access under the revoked capability should be permitted. A capability table can contain pointers to the active capabilities spawned under it so that the operating system can trace what access rights should be deleted if a capability is revoked. A similar problem is deleting capabilities for users who are no longer active.

Procedure-Oriented Access Control

One goal of access control is restricting not just what subjects have access to an object, but also what they can *do* to that object. Read versus write access can be controlled rather readily by most operating systems, but more complex control is not so easy to achieve.

By **procedure-oriented** protection, we imply the existence of a procedure that controls access to objects (for example, by performing its own user authentication to strengthen the basic protection provided by the basic operating system). In essence, the procedure forms a capsule around the object, permitting only certain specified accesses.

Procedures can ensure that accesses to an object be made through a trusted interface. For example, neither users nor general operating system routines might be allowed direct access to the table of valid users. Instead, the only accesses allowed might be through three procedures: one to add a user, one to delete a user, and one to check whether a particular name corresponds to a valid user. These procedures, especially add and delete, could use their own checks to make sure that calls to them are legitimate.

Procedure-oriented protection implements the principle of information hiding, because the means of implementing an object are known only to the object's control procedure. Of course, this degree of protection carries a penalty of inefficiency. With procedure-oriented protection, there can be no simple, fast access, even if the object is frequently used.

Our survey of access control mechanisms has intentionally progressed from simple to complex. Historically, as the mechanisms have provided greater flexibility, they have done so with a price of increased overhead. For example, implementing capabilities that must be checked on each access is far more difficult than implementing a simple directory structure that is checked only on a subject's first access to an object. This complexity is apparent both to the user and to the implementer. The user is aware of additional protection features, but the naïve user may be frustrated or intimidated at having to select protection options with little understanding of their usefulness. The implementation complexity becomes apparent in slow response to users. The balance between simplicity and functionality is a continuing battle in security.

4.4 FILE PROTECTION MECHANISMS

Until now, we have examined approaches to protecting a general object, no matter the object's nature or type. But some protection schemes are particular to the type. To see how they work, we focus in this section on file protection. The examples we present are only representative; they do not cover all possible means of file protection on the market.

Basic Forms of Protection

We noted earlier that all multiuser operating systems must provide some minimal protection to keep one user from maliciously or inadvertently accessing or modifying the files of another. As the number of users has grown, so also has the complexity of these protection schemes.

All–None Protection

In the original IBM OS operating systems, files were by default public. Any user could read, modify, or delete a file belonging to any other user. Instead of software- or hardware-based protection, the principal protection involved trust combined with ignorance. System designers supposed that users could be trusted not to read or modify others' files, because the users would expect the same respect from others. Ignorance helped this situation, because a user could access a file only by name; presumably users knew the names only of those files to which they had legitimate access.

However, it was acknowledged that certain system files were sensitive and that the system administrator could protect them with a password. A normal user could exercise this feature, but passwords were viewed as most valuable for protecting operating system files. Two philosophies guided password use. Sometimes, passwords were used to control all accesses (read, write, or delete), giving the system administrator complete control over all files. But at other times passwords would control only write and delete accesses, because only these two actions affected other users. In either case, the password mechanism required a system operator's intervention each time access to the file began.

However, this all-or-none protection is unacceptable for several reasons.

- *Lack of trust.* The assumption of trustworthy users is not necessarily justified. For systems with few users who all know each other, mutual respect might suffice; but in large systems where not every user knows every other user, there is no basis for trust.
- *All or nothing.* Even if a user identifies a set of trustworthy users, there is no convenient way to allow access only to them.
- *Rise of timesharing.* This protection scheme is more appropriate for a batch environment, in which users have little chance to interact with other users and in which users do their thinking and exploring when not interacting with the system. However, on timesharing systems, users interact with other users. Because users choose when to execute programs, they are more likely in a timesharing environment to arrange computing tasks to be able to pass results from one program or one user to another.
- *Complexity.* Because (human) operator intervention is required for this file protection, operating system performance is degraded. For this reason, this type of file protection is discouraged by computing centers for all but the most sensitive data sets.

- *File listings.* For accounting purposes and to help users remember for what files they are responsible, various system utilities can produce a list of all files. Thus, users are not necessarily ignorant of what files reside on the system. Interactive users may try to browse through any unprotected files.

Group Protection

Because the all-or-nothing approach has so many drawbacks, researchers sought an improved way to protect files. They focused on identifying *groups* of users who had some common relationship. In a typical implementation, the world is divided into three classes: the user, a trusted working group associated with the user, and the rest of the users. For simplicity we can call these classes *user*, *group,* and *world.* This form of protection is used on some network systems and the Unix system.

All authorized users are separated into groups. A group may consist of several members working on a common project, a department, a class, or a single user. The basis for group membership is *need to share*. The group members have some common interest and therefore are assumed to have files to share with the other group members. In this approach, no user belongs to more than one group. (Otherwise, a member belonging to groups *A* and *B* could pass along an *A* file to another *B* group member.)

When creating a file, a user defines access rights to the file for the user, for other members of the same group, and for all other users in general. Typically, the choices for access rights are a limited set, such as {read, write, execute, delete}. For a particular file, a user might declare read-only access to the general world, read and write access to the group, and all rights to the user. This approach would be suitable for a paper being developed by a group, whereby the different members of the group might modify sections being written within the group. The paper itself should be available for people outside the group to review but not change.

A key advantage of the group protection approach is its ease of implementation. A user is recognized by two identifiers (usually numbers): a user ID and a group ID. These identifiers are stored in the file directory entry for each file and are obtained by the operating system when a user logs in. Therefore, the operating system can easily check whether a proposed access to a file is requested from someone whose group ID matches the group ID for the file to be accessed.

Although this protection scheme overcomes some of the shortcomings of the all-or-nothing scheme, it introduces some new difficulties of its own.

- *Group affiliation.* A single user cannot belong to two groups. Suppose Tom belongs to one group with Ann and to a second group with Bill. If Tom indicates that a file is to be readable by the group, to which group(s) does this permission refer? Suppose a file of Ann's is readable by the group; does Bill have access to it? These ambiguities are most simply resolved by declaring that every user belongs to exactly one group. (This restriction does not mean that all users belong to the *same* group.)
- *Multiple personalities.* To overcome the one-person one-group restriction, certain people might obtain multiple accounts, permitting them, in effect, to be multiple users. This hole in the protection approach leads to new problems, be-

cause a single person can be only one user at a time. To see how problems arise, suppose Tom obtains two accounts, thereby becoming Tom1 in a group with Ann and Tom2 in a group with Bill. Tom1 is not in the same group as Tom2, so any files, programs, or aids developed under the Tom1 account can be available to Tom2 only if they are available to the entire world. Multiple personalities lead to a proliferation of accounts, redundant files, limited protection for files of general interest, and inconvenience to users.

- *All groups.* To avoid multiple personalities, the system administrator may decide that Tom should have access to all his files any time he is active. This solution puts the responsibility on Tom to control with whom he shares what things. For example, he may be in Group1 with Ann and Group2 with Bill. He creates a Group1 file to share with Ann. But if he is active in Group2 the next time he is logged in, he still sees the Group1 file and may not realize that it is not accessible to Bill, too.
- *Limited sharing.* Files can be shared only within groups or with the world. Users want to be able to identify sharing partners for a file on a per-file basis, for example, sharing one file with ten people and another file with twenty others.

Single Permissions

In spite of their drawbacks, the file protection schemes we have described are relatively simple and straightforward. The simplicity of implementing them suggests other easy-to-manage methods that provide finer degrees of security while associating permission with a single file.

Password or Other Token

We can apply a simplified form of password protection to file protection by allowing a user to assign a password to a file. User accesses are limited to those who can supply the correct password at the time the file is opened. The password can be required for any access or only for modifications (write access).

Password access creates for a user the effect of having a different "group" for every file. However, file passwords suffer from difficulties similar to those of authentication passwords:

- *Loss.* Depending on how the passwords are implemented, it is possible that no one will be able to replace a lost or forgotten password. The operators or system administrators can certainly intervene and unprotect or assign a particular password, but often they cannot determine what password a user has assigned; if the user loses the password, a new one must be assigned.
- *Use.* Supplying a password for each access to a file can be inconvenient and time consuming.
- *Disclosure.* If a password is disclosed to an unauthorized individual, the file becomes immediately accessible. If the user then changes the password to reprotect the file, all the other legitimate users must be informed of the new password because their old password will fail.

- *Revocation.* To revoke one user's access right to a file, someone must change the password, thereby causing the same problems as disclosure.

Temporary Acquired Permission

The Unix operating system provides an interesting permission scheme based on a three-level user–group–world hierarchy. The Unix designers added a permission called **set userid (suid)**. If this protection is set for a file to be executed, the protection level is that of the file's *owner*, not the *executor*. To see how it works, suppose Tom owns a file and allows Ann to execute it with *suid*. When Ann executes the file, she has the protection rights of Tom, not of herself.

This peculiar-sounding permission has a useful application. It permits a user to establish data files to which access is allowed only through specified procedures.

For example, suppose you want to establish a computerized dating service that manipulates a database of people available on particular nights. Sue might be interested in a date for Saturday, but she might have already refused a request from Jeff, saying she had other plans. Sue instructs the service not to reveal to Jeff that she is available. To use the service, Sue, Jeff, and others must be able to read and write (at least indirectly) the file to determine who is available or to post their availability. But if Jeff can read the file directly, he would find that Sue has lied. Therefore, your dating service must force Sue and Jeff (and all others) to access this file only through an access program that would screen the data Jeff obtains. But if the file access is limited to read and write by you as its owner, Sue and Jeff will never be able to enter data into it.

The solution is the Unix SUID protection. You create the database file, giving only you access permission. You also write the program that is to access the database, and save it with the SUID protection. Then, when Jeff executes your program, he temporarily acquires your access permission, but only during execution of the program. Jeff never has direct access to the file because your program will do the actual file access. When Jeff exits from your program, he regains his own access rights and loses yours. Thus, your program can access the file, but the program must display to Jeff only the data Jeff is allowed to see.

This mechanism is convenient for system functions that general users should be able to perform only in a prescribed way. For example, only the system should be able to modify the file of users' passwords, but individual users should be able to change their own passwords any time they wish. With the SUID feature, a password change program can be owned by the system, which will therefore have full access to the system password table. The program to change passwords also has SUID protection, so that when a normal user executes it, the program can modify the password file in a carefully constrained way on behalf of the user.

Per-Object and Per-User Protection

The primary limitation of these file protection schemes is the ability to create meaningful groups of related users who should have similar access to one or more data sets. The access control lists or access control matrices described earlier provide very flexible protection. Their disadvantage is for the user who wants to allow access to many users and to many different data sets; such a user must still specify each data set to be accessed by each user. As a new user is added, that user's special access rights must be specified by all appropriate users.

4.5 USER AUTHENTICATION

An operating system bases much of its protection on knowing who a user of the system is. In real-life situations, people commonly ask for identification from people they do not know: A bank employee may ask for a driver's license before cashing a check, library employees may require some identification before charging out books, and immigration officials ask for passports as proof of identity. In-person identification is usually easier than remote identification. For instance, some universities do not report grades over the telephone because the office workers do not necessarily know the students calling. However, a professor who recognizes the voice of a certain student can release that student's grades. Over time, organizations and systems have developed means of authentication, using documents, voice recognition, fingerprint and retina matching, and other trusted means of identification.

In computing, the choices are more limited and the possibilities less secure. Anyone can attempt to log in to a computing system. Unlike the professor who recognizes a student's voice, the computer cannot recognize electrical signals from one person as being any different from those of anyone else. Thus, most computing authentication systems must be based on some knowledge shared only by the computing system and the user.

Authentication mechanisms use any of three qualities to confirm a user's identity:

1. Something the user *knows*. Passwords, PIN numbers, passphrases, a secret handshake, and mother's maiden name are examples of what a user may know.
2. Something the user *has*. Identity badges, physical keys, a driver's license, or a uniform are common examples of things people have that make them recognizable.
3. Something the user *is*. These authenticators, called **biometrics,** are based on a physical characteristic of the user, such as a fingerprint, the pattern of a person's voice, or a face (picture). These authentication methods are old (we recognize friends in person by their faces or on a telephone by their voices) but are just starting to be used in computer authentications. See Sidebar 4-3 for a glimpse at some of the promising approaches.

Two or more forms can be combined for more solid authentication; for example, a bank card and a PIN combine something the user has with something the user knows.

Use of Passwords

The most common authentication mechanism for user to operating system is a **password**, a "word" known to computer and user. Although password protection seems to offer a relatively secure system, human practice sometimes degrades its quality. In this section we consider passwords, criteria for selecting them, and ways of using them for authentication. We conclude by noting other authentication techniques and by studying problems in the authentication process, notably Trojan horses masquerading as the computer authentication process.

Sidebar 4-3 Biometrics: Ready for Prime Time?

Biometrics are appealing for authentication: in principle they are immune to forgery, cannot be forgotten or misplaced, and compare favorably to passwords in their discrimination.

A biometric authentication should be easy to use, fast, nonthreatening, and discriminating. Of particular interest with biometrics is the balance between false acceptances (incorrectly confirming an authenticity) and false rejections (incorrectly denying).

Let us look at some of the more promising biometric authenticators.

Fingerprints are good discriminators, which is why they are used by law enforcement agencies to track criminals. Several commercial devices on the market operate quickly and reliably. Originally, experts assumed fingerprints to be immune to forgery, but researchers in 2002 [MAT02] showed that they could fool a fingerprint reader with a casting made of gelatin.

Retina pattern is also unique to individuals, so the authentication could be very strong. But it requires a focused light beam to obtain the distinct map of blood vessels from the back of the eyeball. Humans are wary of exposing their eyes to a retina scan device.

Iris pattern is not unique to an individual, but it does offer enough variation to have a high probability of discrimination. The iris pattern can be sensed with a more conventional camera, which makes it more acceptable to human users.

Hand geometry measures the lengths and thicknesses of the fingers of a hand. Although not unique, these measurements are distinctive enough to be acceptable to confirm identity. Devices on the market can authenticate hand geometry in a few seconds.

Voice recognition detects the subtle variations in the speed, pitch, stress, and pronunciation of different people. Two factors limit voice recognition: the ability to record and replay speech and the ability to simulate speech.

Face recognition is readily practiced by humans for people they know, but it is more difficult for computers to implement in the general case.

For all these techniques, the discrimination merely needs to be "close enough." The authentication must distinguish impostors, but it is unlikely that the impostor will be an identical twin. A study by the National Physical Laboratory in England [MAN01] reported that most biometric technologies have an expectable inverse relationship between false acceptance and false rejection: A very low false acceptance rate can be achieved if one is willing to tolerate an enormous false rejection rate. (Curiously, for fingerprint recognition, the false rejection rate is almost flat, between 5 percent and 10 percent for false acceptance rates ranging from 0.001 percent to 10 percent.) For face recognition, hand geometry, fingerprint, and voice recognition, it is possible to hold false rejection below 10% and still achieve a false acceptance rate under 1 percent. False rejection rates on hand geometry and fingerprint recognition improve significantly if three samples are taken.

Biometrics techniques have been used for some time for employee and other insider authentication; now banks and other institutions are beginning to adopt them for outside users. A study by Meridian Research cited by Mearian [MEA02] reported that in 2000, companies spent $127 million on biometric devices. Fingerprint scanners represented over 40 percent of that total, and facial recognition, hand geometry, voice recognition, and iris scanners represented about 10 percent each.

Sidebar 4-3 Biometrics: Ready for Prime Time? (Continued)

Still, as the quality of authentication recognition improves, so also does the quality of simulation. Scientists at MIT [COO02] recently demonstrated a video of a woman speaking new sentences and even singing a song in Japanese, a language she does not speak. Their technique was to record the woman as she spoke in her native tongue and then break the recording down into pieces for each sound.

Passwords are mutually agreed-upon code words, assumed to be known only to the user and the system. In some cases a user chooses passwords; in other cases they are assigned by the system. The length and format of the password also vary from one system to another.

The use of passwords is fairly straightforward. A user enters some piece of identification, such as a name or an assigned user ID; this identification can be available to the public or easy to guess because it does not provide the real security of the system. The system then requests a password from the user. If the password matches that on file for the user, the user is authenticated and allowed access to the system. If the password match fails, the system requests the password again, in case the user mistyped.

Loose-Lipped Systems

So far the process seems secure, but in fact it has some vulnerabilities. To see why, consider the actions of a would-be intruder. Authentication is based on knowing the ⟨*name*, *password*⟩ pair. A complete outsider is presumed to know nothing of the system. Suppose the intruder attempts to access a system in the following manner. (In the following examples, the system messages are in upper case, and the user's responses are in lower case.)

```
WELCOME TO THE XYZ COMPUTING SYSTEMS
ENTER USER NAME: adams
INVALID USER NAME–UNKNOWN USER
ENTER USER NAME:
```

We assumed that the intruder knew nothing of the system, but without having to do much, the intruder found out that *adams* is not the name of an authorized user. The intruder could try other common names, first names, and likely generic names such as *system* or *operator* to build a list of authorized users.

An alternative arrangement of the login sequence is shown below.

```
WELCOME TO THE XYZ COMPUTING SYSTEMS
ENTER USER NAME: adams
ENTER PASSWORD: john
INVALID ACCESS
ENTER USER NAME:
```

This system notifies a user of a failure only after accepting both the user name and the password. The failure message should not indicate whether it is the user name or password that is unacceptable. In this way, the intruder does not know which failed.

These examples also gave a clue as to which computing system is being accessed. The true outsider has no right to know that, and legitimate insiders already know what system they have accessed. In the example below, the user is given no information until the system is assured of the identity of the user.

```
ENTER USER NAME: adams
ENTER PASSWORD: john
INVALID ACCESS
ENTER USER NAME: adams
ENTER PASSWORD: johnq
WELCOME TO THE XYZ COMPUTING SYSTEMS
```

Additional Authentication Information

In addition to the name and password, we can use other information available to authenticate users. Suppose Adams works in the accounting department during the shift between 8:00 a.m. and 5:00 p.m., Monday through Friday. Any legitimate access attempt by Adams should be made during those times, through a terminal in the accounting department offices. By limiting Adams to logging in under those conditions, the system protects against two problems:

- Someone from outside might try to impersonate Adams. This attempt would be thwarted by either the time of access or the port through which the access was attempted.
- Adams might attempt to access the system from home or on a weekend, planning to use resources not allowed or to do something that would be too risky with other people around.

Limiting users to certain terminals or certain times of access can cause complications (as when a user legitimately needs to work overtime, or a person has to access the system while out of town on a business trip). However, some companies use these authentication techniques because the added security they provide outweighs inconveniences.

Attacks on Passwords

How secure are passwords themselves? Passwords are somewhat limited as protection devices because of the relatively small number of bits of information they contain.

Here are some ways you might be able to determine a user's password.

- Try all possible passwords.
- Try many probable passwords.
- Try passwords likely for the user.
- Search for the system list of passwords.
- Ask the user.

These suggestions are arranged in decreasing order of difficulty; the later ones are, or at least should be, less likely to succeed.

Exhaustive Attack

In an **exhaustive** or **brute force attack**, the attacker tries all possible passwords, usually in some automated fashion. Of course, the number of possible passwords depends on the implementation of the particular computing system. For example, if passwords are words consisting of the 26 characters A–Z and can be of any length from 1 to 8 characters, there are 26^1 passwords of 1 character, 26^2 passwords of 2 characters, and 26^8 passwords of 8 characters. Therefore, the system as a whole has $26^1 + 26^2 + ... + 26^8 = 26^9 - 1 \approx 5 * 10^{12}$ or five million million possible passwords. That number seems intractable enough. If we were to use a computer to create and try each password at a rate of one password per millisecond, it would take on the order of 150 years to test all passwords. But if we can speed up the search to one password per microsecond, the work factor drops to about two months. This amount of time is reasonable if the reward is large. For instance, an intruder may try to break the password on a file of credit card numbers or bank account information.

But the break-in time can be made more tractable in a number of ways. Searching for a single particular password does not necessarily require all passwords to be tried; an intruder needs to try only until the correct password is identified. If the set of all possible passwords were evenly distributed, an intruder would likely need to try only half of the password space: the expected number of searches to find any particular password. However, an intruder can also use to advantage the fact that passwords are not evenly distributed. Because a password has to be remembered, people tend to pick simple passwords. This feature reduces the size of the password space.

Probable Passwords

Think of a word.

Is the word you thought of long? Is it uncommon? Is it hard to spell or to pronounce? The answer to all three of these questions is probably no.

Penetrators searching for passwords realize these very human characteristics and use them to their advantage. Therefore, penetrators try techniques that are likely to lead to rapid success. If people prefer short passwords to long ones, the penetrator will plan to try all passwords but to try them in order by length. There are only $26^1 + 26^2 + 26^3 =$ 18,278 passwords of length 3 or less. At the assumed rate of one password per millisecond, all of these passwords can be checked in 18.278 seconds, hardly a challenge with a computer. Even expanding the tries to 4 or 5 characters raises the count only to 475 seconds (about 8 minutes) and 12,356 seconds (about 3.5 hours), respectively.

This analysis assumes that people choose passwords such as *vxlag* and *msms* as often as they pick *enter* and *beer*. However, people tend to choose names or words they can remember. Many computing systems have spelling checkers that can be used to check for spelling errors and typographic mistakes in documents. These spelling checkers sometimes carry online dictionaries of the most common English words. One contains a dictionary of 80,000 words. Trying all of these words as passwords takes only 80 seconds.

Passwords Likely for a User

If Sandy is selecting a password, she is probably not choosing a word completely at random. Most likely Sandy's password is something meaningful to her. People typically choose personal passwords, such as the name of a spouse, a child, a brother or sister, a pet, a street name, or something memorable or familiar. If we restrict our password attempts to just names of people (first names), streets, projects, and so forth, we generate a list of only a few hundred possibilities at most. Trying this number of passwords takes under a second! Even a person working by hand could try ten likely candidates in a minute or two.

Thus, what seemed formidable in theory is in fact quite vulnerable in practice, and the likelihood of successful penetration is frightening. Morris and Thompson [MOR79] confirmed our fears in their report on the results of having gathered passwords from many users, shown in Table 4-2. Figure 4-15 (based on data from that study) shows the characteristics of the 3,289 passwords gathered. The results from that study are distressing, and the situation today is likely to be the same. Of those passwords, 86 percent could be uncovered in about one week's worth of 24-hour-a-day testing, using the very generous estimate of 1 millisecond per password check.

Lest you dismiss these results as dated (they were reported in 1979), Klein repeated the experiment in 1990 [KLE90] and Spafford in 1992 [SPA92]. Each collected approximately 15,000 passwords. Klein reported that 2.7 percent of the passwords were guessed in only 15 minutes of machine time and 21 percent were guessed within a week! Spafford found the average password length was 6.8 characters, and 28.9 percent consisted of only lowercase alphabetic characters. Notice that both these studies were done *after* the Internet worm (described in Chapter 3) succeeded, in part by breaking weak passwords.

Even in 2002, the British online bank Egg found users still choosing weak passwords [BUX02]. A full 50 percent of passwords for their online banking service were family members' names: 23 percent children's names, 19 percent a spouse or partner, and 9 percent their own. Alas, pets came in at only 8 percent, while celebrities and

TABLE 4-2 Distribution of Actual Passwords.

15	0.5%	were a single(!) ASCII character
72	2%	were two ASCII characters
464	14%	were three ASCII characters
477	14%	were four alphabetic letters
706	21%	were five alphabetic letters, all of the same case
605	18%	were six lowercase alphabetic letters
492	15%	were words in dictionaries or lists of names
2831	86%	total of all above categories

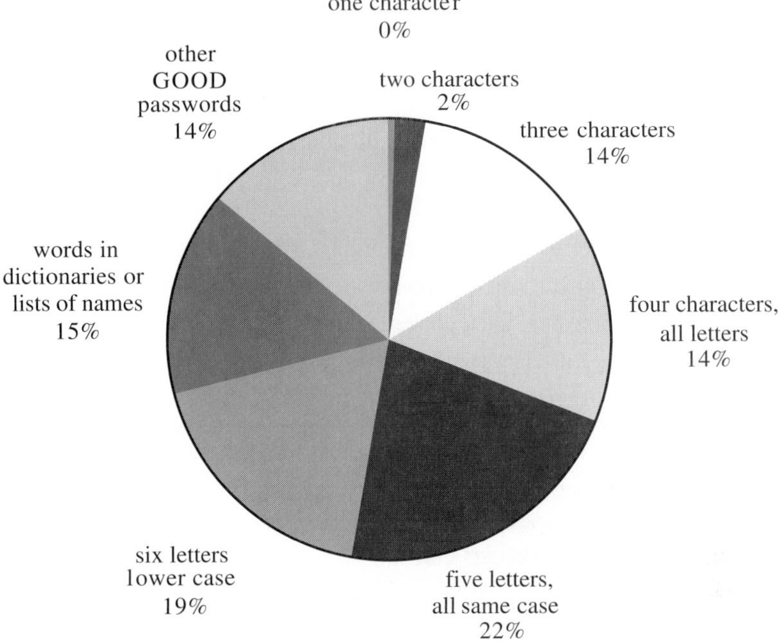

FIGURE 4-15 Users' Password Choices.

football (soccer) stars tied at 9 percent each. And in 1998, Knight and Hartley [KNI98] reported that approximately 35 percent of passwords are deduced from syllables and initials of the account owner's name.

Several network sites post dictionaries of phrases, science fiction characters, places, mythological names, Chinese words, Yiddish words, and other specialized lists. All these lists are posted to help site administrators identify users who have chosen weak passwords, but the same dictionaries can also be used by attackers of sites that do not have such attentive administrators. The COPS [FAR90], Crack [MUF92], and SATAN [FAR95] utilities allow an administrator to scan a system for weak passwords. But these same utilities, or other homemade ones, allow attackers to do the same.

People think they can be clever by picking a simple password and replacing certain characters, such as 0 (zero) for letter O, 1 (one) for letter I or L, 3 (three) for letter E or @ (at) for letter A. But users aren't the only people who could think up these substitutions. Knight and Hartley [KNI98] list, in order, 12 steps an attacker might try to determine a password. These steps are in increasing degree of difficulty (number of guesses), and so they indicate the amount of work to which the attacker must go in order to derive a password. Here are their password guessing steps:

- no password
- the same as the user ID
- is, or is derived from, the user's name

- common word list (e.g., "password," "secret," " private") plus common names and patterns (e.g., "asdfg," "aaaaaa")
- short college dictionary
- complete English word list
- common non-English language dictionaries
- short college dictionary with capitalizations (PaSsWorD) and substitutions (0 for O, and so forth)
- complete English with capitalizations and substitutions
- common non-English dictionaries with capitalization and substitutions
- brute force, lowercase alphabetic characters
- brute force, full character set

Although the last step will always succeed, the steps immediately preceding it are so time consuming that they will deter all but the dedicated attacker for whom time is not a limiting factor.

Plaintext System Password List

To validate passwords, the system must have a way of comparing entries with actual passwords. Rather than trying to guess a user's password, an attacker may instead target the system password file. Why guess when with one table you can determine all passwords with total accuracy?

On some systems, the password list is a file, organized essentially as a two-column table of user IDs and corresponding passwords. This information is certainly too obvious to leave out in the open. Various security approaches are used to conceal this table from those who should not see it.

You might protect the table with strong access controls, limiting access to the operating system. But even this tightening of control is looser than it should be, because not every operating system module needs or deserves access to this table. For example, the operating system scheduler, accounting routines, or storage manager have no need to know the table's contents. Unfortunately, in some systems, there are n+1 known users: n regular users and the operating system. The operating system is not divided, so all its modules have access to all privileged information. This monolithic view of the operating system implies that a user who exploits a flaw in one section of the operating system has access to all the system's deepest secrets. A better approach is to limit table access to the modules that need access: the user authentication module and the parts associated with installing new users, for example.

If the table is stored in plain sight, an intruder can simply dump memory at a convenient time to access it. Careful timing may enable a user to dump the contents of all of memory and, by exhaustive search, find values that look like the password table.

System backups can also be used to obtain the password table. To be able to recover from system errors, system administrators periodically back up the file space onto some auxiliary medium for safe storage. In the unlikely event of a problem, the file system can be reloaded from a backup, with a loss only of changes made since the last backup. Backups often contain only file contents, with no protection mechanism to control file access. (Physical security and access controls to the backups themselves are depended upon to provide security for the contents of backup media.) If a regular user can access the backups, even ones from several weeks, months, or years ago, the password tables stored in them may contain entries that are still valid.

Finally, the password file is a copy of a file stored on disk. Anyone with access to the disk or anyone who can overcome file access restrictions can obtain the password file.

Encrypted Password File

There is an easy way to foil an intruder seeking passwords in plain sight: encrypt them. Frequently, the password list is hidden from view with conventional encryption or one-way ciphers.

With conventional encryption, either the entire password table is encrypted or just the password column. When a user's password is received, the stored password is decrypted, and the two are compared.

Even with encryption, there is still a slight exposure because for an instant the user's password is available in plaintext in main memory. That is, the password is available to anyone who could obtain access to all of memory.

A safer approach uses one-way encryption, defined in Chapter 2. The password table's entries are encrypted by a one-way encryption and then stored. When the user enters a password, it is also encrypted and then compared with the table. If the two values are equal, the authentication succeeds. Of course, the encryption has to be such that it is unlikely that two passwords would encrypt to the same ciphertext, but this characteristic is true for most secure encryption algorithms.

With one-way encryption, the password file can be stored in plain view. For example, the password table for the Unix operating system can be read by any user, unless special access controls have been installed. Because the contents are encrypted, backup copies of the password table are no longer a problem.

There is always the possibility that two people might choose the same password, thus creating two identical entries in the password file. Even though the entries are encrypted, each user will know the plaintext equivalent. For instance, if Bill and Kathy both choose their passwords on April 1, they might choose APRILFOOL as a password. Bill might read the password file and notice that the encrypted version of his password is the same as Kathy's.

Unix circumvents this vulnerability by using a password extension, called the salt. The **salt** is a 12-bit number formed from the system time and the process identifier. Thus, the salt is likely to be unique for each user, and it can be stored in plaintext in the password file. The salt is concatenated to Bill's password (*pw*) when he chooses it; $E(pw+\text{salt}_B)$ is stored for Bill, and his salt value is also stored. When Kathy chooses her password, the salt is different because the time or the process number is different. Call this new one salt_K. For her, $E(pw+\text{salt}_K)$ and salt_K are stored. When either person tries to log in, the system fetches the appropriate salt from the password table and combines that with the password before performing the encryption. The encrypted versions of $(pw+\text{salt})$ are very different for these two users. When Bill looks down the password list, the encrypted version of his password will not look at all like Kathy's.

Storing the password file in a disguised form relieves much of the pressure to secure it. Better still is to limit access to processes that have a legitimate need for access. In this way, the password file is protected to a level commensurate with the protection provided by the password itself. Someone who has broken the controls of the file system has access to data, not just passwords, and that is a serious threat. But if an attacker successfully penetrates the outer security layer, the attacker still must get past the encryption of the password file to access the useful information in it.

Indiscreet Users

Guessing passwords and breaking encryption can be tedious or daunting. But there is a simple way to obtain a password: Get it directly from the user! People often tape a password to the side of a terminal, or write it on a card just inside the top desk drawer. Users are afraid they will forget their passwords, or they cannot be bothered trying to remember them. It is particularly tempting to write the passwords down when users have several accounts.

Users sharing work or data may also be tempted to share passwords. If someone needs a file, it is easier to say "my password is *x*; get the file yourself" than to arrange to share the file. This situation is a result of user laziness, but it may be brought about or exacerbated by a system that makes sharing inconvenient.

Password Selection Criteria

So what can we conclude about passwords? They should be hard to guess and difficult to determine exhaustively. But the degree of difficulty should be appropriate to the security needs of the situation. To these ends, we present several guidelines for password selection:

- *Use characters other than just A–Z.* If passwords are chosen from the letters A–Z, there are only 26 possibilities for each character. Adding digits expands the number of possibilities to 36. Using both uppercase and lowercase letters plus digits expands the number of possible characters to 62. Although this change seems small, the effect is large when someone is testing a full space of all possible combinations of characters. It takes about 100 hours to test all 6-letter words chosen from letters of one case only, but it takes about 2 years to test all 6-symbol passwords from upper- and lowercase letters and digits. Although 100 hours is reasonable, 2 years is oppressive enough to make this attack far less attractive.
- *Choose long passwords.* The combinatorial explosion of passwords begins at length 4 or 5. Choosing longer passwords makes it less likely that a password will be uncovered. Remember that a brute force penetration can stop as soon as the password is found. Some penetrators will try the easy cases—known words and short passwords—and move on to another target if those attacks fail.
- *Avoid actual names or words.* Theoretically, there are 26^6 or about 300 million "words" of length 6, but there are only about 150,000 words in a good collegiate dictionary, ignoring length. By picking one of the 99.95 percent non-

words, you force the attacker to use a longer brute force search instead of the abbreviated dictionary search.

- *Choose an unlikely password.* Password choice is a double bind. To remember the password easily, you want one that has special meaning to you. However, you don't want someone else to be able to guess this special meaning. One easy-to-remember password is 2Brn2B. That unlikely looking jumble is a simple transformation of "to be or not to be." The first letters of a line from a song, a few letters from different words of a private phrase, or a memorable football score are examples of reasonable passwords. But don't be too obvious. Password-cracking tools also test replacements of 0 (zero) for o or O (letter "oh") and 1 (one) for l (letter "ell") or $ for S (letter "ess"). So I10veu is already in the search file.
- *Change the password regularly.* Even if there is no reason to suspect that the password has been compromised, change is advised. A penetrator may break a password system by obtaining an old list or working exhaustively on an encrypted list.
- *Don't write it down.* (Note: This time-honored advice is relevant only if physical security is a serious risk. People who have accounts on many different machines and servers, not to mention bank and charge card PINs, may have trouble remembering all the access codes. Setting all codes the same or using insecure but easy-to-remember passwords may be more risky than writing passwords on a reasonably well protected list.)
- *Don't tell anyone else.* The easiest attack is **social engineering**, in which the attacker contacts the system's administrator or a user to elicit the password in some way. For example, the attacker may phone a user, claim to be "system administration," and ask the user to verify the user's password. Under no circumstances should you ever give out your private password; legitimate administrators can circumvent your password if need be, and others are merely trying to deceive you.

To help users select good passwords, some systems provide meaningless but pronounceable passwords. For example, the VAX VMS system randomly generates five passwords from which the user chooses one. They are pronounceable, so that the user should be able to repeat and memorize them. However, the user may misremember a password because of having interchanged syllables or letters of a meaningless string. (The sound "bliptab" is easily misremembered as "blaptib" or "blabtip.")

Other systems encourage users to change their passwords regularly. The regularity of password change is usually a system parameter, which can be changed for the characteristics of a given installation. Suppose the frequency is set at 30 days. Some systems begin to warn the user after 25 days that the password is about to expire. Others wait until 30 days and inform the user that the password has expired. Some systems nag without end, whereas other systems cut off a user's access if a password has expired. Still others force the user immediately into the password change utility on the first login after 30 days.

Grampp and Morris [GRA84a] argue that this reminder process is not necessarily good. Choosing passwords is not difficult, but under pressure a user may adopt any password, just to satisfy the system's demand for a new password. Furthermore, if this is the only time when a password can be changed, a user who selects a bad password and realizes it cannot change until the next scheduled time.

Sometimes when systems force users to change passwords periodically, users with favorite passwords will alternate between two passwords each time a change is required. To prevent password reuse, Microsoft Windows 2000 systems refuse to accept any of the *k* most recently used passwords. One user of such a system went through 24 password changes each month, just to cycle back to the favorite password.

One-Time Passwords

A **one-time password** is one that changes every time it is used. Instead of assigning a static phrase to a user, the system assigns a static mathematical function. The system provides an argument to the function, and the user computes and returns the function value. Such systems are also called **challenge–response systems** because the system presents a challenge to the user and judges the authenticity of the user by the user's response. Here are some simple examples of one-time password functions; these functions are overly simplified to make the explanation easier. Very complex functions can be used in place of these simple ones for host authentication in a network.

- $f(x) = x + 1$. With this function, the system prompts with a value for x, and the user enters the value $x + 1$. The kinds of mathematical functions used are limited only by the ability of the user to compute the response quickly and easily. Other similar possibilities are $f(x) = 3x^2 - 9x + 2$, $f(x) = p_x$, where p_x is the xth prime number, or $f(x) = d * h$, where d is the date and h is the hour of the current time. (Alas, many users cannot perform simple arithmetic in their heads.)
- $f(x) = r(x)$. For this function, the receiver uses the argument as the seed for a random number generator (available to both the receiver and host). The user replies with the value of the first random number generated. A variant of this scheme uses x as a number of random numbers to generate. The receiver generates x random numbers and sends the xth of these to the host.
- $f(a_1a_2a_3a_4a_5a_6) = a_3a_1a_1a_4$. With this function, the system provides a character string, which the user must transform in some predetermined manner. Again, many different character operations can be used.
- $f(E(x)) = E(\ D(E(x)) + 1)$. In this function, the computer sends an encrypted value, $E(x)$. The user must decrypt the value, perform some mathematical function, and encrypt the result to return it to the system. Clearly, for human use, the encryption function must be something that can be done easily by hand, unlike DES. For machine-to-machine authentication, however, an encryption algorithm such as DES is appropriate.

One-time passwords are very important for authentication because (as becomes clear in Chapter 7) an intercepted password is useless. However, their usefulness is limited by the complexity of algorithms people can be expected to remember. A password generating device, similar to a pocket calculator, can implement more complex functions. Several models are readily available at reasonable prices. They are very effective at countering the threat of transmitting passwords in plaintext across a network. (See Sidebar 4-4 for another dilemma in remote authentication.)

The Authentication Process

Authentication usually operates as described previously. However, users occasionally mistype their passwords. A user who receives a message of INCORRECT LOGIN will carefully retype the login and gain access to the system. Even a user who is a terrible typist should be able to log in successfully in a few tries.

Some authentication procedures are intentionally slow. A legitimate user will not complain if the login process takes 5 or 10 seconds. To a penetrator who is trying an exhaustive search or a dictionary search, however, 5 or 10 seconds per trial makes this class of attack generally infeasible.

Someone who continually fails to log in may not be an authorized user. Systems commonly disconnect a user after a small number of failed logins, forcing the user to reestablish a connection with the system. (This action will slow down a penetrator who is trying to penetrate the system by telephone. After a small number of failures, the penetrator must redial, which takes a few seconds.)

In more secure installations, stopping penetrators is more important than tolerating users' mistakes. For example, some system administrators assume that all legitimate users can type their passwords correctly within three tries. After three successive password failures, the account for that user is disabled and only the security administrator

Sidebar 4-4 Single Sign-On

Authenticating to multiple systems is unpopular with users. Left to their own, users will reuse the same password to avoid having to remember many different passwords. For example, users become frustrated at having to authenticate to a computer, a network, a mail system, an accounting system, and numerous web sites. The panacea for this frustration is called **single sign-on**. A user authenticates once per session, and the system forwards that authenticated identity to all other processes that would require authentication.

Obviously, the strength of single sign-on can be no better than the strength of the initial authentication, and quality diminishes if someone compromises that first authentication or the transmission of the authenticated identity. Trojan horses, sniffers and wiretaps, man-in-the-middle attacks, and guessing can all compromise a single sign-on.

Microsoft has developed a single sign-on solution for its .net users. Called a "passport," the single sign-on mechanism is effectively a folder in which the user can store login credentials for other sites. But, as the market research firm Gartner Group points out [PES01], users are skeptical about using single sign-on for the Internet, and they are especially wary of entrusting the security of credit card numbers to a single sign-on utility.

Although a desired feature, single sign-on raises doubt about what a computer is doing on behalf of or in the name of a user, perhaps without that user's knowledge.

can reenable it. This action identifies accounts that may be the target of attacks by penetrators.

Fixing Flaws in the Authentication Process

Password authentication assumes that anyone who knows a password is the user to whom the password belongs. As we have seen, passwords can be guessed, deduced, or inferred. Some people give out their passwords for the asking. Other passwords have been obtained just by someone watching a user typing in the password. The password can be considered as a preliminary or first-level piece of evidence, but skeptics will want more convincing proof. There are several ways to provide a second level of protection, including another round of passwords or a challenge-response interchange.

Challenge–Response Systems

As we have just seen, the login is usually time invariant. Except when passwords are changed, each login looks like every other. A more sophisticated login requires a user ID and password, followed by a challenge–response interchange. In such an interchange, the system prompts the user for a reply that will be different each time the user logs in. For example, the system might display a four-digit number, and the user would have to correctly enter a function such as the sum or product of the digits. Each user is assigned a different challenge function to compute. Because there are many possible challenge functions, a penetrator who captures the user ID and password cannot necessarily infer the proper function.

A physical device similar to a calculator can be used to implement a more complicated response function. The user enters the challenge number, and the device computes and displays the response for the user to type in order to log in. (For more examples, see Chapter 7's discussion of network authentication.)

Impersonation of Login

In the systems we have described, the proof is one sided. The system demands certain identification of the user, but the user is supposed to trust the system. However, a programmer can easily write a program that displays the standard prompts for user ID and password, captures the pair entered, stores the pair in a file, displays SYSTEM ERROR; DISCONNECTED, and exits. This attack is a type of Trojan horse. The perpetrator sets it up, leaves the terminal unattended, and waits for an innocent victim to attempt a login. The naïve victim may not even suspect that a security breach has occurred.

To foil this type of attack, the user should be sure the path to the system is reinitialized each time the system is used. On some systems, turning the terminal off and on again or pressing the BREAK key generates a clear signal to the computer to halt any running process for the terminal. (Microsoft chose <CTRL><ALT><DELETE> as the path to the secure authorization mechanism for this reason.) Not every computer recognizes power-off or BREAK as an interruption of the current process, though. And computing systems are often accessed through networks, so that physical reinitialization is impossible.

Alternatively, the user can be suspicious of the computing system, just as the system is suspicious of the user. The user will not enter confidential data (such as a password) until convinced that the computing system is legitimate. Of course, the computer acknowledges the user only after passing the authentication process. A computing system can display some information known only by the user and the system. For example, the system might read the user's name and reply "YOUR LAST LOGIN WAS 10 APRIL AT 09:47." The user can verify that the date and time are correct before entering a secret password. If higher security is desired, the system can send an encrypted timestamp. The user decrypts this and discovers that the time is current. The user then replies with an encrypted timestamp and password, to convince the system that a malicious intruder has not intercepted a password from some prior login.

Authentication Other Than Passwords

Some sophisticated authentication devices are now available. These devices include handprint detectors, voice recognizers, and identifiers of patterns in the retina. Authentication with such devices uses unforgeable physical characteristics to authenticate users. The cost continues to fall as these devices are adopted by major markets; the devices are useful in very high security situations.

More normal security needs can be handled by a combination of login and characteristics such as work hours, physical location, or patterns of access. For example, a user who seeks access to files with no justifiable reason might not be authentic. After a system detects this access violation attempt, it might disconnect the user and suspend access until a security administrator clears the matter. Therefore, a penetrator who enters the system as "Jones" has to continue to act like Jones to remain on the system. (See Chapter 7 for more on intrusion and anomaly detection.)

Authentication is essential for an operating system because accurate user identification is the key to individual access rights. Most operating systems and computing system administrators have applied reasonable but stringent security measures to lock out illegal users before they can access system resources. But, as reported in Sidebar 4-5, sometimes an inappropriate mechanism is forced into use as an authentication device.

4.6 SUMMARY OF SECURITY FOR USERS

This chapter has addressed four topics: memory protection, file protection, general object access control, and user authentication. Memory protection in a multiuser setting has evolved with advances in hardware and system design. Fences, base/bounds registers, tagged architecture, paging, and segmentation are all mechanisms designed both for addressing and for protection.

File protection schemes on general-purpose operating systems are often based on a three- or four-level format (for example, user–group–all). This format is reasonably straightforward to implement, but it restricts the granularity of access control to few levels.

Access control in general is addressed by an access control matrix or by lists organized on a per-object or per-user basis. Although very flexible, these mechanisms can be difficult to implement efficiently.

User authentication is a serious issue that becomes even more serious when unacquainted users seek to share facilities by means of computer networks. The traditional

Sidebar 4-5 Using Cookies for Authentication

On the web, cookies are often used for authentication. A cookie is a pair of data items sent to the web browsing software by the web site's server. The data items consist of a key and a value, designed to represent the current state of a session between a user and a web site. Once the cookie is placed on the user's system (usually in a directory with other cookies), the browser continues to use it for subsequent interaction between the user and that web site. Each cookie is supposed to have an expiration date, but that date can be modified later or even ignored.

For example, *The Wall Street Journal*'s web site, wsj.com, creates a cookie when a user first logs in. In subsequent transactions, the cookie acts as an identifier; the user no longer needs a password to access that site. (Other sites use the same or a similar approach.)

It is important that users be protected from exposure and forgery. That is, users may not want the rest of the world to know what sites they have visited. Neither will they want someone to examine information or buy merchandise online by impersonation and fraud. However, Sit and Fu [SIT01] point out that cookies were not designed for protection. There is no way to establish or confirm a cookie's integrity, and not all sites encrypt the information in their cookies.

Sit and Fu also point out that a server's operating system must be particularly vigilant to protect against eavesdropping: "Most HTTP exchanges do not use SSL to protect against eavesdropping; anyone on the network between the two computers can overhear the traffic. Unless a server takes strong precautions, an eavesdropper can steal and reuse a cookie, impersonating a user indefinitely."

authentication device is the password. A plaintext password file presents a serious vulnerability for a computing system. These files are usually either heavily protected or encrypted. The more serious problem, however, is how to convince users to choose strong passwords. Additional protocols are needed to perform mutual authentication in an atmosphere of distrust.

This chapter concentrates on the user's side of protection, presenting protection mechanisms visible to and invoked by users of operating systems. Chapter 5 addresses security from the perspective of the operating system designer. It includes material on how the security features of an operating system are implemented and why security considerations should be a part of the initial design of the operating system.

4.7 TERMS AND CONCEPTS

4.8 WHERE THE FIELD IS HEADED

Operating system research has been popular and important since the 1960s. University research projects have explored approaches that have influenced mainstream commercial operating systems. Two prominent examples have been the Multics project at M.I.T. in the 1960s, which was a precursor to the Unix operating system (albeit as a desire to keep the information-sharing aspects of Multics within a much slimmer, elemental system), and Mach from Carnegie Mellon University, which influenced the Microsoft NT family. Computer security depends heavily on the operating system, so it is important to follow the current research in operating systems to see what its impact will be on security.

In June 2002 Microsoft unveiled a project, code-named Palladium [WAL02]. The company plans to cooperate with designers of computer chips in establishing a memory section protected by hardware to hold security enforcement data. This hardware design is similar to a multistate hardware architecture from two decades earlier. Arbaugh et al. [ARB97] present a similar hardware-enforced protection approach. Interestingly, the simple operating systems of the 1980s (such as MS-DOS) did not use the process separation available on chips in those days. Now, however, the need for separation of security-critical data has become apparent on larger, more complex operating systems that need to implement controlled information sharing. Perhaps next someone will find a need for the four-state architecture common on hardware from machines of Digital Equipment Corporation in the 1980s. The concept of hardware-enforced separation to protect the security-critical code and data in operating systems should expand in the next few years.

Single sign-on and distributed authentication are open topics certain to evolve in the next few years. There is a need to balance user convenience with security because, as has been demonstrated repeatedly, unused security features are worse than no security at all.

4.9 TO LEARN MORE

The survey article by Denning and Denning [DEN77] gives a good background on access control in operating systems, and the paper by Linden [LIN76] describes operating systems components that affect protection. Lampson [LAM71], Graham and Denning [GRA72], Popek [POP74a], and Saltzer and Schroeder [SAL74, SAL75] are good treatments of protection in operating systems.

Capability-based protection is described in Fabry [FAB74] and Wulf [WUL74]. Lampson and Sturgis [LAM76] and Karger and Herbert [KAR84] discuss the subject in general. Password authentication is discussed in [SEE89] and [KNI98].

Several other papers on different aspects of operating system design are noted in the bibliographic notes for Chapter 5.

4.10 EXERCISES

1. Give an example of the use of physical separation for security in a computing environment.
2. Give an example of the use of temporal separation for security in a computing environment.
3. Give an example of an object whose security level may change during execution.
4. Respond to the allegation "An operating system requires no protection for its executable code (in memory) because that code is a duplicate of code maintained on disk."
5. Explain how a fence register is used for relocating a user's program.
6. Can any number of concurrent processes be protected from one another by just one pair of base/bounds registers?
7. The discussion of base/bounds registers implies that program code is execute-only and that data areas are read-write-only. Is this ever not the case? Explain your answer.
8. A design using tag bits presupposes that adjacent memory locations hold dissimilar things: a line of code, a piece of data, a line of code, two pieces of data, and so forth. Most programs do not look like that. How can tag bits be appropriate in a situation in which programs have the more conventional arrangement of code and data?
9. What are some other levels of protection that users might want to apply to code or data, in addition to the common *read, write,* and *execute* permission?
10. If two users share access to a segment, they must do so by the same name. Must their protection rights to it be the same? Why or why not?
11. A problem with either segmented or paged address translation is timing. Suppose a user wishes to read some data from an input device into memory. For efficiency during data transfer, often the actual memory address at which the data are to be placed is provided to an

I/O device. The real address is passed so that time-consuming address translation does not have to be performed during a very fast data transfer. What security problems does this approach bring?

12. A directory is also an object to which access should be controlled. Why is it *not* appropriate to allow users to modify their own directories?

13. Why should the directory of one user not be generally accessible (for read-only access) to other users?

14. Describe each of the following four kinds of access control mechanisms in terms of (a) ease of determining authorized access during execution, (b) ease of adding access for a new subject, (c) ease of deleting access by a subject, and (d) ease of creating a new object to which all subjects by default have access.
    - per-subject access control list (that is, one list for each subject tells all the objects to which that subject has access)
    - per-object access control list (that is, one list for each object tells all the subjects who have access to that object)
    - access control matrix
    - capability

15. Suppose a per-subject access control list is used. Deleting an object in such a system is inconvenient because all changes must be made to the control lists of all subjects who did have access to the object. Suggest an alternative, less costly means of handling deletion.

16. File access control relates largely to the secrecy dimension of security. What is the relationship between an access control matrix and the integrity of the objects to which access is being controlled?

17. One feature of a capability-based protection system is the ability of one process to transfer a copy of a capability to another process. Describe a situation in which one process should be able to transfer a capability to another.

18. Describe a mechanism by which an operating system can enforce *limited* transfer of capabilities. That is, process *A* might transfer a capability to process *B*, but *A* wants to prevent *B* from transferring the capability to any other processes.

    Your design should include a description of the activities to be performed by *A* and *B*, as well as the activities performed by and the information maintained by the operating system.

19. List two disadvantages of using physical separation in a computing system. List two disadvantages of using temporal separation in a computing system.

20. Explain why asynchronous I/O activity is a problem with many memory protection schemes, including base/bounds and paging. Suggest a solution to the problem.

21. Suggest an efficient scheme for maintaining a per-user protection scheme. That is, the system maintains one directory per user, and that directory lists all the objects to which the user is allowed access. Your design should address the needs of a system with 1000 users, of whom no more than 20 are active at any time. Each user has an average of 200 permitted objects; there are 50,000 total objects in the system.

22. (a) If passwords are three uppercase alphabetic characters long, how long (that is, how much time) would it take to determine a particular password, assuming that testing an individual password requires 5 seconds?

    (b) Argue for a particular amount of time as the starting point for "secure." That is, suppose an attacker plans to use a brute force attack to determine a password. For what value of x (the total amount of time to try as many passwords as necessary) would the attacker find this attack prohibitively long?

    (c) If the cutoff between "insecure" and "secure" were x amount of time, how long would a secure password have to be? State and justify your assumptions regarding the character set from which the password is selected and the amount of time required to test a single password.

23. Design a protocol by which two mutually suspicious parties can authenticate each other. Your protocol should be usable the first time these two parties try to authenticate each other.

24. A flaw in the protection system of many operating systems is argument passing. Often a common shared stack is used by all nested routines for arguments as well as the remainder of the context of each calling process.
(a) Explain what vulnerabilities this flaw presents.
(b) Explain how the flaw can be controlled. The shared stack is still to be used for passing arguments and storing context.

25. Outline the design of an authentication scheme that "learns." The authentication scheme would start with certain primitive information about a user, such as name and password. As the use of the computing system continued, the authentication system would gather such information as commonly used programming languages; dates, times, and lengths of computing sessions; and use of distinctive resources. The authentication challenges would become more individualized as the system learned more information about the user.

Your design should include a list of many pieces of information about a user that the system could collect. It is permissible for the system to ask an authenticated user for certain additional information, such as favorite book, to use in subsequent challenges. Your design should also consider the problem of presenting and validating these challenges: Does the would-be user answer a true-false or a multiple-choice question? Does the system interpret natural language prose?

5

Designing Trusted Operating Systems

In this chapter:

- What makes an operating system "secure"? Or "trustworthy"?
- How are trusted systems designed, and which of those design principles carry over naturally to other program development tasks?
- How do we develop "assurance" of the correctness of a trusted operating system?

Operating systems are the prime providers of security in computing systems. They support many programming capabilities, permit multiprogramming and sharing of resources, and enforce restrictions on program and user behavior. Because they have such power, operating systems are also targets for attack, because breaking through the defenses of an operating system gives access to the secrets of computing systems.

In Chapter 4 we considered operating systems from the perspective of users, asking what primitive security services general operating systems provide. We studied these four services:

- memory protection
- file protection
- general object access control
- user authentication

We say that an operating system is **trusted** if we have confidence that it provides these four services in a consistent and effective way. In this chapter, we take the designer's perspective, viewing a trusted operating system in terms of the design and function of components that provide security services. The first four sections of this chapter correspond to the four major underpinnings of a trusted operating system:

- *Policy.* Every system can be described by its requirements: statements of what the system should do and how it should do it. An operating system's security requirements are a set of well-defined, consistent, and implementable rules that have been clearly and unambiguously expressed. If the operating system is implemented to meet these requirements, it meets the user's expectations. To ensure that the requirements are clear, consistent, and effective, the operating system usually follows a stated security policy: a set of rules that lay out what is to be secured and why. We begin this chapter by studying several security policies for trusted operating systems.
- *Model.* To create a trusted operating system, the designers must be confident that the proposed system will meet its requirements while protecting appropriate objects and relationships. They usually begin by constructing a model of the environment to be secured. The model is actually a representation of the policy the operating system will enforce. Designers compare the model with the system requirements to make sure that the overall system functions are not compromised or degraded by the security needs. Then, they study different ways of enforcing that security. In the second part of this chapter we consider several different models for operating system security.
- *Design.* After having selected a security model, designers choose a means to implement it. Thus, the design involves both what the trusted operating system is (that is, its intended functionality) and how it is to be constructed (its implementation). The third major section of this chapter addresses choices to be made during development of a trusted operating system.
- *Trust.* Because the operating system plays a central role in enforcing security, we (as developers and users) seek some basis (assurance) for believing that it will meet our expectations. Our trust in the system is rooted in two aspects: *features* (the operating system has all the necessary functionality needed to enforce the expected security policy) and *assurance* (the operating system has been implemented in such a way that we have confidence it will enforce the security policy correctly and effectively). In the fourth part of this chapter we explore what makes a particular design or implementation worthy of trust.

The chapter ends with some examples of actual trusted operating systems. Several such systems have been written, and more are under development. In some cases, the secure systems were originally designed for security; in others, security features were added to existing operating systems. Our examples show that both approaches can produce a secure operating system.

5.1 WHAT IS A TRUSTED SYSTEM?

Before we begin to examine a trusted operating system in detail, let us look more carefully at the terminology involved in understanding and describing trust. What would it take for us to consider something secure? The word *secure* reflects a dichotomy: Something is either secure or not secure. If secure, it should withstand all attacks, today, tomorrow, and a century from now. And if we claim that it is secure, you either accept our assertion (and buy and use it) or reject it (and either do not use it or use it but do not trust it). How does security differ from quality? If we claim that something is *good*, you are less interested in our claims and more interested in an objective appraisal of whether the thing meets your performance and functionality needs. From this perspective, security is only one facet of goodness or quality; you may choose to balance security with other characteristics (such as speed or user friendliness) to select a system that is best, given the choices you may have. In particular, the system you build or select may be pretty good, even though it may not be as secure as you would like it to be.

For this reason, security professionals prefer to speak of *trusted* instead of *secure* operating systems. A trusted system connotes one that meets the intended security requirements, is of high enough quality, and justifies the user's confidence in that quality. That is, trust is perceived by the system's receiver or user, not by its developer, designer, or manufacturer. As a user, you may not be able to evaluate that trust directly. You may trust the design, a professional evaluation, or the opinion of a valued colleague. But in the end, it is your responsibility to sanction the degree of trust you require.

It is important to realize that there can be degrees of trust; unlike security, trust is not a dichotomy. For example, you trust certain friends with deep secrets, but you trust others only to give you the time of day. Trust is a characteristic that often grows over time, in accordance with evidence and experience. For instance, banks increase their trust in borrowers as the borrowers repay loans as expected; borrowers with good trust (credit) records can borrow larger amounts. Finally, trust is earned, not claimed or conferred. The comparison in Table 5-1 highlights some of these distinctions.

The adjective *trusted* appears many times in this chapter, as in *trusted process* (a process that can affect system security, or a process whose incorrect or malicious execution is capable of violating system security policy), *trusted product* (an evaluated and approved product), *trusted software* (the software portion of a system that can be relied upon to enforce security policy), *trusted computing base* (the set of all protection mechanisms within a computing system, including hardware, firmware, and software, that together enforce a unified security policy over a product or system), or *trusted system* (a system that employs sufficient hardware and software integrity measures to

TABLE 5-1 Qualities of Security and Trustedness.

Secure	Trusted
Either-or: Something either is or is not secure.	*Graded*: There are degrees of "trustworthiness."
Property of *presenter*	Property of *receiver*
Asserted based on product characteristics	*Judged* based on evidence and analysis
Absolute: not qualified as to how, where, when, or by whom used	*Relative*: viewed in context of use
A *goal*	A *characteristic*

allow its use for processing sensitive information). These definitions are paraphrased from [NIS91b]. Common to these definitions are the concepts of

- enforcement of security policy
- sufficiency of measures and mechanisms
- evaluation

In studying trusted operating systems, we examine closely what makes them trustworthy.

5.2 SECURITY POLICIES

To know that an operating system maintains the security we expect, we must be able to state its security policy. A **security policy** is a statement of the security we expect the system to enforce. An operating system (or any other piece of a trusted system) can be trusted only in relation to its security policy, that is, to the security needs the system is expected to satisfy.

We begin our study of security policy by examining military security policy because it has been the basis of much trusted operating system development and is fairly easy to state precisely. Then, we move to security policies that commercial establishments might adopt.

Military Security Policy

Military security policy is based on protecting classified information. Each piece of information is ranked at a particular sensitivity level, such as *unclassified*, *restricted*, *confidential*, *secret*, or *top secret*. The ranks or levels form a hierarchy, and they reflect an increasing order of sensitivity, as shown in Figure 5-1. That is, the information at a given level is less sensitive than the information in the level above it and more sensitive than the level below it. For example, restricted information is more sensitive than unclassified but more sensitive than confidential. We can denote the sensitivity of an object O by $rank_o$. In the rest of this chapter we assume these five sensitivity levels.

Information access is limited by the **need-to-know** rule: Access to sensitive data is allowed only to subjects who need to know those data to perform their jobs. Each piece of classified information may be associated with one or more projects, called **compartments**, describing the subject matter of the information. For example, the *alpha* project may use secret information, as may the *beta* project, but staff on *alpha* do not need access to the information on *beta*. In other words, both projects use secret information, but each is restricted to only the secret information needed for its particular project. In this way, compartments help enforce need-to-know restrictions so that people obtain access only to information that is relevant to their jobs. A compartment may cover information at only one sensitivity level, or it may include information at several sensitivity levels. The relationship between compartments and sensitivity levels is shown in Figure 5-2.

We can assign names to identify the compartments, such as *snowshoe*, *crypto*, and *Sweden*. A single piece of information can be coded with zero, one, two, or more compartment names, depending on the categories to which it relates. The association of information and compartments is shown in Figure 5-3. For example, one piece of

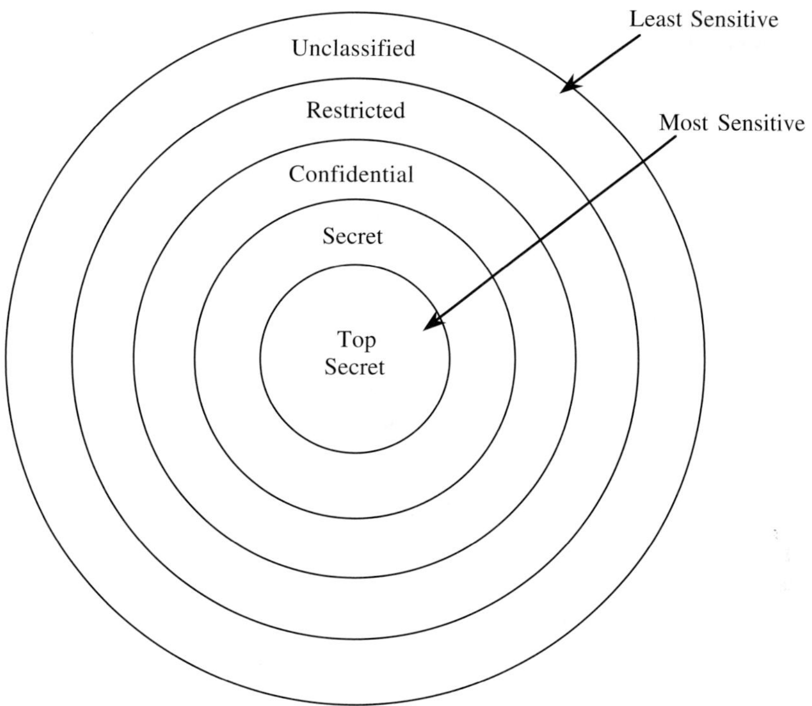

FIGURE 5-1 Hierarchy of Sensitivities.

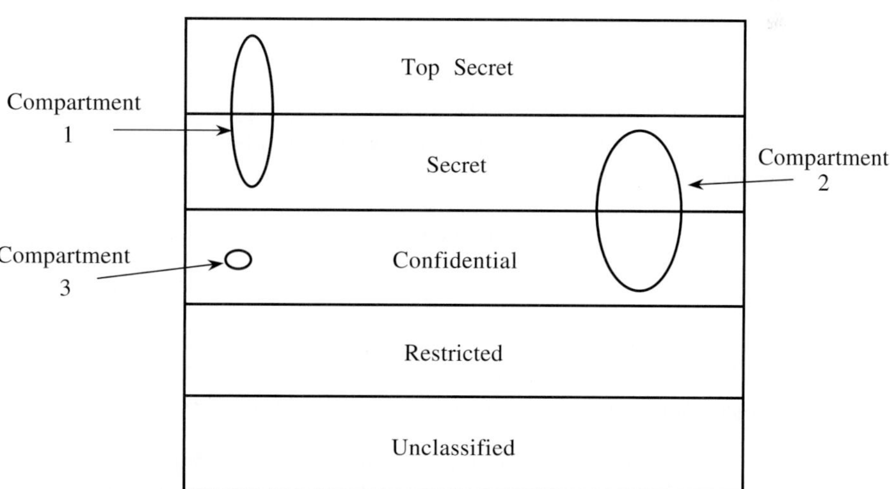

FIGURE 5-2 Compartments and Sensitivity Levels.

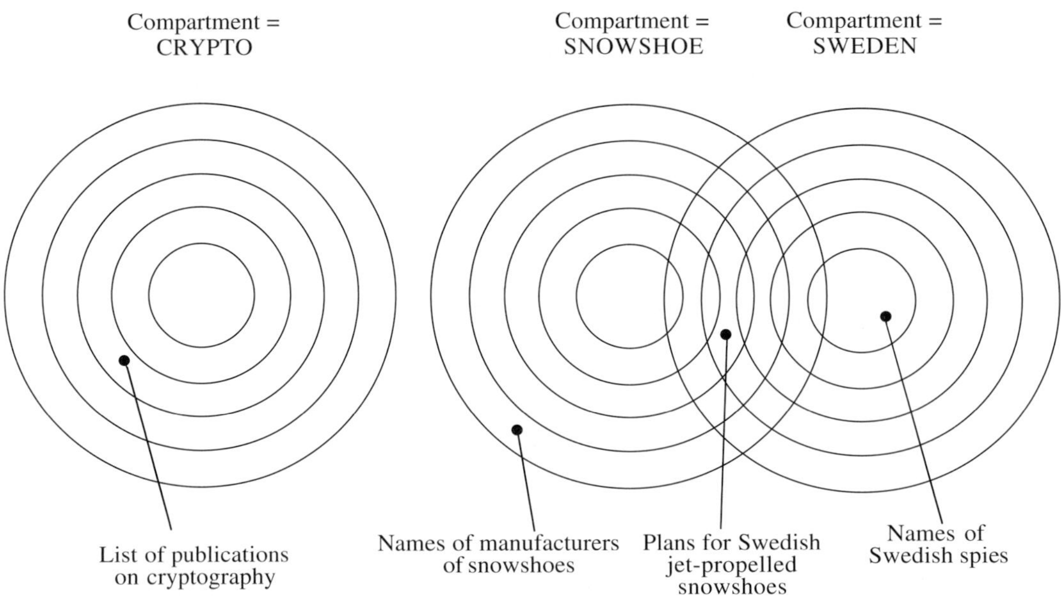

FIGURE 5-3 Association of Information and Compartments.

information may be a list of publications on cryptography, whereas another may describe development of snowshoes in Sweden. The compartment of this first piece of information is {*crypto*}; the second is {*snowshoe, Sweden*}.

The combination ⟨*rank*; *compartments*⟩ is called the **class** or **classification** of a piece of information. By designating information in this way, we can enforce need-to-know both by security level and by topic.

A person seeking access to sensitive information must be cleared. A **clearance** is an indication that a person is trusted to access information up to a certain level of sensitivity and that the person needs to know certain categories of sensitive information. The clearance of a subject is expressed as a combination ⟨*rank*; *compartments*⟩. This combination has the same form as the classification of a piece of information.

Now we introduce a relation ≤, called **dominance**, on the sets of sensitive objects and subjects. For a subject *s* and an object *o*,

$$\begin{aligned} s \leq o \text{ if and only if} \\ rank_s \leq rank_o \text{ and} \\ compartments_s \subseteq compartments_o \end{aligned}$$

We say that *o* **dominates** *s* (or *s* **is dominated by** *o*) if $s \leq o$; the relation ≥ is defined correspondingly. Dominance is used to limit the sensitivity and content of information a subject can access. A subject can read an object only if

- the clearance level of the subject is *at least as high* as that of the information, and
- the subject has a need to know about *all* compartments for which the information is classified.

These conditions are equivalent to saying that the subject dominates the object.

To see how the dominance relation works, consider the concentric circles in Figure 5-3. According to the relationships depicted there, information classified as ⟨*secret*;{Sweden}⟩ could be read by someone cleared for access to ⟨*top secret*;{Sweden}⟩ or ⟨*secret*;{Sweden,crypto}⟩, but not by someone with a ⟨*top secret*;{crypto}⟩ clearance or someone cleared for ⟨*confidential*;{Sweden}⟩ or ⟨*secret*;{France}⟩.

Military security enforces both sensitivity requirements and need-to-know requirements. Sensitivity requirements are known as **hierarchical** requirements because they reflect the hierarchy of sensitivity levels; need-to-know restrictions are **nonhierarchical** because compartments do not necessarily reflect a hierarchical structure. This combinational model is appropriate for a setting in which access is rigidly controlled by a central authority. Someone, often called a security officer, controls clearances and classifications, which are not generally up to individuals to alter.

Commercial Security Policies

Commercial enterprises have significant security concerns. They worry that industrial espionage will reveal information to competitors about new products under development. Likewise, corporations are often eager to protect information about the details of corporate finance. So even though the commercial world is usually less rigidly and less hierarchically structured than the military world, we still find many of the same concepts in commercial security policies. For example, a large organization, such as a corporation or a university, may be divided into groups or departments, each responsible for a number of disjoint projects. There may also be some corporate-level responsibilities, such as accounting and personnel activities. Data items at any level may have different degrees of sensitivity, such as *public*, *proprietary*, or *internal*; here, the names may vary among organizations, and no universal hierarchy applies.

Let us assume that *public* information is less sensitive than *proprietary*, which in turn is less sensitive than *internal*. Projects and departments tend to be fairly well separated, with some overlap as people work on two or more projects. Corporate-level responsibilities tend to overlie projects and departments, as people throughout the corporation may have need for accounting or personnel data. However, even corporate data may have degrees of sensitivity. Projects themselves may introduce a degree of sensitivity: Staff members on project *old-standby* have no need to know about project *new-product*, while staff members on *new-product* may have access to all data on *old-standby*. For these reasons, a commercial layout of data might look like Figure 5-4.

Two significant differences exist between commercial and military information security. First, outside the military, there is usually no formalized notion of clearances: A person working on a commercial project does not require approval for project MARS access by a central security officer. Typically, an employee is not conferred a different degree of trust by being allowed access to *internal* data. Second, because there is no formal concept of a clearance, the rules for allowing access are less regularized. For example, if a senior manager decides that a person needs access to a piece of MARS *internal* data, the manager will instruct someone to allow the access, either one-time or continuing. Thus, there is no *dominance* function for most commercial information access because there is no formal concept of a commercial clearance.

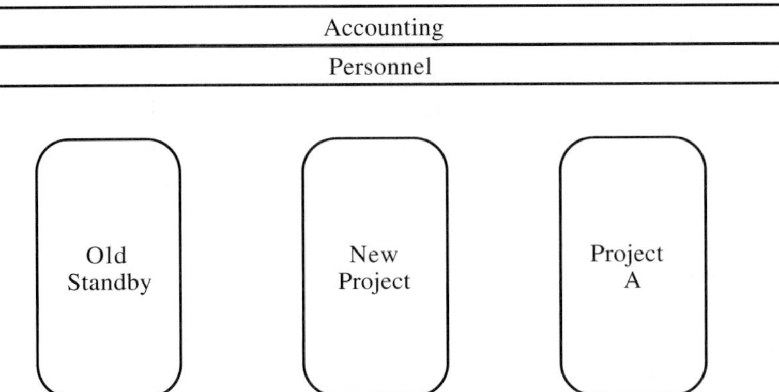

FIGURE 5-4 Commercial View of Sensitive Information.

So far, much of our discussion has focused only on read access, which addresses *confidentiality* in security. In fact, this narrow view holds true for much of the existing work in computer security. However, integrity and availability are at least as important as confidentiality in many instances. Policies for integrity and availability are significantly less well formulated than those for confidentiality, in both military and commercial realms. In the two examples that follow, we explore some instances of integrity concerns.

Clark–Wilson Commercial Security Policy

In many commercial applications, integrity can be at least as important as confidentiality. The correctness of accounting records, the accuracy of legal work, and the proper timing of medical treatments are the essence of their fields. Clark and Wilson [CLA87] proposed a policy for what they call *well-formed transactions*, which they assert are as important in their field as is confidentiality in a military realm.

To see why, consider a company that orders and pays for materials. A representation of the procurement process might be this:

1. A purchasing clerk creates an order for a supply, sending copies of the order to both the supplier and the receiving department.
2. The supplier ships the goods, which arrive at the receiving department. A receiving clerk checks the delivery, ensures that the correct quantity of the right item has been received, and signs a delivery form. The delivery form and the original order go to the accounting department.
3. The supplier sends an invoice to the accounting department. An accounting clerk compares the invoice with the original order (as to price and other terms) and the delivery form (as to quantity and item) and issues a check to the supplier.

The sequence of activities is important. A receiving clerk will not sign a delivery form without already having received a matching order (because suppliers should not be allowed to ship any quantities of any items they want and be paid), and an accounting clerk will not issue a check without already having received a matching order and delivery form (because suppliers should not be paid for goods not ordered or received). Furthermore, in most cases, both the order and the delivery form must be signed by an authorized individual. Performing the steps in order, performing exactly the steps listed, and authenticating the individuals who perform the steps constitute a **well-formed transaction**. The goal of the Clark–Wilson policy is to maintain consistency between the internal data and the external (users') expectations of those data.

Clark and Wilson present their policy in terms of **constrained data items**, which are processed by **transformation procedures**. A transformation procedure is like a monitor in that it performs only particular operations on specific kinds of data items; these data items are manipulated only by transformation procedures. The transformation procedures maintain the integrity of the data items by validating the processing to be performed. Clark and Wilson propose defining the policy in terms of **access triples**: $\langle userID, TP_i, \{CDI_j, CDI_k, ...\}\rangle$, combining a transformation procedure, one or more constrained data items, and the identification of a user who is authorized to operate on those data items by means of the transaction procedure.

Separation of Duty

A second commercial security policy involves separation of responsibility. Clark and Wilson [CLA87] raised this issue in their analysis of commercial security requirements, and Lee [LEE88] and Nash and Poland [NAS90] added to the concept.

To see how it works, we continue our example of a small company ordering goods. In the company, several people might be authorized to issue orders, receive goods, and write checks. However, we would not want the same person to issue the order, receive the goods, and write the check, because there is potential for abuse. Therefore, we might want to establish a policy that specifies that three separate individuals issue the order, receive the goods, and write the check, even though any of the three might be authorized to do any of these tasks. This required division of responsibilities is called **separation of duty**.

Separation of duty is commonly accomplished manually by means of dual signatures. Clark and Wilson triples are "stateless," meaning that a triple does not have a context of prior operations; triples are incapable of passing control information to other triples. Thus, if one person is authorized to perform operations TP_1 and TP_2, the Clark and Wilson triples cannot prevent the same person from performing both TP_1 and TP_2 on a given data item. However, it is quite easy to implement distinctness if it is stated as a policy requirement.

Chinese Wall Security Policy

Brewer and Nash [BRE89] defined a security policy called the Chinese Wall that reflects certain commercial needs for information access protection. The security requirements reflect issues relevant to those people in legal, medical, investment, or accounting firms who might be subject to conflict of interest. A conflict of interest exists when a person in one company can obtain sensitive information about people, products, or services in competing companies.

The security policy builds on three levels of abstraction.

- *Objects.* At the lowest level are elementary objects, such as files. Each file contains information concerning only one company.
- *Company groups.* At the next level, all objects concerning a particular company are grouped together.
- *Conflict classes.* At the highest level, all groups of objects for competing companies are clustered.

With this model, each object belongs to a unique company group, and each company group is contained in a unique conflict class. A conflict class may contain one or more company groups. For example, suppose you are an advertising company with clients in several fields: chocolate companies, banks, and airlines. You might want to store data on chocolate companies Suchard and Cadbury; on banks Citicorp, Deutsche Bank, and Credit Lyonnais; and on airline SAS. Using the Chinese Wall hierarchy, you would form six company groups (one for each company) and three conflict classes: {Suchard, Cadbury}, {Citicorp, Deutsche Bank, Credit Lyonnais}, and {SAS}.

The hierarchy guides a simple access control policy: A person can access any information as long as that person has never accessed information from a different company in the same conflict class. That is, access is allowed if either the object requested is in the same company group as an object that has previously been accessed or the object requested belongs to a conflict class that has never before been accessed. In our example, initially you can access any objects. Suppose you read from a file on Suchard. A subsequent request for access to any bank or to SAS would be granted, but a request to access Cadbury files would be denied. Your next access, of SAS data, does not affect future accesses. But if you then access a file on Credit Lyonnais, you will be blocked from future accesses to Deutsche Bank or Citicorp. From that point on, as shown in Figure 5-5, you can access objects only concerning Suchard, SAS, Credit Lyonnais, or a newly defined conflict class.

The Chinese Wall is a commercially inspired confidentiality policy. It is unlike most other commercial policies, which focus on integrity. It is also interesting because access permissions change dynamically: As a subject accesses some objects, other objects that would previously have been accessible are subsequently denied.

5.3 MODELS OF SECURITY

In security and elsewhere, models are often used to describe, study, or analyze a particular situation or relationship. In particular, security models are used to

- test a particular policy for completeness and consistency
- document a policy
- help conceptualize and design an implementation
- check whether an implementation meets its requirements

We assume that some access control policy dictates whether a given user can access a particular object. We also assume that this policy is established outside any model.

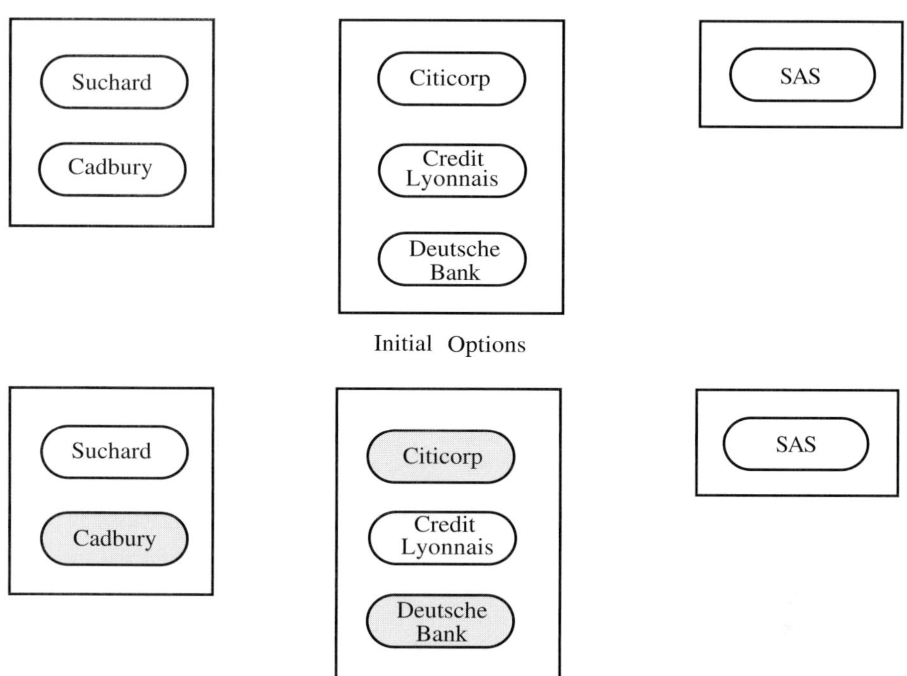

FIGURE 5-5 Chinese Wall Security Policy.

That is, a policy decision determines whether a specific user should have access to a specific object; the model is only a mechanism that enforces that policy. Thus, we begin studying models by considering simple ways to control access by one user.

Multilevel Security

Ideally, we want to build a model to represent a range of sensitivities and to reflect the need to separate subjects rigorously from objects to which they should not have access. For instance, consider an election and the sensitivity of data involved in the voting process. The names of the candidates are probably not sensitive. If the results have not yet been released, the name of the winner is somewhat sensitive. If one candidate received an embarrassingly low number of votes, the vote count may be more sensitive. Finally, the way a particular individual voted is extremely sensitive. Users can also be ranked by the degree of sensitivity of information to which they can have access.

For obvious reasons, the military has developed extensive procedures for securing information. A generalization of the military model of information security has also been adopted as a model of data security within an operating system. Bell and La Padula [BEL73] were first to describe the properties of the military model in mathematical notation, and Denning [DEN76a] first formalized the structure of this model. The generalized model is called the **lattice model** of security because its elements form a mathematical structure called a lattice. (See Sidebar 5-1.) In this section, we describe the military example and then use it to explain the lattice model.

Lattice Model of Access Security

The military security model is a representative of a more general scheme, called a lattice. The dominance relation $\leq$ defined in the military model is the relation for the lattice. The relation $\leq$ is transitive and antisymmetric. The largest element of the lattice is the classification ⟨*top secret*; *all compartments*⟩, and the smallest element is ⟨*unclassified*; *no compartments*⟩; these two elements respectively dominate and are dominated by all elements. Therefore, the military model is a lattice.

Many other structures are lattices. For example, we noted earlier that a commercial security policy may contain data sensitivities such as *public*, *proprietary*, and *internal*,

Sidebar 5-1 What Is a Lattice?

A **lattice** is a mathematical structure of elements organized by a relation among them, represented by a **relational operator.** We use the notation $\leq$ to denote this relation, and we say that $b \geq a$ means the same thing as $a \leq b$. A relation is called a **partial ordering** when it is both transitive and antisymmetric. These terms mean that for every three elements a, b, and c, the following two rules hold:

transitive: If $a \leq b$ and $b \leq c$, then $a \leq c$
antisymmetric: If $a \leq b$ and $b \leq a$, then $a = b$

In a lattice, not every pair of elements needs to be comparable; that is, there may be elements a and b for which neither $a \leq b$ nor $b \leq a$. However, every pair of elements possesses an **upper bound**, namely, an element at least as large as ($\geq$) both a and b. In other words, even though a and b may be noncomparable under $\leq$, in a lattice there is an upper bound element u such that $a \leq u$ and $b \leq u$. Furthermore, in a lattice, every pair of elements possesses a **lower bound**, an element l dominated by both a and b; that is, $l \leq a$ and $l \leq b$.

Consider the lattice in Figure 5-6, which represents all factors of the number 60. The relational operator represents the relationship "is a factor of." Thus, the notation $a \leq b$ means that a divides b. The lattice shows us that the number 60 dominates all other elements; 12 dominates 4, 6, 2, 3, and 1; 20 dominates 4, 10, and 5; and so on. We can also see that some elements are not comparable. For instance, 2 and 5 are not comparable and therefore are not directly connected by lines in the diagram.

Lattices are helpful for depicting relationships, and they appear most commonly when the relationship shows a difference in power, substance, or value. But many typical relationships form only half a lattice. In the relationships "is less than," "is a subset of," "reports to (for employees)," or "is a descendant of," there is a unique least upper bound (for example, a common ancestor) but not a greatest lower bound for each pair.

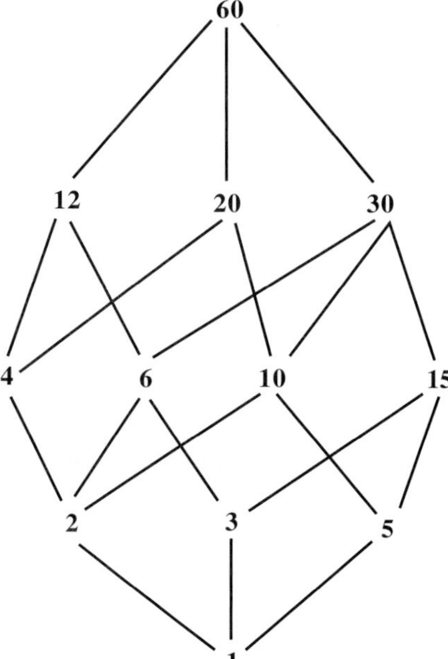

FIGURE 5-6 Sample Lattice.

with the natural ordering that *public* data are less sensitive than *proprietary*, which are less sensitive than *internal*. These three levels also form a lattice.

Security specialists have chosen to base security systems on a lattice because it naturally represents increasing degrees. A security system designed to implement lattice models can be used in a military environment. However, it can also be used in commercial environments with different labels for the degrees of sensitivity. Thus, lattice representation of sensitivity levels applies to many computing situations.

Bell–La Padula Confidentiality Model

The Bell and La Padula model [BEL73] is a formal description of the allowable paths of information flow in a secure system. The model's goal is to identify allowable communication when maintaining secrecy is important. The model has been used to define security requirements for systems concurrently handling data at different sensitivity levels. This model is a formalization of the military security policy and was central to the U.S. Department of Defense's evaluation criteria, described later in this chapter.

We are interested in secure information flows because they describe acceptable connections between subjects and objects of different levels of sensitivity. One purpose for security-level analysis is to enable us to construct systems that can perform concurrent computation on data at two different sensitivity levels. For example, we may want to use one machine for top-secret and confidential data at the same time. The programs processing top-secret data would be prevented from leaking top-secret data to the confidential data, and the confidential users would be prevented from accessing the top-secret data. Thus, the Bell–La Padula model is useful as the basis for the design of systems that handle data of multiple sensitivities.

To understand how the Bell-La Padula model works, consider a security system with the following properties. The system covers a set of subjects S and a set of objects O. Each subject s in S and each object o in O has a fixed security class $C(s)$ and $C(o)$ (denoting clearance and classification level). The security classes are ordered by a relation $\leq$. (Note: The classes may form a lattice, even though the Bell–La Padula model can apply to even less restricted cases.)

Two properties characterize the secure flow of information.

Simple Security Property. A subject s may have *read* access to an object o only if $C(o) \leq C(s)$.

In the military model, this property says that the security class (clearance) of someone receiving a piece of information must be at least as high as the class (classification) of the information.

$*$-Property. A subject s who has *read* access to an object o may have *write* access to an object p only if $C(o) \leq C(p)$.

In the military model, this property says that the contents of a sensitive object can be written only to objects at least as high.

In the military model, one interpretation of the $*$-property is that a person obtaining information at one level may pass that information along only to people at levels no lower than the level of the information. The $*$-property is used to prevent **write-down**, which occurs when a subject with access to high-level data transfers that data by writing it to a low-level object.

Literally, the $*$-property requires that a person receiving information at one level not talk with people cleared at levels lower than the level of the information—not even about the weather! This example points out that this property is stronger than necessary to ensure security; the same is also true in computing systems.

The implications of these two properties are shown in Figure 5-7. The classifications of subjects (represented by squares) and objects (represented by circles) are indicated by their positions: As the classification of an item increases, it is shown higher in the figure. The flow of information is generally horizontal (to and from the same level) and upward (from lower levels to higher). A downward flow is acceptable only if the highly cleared subject does not pass any high-sensitivity data to the lower-sensitivity object.

For computing systems, downward flow of information is difficult because a computer program cannot readily distinguish between having read a piece of information and having read a piece of information that influenced what was later written. (McLean [MCL90b], in work related to Goguen and Meseguer [GOG82], presents an interesting counter to the $*$-property of Bell and La Padula. He suggests considering noninterference, which can be loosely described as tracing the *effects* of inputs on outputs. If we can trace all output effects, we can determine conclusively whether a particular low-level output was "contaminated" with high level input.)

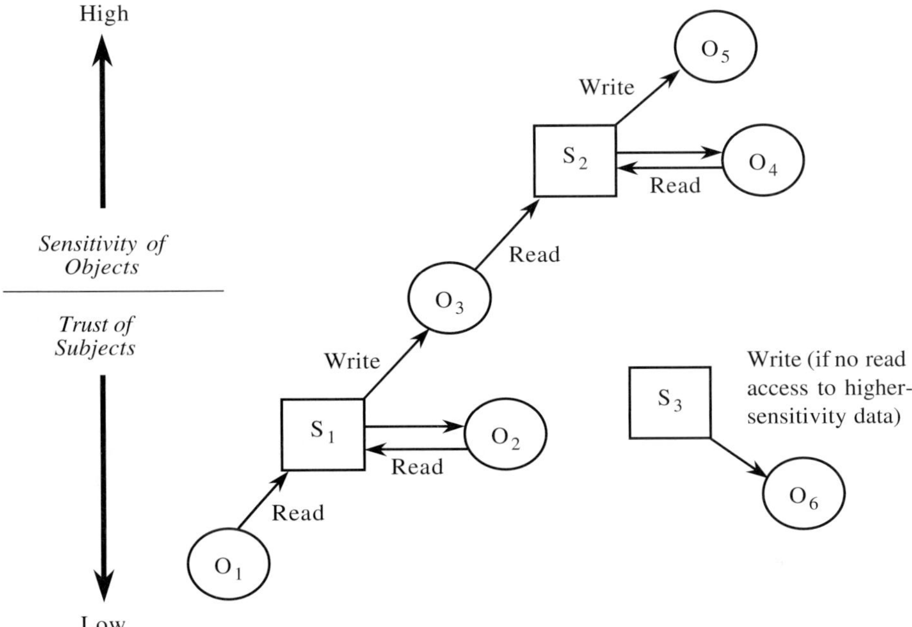

FIGURE 5-7 Secure Flow of Information.

Biba Integrity Model

The Bell–La Padula model applies only to secrecy of information: The model identifies paths that could lead to inappropriate *disclosure* of information. However, the integrity of data is important, too. Biba [BIB77] constructed a model for preventing inappropriate modification of data.

The Biba model is the counterpart (sometimes called the dual) of the Bell–La Padula model. Biba defines "integrity levels," which are analogous to the sensitivity levels of the Bell–La Padula model. Subjects and objects are ordered by an integrity classification scheme, denoted $I(s)$ and $I(o)$. The properties are

Simple Integrity Property. Subject s can modify (have *write* access to) object o only if $I(s) \geq I(o)$

Integrity $*$-Property. If subject s has *read* access to object o with integrity level $I(o)$, s can have *write* access to object p only if $I(o) \geq I(p)$

These two rules cover untrustworthy information in a natural way. Suppose John is known to be untruthful. If John can create or modify a document, other people should distrust the truth of the statements in that document. Thus, an untrusted subject who has write access to an object reduces the integrity of that object. Similarly, people are rightfully skeptical of a report based on unsound evidence. The low integrity of a source object implies low integrity for any object based on the source object.

This model addresses the integrity issue that the Bell–La Padula model ignores. However, in doing so, the Biba model ignores secrecy. Secrecy-based security systems have been much more fully studied than have integrity-based systems. The current trend is to join secrecy and integrity concerns in security systems, although no widely-accepted formal models achieve this compromise.

Models Proving Theoretical Limitations of Security Systems

Models are also useful for demonstrating the feasibility of an approach. Consider the security properties that we want a system to have. We want to build a model that tells us (before we invest in design, code, and testing) whether the properties can actually be achieved. This new class of models is based on the general theory of computability, which you may have studied in your computer science classes. Computability helps us determine decidability: If we pose a question, we want to know if we ever will be able to decide what the answer is. The results of these computability-based models show us the limitations of abstract security systems.

Graham–Denning Model

Lampson [LAM71] and Graham and Denning [GRA72] introduced the concept of a formal system of protection rules. Graham and Denning constructed a model having generic protection properties. This model forms the basis for two later models of security systems.

The Graham–Denning model operates on a set of subjects S, a set of objects O, a set of rights R, and an access control matrix A. The matrix has one row for each subject and one column for each subject and each object. The rights of a subject on another subject or an object are shown by the contents of an element of the matrix. For each object, one subject designated the "owner" has special rights; for each subject, another subject designated the "controller" has special rights.

In the Graham–Denning model, there are eight primitive protection rights. These rights are phrased as commands that can be issued by subjects, with effects on other subjects or objects.

- *Create object* allows the commanding subject to introduce a new object to the system.
- *Create subject, delete object,* and *delete subject* have the similar effect of creating or destroying a subject or object.
- *Read access right* allows a subject to determine the current access rights of a subject to an object.
- *Grant access right* allows the *owner* of an object to convey any access rights for an object to another subject.
- *Delete access right* allows a subject to delete a right of another subject for an object, provided that the deleting subject either is the owner of the object or controls the subject from which access should be deleted.

- *Transfer access right* allows a subject to transfer one of its rights for an object to another subject. Each right can be transferable or nontransferable. If a subject receives a transferable right, the subject can then transfer that right (either transferable or not) to other subjects. If a subject receives a nontransferable right, it can use the right but cannot transfer that right to other subjects.

These rules are shown in Table 5-2 (for more details see [GRA72]), which shows prerequisite conditions for executing each command and its effect. The access control matrix is A[*s*,*o*], where *s* is a subject and *o* is an object. The subject executing each command is denoted *x*. A transferable right is denoted *r**; a nontransferable right is written *r*.

This set of rules provides the properties necessary to model the access control mechanisms of a protection system. For example, this mechanism can represent a reference monitor or a system of sharing between two untrustworthy, mutually suspicious subsystems.

Harrison–Ruzzo–Ullman Results

Harrison, Ruzzo, and Ullman [HAR76] proposed a variation on the Graham–Denning model. This revised model answered several questions concerning the kinds of protection a given system can offer. Suppose you are about to use a particular operating system and you want to know if a given user can ever be granted a certain kind of access. For example, you may be establishing protection levels in Windows or MVS. You set up the access controls and then ask whether user *X* will ever have access to object *Y*. The three researchers developed their model so that we might be able to answer questions like this one.

TABLE 5-2 Protection System Commands.

Command	Precondition	Effect
Create object *o*	—	Add column for *o* in A; place *owner* in A[*x*,*o*]
Create subject *s*	—	Add row for *s* in A; place *control* in A[*x*,*s*]
Delete object *o*	*Owner* in A[*x*,*o*]	Delete column *o*
Delete subject *s*	*Control* in A[*x*,*s*]	Delete row *s*
Read access right of *s* on *o*	*Control* in A[*x*,*s*] or *owner* in A[*x*,*o*]	Copy A[*s*,*o*] to *x*
Delete access right *r* of *s* on *o*	*Control* in A[*x*,*s*] or *owner* in A[*x*,*o*]	Remove *r* from A[*s*,*o*]
Grant access right *r* to *s* on *o*	*Owner* in A[*x*,*o*]	Add *r* to A[*s*,*o*]
Transfer access right *r* or *r** to *s* on *o*	*r** in A[*x*,*o*]	Add *r* or *r** to A[*s*,*o*]

The Harrison–Ruzzo–Ullman model (called the HRU model) is based on **commands**, where each command involves **conditions** and **primitive operations**. The structure of a command is as follows.

```
command name(o1,o2,...,ok)
        if      r1 in A[s1,o1] and
                r2 in A[s2,o2] and
                   ...
                rm in A[sm,om]
        then
                op1
                op2
                ...
                opn
end
```

This command is structured like a procedure, with parameters o_1 through o_k. The notation of the HRU model is slightly different from the Graham–Denning model; in HRU every subject is an object, too. Thus, the columns of the access control matrix are all the subjects *and* all the objects that are not subjects. For this reason, all the parameters of a command are labeled *o*, although they could be either subjects or nonsubject objects. Each *r* is a generic right, as in the Graham–Denning model. Each *op* is a primitive operation, defined in the following list. The access matrix is shown in Table 5-3.

The primitive operations *op*, similar to those of the Graham–Denning model, are as follows:

- create subject *s*
- create object *o*
- destroy subject *s*
- destroy object *o*
- enter right *r* into A[*s*,*o*]
- delete right *r* from A[*s*,*o*]

The interpretations of these operations are what their names imply. A **protection system** is a set of subjects, objects, rights, and commands.

TABLE 5-3 Access Matrix in HRU Model.

	Objects					
Subjects	S_1	S_2	S_3	O_1	O_2	O_3
S_1	Control	Own, Suspend, Resume		Own	Own	Read, Propagate
S_2		Control			Extend	Own
S_3			Control	Read, Write	Write	Read

Harrison et al. demonstrate that these operations are adequate to model several examples of protection systems, including the Unix protection mechanism and an *indirect* access mode introduced by Graham and Denning [GRA72]. Thus, like the Graham–Denning model, the HRU model can represent "reasonable" interpretations of protection.

Two important results derived by Harrison et al. have major implications for designers of protection systems. We omit the complete proofs of these results, but we outline them in Sidebar 5-2 to give you an idea of what is involved.

The first result from HRU indicates that

> In the modeled system, in which commands are restricted to a single operation each, it *is* possible to decide whether a given subject can ever obtain a particular right to an object.

Sidebar 5-2 Proving the HRU Results

The first HRU result applies when commands are restricted to containing just one operation each. In this case, it is possible to decide whether a given protection system, started with a given initial configuration of the access control matrix, can allow a given user a given access right to a given object. In other words, suppose you want to know whether a particular protection system can allow a subject *s* to obtain access right *r* to object *o*. (Harrison et al. say that such a system **leaks** the access right.)

As long as each command consists of only a single operation, there is an algorithm that can answer this question. The proof involves analyzing the minimum number of commands by which a right can be conferred. Certain operations, such as *delete* and *destroy*, have no effect on expanding access rights; they can be ignored. The shortest sequence of commands by which such a right can be conferred contains at most $m = |r| * (|s|+1) * (|o|+1) + 1$ commands, where $|r|$ is the number of rights, $|s|$ is the number of subjects, and $|o|$ is the number of objects in the protection system. The algorithm calls for testing all sequences of commands of length up to *m*. (There are 2^{km} such sequences, for some constant *k*.) If the right is conferred, it will be in one of the sequences.

The proof of the second HRU result uses commands of an HRU protection system to represent operations of a formal system called a Turing machine. Turing machines are general models of computing devices, expressed as a machine reading a tape that has a string of zeros and ones. The decidability problems we want to solve are often framed so that the result we seek is true if we can decide whether the Turing machine will ever halt when reading commands from the tape. Any conventional computing system and program can be modeled with a Turing machine. Several decidable results about Turing machines are well known, including one that shows it is impossible to develop a general procedure to determine whether a given Turing machine will halt when performing a given computation. The proof of the second HRU result follows by the demonstration that a decision procedure for protection systems would also solve the halting problem for Turing machines, which is known to be unsolvable.

Therefore, we can decide (that is, we can know in advance) whether a low-level subject can ever obtain *read* access to a high-level object, for example.

The second result is less encouraging. Harrison et al. show that

> If commands are *not* restricted to one operation each, it is *not* always decidable whether a given protection system can confer a given right.

Thus, we cannot determine in general whether a subject can obtain a particular right to an object.

As an example, consider protection in the Unix operating system. The Unix protection scheme is relatively simple; other protection systems are more complex. Because the Unix protection scheme requires more than one operation per command in the HRU model, there can be no general procedure to determine whether a certain access right can be given to a subject.

The HRU result is important but bleak. In fact, the HRU result can be extended. There may be an algorithm to decide the access right question for a particular collection of protection systems, but even an infinite number of algorithms *cannot* decide the access right question for all protection systems. However, the negative results do not say that no decision process exists for any protection system. In fact, for certain specific protection systems, it is decidable whether a given access right can be conferred. Therefore, the HRU results are negative for general procedures but do not rule out the possibility of making decisions about particular protection systems.

Take–Grant Systems

One final model of a protection system is the **take–grant** system, introduced by Jones [JON78a] and expanded by Lipton and Snyder [LIP77], [SNY81].

This model has only four primitive operations: create, revoke, take, and grant. Create and revoke are similar to operations from the Graham–Denning and HRU models; take and grant are new types of operations. These operations are presented most naturally through the use of graphs.

As in other systems, let S be a set of subjects and O be a set of objects; objects can be either active (subjects) or passive (nonsubject objects). Let R be a set of rights. Each subject or object is denoted by a node of a graph; the rights of a particular subject to a particular object are denoted by a labeled, directed edge from the subject to the object. Figure 5-8 shows an example of subject, object, and rights.

Let s be the subject performing each of the operations. The four operations are defined as follows. The effects of these operations are shown in Figure 5-9.

- *Create(o,r).* A new node with label o is added to the graph. From s to o is a directed edge with label r, denoting the rights of s on o.

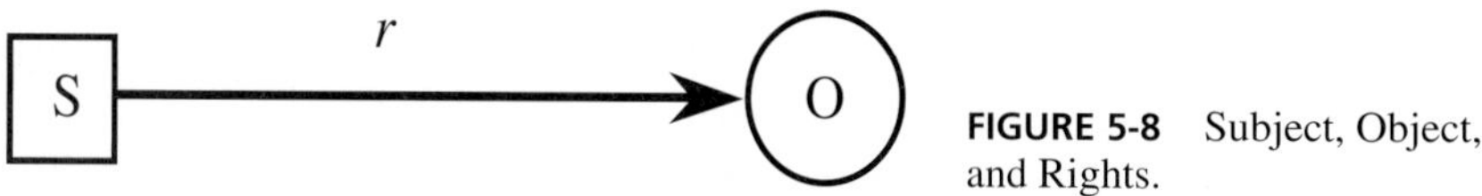

FIGURE 5-8 Subject, Object, and Rights.

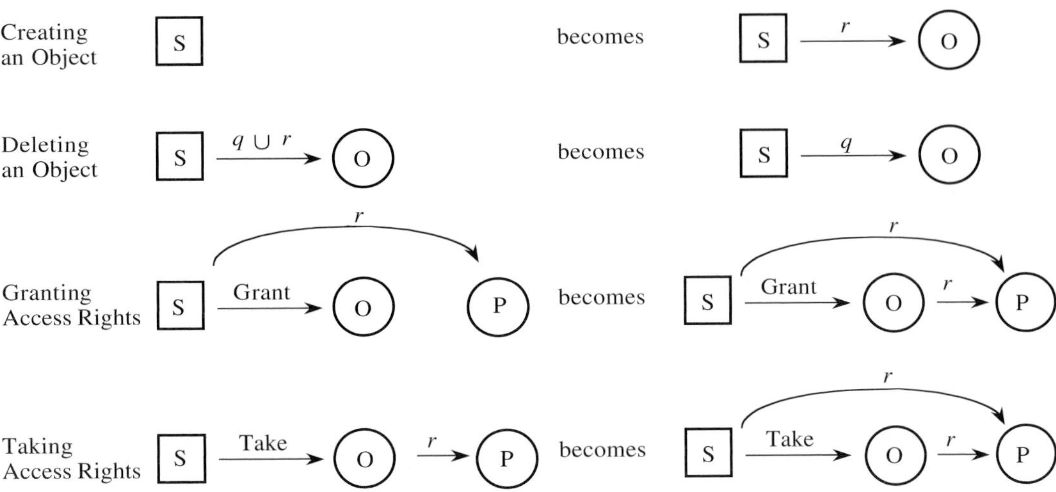

FIGURE 5-9 Creating an Object; Revoking, Granting, and Taking Access Rights.

- *Revoke(o,r).* The rights r are revoked from s on o. The edge from s to o was labeled $q \cup r$; the label is replaced by q. Informally, we say that s can revoke its rights to do r on o.
- *Grant(o,p,r).* Subject s grants to o access rights r on p. A specific right is *grant.* Subject s can grant to o access rights r on p only if s has *grant* rights on o and s has r rights on p. Informally, s can grant (share) any of its rights with o, as long as s has the right to grant privileges to o. An edge from o to p is added, with label r.
- *Take(o,p,r).* Subject s takes from o access rights r on p. A specific right is *take.* Subject s can take from o access rights r on p only if s has *take* right on o and o has r rights on p. Informally, s can take any rights o has, as long as s has the right to take privileges from o. An edge from s to p is added, with label r.

This set of operations is even shorter than the operations of either of the two previous models. However, *take* and *grant* are more complex rights.

Snyder shows that in this system certain protection questions are decidable; furthermore, they are decidable in reasonable (less than exponential) time. In [SNY81], Snyder considers two questions:

1. Can we decide whether a given subject can share an object with another subject?
2. Can we decide whether a given subject can steal access to an object from another subject?

Clearly, these are important questions to answer about a protection system, for they show whether the access control mechanisms are secure against unauthorized disclosure.

The answer to Snyder's first question is yes. Sharing can occur only if several other subjects together have the desired access to the object and the first subject is connected to each of the group of other subjects by a path of edges having a particular form. An algorithm that detects sharability runs in time proportional to the size of the graph of the particular case.

Snyder also answers the second question affirmatively, in a situation heavily dependent on the ability to share. Thus, an algorithm can decide whether access can be stolen by direct appeal to the algorithm to decide sharability.

Landwehr [LAN81] points out that the take–grant model assumes the worst about users: If a user *can* grant access rights, the model assumes that the user will. Suppose a user can create a file and grant access to it to everyone. In that situation, every user could allow access to every object by every other user. This worst-case assumption limits the applicability of the model to situations of controlled sharing of information. In general, however, the take–grant model is useful because it identifies conditions under which a user can obtain access to an object.

Summary of Models of Protection Systems

There are two purposes to studying models of computer security. First, models are important in determining the policies a secure system should enforce. For example, the Bell–La Padula and Biba models identify specific conditions we must enforce so that we can ensure secrecy or integrity. Second, the study of abstract models can lead to an understanding of the properties of protection systems. For example, the HRU model states certain characteristics that can or cannot be decided by an arbitrary protection system. These characteristics are important for designers of protection systems to know.

Building and analyzing models are essential to designing a trusted operating system. We use models of protection systems to establish our security policies, determining what is feasible and desirable from what is not. From the policies we move to the operating system design itself. In the next section, we look closely at trusted operating system design.

5.4 TRUSTED OPERATING SYSTEM DESIGN

Operating systems by themselves (regardless of their security constraints) are very difficult to design. They handle many duties, are subject to interruptions and context switches, and must minimize overhead so as not to slow user computations and interactions. Adding the responsibility for security enforcement to the operating system substantially increases the difficulty of designing an operating system.

Nevertheless, the need for effective security is becoming more pervasive, and good software engineering principles tell us that it is better to design the security in at the beginning than to shoehorn it in at the end. (See Sidebar 5-3 for more about good design principles.) Thus, this section focuses on the design of operating systems for a high degree of security. First, we examine the basic design of a standard multipurpose operating system. Then, we consider isolation, through which an operating system supports both sharing and separating user domains. We look in particular at the design of

Sidebar 5-3 The Importance of Good Design Principles

Every design, whether it be for hardware or software, must begin with a design philosophy and guiding principles. These principles suffuse the design, are built in from the beginning, and are preserved (according to the design philosophy) as the design evolves.

The design philosophy expresses the overall intentions of the designers, not only in terms of how the system will look and act but also in terms of how it will be tested and maintained. Most systems are not built for short-term use. They grow and evolve as the world changes over time. Features are enhanced, added or deleted. Supporting or communicating hardware and software change. The system is fixed as problems are discovered and their causes rooted out. The design philosophy explains how the system will "hang together," maintaining its integrity through all these changes. A good design philosophy will make a system easy to test and easy to change.

The philosophy suggests a set of good design principles. Modularity, information hiding, and other notions discussed in Chapter 3 form guidelines that enable designers to meet their goals for software quality. Since security is one of these goals, it is essential that security policy be consistent with the design philosophy and that the design principles enable appropriate protections to be built into the system.

When the quality of the design is not considered up front and embedded in the development process, the result can be a sort of software anarchy. The system may run properly at first, but as changes are made, the software degrades quickly and in a way that makes future changes more difficult and time consuming. The software becomes brittle, failing more often and sometimes making it impossible to add or change features, including security. Equally important, brittle and poorly designed software can easily hide vulnerabilities, because the software is so difficult to understand and the execution states so hard to follow, reproduce, and test. Thus, good design is in fact a security issue, and secure software must be designed well.

an operating system's kernel; how the kernel is designed suggests whether security will be provided effectively. We study two different interpretations of the kernel, and then we consider layered or ring-structured designs.

Trusted System Design Elements

That security considerations pervade the design and structure of operating systems implies two things. First, an operating system controls the interaction between subjects and objects, so security must be considered in every aspect of its design. That is, the operating system design must include definitions of which objects will be protected in what way, what subjects will have access and at what levels, and so on. There must be a clear mapping from the security requirements to the design, so that all developers can see how the two relate. Moreover, once a section of the operating system has been designed, it must be checked to see that the degree of security that it is supposed to enforce or provide has actually been designed correctly. This checking can be done in many ways, including formal reviews or simulations. Again, a mapping is necessary, this time from the requirements to design to tests, so that developers can affirm that each aspect of operating system security has been tested and shown to work correctly.

Second, because security appears in every part of an operating system, its design and implementation cannot be left fuzzy or vague until the rest of the system is working and being tested. It is extremely hard to retrofit security features to an operating system designed with inadequate security. Leaving an operating system's security to the last minute is much like trying to install plumbing or wiring in a house whose foundation is set, structure defined, and walls already up and painted; not only must you destroy most of what you have built, but you may also find that the general structure can no longer accommodate all that is needed (and so some has to be left out or compromised). Thus, security must be an essential part of the initial design of a trusted operating system. Indeed, the security considerations may shape many of the other design decisions, especially for a system with complex and constraining security requirements. For the same reasons, the security and other design principles must be carried throughout implementation, testing, and maintenance.

Good design principles are always good for security, as we have noted above. But several important design principles are quite particular to security and essential for building a solid, trusted operating system. These principles have been articulated well by Saltzer [SAL74] and Saltzer and Schroeder [SAL75]:

- *Least privilege.* Each user and each program should operate by using the fewest privileges possible. In this way, the damage from an inadvertent or malicious attack is minimized.
- *Economy of mechanism.* The design of the protection system should be small, simple, and straightforward. Such a protection system can be carefully analyzed, exhaustively tested, perhaps verified, and relied on.
- *Open design.* The protection mechanism must not depend on the ignorance of potential attackers; the mechanism should be public, depending on secrecy of relatively few key items, such as a password table. An open design is also available for extensive public scrutiny, thereby providing independent confirmation of the design security.
- *Complete mediation.* Every access attempt must be checked. Both direct access attempts (requests) and attempts to circumvent the access checking mechanism should be considered, and the mechanism should be positioned so that it cannot be circumvented.
- *Permission based.* The default condition should be denial of access. A conservative designer identifies the items that *should* be accessible, rather than those that should *not.*
- *Separation of privilege.* Ideally, access to objects should depend on more than one condition, such as user authentication plus a cryptographic key. In this way, someone who defeats one protection system will not have complete access.
- *Least common mechanism.* Shared objects provide potential channels for information flow. Systems employing physical or logical separation reduce the risk from sharing.

- *Ease of use.* If a protection mechanism is easy to use, it is unlikely to be avoided.

Although these design principles were suggested several decades ago, they are as accurate now as they were when originally written. The principles have been used repeatedly and successfully in the design and implementation of numerous trusted systems. More importantly, when security problems have been found in operating systems in the past, they almost always derive from failure to abide by one or more of these principles.

Security Features of Ordinary Operating Systems

As described in Chapter 4, a multiprogramming operating system performs several functions that relate to security. To see how, examine Figure 5-10, which illustrates how an operating system interacts with users, provides services, and allocates resources.

We can see that the system addresses several particular functions that involve computer security:

- *Authentication of users.* The operating system must identify each user who requests access and ascertain that the user is actually who he or she purports to be. The most common authentication mechanism is password comparison.

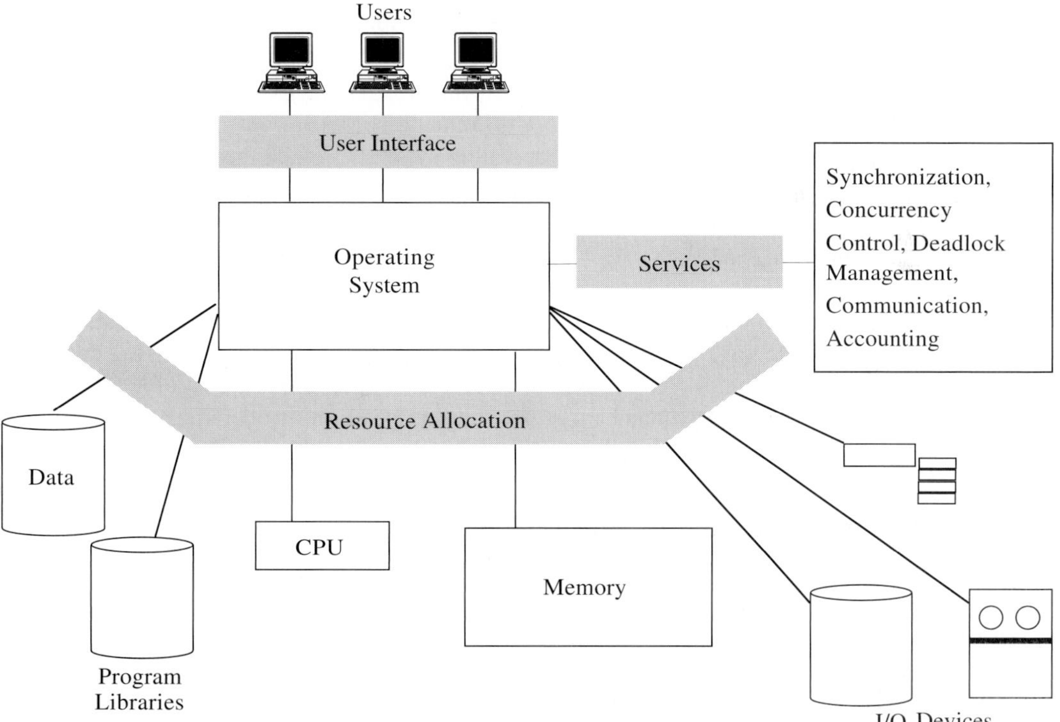

FIGURE 5-10 Overview of an Operating System's Functions.

- *Protection of memory.* Each user's program must run in a portion of memory protected against unauthorized accesses. The protection will certainly prevent outsiders' accesses, and it may also control a user's own access to restricted parts of the program space. Differential security, such as read, write, and execute, may be applied to parts of a user's memory space. Memory protection is usually performed by hardware mechanisms, such as paging or segmentation.
- *File and I/O device access control.* The operating system must protect user and system files from access by unauthorized users. Similarly, I/O device use must be protected. Data protection is usually achieved by table lookup, as with an access control matrix.
- *Allocation and access control to general objects.* Users need general objects, such as constructs to permit concurrency and allow synchronization. However, access to these objects must be controlled so that one user does not have a negative effect on other users. Again, table lookup is the common means by which this protection is provided.
- *Enforcement of sharing.* Resources should be made available to users as appropriate. Sharing brings about the need to guarantee integrity and consistency. Table lookup, combined with integrity controls such as monitors or transaction processors, is often used to support controlled sharing.
- *Guarantee of fair service.* All users expect CPU usage and other service to be provided so that no user is indefinitely starved from receiving service. Hardware clocks combine with scheduling disciplines to provide fairness. Hardware facilities and data tables combine to provide control.
- *Interprocess communication and synchronization.* Executing processes sometimes need to communicate with other processes or to synchronize their accesses to shared resources. Operating systems provide these services by acting as a bridge between processes, responding to process requests for asynchronous communication with other processes or synchronization. Interprocess communication is mediated by access control tables.
- *Protection of operating system protection data.* The operating system must maintain data by which it can enforce security. Obviously if these data are not protected against unauthorized access (read, modify, and delete), the operating system cannot provide enforcement. Various techniques, including encryption, hardware control, and isolation, support isolation of operating system protection data.

Security Features of Trusted Operating Systems

Unlike regular operating systems, trusted systems incorporate technology to address both **features** and **assurance**. The design of a trusted system is delicate, involving selection of an appropriate and consistent set of features together with an appropriate degree of assurance that the features have been assembled and implemented correctly. Figure 5-11 illustrates how a trusted operating system differs from an ordinary one. Compare it with Figure 5-10. Notice how objects are accompanied or surrounded by an access control mechanism, offering far more protection and separation than does a con-

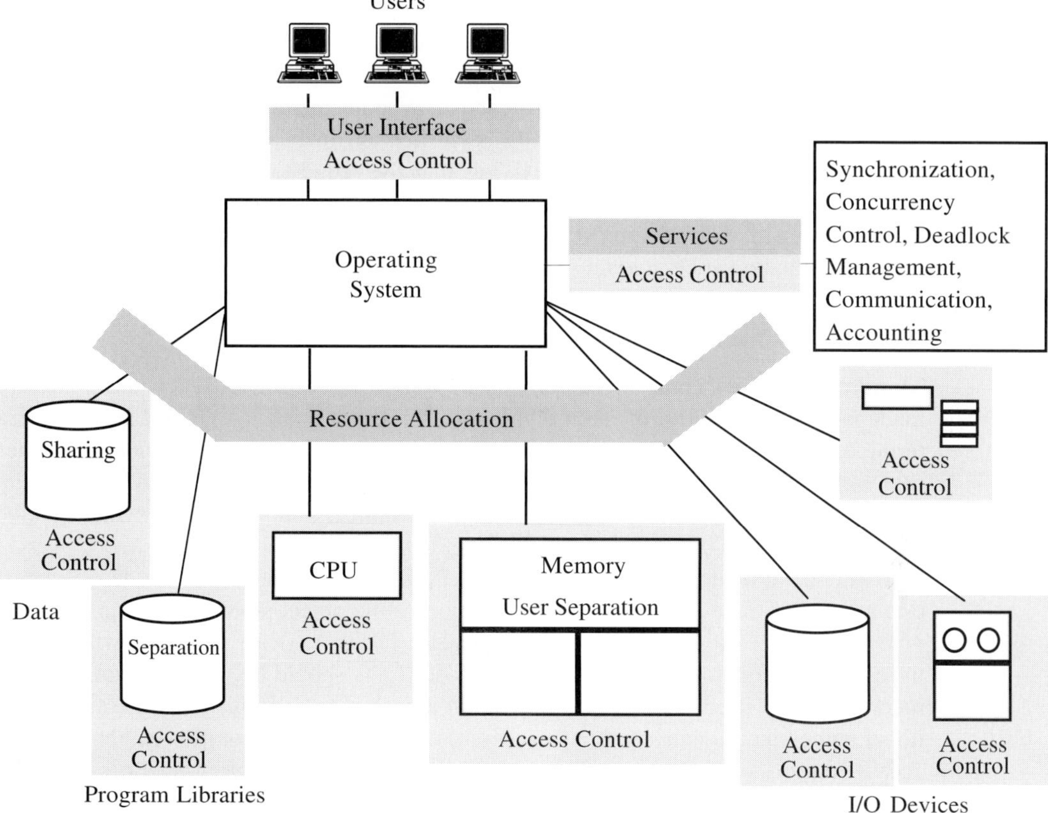

FIGURE 5-11 Security Functions of a Trusted Operating System.

ventional operating system. In addition, memory is separated by user, and data and program libraries have controlled sharing and separation.

In this section, we consider in more detail the key features of a trusted operating system, including these:

- user identification and authentication
- mandatory access control
- discretionary access control
- object reuse protection
- complete mediation
- trusted path
- audit
- audit log reduction
- intrusion detection

We consider each of these features in turn.

Identification and Authentication

Identification is at the root of much of computer security. We must be able to tell who is requesting access to an object, and we must be able to verify the subject's identity. As we shall see shortly, most access control, whether mandatory or discretionary, is based on accurate identification. Thus, identification involves two steps: finding out who the access requester is and verifying that the requester is indeed who he/she/it claims to be. That is, we want to establish an identity and then authenticate or verify that identity. Trusted operating systems require secure identification of individuals, and each individual must be uniquely identified.

Mandatory and Discretionary Access Control

Mandatory access control (MAC) means that access control policy decisions are made beyond the control of the individual owner of an object. A central authority determines what information is to be accessible by whom, and the user cannot change access rights. An example of MAC occurs in military security, where an individual data owner does not decide who has a top-secret clearance; neither can the owner change the classification of an object from top secret to secret.

By contrast, **discretionary access control (DAC)**, as its name implies, leaves a certain amount of access control to the discretion of the object's owner or to anyone else who is authorized to control the object's access. The owner can determine who should have access rights to an object and what those rights should be. Commercial environments typically use DAC to allow anyone in a designated group, and sometimes additional named individuals, to change access. For example, a corporation might establish access controls so that the accounting group can have access to personnel files. But the corporation may also allow Ana and Jose to access those files, too, in their roles as directors of the Inspector General's office. Typically DAC access rights can change dynamically. The owner of the accounting file may add Renee and remove Walter from the list of allowed accessors, as business needs dictate.

MAC and DAC can both be applied to the same object. MAC has precedence over DAC, meaning that of all those who are approved for MAC access, only those who also pass DAC will actually be allowed to access the object. For example, a file may be classified secret, meaning that only people cleared for secret access can potentially access the file. But of those millions of people granted secret access by the government, only people on project "deer park" or in the "environmental" group or at location "Fort Hamilton" are actually allowed access.

Object Reuse Protection

One way that a computing system maintains its efficiency is to reuse objects. The operating system controls resource allocation, and as a resource is freed for use by other users or programs, the operating system permits the next user or program to access the resource. But reusable objects must be carefully controlled, lest they create a serious vulnerability. To see why, consider what happens when a new file is created. Usually, space for the file comes from a pool of freed, previously used space on a disk or other storage device. Released space is returned to the pool "dirty," that is, still containing the data from the previous user. Because most users would write to a file before trying to read from it, the new user's data obliterate the previous owner's, so there is no inappropriate disclosure of the previous user's information. However, a malicious user may claim a large amount of disk space and then scavenge for sensitive data. This kind of attack is called **object reuse**. The problem is not limited to disk; it can occur with main memory, processor registers and storage, other magnetic media (such as disks and tapes), or any other reusable storage medium.

To prevent object reuse leakage, operating systems clear (that is, overwrite) all space to be reassigned before allowing the next user to have access to it. Magnetic media are particularly vulnerable to this threat. Very precise and expensive equipment can sometimes separate the most recent data from the data previously recorded, from the data before that, and so forth. This threat, called **magnetic remanence**, is beyond the scope of this book. For more information, see [NCS91a]. In any case, the operating system must take responsibility for "cleaning" the resource before permitting access to it.

Complete Mediation

For mandatory or discretionary access control to be effective, *all* accesses must be controlled. It is insufficient to control access only to files if the attack will acquire access through memory or an outside port or a network or a covert channel. The design and implementation difficulty of a trusted operating system rises significantly as more paths for access must be controlled. Highly trusted operating systems perform **complete mediation**, meaning that all accesses are checked.

Trusted Path

One way for a malicious user to gain inappropriate access is to "spoof" users, making them think they are communicating with a legitimate security enforcement system when in fact their keystrokes and commands are being intercepted and analyzed. For example, a malicious spoofer may place a phony user ID and password system in between the user and the legitimate system. As the illegal system queries the user for identification information, the spoofer captures the real user ID and password; the spoofer can use these bona fide entry data to access the system later on, probably for malicious intent. Thus, for critical operations such as setting a password or changing access permissions, users want an unmistakable communication, called a **trusted path**, to ensure that they are supplying important, protected information only to a legitimate receiver. On some trusted systems, the user invokes a trusted path by pressing a unique key sequence that, by design, is intercepted directly by the security enforcement software; on other trusted systems, security-relevant changes can be made only at system startup, before any processes other than the security enforcement code run.

Accountability and Audit

A security-relevant action may be as simple as an individual access to an object, such as a file, or it may be as major as a change to the central access control database affecting all subsequent accesses. Accountability usually entails maintaining a log of security-relevant events that have occurred, listing each event and the person responsible for the addition, deletion, or change. This audit log must obviously be protected from outsiders, and every security-relevant event must be recorded.

Audit Log Reduction

Theoretically, the general notion of an audit log is appealing, because it allows responsible parties to evaluate all actions that affect all protected elements of the system. But in practice an audit log may be too difficult to handle, owing to volume and analysis. To see why, consider what information would have to be collected and analyzed. In the extreme (such as where the data involved can affect a business' viability or a nation's security), we might argue that every modification or even each character read from a file is potentially security relevant; the modification could affect the integrity of data, or the single character could divulge the only really sensitive part of an entire file. And because the path of control through a program is affected by the data the program processes, the sequence of individual instructions is also potentially security relevant. If an audit record were to be created for every access to a single character from a file and for every instruction executed, the audit log would be enormous. (In fact, it would be impossible to audit every instruction, because then the audit commands themselves would have to be audited. In turn, these commands would be implemented by instructions that would have to be audited, and so on forever.)

In most trusted systems, the problem is simplified by an audit of only the opening (first access to) and closing of (last access to) files or similar objects. Similarly, objects such as individual memory locations, hardware registers, and instructions are not audited. Even with these restrictions, audit logs tend to be very large. Even a simple word processor may open fifty or more support modules (separate files) when it begins, it may create and delete a dozen or more temporary files during execution, and it may open many more drivers to handle specific tasks such as complex formatting or printing. Thus, one simple program can easily cause a hundred files to be opened and closed, and complex systems can cause thousands of files to be accessed in a relatively short time. On the other hand, some systems continuously read from or update a single file. A bank teller may process transactions against the general customer accounts file throughout the entire day; what is significant is not that the teller accessed the accounts file, but *which entries* in the file were accessed. Thus, audit at the level of file opening and closing is in some cases too much data and in other cases not enough to meet security needs.

A final difficulty is the "needle in a haystack" phenomenon. Even if the audit data could be limited to the right amount, there will typically be many legitimate accesses and perhaps one attack. Finding the one attack access out of a thousand legitimate accesses can be difficult. A corollary to this problem is the one of determining who or what does the analysis. Does the system administrator sit and analyze all data in the audit log? Or do the developers write a program to analyze the data? If the latter, how can we automatically recognize a pattern of unacceptable behavior? These issues are open questions being addressed not only by security specialists but also by experts in artificial intelligence and pattern recognition.

Sidebar 5-4 illustrates how the volume of audit log data can get out of hand very quickly. Some trusted systems perform **audit reduction**, using separate tools to reduce the volume of the audit data. In this way, if there is an event, all the data have been

Sidebar 5-4 Theory vs. Practice: Audit Data Out of Control

In the 1980s, the U.S. State Department was enhancing the security of the automated systems that handled diplomatic correspondence among its embassies worldwide. One of the security requirements for an operating system enhancement requested an audit log of every transaction related to protected documents. The requirement included the condition that the system administrator was to review the audit log daily, looking for signs of malicious behavior.

In theory, this requirement was sensible, since revealing the contents of protected documents could at least embarrass the nation, even endanger it. But, in fact, the requirement was impractical. The State Department ran a test system with five users, printing out the audit log for ten minutes. At the end of the test period, the audit log generated a stack of paper more than a foot high! Because the actual system involved thousands of users working around the clock, the test demonstrated that it would have been impossible for the system administrator to review the log—even if that were all the system administrator had to do each day.

The State Department went on to consider other options for detecting malicious behavior, including audit log reduction and automated review of the log's contents.

recorded and can be consulted directly. However, for most analysis, the reduced audit log is enough to review.

Intrusion Detection

Closely related to audit reduction is the ability to detect security lapses, ideally while they occur. As we have seen in the State Department example, there may well be too much information in the audit log for a human to analyze, but the computer can help correlate independent data. **Intrusion detection** software builds patterns of normal system usage, triggering an alarm any time the usage seems abnormal. After a decade of promising research results in intrusion detection, products are now commercially available. Some trusted operating systems include a primitive degree of intrusion detection software. See Chapter 7 for a more detailed description of intrusion detection systems.

Although the problems are daunting, there have been many successful implementations of trusted operating systems. In the following section, we examine some of them. In particular, we consider three properties: kernelized design (a result of least privilege and economy of mechanism), isolation (the logical extension of least common mechanism), and ring-structuring (an example of open design and complete mediation).

Kernelized Design

A **kernel** is the part of an operating system that performs the lowest-level functions. In standard operating system design, the kernel implements operations such as synchronization, interprocess communication, message passing, and interrupt handling. The kernel is also called a **nucleus** or **core**. The notion of designing an operating system around a kernel is described by Lampson and Sturgis [LAM76] and by Popek and Kline [POP78].

A **security kernel** is responsible for enforcing the security mechanisms of the entire operating system. The security kernel provides the security interfaces among the hardware, operating system, and other parts of the computing system. Typically, the operating system is designed so that the security kernel is contained within the operating system kernel. Security kernels are discussed in detail by Ames [AME83].

There are several good design reasons why security functions may be isolated in a security kernel.

- *Coverage.* Every access to a protected object must pass through the security kernel. In a system designed in this way, the operating system can use the security kernel to ensure that every access is checked.
- *Separation.* Isolating security mechanisms both from the rest of the operating system and from the user space makes it easier to protect those mechanisms from penetration by the operating system or the users.
- *Unity.* All security functions are performed by a single set of code, so it is easier to trace the cause of any problems that arise with these functions.
- *Modifiability.* Changes to the security mechanisms are easier to make and easier to test.
- *Compactness.* Because it performs only security functions, the security kernel is likely to be relatively small.
- *Verifiability.* Being relatively small, the security kernel can be analyzed rigorously. For example, formal methods can be used to ensure that all security situations (such as states and state changes) have been covered by the design.

Notice the similarity between these advantages and the design goals of operating systems that we described earlier. These characteristics also depend in many ways on modularity, as described in Chapter 3.

On the other hand, implementing a security kernel may degrade system performance because the kernel adds yet another layer of interface between user programs and operating system resources. Moreover, the presence of a kernel does not guarantee that it contains *all* security functions or that it has been implemented correctly. And in some cases a security kernel can be quite large.

How do we balance these positive and negative aspects of using a security kernel? The design and usefulness of a security kernel depend somewhat on the overall approach taken to the operating system's design. There are many design choices, each of which falls into one of two types: Either the kernel is designed as an addition to the operating system, or it is the basis of the entire operating system. Let us look more closely at each design choice.

Reference Monitor

The most important part of a security kernel is the **reference monitor**, the portion that controls accesses to objects [AND72, LAM71]. A reference monitor is not necessarily a single piece of code; rather, it is the collection of access controls for devices, files, memory, interprocess communication, and other kinds of objects. As shown in Figure 5-12, a reference monitor acts like a brick wall around the operating system or trusted software. It must be:

- tamperproof
- always invoked when access to any object is required
- small enough to be subjected to analysis and testing, the completeness of which can be ensured

A reference monitor can control access effectively only if it cannot be modified or circumvented by a rogue process, and it is the single point through which all access requests must pass. Furthermore, the reference monitor must function correctly if it is to fulfill its crucial role in enforcing security. Because the likelihood of correct behavior decreases as the complexity and size of a program increase, the best assurance of correct policy enforcement is to build a small, simple, understandable reference monitor.

The reference monitor is not the only security mechanism of a trusted operating system. Other parts of the security suite include audit, identification, and authentication processing, as well as the setting of enforcement parameters, such as who the allowable subjects are and what objects they are allowed to access. These other security parts interact with the reference monitor, receiving data from the reference monitor or providing it with the data it needs to operate.

The reference monitor concept has been used for many trusted operating systems and also for smaller pieces of trusted software. The validity of this concept is well supported both in research and in practice.

Trusted Computing Base (TCB)

The **trusted computing base** or **TCB** is the name we give to everything in the trusted operating system necessary to enforce the security policy. Alternatively, we say that the TCB consists of the parts of the trusted operating system on which we depend for correct enforcement of policy. We can think of the TCB as a coherent whole in the follow-

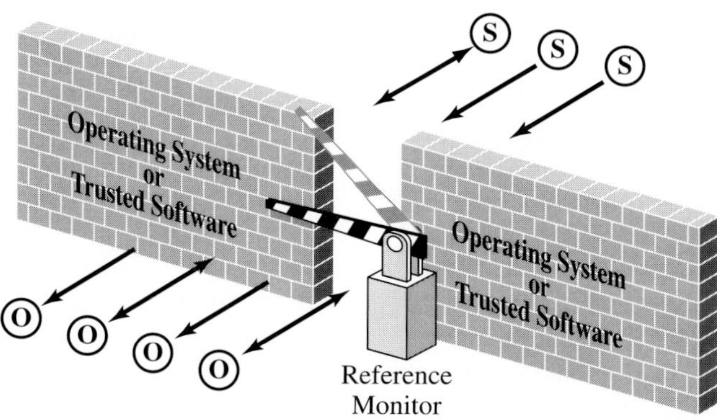

FIGURE 5-12 Reference Monitor.

ing way. Suppose you divide a trusted operating system into the parts that are in the TCB and those that are not, and you allow the most skillful malicious programmers to write all the *non*-TCB parts. Since the TCB handles all the security, there is nothing the malicious non-TCB parts can do to impair the correct security policy enforcement of the TCB. This definition gives you a sense that the TCB forms the fortress-like shell that protects whatever in the system needs protection. But the analogy also clarifies the meaning of *trusted* in *trusted operating system*: Our trust in the security of the whole system depends on the TCB.

It is easy to see that it is essential for the TCB to be both correct and complete. Thus, to understand how to design a good TCB, we focus on the division between the TCB and non-TCB elements of the operating system and spend our effort on ensuring the correctness of the TCB.

TCB Functions

Just what constitutes the TCB? We can answer this question by listing system elements on which security enforcement could depend:

- *hardware*, including processors, memory, registers, and I/O devices
- some notion of *processes*, so that we can separate and protect security-critical processes
- primitive *files*, such as the security access control database and identification/authentication data
- *protected memory*, so that the reference monitor can be protected against tampering
- some *interprocess communication*, so that different parts of the TCB can pass data to and activate other parts. For example, the reference monitor can invoke and pass data securely to the audit routine.

It may seem as if this list encompasses most of the operating system, but in fact the TCB is only a small subset. For example, although the TCB requires access to files of enforcement data, it does not need an entire file structure of hierarchical directories, virtual devices, indexed files, and multidevice files. Thus, the TCB might contain a primitive file manager to handle only the small, simple files needed for the TCB. The more complex file manager to provide externally visible files could be outside the TCB. Figure 5-13 shows a typical division into TCB and non-TCB sections.

The TCB, which must maintain the secrecy and integrity of each domain, monitors four basic interactions.

- *Process activation.* In a multiprogramming environment, activation and deactivation of processes occur frequently. Changing from one process to another requires a complete change of registers, relocation maps, file access lists, process status information, and other pointers, much of which is security-sensitive information.

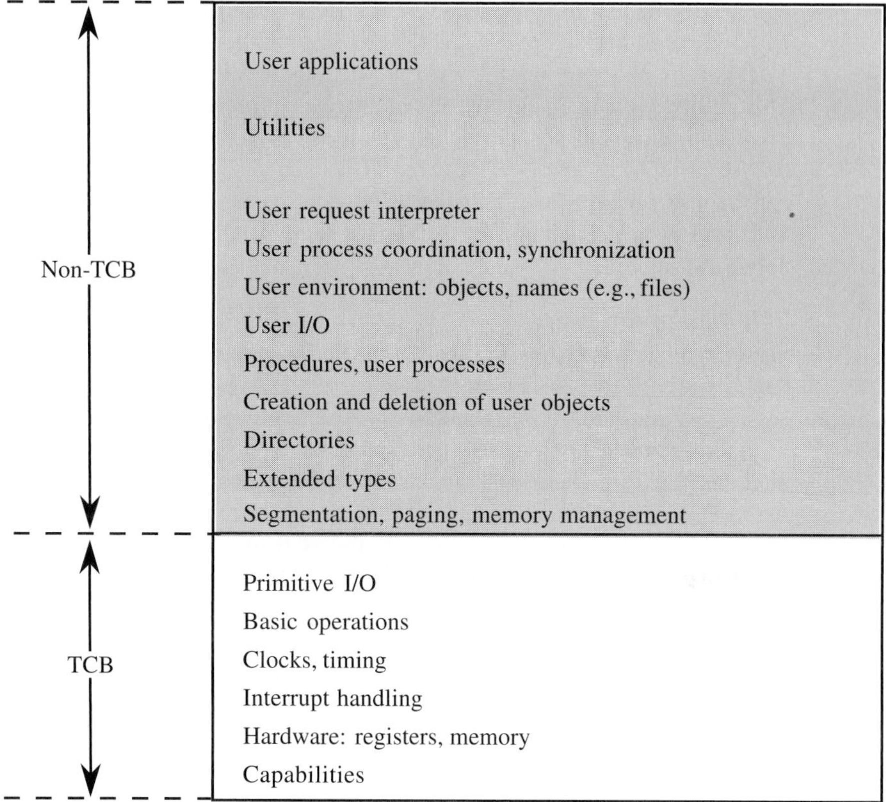

FIGURE 5-13 TCB and Non-TCB Code.

- *Execution domain switching.* Processes running in one domain often invoke processes in other domains to obtain more sensitive data or services.
- *Memory protection.* Because each domain includes code and data stored in memory, the TCB must monitor memory references to ensure secrecy and integrity for each domain.
- *I/O operation.* In some systems, software is involved with each character transferred in an I/O operation. This software connects a user program in the outermost domain to an I/O device in the innermost (hardware) domain. Thus, I/O operations can cross all domains.

TCB Design

The division of the operating system into TCB and non-TCB aspects is convenient for designers and developers because it means that all security-relevant code is located in one (logical) part. But the distinction is more than just logical. To ensure that the security enforcement cannot be affected by non-TCB code, TCB code must run in some protected state that distinguishes it. Thus, the structuring into TCB and non-TCB must be done consciously. However, once this structuring has been done, code outside the TCB can be changed at will, without affecting the TCB's ability to enforce security. This ability to change helps developers because it means that major sections of the operating system—utilities, device drivers, user interface managers, and the like—can be revised or replaced any time; only the TCB code must be controlled more carefully. Finally, for anyone evaluating the security of a trusted operating system, a division into TCB and non-TCB simplifies evaluation substantially, because non-TCB code need not be considered.

TCB Implementation

Security-related activities are likely to be performed in different places. Security is potentially related to every memory access, every I/O operation, every file or program access, every initiation or termination of a user, and every interprocess communication. In modular operating systems, these separate activities can be handled in independent modules. Each of these separate modules, then, has both security-related and other functions.

Collecting all security functions into the TCB may destroy the modularity of an existing operating system. A unified TCB may also be too large to be analyzed easily. Nevertheless, a designer may decide to separate the security functions of an existing operating system, creating a security kernel. This form of kernel is depicted in Figure 5-14.

A more sensible approach is to design the security kernel first and then design the operating system around it. This technique was used by Honeywell in the design of a

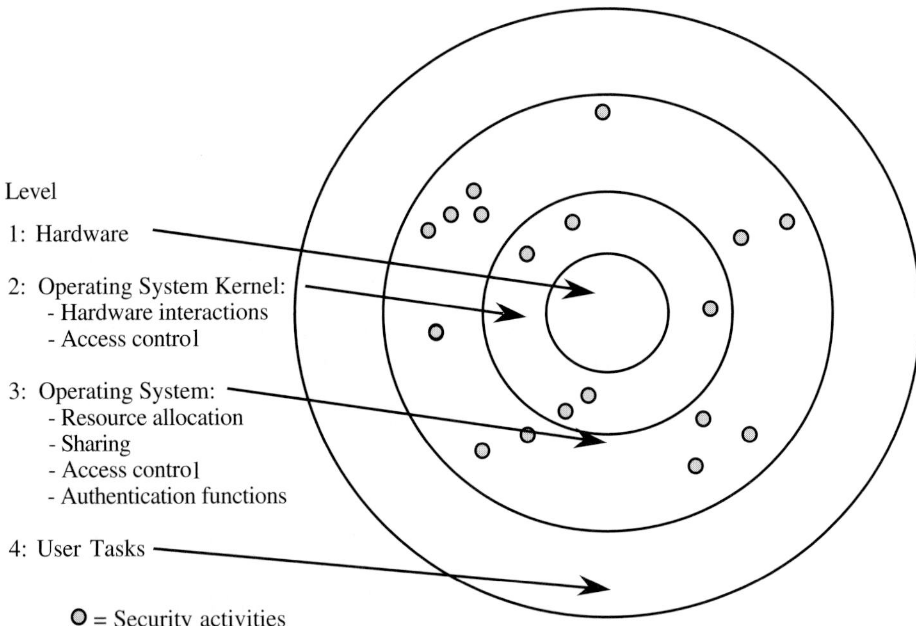

FIGURE 5-14 Combined Security Kernel/Operating System.

prototype for its secure operating system, Scomp. That system contained only twenty modules to perform the primitive security functions, and it consisted of fewer than 1,000 lines of higher-level-language source code. Once the actual security kernel of Scomp was built, its functions grew to contain approximately 10,000 lines of code.

In a security-based design, the security kernel forms an interface layer, just atop system hardware. The security kernel monitors all operating system hardware accesses and performs all protection functions. The security kernel, which relies on support from hardware, allows the operating system itself to handle most functions not related to security. In this way, the security kernel can be small and efficient. As a byproduct of this partitioning, computing systems have at least three execution domains: security kernel, operating system, and user. See Figure 5-15.

Separation/Isolation

Recall from Chapter 4 that Rushby and Randell [RUS83] list four ways to separate one process from others: physical separation, temporal separation, cryptographic separation, and logical separation. With **physical separation**, two different processes use two different hardware facilities. For example, sensitive computation may be performed on a reserved computing system; nonsensitive tasks are run on a public system. Hardware separation offers several attractive features, including support for multiple independent threads of execution, memory protection, mediation of I/O, and at least three different degrees of execution privilege. **Temporal separation** occurs when different processes are run at different times. For instance, some military systems run nonsensitive jobs be-

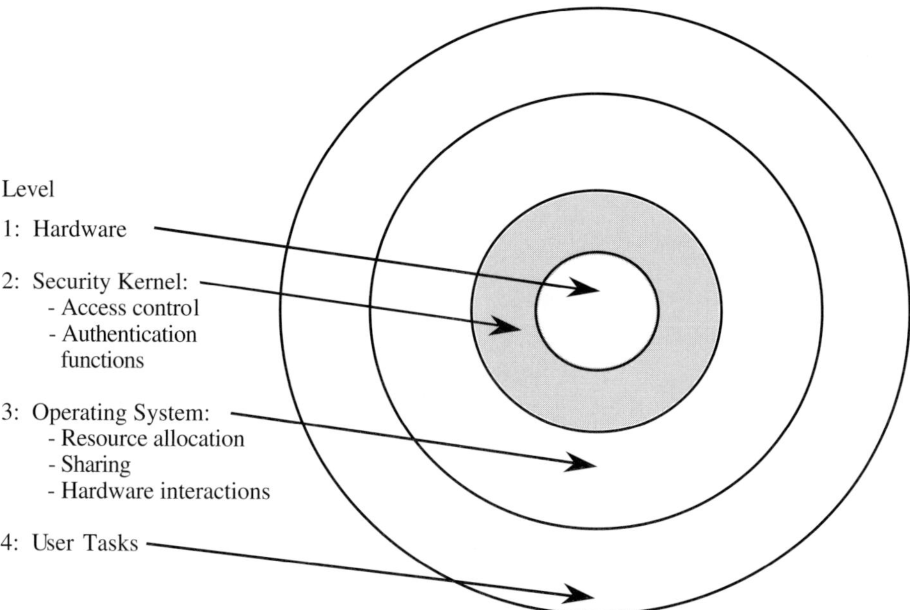

FIGURE 5-15 Separate Security Kernel.

tween 8:00 a.m. and noon, with sensitive computation only from noon to 5:00 p.m. Encryption is used for **cryptographic separation**, so two different processes can be run at the same time because unauthorized users cannot access sensitive data in a readable form. **Logical separation**, also called **isolation**, is provided when a process such as a reference monitor separates one user's objects from those of another user. Secure computing systems have been built with each of these forms of separation.

Multiprogramming operating systems should isolate each user from all others, allowing only carefully controlled interactions between the users. Most operating systems are designed to provide a single environment for all. In other words, one copy of the operating system is available for use by many users, as shown in Figure 5-16. The operating system is often separated into two distinct pieces, located at the highest and lowest addresses of memory.

Virtualization

Virtualization is a powerful tool for trusted system designers because it allows users to access complex objects in a carefully controlled manner. By **virtualization** we mean that the operating system emulates or simulates a collection of a computer system's resources. We say that a **virtual machine** is a collection of real or simulated hardware facilities: a [central] processor that runs an instruction set, an amount of directly addressable storage, and some I/O devices. These facilities support the execution of programs.

Obviously, virtual resources must be supported by real hardware or software, but the real resources do not have to be the same as the simulated ones. There are many examples of this type of simulation. For instance, printers are often simulated on direct access devices for sharing in multiuser environments. Several small disks can be simu-

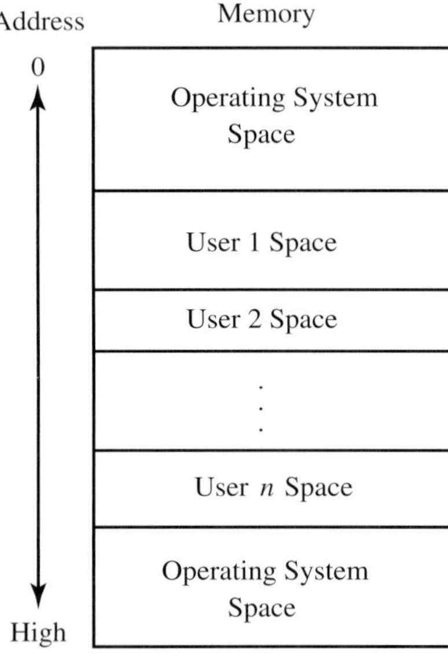

FIGURE 5-16 Conventional Multiuser Operating System Memory.

lated with one large one. With demand paging, some noncontiguous memory can support a much larger contiguous virtual memory space. And it is common even on PCs to simulate space on slower disks with faster memory. In these ways, the operating system provides the virtual resource to the user, while the security kernel precisely controls user accesses.

Multiple Virtual Memory Spaces

The IBM MVS/ESA operating system uses virtualization to provide logical separation that gives the user the impression of physical separation. IBM MVS/ESA is a paging system such that each user's logical address space is separated from that of other users by the page mapping mechanism. Additionally, MVS/ESA includes the operating system in each user's logical address space, so a user runs on what seems to be a complete, separate machine.

Most paging systems present to a user only the user's virtual address space; the operating system is outside the user's virtual addressing space. However, the operating system is part of the logical space of each MVS/ESA user. Therefore, to the user MVS/ESA seems like a single-user system, as shown in Figure 5-17.

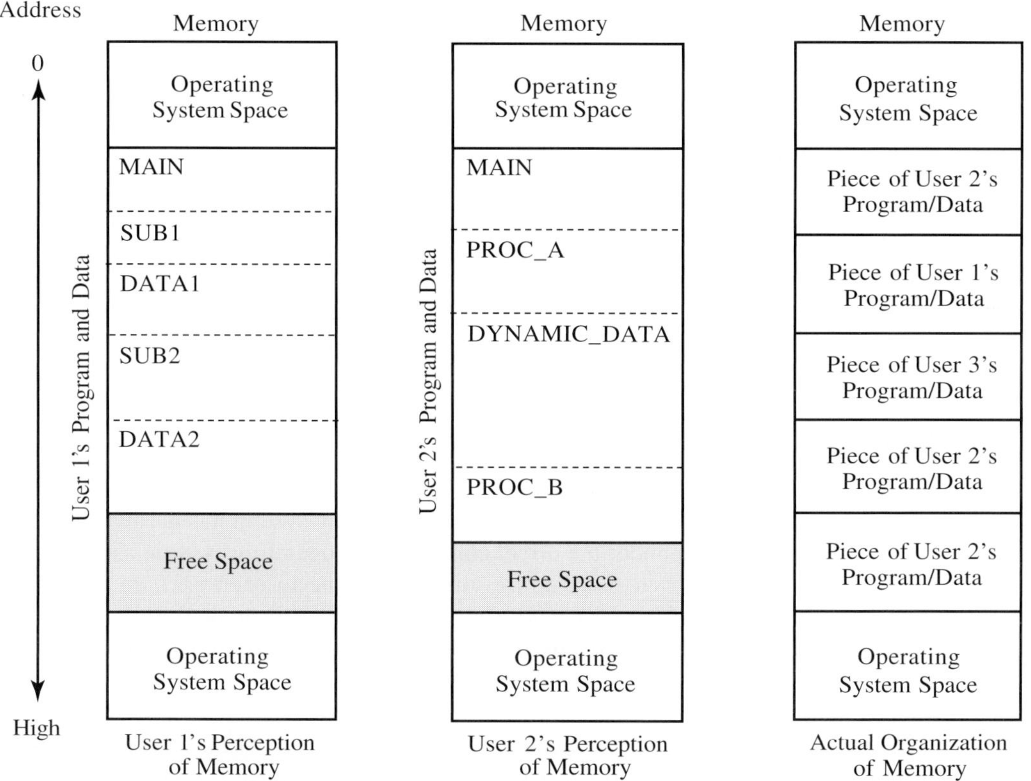

FIGURE 5-17 Multiple Virtual Addressing Spaces.

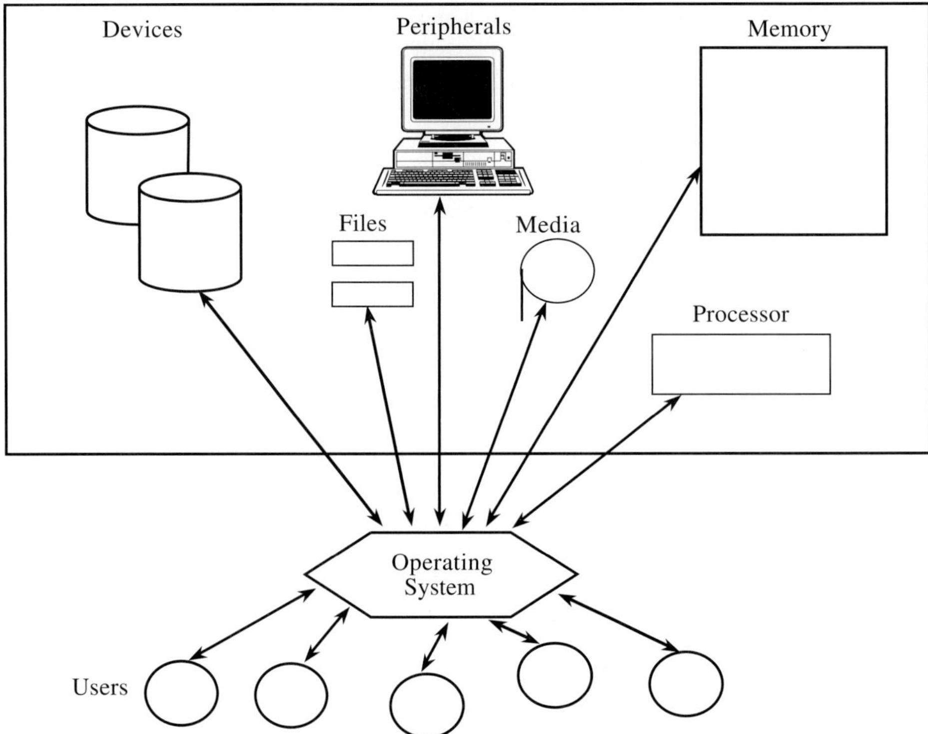

FIGURE 5-18 Conventional Operating System.

A primary advantage of MVS/ESA is memory management. Each user's virtual memory space can be as large as total addressable memory, in excess of 16 million bytes. And protection is a second advantage of this representation of memory. Because each user's logical address space includes the operating system, the user's perception is of running on a separate machine, which could even be true.

Virtual Machines

The IBM Processor Resources/System Manager (PR/SM) system provides a level of protection that is stronger still. A conventional operating system has hardware facilities and devices that are under the direct control of the operating system, as shown in Figure 5-18. PR/SM provides an entire virtual machine to each user, so that each user has not only logical memory but also logical I/O devices, logical files, and other logical resources. PR/SM performs this feat by strictly separating resources. (The PR/SM system is not a conventional operating system, as we will see later in this chapter.)

The PR/SM system is a natural extension of the concept of virtual memory. Virtual *memory* gives the user a memory space that is logically separated from real memory; a virtual memory space is usually larger than real memory, as well. A virtual *machine*

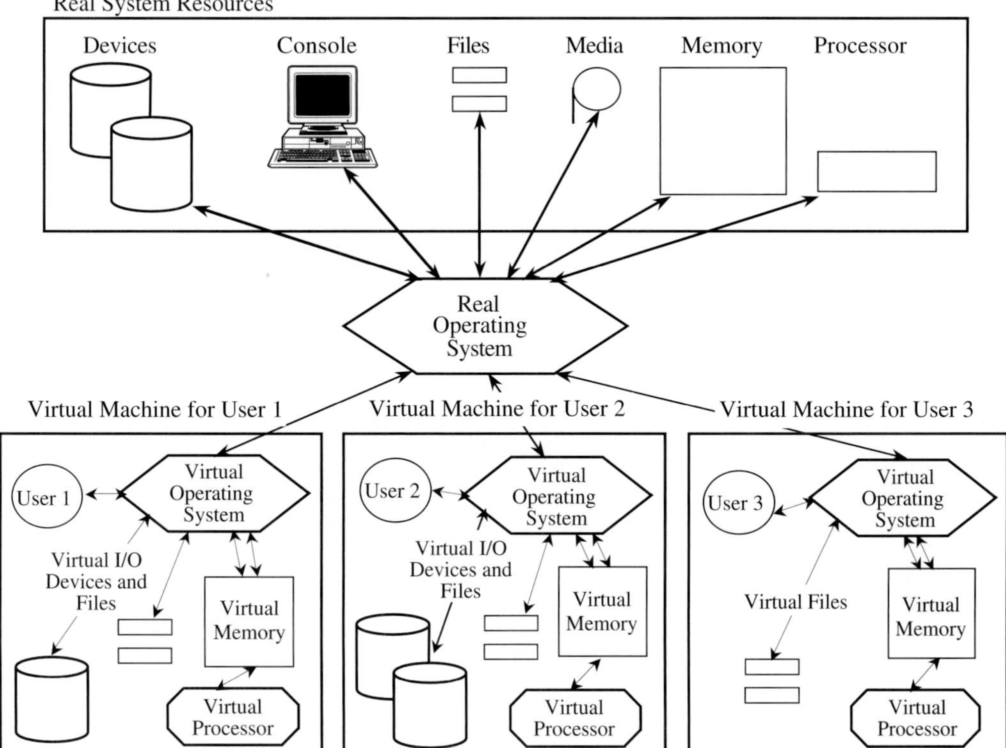

FIGURE 5-19 Virtual Machine.

gives the user a full set of hardware features, that is, a complete machine that may be substantially different from the real machine. These virtual hardware resources are also logically separated from those of other users. The relationship of virtual machines to real ones is shown in Figure 5-19.

Both MVS/ESA and PR/SM improve the isolation of each user from other users and from the hardware of the system. Of course, this added complexity increases the overhead incurred with these levels of translation and protection. In the next section we study alternative designs that reduce the complexity of providing security in an operating system.

Layered Design

As described previously, a kernelized operating system consists of at least four levels: hardware, kernel, operating system, and user. Each of these layers can itself include sublayers. For example, in [SCH83b], the kernel has five distinct layers. At the user level, it is not uncommon to have quasi-system programs, such as database managers or user interface shells, that constitute separate layers of security themselves.

Layered Trust

As we have seen earlier in this chapter (in Figure 5-15), the layered view of a secure operating system can be depicted as a series of concentric circles, with the most sensitive operations in the innermost layers. Then, the trustworthiness and access rights of a process can be judged by the process's proximity to the center: The more trusted processes are closer to the center. But we can also depict the trusted operating system in layers as a stack, with the security functions closest to the hardware. Such a system is shown in Figure 5-20.

In this design, some activities related to protection functions are performed outside the security kernel. For example, user authentication may include accessing a password table, challenging the user to supply a password, verifying the correctness of the password, and so forth. The disadvantage of performing all of these operations inside the security kernel is that some of them (such as formatting the user–terminal interaction and searching for the user in a table of known users) do not warrant high security.

Alternatively, we can implement a single logical function in several different modules; we call this a **layered design**. Trustworthiness and access rights are the basis of the layering. In other words, a single function may be performed by a set of modules operating in different layers, as shown in Figure 5-21. The modules of each layer perform operations of a certain degree of sensitivity.

Neumann [NEU86] describes the layered structure used for the Provably Secure Operating System (PSOS). As shown in Table 5-4, some lower-level layers present

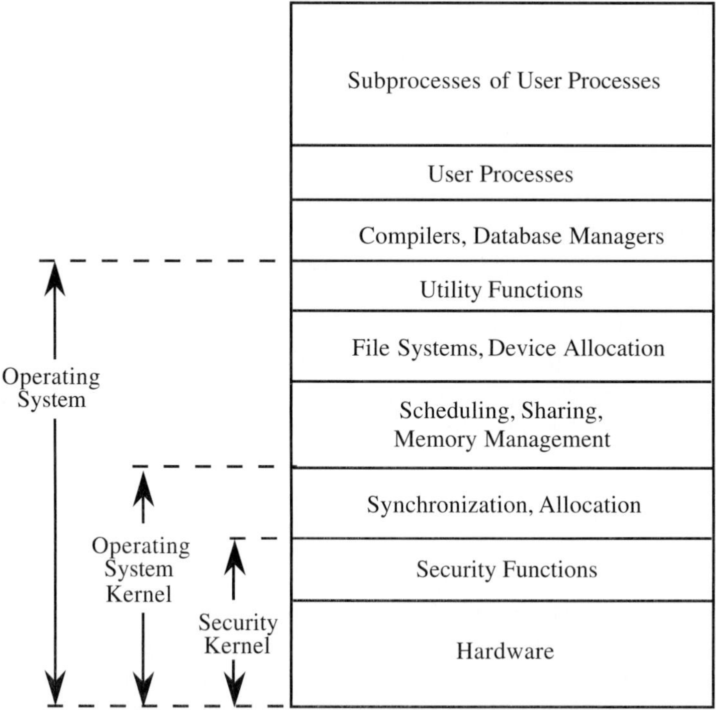

FIGURE 5-20 Layered Operating System.

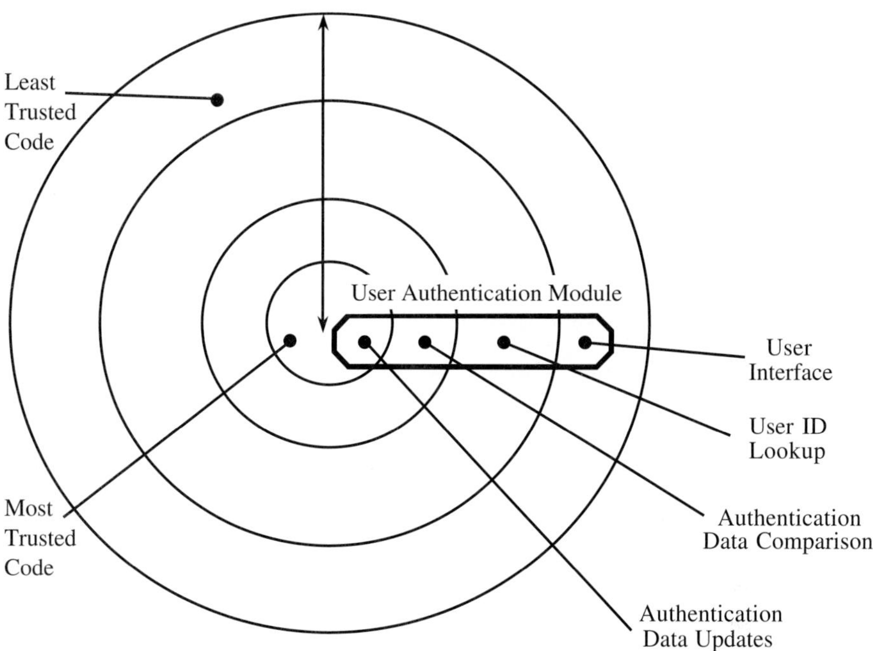

FIGURE 5-21 Modules Operating in Different Layers.

some or all of their functionality to higher levels, but each layer properly encapsulates those things below itself.

A layered approach is another way to achieve encapsulation, discussed in Chapter 3. Layering is recognized as a good operating system design. Each layer uses the more central layers as services, and each layer provides a certain level of functionality to the layers farther out. In this way, we can "peel off" each layer and still have a logically complete system with less functionality. Layering presents a good example of how to trade off and balance design characteristics.

Another justification for layering is damage control. To see why, consider Neumann's [NEU86] two examples of risk, shown in Tables 5-5 and 5-6. In a conventional, nonhierarchically designed system (shown in Table 5-5), any problem—hardware failure, software flaw, or unexpected condition, even in a supposedly non-security-relevant portion—can cause disaster because the effect of the problem is unbounded and because the system's design means that we cannot be confident that any given function has no (indirect) security effect.

By contrast, as shown in Table 5-6, hierarchical structuring has two benefits:

- Hierarchical structuring permits identification of the most critical parts, which can then be analyzed intensely for correctness, so that the number of problems should be smaller.
- Isolation limits effects of problems to the hierarchical levels at and above the point of the problem, so that the effects of many problems should be confined.

TABLE 5-4 PSOS Design Hierarchy.

Level	Function	Hidden by Level	Visible to User
16	User request interpreter		Yes
15	User environments and name spaces		Yes
14	User I/O		Yes
13	Procedure records		Yes
12	User processes and visible I/O		Yes
11	Creation and deletion of user objects		Yes
10	Directories	11	Partially
9	Extended types	11	Partially
8	Segments	11	Partially
7	Paging	8	No
6	System processes and I/O	12	No
5	Primitive I/O	6	No
4	Arithmetic and other basic operations		Yes
3	Clocks	6	No
2	Interrupts	6	No
1	Registers and addressable memory	7	Partially
0	Capabilities		Yes

From [NEU86], © IEEE, 1986. Used with permission.

These design properties—the kernel, separation, isolation, and hierarchical structure—have been the basis for many trustworthy system prototypes. They have stood the test of time as best design and implementation practices. (They are also being used in a different form of trusted operating system, as described in Sidebar 5-5.)

In the next section, we look at what gives us confidence in an operating system's security.

TABLE 5-5 Conventionally (Nonhierarchically) Designed System.

Level	Functions	Risk
All	Noncritical functions	Disaster possible
All	Less critical functions	Disaster possible
All	Most critical functions	Disaster possible

TABLE 5-6 Hierarchically Designed System.

Level	Functions	Risk
2	Noncritical functions	Few disasters likely from noncritical software
1	Less critical functions	Some failures possible from less critical functions, but because of separation, effect limited
0	Most critical functions	Disasters possible but unlikely if system simple enough to be analyzed extensively

5.5 ASSURANCE IN TRUSTED OPERATING SYSTEMS

This chapter has moved our discussion from the general to the particular. We began by studying different models of protection systems. By the time we reached the last section, we examined three principles—isolation, security kernel, and layered structure—used in designing secure operating systems, and we looked in detail at the approaches taken by designers of particular operating systems. Now, we suppose that an operating system provider has taken these considerations into account and claims to have a secure design. It is time for us to consider **assurance**, ways of convincing others that a model, design, and implementation are correct.

What does it mean to have confidence in the security features of an operating system? That is, what justifies our confidence in the system? And if someone else has evaluated the system, how have the confidence levels of operating systems been rated? In our assessment, we must recognize that operating systems are used in different environments; in some applications, less secure operating systems may be acceptable. Overall, then, we need ways of determining whether a particular operating system is

Sidebar 5-5 An Operating System for the Untrusting

The U.K. Regulation of Investigatory Powers Act (RIPA) was intended to broaden government surveillance capabilities, but privacy advocates worry that it can permit too much government eavesdropping.

Peter Fairbrother, a British mathematician, is programming a new operating system he calls M-o-o-t to keep the government at bay by carrying separation to the extreme. As described in *The New Scientist* [KNI02], Fairbrother's design has all sensitive data stored in encrypted form on servers outside the U.K. government's jurisdiction. Encrypted communications will protect the file transfers from server to computer and back again. Each encryption key will be used only once and won't be known by the user. Under RIPA the government will have the power to require any user to produce the key for any message that user has encrypted. But if the user does not know the key, the user cannot surrender it.

Fairbrother admits that in the wrong hands M-o-o-t could benefit criminals, but he thinks the personal privacy benefits outweigh this harm.

appropriate for a certain set of needs. Both in Chapter 4 and in the previous section, we looked at design and process techniques for building confidence in the quality and correctness of a system. In this section, we explore ways to actually demonstrate the security of an operating system, using techniques such as testing, formal verification, and informal validation.

Typical Operating System Flaws

Periodically throughout our analysis of operating system security features, we have used the phrase "exploit a vulnerability." Throughout the years, many vulnerabilities have been uncovered in many operating systems. They have gradually been corrected, and the body of knowledge about likely weak spots has grown.

Known Vulnerabilities

In this section, we discuss typical vulnerabilities that have been uncovered in operating systems. Our goal is not to provide a "how to" guide for potential penetrators of operating systems. Rather, we study these flaws to understand the careful analysis necessary in designing and testing operating systems.

I/O processing is the largest single source of operating system vulnerabilities, for several reasons:

- I/O is performed by independent, intelligent hardware subsystems. (A so-called intelligent device can take some independent action on its own, such as reordering disk requests to optimize head movement or executing a series of I/O operations asynchronously from the central processor.) These independent units often fall outside the security kernel or security restrictions implemented by an operating system.
- The code to perform I/O is often much more complex and much more dependent on the specific device hardware than code for any other component of the computing system. For these reasons, it is harder to review I/O device drivers, access code, and service routines for correctness, let alone to verify them formally.
- I/O activity sometimes bypasses other operating system functions, such as page or segment address translation, in the interest of fast data transfer. Thus, it may also bypass the protection features associated with those functions.
- I/O operations are often character oriented. Again, in the interest of fast data transfer, the operating systems designers may have tried to take shortcuts by limiting the number of instructions executed by the operating system during actual data transfer. Sometimes the instructions eliminated are those that enforce security policies as each character is transferred.

A second prominent weakness in operating system security reflects an *ambiguity in access policy*. On one hand, we want to separate users and protect their individual resources. On the other hand, users depend on shared access to libraries, utility programs, common data, and system tables. The distinction between isolation and sharing is not always clear at the policy level, so the distinction cannot be sharply drawn at implementation.

A third potential problem area is *incomplete mediation*. Recall that Saltzer [SAL74] recommended an operating system design in which every requested access was checked for proper authorization. However, some systems check access only once per I/O operation, per process execution, or per machine interval. The mechanism is available to implement full protection, but the policy decision on when to invoke the mechanism is not complete. Therefore, in the absence of any explicit requirement, system designers adopt the "most efficient" enforcement, that is, the one that will lead to the least use of machine resources.

Generality is a fourth protection weakness, especially among commercial operating systems for large computing systems. Implementers try to provide a means for users to customize their operating system installation and to allow installation of software packages written by other companies. Some of these packages, which operate as part of the operating system themselves, must execute with the same access privileges as the operating system. For example, there are programs that provide stricter access control than the standard control available from the operating system. The "hooks" by which these packages are installed are also trapdoors for any user to penetrate the operating system.

Thus, there are several well-known points of security weakness common to many commercial operating systems. Let us consider several examples of actual vulnerabilities that have been exploited to penetrate operating systems.

Examples of Exploitations

Earlier, we discussed why I/O is a weak point in many major operating systems. We begin our examples by exploring this weakness in greater detail. On some systems, after access has been checked to initiate an I/O operation, the operation continues without subsequent checking, leading to classic time-of-check to time-of-use flaws. Checking access permission with each character transferred is a substantial overhead for the protection system. The I/O command often resides in the user's memory space. Any user can alter the source or destination address of the command after the I/O operation has commenced. Because access has already been checked once, the new address will be used without further checking—it is not checked each time a piece of data is transferred. By exploiting this flaw, users have been able to transfer data to or from any memory address they desire. Similarly, in demand paging systems, when I/O begins, a memory page frame may be occupied by data from one user, for whom I/O is performed. However, while the I/O is in progress, the system may reassign that page frame to another user without necessarily notifying the I/O subsystem. Complete mediation would have prevented these attacks.

I/O can also be involved in other ways in malicious behavior. For instance, knowing that the operating system uses a common system buffer to retain data scheduled for delivery to all users, any user can search this buffer and extract data that would have been more carefully protected if they had been transferred to the user. In a particular attack, the data were for user authentication, showing user IDs and passwords waiting to be read and validated by the operating system. Again, complete mediation would have eliminated this vulnerability.

Another example of exploitation involves a procedural problem. In one system a special supervisor function was reserved for the installation of other security packages.

When executed, this supervisor call returned control to the user in privileged mode. The operations allowable in that mode were not monitored closely, so the supervisor call could be used for access control or for any other high-security system access. The particular supervisor call required some effort to execute, but it was fully available on the system. Additional checking should have been used to authenticate the program executing the supervisor request. As an alternative, the access rights for any subject entering under that supervisor request could have been limited to the objects necessary to perform the function of the added program.

The time-of-check to time-of-use mismatch described in Chapter 3 can introduce security problems, too. In an attack based on this vulnerability, access permission is checked for a particular user to access an object, such as a buffer. But between the time the access is approved and the access actually occurs, the user changes the designation of the object, so that instead of accessing the approved object, the user now accesses another, unacceptable, one.

Other penetrations have occurred by exploitation of more complex combinations of vulnerabilities. In general, however, security flaws in trusted operating systems have resulted from a faulty analysis of a complex situation, such as I/O, or from an ambiguity or omission in the security policy. When simple security mechanisms are used to implement clear and complete security policies, the number of penetrations falls dramatically.

Assurance Methods

Once we understand the potential vulnerabilities in a system, we can apply assurance techniques to seek out the vulnerabilities and mitigate or eliminate their effects. In this section, we consider three such techniques, showing how they give us confidence in a system's correctness: testing, verification, and validation. None of these is complete or foolproof, and each has advantages and disadvantages. However, used with understanding, each can play an important role in deriving overall assurance of the systems' security.

Testing

Testing is the most widely accepted assurance technique. As Boebert [BOE92] observes, conclusions from testing are based on the actual product being evaluated, not on some abstraction or precursor of the product. This realism is a security advantage. However, conclusions based on testing are necessarily limited, for the following reasons:

- Testing can demonstrate the *existence* of a problem, but passing tests does not demonstrate the absence of problems.
- It is hard to achieve adequate test coverage within reasonable time or effort because the combinatorial explosion of inputs and internal states makes testing very complex.
- Testing based only on observable effects, not on the internal structure of a product, does not ensure any degree of completeness.

- Testing based on the internal structure of a product involves modifying the product by adding code to extract and display internal states. That extra functionality affects the product's behavior and can itself be a source of vulnerabilities or mask other vulnerabilities.
- In testing real-time systems, it is difficult to keep track of all states and triggers. This problem makes it hard to reproduce and analyze problems reported as testers proceed.

Ordinarily, we think of testing in terms of the developer: unit testing a module, integration testing to ensure that modules function properly together, function testing to trace correctness across all aspects of a given function, and system testing to combine hardware with software. Likewise, regression testing is performed to make sure a change to one part of a system does not degrade any other functionality. But for other tests, including acceptance tests, the user or customer administers tests to determine if what was ordered is what is delivered. Thus, an important aspect of assurance is considering whether the tests run are appropriate for the application and level of security. The nature and kinds of testing reflect the developer's testing strategy: which tests address what issues.

Similarly, it is important to recognize that testing is almost always constrained by a project's budget and schedule. The constraints usually mean that testing is incomplete in some way. For this reason, we consider notions of test coverage, test completeness, and testing effectiveness in a testing strategy. The more complete and effective our testing, the more confidence we have in the software. More information on testing can be found in Pfleeger [PFL01].

Penetration Testing

A testing strategy often used in computer security is called **penetration testing**, **tiger team analysis**, or **ethical hacking**. In this approach, a team of experts in the use and design of operating systems tries to crack the system being tested. (See, for example, [RUB01] or [PAL01].) The tiger team knows well the typical vulnerabilities in operating systems and computing systems, as described in previous sections and chapters. With this knowledge, the team attempts to identify and exploit the system's particular vulnerabilities.

Using penetration testing is much like asking a mechanic to look over a used car on a sales lot. The mechanic knows potential weak spots and checks as many of them as possible. There is likelihood that the mechanic will find a problem, but finding a problem (and fixing it) is no guarantee that no other problems are lurking in other parts of the system. For instance, if the mechanic checks the fuel system, the cooling system, and the brakes, there is no guarantee that the muffler is good. In the same way, an operating system that fails a penetration test is known to have faults, but a system that does not fail is not guaranteed to be fault-free. Nevertheless, penetration testing is useful and often finds faults that might have been overlooked by other forms of testing. One possible reason for the success of penetration testing is its use under real-life conditions. Users often exercise a system in ways that its designers never anticipated or intended.

So penetration testers can exploit this real-life environment and knowledge to make certain kinds of problems visible.

Formal Verification

The most rigorous method of analyzing security is through formal verification. Formal verification uses rules of mathematical logic to demonstrate that a system has certain security properties. In formal verification, the operating system is modeled and the operating system principles are described as assertions. The collection of models and assertions is viewed as a theorem, which is then proven. The theorem asserts that the operating system is correct. That is, formal verification confirms that the operating system provides the security features it should and nothing else.

Proving correctness of an entire operating system is a formidable task, often requiring months or even years of effort by several people. Computer programs called **theorem provers** can assist in this effort, although much human activity is still needed. The amount of work required and the methods used are well beyond the scope of this book. However, we illustrate the general principle of verification by presenting a simple example that uses proofs of correctness. You can find more extensive coverage of this topic in [BOW95], [CHE81], [GRI81], [HAN76], [PFL01], and [SAI96].

Consider the flow diagram of Figure 5-22, illustrating the logic in a program to determine the smallest of a set of n values, $A[1]$ through $A[n]$. The flow chart has a single

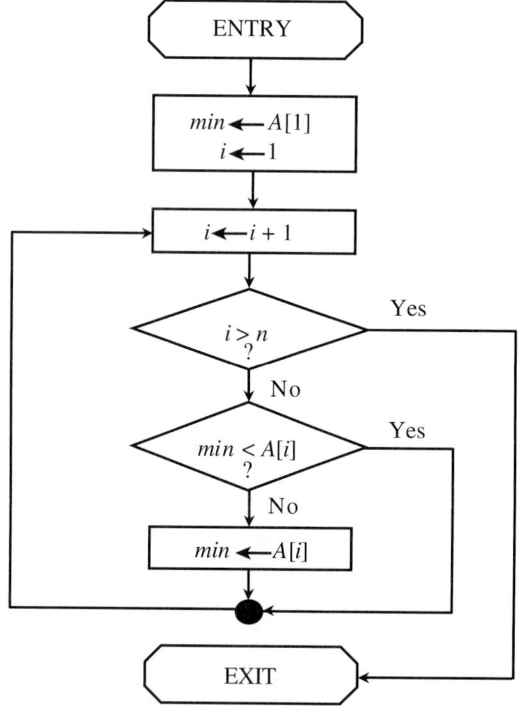

FIGURE 5-22 Flow Diagram for Finding the Minimum Value.

identified beginning point, a single identified ending point, and five internal blocks, including an if-then structure and a loop.

In program verification, we rewrite the program as a series of assertions about the program's variables and values. The initial assertion is a statement of conditions on entry to the module. Next, we identify a series of intermediate assertions associated with the work of the module. We also determine an ending assertion, a statement of the expected result. Finally, we show that the initial assertion leads logically to the intermediate assertions that in turn lead logically to the ending assertion.

We can formally verify the example in Figure 5-22 by using four assertions. The first assertion, *P*, is a statement of initial conditions, assumed to be true on entry to the procedure.

$$n > 0 \qquad (P)$$

The second assertion, *Q*, is the result of applying the initialization code in the first box.

$$\begin{aligned} &n > 0 \text{ and} \\ &1 \le i \le n \text{ and} \\ &min \le \mathrm{A}[1] \end{aligned} \qquad (Q)$$

The third assertion, *R*, is the loop assertion. It asserts what is true at the start of each iteration of the loop.

$$\begin{aligned} &n > 0 \text{ and} \\ &1 \le i \le n \text{ and} \\ &\text{for all } j,\ 1 \le j \le i-1,\ min \le A[j] \end{aligned} \qquad (R)$$

The final assertion, *S*, is the concluding assertion, the statement of conditions true at the time the loop exit occurs.

$$\begin{aligned} &n > 0 \text{ and} \\ &i = n + 1 \text{ and} \\ &\text{for all } j,\ 1 \le j \le n,\ min \le A[j] \end{aligned} \qquad (S)$$

These four assertions, shown in Figure 5-23, capture the essence of the flow chart. The next step in the verification process involves showing the logical progression of these four assertions. That is, we must show that, assuming *P* is true on entry to this procedure, *Q* is true after completion of the initialization section, *R* is true the first time the loop is entered, *R* is true each time through the loop, and the truth of *R* implies that *S* is true at the termination of the loop.

Clearly, *Q* follows from *P* and the semantics of the two statements in the second box. When we enter the loop for the first time, $i = 2$, so $i - 1 = 1$. Thus, the assertion about *min* applies only for $j = 1$, which follows from *Q*. To prove that *R* remains true with each execution of the loop, we can use the principle of mathematical induction. The basis of the induction is that *R* was true the first time through the loop. With each iteration of the loop the value of *i* increases by 1, so it is necessary to show only that $min \le A[i]$ for this new value of *i*. That proof follows from the meaning of the compari-

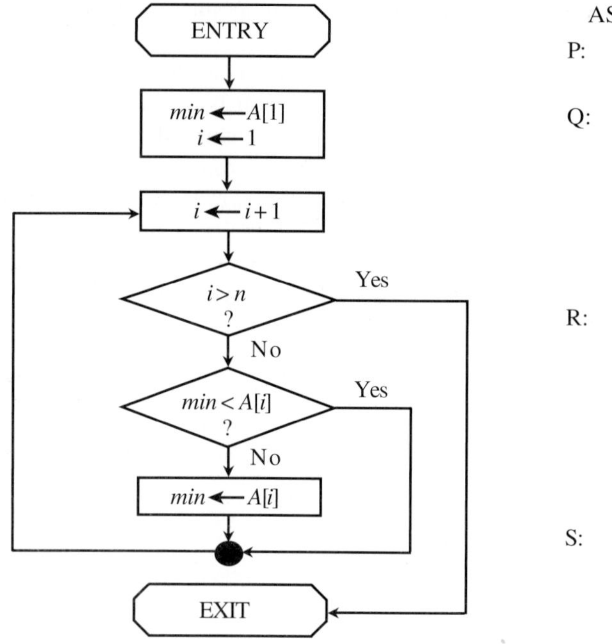

ASSERTIONS

P: $n > 0$

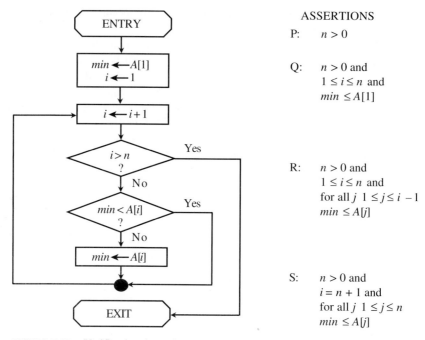

Q: $n > 0$ and $1 \le i \le n$ and $min \le A[1]$

R: $n > 0$ and $1 \le i \le n$ and for all j $1 \le j \le i - 1$ $min \le A[j]$

S: $n > 0$ and $i = n + 1$ and for all j $1 \le j \le n$ $min \le A[j]$

FIGURE 5-23 Verification Assertions.

son and replacement statements. Therefore, *R* is true with each iteration of the loop. Finally, *S* follows from the final iteration value of *R*. This step completes the formal verification that this flow chart exits with the smallest value of $A[1]$ through $A[n]$ in *min*.

The algorithm (*not* the verification) shown here is frequently used as an example in the first few weeks of introductory programming classes. It is quite simple; in fact, after studying the algorithm for a short time, most students convince themselves that the algorithm is correct. The verification itself takes much longer to explain; it also takes far longer to write than the algorithm itself. Thus, this proof-of-correctness example highlights two principal difficulties with formal verification methods:

- *Time.* The methods of formal verification are time consuming to perform. Stating the assertions at each step and verifying the logical flow of the assertions are both slow processes.
- *Complexity.* Formal verification is a complex process. For some systems with large numbers of states and transitions, it is hopeless to try to state and verify the assertions. This situation is especially true for systems that have not been designed with formal verification in mind.

These two difficulties constrain the situations in which formal verification can be used successfully. Gerhart [GER89] succinctly describes the advantages and disadvantages of using formal methods, including proof of correctness. As Schaefer [SCH89a] points out, too often people focus so much on the formalism and on deriving a formal proof that they ignore the underlying security properties to be ensured.

Validation

Formal verification is a particular instance of the more general approach to assuring correctness: **verification**. As we have seen in Chapter 3, there are many ways to show that each of a system's functions works correctly. **Validation** is the counterpart to verification, assuring that the system developers have implemented all requirements. Thus, validation makes sure that the developer is building the right product (according to the specification), and verification checks the quality of the implementation. [PFL01] There are several different ways to validate an operating system.

- *Requirements checking.* One technique is to cross-check each operating system requirement with the system's source code or execution-time behavior. The goal is to demonstrate that the system does each thing listed in the functional requirements. This process is a narrow one, in the sense that it demonstrates only that the system does everything it should do. In security, we are equally concerned about prevention: making sure the system does *not* do the things it is not supposed to do. Requirements checking seldom addresses this aspect of requirements compliance.
- *Design and code reviews.* As described in Chapter 3, design and code reviews usually address system correctness (that is, verification). But a review can also address requirements implementation. To support validation, the reviewers scrutinize the design or the code to assure traceability from each requirement to design and code components, noting problems along the way (including faults, incorrect assumptions, incomplete or inconsistent behavior, or faulty logic). The success of this process depends on the rigor of the review.
- *System testing.* The programmers or an independent test team select data to check the system. These test data can be organized much like acceptance testing, so behaviors and data expected from reading the requirements document can be confirmed in the actual running of the system. The checking is done in a methodical manner to assure completeness.

Open Source

A debate has opened in the software development community over so-called **open source** operating systems (and other programs), ones for which the source code is freely released for public analysis. The arguments are predictable: With open source, many critics can peruse the code, presumably finding flaws, whereas closed (proprietary) source makes it more difficult for attackers to find and exploit flaws.

The Linux operating system is the prime example of open source software, although the source of its predecessor Unix was also widely available. The open source idea is catching on: According to a survey by IDG Research, reported in the *Washington Post* [CHA01], 27 percent of high-end servers now run Linux, as opposed to 41 percent for a Microsoft operating system, and open source Apache web server outruns Microsoft Internet Information Server by 63 percent to 20 percent.

Lawton [LAW02] lists additional benefits of open source:

- *Cost*: Because the source code is available to the public, if the owner charges a high fee, the public will trade the software unofficially.
- *Quality*: The code can be analyzed by many reviewers who are unrelated to the development effort or the firm that developed the software.
- *Support*: As the public finds flaws, it may also be in the best position to propose the fixes for those flaws.
- *Extensibility*: The public can readily figure how to extend code to meet new needs and can share those extensions with other users.

Opponents of public release argue that giving the attacker knowledge of the design and implementation of a piece of code allows a search for shortcomings and provides a blueprint for their exploitation. Many commercial vendors have opposed open source for years, and Microsoft is currently being quite vocal in its opposition. Craig Mundie, Senior Vice President of Microsoft, says open source software "puts at risk the continued vitality of the independent software sector." [CHA01] Microsoft favors a scheme under which it would share source code of some of its products with selected partners, while still retaining intellectual property rights. The Alexis de Tocqueville Institution argues that "terrorists trying to hack or disrupt U.S. computer networks might find it easier if the Federal government attempts to switch to 'open source' as some groups propose," citing threats against air traffic control or surveillance systems [BRO02].

But noted computer security researchers argue that open or closed source is not the real issue to examine. Marcus Ranum, President of Network Flight Recorder, has said, "I don't think making [software] open source contributes to making it better at all. What makes good software is single-minded focus." Eugene Spafford of Purdue University [LAW02] agrees, saying, "What really determines whether it is trustable is quality and care. Was it designed well? Was it built using proper tools? Did the people who built it use discipline and not add a lot of features?" Ross Anderson of Cambridge University [AND02] argues that "there are more pressing security problems for the open source community. The interaction between security and openness is entangled with attempts to use security mechanisms for commercial advantage, to entrench monopolies, to control copyright, and above all to control interoperability."

Anderson presents a statistical model of reliability that shows that after open or closed testing the two approaches are equivalent in expected failure rate. This is an initial result, and more work is required to develop both theoretical and empirical results on the quality of these two approaches.

Evaluation

Most system consumers (that is, users or system purchasers) are not security experts. They need the security functions, but they are not usually capable of verifying the accuracy or adequacy of test coverage, checking the validity of a proof of correctness, or determining in any other way that a system correctly implements a security policy. Thus, it is useful (and sometimes essential) to have an independent third party evaluate an operating system's security. Independent experts can review the requirements, design, implementation, and evidence of assurance for a system. Because it is helpful to have a standard approach for an evaluation, several schemes have been devised for structuring an independent review. In this section, we examine three different approaches: from the United States, from Europe, and a scheme that combines several known approaches.

U.S. "Orange Book" Evaluation

In the late 1970s, the U.S. Department of Defense (DoD) defined a set of distinct, hierarchical levels of trust in operating systems. Published in a document [DOD85] that has become known informally as the "Orange Book," the *Trusted Computer System Evaluation Criteria* (TCSEC) provides the criteria for an independent evaluation. The National Computer Security Center (NCSC), an organization within the National Security Agency, guided and sanctioned the actual evaluations.

The levels of trust are described as four divisions, A, B, C, and D, where A has the most comprehensive degree of security. Within a division, additional distinctions are denoted with numbers; the higher numbers indicate tighter security requirements. Thus, the complete set of ratings ranging from lowest to highest assurance is D, C1, C2, B1, B2, B3, and A1. Table 5-7 (from Appendix D of [DOD85]) shows the security requirements for each of the seven evaluated classes of NCSC certification. (Class D has no requirements because it denotes minimal protection.)

The table's pattern reveals that there are really four clusters of ratings:

- D, with no requirements
- C1/C2/B1, requiring security features common to many commercial operating systems
- B2, requiring a precise proof of security of the underlying model and a narrative specification of the trusted computing base
- B3/A1, requiring more precisely proven descriptive and formal designs of the trusted computing base

These clusters do not imply that classes C1, C2, and B1 are equivalent. However, there are substantial increases of stringency between B1 and B2, and between B2 and B3 (especially in the assurance area). To see why, consider the requirements for C1, C2, and B1. An operating system developer might be able to add security measures to an existing operating system in order to qualify for these ratings. However, security must be included in the *design* of the operating system for a B2 rating. Furthermore, the design of a B3 or A1 system must begin with construction and proof of a formal *model* of security. Thus, the distinctions between B1 and B2 and between B2 and B3 are significant.

Let us look at each class of security described in the TCSEC. In our descriptions, terms in quotation marks have been taken directly from the Orange Book to convey the spirit of the evaluation criteria.

Class D: Minimal Protection

This class is applied to systems that have been evaluated for a higher category but have failed the evaluation. No security characteristics are needed for a D rating.

TABLE 5-7 Trusted Computer System Evaluation Criteria.

Criteria	D	C1	C2	B1	B2	B3	A1
Security Policy							
Discretionary access control	–	⊗	⊗	⇒	⇒	⊗	⇒
Object reuse	–	–	⊗	⇒	⇒	⇒	⇒
Labels	–	–	–	⊗	⊗	⇒	⇒
Label integrity	–	–	–	⊗	⇒	⇒	⇒
Exportation of labeled information	–	–	–	⊗	⇒	⇒	⇒
Labeling human-readable output	–	–	–	⊗	⇒	⇒	⇒
Mandatory access control	–	–	–	⊗	⊗	⇒	⇒
Subject sensitivity labels	–	–	–	–	⊗	⇒	⇒
Device labels	–	–	–	–	⊗	⇒	⇒
Accountability							
Identification and authentication	–	⊗	⊗	⊗	⇒	⇒	⇒
Audit	–	–	⊗	⊗	⊗	⊗	⇒
Trusted path	–	–	–	–	⊗	⊗	⇒
Assurance							
System architecture	–	⊗	⊗	⊗	⊗	⊗	⇒
System integrity	–	⊗	⇒	⇒	⇒	⇒	⇒
Security testing	–	⊗	⊗	⊗	⊗	⊗	⊗
Design specification and verification	–	–	–	⊗	⊗	⊗	⊗
Covert channel analysis	–	–	–	–	⊗	⊗	⊗
Trusted facility management	–	–	–	–	⊗	⊗	⇒
Configuration management	–	–	–	–	⊗	⇒	⊗
Trusted recovery	–	–	–	–	–	⊗	⇒
Trusted distribution	–	–	–	–	–	–	⊗
Documentation							
Security features user's guide	–	⊗	⇒	⇒	⇒	⇒	⇒
Trusted facility manual	–	⊗	⊗	⊗	⊗	⊗	⇒
Test documentation	–	⊗	⇒	⇒	⊗	⇒	⊗
Design documentation	–	⊗	⇒	⊗	⊗	⊗	⊗

Legend: –: no requirement; ⇒: same requirement as previous class; ⊗: additional requirement

Class C1: Discretionary Security Protection

C1 is intended for an environment of cooperating users processing data at the same level of sensitivity. A system evaluated as C1 provides a separation of users from data. There must be controls that appear sufficient to implement access limitation, to allow users to protect their own data. The controls of a C1 system may not have been stringently evaluated; the evaluation may be based more on the presence of certain features. To qualify for a C1 rating, a system must have a domain that includes security functions and that is protected against tampering. A key word in the classification is "discretionary." A user is "allowed" to decide when the controls apply, when they do not, and which named individuals or groups are allowed access.

Class C2: Controlled Access Protection

A C2 system still implements discretionary access control, although the granularity of control is finer. The audit trail must be capable of tracking each individual's access (or attempted access) to each object.

Class B1: Labeled Security Protection

All certifications in the B division include *nondiscretionary* access control. At the B1 level, each controlled subject and object must be assigned a security level. (For class B1, the protection system does not need to control every object.)

Each controlled object must be individually labeled for security level, and these labels must be used as the basis for access control decisions. The access control must be based on a model employing both hierarchical levels and nonhierarchical categories. (The military model is an example of a system with hierarchical levels—unclassified, classified, secret, top secret—and nonhierarchical categories—need-to-know category sets.) The mandatory access policy is the Bell–La Padula model. Thus, a B1 system must implement Bell–La Padula controls for all accesses, with user discretionary access controls to further limit access.

Class B2: Structured Protection

The major enhancement for B2 is a design requirement: The design and implementation of a B2 system must enable a more thorough testing and review. A verifiable top-level design must be presented, and testing must confirm that the system implements this design. The system must be internally structured into "well-defined largely independent modules." The principle of least privilege is to be enforced in the design. Access control policies must be enforced on all objects and subjects, including devices. Analysis of covert channels is required.

Class B3: Security Domains

The security functions of a B3 system must be small enough for extensive testing. A high-level design must be complete and conceptually simple, and a "convincing argument" must exist that the system implements this design. The implementation of the design must "incorporate significant use of layering, abstraction, and information hiding."

The security functions must be tamperproof. Furthermore, the system must be "highly resistant to penetration." There is also a requirement that the system audit facility be able to identify when a violation of security is imminent.

Class A1: Verified Design

Class A1 requires a formally verified system design. The capabilities of the system are the same as for class B3. But in addition there are five important criteria for class A1 certification: (1) a formal model of the protection system and a proof of its consistency and adequacy, (2) a formal top-level specification of the protection system, (3) a demonstration that the top-level specification corresponds to the model, (4) an implementation "informally" shown to be consistent with the specification, and (5) formal analysis of covert channels.

European ITSEC Evaluation

The TCSEC was developed in the United States, but representatives from several European countries also recognized the need for a criterion and methodology for evaluating security-enforcing products. The European efforts culminated in the ITSEC, the *Information Technology Security Evaluation Criteria* [ITS91b].

Origins of the ITSEC

England, Germany, and France independently began work on evaluation criteria at approximately the same time. Both England and Germany published their first drafts in 1989; France had its criteria in limited review when these three nations, joined by the Netherlands, decided to work together to develop a common criteria document. We examine Britain and Germany's efforts separately, followed by their combined output.

German Green Book

The (then West) German Information Security Agency (GISA) produced a catalog of criteria [GIS88] five years after the first use of the U.S. TCSEC. Keeping with tradition, the security community began to call the document the German Green Book because of its green cover. The German criteria identified eight basic security functions, deemed sufficient to enforce a broad spectrum of security policies:

- *identification and authentication*: unique and certain association of an identity with a subject or object
- *administration of rights*: the ability to control the assignment and revocation of access rights between subjects and objects
- *verification of rights*: mediation of the attempt of a subject to exercise rights with respect to an object
- *audit*: a record of information on the successful or attempted unsuccessful exercise of rights
- *object reuse*: resetting reusable resources in such a way that no information flow occurs in contradiction to the security policy
- *error recovery*: identification of situations from which recovery is necessary, and invocation of an appropriate action
- *continuity of service*: identification of functionality that must be available in the system and what degree of delay or loss (if any) can be tolerated

- *data communication security*: peer entity authentication, control of access to communications resources, data confidentiality, data integrity, data origin authentication, and nonrepudiation

Note that the first five of these eight functions closely resemble the U.S. TCSEC, but the last three move into entirely new areas: integrity of data, availability, and a range of communications concerns.

Like the U.S. DoD, GISA did not expect ordinary users (that is, those who were not security experts) to select appropriate sets of security functions, so ten functional classes were defined. Classes F1 through F5 corresponded closely to the functionality requirements of U.S. classes C1 through B3. (Recall that the *functionality* requirements of class A1 are identical to those of B3.) Class F6 was for high data and program integrity requirements, class F7 was appropriate for high availability, and classes F8 through F10 relate to data communications situations. The German method addressed assurance by defining eight quality levels, Q0 through Q7, corresponding roughly to the assurance requirements of U.S. TCSEC levels D through A1, respectively. For example,

- The evaluation of a Q1 system is merely intended to ensure that the implementation more or less enforces the security policy and that no major errors exist.
- The goal of a Q3 evaluation is to show that the system is largely resistant to simple penetration attempts.
- To achieve assurance level Q6, it must be formally proven that the highest specification level meets all the requirements of the formal security policy model. In addition, the source code is analyzed very precisely.

These functionality classes and assurance levels can be combined in any way, producing potentially 80 different evaluation results, as shown in Table 5-8. The region in the upper-right portion of the table represents requirements in excess of U.S. TCSEC requirements, showing higher assurance requirements for a given functionality class. Even though assurance and functionality can be combined in any way, there may be limited applicability for a low-assurance, multilevel system (e.g., F5, Q1) in usage. The Germans did not assert that all possibilities would necessarily be useful, however.

Another significant contribution of the German approach was to support evaluations by independent, commercial evaluation facilities.

British Criteria

The British criteria development was a joint activity between the U.K. Department of Trade and Industry (DTI) and the Ministry of Defence (MoD). The first public version, published in 1989 [DTI89a], was issued in several volumes.

The original U.K. criteria were based on the "claims" language, a metalanguage by which a vendor could make claims about functionality in a product. The claims language consisted of lists of action phrases and target phrases with parameters. For example, a typical action phrase might look like this:

> This *product* can [not] determine ... [using the mechanism described in paragraph *n* of this document]...

TABLE 5-8 Relationship of German and U.S. Evaluation Criteria.

	Q0	Q1	Q2	Q3	Q4	Q5	Q6	Q7
F1		=US C1						Beyond US A1
F2			=US C2					Beyond US A1
F3				=US B1				Beyond US A1
F4					=US B2			Beyond US A1
F5						=US B3	=US A1	Beyond US A1
F6	New functional class							
F7	New functional class							
F8	New functional class							
F9	New functional class							
F10	New functional class							

The parameters *product* and *n* are, obviously, replaced with specific references to the product to be evaluated. An example of a target phrase is

> … the *access-type* granted to a [*user*, *process*] in respect of a(n) *object*.

These two phrases can be combined and parameters replaced to produce a claim about a product.

> This **access control subsystem** can determine the **read access** granted to **all subjects** in respect to **system files**.

The claims language was intended to provide an open-ended structure by which a vendor could assert qualities of a product and independent evaluators could verify the truth of those claims. Because of the generality of the claims language, there was no direct correlation of U.K. and U.S. evaluation levels.

In addition to the claims language, there were six levels of assurance evaluation, numbered L1 through L6, corresponding roughly to U.S. assurance C1 through A1 or German Q1 through Q6.

The claims language was intentionally open-ended because the British felt it was impossible to predict which functionality manufacturers would choose to put in their products. In this regard, the British differed from Germany and the United States, who thought manufacturers needed to be guided to include specific functions with precise functionality requirements. The British envisioned certain popular groups of claims being combined into bundles that could be reused by many manufacturers.

The British defined and documented a scheme for Commercial Licensed Evaluation Facilities (CLEFs) [DTI89b], with precise requirements for the conduct and process of evaluation by independent commercial organizations.

Other Activities

As if these two efforts were not enough, Canada, Australia, and France were also working on evaluation criteria. The similarities among these efforts were far greater than their differences. It was as if each profited by building upon the predecessors' successes.

Three difficulties, which were really different aspects of the same problem, became immediately apparent.

- *Comparability*. It was not clear how the different evaluation criteria related. A German F2/E2 evaluation was structurally quite similar to a U.S. C2 evaluation, but an F4/E7 or F6/E3 evaluation had no direct U.S. counterpart. It was not obvious what U.K. claims would correspond to a particular U.S. evaluation level.
- *Transferability*. Would a vendor get credit for a German F2/E2 evaluation in a context requiring a U.S. C2? Would the stronger F2/E3 or F3/E2 be accepted?
- *Marketability*. Could a vendor be expected to have a product evaluated independently in the United States, Germany, Britain, Canada, and Australia? How many evaluations would a vendor support? (Many vendors suggested that they would be interested in at most one, because the evaluations were costly and time consuming.)

For reasons including these problems, Britain, Germany, France, and the Netherlands decided to pool their knowledge and synthesize of their work.

ITSEC: Information Technology Security Evaluation Criteria

In 1991 the Commission of the European Communities sponsored the work of these four nations to produce a harmonized version for use by all European Union member nations. The result was a good amalgamation.

The ITSEC preserved the German functionality classes F1–F10, while at the same time allowing the flexibility of the British claims language. There is similarly an **effectiveness** component to the evaluation, corresponding roughly to the U.S. notion of assurance and to the German E0–E7 effectiveness levels.

A vendor (or other "sponsor" of an evaluation) has to define a **target of evaluation** (TOE), the item that is the evaluation's focus. The TOE is considered in the context of an operational environment (that is, an expected set of threats) and security enforcement requirements. An evaluation can address either a *product* (in general distribution, for use in a variety of environments) or a *system* (designed and built for use in a specified setting). The sponsor or vendor states the following information.

- *system security policy* or *rationale*: why this product (or system) was built
- specification of *security-enforcing functions*: security properties of the product (or system)

- definition of the *mechanisms* of the product (or system) by which security is enforced
- a claim about the *strength* of the mechanisms
- the target *evaluation level* in terms of functionality and effectiveness

The evaluation proceeds to determine the following aspects.

- *suitability of functionality*: whether the chosen functions implement the desired security features
- *binding of functionality*: whether the chosen functions work together synergistically
- *vulnerabilities*: whether vulnerabilities exist either in the construction of the TOE or how it will work in its intended environment
- *ease of use*
- *strength of mechanism*: the ability of the TOE to withstand direct attack

The results of these subjective evaluations determine whether the evaluators agree that the product or system deserves its proposed functionality and effectiveness rating.

Significant Departures from the Orange Book

The European ITSEC offers the following significant changes compared with the Orange Book. These variations have both advantages and disadvantages, as listed in Table 5-9.

TABLE 5-9 Advantages and Disadvantages of ITSEC Approach vs. TCSEC.

Quality	Advantages of ITSEC over TCSEC	Disadvantages of ITSEC Compared with TCSEC
New functionality requirement classes	• Surpasses traditional confidentiality focus of TCSEC • Shows additional areas in which products are needed	• Complicates user's choice
Decoupling of features and assurance	• Allows low-assurance or high-assurance product	• Requires user sophistication to decide when high assurance is needed • Some functionality may inherently require high assurance but not guarantee receiving it
Permitting new feature definitions; independence from specific security policy	• Allows evaluation of any kind of security-enforcing product • Allows vendor to decide what products the market requires	• Complicates comparison of evaluations of differently described but similar products • Requires vendor to formulate requirements to highlight product's features • Preset feature bundles not necessarily hierarchical
Commercial evaluation facilities	• Subject to market forces for time, schedule, price	• Government does not have direct control of evaluation • Evaluation cost paid by vendor

U.S. Combined Federal Criteria

In 1992, partly in response to other international criteria efforts, the United States began a successor to the TCSEC, which had been written over a decade earlier. This successor, the *Combined Federal Criteria* [NSA92], was produced jointly by the National Institute for Standards and Technology (NIST) and the National Security Agency (NSA) (which formerly handled criteria and evaluations through its National Computer Security Center, the NCSC).

The team creating the *Combined Federal Criteria* was strongly influenced by Canada's criteria [CSS93], released in draft status just before the combined criteria effort began. Although many of the issues addressed by other countries' criteria were the same for the United States, there was a compatibility issue that did not affect the Europeans, namely, the need to be fair to vendors that had already passed U.S. evaluations at a particular level or that were planning for or in the middle of evaluations. Within that context, the new U.S. evaluation model was significantly different from the TCSEC. The combined criteria draft resembled the European model, with some separation between features and assurance.

The *Combined Federal Criteria* introduced the notions of security target (not to be confused with a target of evaluation, or TOE) and protection profile. A user would generate a **protection profile** to detail the protection needs, both functional and assurance, for a specific situation or a generic scenario. This user might be a government sponsor, a commercial user, an organization representing many similar users, a product vendor's marketing representative, or a product inventor. The protection profile would be an abstract specification of the security aspects needed in an information technology (IT) product. The protection profile would contain the elements listed in Table 5-10.

In response to a protection profile, a vendor might produce a product that, the vendor would assert, met the requirements of the profile. The vendor would then map the requirements of the protection profile in the context of the specific product onto a statement called a **security target**. As shown in Table 5-11, the security target matches the elements of the protection profile.

The security target then becomes the basis for the evaluation. The target details which threats are countered by which features, to what degree of assurance and using what mechanisms. The security target outlines the convincing argument that the product satisfies the requirements of the protection profile. Whereas the protection profile is an abstract description of requirements, the security target is a detailed specification of *how* each of those requirements is met in the specific product.

The criteria document also included long lists of potential requirements (a subset of which could be selected for a particular protection profile), covering topics from object reuse to accountability and from covert channel analysis to fault tolerance. Much of the work in specifying precise requirement statements came from the draft version of the Canadian criteria.

The U.S. *Combined Federal Criteria* was issued only once, in initial draft form. After receiving a round of comments, the editorial team announced that the United States had decided to join forces with the Canadians and the editorial board from the ITSEC to produce the *Common Criteria* for the entire world.

TABLE 5-10 Protection Profile.

Protection Profile
Rationale
Protection policy and regulations
Information protection philosophy
Expected threats
Environmental assumptions
Intended use
Functionality
Security features
Security services
Available security mechanisms (optional)
Assurance
Profile-specific assurances
Profile-independent assurances
Dependencies
Internal dependencies
External dependencies

Common Criteria

The *Common Criteria* [CCE94, CCE98] approach closely resembles the U.S. *Federal Criteria* (which, of course, was heavily influenced by the ITSEC and Canadian efforts). It preserves the concepts of security targets and protections profiles. The U.S. *Federal Criteria* were intended to have packages of protection requirements that were complete and consistent for a particular type of application, such as a network communications switch, a local area network, or a stand-alone operating system. The example packages received special attention in the *Common Criteria*.

The *Common Criteria* defined topics of interest to security, shown in Table 5-12.

Under each of these classes, they defined families of functions or assurance needs, and from those families, they defined individual components, as shown in Figure 5-24.

Individual components were then combined into packages of components that met some comprehensive requirement (for functionality) or some level of trust (for assurance), as shown in Figure 5-25.

Finally, the packages were combined into requirements sets, or assertions, for specific applications or products, as shown in Figure 5-26.

TABLE 5-11 Security Target.

Security Target
Rationale
Implementation fundamentals
Information protection philosophy
Countered threats
Environmental assumptions
Intended use
Functionality
Security features
Security services
Security mechanisms selected
Assurance
Target-specific assurances
Target-independent assurances
Dependencies
Internal dependencies
External dependencies

TABLE 5-12 Classes in Common Criteria.

Functionality	Assurance
Identification and authentication	Development
Trusted path	Testing
Security audit	Vulnerability assessment
Invocation of security functions	Configuration management
User data protection	Life-cycle support
Resource utilization	Guidance documents
Protection of the trusted security functions	Delivery and operation
Privacy	
Communication	

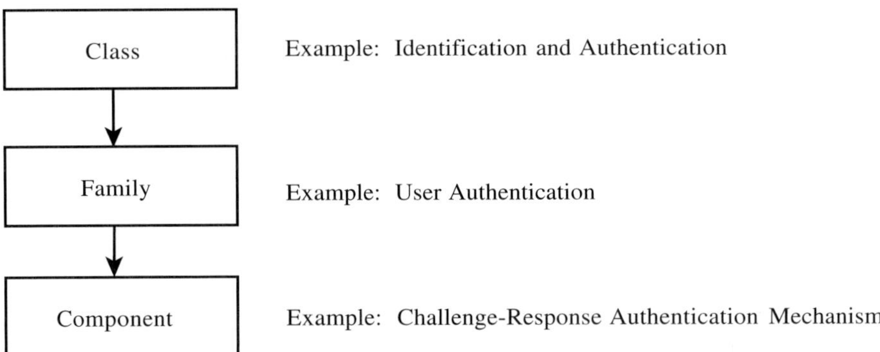

FIGURE 5-24 Classes, Families, and Components in *Common Criteria*.

Summary of Evaluation Criteria

The criteria were intended to provide independent security assessments in which we could have some confidence. Have the criteria development efforts been successful? For some, it is too soon to tell. For others, the answer lies in the number and kinds of products that have passed evaluation and how well the products have been accepted in the marketplace.

However, we can examine the evaluation process itself, using our own set of objective criteria. For instance, it is fair to say that there are several desirable qualities we would like to see in an evaluation, including:

- *Extensibility*: Can the evaluation be extended as the product is enhanced?
- *Granularity*: Does the evaluation look at the product at the right level of detail?
- *Speed*: Can the evaluation be done quickly enough to allow the product to compete in the marketplace?
- *Thoroughness*: Does the evaluation look at all relevant aspects of the product?

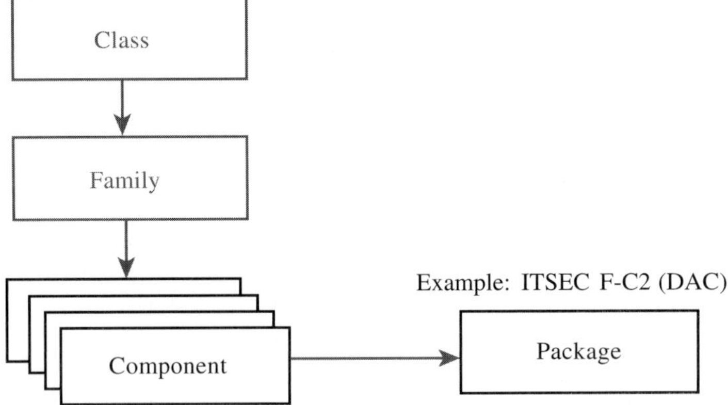

FIGURE 5-25 Functionality or Assurance Packages in *Common Criteria*.

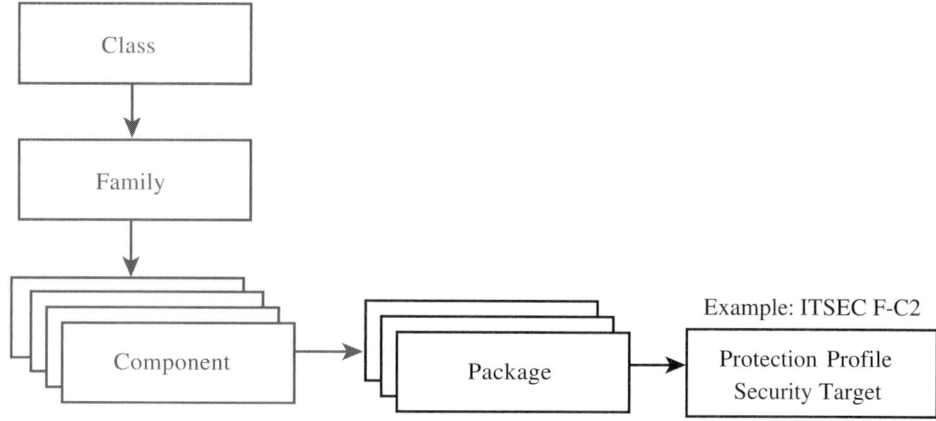

FIGURE 5-26 Protection Profiles and Security Targets in *Common Criteria.*

- *Objectivity*: Is the evaluation independent of the reviewer's opinions? That is, will two different reviewers give the same rating to a product?
- *Portability*: Does the evaluation apply to the product no matter what platform the product runs on?
- *Consistency*: Do similar products receive similar ratings? Would one product evaluated by different teams receive the same results?
- *Compatibility*: Could a product be evaluated similarly under different criteria? That is, does one evaluation have aspects that are not examined in another?
- *Exportability*: Could an evaluation under one scheme be accepted as meeting all or certain requirements of another scheme?

Using these characteristics, we can see that the applicability and extensibility of the TCSEC are somewhat limited. Compatibility is being addressed by combination of criteria, although the experience with the ITSEC has shown that simply combining the words of criteria documents does not necessarily produce a consistent understanding of them. Consistency has been an important issue, too. It was unacceptable for a vendor to receive different results after bringing the same product to two different evaluation facilities or to one facility at two different times. For this reason, the British criteria documents stressed consistency of evaluation results; this characteristic was carried through to the ITSEC and its companion evaluation methodology, the ITSEM. Even though speed, thoroughness, and objectivity are considered to be three essential qualities, in reality evaluations still take a long time relative to a commercial computer product delivery cycle of 6 to 18 months.

Evaluation criteria continue to be developed and refined. If you are interested in doing evaluations, in buying an evaluated product, or in submitting a product for evaluation, you should follow events closely in the evaluation community. You can use the evaluation goals listed above to help you decide whether an evaluation is appropriate and which kind of evaluation it should be.

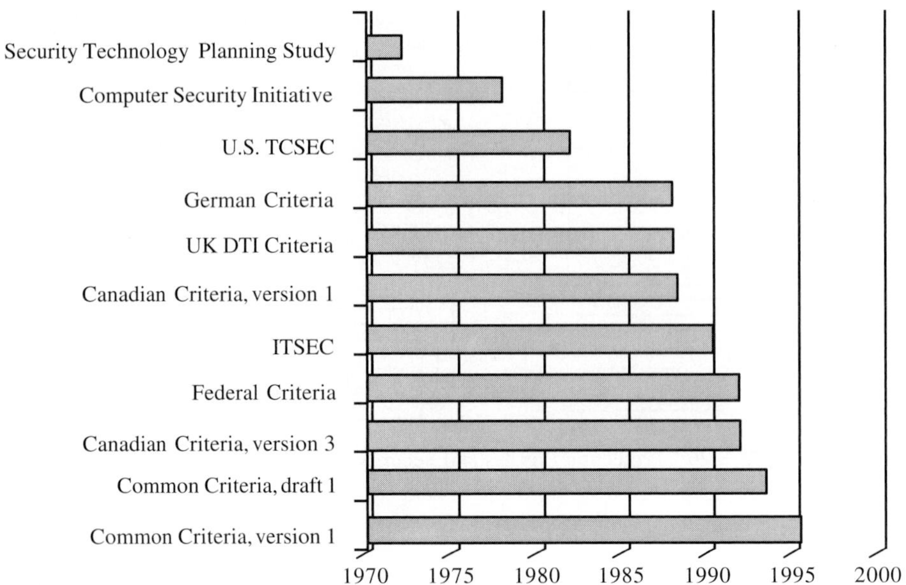

FIGURE 5-27 Criteria Development Efforts.

It is instructive to look back at the evolution of evaluation criteria documents, too. Figure 5-27 shows the timeline for different criteria publications; remember that the writing preceded the publication by one or more years. The figure begins with Anderson's original Security Technology Planning Study [AND72], calling for methodical, independent evaluation. To see whether progress is being made, look at the dates when different criteria documents were published; earlier documents had influence on the contents and philosophy of later ones.

The criteria development activities have made significant progress since 1983. The U.S. TCSEC was based on the state of best practice known around 1980. For this reason, it draws heavily from the structured programming paradigm that was popular throughout the 1970s. Its major difficulty was its very prescriptive manner; it forced its model on all developments and all types of products. The TCSEC applied most naturally to monolithic, stand-alone, multiuser operating systems, not to the heterogeneous, distributed, networked environment based largely on individual intelligent workstations that followed in the next decade.

To date, criteria efforts have been paid attention by the military, but those efforts have not led to much commercial acceptance of trusted products. The computer security research community is heavily dominated by defense needs because much of the funding for security research is derived from defense departments. Ware [WAR95] points out the following about the initial TCSEC:

- It was driven by the U.S. Department of Defense.
- It focused on threat as perceived by the U.S. Department of Defense.

- It was based on a U.S. Department of Defense concept of operations, including cleared personnel, strong respect for authority and management, and generally secure physical environments.
- It had little relevance to networks, LANs, WANs, Internets, client-server distributed architectures, and other more recent modes of computing.

When the TCSEC was introduced, there was an implicit contract between the U.S. government and vendors, saying that if vendors built products and had them evaluated, the government would buy them. Anderson [AND82] warned how important it was for the government to keep its end of this bargain. The vendors did their part by building numerous products: KSOS, PSOS, Scomp, KVM, and Multics. But unfortunately, the products are now only of historical interest because the U.S. government did not follow through and create the market that would encourage those vendors to continue and other vendors to join. If there had been many evaluated products on the market, support and usability would have been more adequately addressed, and there would have been a good chance for commercial adoption. Without government support or perceived commercial need, there has been almost no commercial acceptance of any of these products, even though they have been developed to some of the highest quality standards.

On the other hand, some major vendors are actively embracing low assurance evaluations. Some have announced corporate commitments to evaluation, noting that independent evaluation is a mark of quality that will always be a stronger selling point than so-called emphatic assertion (when a vendor makes loud claims about the strength of a product, with no independent evidence to substantiate those claims). Current efforts in criteria-writing support objectives, such as integrity and availability, as strongly as confidentiality. This approach can allow a vendor to identify a market niche and build a product for it, rather than building a product for a paper need (that is, the dictates of the evaluation criteria) not matched by purchases. Thus, there is reason for optimism regarding criteria and evaluations. But realism requires everyone to accept that the market—not a criteria document—will dictate what is desired and delivered.

It is generally believed that the market will eventually choose quality products. The evaluation principles described above were derived over time; empirical evidence shows us that they can produce high-quality, reliable products deserving our confidence. Thus, evaluation criteria and related efforts have not been in vain, especially as we see dramatic increases in security threats and the corresponding increased need for trusted products. However, it is often easier and cheaper for product proponents to speak loudly than to present clear evidence of trust. We caution you to look for solid support for the trust you seek, whether that support be in test and review results, evaluation ratings, or specialized assessment.

5.6 IMPLEMENTATION EXAMPLES

This chapter has focused on designing the security aspects of operating systems, which in turn can contribute to the overall security of a computing system. Fortunately, not every application requires A1- or F–A1/E6-quality security; few operating systems have the features needed to make them A1 or have been built with the care and discipline necessary to be judged E6.

In this section, we examine several commonly used operating systems, looking at features such as access control, security kernel, and design. Two examples are drawn from the general commercial world, and two more from the restricted world of TCSEC-inspired systems. We cover only features relevant to security, and then only some of those features.

General-Purpose Operating Systems

Several general-purpose operating systems are in wide use, affecting not only the development we do but also the applications we run as professionals and consumers. Unix is one such system, and we explore some of its design and development characteristics that have had an impact on its security. We also look at IBM's PR/SM, in widespread use on mainframe computers and whose origin and development have influenced its security.

Unix

The Unix operating system was never intended to have a high degree of security. It was designed in 1969 by two programmers, Ken Thompson and Dennis Ritchie, primarily for their own use in developing, testing, and maintaining programs. The system was intended for use in "nonhostile" environments, such as research laboratories and universities, where the advantages of easy object sharing far outweighed the possibility of unfriendly access.

As a result, sharing of files, data, devices, and storage volumes is relatively simple, unencumbered by a strong protection mechanism. The Unix system administrator is assumed to be a programmer too, who administers only part of the time and who does not, cannot, or should not perform many security functions.

Unix grew essentially without plan. When Bell Laboratories decided to withdraw from the Multics project, the early Unix designers, Thompson, Ritchie, Doug McIlroy, and J. F. Ossanna, were programmers there. Multics had provided them with interactive use of a computing utility, so they searched for another available machine on which to write their system. The philosophy and structure of Unix derived largely from Thompson, who designed the initial version and was heavily involved in the system's development for over a decade.

Thompson's goal was to provide a simple toolbox in which a user could store and access a variety of tools, combining them as needed for individual uses. Generality and compactness were prominent in the design of the elementary Unix functions, still a hallmark of the operating system today. Unix was intended to be extensible, even though this freedom brought security problems. If each user could add to the functionality of Unix, so could a malicious user. Simplicity and economy of design are virtues for the users, but they are a nightmare to the designer of a secure system. Thus, security side effects accompany many of the Unix commands.

There is one identified user, called the superuser, who can perform essentially any operation in the system. Because the superuser is all-powerful, most system attacks are aimed at obtaining superuser rights. Having obtained this right once, even for only a few seconds, a penetrator can establish a trapdoor that permits superuser access at any time in the future.

A user sharing access to a system program can obtain high security rights if the system program runs in *setuid* mode. As we noted earlier in this chapter, when a user executes such a program, the file access rights during program execution are the rights of the program's owner, not the program's user. The intended purpose of this feature is to allow a user to use a utility program, such as *mail*, and through the program access files at the level of *mail*. However, most sensitive utility programs are "owned" by the superuser, so that a security flaw exploited in one utility program gives very wide access.

From the point of view of the Unix operating system, all objects—directories, I/O devices, even parts of memory—are files, and they are accessed with the same structure. Again, this simplicity is good for the user, but it makes security difficult. File access permission is checked only once, when the file is opened. By changing the characteristics of the file or device after it has been opened, a user can obtain unchecked access permission.

Unix is distributed in modular form: An individual installation decides which features or modules it wants to use. Administrators can acquire modules from a wide range of external providers or even write their own and link them into the Unix operating system. A user can also build an individual environment of commands and functions. Of course, for Unix to support additions and replacements, all Unix interfaces must be clearly and completely documented, which they usually are. This ability to change is an advantage to attackers, who can replace practically any functions, including login, password management, object-level access control, and auditing, often without the knowledge of administrators or users.

Unix provides reasonable security for the environment for which it was designed: essentially a friendly environment. However, the inherent lack of security in the basic Unix system is evident from the fact that Unix-based secure operating systems have actually been implemented by substantial rewrites of the Unix kernel, to provide a system that has the outward functionality of Unix with a different internal structure. Sibert et al. [SIB87] describe the difficulties that would occur if Unix were to be evaluated for B2 certification.

PR/SM

Strictly speaking, the IBM Processor Resources/System Manager (PR/SM) is not really an operating system. Rather, it is a resource manager that provides strong separation and strictly controlled sharing of virtual machines. PR/SM does not support ordinary user tasks; instead, its "users" are other operating systems. PR/SM derives from a long line of IBM mainframe virtual machine operating systems, including VM/370 and MVS. It consists of a **logical partition manager** (LPAR) that maps physical devices and hardware interactions to signals passed between LPAR and each subject operating system.

PR/SM implements a very simple security policy: strict separation. All resources are partitioned into separate domains so that resources and processes running in one domain are unaware of and perceive no effect from resources and processes in other domains. PR/SM manages all hardware resources, which are shared only serially. In other words, before each resource (such as memory or processor registers) is to be reallocated to another operating system, the resource is completely purged of data. Other resources, such as direct access storage devices, are allocated to just one domain.

PR/SM was intended to support two or more different operating systems on a single computing system. Such a system might be desirable during a gradual changeover from one operating system to another so that both systems could be available at the same time. Or we may want to be able to change and test one operating system in an environment in which a system error in one (virtual) machine would not affect other users.

Virtualization was originally designed to provide flexibility in addressing and memory management; security was achieved as a bonus. PR/SM turned out to have a security advantage as well. Because LPAR performs all actual interaction with hardware, it acts as a second security layer between the operating system and the hardware.

To see how, suppose a user identifies and exploits a vulnerability in the operating system (that is, in the operating system running in the user's virtual machine, such as MVS/ESA). Under PR/SM, the user might extend outside the user domain and reach the operating system domain (where MVS/ESA is run). Even so, the user still does not have access to the actual machine hardware nor to users or domains running on other operating systems on other virtual machines. To penetrate another user or operating system, the user would have to find and exploit yet another vulnerability, this one in the security mechanism of PR/SM itself.

The separation advantages reach beyond security concerns. Strictly separate domains permit an installation to run a testing environment without risking interference with a domain supporting commercial needs. Separate domains can also serve as redundant backup capabilities, ready to take over instantly in the event of a hardware or software failure. Finally, separate domains can run different operating systems for separate communities of users.

PR/SM security capabilities include extensive hardware and software support for domain separation, strong role-based security management for such actions as configuring the partitioning of resources to domains, audit of actions of security administrators, and a secure communications path to PR/SM from security administrators and from the domains.

Operating Systems Designed for Security

Commercial operating systems such as Unix and PR/SM meet well-defined security needs. For example, Unix supposes an environment of trustworthy collaborators, and PR/SM anticipates situations requiring protection against inadvertent or malicious attempts by a process in one domain to interfere with one in another domain. Unix's degree of security is moderate, but PR/SM's is high, implemented largely by hardware to avoid a major performance penalty. Each approach is appropriate; the security requirements for these systems are commensurate with the degree of threat expected.

We must also consider operating systems designed for environments having far greater security needs. In the 1970s and 1980s, much effort was invested in the research, design and implementation of trusted operating systems. Projects such as KVM [GOL77, GOL84], KSOS [MCC79], Scomp [FRA83], Multics [SAL74], and TMach [BRA89, TIS97] were noble research efforts that never had enough commercial impact to keep their products alive. In these cases, the design addressed security as the foremost requirement, with such factors as usability and efficiency having lower importance. Regardless of past disappointments, such systems have great potential for government security applications, diplomatic communication, or projects in which the value of the system assets is high. The VAX security kernel was one such system, intended to meet both high security and ordinary commercial requirements.

VAX Security Kernel

The VAX Security Kernel, a project of Digital Equipment Corporation, targeted the A1 level of the TCSEC. It would have led to a very high assurance (A1) security kernel supporting the widely used commercial operating systems VMS and Ultrix. Standard VMS utilities and other software would have run on the security kernel, so it would have had a large number of widely used, well-supported applications. This kernel would have been the bridge between high assurance and mainstream commercial operating systems.

The security kernel faithfully emulated the underlying VAX hardware, including exporting all privilege states (virtualized versions), virtualized I/O (through monitoring of specific memory locations that reflect I/O data and status registers), and virtualized memory. The security kernel concurrently enforced Bell–La Padula mandatory confidentiality *and* Biba mandatory integrity.

The design of the security kernel was carefully constructed in 16 layers, each of which exported a capability to the layers above but depended on only layers below. This layered structure simplified debugging and imposed an order on the system's data and control flows. The layers protected themselves from above.

The A1 requirements dictated a development philosophy and methodology, starting with a formal model of security policy, a formal presentation of the highest-level design, and an argument that the formal design carried through to the implementation. The VAX security kernel was developed with rigid configuration control. In fact, it was built twice, once as a research and learning vehicle and once for real. Performance was significantly better in the second version.

The project began as a proposal for a research prototype in 1981, which was implemented between 1982 and 1984. This first version was redone as a production quality system by 1988. Tuning, additional development, and final documentation and preparation for the evaluation took place between 1988 and 1990. But in 1990 the project was terminated. Two reasons have been cited for the termination: corporate unwillingness to support multiple versions of the VAX family of operating systems (one for the security kernel and the other for general—not A1—distribution) and export control restrictions.

Nevertheless, the VAX virtual machine monitor project remains an outstanding example of high-quality development of trusted systems. Excellent descriptions of this project, especially of the security design issues, can be found in [KAR90, KAR91a]. Among other things, the project demonstrates the importance of building in security from the beginning of the development process. By contrast, most of the many examples of inserting security after the fact end in disappointment and unsatisfactory compromise. Sidebar 5-6 tells one of these tales.

Sidebar 5-6 Security As an Add-On

In the 1980s, the U.S. State Department handled its diplomatic office functions with a network of Wang computers. Each American embassy had at least one Wang system, with specialized word processing software to create documents, modify them, store and retrieve them, and send them from one location to another. Supplementing Wang's office automation software was the State Department's own Foreign Affairs Information System (FAIS).

In the mid-1980s, the State Department commissioned a private contractor to add security to FAIS. Diplomatic and other correspondence was to be protected by a secure "envelope" surrounding sensitive materials. The added protection was intended to prevent unauthorized parties from "opening" an envelope and reading the contents.

To design and implement the security features, the contractor had to supplement features offered by Wang's operating system and utilities. The security design depended on the current Wang VS operating system design, including the use of unused words in operating system files. As designed and implemented, the new security features worked properly and met the State Department requirements. But the system was bound for failure because the evolutionary goals of VS were different from those of the State Department. That is, Wang could not guarantee that future modifications to VS would preserve the functions and structure required by the contractor's security software. Eventually, there were fatal clashes of intent and practice.

5.7 SUMMARY OF SECURITY IN OPERATING SYSTEMS

We study operating systems in depth because they are at the heart of security systems for modern computers. They must provide mechanisms for both separation and sharing, mechanisms that must be robust and yet easy to use.

Developing secure operating systems involves four activities. First, the environment to be protected must be well understood. Through policy statements and models, the essential components of systems are identified, and the interactions among components can be studied. This chapter has presented a variety of policies and models of security. Whereas the policies covered confidentiality and integrity, the models ranged from reference monitors and information flow filters to multilevel security and integrity models. Models such as that of Bell and La Padula describe permissible access in a multilevel environment, and the HRU model demonstrates the limits of computer security.

After an environment is understood, a system to implement it must be designed to provide the desired protection. We have seen how certain design principles for secure operating systems help us meet that design goal. Not surprisingly, features such as least privilege, openness of design, and economy of mechanism are quite similar to the software engineering design principles described in Chapter 3; characteristics that lead to good design of an operating system apply to the design of other programs as well. We studied security-specific design principles in some detail, including isolation or separation, layered design, and the notion of a security kernel.

It is not enough to have a good operating system design. We also want assurance that the design and its implementation are correct. This chapter considered three methods to demonstrate correctness: formal verification, validation, and penetration testing. Because there are many formal evaluation schemes for assigning a security rating to software, we also examined several evaluation criteria in detail; they represent the current standard for certifying trusted computing systems.

Finally, we looked at several implementations of secure operating systems. These examples included both widely available commercial systems and those designed specifically for their security features.

Next, we turn from operating systems to major applications or subsystems, looking in particular at database management systems as an example of how to deal with data that must be protected. In Chapter 6, we study secure database management systems. We will see that database systems have many of the same requirements as operating systems: access control, availability, and multilevel security. Indeed, since database management systems are implemented on top of operating systems, they use some of the services provided by operating systems. However, integrity and granularity are substantially different, and we look at novel ways of dealing with these issues.

5.8 TERMS AND CONCEPTS

secure, 230
trust, 231
trusted process, 231
trusted software, 231
trusted system, 231
security policy, 232
military security policy, 232
sensitivity level, 232
object, 232
need-to-know rule, 232
compartment, 232
classification, 234
clearance, 234
dominance, 234
subject, 234
hierarchical security, 235
nonhierarchical security, 235
Clark–Wilson policy, 236
well-formed transaction, 237
constrained data item, 237
transformation procedure, 237
access triple, 237
separation of duty, 237
Chinese wall policy, 237
lattice model, 239
Bell–La Padula model, 241
simple security property, 242
∗-property, 242
write-down, 242
Biba model, 243
simple integrity policy, 243
integrity ∗-property, 243
Graham–Denning model, 244
Harrison–Ruzzo–Ullman model, 245
take–grant system, 248
least privilege, 252
economy of mechanism, 252
open design, 252
complete mediation, 252
permission-based access, 252
separation of privilege, 252
least common mechanism, 252
ease of use, 253
user authentication, 253
memory protection, 254
object access control, 254
enforced sharing, 254
fair service, 254

interprocess communication, 254
synchronization, 254
protected control data, 254
user identification and authentication, 256
mandatory access control, 256
discretionary access control, 256
object reuse, 256
magnetic remanence, 257
trusted path, 257
audit, 257
audit log reduction, 258
accountability, 258
intrusion detection, 259
kernel, 259
nucleus, 259
core, 259
security kernel, 260
reference monitor, 260
tamperproofness, 261
unbypassability, 261
analyzability, 261
trusted computing base (TCB), 261
process activation, 262
execution domain switching, 263
memory protection, 263
physical separation, 265
temporal separation, 265
cryptographic separation, 266
logical separation, 266
virtualization, 266
virtual machine, 266
virtual memory, 267
layering, 269
hierarchically structured operating system, 271
assurance, 273
flaw exploitation, 274
I/O processing flaw, 274
access ambiguity flaw, 274
incomplete mediation flaw, 275
generality flaw, 274
time-of-check to time-of-use flaw, 275
testing, 276
test coverage, 276
penetration testing, 276
formal verification, 278
proof of correctness, 278
theorem prover, 278
validation, 281
requirements checking, 281
design and code review, 281
module and system testing, 281
open source, 281
evaluation, 282
Orange Book (TCSEC), 283
D, C1, C2, B1, B2, B3, A1 rating, 283
German Green Book, 286
functionality class, 287
assurance level, 287
British evaluation criteria, 287
claims language, 287
action phrase, 287
target phrase, 288
CLEF, 289
comparable evaluation, 289
transferable evaluation, 289
ITSEC, 289
effectiveness, 289
target of evaluation, 289
security-enforcing function, 289
mechanism, 290
strength of mechanism, 290
target evaluation level, 290
suitability of functionality, 290
binding of functionality, 290
vulnerabilities, 290
Combined Federal Criteria, 291
protection profile, 291
security target, 291
Common Criteria, 292
extensibility, 294
granularity, 294
objectivity, 295
portability, 295
emphatic assertion, 297
Unix, 298
PR/SM, 299
logical partition manager, 300
domain, 300
VAX Security Kernel, 301

5.9 WHERE THE FIELD IS HEADED

The field of trusted operating systems advanced significantly during the 1970s and early 1980s due to major investment by the U.S. government and other governments, especially the defense departments. Progress slowed when funding stopped. Trusted, trustworthy, or secure operating systems do not seem to be commercially viable, and without a large government market to spur the new products and approaches, little innovation occurs. In a move reminiscent of the 1978 Computer Security Act (leading to the Orange book) and the later "C2 by '92" directive (requiring all computing systems for U.S. Defense Department use to have passed at least a C2 evaluation), the U.S. Defense Department has required national security organizations to use the Common Criteria to evaluate information assurance products by July 2002. As a result, the market for Common Criteria evaluations is heating up again. Continuing refinement is likely for evaluation standards, evaluation processes, and protection profiles for specific purposes and product types.

Composition has always been the next problem after evaluation: If you combine two evaluated products, what can you say about their security when those products run together? Consider, for example, a database management system running on an operating system, or an operating system on a network infrastructure. Is a high-assurance product degraded by being combined with a lower assurance one? Does one high-assurance component compensate for shortcomings in a lower-assurance one? Examples can show that simple algebra does not hold: good+good is not always good, and bad+bad is not necessarily worse. Ross [FRA02] acknowledges that solving the composition problem—building secure or high-assurance systems composed from evaluated products—is not easy. And Schell [SCH01] observed "Even though there has been wishful thinking that it would be nice to discover a means of 'building trustworthy systems from untrustworthy components, [NAS98]' to the current state of science this appears to be intractable."

5.10 TO LEARN MORE

The topic of secure computing systems includes fundamental papers such as Lampson [LAM71], Popek [POP74a], Hoare [HOA74], Graham [GRA68], Saltzer and Schroeder [SAL75], and Jones [JON78a]. Landwehr [LAN81] provides a good overview of models of protection systems. Additional information on policy and models of security is provided by Bell [BEL83], Harrison [HAR85], Goguen and Meseguer [GOG82], Clark and Wilson [CLA87], Badger [BAD89], Karger [KAR88], Brewer and Nash [BRE89].

The design of secure systems is discussed by Gasser [GAS88], Ames [AME83], and Landwehr [LAN83]. Certification of security-enforcing systems is discussed by Neumann [NEU78] and Neugent [NEU82]. Criteria documents are the easiest to locate: in [CCE94], [NSA92], [ITS91a, ITS91b], [CSS93], [DTI89a, DTI89b, DTI89c], and [GIS88]. Also read commentary by Neumann [NEU90a, NEU90b] and Ware [WAR95].

5.11 EXERCISES

1. A principle of the Bell–La Padula model was not mentioned in this chapter. Called the **tranquillity principle**, it states that the classification of a subject or object does not change

while it is being referenced. Explain the purpose of the tranquillity principle. What are the implications of a model in which the tranquillity principle is *not* true?

2. Subjects can access objects, but they can also access other subjects. Describe how a reference monitor would control access in the case of a subject acting on another subject. Describe how a reference monitor would control access in the case of two subjects interacting.
3. List the source and end of all information flows in each of the following statements.
   (a) `sum := a+b+c;`
   (b) `if a+b < c+d then q:=0 else q:=1;`
   (c) `write (a,b,c);`
   (d) `read (a,b,c);`
   (e)
   ```
   case (k) of
          0: d:= 10;
          1,2: d:= 20;
          other: d:= 30;
     end; /* case */
   ```
   (f) `for i:=min to max do k:=2*k+1;`
   (g)
   ```
   repeat
          a[i]:=0;
          i:=i-1;
          until i ≤ 0;
   ```
4. Does the system of all subsets of a finite set under the operation "subset of" ($\subseteq$) form a lattice? Why or why not?
5. Can a user cleared for ⟨*secret*;{dog, cat, pig}⟩ have access to documents classified in each of the following ways under the military security model?
   (a) ⟨*top secret*;dog⟩
   (b) ⟨*secret*;{dog}⟩
   (c) ⟨*secret*;{dog,cow}⟩
   (d) ⟨*secret*;{moose}⟩
   (e) ⟨*confidential*;{dog,pig,cat}⟩
   (f) ⟨*confidential*;{moose}⟩
6. According to the Bell–La Padula model, what restrictions are placed on two active subjects (for example, two processes) that wish to send and receive signals to each other? Justify your answer.
7. Write a set of rules combining the secrecy controls of the Bell–La Padula model with the integrity controls of the Biba model.
8. Demonstrate a method for limited transfer of rights in the Graham–Denning model. A limit of one is adequate. That is, give a method by which *A* can transfer to *B* right *R*, with the provision that *B* can transfer that right to any one other subject. The subject to which *B* transfers the right cannot transfer the right, nor can *B* transfer it again.
9. Explain what is necessary to provide temporal separation. That is, what conditions must be met in order for two processes to be adequately separated?
10. Does the standard Unix operating system use a nondiscretionary access control? Explain your answer.
11. Why is labeling of objects a security requirement? That is, why cannot the trusted computing base just maintain an access control table with entries for each object and each subject?
12. Label integrity is a technique that ensures that the label on each object is changed only by the trusted computing base. Suggest a method to implement label integrity for a data file. Suggest a method to implement label integrity for a callable procedure.
13. Describe a situation in which you might want to allow the security kernel to violate one of the security properties of the Bell–La Padula model.

14. Explain the meaning of the term *granularity* in reference to access control. Discuss the trade-off between granularity and efficiency.

15. Explain how a semaphore could be used to implement a covert channel in concurrent processing. Explain how concurrent processing primitives, such as *fork* and *join*, could be used to implement a covert channel in concurrent processing.

16. The Unix operating system structures files by using a tree. Each file is at a leaf of the tree, and the file is identified by the (unique) path from the root to the leaf. Each interior node is a "subdirectory," which specifies the names of the paths leading from that node. A user can block access through a node by restricting access to the subdirectory. Devise a method that uses this structure to implement a discretionary access policy.

17. In the Unix file system described in this chapter, could a nondiscretionary access policy be defined so that a user has access to a file only if the user has access to all subdirectories higher (closer to the root) in the file structure? What would be the effect of this policy?

18. I/O appears as the source of several successful methods of penetration. Discuss why I/O is hard to secure in a computing system.

6

Database Security

In this chapter:

- Integrity for databases: record integrity, data correctness, update integrity
- Security for databases: access control, inference, and aggregation
- Multilevel secure databases: partitioned, cryptographically sealed, filtered

Protecting data is at the heart of many secure systems, and many users (people, programs, or systems) rely on a database management system (DBMS) to manage the protection. For this reason, we devote this chapter to the security of database management systems, as an example of how application security can be designed and implemented for a specific task. There is substantial current interest in DBMS security because databases are newer than programming and operating systems. Databases are essential to many business and government organizations, holding data that reflect the organization's core competencies. Often, when business processes are reengineered to make them more effective and more in tune with new or revised goals, one of the first systems to receive careful scrutiny is the set of databases supporting the business processes. Thus, databases are more than software-related repositories. Their organization and contents are considered valuable corporate assets that must be carefully protected.

However, the protection provided by database management systems has had mixed results. Over time, we have improved our understanding of database security problems, and several good controls have been developed. But, as you will see, there are still more security concerns for which there are no available controls.

We begin this chapter with a brief summary of database terminology. Then we consider the security requirements for database management systems. Two major security problems—integrity and secrecy—are explained in a database context. The chapter concludes by studying two major (but related) database security problems, the inference problem and the multilevel problem. Both problems are complex, and there are no immediate solutions. However, by understanding the problems, we become more sensitive to ways of reducing potential threats to the data.

6.1 INTRODUCTION TO DATABASES

We begin by describing a database and defining terminology related to its use. We draw on examples from what is called the relational database because it is one of the most widely used types. However, all of the concepts described here apply to any type of database. We first define the basic concepts and then use them to discuss security concerns.

Concept of a Database

A **database** is a collection of *data* and a set of *rules* that organize the data by specifying certain relationships among the data. Through these rules, the user describes a *logical* format for the data. The data items are stored in a file, but the precise *physical* format of the file is of no concern to the user. A **database administrator** is a person who defines the rules that organize the data and also controls who should have access to what parts of the data. The user interacts with the database through a program called a **database manager** or a **database management system (DBMS)**, informally known as a **front end.**

Components of Databases

The database file consists of **records,** each of which contains one related group of data. As shown in the example in Table 6-1, a record in a name and address file consists of one name and address. Each record contains **fields** or **elements,** the elementary data items themselves. The fields in the name and address record are NAME, ADDRESS, CITY, STATE, and ZIP (where ZIP is the U.S. postal code). This database can be viewed as a two-dimensional table, where a record is a row and each field of a record is an element of the table.

Not every database is easily represented as a single, compact table. The database in Figure 6-1 logically consists of three files with possibly different uses. These three files could be represented as one large table, but that depiction may not improve the utility of or access to the data.

The logical structure of a database is called a **schema.** A particular user may have access to only part of the database, called a **subschema.** The overall schema of the database in Figure 6-1 is detailed in Table 6-2. The three separate blocks of the figure are examples of subschemas, although other subschemas of this database can be defined. We can use schemas and subschemas to present to users only those elements they wish or need to see. For example, if Table 6-1 represents the employees at a company, the subschema on the lower left can list employee names without revealing personal information such as home address.

TABLE 6-1 Example of a Database.

ADAMS	212 Market St.	Columbus	OH	43210
BENCHLY	501 Union St.	Chicago	IL	60603
CARTER	411 Elm St.	Columbus	OH	43210

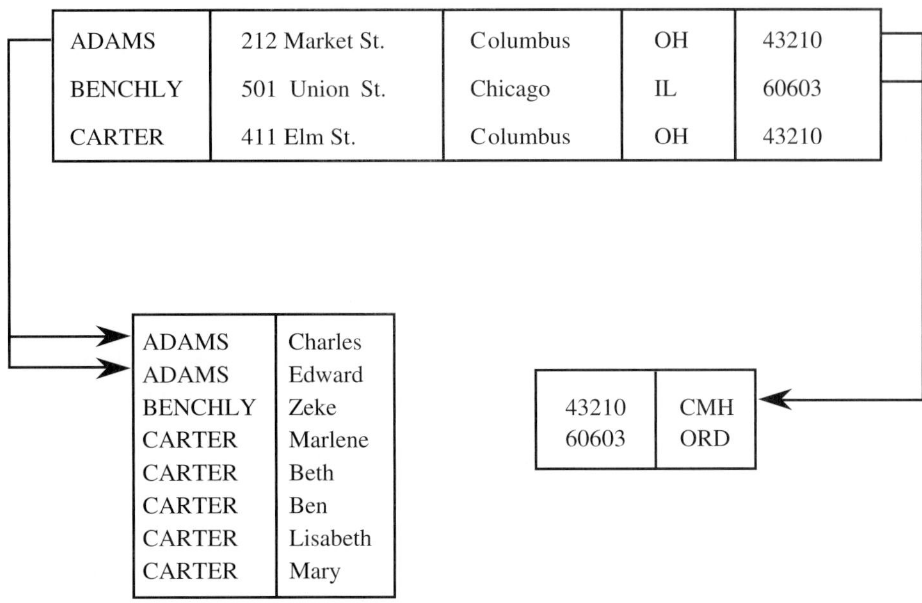

FIGURE 6-1 Related Parts of a Database.

The rules of a database identify the columns with names. The name of each column is called an **attribute** of the database. A **relation** is a set of columns. For example, using the database in Table 6-2, we see that NAME–ZIP is a relation formed by taking the NAME and ZIP columns, as shown in Table 6-3. The relation specifies clusters of related data values, in much the same way that the relation "mother of" specifies a relationship among pairs of humans. In this example, each cluster contains a pair of ele-

TABLE 6-2 Schema of Database Shown in Figure 6-1.

Name	First	Address	City	State	Zip	Airport
ADAMS	Charles	212 Market St.	Columbus	OH	43210	CMH
ADAMS	Edward	212 Market St.	Columbus	OH	43210	CMH
BENCHLY	Zeke	501 Union St.	Chicago	IL	60603	ORD
CARTER	Marlene	411 Elm St.	Columbus	OH	43210	CMH
CARTER	Beth	411 Elm St.	Columbus	OH	43210	CMH
CARTER	Ben	411 Elm St.	Columbus	OH	43210	CMH
CARTER	Lisabeth	411 Elm St.	Columbus	OH	43210	CMH
CARTER	Mary	411 Elm St.	Columbus	OH	43210	CMH

TABLE 6-3 Relation in a Database.

Name	Zip
ADAMS	43210
BENCHLY	60603
CARTER	43210

ments, a NAME and a ZIP. Other relations can have more columns, so each cluster may be a triple, a 4-tuple, or an n-tuple (for some value n) of elements.

Queries

Users interact with database managers through commands to the DBMS that retrieve, modify, add, or delete fields and records of the database. A command is called a **query.** Database management systems have precise rules of syntax for queries. Most query languages use an English-like notation, and many are based on SQL, a structured query language originally developed by IBM. We have written the example queries in this chapter to resemble English sentences, so that they are easy to understand. For example, the query

```
SELECT NAME = 'ADAMS'
```

retrieves all records having the value *ADAMS* in the NAME field.

The result of executing a query is a subschema. One way to form a subschema of a database is by selecting records meeting certain conditions. For example, we might select records in which ZIP=43210, producing the result shown in Table 6-4.

TABLE 6-4 Result of Select Query.

Name	First	Address	City	State	Zip	Airport
ADAMS	Charles	212 Market St.	Columbus	OH	43210	CMH
ADAMS	Edward	212 Market St.	Columbus	OH	43210	CMH
CARTER	Marlene	411 Elm St.	Columbus	OH	43210	CMH
CARTER	Beth	411 Elm St.	Columbus	OH	43210	CMH
CARTER	Ben	411 Elm St.	Columbus	OH	43210	CMH
CARTER	Lisabeth	411 Elm St.	Columbus	OH	43210	CMH
CARTER	Mary	411 Elm St.	Columbus	OH	43210	CMH

Other, more complex, selection criteria are possible, with logical operators such as *and* (∧) and *or* (∨), and comparisons such as *less than* (<). An example of a select query is

```
SELECT (ZIP='43210') ∧ (NAME='ADAMS')
```

After having selected records, we may **project** these records onto one or more attributes. The select operation extracts certain rows from the database, and a project operation extracts the values from certain fields (columns) of those records. The result of a select-project operation is the set of values of specified attributes for the selected records. For example, we might select records meeting the condition ZIP=43210 and project the results onto the attributes NAME and FIRST, as in Table 6-5. The result is the list of first and last names of people whose addresses have zip code 43210.

Notice that you do not have to project onto the same attribute(s) on which the selection is done. For example, we can build a query using ZIP and NAME but project the result onto FIRST:

```
SHOW FIRST WHERE (ZIP='43210') ∧ (NAME='ADAMS')
```

The result would be a list of the first names of people whose last names are *ADAMS* and ZIP is *43210*.

We can also merge two subschema on a common element by using a **join** query. The result of this operation is a subschema whose records have the same value for the common element. For example, Figure 6-2 shows that the subschema NAME–ZIP and the subschema ZIP–AIRPORT can be joined on the common field ZIP to produce the subschema NAME–AIRPORT.

Advantages of Using Databases

The logical idea behind a database is this: A database is a single collection of data, stored and maintained at one central location, to which many people have access as needed. However, the actual implementation may involve some other physical storage

TABLE 6-5 Results of Select-Project Query.

ADAMS	Charles
ADAMS	Edward
CARTER	Marlene
CARTER	Beth
CARTER	Ben
CARTER	Lisabeth
CARTER	Mary

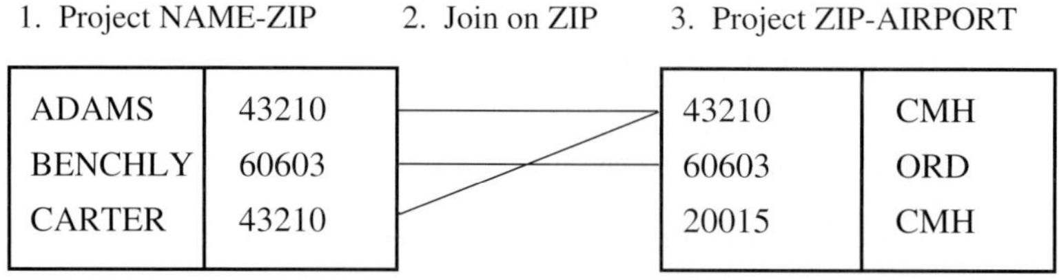

4. Result

ADAMS	CMH
BENCHLY	ORD
CARTER	CMH

FIGURE 6-2 Results of Select-Project-Join Query.

arrangement or access. The essence of a good database is that the users are unaware of the physical arrangements; the unified logical arrangement is all they see. As a result, a database offers many advantages over a simple file system:

- *shared access,* so that many users can use one common, centralized set of data
- *minimal redundancy,* so that individual users do not have to collect and maintain their own sets of data
- *data consistency,* so that a change to a data value affects all users of the data value
- *data integrity,* so that data values are protected against accidental or malicious undesirable changes
- *controlled access,* so that only authorized users are allowed to view or to modify data values

A DBMS is designed to provide these advantages efficiently. However, as often happens, the objectives can conflict with each other. In particular, as we shall see, security interests can conflict with performance. This clash is not surprising, because measures taken to enforce security often increase the computing system's size or complexity. What is surprising, though, is that security interests may also reduce the system's ability to provide data to users by limiting certain queries that would otherwise seem innocuous.

6.2 SECURITY REQUIREMENTS

The basic security requirements of database systems are not unlike those of other computing systems we have studied. The basic problems—access control, exclusion of spurious data, authentication of users, and reliability—have appeared in many contexts so far in this book. Following is a list of requirements for database security.

- *Physical database integrity.* The data of a database are immune to physical problems, such as power failures, and someone can reconstruct the database if it is destroyed through a catastrophe.
- *Logical database integrity.* The structure of the database is preserved. With logical integrity of a database, a modification to the value of one field does not affect other fields, for example.
- *Element integrity.* The data contained in each element are accurate.
- *Auditability.* It is possible to track who or what has accessed (or modified) the elements in the database.
- *Access control.* A user is allowed to access only authorized data, and different users can be restricted to different modes of access (such as read or write).
- *User authentication.* Every user is positively identified, both for the audit trail and for permission to access certain data.
- *Availability.* Users can access the database in general and all the data for which they are authorized.

We briefly examine each of these requirements.

Integrity of the Database

If a database is to serve as a central repository of data, users must be able to trust the accuracy of the data values. This condition implies that the database administrator must be assured that updates are performed only by authorized individuals. It also implies that the data must be protected from corruption, either by an outside illegal program action or by an outside force such as fire or a power failure. Two situations can affect the integrity of a database: when the whole database is damaged (as happens, for example, if its storage medium is damaged), or when individual data items are unreadable.

Integrity of the database as a whole is the responsibility of the DBMS, the operating system, and the computing system manager. From the perspective of the operating system and the computing system manager, databases and DBMSs are files and programs, respectively. Therefore, one way of protecting the database as a whole is to regularly back up all files on the system. These periodic backups can be adequate controls against catastrophic failure.

Sometimes it is important to be able to reconstruct the database at the point of a failure. For instance, when the power fails suddenly, a bank's clients may be in the middle of making transactions or students may be in the midst of registering online for their classes. In these cases, we want to be able to restore the systems to a stable point without forcing users to redo their recent transactions. To handle these situations, the DBMS must maintain a log of transactions. For example, suppose the banking system is designed so that a message is generated in a log (electronic or paper or both) each time a transaction is processed. In the event of a system failure, the system can obtain accurate account balances by reverting to a backup copy of the database and reprocessing all later transactions from the log.

Element Integrity

The **integrity** of database elements is their correctness or accuracy. Ultimately, authorized users are responsible for entering correct data in databases. However, users and programs make mistakes collecting data, computing results, and entering values. Therefore, DBMSs sometimes take special action to help catch errors as they are made and to correct errors after they are inserted.

This corrective action can be taken in three ways. First, the DBMS can apply **field checks,** activities that test for appropriate values in a position. A field might be required to be numeric, an uppercase letter, or one of a set of acceptable characters. The check ensures that a value falls within specified bounds or is not greater than the sum of the values in two other fields. These checks prevent simple errors as the data are entered. (Sidebar 6-1 demonstrates the importance of element integrity.)

A second integrity action is provided by **access control.** To see why, consider life before databases. Data files may contain data from several sources, and redundant data may be stored in several different places. For example, a student's home address may be stored in many different campus files: at class registration, for dining hall privileges, at the bookstore, and in the financial aid office. Indeed, the student may not even be aware that each separate office has the address on file. If the student moves from one residence to another, each of the separate files requires correction. Without a database, there are several risks to the data's integrity. First, at a given time, there could be some data files with the old address (they have not yet been updated) and some simultaneously with the new address (they have already been updated). Second, there is always the possibility that the data fields were changed incorrectly, again leading to files with incorrect information. Third, there may be files of which the student is unaware, so he or she does not know to notify the file owner about updating the address information. These problems are solved by databases. They enable collection and control of this data at one central source, ensuring the student and users of having the correct address.

Sidebar 6-1 Element Integrity Failure Crashes Network

Crocker and Bernstein [CRO89] studied catastrophic failures of what was then known as the ARPANET, the predecessor of today's Internet. Several failures came from problems with the routing tables used to direct traffic through the network.

A 1971 error was called the "black hole." A hardware failure caused one node to declare that it was the best path to every other node in the network. This node sent this declaration to other nodes, which soon propagated the erroneous posting throughout the network. This node immediately became the black hole of the network because all traffic was routed to it but never made it to the real destination.

The ARPANET used simple tables, not a full-featured database management system, so there was no checking of new values prior to their being installed in the distributed routing tables. Had there been a database, integrity checking software could have performed error checking on the newly distributed values and raised a flag for human review.

However, the centralization is easier said than done. Who owns this shared central file? Who has authorization to update which elements? What if two people apply conflicting modifications? What if modifications are applied out of sequence? How are duplicate records detected? What action is taken when duplicates are found? These are policy questions that must be resolved by the database administrator. Sidebar 6-2

Sidebar 6-2 Configuration Management and Access Control

Software engineers must address access control when they manage the configurations of large computer systems. The code of a major system and changes to it over time are actually a database. There are many instances when multiple programmers are making changes to a system at the same time; the configuration management database must help ensure that the correct and most recent changes are stored.

There are three primary ways to control the proliferation of versions and releases. [PFL01a]

- *Separate files*: A separate file can be kept for each different version or release. For instance, version 1 may exist for machines that store all data in main memory, and version 2 is for machines that must put some data out to a disk. Suppose the common functions are the same in both versions, residing in components C_1 through C_k, but memory management is done by component M_1 for version 1 and M_2 for version 2. If new functionality is to be added to the memory management routines, keeping both versions current and correct may be difficult; the results must be the same from the user's point of view.
- *Deltas*: One version of the system is deemed the main version, and all other versions are considered to be variations from the main version. The database keeps track only of the differences, in a file called a *delta* file. The delta contains commands that are "applied" to the main version to transform it into the alternative version. This approach saves storage space but can become unwieldy.
- *Conditional compilation*: All versions are handled by a single file, and conditional statements are used to determine which statements apply under which conditions. In this case, shared code appears only once, so only one correction is needed if a problem is found. But the code in this single file can be very complex and difficult to maintain.

In any of these three cases, it is essential to control access to the configuration files. It is common practice for two different programmers fixing different problems to need to make changes to the same component. If care is not taken in controlling access, then the second programmer can inadvertently "undo" the changes made by the first programmer, resulting in not only recurrence of the initial problems but also introduction of additional problems. For this reason, files are controlled in several ways, including being locked while changes are made by one programmer, and being subject to a group of people called a configuration control board who ensure that no changed file is put back into production without the proper checking and testing. More information about these techniques is found in [PFL01a].

describes how these issues are addressed for managing the configuration of programs; similar formal processes are needed for managing changes in databases.

The third means of providing database integrity is maintaining a **change log** for the database. A change log lists every change made to the database; it contains both original and modified values. Using this log, a database administrator can undo any changes that were made in error. For example, a library fine might erroneously be posted against Charles W. Robertson, instead of Charles M. Robertson, flagging Charles W. Robertson as ineligible to participate in varsity athletics. Upon discovering this error, the database administrator obtains Charles W.'s original eligibility value from the log and corrects the database.

Auditability

For some applications it may be desirable to generate an audit record of all access (read or write) to a database. Such a record can help to maintain the database's integrity, or at least to discover after the fact who had affected what values and when. A second advantage, as we will see later, is that users can access protected data incrementally; that is, no single access reveals protected data, but a set of sequential accesses viewed together reveals the data, much like discovering the clues in a detective novel. In this case, an audit trail can identify which clues a user has already been given, as a guide to whether to tell the user more.

As we noted in Chapters 4 and 5, granularity becomes an impediment in auditing. Audited events in operating systems are actions like *open file* or *call procedure*; they are seldom as specific as *write record* 3 or *execute instruction* I. To be useful for maintaining integrity, database audit trails should include accesses at the record, field, and even element levels. This detail is prohibitive for most database applications.

Furthermore, it is possible for a record to be accessed but not reported to a user, as when the user performs a select operation. (Accessing a record or an element without transferring to the user the data received is called the **pass-through problem**.) Also, you can determine the values of some elements without accessing them directly. (For example, you can ask for the average salary in a group of employees when you know the number of employees in the group is only one.) Thus, a log of all records accessed directly may both overstate and understate what a user actually knows.

Access Control

Databases are often separated logically by user access privileges. For example, all users can be granted access to general data, but only the personnel department can obtain salary data and only the marketing department can obtain sales data. Databases are very useful because they centralize the storage and maintenance of data. Limited access is both a responsibility and a benefit of this centralization.

The database administrator specifies who should be allowed access to which data, at the view, relation, field, record, or even element level. The DBMS must enforce this policy, granting access to all specified data or no access where prohibited. Furthermore, the number of modes of access can be many. A user or program may have the right to read, change, delete, or append to a value, add or delete entire fields or records, or reorganize the entire database.

Superficially, access control for a database seems like access control for operating systems or any other component of a computing system. However, the database problem is more complicated, as we see throughout this chapter. Operating system objects, such as files, are unrelated items, whereas records, fields, and elements are related. Although a user cannot determine the contents of one file by reading others, a user might be able to determine one data element just by reading others. The problem of obtaining data values from others is called **inference**, and we consider it in depth later in this chapter.

It is important to notice that you can access data by inference without needing direct access to the secure object itself. Restricting inference may mean prohibiting certain paths to prevent possible inferences. However, restricting access to control inference also limits queries from users who do not intend unauthorized access to values. Moreover, attempts to check requested accesses for possible unacceptable inferences may actually degrade the DBMS's performance.

Finally, size or granularity is different between operating system objects and database objects. An access control list of several hundred files is much easier to implement than an access control list for a database with several hundred files of perhaps a hundred fields each. Size affects the efficiency of processing.

User Authentication

The DBMS can require rigorous user authentication. For example, a DBMS might insist that a user pass both specific password and time-of-day checks. This authentication supplements the authentication performed by the operating system. Typically, the DBMS runs as an application program on top of the operating system. This system design means that there is no trusted path from the DBMS to the operating system, so the DBMS must be suspicious of any data it receives, including user authentication. Thus, the DBMS is forced to do its own authentication.

Availability

A DBMS has aspects of both a program and a system. It is a program that uses other hardware and software resources, yet to many users it is the only application run. Users often take the DBMS for granted, employing it as an essential tool with which to perform particular tasks. But when the system is not available—busy serving other users or down to be repaired or upgraded—the users are very aware of a DBMS's unavailability. For example, two users may request the same record, and the DBMS must arbitrate; one user is bound to be denied access for a while. Or the DBMS may withhold unprotected data to avoid revealing protected data, leaving the requesting user unhappy. We examine these problems in more detail later in this chapter. Problems like these result in high availability requirements for a DBMS.

Integrity/Confidentiality/Availability

The three aspects of computer security—integrity, confidentiality, and availability—clearly relate to database management systems. As we have described, integrity applies to the individual elements of a database as well as to the database as a whole. Thus, integrity is a major concern in the design of database management systems. We look more closely at integrity issues in the next section.

Confidentiality is a key issue with databases because of the inference problem, whereby a user can access sensitive data indirectly. Inference and access control are covered later in this chapter.

Finally, availability is important because of the shared access motivation underlying database development. However, availability conflicts with confidentiality. The last sections of the chapter address availability in an environment in which confidentiality is also important.

6.3 RELIABILITY AND INTEGRITY

Databases amalgamate data from many sources, and users expect a DBMS to provide access to the data in a reliable way. When software engineers say that software is **reliable**, they mean that the software runs for very long periods of time without failing. Users certainly expect a DBMS to be reliable, since the data usually are key to business or organizational needs. Moreover, users entrust their data to a DBMS and rightly expect it to protect the data from loss or damage. Concerns for reliability and integrity are general security issues, but they are more highly apparent with databases.

There are several ways that a DBMS guards against loss or damage, and we study them in this section. However, the controls we consider are not absolute: No control can prevent an authorized user from inadvertently entering an acceptable but incorrect value.

Database concerns about reliability and integrity can be viewed from three dimensions:

- *Database integrity:* concern that the database as a whole is protected against damage, as from the failure of a disk drive or the corruption of the master database index. These concerns are addressed by operating system integrity controls and recovery procedures.
- *Element integrity:* concern that the value of a specific data element is written or changed only by authorized users. Proper access controls protect a database from corruption by unauthorized users.
- *Element accuracy:* concern that only correct values are written into the elements of a database. Checks on the values of elements can help to prevent insertion of improper values. Also, constraint conditions can detect incorrect values.

Protection Features from the Operating System

In Chapter 4 we discussed the protection an operating system provides for its users. When a system is administered responsibly, the files of a database are backed up periodically, as are other user files. The files are protected during normal execution against outside access by the operating system's standard access control facilities. Finally, the operating system performs certain integrity checks for all data as a part of normal read and write operations for I/O devices. These controls provide basic security for databases, but the database manager must enhance them.

Two-Phase Update

A serious problem for a database manager is the failure of the computing system in the middle of modifying data. If the data item to be modified was a long field, half of the field might show the new value, while the other half would contain the old. Even if errors of this type were spotted easily (which they are not), a more subtle problem occurs when several fields are updated and no single field appears to be in obvious error. The solution to this problem, proposed first by Lampson and Sturgis [LAM76] and adopted by most DBMSs, uses a two-phase update.

Update Technique

During the first phase, called the **intent** phase, the DBMS gathers the resources it needs to perform the update. It may gather data, create dummy records, open files, lock out other users, and calculate final answers; in short, it does everything to prepare for the update, but it makes no changes to the database. The first phase is repeatable an unlimited number of times because it takes no permanent action. If the system fails during execution of the first phase, no harm is done, because all these steps can be restarted and repeated after the system resumes processing.

The last event of the first phase, called **committing,** involves the writing of a **commit flag** to the database. The commit flag means that the DBMS has passed the point of no return: After committing, the DBMS begins making permanent changes.

The second phase makes the permanent changes. During the second phase, no actions from before the commit can be repeated, but the update activities of phase two can also be repeated as often as needed. If the system fails during the second phase, the database may contain incomplete data, but the system can repair these data by performing all activities of the second phase. After the second phase has been completed, the database is again complete.

Two-Phase Update Example

Suppose a database contains an inventory of a company's office supplies. The company's central stockroom stores paper, pens, paper clips, and the like, and the different departments requisition items as they need them. The company buys in bulk to obtain the best prices. Each department has a budget for office supplies, so there is a charging mechanism by which the cost of supplies is recovered from the department. Also, the central stockroom monitors quantities of supplies on hand so as to order new supplies when the stock becomes low.

Suppose the process begins with a requisition from the accounting department for 50 boxes of paper clips. Assume that there are 107 boxes in stock and a new order is placed if the quantity in stock ever falls below 100. Here are the steps followed after the stockroom receives the requisition.

1. The stockroom checks the database to determine that 50 boxes of paper clips are on hand. If not, the requisition is rejected and the transaction is finished.
2. If enough paper clips are in stock, the stockroom deducts 50 from the inventory figure in the database (107 – 50 = 57).

3. The stockroom charges accounting's supplies budget (also in the database) for 50 boxes of paper clips.
4. The stockroom checks its remaining quantity on hand (57) to determine whether the remaining quantity is below the reorder point. Because it is, a notice to order more paper clips is generated, and the item is flagged as "on order" in the database.
5. A delivery order is prepared, enabling 50 boxes of paper clips to be sent to accounting.

All five of these steps must be completed in the order listed for the database to be accurate and for the transaction to be processed correctly.

Suppose a failure occurs while these steps are being processed. If the failure occurs before step 1 is complete, there is no harm because the entire transaction can be restarted. However, during steps 2, 3, and 4, changes are made to elements in the database. If a failure occurs then, the values in the database are inconsistent. Worse, the transaction cannot be reprocessed because a requisition would be deducted twice, or a department would be charged twice, or two delivery orders would be prepared.

When a two-phase commit is used, **shadow values** are maintained for key data points. A shadow data value is computed and stored locally during the intent phase, and it is copied to the actual database during the commit phase. The operations on the database would be performed as follows for a two-phase commit.

Intent:

1. Check the value of COMMIT-FLAG in the database. If it is set, this phase cannot be performed. Halt or loop, checking COMMIT-FLAG until it is not set.
2. Compare number of boxes of paper clips on hand to number requisitioned; if more are requisitioned than are on hand, halt.
3. Compute TCLIPS = ONHAND – REQUISITION.
4. Obtain BUDGET, the current supplies budget remaining for accounting department. Compute TBUDGET = BUDGET – COST, where COST is the cost of 50 boxes of clips.
5. Check whether TCLIPS is below reorder point; if so, set TREORDER = TRUE; else set TREORDER = FALSE.

Commit:

1. Set COMMIT-FLAG in database.
2. Copy TCLIPS to CLIPS in database.
3. Copy TBUDGET to BUDGET in database.
4. Copy TREORDER to REORDER in database.
5. Prepare notice to deliver paper clips to accounting department. Indicate transaction completed in log.
6. Unset COMMIT-FLAG.

With this example, each step of the intent phase depends only on unmodified values from the database and the previous results of the intent phase. Each variable beginning with T is a shadow variable used only in this transaction. The steps of the intent phase can be repeated an unlimited number of times without affecting the integrity of the database.

Once the DBMS begins the commit phase, it writes a COMMIT flag. When this flag is set, the DBMS will not perform any steps of the intent phase. Intent steps cannot be performed after committing because database values are modified in the commit phase. Notice, however, that the steps of the commit phase can be repeated an unlimited number of times, again with no negative effect on the correctness of the values in the database.

The one remaining flaw in this logic occurs if the system fails after writing the "transaction complete" message in the log but before clearing the commit flag in the database. It is a simple matter to work backward through the transaction log to find completed transactions for which the commit flag is still set and to clear those flags.

Redundancy/Internal Consistency

Many DBMSs maintain additional information to detect internal inconsistencies in data. The additional information ranges from a few check bits to duplicate or shadow fields, depending on the importance of the data.

Error Detection and Correction Codes

One form of redundancy is error detection and correction codes, such as parity bits, Hamming codes, and cyclic redundancy checks. These codes can be applied to single fields, records, or the entire database. Each time a data item is placed in the database, the appropriate check codes are computed and stored; each time a data item is retrieved, a similar check code is computed and compared to the stored value. If the values are unequal, they signify to the DBMS that an error has occurred in the database. Some of these codes point out the place of the error; others show precisely what the correct value should be. The more information provided, the more space required to store the codes.

Shadow Fields

Entire attributes or entire records can be duplicated in a database. If the data are irreproducible, this second copy can provide an immediate replacement if an error is detected. Obviously, redundant fields require substantial storage space.

Recovery

In addition to these error correction processes, a DBMS can maintain a log of user accesses, particularly changes. In the event of a failure, the database is reloaded from a backup copy and all later changes are then applied from the audit log.

Concurrency/Consistency

Database systems are often multiuser systems. Accesses by two users sharing the same database must be constrained so that neither interferes with the other. Simple locking is done by the DBMS. If two users attempt to read the same data item, there is no conflict because both obtain the same value.

If both users try to modify the same data items, we often assume that there is no conflict because each knows what to write; the value to be written does not depend on the previous value of the data item. However, this supposition is not quite accurate.

To see how concurrent modification can get us into trouble, suppose that the database consists of seat reservations for a particular airline flight. Agent A, booking a seat for passenger Mock, submits a query to find what seats are still available. The agent knows that Mock prefers a right aisle seat, and the agent finds that seats 5D, 11D, and 14D are open. At the same time, Agent B is trying to book seats for a family of three traveling together. In response to a query, the database indicates that 8A–B–C and 11D–E–F are the two remaining groups of three adjacent unassigned seats. Agent A submits the update command

```
SELECT (SEAT-NO = '11D')
ASSIGN 'MOCK,E' TO PASSENGER-NAME
```

while Agent B submits the update sequence

```
SELECT (SEAT-NO = '11D')
ASSIGN 'EHLERS,P' TO PASSENGER-NAME
```

as well as commands for seats 11E and 11F. Then two passengers have been booked into the same seat (which would be uncomfortable, to say the least).

Both agents have acted properly: Each sought a list of empty seats, chose one seat from the list, and updated the database to show to whom the seat was assigned. The difficulty in this situation is the time delay between reading a value from the database and writing a modification of that value. During the delay time, another user has accessed the same data.

To resolve this problem, a DBMS treats the entire query–update cycle as a single atomic operation. The command from the agent must now resemble "read the current value of seat PASSENGER-NAME for seat 11D; if it is 'UNASSIGNED', modify it to 'MOCK,E' (or 'EHLERS,P')." The read–modify cycle must be completed as an uninterrupted item without allowing any other users access to the PASSENGER-NAME field for seat 11D. The second agent's request to book would not be considered until after the first agent's had been completed; at that time, the value of PASSENGER-NAME would no longer be 'UNASSIGNED.'

A final problem in concurrent access is read–write. Suppose one user is updating a value when a second user wishes to read it. If the read is done while the write is in progress, the reader may receive data that are only partly updated. Consequently, the DBMS locks any read requests until a write has been completed.

Monitors

The **monitor** is the unit of a DBMS responsible for the structural integrity of the database. A monitor can check values being entered to ensure their consistency with the rest of the database or with characteristics of the particular field. For example, a monitor might reject alphabetic characters for a numeric field. We discuss several forms of monitors.

Range Comparisons

A range comparison monitor tests each new value to ensure that the value is within an acceptable range. If the data value is outside the range, it is rejected and not entered into the database. For example, the range of dates might be 1–31, "/," 1–12, "/," 1900–2099. An even more sophisticated range check might limit the day portion to 1–30 for months with 30 days, or it might take into account leap year for February.

Range comparisons are also convenient for numeric quantities. For example, a salary field might be limited to $200,000, or the size of a house might be constrained to be between 500 and 5,000 square feet. Range constraints can also apply to other data having a predictable form.

Range comparisons can be used to ensure the internal consistency of a database. When used in this manner, comparisons are made between two database elements. For example, a grade level from K–8 would be acceptable if the record described a student at an elementary school, whereas only 9–12 would be acceptable for a record of a student in high school. Similarly, a person could be assigned a job qualification score of 75–100 only if the person had completed college or had had at least ten years of work experience.

Checks of these types can control the data allowed in the database. They can also be used to test existing values for reasonableness. If you suspect that the data in a database have been corrupted, a range check of all records could identify those having suspicious values.

State Constraints

State constraints describe the condition of the entire database. At no time should the database values violate these constraints. Phrased differently, if these constraints are not met, some value of the database is in error.

In the section on two-phase updates, we saw how to use a commit flag, which is set at the start of the commit phase and cleared at the completion of the commit phase. The commit flag can be considered a state constraint because it is used at the end of every transaction for which the commit flag set is not set. Earlier in this chapter, we described a process to reset the commit flags in the event of a failure after a commit phase. In this way, the status of the commit flag is an integrity constraint on the database.

For another example of a state constraint, consider a database of employees' classifications. At any time, at most one employee is classified as "president." Furthermore, each employee has an employee number different from that of every other employee. If a mechanical or software failure causes portions of the database file to be duplicated, one of these uniqueness constraints might be violated. By testing the state of the database, the DBMS could identify records with duplicate employee numbers or two records classified as "president."

Transition Constraints

State constraints describe the state of a correct database. **Transition constraints** describe conditions necessary before changes can be applied to a database. For example, before a new employee can be added to the database, there must be a position number in the database with status "vacant." (That is, an empty slot must exist.) Furthermore, after the employee is added, exactly one slot must be changed from "vacant" to the number of the new employee.

Simple range checks can be implemented within most database management systems. However, the more sophisticated state and transition constraints can require special procedures for testing. Such user-written procedures are invoked by the DBMS each time an action must be checked.

Summary of Data Reliability

Reliability, correctness, and integrity are three closely related concepts in databases. Users trust the DBMS to maintain their data correctly, so integrity issues are very important to database security.

6.4 SENSITIVE DATA

Some databases contain what is called sensitive data. As a working definition, let us say that **sensitive data** are data that should not be made public. Determining which data items and fields are sensitive depends both on the individual database and the underlying meaning of the data. Obviously, some databases, such as a public library catalog, contain no sensitive data; other databases, such as defense-related ones, are totally sensitive. These two cases—nothing sensitive and everything sensitive—are the easiest to handle, because they can be covered by access controls to the database itself. Someone either is or is not an authorized user. These controls are provided by the operating system.

The more difficult problem, which is also the more interesting one, is the case in which *some but not all* of the elements in the database are sensitive. There may be varying degrees of sensitivity. For example, a university database might contain student data consisting of name, financial aid, dorm, drug use, sex, parking fines, and race. Name and dorm are probably the least sensitive; financial aid, parking fines, and drug use the most; sex and race somewhere in between. That is, many people may have legitimate access to name, some to sex and race, and relatively few to financial aid, parking fines, or drug use. Indeed, knowledge of the existence of some fields, such as drug use, may itself be sensitive. Thus, security concerns not only the data elements but their context and meaning. An example of this database is shown in Table 6-6.

Furthermore, we must take into account different degrees of sensitivity. For instance, although they are all highly sensitive, the financial aid, parking fines, and drug-use fields may not have the same kinds of access restrictions. Our security requirements may demand that a few people be authorized to see each field, but no one be authorized to see all three. The challenge of the access control problem is to limit users' access so that they can obtain only the data to which they have legitimate access. Alternatively, the access control problem forces us to ensure that sensitive data are not to be released to unauthorized people.

Several factors can make data sensitive.

- *Inherently sensitive.* The value itself may be so revealing that it is sensitive. Examples are the locations of defensive missiles or the median income of barbers in a town with only one barber.

TABLE 6-6 Sample Database.

Name	Sex	Race	Aid	Fines	Drugs	Dorm
Adams	M	C	5000	45.	1	Holmes
Bailey	M	B	0	0.	0	Grey
Chin	F	A	3000	20.	0	West
Dewitt	M	B	1000	35.	3	Grey
Earhart	F	C	2000	95.	1	Holmes
Fein	F	C	1000	15.	0	West
Groff	M	C	4000	0.	3	West
Hill	F	B	5000	10.	2	Holmes
Koch	F	C	0	0.	1	West
Liu	F	A	0	10.	2	Grey
Majors	M	C	2000	0.	2	Grey

- *From a sensitive source.* The source of the data may indicate a need for confidentiality. An example is information from an informer whose identity would be compromised if the information were disclosed.
- *Declared sensitive.* The database administrator or the owner of the data may have declared the data to be sensitive. Examples are classified military data or the name of the anonymous donor of a piece of art.
- Part of a sensitive *attribute* or a sensitive *record.* In a database, an entire attribute or record may be classified as sensitive. Examples are the salary attribute of a personnel database or a record describing a secret space mission.
- Sensitive *in relation to previously disclosed information.* Some data become sensitive in the presence of other data. For example, the longitude coordinate of a secret gold mine reveals little, but the longitude coordinate in conjunction with the latitude coordinate pinpoints the mine.

All of these factors must be considered to determine the sensitivity of the data.

Access Decisions

Remember that a database administrator is a *person* who decides *what* data should be in the database and *who* should have access to it. The database administrator considers the need for different users to know certain information and decides who should have what access. Decisions of the database administrator are based on an access *policy.*

The database manager or DBMS is a *program* that operates on the database and auxiliary control information to implement the decisions of the access policy. We say that the database manager decides to permit user x to access data y. Clearly, a program or machine cannot decide anything; it is more precise to say that the program performs the instructions by which x accesses y as a way of implementing the policy established by the database administrator. (Now you see why we use the simpler wording.) To keep explanations concise, we occasionally describe programs as if they can carry out human thought processes.

The DBMS may consider several factors when deciding whether to permit an access. These factors include availability of the data, acceptability of the access, and authenticity of the user. We expand on these three factors below.

Availability of Data

One or more required elements may be inaccessible. For example, if a user is updating several fields, other users' accesses to those fields must be blocked temporarily. This blocking ensures that users do not receive inaccurate information, such as a new street address with an old city and state, or a new code component with old documentation. Blocking is usually temporary. When performing an update, a user may have to block access to several fields or several records to ensure the consistency of data for others.

Notice, however, that if the updating user aborts the transaction while the update is in progress, the other users may be permanently blocked from accessing the record. This indefinite postponement is also a security problem, resulting in denial of service.

Acceptability of Access

One or more values of the record may be sensitive and not accessible by the general user. A DBMS should not release sensitive data to unauthorized individuals.

Deciding what is sensitive, however, is not as simple as it sounds, because the fields may not be directly requested. A user may have asked for certain records that contain sensitive data, but the user's purpose may have been only to project the values from particular fields that are not sensitive. For example, a user of the database shown in Table 6-6 may request the NAME and DORM of any student for whom FINES is not 0. The exact value of the sensitive field FINES is not disclosed, although "not 0" is a partial disclosure. Even when a sensitive value is not explicitly given, the database manager may deny access on the grounds that it reveals information the user is not authorized to have.

Alternatively, the user may want to derive a nonsensitive statistic from the sensitive data; for example, if the average financial aid value does not reveal any individual's financial aid value, the database management system can safely return the average. However, the average of one data value discloses that value.

Assurance of Authenticity

Certain characteristics of the user external to the database may also be considered when permitting access. For example, to enhance security, the database administrator may permit someone to access the database only at certain times, such as during working hours. Previous user requests may also be taken into account; repeated requests for the same data or requests that exhaust a certain category of information may be used to find out all elements in a set when a direct query is not allowed. As we shall see, sensitive data can sometimes be revealed by combined results from several less sensitive queries.

Types of Disclosures

Data can be sensitive, but so can their characteristics. In this section, we see that even descriptive information about data (such as their existence or whether they have an element that is zero) is a form of disclosure.

Exact Data

The most serious disclosure is the *exact value of a sensitive data item* itself. The user may know that sensitive data are being requested, or the user may request general data without knowing that some of it is sensitive. A faulty database manager may even deliver sensitive data by accident, without the user's having requested it. In all of these cases the result is the same: The security of the sensitive data has been breached.

Bounds

Another exposure is disclosing bounds on a sensitive value, that is, indicating that a sensitive value, y, is between two values, L and H. Sometimes, by using a narrowing technique not unlike the binary search, the user may first determine that $L \leq y \leq H$ and then see whether $L \leq y \leq H/2$, and so forth, thereby permitting the user to determine y to any desired precision. In another case, merely revealing that a value such as the athletic scholarship budget or the number of CIA agents exceeds a certain amount may be a serious breach of security.

Sometimes, however, bounds are a useful way to present sensitive data. It is common to release upper and lower bounds for data without identifying the specific records. For example, a company may announce that its salaries for programmers range from $50,000 to $82,000. If you are a programmer earning $79,700, you can presume that you are fairly well off, so you have the information you want; however, the announcement does not disclose who are the highest- and lowest-paid programmers.

Negative Result

Sometimes we can word a query to determine a negative result. That is, we can learn that z is *not* the value of y. For example, knowing that 0 is not the total number of felony convictions for a person reveals that the person was convicted of a felony. The distinction between 1 and 2 or 46 and 47 felonies is not as sensitive as the distinction between 0 and 1. Therefore, disclosing that a value is not 0 is a significant disclosure. Similarly, if a student does not appear on the honors list, you can infer that the person's grade point average is below 3.50. This information is not too revealing, however, because the range of grade point averages from 0.0 to 3.49 is rather wide.

Existence

In some cases, the existence of data is itself a sensitive piece of data, regardless of the actual value. For example, an employer may not want employees to know that their use of long distance telephone lines is being monitored. In this case, discovering a LONG DISTANCE field in a personnel file would reveal sensitive data.

Probable Value

Finally, it may be possible to determine the probability that a certain element has a certain value. To see how, suppose you want to find out whether the president of the United States is registered in the Tory party. Knowing that the president is in the database, you submit two queries to the database:

> How many people have 1600 Pennsylvania Avenue as their official residence? (Response: 4)
>
> How many people have 1600 Pennsylvania Avenue as their official residence and have YES as the value of TORY? (Response: 1)

From these queries you conclude there is a 25 percent likelihood that the president is a registered Tory.

Summary of Partial Disclosure

We have seen several examples of how a security problem can result if characteristics of sensitive data are revealed. Notice that some of the techniques we presented used information *about* the data, rather than direct access to the data, to infer sensitive results. A successful security strategy must protect from both direct and indirect disclosure.

Security versus Precision

Our examples have illustrated how difficult it is to determine what data are sensitive and how to protect them. The situation is complicated by a desire to share nonsensitive data. For reasons of confidentiality we want to disclose only those data that are not sensitive. Such an outlook encourages a conservative philosophy in determining what data to disclose: less is better than more.

On the other hand, consider the users of the data. The conservative philosophy suggests rejecting any query that mentions a sensitive field. We may thereby reject many reasonable and nondisclosing queries. For example, a researcher may want a list of grades for all students using drugs, or a statistician may request lists of salaries for all men and for all women. These queries probably do not compromise the identity of any individual. We want to disclose as much data as possible so that users of the database have access to the data they need. This goal, called **precision,** aims to protect all sensitive data while revealing as much nonsensitive data as possible.

We can depict the relationship between security and precision with concentric circles. As Figure 6-3 shows, the sensitive data in the central circle should be carefully

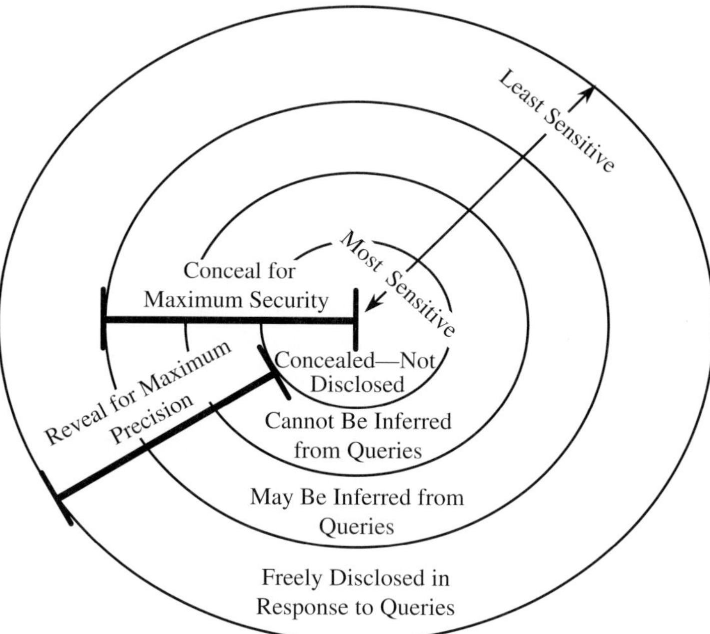

FIGURE 6-3 Security versus Precision.

concealed. The outside band represents data we willingly disclose in response to queries. But we know that the user may put together pieces of disclosed data and infer other, more deeply hidden, data. The figure shows us that beneath the outer layer may be yet more nonsensitive data that the user cannot infer.

The ideal combination of security and precision allows us to maintain perfect confidentiality with maximum precision; in other words, we disclose all and only the nonsensitive data. But achieving this goal is not as easy as it might seem, as we show in the next section. Sidebar 6-3 gives an example of using imprecise techniques to improve accuracy. In the next section, we consider ways in which sensitive data can be obtained from queries that appear harmless.

6.5 INFERENCE

The **inference problem** is a way to infer or derive sensitive data from nonsensitive data. The inference problem is a subtle vulnerability in database security.

The database in Table 6-7 can help illustrate the inference problem. Recall that AID is the amount of financial aid a student is receiving. FINES is the amount of parking fines still owed. DRUGS is the result of a drug-use survey: 0 means never used and 3 means frequent user. Obviously this information should be kept confidential. We assume that AID, FINES, and DRUGS are sensitive fields, although only when the values are related to a specific individual. In this section, we look at ways to determine sensitive data values from the database.

Sidebar 6-3 Accuracy and Imprecision

Article I of the U.S. Constitution charges Congress with determining the "respective numbers... of free...and all other persons...within every...term of ten years." This count is used for many things, including apportioning the number of representatives to Congress and distributing funds fairly to the states. Although difficult in 1787, this task has become increasingly challenging. The count cannot simply be based on residences because some homeless people would be missed. A fair count cannot be obtained solely by sending a questionnaire for each person to complete and return because some people cannot read and, more significantly, many people do not return such forms. And there is always the possibility that a form would be lost in the mail.

For the 2000 census the U.S. Census Bureau proposed using statistical sampling and estimating techniques to approximate the population. With these techniques they would select certain areas in which to take two counts: a regular count and a second, especially diligent search for every person residing in the area. In this way the bureau could determine the "undercount," the number of people missed in the regular count. They could then use this undercount factor to adjust the regular count in other similar areas and thus obtain a more accurate, although less precise, count.

The Supreme Court ruled that statistical sampling techniques were acceptable for determining revenue distribution to the states but not for allocating representatives in Congress. As a result, the census can never get an exact, accurate count of the number of people in the United States or even in a major U.S. city. At the same time, concerns about precision and privacy prevent the Census Bureau from releasing information about any particular individual living in the United States.

Does this lack of accuracy and exactness mean that the census is not useful? No. We may not know exactly how many people live in Washington D.C. or the exact information about a particular resident of Washington D.C., but we can use the census information to characterize the residents of Washington D.C. For example, we can determine the maximum, minimum, mean, and median ages or incomes, and we can investigate the relationships among characteristics, such as between education level and income. So accuracy and precision help to reflect the balance between protection and need to know.

Direct Attack

In a direct attack, a user tries to determine values of sensitive fields by seeking them directly with queries that yield few records. The most successful technique is to form a query so specific that it matches exactly one data item.

In Table 6-7, a sensitive query might be

```
List NAME where
      SEX=M ∧ DRUGS=1
```

This query discloses that for record ADAMS, DRUGS=1. However, it is an obvious attack because it selects people for whom DRUGS=1.

TABLE 6-7 Sample Database (repeated).

Name	Sex	Race	Aid	Fines	Drugs	Dorm
Adams	M	C	5000	45.	1	Holmes
Bailey	M	B	0	0.	0	Grey
Chin	F	A	3000	20.	0	West
Dewitt	M	B	1000	35.	3	Grey
Earhart	F	C	2000	95.	1	Holmes
Fein	F	C	1000	15.	0	West
Groff	M	C	4000	0.	3	West
Hill	F	B	5000	10.	2	Holmes
Koch	F	C	0	0.	1	West
Liu	F	A	0	10.	2	Grey
Majors	M	C	2000	0.	2	Grey

A less obvious query is

```
List NAME where
      (SEX=M ∧ DRUGS=1) ∨
      (SEX≠M ∧ SEX≠F) ∨
      (DORM=AYRES)
```

On the surface, this query looks as if it should conceal drug usage by selecting other non-drug-related records as well. However, this query still retrieves only one record, revealing a name that corresponds to the sensitive DRUG value. The DBMS needs to know that SEX has only two possible values, so that the second clause will select no records. Even if that were possible, the DBMS would also need to know that no records exist with DORM=AYRES, even though AYRES might in fact be an acceptable value for DORM.

Organizations that publish personal statistical data, such as the U.S. Census Bureau, do not reveal results when a small number of people make up a large proportion of a category. The rule of "*n* items over *k* percent" means that data should be withheld if *n* items represent over *k* percent of the result reported. In the previous case, the one person selected represents 100 percent of the data reported, so that there would be no ambiguity about which person matches the query.

Indirect Attack

Another procedure, used by the U.S. Census Bureau and other organizations that gather sensitive data, is to release only statistics. The organizations suppress individual names, addresses, or other characteristics by which a single individual can be recognized. Only neutral statistics, such as count, sum, and mean, are released.

The indirect attack seeks to infer a final result based on one or more intermediate statistical results. But this approach requires work outside the database itself. In particular, a statistical attack seeks to use some apparently anonymous statistical measure to infer individual data. In the following sections, we present several examples of indirect attacks on databases that report statistics.

Sum

An attack by sum tries to infer a value from a reported sum. For example, with the sample database in Table 6-7, it might seem safe to report student aid total by sex and dorm. Such a report is shown in Table 6-8. This seemingly innocent report reveals that no female living in Grey is receiving financial aid. Thus, we can infer that any female living in Grey (such as Liu) is certainly not receiving financial aid. This approach often allows us to determine a negative result.

Count

The count can be combined with the sum to produce some even more revealing results. Often these two statistics are released for a database to allow users to determine average values. (Conversely, if count and mean are released, sum can be deduced.)

Table 6-9 shows the count of records for students by dorm and sex. This table is innocuous by itself. Combined with the sum table, however, this table demonstrates that the two males in Holmes and West are receiving financial aid in the amount of $5000 and $4000, respectively. We can obtain the names by selecting the subschema of NAME, DORM, which is not sensitive because it delivers only low-security data on the entire database.

Median

By a slightly more complicated process, we can determine an individual value from medians. The attack requires finding selections having one point of intersection that happens to be exactly in the middle, as shown in Figure 6-4.

For example, in our sample database, there are five males and three persons whose drug use value is 2. Arranged in order of aid, these lists are shown in Table 6-10. Notice that Majors is the only name common to both lists, and conveniently that name is

TABLE 6-8 Sums of Financial Aid by Dorm and Sex.

	Holmes	Grey	West	Total
M	5000	3000	4000	12000
F	7000	0	4000	11000
Total	12000	3000	8000	23000

TABLE 6-9 Count of Students by Dorm and Sex.

	Holmes	Grey	West	Total
M	1	3	1	5
F	2	1	3	6
Total	3	4	4	11

in the middle of each list. Someone working at the Health Clinic might be able to find out that Majors is a white male whose drug-use score is 2. That information identifies Majors as the intersection of these two lists and pinpoints Majors' financial aid as $2000. In this example, the queries

```
q = median(AID where SEX = M)
p = median(AID where DRUGS = 2)
```

reveal the exact financial aid amount for Majors.

Tracker Attacks

As already explained, database management systems may conceal data when a small number of entries make up a large proportion of the data revealed. A **tracker attack** can fool the database manager into locating the desired data by using additional queries that

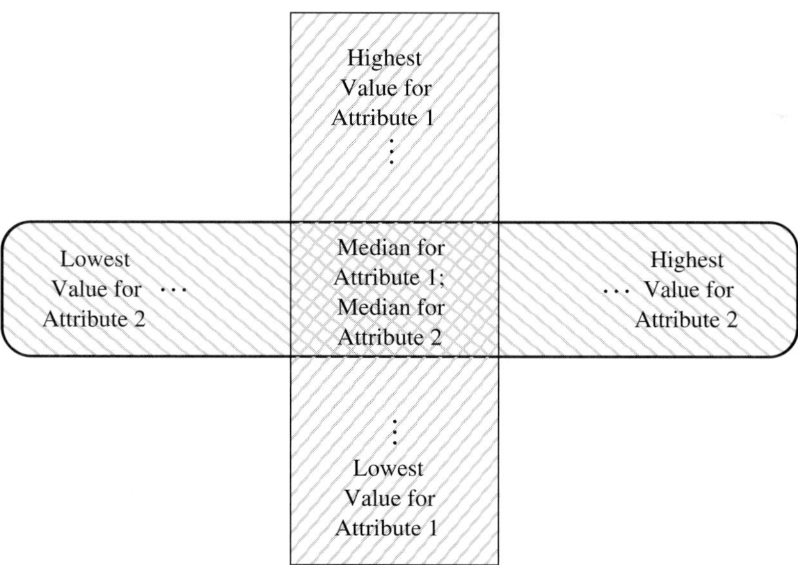

FIGURE 6-4 Intersecting Medians.

TABLE 6-10 Inference from Median of Two Lists.

Name	Sex	Drugs	Aid
Bailey	M	0	0
Dewitt	M	3	1000
Majors	M	2	2000
Groff	M	3	4000
Adams	M	1	5000
Liu	F	2	0
Majors	M	2	2000
Hill	F	2	5000

produce small results. The tracker adds additional records to be retrieved for two different queries; the two sets of records cancel each other out, leaving only the statistic or data desired. The approach is to use intelligent padding of two queries. In other words, instead of trying to identify a unique value, we request $n - 1$ other values (where there are n values in the database). Given n and $n - 1$, we can easily compute the desired single element.

For instance, suppose we wish to know how many female Caucasians live in Holmes Hall. A query posed might be

```
count ((SEX=F) ∧ (RACE=C) ∧ (DORM=Holmes))
```

The database management system might consult the database, find that the answer is 1, and refuse to answer that query because one record dominates the result of the query. However, further analysis of the query allows us to track sensitive data through nonsensitive queries.

The query

```
q=count((SEX=F) ∧ (RACE=C) ∧ (DORM=Holmes))
```

is of the form

```
q = count(a ∧ b ∧ c)
```

By using the rules of logic and algebra, we can transform this query to

```
q = count(a ∧ b ∧ c) = count(a) - count(a ∧ ¬ (b ∧ c))
```

Thus, the original query is equivalent to

```
count (SEX=F)
```

minus

```
count ((SEX=F) ∧ ((RACE≠C) ∨ (DORM≠Holmes)))
```

Because count(a) = 6 and count($a \wedge \neg (b \wedge c)$) = 5, we can determine the suppressed value easily: 6 – 5 = 1. Furthermore, neither 6 nor 5 is a sensitive count.

Linear System Vulnerability

A tracker is a specific case of a more general vulnerability. With a little logic, algebra, and luck in the distribution of the database contents, it may be possible to determine a series of queries that returns results relating to several different sets. For example, the following system of five queries does not overtly reveal any single c value from the database. However, the queries' equations can be solved for each of the unknown c values, revealing them all.

$$\begin{aligned} q_1 &= c_1 + c_2 + c_3 + c_4 + c_5 \\ q_2 &= c_1 + c_2 + c_4 \\ q_3 &= c_3 + c_4 \\ q_4 &= c_4 + c_5 \\ q_5 &= c_2 + c_5 \end{aligned}$$

To see how, use basic algebra to note that $q_1 - q_2 = c_3 + c_5$, and $q_3 - q_4 = c_3 - c_5$. Then, subtracting these two equations, we obtain $c_5 = ((q_1 - q_2) - (q_3 - q_4))/2$. Once we know c_5, we can derive the others.

In fact, this attack can also be used to obtain results *other than* numerical ones. Recall that we can apply logical rules to *and* ($\wedge$) and *or* ($\vee$), typical operators for database queries, to derive values from a series of logical expressions. For example, each expression might represent a query asking for precise data instead of counts, such as the equation

$$q_1 = s_1 \vee s_2 \vee s_3 \vee s_4 \vee s_5$$

The result of the query is a set of records. Using logic and set algebra in a manner similar to our numerical example, we can carefully determine the actual values for each of the s_i.

Controls for Statistical Inference Attacks

Denning and Schlörer [DEN83a] present a very good survey of techniques for maintaining security in databases. The controls for all statistical attacks are similar. Essentially, there are two ways to protect against inference attacks: Either controls are applied to the queries or controls are applied to individual items within the database. As we have seen, it is difficult to determine whether a given query discloses sensitive data. Thus, query controls are effective primarily against direct attacks.

Suppression and concealing are two controls applied to data items. With **suppression,** sensitive data values are not provided; the query is rejected without response. With **concealing,** the answer provided is *close to* but not exactly the actual value.

These two controls reflect the contrast between security and precision. With suppression, any results provided are correct, yet many responses must be withheld to maintain security. With concealing, more results can be provided, but the precision of the results is lower. The choice between suppression and concealing depends on the context of the database. Examples of suppression and concealing follow.

TABLE 6-11 Students by Dorm and Sex.

	Holmes	Grey	West	Total
M	1	3	1	5
F	2	1	3	6
Total	3	4	4	11

Limited Response Suppression

The n-item k-percent rule eliminates certain low-frequency elements from being displayed. It is not sufficient to delete them, however, if their values can also be inferred. To see why, consider Table 6-11, which shows counts of students by dorm and sex.

The data in this table suggest that the cells with counts of 1 should be suppressed; their counts are too revealing. But it does no good to suppress the Male–Holmes cell when the value 1 can be determined by subtracting Female–Holmes (2) from the total (3) to determine 1, as shown in Table 6-12.

When one cell is suppressed in a table with totals for rows and columns, it is necessary to suppress at least one additional cell on the row and one on the column to provide some confusion. Using this logic, all cells (except totals) would have to be suppressed in this small sample table. When totals are not provided, single cells in a row or column can be suppressed.

Combined Results

Another control combines rows or columns to protect sensitive values. For example, Table 6-13 shows several sensitive results that identify single individuals. (Even though these counts may not seem sensitive, they can be used to infer sensitive data such as NAME; therefore, we consider them to be sensitive.)

These counts, combined with other results such as sum, permit us to infer individual drug-use values for the three males, as well as to infer that no female was rated 3 for drug use. To suppress such sensitive information, it is possible to combine the attribute values for 0 and 1, and also for 2 and 3, producing the less sensitive results shown in Table 6-14. In this instance, it is impossible to identify any single value.

Another way of combining results is to present values in ranges. For example, instead of releasing exact financial aid figures, results can be released for the ranges $0–1999, $2000–3999, and $4000 and above. Even if there is only one record represented by a single result, the exact value of that record is not known. Similarly, the highest and lowest financial aid values are concealed.

Yet another method of combining is by rounding. This technique is actually a fairly well known example of combining by range. If numbers are rounded to the nearest 10, the effective ranges are 0–5, 6–15, 16–25, and so on. Actual values are rounded up or down to the nearest multiple of some base.

TABLE 6-12 Students by Dorm and Sex, with Low Count Suppression.

	Holmes	Grey	West	Total
M	–	3	–	5
F	2	–	3	6
Total	3	4	4	11

Random Sample

With random sample control, a result is not derived from the whole database; instead the result is computed on a random sample of the database. The sample chosen is large enough to be valid. Because the sample is not the whole database, a query against this sample will not necessarily match the result for the whole database. Thus, a result of 5 percent for a particular query means that 5 percent of the records chosen for the sample for this query had the desired property. You would expect that approximately 5 percent of the entire database will have the property in question, but the actual percentage may be quite different.

So that averaging attacks from repeated, equivalent queries are prevented, the same sample set should be chosen for equivalent queries. In this way, all equivalent queries will produce the same result, although that result will be only an approximation for the entire database.

Random Data Perturbation

It is sometimes useful to perturb the values of the database by a small error. For each x_i that is the true value of data item i in the database, we can generate a small random error term ε_i and add it to x_i for statistical results. The ε values are both positive and negative, so that some reported values will be slightly higher than their true values and other reported values will be lower. Statistical measures such as sum and mean will be close but not necessarily exact. Data perturbation is easier to use than random sample selection because it is easier to store all the ε values in order to produce the same result for equivalent queries.

TABLE 6-13 Students by Sex and Drug Use.

	Drug Use			
Sex	**0**	**1**	**2**	**3**
M	1	1	1	2
F	2	2	2	0

TABLE 6-14 Suppression by Combining Revealing Values.

Sex	Drug Use: 0 or 1	Drug Use: 2 or 3
M	2	3
F	4	2

Query Analysis

A more complex form of security uses query analysis. Here, a query and its implications are analyzed to determine whether a result should be provided. As noted earlier, query analysis can be quite difficult. One approach involves maintaining a query history for each user and judging a query in the context of what inferences are possible given previous results.

Conclusion on the Inference Problem

There are no perfect solutions to the inference problem. The approaches to controlling it follow the three paths listed below. The first two methods can be used either to limit queries accepted or to limit data provided in response to a query. The last method applies only to data released.

- *Suppress obviously sensitive information.* This action can be taken fairly easily. The tendency is to err on the side of suppression, thereby restricting the usefulness of the database.
- *Track what the user knows.* Although possibly leading to the greatest safe disclosure, this approach is extremely costly. Information must be maintained on all users, even though most are not trying to obtain sensitive data. Moreover, this approach seldom takes into account what any two people may know together and cannot address what a single user can accomplish by using multiple IDs.
- *Disguise the data.* Random perturbation and rounding can inhibit statistical attacks that depend on exact values for logical and algebraic manipulation. The users of the database receive slightly incorrect or possibly inconsistent results.

It is unlikely that research will reveal a simple, easy-to-apply measure that determines exactly which data can be revealed without compromising sensitive data.

Nevertheless, an effective control for the inference problem is just knowing that it exists. As with other problems in security, recognition of the problem leads to understanding of the purposes of controlling the problem and to sensitivity to the potential difficulties caused by the problem. However, just knowing of possible database attacks does not necessarily mean people will protect against those attacks, as explained in Sidebar 6-4. It is also noteworthy that much of the research on database inference was done in the early 1980s, but this proposal appeared almost two decades later.

Sidebar 6-4 Iceland Protects Privacy Against Inference

In 1998, Iceland authorized the building of a database of citizens' medical records, genealogy, and genetic information. Ostensibly, this database would provide data on genetic diseases to researchers—medical professionals and drug companies. Iceland is especially interesting for genetic disease research because the gene pool has remained stable for a long time; few outsiders have moved to Iceland and few Icelanders have emigrated. For privacy, all identifying names or numbers would be replaced by a unique pseudonym. The Iceland health department asked computer security expert Ross Anderson to analyze the security aspects of this approach.

Anderson found several flaws with the proposed approach [AND98]:

- Inclusion in the genealogical database complicates the task of maintaining individuals' anonymity because there are distinctive family features. Moreover, parts of the genealogical database are already public, because information about individuals is published in their birth and death records. It would be rather easy to identify someone in a family of three children born, respectively, in 1910, 1911, and 1929.
- Even a life's history of medical events may identify an individual. Many people would know that a person broke her leg skiing in one winter and contracted a skin disease the following summer.
- Even small sample set restrictions on queries would fail to protect against algebraic attacks.
- To analyze the genetic data, which by its nature is necessarily of very fine detail, researchers would require the ability to make complex and specific queries. This same powerful query capability could lead to arbitrary selection of combinations of results.

For these reasons (and others), Anderson recommended against continuing to develop the public database. In spite of these problems, the Iceland Parliament voted to proceed with its construction and public release [JON00].

Aggregation

Related to the inference problem is **aggregation**, which means building sensitive results from less sensitive inputs. We saw earlier that knowing either the latitude or longitude of a gold mine does you no good. But if you know both latitude and longitude, you can pinpoint the mine. For a more realistic example, consider how police use aggregation frequently in solving crimes: They determine who had a motive for committing the crime, when the crime was committed, who had alibis covering that time, who had the skills, and so forth. Typically, you think of police investigation as starting with the entire population and narrowing the analysis to a single person. But if the police officers work in parallel, one may have a list of possible suspects, another may have a list with possible motive, and another may have a list of capable persons. When the intersection of these lists is a single person, the police have their prime suspect.

Addressing the aggregation problem is difficult because it requires the database management system to track what results each user had already received and conceal any result that would let the user derive a more sensitive result. Aggregation is especially difficult to counter because it can take place outside the system. For example, suppose the security policy is that anyone can have *either* the latitude or longitude of the mine, but not both. Nothing prevents you from getting one, your friend from getting the other, and the two of you talking to each other.

Recent interest in data mining has raised concern again about aggregation. **Data mining** is the process of sifting through multiple databases and correlating multiple data elements to find useful information. Marketing companies use data mining extensively to find consumers likely to buy a product. As Sidebar 6-5 points out, it is not only marketers who are interested in aggregation through data mining.

Aggregation was of interest to database security researchers at the same time as was inference. As we have seen, some approaches to inference have proven useful and are currently being used. But there have been few proposals for countering aggregation. We will consider the privacy aspects of data mining in Chapter 9.

Sidebar 6-5 Who Wrote Shakespeare's Plays?

Most people would answer "Shakespeare" when asked who wrote any of the plays attributed to the bard. But for 150 years literary scholars have had their doubts. In 1852 it was suggested that Edward de Vere, Earl of Oxford wrote at least some of the works. For decades scholarly debate raged, citing what was known of Shakespeare's education, travels, work schedule, and the few other facts known about him.

In the 1980s a new analytic technique was developed: computerized analysis of text. Different researchers studied qualities such as word choice, images used in different plays, word pairs, sentence structure, and the like: any structural element that could show similarity or dissimilarity. (See, for example, [FAR96a] and [KAR01], as well as *www.shakespearefellowship.org.*) The debate continues as researchers develop more and more qualities to correlate among databases (the language of the plays and other works attributed to Shakespeare). The debate will probably never be settled.

But the technique has proven useful. In 1996 an author called Anonymous published the novel *Primary Colors.* Many people tried to determine who the author was. But Donald Foster, a professor at Vassar College, aided by some simple computer tools, attributed the novel to Joe Klein, who later admitted being the author. Neumann [NEU96] in the Risks forum, notes how hard it is lie convincingly, even having tried to alter your writing style, given "telephone records, credit-card records, airplane reservation databases, library records, snoopy neighbors, coincidental encounters, etc."—in short, given aggregation.

The approach has uses outside the literary field. In 2002 the SAS Institute, vendors of statistical analysis software, introduced data mining software intended to find patterns in old e-mail messages and other masses of text. The company suggests the tool might be useful in identifying and blocking spam. Another possible use is detecting lies, or perhaps just flagging potential inconsistencies. It could also help locate the author of malicious code.

6.6 MULTILEVEL DATABASES

So far, we have considered data in only two categories: either sensitive or nonsensitive. We have alluded to some data items being more sensitive than others, but we have allowed only yes-or-no access. Our presentation may have implied that sensitivity was a function of the *attribute,* the column in which the data appeared, although nothing we have done depended on this interpretation of sensitivity. Such a model appears in Table 6-15, where two columns are identified (by shading) as sensitive. In fact, though, sensitivity is determined not just by attribute but also in ways that we investigate in the next section.

The Case for Differentiated Security

Consider a database containing data on U.S. government expenditures. Some of the expenditures are for paper clips, which is not sensitive information. Some salary expenditures are subject to privacy requirements. Individual salaries are sensitive, but the aggregate (for example, the total Agriculture Department payroll, which is a matter of public record) is not sensitive. Expenses of certain military operations are more sensitive, for example, the total amount the United States spends for ballistic missiles, which is not public. There are even operations known only to a few people, and so the amount spent on these operations, or even the fact that anything was spent on such an operation, is highly sensitive.

Table 6-15 lists employee information. It may in fact be the case that Davis is a temporary employee hired for a special project, and her whole record has a different sensitivity from the others. Perhaps the phone shown for Garland is her private line, not available to the public. We can refine the sensitivity of the data by depicting it as shown in Table 6-16.

From this description, three characteristics of database security emerge.

- The security of a single element may be different from the security of other elements of the same record or from other values of the same attribute. That is, the security of one element may be different from that of other elements of the same row or column. This situation implies that security should be implemented for each individual element.

TABLE 6-15 Attribute-Level Sensitivity. (Sensitive attributes are shaded.)

Name	Department	Salary	Phone	Performance
Rogers	training	43,800	4-5067	A2
Jenkins	research	62,900	6-4281	D4
Poling	training	38,200	4-4501	B1
Garland	user services	54,600	6-6600	A4
Hilten	user services	44,500	4-5351	B1
Davis	administration	51,400	4-9505	A3

TABLE 6-16 Data and Attribute Sensitivity.

Name	Department	Salary	Phone	Performance
Rogers	training	43,800	4-5067	A2
Jenkins	research	62,900	6-4281	D4
Poling	training	38,200	4-4501	B1
Garland	user services	54,600	6-6600	A4
Hilten	user services	44,500	4-5351	B1
Davis	administration	51,400	4-9505	A3

- Two levels—sensitive and nonsensitive—are inadequate to represent some security situations. Several grades of security may be needed. These grades may represent ranges of allowable knowledge, which may overlap. Typically, the security grades form a lattice.
- The security of an aggregate—a sum, a count, or a group of values in a database—may be different from the security of the individual elements. The security of the aggregate may be higher or lower than that of the individual elements.

These three principles lead to a model of security not unlike the military model of security encountered in Chapter 5, in which the sensitivity of an object is defined as one of n levels and is further separated into compartments by category.

Granularity

Recall that the military classification model applied originally to paper documents and was adapted to computers. It is fairly easy to classify and track a single sheet of paper or, for that matter, a paper file, a computer file, or a single program or process. It is entirely different to classify individual data items.

For obvious reasons, an entire sheet of paper is classified at one level, even though certain words, such as *and*, *the*, or *of*, would be innocuous in any context, and other words, such as codewords like *Manhattan project*, might be sensitive in any context. But defining the sensitivity of each value in a database is similar to applying a sensitivity level to each individual word of a document.

And the problem is still more complicated. The word *Manhattan* by itself is not sensitive, nor is *project*. However, the combination of these words produces the sensitive codeword *Manhattan project*. A similar situation occurs in databases. Therefore, not only can every *element* of a database have a distinct sensitivity, every *combination of elements* can also have a distinct sensitivity. Furthermore, the combination can be more or less sensitive than any of its elements.

So what would we need in order to associate a sensitivity level with each value of a database? First, we need an access control policy to dictate which users may have access to what data. Typically, to implement this policy each data item is marked to show its access limitations. Second, we need a means to guarantee that the value has not been changed by an unauthorized person. These two requirements address both confidentiality and integrity.

Security Issues

In Chapter 1, we introduced three general security concerns: confidentiality, integrity, and availability. In this section, we extend these concepts to include their special roles for multilevel databases.

Integrity

Even in a single-level database in which all elements have the same degree of sensitivity, integrity is a tricky problem. In the case of multilevel databases, integrity becomes both more important and more difficult to achieve. Because of the $*$-property for access control, a process that reads high-level data is not allowed to write a file at a lower level. Applied to databases, however, this principle says that a high-level user should not be able to write a lower-level data element.

The problem with this interpretation arises when the DBMS must be able to read all records in the database and write new records for any of the following purposes: to do backups, to scan the database to answer queries, to reorganize the database according to a user's processing needs, or to update all records of the database.

When people encounter this problem, they handle it by using trust and common sense. People who have access to sensitive information are careful not to convey it to uncleared individuals. In a computing system, there are two choices: either the process cleared at a high level cannot write to a lower level, or the process must be a "trusted process," the computer equivalent of a person with a security clearance.

Confidentiality

Users trust that a database will provide correct information, meaning that the data are consistent and accurate. As indicated earlier, some means of protecting confidentiality may result in small changes to the data. Although these perturbations should not affect statistical analyses, they may produce two different answers representing the same underlying data value in response to two differently formed queries. In the multilevel case, two different users operating at two different levels of security might get two different answers to the same query. In order to preserve confidentiality, precision is sacrificed.

Enforcing confidentiality also leads to unknowing redundancy. Suppose a personnel specialist works at one level of access permission. The specialist knows that Bob Hill works for the company. However, Bob's record does not appear on the retirement payment roster. The specialist assumes this omission is an error and creates a record for Bob.

The reason that no record for Bob appears is that Bob is a secret agent, and his employment with the company is not supposed to be public knowledge. There actually is a record on Bob in the file but, because of his special position, his record is not accessible to the personnel specialist. The creation of the new record means that there are now two records for Bob Hill: one sensitive and one not, as shown in Table 6-17. This situation is called **polyinstantiation,** meaning that one record can appear (be instantiated) many times, with a different level of confidentiality each time.

TABLE 6-17 Polyinstantiated Records.

Name	Sensitivity	Assignment	Location
Hill, Bob	C	Program Mgr	London
Hill, Bob	TS	Secret Agent	South Bend

This problem is exacerbated because Bob Hill is a common enough name that there might be two different people in the database with that name. Thus, merely scanning the database (from a high-sensitivity level) for duplicates is not a satisfactory way to find records entered unknowingly by people with only low clearances.

We might also find other reasons, unrelated to sensitivity level, that result in polyinstantiation. For example, Mark Thyme worked for Acme Corporation for 30 years and retired. He is now drawing a pension from Acme, so he appears as a retiree in one personnel record. But Mark tires of being home and is rehired as a part-time contractor; this new work generates a second personnel record for Mark. Each is a legitimate employment record. In our zeal to reduce polyinstantiation, we must be careful not to eliminate legitimate records such as these.

6.7 PROPOSALS FOR MULTILEVEL SECURITY

As you can already tell, implementing multilevel security for databases is difficult, probably more so than in operating systems, because of the small granularity of the items being controlled. In the remainder of this chapter, we study approaches to multilevel security for databases.

Separation

As we have already seen, separation is necessary to limit access. In this section, we study mechanisms to implement separation in databases. Then, we see how these mechanisms can help to implement multilevel security for databases.

Partitioning

The obvious control for multilevel databases is partitioning. The database is divided into separate databases, each at its own level of sensitivity. This approach is similar to maintaining separate files in separate file cabinets.

This control destroys a basic advantage of databases: elimination of redundancy and improved accuracy through having only one field to update. Furthermore, it does not address the problem of a high-level user who needs access some low-level data combined with high-level data.

Nevertheless, because of the difficulty of establishing, maintaining, and using multilevel databases, many users with data of mixed sensitivities handle their data by using separate, isolated databases.

Encryption

If sensitive data are encrypted, a user who accidentally receives them cannot interpret the data. Thus, each level of sensitive data can be stored in a table encrypted under a key unique to the level of sensitivity. But encryption has certain disadvantages.

First, a user can mount a chosen plaintext attack. Suppose party affiliation of REP or DEM is stored in encrypted form in each record. A user who achieves access to these encrypted fields can easily decrypt them by creating a new record with party=DEM and comparing the resulting encrypted version to that element in all other records. Worse, if authentication data are encrypted, the malicious user can substitute the encrypted form of his or her own data for that of any other user. Not only does this provide access for the malicious user, but it also excludes the legitimate user whose authentication data have been changed to that of the malicious user. These possibilities are shown in Figures 6-5 and 6-6.

Using a different encryption key for each record overcomes these defects. Each record's fields can be encrypted with a different key, or all fields of a record can be cryptographically linked, as with cipher block chaining.

The disadvantage, then, is that each field must be decrypted when users perform standard database operations such as "select all records with SALARY > 10,000." Decrypting the SALARY field, even on rejected records, increases the time to process a

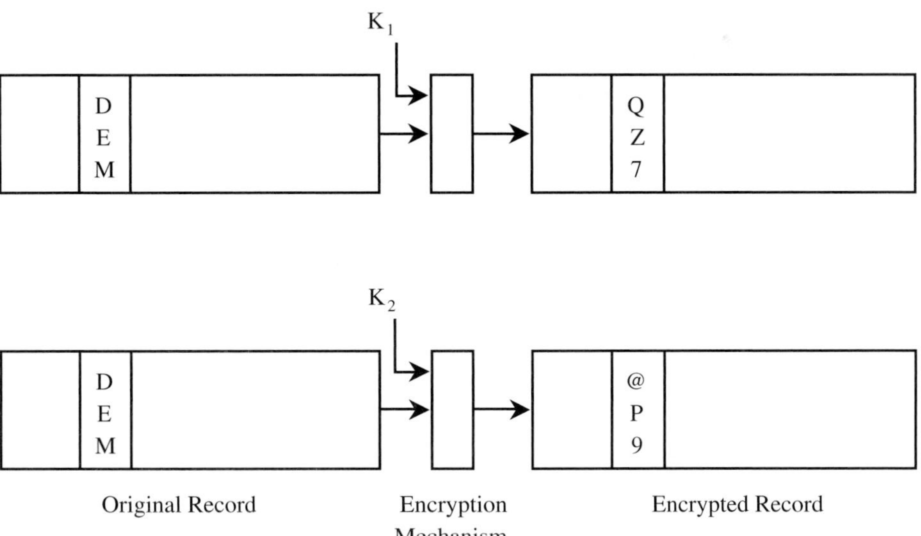

FIGURE 6-5 Cryptographic Separation: Different Encryption Keys.

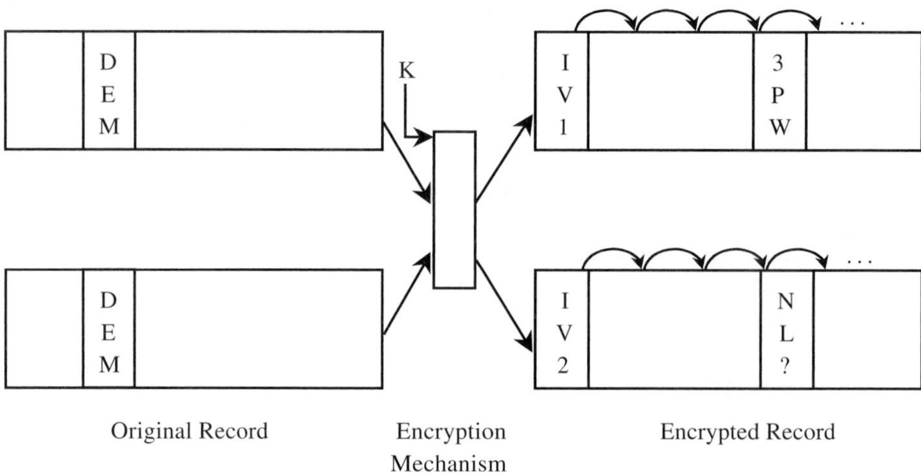

FIGURE 6-6 Cryptographic Separation: Block Chaining.

query. (Consider the query that selects just one record but that must decrypt and compare one field of each record to find the one that satisfies the query.) Thus, encryption is not often used to implement separation in databases.

Integrity Lock

The **integrity lock** was first proposed at the U.S. Air Force Summer Study on Data Base Security [AFS83]. The lock is a way to provide both integrity and limited access for a database. The operation was nicknamed "spray paint" because each element is figuratively painted with a color that denotes its sensitivity. The coloring is maintained with the element, not in a master database table.

A model of the basic integrity lock is shown in Figure 6-7. As illustrated, each apparent data item consists of three pieces: the actual data item itself, a sensitivity label, and a checksum. The sensitivity label defines the sensitivity of the data, and the checksum is computed across both data and sensitivity label to prevent unauthorized modification of the data item or its label. The actual data item is stored in plaintext, for

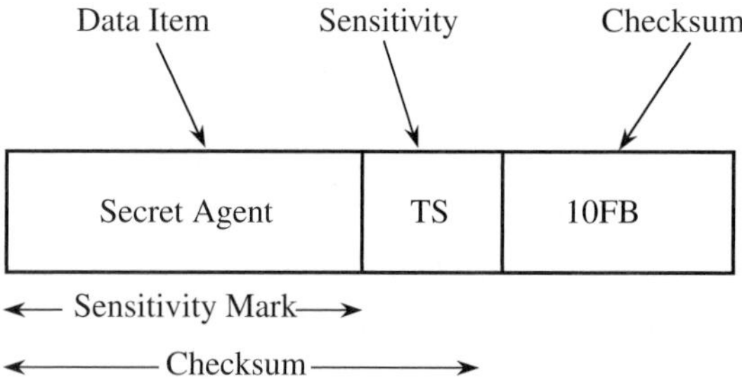

FIGURE 6-7 Integrity Lock.

efficiency because the DBMS may need to examine many fields when selecting records to match a query.

The sensitivity label should be

- *unforgeable,* so that a malicious subject cannot create a new sensitivity level for an element
- *unique,* so that a malicious subject cannot copy a sensitivity level from another element
- *concealed,* so that a malicious subject cannot even determine the sensitivity level of an arbitrary element

The third piece of the integrity lock for a field is an error-detecting code, called a **cryptographic checksum**. To guarantee that a data value or its sensitivity classification has not been changed, this checksum must be unique for a given element, and must contain both the element's data value and something to tie that value to a particular position in the database. As shown in Figure 6-8, an appropriate cryptographic checksum includes something unique to the record (the record number), something unique to this data field within the record (the field attribute name), the value of this element, and the sensitivity classification of the element. These four components guard against anyone's changing, copying, or moving the data. The checksum can be computed with a strong encryption algorithm such as the Data Encryption Standard (DES).

Sensitivity Lock

The sensitivity lock shown in Figure 6-9 was designed by Graubert and Kramer [GRA84b] to meet these principles. A **sensitivity lock** is a combination of a unique identifier (such as the record number) and the sensitivity level. Because the identifier is unique, each lock relates to one particular record. Many different elements will have the same sensitivity level. A malicious subject should not be able to identify two elements having identical sensitivity levels or identical data values just by looking at the sensitivity level portion of the lock. Because of the encryption, the lock's contents, especially the sensitivity level, are concealed from plain view. Thus, the lock is associated with one specific record, and it protects the secrecy of the sensitivity level of that record.

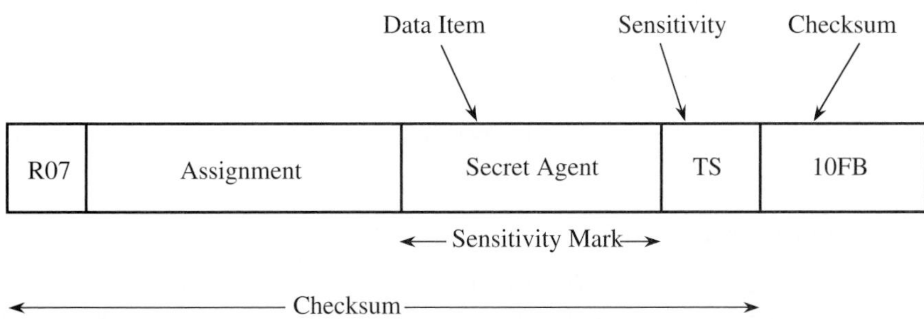

FIGURE 6-8 Cryptographic Checksum.

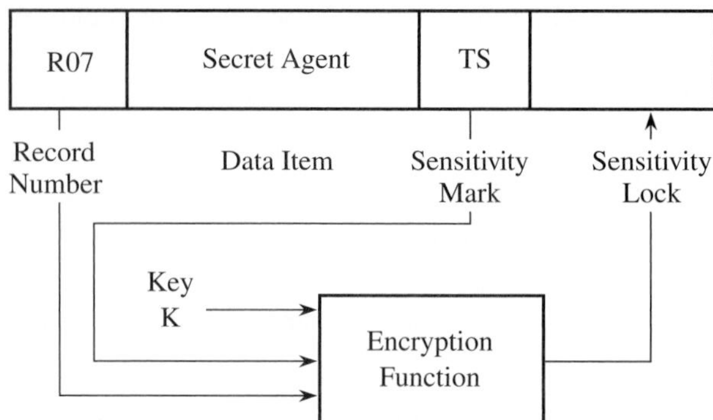

FIGURE 6-9 Sensitivity Lock.

Designs of Multilevel Secure Databases

This section covers different designs for multilevel secure databases. These designs show the trade-offs among efficiency, flexibility, simplicity, and trustworthiness.

Integrity Lock

The integrity lock DBMS was invented as a short-term solution to the security problem for multilevel databases. The intention was to be able to use any (untrusted) database manager with a trusted procedure that handles access control. The sensitive data were obliterated or concealed with encryption that protected both a data item and its sensitivity. In this way, only the access procedure would need to be trusted because only it would be able to achieve or grant access to sensitive data. The structure of such a system is shown in Figure 6-10.

The efficiency of integrity locks is a serious drawback. The space needed for storing an element must be expanded to contain the sensitivity label. Because there are several pieces in the label and one label for every element, the space required is significant.

Problematic, too, is the processing time efficiency of an integrity lock. The sensitivity label must be decoded every time a data element is passed to the user in order to verify that the user's access is allowable. Also, each time a value is written or modified, the label must be recomputed. Thus, substantial processing time is consumed. If the database file can be sufficiently protected, the data values of the individual elements can be left in plaintext. That approach benefits select and project queries across sensitive fields because an element need not be decrypted just to determine whether it should be selected.

A final difficulty with this approach is that the untrusted database manager sees all data, so it is subject to Trojan horse attacks by which data can be leaked through covert channels.

Trusted Front End

The model of a **trusted front-end** process is shown in Figure 6-11. A trusted front end is also known as a **guard** and operates much like the reference monitor of Chapter 5. This approach, originated by Hinke and Schaefer [HIN75], recognizes that many

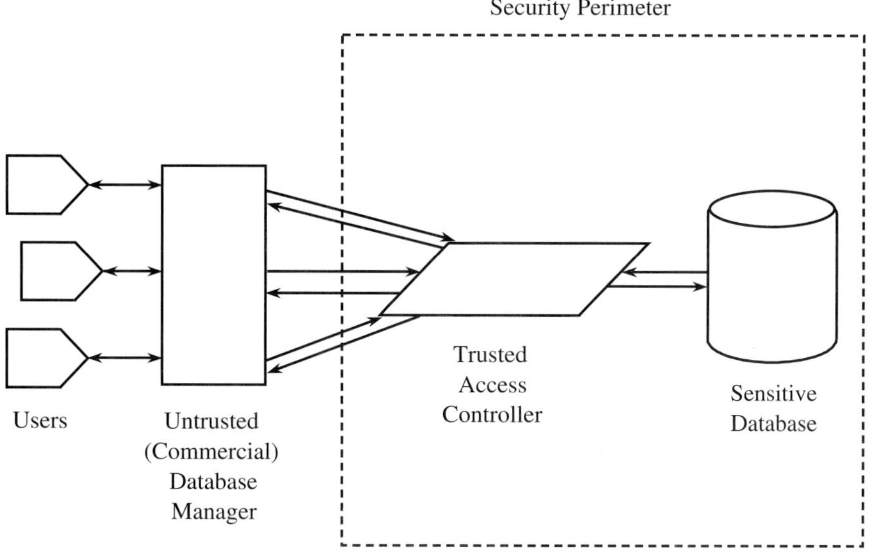

FIGURE 6-10 Trusted Database Manager.

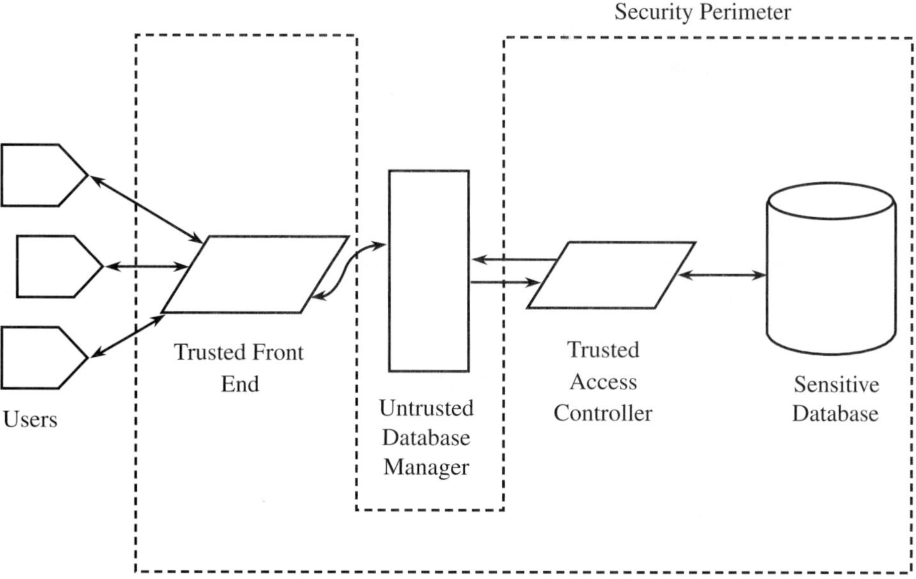

FIGURE 6-11 Trusted Front End.

DBMSs have been built and put into use without consideration of multilevel security. Staff members are already trained in using these DBMSs, and they may in fact use them frequently. The front-end concept takes advantage of existing tools and expertise, enhancing the security of these existing systems with minimal change to the system. The interaction between a user, a trusted front end, and a DBMS involves the following steps.

1. A user identifies himself or herself to the front end; the front end authenticates the user's identity.
2. The user issues a query to the front end.
3. The front end verifies the user's authorization to data.
4. The front end issues a query to the database manager.
5. The database manager performs I/O access, interacting with low-level access control to achieve access to actual data.
6. The database manager returns the result of the query to the trusted front end.
7. The front end analyzes the sensitivity levels of the data items in the result and selects those items consistent with the user's security level.
8. The front end transmits selected data to the untrusted front end for formatting.
9. The untrusted front end transmits formatted data to the user.

The trusted front end serves as a one-way filter, screening out results the user should not be able to access. But the scheme is inefficient because potentially much data is retrieved and then discarded as inappropriate for the user.

Commutative Filters

The notion of a commutative filter was proposed by Denning [DEN85] as a simplification of the trusted interface to the DBMS. Essentially, the filter screens the user's request, reformatting it if necessary, so that only data of an appropriate sensitivity level are returned to the user.

A **commutative filter** is a process that forms an interface between the user and a DBMS. However, unlike the trusted front end, the filter tries to capitalize on the efficiency of most DBMSs. The filter reformats the query so that the database manager does as much of the work as possible, screening out many unacceptable records. The filter then provides a second screening to select only data to which the user has access.

Filters can be used for security at the record, attribute, or element level.

- When used at the record level, the filter requests desired data plus cryptographic checksum information; it then verifies the accuracy and accessibility of data to be passed to the user.
- At the attribute level, the filter checks whether all attributes in the user's query are accessible to the user and, if so, passes the query to the database manager. On return, it deletes all fields to which the user has no access rights.
- At the element level, the system requests desired data plus cryptographic checksum information. When these are returned, it checks the classification level of every element of every record retrieved against the user's level.

Suppose a group of physicists in Washington works on very sensitive projects, so the current user should not be allowed to access the physicists' names in the database. This restriction presents a problem with this query:

```
retrieve NAME where ((OCCUP=PHYSICIST) ∧ (CITY=WASHDC))
```

Suppose, too, that the current user is prohibited from knowing anything about any people in Moscow. Using a conventional DBMS, the query might access all records, and the DBMS would then pass the results on to the user. However, as we have seen, the user might be able to infer things about Moscow employees or Washington physicists working on secret projects without even accessing those fields directly.

The commutative filter reforms the original query in a trustable way so that sensitive information is never extracted from the database. Our sample query would become

```
retrieve NAME where ((OCCUP=PHYSICIST) ∧ (CITY=WASHDC))
from all records R where
      (NAME-SECRECY-LEVEL (R) ≤ USER-SECRECY-LEVEL) ∧
      (OCCUP-SECRECY-LEVEL (R) ≤ USER-SECRECY-LEVEL) ∧
      (CITY-SECRECY-LEVEL (R) ≤ USER-SECRECY-LEVEL))
```

The filter works by restricting the query to the DBMS and then restricting the results before they are returned to the user. In this instance, the filter would request NAME, NAME-SECRECY-LEVEL, OCCUP, OCCUP-SECRECY-LEVEL, CITY, and CITY-SECRECY-LEVEL values and would then filter and return to the user only those fields and items that are of a secrecy level acceptable for the user. Although even this simple query becomes complicated because of the added terms, these terms are all added by the front-end filter, invisible to the user.

An example of this query filtering in operation is shown in Figure 6-12. The advantage of the commutative filter is that it allows query selection, some optimization, and

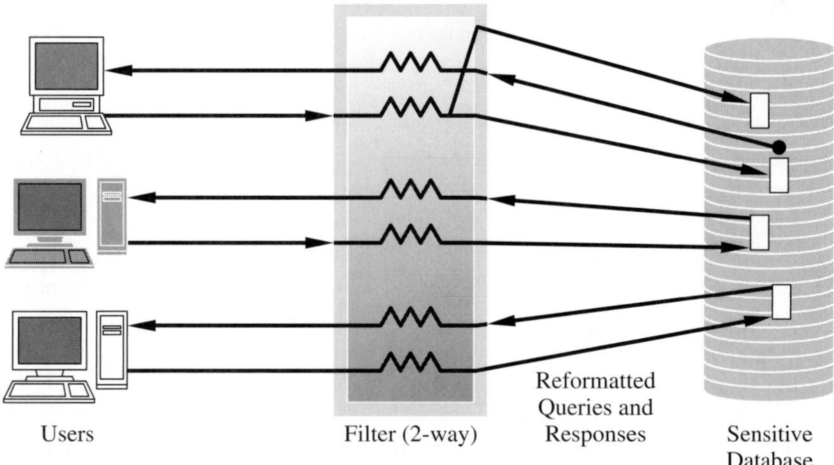

FIGURE 6-12 Commutative Filters.

some subquery handling to be done by the DBMS. This delegation of duties keeps the size of the security filter small, reduces redundancy between it and the DBMS, and improves the overall efficiency of the system.

Distributed Databases

The **distributed** or **federated database** is a fourth design for a secure multilevel database. In this case, a trusted front end controls access to two unmodified commercial DBMSs: one for all low-sensitivity data and one for all high-sensitivity data.

The front end takes a user's query and formulates single-level queries to the databases as appropriate. For a user cleared for high-sensitivity data the front end submits queries to both the high- and low-sensitivity databases. But if the user is not cleared for high-sensitivity data, the front end submits a query to only the low-sensitivity database. If the result is obtained from either back-end database alone, the front end passes the result back to the user. If the result comes from both databases, the front end has to combine the results appropriately. For example, if the query is a join query having some high-sensitivity terms and some low, the front end has to perform the equivalent of a database join itself.

The distributed database design is not popular because the front end, which must be trusted, is complex, potentially including most of the functionality of a full DBMS itself. In addition, the design does not scale well to many degrees of sensitivity; each sensitivity level of data must be maintained in its own separate database.

Window/View

Traditionally, one of the advantages of using a DBMS for multiple users of different interests (but not necessarily different sensitivity levels) is the ability to create a different view for each user. That is, each user is restricted to a picture of the data reflecting only what the user needs to see. For example, the registrar may see only the class assignments and grades of each student at a university, not needing to see extracurricular activities or medical records. The university health clinic, on the other hand, needs medical records and drug-use information but not scores on standardized academic tests.

The notion of a **window** or a **view** can also be an organizing principle for multilevel database access. A window is a subset of a database, containing exactly the information that a user is entitled to access. Denning [DEN87a] surveys the development of views for multilevel database security.

A view can represent a single user's subset database so that all of a user's queries access only that database. This subset guarantees that the user does not access values outside the permitted ones, because nonpermitted values are not even in the user's database. The view is specified as a set of relations in the database, so that the data in the view subset change as data change in the database.

For example, a travel agent might have access to part of an airline's flight information database. Records for cargo flights would be excluded, as would the pilot's name and the serial number of the plane for every flight. Suppose the database contained an attribute TYPE whose value was either CARGO or PASS (for passenger). Other attributes might be flight number, origin, destination, departure time, arrival time, capacity, pilot, and tail number.

Now suppose the airline created some passenger flights with lower fares that could be booked only directly through the airline. The airline might assign their flight numbers a more sensitive rating to make these flights unavailable to travel agents. The whole database, and the agent's view, might have the logical structure shown in Table 6-18.

The travel agent's view of the database is expressed as

```
view AGENT-INFO
      FLTNO:=MASTER.FLTNO
      ORIG:=MASTER.ORIG
      DEST:=MASTER.DEST
      DEP:=MASTER.DEP
      ARR:=MASTER.ARR
      CAP:=MASTER.CAP
            where MASTER.TYPE='PASS'
      class AGENT
      auth retrieve
```

Because the access class of this view is AGENT, more sensitive flight numbers (flights booked only through the airline) do not appear in this view. Alternatively, we could have eliminated the entire records for those flights by restricting the record selection with a *where* clause. A view may involve computation or complex selection criteria to specify subset data.

The data presented to a user is obtained by **filtering** of the contents of the original database. Attributes, records, and elements are stripped away so that the user sees only

TABLE 6-18 Airline Database.

(a) Airline's View.

FLT#	ORIG	DEST	DEP	ARR	CAP	TYPE	PILOT	TAIL
362	JFK	BWI	0830	0950	114	PASS	Dosser	2463
397	JFK	ORD	0830	1020	114	PASS	Bottoms	3621
202	IAD	LGW	1530	0710	183	PASS	Jevins	2007
749	LGA	ATL	0947	1120	0	CARGO	Witt	3116
286	STA	SFO	1020	1150	117	PASS	Gross	4026
...								
...								

(b) Travel Agent's View.

FLT#	ORIG	DEST	DEP	ARR	CAP
362	JFK	BWI	0830	0950	114
397	JFK	ORD	0830	1020	114
202	IAD	LGW	1530	0710	183
286	STA	SFO	1020	1150	117
...					
...					

acceptable items. Any attribute (column) is withheld unless the user is authorized to access at least one element. Any record (row) is withheld unless the user is authorized to access at least one element. Then, for all elements that still remain, if the user is not authorized to access the element, it is replaced by UNDEFINED. This last step does not compromise any data because the user knows the existence of the attribute (there is at least one element that the user can access) and the user knows the existence of the record (again, at least one accessible element exists in the record).

In addition to elements, a view includes relations on attributes. Furthermore, a user can create new relations from new and existing attributes and elements. These new relations are accessible to other users, subject to the standard access rights. A user can operate on the subset database defined in a view only as allowed by the operations authorized in the view. As an example, a user might be allowed to retrieve records specified in one view or to retrieve and update records as specified in another view. For instance, the airline in our example may restrict travel agents to retrieving data.

The Sea Views project described in [DEN87a, LUN90a] is the basis for a system that integrates a trusted operating system to form a trusted database manager. The layered implementation as described is shown in Figure 6-13. The lowest layer, the reference monitor, performs file interaction, enforcing the Bell–La Padula access controls, and does user authentication. Part of its function is to filter data passed to higher levels. The second level performs basic indexing and computation functions of the database. The third level translates views into the base relations of the database. These three lay-

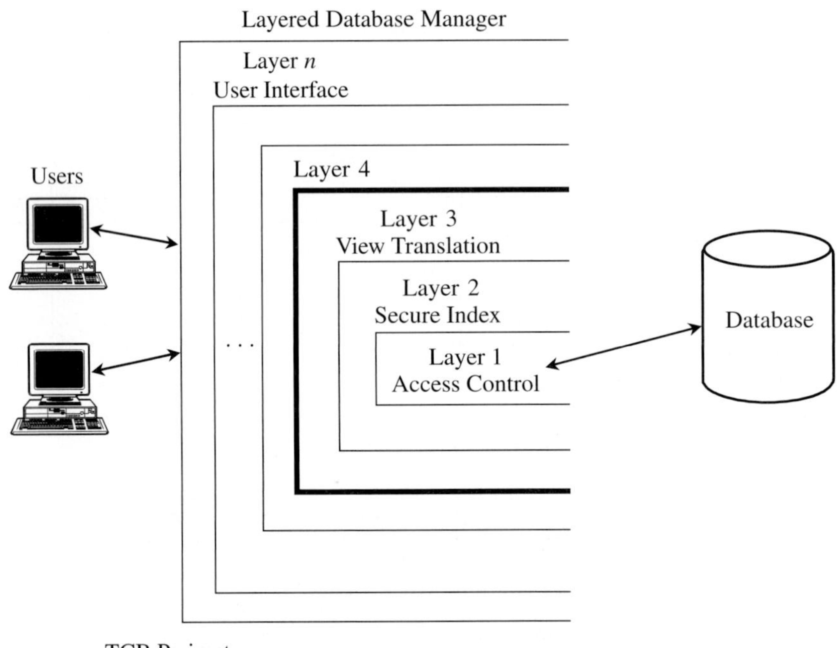

FIGURE 6-13 Secure Database Decomposition.

ers make up the trusted computing base (TCB) of the system. The remaining layers implement normal DBMS functions and user interface.

This layered approach makes views both a logical division of a database and a functional one. The approach is an important step toward the design and implementation of a trustable database management system.

Concluding Remarks

The multilevel security problem for databases has been studied since the 1970s. Several promising research results have been identified, as we have seen in this chapter. However, as with trusted operating systems, the consumer demand has not been sufficient to support many products. Civilian users have not liked the inflexibility of the military multilevel security model, and there have been too few military users. Consequently, multilevel secure databases are primarily of research and historical interest.

6.8 SUMMARY OF DATABASE SECURITY

This chapter has addressed three aspects of security for database management systems: confidentiality and integrity problems specific to database applications, the inference problem for statistical databases, and problems of including users and data of different sensitivity levels in one database.

Both confidentiality and integrity are important to users of databases. Confidentiality can be broken by indirect disclosure of a negative result or of the bounds of a value. Integrity of the entire database is a responsibility of the DBMS software; this problem is handled by most major commercial systems through backups, redundancy, change logs, and two-step updates. Integrity of an individual element of the database is the responsibility of the database administrator, who defines the access policy.

The inference problem in a statistical database arises from the mathematical relationships between data elements and query results. We studied controls to prevent statistical inference, including limited response suppression, perturbation of results, and query analysis. One very complex control involves monitoring all data provided to a user in order to prevent inference from independent queries.

Multilevel secure databases must provide both confidentiality and integrity. Separation can be implemented physically, logically, or cryptographically. We explored five approaches to assuring confidentiality in multilevel secure databases: integrity lock, trusted front end, commutative filters, distributed databases, and restricted views. Other solutions are likely to evolve as the problem is studied further.

Many of the techniques discussed in this chapter are particular to database management systems. But the analysis of the problems and the derivation of techniques are typical of how we analyze security needs in any software application. In a sense, we must do a threat analysis, trying to imagine ways in which the security of the application can be breached. Once we conjecture ways to destroy integrity, confidentiality, or availability, we conjure up designs to help us build the security into the application's design, rather than after the fact. In the next chapter, we examine the security implications of another specialized form of application, networks.

6.9 TERMS AND CONCEPTS

database management system (DBMS), 310
front end, 310
field, 310
element, 310
record, 310
attribute, 310
schema, 310
subschema, 310
relation, 311
query, 312
project, 313
select, 313
join, 313
database integrity, 315
element integrity, 315
access control, 315
user authentication, 315
auditability, 318
availability, 319
sensitive data, 319
availability of data, 319
access control decision, 319
disclosure, 326
exact disclosure, 329
bounded disclosure, 329
negative disclosure, 329
probable value disclosure, 330
disclosure of existence, 330
security, 330
precision, 330
revealed data, 330
retrieved data, 330
requested data, 330
allowed data, 330
inference, 331
direct inference, 332
indirect inference, 333
inference by sum, 334
inference by count, 334
inference by median, 334
tracker inference, 335
linear system inference, 337
statistical inference, 337
limited response suppression, 338
combining results to suppress, 338
revealing a random sample, 339
random perturbation of data, 339
restricting output by query analysis, 340
aggregation, 341
multilevel databases, 343
granularity of control, 344
multilevel integrity, 345
multilevel secrecy, 345
polyinstantiation, 345
partitioned database, 346
encryption, 347
integrity lock, 348
sensitivity lock, 349
trusted front end, 350
commutative filter, 352
query modification, 352
window, 354
view, 354

6.10 WHERE THE FIELD IS HEADED

Database security has been receiving renewed interest, in part because of privacy concerns related to information gathering to counter terrorism.

Privacy concerns (for more discussion of which see Chapter 9) will lead to more investigation of ways to protect privacy while allowing the power of databases to track targeted individuals. Because most targets become such only when their profile emerges from a database, many of these controls will have to be procedural, to ensure that sensitive information is not misused, rather than technical, to restrict access to potentially sensitive information. Controls are especially needed for the field of data mining, the practice of pulling closely focused results from large and perhaps only partially structured data. Agrawal and Srikant [AGR00] present an approach that could address both needs.

A second trend in database technology that should be of interest is decentralization. Segmentation, replication, and mirroring of databases are all methods that can improve performance, usability, and reliability in databases. Yet in the decentralization, data are also subject to inadvertent and nonmalicious integrity failures, as well as malicious ones. The well-studied topic of Byzantine failures has been applied to cooperating processes [LAM82]. (The problem, simply stated, is how to protect the correctness of a compound system against one or more compromised subsystems.) A similar approach will need to be applied to distributed databases. Work in this area is already underway at Xerox PARC [TER98] and other places.

6.11 TO LEARN MORE

Date [DAT81] addresses general topics of database management, and the second volume [DAT83] covers recovery, integrity, concurrency, and security (secrecy). Fernandez et al. [FER81] also cover basic security issues for databases. The state of the art is surveyed by Lunt and Fernandez [LUN90] and Schaefer [SCH90a].

The inference problem dates back at least to [HOF70]. Denning and Schlörer [DEN83a] and Smith [SMI88b] survey the problems and controls for inference in databases. Burns [BUR90] raises an issue of the secrecy/integrity trade-off. Lunt [LUN89] clarifies several issues regarding aggregation and inference. Adam and Wortmann [ADA89] cover statistical databases, and Denning et al. [DEN79b] describe tracker attacks. Access control is first proposed by Stonebraker and Wong [STO74].

The best description of the multilevel security problem for databases is [AFS83], the "Wood's Hole" report of the Air Force Studies Board of the National Academy of Sciences. Multilevel security issues for databases have been explored by Denning [DEN85, DEN86, and DEN87a], Lunt [LUN90a], and Graubert [GRA84b, GRA85].

6.12 EXERCISES

1. In an environment in which several users are sharing access to a single database, how can indefinite postponement occur? Describe a scenario in which two users could cause the indefinite postponement of each other. Describe a scenario in which a single user could cause the indefinite postponement of all users.
2. Using the two-step commit presented in the beginning of this chapter, describe how to avoid assigning one seat to two people, as in the airline example. That is, list precisely which steps the database manager should follow in assigning passengers to seats.
3. UNDO is a recovery operation for databases. It is a command that obtains information from a transaction log and resets the elements of a database to their values *before* a particular transaction is performed. Describe a situation in which an UNDO command would be useful.

4. The UNDO operation described in the previous exercise must be repeatable. That is, if x is the original value of a database and x' is an incorrectly modified version, we want

```
UNDO(x') = x,
```

but also

```
UNDO(x) = x
```

and

```
UNDO(UNDO(x')) = x
```

(a) Why must `UNDO(x) = x`?
(b) Why must `UNDO(UNDO(x')) = x`?

5. Suppose a database manager were to allow nesting of one transaction inside another. That is, after having updated part of one record, the DBMS would allow you to select another record, update it, and then perform further updates on the first record. What effect would nesting have on the integrity of a database? Suggest a mechanism by which nesting could be allowed.

6. Can a database contain two identical records without a negative effect on the integrity of the database? Why or why not?

7. Some operating systems perform buffered I/O. In this scheme, an output request is accepted from a user and the user is informed of the normal I/O completion. However, the actual physical write operation is performed later, at a time convenient to the operating system. Discuss the effect of buffered I/O on integrity in a DBMS.

8. A database transaction implements the command "set STATUS to 'CURRENT' in all records where BALANCE-OWED = 0." (a) Describe how that transaction would be performed with the two-step commit described in this chapter. (b) Suppose the relations from which that command was formed are (CUSTOMER-ID,STATUS) and (CUSTOMER-ID,BALANCE-OWED). How would the transaction be performed? (c) Suppose the relations from which that command was formed are (CUSTOMER-ID,STATUS), (CREDIT-ID,CUSTOMER-ID), (CREDIT-ID, BALANCE-OWED). How would the transaction be performed?

9. Show that if longitudinal parity is used as an error detection code, values in a database can still be modified without detection. (Longitudinal parity is computed for the *n*th bit of each byte; that is, one parity bit is computed and retained for all bits in the 0th position, another parity bit for all bits in the 1st position, etc.)

10. Suppose query Q_1 obtains the median m_1 of a set S_1 of values. Suppose query Q_2 obtains the median m_2 of a subset S_2 of S_1. If $m_1 < m_2$, what can be inferred about S_1, S_2, and the elements of S_1 not in S_2?

11. Disclosure of the sum of all financial aid for students in Smith dorm is not sensitive because no individual student is associated with an amount. Similarly, a list of names of students receiving financial aid is not sensitive because no amounts are specified. However, the combination of these two lists reveals the amount for an individual student if only one student in Smith dorm receives aid. What computation would a database management system have to perform to determine that the list of names might reveal sensitive data? What records would the database management system have to maintain on what different users know in order to determine that the list of names might reveal sensitive data?

12. One approach suggested to ensure privacy is the small result rejection, in which the system rejects (returns no result from) any query, the result of which is derived from a small number, for example, five, of records. Show how to obtain sensitive data by using only queries derived from six records.

13. The response "sensitive value; response suppressed" is itself a disclosure. Suggest a manner in which a database management system could suppress responses that reveal sensitive information without disclosing that the responses to certain queries are sensitive.

14. Cite a situation in which the sensitivity of an aggregate is greater than that of its constituent values. Cite a situation in which the sensitivity of an aggregate is less than that of its constituent values.
15. Explain the disadvantages of partitioning as a means of implementing multilevel security for databases.
16. A database management system is implemented under an operating system trusted to provide multilevel separation of users. (a) What security features of the operating system can be used to simplify the design of the database management system? (b) Suppose the operating system has rating *r*, where *r* is C2 or B1 or B3, and so on. State and defend a policy for the degree of trust in the database management system, based on the trust of the operating system.
17. What is the purpose of encryption in a multilevel secure database management system?

7

Security in Networks

In this chapter:

- How networks differ from and are similar to single, stand-alone applications and environments
- Threats against networked applications, including denial of service, web site defacements, malicious mobile code, and protocol attacks
- Controls against network attacks: physical security, policies and procedures, and a range of technical controls
- Firewalls: design, capabilities, limitations
- Intrusion detection systems
- Private e-mail: PGP and S/MIME

Networks—their design, development, and usage—are critical to computing, at least for the next few years. We interact with networks daily, if not more frequently, when we perform banking transactions, make telephone calls, or ride trains and planes. The utility companies use networks to track electricity or water usage and bill for it. When we pay for groceries or gasoline, networks enable our credit or debit card transactions and billing. Life without networks would be considerably less convenient, and many activities would be impossible. Not surprisingly, then, computing networks are attackers' present and future targets of choice. Because of their actual and potential impact, network attacks attract the attention of journalists, managers, auditors, and the general public. For example, when you read the daily newspapers, you are likely to find a story about a network-based attack at least every month. The coverage itself evokes a sense of evil, using terms such as hijacking, distributed denial of service, and our familiar friends viruses, worms, and Trojan horses. Because any large-scale attack is likely to put thousands of computing systems at risk, with potential losses well into the millions of dollars, network attacks make good copy.

The media coverage is more than hype; network attacks are critical problems. Fortunately, your bank, your utility company, and even your Internet service provider take network security very seriously. Because they do, they are vigilant about applying the most current and most effective controls to their systems. Of equal importance, these organizations continually assess their risks and learn about the latest attack types and defense mechanisms, so that they can maintain the protection of their networks.

In this chapter we describe what makes a network similar to and different from an application program or an operating system, which you have studied in earlier chapters. In investigating networks, you will learn how the concepts of confidentiality, integrity, and availability apply in networked settings. At the same time, you will see that the basic notions of identification and authentication, access control, accountability, and assurance are the basis for network security, just as they have been in other settings.

Networking is growing and changing perhaps even faster than other computing disciplines. Consequently, this chapter is unlikely to present you with the most current technology, the latest attack, or the newest defense mechanism; you can read about those in daily newspapers and at web sites. But the novelty and change build on what we know today: the fundamental concepts, threats, and controls for networks. By developing an understanding of the basics, you can absorb the most current news quickly and easily. More importantly, your understanding can assist you in building, protecting, and using networks.

7.1 NETWORK CONCEPTS

To study network threats and controls, we first must review some of the relevant networking terms and concepts. This review does not attempt to provide the depth of a classic networking reference, such as [GAL99] or [TAN03]. In earlier chapters, our study of security focused on the individual pieces of a computing system, such as a single application, an operating system, or a database. Networks involve not only the pieces but also—importantly—the connections among them.

Networks are both fragile and strong. To see why, think about the power, cable television, telephone, or water network that serves your home. If a falling tree branch breaks the power line to your home, you are without electricity until that line is repaired; you are vulnerable to what is called a **single point of failure**, because one cut to the network destroys electrical functionality for your entire home. Similarly, there may be one telephone trunk line or water main that serves your home and those nearby; a failure can leave your building, street, or neighborhood without service. But we have ways to keep the entire network from failing. If we trace back through the network from your home to the source of what flows through it, we are likely to see that several main distribution lines support an entire city or campus. That is, there is more than one way to get from the source to your neighborhood, enabling engineers to redirect the flow along alternative paths. Redundancy makes it uncommon for an entire city to lose service from a single failure. For this reason, we say that such a network has **resilience** or **fault tolerance.**

Complex routing algorithms reroute the flow not just around failures but also around overloaded segments. The routing is usually done automatically; the control program is often supplemented by human supervision or intervention. Many types of networks have very high reliability by design, not by accident. But because there often is less redundancy near a network's endpoints than there is elsewhere, we say that the network has great strength in the middle and fragility at the perimeter.

From the user's perspective, a network is sometimes designed so that it looks like two endpoints with a single connection in the middle. For example, the municipal water supply may appear to be little more than a reservoir (the source), the pipes (the transmission or communication medium), and the water faucet (the destination). Although this simplistic view is functionally correct, it ignores the complex design, implementation, and management of the "pipes." In a similar way, we describe computer networks in this chapter in ways that focus on the security concepts but present the networks themselves in a simplistic way, to highlight the role of security and prevent the complexity of the networks from distracting our attention. Please keep in mind that our network descriptions are often abstractions of a more complex actuality.

The Network

Figure 7-1 shows a network in its simplest form, as two devices connected across some medium by hardware and software that enable the communication. In some cases, one device is a computer (sometimes called a "server") and the other is a simpler device (sometimes called a "client") enabled only with some means of input (such as a keyboard) and some means of output (such as a screen). For example, a powerful computer can be a server, but a handheld personal digital assistant (PDA) or a cell phone might be a network client.

Although this model defines a basic network, the actual situation is frequently significantly more complicated.

- The simpler client device, employed for user-to-computer communication, is often a PC or workstation, so the client has considerable storage and processing capability.
- A network can be configured as just a single client connected to a single server. But more typically, many clients interact with many servers.
- The network's services are often provided by many computers. As a single user's communication travels back and forth from client to server, it may merely pass through some computers but pause at others for significant interactions.
- The end user is usually unaware of many of the communications and computations taking place in the network on the user's behalf.

Most real-world situations are more like Figure 7-2. In this second view, the user at one of the lettered client machines may send a message to System 3, unaware that

FIGURE 7-1 Simple View of Network.

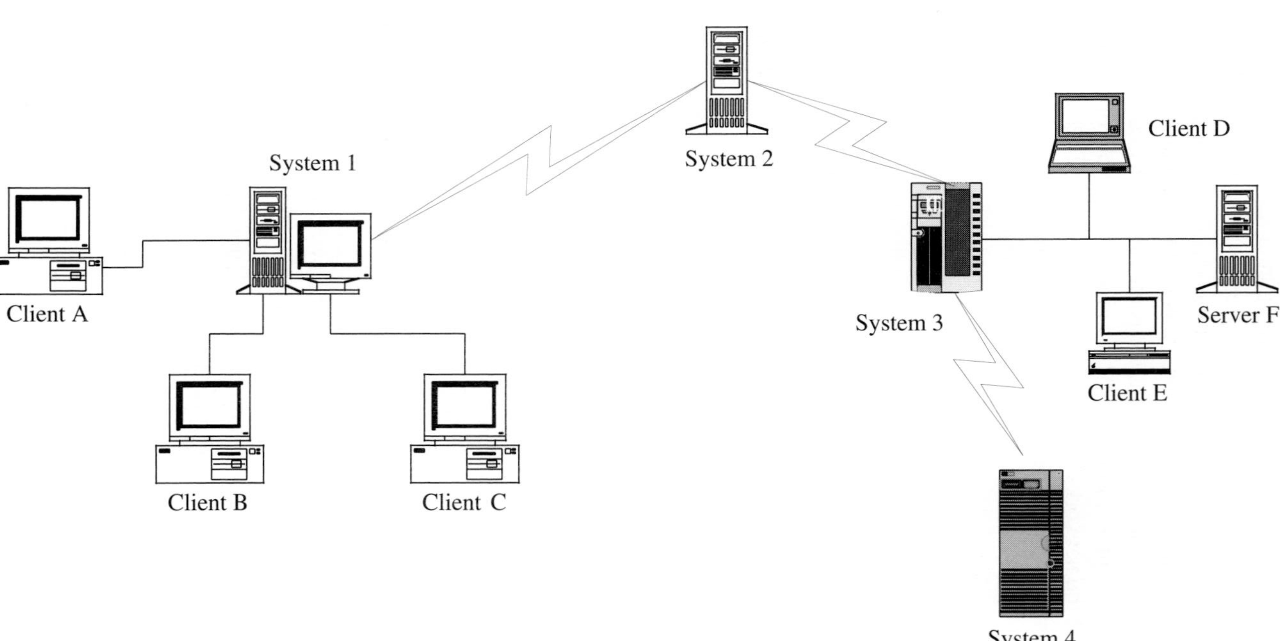

FIGURE 7-2 More Complex but More Typical View of Networks.

communication is actually passing through the active Systems 1 and 2. In fact, the user may be unaware that System 3 sometimes passes work to System 4.

A single computing system in a network is often called a **node**, and its processor (computer) is called a **host**. A connection between two hosts is known as a **link**. Network computing consists of users, communications media, visible hosts, and systems not generally visible to end users. In Figure 7-2, Systems 1 through 4 are nodes. In our figure the users are at the lettered client machines, perhaps interacting with Server F.

Users communicate with networked systems by interacting directly with terminals, workstations, and computers. A **workstation** is an end-user computing device, usually designed for a single user at a time. Workstations often have powerful processors and good-sized memory and storage so that they can do sophisticated data manipulation (such as converting coded data to a graphical format and displaying the picture). A system is a collection of processors, perhaps including a mixture of workstations and independent processors, typically with more processing power and more storage capacity than a workstation.

Environment of Use

The biggest difference between a network and a stand-alone device is the environment in which each operates. Although some networks are located in protected spaces (for example, a local area network in a single laboratory or office), at least some portion of most networks is exposed, often to total strangers. The relatively simple network in Figure 7-2 is a good example. Systems 2, 3, and 4 are remote from System 1, and they may be under different ownership or control.

Networks can be described by several typical characteristics:

- *Anonymity*. A cartoon image shows a dog typing at a workstation, and saying to another dog, "On the Internet, nobody knows you're a dog." A network removes most of the clues, such as appearance, voice, or context, by which we recognize acquaintances.
- *Automation*. In some networks, one or both endpoints, as well as all intermediate points, involved in a given communication may be machines with only minimal human supervision.
- *Distance*. Many networks connect endpoints that are physically far apart. Although not all network connections involve distance, the speed of communication is fast enough that humans usually cannot tell whether a remote site is near or far.
- *Opaqueness*. Because the dimension of distance is hidden, users cannot tell whether a remote host is in the room next door or in a different country. In the same way, users cannot distinguish whether they are connected to a node in an office, school, home, or warehouse, or whether the node's computing system is large or small, modest or powerful. In fact, users cannot tell if the current communication involves the same host with which they communicated the last time.
- *Routing diversity*. To maintain or improve reliability and performance, routings between two endpoints are usually dynamic. That is, the same interaction may

follow one path through the network the first time and a very different path the second time. In fact, a query may take a different path from the response that follows a few seconds later.

Shape and Size

The way a network is configured, in terms of nodes and connections, is called the network **topology**. You can think of the topology as the shape of the network. The topology ranges from very simple, such as two hosts connected by one path, to very complex, such as the Internet. These two extremes highlight three dimensions of networks that have particular bearing on a network's security.

- *Boundary*. The boundary distinguishes an element of the network from an element outside it. For a simple network, we can easily list all the components and draw an imaginary line around it to separate what is in the network from what is outside. But listing all the hosts connected to the Internet is practically impossible. For example, a line surrounding the Internet would have to surround the entire globe today, and Internet connections also pass through satellites in orbit around the earth. Moreover, as people and organizations choose to be connected or not, the number and type of hosts change almost second by second, with the number generally increasing over time.
- *Ownership*. It is often difficult to know who owns each host in a network. The network administrator's organization may own the network infrastructure, including the cable and network devices. However, certain hosts may be connected to a network for convenience, not necessarily implying ownership.
- *Control*. Finally, if ownership is uncertain, control must be, too. To see how, pick an arbitrary host. Is it part of network A? If yes, is it under the control of network A's administrator? Does that administrator establish access control policies for the network, or determine when its software must be upgraded and to what version? Indeed, does the administrator even know what version of software that host runs?

The truth is that, for many networks, it is difficult and at times impossible to tell which hosts are part of that network, who owns the hosts, and who controls them. Even for networks significantly smaller than the Internet, major corporate, university, or government networks are hard to understand and are not even well known by their system administrators. Although it seems contrary to common sense, many corporations today have no accurate picture of how their networks are configured. To understand why, consider a network of automated teller machines for a multinational bank. The bank may have agreements with other banks to enable customers to withdraw money anywhere in the world. The multinational bank may understand its own bank's network, but it may have no conception of how the connecting banks' networks are configured; there is no "big picture" of how the combined networks look or operate. Similarly, a given host may be part of more than one network. In such a situation, suppose a host has two network interfaces. Whose rules does that host (and that host's administrator) have to follow?

Depicting, configuring, and administering networks are not easy tasks.

Mode of Communication

A computer network implements communication between two endpoints. Data are communicated either in **digital** format (in which data items are expressed as discrete binary values) or **analog** (in which data items are expressed as points in a continuous range, using a medium like sound or electrical voltage). Computers typically store and process digital data, but some telephone and similar cable communications are in analog form (because telephones were originally designed to transmit voice). When the transmission medium expects to transfer analog data, the digital signals must be converted to analog for transmission and then back to digital for computation at the receiving end. Some mostly analog networks may even have some digital segments, so the analog signals are digitized more than once. These conversions are performed by a **modem** (the term is derived from *mo*dulator-*dem*odulator), which converts a digital data stream to tones and back again.

Media

Communication is enabled using several kinds of media. We can choose among several types, such as along copper wires or optical fiber, or through the air, as with cellular phones. Let us look at each type in turn.

Cable

Because much of our computer communication has historically been done over telephone lines, the most common network communication medium today is **wire**. Inside our homes and offices, we use a pair of insulated copper wires, called a **twisted pair** or **unshielded twister pair (UTP)**. Copper has good transmission properties at a relatively low cost. The bandwidth of UTP is limited to under 10 megabits per second (Mbps),[1] so engineers cannot transmit a large number of communications simultaneously on a single line. Moreover, the signal strength degrades as it travels through the copper wire, and it cannot travel long distances without a boost. Thus, for many networks, line lengths are limited to approximately 300 feet. Single twisted pair service is most often used locally, within a building or up to a local communications drop (that is, the point where the home or office service is connected to the larger network, such as the commercial telephone system). Although regular copper wire can transmit signals, the twisting reduces crossover (interference and signal transfer) between adjacent wires.

Another choice for network communication is **coaxial (coax) cable,** the kind used for cable television. Coax cable is constructed with a single wire surrounded by an insulation jacket. The jacket is itself surrounded by a braided or spiral-wound wire. The inner wire carries the signal, and the outer braid acts as a ground. The most widely used computer communication coax cable is **Ethernet**, carrying up to 100 Mbps over distances of up to 1500 feet.

[1] The figures in this section were accurate when they were written, but technology is constantly changing. However, as speeds or capacities change, the basic ranking of two technologies tends to remain the same.

Coax cable also suffers from degradation of signal quality over distance. **Repeaters** (for digital signals) or **amplifiers** (for analog signals) can be spaced periodically along the cable to pick up the signal, amplify it, remove spurious signals called "noise," and retransmit it.

Optical Fiber

A newer form of cable is made of very thin strands of glass. Instead of carrying electrical energy, these fibers carry pulses of light. The bandwidth of optical fiber is up to 1000 Mbps, and the signal degrades less over fiber than over wire or coax; the fiber is good for a run of approximately 2.5 miles. Optical fiber involves less interference, less crossover between adjacent media, lower cost, and less weight than copper. Thus, optical fiber is generally a much better transmission medium than copper. Consequently, as copper ages, it is being replaced by optical fiber in most communication systems. In particular, most long distance communication lines are now fiber.

Wireless

Radio signals can also carry communications. Similar to pagers, wireless microphones, garage door openers, and portable telephones, wireless radio can be used in networks, following a protocol developed for short-range telecommunications, designated the 802.11 family of standards. The wireless medium is used for short distances; it is especially useful for networks in which the nodes are physically close together, such as in an office building or at home. Many 802.11 devices are becoming available for home and office wireless networks.

Microwave

Microwave is a form of radio transmission especially well suited for outdoor communication. Microwave has a channel capacity similar to coax cable; that is, it carries similar amounts of data. Its principal advantage is that the signal is strong from point of transmission to point of receipt. Therefore, microwave signals do not need to be regenerated with repeaters, as do signals on cable.

However, a microwave signal travels in a straight line, presenting a problem because the earth curves. Microwave signals travel by line of sight: The transmitter and receiver must be in a straight line with one another, with no intervening obstacles, such as mountains. As shown in Figure 7-3, a straight microwave signal transmitted between towers of reasonable height can travel a distance of only about 30 miles because of the earth's curvature. Thus, microwave signals are "bounced" from receiver to receiver, spaced less than 30 miles apart, to cover a longer distance.

Infrared

Infrared communication carries signals for short distances (up to 9 miles) and also requires a clear line of sight. Because it does not require cabling, it is convenient for portable objects, such as laptop computers and connections to peripherals. An infrared signal is difficult to intercept because it is a point-to-point signal. However, it is subject to "in the middle" attacks in which the interceptor functions like a repeater, receiving

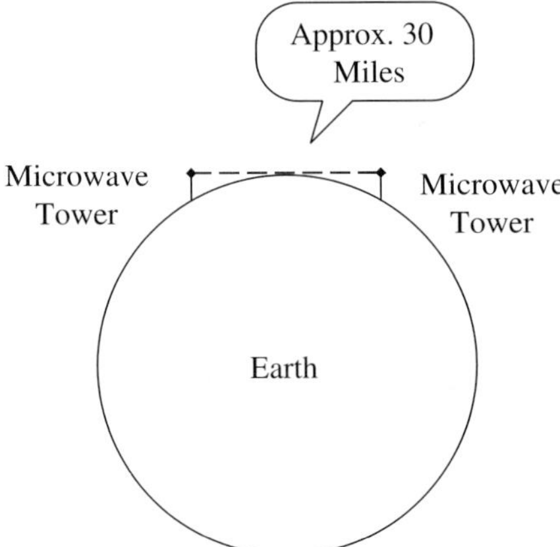

FIGURE 7-3 Microwave Transmission.

the signal, extracting any desired data, and retransmitting to the original destination the original signal or a modified version. Because of line-of-sight requirements and limited distance, infrared is typically used in a protected space, such as an office, in which in-the-middle attacks would be difficult to conceal.

Satellite

Many communications, such as international telephone calls, must travel around the earth. In the early days of telephone technology, telephone companies ran huge cables along the ocean's bottom, enabling calls to travel from one continent to another. Today, we have other alternatives. The communication companies place satellites in orbits that are synchronized with the rotation of the earth (called **geosynchronous orbits**), so the satellite appears to hover in a fixed position 22,300 miles above the earth. Although the satellite can be expensive to launch, once in space it is essentially maintenance free. Furthermore, the quality of a satellite communication link is often better than an earth-bound wire cable.

Satellites act as naïve transponders: Whatever they receive they broadcast out again. Thus, satellites are really sophisticated receivers, in that their sole function is to receive and repeat signals. From the user's point of view, the signal essentially "bounces" off the satellite and back to earth. For example, a signal from North America travels 22,300 miles into the sky and the same distance back to a point in Europe. The process of bouncing a signal off a satellite is shown in Figure 7-4.

We can project a signal to a satellite with reasonable accuracy, but the satellite is not expected to have the same level of accuracy when it sends the signal back to earth. Thus, to reduce complexity and eliminate beam focusing, satellites typically spread their transmissions over a very wide area. A rather narrow angle of dispersion from the satellite's transmitter produces a fairly broad pattern (called the **footprint**) on the surface of the earth because of the 22,300-mile distance from the satellite to earth. Thus, a typical satellite transmission can be received over a path several hundred miles wide; some cover the width of the entire continental United States in a single transmission.

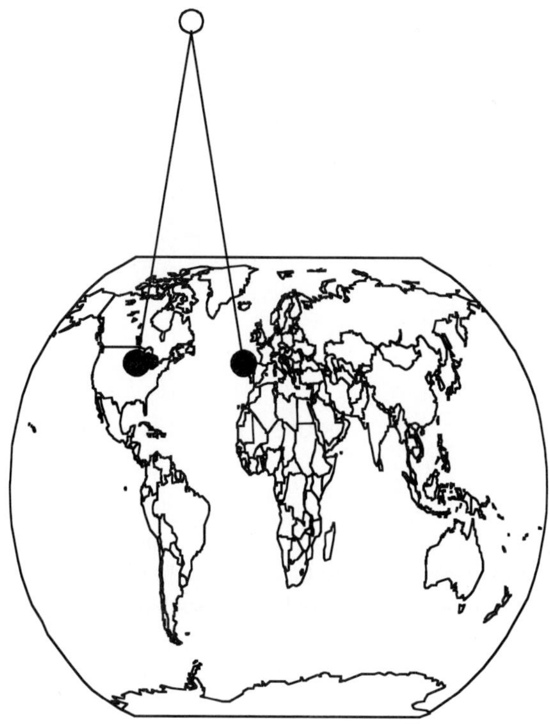

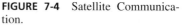

FIGURE 7-4 Satellite Communication.

For some applications, such as satellite television, a broad footprint is desirable. But for secure communications, the smaller the footprint, the less the risk of interception.

Protocols

When we use a network, the communication media are usually transparent to us. That is, most of us do not know whether our communication is carried over copper wire, optical fiber, satellite, microwave, or some combination. In fact, the communication medium may change from one transmission to the next. This ambiguity is actually a positive feature of a network: its *independence*. That is, the communication is separated from the actual medium of communication. Independence is possible because we have defined **protocols** that allow a user to view the network at a high, abstract level of communication (viewing it in terms of user and data); the details of *how* the communication is accomplished are hidden within software and hardware at both ends. The software and hardware enable us to implement a network according to a **protocol stack**, a layered architecture for communications. Each layer in the stack is much like a language for communicating information relevant at that layer.

Two popular protocol stacks are used frequently for implementing networks: the Open Systems Interconnection (OSI) and the Transmission Control Protocol and Internet Protocol (TCP/IP) architecture. We examine each one in turn.

ISO OSI Reference Model

The International Standards Organization (ISO) Open Systems Interconnection (OSI) model consists of layers by which a network communication occurs. The OSI reference model contains the seven layers listed in Table 7-1.

How communication works across the different layers is depicted in Figure 7-5. We can think of the layers as creating an assembly line, in which each layer adds its own service to the communication. In concert, the layers represent the different activities that must be performed for actual transmission of a message. Separately, each layer serves a purpose; equivalent layers perform similar functions for the sender and receiver. For example, the sender's layer four affixes a header to a message, designating the sender, the receiver, and relevant sequence information. On the receiving end, layer four reads the header to verify that the message is for the intended recipient, and then removes this header.

Each layer passes data in three directions: *above* with a layer communicating more abstractly, *parallel* or *across* to the same layer in another host, and *below* with a layer handling less abstract (that is, more fundamental) data items. The communications above and below are actual interactions, while the parallel one is a virtual communication path. Parallel layers are called "peers."

Let us look at a simple example of protocol transmission. Suppose that, to send e-mail to a friend, you run an application such as Eudora, Outlook, or Unix mail. You type a message, using the application's editor, and the application formats the message into two parts: a header that shows to whom the message is intended (as well as other things, such as sender and time sent), and a body that contains the text of your message. The application reformats your message into a standard format so that even if you and your friend use different mail applications, you can still exchange e-mail. This transformation is shown in Figure 7-6.

However, the message is not transmitted exactly as you typed it, as raw text. Raw text is a very inefficient coding, because an alphabet uses relatively few of the 255 possible characters for an 8-bit byte. Instead, the presentation layer is likely to change the

TABLE 7-1 OSI Protocol Layer Levels.

Layer	Name	Activity
7	Application	User-level data
6	Presentation	Standardized data appearance, blocking, text compression
5	Session	Sessions or logical connections between parts of an application; message sequencing, recovery
4	Transport	Flow control, end-to-end error detection and correction, priority service
3	Network	Routing, message blocking into uniformly sized packets
2	Data Link	Reliable data delivery over physical medium; transmission error recovery, separating packets into uniformly sized frames
1	Physical	Actual communication across physical medium; individual bit transmission

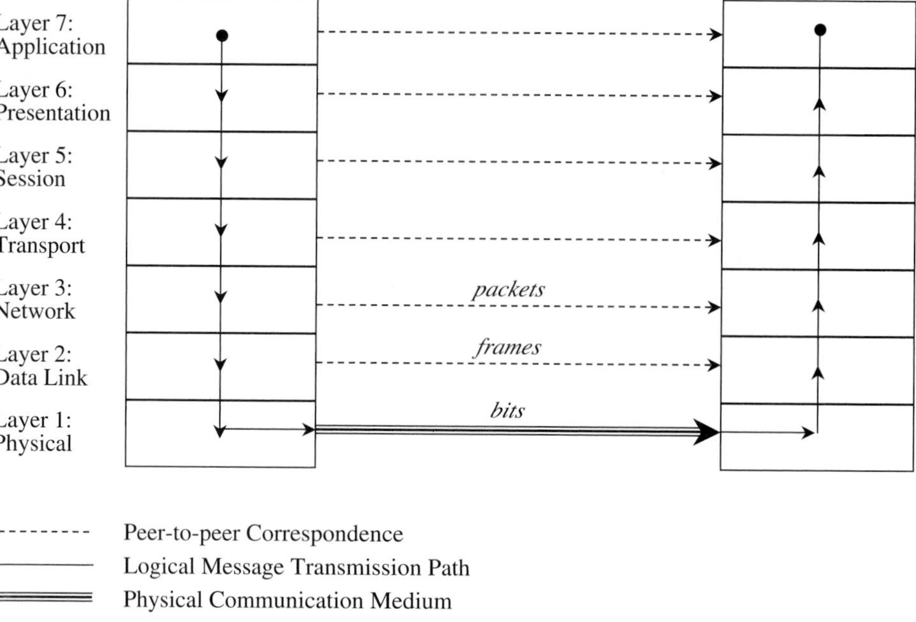

FIGURE 7-5 ISO OSI Network Model.

raw text into something else. It may do compression, character conversions, and even some cryptography. An e-mail message is a one-way transfer (from sender to receiver), so it is not initiating a session in which data fly back and forth between the two endpoints. Because the notion of a communication session is not directly relevant in this scenario, we ignore the session layer for now. Occasionally, spurious signals intrude in a communication channel, as when static rustles a telephone line or interference intrudes on a radio or television signal. To address this, the transport layer adds error detection and correction coding to filter out these spurious signals.

Addressing

Suppose your message is addressed to yourfriend@somewhere.net. This notation means that "somewhere.net" is the name of a destination host (or more accurately, a destination network). At the network layer, a hardware device called a **router** will actually send the message from your network to a router on the network somewhere.net. The network layer adds two headers to show your computer's address as the source and somewhere.net's address as the destination. Logically, your message is prepared to move from your machine to your router to your friend's router to your friend's computer. (In fact, between the two routers there may be many other routers in a path through the networks from you to your friend.) Together, the network layer structured with destination address, source address, and data is called a **packet**. The basic network layer protocol transformation is shown in Figure 7-7.

The message must travel from your computer to your router. Every computer connected to a network has a **network interface card (NIC)** with a unique physical ad-my computer security class - Message (Rich Text)

File Edit View Insert Format Tools Actions Help

Tahoma 10 A B I U

To... yourfriend@somewhere.net

Cc...

Subject: my computer security class

Mon ami,
Enfin nous arrivons au sujet de la sécurité des reseaux.
On va étudier les bretelles, la mystification, le déni de service, comment se déguiser, et les attaques de rejeu.
J'aurais beaucoup plus à te dire après avoir étudié un peu.
--Ciao

header

To:	yourfriend@somewhere.net
From:	myself@myhost.myISP.com
Subject:	my computer security class
Date:	24-Oct-2002 14:02:31 (GMT-0500)
Mailer:	MS Outlook v 4.3

body

Mon ami,
Enfin nous arrivons au sujet de la sécurité...

FIGURE 7-6 Transformation.

dress, called a **MAC address** (for Media Access Control). At the data link level, two more headers are added, one for your computer's NIC address (the source MAC) and one for your router's NIC address. A data link layer structure with destination MAC, source MAC, and data is called a **frame**. Every NIC selects from the network those frames with its own address as a destination address. As shown in Figure 7-8, the data link layer adds the structure necessary for data to get from your computer to another computer (a router is just a dedicated computer) on your network.

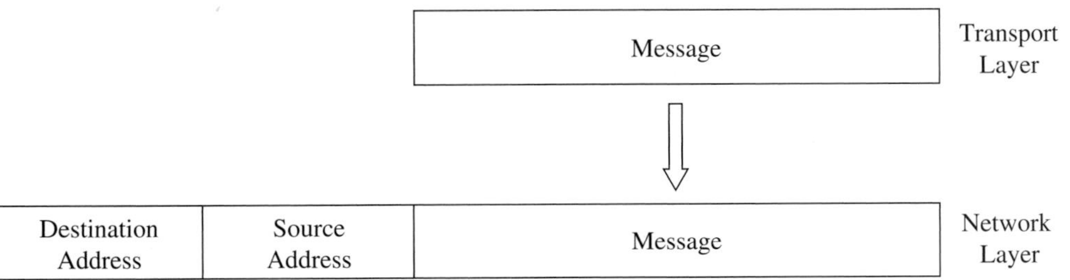

FIGURE 7-7 Network Layer Transformation.

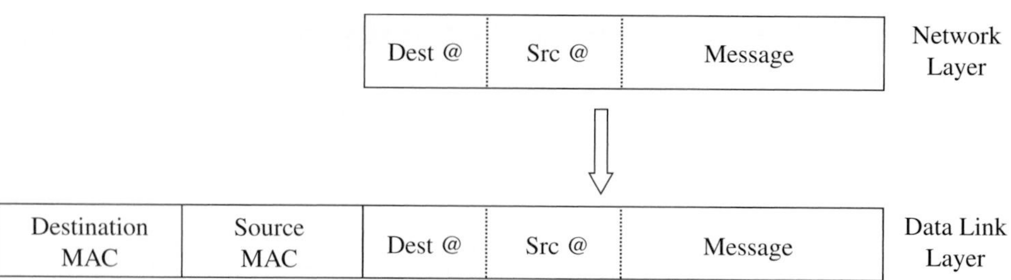

FIGURE 7-8 Data Link Layer Transformation.

Finally, the message is ready to be sent out as a string of bits. We noted earlier that analog transmissions communicate bits by using voltage or tone changes, and digital transmissions communicate them as discrete pulses. The physics and electronics of how bits are actually sent are handled at the physical layer.

On the receiving (destination) side, this process is exercised in reverse: Analog or digital signals are converted to digital data. The NIC card receives frames destined for it. The recipient network layer checks that the packet is really addressed to it. Packets may not arrive in the order in which they were sent (because of network delays or differences in paths through the network), so the session layer may have to reorder packets. The presentation layer removes compression and sets the appearance appropriate for the destination computer. Finally, the application layer formats and delivers the data as an e-mail message to your friend.

The layering and coordinating are a lot of work, and each protocol layer does its own part. But the work is worth the effort because the different layers are what enable Outlook running on an IBM PC on an Ethernet network in Washington D.C. to communicate with a user running Eudora on an Apple computer via a dial-up connection in Prague. Moreover, the separation by layers helps the network staff troubleshoot when something goes awry.

Layering

Each layer reformats the transmissions and exchanges information with its peer layer. Let us summarize what each layer contributes. Figure 7-9 shows a typical message that has been acted upon by the seven layers in preparation for transmission. Layer 6 breaks the original message data into blocks. At the session layer (5), a session header is added to show the sender, the receiver, and some sequencing information. Layer 4 adds information concerning the logical connection between the sender and receiver. The network layer (3) adds routing information and divides the message into units called packets, the standard units of communication in a network. The data link layer (2) adds both a header and a trailer to ensure correct sequencing of the message blocks and to detect and correct transmission errors. The individual bits of the message and the control information are transmitted on the physical medium by level 1. All additions to the message are checked and removed by the corresponding layer on the receiving side.

The OSI model is one of several transmission models. Different network designers implement network activities in slightly different combinations, although there is

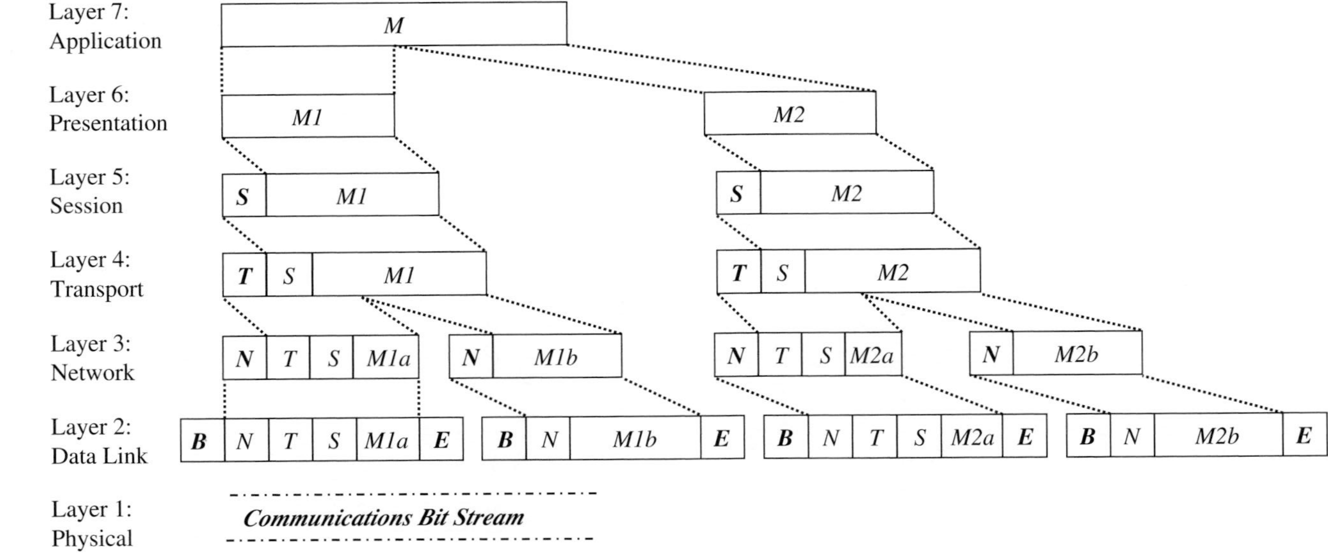

FIGURE 7-9 Message Prepared for Transmission.

always a clear delineation of responsibility. Some designers argue that the OSI model is overly complex—it has too many levels—and so other models are typically shorter.

TCP/IP

The OSI model is a conceptual one; it shows the different activities required for sending a communication. However, full implementation of a seven-layer transmission carries too much overhead for megabit-per-second communications; the OSI protocol slows things down to unacceptable levels. For this reason, TCP/IP (Transmission Control Protocol/Internet Protocol) is the protocol stack used for most wide area network communications. TCP/IP was invented for what became the Internet. TCP/IP is defined by protocols, not layers, but we can think of it in terms of four layers: application, host-to-host (end-to-end) transport, Internet, and physical. In particular, an application program deals only with abstract data items meaningful to the application user. Although TCP/IP is often used as a single acronym, it really denotes two different protocols: TCP implements a connected communications session on top of the more basic IP transport protocol. In fact, a third protocol, UDP (user datagram protocol) is also an essential part of the suite.

The transport layer receives variable-length messages from the application layer; the transport layer breaks them down into units of manageable size, transferred in **packets**. The Internet layer transmits application layer packets in **datagrams**, passing them to different physical connections based on the data's destination (provided in an address accompanying the data). The physical layer consists of device drivers to perform the actual bit-by-bit data communication. Table 7-2 shows how each layer contributes to the complete interaction.

The TCP protocol must ensure the correct sequencing of packets as well as the integrity (correct transmission) of data within packets. The protocol will put out-of-sequence packets in proper order, call for retransmitting a missing packet, and obtain a fresh copy of a damaged packet. In this way, TCP hands a stream of correct data in proper order to the invoking application. But this service comes at a price. Recording and checking sequence numbers, verifying integrity checks, and requesting and waiting for retransmissions of faulty or missing packets take time and induce overhead. Most applications expect a flawless stream of bits, but some applications can tolerate a less accurate stream of data if speed or efficiency is critical.

A TCP packet is a data structure that includes a sequence number, an acknowledgment number for connecting the packets of a communication session, flags, and source

TABLE 7-2 Internet Communication Layers.

Layer	Action	Responsibilities
Application	Prepare messages from user interactions	User interaction, addressing
Transport	Convert messages to packets	Sequencing, reliability (integrity), error correction
Internet	Convert packets to datagrams	Flow control, routing
Physical	Transmit datagrams as individual bits	Data communication

and destination **port** numbers. A port is a number designating a particular application running on a computer. For example, if Jose and Walter begin a communication, they establish a unique channel number by which their computers can route their respective packets to each of them. The channel number is called a port. Each service uses a well-known port, such as port 80 for HTTP (web pages), 23 for Telnet (remote terminal connection), 25 for SMTP (e-mail), or 161 for SNMP (network management). More precisely, each of these services has a waiting process that monitors the specified port number and tries to perform its service on any data passed to the port.

The UDP protocol does not provide the error-checking and correcting features of TCP, but it is a much smaller, faster protocol. For instance, a UDP datagram adds 8 bytes for control information, whereas the more complex TCP packet adds at least 24 bytes.

Most applications do not interact directly in TCP or UDP themselves. Instead, they operate on data structured by an application-level protocol applied on top of TCP or UDP. Some of the more common Internet protocols are shown in Table 7-3.

Whatever the model, a layer will typically subdivide data it receives from a higher layer and then add header and/or trailer information to the data before passing it to a lower layer. Each layer encapsulates the higher layer, so that higher layer headers and trailers are seen simply as part of the data to be transmitted.

Addressing Scheme

For communication to occur, the bits have to be directed *to* somewhere. All networks use an addressing scheme so that data can be directed to the expected recipient. Because it is the most common, we use the Internet addressing scheme known as IP addresses in our examples, since it is the addressing handled by the IP protocol.

All network models implement an addressing scheme. An address is a unique identifier for a single point in the network. For obvious reasons, addressing in shared, wide

TABLE 7-3 Internet Services.

Layer	TCP Protocols	UDP Protocols
Application Protocol	SMTP (Simple Mail Transfer Protocol): used for communicating e-mail HTTP (Hypertext Transfer Protocol): used for communicating web pages FTP (File Transfer Protocol): used for receiving or sending files Telnet (Terminal Emulation Protocol): used for performing remote operations as if directly connected to the host from a terminal *and others*	SNMP (Simple Network Monitoring Protocol): used for controlling network devices Syslog (System Audit Log): used for entering records in the system log Time: used for communicating and synchronizing time among network devices *and others*
Transport	TCP	UDP
Internet	IP	IP
Physical	Data communication	Data communication

area networks follows established rules, while addressing in local area networks is less constrained.

Starting at the local area network, each node has a unique address, defined in hardware on the network connector device (such as a network interface card) or its software driver. A network administrator may choose network addresses to be easy to work with, such as 1001, 1002, 1003 for nodes on one LAN, and 2001, 2002, and so forth on another.

A host on a TCP/IP wide area network has a 32-bit address,[2] called an **IP address**. An IP address is expressed as four 8-bit groups in decimal notation, separated by periods, such as 100.24.48.6. People prefer speaking in words or pseudowords, so network addresses are also known by names, such as ATT.COM or CAM.AC.UK. Addressing tables convert these acronyms to numeric format.

An IP address is parsed from right to left. The rightmost portion, such as .COM, .EDU, .NET, .ORG, or .GOV, or one of the two-letter country specific codes, such as .UK, .FR, .JP, or .DE, is called a **top-level domain**. A small set of organizations called the Internet Registrars controls these top-level domains; the registrars also control the registration of second-level domains, such as ATT in ATT.COM. Essentially, the registrars publish addresses of hosts that maintain tables of the second-level domains contained in the top-level domain. A host connected to the Internet queries one of these tables to find the numeric IP address of ATT in the .COM domain. AT&T, the company owning the ATT Internet site, must maintain its own host to resolve addresses within its own domain, such as MAIL.ATT.COM. You may find that the first time you try to resolve a fully qualified domain name to its IP address, your system performs a lookup starting at the top; for subsequent attempts, your system maintains a cache of domain name records that lets it resolve addresses locally. Finally, a domain name is translated into a 32-bit, four-octet address, and that address is included in the IP packets destined for that address. (We return to name resolution later in this chapter because it can be used in network attacks.)

Routing Concepts

A host needs to know how to direct a packet from its own IP address. Each host knows to what other hosts it is directly connected, and hosts communicate their connections to their neighbors. For the example network of Figure 7-2, System 1 would inform System 2 that it was one hop away from Clients A, B, and C. In turn, System 2 would inform its other neighbor, System 3, that it (System 2) was two hops away from Clients A, B, and C. From System 3, System 2 would learn that System 3 was one hop away from Clients D and E, Server F, and System 4, which System 2 would then pass to System 1 as being a distance of two hops. The routing protocols are actually more complex than this description, but the concepts are the same; hosts advertise to their neighbors to describe to which hosts (addresses) they can route traffic and at what cost (number of hops). Each host routes traffic to a neighbor that offers a path at the cheapest cost.

[2] Note: The world's networks are running out of unique addresses. This 32-bit standard address is being increased to 128 bits in a scheme called IPv6. But because 32-bit addresses will remain for some time, we focus on the older version.

Types of Networks

A network is a collection of communicating hosts. But to understand the network and how it works, we have several key questions to ask, such as How many hosts? Communicating by what means? To answer these questions, we are helped by an understanding of several types of subclasses of networks, since they commonly combine into larger networks. The subclasses are general notions, not definitive distinctions. But since the terms are commonly used, we present several common network subclasses that have significant security properties.

Local Area Networks

As the name implies, a **local area network** (or **LAN**) covers a small distance, typically within a single building. Usually a LAN connects several small computers, such as personal computers, as well as printers and perhaps some dedicated file storage devices. Figure 7-10 shows the arrangement of a typical LAN. The primary advantage of a LAN is the opportunity for its users to share data and programs and to share access to devices such as printers.

Most LANs have the following characteristics.

- *Small.* Typically, fewer than 100 users share a single LAN, within a distance less than 3 kilometers, or 2 miles. More commonly, a LAN is much smaller, stretching less than 1 kilometer inside a single building.
- *Locally controlled.* The equipment is owned and managed by a single organization. The users all are affiliated with a single organization, such as a company, a department, a workgroup, or a physical proximity.
- *Physically protected.* The LAN is on the premises of a company or other organization, so malicious outsiders usually cannot readily get to the LAN equipment.

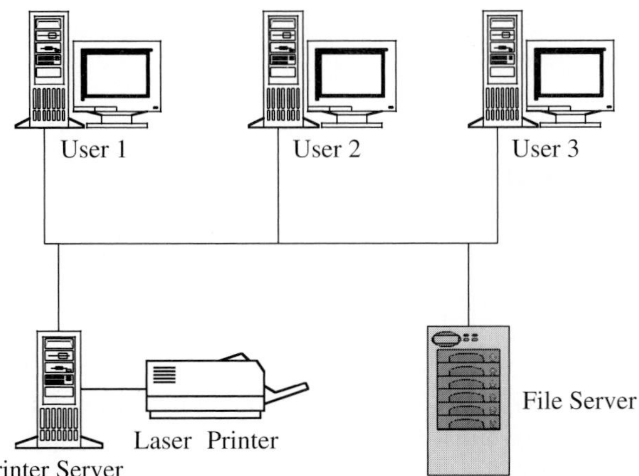

FIGURE 7-10 Typical LAN.

- *Limited scope.* Many LANs support a single group, department, floor, activity, or other geographical or administrative unit. As a result, each has a narrowly scoped set of function it performs.

Wide Area Networks

A **wide area network**, or **WAN**, differs from a local area network in terms of both size or distance (as its name implies, it covers a wider geographic area than does a LAN) and control or ownership (it is more likely *not* to be owned or controlled by a single body). Still, there tends to be some unifying principle to a WAN. The hosts on a WAN may all belong to a company with many offices, perhaps even in different cities or countries, or they may be a cluster of independent organizations within a few miles of each other, who share the cost of networking hardware. These examples also show how WANs themselves differ. Some are under close control and maintain a high degree of logical and physical isolation (typically, these are WANs controlled by one organization), while others are only marriages of convenience. Typical characteristics of WANs are these.

- *Single control.* Typically, a single organization is responsible for and controls a wide area network. Even if a network is shared by several unrelated subscribers, one organization usually determines who may join the network.
- *Covers a significant distance.* A WAN generally serves a distance greater than a LAN can cover, typically from a few miles to the entire globe.
- *Physically exposed* (often, but not always). Most wide area networks use publicly available communications media, which are relatively exposed. However, the fact that many subscribers share those media helps protect the privacy of any one subscriber.

Other network types include campus area networks (CANs) and metropolitan area networks (MANs). A CAN is usually under the control of a single organization, such as a university or company, and covers the adjacent buildings of one site of that organization. A MAN often covers a city, with the communication offering of one provider in that area. CANs, MANs, and WANs cover a wide range of possibilities; they loosely characterize everything between LANs and Internets, the two extremes of the networking spectrum.

Internetworks (Internets)

Networks of networks, or internetwork networks, are sometimes called **internets**. An internet is a connection of two or more separate networks, in that they are separately managed and controlled. The most significant internetwork is known as the **Internet**, because it connects so many of the other public networks.

The Internet is, in fact, a federation of networks, loosely controlled by the Internet Society. The Internet Society enforces certain minimal rules of fair play to ensure that all users are treated equitably, and it supports standard protocols so that users can communicate. These are the characteristics of the Internet.

- *Federation.* Almost no general statements can be made about Internet users or even network service providers. Some may access the network through businesses or government organizations whose memberships are very restrictive, while others may obtain access simply by paying a small monthly fee.
- *Enormous.* No one really knows how large the Internet is. Our knowledge is incomplete in part because new hosts are added daily, in part because one Internet access point can support hundreds or thousands of machines connected through that single access point, and in part because nobody has laid the basis for an accurate census. The Internet connects many thousands of networks. In 2002, there were almost 200 million Internet hosts and well over 700 million users.[3] Based on past history, we can expect the size of the Internet to double each year. Sidebar 7-1 describes the large number of outside accesses just to one site at the University of Illinois.
- *Heterogeneous.* Probably at least one of every kind of commercially available hardware and software is connected to the Internet. Unix is popular as the operating system at the Internet connection point, although most other multiuser operating systems could support access.
- *Physically and logically exposed.* Since there is no global access control, practically any attacker can access the Internet and, because of its complex connectivity, reach practically any resource on the net.

Topologies

The topology of a network can affect its security. Three basic patterns come from LANs, but the structures describe wider networks, or parts of wider networks, as well. These three patterns are depicted in Figure 7-11.

Common Bus

Conceptually, a **common bus** is a single wire to which each node of a LAN is connected. Timing signals on the bus help the nodes communicate. This medium is especially convenient for LANs, since users and machines are frequently rearranged and new connections can be added easily.

Nodes must continually monitor the bus to retrieve communications addressed for them. In that respect, every communication is accessible to every node, not just the designated addressee. Each host acts cooperatively but autonomously.

Star or Hub

In a **star** or **hub** network, each node is connected to a central "traffic controller" node. All transmissions flow from the source node to the traffic controller and then from the traffic controller to the destination node. Such a central node can monitor and control traffic to defeat covert channels.

[3] Counting the number of hosts or users is obviously difficult. But from a security perspective, even if these numbers are too high and if only a small percentage of hosts and users are malicious, the number of possible attacks is still large enough to be worth attention.

Sidebar 7-1 Traffic at a Typical Web Site

The University of Illinois at Urbana-Champaign tracks the usage of its web site over time. On one summer day (26 August 2001) browsers were used by 6,817 hosts in 57 countries making 75,062 accesses to the university's Engineering Workstations World Wide Web server. This volume and diversity are usual for a site that is not a popular public site like Google or Yahoo. The latest statistics are available at *http://www.cen.uiuc.edu/bstats/latest.html*.

The network administrators look not only at where the accesses come from but also at what the users are trying to do. Most of the accesses to this server were for viewing the home pages of engineering students who had posted information at the site. Many sites gather statistics on local and remote accesses for performance and security.

But these statistics count all traffic, not just the security-relevant activity. The security company ISS (Internet Security Systems) tracks the status of actual Internet security risk. Its four-point scale goes from 1 (normal risk from random malicious attacks experienced by all site administrators) to 4 (actual or potential catastrophic security event requiring immediate defense). During a period from April to June 2002, ISS reported 56 days at level 1, 22 at level 2, and 7 at level 3 [ISS02].

Each message is read only by the traffic controller (presumably for address only) and the intended recipient. There is a unique path between any two nodes, and this path is inaccessible to any others.

Ring

In a **ring topology**, each node receives many messages, scans each, removes ones designated for it, adds any more it wants to transmit, and sends the pack of messages to the next node.

As with the bus, there is no central control. In this topology, however, each node has greater responsibility to the others because a single node's failure to pass along all the messages it has received would deny data to other nodes.

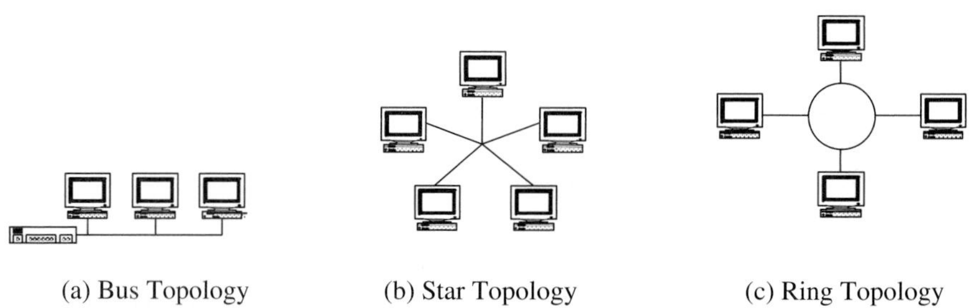

FIGURE 7-11 Network Topologies.

Distributed Systems

Distributed systems are related to networks. A **distributed system** is one in which computation is spread across two or more computers. From a security point of view, we are most interested in the type of distributed system in which one computer invokes a process on another computer without the direct participation of, or necessarily even the knowledge of, the user. For example, a user task on one machine might require data or specialized processing from another machine, such as a central machine on which a database is maintained. Alternatively, several machines may share tasks, depending on the current workload to optimize performance for all users.

For our purposes, the significant characteristic of a distributed system is its use of multiple, independent, and physically separated computers. The computers may be directly connected to one another, nodes on a LAN, or connected to a wider network.

In a **client server architecture** one host, the client, requests services from another, the server. A **peer-to-peer** system is a collection of equals, in which no one host consistently seeks or provides services from or to any other; all hosts could be called servers to the others. A distinction often inferred between clients and servers is that servers are expected to be more trustworthy than clients, meaning that a server must protect itself from any faulty data or processing requests from its client. On the other hand, the client, often a networking end user's workstation, does little to protect itself from potential rogue servers. Clearly, this distinction is flawed; as we will see, a client should not assume that all servers are trustworthy and should apply prudent protection measures.

APIs

Applications Programming Interfaces or **APIs** are definitions of interfaces to modules or systems. More and more frequently, software systems are not written from scratch. Instead, they are composed of components, some of which are new but many of which are purchased or modified from other applications. For example, developers may purchase graph-drawing routines, statistics packages, or sorts and searches, rather than write their own. In many cases, the services provided by the components are not embedded in a given application but are invoked from software resident on another machine. That is, the software is in a sense networked among several places, so we need standard, controlled ways to invoke services and routines. An API is the specification of what parameters in what forms must be passed to a routine, as well as what results that routine will provide. With an API, a developer need know only enough about a routine to be able to invoke it, without needing to understand how it operates or is structured internally.

GSSAPI or **Generic Security Services API** [LIN97] is a template for the many kinds of security services that a routine could provide. The template is independent of the mechanisms or structures that actually implement the security services. It is based on the notion that callers have credentials denoting their identities or authorizations to view and manipulate data. With these credentials, callers establish contexts or environments with security permissions. A caller with credentials operating in a particular context can invoke security services to implement confidentiality or integrity. GSSAPI defines calls to manage credentials, establish and destroy contexts, and obtain security services.

CAPI or **Cryptographic API** [COL96] is a Microsoft API for cryptographic services. Such APIs are useful because they let us separate the actual cryptographic implementation from a routine that needs cryptographic service; in this way, a user can invoke cryptographic algorithms of different strengths as they are needed. CAPI is a procedure that calls for generic cryptographic services, without specifying implementation or particular algorithm.

Advantages of Computing Networks

Computer networks offer several advantages over single-processor systems.

- *Resource sharing.* Network users can access a variety of resources through the network, rather than having them at hand locally. For instance, sharing databases, data and program files, and other resources reduces maintenance and storage costs while providing each user with improved access. For a single individual, usage may be too low to justify buying a specialized or expensive device. However, being able to share the device with many network users may justify its purchase.
- *Distributing the workload.* A single system's usage varies as users join and leave a system. The degree of workload fluctuation for a single system can be moderated in a network, shifting the workload from a heavily loaded system to an underutilized one.
- *Increased reliability.* Since a computing network consists of more than one computing system, the failure of one system or of just one component need not necessarily block users from continuing to compute. If similar systems exist, users can move their computing tasks to other systems when one system fails.
- *Expandability.* Network systems can be expanded easily by addition of new nodes. This expansion of the user base can occur without the manager of any single system having to take special action.

In earlier chapters, we considered computing systems as self-contained entities. A single security policy is associated with each computing system, addressing integrity of data, secrecy of data, and availability of service. A single operating system enforces the security policy; hardware controls assist the operating system; and some users augment the controls from the operating system with security features in individual applications programs. In general, users trust the operating system to provide a certain level of protection. In particular, the operating system can protect resources because it exercises complete control over those resources.

Computing networks have similar characteristics. The network must ensure integrity of data, secrecy of data, and availability of service. Each user accesses the network through a single operating system, which also includes network interface responsibilities. Users still expect the operating systems to enforce the security policies of the network. However, in a network the operating systems at the two ends of the communication, as well as the operating systems of all computers in between, must cooperate to enforce security.

We cannot always protect the whole network because its distant points are not under our control. However, we can consider our computer's or system's relationship to the rest of the network and focus on local users' accesses to the network, data received from and sent to the network, and possible accesses by other more distant users. In the next section we analyze the security ramifications of these network aspects.

7.2 THREATS IN NETWORKS

Up to now, we have reviewed network concepts with very little discussion of their security implications. But our earlier discussion of threats and vulnerabilities, as well as outside articles and your own experiences, probably have you thinking about the many possible attacks against networks. This section describes some of the threats you have already hypothesized and perhaps presents you with some new ones. But the general thrust is the same: threats aimed to compromise confidentiality, integrity, or availability, applied against data, software, and hardware by nature, accidents, nonmalicious humans, and malicious attackers.

What Makes a Network Vulnerable?

An isolated home user or a stand-alone office with a few employees is an unlikely target for many attacks. But add a network to the mix and the risk rises sharply. Consider how a network differs from a stand-alone environment:

- *Anonymity*. An attacker can mount an attack from thousands of miles away and never come into direct contact with the system, its administrators, or users. The potential attacker is thus safe behind an electronic shield. The attack can be passed through many other hosts in an effort to disguise the attack's origin. And computer-to-computer authentication is not the same for computers as it is for humans; as illustrated by Sidebar 7-2, secure distributed authentication requires thought and attention to detail.
- *Many points of attack—both targets and origins*. A simple computing system is a self-contained unit. Access controls on one machine preserve the confidentiality of data on that processor. However, when a file is stored in a network host remote from the user, the data or the file itself may pass through many hosts to get to the user. One host's administrator may enforce rigorous security policies, but that administrator has no control over other hosts in the network. Thus, the user must depend on the access control mechanisms in each of these systems. An attack can come from any host to any host, so that a large network offers many points of vulnerability.
- *Sharing*. Because networks enable resource and workload sharing, more users have the potential to access networked systems than on single computers. Perhaps worse, access is afforded to *more systems,* so that access controls for single systems may be inadequate in networks.
- *Complexity of system*. In Chapter 4 we saw that an operating system is a complicated piece of software. Reliable security is difficult, if not impossible, on a large operating system, especially one not designed specifically for security. A

Sidebar 7-2 Distributed Authentication in Windows NT and 2000

Authentication must be handled carefully and correctly in a network because a network involves authentication not just of people but of processes, servers, and services only loosely associated with a person. And for a network, the authentication process and database are often distributed for performance and reliability. Consider Microsoft's authentication scheme for its Windows operating systems. In Windows NT 4.0, the authentication database is distributed among several domain controllers. Each domain controller is designated as a primary or backup controller. All changes to the authentication database must be made to the (single) primary domain controller; then the changes are replicated from the primary to the backup domain controllers.

In Windows 2000, there no longer is a concept of primary and backup domain controllers. Instead, the network views the controllers as equal trees in a forest, in which any domain controller can update the authentication database. This scheme reflects Microsoft's notion that the system is "multimaster": only one controller can be master at a given time, but any controller can be a master. Once changes are made to a master, they are automatically replicated to the remaining domain controllers in the forest.

This approach is more flexible and robust than the primary-secondary approach, because it allows any controller to take charge—especially useful if one or more controllers have failed or are out of service for some reason. But the multimaster approach introduces a new problem. Because any domain controller can initiate changes to the authentication database, any hacker able to dominate a domain controller can alter the authentication database. And, what's worse, the changes are then replicated throughout the remaining forest. Theoretically, the hacker could access anything in the forest that relies on Windows 2000 for authentication.

When we think of attackers, we usually think of threats from outside the system. But in fact the multimaster approach can tempt people inside the system, too. A domain administrator in any domain in the forest can access domain controllers within that domain. Thanks to multimaster, the domain administrator can also modify the authentication database to access anything else in the forest.

For this reason, system administrators must consider how they define domains and their separation in a network. Otherwise, we can conjure up scary but possible scenarios. For instance, suppose one domain administrator is a bad apple. She works out a way to modify the authentication database to make herself an administrator for the entire forest. Then she can access any data in the forest, turn on services for some users, and turn off services for other users.

network combines two or more possibly dissimilar operating systems. Therefore, a network operating/control system is likely to be more complex than an operating system for a single computing system. Furthermore, the ordinary desktop computer today has greater computing power than did many office computers in the last two decades. The attacker can use this power to advantage by causing the victim's computer to perform part of the attack's computation. And because an average computer is so powerful, most users do not know what their computers are really doing at any moment: What processes are active in the background while you are playing Invaders from Mars? This complexity diminishes confidence in the network's security.

- *Unknown perimeter.* A network's expandability also implies uncertainty about the network boundary. One host may be a node on two different networks, so resources on one network are accessible to the users of the other network as well. Although wide accessibility is an advantage, this unknown or uncontrolled group of possibly malicious users is a security disadvantage. A similar problem occurs when new hosts can be added to the network. Every network node must be able to react to the possible presence of new, untrustable hosts. Figure 7-12 points out the problems in defining the boundaries of a network. Notice, for example, that a user on a host in network D may be unaware of the potential connections from users of networks A and B. And the host in the middle of networks A and B in fact belongs to A, B, C, and E. If there are different security rules for these networks, to what rules is that host subject?
- *Unknown path.* Figure 7-13 illustrates that there may be many paths from one host to another. Suppose that a user on host A1 wants to send a message to a user on host B3. That message might be routed through hosts C or D before arriving at host B3. Host C may provide acceptable security, but not D. Network users seldom have control over the routing of their messages.

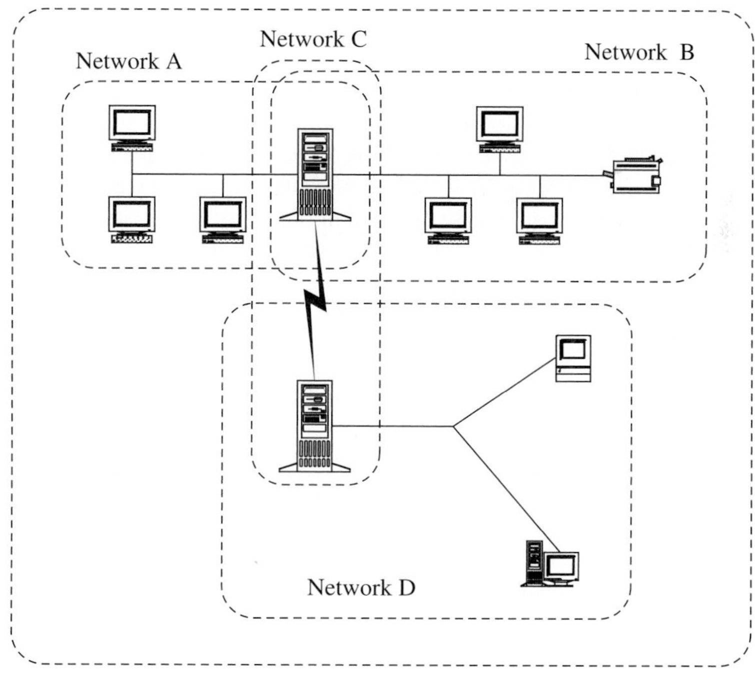

FIGURE 7-12 Unclear Network Boundaries.

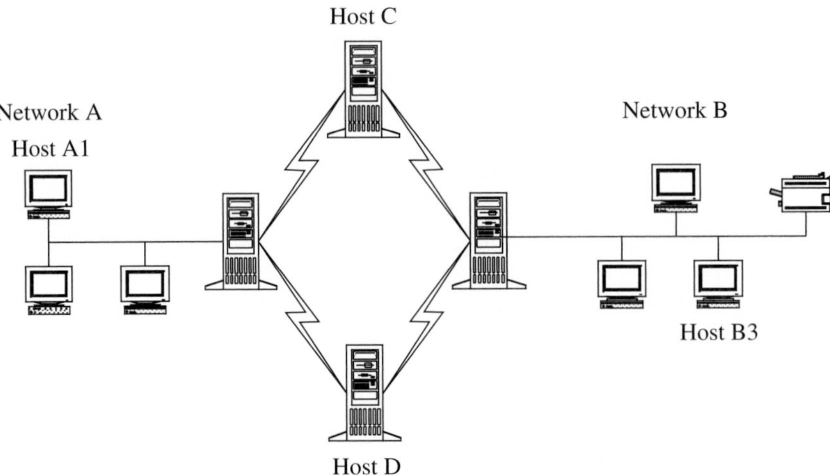

FIGURE 7-13 Uncertain Message Routing in a Network.

Thus, a network differs significantly from a stand-alone, local environment. Network characteristics significantly increase the security risk.

Who Attacks Networks?

Who are the attackers? We cannot list their names, just as we cannot know who all the criminals in our city, country, or the world are. Even if we knew who they were, we do not know if we could stop their behavior. (See Sidebar 7-3 for a first, tenuous link between psychological traits and hacking.) To have some idea of who the attackers might be, we return to concepts introduced in Chapter 1, where we described the three necessary components of an attack: method, opportunity, and motive.

In the next sections we explore method: tools and techniques the attackers use. Here we consider first the motives of attackers. Focusing on motive may give us some idea of who might attack a networked host or user. Four important motives are challenge or power, fame, money, and ideology.

Challenge

Why do people do dangerous or daunting things, like climb mountains or swim across the English Channel or engage in extreme sports? Because of the challenge. The situation is no different for someone skilled in writing or using programs. The single most significant motivation for a network attacker is the intellectual challenge. He or she is intrigued with knowing the answers to Can I defeat this network? What would happen if I tried this approach or that technique?

Some attackers enjoy the intellectual stimulation of defeating the supposedly undefeatable. For example, Robert Morris, who perpetrated the Internet worm in 1988 (described in Chapter 3), attacked supposedly as an experiment to see if he could exploit a particular vulnerability. Other attackers, such as the Cult of the Dead Cow, seek to

Sidebar 7-3 An Attacker's Psychological Profile?

Temple Grandin, a professor of animal science at Colorado State University and a sufferer from a mental disorder called Asperger syndrome (AS), thinks that Kevin Mitnick and several other widely described hackers show classic symptoms of Asperger syndrome. Although quick to point out that no research has established a link between AS and hacking, Grandin notes similar behavior traits among Mitnick, herself, and other AS sufferers. An article in *USA Today* (29 March 2001) lists the following AS traits:

- Poor social skills, often associated with being loners during childhood; the classic "computer nerd"
- Fidgeting, restlessness, inability to make eye contact, unresponsive to cues in social interaction, such as facial expressions or body language
- Exceptional ability to remember long strings of numbers
- Ability to focus on a technical problem intensely and for a long time, although easily distracted on other problems and unable to manage several tasks at once
- Deeply honest and law abiding

Donn Parker [PAR98] has studied hacking and computer crime for over 20 years. He states "hackers are characterized by an immature, excessively idealistic attitude... They delight in presenting themselves to the media as idealistic do-gooders, champions of the underdog."

Consider the following excerpt from an interview [SHA00] with "Mixter," the German programmer who admitted he was the author of the denial-of-service attacks called Tribal Flood Network (TFN) and its sequel TFN2K:

Q: Why did you write the software?

A: *I first heard about Trin00 [another denial of service attack] in July '99 and I considered it as interesting from a technical perspective, but also potentially powerful in a negative way. I knew some facts of how Trin00 worked, and since I didn't manage to get Trin00 sources or binaries at that time, I wrote my own server-client network that was capable of performing denial of service.*

Q: Were you involved ... in any of the recent high-profile attacks?

A: *No. The fact that I authored these tools does in no way mean that I condone their active use. I must admit I was quite shocked to hear about the latest attacks. It seems that the attackers are pretty clueless people who misuse powerful resources and tools for generally harmful and senseless activities just "because they can."*

Notice that from some information about denial-of-service attacks, he wrote his own server-client network and then a denial-of-service attack. But he was "quite shocked" to hear they were used for harm.

More research is needed before we will be able to define the profile of a hacker. And even more work will be needed to extend from that profile to the profile of a (malicious) attacker. Not all hackers become attackers; some hackers become extremely dedicated and conscientious system administrators, developers, or security experts. But some psychologists see in AS the rudiments of a hacker's profile.

demonstrate weaknesses in security defenses so that others will pay attention to strengthening security. Still other attackers are unnamed, unknown individuals working persistently just to see how far they can go in performing unwelcome activities.

However, as we will soon see, only a few attackers find previously unknown flaws. The vast majority of attackers repeat well-known and even well-documented attacks, sometimes only to see if they work against different hosts. In these cases, intellectual stimulation is certainly not the driving force, when the attacker is merely pressing [run] to activate an attack discovered, designed, and implemented by someone else.

Fame

The challenge of accomplishment is enough for some attackers. But other attackers seek recognition for their activities. That is, part of the challenge is doing the deed; another part is taking credit for it. In many cases, we do not know who the attackers really are, but they leave behind a "calling card" with a recognizable name: Mafiaboy, Kevin Mitnick, and members of the Chaos Computer Club, for example. The actors often retain some anonymity by using pseudonyms, but they achieve fame nevertheless. They may not be able to brag too openly, but they enjoy the personal thrill of seeing their attacks written up in the news media.

Money and Espionage

As in other settings, financial reward motivates attackers, too. Some attackers perform industrial espionage, seeking information on a company's products, clients, or long-range plans. We know industrial espionage has a role when we read about laptops and sensitive papers having been lifted from hotel rooms when other more valuable items were left behind. Some countries are notorious for using espionage to aid their state-run industries.

Sometimes industrial espionage is responsible for seemingly strange corporate behavior. For example, in July 2002, newspapers reported that a Yale University security audit had revealed that admissions officers from rival Princeton University broke into Yale's online admissions notification system. The Princeton snoops admitted looking at the confidential decisions about eleven students who had applied to both schools but who had not yet been told of their decisions by Yale. In another case, a startup company was about to activate its first application on the web. Two days before the application's unveiling, the head offices were burglarized. The only item stolen was the one computer containing the application's network design. Corporate officials had to make a difficult choice: go online knowing that a competitor might then take advantage of knowing the internal architecture or delay the product's rollout until the network design was changed. They chose the latter. Similarly, the chief of security for a major manufacturing company has reported privately to us of evidence that one of the company's competitors had stolen information. But he could take no action because he could not determine which of three competitors was the actual culprit.

Industrial espionage is illegal, but it occurs, in part because of the high potential gain. Its existence and consequences can be embarrassing for the target companies. Thus, many incidents go unreported, and there are few reliable statistics on how much industrial espionage and "dirty tricks" go on. Yearly since 1997, the Computer Security Institute and the U.S. Federal Bureau of Investigation have surveyed security professionals from companies, government agencies, universities, and organizations, asking them to report perceptions of computer incidents. About 500 responses are received for each survey. One question asks about sources of attacks, and a respondent can answer "yes" to more than one category, indicating more than one apparent attack. For the period between 1997 and 2002, between 72 percent and 81 percent indicated they had been attacked by an independent hacker. In addition, 38 percent to 53 percent reported they were attacked by a U.S. competitor and 23 percent to 31 percent by a foreign corporation. (For full details on the survey see [CSI02].) Clearly, security administrators believe there is a serious degree of industrial espionage; that is, not all security attacks come from individual hackers.

Ideology

In the last few years, we are starting to find cases in which attacks are perpetrated to advance ideological ends. For example, many security analysts believe that the Code Red worm of 2001 was launched by a group motivated by the tension in U.S.–China relations. Dorothy Denning [DEN99a] has distinguished between two types of related behaviors, hactivism and cyberterrorism. **Hactivism** involves "operations that use hacking techniques against a target's [network] with the intent of disrupting normal operations but not causing serious damage." In some cases, the hacking is seen as giving voice to a constituency that might otherwise not be able to be heard by the company or government organization. For example, Denning describes activities such as virtual sit-ins, in which an interest group floods an organization's web site with traffic to demonstrate support of a particular position. **Cyberterrorism** is more dangerous than hactivism: "politically motivated hacking operations intended to cause grave harm such as loss of life or severe economic damage."

Threat Precursors

Now that we have listed many motives for attacking, we will turn to how attackers perpetrate their attacks. Attackers do not ordinarily sit down at a terminal and launch an attack. A clever attacker investigates and plans before acting. Just as you might invest time in learning about a jewelry store before entering to steal from it, a network attacker learns a lot about a potential target before beginning the attack. We study the precursors to an attack so that if we can recognize characteristic behavior, we may be able to block the attack before it is launched.

Because most vulnerable networks are connected to the Internet, the attacker begins preparation by finding out as much as possible about the target. An example of information gathering is given in [HOB97].

Port Scan

An easy way to gather network information is to use a **port scan**, a program that, for a particular IP address, reports which ports respond to messages and which of several known vulnerabilities seem to be present.

A port scan is much like a routine physical examination from a doctor, particularly the initial questions used to determine a medical history. The questions and answers by themselves may not seem significant, but they point to areas that suggest further investigation.

Port scanning tells an attacker three things: which standard ports or services are running and responding on the target system, what operating system is installed on the target system, and what applications and versions of applications are present. This information is readily available for the asking from a networked system; it can be obtained quietly, anonymously, without identification or authentication, drawing little or no attention to the scan.

Port scanning tools are readily available, and not just to the underground community. The nmap scanner by Fyodor at *www.insecure.org/nmap* is a useful tool that anyone can download. Given an address, nmap will report all open ports, the service they support, and the owner (user ID) of the daemon providing the service. (The owner is significant because it implies what privileges would descend upon someone who compromised that service.) Another readily available scanner is netcat, written by Hobbit at *www.l0pht.com/users/l0pht*. (That URL is "letter ell," "digit zero," p-h-t.) Commercial products are a little more costly, but not prohibitive. Well-known commercial scanners are Nessus (Nessus Corp.), CyberCop Scanner (Network Associates), Secure Scanner (Cisco), and Internet Scanner (Internet Security Systems).

Social Engineering

The port scan gives an external picture of a network—where are the doors and windows, of what are they constructed, to what kinds of rooms do they open? The attacker also wants to know what is inside the building. What better way to find out than to ask?

Suppose, while sitting at your workstation, you receive a phone call. "Hello, this is John Davis from IT support. We need to test some connections on the internal network. Could you please run the command ipconfig/all on your workstation and read to me the addresses it displays?" The request sounds innocuous. But unless you know John Davis and his job responsibilities well, the caller could be an attacker gathering information on the inside architecture.

Social engineering involves using social skills and personal interaction to get someone to reveal security-relevant information and perhaps even to do something that permits an attack. The point of social engineering is to persuade the victim to be helpful. The attacker often impersonates someone inside the organization who is in a bind: "My laptop has just been stolen and I need to change the password I had stored on it," or "I have to get out a very important report quickly and I can't get access to the following thing." This attack works especially well if the attacker impersonates someone in a high position, such as the division vice president or the head of IT security. (Their names can sometimes be found on a public web site, in a network registration with the Internet registry, or in publicity and articles.) The attack is often directed at someone low enough to be intimidated or impressed by the high-level person. A direct phone call and expressions of great urgency can override any natural instinct to check out the story.

Because the victim has helped the attacker (and the attacker has profusely thanked the victim), the victim will think nothing is wrong and not report the incident. Thus, the damage may not be known for some time.

An attacker has little to lose in trying a social engineering attack. At worst it will raise awareness of a possible target. But if the social engineering is directed against someone who is not skeptical, especially someone not involved in security management, it may well succeed. We as humans like to help others when asked politely.

Reconnaissance

From a port scan the attacker knows what is open. From social engineering, the attacker knows certain internal details. But a more detailed floor plan would be nice. **Reconnaissance** is the general term for collecting information. In security it often refers to gathering discrete bits of information from various sources and then putting them together like the pieces of a puzzle.

One commonly used reconnaissance technique is called "dumpster diving." It involves looking through items that have been discarded in rubbish bins or recycling boxes. It is amazing what we throw away without thinking about it. Mixed with the remains from lunch might be network diagrams, printouts of security device configurations, system designs and source code, telephone and employee lists, and more. Even outdated printouts may be useful. Seldom will the configuration of a security device change completely. More often only one rule is added or deleted or modified, so an attacker has a high probability of a successful attack based on the old information.

Reconnaissance may also involve eavesdropping. Trained spies may follow employees to lunch and listen in from nearby tables as coworkers discuss security matters. Or spies may befriend key personnel in order to co-opt, coerce, or trick them into passing on useful information.

Most reconnaissance techniques require little training and minimal investment of time. If an attacker has targeted a particular organization, spending a little time to collect background information yields a big payoff.

Operating System and Application Fingerprinting

The port scan supplies the attacker with very specific information. For instance, an attacker can use one to find out that port 80 is open and supports HTTP, the protocol for transmitting web pages. But the attacker is likely to have many related questions, such as which commercial server application is running, what version, and what the underlying operating system and version are. Once armed with this additional information, the attacker can consult a list of specific software's known vulnerabilities to determine which particular weaknesses to try to exploit.

How can the attacker answer these questions? The network protocols are standard and vendor independent. Still, each vendor's code is implemented independently, so there may be minor variations in interpretation and behavior. The variations do not make the software noncompliant with the standard, but they are different enough to make each version distinctive. For example, each version may have different sequence numbers, TCP flags, and new options. To see why, consider that sender and receiver must coordinate with sequence numbers to implement the connection of a TCP session. Some implementations respond with a given sequence number, others respond with the number one greater, and others respond with an unrelated number. Likewise, certain flags in one version are undefined or incompatible with others. How a system responds to a prompt (for instance, by acknowledging it, requesting retransmission, or ignoring it) can also reveal the system and version. Finally, new features offer a strong clue: A new version will implement a new feature but an old version will reject the request. All these peculiarities, sometimes called the operating system or application **fingerprint**, can mark the manufacturer and version.

For example, in addition to performing its port scan, the nmap scanner will respond with a guess at the target operating system. For more information about how this is done, see the paper at *www.insecure.org/nmap/nmap-fingerprinting-article.html.*

Sometimes the application identifies itself. Usually a client-server interaction is handled completely within the application according to protocol rules: "Please send me this page; OK but run this support code; thanks, I just did." But the application cannot respond to a message that does not follow the expected form. For instance, the attacker might use a Telnet application to send meaningless messages to another application. Ports such as 80 (HTTP), 25 (SMTP), 110 (POP), and 21 (FTP) may respond with something like

```
Server: Netscape-Commerce/1.12
Your browser sent a non-HTTP compliant message.
```

or

```
Microsoft ESMTP MAIL Service, Version: 5.0.2195.3779
```

This reply tells the attacker which application and version are running.

Bulletin Boards and Chats

The Internet is probably the greatest tool for sharing knowledge since the invention of the printing press. It is probably also the most dangerous tool for sharing knowledge.

Numerous underground bulletin boards and chat rooms support exchange of information. Attackers can post their latest exploits and techniques, read what others have done, and search for additional information on systems, applications, or sites. Remember that, as with everything on the Internet, anyone can post anything, so there is no guarantee that the information is reliable or accurate. And you never know who is reading from the Internet. (See Sidebar 7-4 on law enforcement officials' "going underground" to catch malicious hackers.)

Availability of Documentation

The vendors themselves sometimes distribute information that is useful to an attacker. For example, Microsoft produces a resource kit by which application vendors can investigate a Microsoft product in order to develop compatible, complementary applications. This toolkit also gives attackers tools to use in investigating a product that can subsequently be the target of an attack.

Reconnaissance: Concluding Remarks

A good thief, that is, a successful one, spends time understanding the context of the target. To prepare for perpetrating a bank theft, the thief might monitor the bank, seeing

Sidebar 7-4 To Catch a Thief

The U.S. FBI launched a program in 1999 to identify and arrest malicious hackers. Led by William Swallow, the FBI set up a classic sting operation in which it tracked hackers. Swallow chose an online identity and began visiting hackers' web sites and chat rooms. At first the team merely monitored what the hackers posted. To join the hacker underground community, Swallow had to share knowledge with other hackers. He and his team decided what attack techniques they could post without compromising the security of any sites; they reposted details of attacks that they picked up from other sites or combined known methods to produce shortcuts.

But, to be accepted into "the club," Swallow had to demonstrate that he personally had hacker skills—that he was not just repeating what others had done. This situation required that Swallow pursue real exploits. With permission, he conducted more than a dozen defacements of government web sites to establish his reputation. Sharing information with the hackers gave Swallow credibility. He became "one of them."

During the eighteen-month sting operation, Swallow and his team gathered critical evidence on several people, including "Mafiaboy," the 17-year old hacker who pled guilty to 58 charges related to a series of denial-of-service attacks in February 2000 against companies such as Amazon.com, eBay, and Yahoo.

Proving the adage that "on the Internet, nobody knows you're a dog," Swallow, in his 40s, was able to befriend attackers in their teens.

how many guards there are, when they take breaks, when cash shipments arrive, and so forth.

Remember that time is usually on the side of the attacker. In the same way that a bank might notice someone loitering around the entrance, a computing site might notice exceptional numbers of probes in a short time. But the clever thief or attacker will collect a little information, go dormant for a while, and resurface to collect more. So many people walk past banks and peer in the windows, or scan and probe web hosts that individual peeks over time are hard to correlate.

The best defense against reconnaissance is silence. Give out as little information about your site as possible, whether by humans or machines.

Threats in Transit: Eavesdropping and Wiretapping

By now, you can see that an attacker can gather a significant amount of information about a victim before beginning the actual attack. Once the planning is done, the attacker is ready to proceed. In this section we turn to the kinds of attacks that can occur. Recall from Chapter 1 that there are many ways by which an attacker can do harm in a computing environment: loss of confidentiality, integrity, or availability to data, hardware or software, processes, or other assets. Because a network involves data in transit, we look first at the harm that can occur in between a sender and a receiver.

The easiest way to attack is simply to listen in. An attacker can pick off the content of a communication passing in the clear. The term **eavesdrop** implies overhearing without expending any extra effort. For example, we might say that an attacker (or a system administrator) is eavesdropping by monitoring all traffic passing through a node. The administrator might have a legitimate purpose, such as watching for inappropriate use of resources (for instance, visiting non-work-related web sites from a company network) or communicating with inappropriate parties (for instance, passing files to an enemy from a military computer).

A more hostile term is **wiretap**, which means intercepting communications through some effort. **Passive wiretapping** is just "listening," much like eavesdropping. But **active wiretapping** means injecting something into the communication. For example, Marvin could replace Manny's communications with his own or create communications purported to be from Manny. Originally derived from listening in on telegraph and telephone communications, the term wiretapping usually conjures up a physical act by which a device extracts information as it flows over a wire. But in fact no actual contact is necessary. A wiretap can be done covertly so that neither the sender nor the receiver of a communication will know that the contents have been intercepted.

Wiretapping works differently depending on the communication medium used. Let us look more carefully at each possible choice.

Cable

At the most local level, all signals in an Ethernet or other LAN are available on the cable for anyone to intercept. Each LAN connector (such as a computer board) has a unique address; each board and its drivers are programmed to label all packets from its host with its unique address (as a sender's "return address") and to take from the net only those packets addressed to its host.

But removing only those packets addressed to a given host is mostly a matter of politeness; there is little to stop a program from examining each packet as it goes by. A device called a **packet sniffer** can retrieve all packets on the LAN. Alternatively, one of the interface cards can be reprogrammed to have the supposedly unique address of another existing card on the LAN so that two different cards will both fetch packets for one address. (To avoid detection, the rogue card will have to put back on the net copies of the packets it has intercepted.) Fortunately (for now), LANs are usually used only in environments that are fairly friendly, so these kinds of attacks occur infrequently.

Clever attackers can take advantage of a wire's properties and read packets without any physical manipulation. Ordinary wire (and many other electronic components) emit radiation. By a process called **inductance** an intruder can tap a wire and read radiated signals without making physical contact with the cable. A cable's signals travel only short distances, and they can be blocked by other conductive materials. The equipment needed to pick up signals is inexpensive and easy to obtain, so inductance threats are a serious concern for cable-based networks. For the attack to work, the intruder must be fairly close to the cable; this form of attack is thus limited to situations with reasonable physical access.

If the attacker is not close enough to take advantage of inductance, then more hostile measures may be warranted. The easiest form of intercepting a cable is by direct cut. If a cable is severed, all service on it stops. As part of the repair, an attacker can easily splice in a secondary cable that then receives a copy of all signals along the primary cable. There are ways to be a little less obvious but accomplish the same goal. For example, the attacker might carefully expose some of the outer conductor, connect to it, then carefully expose some of the inner conductor and connect to it. Both of these operations alter the resistance, called the **impedance**, of the cable. In the first case, the repair itself alters the impedance, and the impedance change can be explained (or concealed) as part of the repair. In the second case, a little social engineering can explain the change. ("Hello, this is Matt, a technician with Alphanetworks. We are changing some equipment on our end, and so you might notice a change in impedance.")

Signals on a network are **multiplexed**, meaning that more than one signal is transmitted at a given time. For example, two analog (sound) signals can be combined, like two tones in a musical chord, and two digital signals can be combined by interleaving, like playing cards being shuffled. A LAN carries distinct packets, but data on a WAN may be heavily multiplexed as it leaves its sending host. Thus, a wiretapper on a WAN needs to be able not only to intercept the desired communication but also to extract it from the others with which it is multiplexed. While this can be done, the effort involved means it will be used sparingly.

Microwave

Microwave signals are not carried along a wire; they are broadcast through the air, making them more accessible to outsiders. Typically, a transmitter's signal is focused on its corresponding receiver. The signal path is fairly wide, to be sure of hitting the receiver, as shown in Figure 7-14. From a security standpoint, the wide swath is an invitation to mischief. Not only can someone intercept a microwave transmission by interfering with the line of sight between sender and receiver, someone can also pick up an entire transmission from an antenna located close to but slightly off the direct focus point.

A microwave signal is usually not shielded or isolated to prevent interception. Microwave is, therefore, a very insecure medium. However, because of the large volume of traffic carried by microwave links, it is unlikely—but not impossible—that someone will be able to separate an individual transmission from all the others interleaved with

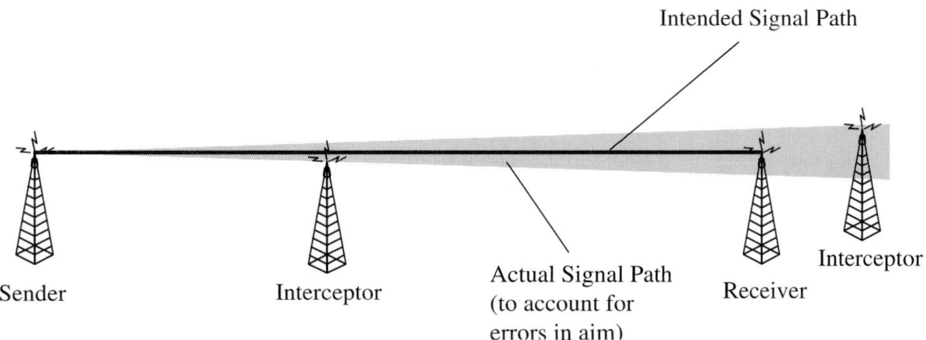

FIGURE 7-14 Path of Microwave Signals.

it. A privately owned microwave link, carrying only communications for one organization, is not so well protected by volume.

Satellite Communication

Satellite communication has a similar problem of being dispersed over an area greater than the intended point of reception. Different satellites have different characteristics, but some signals can be intercepted in an area several hundred miles wide and a thousand miles long. Therefore, the potential for interception is even greater than with microwave signals. However, because satellite communications are generally heavily multiplexed, the risk is small that any one communication will be intercepted.

Optical Fiber

Optical fiber offers two significant security advantages over other transmission media. First, the entire optical network must be tuned carefully each time a new connection is made. Therefore, no one can tap an optical system without detection. Clipping just one fiber in a bundle will destroy the balance in the network.

Second, optical fiber carries light energy, not electricity. Light does not emanate a magnetic field as electricity does. Therefore, an inductive tap is impossible on an optical fiber cable.

Just using fiber, however, does not guarantee security, any more than does using encryption. The repeaters, splices, and taps along a cable are places at which data may be available more easily than in the fiber cable itself. The connections from computing equipment to the fiber may also be points for penetration. By itself, fiber is much more secure than cable, but it has vulnerabilities too.

Wireless

Wireless networking is becoming very popular, with good reason. With wireless, people are not tied to a wired connection; they are free to roam throughout an office, house, or building while maintaining a connection. Universities, offices, and even home users like being able to connect to a network without the cost, difficulty, and inconvenience of running wires. The difficulties of wireless arise in the ability of intruders to intercept and spoof a connection.

As we noted earlier, wireless communications travel by radio. In the United States, wireless computer connections share the same frequencies as garage door openers, local radios (typically used as baby monitors), some cordless telephones, and other very short distance applications. Although the frequency band is crowded, few applications are expected to be on the band from any single user, so contention or interference is not an issue.

But the major threat is not interference; it is interception. A wireless signal is strong for approximately 100 to 200 feet. To appreciate those figures, picture an ordinary ten-story office building, ten offices "wide" by five offices "deep," similar to many buildings in office parks or on university campuses. Assume you set up a wireless base station (receiver) in the corner of the top floor. That station could receive signals transmitted from the opposite corner of the ground floor. If there were a similar building adjacent, the signal could also be received throughout that building, too. Few people would care to listen to someone else's baby monitor, but many people could and do take advantage of a passive or active wiretap of a network connection.

A strong signal can be picked up easily. And with an inexpensive, tuned antenna, a wireless signal can be picked up several miles away. In other words, someone who wanted to pick up your particular signal could do so from several streets away. Parked in a truck or van, the interceptor could monitor your communications for quite some time without arousing suspicion.

Interception

Interception of wireless traffic is always a threat, through either passive or active wiretapping. Sidebar 7-5 illustrates how software faults may make interception easier than you might think. You may react to that threat by assuming that encryption will address it. Unfortunately, encryption is not always used for wireless communication, and the encryption built into some wireless devices is not as strong as it should be to deter a dedicated attacker.

The wireless communication standards are 802.11b, 802.11a, and 802.11g. The -b and -a standards are very similar, differing primarily in which frequency they use and what transfer rate they can support. The -b standard can currently support up to 10 Mbps (million bits per second), and -a slightly over 50 Mbps.

The encryption standard is Wired Equivalent Privacy (WEP). WEP is a classical stream cipher using a 40- or 104-bit key. As we noted in Chapter 2, a 40-bit key can be easily discerned by any interested attacker. But surveys reveal that WEP has been disabled in 85 percent (!) of wireless installations, probably because it is difficult for the administrator to configure and manage encryption. Moreover, even when encryption is used, the design of the encryption solution sometimes makes it easy to crack.

Theft of Service

Wireless also admits a second problem: the possibility of rogue use of a network connection. Many hosts run the Dynamic Host Configuration Protocol (DHCP), by which a client negotiates a one-time IP address and connectivity with a host. This protocol is useful in office or campus settings, where not all users (clients) are active at any time. A small number of IP addresses can be shared among users. Essentially the addresses are available in a pool. A new client requests a connection and an IP address through DHCP, and the server assigns one from the pool.

This scheme admits a big problem with authentication. Unless the host authenticates users before assigning a connection, any requesting client is assigned an IP address and network access. (Typically, this assignment occurs before the user on the client workstation actually identifies and authenticates to a server, so there may not be an authenticable identity that the DHCP server can demand.) The situation is so serious that in some metropolitan areas a map is available, showing many accepting wireless connections. A user wanting free Internet access can often get it simply by finding a wireless LAN offering DHCP service.

Summary of Wiretapping

There are many points of which network traffic is available to an interceptor. Figure 7-15 illustrates how communications are exposed from their origin to their destination.

Sidebar 7-5 Wireless Vulnerabilities

The New Zealand Herald [GRI02] reports that a major telecommunications company was forced to shut down its mobile e-mail service because of a security flaw in its wireless network software. The flaw affected users on the company's CDMA network who were sending e-mail on their WAP-enabled (wireless applications protocol) mobile phones.

The vulnerability occurred when the user finished an e-mail session. In fact, the software did not end the WAP session for 60 more seconds. If a second network customer were to initiate an e-mail session within those 60 seconds and be connected to the same port as the first customer, the second customer could then view the first customer's message.

The company blamed the third-party software provided by a mobile portal. Nevertheless, the company was highly embarrassed, especially because it "perceived security issues with wireless networks" to be "a major factor threatening to hold the [wireless] technology's development back." [GRI02]

But perceived—and real—security issues *should* hold back widespread use of wireless. It is estimated that 85 percent of wireless users do not enable encryption on their access points, and weaknesses in the WEP protocol leave many of the remaining 15 percent vulnerable.

Anyone with a wireless network card can search for an available network. Security consultant Chris O'Ferrell has been able to connect to wireless networks in Washington D.C. from outside a Senate office building, the Supreme Court, and the Pentagon [NOG02]; others join networks in airports, on planes, and at coffee shops. Internet bulletin boards have maps of metropolitan areas with dots showing wireless access points. The so-called parasitic grid movement is an underground attempt to allow strangers to share wireless Internet access in metropolitan areas. A listing of some of the available wireless access points by city is maintained at *www.guerilla.net/freenets.html.* Products like AirMagnet from AirMagnet, Inc., Observer from Network Instruments, and IBM's Wireless Security Analyzer can locate open wireless connections on a network so that a security administrator can know a network is open to wireless access.

And then there are wireless LAN users who refuse to shut off their service. Retailer BestBuy was embarrassed by a customer who bought a wireless product. While in the parking lot, he installed it in his laptop computer. Much to his surprise, he found he could connect to the store's wireless network. BestBuy subsequently took all its wireless cash registers offline. But the CVS pharmacy chain announced plans to continue use of wireless networks in all 4100 of its stores, arguing "We use wireless technology strictly for internal item management. If we were to ever move in the direction of transmitting [customer] information via in-store wireless LANs, we would encrypt the data" [BRE02].

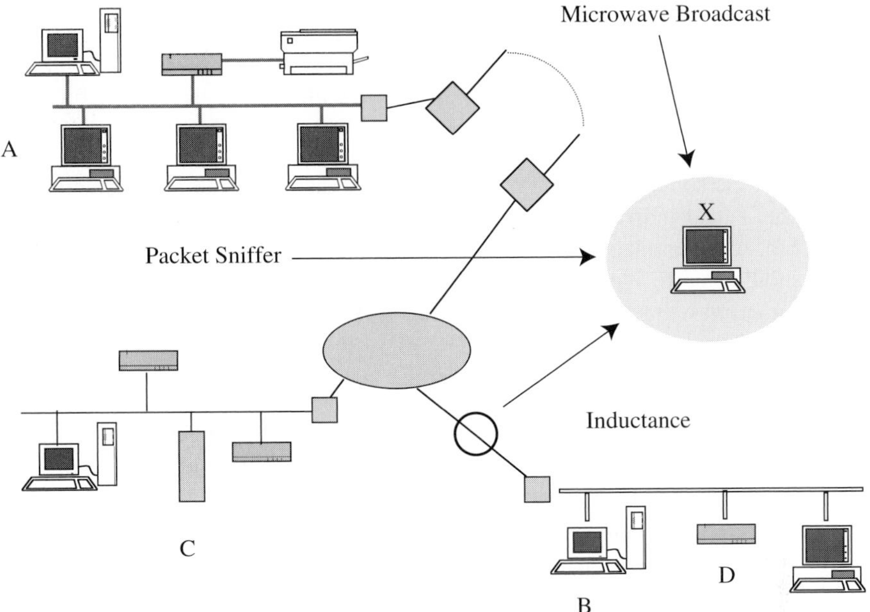

FIGURE 7-15 Wiretap Vulnerabilities.

From a security standpoint, you should assume that *all* communication links between network nodes can be broken. For this reason, commercial network users employ encryption to protect the confidentiality of their communications, as we demonstrate later in this chapter. Local network communications can be encrypted, although for performance reasons it may be preferable to protect local connections with strong physical and administrative security instead.

Protocol Flaws

Internet protocols are publicly posted for scrutiny by the entire Internet community. Each accepted protocol is known by its Request for Comment (**RFC**) number. Many problems with protocols have been identified by sharp reviewers and corrected before the protocol was established as a standard.

But protocol definitions are made and reviewed by fallible humans. Likewise, protocols are implemented by fallible humans. For example, TCP connections are established through sequence numbers. The client (initiator) sends a sequence number to open a connection, the server responds with that number and a sequence number of its own, and the client responds with the server's sequence number. Suppose (as pointed out by Morris [MOR85]) someone can guess a client's next sequence number. That person could impersonate the client in an interchange. Sequence numbers are incremented regularly, so it can be easy to predict the next number. (Similar protocol problems are summarized in [BEL89].)

Impersonation

In many instances, there is an easier way than wiretapping for obtaining information on a network: impersonate another person or process. Why risk tapping a line, or why bother extracting one communication out of many, if you can obtain the same data directly?

Impersonation is a more significant threat in a wide area network than in a local one. Local individuals often have better ways to obtain access as another user; they can, for example, simply sit at an unattended workstation. Still, impersonation attacks should not be ignored even on local area networks, because local area networks are sometimes attached to wider area networks without anyone's first thinking through the security implications.

In an impersonation, an attacker has several choices:

- Guess the identity and authentication details of the target.
- Pick up the identity and authentication details of the target from a previous communication or from wiretapping.
- Circumvent or disable the authentication mechanism at the target computer.
- Use a target that will not be authenticated.
- Use a target whose authentication data are known.

Let us look at each choice.

Authentication Foiled by Guessing

Chapter 4 reported the results of several studies showing that many users choose easy-to-guess passwords. In Chapter 3, we saw that the Internet worm of 1988 capitalized on exactly that flaw. Morris's worm tried to impersonate each user on a target machine by trying, in order, a handful of variations of the user name, a list of about 250 common passwords and, finally, the words in a dictionary. Sadly, many users' accounts are still open to these easy attacks.

A second source of password guesses is default passwords. Many systems are initially configured with default accounts having GUEST or ADMIN as login IDs; accompanying these IDs are well-known passwords such as "guest" or "null" or "password" to enable the administrator to set up the system. Administrators often forget to delete or disable these accounts, or at least to change the passwords.

In a trustworthy environment, such as an office LAN, a password may simply be a signal that the user does not want others to use the workstation or account. Sometimes the password-protected workstation contains sensitive data, such as employee salaries or information about new products. Users may think that the password is enough to keep out a curious colleague; they see no reason to protect against concerted attacks. However, if that trustworthy environment is connected to an untrustworthy wider-area network, all users with simple passwords become easy targets. Indeed, some systems are not originally connected to a wider network, so their users begin in a less exposed situation that clearly changes when the connection occurs.

Dead accounts offer a final source of guessable passwords. To see how, suppose Professor Romine, a faculty member, takes leave for a year to teach at another university. The existing account may reasonably be kept on hold, awaiting the professor's return. But an attacker, reading a university newspaper online, finds out that the user is away. Now the attacker uses social engineering on the system administration ("Hello, this is Professor Romine calling from my temporary office at State University. I haven't used my account for quite a while, but now I need something from it urgently. I have forgotten the password. Can you please reset it to ICECREAM?") Alternatively, the attacker can try several passwords until the password guessing limit is exceeded. The system then locks the account administratively, and the attacker uses a social engineering attack. In all these ways the attacker may succeed in resetting or discovering a password.

Authentication Thwarted by Eavesdropping or Wiretapping

Because of the rise in distributed and client-server computing, some users have access privileges on several connected machines. To protect against arbitrary outsiders using these accesses, authentication is required between hosts. This access can involve the user directly, or it can be done automatically on behalf of the user through a host-to-host authentication protocol. In either case, the account and authentication details of the subject are passed to the destination host. When these details are passed on the network, they are exposed to anyone observing the communication on the network. These same authentication details can be reused by an impersonator until they are changed.

Because transmitting a password in the clear is a significant vulnerability, protocols have been developed so that the password itself never leaves a user's workstation. But, as we have seen in several other places, the details are important.

Microsoft LAN Manager was an early method for implementing networks. It had a password exchange mechanism in which the password itself was never transmitted in the clear; instead only a cryptographic hash of it was transmitted. A password could consist of up to 14 characters. It could include upper- and lowercase letters, digits, and special characters, for 67 possibilities in any one position, and 67^{14} possibilities for a whole 14-character password—quite a respectable work factor. However, those 14 characters were not diffused across the entire hash; they were sent in separate substrings, representing characters 1–7 and 8–14. A 7-character or shorter password had all nulls in the second substring and was instantly recognizable. An 8-character password had 1 character and 6 nulls in the second substring, so 67 guesses would find the one character. Even in the best case, a 14-character password, the work factor fell from 67^{14} to $67^7 + 67^7 = 2 * 67^7$. These work factors differ by a factor of approximately 10 billion. (See [MUD97] for details.) LAN Manager authentication was preserved in many later systems (including Windows NT) as an option to support backward compatibility with systems such as Windows 95/98. This lesson is a good example of why security and cryptography are very precise and must be monitored by experts from concept through design and implementation.

Authentication Foiled by Avoidance

Obviously, authentication is effective only when it works. A weak or flawed authentication allows access to any system or person who can circumvent the authentication.

In a classic operating system flaw, the buffer for typed characters in a password was of fixed size, counting all characters typed, including backspaces for correction. If a user typed more characters than the buffer would hold, the overflow caused the operating system to bypass password comparison and act as if a correct authentication had been supplied. These flaws or weaknesses can be exploited by anyone seeking access.

Many network hosts, especially those that connect to wide area networks, run variants of Unix System V or BSD Unix. In a local environment, many users are not aware of which networked operating system is in use; still fewer would know of, be capable of, or be interested in exploiting flaws. However, some hackers regularly scan wide area networks for hosts running weak or flawed operating systems. Thus, connection to a wide area network, especially the Internet, exposes these flaws to a wide audience intent on exploiting them.

Nonexistent Authentication

If two computers are used by the same users to store data and run processes and if each has authenticated its users on first access, you might assume that computer-to-computer or local user-to-remote process authentication is unnecessary. These two computers and their users are a trustworthy environment in which the added complexity of repeated authentication seems excessive.

However, this assumption is not valid. To see why, consider the Unix operating system. In Unix, the file *.rhosts* lists trusted hosts and *.rlogin* lists trusted users who are allowed access without authentication. The files are intended to support computer-to-computer connection by users who have already been authenticated at their primary hosts. These "trusted hosts" can also be exploited by outsiders who obtain access to one system through an authentication weakness (such as a guessed password) and then transfer to another system that accepts the authenticity of a user who comes from a system on its trusted list.

An attacker may also realize that a system has some identities requiring no authentication. Some systems have "guest" or "anonymous" accounts to allow outsiders to access things the systems want to release to anyone. For example, a bank might post a current listing of foreign currency rates, a library with an online catalog might make that catalog available for anyone to search, or a company might allow access to some of its reports. A user can log in as "guest" and retrieve publicly available items. Typically, no password is required, or the user is shown a message requesting that the user type "GUEST" (or *your name*, which really means any string that looks like a name) when asked for a password. Each of these accounts allows access to unauthenticated users.

Well-Known Authentication

Authentication data should be unique and difficult to guess. But unfortunately, the convenience of one, well-known authentication scheme sometimes usurps the protection. For example, one computer manufacturer planned to use the same password to allow its remote maintenance personnel to access any of its computers belonging to any of its customers throughout the world. Fortunately, security experts pointed out the potential danger before that idea was put in place.

The system network management protocol (SNMP) is widely used for remote management of network devices, such as routers and switches, that support no ordinary users. SNMP uses a "community string," essentially a password for the community of devices that can interact with one another. But network devices are designed especially for quick installation with minimal configuration, and many network administrators do not change the default community string installed on a router or switch. This laxity makes these devices on the network perimeter open to many SNMP attacks.

Some vendors still ship computers with one system administration account installed, having a default password. Or the systems come with a demonstration or test account, with no required password. Some administrators fail to change the passwords or delete these accounts.

Trusted Authentication

Finally, authentication can become a problem when identification is delegated to other trusted sources. For instance, a file may indicate who can be trusted on a particular host. Or the authentication mechanism for one system can "vouch for" a user. We noted earlier how the Unix *.rhosts, .rlogin,* and */etc/hosts/equiv* files indicate hosts or users that are trusted on other hosts. While these features are useful to users who have accounts on multiple machines or for network management, maintenance, and operation, they must be used very carefully. Each of them represents a potential hole through which a remote user—or a remote attacker—can achieve access.

Spoofing

Guessing or otherwise obtaining the network authentication credentials of an entity (a user, an account, a process, a node, a device) permits an attacker to create a full communication under the entity's identity. Impersonation falsely represents a valid entity in a communication. Closely related is **spoofing**, when an attacker falsely carries on one end of a networked interchange. Examples of spoofing are masquerading, session hijacking, and man-in-the-middle attacks.

Masquerade

In a **masquerade** one host pretends to be another. A common example is URL confusion. Domain names can easily be confused, or someone can easily mistype certain names. Thus xyz.com, xyz.org, and xyz.net might be three different organizations, or one bona fide organization (for example, xyz.com) and two masquerade attempts from someone who registered the similar domain names. Names with or without hyphens (coca-cola.com versus cocacola.com) and easily mistyped names (l0pht.com versus lopht.com, or citibank.com versus citybank.com) are candidates for masquerading.

From the attacker's point of view, the fun in masquerading comes before the mask is removed. For example, suppose you want to attack a real bank, First Blue Bank of Chicago. The actual bank has the domain name Blue-Bank.com, so you register the domain name BlueBank.com. Next, you put up a web page at BlueBank.com, perhaps using the real Blue Bank logo that you downloaded to make your site look as much as possible like that of the Chicago bank. Finally, you ask people to log in with their name, account number, and password or PIN. (This redirection can occur in many ways. For example, you can pay for a banner ad that links to your site instead of the real bank's, or you can send e-mail to Chicago residents and invite them to visit your site.) After collecting personal data from several bank users, you can drop the connection, pass the connection on to the real Blue Bank, or continue to collect more information. You may even be able to transfer this connection smoothly to an authenticated access to the real Blue Bank so that the user never realizes the deviation.

There are no known cases of this kind of fraudulent connection involving banks or finance. But there are two U.S. web sites that are easily confused: *www.whitehouse.com* and *www.whitehouse.gov*; only the latter is maintained by the U.S. government.

In another version of a masquerade, the attacker exploits a flaw in the victim's web server and is able to overwrite the victim's web pages. Although there is some public humiliation at having one's site replaced, perhaps with obscenities or strong messages opposing the nature of the site (for example, a plea for vegetarianism on a slaughterhouse web site), most people would not be fooled by a site displaying a message absolutely contrary to its aims. However, a clever attacker can be more subtle. Instead of differentiating from the real site, the attacker can try to build a false site that resembles the real one, perhaps to obtain sensitive information (names, authentication numbers, credit card numbers) or to induce the user to enter into a real transaction. For example, if one bookseller's site, call it Books-R-Us, were overtaken subtly by another, called Books Depot, the orders may actually be processed, filled, and billed to the naïve users by Books Depot.

Session Hijacking

Session hijacking is intercepting and carrying on a session begun by another entity. Suppose two entities have entered into a session but then a third entity intercepts the traffic and carries on the session in the name of the other. Our example of Books-R-Us could be an instance of this technique. If Books Depot used a wiretap to intercept packets between you and Books-R-Us, Books Depot could simply monitor the information flow, letting Books-R-Us do the hard part of displaying titles for sale and convincing the user to buy. Then, when the user has completed the order, Books Depot intercepts the "I'm ready to check out" packet, and finishes the order with the user, obtaining shipping address, credit card details, and so forth. To Books-R-Us, the transaction would look like any other incomplete transaction: The user was browsing but for some reason decided to go elsewhere before purchasing. We would say that Books Depot had hijacked the session.

A different type of example involves an interactive session, for example, using Telnet. If a system administrator logs in remotely to a privileged account, a session hijack utility could intrude in the communication and pass commands as if they came from the administrator.

Man-in-the-Middle Attack

Our hijacking example requires a third party involved in a session between two entities. A **man-in-the-middle** attack is a similar form of attack, in which one entity intrudes between two others. The difference between man-in-the-middle and hijacking is that a man-in-the-middle usually participates from the start of the session, whereas a session hijacking occurs after a session has been established. The difference is largely semantic and not too significant.

Man-in-the-middle attacks are frequently described in protocols. To see how, suppose you want to exchange encrypted information with your friend. You contact the key server and ask for a secret key with which to communicate with your friend. The key server responds by sending a key to you and your friend. One man-in-the-middle attack assumes someone can see and enter into all parts of this protocol. A malicious middleman intercepts the response key and can then eavesdrop on, or even decrypt, modify, and reencrypt any subsequent communications between you and your friend. This attack is depicted in Figure 7-16.

This attack would be foiled with public keys, because the man-in-the-middle would not have the private key to be able to decrypt messages encrypted under your friend's public key. The man-in-the-middle attack now becomes more of the three-way interchange its name implies. The man-in-the-middle intercepts your request to the key server and instead asks for your friend's public key. The man-in-the-middle passes to you his own public key, not your friend's. You encrypt using the public key you received (from the man-in-the-middle); the man-in-the-middle intercepts and decrypts, reads, and reencrypts, using your friend's public key; and your friend receives. In this way, the man-in-the-middle reads the messages and neither you nor your friend is

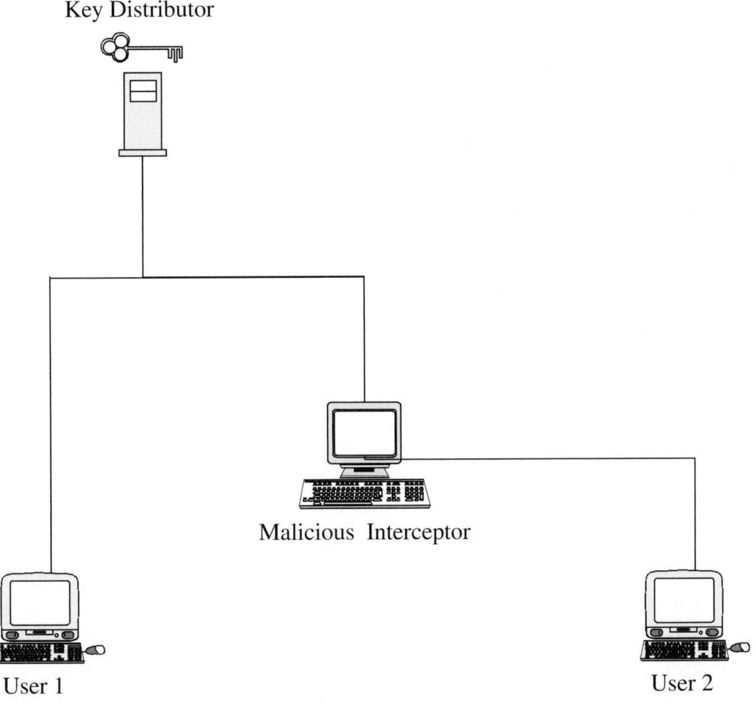

FIGURE 7-16 Key Interception by a Man-in-the-Middle Attack.

aware of the interception. A slight variation of this attack works for secret key distribution under a public key.

Message Confidentiality Threats

An attacker can easily violate message confidentiality (and perhaps integrity) because of the public nature of networks. Eavesdropping and impersonation attacks can lead to a confidentiality or integrity failure. Here we consider several other vulnerabilities that can affect confidentiality.

Misdelivery

Sometimes messages are misdelivered because of some flaw in the network hardware or software. Most frequently, messages are lost entirely, which is an integrity or availability issue. Occasionally, however, a destination address will be modified or some handler will malfunction, causing a message to be delivered to someone other than the intended recipient. All of these "random" events are quite uncommon.

More frequent than network flaws are human errors. It is far too easy to mistype an address such as 100064,30652 as 10064,30652 or 100065,30642, or to type "idw" or "iw" instead of "diw" for David Ian Walker, who is called Ian by his friends. There is simply no justification for a computer network administrator to identify people by meaningless long numbers or cryptic initials when "iwalker" would be far less prone to human error.

Exposure

To protect the confidentiality of a message, we must track it all the way from its creation to its disposal. Along the way, the content of a message may be exposed in temporary buffers; at switches, routers, gateways, and intermediate hosts throughout the network; and in the workspaces of processes that build, format, and present the message. In earlier chapters, we considered confidentiality exposures in programs and operating systems. All of these exposures apply to networked environments as well. Furthermore, a malicious attacker can use any of these exposures as part of a general or focused attack on message confidentiality.

Passive wiretapping is one source of message exposure. So also is subversion of the structure by which a communication is routed to its destination. Finally, intercepting the message at it source, destination, or at any intermediate node can lead to its exposure.

Traffic Flow Analysis

Sometimes not only is the message itself sensitive but the fact that a message *exists* is also sensitive. For example, if the enemy during wartime sees a large amount of network traffic between headquarters and a particular unit, the enemy may be able to infer that significant action is being planned involving that unit. In a commercial setting, messages sent from the president of one company to the president of a competitor could lead to speculation about a takeover or conspiracy to fix prices. Or communications from the prime minister of one country to another with whom diplomatic relations were suspended could lead to inferences about a rapprochement between the countries. In these cases, we need to protect both the *content* of messages and the *header* information that identifies sender and receiver.

Message Integrity Threats

In many cases, the *integrity* or correctness of a communication is at least as important as its confidentiality. In fact for some situations, such as passing authentication data, the integrity of the communication is paramount. In other cases, the need for integrity is less obvious. Next we consider threats based on failures of integrity in communication.

Falsification of Messages

Increasingly, people depend on electronic messages to justify and direct actions. For example, if you receive a message from a good friend asking you to meet at the pub for a drink next Tuesday evening, you will probably be there at the appointed time. Likewise, you will comply with a message from your supervisor telling you to stop work on project A and devote your energy instead to project B. As long as it is reasonable, we tend to act on an electronic message just as we would on a signed letter, a telephone call, or a face-to-face communication.

However, an attacker can take advantage of our trust in messages to mislead us. In particular, an attacker may

- change some or all of the content of a message
- replace a message entirely, including the date, time, and sender/receiver identification
- reuse (**replay**) an old message
- combine pieces of different messages into one
- change the apparent source of a message
- redirect a message
- destroy or delete a message

These attacks can be perpetrated in the ways we have already examined, including:

- active wiretap
- Trojan horse
- impersonation
- preempted host
- preempted workstation

Noise

Signals sent over communications media are subject to interference from other traffic on the same media, as well as from natural sources, such as lightning, electric motors, and animals. Such unintentional interference is called **noise**. These forms of noise are inevitable, and they can threaten the integrity of data in a message.

Fortunately, communications protocols have been intentionally designed to overcome the negative effects of noise. For example, the TCP/IP protocol suite ensures detection of almost all transmission errors. Processes in the communications stack detect errors and arrange for retransmission, all invisible to the higher-level applications. Thus, noise is scarcely a consideration for users in security-critical applications.

Web Site Defacement

One of the most widely known attacks is the web site defacement attack. Because of the large number of sites that have been defaced and the visibility of the result, the attacks are often reported in the popular press.

A defacement is common not only because of its visibility but also because of the ease with which one can be done. Web sites are designed so that their code is downloaded, enabling an attacker to obtain the full hypertext document and all programs directed to the client in the loading process. An attacker can even view programmers' comments left in as they built or maintained the code. The download process essentially gives the attacker the blueprints to the web site.

The ease and appeal of a defacement are enhanced by the seeming plethora of vulnerabilities that web sites offer an attacker. For example, between December 1999 and June 2001 (the first 18 months after its release), Microsoft provided 17 *security* patches for its web server software, Internet Information Server (IIS) version 4.0. And version 4.0 was an upgrade for three previous versions, so theoretically Microsoft had a great deal of time earlier to work out its security flaws.

The web site vulnerabilities enable attacks known as buffer overflows, dot-dot problems, application code errors, and server-side include problems.

Buffer Overflows

Buffer overflow is alive and well on web pages, too. It works exactly the same as described in Chapter 3: The attacker simply feeds a program far more data than it expects to receive. A buffer size is exceeded, and the excess data spill over into adjoining code and data locations.

Perhaps the best-known web server buffer overflow is the file name problem known as iishack. This attack is so well known that is has been written into a procedure (see *http://www.technotronic.com*). To execute the procedure, an attacker supplies as parameters the site to be attacked and the URL of a program the attacker wants that server to execute.

Other web servers are vulnerable to extremely long parameter fields, such as passwords of length 10,000 or a long URL padded with space or null characters.

Dot-Dot and Address Problems

Web server code should always run in a constrained environment. Ideally, the web server should never have editors, xterm and Telnet programs, or even most system utilities loaded. By constraining the environment in this way, even if an attacker escapes from the web server application, no other executable programs will help the attacker use the web server's computer and operating system to extend the attack. The code and data for web applications can be transferred manually to a web server or pushed as a raw image.

But many web applications programmers are naïve. They expect to need to edit a web application in place, so they expect to need editors and system utilities to give them a complete environment in which to program.

A second, less desirable, condition for preventing an attack is to create a fence confining the web server application. With such a fence, the server application cannot escape from its area and access other potentially dangerous system areas (such as editors and utilities). The server begins in a particular directory subtree, and everything the server needs is in that same subtree.

Enter the dot-dot. In both Unix and Windows, '..' is the directory indicator for "predecessor." And '../..' is the grandparent of the current location. So someone who can enter file names can travel back up the directory tree one .. at a time. Cerberus Information Security analysts found just that vulnerability in the webhits.dll extension for the Microsoft Index Server. For example, passing the following URL causes the server to return the requested file, autoexec.nt, enabling an attacker to modify or delete it.

```
http://URL/null.htw?CiWebHitsFile=
/../../../../../winnt/system32/autoexec.nt
```

Application Code Errors

A user's browser carries on an intricate, undocumented protocol interchange with the web server. To make its job easier, the web server passes context strings to the user, making the user's browser reply with full context. A problem arises when the user can modify that context.

To see why, consider our fictitious shopping site called CDs-R-Us, selling compact disks. At any given time, a server at that site may have a thousand or more transactions in various states of completion. The site displays a page of goods to order, the user selects one, the site displays more items, the user selects another, the site displays more items, the user selects two more, and so on until the user is finished selecting. Many people go on to complete the order by specifying payment and shipping information. But other people use web sites like this one as an online catalog or guide, with no real intention of ordering. For instance, they can use this site to find out the price of the latest CD from Cherish the Ladies; they can use an online book service to determine how many books by Iris Murdoch are in print. And even if the user is a bona fide customer, sometimes web connections fail, leaving the transaction incomplete. For these reasons, the web server often keeps track of the status of an incomplete order in parameter fields appended to the URL. These fields travel from the server to the browser and back to the server with each user selection or page request.

Assume you have selected one CD and are looking at a second web page. The web server has passed you a URL similar to

```
http://www.CDs-r-us.com/page4&i1=459012&p1=1599
```

This URL means you have chosen CD number 459012, and its price is $15.99. You now select a second and the URL becomes

```
http://www.CDs-r-us.com/
page7&i1=459012&p1=1599&i2=365217&p2=1499
```

But if you are a clever attacker, you realize that you can edit the URL in the address window of your browser. Consequently, you change each of 1599 and 1499 to 199. And when the server totals up your order, lo and behold, your two CDs cost only $1.99 each.

This failure is an example of the time-of-check to time-of-use flaw that we discussed in Chapter 3. The server sets (checks) the price of the item when you first display the price, but then it loses control of the checked data item and never checks it again. This situation arises frequently in server application code because application programmers are generally not aware of security (they haven't read Chapter 3!) and typically do not anticipate malicious behavior.

Server-Side Include

A potentially more serious problem is called a **server-side include**. The problem takes advantage of the fact that web pages can be organized to invoke a particular function automatically. For example, many pages use web commands to send an e-mail message in the "contact us" part of the displayed page. The commands, such as e-mail, if, goto, and include, are placed in a field that is interpreted in HTML.

One of the server-side include commands is exec, to execute an arbitrary file on the server. For instance, the server-side include command

```
<!-#exec cmd="/usr/bin/telnet &"->
```

will open a Telnet session from the server running in the name of (that is, with the privileges of) the server. An attacker may find it interesting to execute commands such as chmod (change access rights to an object), sh (establish a command shell), or cat (copy to a file).

Denial of Service

So far, we have discussed attacks that lead to failures of confidentiality or integrity—problems we have also seen in the contexts of operating systems, databases, and applications. Availability attacks, sometimes called **denial-of-service** or **DOS** attacks, are much more significant in networks than in other contexts. There are many accidental and malicious threats to availability or continued service.

Transmission Failure

Communications fail for many reasons. For instance, a line is cut. Or network noise makes a packet unrecognizable or undeliverable. A machine along the transmission path fails for hardware or software reasons. A device is removed from service for repair or testing. A device is saturated and rejects incoming data until it can clear its overload. Many of these problems are temporary or automatically fixed (circumvented) in major networks, including the Internet.

However, some failures cannot be easily repaired. A break in the single communications line to your computer (for example, from the network to your network interface card or the telephone line to your modem) can be fixed only by establishment of an alternative link or repair of the damaged one. The network administrator will say "service to the rest of the network was unaffected," but that is of little consolation to you.

From a malicious standpoint, you can see that anyone who can sever, interrupt, or overload capacity to you can deny you service. The physical threats are pretty obvious. We consider instead several electronic attacks that can cause a denial of service.

Connection Flooding

The most primitive denial-of-service attack is flooding a connection. If an attacker sends you as much data as your communications system can handle, you are prevented from receiving any other data. Even if an occasional packet reaches you from someone else, communication to you will be seriously degraded.

More sophisticated attacks use elements of Internet protocols. In addition to TCP and UDP, there is a third class of protocols, called **ICMP** or **Internet Control Message Protocols**. Normally used for system diagnostics, these protocols do not have associated user applications. ICMP protocols include:

- *ping*, which requests a destination to return a reply, intended to show that the destination system is reachable and functioning
- *echo*, which requests a destination to return the data sent to it, intended to show that the connection link is reliable (ping is actually a version of echo)
- *destination unreachable*, which indicates that a destination address cannot be accessed
- *source quench*, which means that the destination is becoming saturated and the source should suspend sending packets for a while

These protocols have important uses for network management. But they can also be used to attack a system. The protocols are handled within the network stack, so the attacks may be difficult to detect or block on the receiving host. We examine how two of these protocols can be used to attack a victim.

Echo-Chargen

This attack works between two hosts. Chargen is a protocol that generates a stream of packets; it is used to test the network's capacity. The attacker sets up a chargen process on host A that generates its packets as echo packets with a destination of host B. Then, host A produces a stream of packets to which host B replies by echoing them back to host A. This series puts the network infrastructures of A and B into an endless loop. If the attacker makes B both the source and destination address of the first packet, B hangs in a loop, constantly creating and replying to its own messages.

Ping of Death

A **ping of death** is a simple attack. Since ping requires the recipient to respond to the ping request, all the attacker needs to do is send a flood of pings to the intended victim. The attack is limited by the smallest bandwidth on the attack route. If the attacker is on a 10-megabyte (MB) connection and the path to the victim is 100 MB or more, the attacker cannot mathematically flood the victim alone. But the attack succeeds if the numbers are reversed: The attacker on a 100-MB connection can easily flood a 10-MB victim. The ping packets will saturate the victim's bandwidth.

Smurf

The **smurf** attack is a variation of a ping attack. It uses the same vehicle, a ping packet, with two extra twists. First, the attacker chooses a network of unwitting victims. The attacker spoofs the source address in the ping packet so that it appears to come from the victim. Then, the attacker sends this request to the network in **broadcast mode** by setting the last byte of the address to all 1s; broadcast mode packets are distributed to all hosts on the network. The attack is shown in Figure 7-17.

Syn Flood

Another popular denial-of-service attack is the **syn flood**. This attack uses the TCP protocol suite, making the session-oriented nature of these protocols work against the victim.

For a protocol such as Telnet, the protocol peers establish a virtual connection, called a **session**, to synchronize the back-and-forth, command-response nature of the Telnet terminal emulation. A session is established with a three-way TCP handshake. Each TCP packet has flag bits, two of which are denoted SYN and ACK. To initiate a TCP connection, the originator sends a packet with the SYN bit on. If the recipient is ready to establish a connection, it replies with a packet with both the SYN and ACK bits on. The first party then completes the exchange to demonstrate a clear and complete communication channel by sending a packet with the ACK bit on, as shown in Figure 7-18.

Occasionally packets get lost or damaged in transmission. The destination maintains a queue called the **SYN_RECV** connections, tracking those items for which a SYN–ACK has been sent but no corresponding ACK has yet been received. Normally, these connections are completed in a short time. If the SYN–ACK (2) or the ACK (3) packet is lost, eventually the destination host will time out the incomplete connection and discard it from its waiting queue.

The attacker can deny service to the target by sending many SYN requests and never responding with ACKs, thereby filling the victim's SYN_RECV queue. Typically, the SYN_RECV queue is quite small, such as 10 or 20 entries. Because of potential routing delays in the Internet, typical holding times for the SYN_RECV queue can

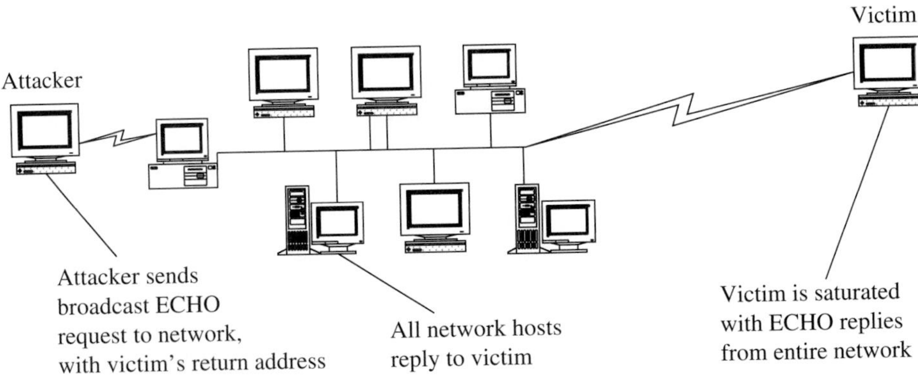
Victim
Attacker
Attacker sends broadcast ECHO request to network, with victim's return address
All network hosts reply to victim
Victim is saturated with ECHO replies from entire network

FIGURE 7-17 Smurf Attack.

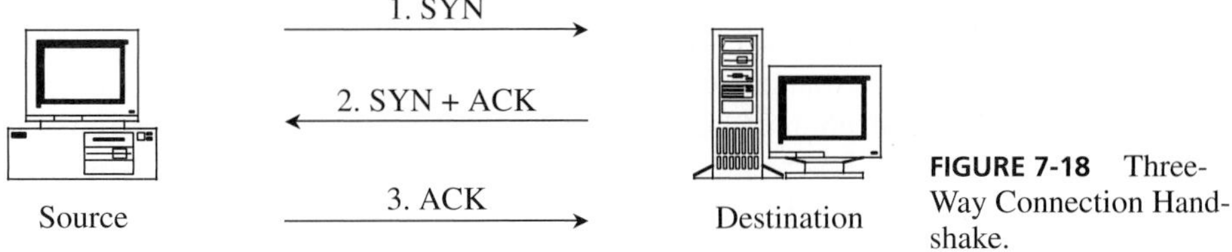

FIGURE 7-18 Three-Way Connection Handshake.

be minutes. So the attacker needs only to send a new SYN request every few seconds and it will fill the queue.

Attackers using this approach usually do one more thing: They spoof the nonexistent return address in the initial SYN packet. Why? For two reasons. First, the attacker does not want to disclose the real source address in case someone should inspect the packets in the SYN_RECV queue to try to identify the attacker. Second, the attacker wants to make the SYN packets indistinguishable from legitimate SYN packets to establish real connections. Choosing a different (spoofed) source address for each one makes them unique. A SYN–ACK packet to a nonexistent address will result in an ICMP Destination Unreachable result, but this will not be the ACK for which the TCP connection is waiting. (Remember that TCP and ICMP are different protocol suites, so an ICMP reply does not necessarily get back to the sender's TCP handler.)

For more on these and other denial of service threats, see [CER99].

Traffic Redirection

As we saw earlier, at the network layer, a router is a device that forwards traffic on its way through intermediate networks between a source host's network and a destination's. So if an attacker can corrupt the routing, traffic can disappear.

Routers use complex algorithms to decide how to route traffic. No matter the algorithm, they essentially seek the best path (where "best" is measured in some combination of distance, time, cost, quality, and the like). Routers are aware only of the routers with which they share a direct network connection, and they use gateway protocols to share information about their capabilities. Each router advises its neighbors about how well it can reach other network addresses. This characteristic allows an attacker to disrupt the network.

To see how, keep in mind that, in spite of its sophistication, a router is simply a computer with two or more network interfaces. Suppose a router advertises to its neighbors that it has the best path to every other address in the whole network. Soon all routers will direct all traffic to that one router. The one router may become flooded, or it may simply drop much of its traffic. In either case, a lot of traffic never makes it to the intended destination.

DNS Attacks

Our final denial-of-service attack is actually a class of attacks based on the concept of domain name server. A **domain name server (DNS)** is a table that converts domain names like ATT.COM into network addresses like 211.217.74.130; this process is called resolving the domain name. A domain name server queries other name servers to resolve domain names it does not know. For efficiency, it caches the answers it receives so it can resolve that name more rapidly in the future.

In the most common implementations of Unix, name servers run software called **Berkeley Internet Name Domain** or **BIND** or **named** (a shorthand for "name daemon"). There have been numerous flaws in BIND, including the now-familiar buffer overflow.

By overtaking a name server or causing it to cache spurious entries, an attacker can redirect the routing of any traffic, with an obvious implication for denial of service.

Distributed Denial of Service

The denial-of-service attacks we have listed are powerful by themselves, and Sidebar 7-6 shows us that many are launched. But an attacker can construct a two-stage attack that multiplies the effect many times. This multiplicative effect gives power to distributed denial of service.

To perpetrate a **distributed denial-of-service** (or **DDoS)** attack, an attacker does two things, as illustrated in Figure 7-19. In the first stage, the attacker uses any convenient attack (such as exploiting a buffer overflow or tricking the victim to open and

Sidebar 7-6 How Much Denial-of-Service Activity Is There?

Researchers at the University of California, San Diego (UCSD) studied the amount of denial-of-service activity on the Internet [UCS01]. Because many DOS attacks use a fictitious return address, the researchers asserted that traffic to nonexistent addresses was indicative of the amount of denial-of-service attacking. They monitored a large, unused address space on the Internet for a period of three weeks. They found:

- More than 12,000 attacks were aimed at more than 5,000 targets during the three-week period.
- Syn floods likely accounted for more than half of the attacks.
- Half the attacks lasted less than ten minutes, and 90 percent of attacks lasted less than an hour.

Steve Gibson of Gibson Research Corporation (GRC) experienced several denial-of-service attacks in mid-2001. He collected data for his own forensic purposes [GIB01]. The first attack lasted 17 hours, at which point he was able to reconfigure the router connecting him to the Internet so as to block the attack. During those 17 hours he found his site was attacked by 474 Windows-based PCs. A later attack lasted 6.5 hours before it stopped by itself. These attacks were later found to have been launched by a 13-year old from Kenosha, Wisconsin.

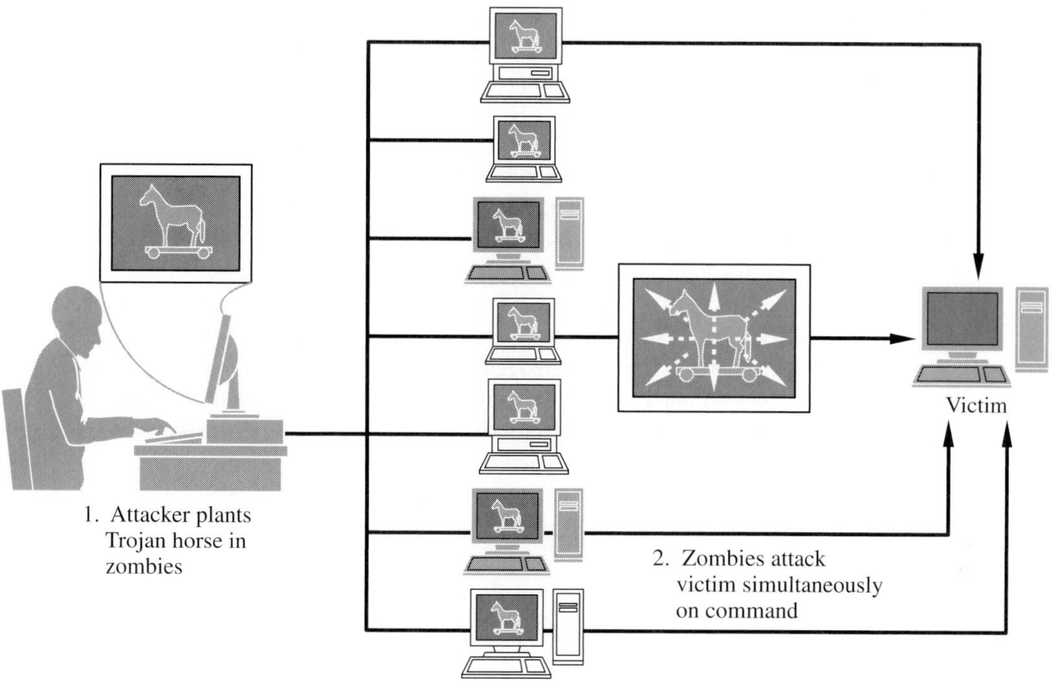

FIGURE 7-19 Distributed Denial-of-Service Attack.

install unknown code from an e-mail attachment) to plant a Trojan horse on a target machine. That Trojan horse does not necessarily cause any harm to the target machine, so it may not be noticed. The Trojan horse file may be named for a popular editor or utility, bound to a standard operating system service, or entered into the list of processes (daemons) activated at startup. No matter how it is situated within the system, it will probably not attract any attention.

The attacker repeats this process with many targets. Each of these target systems then becomes what is known as a **zombie**. The target systems carry out their normal work, unaware of the resident zombie.

At some point the attacker chooses a victim and sends a signal to all the zombies to launch the attack. Then, instead of the victim's trying to defend against one denial-of-service attack from one malicious host, the victim must try to counter *n* attacks from the *n* zombies all acting at once. Not all of the zombies need to use the same attack; for instance, some can use smurf attacks and others syn floods to address different potential weaknesses.

In addition to their tremendous multiplying effect, distributed denial-of-service attacks are a serious problem because they are easily launched from scripts. Given a collection of denial-of-service attacks and a Trojan horse propagation method, one can easily write a procedure to plant a Trojan horse that can launch any or all of the denial-of-service attacks. DDoS attack tools first appeared in mid-1999. Some of the original

DDoS tools include **Tribal Flood Network** (**TFN**), **Trin00**, and **TFN2K** (Tribal Flood Network, year 2000 edition). As new vulnerabilities are discovered that allow Trojan horses to be planted and as new denial-of-service attacks are found, new combination tools appear. For more details on this topic, see [HAN00a].

According to the U.S. Computer Emergency Response Team (CERT) [HOU01], scanning to find a vulnerable host (potential zombie) is now being included in combination tools; a single tool now identifies its zombie, installs the Trojan horse, and activates the zombie to wait for an attack signal. Recent target (zombie) selection has been largely random, meaning that attackers do not seem to care which zombies they infect. This revelation is actually bad news, because it means that no organization or accessible host is safe from attack. Perhaps because they are so numerous and because their users are assumed to be less knowledgeable about computer management and protection, Windows-based machines are becoming more popular targets for attack than other systems. Most frightening is the CERT finding that the time is shrinking between discovery of a vulnerability and its widespread exploitation.

Threats to Active or Mobile Code

Active code or **mobile code** is a general name for code that is pushed to the client for execution. Why should the web server waste its precious cycles and bandwidth doing simple work that the client's workstation can do? For example, suppose you want your web site to have bears dancing across the top of the page. To download the dancing bears, you could download a new image for each movement the bears take: one bit forward, two bits forward, and so forth. However, this approach uses far too much server time and bandwidth to compute the positions and download new images. A more efficient use of (server) resources is to download a program that runs on the client's machine and implements the movement of the bears.

Since you have been studying security and are aware of vulnerabilities, you probably are saying to yourself, "You mean a site I don't control, which could easily be hacked by teenagers, is going to push code to my machine that will execute without my knowledge, permission, or oversight?" Welcome to the world of (potentially malicious) mobile code. In fact, there are many different kinds of active code, and in this section we look at the related potential vulnerabilities.

Cookies

Strictly speaking, cookies are not active code. They are data files that can be stored and fetched by a remote server. However, cookies can be used to cause unexpected data transfer from a client to a server, so they have a role in a loss of confidentiality.

A **cookie** is a data object that can be held in memory (a **per-session** cookie) or stored on disk for future access (a **persistent** cookie). Cookies can store anything about a client that the browser can determine: keystrokes the user types, the machine name, connection details (such as IP address), date and type, and so forth. On command a browser will send to a server the cookies saved for it. Per-session cookies are deleted when the browser is closed, but persistent cookies are retained until a set expiration date, which can be years in the future.

Cookies provide context to a server. Using cookies, certain web pages can greet you with "Welcome back, James Bond" or reflect your preferences, as in "Shall I ship this order to you at 135 Elm Street?" But as these two examples demonstrate, anyone possessing someone's cookie becomes that person in some contexts. Thus, anyone intercepting or retrieving a cookie can impersonate the cookie's owner.

What information about you does a cookie contain? Even though it is your information, most of the time you cannot tell what is in a cookie, because the cookie's contents are encrypted under a key from the server.

So a cookie is something that takes up space on your disk, holding information about you that you cannot see, forwarded to servers you do not know whenever the server wants it, without informing you. The philosophy behind cookies seems to be "Trust us, it's good for you."

Scripts

Clients can invoke services by executing scripts on servers. Typically, a web browser displays a page. As the user interacts with the web site via the browser, the browser organizes user inputs into parameters to a defined script; it then sends the script and parameters to a server to be executed. But all communication is done through HTML. The server cannot distinguish between commands generated from a user at a browser completing a web page, and a user's handcrafting a set of orders. The malicious user can monitor the communication between a browser and a server to see how changing a web page entry affects what the browser sends and then how the server reacts. With this knowledge, the malicious user can manipulate the server's actions.

To see how easily this manipulation is done, remember that programmers do not often anticipate malicious behavior; instead, programmers assume that users will be benign and will use a program in the way it was intended to be used. For this reason, programmers neglect to filter script parameters to ensure that they are reasonable for the operation and safe to execute. Some scripts allow arbitrary files to be included or arbitrary commands to be executed. An attacker can see the files or commands in a string and experiment with changing them.

A well-known attack against web servers is the **escape-character** attack. A common scripting language for web servers, **CGI** (**Common Gateway Interface**), defines a machine-independent way to encode communicated data. The coding convention uses %nn to represent ASCII special characters. However, special characters may be interpreted by CGI script interpreters. So, for example, %0A (end-of-line) instructs the interpreter to accept the following characters as a new command. The following command requests a copy of the server's password file:

```
http://www.test.com/cgi-bin/query?%0a/bin/cat%20/etc/passwd
```

CGI scripts can also initiate actions directly on the server. For example, an attacker can observe a CGI script that includes a string of this form:

```
<!-#action arg1=value arg2=value ...>
```

and submit a subsequent command where the string is replaced by

```
<!-#exec cmd="rm *">
```

to cause a command shell to execute a command to remove all files in the shell's current directory.

Microsoft uses **active server pages (ASP)** as its scripting capability. Such pages instruct the browser on how to display files, maintain context, and interact with the server. These pages can also be viewed at the browser end, so any programming weaknesses in the ASP code are available for inspection and attack.

The server should never trust anything received from a client, because the remote user can send the server a string crafted by hand, instead of one generated by a benign procedure the server sent the client. As with so many cases of remote access, these examples demonstrate that if you allow someone else to run a program on your machine, you can no longer have confidence that your machine is secure.

Active Code

Displaying web pages started simply with a few steps: generate text, insert images, and register mouse clicks to fetch new pages. Soon, people wanted more elaborate action at their web sites: toddlers dancing atop the page, a three-dimensional rotating cube, images flashing on and off, colors changing, totals appearing. Some of these tricks, especially those involving movement, take significant computing power; they require a lot of time and communication to download from a server. But typically, the client has a capable and underutilized processor, so the timing issues are irrelevant.

To take advantage of the processor's power, the server may download code to be executed on the client. This executable code is called **active code**. The two main kinds of active code are **Java code** and **ActiveX controls**.

Java Code

Sun Microsystems [GOS96] designed and promoted Java as a truly machine-independent programming language. A Java program consists of Java bytecode executed on a Java virtual machine (JVM). The bytecode programs are machine independent, and only the JVM needs to be implemented on each class of machine to achieve program portability. The JVM contains a built-in security manager that enforces a security policy. A Java program runs in a Java "sandbox," a constrained resource domain from which the program cannot escape. The Java programming language is strongly typed, meaning that the content of a data item must be of the appropriate type for which it is to be used (for example, a text string cannot be used as a numeric).

The original specification, called Java 1.1, was very solid, very restrictive, and hence very unpopular. In it, a program could not write permanently to disk, nor could it invoke arbitrary procedures that had not been included in the sandbox by the security manager's policy. Thus, the sandbox was a collection of resources the user was willing to sacrifice to the uncertainties of Java code. Although very strong, the Java 1.1 definition proved unworkable. As a result, the original restrictions on the sandbox were relaxed, to the detriment of security.

The Java 1.2 specification opened the sandbox to more resources, particularly to stored disk files and executable procedures. (See, for example, [GON96, GON97].) Although it is still difficult to break its constraints, the Java sandbox contains many new toys, enabling more interesting computation but opening the door to exploitation of more serious vulnerabilities. (For more information, see [DEA96] and review the work of the Princeton University Secure Internet Programming group, *http://www.cs.princeton.edu/sip/history/index.php3*.)

Does this mean that Java's designers made bad decisions? No. As we have seen many times before, a product's security flaw is not necessarily a design flaw. Sometimes the designers choose to trade some security for increased functionality or ease of use. In other cases, the design is fine, but implementers fail to uphold the high security standards set out by designers. The latter is certainly true for Java. There have been problems with implementations of Java virtual machines for different platforms and in different components. For example, a version of Netscape browser failed to implement type checking on all data types, as is required in the Java specifications. A similar vulnerability affected Microsoft Internet Explorer. Although these vulnerabilities have been patched, other problems could occur with subsequent releases.

A **hostile applet** is downloadable Java code that can cause harm on the client's system. Because an applet is not screened for safety when it is downloaded and because it typically runs with the privileges of its invoking user, a hostile applet can cause serious damage. Dean et al. [DEA96] list necessary conditions for secure execution of applets:

- The system must control applets' access to sensitive system resources, such as the file system, the processor, the network, the user's display, and internal state variables.
- The language must protect memory by preventing forged memory pointers and array (buffer) overflows.
- The system must prevent object reuse by clearing memory contents for new objects; the system should perform garbage collection to reclaim memory that is no longer in use.
- The system must control interapplet communication as well as applets' effects on the environment outside the Java system through system calls.

ActiveX

Microsoft's answer to Java technology is ActiveX. Using ActiveX, objects of arbitrary type can be downloaded to a client. If the client has a viewer or handler for the object's type, that viewer is invoked to present the object. For example, downloading a Microsoft Word .doc file would invoke Microsoft Word on a system on which it is installed. Files for which the client has no handler cause other code to be downloaded. Thus, in theory, an attacker could invent a type, called .bomb, and cause any unsuspecting user who downloaded a web page with a .bomb file also to download code that would execute .bombs.

To prevent arbitrary downloads, Microsoft uses an authentication scheme under which downloaded code is cryptographically signed and the signature is verified before execution. But the authentication verifies only the source of the code, not its correctness or safety. Code from Microsoft (or Netscape or any other manufacturer) is not inherently safe, and code from an unknown source may be more or less safe than that from a known source. Proof of origin shows where it came from, not how good or safe it is. And some vulnerabilities allow ActiveX to bypass the authentication.

Auto Exec by Type

Data files are processed by programs. For some products, the file type is implied by the file extension, such as .doc for a Word document, .pdf (Portable Document Format) for an Adobe Acrobat file, or .exe for an executable file. On many systems, when a file arrives with one of these extensions, the operating system automatically invokes the appropriate processor to handle it.

By itself, a Word document is unintelligible as an executable file. To prevent someone from running a file temp.doc by typing that name as a command, Microsoft embeds within a file what type it really is. Double-clicking the file in a Windows Explorer window brings up the appropriate program to handle that file.

But, as we noted in Chapter 3, this scheme presents an opportunity to an attacker. A malicious agent might send you a file named innocuous.doc, which you would expect to be a Word document. Because of the .doc extension, Word would try to open it. Suppose that file is renamed "innocuous" (without a .doc). If the embedded file type is .doc, then double-clicking innocuous also brings the file up in Word. The file might contain malicious macros or invoke the opening of another, more dangerous file.

Generally, we recognize that executable files can be dangerous, text files are likely to be safe, and files with some active content, such as .doc files, fall in between. If a file has no apparent file type and will be opened by its built-in file handler, we are treading on dangerous ground. An attacker can disguise a malicious active file under a nonobvious file type.

Complex Attacks

As if these vulnerabilities were not enough, two other phenomena multiply the risk. Scripts let people perform attacks even if they do not understand what the attack is or how it is performed. Building blocks let people combine components of an attack, almost like building a house from prefabricated parts.

Script Kiddies

Attacks can be scripted. A simple smurf denial-of-service attack is not hard to implement. But an underground establishment has written scripts for many of the popular attacks. With a script, attackers need not understand the nature of the attack nor even the concept of a network. The attackers merely download the attack script (no more difficult than downloading a newspaper story from a list of headlines) and execute it. The script takes care of selecting an appropriate (that is, vulnerable) victim and launching the attack.

The hacker community is active in creating scripts for known vulnerabilities. For example, within three weeks of a CERT advisory for a serious SNMP vulnerability in February 2002 [CER02], scripts had appeared. These scripts probed for the vulnerability's existence in specific brands and models of network devices; then they executed attacks when a vulnerable host was found.

People who download and run attack scripts are called **script kiddies**. As the rather derogatory name implies, script kiddies are not well respected in the attacker community because the damage they do requires almost no creativity or innovation. Nevertheless, script kiddies can cause serious damage, sometimes without even knowing what they do.

Building Blocks

This chapter's attack types do not form an exhaustive list, but they are representative of the kinds of vulnerabilities being exploited, their sources, and their severity. A good attacker knows these vulnerabilities and many more.

An attacker simply out to cause minor damage to a randomly selected site could use any of the techniques we have described, perhaps under script control. A dedicated attacker who targets one location can put together several pieces of an attack in order to compound the damage. Often, the attacks are done in series so that each part builds on the information gleaned from previous attacks. For example, a wiretapping attack may yield reconnaissance information with which to form an ActiveX attack that transfers a Trojan horse that monitors for sensitive data in transmission. Putting the attack pieces together like building blocks expands the number of targets and increases the degree of damage.

Summary of Network Vulnerabilities

A network has many different vulnerabilities, but all derive from an underlying model of computer, communications, and information systems security. Threats are raised against the key aspects of security: confidentiality, integrity, and availability, as shown in Table 7-4.

7.3 NETWORK SECURITY CONTROLS

The list of security attacks is very long, and the news media carry frequent accounts of serious security incidents. From these, you may be ready to conclude that network security is hopeless. Fortunately, that is not the case. Previous chapters have presented several strategies for addressing security concerns, such as encryption for confidentiality and integrity, reference monitors for access control, and overlapping controls for defense in depth. These strategies are also useful in protecting networks. This section presents many excellent defenses available to the network security engineer. Subsequent sections provide detailed explanations for three particularly important controls—firewalls, intrusion detection systems, and encrypted e-mail.

Security Threat Analysis

Recall the three steps of a security threat analysis in other situations. First, we scrutinize all the parts of a system so that we know what each part does and how it interacts with other parts. Next, we consider possible damage to confidentiality, integrity, and availability. Finally, we hypothesize the kinds of attacks that could cause this damage. We can take the same steps with a network. We begin by looking at the individual parts of a network:

TABLE 7-4 Network Vulnerabilities.

Target	Vulnerability
Precursors to attack	• Port scan • Social engineering • Reconnaissance • OS and application fingerprinting
Authentication failures	• Impersonation • Guessing • Eavesdropping • Spoofing • Session hijacking • Man-in-the-middle attack
Programming flaws	• Buffer overflow • Addressing errors • Parameter modification, time-of-check to time-of-use errors • Server-side include • Cookie • Malicious active code: JavaScript, ActiveX • Malicious code: virus, worm, Trojan horse • Malicious typed code
Confidentiality	• Protocol flaw • Eavesdropping • Passive wiretap • Misdelivery • Exposure within the network • Traffic flow analysis • Cookie
Integrity	• Protocol flaw • Active wiretap • Impersonation • Falsification of message • Noise • Web site defacement • DNS attack
Availability	• Protocol flaw • Transmission or component failure • Connection flooding, e.g., echo-chargen, ping of death, smurf, syn flood • DNS attack • Traffic redirection • Distributed denial of service

- *local nodes* connected via
- *local communications links* to a
- *local area network,* which also has
- *local data storage,*
- *local processes,* and
- *local devices.*

The local network is also connected to a

- *network gateway* which gives access via
- *network communications links* to
- *network control resources,*
- *network routers,* and
- *network resources*, such as databases.

These functional needs are typical for network users. But now we look again at these parts, this time conjuring up the negative effects threat agents can cause. We posit a malicious agent—call him Hector—who wants to attack networked communications between two users, Andy and Bo. What might Hector do?

- *Read communications*. The messages sent and received are exposed inside Andy's machine, at all places through the network, and inside Bo's machine. Thus, a confidentiality attack can be mounted from practically any place in the network.
- *Modify communications* from Andy to Bo. Again, the messages are exposed at all places through the network.
- *Forge communications* allegedly from Andy to Bo. This action is even easier than modifying a communication because a forgery can be inserted at any place in the network. It need not originate with the ostensible sender, and it does not require catching a communication in transit. Since Andy does not deliver his communications personally and since Bo might even never have met Andy, Bo has little basis for judging whether a communication purportedly sent by Andy is authentic.
- *Inhibit communications* from Andy to Bo. Here again, Hector can achieve this result by invading Andy's machine, Bo's machine, routers between them, or communications links. He can also disrupt communications in general by flooding the network or disrupting any unique path on the network.
- *Inhibit all communications* passing through a point. If the point resides on a unique path to or from a node, all traffic to or from that node is blocked. If the path is not unique, blocking it will shift traffic to other nodes, perhaps overburdening them.
- *Read data* at some machine C between Andy and Bo. Hector can impersonate Andy (who is authorized to access data at C). Bo might question a message that seems out of character for Andy, but machine C will nevertheless apply the access controls for Andy. Alternatively, Hector can invade (run a program on) machine C to override access controls. Finally, he can search the network for machines that have weak or improperly administered access controls.

- *Modify* or *destroy data* at C. Here again Hector can impersonate Andy and do anything Andy could. Similarly, Hector can try to circumvent controls.

We summarize these threats with a list:

- intercepting data in traffic
- accessing programs or data at remote hosts
- modifying programs or data at remote hosts
- modifying data in transit
- inserting communications
- impersonating a user
- inserting a repeat of a previous communication
- blocking selected traffic
- blocking all traffic
- running a program at a remote host

Why are all these attacks possible? Size, anonymity, ignorance, misunderstanding, complexity, dedication, and programming all contribute. But we have help at hand; we look next at specific threats and their countermeasures. Later in this chapter we investigate how these countermeasures fit together into specific tools.

Design and Implementation

Throughout this book we have discussed good principles of system analysis, design, implementation, and maintenance. Chapter 3, in particular, presented techniques that have been developed by the software engineering community to improve requirements, design, and code quality. Concepts from the work of the early trusted operating systems projects (presented in Chapter 5) have natural implications for networks as well. And assurance, also discussed in Chapter 5, relates to networked systems. In general, the Open Web Applications project [OWA02] has documented many of the techniques people can use to develop secure web applications. Thus, having addressed secure programming from several perspectives already, we do not belabor the points now.

Architecture

As with so many of the areas we have studied, planning can be the strongest control. In particular, when we build or modify computer-based systems, we can give some thought to their overall architecture and plan to "build in" security as one of the key constructs. Similarly, the architecture or design of a network can have a significant effect on its security.

Segmentation

Just as segmentation was a powerful security control in operating systems, it can limit the potential for harm in a network in two important ways: Segmentation reduces the number of threats, and it limits the amount of damage a single vulnerability can allow.

Assume your network implements electronic commerce for users of the Internet. The fundamental parts of your network may be

- a web server, to handle users' HTTP sessions
- application code, to present your goods and services for purchase
- a database of goods, and perhaps an accompanying inventory to the count of stock on hand and being requested from suppliers
- a database of orders taken

If all these activities were to run on one machine, your network would be in trouble: Any compromise or failure of that machine would destroy your entire commerce capability.

A more secure design uses multiple segments, as shown in Figure 7-20. Suppose one piece of hardware is to be a web server box exposed to access by the general public. To reduce the risk of attack from outside the system, that box should not also have other, more sensitive, functions on it, such as user authentication or access to a sensitive data repository. Separate segments and servers—corresponding to the principles of least privilege and encapsulation—reduce the potential harm should any subsystem be compromised.

Separate access is another way to segment the network. For example, suppose a network is being used for three purposes: using the "live" production system, testing the next production version, and developing subsequent systems. If the network is well

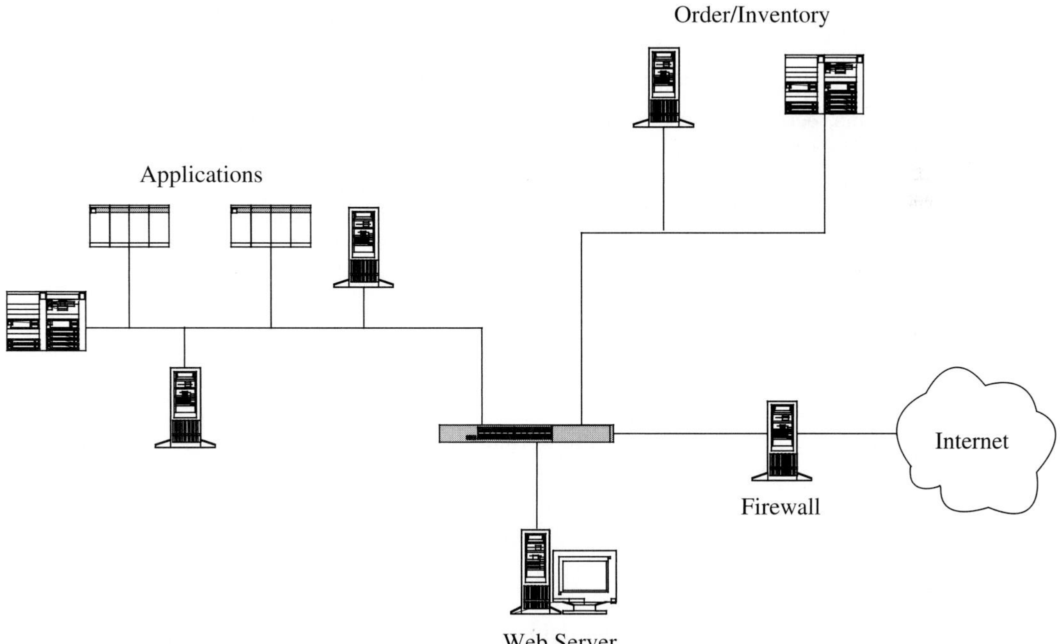

FIGURE 7-20 Segmented Architecture.

segmented, external users should be able to access only the live system, testers should access only the test system, and developers should access only the development system. Segmentation permits these three populations to coexist without risking that, for instance, a developer will inadvertently change the production system.

Redundancy

Another key architectural control is redundancy: allowing a function to be performed on more than one node, to avoid "putting all the eggs in one basket." For example, the design of Figure 7-20 has only one web server; lose it and all connectivity is lost. A better design would have two servers, using what is called failover mode. In **failover mode** the servers communicate with each other periodically, each determining if the other is still active. If one fails, the other takes over processing for both of them. Although performance is cut approximately in half when a failure occurs, at least some processing is being done.

Single Points of Failure

Ideally, the architecture should make the network immune to failure. In fact, the architecture should at least make sure that the system tolerates failure in an acceptable way (such as slowing down but not stopping processing, or recovering and restarting incomplete transactions). One way to evaluate the network architecture's tolerance of failure is to look for **single points of failure**. That is, we should ask if there is a single point in the network that, if it were to fail, could deny access to all or a significant part of the network. So, for example, a single database in one location is vulnerable to all the failures that could affect that location. Good network design eliminates single points of failure. Distributing the database—placing copies of it on different network segments, perhaps even in different physical locations—can reduce the risk of serious harm from a failure at any one point. There is often substantial overhead in implementing such a design; for example, the independent databases must be synchronized. But usually we can deal with the failure-tolerant features more easily than with the harm caused by a failed single link.

Architecture plays a role in implementing many other controls. We point out architectural features as we introduce other controls throughout the remainder of this chapter.

Encryption

Encryption is probably the most important and versatile tool for a network security expert. We have seen in earlier chapters that encryption is powerful for providing privacy, authenticity, integrity, and limited access to data. Because networks often involve even greater risks, they often secure data with encryption, perhaps in combination with other controls.

In network applications, encryption can be applied either between two hosts (called link encryption) or between two applications (called end-to-end encryption). We consider each below. With either form of encryption, key distribution is always a problem. Encryption keys must be delivered to the sender and receiver in a secure manner. In this section, we also investigate techniques for safe key distribution in networks. Finally, we study a cryptographic facility for a network computing environment.

Link Encryption

In **link encryption**, data are encrypted just before the system places them on the physical communications link. In this case, encryption occurs at layer 1 or 2 in the OSI model. (A similar situation occurs with TCP/IP protocols.) Similarly, decryption occurs just as the communication arrives at and enters the receiving computer. A model of link encryption is shown in Figure 7-21.

Encryption protects the message in transit between two computers, but the message is in plaintext inside the hosts. (A message in plaintext is said to be "in the clear.") Notice that because the encryption is added at the bottom protocol layer, the message is exposed in all other layers of the sender and receiver. If we have good physical security, we may not be too concerned about this exposure; the exposure occurs on the sender's or receiver's host or workstation, protected by alarms or locked doors, for example. Nevertheless, you should notice that the message is exposed in two layers of all intermediate hosts through which the message may pass. This exposure occurs because routing and addressing are not read at the bottom layer, but only at higher layers. The message is in the clear in the intermediate hosts, and one of these hosts may not be especially trustworthy.

Link encryption is invisible to the user. The encryption becomes a transmission service performed by a low-level network protocol layer, just like message routing or transmission error detection. Figure 7-22 shows a typical link encrypted message, where the shaded fields are encrypted. Because some of the data link header and trailer is applied before the block is encrypted, part of each of those blocks is shaded. As the

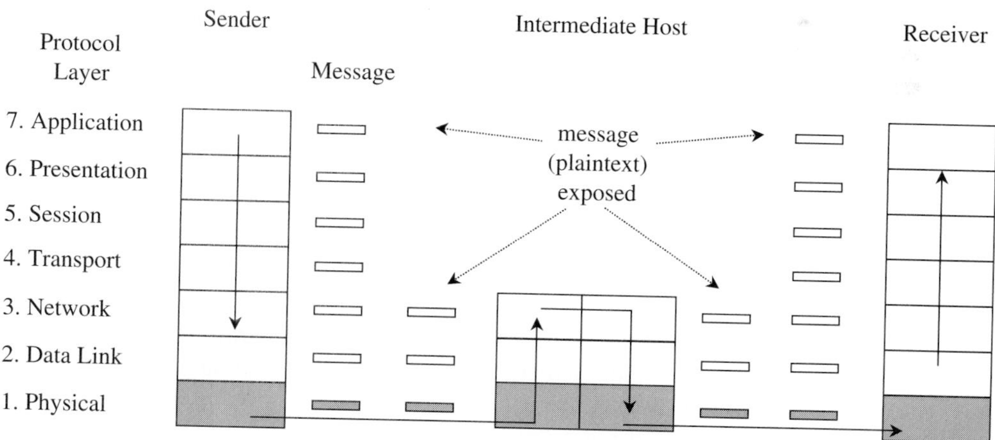

FIGURE 7-21 Link Encryption.

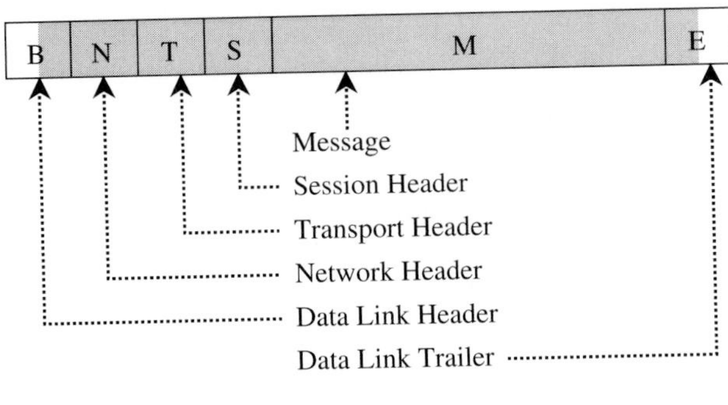

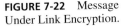

FIGURE 7-22 Message Under Link Encryption.

message M is handled at each layer, header and control information is added on the sending side and removed on the receiving side. Hardware encryption devices operate quickly and reliably; in this case, link encryption is invisible to the operating system as well as to the operator.

Link encryption is especially appropriate when the transmission line is the point of greatest vulnerability. If all hosts on a network are reasonably secure but the communications medium is shared with other users or is not secure, link encryption is an easy control to use.

End-to-End Encryption

As its name implies, **end-to-end encryption** provides security from one end of a transmission to the other. The encryption can be applied by a hardware device between the user and the host. Alternatively, the encryption can be done by software running on the host computer. In either case, the encryption is performed at the highest levels (layer 7, application, or perhaps at layer 6, presentation) of the OSI model. A model of end-to-end encryption is shown in Figure 7-23.

Since the encryption precedes all the routing and transmission processing of the layer, the message is transmitted in encrypted form throughout the network. The encryption addresses potential flaws in lower layers in the transfer model. If a lower layer should fail to preserve security and reveal data it has received, the data's confidentiality is not endangered. Figure 7-24 shows a typical message with end-to-end encryption, again with the encrypted field shaded.

When end-to-end encryption is used, messages sent through several hosts are protected. The data content of the message is still encrypted, as shown in Figure 7-25, and the message is encrypted (protected against disclosure) while in transit. Therefore, even though a message must pass through potentially insecure nodes (such as C through G) on the path between A and B, the message is protected against disclosure while in transit.

Comparison of Encryption Methods

Simply encrypting a message is not absolute assurance that it will not be revealed during or after transmission. In many instances, however, the strength of encryption is ad-

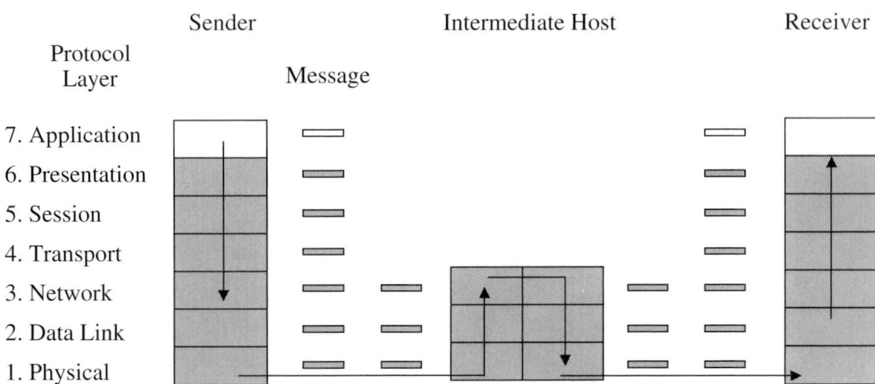

FIGURE 7-23 End-to-End Encryption.

equate protection, considering the likelihood of the interceptor's breaking the encryption and the timeliness of the message. As with many aspects of security, we must balance the strength of protection with the likelihood of attack. (You will learn more about managing these risks in Chapter 8.)

With link encryption, encryption is invoked for all transmissions along a particular link. Typically, a given host has only one link into a network, meaning that all network traffic initiated on that host will be encrypted by that host. But this encryption scheme implies that every other host receiving these communications must also have a cryptographic facility to decrypt the messages. Furthermore, all hosts must share keys. A message may pass through one or more intermediate hosts on the way to its final destination. If the message is encrypted along some links of a network but not others, then part of the advantage of encryption is lost. Therefore, link encryption is usually performed on all links of a network if it is performed at all.

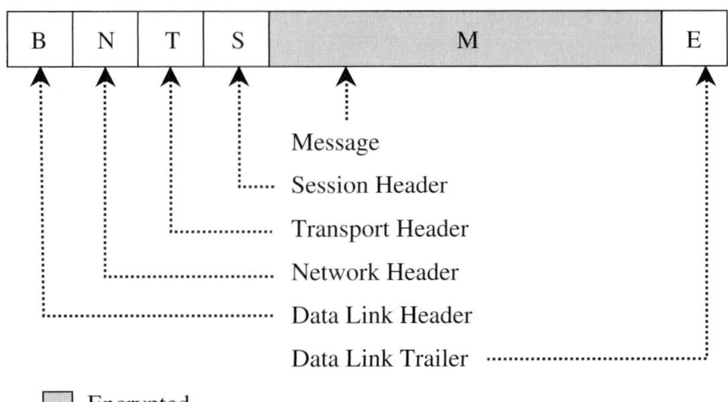

FIGURE 7-24 End-to-End Encrypted Message.

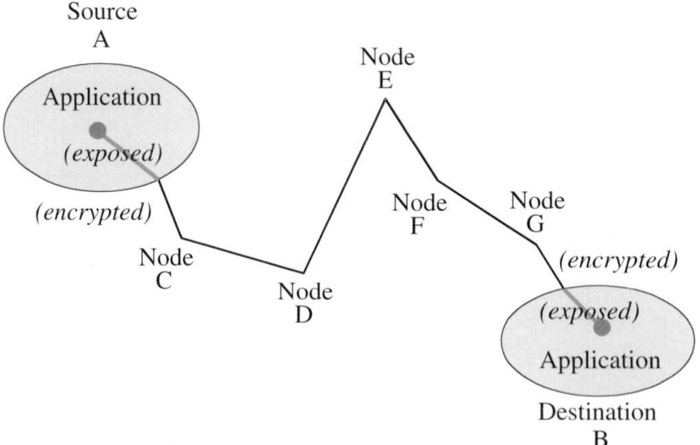

FIGURE 7-25 Encrypted Message Passing Through a Host.

By contrast, end-to-end encryption is applied to "logical links," which are channels between two processes, at a level well above the physical path. Since the intermediate hosts along a transmission path do not need to encrypt or decrypt a message, they have no need for cryptographic facilities. Thus, encryption is used only for those messages and applications for which it is needed. Furthermore, the encryption can be done with software, so we can apply it selectively, one application at a time or even to one message within a given application.

The selective advantage of end-to-end encryption is also a disadvantage regarding encryption keys. Under end-to-end encryption, there is a virtual cryptographic channel between each pair of users. To provide proper security, each pair of users should share a unique cryptographic key. The number of keys required is thus equal to the number of pairs of users, which is $n * (n - 1)/2$ for n users. This number increases rapidly as the number of users increases. However, this count assumes that single key encryption is used. With a public key system, only one pair of keys is needed per recipient.

As shown in Table 7-5, link encryption is faster, easier for the user, and uses fewer keys. End-to-end encryption is more flexible, can be used selectively, is done at the user level, and can be integrated with the application. Neither form is right for all situations.

In some cases, both forms of encryption can be applied. A user who does not trust the quality of the link encryption provided by a system can apply end-to-end encryption as well. A system administrator who is concerned about the security of an end-to-end encryption scheme applied by an applications program can also install a link encryption device. If both encryptions are relatively fast, this duplication of security will have little negative effect.

Virtual Private Networks

Link encryption can be used to give a network's users the sense that they are on a private network, even when it is part of a public network. For this reason, the approach is called a **virtual private network** (or **VPN**).

TABLE 7-5 Comparison of Link and End-to-End Encryption.

Link Encryption	End-to-End Encryption
Security within hosts	
Data exposed in sending host	Data encrypted in sending host
Data exposed in intermediate nodes	Data encrypted in intermediate nodes
Role of user	
Applied by sending host	Applied by sending process
Invisible to user	User applies encryption
Host maintains encryption	User must find algorithm
One facility for all users	User selects encryption
Typically done in hardware	Either software or hardware implementation
All or no data encrypted	User chooses to encrypt or not, for each data item
Implementation concerns	
Requires one key per host pair	Requires one key per user pair
Provides node authentication	Provides user authentication

Typically, physical security and administrative security are strong enough to protect transmission inside the perimeter of a network. Thus, the greatest exposure for a user is between the user's workstation or client and the perimeter of the host network or server.

A firewall is an access control device that sits between two networks or two network segments. It filters all traffic between the protected or "inside" network and a less trustworthy or "outside" network or segment. (We examine firewalls in detail later in this chapter.)

Many firewalls can be used to implement a VPN. When a user first establishes a communication with the firewall, the user can request a VPN session with the firewall. The user's client and the firewall negotiate a session encryption key, and the firewall and the client subsequently use that key to encrypt all traffic between the two. In this way, the larger network is restricted only to those given special access by the VPN. In other words, it feels to the user that the network is private, even though it is not. With the VPN, we say that the communication passes through an **encrypted tunnel** or **tunnel**. Establishment of a VPN is shown in Figure 7-26.

Virtual private networks are created when the firewall interacts with an authentication service inside the perimeter. The firewall may pass user authentication data to the authentication server and, upon confirmation of the authenticated identity, the firewall provides the user with appropriate security privileges. For example, a known trusted person, such as an employee or a system administrator, may be allowed to access resources not available to general users. The firewall implements this access control on

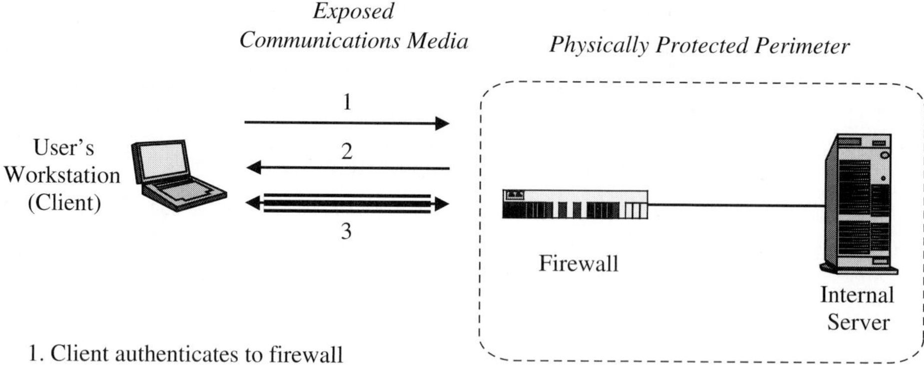

FIGURE 7-26 Establishing a Virtual Private Network.

the basis of the VPN. A VPN with privileged access is shown in Figure 7-27. In that figure, the firewall passes to the internal server the (privileged) identity of User 2.

PKI and Certificates

A **public key infrastructure**, or **PKI**, is a process created to enable users to implement public key cryptography, usually in a large (and frequently, distributed) setting. PKI offers each user a set of services, related to identification and access control, as follows:

- create certificates associating a user's identity with a (public) cryptographic key
- give out certificates from its database
- sign certificates, adding its credibility to the authenticity of the certificate

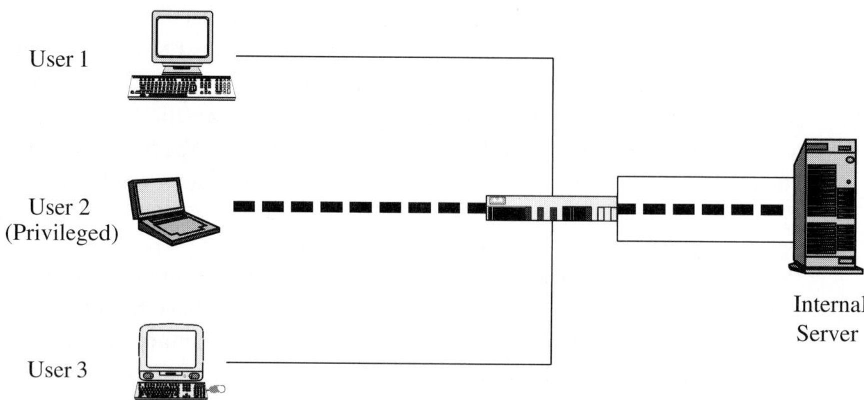

FIGURE 7-27 VPN to Allow Privileged Access.

- confirm (or deny) that a certificate is valid
- invalidate certificates for users who no longer are allowed access or whose private key has been exposed

PKI is often considered to be a standard, but in fact it is a set of policies, products, and procedures that leave some room for interpretation. The policies define the rules under which the cryptographic systems should operate. In particular, the policies specify how to handle keys and valuable information and how to match level of control to level of risk. The procedures dictate how the keys should be generated, managed, and used. Finally, the products actually implement the policies, and they generate, store, and manage the keys.

PKI sets up entities, called **certificate authorities**, that implement the PKI policy on certificates. The general idea is that a certificate authority is trusted, so users can delegate the construction, issuance, acceptance, and revocation of certificates to the authority, much as one would use a trusted bouncer to allow only some people to enter a restricted nightclub. The specific actions of a certificate authority include the following:

- managing public key certificates for their whole life cycle
- issuing certificates by binding a user's or system's identity to a public key with a digital signature
- scheduling expiration dates for certificates
- ensuring that certificates are revoked when necessary by publishing certificate revocation lists

The functions of a certificate authority can be done in-house or by a commercial service or a trusted third party.

PKI also involves a registration authority that acts as an interface between a user and a certificate authority. The registration authority captures and authenticates the identity of a user and then submits a certificate request to the appropriate certificate authority. In this sense, the registration authority is much like the U.S. Postal Service; the Postal Service acts as an agent of the U.S. State Department to enable U.S. citizens to obtain passports (official U.S. authentication) by providing the appropriate forms, verifying identity, and requesting the actual passport (akin to a certificate) from the appropriate passport-issuing office (the certificate authority). As with passports, the quality of registration authority determines the level of trust that can be placed in the certificates that are issued.

PKI efforts are under way in many countries to enable companies and government agencies to implement PKI and interoperate. For example, a Federal PKI Initiative in the United States will eventually allow any U.S. government agency to send secure communication to any other U.S. government agency, when appropriate. The initiative also specifies how commercial PKI-enabled tools should operate, so agencies can buy ready-made PKI products rather than build their own. Sidebar 7-7 describes the commercial use of PKI in a major U.K. bank. Major PKI solutions vendors include Baltimore Technologies, Northern Telecom/Entrust, and Identrus.

Sidebar 7-7 Using PKI at Lloyd's Bank

Lloyd's TSB is a savings bank based in the United Kingdom. With 16 million customers and over 2,000 branches, Lloyd's has 1.2 million registered Internet customers. In fact, *lloydstsb.com* is the most visited financial web site in the United Kingdom. [ACT02] In 2002, Lloyd's implemented a pilot project using smart cards for online banking services. Called the Key Online Banking (KOB) program, it is the first large-scale deployment of smart-card-based PKI for Internet banking. Market research revealed that 75 percent of the bank's clients found appealing the enhanced security offered by KOB.

To use KOB, customers will insert the smart card into an ATM-like device and then supply a unique PIN. Thus, authentication is a two-step approach required before any financial transaction can be conducted. The smart card contains PKI key pairs and digital certificates. When the customer is finished, he or she logs out and removes the smart card to end the banking session.

According to Alan Woods, Lloyd's TSB's business banking director of distribution, "The beauty of the Key Online Banking solution is that it reduces the risk of a business' digital identity credentials from being exposed. This is because—unlike standard PKI systems—the user's private key is not kept on their desktop but is issued, stored, and revoked on the smart card itself. This Key Online Banking smart card is kept with the user at all times."

The benefits of this system are clear to customers, who can transact their business more securely. But the bank has an added benefit as well. The use of PKI protects issuing banks and financial institutions against liability under U.K. law.

Most PKI processes use certificates that bind identity to a key. But research is being done to expand the notion of certificate to a broader characterization of credentials. For instance, a credit card company may be more interested in verifying your financial status than your identity; a PKI scheme may involve a certificate that is based on binding the financial status with a key. The Simple Distributed Security Infrastructure (SDSI) takes this approach, including identity certificates, group membership certificates, and name-binding certificates. As of this writing, there are drafts of two related standards: ANSI standard X9.45 and the Simple Public Key Infrastructure (SPKI); the latter has only a set of requirements and a certificate format.

PKI is not yet a mature process. Many issues must be resolved, especially since PKI has yet to be implemented on a large scale. Table 7-6 lists several issues to be addressed as we learn more about PKI. However, some things have become clear. First, the certificate authority should be approved and verified by an independent body. The certificate authority's private key should be stored in a tamper-resistant security module. Then, access to the certificate and registration authorities should be tightly controlled, by means of strong user authentication such as smart cards.

The security involved in protecting the certificates involves administrative procedures. For example, more than one operator should be required to authorize certification requests. Controls should be put in place to detect hackers and prevent them from

TABLE 7-6 Issues Relating to PKI.

Issue	Questions
Flexibility	How do we implement interoperability and stay consistent with other PKI implementations? • Open, standard interfaces? • Compatible security policies? How do we register certificates? • Face-to-face, e-mail, web, network? • Single or batch (e.g., national identity cards, bank cards)?
Ease of use	How do we train people to implement, use, maintain PKI? How do we configure and integrate PKI? How do we incorporate new users? How do we do backup and disaster recovery?
Support for security policy	How does PKI implement an organization's security policy? Who has which responsibilities?
Scalability	How do we add more users? Add more applications? Add more certificate authorities? Add more registration authorities? How do we expand certificate types? How do we expand registration mechanisms?

issuing bogus certificate requests. These controls might include digital signatures and strong encryption. Finally, a secure audit trail is necessary for reconstructing certificate information should the system fail and for recovering if a hacking attack does indeed corrupt the authentication process.

SSH Encryption

SSH (secure shell) is a pair of protocols (versions 1 and 2), originally defined for Unix but also available under Windows 2000, that provides an authenticated and encrypted path to the shell or operating system command interpreter. Both SSH versions replace Unix utilities such as Telnet, rlogin, and rsh for remote access. SSH protects against spoofing attacks and modification of data in communication.

The SSH protocol involves negotiation between local and remote sites for encryption algorithm (for example, DES, IDEA, AES) and authentication (including public key and Kerberos).

SSL Encryption

The **SSL (Secure Sockets Layer)** protocol was originally designed by Netscape to protect communication between a web browser and server. It is also known now as **TLS,** for **transport layer security**. SSL interfaces between applications (such as browsers) and the TCP/IP protocols to provide server authentication, optional client authentication, and an encrypted communications channel between client and server. Client and server negotiate a mutually supported suite of encryption for session encryption and hashing; possibilities include triple DES and SHA1, or RC4 with a 128-bit key and MD5.

To use SSL, the client requests an SSL session. The server responds with its public key certificate so that the client can determine the authenticity of the server. The client returns part of a symmetric session key encrypted under the server's public key. Both the server and client compute the session key, and then they switch to encrypted communication, using the shared session key.

The protocol is simple but effective, and it is the most widely used secure communication protocol on the Internet.

IPSec

As noted previously, the address space for the Internet is running out. As domain names and equipment proliferate, the original, 30-year old, 32-bit address structure of the Internet is filling up. A new structure, called **IPv6** (version 6 of the IP protocol suite), solves the addressing problem. This restructuring also offered an excellent opportunity for the Internet Engineering Task Force (IETF) to address serious security requirements.

As a part of the IPv6 suite, the IETF adopted **IPSec**, or the **IP Security Protocol Suite**. Designed to address fundamental shortcomings such as being subject to spoofing, eavesdropping, and session hijacking, the IPSec protocol defines a standard means for handling encrypted data. IPSec is implemented at the IP layer, so it affects all layers above it, in particular TCP and UDP. Therefore, IPSec requires no change to the existing large number of TCP and UDP protocols.

IPSec is somewhat similar to SSL, in that it supports authentication and confidentiality in a way that does not necessitate significant change either above it (in applications) or below it (in the TCP protocols). Like SSL, it was designed to be independent of specific cryptographic protocols and to allow the two communicating parties to agree on a mutually supported set of protocols.

The basis of IPSec is what is called a **security association**, which is essentially the set of security parameters for a secured communication channel. It is roughly comparable to an SSL session. A security association includes

- encryption algorithm and mode (for example, DES in block chaining mode)
- encryption key
- encryption parameters, such as the initialization vector
- authentication protocol and key
- lifespan of the association, to permit long-running sessions to select a new cryptographic key as often as needed
- address of the opposite end of association
- sensitivity level of protected data (usable for classified data)

A host, such as a network server or a firewall, might have several security associations in effect for concurrent communications with different remote hosts. A security association is selected by a **security parameter index (SPI)**, a data element that is essentially a pointer into a table of security associations.

The fundamental data structures of IPSec are the **AH (authentication header)** and the **ESP (encapsulated security payload)**. The ESP replaces (includes) the conventional TCP header and data portion of a packet, as shown in Figure 7-28. The physical

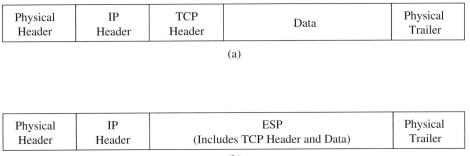

Physical Header	IP Header	TCP Header	Data	Physical Trailer

(a)

Physical Header	IP Header	ESP (Includes TCP Header and Data)	Physical Trailer

(b)

FIGURE 7-28 Packets: (a) Conventional Packet; (b) IPSec Packet.

header and trailer depend on the data link and physical layer communications medium, such as Ethernet.

The ESP contains both an authenticated portion and an encrypted portion, as shown in Figure 7-29. The sequence number is incremented by one for each packet transmitted to the same address using the same SPI, to preclude packet replay attacks. The payload data is the actual data of the packet. Because some encryption or other security mechanisms require blocks of certain sizes, the padding factor and padding length

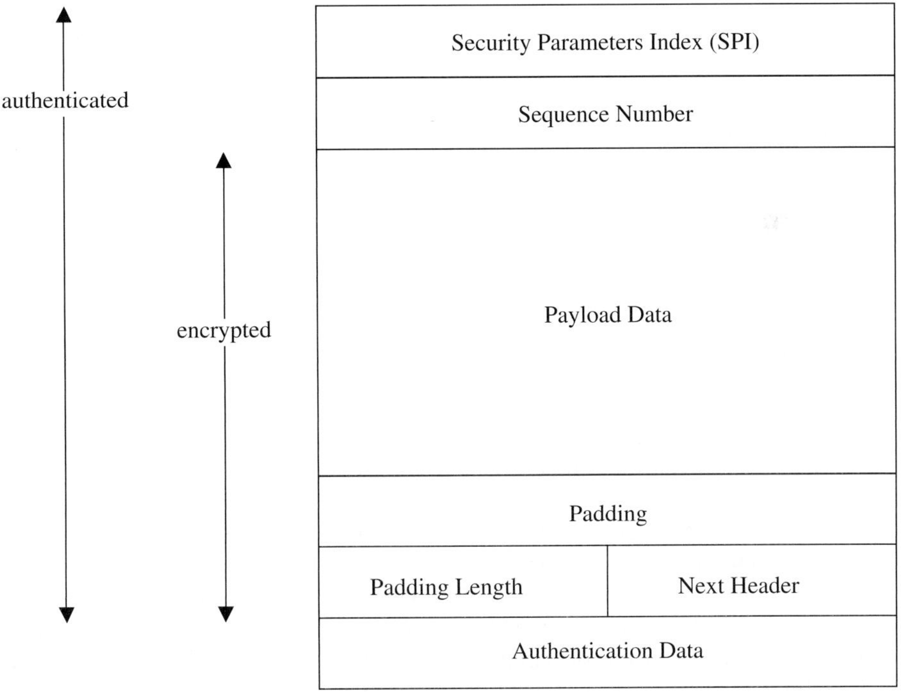

FIGURE 7-29 Encapsulated Security Packet.

fields contain padding and the amount of padding to bring the payload data to an appropriate length. The next header indicates the type of payload data. The authentication field is used for authentication of the entire object.

As with most cryptographic applications, the critical element is key management. IPSec addresses this need with **ISAKMP** or **Internet Security Association Key Management Protocol**. Like SSL, ISAKMP requires that a distinct key be generated for each security association. The ISAKMP protocol is simple, flexible, and scalable. In IPSec, ISAKMP is implemented through **IKE** or ISAKMP **key exchange**. IKE provides a way to agree on and manage protocols, algorithms, and keys. IKE uses the Diffie–Hellman scheme for key exchange. In Diffie–Hellman, each of the two parties to the key exchange chooses a large prime and sends a number g raised to the power of the prime to the other. That is, one sends g^x and the other sends g^y. They both raise what they receive to the power they kept: Y raises g^x to $(g^x)^y$ and X raises g^y to $(g^y)^x$, which are both the same; voilà, they share a secret $(g^x)^y = (g^y)^x$. (The computation is slightly more complicated, being done in a finite field $mod(n)$, which makes this a public key algorithm.) With that secret, the two parties now exchange identities and certificates to authenticate those identities. Finally, they derive a shared cryptographic key and enter a security association.

The key exchange is very efficient: The exchange can be accomplished in two messages, with an optional two more messages for authentication. Because this is a public key method, only two keys are needed for each pair of communicating parties. IKE has submodes for authentication (initiation) and for establishing new keys in an existing security association.

IPSec can be used to establish cryptographic sessions with many purposes, including VPNs, applications, and lower-level network management (such as routing). The protocols of IPSec have been published and extensively scrutinized. Work on the protocols began in 1992. They were first published in 1995, and they were finalized in 1998 (RFCs 2401–2409). [KEN98]

Signed Code

As we have seen, someone can place malicious active code on a web site to be downloaded by unsuspecting users. Running with the privilege of whoever downloads it, such active code can do serious damage, from deleting files to sending e-mail messages to fetching Trojan horses to performing subtle and hard-to-detect mischief. Today's trend is to allow applications and updates to be downloaded from central sites, so the risk of downloading something malicious is growing.

A partial—not complete—approach to reducing this risk is to use **signed code**. A trustworthy third party appends a digital signature to a piece of code, supposedly connoting more trustworthy code. A signature structure in a PKI helps to validate the signature.

Who might the trustworthy party be? A well-known manufacturer would be recognizable as a code signer. But what of the small and virtually unknown manufacturer of a device driver or a code add-in? If the code vendor is unknown, it does not help that the vendor signs its own code; miscreants can post their own signed code, too.

Note, however, that in March 2001, Verisign announced it had erroneously issued two code-signing certificates under the name of Microsoft Corp. to someone who purported to be—but was not—a Microsoft employee. These certificates were in circulation for almost two months before the error was detected. Even after Verisign detected the error and cancelled the certificates, someone would know the certificates had been revoked only by checking Verisign's list. Most people would not question a code download signed by Microsoft.

Encrypted E-Mail

An electronic mail message is much like the back of a post card. The mail carrier (and everyone in the postal system through whose hands the card passes) can read not just the address but also everything in the message field. To protect the privacy of the message and routing information, we can use encryption to protect the confidentiality of the message and perhaps its integrity.

As we have seen in several other applications, the encryption is the easy part; key management is the more difficult issue. The two dominant approaches to key management are using a hierarchical, certificate-based PKI solution for key exchange and using a flat, individual-to-individual exchange method. The hierarchical method is called S/MIME and is employed by many commercial mail handling programs, such as Microsoft Exchange or Eudora. The individual method is called PGP and is a commercial add-on. We look more carefully at encrypted e-mail in a later section of this chapter.

Content Integrity

Content integrity comes as a bonus with cryptography. No one can change encrypted data in a meaningful way without breaking the encryption. This does not say, however, that encrypted data cannot be modified. Changing even one bit of an encrypted data stream will affect the result after decryption, often in a way that seriously alters the resulting plaintext. We need to consider three potential threats:

- malicious modification that changes content in a meaningful way
- malicious or nonmalicious modification that changes content in a way that is not necessarily meaningful
- nonmalicious modification that changes content in a way that will not be detected

Encryption addresses the first of these threats very effectively. To address the others, we can use other controls.

Error Correcting Codes

We can use **error detection** and **error correction codes** to guard against modification in a transmission. The codes work as their names imply: Error detection codes detect when an error has occurred, and error correction codes can actually correct errors without requiring retransmission of the original message. The error code is transmitted along with the original data, so the recipient can recompute the error code and check whether the received result matches the expected value.

The simplest error detection code is a **parity check**. An extra bit is added to an existing group of data bits depending on their sum or an exclusive OR. The two kinds of parity are called even and odd. With **even parity** the extra bit is 0 if the sum of the data bits is even and 1 if the sum is odd; that is, the parity bit is set so that the sum of all data bits plus the parity bit is even. **Odd parity** is the same except the sum is odd. For example, the data stream 01101101 would have an even parity bit of 1 (and an odd parity bit of 0) because 0+1+1+0+1+1+0+1 = 5 + 1 = 6 (or 5 + 0 = 5 for odd parity). A parity bit can reveal the modification of a single bit. However, parity does not detect two-bit errors—cases in which two bits in a group are changed. That is, the use of a parity bit relies on the assumption that single-bit errors will occur infrequently, so it is very unlikely that two bits would be changed. Parity signals only that a bit has been changed; it does not identify which bit has been changed.

There are other kinds of error detection codes, such as **hash codes** and **Huffman codes**. Some of the more complex codes can detect multiple-bit errors (two or more bits changed in a data group) and may be able to pinpoint which bits have been changed.

Parity and simple error detection and correction codes are used to detect nonmalicious changes in situations in which there may be faulty transmission equipment, communications noise and interference, or other sources of spurious changes to data.

Cryptographic Checksum

Malicious modification must be handled in a way that prevents the attacker from modifying the error detection mechanism as well as the data bits themselves. One way to do this is to use a technique that shrinks and transforms the data, according to the value of the data bits.

To see how such an approach might work, consider an error detection code as a many-to-one transformation. That is, any error detection code reduces a block of data to a smaller digest whose value depends on each bit in the block. The proportion of reduction (that is, the ratio of original size of the block to transformed size) relates to the code's effectiveness in detecting errors. If a code reduces an eight-bit data block to a one-bit result, then half of the 2^8 input values map to 0 and half to 1, assuming a uniform distribution of outputs. In other words, there are $2^8/2 = 2^7 = 128$ different bit patterns that all produce the same one-bit result. The fewer inputs that map to a particular output, the fewer ways the attacker can change an input value without affecting its output. Thus, a one-bit result is too weak for many applications. If the output is three bits instead of one, then each output result comes from $2^8/2^3$ or $2^5 = 32$ inputs. The smaller number of inputs to a given output is important for blocking malicious modification.

A **cryptographic checksum** (sometimes called a **message digest**) is a cryptographic function that produces a checksum. The cryptography prevents the attacker from changing the data block (the plaintext) and also changing the checksum value (the ciphertext) to match.

Strong Authentication

As we have seen in earlier chapters, operating systems and database management systems enforce a security policy that specifies who—which individuals, groups, subjects—can access which resources and objects. Central to that policy is authentication: knowing and being assured of the accuracy of identities.

Networked environments need authentication, too. In the network case, however, authentication may be more difficult to achieve securely because of the possibility of eavesdropping and wiretapping, which are less common in nonnetworked environments. Also, both ends of a communication may need to be authenticated to each other: Before you send your password across a network, you want to know that you are really communicating with the remote host you expect. Lampson [LAM00] presents the problem of authentication in autonomous, distributed systems; the real problem, he points out, is how to develop trust of network entities with whom you have no basis for a relationship. Let us look more closely at authentication methods appropriate for use in networks.

One-Time Password

The wiretap threat implies that a password could be intercepted from a user who enters a password across an unsecured network. A one-time password can guard against wiretapping and spoofing of a remote host.

As the name implies, a **one-time password** is good for one use only. To see how it works, consider the easiest case, in which the user and host both have access to identical lists of passwords, like the one-time pad for cryptography from Chapter 2. The user would enter the first password for the first login, the next one for the next login, and so forth. As long as the password lists remained secret and as long as no one could guess one password from another, a password obtained through wiretapping would be useless. However, as with the one-time cryptographic pads, humans have trouble maintaining these password lists.

To address this problem, we can use a **password token,** a device that generates a password that is unpredictable but that can be validated on the receiving end. The simplest form of password token is a synchronous one, such as the SecurID device from Security Dynamics. This device displays a random number, generating a new number every minute. Each user is issued a different device (that generates a different key sequence). The user reads the number from the device's display and types it in as a one-time password. The computer on the receiving end executes the algorithm to generate the password appropriate for the current minute; if the user's password matches the one computed remotely, the user is authenticated. Because the devices may get out of alignment if one clock runs slightly faster than the other, these devices use fairly natural rules to account for minor drift.

What are the advantages and disadvantages of this approach? First, it is easy to use. It largely counters the possibility of a wiretapper reusing a password. With a strong password-generating algorithm, it is immune to spoofing. However, the system fails if the user loses the generating device or, worse, if the device falls into an attacker's hands. Because a new password is generated only once a minute, there is a small (one minute) window of vulnerability during which an eavesdropper can reuse an intercepted password.

Challenge–Response Systems

To counter the loss and reuse problems, a more sophisticated one-time password scheme uses challenge and response, as we first studied in Chapter 4. A challenge and response device looks like a simple pocket calculator. The user first authenticates to the device, usually by means of a PIN. The remote system sends a random number, called the "challenge," which the user enters into the device. The device responds to that number with another number, which the user then transmits to the system.

The system prompts the user with a new challenge for each use. Thus, this device eliminates the small window of vulnerability in which a user could reuse a time-sensitive authenticator. A generator that falls into the wrong hands is useless without the PIN. However, the user must always have the response generator to log in, and a broken device denies service to the user. Finally, these devices do not address the possibility of a rogue remote host.

Digital Distributed Authentication

In the 1980s, Digital Equipment Corporation recognized the problem of needing to authenticate nonhuman entities in a computing system. For example, a process might retrieve a user query, which it then reformats, perhaps limits, and submits to a database manager. Both the database manager and the query processor want to be sure that a particular communication channel is authentic between the two. Neither of these servers is running under the direct control or supervision of a human (although each process was, of course, somehow initiated by a human). Human forms of access control are thus inappropriate.

Digital [GAS89, GAS90] created a simple architecture for this requirement, effective against the following threats:

- *impersonation* of a server by a rogue process, for either of the two servers involved in the authentication
- *interception or modification* of data exchanged between servers
- *replay* of a previous authentication

The architecture assumes that each server has its own private key and that the corresponding public key is available to or held by every other process that might need to establish an authenticated channel. To begin an authenticated communication between server A and server B, A sends a request to B, encrypted under B's public key. B decrypts the request and replies with a message encrypted under A's public key. To avoid replay, A and B can append a random number to the message to be encrypted.

A and B can establish a private channel by one of them choosing an encryption key (for a secret key algorithm) and sending it to the other in the authenticating message. Once the authentication is complete, all communication under that secret key can be assumed to be as secure as was the original dual public key exchange. To protect the privacy of the channel, Gasser recommends a separate cryptographic processor, such as a smart card, so that private keys are never exposed outside the processor.

Two implementation difficulties remain to be solved: (a) How can a potentially large number of public keys be distributed and (b) how can the public keys be distributed in a way that ensures the secure binding of a process with the key? Digital recognized that a key server (perhaps with multiple replications) was necessary to distribute keys. The second difficulty is addressed with certificates and a certification hierarchy, as described in Chapter 2.

Both of these design decisions are to a certain degree implied by the nature of the rest of the protocol. A different approach was taken by Kerberos, as we see in the following sections.

Kerberos

Kerberos is a system that supports authentication in distributed systems. Originally designed to work with secret key encryption, Kerberos, in its latest version, uses public key technology to support key exchange. The Kerberos system was designed at Massachusetts Institute of Technology. [STE88, KOH93]

Kerberos is used for authentication between intelligent processes, such as client-to-server tasks, or a user's workstation to other hosts. Kerberos is based on the idea that a central server provides authenticated tokens, called **tickets**, to requesting applications. A ticket is an unforgeable, nonreplayable, authenticated object. That is, it is an encrypted data structure naming a user and a service that user is allowed to obtain. It also contains a time value and some control information.

The first step in using Kerberos is to establish a session with the Kerberos server, as shown in Figure 7-30. A user's workstation sends the user's identity to the Kerberos server when a user logs in. The Kerberos server verifies that the user is authorized. The Kerberos server sends two messages:

1. to the user's workstation, a session key S_G for use in communication with the ticket-granting server (G) and a ticket T_G for the ticket-granting server; S_G is encrypted under the user's password: $E(S_G + T_G, pw)$[4]
2. to the ticket-granting server, a copy of the session key S_G and the identity of the user (encrypted under a key shared between the Kerberos server and the ticket-granting server)

If the workstation can decrypt $E(S_G + T_G, pw)$ using pw, the password typed by the user, then the user has succeeded in an authentication with the workstation.

Notice that passwords are stored at the Kerberos server, *not* at the workstation, and that the user's password did not have to be passed across the network, even in encrypted form. Holding passwords centrally but not passing them across the network is a security advantage.

Next, the user will want to exercise some other services of the distributed system, such as accessing a file. Using the key S_G provided by the Kerberos server, the user U requests a ticket to access file F from the ticket-granting server. As shown in Figure 7-31, after the ticket-granting server verifies U's access permission, it returns a ticket and a session key. The ticket contains U's authenticated identity (in the ticket U obtained from the Kerberos server), an identification of F (the file to be accessed), the access rights (for example, to read), a session key S_F for the file server to use while communicating this file to U, and an expiration date for the ticket. The ticket is encrypted under a key shared exclusively between the ticket-granting server and the file server. This ticket cannot be read, modified, or forged by the user U (or anyone else). The ticket-

[4] In Kerberos version 5, only S_G is encrypted; in Kerberos version 4, both the session key and the ticket were encrypted when returned to the user.

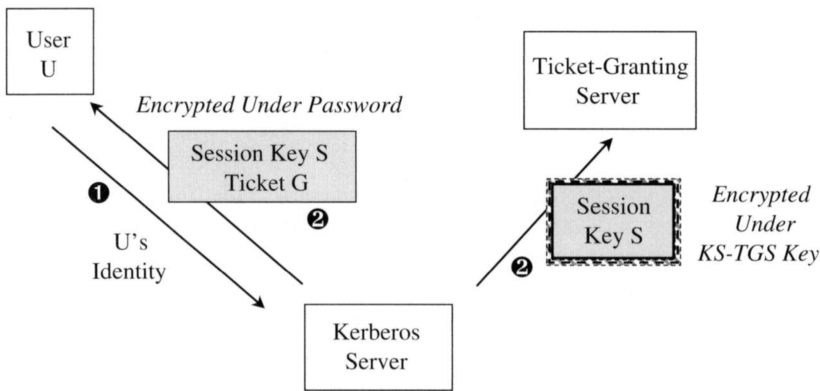

FIGURE 7-30 Initiating a Kerberos Session.

granting server must, therefore, also provide U with a copy of S_F, the session key for the file server. Requests for access to other services and servers are handled similarly.

Kerberos was carefully designed to withstand attacks in distributed environments:

- *No passwords communicated on the network*. As already described, a user's password is stored only at the Kerberos server. The user's password is not sent from the user's workstation when the user initiates a session. (Obviously, a user's initial password must be sent outside the network, such as in a letter.)
- *Cryptographic protection against spoofing*. Each access request is mediated by the ticket-granting server, which knows the identity of the requester, based on the authentication performed initially by the Kerberos server and on the fact that the user was able to present a request encrypted under a key that had been encrypted under the user's password.

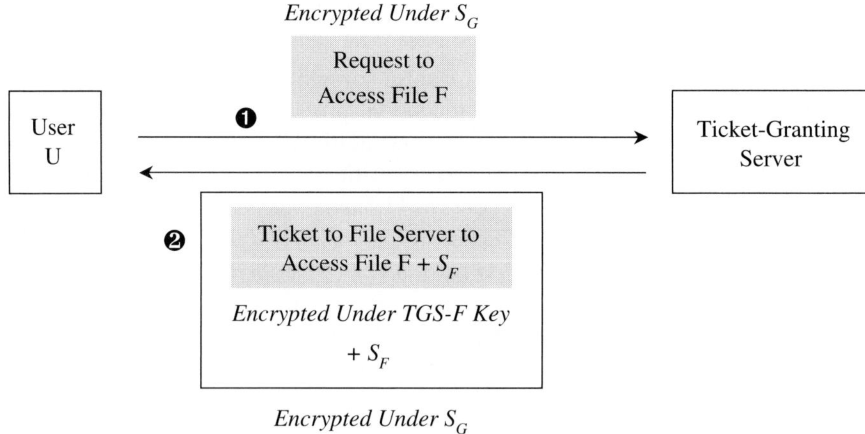

FIGURE 7-31 Obtaining a Ticket to Access a File.

- *Limited period of validity.* Each ticket is issued for a limited time period; the ticket contains a timestamp with which a receiving server will determine the ticket's validity. In this way, certain long-term attacks, such as brute force cryptanalysis, will usually be neutralized because the attacker will not have time to complete the attack.
- *Timestamps to prevent replay attacks.* Kerberos requires reliable access to a universal clock. Each user's request to a server is stamped with the time of the request. A server receiving a request will compare this time to the current time and fulfill the request only if the time is reasonably close to the current time. This time-checking prevents most replay attacks, since the attacker's presentation of the ticket will be delayed too long.
- *Mutual authentication.* The user of a service can be assured of any server's authenticity by requesting an authenticating response from the server. The user sends a ticket to a server and then sends the server a request encrypted under the session key for that server's service; the ticket and the session key were provided by the ticket-granting server. The server can decrypt the ticket only if it has the unique key it shares with the ticket-granting server. Inside the ticket is the session key, which is the only means the server has of decrypting the user's request. If the server can return to the user a message encrypted under this same session key but containing 1 + the user's timestamp, the server must be authentic. Because of this mutual authentication, a server can provide a unique channel to a user and the user may not need to encrypt communications on that channel to ensure continuous authenticity. Avoiding encryption saves time in the communication.

Kerberos is not a perfect answer to security problems in distributed systems.

- *Kerberos requires continuous availability of a trusted ticket-granting server.* Because the ticket-granting server is the basis of access control and authentication, constant access to that server is crucial. Both reliability (hardware or software failure) and performance (capacity and speed) problems must be addressed.
- *Authenticity of servers requires a trusted relationship between the ticket-granting server and every server.* The ticket-granting server must share a unique encryption key with each "trustworthy" server. The ticket-granting server (or that server's human administrator) must be convinced of the authenticity of that server. In a local environment, this degree of trust is warranted. In a widely distributed environment, an administrator at one site can seldom justify trust in the authenticity of servers at other sites.
- *Kerberos requires timely transactions.* To prevent replay attacks, Kerberos limits the validity of a ticket. A replay attack could succeed during the period of validity, however. And setting the period fairly is hard: Too long increases the exposure to replay attacks, while too short requires prompt user actions and risks providing the user with a ticket that will not be honored when presented to a server. Similarly, subverting a server's clock allows reuse of an expired ticket.
- *A subverted workstation can save and later replay user passwords.* This vulnerability exists in any system in which passwords, encryption keys, or other

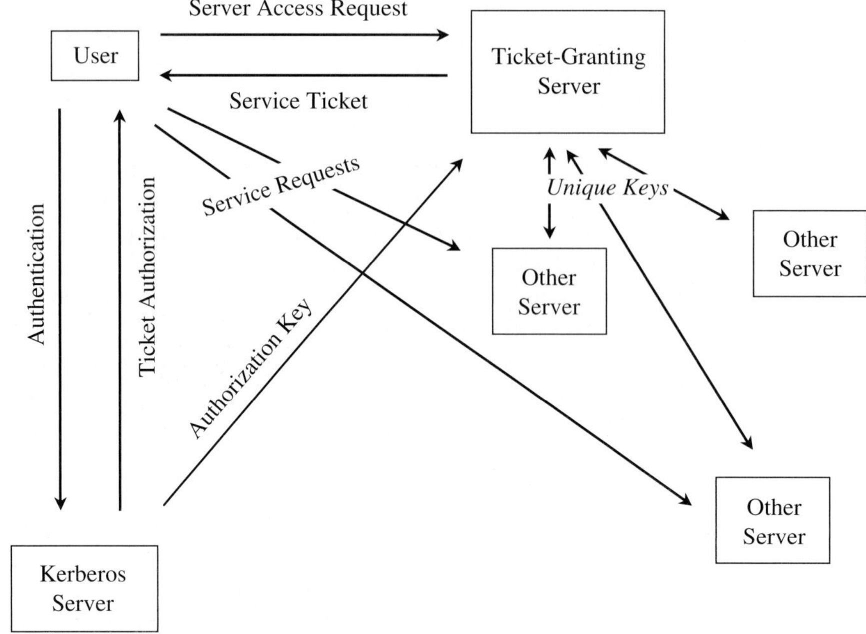

FIGURE 7-32 Access to Services and Servers in Kerberos.

constant, sensitive information is entered in the clear on a workstation that might be subverted.

- *Password guessing works.* A user's initial ticket is returned under the user's password. An attacker can submit an initial authentication request to the Kerberos server and then try to decrypt the response by guessing at the password.
- *Kerberos does not scale well.* The architectural model of Kerberos, shown in Figure 7-32, assumes one Kerberos server and one ticket-granting server, plus a collection of other servers, each of which shares a unique key with the ticket-granting server. Adding a second ticket-granting server, for example, to enhance performance or reliability, would require duplicate keys or a second set for all servers. Duplication increases the risk of exposure and complicates key updates, and second keys more than double the work for each server to act on a ticket.
- *Kerberos is a complete solution.* All applications must use Kerberos authentication and access control. Currently, few applications use Kerberos authentication, and so integration of Kerberos into an existing environment requires modification of existing applications, which is not feasible.

Access Controls

Authentication deals with the *who* of security policy enforcement; access controls enforce the *what* and *how*.

ACLs on Routers

Routers perform the major task of directing network traffic either to subnetworks they control or to other routers for subsequent delivery to other subnetworks. Routers convert external IP addresses into internal MAC addresses of hosts on a local subnetwork.

Suppose a host is being spammed (flooded) with packets from a malicious rogue host. Routers can be configured with access control lists to deny access to particular hosts from particular hosts. So, a router could delete all packets with a source address of the rogue host and a destination address of the target host.

This approach has three problems, however. First, routers in large networks perform a lot of work: They have to handle every packet coming into and going out of the network. Adding ACLs to the router requires the router to compare every packet against the ACLs. One ACL adds work, degrading the router's performance; as more ACLs are added, the router's performance may become unacceptable. The second problem is also an efficiency issue: Because of the volume of work they perform, routers are designed to perform only essential services. Logging of activity is usually not done on a router because of the volume of traffic and the performance penalty logging would entail. With ACLs, it would be useful to know how many packets were being deleted, to know if a particular ACL could be removed (thereby improving performance). But without logging it is impossible to know whether an ACL is being used. These two problems together imply that ACLs on routers are most effective against specific known threats but that they should not be used indiscriminately.

The final limitation on placing ACLs on routers concerns the nature of the threat. A router inspects only source and destination addresses. An attacker will usually not reveal an actual source address. To reveal the real source address would be equivalent to a bank robber's leaving his home address and a description of where he plans to store the stolen money.

Because someone can easily forge any source address on a UDP datagram, many attacks use UDP protocols with false source addresses so that the attack cannot be blocked easily by a router with an ACL. Router ACLs are useful only if the attacker sends many datagrams with the same forged source address.

In principle, a router is an excellent point of access control because it handles every packet coming into and going out of a subnetwork. In specific situations, primarily for internal subnetworks, ACLs can be used effectively to restrict certain traffic flows, for example, to ensure that only certain hosts (addresses) have access to an internal network management subnetwork. But for large-scale, general traffic screening, routers are less useful than firewalls.

Firewalls

A firewall is designed to do the screening that is less appropriate for a router to do. A router's primary function is addressing, whereas a firewall's primary function is filtering. Firewalls can also do auditing. Even more important, firewalls can examine an entire packet's contents, including the data portion, whereas a router is concerned only with source and destination MAC and IP addresses. Because they are an extremely important network security control, we study firewalls in an entire section later in this chapter.

Alarms and Alerts

The logical view of network protection looks like Figure 7-33, in which both a router and a firewall provide layers of protection for the internal network. Now let us add one more layer to this defense.

An **intrusion detection system** is a device that is placed inside a protected network to monitor what occurs within the network. If an attacker is able to pass through the router and pass through the firewall, an intrusion detection system offers the opportunity to detect the attack at the beginning, in progress, or after it has occurred. Intrusion detection systems activate an alarm, which can take defensive action. We study intrusion detection systems in more detail later in this chapter.

Honeypots

How do you catch a mouse? You set a trap with bait (food the mouse finds attractive) and catch the mouse after it is lured into the trap. You can catch a computer attacker the same way.

In a very interesting book, Cliff Stoll [STO89] details the story of attracting and monitoring the actions of an attacker. Cheswick [CHE02] and Bellovin [BEL92c] tell a similar story. These two cases describe the use of a **honeypot**: a computer system open to attackers.

You put up a honeypot for several reasons:

- to watch what attackers do, in order to learn about new attacks (so that you can strengthen your defenses against these new attacks)
- to lure an attacker to a place in which you may be able to learn enough to identify and stop the attacker
- to provide an attractive but diversionary playground, hoping that the attacker will leave your real system alone

A honeypot has no special features. It is just a computer system or a network segment, loaded with servers and devices and data. It may be protected with a firewall, although you want the attackers to have some access. There may be some monitoring capability, done carefully so that the monitoring is not evident to the attacker.

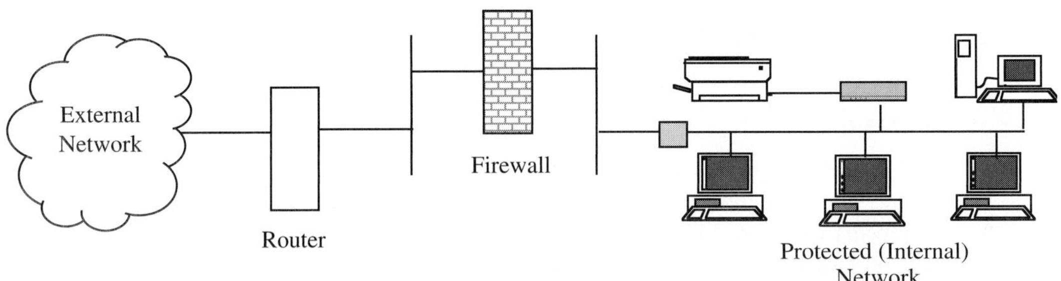

FIGURE 7-33 Layered Network Protection.

Traffic Flow Security

So far, we have looked at controls that cover the most common network threats: cryptography for eavesdropping, authentication methods for impersonation, intrusion detection systems for attacks in progress, architecture for structural flaws. Earlier in this chapter, we listed threats, including a threat of traffic flow inference. If the attacker can detect an exceptional volume of traffic between two points, the attacker may infer the location of an event about to occur.

The countermeasure to traffic flow threats is to disguise the traffic flow. One way to disguise traffic flow, albeit costly and perhaps crude, is to ensure a steady volume of traffic between two points. If traffic between A and B is encrypted so that the attacker can detect only the number of packets flowing, A and B can agree to pass recognizable (to them) but meaningless encrypted traffic. When A has much to communicate to B, there will be few meaningless packets; when communication is light, A will pad the traffic stream with many spurious packets.

A more sophisticated approach to traffic flow security is called **onion routing** [SYV97]. Consider a message that is covered in multiple layers, like the layers of an onion. A wants to send a message to B but doesn't want anyone in or intercepting traffic on the network to know A is communicating with B. So A takes the message to B, wraps it in a package for D to send to B. Then, A wraps that package in another package for C to send to D. Finally, A sends this package to C. This process is shown in Figure 7-34. The internal wrappings are all encrypted under a key appropriate for the intermediate recipient.

Receiving the package, C knows it came from A, although C does not know if A is the originator or an intermediate point. C then unwraps the outer layer and sees it should be sent to D. At this point, C cannot know if D is the final recipient or merely an intermediary. C sends the message to D, who unwraps the next layer. D knows neither where the package originally came from nor where its final destination is. D forwards the package to B, its ultimate recipient.

With this scheme, any intermediate recipients—those other than the original sender and ultimate receiver—know neither where the package originated nor where it will end up. This scheme provides confidentiality of content, source, destination, and routing.

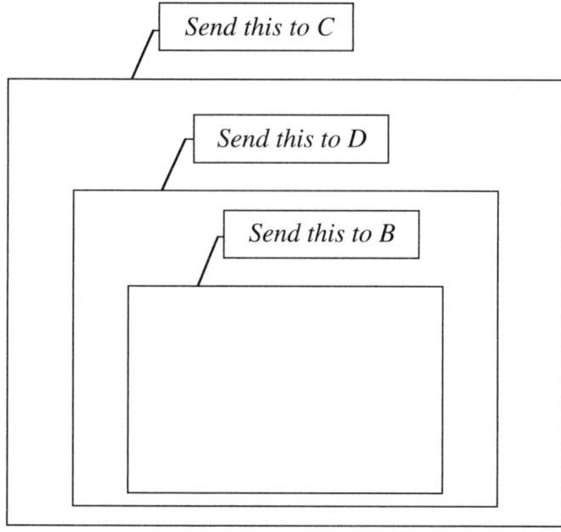

FIGURE 7-34 Onion Routing.

Controls Review

At the end of our earlier discussion on threats in networks, we listed in a table many of the vulnerabilities present in networks. Now that we have surveyed the controls available for networks, we repeat that table as Table 7-7, adding a column to show the controls that can protect against each vulnerability. (Note: This table is not exhaustive; other controls can be used against some of vulnerabilities.)

TABLE 7-7 Network Vulnerabilities and Controls.

Target	Vulnerability	Control
Precursors to attack	• Port scan	• Firewall • Intrusion detection system • Running as few services as possible • Services that reply with only what is necessary
	• Social engineering	• Education, user awareness • Policies and procedures • Systems in which two people must agree to perform certain security-critical functions
	• Reconnaissance	• Firewall • "Hardened" (self-defensive) operating system and applications • Intrusion detection system
	• OS and application fingerprinting	• Firewall • "Hardened" (self-defensive) applications • Programs that reply with only what is necessary • Intrusion detection system
Authentication failures	• Impersonation	• Strong, one-time authentication
	• Guessing	• Strong, one-time authentication • Education, user awareness
	• Eavesdropping	• Strong, one-time authentication • Encrypted authentication channel
	• Spoofing	• Strong, one-time authentication
	• Session hijacking	• Strong, one-time authentication • Encrypted authentication channel • Virtual private network
	• Man-in-the-middle attack	• Strong, one-time authentication • Virtual private network • Protocol analysis
Programming flaws	• Buffer overflow	• Programming controls • Intrusion detection system • Controlled execution environment • Personal firewall

(continued)

TABLE 7-7 Network Vulnerabilities and Controls. (Continued)

Target	Vulnerability	Control
	• Addressing errors	• Programming controls • Intrusion detection system • Controlled execution environment • Personal firewall • Two-way authentication
	• Parameter modification, time-of-check to time-of-use errors	• Programming controls • Intrusion detection system • Controlled execution environment • Intrusion detection system • Personal firewall
	• Server-side include	• Programming controls • Personal firewall • Controlled execution environment • Intrusion detection system
	• Cookie	• Firewall • Intrusion detection system • Controlled execution environment • Personal firewall
	• Malicious active code: JavaScript, ActiveX	• Intrusion detection system • Programming controls • Signed code
	• Malicious code: virus, worm, Trojan horse	• Intrusion detection system • Signed code • Controlled execution environment • Intrusion detection system
	• Malicious typed code	• Signed code • Intrusion detection system • Controlled execution environment
Confidentiality		
	• Protocol flaw	• Programming controls • Controlled execution environment
	• Eavesdropping	• Encryption
	• Passive wiretap	• Encryption
	• Misdelivery	• Encryption
	• Exposure within the network	• End-to-end encryption
	• Traffic flow analysis	• Encryption • Traffic padding • Onion routing
	• Cookie	• Firewall • Intrusion detection system • Controlled execution environment

(continued)

TABLE 7-7 Network Vulnerabilities and Controls. (Continued)

Target	Vulnerability	Control
Integrity	• Protocol flaw	• Firewall • Controlled execution environment • Intrusion detection system • Protocol analysis • Audit
	• Active wiretap	• Encryption • Error detection code • Audit
	• Impersonation	• Firewall • Strong, one-time authentication • Encryption • Error detection code • Audit
	• Falsification of message	• Firewall • Encryption • Strong authentication • Error detection code • Audit
	• Noise	• Error detection code
	• Web site defacement	• Error detection code • Intrusion detection system • Controlled execution environment • Hardened host • Honeypot • Audit
	• DNS attack	• Firewall • Intrusion detection system • Strong authentication for DNS changes • Audit
Availability	• Protocol flaw	• Firewall • Redundant architecture
	• Transmission or component failure	• Architecture
	• Connection flooding, e.g., echo-chargen, ping of death, smurf, syn flood	• Firewall • Intrusion detection system • ACL on border router • Honeypot
	• DNS attack	• Firewall • Intrusion detection system • ACL on border router • Honeypot

(continued)

TABLE 7-7 Network Vulnerabilities and Controls. (Continued)

Target	Vulnerability	Control
	• Traffic redirection	• Encryption • Audit
	• Distributed denial of service	• Firewall • Intrusion detection system • ACL on border router • Honeypot

As this table shows, network security designers have many successful tools at their disposal. Some of these, such as encryption, access control and authentication, and programming controls, are familiar from previous chapters in this book.

But three are specific to networked settings, and we explore them now in greater depth: firewalls, intrusion detection systems, and encrypted e-mail. Firewalls control traffic flow into and out of protected network segments. Intrusion detection systems monitor traffic within a network to spot potential attacks under way or about to occur. And encrypted e-mail uses encryption to enhance the confidentiality or authenticity of e-mail messages.

7.4 FIREWALLS

Firewalls were officially invented in the early 1990s, but the concept really reflects the reference monitor (described in Chapter 5) from two decades earlier. The first reference to a firewall by that name may be [RAN92]; other early references to firewalls are the Trusted Information Systems firewall toolkit [RAN94] and the book by Cheswick and Bellovin [CHE94, updated as CHE02].

What Is a Firewall?

A firewall is a device that filters all traffic between a protected or "inside" network and a less trustworthy or "outside" network. Usually a firewall runs on a dedicated device; because it is a single point through which traffic is channeled, performance is important, which means nonfirewall functions should not be done on the same machine. Because a firewall is executable code, the attacker could compromise that code and execute from the firewall's device. Thus, the fewer pieces of code on the device, the fewer tools the attacker would have by compromising the firewall. Firewall code usually runs on a proprietary or carefully minimized operating system.

The purpose of a firewall is to keep "bad" things outside a protected environment. To accomplish that, firewalls implement a security policy that is specifically designed to address what bad things might happen. For example, the policy might be to prevent any access from outside (while still allowing traffic to pass *from* the inside *to* the outside). Alternatively, the policy might permit accesses only from certain places, from certain users, or for certain activities. Part of the challenge of protecting a network with a firewall is determining which security policy meets the needs of the installation.

People in the firewall community (users, developers, and security experts) disagree about how a firewall should work. In particular, the community is divided about a firewall's default behavior. We can describe the two schools of thought as "that which is not expressly forbidden is permitted" (default permit) and "that which is not expressly permitted is forbidden" (default deny). Users, always interested in new features, prefer the former. Security experts, relying on several decades of experience, strongly counsel the latter. An administrator implementing or configuring a firewall must choose one of the two approaches, although the administrator can often broaden the policy by setting the firewall's parameters.

Design of Firewalls

Remember from Chapter 5 that a reference monitor must be

- always invoked
- tamperproof
- small and simple enough for rigorous analysis

A firewall is a special form of reference monitor. By carefully positioning a firewall within a network, we can ensure that all network accesses that we want to control must pass through it. This restriction meets the "always invoked" condition. A firewall is typically well isolated, making it highly immune to modification. Usually a firewall is implemented on a separate computer, with direct connections only to the outside and inside networks. This isolation is expected to meet the "tamperproof" requirement. And firewall designers strongly recommend keeping the functionality of the firewall simple.

Types of Firewalls

Firewalls have a wide range of capabilities. Types of firewalls include

- packet filtering gateways or screening routers
- stateful inspection firewalls
- application proxies
- guards
- personal firewalls

Each type does different things; no one is necessarily "right" and the others "wrong." In this section, we examine each type to see what it is, how it works, and what its strengths and weaknesses are. In general, screening routers tend to implement rather simplistic security policies, whereas guards and proxy gateways have a richer set of choices for security policy. Simplicity in a security policy is not a bad thing; the important question to ask when choosing a type of firewall is what threats an installation needs to counter.

Because a firewall is a type of host, it often is as programmable as a good-quality workstation. While a screening router *can* be fairly primitive, the tendency is to host even routers on complete computers with operating systems because editors and other programming tools assist in configuring and maintaining the router. However, firewall developers are minimalists: They try to eliminate from the firewall all that is not strictly necessary for the firewall's functionality. There is a good reason for this minimal constraint: to give as little assistance as possible to a successful attacker. Thus, firewalls tend not to have user accounts so that, for example, they have no password file to conceal. Indeed, the most desirable firewall is one that runs contentedly in a back room; except for periodic scanning of its audit logs, there is seldom reason to touch it.

Packet Filtering Gateway

A **packet filtering gateway** or **screening router** is the simplest, and in some situations, the most effective type of firewall. A packet filtering gateway controls access to packets based on packet address (source or destination) or specific transport protocol type (such as HTTP web traffic). As described earlier in this chapter, putting ACLs on routers may severely impede their performance. But a separate firewall behind (on the local side) of the router can screen traffic before it gets to the protected network. Figure 7-35 shows a packet filter that blocks access from (or to) addresses in one network; the filter allows HTTP traffic but blocks traffic using the Telnet protocol.

For example, suppose an international company has three LANs at three locations throughout the world, as shown in Figure 7-36. In this example, the router has two sides: inside and outside. We say that the local LAN is on the inside of the router, and the two connections to distant LANs through wide area networks are on the outside. The company might want communication *only* among the three LANs of the corporate network. It could use a screening router on the LAN at 100.24.4.0 to allow *in* only communications destined to the host at 100.24.4.0 and to allow *out* only communications addressed either to address 144.27.5.3 or 192.19.33.0.

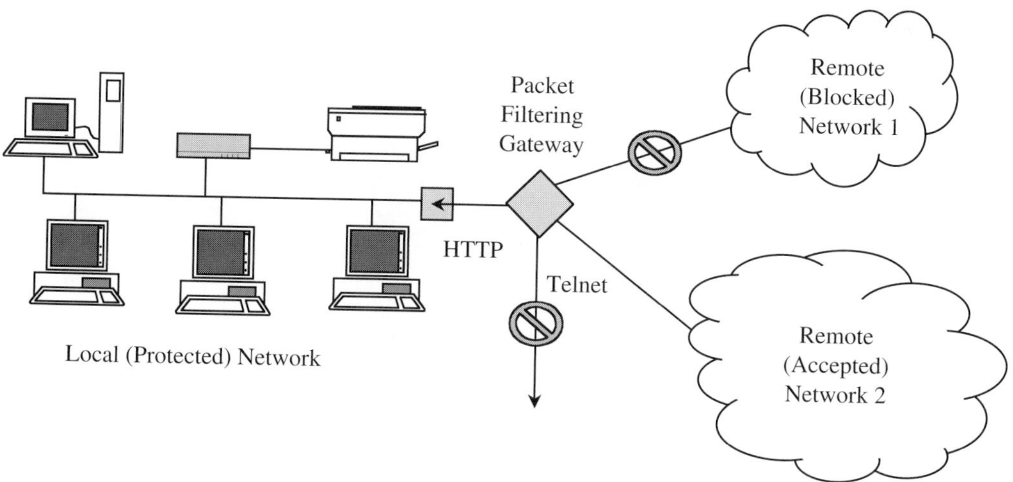

FIGURE 7-35 Packet Filter Blocking Addresses and Protocols.

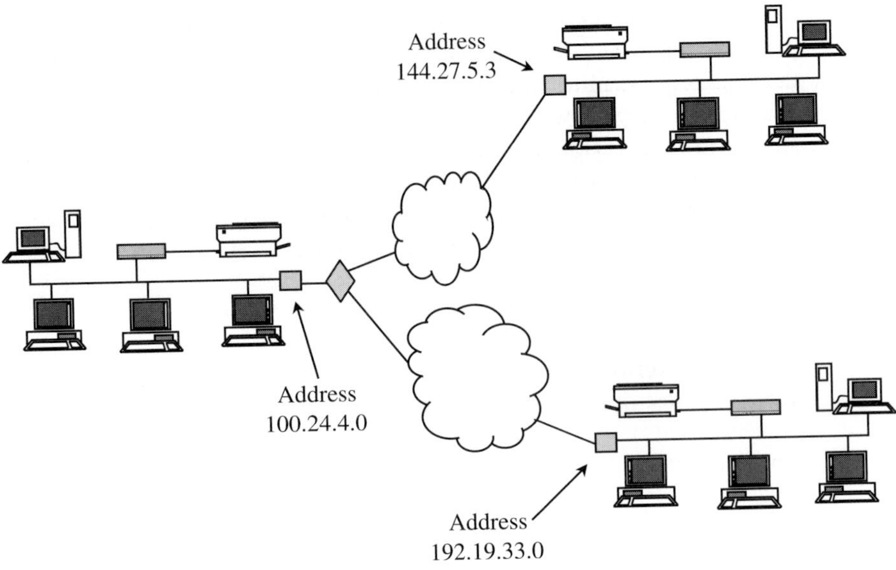

FIGURE 7-36 Three Connected LANs.

Packet filters do not "see inside" a packet; they block or accept packets solely on the basis of the IP addresses and ports. Thus, any details in the packet's data field (for example, allowing certain Telnet commands while blocking other services) is beyond the capability of a packet filter.

Packet filters can perform the very important service of ensuring the validity of inside addresses. Inside hosts typically trust other inside hosts for all the reasons described as characteristics of LANs. But the only way an inside host can distinguish another inside host is by the address shown in the source field of a message. Source addresses in packets can be forged, so an inside application might think it was communicating with another host on the inside instead of an outside forger. A packet filter sits

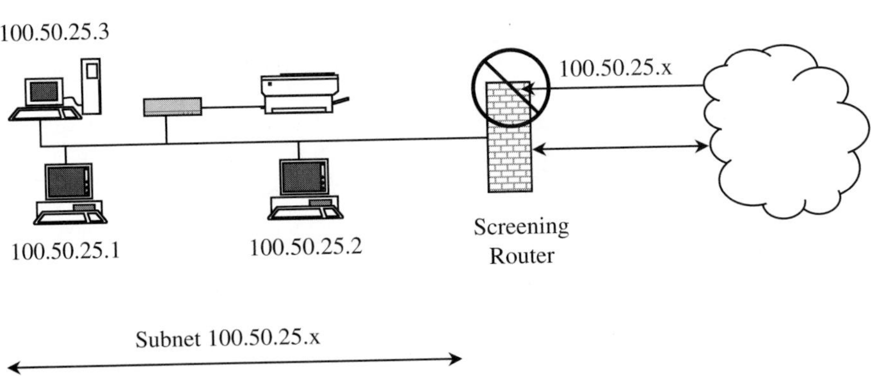

FIGURE 7-37 Filter Screening Outside Addresses.

between the inside network and the outside net, so it can know if a packet from the outside is forging an inside address, as shown in Figure 7-37. A screening packet filter might be configured to block all packets from the *outside* that claimed their source address was an *inside* address. In this example, the packet filter blocks all packets claiming to come from any address of the form 100.50.25.*x* (but, of course, it permits in any packets with *destination* 100.50.25.*x*).

The primary disadvantage of packet filtering routers is a combination of simplicity and complexity. The router's inspection is simplistic; to perform sophisticated filtering, the filtering rules set needs to be very detailed. A detailed rules set will be complex and therefore prone to error. For example, blocking all port 23 traffic (Telnet) is simple and straightforward. But if some Telnet traffic is to be allowed, each IP address from which it is allowed must be specified in the rules; in this way, the rule set can become very long.

Stateful Inspection Firewall

Filtering firewalls work on packets one at a time, accepting or rejecting each packet and moving on to the next. They have no concept of "state" or "context" from one packet to the next. A **stateful inspection firewall** maintains state information from one packet to another in the input stream.

One classic approach used by attackers is breaking an attack into multiple packets by forcing some packets to have very short lengths so that a firewall will not be able to detect the signature of an attack split across two or more packets. (Remember that with the TCP protocols, packets can arrive in any order, and the protocol suite is responsible for reassembling the packet stream in proper order before passing it along to the application.) A stateful inspection firewall would track the sequence of packets and conditions from one packet to another to thwart such an attack.

Application Proxy

Packet filters look only at the headers of packets, not at the data *inside* the packets. Therefore, a packet filter would pass anything to port 25, assuming its screening rules allow inbound connections to that port. But applications are complex and sometimes contain errors. Worse, applications (such as the e-mail delivery agent) often act on behalf of all users, so they require privileges of all users (for example, to store incoming mail messages so that inside users can read them). A flawed application, running with all users' privileges, can cause much damage.

An **application proxy gateway**, also called a **bastion host**, is a firewall that simulates the (proper) effects of an application so that the application will receive only requests to act properly. A proxy gateway is a two-headed device: It looks to the inside as if it is the outside (destination) connection, while to the outside it responds just as the insider would.

An application proxy runs pseudoapplications. For instance, when electronic mail is transferred to a location, a sending process at one site and a receiving process at the destination communicate by a protocol that establishes the legitimacy of a mail transfer and then actually transfers the mail message. The protocol between sender and destination is carefully defined. A proxy gateway essentially intrudes in the middle of this protocol exchange, seeming like a destination in communication with the sender that is outside the firewall, and seeming like the sender in communication with the real destination on the inside. The proxy in the middle has the opportunity to screen the mail transfer, ensuring that only acceptable e-mail protocol commands are sent to the destination.

As an example of application proxying, consider the FTP (file transfer) protocol. Specific protocol commands fetch (get) files from a remote location, store (put) files onto a remote host, list files (ls) in a directory on a remote host, and position the process (cd) at a particular point in a directory tree on a remote host. Some administrators might want to permit gets but block puts, and to list only certain files or prohibit changing out of a particular directory (so that an outsider could retrieve only files from a prespecified directory). The proxy would simulate both sides of this protocol exchange. For example, the proxy might accept get commands, reject put commands, and filter the local response to a request to list files.

To understand the real purpose of a proxy gateway, let us consider several examples.

- A company wants to set up an online price list so that outsiders can see the products and prices offered. It wants to be sure that (a) no outsider can change the prices or product list and (b) outsiders can access only the price list, not any of the more sensitive files stored inside.
- A school wants to allow its students to retrieve any information from World Wide Web resources on the Internet. To help provide efficient service, it wants to know what sites have been visited, and what files from those sites have been fetched; particularly popular files will be cached locally.
- A government agency wants to respond to queries through a database management system. However, because of inference attacks against databases, the agency wants to restrict queries that return the mean of a set of fewer than five values.
- A company with multiple offices wants to encrypt the data portion of all e-mail to addresses at its other offices. (A corresponding proxy at the remote end will remove the encryption.)
- A company wants to allow dial-in access by its employees, without exposing its company resources to login attacks from remote nonemployees.

Each of these requirements can be met with a proxy. In the first case, the proxy would monitor the file transfer protocol *data* to ensure that only the price list file was accessed, and that file could only be read, not modified. The school's requirement could be met by a logging procedure as part of the web browser. The agency's need could be satisfied by a special-purpose proxy that interacted with the database management system, performing queries but also obtaining the number of values from which the response was computed and adding a random minor error term to results from small sample sizes. The requirement for limited login could be handled by a specially written proxy that required strong user authentication (such as a challenge–response system), which many operating systems do not require. These functions are shown in Figure 7-38.

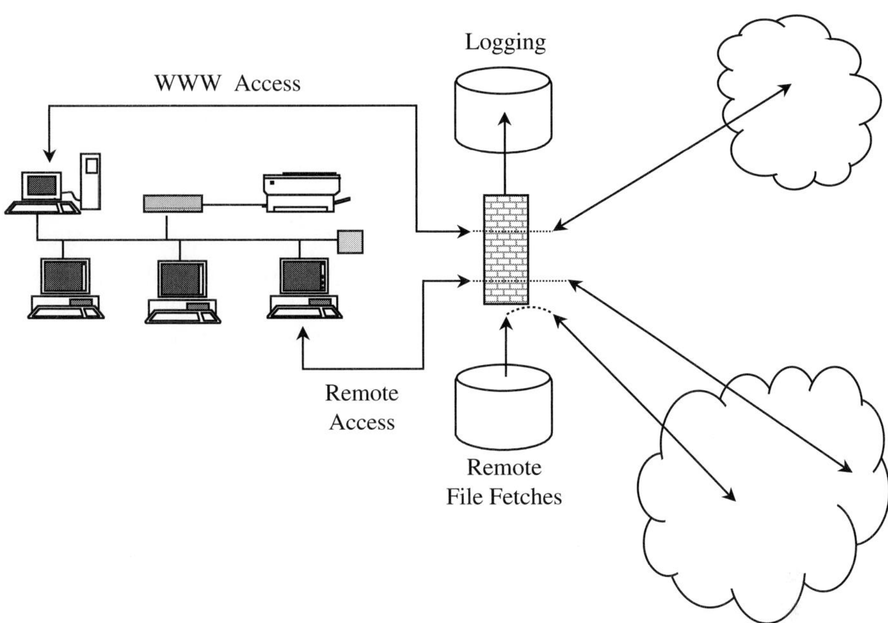

FIGURE 7-38 Actions of Firewall Proxies.

The proxies on the firewall can be tailored to specific requirements, such as logging details about accesses. They can even present a common user interface to what may be dissimilar internal functions. Suppose the internal network has a mixture of operating system types, none of which support strong authentication through a challenge–response token. The proxy can demand strong authentication (name, password, and challenge–response), validate the challenge–response itself, and then pass on only simple name and password authentication details in the form required by a specific internal host's operating system.

The distinction between a proxy and a screening router is that the proxy interprets the protocol stream to an application, to control actions through the firewall on the basis of things visible *within* the protocol, not just on external header data.

Guard

A guard is a sophisticated firewall. Like a proxy firewall, it receives protocol data units, interprets them, and passes through the same or different protocol data units that achieve either the same result or a modified result. The guard decides what services to perform on the user's behalf in accordance with its available knowledge, such as whatever it can reliably know of the (outside) user's identity, previous interactions, and so forth. The degree of control a guard can provide is limited only by what is computable. But guards and proxy firewalls are similar enough that the distinction between them is sometimes fuzzy. That is, we can add functionality to a proxy firewall until it starts to look a lot like a guard.

Guard activities can be quite sophisticated, as illustrated in the following examples:

- A university wants to allow its students to use e-mail up to a limit of so many messages or so many characters of e-mail in the last so many days. Although this result could be achieved by modifying e-mail handlers, it is more easily done by monitoring the common point through which all e-mail flows, the mail transfer protocol.
- A school wants its students to be able to access the World Wide Web but, because of the slow speed of its connection to the web, it will allow only so many characters per downloaded image (that is, allowing text mode and simple graphics, but disallowing complex graphics, animation, music, or the like).
- A library wants to make available certain documents but, to support fair use of copyrighted matter, it will allow a user to retrieve only the first so many characters of a document. After that amount, the library will require the user to pay a fee that will be forwarded to the author.
- A company wants to allow its employees to fetch files via *ftp*. However, to prevent introduction of viruses, it will first pass all incoming files through a virus scanner. Even though many of these files will be nonexecutable text or graphics, the company administrator thinks that the expense of scanning them (which should pass) will be negligible.

Each of these scenarios can be implemented as a modified proxy. Because the proxy decision is based on some quality of the communication data, we call the proxy a guard. Since the security policy implemented by the guard is somewhat more complex than the action of a proxy, the guard's code is also more complex and therefore more exposed to error. Simpler firewalls have fewer possible ways to fail or be subverted.

Personal Firewalls

Firewalls typically protect a (sub)network of multiple hosts. University students and employees in offices are behind a real firewall. Increasingly, home users, individual workers, and small businesses use cable modems or DSL connections with unlimited, always-on access. These people need a firewall, but a separate firewall computer to protect a single workstation can seem too complex and expensive. These people need a firewall's capabilities at a lower price.

A **personal firewall** is an application program that runs on a workstation to block unwanted traffic, usually from the network. A personal firewall can complement the work of a conventional firewall by screening the kind of data a single host will accept, or it can compensate for the lack of a regular firewall, as in a private DSL or cable modem connection.

Just as a network firewall screens incoming and outgoing traffic for that network, a personal firewall screens traffic on a single workstation. A workstation could be vulnerable to malicious code or malicious active agents (ActiveX or Java applets), leakage of personal data stored on the workstation, and vulnerability scans to identify potential weaknesses. Commercial implementations of personal firewalls include Norton Personal Firewall from Symantec, McAfee Personal Firewall, and Zone Alarm from Zone Labs.

The personal firewall is configured to enforce some policy. For example, the user may decide that certain sites, such as computers on the company network, are highly trustworthy, but most other sites are not. The user defines a policy permitting download of code, unrestricted data sharing, and management access from the corporate segment, but not from other sites. Personal firewalls can also generate logs of accesses, which can be useful to examine in case something harmful does slip through the firewall.

Combining a virus scanner with a personal firewall is both effective and efficient. Typically, users forget to run virus scanners daily, but they do remember to run them occasionally, such as sometime during the week. However, leaving the virus scanner execution to the user's memory means that the scanner detects a problem only after the fact—such as when a virus has been downloaded in an e-mail attachment. With the combination of a virus scanner and a personal firewall, the firewall directs all incoming e-mail to the virus scanner, which examines every attachment the moment it reaches the target host and before it is opened.

A personal firewall runs on the very computer it is trying to protect. Thus, a clever attacker is likely to attempt an undetected attack that would disable or reconfigure the firewall for the future. Still, especially for cable modem, DSL, and other "always on" connections, the static workstation is a visible and vulnerable target for an ever-present attack community. A personal firewall can provide reasonable protection to clients that are not behind a network firewall.

Comparison of Firewall Types

We can summarize the differences among the several types of firewalls we have studied in depth. The comparisons are shown in Table 7-8.

TABLE 7-8 Comparison of Firewall Types.

Packet Filtering	Stateful Inspection	Application Proxy	Guard	Personal Firewall
Simplest	More complex	Even more complex	Most complex	Similar to packet filtering firewall
Sees only addresses and service protocol type	Can see either addresses or data	Sees full data portion of packet	Sees full text of communication	Can see full data portion of packet
Auditing difficult	Auditing possible	Can audit activity	Can audit activity	Can—and usually does—audit activity
Screens based on connection rules	Screens based on information across packets—in either header or data field	Screens based on behavior of proxies	Screens based on interpretation of message content	Typically, screens based on information in a single packet, using header or data
Complex addressing rules can make configuration tricky	Usually preconfigured to detect certain attack signatures	Simple proxies can substitute for complex addressing rules	Complex guard functionality can limit assurance	Usually starts in "deny all inbound" mode, to which user adds trusted addresses as they appear

Example Firewall Configurations

Let us look at several examples to understand how to use firewalls. We present situations designed to show how a firewall complements a sensible security policy and architecture.

The simplest use of a firewall is shown in Figure 7-39. This environment has a screening router positioned between the internal LAN and the outside network connection. In many cases, this installation is adequate when we need only screen the address of a router.

However, to use a proxy machine, this organization is not ideal. Similarly, configuring a router for a complex set of approved or rejected addresses is difficult. If the firewall router is successfully attacked, then all traffic on the LAN to which the firewall is connected is visible. To reduce this exposure, a proxy firewall is often installed on its own LAN, as shown in Figure 7-40. In this way the only traffic visible on that LAN is the traffic going into and out of the firewall.

For even more protection, we can add a screening router to this configuration, as shown in Figure 7-41. Here, the screening router ensures address correctness to the proxy firewall (so that the proxy firewall cannot be fooled by an outside attacker forging an address from an inside host); the proxy firewall filters traffic according to its proxy rules. Also, if the screening router is subverted, only the traffic to the proxy firewall is visible—not any of the sensitive information on the internal protected LAN.

Although these examples are simplifications, they show the kinds of configurations firewalls protect. Next, we review the kinds of attacks against which firewalls can and cannot protect.

What Firewalls Can—and Cannot—Block

As we have seen, firewalls are not complete solutions to all computer security problems. A firewall protects only the perimeter of its environment against attacks from outsiders who want to execute code or access data on the machines in the protected environment. Keep in mind these points about firewalls.

- Firewalls can protect an environment only if the firewalls control the entire perimeter. That is, firewalls are effective only if no unmediated connections breach the perimeter. If even one inside host connects to an outside address, by a modem for example, the entire inside net is vulnerable through the modem and its host.

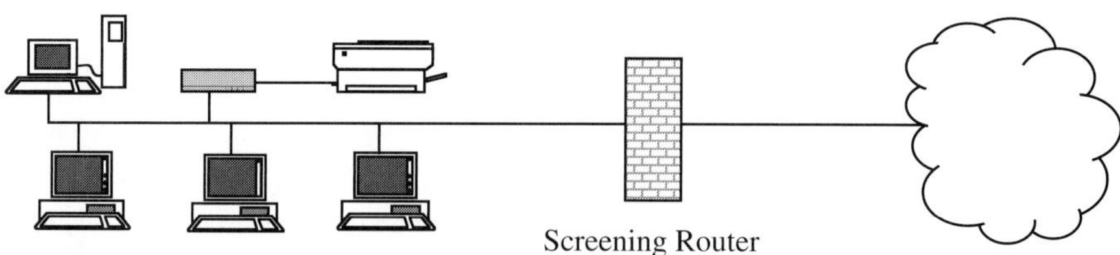

FIGURE 7-39 Firewall with Screening Router.

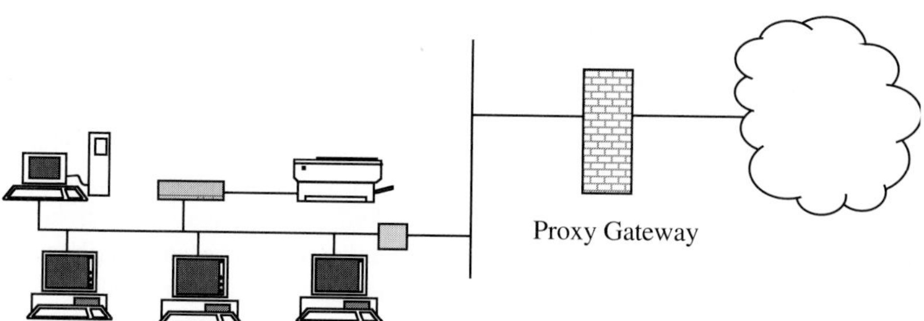

FIGURE 7-40 Firewall on Separate LAN.

- Firewalls do not protect data outside the perimeter; data that have properly passed (outbound) through the firewall are just as exposed as if there were no firewall.
- Firewalls are the most visible part of an installation to the outside, so they are the most attractive target for attack. For this reason, several different layers of protection, called **defense in depth**, are better than relying on the strength of just a single firewall.
- Firewalls must be correctly configured, that configuration must be updated as the internal and external environment changes, and firewall activity reports must be reviewed periodically for evidence of attempted or successful intrusion.
- Firewalls are targets for penetrators. While a firewall is designed to withstand attack, it is not impenetrable. Designers intentionally keep a firewall small and simple so that even if a penetrator breaks it, the firewall does not have further tools, such as compilers, linkers, loaders, and the like, to continue an attack.
- Firewalls exercise only minor control over the content admitted to the inside, meaning that inaccurate data or malicious code must be controlled by other means inside the perimeter.

Firewalls are important tools in protecting an environment connected to a network. However, the environment must be viewed as a whole, all possible exposures must be considered, and the firewall must fit into a larger, comprehensive security strategy. Firewalls alone cannot secure an environment.

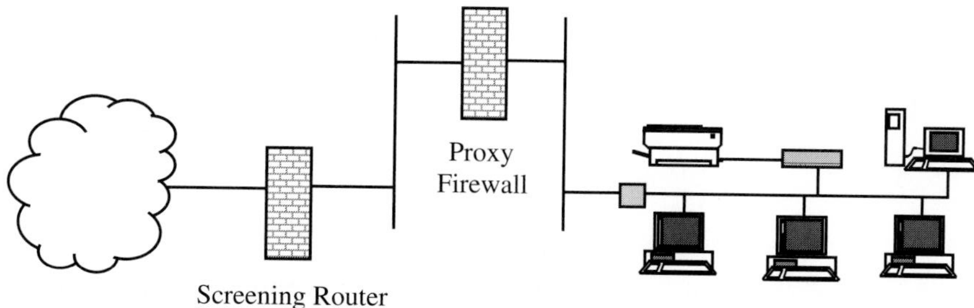

FIGURE 7-41 Firewall with Proxy and Screening Router.

7.5 INTRUSION DETECTION SYSTEMS

After the perimeter controls, firewall, and authentication and access controls block certain actions, some users are admitted to use a computing system. Most of these controls are preventive: they block known bad things from happening. Many studies (for example, see [DUR99]) have shown that most computer security incidents are caused by insiders, people who would not be blocked by a firewall. And insiders require access with significant privileges to do their daily jobs. The vast majority of harm from insiders is not malicious; it is honest people making honest mistakes. Then, too, there are the potential malicious outsiders who have somehow passed the screens of firewalls and access controls. Prevention, although necessary, is not a complete computer security control; detection during an incident copes with harm that cannot be prevented in advance. Halme and Bauer [HAL95] survey the range of controls to address intrusions.

Intrusion detection systems complement these preventive controls as the next line of defense. An **intrusion detection system (IDS)** is a device, typically another separate computer, that monitors activity to identify malicious or suspicious events. An IDS is a sensor, like a smoke detector, that raises an alarm if specific things occur. A model of an IDS is shown in Figure 7-42. The components in the figure are the four basic elements of an intrusion detection system, based on the Common Intrusion Detection Framework of [STA96]. An IDS receives raw inputs from sensors. It saves those inputs, analyzes them, and takes some controlling action.

IDSs perform a variety of functions:

- monitoring users and system activity
- auditing system configuration for vulnerabilities and misconfigurations
- assessing the integrity of critical system and data files
- recognizing known attack patterns in system activity
- identifying abnormal activity through statistical analysis
- managing audit trails and highlighting user violation of policy or normal activity
- correcting system configuration errors
- installing and operating traps to record information about intruders

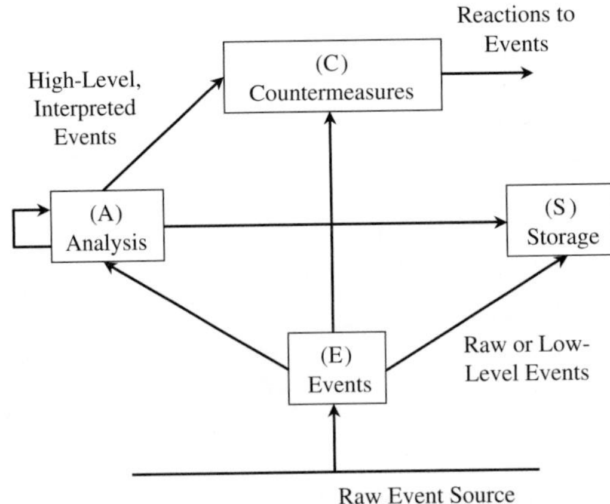

FIGURE 7-42 Common Components of an Intrusion Detection Framework.

No one IDS performs all of these functions. Let us look more closely at the kinds of IDSs and their use in providing security.

Types of IDSs

The two general types of intrusion detection systems are signature based and heuristic. **Signature-based** intrusion detection systems perform simple pattern-matching and report situations that match a pattern corresponding to a known attack type. **Heuristic** intrusion detection systems, also known as **anomaly based**, build a model of acceptable behavior and flag exceptions to that model; for the future, the administrator can mark a flagged behavior as acceptable so that the heuristic IDS will now treat that previously unclassified behavior as acceptable.

Intrusion detection devices can be network based or host based. A **network-based** IDS is a stand-alone device attached to the network to monitor traffic throughout that network; a **host-based** IDS runs on a single workstation or client or host, to protect that one host.

Early intrusion detection systems (for example, [LUN90b, FOX90]) worked after the fact, by reviewing logs of system activity to spot potential misuses that had occurred. The administrator could review the results of the IDS to find and fix weaknesses in the system. Now, however, intrusion detection systems operate in real time (or near real time), watching activity and raising alarms in time for the administrator to take protective action.

Signature-Based Intrusion Detection

A simple signature for a known attack type might describe a series of TCP SYN packets sent to many different ports in succession and at times close to one another, as would be the case for a port scan. An intrusion detection system would probably find nothing unusual in the first SYN, say, to port 80, and then another (from the same source address) to port 25. But as more and more ports receive SYN packets, especially ports that are not open, this pattern reflects a possible port scan. Similarly, some implementations of the protocol stack fail if they receive an ICMP packet with a data length of 65535 bytes, so such a packet would be a pattern for which to watch.

The problem with signature-based detection is the signatures themselves. An attacker will try to modify a basic attack in such a way that it will not match the known signature of that attack. For example, the attacker may convert lowercase to uppercase letters or convert a symbol such as "blank space" to its character code equivalent %20. The IDS must necessarily work from a canonical form of the data stream in order to recognize that %20 matches a pattern with a blank space. The attacker may insert malformed packets that the IDS will see, to intentionally cause a pattern mismatch; the protocol handler stack will discard the packets because of the malformation. Each of these variations could be detected by an IDS, but more signatures require additional work for the IDS, which reduces performance.

Of course, signature-based IDSs cannot detect a new attack for which a signature is not yet installed in the database. Every attack starts as a new attack at some time, and the IDS is helpless to warn of its existence.

Ideally, signatures should match every instance of an attack, match subtle variations of the attack, but not match traffic that is not part of an attack. However, this goal is grand but unreachable.

Heuristic Intrusion Detection

Because signatures are limited to specific, known attack patterns, another form of intrusion detection becomes useful. Instead of looking for matches, heuristic intrusion detection looks for behavior that is out of the ordinary. The original work in this area (for example, [TEN90]) focused on the individual, trying to find characteristics of that person that might be helpful in understanding normal and abnormal behavior. For example, one user might always start the day by reading e-mail, write many documents using a word processor, and occasionally back up files. These actions would be normal. This user does not seem to use many administrator utilities. If that person tried to access sensitive system management utilities, this new behavior might be a clue that someone else was acting under the user's identity. The approach has been extended to networks in [MUK94]. Later work (for example, [FOR96]) sought to build a dynamic model of behavior, to accommodate variation and evolution in a person's actions over time. The technique compares real activity with a known representation of normality.

Alternatively, intrusion detection can work from a model of known bad activity. For example, except for a few utilities (login, change password, create user), any other attempt to access a password file is suspect. This form of intrusion detection is known as **misuse intrusion detection**. In this work, the real activity is compared against a known suspicious area.

All heuristic intrusion detection activity is classified in one of three categories: good/benign, suspicious, or unknown. Over time, specific kinds of actions can move from one of these categories to another, corresponding to the IDS's learning whether certain actions are acceptable or not.

As with pattern-matching, heuristic intrusion detection is limited by the amount of information the system has seen (to classify actions into the right category) and how well the current actions fit into one of these categories.

Stealth Mode

An IDS is a network device (or, in the case of a host-based IDS, a program running on a network device). Any network device is potentially vulnerable to network attacks. How useful would an IDS be if it itself were deluged with a denial-of-service attack? If an attacker succeeded in logging in to a system within the protected network, wouldn't trying to disable the IDS be the next step?

To counter those problems, most IDSs run in **stealth mode**, whereby an IDS has two network interfaces: one for the network (or network segment) being monitored and the other to generate alerts and perhaps other administrative needs. The IDS uses the monitored interface as input only; it *never* sends packets out through that interface. Often, the interface is configured so that the device has no published address through the monitored interface; that is, a router cannot route anything to that address directly, because the router does not know such a device exists. It is the perfect passive wiretap.

If the IDS needs to generate an alert, it uses only the alarm interface on a completely separate control network. Such an architecture is shown in Figure 7-43.

Other IDS Types

Some security engineers consider other devices to be IDSs as well. For instance, to detect unacceptable code modification, programs can compare the active version of a software code with a saved version of a digest of that code. The *tripwire* program [KIM98] is the most well known software (or static data) comparison program. You run *tripwire* on a new system, and it generates a hash value for each file; then you save these hash values in a secure place (offline, so that no intruder can modify them while modifying a system file). If you later suspect your system may have been compromised, you rerun *tripwire*, providing it the saved hash values. It recomputes the hash values and reports any mismatches, which would indicate files that were changed.

System vulnerability scanners, such as *ISS Scanner* or *Nessus*, can be run against a network. They check for known vulnerabilities and report flaws found.

As we have seen, a honeypot is a faux environment intended to lure an attacker. It can be considered an IDS, in the sense that the honeypot may record an intruder's actions and even attempt to trace who the attacker is from actions, packet data, or connections.

Goals for Intrusion Detection Systems

The two styles of intrusion detection—pattern-matching and heuristic—represent different approaches, each of which has advantages and disadvantages. Actual IDS products often blend the two approaches.

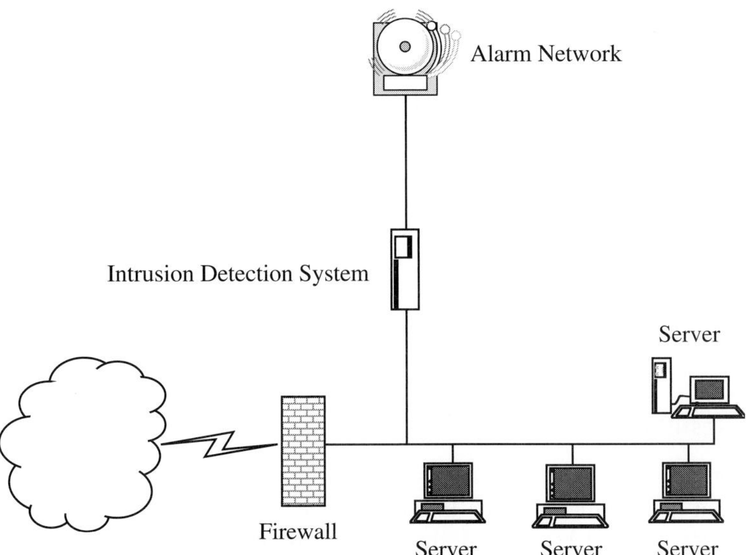

FIGURE 7-43 Stealth Mode IDS Connected to Two Networks.

Ideally, an IDS should be fast, simple, and accurate, while at the same time being complete. It should detect all attacks with little performance penalty. An IDS could use some—or all—of the following design approaches:

- filter on packet headers
- filter on packet content
- maintain connection state
- use complex, multipacket signatures
- use minimal number of signatures with maximum effect
- filter in real time, online
- hide its presence
- use optimal sliding time window size to match signatures

Responding to Alarms

Whatever the type, an intrusion detection system raises an alarm when it finds a match. The alarm can range from something modest, such as writing a note in an audit log, to something significant, such as paging the system security administrator. Particular implementations allow the user to determine what action the system should take on what events.

What are possible responses? The range is unlimited and can be anything the administrator can imagine (and program). In general, responses fall into three major categories (any or all of which can be used in a single response):

- monitor, collect data, perhaps increase amount of data collected
- protect, act to reduce exposure
- call a human

Monitoring is appropriate for an attack of modest (initial) impact. Perhaps the real goal is to watch the intruder, to see what resources are being accessed or what attempted attacks are tried. Another monitoring possibility is to record all traffic from a given source for future analysis. This approach should be invisible to the attacker. Protecting can mean increasing access controls and even making a resource unavailable (for example, shutting off a network connection or making a file unavailable). The system can even sever the network connection the attacker is using. In contrast to monitoring, protecting may be very visible to the attacker. Finally, calling a human allows individual discrimination. The IDS can take an initial defensive action immediately while also generating an alert to a human who may take seconds, minutes, or longer to respond.

False Results

Intrusion detection systems are not perfect, and mistakes are their biggest problem. Although an IDS might detect an intruder correctly most of the time, it may stumble in two different ways: by raising an alarm for something that is not really an attack (called a false positive, or type I error in the statistical community), or not raising an alarm for a real attack (a false negative, or type II error). Too many false positives means the administrator will be less confident of the IDS's warnings, perhaps leading to a real alarm's being ignored. But false negatives mean that real attacks are passing the IDS without action. We say that the degree of false positives and false negatives represents the sensitivity of the system. Most IDS implementations allow the administrator to tune the system's sensitivity, to strike an acceptable balance between false positives and negatives.

IDS Strengths and Limitations

Intrusion detection systems are evolving products. Research began in the mid-1980s and products had appeared by the mid-1990s. However, this area continues to change as new research influences the design of products.

On the up side, IDSs detect an ever-growing number of serious problems. And as we learn more about problems, we can add their signatures to the IDS model. Thus, over time, IDSs continue to improve. At the same time, they are becoming cheaper and easier to administer.

On the down side, avoiding an IDS is a first priority for successful attackers. An IDS that is not well defended is useless. Fortunately, stealth mode IDSs are difficult even to find on an internal network, let alone to compromise.

IDSs look for known weaknesses, whether through patterns of known attacks or models of normal behavior. Similar IDSs may have identical vulnerabilities, and their selection criteria may miss similar attacks. Knowing how to evade a particular model of IDS is an important piece of intelligence passed within the attacker community. Of course, once manufacturers become aware of a shortcoming in their products, they try to fix them. Fortunately, commercial IDSs are pretty good at identifying attacks.

Another IDS limitation is its sensitivity, which is difficult to measure and adjust. IDSs will never be perfect, so finding the proper balance is critical.

A final limitation is not of IDSs *per se*, but is one of their use. An IDS does not run itself; someone has to monitor its track record and respond to its alarms. An administrator is foolish to buy and install an IDS and then ignore it.

In general, IDSs are excellent additions to a network's security. Firewalls block traffic to particular ports or addresses; they also constrain certain protocols to limit their impact. But by definition, firewalls have to allow some traffic to enter a protected area. Watching what that traffic actually does inside the protected area is an IDS's job, which it does quite well.

7.6 SECURE E-MAIL

The final control we consider in depth is secure e-mail. Think about how much you use e-mail and how much you rely on the accuracy of its contents. How would you react if you received a message from your instructor saying that because you had done so well in your course so far, you were excused from doing any further work in it? What if that message were a joke from a classmate? We rely on e-mail's confidentiality and integrity for sensitive and important communications, even though ordinary e-mail has almost no confidentiality or integrity. In this section we investigate how to add confidentiality and integrity protection to ordinary e-mail.

Security for E-Mail

E-mail is vital for today's commerce, as well a convenient medium for communications among ordinary users. But, as we noted earlier, e-mail is very public, exposed at every point from the sender's workstation to the recipient's screen. Just as you would not put sensitive or private thoughts on a postcard, you must also acknowledge that e-mail messages are exposed and available for others to read.

Sometimes we would like e-mail to be more secure. To define and implement a more secure form, we begin by examining the exposures of ordinary e-mail.

Threats to E-Mail

Consider threats to electronic mail:

- message interception (confidentiality)
- message interception (blocked delivery)
- message interception and subsequent replay
- message content modification
- message origin modification
- message content forgery by outsider
- message origin forgery by outsider
- message content forgery by recipient
- message origin forgery by recipient
- denial of message transmission

Confidentiality and content forgery are often handled by encryption. Encryption can also help in a defense against replay, although we would also have to use a protocol in which each message contains something unique that is encrypted. Symmetric encryption cannot protect against forgery by a recipient, since both sender and recipient share a common key; however, public key schemes can let a recipient decrypt but not encrypt. Because of lack of control over the middle points of a network, senders or receivers generally cannot protect against blocked delivery.

Requirements and Solutions

If we were to make a list of the requirements for secure e-mail, our wish list would include the following protections.

- *message confidentiality* (the message is not exposed en route to the receiver)
- *message integrity* (what the receiver sees is what was sent)
- *sender authenticity* (the receiver is confident who the sender was)
- *nonrepudiation* (the sender cannot deny having sent the message)

Not all of these qualities are needed for every message, but an ideal secure e-mail package would allow these capabilities to be invoked selectively.

Designs

The standard for encrypted e-mail was developed by the Internet Society, through its architecture board (IAB) and research (IRTF) and engineering (IETF) task forces. The encrypted e-mail protocols are documented as an Internet standard in documents 1421, 1422, 1423, and 1424 [LIN93, KEN93, BAL93, KAL93a]. This standard is actually the third refinement of the original specification.

One of the design goals for encrypted e-mail was allowing security-enhanced messages to travel as ordinary messages through the existing Internet e-mail system. This requirement ensures that the large existing e-mail network would not require change to accommodate security. Thus, all protection occurs within the body of a message.

Confidentiality

Because the protection has several aspects, we begin our description of them by looking first at how to provide confidentiality enhancements. The sender chooses a (random) symmetric algorithm encryption key. Then, the sender encrypts a copy of the entire message to be transmitted, including FROM:, TO:, SUBJECT:, and DATE: headers. Next, the sender prepends plaintext headers. For key management, the sender encrypts the message key under the recipient's public key, and attaches that to the message as well. The process of creating an encrypted e-mail message is shown in Figure 7-44.

Encryption can potentially yield any string as output. Many e-mail handlers expect that message traffic will not contain characters other than the normal printable characters. Network e-mail handlers use unprintable characters as control signals in the traffic stream. To avoid problems in transmission, encrypted e-mail converts the entire ciphertext message to printable characters. An example of an encrypted e-mail message is

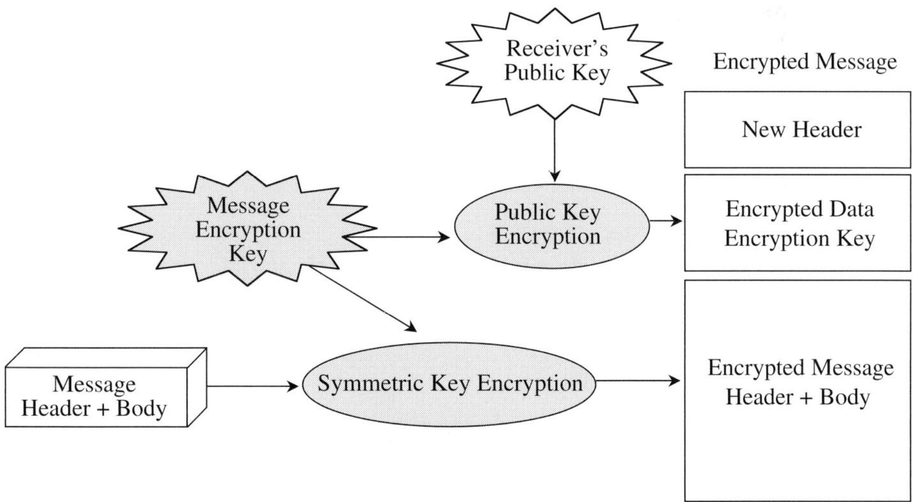

FIGURE 7-44 Overview of Encrypted E-Mail Processing.

shown in Figure 7-45. Notice the three portions: an external (plaintext) header, a section by which the message encryption key can be transferred, and the encrypted message itself. (The encryption is shown with shading.)

The encrypted e-mail standard works most easily as just described, using both symmetric and asymmetric encryption. The standard is also defined for symmetric encryption only: To use symmetric encryption, the sender and receiver must have previously established a shared secret encryption key. The processing type ("Proc-Type") field tells what privacy enhancement services have been applied. In the data exchange key field ("DEK-Info"), the kind of key exchange (symmetric or asymmetric) is shown. The key exchange ("Key-Info") field contains the message encryption key, encrypted under this shared encryption key. The field also identifies the originator (sender) so that the receiver can determine which shared symmetric key was used. If the key exchange technique were to use asymmetric encryption, the key exchange field would contain the message encryption field, encrypted under the recipient's public key. Also included could be the sender's certificate (used for determining authenticity and for generating replies).

The encrypted e-mail standard is designed to support multiple encryption algorithms, using popular algorithms such as DES, triple DES, and AES for message confidentiality, and RSA and Diffie–Hellman for key exchange.

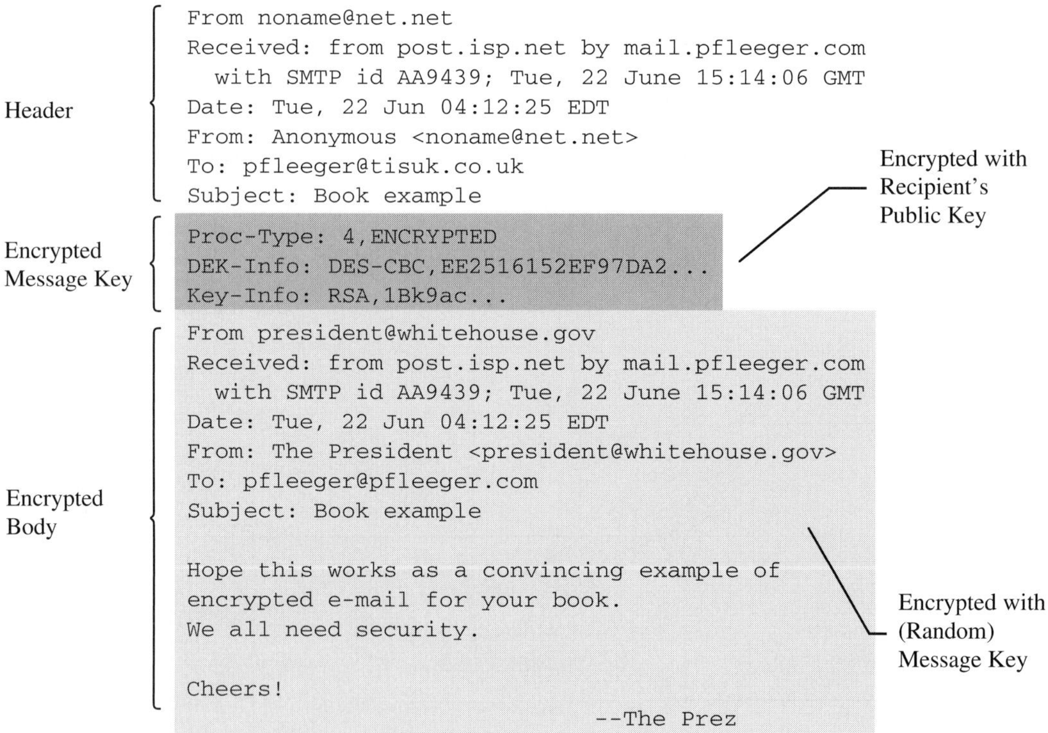

FIGURE 7-45 Encrypted E-Mail–Secured Message.

Other Security Features

In addition to confidentiality, we may want various forms of integrity for secure e-mail.

Encrypted e-mail messages always carry a digital signature, so the authenticity and nonrepudiability of the sender is assured. The integrity is also assured because of a hash function (called a **message integrity check**, or **MIC**) in the digital signature. Optionally, encrypted e-mail messages can be encrypted for confidentiality.

Notice in Figure 7-45 that the header inside the message (in the encrypted portion) differs from that outside. A sender's identity or the actual subject of a message can be concealed within the encrypted portion.

The encrypted e-mail processing can integrate with ordinary e-mail packages, so a person can send both enhanced and nonenhanced messages, as shown in Figure 7-46. If the sender decides to add enhancements, an extra bit of encrypted e-mail processing is invoked on the sender's end; the receiver must also remove the enhancements. But without enhancements, messages flow through the mail handlers as usual.

S/MIME (discussed later in this section) can accommodate the exchange of other than just text messages: support for voice, graphics, video, and other kinds of complex message parts.

Encryption for Secure E-Mail

The major problem with encrypted e-mail is key management. The certificate scheme described in Chapter 2 is excellent for exchanging keys and for associating an identity with a public encryption key. The difficulty with certificates is building the hierarchy.

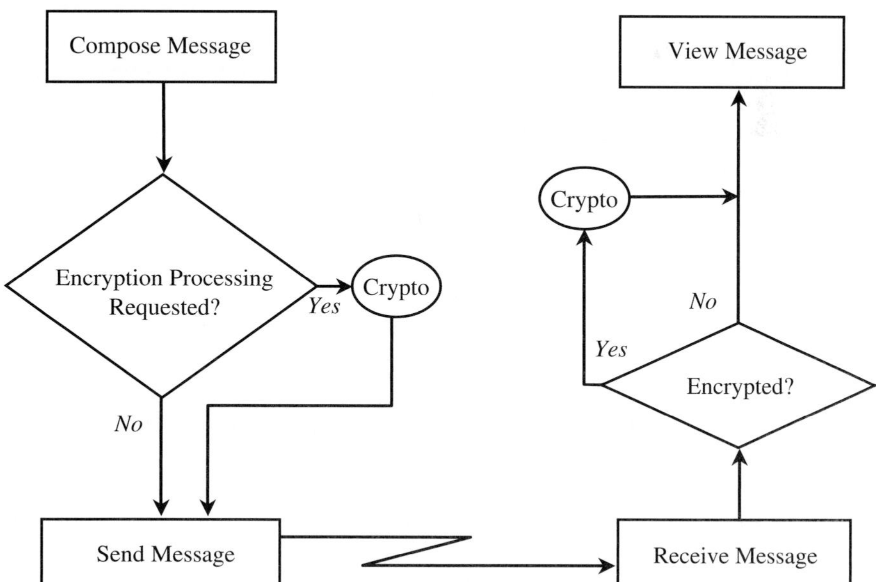

FIGURE 7-46 Encrypted E-Mail Processing in Message Transmission.

Many organizations have hierarchical structures. The encrypted e-mail dilemma is moving beyond the single organization to an interorganizational hierarchy. Precisely because of the problem of imposing a hierarchy on a nonhierarchical world, PGP was developed as a simpler form of encrypted e-mail.

Encrypted e-mail provides strong end-to-end security for electronic mail. Triple DES, AES, and RSA cryptography are quite strong, especially if RSA is used with a long bit key (1024 bits or more). The vulnerabilities remaining with encrypted e-mail come from the points not covered: the endpoints. An attacker with access could subvert a sender's or receiver's machine, modifying the code that does the privacy enhancements or arranging to leak a cryptographic key.

Example Secure E-Mail Systems

Encrypted e-mail programs are available from many sources. Several universities (including Cambridge University in England and the University of Michigan in the United States) and companies (BBN, RSA-DSI, and Trusted Information Systems) have developed either prototype or commercial versions of encrypted e-mail.

PGP

PGP stands for Pretty Good Privacy. It was invented by Phil Zimmerman in 1991. Originally a free package, it became a commercial product after being bought by Network Associates in 1996. A freeware version is still available. PGP is widely available, both in commercial versions and freeware, and it is heavily used by individuals exchanging private e-mail.

PGP addresses the key distribution problem with what is called a "ring of trust" or a user's "keyring." One user directly gives a public key to another, or the second user fetches the first's public key from a server. Some people include their PGP public keys at the bottom of e-mail messages. And one person can give a second person's key to a third (and a fourth, and so on). Thus, the key association problem becomes one of caveat emptor: "let the buyer beware." If I am reasonably confident that an e-mail message really comes from you and has not been tampered with, I will use your attached public key. If I trust you, I may also trust the keys you give me for other people. The model breaks down intellectually when you give me all the keys you received from people, who in turn gave you all the keys they got from still other people, who gave them all their keys, and so forth.

You sign each key you give me. The keys you give me may also have been signed by other people. I decide to trust the veracity of a key-and-identity combination, based on who signed the key.

PGP does not mandate a policy for establishing trust. Rather, each user is free to decide how much to trust each key received.

The PGP processing performs some or all of the following actions, depending on whether confidentiality, integrity, authenticity, or some combination of these is selected:

- Create a random session key for a symmetric algorithm.
- Encrypt the message, using the session key (for message confidentiality).

- Encrypt the session key under the recipient's public key.
- Generate a message digest or hash of the message; sign the hash by encrypting it with the sender's private key (for message integrity and authenticity).
- Attach the encrypted session key to the encrypted message and digest.
- Transmit the message to the recipient.

The recipient reverses these steps to retrieve and validate the message content.

S/MIME

An Internet standard governs how e-mail is sent and received. The general MIME specification defines the format and handling of e-mail attachments. **S/MIME** (Secure Multipurpose Internet Mail Extensions) is the Internet standard for secure e-mail attachments.

S/MIME is very much like PGP and its predecessors, PEM (Privacy-Enhanced Mail) and RIPEM [LIN93, KEN93, BAL93, KAL93a]. The Internet standards documents defining S/MIME (version 3) are described in [HOU99] and [RAM99]. S/MIME has been adopted in commercial e-mail packages, such as Eudora and Microsoft Outlook.

The principal difference between S/MIME and PGP is the method of key exchange. Basic PGP depends on each user's exchanging keys with all potential recipients and establishing a ring of trusted recipients; it also requires establishing a degree of trust in the authenticity of the keys for those recipients. S/MIME uses hierarchically validated certificates, usually represented in X.509 format, for key exchange. Thus, with S/MIME, the sender and recipient do not need to have exchanged keys in advance as long as they have a common certifier they both trust.

S/MIME works with a variety of cryptographic algorithms, such as DES, AES, and RC2 for symmetric encryption.

S/MIME performs security transformations very similar to those for PGP. PGP was originally designed for plaintext messages, but S/MIME handles (secures) all sorts of attachments, such as data files (for example, spreadsheets, graphics, presentations, movies, and sound). Because it is integrated into many commercial e-mail packages, S/MIME is likely to dominate the secure e-mail market.

7.7 SUMMARY OF NETWORK SECURITY

This chapter covers a very large and important area of computer security: networks and distributed applications. As the world becomes more connected by networks, the significance of network security will certainly continue to grow. Security issues for networks are visible and important, but their analysis is similar to the analysis done for other aspects of security. That is, we ask questions about what we are protecting and why we are protecting it. In particular, we ask

- What are the assets?
- What are the threats?
- Who are the threat agents?

- What are the controls?
- What is the residual, uncontrolled risk?

Network assets include the network infrastructure, applications programs and, most importantly, data. Recall that threats are actions or situations that offer potential harm to or loss of confidentiality, integrity, or availability, in the form of interception (eavesdropping or passive wiretapping), modification (active wiretapping, falsification, and compromise of authenticity), and denial of service. In stand-alone computing, most agents have a strong motive for an attack. But in networks we see new threat agents; anyone can be a victim of essentially a random attack. The strongest network controls are solid authentication, access control, and encryption.

Networks usually employ many copies of the same or similar software, with a copy on each of several (or all) machines in the network. This similarity, combined with connectivity, means that any fault in one copy of a program can create vulnerabilities spread across many machines. Mass market software often has flaws, and each flaw can be studied and exploited by an attacker. In large networks, a huge number of potential attackers can probe the software extensively; the result is that a network often includes many identified faults and software patches to counter them.

In a sense, security in networks is the combination and culmination of everything we know about security, and certainly everything we have discussed in this book so far. A network's security depends on all the cryptographic tools at our disposal, good program development processes, operating system controls, trust and evaluation and assurance methods, and inference and aggregation controls.

Networks and their security remind us that good software engineering practices can go a long way toward making software difficult to attack. When a network and its components are structured, designed, and architected well, the resulting system presents solid defenses and avoids potential single points of failure. And a well-engineered network is easy to change as it evolves; because it is easier to understand, changes seldom introduce unintentional flaws.

Many of the controls useful for stand-alone systems are also useful in networks. But three controls are specific to networks: firewalls, intrusion detection systems, and secure e-mail. These controls have evolved from many years of research, both in security and in other computer science realms. They emphasize why we should know not only the history of security but also the relevance of other computing research. For example, firewalls are just an updated form of reference monitor. Similarly, intrusion detection profits from more fundamental research into pattern-matching and expert systems. And secure e-mail is really a carefully designed application of cryptography. You might think that controls such as these are the result of strokes of genius. But in fact, they reflect the long-term nature of knowledge and engineering practice; new ways to provide security build on a growing base of understanding and experience.

Until now we have stressed technical controls, which can be very effective in protecting our computing assets. But many security losses come from trusted insiders—either honest people making honest, human mistakes or dishonest insiders able to capitalize on their knowledge or privileges. In the next chapter we consider administrative controls, such as security policies, user awareness, and risk analysis, as a way to address the insider threat.

7.8 TERMS AND CONCEPTS

single point of failure, 364
resilience, 364
fault tolerance, 364
server, 365
client, 365
node, 367
host, 367
link, 367
workstation, 367
network boundary, 368
network control, 368
network ownership, 368
topology, 368
digital, 369
analog, 369
modem, 369
twisted pair, 369
unshielded twisted pair, 369
bandwidth, 369
coaxial cable, 369
Ethernet, 369
repeater, 370
amplifier, 370
optical fiber, 370
wireless LAN, 370
802.11, 370
microwave, 370
infrared, 370
satellite, 371
geosynchronous orbit, 371
transponder, 371
transceiver, 371
footprint, 371
protocol, 372
ISO reference model, 373
OSI model, 373
application layer, 373
presentation layer, 373
session layer, 373
transport layer, 373
network layer, 373
data link layer, 373
physical layer, 373
peer, 373
router, 374
packet, 374
network interface card, 374
MAC address, 375
frame, 375
session header, 376
logical connection, 376
sequencing, 376
TCP, 378
IP, 378
UDP, 378
application layer, 378
transport layer, 378
Internet layer, 378
physical layer, 378
port, 379
SMTP, 379
HTTP, 379
FTP, 379
SNMP, 379
IP address, 379
domain, 380
top-level domain, 380
local area network, 381
LAN, 381
wide area network, 382
Internet Society, 382
heterogeneous network, 383
network topology, 383
common bus architecture, 383
star or hub architecture, 383
ring topology, 384
distributed system, 385
applications programming interface (API), 385
GSSAPI, 385
CAPI, 386
reliability, 386
expandability, 386
anonymity, 387
motivation for attack, 390
challenge, 390
fame, 392
money, 392

espionage, 392
ideology, 393
port scan, 393
social engineering, 394
reconnaissance, 395
fingerprinting, 395
eavesdrop, 397
passive wiretap, 398
active wiretap, 398
packet sniffer, 398
inductance, 398
impedance, 399
multiplexed signals, 399
interception, 401
theft of service, 401
RFC (request for comments), 403
impersonation, 404
authentication, 404
guess, 404
nonexistent authentication, 406
well-known authentication, 406
trusted authentication, 407
spoof, 407
masquerade, 407
session hijacking, 408
man-in-the-middle attack, 408
mobile computing, 409
misdelivery, 410
message exposure, 410
traffic flow analysis, 410
message falsification, 411
message replay, 411
message fabrication, 411
noise, 411
web site defacement, 412
buffer overflow, 412
dot-dot attack, 412
address resolution, 413
application code attack, 413
server-side include, 414
denial-of-service attack, 414
transmission failure, 414
connection flooding, 415
ICMP, 415
ping, 415
echo, 415
chargen, 415
ping of death, 415
smurf, 416
syn flood, 416
syn, 416
ack, 416
DNS attack, 417
distributed denial of service, 418
zombie, 419
tribal flood network, 420
trin00, 420
tfn2k, 420
active code, 420
mobile code, 420
cookie, 420
script, 421
escape-character attack, 421
active server page, 422
JavaScript, 422
sandbox, 422
Java virtual machine, 422
hostile applet, 423
ActiveX, 423
script kiddie, 424
building block attack, 425
network segmentation, 428
redundancy, 430
failover mode, 430
single point of failure, 430
link encryption, 431
end-to-end encryption, 432
virtual private network, 434
PKI (public key infrastructure), 436
certificate, 436
certificate authority, 437
SSH, 439
SSL, 439
IPSec, 440
authentication header, 440
encapsulated security payload, 440
security association, 440
ISAKMP, 442
ISAKMP key exchange, 442
signed code, 442
content integrity, 443
error correcting code, 443

parity, 443
even parity, 444
odd parity, 444
hash code, 444
cryptographic checksum, 444
message digest, 444
strong authentication, 444
one-time password, 445
password token, 445
challenge–response system, 445
Digital Distributed Authentication, 446
Kerberos, 447
ticket-granting server, 447
ticket, 447
router ACL, 451
honeypot, 452
traffic flow security, 453
firewall, 457
reference monitor, 458
packet filtering gateway, 459
screening router, 459
stateful inspection, 461
application proxy, 461
bastion host, 461
guard, 463
personal firewall, 464
layered protection, 467
defense in depth, 467
intrusion detection system, 468
network-based IDS, 469
host-based IDS, 469
signature-based IDS, 469
anomaly detection, 470
heuristic intrusion detection, 470
misuse detection, 470
stealth mode, 470
scanner, 471
IDS alarm, 472
false positive, 472
false negative, 473
secure e-mail, 473
message confidentiality, 475
message integrity check, 477
sender authenticity, 477
sender nonrepudiation, 477
key management, 478
PGP, 478
key ring, 478
S/MIME, 479

7.9 WHERE THE FIELD IS HEADED

Much work is being done to enhance the security of networks. Research by vendor companies will lead to more flexible and secure boxes, while more fundamental research will look into the fundamental problems of networking: authentication, access types, and authorizations. A particular problem of security in networks is one of speed: As the speed, capacity, bandwidth, and throughput of networks and network devices continue to increase, security devices have to keep pace, which is always a challenge.

A second security challenge with networks is ubiquity: As automobiles, cell phones, personal digital assistants, and even refrigerators become network enabled, they need security. The need for a firewall for a cell phone will become apparent the first time a cell phone is subject to a denial-of-service attack. Once again, security will be called upon to protect after a product is in use.

Joshi et al. [JOS01] present seven different models that could be used for access control in networked applications. These models include the decades-old mandatory and discretionary access control, about which literally hundreds of research results have been published, and more recent task- and agent-based models. The article is an excellent analysis of the models and their applicability in different network situations.

But the article clearly shows the immaturity of network security if after three decades into networking we still need to analyze which security models are appropriate for networking.

Protocol development continues as new networked applications arise. The challenge is to ensure that protocols are scrutinized for security flaws and that security measures are incorporated as needed. An example of a new protocol that addresses interesting security needs is Stajano and Anderson's "resurrecting duckling" protocol [STA02]. This protocol invents the concept of a "secure transient association," to describe a connection that must be created, acquire security properties, operate, and terminate, perhaps passing those properties to other entities. This work is a good example of development of the protection model before the need arises.

The firewall technology has matured nicely in the past decade. The pace of innovation in firewalls has slowed, and it seems as if freestanding firewalls have gone about as far as they can. But we can expect to see more firewall features incorporated into applications, appliances, and devices. The personal firewall to protect a single workstation is a good example of how security technology is extended to new domains of use.

Intrusion detection systems have a much longer history than firewalls, but they also have further to go. Interesting new work is underway to define "good" or "safe" behavior and to restrict access rights. (See, for example, [KO97, FOR96].) The next big challenge for IDS products is to integrate data from more sources to be able to infer a threat picture from many individually insignificant clues.

Denning [DEN99] has done very thorough and thoughtful study of the potential for misuse of the Internet for political purposes or terrorism. Because it is becoming so much a part of the essential infrastructure for commerce, education, and personal interaction, protection of the Internet is very important to society. But because of its necessarily open structure, protecting it is often inconsistent with promoting its use. Denning carefully explores these issues, as well as the possibility of using the Internet for harm.

The security of mobile code will become a larger issue as remote updates and patches and downloading of agents continue to increase. The classic security problem of demonstrating assurance is exacerbated by the anonymity of networking. Rubin and Geer [RUB98] provide a good overview of the field. Proof-carrying code [NEC96], code signing, type checking [VOL96], and constrained execution [GON96, GON97] are possibilities that have been proposed. (Interestingly, these approaches build on the use of the compiler to enforce security, a technique first suggested by Denning and Denning [DEN77].)

7.10 TO LEARN MORE

Network security is a rapidly changing field, but there are many current works and some classics everyone should read. Garfinkel and Spafford [GAR96] is an excellent place to start. For depth on hackers' tools and techniques, read Scambrey et al. [SCA01]. Some of the early works on network security have been reprinted in Davies and Price [DAV89] and Abrams and Podell [ABR87].

Anderson [AND01] presents a well-thought-out approach to putting the pieces together securely. Schneier [SCH00] presents the concepts of network security clearly.

For firewalls, Cheswick and Bellovin [CHE02] and Chapman and Zwicky [CHA00] are recent revisions of two standards. For intrusion detection systems, Northcutt [NOR00] is recommended; Allen [ALL99] and Kemmerer and Vigna [KEM02] also give good surveys of the state of the field.

7.11 EXERCISES

1. Does a gasoline engine have a single point of failure? Does a motorized fire engine? Does a fire department? How does each of the last two compensate for single points of failure in the previous one(s)? Explain your answers.
2. Telecommunications network providers and users are concerned about the single point of failure in "the last mile," which is the single cable from the network provider's last switching station to the customer's premises. How can a customer protect against that single point of failure? Comment on whether your approach presents a good cost-benefit trade-off.
3. You are designing a business in which you will host companies' web sites. What issues can you see as single points of failure? List the resources that could be involved. State ways to overcome each resource's being a single point of failure.
4. The human body exhibits remarkable resilience. State three examples in which the body compensates for failure of single body parts.
5. How can hardware be designed for fault tolerance? Are these methods applicable to software? Why or why not?
6. The old human telephone "switches" were quaint but very slow. You would signal the operator and say you wanted to speak to Jill, but the operator, knowing Jill was visiting Sally, would connect you there. Other than slowness or inefficiency, what are two other disadvantages of this scheme?
7. An (analog) telephone call is "circuit based," meaning that the system chooses a wire path from sender to receiver and that path or circuit is dedicated to the call until it is complete. What are two disadvantages of circuit switching?
8. The OSI model is inefficient; each layer must take the work of higher layers, add some result, and pass the work to lower layers. This process ends with the equivalent of a gift inside seven nested boxes, each one wrapped and sealed. Surely this wrapping (and unwrapping) is inefficient. From reading earlier chapters of this book, cite a security *advantage* of the layered approach.
9. Obviously, the physical layer has to be at the bottom of the OSI stack, with applications at the top. Justify the order of the other five layers as moving from low to high abstraction.
10. List the major security issues dealt with at each level of the OSI protocol stack.
11. What security advantage occurs from a packet's containing the source NIC address and not just the destination NIC address?
12. TCP is a robust protocol: Sequencing and error correction are ensured, but there is a penalty in overhead (for example, if no resequencing or error correction is needed). UDP does not provide these services but is correspondingly simpler. Cite specific situations in which the lightweight UDP protocol could be acceptable, that is, when error correction or sequencing is not needed.
13. Assume no FTP protocol exists. You are asked to define a function analogous to the FTP PUT for exchange of files. List three security features or mechanisms you would include in your protocol.
14. A 32-bit IP addressing scheme affords approximately 4 billion addresses. Compare this number to the world's population. Every additional bit doubles the number of potential addresses. Although 32 bits is becoming too small, 128 bits seems excessive, even allowing for

significant growth. But not all bits have to be dedicated to specifying an address. Cite a security use for a few bits in an address.

15. Sidebar 7-1 on usage of the University of Illinois site states that on a particular day, the site had been visited by hosts in 57 different countries. How do they know? Describe a means that an attacker could make it seem as if there were accesses from 57 countries. In your answer, cover both an actual number smaller than 57 and greater than 57. (You may treat these two cases separately.)
16. When a new domain is created, for example, yourdomain.com, a table in the .com domain has to receive an entry for yourdomain. What security attack might someone try against the registrar of .com (the administrator of the .com table) during the creation of yourdomain.com?
17. Describe a social engineering attack you could use to obtain a user's password.
18. Is a social engineering attack more likely to succeed in person, over the telephone, or through e-mail? Justify your answer.
19. A port scanner is a tool useful to an attacker to identify possible vulnerabilities in a potential victim's system. Cite a situation in which someone who is not an attacker could use a port scanner for a nonmalicious purpose.
20. One argument in the security community is that lack of diversity is itself a vulnerability. For example, the two dominant browsers, Netscape Navigator and Microsoft Internet Explorer, are used by probably 95 percent of Internet users. What security risk does this control of the market introduce? Suppose there were three (each with a significant share of the market). Would three negate that security risk?
21. Compare copper wire, microwave, optical fiber, infrared, and (radio frequency) wireless in their resistance to passive and active wiretapping.
22. How many 4-digit numeric PINs are there? Suppose a ban prohibits "obvious" PINs like 0000 and 1234. What would you define as "obvious," and how many PINs would that disallow? Now assume people choose PINs not for their numeric significance but because they are all or the first four letters of a word as on a telephone keypad: A,B,C=2, D,E,F=3, etc. Using the cryptanalysis lessons from Chapter 2, estimate how many 4-digit PINs that people might choose would really exist. The goal of this exercise is not to obtain the definitive answer but to present a reasonable analysis. In what network settings is a PIN still justified as an authenticator, in spite of the small numbers you obtain in this exercise?
23. What is a "man-in-the-middle" attack? Cite a real-life example (not from computer networking) of such an attack. Suggest a means by which sender and receiver can preclude a man-in-the-middle attack. (a) Cite a means not requiring cryptography. (b) Cite a means involving cryptography but also ensuring that the man in the middle cannot get in the middle of the key exchange.
24. Suggest a countermeasure for traffic flow analysis.
25. A problem with pattern matching is synonyms. If the current directory is bin, and . denotes the current directory and .. its parent, then bin, ../bin, ../bin/., .././bin/../bin all denote the same directory. If you are trying to block access to the bin directory in a command script, you need to consider all these variants (and an infinite number more). Cite a means by which a pattern-matching algorithm copes with synonyms.
26. The HTTP protocol is by definition stateless, meaning that it has no mechanism for "remembering" data from one interaction to the next. (a) Suggest a means by which you can preserve state between two HTTP calls. For example, you may send the user a page of books and prices matching a user's query, and you want to avoid having to look up the price of each book again once the user chooses one to purchase. (b) Suggest a means by which you can preserve some notion of state between two web accesses many days apart. For example, the user may prefer prices quoted in euros instead of dollars, and you want to present prices in the preferred currency next time without asking the user.

27. How can a web site distinguish between lack of capacity and a denial-of-service attack? For example, web sites often experience a tremendous increase in volume of traffic right after an advertisement with the site's URL is shown on television during the broadcast of a popular sporting event. That spike in usage is the result of normal access that happens to occur at the same time. How can a site determine that high traffic is reasonable?

28. Syn flood is the result of some incomplete protocol exchange: The client initiates an exchange but does not complete it. Unfortunately, these situations can also occur normally. Describe a benign situation that could cause a protocol exchange to be incomplete.

29. A distributed denial-of-service attack requires zombies running on numerous machines to perform part of the attack simultaneously. If you were a system administrator looking for zombies on your network, what would you look for?

30. Signing of mobile code is a suggested approach for addressing the vulnerability of hostile code. Outline what a code-signing scheme would have to do.

31. The system must control applets' accesses to sensitive system resources, such as the file system, the processor, the network, and internal state variables. But the term "the file system" is very broad, and useful applets usually need some persistent storage. Suggest controls that could be placed on access to the file system. Your answer has to be more specific than "allow all reads" or "disallow all writes." Your answer should essentially differentiate between what is "security critical" and not, or "harmful" and not.

32. Suppose you have a high-capacity network connection coming into your home, and you also have a wireless network access point. Also suppose you do not use the full capacity of your network connection. List three reasons you might still want to prevent an outsider from obtaining free network access by intruding into your wireless network.

33. Why is segmentation recommended for network design? That is, what makes it better to have a separate network segment for web servers, one for the back-end office processing, one for testing new code, and one for system management?

34. For large applications, some web sites use devices called "load balancers" to distribute traffic evenly among several equivalent servers. For example, a search engine might have a massive database of content and URLs, and several front-end processors that formulate queries to the database manager and format results to display to an inquiring client. A load balancer would assign each incoming client request to the least busy processor. What is a security advantage of using a load balancer?

35. Can link and end-to-end encryption both be used on the same communication? What would be the advantage of that? Cite a situation in which both forms of encryption might be desirable.

36. Does a VPN use link encryption or end-to-end? Justify your answer.

37. Why is a firewall a good place to implement a VPN? Why not implement it at the actual server(s) being accessed?

38. Does a VPN use symmetric or asymmetric encryption? Explain your answer.

39. Does a PKI perform encryption? Explain your answer.

40. Does a PKI use symmetric or asymmetric encryption? Explain your answer.

41. Should a PKI be supported on a firewall (meaning that the certificates would be stored on the firewall and the firewall would distribute certificates on demand)? Explain your answer.

42. Why does a PKI need a means to cancel or invalidate certificates? Why is it not sufficient for the PKI to stop distributing a certificate after it becomes invalid?

43. Some people think the certificate authorities for a PKI should be the government, but others think certificate authorities should be private entities, such as banks, corporations, or schools. What are the advantages and disadvantages of each approach?

44. If you live in country A and receive a certificate signed by a government certificate authority in country B, what conditions would cause you to trust that signature as authentic?

45. A certificate contains an identity, a public key, and signatures attesting that the public key belongs to the identity. Other fields that may be present include the organization (for example, university, company, or government) to which that identity belongs and perhaps suborganizations (college, department, program, branch, office). What security purpose do these other fields serve, if any? Explain your answer.
46. What is the security purpose for the fields, such as sequence number, of an IPSec packet?
47. Discuss the trade-offs between a manual challenge response system (one to which the user computes the response by hand or mentally) and a system that uses a special device, like a calculator.
48. A synchronous password token has to operate at the same pace as the receiver. That is, the token has to advance to the next random number at the same time the receiver advances. Because of clock imprecision, the two units will not always be perfectly together; for example, the token's clock might run 1 second per day slower than the receiver's. Over time, the accumulated difference can be significant. Suggest a means by which the receiver can detect and compensate for clock drift on the part of the token.
49. The workstation is a weak link in systems like PKI and Kerberos: A compromised workstation can collect and transmit cleartext passwords and encryption keys. Suggest a means to prevent compromise of a workstation from, for example, a Trojan horse.
50. This chapter listed several disadvantages to ACLs on routers as a network access control method. List two *advantages.*
51. List a situation in which you might want to block (reject) certain traffic through an ACL on a router; that is, a situation in which the performance penalty would not be the deciding factor.
52. What information might a stateful inspection firewall want to examine from multiple packets?
53. Recall that packet reordering and reassembly occur at the transport level of the TCP/IP protocol suite. A firewall will operate at a lower layer, either the Internet or data layer. How can a stateful inspection firewall determine anything about a traffic stream when the stream may be out of order or damaged?
54. Do firewall rules have to be symmetric? That is, does a firewall have to block a particular traffic type both inbound (to the protected site) and outbound (from the site)? Why or why not?
55. The FTP protocol is relatively easy to proxy; the firewall decides, for example, whether an outsider should be able to access a particular directory in the file system and issues a corresponding command to the inside file manager or responds negatively to the outsider. Other protocols are not feasible to proxy. List three protocols that it would be prohibitively difficult or impossible to proxy. Explain your answer.
56. How would the content of the audit log differ for a screening router versus an application proxy firewall?
57. Cite a reason why an organization might want two or more firewalls on a single network.
58. Firewalls are targets for penetrators. Why are there few compromises of firewalls?
59. Should a network administrator put a firewall in front of a honeypot? Why or why not?
60. Can a firewall block attacks using server scripts, such as the attack in which the user could change a price on an item offered by an e-commerce site? Why or why not?
61. Why does a stealth mode IDS need a separate network to communicate alarms and to accept management commands?
62. One form of IDS starts operation by generating an alert for every action. Over time, the administrator adjusts the setting of the IDS so that common, benign activities do not generate alarms. What are the advantages and disadvantages of this design for an IDS?

63. Can encrypted e-mail provide verification to a sender that a recipient has read an e-mail message? Why or why not?

64. Can message confidentiality and message integrity protection be applied to the same message? Why or why not?

65. What are the advantages and disadvantages of an e-mail program (such as Eudora or Outlook) that automatically applies and removes protection to e-mail messages between sender and receiver?

8

Administering Security

In this chapter:

- Security planning
- Risk analysis
- Security policies
- Physical security

In reading this book you may have concluded by now that security is achieved through technology. You may think that the important activities in security are picking the right IDS, configuring your firewall properly, encrypting your wireless link, and deciding whether fingerprint readers are better than retina scanners. These are important matters. But not all of security is addressed by technology. Focusing on the firewall alone is like choosing a car by the shape of the headlight. Before you get to the headlights, there are some more fundamental questions to answer, such as how you intend to use the car, how much you can afford, and whether you have other transportation choices.

Security is a combination of technical, administrative, and physical controls, as we first pointed out in Chapter 1. So far, we have considered technical controls almost exclusively. But stop and think for a moment: What good is a firewall if there is no power to run it? How effective is a public key infrastructure if someone can walk off with the certificate server? And why have elaborate access control mechanisms if your employee mails a sensitive document to a competitor? The administrative and physical controls may be less glamorous than the technical ones, but they are surely as important.

In this chapter we complete our study of security controls by considering administrative and physical aspects. We look at four related areas:

- *Planning*. What advance preparation and study let us know that our implementation meets our security needs for today and tomorrow?
- *Risk analysis*. How do we weigh the benefits of controls against their costs, and how do we justify any controls?
- *Policy*. How do we establish a framework to see that our computer security needs continue to be met?

- *Physical control.* What aspects of the computing environment have an impact on security?

These four areas are essential for understanding computer security completely.

8.1 SECURITY PLANNING

Years ago, when most computing was done on mainframe computers, data processing centers were responsible for protection. Responsibility for security rested neither with the programmers nor the users but instead with the computing centers themselves. These centers developed expertise in security, and they implemented many protection activities in the background, without users having to be conscious of protection needs and practices.

Since the early 1980s, the introduction of personal computers and the general ubiquity of computing have changed the way many of us work and interact with computers. In particular, a significant amount of the responsibility for security has shifted to the user and away from the computing center. But many users are unaware of (or choose to ignore) this responsibility, so they do not deal with the risks posed or do not implement simple measures to prevent or mitigate problems.

Unfortunately, there are many common examples of this neglect. Moreover, it is exacerbated by the seemingly hidden nature of important data: Things we would protect if they were on paper are ignored when they are stored electronically. For example, a person who carefully locks up paper copies of company confidential records overnight may leave running a personal computer or terminal on an assistant's or manager's desk. In this situation, a curious or malicious person walking past can retrieve confidential memoranda and data. Similarly, the data on laptops and workstations are often more easily available than on older, more isolated systems. For instance, the large and cumbersome disk packs and tapes from a few years ago have been replaced by media such as diskettes, zip disks, and CDs, which hold a similar volume of data but fit easily in a pocket or briefcase. Moreover, we all recognize that a box of CDs or diskettes may contain many times more data than a printed report. But since the report is an apparent, visible exposure and the CD or diskette is not, we leave the computer media in plain view, easy to borrow or steal.

In all cases, whether the user initiates some computing action or simply interacts with an active application, every application has confidentiality, integrity, and availability requirements that relate to the data, programs, and computing machinery. In these situations, users suffer from lack of sensitivity: They often do not appreciate the security risks associated with using computers.

For these reasons, every organization using computers to create and store valuable assets should perform thorough and effective security planning. A **security plan** is a document that describes how an organization will address its security needs. The plan is subject to periodic review and revision as the organization's security needs change.

A good security plan is an official record of current security practices, plus a blueprint for orderly change to improve those practices. By following the plan, developers and users can measure the effect of proposed changes, leading eventually to further improvements. The impact of the security plan is important, too. A carefully written plan, supported by management, notifies employees that security is important to management (and therefore to everyone). Thus, the security plan has to have the appropriate content and produce the desired effects.

In this section we study how to define and implement a security plan. We focus on three aspects of writing a security plan: what it should contain, who writes it, and how to obtain support for it. Then, we address two specific cases of security plans: business continuity plans, to ensure that an organization continues to function in spite of a computer security incident, and incident response plans, to organize activity to deal with the crisis of an incident.

Contents of a Security Plan

A security plan identifies and organizes the security activities for a computing system. The plan is both a description of the current situation and a plan for improvement. Every security plan must address seven issues.

- *policy,* indicating the goals of a computer security effort and the willingness of the people involved to work to achieve those goals
- *current state,* describing the status of security at the time of the plan
- *requirements,* recommending ways to meet the security goals
- *recommended controls*, mapping controls to the vulnerabilities identified in the policy and requirements
- *accountability,* describing who is responsible for each security activity
- *timetable,* identifying when different security functions are to be done
- *continuing attention,* specifying a structure for periodically updating the security plan

There are many approaches to creating and updating a security plan. Some organizations have a formal, defined security planning process, much as they might have a defined and accepted development or maintenance process. Others look to security professionals for guidance on how to perform security planning. For example, Sidebar 8-1 describes a security planning methodology suggested by the U.S. Software Engineering Institute and made available on its web site. But every security plan contains the same basic material, no matter the format. The following sections expand on the seven parts of a security plan.

1. Policy

A security plan must state the organization's policy on security. A security policy is a high-level statement of purpose and intent. Initially, you might think that all policies would be the same: to prevent security breaches. But in fact the policy is one of the most difficult sections to write well. As we discuss later in this chapter, there are tradeoffs among the strength of the security, the cost, the inconvenience to users, and more. For example, we must decide whether to implement very stringent—and possibly unpopular—controls that prevent all security problems or simply mitigate the effects of security breaches once they happen. For this reason, the policy statement must answer three essential questions:

Sidebar 8-1 The OCTAVE[SM] Methodology

The Software Engineering Institute at Carnegie Mellon University has created a framework for building a security plan. (See [ALB99].) The framework, called OCTAVE, includes eight steps:

1. Identify enterprise knowledge.
2. Identify operational area knowledge.
3. Identify staff knowledge.
4. Establish security requirements.
5. Map high-priority information assets to information infrastructure.
6. Perform an infrastructure vulnerability evaluation.
7. Conduct a multidimensional risk analysis.
8. Develop a protection strategy.

These steps lead a project manager or security analyst in determining the security risks and finding controls to address them. The OCTAVE web site (*www.cert.org/octave*) contains detailed information and checklists to guide the planning process.

- *Who* should be allowed access?
- To what system and organizational *resources* should access be allowed?
- What *types* of access should each user be allowed for each resource?

The policy statement should specify the following:

- The organization's *goals* on security. For example, should the system protect data from leakage to outsiders, protect against loss of data due to physical disaster, protect the data's integrity, or protect against loss of business when computing resources fail? What is the higher priority: serving customers or securing data?
- Where the *responsibility* for security lies. For example, should the responsibility rest with a small computer security group, with each employee, or with relevant managers?
- The organization's *commitment* to security. For example, who provides security support for staff, and where does security fit into the organization's structure?

2. Current Security Status

To be able to plan for security, an organization must understand the vulnerabilities to which it may be exposed. The organization can determine the vulnerabilities by performing a **risk analysis**: a careful investigation of the system, its environment, and the things that might go wrong. The risk analysis forms the basis for describing the current status of security. The status can be expressed as a listing of organizational assets, the security threats to the assets, and the controls in place to protect the assets. We look at risk analysis in more detail later in this chapter.

The status portion of the plan also defines the limits of responsibility for security. It describes not only which assets are to be protected but also who is responsible for protecting them. The plan may note that some groups may be excluded from responsibility; for example, joint ventures with other organizations may designate one organization to provide security for all member organizations. The plan also defines the boundaries of responsibility, especially when networks are involved. For instance, the plan should clarify who provides the security for a network router or for a leased line to a remote site.

Even though the security plan should be thorough, there will necessarily be vulnerabilities that are not considered. These vulnerabilities are not always the result of ignorance or naïveté; rather, they can arise from the addition of new equipment or data as the system evolves. They can also result from new situations, such as when a system is used in ways not anticipated by its designers. The security plan should detail the process to be followed when someone identifies a new vulnerability. In particular, instructions should explain how to integrate controls for that vulnerability into the existing security procedures.

3. Requirements

The heart of the security plan is its set of **security requirements**: functional or performance demands placed on a system to ensure a desired level of security. The requirements are usually derived from organizational needs. Sometimes these needs include the need to conform to specific security requirements imposed from outside, such as by a government agency or a commercial standard.

Pfleeger [PFL91] points out that we must distinguish the requirements from constraints and controls. A **constraint** is an aspect of the security policy that constrains, circumscribes, or directs the implementation of the requirements. As we learned in Chapter 1, a **control** is an action, device, procedure, or technique that removes or reduces a vulnerability. To see the difference among the three, consider the six "requirements" of the U.S. Department of Defense's TCSEC, introduced in Chapter 5. These six items are listed in Table 8-1.

Given our definitions of requirement, constraint, and control, it is easy to see that the first "requirement" of the TCSEC is really a constraint: the security policy. The second and third "requirements" describe mechanisms for enforcing security, not descriptions of required behaviors. That is, the second and third "requirements" describe explicit implementations, not a general characteristic or property that the system must have. However, the fourth, fifth, and sixth TCSEC "requirements" are indeed true requirements. They state that the system must have certain characteristics, but they do not enforce a particular implementation.

These distinctions are important because the requirements explain *what* should be accomplished, not *how*. That is, the requirements should always leave the implementation details to the designers, whenever possible. For example, rather than writing a requirement that certain data records should require passwords for access (an implementation decision), a security planner should state only that access to the data records should be restricted (and note to whom the access should be restricted). This more flexible requirement allows the designers to decide among several other access

TABLE 8-1 The Six "Requirements" of the TCSEC.

Security policy	There must be an explicit and well-defined security policy enforced by the system.
Identification	Every subject must be uniquely and convincingly identified. Identification is necessary so that subject/object access can be checked.
Marking	Every object must be associated with a label that indicates its security level. The association must be done so that the label is available for comparison each time an access to the object is requested.
Accountability	The system must maintain complete, secure records of actions that affect security. Such actions include introducing new users to the system, assigning or changing the security level of a subject or an object, and denying access attempts.
Assurance	The computing system must contain mechanisms that enforce security, and it must be possible to evaluate the effectiveness of these mechanisms.
Continuous protection	The mechanisms that implement security must be protected against unauthorized change.

controls (such as access control lists) and to balance the security requirements with other system requirements, such as performance and reliability. Figure 8-1 illustrates how the different aspects of system analysis support the security planning process.

As with the general software development process, the security planning process must allow customers or users to specify desired functions, independent of the implementation. The requirements should address all aspects of security: confidentiality, integrity, and availability. They should also be reviewed to make sure that they are of appropriate quality. In particular, we should make sure that the requirements have these characteristics:

- *Correctness*: Are the requirements understandable? Are they stated without error?
- *Consistency*: Are there any conflicting or ambiguous requirements?
- *Completeness*: Are all possible situations addressed by the requirements?

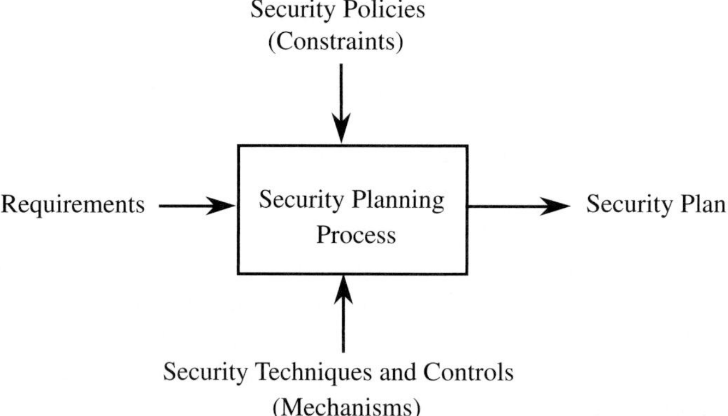

FIGURE 8-1 Inputs to the Security Plan.

- *Realism*: Is it possible to implement what the requirements mandate?
- *Need*: Are the requirements unnecessarily restrictive?
- *Verifiability*: Can tests be written to demonstrate conclusively and objectively that the requirements have been met? Can the system or its functionality be measured in some way that will assess the degree to which the requirements are met?
- *Traceability*: Can each requirement be traced to the functions and data related to it so that changes in a requirement can lead to easy reevaluation?

The requirements may then be constrained by budget, schedule, performance, policies, governmental regulations, and more. Given the requirements and constraints, the developers then choose appropriate controls.

4. Recommended Controls

The security requirements lay out the system's needs in terms of what should be protected. The security plan must also recommend what controls should be incorporated into the system to meet those requirements. Throughout this book you have seen many examples of controls, so we do not need to review them here. As we see later in this chapter, we can use risk analysis to create a map from vulnerabilities to controls. The mapping tells us how the system will meet the security requirements. That is, the recommended controls address implementation issues: how the system will be designed and developed to meet stated security requirements.

5. Responsibility for Implementation

A section of the security plan should identify which people are responsible for implementing the security requirements. This documentation assists those who must coordinate their individual responsibilities with those of other developers. At the same time, the plan makes explicit who is accountable should some requirement not be met or some vulnerability not be addressed. That is, the plan notes who is responsible for implementing controls when a new vulnerability is discovered or a new kind of asset is introduced.

Many roles are played by people building, using, and maintaining the system. Each role can take some responsibility for one or more aspects of security. Consider, for example, the groups listed below.

- *Personal computer users* may be responsible for the security of their own machines. Alternatively, the security plan may designate one person or group to be coordinator of personal computer security.
- *Project leaders* may be responsible for the security of data and computations.
- *Managers* may be responsible for seeing that the people they supervise implement security measures.
- *Database administrators* may be responsible for the access to and integrity of data in their databases.

- *Information officers* may be responsible for overseeing the creation and use of data; these officers may also be responsible for retention and proper disposal of data.
- *Personnel staff members* may be responsible for security involving employees, for example, screening potential employees for trustworthiness and arranging security training programs.

6. Timetable

A comprehensive security plan cannot be executed instantly. The security plan includes a timetable that shows how and when the elements of the plan will be performed. These dates also give milestones so that management can track the progress of implementation.

If the implementation is to be a phased development (that is, the system will be implemented partially at first, and then changed functionality or performance will be added in later releases), the plan should also describe how the security requirements will be implemented over time. Even when overall development is not phased, it may be desirable to implement the security aspects of the system over time. For example, if the controls are expensive or complicated, they may be acquired and implemented gradually. Similarly, procedural controls may require staff training to ensure that everyone understands and accepts the reason for the control.

The plan should specify the order in which the controls are to be implemented so that the most serious exposures are covered as soon as possible. A timetable also gives milestones by which to judge the progress of the security program.

Furthermore, the plan must be extensible. Conditions will change: New equipment will be acquired, new degrees and modes of connectivity will be requested, and new threats will be identified. The plan must include a procedure for change and growth, so that the security aspects of changes are considered as a part of preparing for the change, not for adding security after the change has been made. The plan should also contain a schedule for periodic review. Even though there may have been no obvious, major growth, most organizations experience modest change on a daily basis. At some point the cumulative impact of the change is enough to require the plan to be modified.

7. Continuing Attention

Good intentions are not enough when it comes to security. We must not only take care in defining requirements and controls, but we must also find ways for evaluating a system's security to be sure that the system is as secure as we intend it to be. Thus, the security plan must call for reviewing the security situation periodically. As users, data, and equipment change, new exposures may develop. In addition, the current means of control may become obsolete or ineffective (such as when faster processor times enable attackers to break an encryption algorithm). The inventory of objects and the list of controls should periodically be scrutinized and updated, and risk analysis performed anew. The security plan should set times for these periodic reviews, based either on calendar time (such as, review the plan every nine months) or on the nature of system changes (such as, review the plan after every major system release).

Security Planning Team Members

Who performs the security analysis, recommends a security program, and writes the security plan? As with any such comprehensive task, these activities are likely to be performed by a committee that represents all the interests involved. The size of the committee depends on the size and complexity of the computing organization and the degree of its commitment to security. Organizational behavior studies suggest that the optimum size for a working committee is between five and nine members. Sometimes a larger committee may serve as an oversight body to review and comment on the products of a smaller working committee. Alternatively, a large committee might designate subcommittees to address various sections of the plan.

The membership of a computer security planning team must somehow relate to the different aspects of computer security described in this book. Security in operating systems and networks requires the cooperation of the systems administration staff. Program security measures can be understood and recommended by applications programmers. Physical security controls are implemented by those responsible for general physical security, both against human attacks and natural disasters. Finally, because controls affect system users, the plan should incorporate users' views, especially with regard to usability and the general desirability of controls.

Thus, no matter how it is organized, a security planning team should represent each of the following groups.

- computer hardware group
- system administrators
- systems programmers
- applications programmers
- data entry personnel
- physical security personnel
- representative users

In some cases, a group can be adequately represented by someone who is consulted at appropriate times, rather than a committee member from each possible constituency being enlisted.

Assuring Commitment to a Security Plan

After the plan is written, it must be accepted and its recommendations carried out. Acceptance by the organization is key; a plan that has no organizational commitment is simply a plan that collects dust on the shelf. Commitment to the plan means that security functions will be implemented and security activities carried out. Three groups of people must contribute to making the plan a success.

- The planning team must be sensitive to the needs of each group affected by the plan.
- Those affected by the security recommendations must understand what the plan means for the way they will use the system and perform their business activi-

ties. In particular, they must see how what they do can affect other users and other systems.
- Management must be committed to using and enforcing the security aspects of the system.

Education and publicity can help people to understand and accept a security plan. Acceptance involves not only the letter but also the spirit of the security controls. Recall from Chapter 4 the employee who went through 24 password changes at a time to get back to a favorite password, in a system that prevented use of any of the 23 most recently used passwords. Clearly, the employee either did not understand or did not agree with the reason for restrictions on passwords. If people understand the need for recommended controls and accept them as sensible, they will use the controls properly and effectively. If people think the controls are bothersome, capricious, or counterproductive, they will work to avoid or subvert them.

Management commitment is obtained through understanding. But this understanding is not just a function of what makes sense technologically; it also involves knowing the cause and the potential effects of lack of security. Managers must also weigh trade-offs in terms of convenience and cost. The plan must present a picture of how cost effective the controls are, especially when compared to potential losses if security is breached without the controls. Thus, proper presentation of the plan is essential, in terms that relate to management as well as technical concerns.

Remember that some managers are not computing specialists. Instead, the system supports a manager who is an expert in some other business function, such as banking, medical technology, or sports. In such cases, the security plan must present security risks in language that the managers understand. It is important to avoid technical jargon and to educate the readers about the nature of the perceived security risks in the context of the business the system supports. Sometimes outside experts can bridge the gap between the managers' business and security.

Management is often reticent to allocate funds for controls until the value of those controls is explained. As we note in the next section, the results of a risk analysis can help communicate the financial trade-offs and benefits of implementing controls. By describing vulnerabilities in financial terms and in the context of ordinary business activities (such as leaking data to a competitor or an outsider), security planners can help managers understand the need for controls.

The plans we have just discussed are part of normal business. They address how a business handles computer security needs. Similar plans might address how to increase sales or improve product quality, so these planning activities should be a natural part of management.

Next we turn to two particular kinds of business plans that address specific security problems: coping with and controlling activity during security incidents.

Business Continuity Plans

Small companies working on a low profit margin can literally be put out of business by a computer incident. Large, financially sound businesses can weather a modest incident that interrupts their use of computers for a while, although it is painful to them.

But even rich companies do not want to spend money unnecessarily. The analysis is sometimes as simple as *no computers means no customers means no sales means no profit.*

Government agencies, educational institutions, and nonprofit organizations also have limited budgets, which they want to use to further their needs. They may not have a direct profit motive, but being able to meet the needs of their customers—the public, students, and constituents—partially determines how well they will fare in the future. All kinds of organizations must plan for ways to cope with emergency situations.

A **business continuity plan**[1] documents how a business will continue to function during a computer security incident. An ordinary security plan covers computer security during normal times and deals with protecting against a wide range of vulnerabilities from the usual sources. A business continuity plan deals with situations having two characteristics:

- *catastrophic situations,* in which all or a major part of a computing capability is suddenly unavailable
- *long duration,* in which the outage is expected to last for so long that business will suffer

There are many situations in which a business continuity plan would be helpful. Here are some examples that typify what you might find in reading your daily newspaper:

- A fire destroys a company's entire network.
- A seemingly permanent failure of a critical software component renders the computing system unusable.
- A business must deal with the abrupt failure of its supplier of electricity, telecommunications, network access, or other critical service.
- A flood prevents the essential network support staff from getting to the operations center.

As you can see, these examples are likely to recur, and each disables a vital function.

You may also have noticed how often "the computer" is blamed for an inability to provide a service or product. For instance, the clerk in a shop is unable to use the cash register because "the computer is down." You may have a CD in your hand, plus exactly the cash to pay for it. But the clerk will not take your money and send you on your way. Often, computer service is restored shortly. But sometimes it is not. Once we were delayed for over an hour in an airport because of an electrical storm that caused a power failure and disabled the airlines' computers. Although our tickets showed clearly our reservations on a particular flight, the airline agents refused to let anyone board because they could not assign seats. As the computer remained down, the agents were frantic[2] because the technology was delaying the flight and, more importantly, disrupting hundreds of connections.

---

[1] The standard terminology is "business continuity plan," even though such a plan is needed by and applies to a university's "business" of educating students or a government's "business" of serving the public.

[2] The obvious, at least to us, idea of telling passengers to "sit in any seat" seemed to be against airline policy.

The key to coping with such disasters is advance planning and preparation, identifying activities that will keep a business viable when the computing technology is disabled. The steps in business continuity planning are these:

- Assess the business impact of a crisis.
- Develop a strategy to control impact.
- Develop and implement a plan for the strategy

Assess Business Impact

To assess the impact of a failure on your business, you begin by asking two key questions:

- What are the *essential assets*? What are the things that will prevent the business from doing business? Answers are typically of the form "the network," "the customer reservations database," or "the system controlling traffic lights."
- What could *disrupt use* of these assets? The vulnerability is more important than the threat agent. For example, whether destroyed by a fire or zapped in an electrical storm, the network is nevertheless down. Answers might be "failure," "corrupted," or "loss of power."

You probably will find only a handful of key assets when doing this analysis.

Do not overlook people and the things they need for support, such as documentation and communications equipment. Another way to think about your assets is to ask yourself, "What is the minimum set of things or activities needed to keep business operational, at least to some degree?" If a manual system would compensate for a failed computer system, albeit inefficiently, you may want to consider building such a manual system as a potential critical asset. Think of the airline unable to assign seats from a chart of the cabin.

Later in this chapter we study risk analysis, a comprehensive examination of assets, vulnerabilities, and controls. For business continuity planning we do not need a full risk analysis. Instead, we focus on only those things that are critical to continued operation. We also look at larger classes of objects, such as "the network," whose loss or compromise can have catastrophic effect.

Develop Strategy

The continuity strategy investigates how the key assets can be safeguarded. In some cases, a backup copy of data or redundant hardware or an alternative manual process is good enough. Sometimes, the most reasonable answer is reduced capacity. For example, a planner might conclude that if the call center in London fails, the business can divert all calls to Tokyo. It is possible, though, that the staff in Tokyo cannot handle the full load of the London traffic; this situation may result in irritated or even lost customers, but at least some business can be transacted.

Ideally, you would like to continue business with no loss. But with catastrophic failures, usually only a portion of the business function can be preserved. In this case, you must develop a strategy appropriate for your business and customers. For instance, you can decide whether it is better to preserve half of function A and half of B, or most of A and none of B.

You also must consider the time frame in which business is done. Some catastrophes last longer than others. For example, rebuilding after a fire is a long process and implies a long time in disaster mode. Your strategy may have several steps, each dependent on how long the business is disabled. Thus, you may take one action in response to a one-hour outage, and another if the outage might last a day or longer.

Because you are planning in advance, you have the luxury of being able to think about possible circumstances and evaluate alternatives. For instance, you may realize that if the Tokyo site takes on work for the disabled London site, there will be a significant difference in time zones. It may be better to divert morning calls to Tokyo and afternoon ones to Dallas, to avoid asking Tokyo workers to work extra hours.

The result of a strategy analysis is a selection of the best actions, organized by circumstances. The strategy can then be used as the basis for your business continuity plan.

Develop Plan

The business continuity plan specifies several important things:

- who is in charge when an incident occurs
- what to do
- who does it

The plan justifies making advance arrangements, such as acquiring redundant equipment, arranging for data backups, and stockpiling supplies, before the catastrophe. The plan also justifies advance training so that people know how they should react. In a catastrophe there will be confusion; you do not want to add confused people to the already severe problem.

The person in charge declares the state of emergency and instructs people to follow the procedures documented in the plan. The person in charge also declares when the emergency is over and conditions can revert to normal.

Thus, the business continuity planning addresses how to maintain some degree of critical business activity in spite of a catastrophe. Its focus is on keeping the business viable. It is based on the asset survey, which focuses on only a few critical assets and serious vulnerabilities that could threaten operation for a long or undetermined period of time.

The focus of the business continuity plan is to keep the business going while someone else addresses the crisis. That is, the business continuity plan does not include calling the fire department or evacuating the building, important though those steps are. The focus of a business continuity plan is the *business* and how to keep it functioning to the degree possible in the situation. Handling the emergency is someone else's problem.

Now we turn to a different plan that deals specifically with computer crises.

Incident Response Plans

An **incident response plan** tells the staff how to deal with a security incident. In contrast to the business continuity plan, the goal of incident response is handling the current security incident, without regard for the business issues. The security incident may at the same time be a business catastrophe, as addressed by the business continuity plan. But as a specific security event, it might be less than catastrophic (that is, it may not interrupt business severely) but could be a serious breach of security, such as a hacker attack or a case of internal fraud. An incident could be a single event, a series of events, or an ongoing problem.

An incident response plan should

- define what constitutes an *incident*
- identify who is responsible for *taking charge* of the situation
- describe the plan of *action*

The plan usually has three phases: advance planning, triage, and running the incident. A fourth phase, review, is useful after the situation abates so that this incident can lead to improvement for future incidents.

Advance Planning

As with all planning functions, advance planning works best because people can think logically, unhurried, and without pressure. What constitutes an incident may be vague. We cannot know the details of an incident in advance. Typical characteristics include harm or risk of harm to computer systems, data, or processing; initial uncertainty as to the extent of damage; and similar uncertainty as to the source or method of the incident. For example, you can see that the file is missing or the home page has been defaced, but you do not know how or by whom or what other damage there may be.

In organizations that have not done incident planning, chaos may develop at this point. Someone calls the network manager. Someone sends e-mail to the help desk. Someone calls the FBI, the CERT, the newspapers, or the fire department. People start to investigate on their own, without coordinating with the relevant staff in other departments, agencies, or businesses. And there is a lot of conversation, rumor, and misinformation: more heat than light.

With an incident response plan in place, everybody is trained in advance to call the designated leader. There is an established list of people to call, in order, in case the first person is unavailable. The leader decides what to do next, and he or she begins by determining if this is a real incident or a false alarm. Indeed, natural events sometimes look like incidents, and the facts of the situation should be established first. If the leader decides this may be a real incident, he or she invokes the response team.

Response Team

The response team is the set of people charged with responding to the incident. The response team may include

- *director*: person in charge of the incident, who decides what actions to take and when to terminate the response. The director is typically a management employee.
- *lead technician*: person who directs and coordinates the response. The lead technician decides where to focus attention, analyzes situation data, documents

the incident and how it was handled, and calls for other technical people to assist with the analysis.

- *advisor(s)*: legal, human resources, or public relations staff members as appropriate.

In a small incident a single person can handle more than one of these roles. Nevertheless, it is important that there be a single person in charge, a single person who directs the response work, a single point of contact for "insiders" (employees, users), and a single point of contact for "the public."

To develop policy and identify a response team, you need to consider certain matters.

- *Legal issues*: An incident has legal ramifications. In some countries, computer intrusions are illegal, so law enforcement officials must be involved in the investigation. In other places, you have discretion in deciding whether to ask law enforcement to participate. In addition to criminal action, you may be able to bring a civil case. Both kinds of legal action have serious implications for the response. For example, evidence must be gathered and maintained in specific ways in order to be usable in court. Similarly, laws may limit what you can do against the alleged attacker: Cutting off a connection is probably acceptable, but launching a retaliatory denial-of-service attack may not be.
- *Preserving evidence*: The most common reaction in an incident is to assume the cause was internal or accidental. For instance, you may surmise that the hardware has failed or that the software isn't working correctly. The staff may be directed to change the configuration, reload the software, reboot the system, or similarly attempt to resolve the problem by adjusting the software. Unfortunately, each of these acts can irreparably distort or destroy evidence. When dealing with a possible incident, do as little as possible before "dusting for fingerprints."
- *Records*: It may be difficult to remember what you have already done: Have you already reloaded a particular file? What steps got you to the prompt asking for the new DNS server's address? If you call in an outside forensic investigator or the police, you will need to tell exactly what you have already done.
- *Public relations*: In handling an incident your organization should speak with one voice. You risk sending confusing messages if too many people speak. It is especially important that only one person speak publicly if legal action may be taken. An unguarded comment may tip off the attacker or have a negative effect on the case. You can simply say that an incident occurred, tell briefly and generally what it was, and state that the incident is now under control and normal operation is resuming.

After the Incident Is Resolved

Eventually, the incident response team closes the case. At this point it will hold a review after the incident to consider two things:

- *Is any security control action to be taken?* Did an intruder compromise a system because security patches were not up to date; if so, should there be a procedure to ensure that patches are applied when they become available? Was access obtained because of a poorly chosen password; if so, should there be a campaign to educate users on how to strong passwords? If there were control failures, what should be done to prevent similar attacks in the future?

- *Did the incident response plan work?* Did everyone know whom to notify? Did the team have needed resources? Was the response fast enough? What should be done differently next time?

The incident response plan ensures that incidents are handled promptly, efficiently, and with minimal harm.

8.2 RISK ANALYSIS

Good, effective security planning includes a careful risk analysis. A **risk** is a potential problem that the system or its users may experience. We distinguish a risk from other project events by looking for three things, as suggested by Rook [ROO93]:

1. *A loss associated with an event.* The event must generate a negative effect: compromised security, lost time, diminished quality, lost money, lost control, lost understanding, and so on. This loss is called the **risk impact**.
2. *The likelihood that the event will occur.* There is a probability of occurrence associated with each risk, measured from 0 (impossible) to 1 (certain). When the risk probability is 1, we say we have a **problem**.
3. *The degree to which we can change the outcome.* We must determine what, if anything, we can do to avoid the impact or at least reduce its effects. **Risk control** involves a set of actions to reduce or eliminate the risk. Many of the security controls we describe in this book are examples of risk control.

We usually want to weigh the pros and cons of different actions we can take to address each risk. To that end, we can quantify the effects of a risk by multiplying the risk impact by the risk probability, yielding the **risk exposure**. For example, if the likelihood of virus attack is 0.3 and the cost to clean up the affected files is $10,000, then the risk exposure is $3,000. So we may use a calculation like this one to decide that a virus checker is worth an investment of $100, since it will prevent a much larger potential loss. Clearly, risk probabilities can change over time, so it is important to track them and plan for events accordingly.

In general, there are three strategies for risk reduction:

1. *avoiding* the risk, by changing requirements for security or other system characteristics
2. *transferring* the risk, by allocating the risk to other systems, people, organizations, or assets; or by buying insurance to cover any financial loss should the risk become a reality
3. *assuming* the risk, by accepting it, controlling it with available resources, and preparing to deal with the loss if it occurs

Thus, costs are associated not only with the risk's potential impact but also with reducing it. **Risk leverage** is the difference in risk exposure divided by the cost of reducing the risk. In other words, risk leverage is

$$\frac{\text{(risk exposure before reduction)} - \text{(risk exposure after reduction)}}{\text{(cost of risk reduction)}}$$

If the leverage value of a proposed action is not high enough, then we look for alternative but less costly actions or more effective reduction techniques.

Risk analysis is the process of examining a system and its operational context to determine possible exposures and the potential harm they can cause. Thus, the first step in a risk analysis is to identify and list all exposures in the computing system of interest. Then, for each exposure, we identify possible controls and their costs. The last step is a cost–benefit analysis: Does it cost less to implement a control or to accept the expected cost of the loss? In the remainder of this section, we describe risk analysis, present examples of risk analysis methods, and discuss some of the drawbacks to performing risk analysis.

The Nature of Risk

In our everyday lives, we take risks. In crossing the road, eating oysters, or playing the lottery, we take the chance that our actions may result in some negative result—such as being injured, getting sick, or losing money. Consciously or unconsciously, we weigh the benefits of taking the action with the possible losses that might result. Just because there is a risk to a certain act we do not necessarily avoid it; we may look both ways before crossing the street, but we do cross it. In building and using computing systems, we must take a more organized and careful approach to assessing our risks. Many of the systems we build and use can have a dramatic impact on life and health if they fail. For this reason, risk analysis is an essential part of security planning.

We cannot guarantee that our systems will be risk free; that is why our security plans must address actions needed should an unexpected risk become a problem. And some risks are simply part of doing business; for example, as we have seen, we must plan for disaster recovery, even though we take many steps to avoid disasters in the first place.

When we acknowledge that a significant problem cannot be prevented, we can use controls to reduce the seriousness of a threat. For example, you can back up files on your computer as a defense against the possible failure of a file storage device. But as our computing systems become more complex and more distributed, complete risk analysis becomes more difficult and time consuming—and more essential.

Steps of a Risk Analysis

Risk analysis is performed in many different contexts; for example, environmental and health risks are analyzed for activities such as building dams, disposing of nuclear waste, or changing a manufacturing process. Risk analysis for security is adapted from more general management practices, placing special emphasis on the kinds of problems likely to arise from security issues. By following well-defined steps, we can analyze the security risks in a computing system.

The basic steps of risk analysis are listed below.

1. Identify assets.
2. Determine vulnerabilities.
3. Estimate likelihood of exploitation.
4. Compute expected annual loss.
5. Survey applicable controls and their costs.
6. Project annual savings of control.

Sidebar 8-2 illustrates how different organizations take slightly different approaches, but the basic activities are still the same. These steps are described in detail in the following sections.

Step 1: Identify Assets

Before we can identify vulnerabilities, we must first decide what we need to protect. Thus, the first step of a risk analysis is to identify the assets of the computing system. The assets can be considered in categories, as listed below. The first three categories are the assets identified in Chapter 1 and described throughout this book. The remain-

Sidebar 8-2 Alternative Steps in Risk Analysis

There are many formal approaches to performing risk analysis. For example, the U.S. Army used its Operations Security (OPSEC) guidelines during the Vietnam War. [SEC99] The guidelines involve five steps:

1. Identify the critical information to be protected.
2. Analyze the threats.
3. Analyze the vulnerabilities.
4. Assess the risks.
5. Apply countermeasures.

Similarly, the U.S. Air Force uses an Operational Risk Management procedure to support its decision making. [AIR2000] The steps are:

1. Identify hazards.
2. Assess hazards.
3. Make risk decisions.
4. Implement controls.
5. Supervise.

As you can see, the steps are similar, but their details are always tailored to the particular situation at hand. For this reason, it is useful to use someone else's risk analysis process as a framework, but it is important to change it to match your own situation.

ing items are not strictly a part of a computing system but are important to its proper functioning.

- *hardware:* processors, boards, keyboards, monitors, terminals, microcomputers, workstations, tape drives, printers, disks, disk drives, cables, connections, communications controllers, and communications media
- *software:* source programs, object programs, purchased programs, in-house programs, utility programs, operating systems, systems programs (such as compilers), and maintenance diagnostic programs
- *data:* data used during execution, stored data on various media, printed data, archival data, update logs, and audit records
- *people:* skills needed to run the computing system or specific programs
- *documentation:* on programs, hardware, systems, administrative procedures, and the entire system
- *supplies:* paper, forms, laser cartridges, magnetic media, and printer fluid

It is essential to tailor this list to your own situation. No two organizations will have the same assets to protect, and something that is valuable in one organization may not be as valuable to another. For example, if a project has one key designer, then that designer is an essential asset; on the other hand, if a similar project has ten designers, any of whom could do the project's design, then each designer is not as essential because there are nine easily available replacements. Thus, you must add to the list of assets the other people, processes, and things that must be protected. For example, RAND Corporation's Vulnerability Assessment and Mitigation (VAM) methodology [ANT02] includes additional assets, such as

- the enabling infrastructure
- the building or vehicle in which the system will reside
- the power, water, air, and other environmental conditions necessary for proper functioning
- human and social assets, such as policies, procedures, and training

The VAM methodology is a process supported by a tool to help people identify assets, vulnerabilities, and countermeasures. We use other aspects of VAM as an example technique in later risk analysis steps.

In a sense, the list of assets is an inventory of the system, including intangibles and human resource items. For security purposes, this inventory is more comprehensive than the traditional inventory of hardware and software often performed for configuration management or accounting purposes. The point is to identify all assets necessary for the system to be usable.

Step 2: Determine Vulnerabilities

The next step in risk analysis is to determine the vulnerabilities of these assets. This step requires imagination; we want to predict what damage might occur to the assets and from what sources. We can enhance our imaginative skills by developing a clear idea of the nature of vulnerabilities. This nature derives from the need to ensure the three basic goals of computer security: confidentiality, integrity, and availability. Thus, a vulnerability is any situation that could cause loss of confidentiality, integrity, and availability. We want to use an organized approach to considering situations that could cause these losses for a particular object.

Software engineering offers us several techniques for investigating possible problems. Hazard analysis, described in Sidebar 8-3, explores failures that may occur and faults that may cause them. These techniques have been used successfully in analyzing

Sidebar 8-3 Hazard Analysis Techniques

Hazard analysis is a set of systematic but informal techniques intended to expose potentially hazardous system states. Using hazard analysis helps us find strategies to prevent or mitigate harm once we understand what problems can occur. That is, hazard analysis ferrets out not only the effects of problems but also their likely causes so that we can then apply an appropriate technique for preventing a problem or softening its consequences. Hazard analysis usually involves creating hazard lists as well as procedures for exploring "what if" scenarios to trigger consideration of nonobvious hazards. The problems' sources can be lurking in any artifacts of the development or maintenance process, not just in the code. There are many kinds of problems, ranging from incorrect information or code, to unclear consequences of a particular action. A good hazard analysis takes all of them into account.

A variety of techniques support the identification and management of potential hazards in complex critical systems. Among the most effective are *hazard and operability studies* (HAZOP), *failure modes and effects analysis* (FMEA), and *fault tree analysis* (FTA). HAZOP is a structured analysis technique originally developed for the process control and chemical plant industries. FMEA is a bottom-up technique applied at the system component level. A team identifies each component's possible faults or fault modes; then, it determines what could trigger the fault and what systemwide effects each fault might have. By keeping system consequences in mind, the team often finds possible system failures that are not made visible by other analytical means. FTA complements FMEA. It is a top-down technique that begins with a postulated hazardous system malfunction. Then, the FTA team works backward to identify the possible precursors to the mishap. By tracing from a specific hazardous malfunction, the team can derive unexpected contributors to mishaps and identify opportunities to mitigate the risk of mishaps.

We decide which technique is most appropriate by understanding how much we know about causes and effects. When we know the cause and effect of a given problem, we can strengthen the description of how the system should behave. If we can describe a known effect with unknown cause, then we use deductive techniques such as FTA to help us understand the likely causes of the unwelcome behavior. Conversely, we may know the cause of a problem but not understand all the effects; here, we use inductive techniques such as FMEA to help us trace from cause to all possible effects. Finally, to find problems about which we may not yet be aware, we perform an exploratory analysis such as a HAZOP study.

TABLE 8-2 Assets and Security Properties.

Asset	Confidentiality	Integrity	Availability
Hardware			
Software			
Data			
People			
Documentation			
Supplies			

safety-critical systems. However, additional techniques are tailored specifically to security concerns; we address those techniques in this and following sections.

To organize the way we consider threats and assets we can use a matrix, such as the one shown in Table 8-2. One vulnerability can affect more than one asset or cause more than one type of loss. The table is a guide to stimulate thinking, but its format is not rigid.

In thinking about the contents of each matrix entry, we can ask the following questions.

- What are the effects of unintentional errors? Consider typing the wrong command, entering the wrong data, using the wrong data item, discarding the wrong listing, and disposing of output insecurely.
- What are the effects of willfully malicious insiders? Consider disgruntled employees, bribery, and curious browsers.
- What are the effects of outsiders? Consider network access, dial-in access, hackers, people walking through the building, and people sifting through the trash.
- What are the effects of natural and physical disasters? Consider fires, storms, floods, power outages, and component failures.

Table 8-3 is a version of the previous table with some of the entries filled in. It shows that certain general problems can affect the assets of a computing system. In a given installation, it is necessary to determine what can happen to specific hardware, software, data items, and other assets.

Some organizations use other approaches to determining vulnerabilities and assessing their importance. For example, Sidebar 8-4 describes the U.S. Navy's approach to vulnerability evaluation.

Alas, there is no simple checklist or easy procedure to list all vulnerabilities. But from the earlier chapters of this book you have seen many examples of vulnerabilities to assets, and your mind has been trained to think of harm that can occur. Tools can help us conceive of vulnerabilities by providing a structured way to think. For example, RAND's VAM methodology suggests that assets have certain properties that make

TABLE 8-3 Assets and Attacks.

Asset	Secrecy	Integrity	Availability
Hardware		overloaded destroyed tampered with	failed stolen destroyed unavailable
Software	stolen copied pirated	impaired by Trojan horse modified tampered with	deleted misplaced usage expired
Data	disclosed accessed by outsider inferred	damaged - software error - hardware error - user error	deleted misplaced destroyed
People			quit retired terminated on vacation
Documentation			lost stolen destroyed
Supplies			lost stolen damaged

Sidebar 8-4 Integrated Vulnerability Assessments and CARVER

The U.S. Navy (see *http://www.safetycenter.navy.mil/orm/generalorm/introduction/default.htm*) performs Integrated Vulnerability Assessments (IVAs) as part of its risk analysis process. An IVA uses checklists to review system vulnerabilities and suggest appropriate mitigative strategies. The steps in an IVA include:

1. identifying vulnerabilities
2. assigning priorities to the vulnerabilities
3. brainstorming countermeasures
4. assessing the risks

The Criticality, Accessibility, Recuperability, Vulnerability, Effect, and Recognizability (CARVER) method is employed to assign priorities to the vulnerabilities. Numeric ratings are applied to each vulnerability, and the sum represents a vulnerability score. However, the summation procedure blurs the distinctions among different types of risks, so the value of the overall score is questionable. Nevertheless, IVAs and CARVER may be useful in helping make security planning issues more visible.

TABLE 8-4 Attributes Contributing to Vulnerabilities.[3]

Design/Architecture	Behavioral	General

• Singularity
  • Uniqueness
  • Centrality
  • Homogeneity
• Separability
• Logic/implementation errors; fallibility
• Design sensitivity, fragility, limits, finiteness
• Unrecoverability
	• Behavioral sensitivity/fragility
	• Malevolence
	• Rigidity
	• Malleability
	• Gullibility, deceivability, naïveté
	• Complacency
	• Corruptibility, co ntrollability
		• Accessible, detectable, identifiable, transparent, interceptable
		• Hard to manage or control
		• Self-unawareness and unpredictability
		• Predictability

them vulnerable. The properties exist in three categories: aspects of the design or architecture, aspects of behavior, and general attributes. Table 8-4 lists these properties in more detail. Notice that the properties apply to many kinds of systems and at various places within a given system.

These attributes can be used to build a matrix, each of whose entries may suggest one or more vulnerabilities. An example of such a matrix is shown in Figure 8-2. Using that matrix, for example, the design attribute *limits, finiteness* applied to a *cyber object*, a *software program*, could lead you to suspect buffer overflow vulnerabilities, or *uniqueness* for a *hardware object* could signal a single point of failure. To use this methodology you would work through the matrix, thinking of each contributing attribute on each asset class to derive the set of vulnerabilities.

Antón et al. [ANT02] point out that it is not enough to fill in the matrix cells. We must also consider combinations of situations that might enable certain vulnerabilities. For example, as Figure 8-3 shows, at least six attributes can allow a successful attack by Trojan horse. The homogeneity of the design or architecture may encourage an attacker to place a Trojan horse in a well-understood location. The horse may be loaded by a gullible user who downloads a seemingly benign file. To do this, the attacker must have some control over users and their machines; in general, this is a manifestation of the accessibility of systems, especially on the Internet, and the lack of user awareness when a remote site sends data to an unsuspecting system.

Step 3: Estimate Likelihood of Exploitation

The third step in conducting a risk analysis is determining how often each exposure is likely to be exploited. Likelihood of occurrence relates to the stringency of the existing controls and the likelihood that someone or something will evade the existing controls. Sidebar 8-5 describes several approaches to computing the probability that an event will occur: classical, frequency, and subjective. Each approach has its advantages and disadvantages, and we must choose the approach that best suits the situation (and its available information).

[3] From [ANT02], copyright © RAND 2002, reprinted by permission.

		Object of Vulnerability			
		Physical	Cyber	Human / Social	Enabling Infrastructure
	Attributes:	Hardware (Data Storage, Input/Output, Clients, Servers), Network and Communications, Lottery	Software, Data, Information, Knowledge	Staff, Command, Management, Policies, Procedure, Training, Authentication	Ship, Building, Power, Water, Air, Environment
Design / Architecture	Singularity				
	Uniqueness				
	Centrality				
	Homogeneity				
	Separability				
	Logic/ Implementation Errors; Fallibility				
	Design Sensitivity/ Fragility/Limits/ Finiteness				
	Unrecoverability				
Behavior	Behavioral Sensitivity /Fragility				
	Malevolence				
	Rigidity				
	Malleability				
	Gullibility/ Deceivability/Naiveté				
	Complacency				
	Corruptibility/ Controllability				
General	Accessible/ Detectable/ Identifiable/ Transparent/ Interceptable				
	Hard to Manage or Control				
	Self Unawareness and Unpredictability				
	Predictability				

FIGURE 8-2 Vulnerabilities Suggested by Attributes and Objects.[4]

[4] From [ANT02], copyright © RAND 2002, reprinted by permission.

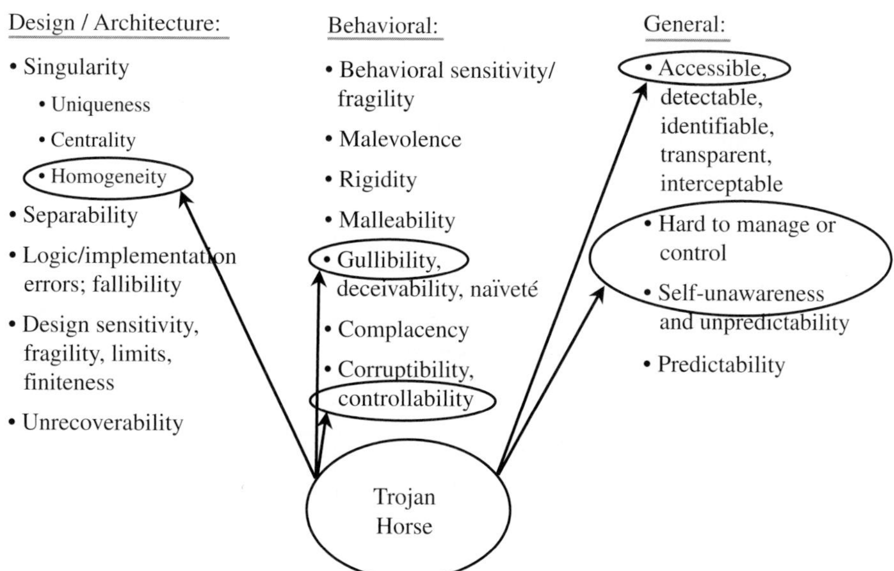

FIGURE 8-3 Vulnerabilities Enabling a Trojan Horse Attack.[5]

In security, it is often not possible to directly evaluate an event's probability by using classical techniques. However, we can try to apply frequency probability by using observed data for a specific system. Local failure rates are fairly easy to record, and we can identify which failures resulted in security breaches or created new vulnerabilities. In particular, operating systems can track data on hardware failures, failed login attempts, numbers of accesses, and changes in the sizes of data files.

Another alternative is to estimate the number of occurrences in a given time period. We can ask an analyst familiar with the system to approximate the number of times a described event occurred in the last year, for example. Although the count is not exact (because the analyst is unlikely to have complete information), the analyst's knowledge of the system and its usage may yield reasonable estimates.

Of course, the two methods described depend on the fact that a system is already built and has been in use for some period of time. In many cases, and especially for proposed systems, the usage data are not available. In this case, we may ask an analyst to estimate likelihood by reviewing a table based on a similar system; this approach is incorporated in several formal security risk processes. For example, the analyst may be asked to choose one of the ratings shown in Table 8-5. Completing this analysis depends on the rater's professional expertise. The table provides the rater with a framework within which to consider each likelihood. Differences between close ratings are not very significant. A rater should be able to distinguish between something that happens once a year and once a month.

[5] From [ANT02], copyright © RAND 2002, reprinted by permission.

Sidebar 8-5 Three Approaches to Probability

Normally, we think of probability or likelihood as one concept. But in fact there are many ways to think about and derive probabilities. The approach to probability that you use suggests how much confidence you can have in the probability numbers you derive.

Classical probability is the simplest and most theoretical kind. It is based on a model of how the world works. For example, to calculate the probability that a given side of a six-sided die will result from tossing the die, we think of a model of a cube, where each side is equally sized and weighted. This kind of probability requires no empirical data. The answers can be derived from the model itself, and in an objective way. However, classical probability requires knowledge of elementary events and is bound to the model's correctness. It is difficult to use classical probability to handle problems involving infinite sets.

When we cannot use classical probability, we often choose to use *frequency probability*. Here, instead of building a model of a die, we take a real die and toss it many times, recording the result each time. This approach to probability requires historical data and assumes environmental stability and replication. In our example, we assume that the die is weighted properly and the tossing motion is the same each time. Frequency probabilities are never exact. What we hope is that, in their limit, they approach the theoretical probability of an event. Thus, if 100 people each toss a die 100 times, each person's distribution may be slightly different from the others, but in the aggregate the distribution will approach the correct one. Clearly, frequency probability cannot be applied to unique events; for example, we cannot use it to estimate the probability that software will fail in a particular way on a particular day.

When we cannot use classical or frequency probability, we often rely on *subjective probability*, which requires neither data nor formal analysis. Here, we ask experts to give us their opinions on the likelihood of an event, so the probability may differ from one person to another. We sometimes use the Delphi method (described later in this section) to reconcile these differences. The big advantage of subjective probability is that it can be used in all circumstances. However, it is clearly not objective, and it requires a coherent and complete understanding of the situation and its context.

In any given risk analysis we may use two or even all three of these estimating techniques. We prefer classical probability, but we use other techniques as necessary.

The **Delphi approach** is a subjective probability technique originally devised by RAND [HAL67] to deal with public policy decisions. It assumes that experts can make informed estimates based on their experience; the method brings a group of experts to consensus. The first step in using Delphi is to provide each of several experts with information describing the situation surrounding the event under consideration. For example, the experts may be told about the software and hardware architecture, conditions of use, and expertise of users. Then, each expert individually estimates the likelihood of the event. The estimates are collected, reproduced, and distributed to all experts. The individual estimates are listed anonymously, and the experts are usually

TABLE 8-5 Ratings of Likelihood.

Frequency	Rating
More than once a day	10
Once a day	9
Once every three days	8
Once a week	7
Once in two weeks	6
Once a month	5
Once every four months	4
Once a year	3
Once every three years	2
Less than once in three years	1

given some statistical information, such as mean or median. The experts are then asked whether they wish to modify their individual estimates in light of values their colleagues have supplied. If the revised values are reasonably consistent, the process ends with the group's reaching consensus. If the values are inconsistent, additional rounds of revision may occur until consensus is reached.

Step 4: Compute Expected Loss

By this time, we have gained an understanding of the assets we value, their possible vulnerabilities, and the likelihood that the vulnerabilities will be exploited. Next, we must determine the likely loss if the exploitation does indeed occur. As with likelihood of occurrence, this value is difficult to determine. Some costs, such as the cost to replace a hardware item, are easy to obtain. The cost to replace a piece of software can be approximated reasonably well from the initial cost to buy it (or specify, design, and write it). However, we must take care to include hidden costs in our calculations. For instance, there is a cost to others of not having a piece of hardware or software. Similarly, there are costs in restoring a system to its previous state, reinstalling software, or deriving a piece of information. These costs are substantially harder to measure.

In addition, there may be hidden costs that involve legal fees if certain events take place. For example, some data require protection for legal reasons. Personal data, such as police records, tax information, census data, and medical information, are so sensitive that there are criminal penalties for releasing the data to unauthorized people. Other data are company confidential; their release may give competitors an edge on new products or on likely changes to the stock price. Some financial data, especially when they reflect an adverse event, could seriously affect public confidence in a bank, an insurance company, or a stock brokerage. It is difficult to determine the cost of releasing these data.

If a computing system, a piece of software, or a key person is unavailable, causing a particular computing task to be delayed, there may be serious consequences. If a program that prints paychecks is delayed, employees' confidence in the company may be shaken, or some employees may face penalties from not being able to pay their own bills. If customers cannot make transactions because the computer is down, they may choose to take their business to a competitor. For some time-critical services involving human lives, such as a hospital's life-support systems or a space station's guidance systems, the costs of failure are infinitely high.

Thus, we must analyze the ramifications of a computer security failure. The following questions can prompt us to think about issues of explicit and hidden cost related to security. The answers may not produce precise cost figures, but they will help identify the sources of various types of costs.

- What legal obligations are there in preserving the confidentiality or integrity of a given data item?
- What business requirements and agreements cover the situation? Does the organization have to pay a penalty if it cannot provide a service?
- Could release of a data item cause harm to a person or organization? Would there be the possibility of legal action if harm were done?
- Could unauthorized access to a data item cause the loss of future business opportunity? Might it give a competitor an unfair advantage? What would be the estimated loss in revenue?
- What is the psychological effect of lack of computer service? Embarrassment? Loss of credibility? Loss of business? How many customers would be affected? What is their value as customers?
- What is the value of access to data or programs? Could this computation be deferred? Could this computation be performed elsewhere? How much would it cost to have a third party do the computing elsewhere?
- What is the value to someone else of having access to data or programs? How much would a competitor be willing to pay for access?
- What other problems would arise from loss of data? Could the data be replaced or reconstructed? With what amount of work?

These are not easy costs to evaluate. Nevertheless, they are needed to develop a thorough understanding of the risks. Furthermore, the vulnerabilities in computer security are often considerably higher than managers expect. Realistic estimates of potential harm can raise concern and suggest places in which attention to security is especially needed.

Step 5: Survey and Select New Controls

By this point in our risk analysis, we understand the system's vulnerabilities and the likelihood of exploitation. We turn next to an analysis of the controls to see which ones address the risks we have identified. We want to match each vulnerability with at least

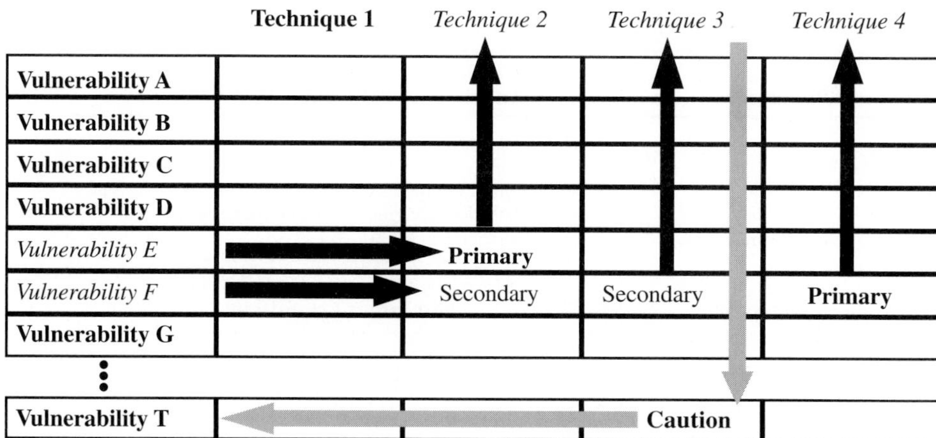

FIGURE 8-4 Mapping Control Techniques to Vulnerabilities.[6]

one appropriate security technique, as shown in Figure 8-4. Once we do that, we can use our expected loss estimates to help us decide which controls, alone or in concert, are the most cost effective for a given situation. Notice that vulnerabilities E and F are countered by primary techniques 2 and 4, respectively. The secondary control techniques 2 and 3 for vulnerability F are good defense in depth. The fact that there is no secondary control for vulnerability E is a minor concern. But vulnerability T is a serious caution, because it has no control whatsoever.

For example, consider the risk of losing data. This loss could be addressed by several of the controls we have discussed in previous chapters: periodic backups, redundant data storage, access controls to prevent unauthorized deletion, physical security to keep someone from stealing a disk, or program development standards to limit the effect of programs on the data. We must determine the effectiveness of each control in a given situation; for instance, using physical security in a building already equipped with guards and limited access may be more effective than sophisticated software-based controls.

What Criteria Are Used for Selecting Controls?

We can also think of controls at a different level. Table 8-6 lists a selection of strategies presented in the VAM methodology; we can use the list to mitigate the effects of a vulnerability. This method reflects a systems approach and also the military defense environment for which VAM was developed.

VAM characterizes controls in terms of four high-level aspects: resilience and robustness; intelligence, surveillance, reconnaissance (ISR), and self-awareness; counterintelligence, denial of ISR, and target acquisition; and deterrence and punishment. Notice that many of these controls are technical but embrace the entire system architecture. For example, heterogeneity is a control that can be implemented only when the

[6] Adapted from [ANT02], copyright © RAND 2002, reprinted by permission.

TABLE 8-6 Categories of Mitigation Techniques.[7]

Resilience and Robustness	Intelligence, Surveillance, Reconnaissance (ISR), and Self-Awareness
• Heterogeneity • Redundancy • Centralization • Decentralization • Verification and validation, software and hardware engineering, evaluation, testing • Control of exposure, access, and output • Trust learning and enforcement systems • Nonrepudiation, so that some agent cannot erase identifying information about who or what took a particular action • Hardening • Fault, uncertainty, validity, and quality tolerance and graceful degradation • Static resource allocation • Dynamic resource allocation • Management • Threat response structures and plans • Rapid reconstitution and recovery • Adaptability and learning • Immunological defense systems • Vaccination	• Intelligence operations • Self-awareness, monitoring, and assessments • Deception for intelligence, surveillance, and reconnaissance • Attack detection, recognition, damage assessment, and forensics (friend and foe) **Counterintelligence, Denial of ISR, and Target Acquisition** • General counterintelligence • Deception for counterintelligence • Denial of ISR and target acquisition **Deterrence and Punishment** • Preventive and retributive information/military operations • Criminal and legal penalties and guarantees • Law enforcement, civil proceedings

system is designed so that it is composed of dissimilar pieces, such as operating systems of different brands. Similarly, redundancy and decentralization are architectural elements, too. Some people think of controls as specific pieces of hardware and software, such as firewalls and virus checkers. But in fact, this broader list takes a software engineering approach to security: Make the system sturdy from the beginning, rather than trying only to patch holes with security-specific, self-contained subsystems.

The VAM methodology takes this table one step further, using it to compare vulnerabilities to possible controls. The matrix in Figure 8-5 lists attributes leading to vulnerabilities (as seen in Table 8-4) along the left side, and the controls of Table 8-6 along the top. Thus, each cell of the matrix corresponds to whether a particular control addresses a given vulnerability.

How Do Controls Affect What They Control?

Controls have positive and negative effects: Encryption, for example, protects confidentiality, but it also takes time and introduces key management issues. Thus, when selecting controls, you have to consider the full impact.

The creators of VAM recognized that sometimes attributes enhance security and other times detract from it. For example, heterogeneity may be useful as a control in preventing the proliferation of the same kind of logic error throughout a system. But heterogeneity can also make the system's design harder to understand and, therefore,

[7] From [ANT02], copyright © RAND 2002, reprinted by permission.

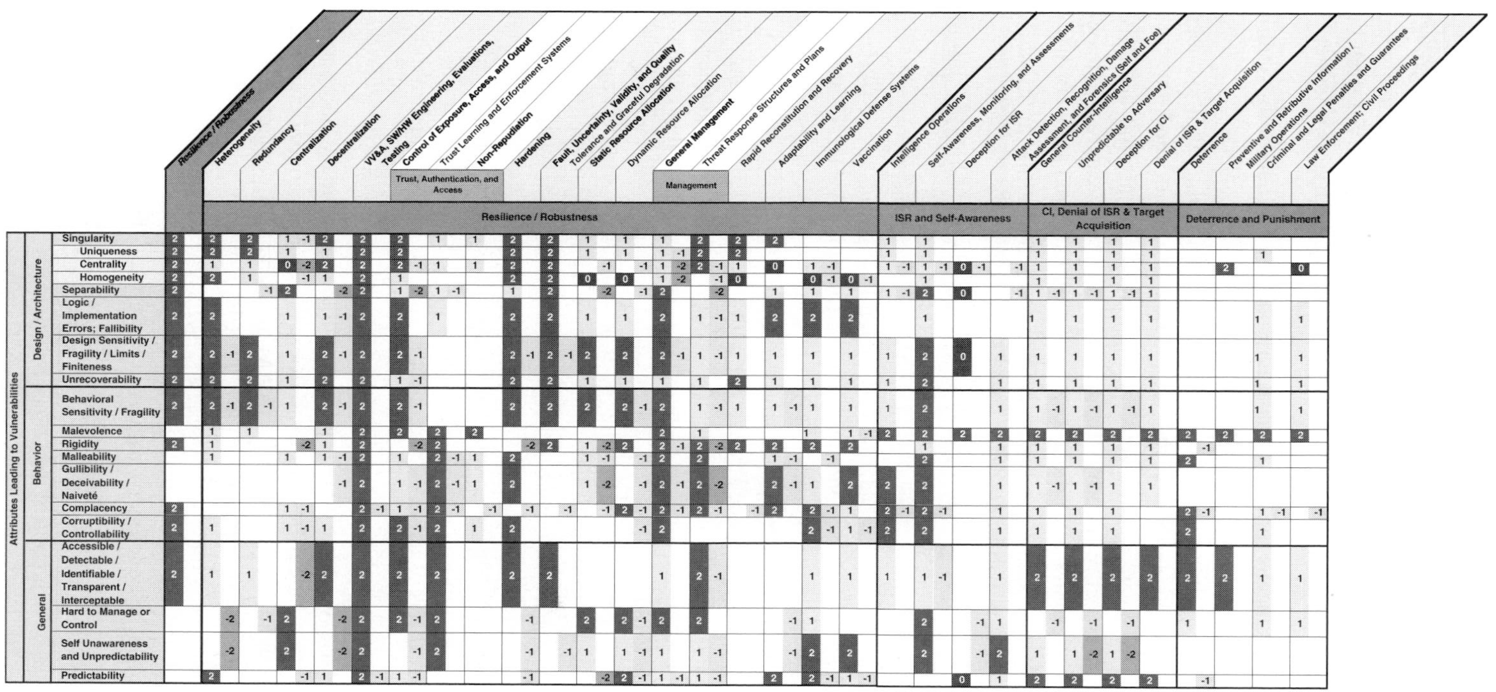

FIGURE 8-5 Matrix of Vulnerabilities and Controls.[8]

[8] From [ANT02], copyright © RAND 2002, reprinted by permission.

harder to maintain; the result can be a fragile design that is easy for an attacker to cause to fail. For this reason, VAM has included a rating scheme to reflect the relationship depicted by each cell of the matrix. A cell relating a vulnerability to a security technique contains a number from –2 to 2, according to this scheme:

- 2 means that the control mitigates the vulnerability significantly and should be a prime candidate for addressing it.
- 1 means that the control mitigates the vulnerability somewhat, but not as well as one labeled 2, so it should be a secondary candidate for addressing it.
- 0 means that the vulnerability may have beneficial side effects that enhance some aspect of security. (Example: homogeneity can facilitate both static and dynamic resource allocation. It can also facilitate rapid recovery and reconstitution.)
- –1 means that the control worsens the vulnerability somewhat or incurs new vulnerabilities.
- –2 means that the control worsens the vulnerability significantly or incurs new vulnerabilities.

The VAM rating scheme is depicted in Figure 8-6; the full explanation of each row name, column name and rating can be found in [ANT02]. The matrix is used to support decisions about controls in the following way. We begin with the rows of the matrix, each of which corresponds to a vulnerability. We follow the row across to look for instances in which a cell is labeled with a 2 (or a 1, if there are no 2s). Then we follow the column up to its heading, to see which security techniques (the column labels) are strong controls for this vulnerability. For example, the matrix indicates that heterogeneity, redundancy, and decentralization are good controls for design sensitivity or fragility. Next, we notice that both heterogeneity and decentralization are also labeled with a –1 in that cell, indicating that by using them, we may enable other vulnerabilities. For instance, heterogeneity can enable several systems to complement each other but can make the overall system harder to maintain. Similarly, decentralization makes it more difficult for an attacker to exploit fragilities, but at the same time it can make the system more fragile due to a need for coordination. In this way, we can look at the implications of using each control to address known vulnerabilities.

Which Controls Are Best?

By now, we have noted a large number of primary and secondary controls to use against our identified vulnerabilities. We need a way to determine the most appropriate controls for a given situation. VAM offers us a refinement process based on three roles: operational, design, and policy. That is, if we are interested in security from the perspective of someone who will be using or managing the system, we take the operational perspective. If instead we view security from an implementation point of view, we take the developer's role. And if we view the system in the larger context of how it provides information processing to relevant organizations, we adopt the policy point of view. VAM provides tables, such as the one shown in Figure 8-7, to identify the relevance of each control to each perspective.

In this matrix, the rows represent security controls, and the columns serve two functions. The first three columns represent the three perspectives for evaluating the rele-

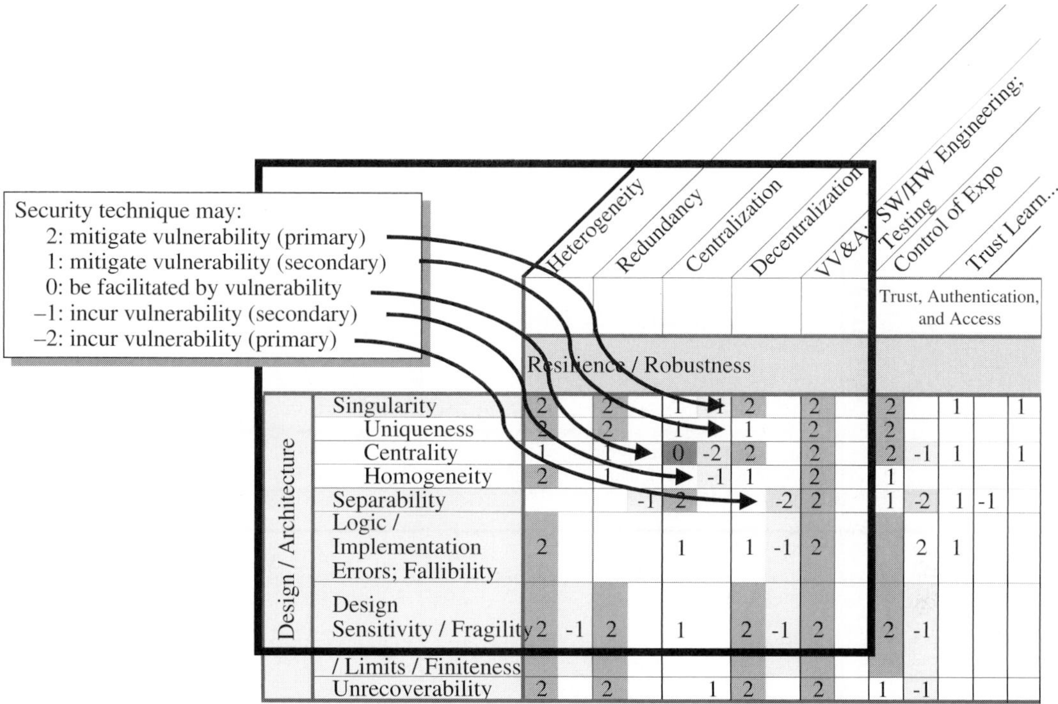

FIGURE 8-6 Valuation of Security Techniques.[9]

vance of the control: operational, developer, and policy. The second five columns note at what stage of an attack the control is most useful: allowing an attacker to have knowledge about the system, enabling access to the system, providing a target for attack, enabling nonretribution, and assessing the extent to which an attack has been successful. In this matrix, the 1s and 2s labeling the cells have a different meaning from the previous matrix. Here, a 1 indicates that the control is weakly relevant to the perspective or attack stage, and a 2 indicates that it is strongly relevant.

Finally, VAM presents a matrix to illustrate the relationships among the attack stages and the vulnerable objects in a system. For example, an attacker can gain knowledge about a system not only by obtaining source code and doing reverse engineering but also by using organizational charts and social engineering.

The VAM approach is comprehensive and effective, supported by a software tool to walk an analyst through the stages of identifying vulnerabilities, selecting controls, and refining choices. [ANT02] contains tables and charts that explain the rating system and the relationships among tables; we have presented some of those tables and charts, courtesy of Antón et al., because they offer good examples that introduce you to the details of selecting controls. Sometimes, however, you can do a much less rigorous analysis

[9] From [ANT02], copyright © RAND 2002, reprinted by permission.

	Apply to Physical, Cyber, Human/ Social, and Infrastructure Components	Useful to these users:			Helps Protect These Attack Stages				
		Operational	Developer	Policy	Knowledge	Access	Target	Non-Retribution	Assess
Intel, Surveillance, & Reconnaissance (ISR) and Self-Awareness	Intelligence Operations	2					1	1	
	Self-Awareness, Monitoring, and Assessments	2	2			1	1	1	
	Deception for ISR	2	2			1	1	1	
	Attack Detection, Recognition, Damage Assessment, and Forensics (Self and Foe)	2	2			1	1	1	
Counter-Intelligence / Denial of ISR & Target Acquisition	General Counter-Intelligence	2	2		2			2	2
	Unpredictable to Adversary	2	2		2			2	2
	Deception for CI	2	2		2			2	2
	Denial of ISR & Target Acquisition	2	2		2		1		
Offense and Retribution	Deterrence	2	2	2				2	
	Preventive and Retributive Information / Military Operations	2		2				2	
	Criminal and Legal Penalties and Guarantees		2	2				2	
	Law Enforcement; Civil Proceedings		2	2				2	

FIGURE 8-7 Relevance of Certain Security Techniques to Roles and Attack Components.[10]

by simply listing the possible controls, assessing the strengths and weaknesses of each, and choosing the one(s) that seem to be most appropriate.

Step 6: Project Savings

By this point in our risk analysis, we have identified controls that address each vulnerability in our list. The next step is to determine whether the costs outweigh the benefits

[10] From [ANT02], copyright © RAND 2002, reprinted by permission.

of preventing or mitigating the risks. Recall that we multiply the risk probability by the risk impact to determine the risk exposure. The risk impact is the loss that we might experience if the risk were to turn into a real problem. There are techniques to help us determine the risk exposure.

The effective cost of a given control is the actual cost of the control (such as purchase price, installation costs, and training costs) minus any expected loss from using the control (such as administrative or maintenance costs). Thus, the true cost of a control may be positive if the control is expensive to administer or introduces new risk in another area of the system. Or the cost can even be negative if the reduction in risk is greater than the cost of the control.

For example, suppose a department has determined that some users have gained unauthorized access to the computing system. It is feared that the intruders might intercept or even modify sensitive data on the system. One approach to addressing this problem is to install a more secure data access control program. Even though the cost of the access control software is high ($25,000), its cost is easily justified when compared to its value, as shown in Table 8-7. Because the entire cost of the package is charged in the first year, even greater benefits are expected for subsequent years.

Another company uses a common carrier to link to a network for certain computing applications. The company has identified the risks of unauthorized access to data and computing facilities through the network. These risks can be eliminated by replacement of remote network access with the requirement to access the system only from a machine operated on the company premises. The machine is not owned; a new one would have to be acquired. The economics of this example are not promising, as shown in Table 8-8.

To supplement this tabular analysis, we can use a graphical depiction to contrast the economics involved in choosing among several strategies. For example, suppose we are considering the use of regression testing after making an upgrade to fix a security flaw. Regression testing means applying tests to verify that all remaining functions are unaffected by the change. It can be an expensive process, especially for large systems that implement many functions. (This example is taken from Pfleeger [PFL01].)

TABLE 8-7 Justification of Access Control Software.

Item	Amount
Risks: disclosure of company confidential data, computation based on incorrect data	
Cost to reconstruct correct data: $1,000,000 @ 10% likelihood per year	$100,000
Effectiveness of access control software: 60%	– 60,000
Cost of access control software	+25,000
Expected annual costs due to loss and controls (100,000 – 60,000 + 25,000)	$65,000
Savings (100,000 – 65,000)	$35,000

TABLE 8-8 Cost/Benefit Analysis for Replacing Network Access.

Item	Amount
Risk: unauthorized access and use	
Access to unauthorized data and programs $100,000 @ 2% likelihood per year	$2,000
Unauthorized use of computing facilities $10,000 @ 40% likelihood per year	4,000
Expected annual loss (2,000 + 4,000)	6,000
Effectiveness of network control: 100%	–6,000
Control cost:	
Hardware (50,000 amortized over 5 years)	+10,000
Software (20,000 amortized over 5 years)	+4,000
Support personnel (each year)	+40,000
Annual cost	54,000
Expected annual loss (6,000 – 6,000 + 54,000)	$54,000
Savings (6,000 – 54,000)	– $48,000

To help us make our decision, we draw a diagram such as that in Figure 8-8. We want to compare the risk impact of doing regression testing with not doing it. Thus, the upper part of the diagram shows the risks in doing regression testing, and the lower part the risks of not doing regression testing. In each of the two cases, one of three things can happen: We find a critical fault, there is a critical fault but we miss finding it, or there are no critical faults to be found. For each possibility, we first calculate the probability of an unwanted outcome, P(UO). Then, we associate a loss with that unwanted outcome, L(UO). Thus, in our example, if we do regression testing and miss a critical fault lurking in the system (a probability of 0.05), the loss could be $30 million. Multiplying the two, we find the risk exposure for that strategy to be $1.5 million. As you can see from the calculations in the figure, it is far safer to do the regression testing than to skip it.

As shown in these examples, risk analysis can be used to evaluate the true costs of proposed controls. In this way, risk analysis can be used as a planning tool. The effectiveness of different controls can be compared on paper before actual investments are made. Risk analysis can thus be used repeatedly, to select an optimum set of controls.

Arguments For and Against Risk Analysis

Risk analysis is a well-known planning tool, used often by auditors, accountants, and managers. In many situations, such as obtaining approval for new drugs, new power plants, and new medical devices, a risk analysis is required by law in many countries. There are many good reasons to perform a risk analysis in preparation for creating a security plan.

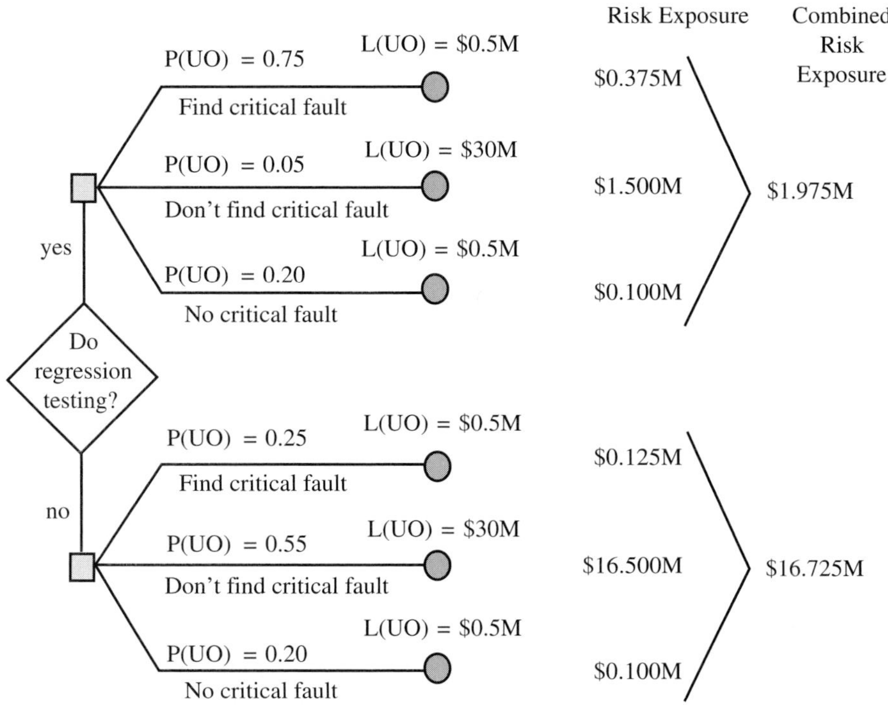

FIGURE 8-8 Risk Calculation for Regression Testing.

- *Improve awareness.* Discussing issues of security can raise the general level of interest and concern among developers and users. Especially when the user population has little expertise in computing, the risk analysis can educate users about the role security plays in protecting functions and data that are essential to user operations and products.
- *Relate security mission to management objectives.* Security is often perceived as a financial drain for no gain. Management does not always see that security helps balance harm and control costs.
- *Identify assets, vulnerabilities, and controls.* Some organizations are unaware of their computing assets, their value to the organization, and the vulnerabilities associated with those assets. A systematic analysis produces a comprehensive list of assets, valuations, and risks.
- *Improve basis for decisions.* A security manager can present an argument such as "I think we need a firewall here" or "I think we should use token-based authentication instead of passwords." Risk analysis augments the manager's judgment as a basis for the decision.
- *Justify expenditures for security.* Some security mechanisms appear to be very expensive and without obvious benefit. A risk analysis can help identify instances where it is worth the expense to implement a major security mecha-

nism. Justification is often derived from examining the much larger risks of *not* spending for security.

However, despite the advantages of risk analysis, there are several arguments against using it to support decision making.

- *False sense of precision and confidence.* The heart of risk analysis is the use of empirical data to generate estimates of risk impact, risk probability, and risk exposure. The danger is that these numbers will give us a false sense of precision, thereby giving rise to an undeserved confidence in the numbers. However, in many cases the numbers themselves are much less important than their relative sizes. Whether an expected loss is $100,000 or $150,000 is relatively unimportant. It is much more significant that the expected loss is far above the $10,000 or $20,000 budget allocated for implementing a particular control. Moreover, anytime a risk analysis generates a large potential loss, the system deserves further scrutiny to see if the root cause of the risk can be addressed.
- *Hard to perform.* Enumerating assets, vulnerabilities, and controls requires creative thinking. Assessing loss frequencies and impact can be difficult and subjective. A large risk analysis will have many things to consider. Risk analysis can be restricted to certain assets or vulnerabilities, however.
- *Immutability.* It is typical on many software projects to view processes like risk analysis as an irritating fact of life—a step to be taken in a hurry so that the developers can get on with the more interesting jobs related to designing, building, and testing the system. For this reason, risk analyses, like contingency plans and five-year plans, have a tendency to be filed and promptly forgotten. But if an organization takes security seriously, it will view the risk analysis as a living document, updating it at least annually or in conjunction with major system upgrades.
- *Lack of accuracy.* Risk analysis is not always accurate, for many reasons. First, we may not be able to calculate the risk probability with any accuracy, especially when we have no past history of similar situations. Second, even if we know the likelihood, we cannot always estimate the risk impact very well. The risk management literature is replete with papers about describing the scenario, showing that presenting the same situation in two different ways to two equivalent groups of people can yield two radically different estimates of impact. And third, we may not be able to anticipate all the possible risks. For example, bridge builders did not know about the risks introduced by torque from high winds until the Tacoma Narrows Bridge twisted in the wind and collapsed. After studying the colossal failure of this bridge and discovering the cause, engineers made mandatory the inclusion of torque in their simulation parameters. Similarly, we may not know enough about software, security, or the context in which the system is to be used, so there may be gaps in our risk analysis that cause it to be inaccurate.

This lack of accuracy is often cited as a deficiency of risk analysis. But this lack is a red herring. Risk analysis is useful as a planning tool, to compare and contrast options. We may not be able to predict events accurately, but we can use risk analysis to weigh the trade-offs between one action and another. When risk analysis is used in security planning, it highlights which security expenditures are likely to be most cost effective. This investigative basis is important for choosing among controls when money available for security is limited. And our risk analysis should improve as we build more systems, evaluate their security, and have a larger experience base from which to draw our estimates.

A risk analysis has many advantages as part of security plan or as a tool for less formal security decision making. It ranges from very subjective and imprecise to highly quantitative. It is useful for generating and documenting thoughts about likely threats and possible countermeasures. Finally, it supports rational decision making about security controls.

Next we turn to another aspect of security planning—developing security policies.

8.3 ORGANIZATIONAL SECURITY POLICIES

A key element of any organization's security planning is an effective security policy. A security policy must answer three questions: *who* can access *which resources* in *what manner*?

A **security policy** is a high-level management document to inform all users of the goals of and constraints on using a system. A policy document is written in broad enough terms that it does not change frequently. The information security policy is the foundation upon which all protection efforts are built. It should be a visible representation of priorities of the entire organization, definitively stating underlying assumptions that drive security activities. The policy should articulate senior management's decisions regarding security as well as asserting management's commitment to security. To be effective, the policy must be understood by everyone as the product of a directive from an authoritative and influential person at the top of the organization.

People sometimes issue other documents, called **procedures** or **guidelines,** to define how the policy translates into specific actions and controls. In this section, we examine how to write a useful and effective security policy.

Purpose

Security policies are used for several purposes, including the following:

- recognizing sensitive information assets
- clarifying security responsibilities
- promoting awareness for existing employees
- guiding new employees

Audience

A security policy addresses several different audiences with different expectations. That is, each group—users, owners, and beneficiaries—uses the security policy in important but different ways.

Users

Users legitimately expect a certain degree of confidentiality, integrity, and continuous availability in the computing resources provided to them. Although the degree varies with the situation, a security policy should reaffirm a commitment to this requirement for service.

Users also need to know and appreciate what is considered acceptable use of their computers, data, and programs. For users, a security policy should define acceptable use.

Owners

Each piece of computing equipment is owned by someone, and the owner may not be a system user. An owner provides the equipment to users for a purpose, such as to further education, support commerce, or enhance productivity. A security policy should also reflect the expectations and needs of owners.

Beneficiaries

A business has paying customers or clients; they are beneficiaries of the products and services offered by that business. At the same time, the general public may benefit in several ways: as a source of employment or by provision of infrastructure. For example, you may not be a client of BellSouth, but when you place a telephone call from London to Atlanta, you benefit from BellSouth's telecommunications infrastructure. In the same way, the government has customers: the citizens of its country, and "guests" who have visas enabling entry for various purposes and times. A university's customers include its students and faculty; other beneficiaries include the immediate community (which can take advantage of lectures and concerts on campus) and often the world population (enriched by the results of research and service).

To varying degrees, these beneficiaries depend, directly or indirectly, on the existence of or access to computers, their data and programs, and their computational power. For this set of beneficiaries, continuity and integrity of computing are very important. In addition, beneficiaries value confidentiality and correctness of the data involved. Thus, the interests of beneficiaries of a system must be reflected in the system's security policy.

Balance Among All Parties

A security policy must relate to the needs of users, owners, and beneficiaries. Unfortunately, the needs of these groups may conflict. A beneficiary might require immediate access to data, but owners or users might not want to bear the expense or inconvenience of providing access at all hours. Continuous availability may be a goal for users, but that goal is inconsistent with a need to perform preventive or emergency maintenance. Thus, the security policy must balance the priorities of all affected communities.

Contents

A security policy must identify its audiences: the beneficiaries, users, and owners. The policy should describe the nature of each audience and their security goals. Several other sections are required, including the purpose of the computing system, the resources needing protection, and the nature of the protection to be supplied. We discuss each one in turn.

Purpose

The policy should state the purpose of the organization's security functions, reflecting the requirements of beneficiaries, users, and owners. For example, the policy may state that the system will "protect customers' confidentiality or preserve a trust relationship," "ensure continual usability," or "maintain profitability." There are typically three to five goals, such as:

- Promote efficient business operation.
- Facilitate sharing of information throughout the organization.
- Safeguard business and personal information.
- Ensure that accurate information is available to support business processes.
- Ensure a safe and productive place to work.
- Comply with applicable laws and regulations.

The security goals should be related to the overall goal or nature of the organization. It is important that the system's purpose be stated clearly and completely because subsequent sections of the policy will relate back to these goals, making the policy a goal-driven product.

Protected Resources

A risk analysis will have identified the assets that are to be protected. These assets should be listed in the policy, in the sense that the policy lays out which items it addresses. For example, will the policy apply to all computers or only to those on the network? Will it apply to all data or only to client or management data? Will security be provided to all programs or only the ones that interact with customers? If the degree of protection varies from one service, product, or data type to another, the policy should state the differences. For example, data that uniquely identify clients may be protected more carefully than the names of cities in which clients reside.

Nature of the Protection

The asset list tells us *what* should be protected. The policy should also indicate *who* should have access to the protected items. It may also indicate *how* that access will be ensured and *how* unauthorized people will be denied access. All the mechanisms described in this book are at your disposal in deciding which controls should protect which objects. In particular, the security policy should state what degree of protection should be provided to which kinds of resources.

Characteristics of a Good Security Policy

If a security policy is written poorly, it cannot guide the developers and users in providing appropriate security mechanisms to protect important assets. Certain characteristics make a security policy a good one.

Coverage

A security policy must be comprehensive: It must either apply to or explicitly exclude all possible situations. Furthermore, a security policy may not be updated as each new situation arises, so it must be general enough to apply naturally to new cases that occur as the system is used in unusual or unexpected ways.

Durability

A security policy must grow and adapt well. In large measure, it will survive the system's growth and expansion without change. If written in a flexible way, the existing policy will be applicable to new situations. However, there are times when the policy must change (such as when government regulations mandate new security constraints), so the policy must be changeable when it needs to be.

An important key to durability is keeping the policy free from ties to specific data or protection mechanisms that almost certainly will change. For example, an initial version of a security policy might require a ten-character password for anyone needing access to data on the Sun workstation in room 110. But when that workstation is replaced or moved, the policy's guidance becomes useless. It is preferable to describe assets needing protection in terms of their function and characteristics, rather than in terms of specific implementation. For example, the policy on Sun workstations could be reworded to mandate strong authentication for access to sensitive student grades or customers' proprietary data. Better still, we can separate the elements of the policy, having one policy statement for student grades and another for customers' proprietary data. Similarly, we may want to define one policy that applies to preserving the confidentiality of relationships, and another protecting the use of system through strong authentication.

Realism

The policy must be realistic. That is, it must be possible to implement the stated security requirements with existing technology. Moreover, the implementation must be beneficial in terms of time, cost, and convenience; the policy should not recommend a control that works but prevents the system or its users from performing their activities and functions. Sidebar 8-6 points out that sometimes the policy writers are seduced by what is fashionable in security at the time of writing. It is important to make economically worthwhile investments in security, just as for any other careful business investment.

Usefulness

An obscure or incomplete security policy will not be implemented properly, if at all. The policy must be written in language that can be read, understood and followed by

Sidebar 8-6 The Economics of Information Security Policy

Anderson [AND02a] asks that we consider carefully the economic aspects of security when we devise our security policy. He points out that the security engineering community tends to overstate security problems because it is in their best interest to do so. "The typical infosec professional is a firewall vendor struggling to meet quarterly sales targets to prop up a sagging stock price, or a professor trying to mine the 'cyberterrorism' industry for grants, or a policeman pitching for the budget to build up a computer crime agency." Thus, they may exaggerate a security problem to meet a more pressing goal.

Moreover, the security community is subject to fads, as in other disciplines. Anderson says that network security is trendy in 2002, which means that vendors are pushing firewalls and encryption, products that have been oversold and address only part of the typical organization's security problems. He suggests that, rather than focusing on what is fashionable, we focus instead on asking for a reasonable return on our investment in security.

Soo Hoo's research indicates that a reasonable number is 20 percent, at a time when companies usually expect a 30 percent return from their investments in information technology. [SOO00] In this context, it may be more worthwhile to implement simple, inexpensive measures such as enabling screen-locking than larger, more complex and expensive measures such as PKI and centralized access control. As Anderson points out, "you could spend a bit less on security if you spend it smarter."

anyone who must implement it or is affected by it. For this reason, the policy should be succinct, clear, and direct.

Examples

To understand the nature of security policies, we study a few examples to illustrate some of the points presented above.

Data Sensitivity Policy

Our first example is from an organization that decided to classify all its data resources into four levels, based on how severe might be the effect if a resource were damaged. These levels are listed in Table 8-9. Then, the required protection was based on the resource's level. Finally, the organization analyzed its threats, their possible severities, and countermeasures, and their effectiveness, within each of the four levels.

Although the phrases describing the degree of damage are open to interpretation, the intent of these levels is clear: All information assets are to be classified as sensitive, personal, confidential, or open, and protection requirements for these four types are detailed in the remainder of the organization's policy document.

TABLE 8-9 Example: Defined Levels of Data Sensitivity.

Name	Description	Examples
Sensitive	Could damage competitive advantage	• business strategy • profit plans
Personal or protected	Could reveal personal, private, or protected information	• personal data: employees' salaries or performance reviews • private data: employee lists • protected data: data obligated to protect, such as those obtained under a nondisclosure agreement
Company confidential	Could damage company's public image	• audit reports, operating plans
Open	No harm	• press releases • white paper • marketing materials

Government Agency IT Security Policy

The U.S. Department of Energy (DOE), like many government units, has established its own security policy. The following excerpt is from the policy on protecting classified material, although the form is appropriate for many unclassified uses as well.

> It is the policy of DOE that classified information and classified ADP [automatic data processing] systems shall be protected from unauthorized access (including the enforcement of need-to-know protections), alteration, disclosure, destruction, penetration, denial of service, subversion of security measures, or improper use as a result of espionage, criminal, fraudulent, negligent, abusive, or other improper actions. The DOE shall use all reasonable measures to protect ADP systems that process, store, transfer, or provide access to classified information, to include but not limited to the following: physical security, personnel security, telecommunications security, administrative security, and hardware and software security measures. This order establishes this policy and defines responsibilities for the development, implementation, and periodic evaluation of the DOE program.

The policy then continues for several more pages to list specific responsibilities for specific people.

The cited paragraph is comprehensive, covering practically every possible source (espionage, crime, fraud, etc.) of practically every possible harm (unauthorized access, alteration, destruction, etc.), and practically every possible kind of control (physical, personnel, etc.). The generality of the header paragraph is complemented by subsequent paragraphs giving specific responsibilities:

- "Each data owner shall determine and declare the required protection level of information..."

- "Each security officer shall...perform a risk assessment to identify and document specific...assets,... threats,...and vulnerability..."
- "Each manager shall...establish procedures to ensure that systems are continuously monitored...to detect security infractions..."

and so on.

Internet Security Policy

The Internet does not have a governing security policy per se, because it is a federation of users. Nevertheless, the Internet Society drafted a security policy for its members [PET91]. The policy contains the following interesting portions.

- Users are individually responsible for understanding and respecting the security policies of the systems (computers and networks) they are using. Users are individually accountable for their own behavior.
- Users have a responsibility to employ available security mechanisms and procedures for protecting their own data. They also have a responsibility for assisting in the protection of the systems they use.
- Computer and network service providers are responsible for maintaining the security of the systems they operate. They are further responsible for notifying users of their security policies and any changes to these policies.
- Vendors and system developers are responsible for providing systems which are sound and which embody adequate security controls.
- Users, service providers, and hardware and software vendors are responsible for cooperating to provide security.
- Technical improvements in Internet security protocols should be sought on a continuing basis. At the same time, personnel developing new protocols, hardware or software for the Internet are expected to include security considerations as part of the design and development process.

These statements clearly state to whom they apply and for what each party is responsible.

Policy Issue Example: Government E-Mail

Organizations develop computer security policies along the lines just described. Generally the policies lead to the familiar assets, vulnerabilities, and controls. But sometimes you have to start with existing policies—which may be formal documents or informal understandings—and consider how they apply in new situations. Is this action consistent with the goals of the policy and therefore acceptable? Applying policies can be like being a judge. As security professionals, we often focus on security policy without remembering the context in which we are making policy decisions. In this section, we look at a real-life issue to see how security policy fits into the broader scope of issues the security must address.

The U.S. government has proposed using network technologies to enhance its ability to interact with American citizens. Some people think that by employing functions such as electronic mail and World Wide Web access, the government could make more information available to citizens more quickly and at the same time be more responsive to citizens' needs. It is also hoped that costs would be reduced, a winning proposition for government and taxpayers alike.

This proposal has clear security implications. Indeed, having read this far in this book, you can probably list dozens of security issues that must be addressed to make this proposal work. The technology to design, build, and support this type of function exists, and the requirements, design, and implementation can easily be done from a technological point of view. But what about the other issues involved in building such a system? Neu et al. [NEU98] point out that the technology must be viewed in the larger institutional, organizational, and administrative contexts.

Much of what the government wants to do is already done. Many federal agencies have web sites providing large amounts of information to citizens, such as regulations, reports, and forms. This type of information is equally accessible to anyone who needs it. But other information exchange is more personalized: submitting completed tax forms, filing required paperwork for licenses and benefits, and asking specific questions about an individual's records, for example. Clearly the last type suggests stringent requirements relating to confidentiality, authentication, and integrity.

[NEU98] points out several security policy issues that must be addressed before such a system could be implemented. These include the following:

- How do the commercial firms' security policies meet the government's security needs?
- To enable secure communication, the government will likely want to use public key encryption. As we noted in Chapter 2, a certificate authority associates a public key with a particular user, establishing the user's identity. But for the government communication system, we must also know who has authority to access information and services and to initiate transactions. The processes required to perform identification are likely to be different from those performing authorization. In particular, identification may require direct interaction with a user, whereas authorization may require links among large databases.
- A citizen may have more than one identity. For example, Jane Doe may be the same person as Mrs. Nathaniel Simmons, who is also the same person as the Trustee for the Estate of Mr. Robert Jones. In turn, each of these identities may have multiple authorities. How will the identification authorities interact with the authorization ones to enable these situations?
- Sometimes the authorization does not need to be tied to a specific identity. For example, a government agency may need to know only that an individual is capable of paying for a service, much as a credit card company provides a credit rating. How will the authorization be able to release the minimum amount of information possible about an individual?
- How will certificate authorities have a high degree of confidence in their identification of individuals?
- How will certificate authorities deal with the need to view certain documents, such as birth certificates and passports, in person? This condition may mean

that certificate authorities may be required to have local offices around the country.

- Should there be a single certificate authority or many? A single provider can minimize the need for multiple keys and might save money by streamlining operations. But a single provider can also monitor all of a citizen's transactions, inviting abuse.

These issues are not trivial. Their solutions, not at all obvious, build on the concepts presented in this book. But they do so in a way that is not just technological. We can easily build a PKI to provide certificates to anyone we want. But how do we connect two certificates, connoting that the digital identities actually belong to the same person? In the real world you can be anonymous by purchasing something with cash; how can you be anonymous digitally?

But in addition to the security issues, there are also broader issues of management, responsibility, and law. [NEU98] points out that, even when the technical issues are resolved, we have still to answer these questions:

- What happens if a certificate authority makes a mistake, either by identifying or authorizing the wrong person or by assigning keys to an impostor? What are the legal and financial implications of such an error? What if the error is made even though the certificate authority followed government guidelines?
- How will citizens create, record, and protect their keys? If smart cards are used to store keys, does that card become a national identity card?
- What legal protections are available to electronic transactions? For example, in the United States today, it is illegal to intercept someone's surface mail, but it is not illegal to intercept someone's electronic mail.
- How do we prove that official electronic communications, such as a summons or subpoena, have been read? Will a citizen be responsible for regularly checking e-mail for official documents?
- If law enforcement officials need to access encrypted electronic communications, how will they be able to perform the decryption? Will there be a method by which they can obtain the key? Does this require the citizen to participate?
- What levels of protection are required for electronic documents? For instance, should medical records have the same level of protection as tax returns or driving violations? How do these levels apply across the different states that have very different laws? How does the protection address international law?
- How will every citizen be provided with an electronic mail address? What happens when an e-mail address changes? What security standards will apply to e-mail boxes and service providers?
- How will the government ensure equal access to electronic government services? Should the government provide help and training to first-time users?
- How will electronic communication be phased in to the current mix of paper and telephone communication?

These questions are not challenges to the technical side of computer security. But they are very much a part of the administrative side. It is not sufficient to know all the latest encryption algorithms; you also have to know how the use of computer security mechanisms fits into the broader context of how they are used and what they support. This example is included to introduce you to the procedural, administrative, policy, and privacy issues that a computer security administrator must consider. These questions highlight the degree to which security planning and policy must fit in with the larger policy issues that we, as individuals, organizations, and societies, must address. For this reason, in the next chapter we turn to the legal and ethical considerations of computer security.

But before we move to those concerns, we must cover one more topic involved in administering security: physical security. Protecting computing systems from physical harm is no less important than protecting data from modification in transit through a network. In the next section we briefly survey physical security vulnerabilities and controls.

8.4 PHYSICAL SECURITY

Much of this book has focused on technical issues in security and their technical solutions: firewalls, encryption techniques, and more. But many threats to security involve human or natural disasters, events that should also be addressed in the security plan. For this reason, in this section we consider how to cope with the nontechnical things that can go wrong. There are two pieces to the process of dealing with nontechnical problems: preventing things that can be prevented and recovering from the things that cannot be prevented. **Physical security** is the term used to describe protection needed outside the computer system. Typical physical security controls include guards, locks, and fences to deter direct attacks. In addition, there are other kinds of protection against less direct disasters, such as floods and power outages; these, too, are part of physical security. As we will see, many physical security measures can be provided simply by good common sense, a characteristic that Mark Twain noted "is a most uncommon virtue."

Natural Disasters

Computers are subject to the same natural disasters that can occur to homes, stores, and automobiles. They can be flooded, burned, melted, hit by falling objects, and destroyed by earthquakes, storms, and tornadoes. Additionally, computers are sensitive to their operating environment, so excessive heat or inadequate power is also a threat. It is impossible to prevent natural disasters, but through careful planning it is possible to reduce the damage they inflict. Some measures can be taken to reduce their impact. Because many of these perils cannot be prevented or predicted, controls focus on limiting possible damage and recovering quickly from a disaster. Issues to be considered include the need for offsite backups, the cost of replacing equipment, the speed with which equipment can be replaced, the need for available computing power, and the cost or difficulty of replacing data and programs.

Flood

Water from a natural flood comes from ground level, rising gradually, and bringing with it mud and debris. Often, there is time for an orderly shutdown of the computing system; at worst, the organization loses some of the processing in progress. At other times, such as when a dam breaks, a water pipe bursts, or the roof collapses in a storm, a sudden flood can overwhelm the system and its users before anything can be saved. Water can come from above, below, or the side. The machinery may be destroyed or damaged by mud and water, but most computing systems are insured and replaceable by the manufacturer. Managers of unique or irreplaceable equipment who recognize the added risk sometimes purchase or lease duplicate redundant hardware systems to ensure against disruption of service.

Even when the hardware can be replaced, we must be concerned about the stored data and programs. The system administrator may choose to label storage media in a way that makes it easy to identify the most important data. For example, green, yellow, and red labels may show which disks are the most sensitive, so that all red disks are moved from the data center during a storm. Similarly, large plastic bags and waterproof tape can be kept near important equipment and media; they are used to protect the hardware and storage media in case of a burst pipe or other sudden flood.

The real issue is protecting data and preserving the ability to compute. The only way to ensure the safety of data is to store backup copies in one or more safe locations.

Fire

Fire is more serious than water; often there is not as much time to react, and human lives are more likely to be in immediate danger. To ensure that system personnel can react quickly, every user and manager should have a plan for shutting down the system in an orderly manner. Such a process takes only a few minutes but can make recovery much easier. This plan should include individual responsibilities for all people: some to halt the system, others to protect crucial media, others to close doors on media cabinets. Provision should be made for secondary responsibilities, so that onsite staff can perform duties for those who are not in the office.

Water is traditionally used to put out fires, but it is not a good idea for use in computer rooms. In fact, more destruction can be the result of sprinklers than of the fires themselves. A fire sensor usually activates many sprinklers, dousing an entire room, even when the fire is merely some ignited paper in a wastebasket and of no threat to the computing system. Many computing centers use carbon dioxide extinguishers or an automatic system that sprays a gas such as Halon to smother a fire but leave no residue. Unfortunately, these gas systems work by displacing the oxygen in the room, choking the fire but leaving humans unable to breathe. Consequently, when these protection devices are activated, humans must leave, disabling efforts to protect media.

The best defense for situations like these is careful placement of the computing facility. A windowless location with fire-resistant access doors and nonflammable full-height walls can prevent some fires from spreading from adjacent areas to the computing room. With a fire- and smoke-resistant facility, personnel merely shut down the system and leave, perhaps carrying out the most important media.

Fire prevention is quite effective, especially because most computer goods are not especially flammable. Advance planning, reinforced with simulation drills, can help make good use of the small amount of time available before evacuation is necessary.

Other Natural Disasters

Computers are subject to storms, earthquakes, volcanoes, and similar events. Although not natural disasters, building collapse, explosion, and damage from falling objects can be considered in the same category. These kinds of catastrophes are difficult to predict or estimate.

But we know these catastrophes will occur. Security managers cope with them in several ways:

- developing contingency plans so that people know how to react in emergencies and business can continue
- insuring physical assets—computers, buildings, devices, supplies—against harm
- preserving sensitive data by maintaining copies in physically separated locations

Power Loss

Computers need their food—electricity—and they require a constant, pure supply of it. With a direct power loss, all computation ceases immediately. Because of possible damage to media by sudden loss of power, many disk drives monitor the power level and quickly retract the recording head if power fails. For certain time-critical applications, loss of service from the system is intolerable; in these cases, alternative complete power supplies must be instantly available.

Uninterruptible Power Supply

One protection against power loss is an **uninterruptible power supply.** This device stores energy during normal operation so that it can return the backup energy if power fails. One form of uninterruptible power supply uses batteries that are continually charged when the power is on but which then provide power when electricity fails. However, size, heat, flammability, and low output can be problems with batteries.

Some uninterruptible power supplies use massive wheels that are kept in continuous motion when electricity is available. When the power fails, the inertia in the wheels operates generators to produce more power. Size and limited duration of energy output are problems with this variety of power supply. Both forms of power supplies are intended to provide power for a limited time, just long enough to allow the current state of the computation to be saved so that no computation is lost.

Surge Suppressor

Another problem with power is its "cleanness." Although most people are unaware of it, a variation of 10 percent from the stated voltage of a line is considered acceptable, and some power lines vary even more. A particular power line may always be 10 percent high or low.

In many places, lights dim momentarily when a large appliance, such as an air conditioner, begins operation. When a large motor starts, it draws an exceptionally large amount of current, which reduces the flow to other devices on the line. When a motor stops, the sudden termination of draw can send a temporary surge along the line. Similarly, lightning strikes may send a momentary large pulse. Thus, instead of being constant, the power delivered along any electric line shows many brief fluctuations, called **drops, spikes,** and **surges**. A drop is a momentary reduction in voltage, and a spike or surge is a rise. For computing equipment, a drop is less serious than a surge. Most electrical equipment is tolerant of rather large fluctuations of current.

These variations can be destructive to sensitive electronic equipment, however. Simple devices called "surge suppressors" filter spikes from an electric line, blocking fluctuations that would affect computers. These devices cost from $20 to $100; they should be installed on every computer, printer, or other connected component. More sensitive models are typically used on larger systems.

As mentioned previously, a lightning strike can send a surge through a power line. To increase protection, personal computer users usually unplug their machines when they are not in use, as well as during electrical storms. Another possible source of destruction is lightning striking a telephone line. Because the power surge can travel along the phone line and into the computer or peripherals, the phone line should be disconnected from the modem during storms. These simple measures may save much work as well as valuable equipment.

Human Vandals

Because computers and their media are sensitive to a variety of disruptions, a vandal can destroy hardware, software, and data. Human attackers may be disgruntled employees, bored operators, saboteurs, people seeking excitement, or unwitting bumblers. If physical access is easy to obtain, crude attacks using axes or bricks can be very effective. One man recently shot a computer that he claimed had been in the shop for repairs many times without success.

Physical attacks by unskilled vandals are often easy to prevent; a guard can stop someone approaching a computer installation with a threatening or dangerous object. When physical access is difficult, more subtle attacks can be tried, resulting in quite serious damage. People with only some sophisticated knowledge of a system can short-circuit a computer with a car key or disable a disk drive with a paper clip. These items are not likely to attract attention until the attack is completed.

Unauthorized Access and Use

Films and newspaper reports exaggerate the ease of gaining access to a computing system. Still, as distributed computing systems become more prevalent, protecting the system from outside access becomes more difficult and more important. Interception is a form of unauthorized access; the attacker intercepts data and either breaks confidentiality or prevents the data from being read or used by others. In this context, interception is a passive attack. But we must also be concerned about active interception, in the sense that the attacker can change or insert data before allowing it to continue to its destination.

Theft

It is hard to steal a large mainframe computer. Not only is carrying it away difficult, but finding a willing buyer and arranging installation and maintenance also require special assistance. However, printed reports, tapes, or disks can be carried easily. If done well, the loss may not be detected for some time.

Personal computers, laptops, and personal digital assistants (PDAs, such as Palms or BlackBerries) are designed to be small and portable. Diskettes and tape backup cartridges are easily carried in a shirt pocket or briefcase. Computers and media that are easy to carry are also easy to conceal.

We can take one of three approaches to preventing theft: preventing access, preventing portability, or detecting exit.

Preventing Access

The surest way to prevent theft is to keep the thief away from the equipment. However, thieves can be either insiders or outsiders. Therefore, access control devices are needed both to prevent access by unauthorized individuals and to record access by those authorized. A record of accesses can help identify who committed a theft.

The oldest access control is a guard, not in the database management system sense we discussed in Chapter 6 but rather in the sense of a human being stationed at the door to control access to a room or to equipment. Guards offer traditional protection; their role is well understood, and the protection they offer is adequate in many situations. However, guards must be on duty continuously in order to be effective; providing breaks implies at least four guards for a 24-hour operation, with extras for vacation and illness. A guard must personally recognize someone or recognize an access token, such as a badge. People can lose or forget badges; terminated employees and forged badges are also problems. Unless the guard makes a record of everyone who has entered a facility, there is no way to know who (employee or visitor) has had access in case a problem is discovered.

The second oldest access control is a lock. This device is even easier, cheaper, and simpler to manage than a guard. However, it too provides no record of who has had access, and difficulties arise when keys are lost or duplicated. At computer facilities, it is inconvenient to fumble for a key when your hands are filled with tapes or disks, which might be ruined if dropped. There is also the possibility of piggybacking: a person walks through the door that someone else has just unlocked. Still, guards and locks provide simple, effective security for access to facilities such as computer rooms.

More exotic access control devices employ cards with radio transmitters, magnetic stripe cards (similar to 24-hour bank cards), and smart cards with chips containing electronic circuitry that makes them difficult to duplicate. Because each of these devices interfaces with a computer, it is easy for the computer to capture identity information, generating a list of who entered and left the facility, when, and by which routes. Some of these devices operate by proximity, so that a person can carry the device in a pocket or clipped to a collar; the person obtains easy access even when hands are full. Because these devices are computer controlled, it is easy to invalidate an access authority when someone quits or reports the access token lost or stolen.

The nature of the application or service determines how strict the access control needs to be. Working in concert with computer-based authentication techniques, the access controls can be part of defense in depth—using multiple mechanisms to provide security.

Preventing Portability

Portability is a mixed blessing. We can now carry around in our pockets devices that provide as much computing power as mainframes did twenty years ago. Portability is in fact a necessity in devices such as PDAs and mobile phones. And we do not want to permanently affix our personal computers to our desks, in case they need to be removed for repair or replacement. Thus, we need to find ways to enable portability without promoting theft.

One antitheft device is a pad connected to cable, similar to those used to secure bicycles. The pad is glued to the desktop with extremely strong adhesive. The cables loop around the equipment and are locked in place. Releasing the lock permits the equipment to be moved. An alternative is to couple the base of the equipment to a secure pad, in much the same way that televisions are locked in place in hotel rooms. Yet a third possibility is a large, lockable cabinet in which the personal computer and its peripherals are kept when they are not in use. Some people argue that cables, pads, and cabinets are unsightly and, worse, they make the equipment inconvenient to use.

Another alternative is to use movement-activated alarm devices when the equipment is not in use. Small alarms are available that can be locked to a laptop or PDA. When movement is detected, a loud, annoying whine or whistle warns that the equipment has been disturbed. Such an alarm is especially useful when laptops must be left in meeting or presentation rooms overnight or during a break. Used in concert with guards, the alarms can offer reasonable protection at reasonable cost.

Detecting Theft

For some devices, protection is more important than detection. We want to keep someone from stealing certain systems or information at all costs. But for other devices, it may be enough to detect that an attempt has been made to access or steal hardware or software. For example, chaining down a disk makes it unusable. Instead, we try to detect when someone tries to leave a protected area with the disk or other protected object. In these cases, the protection mechanism should be small and unobtrusive.

One such mechanism is similar to the protection used by many libraries, bookstores, or department stores. Each sensitive object is marked with a special label. Although the label looks like a normal pressure-sensitive one, its presence can be detected by a machine at the exit door if the label has not been disabled by an authorized party, such as a librarian or sales clerk. Similar security code tags are available for vehicles, people, machinery, and documents. Some tags are enabled by radio transmitters. When the detector sounds an alarm, someone must apprehend the person trying to leave with the marked object.

Interception of Sensitive Information

When disposing of a draft copy of a confidential report containing its sales strategies for the next five years, a company wants to be especially sure that the report is not reconstructable by one of its competitors. When the report exists only as hard copy, destroying the report is straightforward, usually accomplished by shredding or burning. But when the report exists digitally, destruction is more problematic. There may be many copies of the report in digital and paper form and in many locations (including on the computer and on storage media). There may also be copies in backups and archived in e-mail files. In this section, we look at several ways to dispose of sensitive information.

Shredding

Shredders have existed for a long time, as devices used by banks, government agencies, and others organizations to dispose of large amounts of confidential data. Although most of the shredded data is on paper, shredders can also be used for destroying printer ribbons and some types of disks and tapes. Shredders work by converting their input to thin strips or pulp, with enough volume to make it infeasible for most people to try to reconstruct the original from its many pieces. When data are extremely sensitive, some organizations burn the shredded output for added protection.

Overwriting Magnetic Data

Magnetic media present a special problem for those trying to protect the contents. When data are stored on magnetic disks, the ERASE or DELETE functions often simply change a directory pointer to free up space on the disk. As a result, the sensitive data are still recorded on the medium, and they can be recovered by analysis of the directory. A more secure way to destroy data on magnetic devices is to overwrite the data several times, using a different pattern each time. This process removes enough magnetic residue to prevent most people from reconstructing the original file. However, "cleaning" a disk in this fashion takes time. Moreover, a person using highly specialized equipment might be able to identify each separate message, much like the process of peeling off layers of wallpaper to reveal the wall beneath.

Degaussing

Degaussers destroy magnetic fields. Passing a disk or other magnetic medium through a degausser generates a magnetic flux so forceful that all magnetic charges are instantly realigned, thereby fusing all the separate layers. A degausser is a fast way to cleanse a magnetic medium, although there is still question as to whether it is adequate for use in the most sensitive of applications. (Media that have had the same pattern for a long time, such as a disk saved for archival purposes, may retain traces of the original pattern even after it has been overwritten many times or degaussed.) For most users, a degausser is a fast way to neutralize a disk or tape, permitting it to be reused by others.

Protecting Against Emanation: Tempest

Computer screens emit signals that can be detected from a distance. In fact, any components, including printers, disk drives, and processors, can emit information. **Tempest** is a U.S. government program under which computer equipment is certified as emission-free (that is, no detectable emissions). There are two approaches for preparing a device for Tempest certification: enclosing the device and modifying the emanations.

The obvious solution to preventing emanations is to trap the signals before they can be picked up. Enclosing a device in a conductive case, such as copper, diffuses all the waves by conducting them throughout the case. Copper is a good conductor, and the waves travel much better through copper than through the air outside the case, so the emissions are rendered harmless.

This solution works very well with cable, which is then enclosed in a solid, emanation-proof shield. Typically, the shielded cable is left exposed so that it is easy to inspect visually for any signs of tapping or other tampering. The shielding must be complete. That is, it does little good to shield a length of cable but not also shield the junction box at which that cable is connected to a component. The line to the component and the component itself must be shielded, too.

The shield must enclose the device completely. If top, bottom, and three sides are shielded, emanations are prevented only in those directions. However, a solid copper shield is useless in front of a computer screen. Covering the screen with a fine copper mesh in an intricate pattern carries the emanation safely away. This approach solves the emanation problem while still maintaining the screen's usability.

Entire computer rooms or even whole buildings can be shielded in copper so that large computers inside do not leak sensitive emanations. Although it seems appealing to shield the room or building instead of each component, the scheme has a significant drawbacks. A shielded room is inconvenient because it is impossible to expand the room easily as needs change. The shielding must be done carefully, because any puncture is a possible point of emanation. Furthermore, continuous metal pathways, such as water pipes or heating ducts, act as antennas to convey the emanations away from their source.

Emanations can also be designed in such a way that they cannot be retrieved. This process is similar to generating noise in an attempt to jam or block a radio signal. With this approach, the emanations of a piece of equipment must be modified by addition of spurious signals. Additional processors are added to Tempest equipment specifically to generate signals that fool an interceptor. The exact Tempest modification methods are classified.

As might be expected, Tempest-enclosed components are larger and heavier than their unprotected counterparts. Tempest testing is a rigorous program of the U.S. Department of Defense. Once a product has been approved, even a minor design modification, such as changing from one manufacturer's power supply to an equivalent one from another manufacturer, invalidates the Tempest approval. Therefore, these components are costly, ranging in price from 10 percent to 300 percent more than similar non-Tempest products. They are most appropriate in situations in which the data to be confined are of great value, such as top-level government information. Other groups with less dramatic needs can use other less rigorous shielding.

Contingency Planning

The key to successful recovery is adequate preparation. Seldom does a crisis destroy irreplaceable equipment; most computing systems—personal computers to mainframes—are standard, off-the-shelf systems that can be easily replaced. Data and locally developed programs are more vulnerable because they cannot be quickly substituted from another source. Let us look more closely at what to do after a crisis occurs.

Backup

In many computing systems, some data items change frequently, whereas others seldom change. For example, a database of bank account balances changes daily, but a file of depositors' names and addresses changes much less often. Also the number of changes in a given period of time is different for these two files. These variations in number and extent of change relate to the amount of data necessary to reconstruct these files in the event of a loss.

A **backup** is a copy of all or a part of a file to assist in reestablishing a lost file. In professional computing systems, periodic backups are usually performed automatically, often at night when system usage is low. Everything on the system is copied, including system files, user files, scratch files, and directories, so that the system can be regenerated after a crisis. This type of backup is called a **complete backup**. Complete backups are done at regular intervals, usually weekly or daily, depending on the criticality of the information or service provided by the system.

Major installations may perform **revolving backups**, in which the last several backups are kept. Each time a backup is done, the oldest backup is replaced with the newest one. There are two reasons to perform revolving backups: to avoid problems with corrupted media (so that all is not lost if one of the disks is bad) and to allow users or developers to retrieve old versions of a file. Another form of backup is a **selective backup**, in which only files that have been changed (or created) since the last backup are saved. In this case, fewer files must be saved, so the backup can be done more quickly. A selective backup combined with an earlier complete backup gives the effect of a complete backup in the time needed for only a selective backup. The selective backup is subject to the configuration management techniques described in Chapter 3.

For each type of backup, we need the means to move from the backup forward to the point of failure. That is, we need a way to restore the system in the event of failure. In critical transaction systems, we address this need by keeping a complete record of changes since the last backup. Sometimes, the system state is captured by a combination of computer- and paper-based recording media. For example, if a system handles bank teller operations, the individual tellers duplicate their processing on paper records—the deposit and withdrawal slips that accompany your bank transactions; if the system fails, the staff restores the latest backup version and reapplies all changes from the collected paper copies. Or the banking system creates a paper journal, which is a log of transactions printed just as each transaction completes.

Personal computer users often do not appreciate the need for regular backups. Even minor crises, such as a failed piece of hardware, can seriously affect personal computer users. With a backup, users can simply change to a similar machine and continue work.

Offsite Backup

A backup copy is useless if it is destroyed in the crisis, too. Many major computing installations rent warehouse space some distance from the computing system, far enough away that a crisis is not likely to affect the offsite location at the same time. As a backup is completed, it is transported to the backup site. Keeping a backup version separate from the actual system reduces the risk of its loss. Similarly, the paper trail is also stored somewhere other than at the main computing facility.

Personal computer users concerned with integrity can take home a copy of important disks as protection or send a copy to a friend in another city. If both secrecy and integrity are important, a bank vault, or even a secure storage place in another part of the same building can be used. The worst place to store a backup copy is where it usually is stored: right next to the machine.

Networked Storage

With today's extensive use of networking, using the network to implement backups is a good idea. Storage providers sell space in which you can store data; think of these services as big network-attached disk drives. You rent space just as you would consume electricity: you pay for what you use. The storage provider needs to provide only enough total space to cover everyone's needs, and it is easy to monitor usage patterns and increase capacity as combined needs rise.

Networked storage is perfect for backups of critical data because you can choose a storage provider whose physical storage is not close to your processing. In this way, physical harm to your system will not affect your backup. You do not need to manage tapes or other media and physically transport them offsite.

Cold Site

Depending on the nature of the computation, it may be important to be able to recover from a crisis and resume computation quickly. A bank, for example, might be able to tolerate a four-hour loss of computing facilities during a fire, but it could not tolerate a ten-month period to rebuild a destroyed facility, acquire new equipment, and resume operation.

Most computer manufacturers have several spare machines of most models that can be delivered to any location within 24 hours in the event of a real crisis. Sometimes the machine will come straight from assembly; other times the system will have been in use at a local office. Machinery is seldom the hard part of the problem. Rather, the hard part is deciding where to put the equipment in order to begin a temporary operation.

A **cold site** or **shell** is a facility with power and cooling available, in which a computing system can be installed to begin immediate operation. Some companies maintain their own cold sites, and other cold sites can be leased from disaster recovery companies. These sites usually come with cabling, fire prevention equipment, separate office space, telephone access, and other features. Typically, a computing center can have equipment installed and resume operation from a cold site within a week of a disaster.

Hot Site

If the application is more critical or if the equipment needs are more specialized, a **hot site** may be more appropriate. A hot site is a computer facility with an installed and ready-to-run computing system. The system has peripherals, telecommunications lines, power supply, and even personnel ready to operate on short notice. Some companies maintain their own; other companies subscribe to a service that has available one or more locations with installed and running computers. To activate a hot site, it is necessary only to load software and data from offsite backup copies.

Numerous services offer hot sites equipped with every popular brand and model of system. They provide diagnostic and system technicians, connected communications lines, and an operations staff. The hot site staff also assists with relocation by arranging transportation and housing, obtaining needed blank forms, and acquiring office space.

Because these hot sites serve as backups for many customers, most of whom will not need the service, the annual cost to any one customer is fairly low. The cost structure is like insurance: The likelihood of an auto accident is low, so the premium is reasonable, even for a policy that covers the complete replacement cost of an expensive car. Notice, however, that the first step in being able to use a service of this type is a complete and timely backup.

Physical Security Recap

By no means have we covered all of physical security in this brief introduction. Professionals become experts at individual aspects, such as fire control or power provision. However, this section should have made you aware of the major issues in physical security. We have to protect the facility against many sorts of disasters, from weather to chemical spills and vehicle crashes to explosions. It is impossible to predict what will occur or when. The physical security manager has to consider all assets and a wide range of harm.

Malicious humans seeking physical access are a different category of threat agent. With them, you can consider motive or objective: is it theft of equipment, disruption of processing, interception of data, or access to service? Fences, guards, solid walls, and locks will deter or prevent most human attacks. But you always need to ask where weaknesses remain; a solid wall has a weakness in every door and window.

The primary physical controls are strength and duplication. Strength means overlapping controls implementing a defense-in-depth approach so that if one control fails, the next one will protect. People who built ancient castles practiced this philosophy with moats, walls, drawbridges, and arrow slits. Duplication means eliminating single points of failure. Redundant copies of data protect against harm to one copy from any cause. Spare hardware components protect against failures.

8.5 SUMMARY

The administration of security draws on skills slightly different from the technical skills we developed in the earlier chapters of this book. The security administrator must understand not just security assets, threats, vulnerabilities, and controls, but management and implementation. In this chapter we examined four parts of how security is administered.

First, security planning is a process that drives the rest of security administration. A security plan is a structure that allows things to happen in a studied, organized manner. General security plans explain how the organization will match threats to controls and to assets. Business continuity plans focus on the single issue of maintaining some ability to do business. Incident response plans cover how to keep a security event, such as a breach or attack, from running out of control. All plans offer the advantage that you can think about a situation in advance, with a clear mind, when you can weigh options easily.

Risk assessment is a technique supporting security planning. In a risk assessment, you list vulnerabilities and controls, and then balance the cost of each control against the potential harm it can block. Risk assessments let you calculate the savings of security measures, instead of their costs, as is more frequently the case. Not all risk can be blocked. With a thorough risk assessment, you are able to know what risks you choose to accept.

An organizational security policy is a document that specifies the organization's goals regarding security. It lists policy elements that are statements of actions that must or must not be taken to preserve those goals. Policy documents often lead to implementational procedures. Also, user education and awareness activities ensure that users are aware of policy restrictions.

Physical security concerns the physical aspects of computing: the devices themselves and harm that can come to them because of the buildings in which they are contained. Physical security addresses two branches of threats: natural threats to buildings and the infrastructure, and human threats. Redundancy and physical controls address physical security threats.

The administration of security has a strong human component, from the writing of plans and policies, to the mental work in performing a risk analysis, to the human guards that implement or reinforce many physical controls. In the next chapter we continue our study of the human aspects of computer security as we consider laws, privacy, and ethics.

8.6 TERMS AND CONCEPTS

attributes contributing to vulnerabilities:
- singularity, 513
- separability, 513
- logic errors, 513
- design sensitivity, 513
- unrecoverability, 513
- behavioral sensitivity, 513
- malevolence, 513
- rigidity, 513
- malleability, 513
- gullibility, 513
- complacency, 513
- corruptibility, 513
- accessibility, 513
- difficulty to control, 513
- unpredictability, 513
- predictability, 513

likelihood of exploitation, 515
classical probability, 516
frequency probability, 516
subjective probability, 516
Delphi method, 516
annual loss expectation (ALE), 517
cost/benefit analysis, 525
risk calculation, 525
organizational security policy:
- purpose, 529
- beneficiaries, 530
- users, 530
- owners, 530

balancing interest, 530
policy contents, 531
policy characteristics:
- coverage, 532
- durability, 532
- realism, 532
- usefulness, 532

physical security, 538
natural disaster, 538
fire, 539
power loss, 540
uninterruptible power supply, 540
surge suppressor, 540
drop, 541
spike, 541
surge, 541
intruder, 541
theft prevention, 541
theft detection, 543
disposal of sensitive information, 543
shredder, 544
degausser, 544
emanations, 544
Tempest, 544
backup, 546
complete backup, 546
revolving backup, 546
selective backup, 546
offsite backup, 546
cold disaster recovery site, 547
hot disaster recovery site, 547
networked storage device, 547

8.7 TO LEARN MORE

Basic works on risk analysis are Rook's tutorial [ROO93] and the paper by Fairley and Rook [FAI97].

Two good resources on administering security are Fites [FIT89] and Wood [WOO87b].

For a discussion of the cautions of using risk analysis on software projects, see [PFL00]. This issue of the *Journal of Systems and Software* is a special issue on risk management for software engineering.

8.8 EXERCISES

1. In what ways is denial of service (lack of availability for authorized users) a vulnerability to users of single-user personal computers?
2. Identify the three most probable threats to a personal computing system in an office with fewer than ten employees. That is, identify the three vulnerabilities most likely to be exploited. Estimate the number of times each vulnerability is exploited per year; justify your estimate.
3. Perform the analysis of Exercise 2 for a personal computing system located in a large research laboratory.
4. Perform the analysis of Exercise 2 for a personal computing system located in the library of a major university.
5. List three factors that should be considered when developing a security plan.
6. State a security requirement that is not realistic. State a security requirement that is not verifiable. State two security requirements that are inconsistent.
7. Investigate your university's or employer's security plan to determine whether its security requirements meet all the conditions listed in this chapter. List any that do not. When was the plan written? When was it last reviewed and updated?
8. Cite three controls that could have both positive and negative effects.
9. For an airline, what are its most important assets? What are the minimal computing resources it would need to continue business for a limited period (up to two days)? What other systems or processes could it use during the period of the disaster?
10. Answer Exercise 9 for a bank instead of an airline.
11. Answer Exercise 9 for an oil drilling company instead of an airline.
12. Answer Exercise 9 for a political campaign instead of an airline.
13. When is an incident over? That is, what factors influence whether to continue the work of the incident handling team or to disband it?
14. List five kinds of harm that could occur to your own personal computer. Estimate the likelihood of each, expressed in number of times per year (number of times could be a fraction, for example, 1/2 means could be expected to happen once every two years). Estimate the monetary loss that would occur from that harm. Compute the expected annual loss from these kinds of harm.
15. Cite a risk in computing for which it is impossible or infeasible to develop a classical probability of occurrence.
16. Investigate the computer security policy for your university or employer. Who wrote the policy? Who enforces the policy? Who does it cover? What resources does it cover?
17. List three different sources of water to a computing system, and state a control for each.
18. You discover that your computing system has been infected by a piece of malicious code. You have no idea when the infection occurred. You do have backups performed every week since the system was put into operation but, of course, there have been numerous changes to the system over time. How could you use the backups to construct a "clean" version of your system?

9

Legal, Privacy, and Ethical Issues in Computer Security

In this chapter:

- Program and data protection by patents, copyrights, and trademarks
- Computer crime
- Privacy
- Ethical analysis of computer security situations
- Codes of professional ethics

In this chapter we study human controls applicable to computer security: the legal system and ethics. The legal system has adapted quite well to computer technology by reusing some old forms of legal protection (copyrights and patents) and creating laws where no adequate ones existed (malicious access). Still, the courts are not a perfect form of protection for computer resources, for two reasons. First, the courts tend to be reactive instead of proactive. That is, we have to wait for a transgression to occur and then adjudicate it, rather than try to prevent it in the first place. Second, fixing a problem through the courts can be time consuming (sometimes taking years) and expensive; the latter characteristic prevents all but the wealthy from addressing most security issues.

On the other hand, ethics has not had to change, because ethics is more situational and personal than the law. For example, the privacy of personal information is becoming a very important part of computer security. And although technically this issue is just an aspect of confidentiality, practically it has a long history in both law and ethics. The purpose of this chapter is to round out our study of protection for computing systems by understanding the context in which security is assessed and applied.

Not always are conflicts resolved pleasantly. Some people will think that they have been treated unfairly, and some people do indeed act unfairly. In some countries, a citizen reacts to a wrongful act by going to court. The courts are seen as the ultimate arbiters and enforcers of fairness. But, as most lawyers will tell you, the courts' definition of *fair* may not coincide with yours. Even if you could be sure the courts would side with you, a legal battle can be emotionally draining. Our purpose in this section is not only to understand how the legal system helps protect computer security but also to know how and when to use the legal system wisely.

Law and computer security are related in several ways. First, international, federal, state, and city laws can affect privacy and secrecy. These statutes often apply to the rights of individuals to keep personal matters private. Second, laws regulate the use, development, and ownership of data and programs. Patents, copyrights, and trade secrets are legal devices to protect the rights of developers and owners of programs and data. Similarly, one aspect of computer security is controlling access to programs and data; that access control is supported by these mechanisms of the law. Third, laws affect actions that can be taken to protect the secrecy, integrity, and availability of computer information and service. These basic concerns in computer security are both strengthened and constrained by applicable laws. Thus, legal means interact with other controls to establish computer security.

However, the law does not always provide an adequate control. When computer systems are concerned, the law is slowly evolving because the issues are similar to but not the same as those for property rights. Computers are new, compared to houses, land, horses, or money. As a consequence, the place of computer systems in law is not yet firmly established. As statutes are written and cases decided, the roles of computers and the people, data, and processes involved are becoming more defined in the law. However, laws do not yet address all improper acts committed with computers. Finally, some judges, lawyers, and police officers do not understand computing, so they cannot determine how computing relates to other, more established, parts of the law.

The laws dealing with computer security affect programmers, designers, users, and maintainers of computing systems and computerized data banks. These laws protect, but they also regulate the behavior of people who use computers. Furthermore, computer professionals are among the best qualified advocates for changing old laws and creating new ones regarding computers. Before recommending change, however, professionals must understand the current state of computers and the law. Therefore, we have three motivations for studying the legal section of this chapter:

- to know what protection the law provides for computers and data
- to appreciate laws that protect the rights of others with respect to computers, programs, and data
- to understand existing laws as a basis for recommending new laws to protect computers, data, and people

The next few sections address the following aspects of protection of the security of computers.

- *Protecting computing systems against criminals.* Computer criminals violate the principles of confidentiality, integrity, and availability for computer systems. Preventing the violation is better than prosecuting it after the fact. However, if other controls fail, legal action may be necessary. In this section we study several representative laws to determine what acts are punishable under the law.
- *Protecting code and data.* Copyrights, patents, and trade secrets are all forms of legal protection that can be applied to programs and, sometimes, data. How-

ever, we must understand the fundamental differences between the kind of protection these three provide and the methods of obtaining that protection.

- *Protecting programmers' and employers' rights.* The law protects both programmers and people who employ programmers. Generally, programmers have only limited legal rights to access programs they have written while employed. This section contains a survey of the rights of employees and employers regarding programs written for pay.
- *Protecting private data about individuals.* We also consider the legal right of privacy. The private affairs of every individual are protected by laws. Computer security systems must be adequate to prevent unauthorized disclosure of sensitive data about individuals. This section describes sensitive data that must be protected.
- *Protecting users of programs.* When you buy a program, you expect it to work properly. If it doesn't, you want the legal system to protect your rights as a consumer. This section surveys the legal recourse you have to address faulty programs.

Computer law is complex and emerging rather rapidly as it tries to keep up with the rapid technological advances in and enabled by computing. We present the fundamentals in this book not in their full detail as you would expect by someone with a law degree, but as a situational analysis to heighten the awareness of those who are not lawyers but who must deal with the law's implications. You should consult a lawyer who understands and specializes in computer law in order to apply the material of this section to any specific case. And, as most lawyers will advise, ensuring legal protection by doing things correctly from the beginning is far easier—and cheaper—than hiring a lawyer to sort out a web of conflict after things have gone wrong.

9.1 PROTECTING PROGRAMS AND DATA

Suppose Martha wrote a computer program to play a video game. She invited some friends over to play the game and gave them copies so that they could play at home. Steve took a copy and rewrote parts of Martha's program to improve the quality of the screen display. After Steve shared the changes with her, Martha incorporated them into her program. Now Martha's friends have convinced her that the program is good enough to sell, so she wants to advertise and offer the game for sale by mail.

She wants to know what legal protection she can apply to protect her software. Copyrights, patents, and trade secrets are legal devices that can protect computers, programs, and data. However, in some cases, precise steps must be taken to protect the work before anyone else is allowed access to it. In this section, we explain how each of these forms of protection was originally designed to be used and how each is currently used in computing. We focus primarily on U.S. law, to provide examples of intent and consequence. Readers from other countries or doing business in other countries should consult lawyers in those countries to determine the specific differences and similarities.

Copyrights

In the United States, the basis of copyright protection is presented in the U.S. Constitution. The body of legislation supporting constitutional provisions contains laws that elaborate on or expand the constitutional protections. Relevant statutes include the U.S. copyright law of 1978, which was updated in 1998 as the Digital Millennium Copyright Act specifically to deal with computers and other electronic media such as digital video and music. The 1998 changes brought U.S. copyright law into general conformance with the World Intellectual Property Organization treaty of 1996, an international copyright standard to which 95 countries adhere.

Copyrights are designed to protect the expression of ideas. Thus, a copyright applies to a creative work, such as a story, photograph, song, or pencil sketch. The right to copy an *expression* of an idea is protected by a copyright. Ideas themselves, the law alleges, are free; anyone with a bright mind can think up anything anyone else can, at least in theory. The intention of a copyright is to allow regular and free exchange of ideas.

The author of a book translates ideas into words on paper. The paper embodies the expression of those ideas and is the author's livelihood. That is, an author hopes to earn a living by presenting ideas in such an appealing manner that others will pay to read them. (The same protection applies to pieces of music, plays, films, and works of art, each of which is a personal expression of ideas.) The law protects an individual's right to earn a living, while recognizing that exchanging ideas supports the intellectual growth of society. The copyright says that a particular *way* of expressing an idea belongs to the author. For example, in music, there may be two or three copyrights related to a single creation: a composer can copyright a song, an arranger can copyright an arrangement of that song, and an artist can copyright a specific performance of that arrangement of that song. The price you pay for a ticket to a concert includes compensation for all three creative expressions.

Copyright gives the author the *exclusive* right to make copies of the expression and sell them to the public. That is, only the author (or booksellers or others working as the author's agents) can sell copies of the author's book.

Definition of Intellectual Property

The U.S. copyright law states that a copyright can be registered for "original works of authorship fixed in any tangible medium of expression,...from which they can be perceived, reproduced, or otherwise communicated, either directly or with the aid of a machine or device." Again, the copyright does *not* cover the *idea* being expressed. "In no case does copyright protection for an original work of authorship extend to any idea." The copyright must apply to an *original* work, and it must be in some *tangible* medium of expression.

Only the originator of the expression is entitled to copyright; if an expression has no determinable originator, then copyright cannot be granted. Certain works are considered to be in the **public domain**, owned by the public, by no one in particular. Works of the U.S. government and many other governments are considered to be in the public domain and therefore not subject to copyright. Works generally known, such as the phrase "top o' the mornin' to ye," or the song "Happy Birthday to You," or a recipe for tuna noodle casserole, are also so widely known that it would be very difficult for someone to trace originality and claim a copyright. Finally, copyright lasts for only a limited period of time, so certain very old works, such as the plays of Shakespeare, are in the public domain, their possibility of copyright having expired.

The copyrighted expression must also be in some tangible medium. A story or art work must be written, printed, recorded (on a physical medium such as a plastic record), stored on a magnetic medium (such as a disk or tape), or fixed in some other way. Furthermore, the purpose of the copyright is to promote distribution of the work; therefore, the work must be distributed, even if a fee is charged for a copy.

Originality of Work

The work being copyrighted must be original to the author. As noted previously, some expressions in the public domain are not subject to copyright. A work can be copyrighted even if it contains some public domain material, as long as there is some originality, too. The author does not even have to identify what is public and what is original.

For example, a music historian could copyright a collection of folksongs even if some are in the public domain. To be subject to copyright, something in or *about* the collection has to be original. The historian might argue that collecting the songs, selecting which ones to include, and putting them in order was the original part. In this case, the copyright law would not protect the folk songs (which would be in the public domain) but would instead protect that specific selection and organization. Someone selling a sheet of paper on which just one of the songs was written would likely not be found to have infringed on the copyright of the historian. Dictionaries can be copyrighted in this way, too; the authors do not claim to own the words, just their expression as a particular dictionary.

Fair Use of Material

The copyright law indicates that the copyrighted object is subject to **fair use**. Specifically, the law allows "fair use of a copyrighted work, including such use by reproduction in copies... for purposes such as criticism, comment, news reporting, teaching (including multiple copies for classroom use), scholarship or research." The purpose and effect of the use on the potential market for or value of the work affect the decision of what constitutes fair use. The copyright law usually upholds the author's right to a fair return for the work, while encouraging others to use the underlying ideas. Unfair use of a copyrighted item is called **piracy**.

The invention of the photocopier made it more difficult to enforce fair use. Today many commercial copy shops will copy a portion—sometimes an entire chapter—of a book or a single article out of a journal but refuse to copy an entire volume, citing fair use. With photocopiers, the quality of the copy degrades with each copy, as you know if you have ever tried to read a copy of a copy of a copy of a paper.

The copyright law also has the concept of a **first sale**: after having bought a copyrighted object, the new owner can give away or resell the object. That is, the copyright owner is entitled to control the first sale of the object. This concept works fine for books: an author is compensated when a bookstore sells a book, but the author earns no additional revenue if the book is later resold at a secondhand store.

Requirements for Registering a Copyright

The copyright is easy to obtain, and mistakes in securing a copyright can be corrected. The first step of registration is notice. Any potential user must be made aware that the work is copyrighted. Each copy must be marked with the copyright symbol ©, the word *Copyright*, the year, and the author's name. (At one time, these items were followed by *All rights reserved* to preserve the copyright in certain South American countries. Adding the phrase now is unnecessary but harmless.)

The order of the elements can be changed, and either © or *Copyright* can be omitted (but not both). Each copy distributed must be so marked, although the law will forgive failure to mark copies if a reasonable attempt is made to recall and mark any ones distributed without a mark.

The copyright must also be officially filed. In the United States a form is completed and submitted to the Copyright Office, along with a nominal fee and a copy of the work. Actually, the Copyright Office requires only the first 25 and the last 25 pages of the work, to help it justify a claim in the event of a court case. The filing must be done within three months after the first distribution of the work. The law allows filing up to five years late, but no infringements before the time of filing can be prosecuted.

A U.S. copyright now lasts for 70 years beyond the death of the last surviving author or, if the item was copyrighted by a company or organization, for 95 years after the date of publication.

Copyright Infringement

The holder of the copyright must go to court to prove that someone has infringed on the copyright. The infringement must be substantial, and it must be copying, not independent work. In theory, two people might write identically the same song independently, neither knowing the other. These two people would *both* be entitled to copyright protection for their work. Neither would have infringed on the other, and both would have the right to distribute their work for a fee. Again, copyright is most easily understood for written works of fiction because it is extremely unlikely that two people would express an idea with the same or similar wording.

The independence of nonfiction works is not nearly so clear. Consider, for example, an arithmetic book. Long division can be explained in only so many ways, so two independent books could use similar wording for that explanation. The number of possible alternative examples is limited, so that two authors might independently choose to write the same simple example. However, it is far less likely that two arithmetic textbooks would have the same pattern of presentation and the same examples from beginning to end.

Copyrights for Computer Software

The original copyright law envisioned protection for things such as books, songs, and photographs. People can rather easily detect when these items are copied. The separation between public domain and creativity is fairly clear. And the distinction between an idea (feeling, emotion) and its expression is pretty obvious. Works of nonfiction understandably have less leeway for independent expression. Because of programming language constraints and speed and size efficiency, computer programs have less leeway still.

Can a computer program be copyrighted? Yes. The 1976 copyright law was amended in 1980 to include an explicit definition of computer software. However, copyright protection may not be an especially desirable form of protection for computer works. To see why, consider the algorithm used in a given program. The algorithm is the idea, and the statements of the programming language are the expression of the idea. Therefore, protection is allowed for the program statements themselves, but not for the algorithmic concept: copying the code intact is prohibited, but reimplementing the algorithm is permitted.

A second problem with copyright protection for computer works is the requirement that the work be published. A program may be published by distribution of copies of its object code, for example, on a disk. However, if the source code is not distributed, it has not been published. An alleged infringer cannot have violated a copyright on source code if the source code was never published.

Copyrights for Digital Objects

The **Digital Millennium Copyright Act (DMCA)** of 1998 clarified some issues of digital objects (such as music files, graphics images, data in a database, and also computer programs), but it left others unclear.

Among the provisions of the DMCA are these:

- Digital objects *can be* subject to copyright.
- It is a crime to circumvent or disable antipiracy functionality built into an object.
- It is a crime to manufacture, sell, or distribute devices that disable antipiracy functionality or that copy digital objects.
- However, these devices can be used (and manufactured, sold, or distributed) for research and educational purposes.
- It is acceptable to make a backup copy of a digital object as a protection against hardware or software failure or to store copies in an archive.
- Libraries can make up to three copies of a digital object for lending to other libraries.

So, a user can make reasonable copies of an object in the normal course of its use and to protect against system failures. If a system is regularly backed up and so a digital object (such as a software program) is copied onto many backups, that is not a violation of copyright.

The uncertainty comes in deciding what is considered to be a device to counter piracy. A disassembler or decompiler could support piracy or could be used to study and enhance a program. Someone who decompiles an executable program, studies it to infer its method, and then modifies, compiles, and sells the result is misusing the decompiler. But the distinction is hard to enforce, in part because the usage depends on intent and context. It is as if there were a law saying it is legal to sell a knife to cut vegetables but not to harm people. Knives do not know their uses; the users determine intent and context.

Reaction to the Digital Millennium Copyright Act has not been uniformly favorable. (See, for example, [MAN98].) Some say it limits computer security research. Worse, others point out it can be used to prevent exactly the free interchange of ideas that copyright was intended to promote. In 2001 a Princeton University professor, Edward Felten, and students presented a paper on cryptanalysis of the digital watermarking techniques used to protect digital music files from being copied. They had been pressured not to present in the preceding April by music industry groups who threatened legal action under the DMCA.

Digital objects are more problematic than paper ones because they can be copied exactly. Unlike fifth-generation photocopies, each digital copy of a digital object can be identical to the original.

Copyright protects the right of a creator to profit from a copy of an object, even if no money changes hands. The Napster situation (see Sidebar 9-1) is an interesting case, closely related to computer data. It clearly distinguishes between an object and a copy of that object.

Sidebar 9-1 Napster: No Right to Copy

Napster is a web-based clearinghouse for musical files. To see why its existence was problematic, we must first consider its predecessor, MP3. MP3.com was an archive for digital files of music. Users might obtain the MP3 file of a particular song for their personal listening pleasure. Eventually, one of the users might upload a file to MP3.com, which made it available to others. In May 2000 the courts ruled that MP3.com had illegally copied over 45,000 audio CDs and distributed copyright works illegally.

To address the legal issues, music lovers sought an approach one step away from actual distribution, thereby being legal under U.S. laws. Instead of being a digital archive, Napster was designed to be a clearinghouse for individuals. A person might register with Napster to document that he or she had a digital version of a particular performance by an artist. A second person would express interest in that recording, and Napster would connect the two. Thus, Napster never really touched the file itself. Instead, Napster operated a peer-to-peer file swapping service.

In February 2001 the U.S. 9th Circuit Court ruled that Napster infringed on the copyrights of various artists. The Recording Industry Association of America brought the suit, representing thousands of performers.

The crux of the MP3 and Napster cases is what a person buys when purchasing a CD. The copyright law holds that a person is not buying the music itself, but is buying the right to use the CD. "Using" the CD means playing it, lending it to a friend, giving it to someone else, or even selling it. But the original artist has the right to control distribution of copies of it, under the principle of first sale.

An emerging principle is that software, like music, is acquired in a style more like rental than purchase. You purchase not a piece of software, but the right to use it. Clarifying this position, the U.S. No Electronic Theft (NET) Act of 1997 makes it a criminal offense to reproduce or distribute copyrighted works, such as software or digital recordings, even without charge.

The area of copyright protection applied to computer works continues to evolve and is subject to much interpretation by the courts. Therefore, it is not certain what aspects of a computer work are subject to copyright. Courts have ruled that a computer menu design can be copyrighted but that "look and feel" (such as the Microsoft Windows user interface) cannot.

Therefore, although copyright protection can be applied to computer works, the copyright concept was conceived before the electronic age, and thus the protection may be less than what we desire. Copyrights do not address all the critical computing system elements that require protection. For example, a programmer might want to protect an algorithm, not the way that algorithm was expressed in a particular programming language. Unfortunately, it may be difficult to obtain copyright protection for an algorithm, at least as copyright law is currently interpreted. Because the copyright laws are evolving, we must also take care when copyrights are used as excuses, as we see in Sidebar 9-2.

Patents

Patents are unlike copyrights in that they protect inventions, tangible objects, or ways to make them, not works of the mind. The distinction between patents and copyrights is that patents were intended to apply to the results of science, technology, and engineering, whereas copyrights were meant to cover works in the arts, literature, and written scholarship. A patent can protect a "new and useful process, machine, manufacture, or composition of matter." The U.S. law excludes "newly discovered laws of nature... [and] mental processes." Thus "2+2=4" is not a proper subject for a patent because it is a law of nature. Similarly, that expression is in the public domain and would thus be unsuitable for a copyright. A patent is designed to protect the device or process for *carrying out* an idea, not the idea itself.

Sidebar 9-2 Inappropriate Reference to Copyright Law

Sometimes vendors refer to copyright law inappropriately, to discourage customers from returning a software package. Kaner and Pels [KAN98] explain that some companies do not want to be bothered dealing with returns, especially when the software package it has sold turns out to be defective. The company may publish a policy, posted on the store wall, window, or web site, noting that it cannot accept returns because doing so would violate the copyright act. But in fact the act says nothing about returns. It restricts only software rentals. The case analysis for the lawsuit between Central Point Software, Inc., and Global Software and Accessories, Inc., (resolved in 1995) notes that giving a refund does not turn the sale into a rental.

Requirement of Novelty

If two composers happen to compose the same song independently at different times, copyright law would allow both of them to have copyright. If two inventors devise the same invention, the patent goes to the person who invented it first, regardless of who first filed the patent. A patent can be valid only for something that is truly novel or unique, so there can be only one patent for a given invention.

An object patented must also be nonobvious. If an invention would be obvious to a person ordinarily skilled in the field, it cannot be patented. The law states that a patent *cannot* be obtained "if the differences between the subject matter sought to be patented and the prior art are such that the subject matter as a whole would have been obvious at the time the invention was made to a person having ordinary skill in the art to which said subject matter pertains." For example, a piece of cardboard to be used as a bookmark would not be a likely candidate for a patent because the idea of a piece of cardboard would be obvious to almost any reader.

Procedure for Registering a Patent

One registers a copyright by filing a brief form, marking a copyright notice on the creative work, and distributing the work. The whole process takes less than an hour.

To obtain a patent, an inventor must convince the U.S Patent and Trademark Office that the invention deserves a patent. For a fee, a patent attorney will research the patents already issued for similar inventions. This search accomplishes two things. First, it determines that the invention to be patented has not already been patented (and, presumably, has not been previously invented). Second, the search can help identify similar things that have been patented. These similarities can be useful when describing the unique features of the invention that make it worthy of patent protection. The Patent Office compares an application to those of all other similar patented inventions and decides whether the application covers something truly novel and nonobvious. If the office decides the invention is novel, a patent is granted.

Typically an inventor writes a patent application listing many claims of originality, from very general to very specific. The Patent Office may disallow some of the more general claims while upholding some of the more specific ones. The patent is valid for all the upheld claims. The patent applicant reveals what is novel about the invention in sufficient detail to allow the Patent Office and the courts to judge novelty; that degree of detail may also tell the world how the invention works, thereby opening the possibility of infringement.

The patent owner uses the patented invention by producing products or by licensing others to produce them. Patented objects are sometimes marked with a patent number to warn others that the technology is patented. The patent holder hopes this warning will prevent others from infringing.

Patent Infringement

A patent holder *must* oppose all infringement. With a copyright, the holder can choose which cases to prosecute, ignoring small infringements and waiting for serious infractions where the infringement is great enough to ensure success in court or to justify the cost of the court case. However, failing to sue a patent infringement—even a small one or one the patent holder does not know about—can mean losing the patent rights entirely. But, unlike copyright infringement, a patent holder does not have to prove that the infringer copied the invention; a patent infringement occurs even if someone independently invents the same thing, without knowledge of the patented invention.

Every infringement must be prosecuted. Prosecution is expensive and time consuming, but even worse, suing for patent infringement could cause the patent *holder* to lose the patent. Someone charged with infringement can argue all of the following points as a defense against the charge of infringement.

- *This isn't infringement.* The alleged infringer will claim that the two inventions are sufficiently different that no infringement occurred.
- *The patent is invalid.* If a prior infringement was not opposed, the patent rights may no longer be valid.
- *The invention is not novel.* In this case, the supposed infringer will try to persuade the judge that the Patent Office acted incorrectly in granting a patent and that the invention is nothing worthy of patent.
- *The infringer invented the object first.* If so, the accused infringer, and not the original patent holder, is entitled to the patent.

The first defense does not damage a patent, although it can limit the novelty of the invention. However, the other three defenses can destroy patent rights. Worse, all four defenses can be used every time a patent holder sues someone for infringement. Finally, obtaining and defending a patent can incur substantial legal fees. Patent protection is most appropriate for large companies with substantial research and development (and legal) staffs.

Applicability of Patents to Computer Objects

The Patent Office has not encouraged patents of computer software. For a long time, computer programs were seen as the representation of an algorithm, and an algorithm was a fact of nature, which is not subject to patent. An early software patent case, *Gottschalk v. Benson*, involved a request to patent a process for converting decimal numbers into binary. The Supreme Court rejected the claim, saying it seemed to attempt to patent an abstract idea, in short, an algorithm. But the underlying algorithm is precisely what most software developers would like to protect.

In 1981, two cases (*Diamond v. Bradley* and *Diamond v. Diehr*) won patents for a process that used computer software, a well-known algorithm, temperature sensors, and a computer to calculate the time to cure rubber seals. The court upheld the right to a patent because the claim was not for the software or the algorithm alone, but for the process that happened to use the software as one of its steps. An unfortunate inference is that using the software without using the other patented steps of the process would not be infringement.

Since 1981 the patent law has expanded to include computer software, recognizing that algorithms, like processes and formulas, are inventions. The Patent Office has issued thousands of software patents since these cases. But because of the time and expense involved in obtaining and maintaining a patent, this form of protection may be unacceptable for a small-scale software writer.

Trade Secrets

A trade secret is unlike a patent or copyright in that it must be kept a *secret.* The information has value only as a secret, and an infringer is one who divulges the secret. Once divulged, the information usually cannot be made secret again.

Characteristics of Trade Secrets

A **trade secret** is information that gives one company a competitive edge over others. For example, the formula for a soft drink is a trade secret, as is a mailing list of customers or information about a product due to be announced in a few months.

The distinguishing characteristic of a trade secret is that it must always be kept secret. Employees and outsiders who have access to the secret must be required not to divulge the secret. The owner must take precautions to protect the secret, such as storing it in a safe, encrypting it in a computer file, or making employees sign a statement that they will not disclose the secret.

If someone obtains a trade secret improperly and profits from it, the owner can recover profits, damages, lost revenues, and legal costs. The court will do whatever it can to return the holder to the same competitive position it had while the information was secret and may award damages to compensate for lost sales. However, trade secret protection evaporates in case of independent discovery. If someone else happens to discover the secret independently, there is no infringement and trade secret rights are gone.

Reverse Engineering

Another way trade secret protection can vanish is by reverse engineering. Suppose a secret is the way to pack tissues in a cardboard box to make one pop up as another is pulled out. Anyone can cut open the box and study the process. Therefore, the trade secret is easily discovered. In **reverse engineering**, one studies a finished object to determine how it is manufactured or how it works.

Through reverse engineering someone might discover how a telephone is built; the design of the telephone is obvious from the components and how they are connected. Therefore, a patent is the appropriate way to protect an invention such as a telephone. However, something like a soft drink is not just the combination of its ingredients. Making a soft drink may involve time, temperature, presence of oxygen or other gases, and similar factors that could not be learned from a straight chemical decomposition of the product. The recipe of a soft drink is a closely guarded trade secret. Trade secret protection works best when the secret is not apparent in the product.

Applicability to Computer Objects

Trade secret protection applies very well to computer software. The underlying algorithm of a computer program is novel, but its novelty depends on nobody else's knowing it. Trade secret protection allows distribution of the *result* of a secret (the executable program) while still keeping the program design hidden. Trade secret protection does not cover copying a product (specifically a computer program), so it cannot protect against a pirate who sells copies of someone else's program without permission. However, trade secret protection makes it illegal to steal a secret algorithm and use it in another product.

The difficulty with computer programs is that reverse engineering works. Decompiler and disassembler programs can produce a source version of an executable program. Of course, this source does not contain the descriptive variable names or the comments to explain the code, but it is an accurate version that someone else can study, reuse, or extend.

Difficulty of Enforcement

Trade secret protection is of no help when someone infers a program's design by studying its output or, worse yet, decoding the object code. Both of these are legitimate (that is, legal) activities, and both cause trade secret protection to disappear.

The confidentiality of a trade secret must be ensured with adequate safeguards. If source code is distributed loosely or if the owner fails to impress on people (such as employees) the importance of keeping the secret, any prosecution of infringement will be weakened. Employment contracts typically include a clause stating that the employee will not divulge any trade secrets received from the company, even after leaving a job. Additional protection, such as marking copies of sensitive documents or controlling access to computer files of secret information, may be necessary to impress people with the importance of secrecy.

Protection for Computer Objects

The previous sections have described three forms of protection: the copyright, patent, and trade secret laws. Each of these provides a different form of protection to sensitive things. In this section we consider different kinds of computer objects and describe which forms of protection are most appropriate for each kind. Table 9-1 shows how these three forms of protection compare in several significant ways.

Computer artifacts are new and constantly changing, and they are not yet fully appreciated by the legal system based on centuries of precedent. Perhaps in a few years the issue of what protection is most appropriate for a given computer object will be more clear-cut. Possibly a new form of protection or a new use of an old form will apply specifically to computer objects. For example, the European Union has already enacted model legislation for copyright protection of computer software. However, one of its goals was to promote software that builds on what others have done. Thus, the E.U. specifically exempted a product's interface specification from copyright and permitted others to derive the interface to allow development of new products that could connect via that interface.

Until the law provides protection that truly fits computer goods, here are some guidelines for using the law to protect computer objects.

Protecting Hardware

Hardware, such as chips, disk drives, or floppy disk media, can be patented. The medium itself can be patented, and someone who invents a new process for manufacturing it can obtain a second patent.

TABLE 9-1 Comparing Copyright, Patent, and Trade Secret Protection.

	Copyright	Patent	Trade Secret
Protects	Expression of idea, not idea itself	Invention—the way something works	A secret, competitive advantage
Protected object made public	Yes; intention is to promote publication	Design filed at Patent Office	No
Requirement to distribute	Yes	No	No
Ease of filing	Very easy, do-it-yourself	Very complicated; specialist lawyer suggested	No filing
Duration	Life of human originator plus 70 years, or total of 95 years for a company	19 years	Indefinite
Legal protection	Sue if unauthorized copy sold	Sue if invention copied	Sue if secret improperly obtained

Protecting Firmware

The situation is a little less clear with regard to microcode. Certainly, the physical devices on which microcode is stored can be patented. Also, a special-purpose chip that can do only one specific task (such as a floating-point arithmetic accelerator) can probably be patented. However, the data (instructions, algorithms, microcode, programs) contained in the devices are probably not patentable.

Can they be copyrighted? Are these the expression of an idea in a form that promotes dissemination of the idea? Probably not. And assuming that these devices were copyrighted, what would be the definition of a copy that infringed on the copyright? Worse, would the manufacturer really want to register a copy of the internal algorithm with the Copyright Office? Copyright protection is probably inappropriate for computer firmware.

Trade secret protection seems appropriate for the code embedded in a chip. Given enough time, we can reverse engineer and infer the code from the behavior of the chip. The behavior of the chip does not reveal what algorithm is used to produce that behavior. The original algorithm may have better (or worse) performance (speed, size, fault tolerance) that would not be obvious from reverse engineering.

For example, Apple Computer is enforcing its right to copyright protection for an operating system embedded in firmware. The courts have affirmed that computer software *is* an appropriate subject for copyright protection and that protection should be no less valid when the software is in a chip rather than in a conventional program.

Protecting Object Code Software

Object code is usually copied so that it can be distributed for profit. The code is a work of creativity, and most people agree that object code distribution is an acceptable medium of publication. Thus, copyright protection seems appropriate.

A copyright application is usually accompanied by a copy of the object being protected. With a book or piece of music (printed or recorded), it is easy to provide a copy. The Copyright Office has not yet decided what is an appropriate medium in which to accept object code. A binary listing of the object code will be taken, but the Copyright Office does so without acknowledging the listing to be acceptable or sufficient. The Office will accept a source code listing. Some people argue that a source code listing is not equivalent to an object code listing, in the same way that a French translation of a novel is different from its original language version. It is not clear *in the courts* that registering a source code version provides copyright protection to object code. However, someone should not be able to take the object code of a system, rearrange the order of the individual routines, and say that the result is a new system. Without the original source listings, it would be very difficult to compare two binary files and determine that one was the functional equivalent of the other simply through rearrangement.

Several court cases will be needed to establish acceptable ways of filing object code for copyright protection. Furthermore, these cases will have to develop legal precedents to define the equivalence of two pieces of computer code.

Protecting Source Code Software

Software developers selling to the mass market are reticent to distribute their source code. The code can be treated as a trade secret, although some lawyers also encourage that it be copyrighted. (These two forms of protection are possibly mutually exclusive, although registering a copyright will not hurt.)

Recall that the Copyright Office requires registering at least the first 25 and the last 25 pages of a written document. These pages are filed with the Library of Congress, where they are available for public inspection. This registration is intended to assist the courts in determining which work was registered for copyright protection. However, because they are available for anybody to see, they are not secret, and copyright registration can expose the secrecy of an ingenious algorithm. A copyright protects the right to distribute copies of the *expression* of an idea, not the idea itself. Therefore, a copyright does not prevent someone from reimplementing an algorithm, expressed through a copyrighted computer program.

As just described, source code may be the most appropriate form in which to register a copyright for a program distributed in object form. It is difficult to register source code with the Copyright Office while still ensuring its secrecy. A long computer program can be rearranged so that the first and last 25 pages do not divulge much of the secret part of a source program. Embedding small errors or identifiable peculiarities in the source (or object) code of a program may be more useful in determining copyright infringement. Again, several court cases must be decided in order to establish procedures for protection of computer programs in either source or object form.

Protecting Documentation

If we think of documentation as a written work of nonfiction (or, perhaps, fiction), copyright protection is effective and appropriate for it. Notice that the documentation is distinct from the program. A program and its documentation must be copyrighted separately. Furthermore, copyright protection of the documentation may win a judgment against someone who illegally copies both a program and its documentation.

In cases where a written law is unclear or is not obviously applicable to a situation, the results of court cases serve to clarify or even extend the words of the law. As more unfair acts involving computer works are perpetrated, lawyers will argue for expanded interpretations of the law. Thus, the meaning and use of the law will continue to evolve through judges' rulings. In a sense, computer technology has advanced much faster than the law has been able to.

9.2 INFORMATION AND THE LAW

Source code, object code, and even the "look and feel" of a computer screen are recognizable, if not tangible, objects. The law deals reasonably well, although somewhat belatedly, with these things. But computing is in transition to a new class of object, with new legal protection requirements. Electronic commerce, electronic publishing, electronic voting, electronic banking—these are the new challenges to the legal system. In this section we consider some of these new security requirements.

Information as an Object

The shopkeeper used to stock "things" in the store, such as buttons, automobiles, and pounds of sugar. The buyers were customers. When a thing was sold to a customer, the shopkeeper's stock of that thing was reduced by one, and the customer paid for and left with a thing. Sometimes the customer could resell the thing to someone else, for more or less than the customer originally paid.

But shops also provided services, and the services that could be identified as the "things" were, for example, a haircut, a root canal, a defense for a trial. Some services had a set price (for example, a haircut), although one provider might charge more for that service than another. A "shopkeeper" (hair stylist, dentist, lawyer) essentially sold time. For instance, the price of a haircut generally related to the cost of the stylist's time, and lawyers and accountants charged by the hour for services in which there was no obvious standard item. The value of a service in a free economy was somehow related to its desirability to the buyer and the seller. For example, the dentist was willing to sell a certain amount of time, reserving the rest of the day for other activities. Like a shopkeeper, once a service provider sold some time or service, it could not be sold again to someone else.

But today we must consider a third category for sale: information. No one would argue against the proposition that information is valuable. Students are tempted to pay others for answers during examinations, and businesses pay for credit reports, client lists, and inside information about competitors. But information does not fit the familiar commercial paradigms with which we have dealt for many years. Let us examine why information is different from other commercial things.

Information Is Not Depletable

Unlike tangible things and services, information can be sold again and again without depleting stock or diminishing quality. For example, a credit bureau can sell the same credit report on an individual to an unlimited number of requesting clients. Each client pays for the information in the report. The report may be delivered on some tangible medium, such as paper, but it is the *information*, not the medium, that has the value.

This characteristic separates information from other tangible works, such as books, CDs, or art prints. Each tangible work is a single copy, which can be individually numbered or accounted for. A bookshop can always order more copies of a book if the stock becomes depleted, but it can sell only as many copies as it has.

Information Can Be Replicated

The value of information is what the buyer will pay the seller. But after having bought the information, the buyer can then become a seller and can potentially deprive the original seller of further sales. Because information is not depletable, the buyer can enjoy or use the information and can also sell it many times over, perhaps even making a profit.

Information Has a Minimal Marginal Cost

The **marginal cost** of an item is the cost to produce another one after having produced some already. If a newspaper sold only one copy on a particular day, that one issue would be prohibitively expensive because it would have to cover the day's cost (salary and benefits) of all the writers, editors, and production staff, as well as a share of the cost of all equipment for its production. These are fixed costs needed to produce a first copy. With this model, the cost of the second and subsequent copies is minuscule, representing basically just the cost of paper and ink to print them. Fortunately, newspapers have very large press runs and daily sales, so the fixed costs are spread evenly across a large number of copies printed. More importantly, publishers have a reasonable idea of how many copies will sell, so they adjust their budgets to make a profit at the expected sales volume, and extra sales simply increase the profit. Also, newspapers budget by the month or quarter or year so that the price of a single issue does not fluctuate based on the number of copies sold of yesterday's edition.

In theory, a purchaser of a copy of a newspaper could print and sell other copies of that copy, although doing so would violate copyright law. Few purchasers do that, for four reasons.

- The newspaper is covered by copyright law.
- The cost of reproduction is too high for the average person to make a profit.
- It is not fair to reproduce the newspaper that way.
- There is usually some quality degradation in making the copy.

Unless the copy is truly equivalent to the original, many people would prefer to buy an authentic issue from the news agent, with clear type, quality photos, actual color, and so forth.

The cost of information similarly depends on fixed costs plus costs to reproduce. Typically, the fixed costs are large whereas the cost to reproduce is extremely small, even less than for a newspaper because there is no cost for the raw materials of paper and ink. However, unlike a newspaper, information is far more feasible for a buyer to resell. A copy of digital information can be perfect, indistinguishable from the original, the same being true for copies of copies of copies of copies.

The Value of Information Is Often Time Dependent

If you knew for certain what the trading price of a share of Microsoft stock would be next week, that information would be extremely valuable because you could make an enormous profit on the stock market. Of course, that price cannot be known today. But suppose you knew that Microsoft was certain to announce something next week that would cause the price to rise or fall. That information would be almost as valuable as knowing the exact price, and it could be known in advance. However, knowing *yesterday's* price for Microsoft stock or knowing that *yesterday* Microsoft announced something that caused the stock price to plummet is almost worthless because it is printed in every major financial newspaper. Thus, the value of information may depend on when you know it.

Information Is Often Transferred Intangibly

A newspaper is a printed artifact. The news agent hands it to a customer, who walks away with it. Both the seller and the buyer realize and acknowledge that something has been acquired. Furthermore, it is evident if the newspaper is seriously damaged; if a serious production flaw appears in the middle, the defect is easy to point out.

But times are changing. Increasingly, information is being delivered as bits across a network instead of being printed on paper. If the bits are visibly flawed (that is, if an error detecting code indicates a transmission error), demonstrating that flaw is easy. However, if the copy of the information is accurate but the underlying information is incorrect, useless, or not as expected, it is difficult to justify a claim that the information is flawed.

Legal Issues Relating to Information

These characteristics of information significantly affect its legal treatment. If we want to understand how information relates to copyright, patent, and trademark laws, we must understand these attributes. We can note first that information has some, limited legal basis for the protection. For example, information can be related to trade secrets, in that information is the stock in trade of the information seller. While the seller has the information, trade secret protection applies naturally to the seller's legitimate ability to profit from information. Thus, the courts recognize that information has value.

However, as shown earlier, a trade secret has value only as long as it remains a secret. For instance, the Coca-Cola Company cannot expect to retain trade secret protection for its formula after it sells that formula. Also, the trade secret is not secure if someone else can derive or infer it.

Other forms of protection are offered by copyrights and patents. As we have seen earlier, neither of these applies perfectly to computer hardware or software, and they apply even less well to information. The pace of change in the legal system is slow, helping to ensure that the changes that do occur are fair and well considered. The deliberate pace of change in the legal system is about to be hit by the supersonic rate of change in the information technology industry. Let us look at several examples of situations in which information needs are about to place significant demands on the legal system.

Information Commerce

Information is unlike most other goods traded, even though it has value and is the basis of some forms of commerce. The market for information is still young, and so far the legal community has experienced few problems. Nevertheless, several key issues must be resolved.

For example, we have seen that software piracy involves copying information without offering adequate payment to those who deserve to be paid. Several approaches have been tried to ensure that the software developer or publisher receives just compensation for use of the software: copy protection, freeware, and controlled distribution. More recently, software is being delivered as mobile code or applets, supplied electronically as needed. The applet approach gives the author and distributor more control. Each applet can potentially be tracked and charged for, and each applet can destroy itself after use, so that nothing remains to be passed for free to someone else. But this scheme requires a great deal of accounting and tracking, increasing the costs of what might otherwise be reasonably priced. Thus, none of the current approaches seem ideal, so a legal remedy will often be needed instead of, or in addition to, the technological ones.

Electronic Publishing

Many newspapers and magazines post a version of their content on the Internet, as do wire services and television news organizations. For example, the British Broadcasting Company (BBC) and the Reuters news services have a significant web presence. We should expect that some news and information will eventually be published and distributed exclusively on the Internet. Indeed, encyclopedias such as the Britannica and Expedia are mainly web-based services now, rather than being delivered as the large number of book volumes they used to occupy. Here again the publisher has a problem ensuring that it receives fair compensation for the work. Cryptography-based technical solutions are under development to address this problem. However, these technical solutions must be supported by a legal structure to enforce their use.

Protecting Data in a Database

Databases are a particular form of software that has posed significant problems for legal interpretation. The courts have had difficulty deciding which protection laws apply to databases. How does one determine that a set of data came from a particular database (so that the database owner can claim some compensation)? Who even owns the data in a database if it is public data, such as names and addresses?

Electronic Commerce

Laws related to trade in goods have evolved literally over centuries. Adequate legal protections exist to cover defective goods, fraudulent payment, and failure to deliver when the goods are tangible and are bought through traditional outlets such as stores and catalogs. However, the situation becomes less clear when the goods are traded electronically.

If you order goods electronically, digital signatures and other cryptographic protocols can provide a technical protection for your "money." However, suppose the information you order is not suitable for use, or never arrives, or arrives damaged, or arrives too late to use. How do you prove conditions of the delivery? For catalog sales, you often have receipts or some paper form of acknowledgment of time, date, and location. But for digital sales, such verification may not exist or can be easily modified. These legal issues must be resolved as we move into an age of electronic commerce.

Protecting Information

Clearly, current laws are inadequate for protecting the information itself and for protecting electronically based forms of commerce. So how is information to be protected legally? As described, copyrights, patents, and trade secrets cover some, but not all, issues related to information. Nevertheless, the legal system does not allow free traffic in information; some mechanisms can be useful.

Criminal and Civil Law

Statutes are laws that state explicitly that certain actions are illegal. A statute is the result of a legislative process by which a governing body declares that the new law will be in force after a designated time. For example, the parliament may discuss issues related to taxing Internet transactions and pass a law about when relevant taxes must be paid. Often, a violation of a statute will result in a **criminal** trial, in which the government argues for punishment because an illegal act has harmed the desired nature of society. For example, the government will prosecute a murder case because murder violates a law passed by the government. In the United States, criminal transgressions are severe, and the law requires that the judge or jury find the accused guilty beyond reasonable doubt. For this reason, the evidence must be strong and compelling. The goal of a criminal case is to punish the criminal, usually by depriving him or her of rights in some way (such as putting the criminal in prison or assessing a fine).

Civil law is a different type of law, not requiring such a high standard of proof of guilt. In a **civil** case, an individual, organization, company, or group claims it is has been harmed. The goal of a civil case is restitution: to make the victim "whole" again by repairing the harm. For example, suppose Fred kills John. Because Fred has broken a law against murder, the government will prosecute Fred in criminal court for having broken the law and upsetting the order of society. Abigail, the surviving wife, might be a witness at the criminal trial, hoping to see Fred put in prison. But she may also sue him in civil court for wrongful death, seeking payment to support her surviving children.

Tort Law

Special legal language describes the wrongs treated in a civil case. The language reflects whether a case is based on breaking a law or on countering legal precedents that have evolved over time. In other words, sometime judges may make determinations based on what is reasonable and what has come before, rather than on what is written in legislation. A **tort** is harm not occurring from violation of a statute or from breach of a contract but instead from being counter to the accumulated body of precedents. Thus, statute law is written by legislators and is interpreted by the courts; tort law is unwritten but evolves through court decisions that become precedents for cases that follow. The basic test of a tort is what a reasonable person would do. **Fraud** is a common example of tort law in which, basically, one person lies to another, causing harm.

Computer information is perfectly suited to tort law. The court merely has to decide what is reasonable behavior, not whether a statute covers the activity. For example, taking information from someone without permission and selling it to someone else as your own is fraud. The owner of the information can sue you, even though there may be no statute saying that information theft is illegal. That owner has been harmed by being deprived of the revenue you received from selling the information.

Because tort law is written only as a series of court decisions that evolve constantly, prosecution of a tort case can be difficult. If you are involved in a case based on tort law, you and your lawyer are likely to try two approaches: First, you might argue that your case is a clear violation of the norms of society, that it is not what a fair, prudent person would do. This approach could establish a new tort. Second, you might argue that your case is similar to one or more precedents, perhaps drawing a parallel between a computer program and an art work. The judge or jury would have to decide whether the comparison was apt. In both of these ways, law can evolve to cover new objects.

Contract Law

A third form of protection for computer objects is **contracts**. A contract is an agreement between two parties. A contract must involve three things:

- an offer
- an acceptance
- a consideration

One party offers something: "I will write this computer program for you for this amount of money." The second party can accept the offer, reject it, make a counter offer, or simply ignore it. In reaching agreement with a contract, only an acceptance is interesting; the rest is just the history of how agreement was reached. A contract must include consideration of money or other valuables. The basic idea is that two parties exchange things of value, such as time traded for money or technical knowledge for marketing skills. For example, "I'll wash your car if you feed me dinner" or "Let's trade these two CDs" are offers that define the consideration. It helps for a contract to be in writing, but it does not need to be. A written contract can involve hundreds of pages of terms and conditions qualifying the offer and the consideration.

One final aspect of a contract is its freedom: the two parties have to enter into the contract voluntarily. If I say "sign this contract or I'll break your arm," the contract is not valid, even if leaving your arm intact is a really desirable consideration to you. A contract signed under duress or with fraudulent action is not binding. A contract does not have to be fair, in the sense of equivalent consideration for both parties, as long as both parties freely accept the conditions.

Information is often exchanged under contract. Contracts are ideal for protecting the transfer of information because they can specify any conditions. "You have the right to use but not modify this information," "you have the right to use but not resell this information," or "you have the right to view this information yourself but not allow others to view it" are three potential contract conditions that could protect the commercial interests of an owner of information.

Computer contracts typically involve the development and use of software and computerized data. As we note shortly, there are rules about who has the right to contract for software—employers or employees—and what are reasonable expectations of software's quality.

If the terms of the contract are fulfilled and the exchange of consideration occurs, everyone is happy. Usually. Difficulties arise when one side thinks the terms have been fulfilled and the other side disagrees.

As with tort law, the most common legal remedy in contract law is money. You agreed to sell me a solid gold necklace and I find it is made of brass. I sue you. Assuming the court agreed with me, it might compel you to deliver a gold necklace to me, but more frequently the court will decide I am entitled to a certain sum of money. In the necklace case, I might argue first to get back the money I originally paid you, and then argue for incidental damages from, for example, the doctor I had to see when your brass necklace turned my skin green, or the embarrassment I felt when a friend pointed to my necklace and shouted "Look at the cheap brass necklace!" I might also argue for punitive damages to punish you and keep you from doing such a disreputable thing again. The court will decide which of my claims are valid and what a reasonable amount of compensation is.

Summary of Protection for Computer Artifacts

This section has presented the highlights of law as it applies to computer hardware, software, and data. Clearly these few pages only skim the surface; the law has countless subtleties. Still, by now you should have a general idea of the types of protection available for what things and how to use them. The differences between criminal and civil law are summarized in Table 9-2.

TABLE 9-2 Criminal vs. Civil Law.

	Criminal Law	Civil Law
Defined by	• Statutes	• Contracts • Common law
Cases brought by	• Government	• Government • Individuals and companies
Wronged party	• Society	• Individuals and companies
Remedy	• Jail, fine	• Damages, typically monetary

Contracts help fill the voids among criminal, civil, and tort law. That is, in the absence of relevant statutes, we first see common tort law develop. But people then enhance these laws by writing contracts with the specific protections they want.

Enforcement of civil law—torts or contracts—can be expensive because it requires one party to sue the other. The legal system is informally weighted by money. It is attractive to sue a wealthy party who could pay a hefty judgment. And a big company that can afford dozens of top-quality lawyers will more likely prevail in a suit than an average individual.

9.3 RIGHTS OF EMPLOYEES AND EMPLOYERS

Employers hire employees to generate ideas and make products. The protection offered by copyrights, patents, and trade secrets appeals to employers because it applies to the ideas and products. However, the issue of who owns the ideas and products is complex. Ownership is a computer security concern because it relates to the rights of an employer to protect the secrecy and integrity of works produced by the employees. In this section we study the respective rights of employers and employees to their computer products.

Ownership of Products

Suppose Edye works for a computer software company. As part of her job, she develops a program to manage windows for a computer screen display. The program belongs to her company because it paid Edye to write the program: she wrote it as a part of a work assignment. Thus, Edye cannot market this program herself. She could not sell it even if she worked for a non-software-related company but developed the software as part of her job. Most employees understand this aspect of their responsibilities to their employer.

Instead, suppose Edye develops this program in the evenings at home; it is not a part of her job. Then she tries to market the product herself. If Edye works as a programmer, her employer will probably say that Edye profited from training and experience gained on the job; at the very least, Edye probably conceived or thought about the project while at work. Therefore, the employer has an interest in (that is, owns at least part of) the rights to her program. However, the situation changes if Edye's primary job does not involve programming. If Edye is a television newscaster, her employer may have contributed nothing that relates to her computer product. If her job does not involve programming, she may be free to market any computer product she makes. And if Edye's spare-time program is an application that tracks genealogy, her employer would probably not want rights to her program, since it is far from its area of business. (If you are in such a situation yourself, you should check with your employer to be sure.)

Finally, suppose Edye is not an employee of a company. Rather, she is a consultant who is self-employed and, for a fee, writes customized programs for her clients. Consider her legal position in this situation. She may want to use the basic program design, generalize it somewhat, and market it to others. Edye argues that she thought up, wrote, and tested the program; therefore, it is her work, and she owns it. Her client argues that it paid Edye to develop the program, and it owns the program, just as it would own a bookcase she might be paid to build for the station.

Clearly, these situations differ, and interpreting the laws of ownership is difficult. Let us consider each type of protection in turn.

Ownership of a Patent

The person who owns a work under patent or copyright law is the inventor; in the examples described earlier, the owner is the programmer or the employer. Under patent law, it is important to know who files the patent application. If an employee lets an employer patent an invention, the employer is deemed to own the patent and therefore the rights to the invention.

The employer also has the right to patent if the employee's job functions included inventing the product. For instance, in a large company a scientist may be hired to do research and development, and the results of this inventive work become the property of the employer. Even if an employee patents something, the employer can argue for a right to use the invention if the employer contributed some resources (such as computer time or access to a library or database) in developing the invention.

Ownership of a Copyright

Owning a copyright is similar to owning a patent. The author (programmer) is the presumed owner of the work, and the owner has all rights to an object. However, a special situation known as *work for hire* applies to many copyrights for developing software or other products.

Work for Hire

In a **work for hire** situation, the employer, *not* the employee, is considered the author of a work. Work for hire is not easy to identify and depends in part on the laws of the state in which the employment occurs. The relationship between an employee and employer is considered a work for hire if some or all of the following conditions are true. (The more of these conditions that are true, the more a situation resembles work for hire.)

- The employer has a supervisory relationship, overseeing the manner in which the creative work is done.
- The employer has the right to fire the employee.
- The employer arranges for the work to be done before the work was created (as opposed to the sale of an existing work).
- A written contract between the employer and employee states that the employer has hired the employee to do certain work.

In the situation in which Edye develops a program on her job, her employer will certainly claim a work for hire relationship. Then, the employer owns all copyright rights and should be identified in place of the author on the copyright notice.

Licenses

An alternative to a work for hire arrangement is **licensed software**. In this situation, the programmer develops and retains full ownership of the software. In return for a fee, the programmer grants to a company a license to use the program. The license can be granted for a definite or unlimited period of time, for one copy or for an unlimited number, to use at one location or many, to use on one machine or all, at specified or unlimited times. This arrangement is highly advantageous to the programmer, just as a work for hire arrangement is highly advantageous to the employer. The choice between work for hire and license is largely what the two parties will agree to.

Trade Secret Protection

A trade secret is different from either a patent or a copyright in that there is no registered inventor or author; there is no registration office for trade secrets. In the event a trade secret is revealed, the owner can prosecute the revealer for damages suffered. But first, ownership must be established because only the owner can be harmed.

A company owns the trade secrets of its business-confidential data. As soon as a secret is developed, the company becomes the owner. For example, as soon as sales figures are accumulated, a company has trade secret right to them, even if the figures are not yet compiled, totaled, summarized, printed, or distributed. As with copyrights, an employer may argue about having contributed to the development of trade secrets. If your trade secret is an improved sorting algorithm and part of your job involves investigating and testing sorting algorithms, your employer will probably claim at least partial ownership of the algorithm you try to market.

Employment Contracts

An employment contract often spells out rights of ownership. But sometimes the software developer and possible employer have no contract. Having a contract is desirable both for employees and employers so that both will understand their rights and responsibilities.

Typically, an employment contract specifies that the employee be hired to work as a programmer exclusively for the benefit of the company. The company states that this is a work for hire situation. The company claims all rights to any programs developed, including all copyright rights and the right to market. The contract may further state that the employee is receiving access to certain trade secrets as a part of employment, and the employee agrees not to reveal those secrets to anyone.

More restrictive contracts (from the employee's perspective) assign to the employer rights to all inventions (patents) and all creative works (copyrights), not just those that follow directly from one's job. For example, suppose an employee is hired as an accountant for an automobile company. While on the job, the employee invents a more efficient way to burn fuel in an automobile engine. The employer would argue that the employee used company time to think about the problem, and therefore the company was entitled to this product. An employment contract transferring all rights of inventions to the employer would strengthen the case even more.

An agreement not to compete is sometimes included in a contract. The employee states that simply having worked for one employer will make the employee very valuable to a competitor. The employee agrees not to compete by working in the same field for a set period of time after termination. For example, a programmer who has a very high position involving the design of operating systems would understandably be familiar with a large body of operating system design techniques. The employee might memorize the major parts of a proprietary operating system and be able to write a similar one for a competitor in a very short time. To prevent this, the employer might require the employee not to work for a competitor (including working as an independent contractor). Agreements not to compete are not always enforceable in law; in some states the employee's right to earn a living takes precedence over the employer's rights.

9.4 SOFTWARE FAILURES

So far, we have considered programs, algorithms, and data as objects of ownership. But these objects vary in quality, and some of the legal issues involved with them concern the degree to which they function properly or well. In fact, people have legitimate differences of opinion on what constitutes "fair," "good," and "prudent" as these terms relate to computer software and programmers and vendors. The law applies most easily when there is broad consensus. In this section we look closely at the role that quality plays in various legal disputes. At the same time, we also look at the ethical side of software quality, foreshadowing a broader discussion on ethics later in this chapter.

Program development is a human process of design, creation, and testing, involving a great deal of communication and interaction. For these reasons, there will always be errors in the software we produce. We sometimes expect perfect consumer products, such as automobiles or lawn mowers. At other times, we expect products to be "good enough" for use, in that most instances will be acceptable. We do not mind variation in the amount of cheese in our pizza or a slight flaw in the glaze on a ceramic tile. If an instance of a product is not usable, we expect the manufacturer to provide some appropriate remedy, such as repair or replacement. In fact, the way in which these problems are handled can contribute to a vendor's reputation for quality service; on the rare occasions when there is a problem, the vendor will promptly and courteously make amends.

But the situation with software is very different. To be fair, an operating system is a great deal more complex than many consumer products, and more opportunities for failure exist. For this reason, this section addresses three questions:

- What are the legal issues in selling correct and usable software?
- What are the moral or ethical issues in producing correct and usable software?
- What are the moral or ethical issues in finding, reporting, publicizing, and fixing flaws?

In some ways, the legal issues are evolving. Everyone acknowledges that all vendors *should* produce good software, but that does not always happen. The more difficult concerns arise in the development and maintenance communities about what to do when faults are discovered.

Selling Correct Software

Software is a product. It is built with a purpose and an audience in mind, and it is purchased by a consumer with an intended use in an expected context. And the consumer has some expectations of a reasonable level of quality and function. In that sense, buying software is like buying a radio. If you buy a faulty radio, you have certain legal rights relating to your purchase which you can enforce in court if necessary. You may have three reactions if you find something wrong with the radio: you want your money back, you want a different (not faulty) radio, or you want someone to fix your radio. With software you have the same three possibilities, and we consider each one in turn.

To consider our alternatives with software, we must first investigate the nature of the faulty code. Why was the software bad? One possibility is that it was presented on a defective medium. For example, the CD may have had a flaw and you could not load the software on your computer. In this case, almost any merchant will exchange the faulty copy with a new one with little argument. The second possibility is that the software worked properly, but you don't like it when you try it out. It may not do all it was advertised to do. Or you don't like the "look and feel," or it is slower than you expected it to be, or it works only with European phone numbers, not the phone scheme in your country. The bottom line is that there is some attribute of the software that disappoints you, and you do not want this software.

The final possibility is that the software malfunctions, so you cannot use it with your computer system. Here, too, you do not want the software and hope to return it.

I Want a Refund

If the item were a radio, you would have the opportunity to look at it and listen to it in the shop, to assess its sound quality, measure its size (if it is to fit in a particular space), and inspect it for flaws. Do you have that opportunity with a program? Probably not.

The U.S. Uniform Commercial Code (UCC) governs transactions between buyers and sellers in the United States. Section 2-601 says that "if the goods or the tender of delivery fail in any respect to conform to the contract, the buyer may reject them." You may have had no opportunity to try out the software before purchase, particularly on your computer. Your inspection often could not occur in the store (stores tend to frown on your bringing your own computer, opening their shrink-wrapped software, installing the software on your machine, and checking the features). Even if you could have tried the software in the store, you may not have been able to assess how it works with the other applications with which it must interface. So you take home the software, only to find that it is free from flaws but does not fit your needs. You are entitled to a reasonable period to inspect the software, long enough to try out its features. If you decide within a reasonably short period of time that the product is not for you, you can cite UCC §2-601 to obtain a refund.

More often, though, the reason you want to return the software is because it simply is not of high enough quality. Unfortunately, correctness of software is more difficult to enforce legally.

I Want It to Be Good

Quality demands for mass market software are usually outside the range of legal enforcement for several reasons.

- Mass market software is seldom totally bad. Certain features may not work, and faults may prevent some features from working as specified or as advertised. But the software works for most of its many users, or works most of the time for all of its users.
- The manufacturer has "deep pockets." An individual suing a major manufacturer could find that the manufacturer has a permanent legal staff of dozens of full-time attorneys. The cost to the individual of bringing a suit is prohibitive.
- Legal remedies typically result in monetary awards for damages, not a mandate to fix the faulty software.
- The manufacturer has little incentive to fix small problems. Unless a problem will seriously damage a manufacturer's image or possibly leave the manufacturer open to large damage amounts, there is little justification to fix problems that affect only a small number of users or that do not render the product unfit for general use.

Thus, legal remedies are most appropriate only for a large complaint, such as one from a government or one representing a large class of dissatisfied and vocal users. The "fit for use" provision of the UCC dictates that the product must be usable for its intended purpose; software that doesn't work is clearly not usable. The UCC may help you get your money back, but you may not necessarily end up with working software.

Some manufacturers are very attentive to their customers. When flaws are discovered, the manufacturers promptly investigate the problems and fix serious ones immediately, perhaps holding smaller corrections for a later release. These companies are motivated more by public image or moral obligation than by legal requirement.

Reporting Software Flaws

Who should publicize flaws—the user or the manufacturer? A user might want the recognition of finding a flaw; delaying the release might let someone else get that credit. A manufacturer might want to ignore a problem or fail to credit the user. And either could say the other was wrong. And how should these flaws be reported? Several different viewpoints exist.

What You Don't Know Can Hurt You

The several variants of Code Red in 2001 sparked a debate about whether we should allow full disclosure of the mechanisms that allow malicious code to enter and thrive in our systems. For example, the first variant of Code Red was relatively benign, but the third and fourth variants were powerful. When the first Code Red variant appeared, it was studied by many security analysts, including those at eEye Digital Security in Aliso Viejo, California. In an effort to pressure vendors and software managers to take seriously the threats they represent, eEye practices full disclosure of what it knows about security flaws.

However, some observers claim that such open sharing of information is precisely what enables hackers to learn about vulnerabilities and then exploit them. Several developers suspect that eEye's openness about Code Red enabled the more powerful variants to be written and disseminated. [HUL01]

Scott Culp [CUL01], Microsoft's manager of Windows security, distinguishes between full disclosure and full exposure; he thinks that source code or detailed explanations of a vulnerability's concept should be protected. And many security analysts encourage users and managers to apply patches right away, closing security holes before they can be exploited. But as we saw in Sidebar 3-4, the patches require resources and may introduce other problems while fixing the initial one. Each software-using organization must analyze and balance the risks and cost of not acting with the risks and costs of acting right away.

The Vendor's Interests

Microsoft argues that producing one patch for each discovered vulnerability is inefficient both for the vendor and the user. The vendor might prefer to bundle several patches into a single service pack or, for noncritical vulnerabilities, to hold them until the next version. So, Microsoft would like to control if or when the report of a vulnerability goes public.

Craig Mundie, Microsoft's Chief Technology Officer, suggests a stronger reason to minimize disclosure of vulnerability information. "Every time we become explicit about a problem that exists in a legacy product, the response to our disclosure is to focus the attack. In essence we end up funneling them to the vulnerability." [FIS02a] Scott Culp argued [CUL01] that "a vendor's responsibility is to its customers, not to a self-described security community." He opposed what he called "information anarchy,... the practice of deliberately publishing explicit, step-by-step instructions for exploiting security vulnerabilities without regard for how the information may be used." But he also acknowledged that the process of developing, distributing, and applying patches is imperfect, and his own company "need[s] to make it easier for users to keep their systems secure."

Users' Interests

David Litchfield, a security researcher noted for locating flaws in vendors' programs, announced in May 2002 that he would no longer automatically wait for a vendor's patch before going public with a vulnerability announcement. Citing "lethargy and an unwillingness to patch security problems as and when they are found," [FIS02b] Litchfield criticized the approach of holding fixes of several vulnerabilities until enough had accumulated to warrant a single service pack. He makes the point that publicized or not, the vulnerabilities still exist. If one reporter has found the problem, so too could any number of malicious attackers. For a vendor to fail to provide timely patches to vulnerabilities of which the vendor is aware leaves the users wide open to attacks of which the user may be unaware.

Litchfield's solution is to put pressure on the vendor. He announced he would give vendors one week's notice of a vulnerability before publicizing the vulnerability—but not the details of how to exploit it—to the world.

"Responsible" Vulnerability Reporting

Clearly the conflicting interests of vendors and users must meet at some compromise position. Christey and Wysopal [CHR02] have proposed a vulnerability reporting process that meets constraints of timeliness, fair play, and responsibility. They call the user reporting a suspected vulnerability a "reporter" and the manufacturer the "vendor." A third party—such as a computer emergency response center—called a "coordinator" could also play a role when there is a conflict or power issue between reporter and vendor. Basically, the process requires reporter and vendor to do the following:

- The vendor must acknowledge a vulnerability report confidentially to the reporter.
- The vendor must agree that the vulnerability exists (or argue otherwise) confidentially to the reporter.
- The vendor must inform users of the vulnerability and any available countermeasures within 30 days or request additional time from the reporter as needed.
- After informing users, the vendor may request from the reporter a 30-day quiet period to allow users time to install patches.
- At the end of the quiet period the vendor and reporter should agree upon a date at which time the vulnerability information may be released to the general public.
- The vendor should credit the reporter with having located the vulnerability.
- If the vendor does not follow these steps, the reporter should work with a coordinator to determine a responsible way to publicize the vulnerability.

Such a proposal can only have the status of a commonly agreed-on process, since there is no authority that can enforce adherence on either users or vendors.

Quality Software

Boris Beizer, a consultant, has said, "Software should be shipped with bugs. The zero-defect notion is mythological and theoretically unachievable. That doesn't mean shipping ill-behaved or useless software; it means being open with users about the bugs we find, sending notices or including the bug list, publishing the workarounds when we have for them, and being honest and open about what we have and haven't yet tested and when we do and don't plan to test in the near future." [COF02]

The whole debate over how and when to disclose vulnerabilities avoids the real issue. The world does not need faster patches, it needs better software with fewer vulnerabilities after delivery to the user. Forno [FOR01] says, "The most significant danger and vulnerability facing the Wired World is continuing to accept and standardize corporate and consumer computer environments on technology that's proven time and again to be insecure, unstable, and full of undocumented bugs ('features') that routinely place the Internet community at risk."

In January 2002, Bill Gates, CEO of Microsoft, announced that producing quality software with minimal defects was his highest priority for Microsoft, ahead of new functionality. His manager of development of the XP operating system announced he was requiring programmers involved in development of XP to attend a course in secure programming. Did the initiative work? In one five-day period in June 2002, Microsoft released six separate patches for security vulnerabilities.

The issue is not how promptly a vulnerability is patched or how much detail is released with a vulnerability announcement. The issue is that, as the Anderson report [AND72] noted over three decades ago, "penetrate and patch" is a fatally flawed concept: after a flaw was patched, the penetrators always found other old flaws or new flaws introduced because of or in the patch. The issue is technical, psychological, sociological, managerial, and economic. Until we produce consistently solid software, our entire computing infrastructure is seriously at risk.

9.5 COMPUTER CRIME

The law related to contracts and employment is difficult, but at least employees, objects, contracts, and owners are fairly standard entities for which legal precedents have been developed over centuries. The definitions in copyright and patent law are strained when applied to computing because old forms must be made to fit new objects; for these situations, however, cases being decided now are establishing legal precedents. But crimes involving computers are an area of the law that is even less clear than the other areas. In this section we study computer crime and consider why new laws are needed to address some of its problems.

Why a Separate Category for Computer Crime Is Needed

Crimes can be organized into certain recognized categories, including *murder*, *robbery*, and *littering*. We do not separate crime into categories for different weapons, such as *gun crime* or *knife crime*, but we separate crime victims into categories, depending on whether they are *people* or *other objects*. Nevertheless, driving into your neighbor's picture window can be as bad as driving into his evergreen tree or pet sheep. Let us look at an example to see why these categories are not sufficient, and why we need special laws relating to computers as subjects and objects of crime.

Rules of Property

Parker and Nycom [PAR84] describe the theft of a trade secret proprietary software package. The theft occurred across state boundaries by means of a telephone line; this interstate aspect is important because it means that the crime is subject to federal law as well as state law. The California Supreme Court ruled that this software acquisition was not theft because

> Implicit in the definition of "article" in Section 499c(a) is that it must be something *tangible* ... Based on the record here, the defendant did not carry any tangible thing ... from the computer to his terminal unless the impulses which defendant allegedly

> caused to be transmitted over the telephone wire could be said to be tangible. *It is the opinion of the Court that such impulses are not tangible and hence do not constitute an "article."*

The legal system has explicit rules about what constitutes property. Generally, property is tangible, unlike magnetic impulses. For example, unauthorized use of a neighbor's lawn mower constitutes theft, even if the lawn mower was returned in essentially the same condition as it was when taken. To a computer professional, taking a copy of a software package without permission is clear-cut theft. Fortunately, laws evolve to fit the times, and this interpretation from the 1980s has been refined so that bits are now recognized items of property.

A similar problem arises with computer services. We would generally agree that unauthorized access to a computing system is a crime. For example, if a stranger enters your garden and walks around, even if nothing is touched or damaged, the act is considered trespassing. However, because access by computer does not involve a physical object, not all courts punish it as a serious crime.

Rules of Evidence

Computer printouts have been used as evidence in many successful fraud prosecutions. Under the rules of evidence, courts prefer an original source document to a copy, under the assumption that the copy may be inaccurate or may have been modified in the copying process.

However, magnetic and optical media are often the primary means of storing data today. In some instances, the magnetic copy is the *only* copy; there is no paper copy. Thus, as technology advances, devices such as smart cards, disks, CDs, and memory chips are being accepted as evidence.

The biggest difficulty with computer-based evidence in court is being able to demonstrate the authenticity of the evidence. Law enforcement officials operate under a chain of custody requirement: from the moment a piece of evidence is taken until it is presented in court, they track clearly and completely the order and identities of the people who had personal custody of that object. The reason for the chain of custody is to ensure that nobody has had the opportunity to alter the evidence in any way before its presentation in court. With computer-based evidence, it can be difficult to establish a chain of custody. If a crime occurred on Monday but was not discovered until Wednesday, who can verify that the log file was not altered? In fact, it probably was altered many times as different processes generated log entries. The issue is to demonstrate convincingly that the log entry for 2:37 on Monday does in fact correspond to the event that took place at that time on Monday, not some attempt on Thursday to plant a false clue long after the crime took place.

Threats to Integrity and Confidentiality

The integrity and secrecy of data are also issues in many court cases. Parker and Nycom [PAR84] describe a case in which a trespasser gained remote access to a computing system. The computing system contained confidential records about people, and the integrity of the data was important. The prosecution of this case had to be phrased in terms of theft of computer time and valued as such, even though that was insignificant compared with loss of privacy and integrity. Why? Because the law as written recognized theft of computer time as a loss, but not loss of privacy or destruction of data.

Now, however, several federal and state laws recognize the privacy of data about individuals. For example, disclosing grades or financial information without permission is a crime, and tort law would recognize other cases of computer abuse.

Value of Data

In another computer crime, a person was found guilty of having stolen a substantial amount of data from a computer data bank. However, the court determined that the "value" of that data was the cost of the paper on which it was printed, which was only a few dollars. Because of that valuation, this crime was classified as a misdemeanor and considered to be a minor crime. Fortunately, the courts have since determined that information and other intangibles can have significant value.

The concept of what we value and how we determine its value is key to understanding the problems with computer-based law. In most economies, paper money is accepted as a valuable commodity, even if the paper on which it is printed is worth only a few cents. Cash is easy to value: a dollar bill is worth one dollar. But consider the way we determine the value of a company's assets. Usually, the valuation reflects the amount of money a person or organization is willing to pay for it. For example, the assets of a credit bureau are its files. Banks and insurance companies willingly pay $20 or more for a credit report, even though the paper itself is worth less than a dollar. For a credit bureau, the amount a willing customer will pay for a report is a fair estimate of the report's value; this estimate is called the market value of the report. However, the credit bureau (or any company) has other assets that are not sold but are just as valuable to the company's financially viability. For instance, a confidential list of clients has no market value that can be established but may be essential. Its value is apparent only when a loss is suffered, such as when the secret information is made available to a competitor. Over time, the legal system will find ways to place a value on data that is representative of its value to those who use it. Although these methods of valuation are accepted in civil suits, they have not yet been widely accepted in criminal prosecution.

Acceptance of Computer Terminology

The law is also lagging behind technology in its acceptance of definitions of computing terms. For example, according to a federal statute, it is unlawful to commit arson within a federal enclave (18 USC 81). Part of that act relates to "machinery or building material or supplies" in the enclave, but court decisions have ruled that a motor vehicle located within a federal enclave at the time of the burning was not included under this statute. Because of that ruling, it is not clear whether computer hardware constitutes "machinery" in this context; "supplies" almost certainly does not include software. Computers and their software, media, and data must be understood and accepted by the legal system.

Why Computer Crime Is Hard to Define

From these examples, it is clear that the legal community has not accommodated advances in computers as rapidly as has the rest of society. Some people in the legal process do not understand computers and computing, so crimes involving computers are not always treated properly. Creating and changing laws are slow processes, intended to involve substantial thought about the effects of proposed changes. This deliberate process is very much out of pace with a technology that is progressing as fast as computing.

Adding to the problem of a rapidly changing technology, a computer can perform many roles in a crime. A particular computer can be the subject, object, or medium of a crime. A computer can be attacked (attempted unauthorized access), used to attack (impersonating a legitimate node on a network), and used as a means to commit crime (Trojan horse or fake login). Computer crime statutes must address all of these evils.

Why Computer Crime Is Hard to Prosecute

Even when everyone acknowledges that a computer crime has been committed, computer crime is hard to prosecute for the following reasons.

- *Lack of understanding*. Courts, lawyers, police agents, or jurors do not necessarily understand computers. Many judges began practicing law before the invention of computers, and most began before the widespread use of the personal computer. Fortunately, computer literacy in the courts is improving as judges, lawyers, and police officers use computers in their daily activities.
- *Lack of physical evidence.* Police and courts have for years depended on tangible evidence, such as fingerprints. As readers of Sherlock Holmes know, seemingly minuscule clues can lead to solutions to the most complicated crimes (or so Doyle would have you believe). But with many computer crimes there simply are no fingerprints and no physical clues of any sort.
- *Lack of recognition of assets.* We know what cash is, or diamonds, or even negotiable securities. But are twenty invisible magnetic spots really equivalent to a million dollars? Is computer time an asset? What is the value of stolen computer time if the system would have been idle during the time of the theft?
- *Lack of political impact.* Solving and obtaining a conviction for a murder or robbery is popular with the public, and so it gets high priority with prosecutors and police chiefs. Solving and obtaining a conviction for an obscure high-tech crime, especially one not involving obvious and significant loss, may get less attention. However, as computing becomes more pervasive, the visibility and impact of computer crime will increase.
- *Complexity of Case*. Basic crimes that everyone understands, such as murder, kidnapping, or auto theft, can be easy to prosecute. A complex money-laundering or tax fraud case may be more difficult to present to a jury because jurors have a hard time following a circuitous accounting trail. But the hardest crime to present may be a high-tech crime, described, for example, as root access by a buffer overflow in which memory was overwritten by other instructions, which

allowed the attacker to copy and execute code at will and then delete the code, eliminating all traces of entry (after disabling the audit logging, of course).

- *Juveniles.* Many computer crimes are committed by juveniles. Society understands immaturity and disregards even very serious crimes by juveniles because the juveniles did not understand the impact of their actions. A more serious, related problem is that many adults see juvenile computer crimes as childhood pranks, the modern equivalent of tipping over an outhouse.

Even when there is clear evidence of a crime, the victim may not want to prosecute because of possible negative publicity. Banks, insurance companies, investment firms, the government, and health care groups think their trust by the public will be diminished if a computer vulnerability is exposed. Also, they may fear repetition of the same crime by others: so-called copycat crimes. For all of these reasons, computer crimes are often not prosecuted.

Examples of Statutes

As a few examples from the 1980s have pointed out, in the early days, prosecution of computer crimes was hampered by lack of clear appreciation of the nature or seriousness of crime involving computers. Although theft, harm to persons, and damage to property have been crimes for a long time, in some cases new laws were useful to make it obvious to the courts what computer-related behavior was unacceptable. Most states now have laws covering computer crime of one sort or another. Also, computer-related crimes now appear in sentencing guidelines.

In this section we highlight a few of the laws defining aspects of crime against or using computers.

U.S. Computer Fraud and Abuse Act

The primary federal statute, 18 USC 1030, was enacted in 1984 and has been amended several times since. This statute prohibits

- unauthorized access to a computer containing data protected for national defense or foreign relations concerns
- unauthorized access to a computer containing certain banking or financial information
- unauthorized access, use, modification, destruction, or disclosure of a computer or information in a computer operated on behalf of the U.S. government
- accessing without permission a "protected computer," which the courts now interpret to include any computer connected to the Internet
- computer fraud
- transmitting code that causes damage to a computer system or network
- trafficking in computer passwords

Penalties range from $5,000 to $100,000 or twice the value obtained by the offense, whichever is higher, or imprisonment from 1 year to 20 years, or both.

U.S. Economic Espionage Act

This 1996 act outlaws use of a computer for foreign espionage to benefit a foreign country or business or theft of trade secrets.

U.S. Electronic Funds Transfer Act

This law prohibits use, transport, sale, receipt, or supply of counterfeit, stolen, altered, lost, or fraudulently obtained debit instruments in interstate or foreign commerce.

U.S. Freedom of Information Act

The Freedom of Information Act provides public access to information collected by the executive branch of the federal government. The act requires disclosure of any available data, unless the data fall under one of several specific exceptions, such as national security or personal privacy. The law's original intent was to release to individuals any information the government had collected on them. However, more corporations than individuals file requests for information as a means of obtaining information about the workings of the government. Even foreign governments can file for information. This act applies only to government agencies, although similar laws could require disclosure from private sources. The law's effect is to require increased classification and protection for sensitive information.

U.S. Privacy Act

The Privacy Act of 1974 protects the privacy of personal data collected by the government. An individual is allowed to determine what data have been collected on him or her, for what purpose, and to whom such information has been disseminated. An additional use of the law is to prevent one government agency from accessing data collected by another agency for another purpose. This act requires diligent efforts to preserve the secrecy of private data collected.

U.S. Electronic Communications Privacy Act

This law, enacted in 1986, protects against electronic wiretapping. There are some important qualifications. First, law enforcement agencies are always allowed to obtain a court order to access communications or records of them. And an amendment to the act requires Internet service providers to install equipment as needed to permit these court-ordered wiretaps. Second, the act allows Internet service providers to read the content of communications in order to maintain service or protect the provider itself from damage. So, for example, a provider could monitor traffic for viruses.

USA Patriot Act

Passed in 2001 in reaction to terrorist attacks in the United States, the USA Patriot Act includes a number of provisions supporting law enforcement's access to electronic communications. Under this act, law enforcement needs only to convince a court that a target is probably an agent of a foreign power in order to obtain a wiretap order. The main computer security provision of the Patriot Act is an amendment to the Computer Fraud and Abuse Act:

- Knowingly causing the transmission of code resulting in damage to a protected computer is a felony.
- Recklessly causing damage to a computer system as a consequence of unauthorized access is also a felony.
- Causing damage (even unintentionally) as a consequence of unauthorized access to a protected computer is a misdemeanor.

International Dimensions

So far we have explored laws in the United States. But many people outside the United States will read this book, perhaps wondering why they should learn about laws from a foreign country. This question has two answers.

Technically, computer security laws in the United States are similar to those in many other countries: lawmakers in each country learn about subtle legal points and interpretation or enforcement difficulties from laws passed in other countries. Many other countries, such as Australia, Canada, Brazil, Japan, the Czech Republic, and India, have recently enacted computer crime laws. These laws cover offenses such as fraud, unauthorized computer access, data privacy, and computer misuse. Schjolberg [SCH02] has compiled a survey of different countries' laws to counter unauthorized access.

The second reason to study laws from a foreign country is that the Internet is an international entity. Citizens in one country are affected by users in other countries, and users in one country may be subject to the laws in other countries. Therefore, you need to know which laws may affect you. The international nature of computer crime makes life much more complicated. For example, a citizen of country A may sit in country B, dial into an ISP in country C, use a compromised host in country D, and attack machines in country E (not to mention traveling on communications lines through dozens of other countries). To prosecute this crime may require cooperation of all five countries. The attacker may need to be extradited from B to E to be prosecuted there, but there may be no extradition treaty for computer crimes between B and E. And the evidence obtained in D may be inadmissible in E because of the manner in which it was obtained or stored. And the crime in E may not be a crime in B, so the law enforcement authorities, even if sympathetic, may be unable to act.

Although computer crime is truly international, differing statutes in different jurisdictions inhibit prosecution of international computer crime. In November 2001, the United States, Canada, Japan, and 22 European countries, signed a cybercrime treaty. This treaty makes a crime of activities such as online child pornography, fraud committed using computers and computer networks, and malicious attacks. The significance of this treaty is not so much that these activities are illegal (which most instances of fraud already were) but that the countries acknowledged them as crimes across their borders, making it easier for law enforcement agencies to cooperate and for criminals to be extradited for offenses against one country committed from within another country. But to really support investigation, prosecution, and conviction of computer criminals, more than just these 25 countries will have to be involved.

In the remainder of this section we briefly discuss laws around the world that differ from U.S. laws and that should be of interest to computer security students.

E.U. Data Protection Act

The E.U. Data Protection Act is model legislation for all the countries in the European Union. It establishes privacy rights and protection responsibilities for all citizens of member countries. The act governs the collection and storage of personal data about individuals, such as name, address, and identification numbers. The law requires a business purpose for collecting the data and controls against disclosure. Dating from 1994 in its initial form, this law was one of the first to establish protection requirements for the privacy of personal data. Most significantly, the act requires equivalent protection in non-E.U. countries if organizations in the European Union pass protected data outside the European Union. We look more closely at this act in the next section on privacy.

Restricted Content

Some countries have laws controlling Internet content allowed in their countries. Singapore requires service providers to filter content allowed in. China bans material that disturbs social order or undermines social stability. Tunisia has a law that applies the same controls on critical speech as for other media forms. [HRW99]

Further laws have been proposed to make it illegal to transmit outlawed content *through* a country, regardless of whether the source or destination of the content is in that country. Given the complex and unpredictable routing structure of the Internet, complying with these laws is effectively impossible, let alone enforcing them.

Use of Cryptography

Cryptography is the third major area in which different countries have developed laws. We survey these laws in a subsequent section.

Why Computer Criminals Are Hard to Catch

As if computer crime laws and prosecution were not enough, it is also difficult for law enforcement agencies to catch computer criminals. There are two major reasons for this.

First, computer crime is a multinational activity that must usually be pursued on a national or local level. There are no international laws on computer crime. Even though the major industrial nations cooperate very effectively on tracking computer criminals, criminals know there are "safe havens" from which they cannot be caught. Often, the trail of a criminal stops cold at the boundary of a country. Riptech Inc. [BEL02] studies Internet attack trends by many factors. For the period January–June 2002 the United States led the world in source of Internet attacks (40%) followed by Germany (7%). But when you normalize these data for number of users, a very different pattern emerges. Per Internet user, Israel and Hong Kong lead among those nations with more than 1 million users, and Kuwait and Iran top the list among nations with fewer than 1 million users. Nations all over the globe appear on these lists, which demonstrates that attackers can and do operate from many different countries.

Complexity is an even more significant factor than country of origin. As we have stated throughout this book, networked attacks are hard to trace and investigate because they can involve so many steps. A smart attacker will "bounce" an attack through many places to obscure the trail. Each step along the way makes the investigator complete more legal steps. If the trail leads from server A to B to C, the law enforcement investigators need a search warrant for data at A, and others for B and C. Even after obtaining the search warrants, the investigator has to find the right administrator and serve the warrants to begin obtaining data. In the time the investigator has to get and serve warrants, not to mention follow leads and correlate findings, the attacker has carefully erased the digital evidence.

In a CNET News article, Sandoval [SAN02] says law enforcement agencies are rarely able to track down hackers sophisticated enough to pull off complicated attacks. Sandoval quotes Richard Power, editorial director of the Computer Security Institute: "It's a world class business." Independent investigator Dan Clements says "only about 10 percent of active hackers are savvy enough to work this way consistently, but they are almost always successful."

What Computer Crime Does Not Address

Even with the definitions included in the statutes, the courts must interpret what a computer is. Legislators cannot define precisely what a computer is because computer technology is used in many other devices, such as robots, calculators, watches, automobiles, microwave ovens, and medical instruments. More importantly, we cannot predict what kinds of devices may be invented ten or fifty years from now. Therefore, the language in each of these laws indicates the kinds of devices the legislature seeks to include as computers and leaves it up to the court to rule on a specific case. Unfortunately, it takes a while for courts to build up a pattern of cases, and different courts may rule differently in similar situations. The interpretation of each of these terms will be unsettled for some time to come.

Value presents a similar problem. As noted in some of the cases presented, the courts have trouble separating the intrinsic value of an object (such as a sheet of paper with writing on it) from its cost to reproduce. The courts now recognize that a Van Gogh painting is worth more than the cost of the canvas and paint. But the courts have not agreed on the value of printed computer output. The cost of a blank diskette is miniscule, but it may have taken thousands of hours of data gathering and machine time to produce the data encoded on the diskette. The courts are still striving to determine the fair value of computer objects.

Both the value of a person's privacy and the confidentiality of data about a person are even less settled. In a later section we consider how ethics and individual morality take over where the law stops.

Cryptography and the Law

The law is used to regulate people for their own good and for the greater good of society. Murder, theft, drinking, and smoking are circumscribed by laws. Generally, the balance between personal freedom and the good of society is fairly easy to judge; for example, one's right to fire a gun ends when the bullet hits someone. Cryptography is also a regulated activity, but the issues are a little less clear-cut, in part because there is little open discussion of the subject.

People want to protect their privacy, including the secrecy of communications with others. Businesses want similar confidentiality. Criminals want secrecy so that they can communicate criminal plans in private. Governments want to track illegal activity, both to prevent crime and to apprehend and convict criminals after a crime has been committed. Finally, nations want to know the military and diplomatic plans of other nations. As shown throughout this book, cryptography can be a powerful tool to protect confidentiality, but being able to break cryptography can be a potent tool for government. Phrased differently, it suits governments' interests if people cannot use cryptography that is too good (meaning, unbreakable by the government).

Controls on Use of Cryptography

Closely related to restrictions on content are restrictions on the use of cryptography imposed on users in certain countries. In China, for example, State Council Order 273 requires foreign organizations or individuals to apply for permission to use encryption in China. Pakistan requires that all encryption hardware and software be inspected and approved by the Pakistan Telecommunication Authority. And in Iraq, use of even the Internet is strictly limited, and unauthorized use of encryption carries heavy penalties.

France's encryption policy is probably the most widely discussed. Import of encryption products is subject to a registration requirement: A vendor's registration for a mass market commercial product is valid for all imports of that product. Use of encryption for authentication is unlimited. Use of encryption with a key length up to 128 for confidentiality requires only the vendor's registration. Use of products with a key length greater than 128 bits requires that the key be escrowed with a trusted third party.

Such laws are very difficult to enforce on an individual basis. Cryptography, steganography, and secret writing have been used for centuries. The governments know they cannot prevent two cooperating people from concealing their communications. However, governments can limit widespread computer-based use by limiting cryptography in mass market products. Although policing 50 million computer users is impossible, controlling a handful of major computer manufacturers is feasible, especially ones whose profits would be affected by not being able to sell any products in a particular country. Thus, governments have addressed cryptography use at the source: the manufacturer and vendor.

Controls on Export of Cryptography

Until 1998, the United States led other industrialized nations in controlling cryptography. It did this by controlling export of cryptographic products, using the same category as munitions, such as bombs and atomic missiles. Although the law applied to everyone, in practice it could be enforced reasonably only against mass market software manufacturers. Software makers could export freely[1] any product using symmetric encryption with a key length of 40 bits or less. There were exceptions allowing

[1] That is, they could export to all but a handful of so-called rogue nations subject to stringent controls on munitions.

stronger encryption for financial institutions and for multinational corporations using the encryption for intracompany communication. Cryptography solely for authentication (for example, digital signatures) was also permitted. Although the law did not control the *use* of cryptography, limiting export effectively limited its use because major vendors could not sell products with strong encryption worldwide.

U.S. policy was especially important because most mass market software vendors were based in the United States, and many users were in the United States. The United States could also pressure software vendors not to write programs in such a way that someone could add the cryptography at an overseas location. Although a software vendor could move to or open a subsidiary in an uncontrolled country, a new vendor has a hard time obtaining a significant share of the market against large, established competitors. If such a vendor were able to take a significant amount of business away from U.S. companies, there would be an outcry and possible political pressure from the U.S. government. Thus, U.S. policy on this issue would and did dominate the world market.

Cryptography and Free Speech

Cryptography involves not just products; it involves ideas, too. Although governments effectively control the flow of products across borders, controlling the flow of ideas, either in people's heads or on the Internet, is almost impossible.

In a decision akin to splitting hairs, the U.S. courts ruled that computer object code was subject to the export restrictions, but a printed version of the corresponding source code was an idea that could not be restricted. The case in question involved Phil Zimmermann, the inventor of PGP e-mail encryption. In 1997 Zimmermann "exported" books containing the printed source code to PGP, and volunteers in Europe spent 1000 hours scanning the pages of the book; they then posted this source code publicly on the Internet. To highlight the vacuousness of this distinction, people reduced the object code of the PGP program to a bar code and printed that code on T-shirts with the caption "Warning, this T-shirt may be a controlled munition."

Cryptographic Key Escrow

Although laws enable governments to read encrypted communications, the governments don't really want to read *all* of them. A joking e-mail message or a file with your tax data is seldom a national security concern. But suppose there were evidence of cheating on your taxes or your writings were seditious. In these cases the government could convince a court to allow it to search your home, office, or computer files. It might then have reason and justification for wanting to read your encrypted data. So the government devised a scheme in which your encryption keys would become available only with court authorization.

In 1996 the U.S. government offered to relax the export restriction for so-called **escrowed encryption**, in which the government would be able to obtain the encryption key for any encrypted communication. The key escrow approach was a part of an initiative known under names such as **Clipper**, **Capstone**, and **Fortezza**. Ultimately this approach failed; the public feared what the government could actually access. See [HOF95a] and [DEN99] for more discussion on the key escrow debate.

Current Policy

The U.S. National Research Council (NRC) reported the results of an 18-month study [NRC96] to recommend a cryptographic policy for the U.S. Federal government. The report carefully weighed all the factors affected by cryptographic policy, such as protecting sensitive information for U.S. companies and individuals as well as foreign ones, international commerce, enforcing laws (prevention, investigation, and prosecution), and intelligence gathering. The report's recommendations for policy include the following:

- No law should bar the manufacture, sale, or use of any form of encryption within the United States.
- Export controls on cryptography should be relaxed but not eliminated.
- Products providing confidentiality at a level that meets most general commercial requirements should be easily exportable. In 1996, that level included products that incorporate 56-bit key DES, and so these products should be easily exportable.
- Escrowed encryption should be studied further, but, as it is not yet a mature technology, its use should not be mandated.
- Congress should seriously consider legislation that would impose criminal penalties on the use of encrypted communications in interstate commerce with the intent to commit a crime.
- The U.S. government should develop a mechanism to promote information security in the private sector.

In September 1998, the U.S. government announced that it was opening up export of encryption. Export of single (56-bit) key DES would be allowed to all countries except seven that supported terrorism. Unlimited size encryption would be exportable to 45 major industrial countries for use by financial institutions, medical providers, and e-commerce companies. Furthermore, the process for applying for permission, which had been another formidable deterrent, was simplified to a review taking no more than a week in most cases.

Summary of Legal Issues in Computer Security

This section has described four aspects of the relationship between computing and the law. First, we presented the legal mechanisms of copyright, patent, and trade secret as means to protect the secrecy of computer hardware, software, and data. These mechanisms were designed before the invention of the computer, so their applicability to computing needs is somewhat limited. However, program protection is especially desired, and software companies are pressing the courts to extend the interpretation of these means of protection to include computers.

We also explored the relationship between employers and employees, in the context of writers of software. Well-established laws and precedents control the acceptable access an employee has to software written for a company.

Third, we examined the legal side of software vulnerabilities: Who is liable for errors in software, and how is that liability enforced? Additionally, we considered alternative ways to report software errors.

Fourth, we noted some of the difficulties in prosecuting computer crime. Several examples showed how breaches of computer security are treated by the courts. In general, the courts have not yet granted computers, software, and data appropriate status, considering value of assets and seriousness of crime. The legal system is moving cautiously in its acceptance of computers. We described several important pieces of computer crime legislation that represent slow progress forward.

9.6 PRIVACY

In most of this book we have dealt with protecting "the system" from harm. Our "system" included companies, organizations, governments, and universities; its applications, web pages, infrastructure, computers, and networks; and all its data. "Harm" meant all the threats and threat agents we have studied. Because of the potential for serious harm, we often focused on malicious attacks, for example, by hackers. So the nature of protection has been to safeguard the system.

Now we explore another dimension to information systems security: protecting the individual, nonmalicious user. In particular, we want to investigate the privacy of sensitive data about that user. The user should be protected against the system's misuse of the private data and the system's failure to protect its users' private data against outside attack and disclosure.

In this information age, private data can have value. A new class of crime, called **identity theft**, occurs when one person takes on the identity of another person, perhaps creating massive debt or even perpetrating crimes in the victim's identity. With a victim's credit card details, an attacker can run up huge charges in a short time. An attacker can commit and be convicted of crimes under another name or trade on someone else's education and work experience to get a job. Sorting out who did (or didn't do) what can be a monumental task. People expect privacy for certain aspects of their private lives, such as income, taxes, criminal records, medical data, and even library reading patterns. Since much of this information is now stored electronically, privacy is an important computer security issue.

Sometimes the patterns themselves make the individual data valuable. For example, marketing agencies are eager to acquire lists of likely purchasers. What are private data worth? To most people, it largely depends on whether they are *your* private data or, by extension, whether you could foresee the same loss of privacy coming to you. Although difficult to assess, there certainly is a value to privacy.

In this section first we explore some of the conditions that can cause loss of privacy, and then we examine some of the controls to prevent or limit those losses.

Threats to Privacy

Many of the threats to privacy are not new. Bribing insiders, especially poorly paid ones, has worked for centuries. A break-in usually involves loss of some valuables, such as jewelry, silver, or electronics. But who can say whether the laptop computer was stolen just because it was a computer or because it contained sensitive data? And public records have been, by definition, open to the public. So loss of the privacy in those records is not new. Or is it?

Aggregation and Data Mining

In 1950 you could have gone to the government records office, recorded names of all property owners, recorded the names of all drivers, looked up military veterans, tracked birth announcements in newspapers, and bought magazine subscription lists. Plenty of data was available. A private investigator might have used sources such as these to investigate the background of a single, target individual. But it was too laborious to cross-correlate many large lists to find all veterans who owned homes, drove Chevrolets, and had children under five years old. Details on consumers, especially attributes that can distinguish potential customers, are extremely valuable to marketers.

Database management systems have made large-scale correlation possible. Not only can computers sift, sort, and correlate, there is also much more raw data on which to operate. Often, you don't realize how much information about you can be gleaned from your electronic transactions. For example, your bank, or another bank whose ATM you use, obtains your identity. A toll booth transponder system can record the time and date at which a particular transponder passes the toll booth. (Consider the possibility for the government to mail you a ticket if your transponder passes one receiver and then passes another receiver so soon after that the only way to cover the distance between the two would be to exceed the speed limit.) Credit card transactions or cell phone records demonstrate you are not in your home city. And peaks in your home's electrical usage suggest when you are home and when you are away. In a day, the ordinary person may cause twenty database records to be generated (ignoring records from Internet activity, which is a huge but separate issue.)

Poor System Security

People are the weak link in any security system, and insiders are involved in the majority of computer security incidents [CSI02, DTI02]. Whether through carelessness, poor understanding, pressure, or simple human error, insiders unintentionally expose private data. Personal details are discarded in unprotected trash, inadvertently displayed on web sites, or unknowingly stored in files on a computer (such as in a cookie or as part of a query embedded in a "favorite" URL). Add to that the malicious approaches in which workers are bribed, coerced, or tricked into compromising security.

The vulnerabilities we have studied so far involving loss of confidentiality or integrity can lead to loss of private data. One target of interest to hackers today is credit card numbers. In March 2001 the U.S. FBI said that an estimated 1 million credit card numbers had been stolen from over 40 banking and commerce sites. In August 2001 VISA reported to its member banks a list of 44,000 card numbers that had been exposed. Underground web sites and crime operations sell stolen numbers (see Sidebar 9-3 on credit card theft). Whether these numbers come from compromised web sites or electronic interceptions or some other means is unknown. But system flaws certainly account for some of the loss.

Sidebar 9-3 Playing the Credit Card Numbers Game

On 13 May 2002, *The New York Times* reported Internet sites offering credit card numbers at prices of $100 for 250 numbers, or $1000 for 5000. Prices fluctuate with supply and demand. Because of the worldwide reach of the Internet, these cards are sold to destinations all over the world, especially eastern Europe and Asia. The sites where cards are sold move frequently, frustrating law enforcement. The difficulty in prosecuting a citizen of one country under the laws of another makes the situation even more complex.

The card numbers are used to make purchases over the Internet or to obtain cash advances against the credit card. Although the consumer is typically not responsible for the losses, the issuing banks and card agencies, such as VISA and MasterCard, suffer losses approaching 0.25 percent for online transactions versus 0.10 percent for other kinds of transactions. These costs must be recovered in some way, being passed along to the consumer in higher interest rates or to the merchant in higher transaction fees, which ultimately affect merchants' prices.

Credit card numbers can also be used for extortion. In 2000 an online music distributor was approached by attackers claiming to have extracted its lists of credit card numbers of customers. The attackers threatened to post the numbers publicly unless they were paid $100,000 ransom.

Government Threats

Big Brother is watching. Just as marketers use computers to correlate disparate data and to infer more about you, so also does the government. The taxing authorities would like to know about your spending and banking patterns in order to ensure that you are paying all the taxes you owe. The medical authorities would like to know who has recently traveled to areas where a particular disease may be prevalent and to track that person's health over time. Crime investigators would like to know everyone who passed near a crime scene at the time of commission in order to obtain clues and locate potential witnesses. Everyone (except, perhaps, for criminals) would like the government to have data necessary to protect citizens, prevent crimes, and enforce laws. But citizens want to limit the government's information gathering because of the risk of excesses; in the past, abuses have included taxing authorities subjecting political enemies to unwarranted tax audits or the police harassing innocent people for political purposes.

The government has legitimate reasons to collect personal information about its citizens. Citizens expect the government to safeguard the data's privacy and to not use the data for purposes other than those for which they were rightfully collected.

Computer Use

The biggest risk to individuals' privacy probably is the Internet. Although e-mail and web surfing are two activities in which we engage voluntarily, not everyone is conscious of the enormous volume of data that can be collected.

E-mail is best likened to a post card in the regular mail. From the time the card is placed in the post by the sender to the time it arrives in your mail box, many people have easy access to the card and its message. For example, the mail carrier who delivers the card and every postal worker who handles it in transit could read it. In the same way, the contents of an e-mail message are often open to view by anyone between the sender and receiver. As with the post card analogy, the main thing preventing massive loss of privacy is volume: there are too many e-mail messages for it to be feasible for any group—government, private, or criminal—to read all, or even a substantial proportion, of messages in transit. (See, however, Sidebar 9-4 on the U.S. Carnivore program.) But just because performing large-scale interception or interpretation en route is infeasible today, tomorrow could be different as the speed and storage capacity of computers continues to improve. The places at which privacy is at greatest risk today are the two endpoints: interception at or close to the sender or receiver can make it possible to save and scrutinize all e-mail for that chosen sender or receiver.

Web surfing offers enormous potential for data collection. The server can record which pages you have downloaded, how long you lingered on a single page before clicking to move to another, whether you returned to a starting point or abandoned a line of searching, as well as data you explicitly provided, such as name, address, or other identification. The surfer can be identified by source IP address and perhaps NIC address. The surfer can also be identified by cookies stored from previous visits. Worse, when you download supposedly free software, unwittingly you may also acquire a Trojan horse that can report back to its owner anything about your computer and data or your computing activities. Registration with a service such as the Microsoft Passport allows a personal identity to be linked to a specific machine with a unique serial number and a particular IP address.

Societal Goal: Greatest Good for the Greatest Number

An inherent tension exists between individual privacy and the rights of government to protect its citizens. Your individual privacy rights are superseded by a more compelling need for information if, for example, the government has demonstrable reason to believe you may commit a serious crime. The balance between individual privacy rights and government access swings slowly over time, like a pendulum.

Corporate Rights and Private Business

Companies are free to collect data a government cannot. For example, the courts have held that employees' e-mail messages are the property of the employer, who has the right to read and copy them. A store can operate a security camera that records all movements by all people in the store. And companies can use location-sensitive identity badges to track where employees are within a corporate facility. Although people have certain reasonable expectations of privacy in certain locations, such as rest rooms and public areas, people surrender their privacy rights to the shopkeepers to be protected against shoplifting or other harm.

Privacy for Sale

How much is privacy worth? People have interesting reactions to this question. On the one hand, people argue that privacy is one of the inherent freedoms of a free society

Sidebar 9-4 Carnivore and Big Brother

Carnivore is a project of the U.S. FBI to monitor e-mail traffic. The project collects header data on e-mail messages, but not the body of those messages. The Carnivore device contained secret software that the FBI would install on servers of ISPs. Similar to packet sniffers for Ethernet networks, Carnivore would potentially obtain data on the sender, receiver, size, and date and time for every e-mail message it passes. If Carnivore found traffic in which the FBI was interested and had cause, the FBI would apply to a court for a search warrant; with that warrant, the FBI could begin to collect the content of e-mail messages between named senders and receivers.

The notion and justification of Carnivore are based on legal precedent for telephone communication, in which courts have ruled that without a search warrant the FBI can ask a telephone company to record the phone number called, and date, time, and length of all conversation originating from a particular phone number. To obtain the actual content of the conversations, the FBI needs to apply to a court for a wiretap order, showing the court the basis for believing the wiretap would provide evidence of illegal activity.

Skeptics are concerned about Carnivore. Because the software was held secret, critics charge there is no way to ensure that Carnivore limits its search to headers and not content. Carnivore apparently produces no audit trail, so there is no way to see what addresses the agents are tapping.

When did Carnivore appear? In 1999 EarthLink, a U.S. ISP, was served with a court order to install the EtherPeek packet sniffer on behalf of the FBI. EarthLink refused to comply because it could not ensure that EtherPeek would obtain only headers. Instead, it created and installed a sniffer of its own that it knew would provide only header data, which it agreed to provide to the FBI. In 2000 the FBI again sought to install on an EarthLink server its own software, which it then revealed was not the commercial EtherPeek package but was its own private device named Carnivore. EarthLink challenged the FBI in court and, in a sealed court record, reached an agreement with the FBI.

The FBI tried to allay fears of Carnivore by hiring an independent group of testers to verify the operation of Carnivore, but without access to its source code. The testers concluded that Carnivore appeared to provide only the header data as required. Their report also indicated that Carnivore was vulnerable to the threat of FBI agents intercepting data not covered by a court order because of its lack of audit records.

On 28 May 2002 the FBI acknowledged that its controversial system hampered an investigation into al Qaeda. Before 11 September 2001 an FBI technical agent, reviewing the data obtained by Carnivore, was concerned that it had taken e-mail messages from people not suspected of terrorism. The agent was so concerned by the excess that he deleted all the e-mail, even that properly a part of the investigation.

and that they should not be forced to relinquish it lightly. But offer a consumer a small discount for using a frequent-buyer card (enabling the shopkeeper to track the buying habits of each customer), and the lines extend out the shop's door. So, we voluntarily give away or sell our privacy at many times in many ways.

Think about the annoying telephone calls from telemarketers who interrupt your dinner, trying to interest you in vacation trips or cable TV or another credit card. Could it relate to your use of your frequent-buyer card at the grocery where you buy expensive prepared entrees, higher-priced wines, or large quantities of some items? Buying diapers could put you on a target list for private schools, while buying beer and pizza might attract calls for making money in your spare time.

By accepting and using a frequent-buyer card or having answered a survey on your hobbies or buying habits, you may have sold your privacy rights, and at a small price. But after having sold those rights, you have no control over how they will be used. Even if the store says it intends to use your data only for internal inventory purposes, that intention can change tomorrow without your permission. Or if the store's ownership changes, the rules about your privacy may change, too.

Sometimes selling our privacy is not so obvious. We may, knowingly or not, relinquish our privacy rights in order to obtain something. If you want to join a swim club or purchase an annual pass to an amusement park, you may have to have your photograph taken (and perhaps stored) to generate an access badge. To open a bank or credit account with telephone access you may be asked to provide an ostensibly secret identifier, such as your mother's maiden name. Here the choice of privacy is yours: you can either keep your privacy or join. Usually it is apparent what use is intended to be made of your secret details (for example, serving only as an authenticator). But you have no real control over what is actually done with your private data; for instance, a disreputable clerk could retain your mother's maiden name and impersonate you. (For another means of collecting private data, see Sidebar 9-5.)

Controls Protecting Privacy

Two facts emerge from this exploration of privacy: First, the volume of data collected or that could be collected on individuals is enormous. Collecting that data is perfectly acceptable as long as it is not being used for an illegal purpose, such as prohibited discrimination or harassment. Second, the potential to correlate and mine these data files is also enormous, limited only by the capacities of computers.

And how is personal privacy secured? Sadly, in the United States, not well. Businesses recognize a need to protect the privacy data of their customers. But finding widely acceptable authenticators is difficult. And as we have seen in Chapter 7, the social engineering attack often succeeds against computer network administrators, so why should it not also succeed against bank tellers, customer service agents, or file clerks?

Authentication

Just as with other computer applications, authentication is necessary for establishing the identity of a remote user. But how can two people who have never previously communicated and have few shared secrets authenticate?

Sidebar 9-5 Microsoft Passport

Microsoft has introduced technology it calls Passport. Ostensibly, Passport will collect a user's credentials, making access and commerce on the Internet more user friendly. A user authenticates to Passport, which then shares that authentication with member sites the user visits. Thus, a user does not need to remember different login names and authenticators (passwords) for different sites.

A second convenience, called a Passport Wallet, enables the user to register credit cards, expiration dates, billing addresses, and so forth with Passport, so that the user simply indicates which card to charge, instead of filling out several screens to place an online order.

These two services appeal to many consumers. However, some users are concerned about their privacy. Passport is not implemented as a file stored on the user's computer, like a cookie. Instead, use of Passport involves a data transfer through Microsoft.com. This design gives Microsoft access to a user's browsing and buying habits. Many consumers are wary of providing such information to a commercial third party. Might Microsoft sell to bookseller A the fact that you have recently bought books from booksellers B and C, for a specific amount or of a specific type? Moreover, even if Microsoft promises to limit distribution of this information, it has no control over the companies to which it provides the data.

A second privacy concern involves Microsoft's less-than-perfect record on developing code free from security vulnerabilities. Users worry that a major security vulnerability could expose some or all the private data stored in a Passport, especially in the Wallet.

Understandably, consumers are slow to embrace Passport technology. The single sign-in capability Passport offers is convenient, but is it worth the security risk?

The most commonly used authenticators are name, address, mother's maiden name, birth date, social security or other government identity number, account number (for a business), and preestablished PIN. Name and address are widely available, birth date can often be found from a search of the motor vehicles office (or its web site), mother's maiden name can be found from birth registry records (or its web site), and the social security or government identity number is widely used by employers and banks. Private investigators can obtain these supposedly secret data items quite easily.

The designers of authentication procedures are not creative. Wouldn't it be better to ask "I see from your account that you recently purchased airline tickets. For what airline?" or "What brand of gasoline station do you often use?"

Users are also to blame. Faced with too many PINs, people do the only things sensible: they use the same PIN for access to many places, or they write the PINs down.

As you have already learned, there are some very sound authentication techniques, including challenge–response systems, tokens, biometrics, and one-time passwords. But these approaches seem to be too sophisticated to be widely adopted, and so remote human-to-human and human-to-computer interaction is likely to remain highly subject to spoofing and impersonation.

Anonymity

To protect their privacy, some people use anonymity. For example, whereas a credit card purchase leaves a transaction trail, a cash purchase leaves little record to follow. (Few illegal drug dealers accept credit cards, so a cash transaction protects both the dealer and the buyer.)

Anonymizers are e-mail forwarding services, often located in foreign countries, that remove identifying source information from an e-mail message before forwarding it to its destination. Onion routing, as described in Chapter 7, carries this process further with a series of anonymizers, none of which knows whether this is the first, last, or some other hop. Of course, with anonymizers, one must trust the anonymizers not to retain records.

Chaum [CHA81, CHA82, CHA85] investigated protocols by which anonymous computer transactions could be completed. And several companies, including anonymizer.com, zeroknowledge.com, and siegesoft.com, offer anonymous web access. They intercede in the traffic from a browser to a web site so that the web server cannot determine from what address an access originates. A user can reveal his or her identity, for example, when placing an online order, but to ordinary web sites the user is anonymous.

Computer Voting

Voting is a process in which citizens want anonymity. Although it is easy to achieve with paper ballots (ignoring the possibility of fingerprint tracing or secretly marked ballots), and fairly easy to achieve with machines (assuming usage protocols preclude associating the order in which people voted with a voting log from the machine), it is more difficult with computers. Properties essential to a fair election were enumerated by Shamos [SHA93].

- Each voter's choices must be kept secret.
- Each voter may vote only once and only for allowed offices.
- The voting system must be tamperproof, and the election officials must be prevented from allowing it to be tampered with.
- All votes must be reported accurately.
- The voting system must be available for use throughout the election period.
- An audit trail must be kept to detect irregularities in voting, but without disclosing how any individual voted.

These conditions are challenging in ordinary paper- and machine-based elections; they are even harder to meet in computer-based elections. Privacy of a vote is essential; in some repressive countries, voting for the wrong candidate can be fatal. But public confidence in the validity of the outcome is critical, so there is a similarly strong need to be able to validate the accuracy of the collection and reporting of votes. These two requirements are close to contradictory.

DeMillo and Merritt [DEM83] devised protocols for computerized voting. Hoffman [HOF00] studied the use of computers at polling places to implement casting of votes. Rubin [RUB00] concludes "Given the current state of insecurity of hosts and the vulnerability of the Internet to manipulation and denial-of-service attacks, there is no way that a public election of any significance involving remote electronic voting could be carried out securely." But Tony Blair, British prime minister, announced in July 2002 that in the British 2006 general election, citizens would vote in any of four ways: online (by Internet) from a work or home location, by mail, by touch-tone telephone, or at polling places using online terminals. All the counts of the elections would be done electronically. In 2002 Brazil used a computer network to automate voting in its national election (in which voting was mandatory).

Pseudonymity

Sometimes, full anonymity is not wanted. A person may want to order flower seeds but not be placed on a dozen mailing lists for gardening supplies. But the person does want to be able to place similar orders again, asking for "the same color tulips I bought last time." This situation calls for pseudonyms, unique identifiers that can be used to link records in a server's database but that cannot be used to trace back to a real identity.

The Swiss bank account was a classic example of a pseudonym. Each customer had only a number to access the account. Presumably anyone with that number could perform any transaction on the account. (Obviously there were additional protections against guessing.) While they were in use (their use was discontinued in the early 1990s because of their having been used to hold ill-gotten Nazi gains from World War II), Swiss bank accounts had an outstanding reputation for maintaining the anonymity of the depositor.

Some people register pseudonyms with e-mail providers so that they have anonymous drop boxes for e-mail. Others use pseudonyms in chat rooms or with online dating services.

Legal Controls

Laws are emerging to require reasonable protection of private data. Although of obvious benefit to consumers, these laws are opposed by marketers who want to do data mining with complex collections of data.

The strongest protection of individuals' privacy is undoubtedly the European Union (E.U.) Data Protection Act. For its part, the United States has two major privacy laws, Gramm–Leach–Bliley and HIPAA. We examine each one in turn.

E.U. Data Protection Act

The Data Protection Act of 1998 places requirements on entities—organizations, companies, governments—that collect and save data on individuals. When implemented in legislation in the 15 E.U. member nations, this act requires organizations or companies that maintain records on individuals to do the following:

- Inform individuals of the data collected and the purpose for which it is being held.
- Use the data for that purpose only.
- Give individuals a right to see data about themselves and to correct errors.
- Apply appropriate measures to ensure the privacy of those data.

The requirement to ensure the privacy of the data includes not sharing the data with entities in other countries that do not have data protection laws at least as strong as the E.U. act. Because the United States has few data protection laws, and none as strong as the E.U. requirements, this restriction puts in jeopardy the ability of multinational corporations to share even customer address lists or employees' records with their U.S. branches. Although negotiations continue on this matter and it is unlikely that a large company in Europe would be precluded from exchanging data with its U.S. counterpart, this point of contention will remain between the United States and Europe.

Gramm–Leach–Bliley

The U.S. Gramm–Leach–Bliley Act (Public Law 106-102) of 1999 covers privacy of data for customers of financial institutions. Each institution must have a privacy policy of which it informs its customers, and customers must be given the opportunity to reject any use of the data beyond the necessary business uses for which the private data were collected. The act and its implementation regulations also require financial institutions to undergo a detailed security risk assessment. Based on the results of that assessment, the institution must adopt a comprehensive "information security program" designed to protect against unauthorized access to or use of customers' nonpublic personal information.

HIPAA

In 1996, Public Law 104-191, the Health Insurance Portability and Accountability Act (HIPAA) was passed in the United States. Although the first part of the law concerned the rights of workers to maintain health insurance coverage after their employment was terminated, the second part of the law required protection of the privacy of individuals' medical records. HIPAA, and its associated implementation standards, mandate protection of "individually identifiable healthcare information," that is, medical data that can be associated with an identifiable individual. Health care providers must perform standard security practices to protect the privacy of individuals' health care data, such as the following:

- Enforce need to know.
- Ensure minimum necessary disclosure.
- Designate a privacy officer.
- Document information security practices.
- Track disclosures of information.
- Develop a method for patients' inspection and copying of their information.
- Train staff at least every three years.

Perhaps most far-reaching is the requirement for health care organizations to develop "business associate contracts," which are coordinated agreements on how data shared between entities will be protected. This requirement could affect the sharing and transmittal of patient information among doctors, clinics, laboratories, hospitals, insurers, and any other organizations that handle such data.

9.7 ETHICAL ISSUES IN COMPUTER SECURITY

This final section helps clarify thinking about the ethical issues involved in computer security. We offer no answers. Rather, after listing and explaining some ethical principles, we present several case studies to which the principles can be applied. Each case is followed by a list of possible ethical issues involved, although the list is not necessarily all-inclusive or conclusive. The primary purpose of this section is to explore some of the ethical issues associated with computer security and to show how ethics functions as a control.

Differences Between the Law and Ethics

As we noted earlier, law is not always the appropriate way to deal with issues of human behavior. It is difficult to define a law to preclude only the events we want it to. For example, a law that restricts animals from public places must be refined to *permit* guide dogs for the blind. Lawmakers, who are not computer professionals, are hard pressed to think of all the exceptions when they draft a law. Even when a law is well conceived and well written, its enforcement may be difficult. The courts are overburdened, and prosecuting relatively minor infractions may be excessively time consuming relative to the benefit.

Thus, it is impossible or impractical to develop laws to describe and enforce all forms of behavior acceptable to society. Instead, society relies on **ethics** or **morals** to prescribe generally accepted standards of proper behavior. (In this section the terms ethics and morals are used interchangeably.) An **ethic** is an objectively defined standard of right and wrong. Ethical standards are often idealistic principles because they focus on one objective. In a given situation, however, several moral objectives may be involved, so people have to determine an action that is appropriate, considering all the objectives. Even though religious groups and professional organizations promote certain standards of ethical behavior, ultimately each person is responsible for deciding what to do in a specific situation. Therefore, through our choices, each of us defines a personal set of ethical practices. A set of ethical principles is called an **ethical system**.

An ethic is different from a law in several important ways. First, laws apply to everyone: One may disagree with the intent or the meaning of a law, but that is not an excuse for disobeying the law. Second, the courts have a regular process for determining which law supersedes which if two laws conflict. Third, the laws and the courts identify certain actions as right and others as wrong. From a legal standpoint, anything that is not illegal is right. Finally, laws can be enforced to rectify wrongs done by unlawful behavior.

By contrast, ethics are personal: two people may have different frameworks for making moral judgments. What one person thinks is perfectly justifiable, another would never consider doing. Second, ethical positions can and often do come into conflict. As an example, the value of a human life is very important in most ethical systems. Most people would not cause the sacrifice of one life, but in the right context some would approve of sacrificing one person to save another, or one to save many others. The value of one life cannot be readily measured against the value of others, and many ethical decisions must be founded on precisely this ambiguity. Yet, there is

TABLE 9-3 Contrast of Law vs. Ethics.

Law	Ethics
Described by formal, written documents	Described by unwritten principles
Interpreted by courts	Interpreted by each individual
Established by legislatures representing all people	Presented by philosophers, religions, professional groups
Applicable to everyone	Personal choice
Priority determined by courts if two laws conflict	Priority determined by an individual if two principles conflict
Court is final arbiter of "right"	No external arbiter
Enforceable by police and courts	Limited enforcement

no arbiter of ethical positions: when two ethical goals collide, each person must choose which goal is dominant. Third, two people may assess ethical values differently; no universal standard of right and wrong exists in ethical judgments. Nor can one person simply look to what another has done as guidance for choosing the right thing to do. Finally, there is no enforcement for ethical choices. These differences are summarized in Table 9-3.

Studying Ethics

The study of ethics is not easy because the issues are complex. Sometimes people confuse ethics with religion because many religions supply a framework in which to make ethical choices. However, ethics can be studied apart from any religious connection. Difficult choices would be easier to make if there were a set of universal ethical principles to which everyone agreed. But the variety of social, cultural, and religious beliefs makes the identification of such a set of universal principles impossible. In this section we explore some of these problems and then consider how understanding ethics can help in dealing with issues of computer security.

Ethics and Religion

Ethics is a set of principles or norms for justifying what is right or wrong in a given situation. To understand what ethics *is* we may start by trying to understand what it is *not*. Ethical principles are different from religious beliefs. Religion is based on personal notions about the creation of the world and the existence of controlling forces or beings. Many moral principles are embodied in the major religions, and the basis of a personal morality is a matter of belief and conviction, much the same as for religions. However, two people with different religious backgrounds may develop the same ethical philosophy, while two exponents of the same religion might reach opposite ethical conclusions in a particular situation. Finally, we can analyze a situation from an ethical perspective and reach ethical conclusions without appealing to any particular religion or religious framework. Thus, it is important to distinguish ethics from religion.

Ethical Principles Are Not Universal

Ethical values vary by society, and from person to person within a society. For example, the concept of privacy is important in Western cultures. But in Eastern cultures, privacy is not desirable because people associate privacy with having something to hide. Not only is a Westerner's desire for privacy not understood, but in fact it has a negative connotation. Therefore, the attitudes of people may be affected by culture or background.

Also, an individual's standards of behavior may be influenced by past events in life. A person who grew up in a large family may place greater emphasis on personal control and ownership of possessions than would an only child who seldom had to share. Major events or close contact with others can also shape one's ethical position. Despite these differences, the underlying principles of how to make moral judgment are the same.

Although these aspects of ethics are quite reasonable and understandable, they lead people to distrust ethics because it is not founded on basic principles all can accept. Also, people from a scientific or technical background expect precision and universality.

Ethics Does Not Provide Answers

Ethical pluralism is recognizing or admitting that more than one position may be ethically justifiable—even equally so—in a given situation. Pluralism is another way of noting that two people may legitimately disagree on issues of ethics. We expect and accept disagreement in such areas as politics and religion.

However, in the scientific and technical fields, people expect to find unique, unambiguous, and unequivocal answers. In science one answer must be correct or demonstrable in some sense. Science has provided life with fundamental explanations. Ethics is rejected or misunderstood by some scientists because it is "soft," meaning that it has no underlying framework or it does not depend on fundamental truths.

One need only study the history of scientific discovery to see that science itself is founded largely on temporary truths. For many years the earth was believed to be the center of the solar system. Ptolemy developed a complicated framework of epicycles, orbits within orbits of the planets, to explain the inconsistency of observed periods of rotation. Eventually his theory was superseded by the Copernican model of planets that orbit the sun. Similarly, Einstein's relativity theory opposed the traditional quantum basis of physics. Science is littered with theories that have fallen from favor as we learned or observed more and as new explanations were proposed. As each new theory is proposed, some people readily accept the new proposal, while others cling to the old.

But the basis of science is presumed to be "truth." A statement is expected to be provably true, provably false, or unproven, but a statement can never be both true and false. Scientists are uncomfortable with ethics because ethics does not provide these clean distinctions.

Worse, there is no higher authority of ethical truth. Two people may disagree on their opinion of the ethics of a situation, but there is no one to whom to appeal for a final determination of who is "right." Conflicting answers do not deter one from considering ethical issues in computer security. Nor do they excuse us from making and defending ethical choices.

Ethical Reasoning

Most people make ethical judgments often, perhaps daily. (Is it better to buy from a home-town merchant or from a nationwide chain? Should I spend time with a volunteer organization or with my friends? Is it acceptable to release sensitive data to someone who might not have justification for access to that data?) Because we all engage in ethical choice, we should clarify how we do this so that we can learn to apply the principles of ethics in professional situations, as we do in private life.

Study of ethics can yield two positive results. First, in situations where we already know what is right and what is wrong, ethics should help us justify our choice. Second, if we do not know the ethical action to take in a situation, ethics can help us identify the issues involved so that we can make reasoned judgments.

Examining a Case for Ethical Issues

How, then, can issues of ethical choice in computer security be approached? Here are several steps to making and justifying an ethical choice.

1. *Understand the situation.* Learn the facts of the situation. Ask questions of interpretation or clarification. Attempt to find out whether any relevant forces have not been considered.
2. *Know several theories of ethical reasoning.* To make an ethical choice, you have to know how those choices can be justified.
3. *List the ethical principles involved.* What different philosophies could be applied in this case? Do any of these include others?
4. *Determine which principles outweigh others.* This is a subjective evaluation. It often involves extending a principle to a logical conclusion or determining cases in which one principle clearly supersedes another.

The most important steps are the first and third. Too often people judge a situation on incomplete information, a practice that leads to judgments based on prejudice, suspicion, or misinformation. Considering all the different ethical issues raised forms the basis for evaluating the competing interests of step four.

Examples of Ethical Principles

There are two different schools of ethical reasoning: one based on the good that results from actions and one based on certain prima facie duties of people.

Consequence-Based Principles

The **teleological** theory of ethics focuses on the consequences of an action. The action to be chosen is that which results in the greatest future good and the least harm. For example, if a fellow student asks you to write a program he was assigned for a class, you might consider the good (he will owe you a favor) against the bad (you might get caught, causing embarrassment and possible disciplinary action, plus your friend will not learn the techniques to be gained from writing the program, leaving him deficient). The negative consequences clearly outweigh the positive, so you would refuse. *Teleol-*

ogy is the general name applied to many theories of behavior, all of which focus on the goal, outcome, or consequence of the action.

There are two important forms of teleology. **Egoism** is the form that says a moral judgment is based on the positive benefits to the person taking the action. An egoist weighs the outcomes of all possible acts and chooses the one that produces the most personal good for him or her with the least negative consequence. The effects on other people are not relevant. For example, an egoist trying to justify the ethics of writing shoddy computer code when pressed for time might argue as follows. "If I complete the project quickly, I will satisfy my manager, which will bring me a raise and other good things. The customer is unlikely to know enough about the program to complain, so I am not likely to be blamed. My company's reputation may be tarnished, but that will not be tracked directly to me. Thus, I can justify writing shoddy code."

The principle of **utilitarianism** is also an assessment of good and bad results, but the reference group is the entire universe. The utilitarian chooses that action that will bring the greatest collective good for all people with the least possible negative for all. In this situation, the utilitarian would assess personal good and bad, good and bad for the company, good and bad for the customer, and, perhaps, good and bad for society at large. For example, a developer designing software to monitor smokestack emissions would need to assess its effects on everyone breathing. The utilitarian might perceive greater good to everyone by taking the time to write high-quality code, despite the negative personal consequence of displeasing management.

Rule-Based Principles

Another ethical theory is **deontology**, which is founded in a sense of duty. This ethical principle states that certain things are good in and of themselves. These things that are naturally good are good rules or acts, which require no higher justification. Something just *is* good; it does not have to be judged for its effect.

Examples (from Frankena [FRA73]) of intrinsically good things are

- truth, knowledge, and true opinion of various kinds; understanding, wisdom
- just distribution of good and evil; justice
- pleasure, satisfaction; happiness; life, consciousness
- peace, security, freedom
- good reputation, honor, esteem; mutual affection, love, friendship, cooperation; morally good dispositions or virtues
- beauty, aesthetic experience

Rule-deontology is the school of ethical reasoning that believes certain universal, self-evident, natural rules specify our proper conduct. Certain basic moral principles are adhered to because of our responsibilities to one another; these principles are often stated as rights: the right to know, the right to privacy, the right to fair compensation for work. Sir David Ross [ROS30] lists various duties incumbent on all human beings:

- *fidelity,* or truthfulness
- *reparation,* the duty to recompense for a previous wrongful act

TABLE 9-4 Taxonomy of Ethical Theories.

	Consequence-based	Rule-based
Individual	Based on consequences to individual	Based on rules acquired by the individual—from religion, experience, analysis
Universal	Based on consequences to all of society	Based on universal rules, evident to everyone

- *gratitude,* thankfulness for previous services or kind acts
- *justice,* distribution of happiness in accordance with merit
- *beneficence,* the obligation to help other people or to make their lives better
- *nonmaleficence,* not harming others
- *self-improvement,* to become continually better, both in a mental sense and in a moral sense (for example, by not committing a wrong a second time)

Another school of reasoning is based on rules derived by each individual. Religion, teaching, experience, and reflection lead each person to a set of personal moral principles. The answer to an ethical question is found by weighing values in terms of what a person believes to be right behavior.

Summary of Ethical Theories

We have seen two bases of ethical theories, each applied in two ways. Simply stated, the two bases are consequence-based and rule-based, and the applications are either individual or universal. These theories are depicted in Table 9-4.

In the next section, we apply these theories to analyze certain situations that arise in the ethics of computer security.

9.8 CASE STUDIES OF ETHICS

To understand how ethics affect professional actions, ethicists often study example situations. The remainder of this section consists of several representative examples. These cases are modeled after ones developed by Parker [PAR79] as part of the AFIPS/NSF study of ethics in computing and technology. Each case study is designed to bring out certain ethical points, some of which are listed following the case. You should reflect on each case, determining for yourself what the most influential points are. These cases are suitable for use in a class discussion, during which other values will certainly be mentioned. Finally, each case reaches no conclusion because each individual must assess the ethical situation alone. In a class discussion it may be appropriate to take a vote. Remember, however, that ethics are not determined by majority rule. Those siding with the majority are not "right," and the rest are not "wrong."

Case I: Use of Computer Services

This case concerns deciding what is appropriate use of computer time. Use of computer time is a question both of access by one person and of availability of quality of service to others. The person involved is permitted to access computing facilities for a certain purpose. Many companies rely on an unwritten standard of behavior that governs the actions of people who have legitimate access to a computing system. The ethical issues involved in this case can lead to an understanding of that unwritten standard.

The Case

Dave works as a programmer for a large software company. He writes and tests utility programs such as compilers. His company operates two computing shifts: during the day program development and online applications are run; at night batch production jobs are completed. Dave has access to workload data and learns that the evening batch runs are complementary to daytime programming tasks; that is, adding programming work during the night shift would not adversely affect performance of the computer to other users.

Dave comes back after normal hours to develop a program to manage his own stock portfolio. His drain on the system is minimal, and he uses very few expendable supplies, such as printer paper. Is Dave's behavior ethical?

Values Issues

Some of the ethical principles involved in this case are listed below.

- *Ownership of resources.* The company owns the computing resources and provides them for its own computing needs.
- *Effect on others.* Although unlikely, a flaw in Dave's program could adversely affect other users, perhaps even denying them service because of a system failure.
- *Universalism principle.* If Dave's action is acceptable, it should also be acceptable for others to do the same. However, too many employees working in the evening could reduce system effectiveness.
- *Possibility of detection, punishment.* Dave does not know whether his action would be wrong or right if discovered by his company. If his company decided it was improper use, Dave could be punished.

What other issues are involved? Which principles are more important than others?

Analysis

The utilitarian would consider the total excess of good over bad for all people. Dave receives benefit from use of computer time, although for this application the amount of time is not large. Dave has a possibility of punishment, but he may rate that as unlikely. The company is neither harmed nor helped by this. Thus, the utilitarian could argue that Dave's use is justifiable.

The universalism principle seems as if it would cause a problem because clearly if everyone did this, quality of service would degrade. A utilitarian would say that each new user has to weigh good and bad separately. Dave's use might not burden the machine, and neither might Ann's; but when Bill wants to use the machine, it is heavily enough used that Bill's use *would* affect other people.

Alternative Situations

Would it affect the ethics of the situation if any of the following actions or characteristics were considered?

- Dave began a business managing stock portfolios for many people for profit.
- Dave's salary was below average for his background, implying that Dave was due the computer use as a fringe benefit.
- Dave's employer knew of other employees doing similar things and tacitly approved by not seeking to stop them.
- Dave worked for a government office instead of a private company and reasoned that the computer belonged "to the people."

Case II: Privacy Rights

In this case the central issue is the individual's right to privacy. Privacy is both a legal and an ethical issue because of the pertinent laws discussed in the previous section.

The Case

Donald works for the county records department as a computer records clerk, where he has access to files of property tax records. For a scientific study, a researcher, Ethel, has been granted access to the numerical portion—but not the corresponding names—of some records.

Ethel finds some information that she would like to use, but she needs the names and addresses corresponding with certain properties. Ethel asks Donald to retrieve the names and addresses so she can contact these people for more information and for permission to do further study.

Should Donald release the names and addresses?

Some Principles Involved

Here are some of the ethical principles involved in this case. What are other ethical principles? Which principles are subordinate to which others?

- *Job responsibility.* Donald's job is to manage individual records, not to make determinations of appropriate use. Policy decisions should be made by someone of higher authority.
- *Use.* The records are used for legitimate scientific study, not for profit or to expose sensitive data. (However, Ethel's access is authorized only for the numerical data, not for the private information relating property conditions to individuals.)

- *Possible misuse.* Although he believes Ethel's motives are proper, Donald cannot guarantee that Ethel will use the data only to follow up on interesting data items.
- *Confidentiality.* Had Ethel been intended to have names and addresses, they would have been given initially.
- *Tacit permission.* Ethel has been granted permission to access parts of these records for research purposes, so she should have access to complete her research.
- *Propriety.* Because Ethel has no authority to obtain names and addresses and because the names and addresses represent the confidential part of the data, Donald should deny Ethel's request for access.

Analysis

A rule-deontologist would argue that privacy is an inherent good and that one should not violate the privacy of another. Therefore, Donald should not release the names.

Extensions to the Basic Case

We can consider several possible extensions to the scenario. These extensions probe other ethical issues involved in this case.

- Suppose Donald were responsible for determining allowable access to the files. What ethical issues would be involved in his deciding whether to grant access to Ethel?
- Should Ethel be allowed to contact the individuals involved? That is, should the health department release individuals' names to a researcher? What are the ethical issues for the health department to consider?
- Suppose Ethel contacts the individuals to ask their permission, and one-third of them respond giving permission, one-third respond denying permission, and one-third do not respond. Ethel claims that at least one-half of the individuals are needed to make a valid study. What options are available to Ethel? What are the ethical issues involved in deciding which of these options to pursue?

To show that ethics can be context dependent, let us consider some variations of the situation. Notice that these changes affect the domain of the problem, but not the basic question: access to personal data.

If the domain were medical records, the case would be covered by HIPAA, and so we would first consider a legal issue, not an ethical one. Notice, however, how the case changes subtly depending on the medical condition involved. You may reach one conclusion if the records deal with "ordinary" conditions (colds, broken legs, muscle injuries), but a different conclusion if the cases are for sexually transmitted diseases or AIDS. You may also reach a different conclusion if the research involves genetic conditions of which the subject may be unaware (for example, being a carrier for Huntington's disease or hemophilia).

But change the context once more, and consider web surfing habits. If Donald works for an Internet service provider and could determine all the web sites a person had visited, would that be fair to disclose?

Case III: Denial of Service

This case addresses issues related to the effect of one person's computation on other users. This situation involves people with legitimate access, so standard access controls should not exclude them. However, because of the actions of some, other people are denied legitimate access to the system. Thus, the focus of this case is on the rights of all users.

The Case

Charlie and Carol are students at a university in a computer science program. Each writes a program for a class assignment. Charlie's program happens to uncover a flaw in a compiler that ultimately causes the entire computing system to fail; all users lose the results of their current computation. Charlie's program uses acceptable features of the language; the compiler is at fault. Charlie did not suspect his program would cause a system failure. He reports the program to the computing center and tries to find ways to achieve his intended result without exercising the system flaw.

The system continues to fail periodically, for a total of ten times (beyond the first failure). When the system fails, sometimes Charlie is running a program, but sometimes Charlie is not. The director contacts Charlie, who shows all of his program versions to the computing center staff. The staff concludes that Charlie may have been inadvertently responsible for some, but not all, of the system failures, but that his latest approach to solving the assigned problem is unlikely to lead to additional system failures.

On further analysis, the computing center director notes that Carol has had programs running each of the first eight (of ten) times the system failed. The director uses administrative privilege to inspect Carol's files and finds a file that exploits the same vulnerability as did Charlie's program. The director immediately suspends Carol's account, denying Carol access to the computing system. Because of this, Carol is unable to complete her assignment on time, she receives a D in the course, and she drops out of school.

Analysis

In this case the choices are intentionally not obvious. The situation is presented as a completed scenario, but in studying it you are being asked to suggest alternative actions the players *could have taken.* In this way, you build a repertoire of actions that you can consider in similar situations that might arise.

- What additional information is needed?
- Who has rights in this case? What rights are those? Who has a responsibility to protect those rights? (This step in ethical study is used to clarify who should be considered as the reference group for a deontological analysis.)
- Has Charlie acted responsibly? By what evidence do you conclude so? Has Carol? How? Has the computing center director acted responsibly? How? (In this step you look for past judgments that should be confirmed or wrongs that should be redressed.)

- What are some alternative actions Charlie or Carol or the director could have taken that would have been more responsible?

Case IV: Ownership of Programs

In this case we consider who owns programs: the programmer, the employer, the manager, or all. From a legal standpoint, most rights belong to the employer, as presented earlier in this chapter. However, this case expands on that position by presenting several competing arguments that might be used to support positions in this case. As described in the previous section, legal controls for secrecy of programs can be complicated, time consuming, and expensive to apply. In this case we search for individual ethical controls that can prevent the need to appeal to the legal system.

The Case

Greg is a programmer working for a large aerospace firm, Star Computers, which works on many government contracts; Cathy is Greg's supervisor. Greg is assigned to program various kinds of simulations.

To improve his programming abilities, Greg writes some programming tools, such as a cross-reference facility and a program that automatically extracts documentation from source code. These are not assigned tasks for Greg; he writes them independently and uses them at work, but he does not tell anyone about them. Greg has written them in the evenings, at home, on his personal computer.

Greg decides to market these programming aids by himself. When Star's management hears of this, Cathy is instructed to tell Greg that he has no right to market these products since, when he was employed, he signed a form stating that all inventions become the property of the company. Cathy does not agree with this position because she knows that Greg has done this work on his own. She reluctantly tells Greg that he cannot market these products. She also asks Greg for a copy of the products.

Cathy quits working for Star and takes a supervisory position with Purple Computers, a competitor of Star. She takes with her a copy of Greg's products and distributes it to the people who work with her. These products are so successful that they substantially improve the effectiveness of her employees, and Cathy is praised by her management and receives a healthy bonus. Greg hears of this, and contacts Cathy, who contends that because the product was determined to belong to Star and because Star worked largely on government funding, the products were really in the public domain and therefore they belonged to no one in particular.

Analysis

This case certainly has major legal implications. Probably everyone could sue everyone else and, depending on the amount they are willing to spend on legal expenses, they could keep the cases in the courts for several years. Probably no judgment would satisfy all.

Let us set aside the legal aspects and look at the ethical issues. We want to determine who might have done what, and what changes might have been possible to prevent a tangle for the courts to unscramble.

First, let us explore the principles involved.

- *Rights.* What are the respective rights of Greg, Cathy, Star, and Purple?
- *Basis.* What gives Greg, Cathy, Star, and Purple those rights? What principles of fair play, business, property rights, and so forth are involved in this case?
- *Priority.* Which of these principles are inferior to which others? Which ones take precedence? (Note that it may be impossible to compare two different rights, so the outcome of this analysis may yield some rights that are important but that cannot be ranked first, second, third.)
- *Additional information.* What additional facts do you need in order to analyze this case? What assumptions are you making in performing the analysis?

Next, we want to consider what events led to the situation described and what alternative actions could have prevented the negative outcomes.

- What could Greg have done differently before starting to develop his product? After developing the product? After Cathy explained that the product belonged to Star?
- What could Cathy have done differently when she was told to tell Greg that his products belonged to Star? What could Cathy have done differently to avert this decision by her management? What could Cathy have done differently to prevent the clash with Greg after she went to work at Purple?
- What could Purple have done differently upon learning that it had products from Star (or from Greg)?
- What could Greg and Cathy have done differently after Greg spoke to Cathy at Purple?
- What could Star have done differently to prevent Greg from feeling that he owned his products? What could Star have done differently to prevent Cathy from taking the products to Purple?

Case V: Proprietary Resources

In this case, we consider the issue of access to proprietary or restricted resources. Like the previous one, this case involves access to software. The focus of this case is the rights of a software developer in contrast with the rights of users, so this case concerns determining legitimate access rights.

The Case

Suzie owns a copy of G-Whiz, a proprietary software package she purchased legitimately. The software is copyrighted, and the documentation contains a license agreement that says that the software is for use by the purchaser only. Suzie invites Luis to look at the software to see if it will fit his needs. Luis goes to Suzie's computer and she demonstrates the software to him. He says he likes what he sees, but he would like to try it in a longer test.

Extensions to the Case

So far the actions have all been ethically sound. The next steps are where ethical responsibilities arise. Take each of the following steps as independent; that is, do not assume that any of the other steps has occurred in your analysis of one step.

- Suzie offers to copy the disk for Luis to use.
- Suzie copies the disk for Luis to use, and Luis uses it for some period of time.
- Suzie copies the disk for Luis to use; Luis uses it for some period of time and then buys a copy for himself.
- Suzie copies the disk for Luis to try out overnight, under the restriction that he must bring the disk back to her tomorrow and must not copy it for himself. Luis does so.
- Suzie copies the disk with the same restrictions, but Luis makes a copy for himself before returning it to Suzie.
- Suzie copies the disk with the same restrictions, and Luis makes a copy for himself, but he then purchases a copy.
- Suzie copies the disk with the same restrictions, but Luis does not return it.

For each of these extensions, describe who is affected, which ethical issues are involved, and which principles override which others.

Case VI: Fraud

In previous cases, we have dealt with people acting in situations that were legal or, at worst, debatable. In this case, we consider outright fraud, which is illegal. However, the case really concerns the actions of people who are asked to do fraudulent things.

The Case

Patty works as a programmer in a corporation. David, her supervisor, tells her to write a program to allow people to post entries directly to the company's accounting files ("the books"). Patty knows that ordinarily programs that affect the books involve several steps, all of which have to balance. Patty realizes that with the new program, it will be possible for one person to make changes to crucial amounts, and there will be no way to trace who made these changes, with what justification, or when.

Patty raises these concerns to David, who tells her not to be concerned, that her job is simply to write the programs as he specifies. He says that he is aware of the potential misuse of these programs, but he justifies his request by noting that periodically a figure is mistakenly entered in the books and the company needs a way to correct the inaccurate figure.

Extensions

First, let us explore the options Patty has. If Patty writes this program, she might be an accomplice to fraud. If she complains to David's superior, David or the superior might reprimand or fire her as a troublemaker. If she refuses to write the program, David can clearly fire her for failing to carry out an assigned task. We do not even know that the program is desired for fraudulent purposes; David suggests an explanation that is not fraudulent.

She might write the program but insert extra code that creates a secret log of when the program was run, by whom, and what changes were made. This extra file could provide evidence of fraud, or it might cause trouble for Patty if there is no fraud but David discovers the secret log.

At this point, here are some of the ethical issues involved.

- Is a programmer responsible for the programs he or she writes? Is a programmer responsible for the results of those programs? (In contemplating this question, suppose the program were to adjust dosage in a computer-controlled medical application, and David's request were for a way to override the program controls to cause a lethal dosage. Would Patty then be responsible for the results of the program?)
- Is a programmer merely an employee who follows orders (assigned tasks) unthinkingly?
- What degree of personal risk (such as possible firing) is an employee obliged to accept for opposing an action he or she thinks is improper?
- Would a program to manipulate the books as described here ever be justified? If so, in what circumstances would it be justified?
- What kinds of controls can be placed on such programs to make them acceptable? What are some ways that a manager could legitimately ask an employee to write a program like this?
- Would the ethical issues in this situation be changed if Patty designed and wrote this program herself?

Analysis

The act-deontologist would say that truth is good. Therefore, if Patty thought the purpose of the program was to deceive, writing it would not be a good act. (If the purpose were for learning or to be able to admire beautiful code, then writing it might be justifiable.)

A more useful analysis is from the perspective of the utilitarian. To Patty, writing the program brings possible harm for being an accomplice to fraud, with the gain of having cooperated with her manager. She has a possible item with which to blackmail David, but David might also turn on her and say the program was her idea. On balance, this option seems to have a strong negative slant.

By not writing the program her possible harm is being fired. However, she has a potential gain by being able to "blow the whistle" on David. This option does not seem to bring her much good, either. But fraudulent acts have negative consequences for the stockholders, the banks, and other innocent employees. Not writing the program brings only personal harm to Patty, which is similar to the harm described earlier. Thus, it seems as if not writing the program is the more positive option.

There is another possibility. The program may *not* be for fraudulent purposes. If so, then there is no ethical conflict. Therefore, Patty might try to determine whether David's motives are fraudulent.

Case VII: Accuracy of Information

For our next case, we consider responsibility for accuracy or integrity of information. Again, this is an issue addressed by database management systems and other access control mechanisms. However, as in previous cases, the issue here is access by an *authorized* user, so the controls do not prevent access.

The Case

Emma is a researcher at an institute where Paul is a statistical programmer. Emma wrote a grant request to a cereal manufacturer to show the nutritional value of a new cereal, Raw Bits. The manufacturer funded Emma's study. Emma is not a statistician. She has brought all of her data to Paul to ask him to perform appropriate analyses and to print reports for her to send to the manufacturer. Unfortunately, the data Emma has collected seem to refute the claim that Raw Bits is nutritious, and, in fact, they may indicate that Raw Bits is harmful.

Paul presents his analyses to Emma but also indicates that some other correlations could be performed that would cast Raw Bits in a more favorable light. Paul makes a facetious remark about his being able to use statistics to support either side of any issue.

Ethical Concerns

Clearly, if Paul changed data values in this study he would be acting unethically. But is it any more ethical for him to suggest analyzing correct data in a way that supports two or more different conclusions? Is Paul obligated to present both the positive and the negative analyses? Is Paul responsible for the use to which others put his program results?

If Emma does not understand statistical analysis, is she acting ethically in accepting Paul's positive conclusions? His negative conclusions? Emma suspects that if she forwards negative results to the manufacturer, they will just find another researcher to do another study. She suspects that if she forwards both sets of results to the manufacturer, they will publicize only the positive ones. What ethical principles support her sending both sets of data? What principles support her sending just the positive set? What other courses of action has she?

Case VIII: Ethics of Hacking or Cracking

What behavior is acceptable in cyberspace? Who owns or controls the Internet? Does malicious or nonmalicious intent matter? Legal issues are involved in the answers to these questions, but as we have pointed out previously, laws and the courts cannot protect everything, nor should we expect them to. In this final case study we consider ethical behavior in a shared use computing environment, such as the Internet. The questions are similar to "what behavior is acceptable in outer space?" or "who owns the oceans?"

Goli is a computer security consultant; she enjoys the challenge of finding and fixing security vulnerabilities. Independently wealthy, she does not need to work, and so she has ample spare time in which to test the security of systems.

In her spare time, Goli does three things: First, she aggressively attacks commercial products for vulnerabilities. She is quite proud of the tools and approach she has developed, and she is quite successful at finding flaws. Second, she probes accessible systems on the Internet, and when she finds vulnerable sites, she contacts the owners to offer her services repairing the problems. Finally, she is a strong believer in high-quality pastry, and she plants small programs to slow performance in the web sites of pastry shops that do not use enough butter in their pastries. Let us examine these three actions in order.

Vulnerabilities in Commercial Products

We have already described a current debate regarding the vulnerability reporting process. Now let us explore the ethical issues involved in that debate.

Clearly from a rule-based ethical theory, attackers are wrong to perform malicious attacks. The appropriate theory seems to be one of consequence: who is helped or hurt by finding and publicizing flaws in products? Relevant parties are attackers, the vulnerability finder, the vendor, and the using public. Notoriety or credit for finding the flaw is a small interest. And the interests of the vendor (financial, public relations) are less important than the interests of users to have secure products. But how are the interests of users best served?

- *Full disclosure* helps users assess the seriousness of the vulnerability and apply appropriate protection. But it also gives attackers more information with which to formulate attacks. Early full disclosure—before the vendor has countermeasures ready—may actually harm users by leaving them vulnerable to a now widely known attack.
- *Partial disclosure*—the general nature of the vulnerability but not a detailed exploitation scenario—may forestall attackers. One can argue that the vulnerability details are there to be discovered; when a vendor announces a patch for an unspecified flaw in a product, the attackers will test that product aggressively and study the patch carefully to try to determine the vulnerability. Attackers will then spread a complete description of the vulnerability to other attackers through an underground network, and attacks will start against users who may not have applied the vendor's fix.
- *No disclosure*. Perhaps users are best served by a scheme in which every so often new code is released, sometimes fixing security vulnerabilities, sometimes fixing things that are not security-related, and sometimes adding new features. But without a sense of significance or urgency, users may not install this new code.

Searching for Vulnerabilities and Customers

What are the ethical issues involved in searching for vulnerabilities? Again, the party of greatest interest is the user community and the good or harm that can come from the search.

On the positive side, searching may find vulnerabilities. Clearly, it would be wrong for Goli to report vulnerabilities that were not there, simply to get work, and it would also be wrong to report some but not all vulnerabilities, to be able to use the additional vulnerabilities as future leverage against the client.

But suppose Goli does a diligent search for vulnerabilities and reports them to the potential client. Is that not similar to a service station owner's advising you that a headlight is not operating when you take your car in for gasoline? Not quite, you might say. The headlight flaw can be seen without any possible harm to your car; probing for vulnerabilities might cause your system to fail.

The ethical question seems to be which is greater: the potential for good or the potential for harm? And if the potential for good is stronger, how much stronger does it need to be to override the risk of harm?

This case is also related to the common practice of ostensible nonmalicious probing for vulnerabilities: Hackers see if they can access your system without your permission, perhaps by guessing a password. Spafford [SPA98] points out that many crackers simply want to look around, without damaging anything. As discussed in Sidebar 9-6, Spafford compares this seemingly innocent activity with entry into your house when the door is unlocked. Even when done without malicious intent, cracking can be a serious offense; at its worst, it has caused millions of dollars in damage. Although crackers are prosecuted severely with harsh penalties, cracking continues to be an appealing crime, especially to juveniles.

Politically Inspired Attacks

Finally, consider Goli's interfering with operation of web sites whose actions she opposes. We have purposely phrased the issue in a situation that arouses perhaps only a few gourmands and pâtissiers. We can dismiss the interest of the butter fans as an insignificant minority on an insignificant issue. But you can certainly think of many

Sidebar 9-6 Is Cracking a Benign Practice?

Many people argue that cracking is an acceptable practice because lack of protection means that the owners of systems or data do not really value them. Spafford [SPA98] questions this logic by using the analogy of entering a house.

Consider the argument that an intruder who does no harm and makes no changes is simply learning about how computer systems operate. "Most of these people would never think to walk down a street, trying every door to find one unlocked, then search through the drawers or the furniture inside. Yet, these same people seem to give no second thought to making repeated attempts at guessing passwords to accounts they do not own, and once onto a system, browsing through the files on disk." How would you feel if you knew your home had been invaded, even if no harm was done?

Spafford notes that breaking into a house or a computer system constitutes trespassing. To do so in an effort to make security vulnerabilities more visible is "presumptuous and reprehensible." To enter either a home or a computer system in an unauthorized way, even with benign intent, can lead to unintended consequences. "Many systems have been damaged accidentally by ignorant (or careless) intruders."

other issues that have brought on wars. (See Denning's excellent article on cybercriminals [DEN99a] for real examples of politically motivated computer activity.)

The ethical issues abound in this scenario. Some people will see the (butter) issue as one of inherent good, but is butter use one of the fundamental good principles, such as honesty or fairness or not doing harm to others? Is there universal agreement that butter use is good? Probably there will be a division of the world into the butter advocates (x%), the unrestricted pastry advocates (y%), and those who do not take a position (z%). By how much does x have to exceed y for Goli's actions to be acceptable? What if the value of z is large? Greatest good for the greatest number requires a balance among these three percentages and some measure of benefit or harm.

Is butter use so patently good that is justifies harm to those who disagree? Who is helped and who suffers? Is the world helped if only good, but more expensive, pastries are available, so poor people can no longer afford pastry? Suppose we could determine that 99.9 percent of people in the world agreed that butter use was a good thing. Would that preponderance justify overriding the interests of the other 0.1 percent?

Codes of Ethics

Because of ethical issues such as these, various computer groups have sought to develop codes of ethics for their members. Most computer organizations, such as the Association for Computing Machinery (ACM), the Institute of Electrical and Electronics Engineers (IEEE), and the Data Processing Management Association (DPMA), are voluntary organizations. Being a member of one of these organizations does not certify a level of competence, responsibility, or experience in computing. For these reasons, codes of ethics in these organizations are primarily advisory. Nevertheless, these codes are fine starting points for analyzing ethical issues.

IEEE

The IEEE has produced a code of ethics for its members. The IEEE is an organization of engineers, not limited to computing. Thus, their code of ethics is a little broader than might be expected for computer security, but the basic principles are applicable in computing situations. The IEEE Code of Ethics is shown in Figure 9-1.

ACM

The ACM code of ethics recognizes three kinds of responsibilities of its members: general moral imperatives, professional responsibilities, and leadership responsibilities, both inside the association and in general. The code of ethics has three sections (plus a fourth commitment section), as shown in Figure 9-2.

Computer Ethics Institute

The Computer Ethics Institute is a nonprofit group that aims to encourage people to consider the ethical aspects of their computing activities. The organization has been in existence since the mid-1980s, founded as a joint activity of IBM, the Brookings Insti-

We, the members of the IEEE, in recognition of the importance of our technologies in affecting the quality of life throughout the world, and in accepting a personal obligation to our profession, its members, and the communities we serve, do hereby commit ourselves to conduct of the highest ethical and professional manner and agree

1. to accept responsibility in making engineering decisions consistent with the safety, health, and welfare of the public, and to disclose promptly factors that might endanger the public or the environment;
2. to avoid real or perceived conflicts of interest whenever possible, and to disclose them to affected parties when they do exist;
3. to be honest and realistic in stating claims or estimates based on available data;
4. to reject bribery in all of its forms;
5. to improve understanding of technology, its appropriate application, and potential consequences;
6. to maintain and improve our technical competence and to undertake technological tasks for others only if qualified by training or experience, or after full disclosure of pertinent limitations;
7. to seek, accept, and offer honest criticism of technical work, to acknowledge and correct errors, and to credit properly the contributions of others;
8. to treat fairly all persons regardless of such factors as race, religion, gender, disability, age, or national origin;
9. to avoid injuring others, their property, reputation, or employment by false or malicious action;
10. to assist colleagues and coworkers in their professional development and to support them in following this code of ethics.

FIGURE 9-1 IEEE Code of Ethics. (Reprinted courtesy of the Institute of Electrical and Electronics Engineers © 1996.)

tution, and the Washington Theological Consortium. The group has published its ethical guidance as ten commandments of computer ethics, listed in Figure 9-3.

Many organizations take ethics seriously and produce a document guiding the behavior of its members or employees. Some corporations require new employees to read its code of ethics and sign a promise to abide by it. Others, especially at universities and research centers, have special boards that must approve proposed research and ensure that projects and team members act ethically. As an individual professional, it may be useful for you to review these codes of ethics and compose a code of your own, reflecting your ideas about appropriate behavior in likely situations. A code of ethics can help you assess situations quickly and act in a consistent, comfortable, and ethical manner.

As an ACM member I will . . .

1.1 Contribute to society and human well-being
1.2 Avoid harm to others
1.3 Be honest and trustworthy
1.4 Be fair and take action not to discriminate
1.5 Honor property rights including copyrights and patents
1.6 Give proper credit for intellectual property
1.7 Respect the privacy of others
1.8 Honor confidentiality

As an ACM computing professional I will . . .

2.1 Strive to achieve the highest quality, effectiveness and dignity in both the process and products of professional work
2.2 Acquire and maintain professional competence
2.3 Know and respect existing laws pertaining to professional work
2.4 Accept and provide appropriate professional review
2.5 Give comprehensive and thorough evaluations of computer systems and their impacts, including analysis of possible risks
2.6 Honor contracts, agreements, and assigned responsibilities
2.7 Improve public understanding of computing and its consequences
2.8 Access computing and communication resources only when authorized to do so

As an ACM member and an organization leader, I will . . .

3.1 Articulate social responsibilities of members of an organizational unit and encourage full acceptance of those responsibilities
3.2 Manage personnel and resources
3.3 Acknowledge and support proper and authorized uses of an organization's computing and communication resources
3.4 Ensure that users and those who will be affected by a system have their needs clearly articulated during the assessment and design of requirements; later the system must be validated to meet requirements
3.5 Articulate and support policies that protect the dignity of users and other affected by a computing system
3.6 Create opportunities for members of the organization to learn the principles and limitations of computer systems

As an ACM member, I will . . .

4.1 Uphold and promote the principles of this code
4.2 Treat violations of this code as inconsistent with membership in the ACM

FIGURE 9-2 ACM Code of Ethics and Professional Conduct. (Reprinted courtesy of the Association for Computing Machinery © 1993.)

1. Thou shalt not use a computer to harm other people.
2. Thou shalt not interfere with other people's computer work.
3. Thou shalt not snoop around in other people's computer files.
4. Thou shalt not use a computer to steal.
5. Thou shalt not use a computer to bear false witness.
6. Thou shalt not copy or use proprietary software for which you have not paid.
7. Thou shalt not use other people's computer resources without authorization or proper compensation.
8. Thou shalt not appropriate other people's intellectual output.
9. Thou shalt think about the social consequences of the program you are writing or the system you are designing.
10. Thou shalt always use a computer in ways that insure consideration and respect for your fellow humans.

FIGURE 9-3 The Ten Commandments of Computer Ethics. (Reprinted with permission, Computer Ethics Institute, Washington, D.C.)

Conclusion of Computer Ethics

In this study of ethics, we have tried not to decide right and wrong, or even to brand certain acts as ethical or unethical. The purpose of this section is to stimulate thinking about ethical issues concerned with confidentiality, integrity, and availability of data and computations.

The cases presented show complex, conflicting ethical situations. The important first step in acting ethically in a situation is to obtain the facts, ask about any uncertainties, and acquire any additional information needed. In other words, first one must understand the situation.

The second step is to identify the ethical principles involved. Honesty, fair play, proper compensation, and respect for privacy are all ethical principles. Sometimes these conflict, and then we must determine which principles are more important than others. This analysis may not lead to one principle that obviously overshadows all others. Still, a ranking to identify the major principles involved is needed.

The third step is choosing an action that meets these ethical principles. Making a decision and taking action are difficult, especially if the action has evident negative consequences. However, taking action based on a *personal* ranking of principles is necessary. The fact that other equally sensible people may choose a different action does not excuse you from taking some action.

This section is not trying to force the development of rigid, inflexible principles. Decisions may vary, based on fine differences between two situations. Or a person's views can change over time in response to experience and changing context. Learning to reason about ethical situations is not quite the same as learning "right" from "wrong." Terms such as *right* and *wrong* or *good* and *bad* imply a universal set of values. Yet we know that even widely accepted principles are overridden by some people in some situations. For example, the principle of not killing people may be violated in the case of war or capital punishment. Few, if any, values are held by everyone or in all cases. Therefore, our purpose in introducing this material has been to stimulate you to recognize and think about ethical principles involved in cases related to computer security. Only by recognizing and analyzing principles can you act consistently, thoughtfully, and responsibly.

9.9 TERMS AND CONCEPTS

fairness, 553
legal protection for computers and data, 554
privacy, 555
copyright, 556
intellectual property, 556
originality, 557
fair use, 557
copyright registration, 558
copyright infringement, 558
patent, 561
novelty, 562
patent registration, 562
patent infringement, 562
trade secret, 564
reverse engineering, 564
trade secret enforcement, 565
information, 568
information depletion, 568
information replication, 569
information marginal cost, 569
information timeliness, 570
information tangibility, 570
information commerce, 571
electronic publishing, 571
database, 571
electronic commerce, 571
employer and employee rights, 575
product ownership, 575
patent ownership, 576
copyright ownership, 576
work for hire, 576
license, 577
employment contract, 577
property, 583
rules of evidence, 584
U.S. Computer Fraud and Abuse Act, 587
U.S. Freedom of Information Act, 588
U.S. Privacy Act, 588
USA Patriot Act, 588
cryptography—legality of use, 592
export of cryptography, 592
escrowed encryption, 593
privacy, 595
data mining, 596
Carnivore, 599
anonymity, 602
computer voting, 602
ethics, 605
religion, 606
ethical pluralism, 607
ethical reasoning, 608
teleology, 608
egoism, 609
utilitarianism, 609
deontology, 609
rule-deontology, 609
code of ethics, 622

9.10 TO LEARN MORE

Two excellent and readable works on ethical reasoning are by Frankena [FRA73] and Harris [HAR86]. Harris, especially, is written clearly and concretely.

The ACM devoted a special issue (December 1995) to ethics. The articles by Huff and Martin [HUF95], Johnson and Mulvey [JOH95], and Laudon [LAU95] are thought provoking.

9.11 EXERCISES

1. List the issues involved in the software vulnerability reporting argument. What are the technical issues? What are the psychological/sociological ones? What are the managerial ones? What are the economic ones? What are the ethical ones? Select a vulnerability reporting process that you think is appropriate and explain why it meets more requirements than any other process.
2. Would you hire Goli (the computer security consultant and hacker from case study VIII) to protect your computer system? How would you respond if she came to you describing a vulnerability in your system and offering to help you fix it? Explain your answer.

10

Cryptography Explained

In this chapter:

- Mathematics of encryption
- Cryptanalysis: how encryption systems are "broken"
- Theory of strong symmetric algorithms
- Detailed descriptions of the DES and AES algorithms
- Theory of public key encryption
- Detailed description of the RSA algorithm; details of other public key algorithms
- Digital signatures
- Quantum cryptography

Creating and implementing good cryptography is subtle and difficult, because the goals of a cryptographic algorithm seem to conflict with each other. We want to construct an algorithm that is easy for the legitimate sender and receiver to operate, but difficult—bordering on impossible—for the malicious interceptor to break. As we noted in Chapter 2, the interceptor can use any kind of attack to try to break the encryption: find a weakness in the algorithm, deduce or coerce or guess a key, determine the decryption of a single message or a whole flood of transmissions, exploit a flaw in the algorithm's implementation, or even cut and paste encrypted text without actually knowing the underlying plaintext. Although cryptography is arguably the most important tool a security expert has available, failed or flawed cryptography can give the false illusion of security. For these reasons, the security expert should have both a solid understanding of cryptography and a healthy respect for what can go wrong with its use. This chapter gives you that understanding by explaining in detail the mathematics underpinning different encryption schemes.

If there is one lesson to be learned from the history of cryptography, either before or after computerization, it is that cryptography is best left to experts. By learning the material in this chapter, you will have an advanced understanding of cryptography. But be mindful that understanding is not the same as mastery. You need to learn more than this book offers in order to appreciate cryptography's subtlety. At the end of the chapter, we recommend several references to help you on your way to mastery, should you be interested in it. The information presented in Chapter 2 described the basic concepts of cryptography, addressing what you need to know to understand how to use cryptography in various kinds of security controls. In this chapter, we look more closely at the *how* and *why*, not just the *what*.

Solid cryptography is based on results generated by the disciplines of mathematics and formal computer science. Thus, this chapter begins with discussion from these fields, with enough detail for you to understand the cryptography but not so deep as to be far beyond the scope of this book. Then we progress to the two branches of cryptography introduced in Chapter 2: symmetric (single, secret key), and asymmetric (public key) algorithms. We present details of the DES and AES symmetric systems, and the knapsack, RSA, and El Gamal asymmetric systems. We conclude with quantum cryptography, an interesting but futuristic approach with some emerging commercial products; it is new and untested, so it is not likely to appear in actual cryptosystems in the next few years.

10.1 MATHEMATICS FOR CRYPTOGRAPHY

Encryption is a two-edged sword: We want to encrypt important information relatively easily, but we would like an attacker to have to work very hard to break an encryption—so hard that the attacker will stop trying to break the encryption and focus instead on a different method of attack (or, even better, a different potential victim).

To accomplish these goals, we try to force an interceptor to solve a hard problem, such as figuring out the algorithm that selected one of $n!$ permutations of the original message or data. However, the interceptor may simply generate all possible permutations and scan them visually (or with some computer assistance), looking for probable text. Thus, the interceptor need not solve our hard problem. We noted in Chapter 2 the many ways this could happen. Indeed, the interceptor might solve the easier problem of determining which permutation was used *in this instance.* Remember that the attacker can use any approach that works. Thus, it behooves us as security specialists to make life difficult for the interceptor, no matter what method is used to break the encryption. In this section, we look particularly at how to embed the algorithm in a problem that is extremely difficult to solve. By that, we mean either that there is no conceivable way of determining the algorithm from the ciphertext or that it takes too long to reconstruct the plaintext to be worth the attacker's time.

Complexity

If the encryption algorithm is based on a problem that is known to be difficult to solve and for which the number of possible solutions is very large, then the attacker has a daunting if not impossible task. In this case, even with computer support, an exhaustive brute force solution is expected to be infeasible. Researchers in computer science and applied mathematics help us find these "hard problems" by studying and analyzing the inherent complexity of problems. Their goal is to say not only that a *particular* solution (or algorithm) is time consuming, but also that there simply is *no* easy solution. Much of the important work in this area was done in the early 1970s, under the general name of **computational complexity**. Thus, we begin our study of secure encryption systems by developing a foundation in problem complexity; we also introduce the mathematical concepts we need to understand the theory.

NP-Complete Problems

Cook [COO71] and Karp [KAR72] conducted an important investigation of problem complexity based on what are called **NP-complete** problems. The mathematics of the problems' complexity is daunting, so we present the notions intuitively, by studying three problems. Each of the problems is easy to state, not hard to understand, and straightforward to solve. Each also happens to be NP-complete. After the problems are described and discussed, we develop the precise meaning of NP-completeness.

Satisfiability

Consider the problem of determining whether any given logical formula is satisfiable. That is, for a given formula, we want to know whether there is a way of assigning the values *TRUE* and *FALSE* to the variables so that the result of the formula is *TRUE*. Formally, the problem is presented as follows.

Given a formula that meets these conditions—

- It is composed of the variables $v_1, v_2, \ldots, v_n$ and their logical complements $\neg v_1, \neg v_2, \ldots, \neg v_n$.
- It is represented as a series of clauses in which each clause is the logical *OR* ($\vee$) of variables and their logical complements.
- It is expressed as the logical *AND* ($\wedge$) of the clauses.

—is there a way to assign values to the variables so that the value of the formula is *TRUE*? If there is such an assignment, the formula is said to be **satisfiable.**

For example, the formula

$$(v_1) \wedge (v_2 \vee v_3) \wedge (\neg v_3 \vee \neg v_1)$$

is satisfiable, while

$$(v_1) \wedge (v_2 \vee v_3) \wedge (\neg v_3 \vee \neg v_1) \wedge (\neg v_2)$$

is not. Both of these formulas are in the form prescribed.

Knapsack

The name of the problem relates to placing items into a knapsack. Is there a way to select some of the items to be packed such that their "sum" (the amount of space they take up) exactly equals the knapsack capacity (the target)? We can express the problem as a case of adding integers. Given a set of nonnegative integers and a target, is there a subset of the integers whose sum equals the target?

Formally, given a set $S = \{a_1, a_2, \ldots, a_n\}$ and a target sum T, where each $a_i \geq 0$, we want to know if there is a selection vector, $V = [v_1, v_2, \ldots, v_n]$, each of whose elements is 0 or 1, such that

$$\sum_{i=1}^{n} (a_i * v_i) = T$$

The selection vector V records a 1 for each element chosen for the sum and a 0 for each not chosen. Thus, each element of S can be used once or not at all.

For example, the set S might be {4, 7, 1, 12, 10}. A solution exists for target sum $T = 17$, since $17 = 4 + 1 + 12$. The selection vector is $V = [1,0,1,1,0]$. No solution is possible for $T = 25$.

Clique

Given a graph G and an integer n, is there a subset of n vertices such that every vertex in the subset shares an edge with every other vertex in the subset? (A graph in which each vertex is connected to every other vertex is called a **clique.**)

Formally, we are given a graph $G = (V, E)$ where V is a set of vertices and $E \subseteq V \times V$ is the set of edges, and given a number $n > 0$. The problem is to determine whether there is a subset of n vertices, $V_S \subseteq V$, such that for each pair of vertices v_i, v_j in V_S, the edge (v_i, v_j) is in E.

As an example, consider Figure 10-1. Vertices (v_1, v_2, v_7, v_8) form a clique of size 4, but there are no cliques of 5 vertices.

Characteristics of NP-Complete Problems

These three problems are reasonable representatives of the class of NP-complete problems. Notice that they share the following characteristics.

1. Each problem *is* solvable, and a relatively *simple* approach solves it (although the approach may be time consuming). For each of them, we can simply enumerate all the possibilities: all ways of assigning the logical values of n variables, all subsets of the set S, all subsets of n vertices in G. If there is a solution, it will appear in the enumeration of all possibilities; if there is no solution, testing all possibilities will demonstrate that.
2. There are 2^n cases to consider if we use the approach of enumerating all possibilities (where n depends on the problem). Each possibility can be tested in a relatively small amount of time, so the time to test all possibilities and answer *yes* or *no* is proportional to 2^n.
3. The problems are apparently unrelated, having come from logic, number theory, and graph theory, respectively.

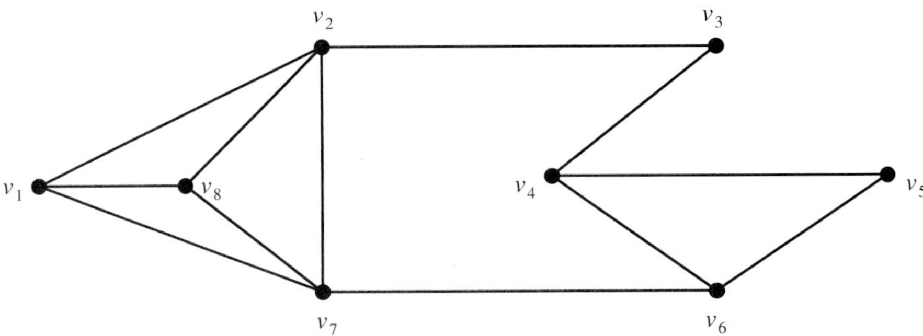

FIGURE 10-1 Clique Subgraphs in a Graph.

4. If it were possible to guess perfectly, we could solve each problem in relatively little time. For example, if someone could guess the correct assignment or the correct subset, we could simply verify that the formula had been satisfied or a correct sum had been determined, or a clique had been identified. The verification process could be done in time bounded by a polynomial function of the size of the problem.

The Classes P and NP

Let **P** be the collection of all problems for which there is a solution that runs in time bounded by a polynomial function of the size of the problem. For example, you can determine if an item is in a list in time proportional to the size of the list (simply by examining each element in the list to determine if it is the correct one), and you can sort all items in a list into ascending order in time bounded by the square of the number of elements in the list (using, for example, the well-known bubble sort algorithm.) There may also be faster solutions; that is not important here. Both the searching problem and the sorting problem are in **P**, since they can be solved in time n and n^2, respectively.

For most problems, polynomial time algorithms reach the limit of feasible complexity. Any problem that could be solved in time $n^{1,000,000,000}$ would be in **P**, even though for large values of n, the time to perform such an algorithm might be prohibitive. Notice also that we do not have to know an explicit algorithm; we just have to be able to say that such an algorithm exists.

By contrast, let **NP** be the set of all problems that can be solved in time bounded by a polynomial function of the size of the problem, *assuming the ability to guess perfectly.* (In the literature, this "guess function" is called an **oracle** or a **nondeterministic Turing machine**). The guessing is called **nondeterminism.**

Of course, no one can guess perfectly. We simulate guessing by cloning an algorithm and applying one version of it to each possible outcome of the guess, as shown in Figure 10-2. Essentially, the idea is equivalent to a computer programming language in which IF statements could be replaced by GUESS statements: Instead of testing a known condition and branching depending on the outcome of the test, the GUESS statements would cause the program to fork, following two or more paths concurrently.

The ability to guess can be useful. For example, instead of deciding whether to assign the value *TRUE* or *FALSE* to variable v_1, the nondeterministic algorithm can proceed in two directions: one assuming *TRUE* had been assigned to v_1 and the other assuming *FALSE.* As the number of variables increases so does the number of possible paths to be pursued concurrently.

Certainly, every problem in **P** is also in **NP**, since the guess function does not have to be invoked. There is also a class **EXP**, which consists of problems for which a deterministic solution exists in exponential time, c^n for some constant c. As noted earlier, every NP-complete problem has such a solution. Every problem in **NP** is also in **EXP**, so $\mathbf{P} \subseteq \mathbf{NP} \subseteq \mathbf{EXP}$.

The Meaning of NP-Completeness

Cook [COO71] showed that the satisfiability problem is **NP-complete,** meaning that it can represent the entire class **NP**. His important conclusion was that *if* there is a *deter-*

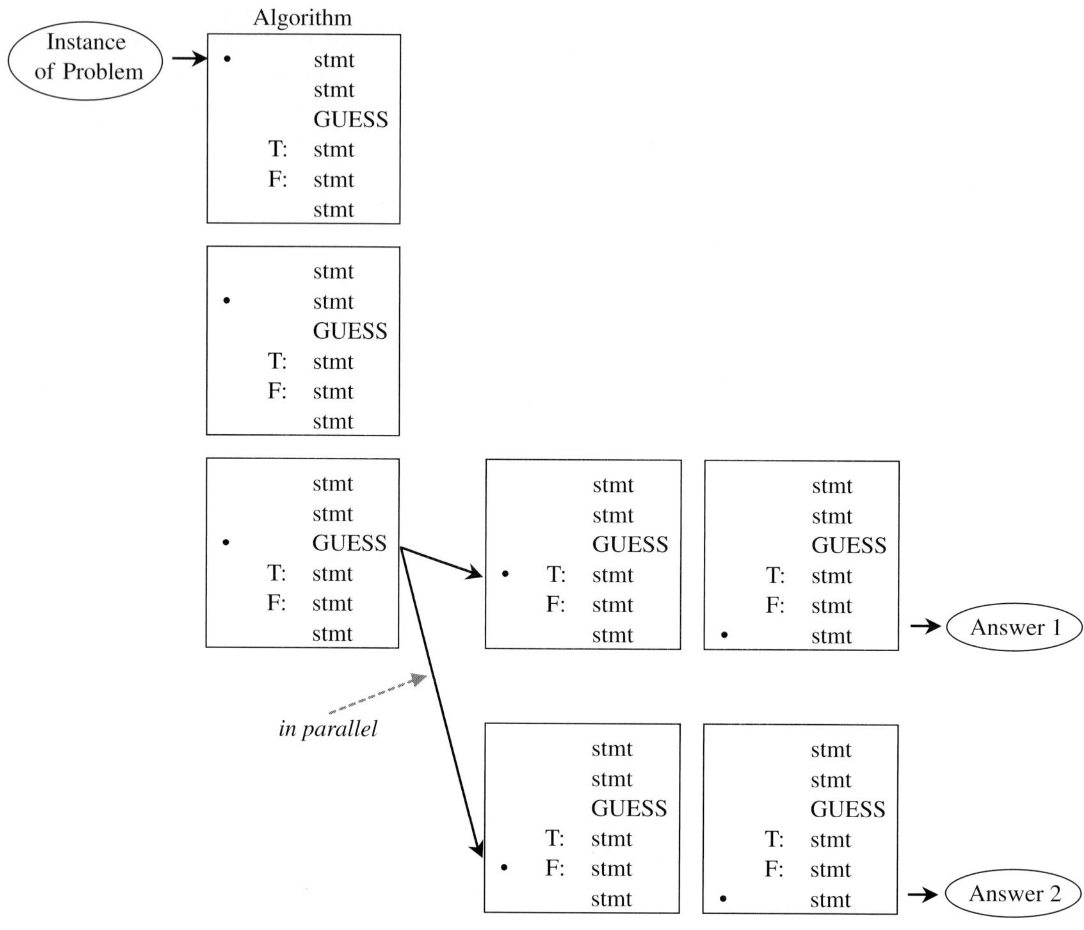

FIGURE 10-2 Simulating Nondeterminism.

ministic, polynomial time algorithm (one without guesses) for the satisfiability problem, then there is a deterministic, polynomial time algorithm for *every* problem in **NP**; that is, **P = NP**.

Karp [KAR72] extended Cook's result by identifying a number of other problems, all of which shared the property that if any *one* of them could be solved in a deterministic manner in polynomial time, then *all* of them could. The knapsack and clique problems were identified by Karp as having this property. The results of Cook and Karp included the converse: If for even *one* of these problems (or any NP-complete problem) it could be shown that there was *no* deterministic algorithm that ran in polynomial time, then no deterministic algorithm could exist for *any* of them.

In discussing problem complexity, we must take care to distinguish between a problem and an instance of a problem. An **instance** is a specific case: one formula, one specific graph, or one particular set S. Certain simple graphs or simple formulas may have solutions that are very easy and fast to identify. A **problem** is more general; it is the description of all instances of a given type. For example, the formal statements of the satisfiability, knapsack, and clique questions are statements of problems, since they tell what each specific instance of that problem must look like. Solving a problem requires finding *one* general algorithm that will solve *every* instance of that problem.

Essentially the problem space (that is, the classification of all problems) looks like Figure 10-3. There are problems known to be solvable deterministically in polynomial time (**P**), and there are problems known *not* to have a polynomial time solution (**EXP** and beyond), so $\mathbf{P} \subseteq \mathbf{EXP}$ and $\mathbf{P} \neq \mathbf{EXP}$, meaning $\mathbf{P} \subset \mathbf{EXP}$. The class **NP** fits somewhere between **P** and **EXP**: $\mathbf{P} \subseteq \mathbf{NP} \subset \mathbf{EXP}$. It may be that $\mathbf{P} = \mathbf{NP}$, or that $\mathbf{P} \neq \mathbf{NP}$.

The significance of Cook's result is that NP-complete problems have been studied for a long time by many different groups of people—logicians, operations research specialists, electrical engineers, number theorists, operating systems specialists, and communications engineers. If there were a practical (polynomial time) solution to any one of these problems, we would hope that someone would have found it by now.

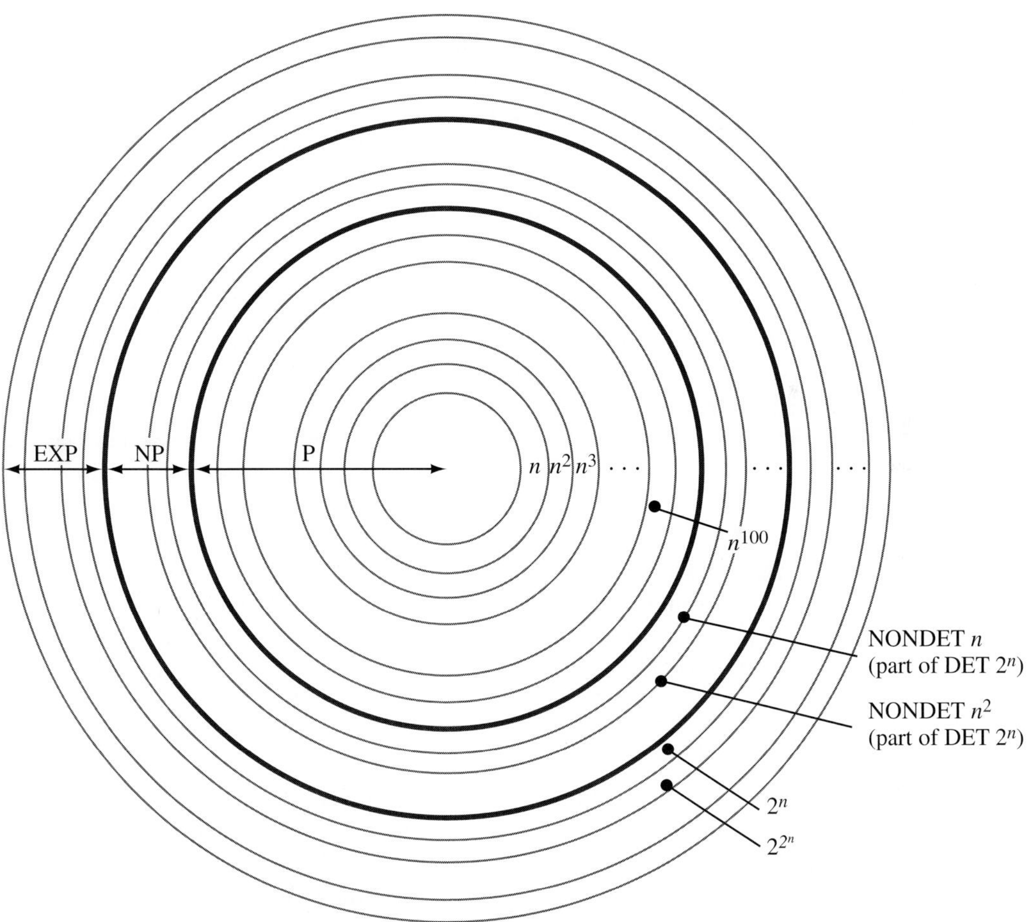

FIGURE 10-3 Hierarchies of Complexity Classes.

Currently, several hundred problems have been identified as NP-complete. (Garey and Johnson [GAR79] catalog many NP-complete problems.) The more problems in the list, the stronger the reason to believe that there is no simple (polynomial time) solution to any (all) of them.

NP-Completeness and Cryptography

Hard-to-solve problems are fundamental to cryptography. Basing an encryption algorithm on one of these hard problems would seem to be a way to require the interceptor to do a prodigious amount of work to break the encryption. Unfortunately, this line of reasoning has four fallacies.

1. An NP-complete problem does not *guarantee* that there is *no* solution easier than exponential; it merely indicates that we are unlikely to find an easier solution. This distinction means that the basis of the difficulty in cracking an encryption algorithm might deteriorate if someone should show that **P** = **NP**. This is the least serious of the fallacies.
2. Every NP-complete problem has a deterministic exponential time solution, that is, one that runs in time proportional to 2^n. For small values of n, 2^n is not large, and so the work of the interceptor using a brute force attack may not be prohibitive. You can get around this difficulty by selecting the algorithm so that the instance of the problem is very large; that is, if n is large, 2^n will be appropriately deterring.
3. Continuing advances in hardware make problems of larger and larger size tractable. For example, parallel processing machines are now being designed with a finite but large number of processors running together. With a GUESS program, two processors could follow the paths from a GUESS point simultaneously. A large number of processors could complete certain nondeterministic programs in deterministic mode in polynomial time. However, we can select the problem's setting so that the value of n is large enough to require an unreasonable number of parallel processors. (What seems unreasonable now may become reasonable in the future, so we need to select n with plenty of room for growth.)
4. Even if an encryption algorithm is based on a hard problem, the interceptor does not always have to solve the hard problem to crack the encryption. In fact, to be useful for encryption, these problems must have a secret, easy solution. An interceptor may look for the easy way instead of trying to solve a hard underlying problem. We study an example of this type of exposure later in this chapter when we investigate the Merkle–Hellman knapsack algorithm.

Other Inherently Hard Problems

Another source of inherently difficult problems is number theory. These problems are appealing because they relate to numeric computation, so their implementation is natural on computers. Since number theory problems have been the subject of much research recently, the lack of easy solutions inspires confidence in their basic complexity. Most of the number theory problems are not NP-complete, but the known algorithms are very time consuming nevertheless.

Two such problems that form the basis for secure encryption systems are computation in Galois fields and factoring large numbers. In the next section we review topics in algebra and number theory that enable us to understand and use these problems.

Properties of Arithmetic

We begin with properties of multiplication and division on integers. In particular, we investigate prime numbers, divisors, and factoring since these topics have major implications in building secure encryption algorithms. We also study a restricted arithmetic system, called a "field." The fields we consider are finite and have convenient properties that make them very useful for representing cryptosystems.

Unless we explicitly state otherwise, this section considers only arithmetic on integers. Also, unless explicitly stated otherwise, we use conventional, *not* mod n, arithmetic in this section.

Inverses

Let • be an operation on numbers. For example, • might be + (addition) or $*$ (multiplication). A number i is called an **identity** for • if $x \bullet i = x$ and $i \bullet x = x$ for every number x. For example, 0 is an identity for +, since $x + 0 = x$ and $0 + x = x$. Similarly, 1 is an identity for $*$.

Let i be an identity for •. The number b is called the **inverse** of a under • if $a \bullet b = i$ and $b \bullet a = i$. An identity holds for an entire operation; an inverse is specific to a single number. The identity element is always its own inverse, since $i \bullet i = i$. The inverse of an element a is sometimes denoted a^{-1}.

Using addition as an example operation, we observe that the inverse of any element a is $(-a)$, since $a + (-a) = 0$. When we consider the operation of multiplication on the rational numbers, the inverse of any element a (except 0) is $1/a$, since $a * (1/a) = 1$. However, under the operation of multiplication on the *integers*, there are no inverses (except 1). Consider, for example, the integer 2. There is no other integer b such that $2 * b = 1$. The positive integers under the operation + have no inverses either.

Primes

To say that one number **divides** another, or that the second is **divisible by** the first, means that the remainder of dividing the second by the first is 0. Thus, we say that 2 divides 10, since 10/2 = 5 with remainder 0. However, 3 does not divide 10, since 10/3 = 3 with remainder 1. Also, the fact that 2 divides 10 does not necessarily mean that 10 divides 2; 2/10 = 0 with remainder 2.

A **prime number** is any number greater than 1 that is divisible (with remainder 0) only by itself and 1.[1] For example, 2, 3, 5, 7, 11, and 13 are primes, whereas 4 $(2 * 2)$, 6 $(2 * 3)$, 8 $(2 * 2 * 2)$, and 9 $(3 * 3)$ are not. A number that is not a prime is a **composite.**

Greatest Common Divisor

The **greatest common divisor** of two numbers, a and b, is the largest integer that divides both a and b. The greatest common divisor is often written $\gcd(a, b)$. For ex-

[1] We disregard -1 as a factor, since $(-1) * (-1) = 1$.

ample, gcd(15, 10) = 5 since 5 divides both 10 and 15, and nothing larger than 5 does. If p is a prime, for any number $q < p$, gcd(p, q) = 1. Clearly, gcd(a, b) = gcd(b, a).

Euclidean Algorithm

The **Euclidean algorithm** is a procedure for computing the greatest common divisor of two numbers. This algorithm exploits the fact that if x divides a and b, x also divides $a - (k * b)$ for every k. To understand why, if x divides both a and b, then $a = x * a_1$ and $b = x * b_1$. But then,

$$\begin{aligned} a - (k * b) &= x * a_1 - (x * k * b_1) \\ &= x * (a_1 - k * b_1) \\ &= x * d \end{aligned}$$

so that x divides (is a factor of) $a - (k * b)$.

This result leads to a simple algorithm for computing the greatest common denominator of two integers. Suppose we want to find x, the gcd of a and b, where $a > b$. Rewrite a as

$$a = m * b + r$$

where $0 \le r < b$. (In other words, compute $m = a/b$ with remainder r.) If x = gcd(a,b), x divides a, x divides b, and x divides r. But gcd(a, b) = gcd(b, r) and $a > b > r \ge 0$. Therefore, we can simplify the search for gcd by working with b and r instead of a and b:

$$b = m' * r + r'$$

where $m' = b/r$ with remainder r'. This result leads to a simple iterative algorithm, which terminates when a remainder 0 is found.

Example

For example, to compute gcd(3615807, 2763323), we take the following steps.

$$\begin{aligned} 3{,}615{,}807 &= (1) * 2{,}763{,}323 + 852{,}484 \\ 2{,}763{,}323 &= (3) * 852{,}484 + 205{,}871 \\ 852{,}484 &= (4) * 205{,}871 + 29{,}000 \\ 205{,}871 &= (7) * 29{,}000 + 2{,}871 \\ 29{,}000 &= (10) * 2{,}871 + 290 \\ 2{,}871 &= (9) * 290 + 261 \\ 290 &= (1) * 261 + 29 \\ 261 &= (9) * 29 + 0 \end{aligned}$$

Thus, gcd(3615807, 2763323) = 29.

Modular Arithmetic

Modular arithmetic offers us a way to confine results to a particular range, just as the hours on a clock face confine us to reporting time relative to 12 or 24. We have seen in earlier chapters how, in some cryptographic applications, we want to perform some arithmetic operations on a plaintext character[2] and guarantee that the result will be an-

[2] Strictly speaking, these operations were on a numeric value associated with the character.

other character. Modular arithmetic enables us to do this; the results stay in the underlying range of numbers. An even more useful property is that the operations +, –, and * can be applied before or after the modulus is taken, with similar results.

Recall that a modulus applied to a nonnegative integer means *remainder after division*, so that 11 mod 3 = 2 since 11/3 = 3 with remainder 2. If a mod $n = b$ then

$$a = c * n + b$$

for some integer c. Two different integers can have the same modulus: 11 mod 3 = 2 and 5 mod 3 = 2. Any two integers are **equivalent** under modulus n if their results mod n are equal. This property is denoted

$$x \equiv_n y \text{ if and only if } (x \bmod n) = (y \bmod n)$$

Equivalently,

$$x \equiv_n y \text{ if and only if } (x - y) = k * n \text{ for some } k$$

In the following sections, unless we use parentheses to indicate otherwise, a modulus applies to a complete expression. Thus, you should interpret $a + b$ mod n as $(a + b)$ mod n, not $a + (b$ mod $n)$.

Properties of Modular Arithmetic

Modular arithmetic on the nonnegative integers forms a construct called a **commutative ring** with operations + and * (addition and multiplication). Furthermore, if every number other than 0 has an inverse under *, the group is called a **Galois field.** All rings have the properties of associativity and distributivity; commutative rings, as their name implies, also have commutativity. Inverses under multiplication produce a Galois field. In particular, the integers mod a prime n are a Galois field. The properties of this arithmetic system are listed here.

Property	Example
associativity	$a + (b + c) \bmod n = (a + b) + c \bmod n$ $a * (b * c) \bmod n = (a * b) * c \bmod n$
commutativity	$a + b \bmod n = b + a \bmod n$ $a * b \bmod n = b * a \bmod n$
distributivity	$a * (b + c) \bmod n = ((a * b) + (a * c)) \bmod n$
existence of identities	$a + 0 \bmod n = 0 + a \bmod n = a$ $a * 1 \bmod n = 1 * a \bmod n = a$
existence of inverses	$a + (-a) \bmod n = 0$ $a * (a^{-1}) \bmod n = 1$ if $a \neq 0$
reducibility	$(a + b) \bmod n = ((a \bmod n) + (b \bmod n)) \bmod n$ $(a * b) \bmod n = ((a \bmod n) * (b \bmod n)) \bmod n$

Example

As an example, consider the field of integers mod 5 shown in the tables below. These tables illustrate how to compute the sum or product of any two integers mod 5. However, the reducibility rule gives a method that you may find easier to use. To compute the sum or product of two integers mod 5, we compute the regular sum or product and then reduce this result by subtracting 5 until the result is between 0 and 4. Alternatively, we divide by 5 and keep only the remainder after division.

+	0	1	2	3	4
0	0	1	2	3	4
1	1	2	3	4	0
2	2	3	4	0	1
3	3	4	0	1	2
4	4	0	1	2	3

*	0	1	2	3	4
0	0	0	0	0	0
1	0	1	2	3	4
2	0	2	4	1	3
3	0	3	1	4	2
4	0	4	3	2	1

For example, let us compute 3 + 4 mod 5. Since 3 + 4 = 7 and 7 − 5 = 2, we can conclude that 3 + 4 mod 5 = 2. This fact is confirmed by the table. Similarly, to compute 4 * 4 mod 5, we compute 4 * 4 = 16. We can compute 16 − 5 = 11 − 5 = 6 − 5 = 1, or we can compute 16/5 = 3 with remainder 1. Either of these two approaches shows that 4 * 4 mod 5 = 1, as noted in the table. Since constructing the tables shown is difficult for large values of the modulus, the remainder technique is especially helpful.

Computing Inverses

In the ordinary system of multiplication on rational numbers, the inverse of any nonzero number a is $1/a$, since $a * (1/a) = 1$. Finding inverses is not quite so easy in the finite fields just described. In this section we learn how to determine the multiplicative inverse of any element.

The inverse of any element a is that element b such that $a * b = 1$. The multiplicative inverse of a can be written a^{-1}. Looking at the table for multiplication mod 5, we find that the inverse of 1 is 1, the inverse of 2 is 3 and, since multiplication is commutative, the inverse of 3 is also 2; finally, the inverse of 4 is 4. These values came from inspection, not from any systematic algorithm.

To perform one of the secure encryptions, we need a procedure for finding the inverse mod n of any element, even for very large values of n. An algorithm to determine a^{-1} directly is likely to be faster than a table search, especially for large values of n. Also, although there is a pattern to the elements in the table, it is not easy to generate the elements of a particular row, looking for a 1 each time we need an inverse. Fortunately, there is an algorithm that is reasonably simple to compute.

Fermat's Theorem

In number theory, Fermat's theorem states that for any prime p and any element $a < p$,

$$a^p \bmod p = a$$

or

$$a^{p-1} \bmod p = 1$$

This result leads to the inverses we want. For a prime p and an element $a < p$, the inverse of a is that element x such that

$$ax \bmod p = 1$$

Combining the last two equations, we obtain

$$ax \bmod p = 1 = a^{p-1} \bmod p$$

so that

$$x = a^{p-2} \bmod p$$

This method is not a complete method for computing inverses, in that it works only for a prime p and an element $a < p$.

Example

We can use this formula to determine the inverse of 3 mod 5:

$$\begin{aligned} 3^{-1} \bmod 5 &= 3^{5-2} \bmod 5 \\ &= 3^3 \bmod 5 \\ &= 27 \bmod 5 \\ &= 2 \end{aligned}$$

as we determined earlier from the multiplication table.

Algorithm for Computing Inverses

Another method to compute inverses is shown in the following algorithm. This algorithm, adapted from [KNU73], is a fast approach that uses Euclid's algorithm for finding the greatest common divisor.

```
{** Compute x = a^-1 mod n given a and n **}
c0 := n
c1 := a
b0 := 0
b1 := 1
i  := 1
repeat
        c(i+1) := c(i-1) mod c(i)
        t := c(i-1) div c(i)
        b(i+1) := b(i-1) - t * b(i)
        i := i + 1
until c(i) = 0
if (b(i-1) ≥ 0) then x := b(i-1) else x := n + b(i-1)
```

We use these mathematical results in the next sections as we examine two encryption systems based on arithmetic in finite fields.

10.2 SYMMETRIC ENCRYPTION

We were introduced to symmetric encryption in Chapter 2. In this section, we begin with a review of the two fundamentals of symmetric encryption, confusion and diffusion, as they are represented in modern algorithms. We also review cryptanalysis so that we can appreciate how encryption can fail. Finally, we study the details of the two main symmetric systems, DES and AES.

Fundamental Concepts

To refresh your memory and prepare you for a detailed description of DES and AES, we present here a review of important points from Chapter 2.

Confusion and Diffusion; Substitution and Permutation

Recall from Chapter 2 that confusion is the act of changing plaintext so that its corresponding plaintext is not apparent. Substitution is the basic tool for confusion; here, we substitute one element of ciphertext for an element of plaintext in some regular manner. Substitution is also the point at which a key is typically introduced in the process. As we noted in Chapter 2, single substitutions can be fairly easy to break, so strong encryption algorithms often employ several different substitutions.

Diffusion is the act of spreading the effect of a change in the plaintext throughout the resulting ciphertext. With poor diffusion, a change to one bit in the plaintext results in a change to only one bit in the ciphertext. A cryptanalyst might trace single bits backward from ciphertext to plaintext, having the effect of reducing 2^n possibilities in an n-bit ciphertext to just n, and thereby reducing the cryptanalytic complexity from exponential to linear. This reduction is not desirable; we always want to make the cryptanalyst work as hard as possible.

Substitution is sometimes represented by so-called S-boxes, which are nothing other than table-driven substitutions. Diffusion can be accomplished by permutations, or "P-boxes." Strong cryptosystems may use several iterations of a substitute-permute cycle. Such a cycle is shown in Figure 10-4. In the figure, a line entering an S-box from the top undergoes a substitution in the box. Then it is sent to another S-box in the line below by permutation of the order in some way; this permutation is represented by the lines spreading out at many angles.

Problems of Symmetric Key Systems

Symmetric key systems present several difficulties.

1. As with all key systems, if the key is revealed (stolen, guessed, bought, or otherwise compromised), the interceptors can immediately decrypt all the encrypted information they have available. Furthermore, an impostor using an intercepted key can produce bogus messages under the guise of a legitimate

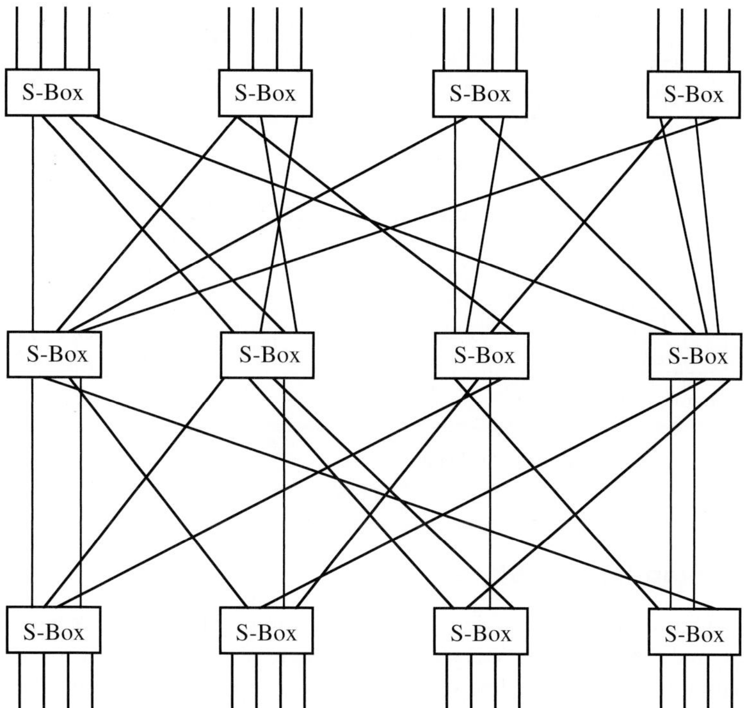

FIGURE 10-4 Substitutions and Permutations.

sender. For this reason, in secure encryption systems, the keys are changed fairly frequently so that a compromised key will reveal only a limited amount of information.

2. Distribution of keys becomes a problem. Keys must be transmitted with utmost security since they allow access to all information encrypted under them. For applications that extend throughout the world, this can be a complex task. Often, couriers are used to distribute the keys securely by hand. Another approach is to distribute the keys in pieces under separate channels so that any one discovery will not produce a full key. (For example, the Clipper program in the United States uses a 2-piece key distribution.) This approach is shown in Figure 10-5.
3. As described earlier, the number of keys increases with the square of the number of people exchanging secret information. This problem is usually contained by having only a few people exchange secrets directly so that the network of interchanges is relatively small. If people in separate networks need to exchange secrets, they can do so through a central "clearing house" or "forwarding office," which accepts secrets from one person, decrypts them, reencrypts them using another person's secret key, and transmits them. This technique is shown in Figure 10-6.

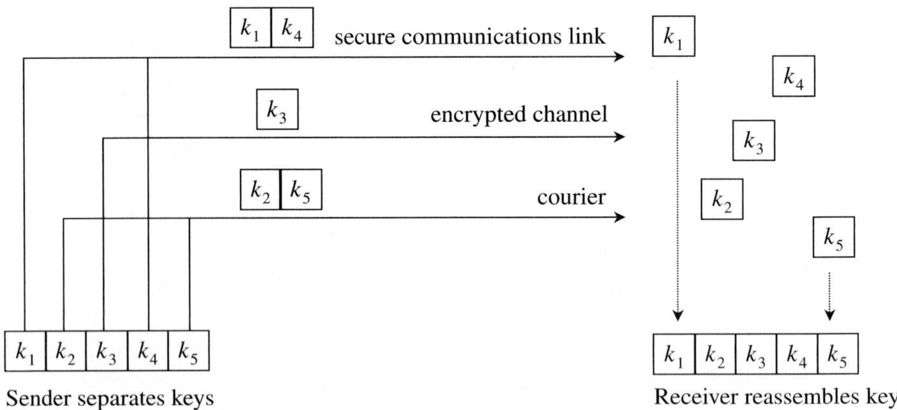

FIGURE 10-5 Key Distribution in Pieces.

Data Encryption Standard (DES)

The symmetric systems provide a two-way channel to their users: A and B share a secret key, and they can both encrypt information to send to the other as well as decrypt information from the other. The symmetry of this situation is a major advantage.

As long as the key remains secret, the system also provides **authentication**, proof that a message received was not fabricated by someone other than the declared sender. Authenticity is ensured because only the legitimate sender can produce a message that will decrypt properly with the shared key.

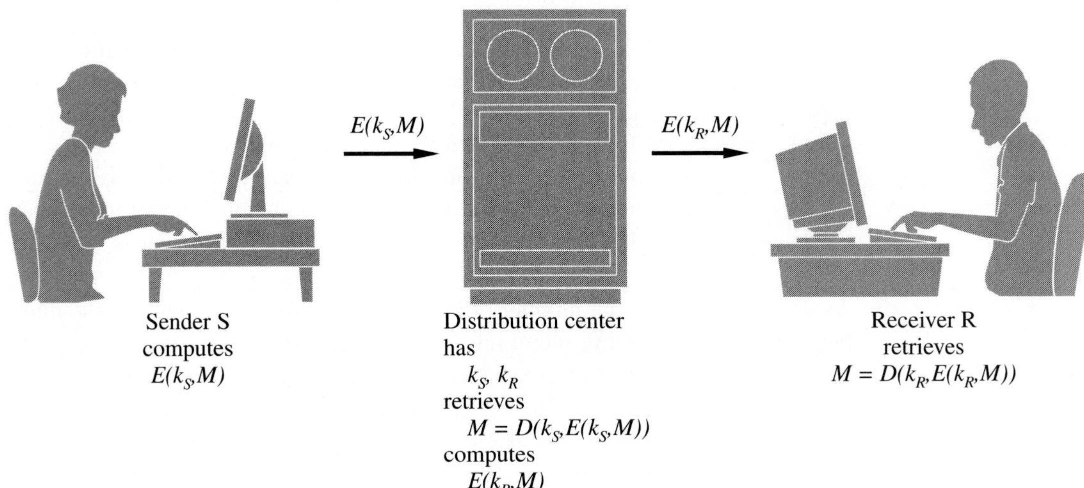

FIGURE 10-6 Distribution Center for Encrypted Information.

As we noted in Chapter 2, the Data Encryption Standard (DES) [NBS77] is a system developed for the U.S. government for use by the general public. It has been officially accepted as a cryptographic standard both in the United States and abroad. Many hardware and software systems use the DES. However, its adequacy has recently been questioned.

Overview of the DES Algorithm

Recall that the strength of the DES algorithm derives from repeated application of substitution and permutation, one on top of the other, for a total of 16 cycles. That is, plaintext is affected by a series of cycles of a substitution then a permutation. The iterative substitutions and permutations are performed as outlined in Figure 10-7.

We noted in Chapter 2 that the algorithm uses only standard arithmetic and logical operations on up to 64-bit numbers, so it is suitable for implementation in software on most current computers. Although complex, the algorithm is repetitive, making it suitable for implementation on a single-purpose chip. In fact, several such chips are available on the market for use as basic components in devices that use DES encryption in an application.

Details of the Encryption Algorithm

The basis of the DES is two different ciphers, applied alternately. Shannon noted that two weak but complementary ciphers can be made more secure by being applied together (called the "product" of the two ciphers) alternately, in a structure called a **product cipher**. The product of two ciphers is depicted in Figure 10-8.

After initialization, the DES algorithm operates on blocks of data. It splits a data block in half, scrambles each half independently, combines the key with one half, and swaps the two halves. This process is repeated 16 times. It is an iterative algorithm using just table lookups and simple bit operations. Although the bit-level manipulations of the algorithm are complex, the algorithm itself can be implemented quite efficiently. The rest of this section identifies the individual steps of the algorithm. In the next section, we describe each step in full detail.

Input to the DES is divided into blocks of 64 bits. The 64 data bits are permuted by a so-called initial permutation. The data bits are transformed by a 64-bit key (of which only 56 bits are used). The key is reduced from 64 bits to 56 bits by dropping bits 8, 16, 24, . . . 64 (where the most significant bit is named bit "1"). These bits are assumed to be parity bits that carry no information in the key.

Next begins the sequence of operations known as a **cycle**. The 64 permuted data bits are broken into a left half and a right half of 32 bits each. The key is shifted left by a number of bits and permuted. The key is combined with the right half, which is then combined with the left half. The result of these combinations becomes the new right half; the old right half becomes the new left half. This sequence of activities, which constitutes a cycle, is shown in Figure 10-9. The cycles are repeated 16 times. After the last cycle is a final permutation, which is the inverse of the initial permutation.

For a 32-bit right half to be combined with a 64-bit key, two changes are needed. First, the algorithm expands the 32-bit half to 48 bits by repeating certain bits, while reducing the 56-bit key to 48 bits by choosing only certain bits. These last two opera-

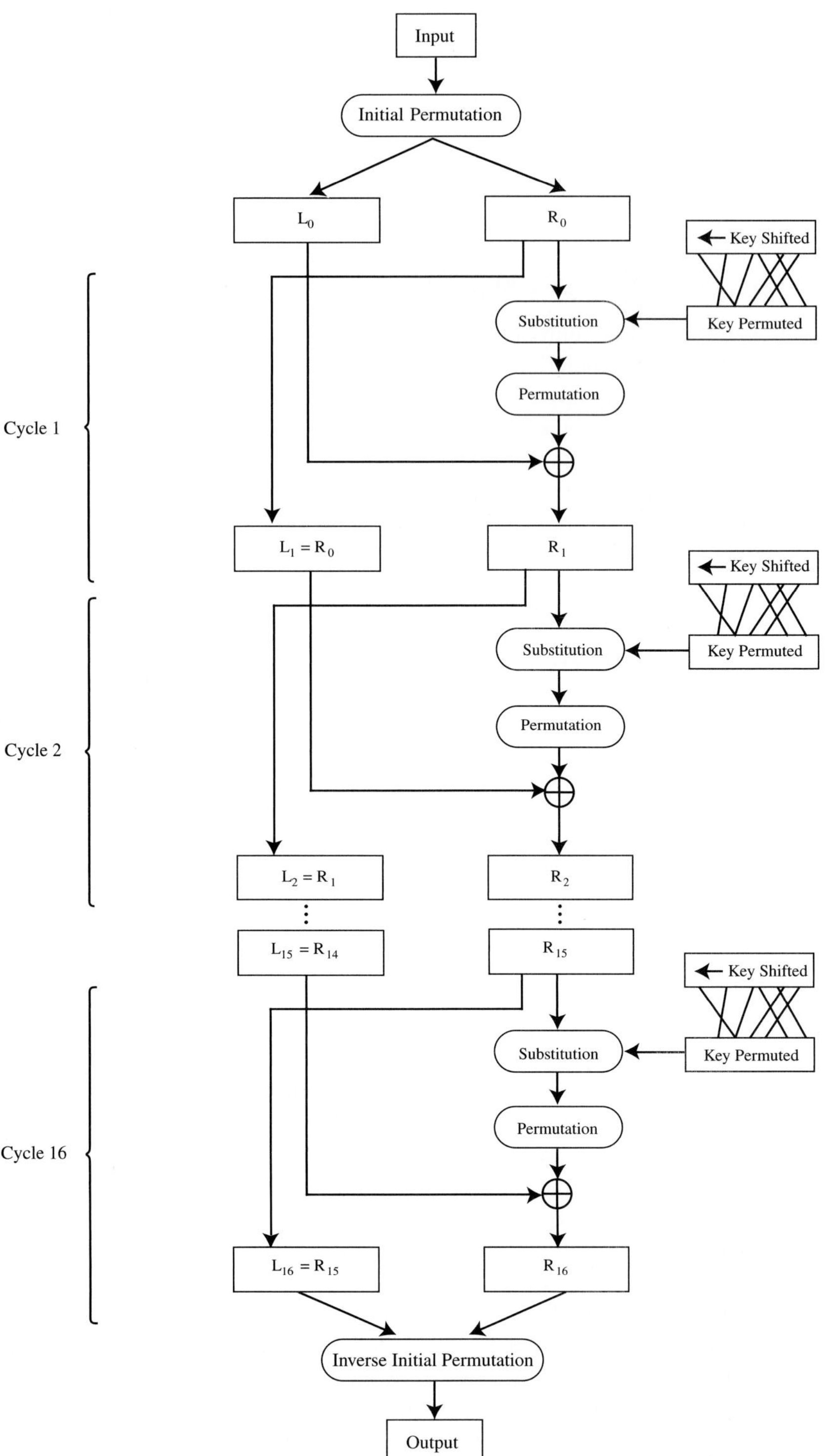

FIGURE 10-7 Cycles of Substitution and Permutation.

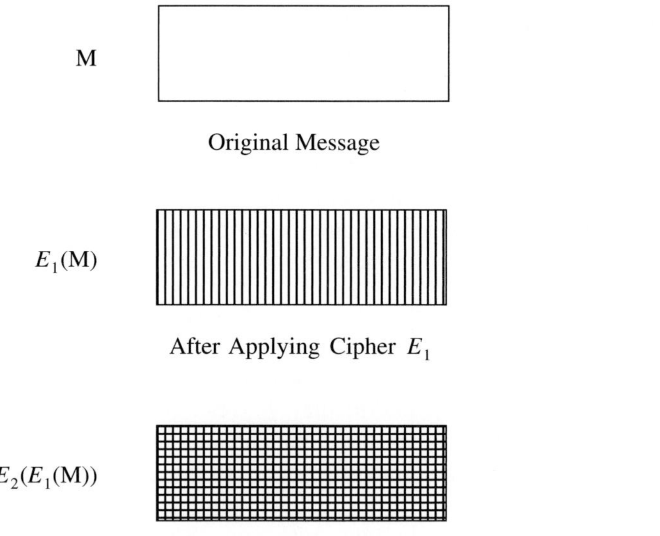

FIGURE 10-8 Product Ciphers.

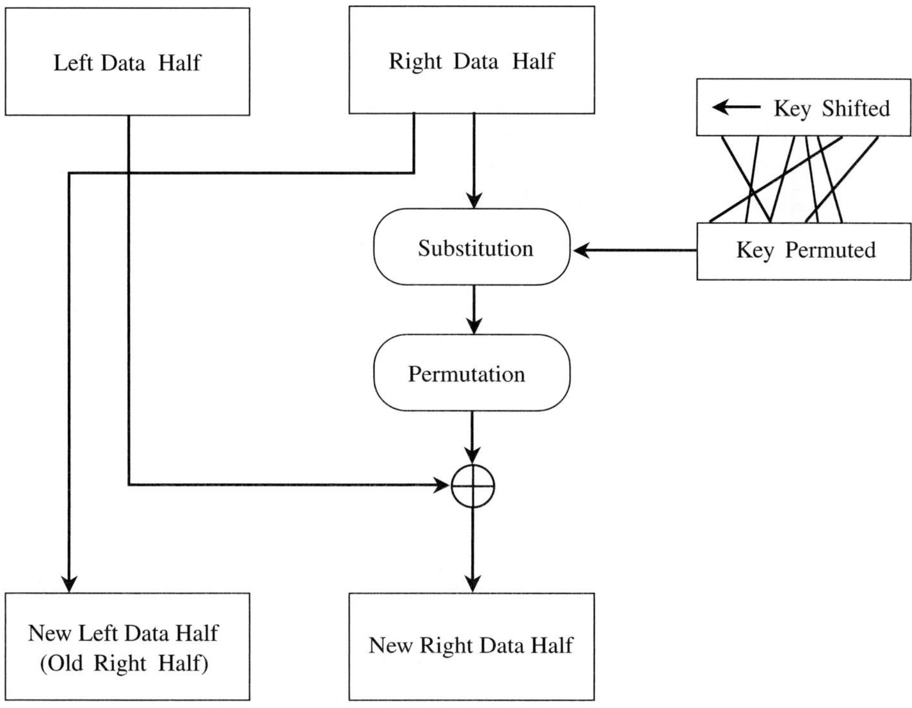

FIGURE 10-9 A Cycle in the DES.

tions, called **expansion permutations** and **permuted choices,** are shown in the diagram of Figure 10-10.

Details of Each Cycle of the Algorithm

Each cycle of the algorithm is really four separate operations. First, a right half is expanded from 32 bits to 48. Then, it is combined with a form of the key. The result of this operation is then substituted for another result and condensed to 32 bits at the same time. The 32 bits are permuted and then combined with the left half to yield a new right half. This whole process is shown in Figure 10-11.

Expansion Permutation

Each right half is expanded from 32 to 48 bits by means of the expansion permutation. The expansion permutes the order of the bits and also repeats certain bits. The expansion has two purposes: to make the intermediate halves of the ciphertext comparable in size to the key and to provide a longer result that can later be compressed.

The expansion permutation is defined by Table 10-1. For each 4-bit block, the first and fourth bits are duplicated, while the second and third are used only once. This table shows *to which* output position(s) the input bits move. Since this is an expansion permutation, some bits move to more than one position. Each row of the table shows the movement of eight bits. The interpretation of this table is that bit 1 moves to positions 2 and 48 of the output, while bit 10 moves to position 15. A portion of the pattern is also shown in Figure 10-12.

Key Transformation

As described above, the 64-bit key immediately becomes a 56-bit key by deletion of every eighth bit. At each step in the cycle, the key is split into two 28-bit halves, the halves are shifted left by a specified number of digits, the halves are then pasted together again, and 48 of these 56 bits are permuted to use as a key during this cycle.

Next, the key for the cycle is combined by an exclusive OR function with the expanded right half. That result moves into the S-boxes we are about to describe.

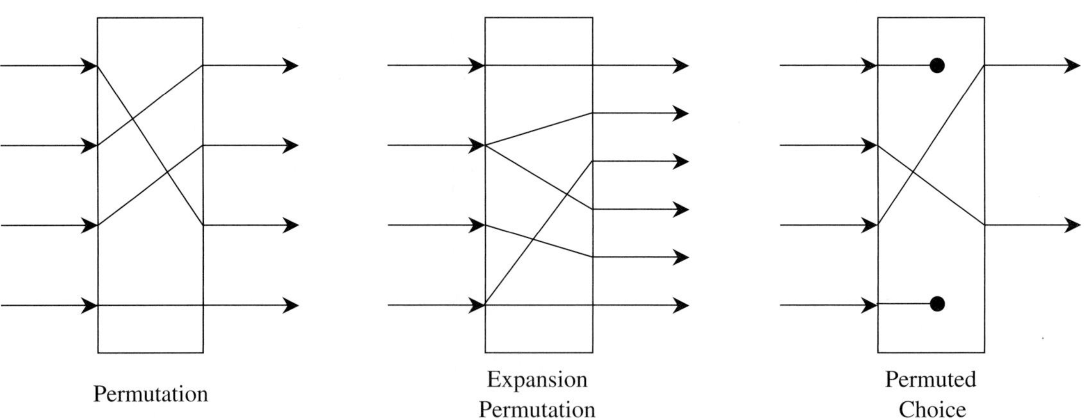

FIGURE 10-10 Types of Permutations.

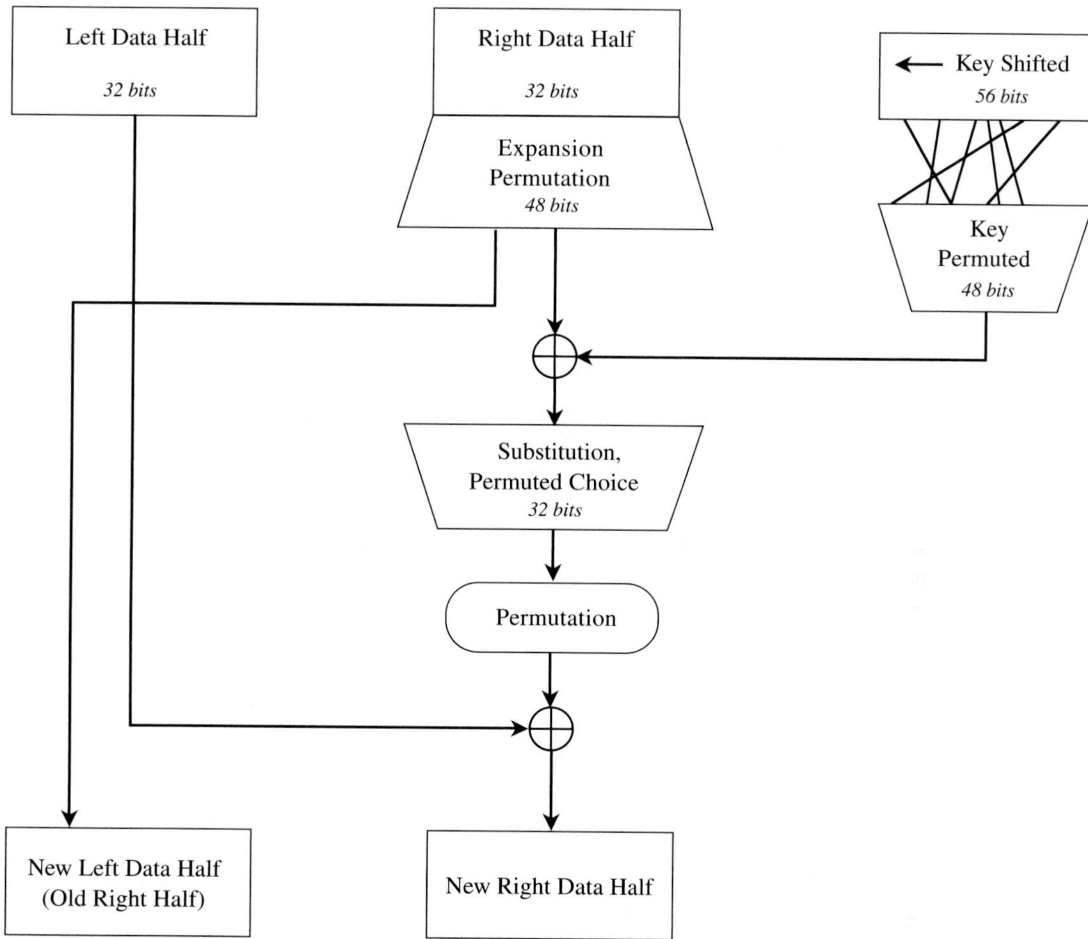

FIGURE 10-11 Details of a Cycle.

TABLE 10-1 Expansion Permutation.

Bit	1	2	3	4	5	6	7	8
Moves to Position	2,48	3	4	5,7	6,8	9	10	11,13
Bit	9	10	11	12	13	14	15	16
Moves to Position	12,14	15	16	17,19	18,20	21	22	23,25
Bit	17	18	19	20	21	22	23	24
Moves to Position	24,26	27	28	29,31	30,32	33	34	35,37
Bit	25	26	27	28	29	30	31	32
Moves to Position	36,38	39	40	41,43	42,44	45	46	47,1

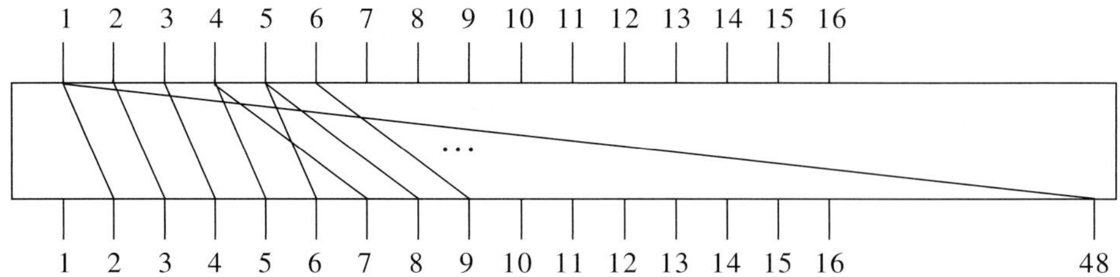

FIGURE 10-12 Pattern of Expansion Permutation.

At each cycle, the halves of the key are independently shifted left circularly by a specified number of bit positions. The number of bits shifted is given in Table 10-2.

After being shifted, 48 of the 56 bits are extracted for the exclusive OR combination with the expanded right half. The choice permutation that selects these 48 bits is shown in Table 10-3. For example, from this table we see that bit 1 of the shifted key goes to output position 5, and bit 9 is ignored in this cycle.

S-Boxes

Substitutions are performed by eight **S-boxes.** An S-box is a permuted choice function by which six bits of data are replaced by four bits. The 48-bit input is divided into eight 6-bit blocks, identified as $B_1B_2 \ldots B_8$; block B_j is operated on by S-box S_j.

The S-boxes are substitutions based on a table of 4 rows and 16 columns. Suppose that block B_j is the six bits $b_1b_2b_3b_4b_5b_6$. Bits b_1 and b_6, taken together, form a two-bit binary number b_1b_6, having a decimal value from 0 to 3. Call this value r. Bits b_2, b_3, b_4, and b_5 taken together form a four-bit binary number $b_2b_3b_4b_5$, having a decimal value from 0 to 15. Call this value c. The substitutions from the S-boxes transform each 6-bit block B_j into the 4-bit result shown in row r, column c of section S_i of Table 10-4. For example, assume that block B_7 in binary is 010011. Then, $r = 01 = 1$ and $c = 1001 = 9$. The transformation of block B_7 is found in row 1, column 9 of section 7 of Table 10-4. The value $3 = 0011$ is substituted for the value 010011.

P-Boxes

After an S-box substitution, all 32 bits of a result are permuted by a straight permutation, P. Table 10-5 shows the position to which bits are moved. Eight bits are shown on each row. For example, bit 1 of the output of the substitution moves to bit 9, while bit 10 moves to position 16.

Initial and Final Permutations

The DES algorithm begins with an **initial permutation** that reorders the 64 bits of each input block. The initial permutation is shown in Table 10-6.

TABLE 10-2 Bits Shifted by Cycle Number.

Cycle Number	Bits Shifted
1	1
2	1
3	2
4	2
5	2
6	2
7	2
8	2
9	1
10	2
11	2
12	2
13	2
14	2
15	2
16	1

TABLE 10-3 Choice Permutation to Select 48 Key Bits.

Key Bit	1	2	3	4	5	6	7	8	9	10	11	12	13	14
Selected for Position	5	24	7	16	6	10	20	18	—	12	3	15	23	1
Key Bit	15	16	17	18	19	20	21	22	23	24	25	26	27	28
Selected for Position	9	19	2	—	14	22	11	—	13	4	—	17	21	8
Key Bit	29	30	31	32	33	34	35	36	37	38	39	40	41	42
Selected for Position	47	31	27	48	35	41	—	46	28	—	39	32	25	44
Key Bit	43	44	45	46	47	48	49	50	51	52	53	54	55	56
Selected for Position	—	37	34	43	29	36	38	45	33	26	42	—	30	40

TABLE 10-4 S-Boxes of DES.

		Column															
Box	**Row**	**0**	**1**	**2**	**3**	**4**	**5**	**6**	**7**	**8**	**9**	**10**	**11**	**12**	**13**	**14**	**15**
S_1																	
	0	14	4	13	1	2	15	11	8	3	10	6	12	5	9	0	7
	1	0	15	7	4	14	2	13	1	10	6	12	11	9	5	3	8
	2	4	1	14	8	13	6	2	11	15	12	9	7	3	10	5	0
	3	15	12	8	2	4	9	1	7	5	11	3	14	10	0	6	13
S_2																	
	0	15	1	8	14	6	11	3	4	9	7	2	13	12	0	5	10
	1	3	13	4	7	15	2	8	14	12	0	1	10	6	9	11	5
	2	0	14	7	11	10	4	13	1	5	8	12	6	9	3	2	15
	3	13	8	10	1	3	15	4	2	11	6	7	12	0	5	14	9
S_3																	
	0	10	0	9	14	6	3	15	5	1	13	12	7	11	4	2	8
	1	13	7	0	9	3	4	6	10	2	8	5	14	12	11	15	1
	2	13	6	4	9	8	15	3	0	11	1	2	12	5	10	14	7
	3	1	10	13	0	6	9	8	7	4	15	14	3	11	5	2	12
S_4																	
	0	7	13	14	3	0	6	9	10	1	2	8	5	11	12	4	15
	1	13	8	11	5	6	15	0	3	4	7	2	12	1	10	14	9
	2	10	6	9	0	12	11	7	13	15	1	3	14	5	2	8	4
	3	3	15	0	6	10	1	13	8	9	4	5	11	12	7	2	14
S_5																	
	0	2	12	4	1	7	10	11	6	8	5	3	15	13	0	14	9
	1	14	11	2	12	4	7	13	1	5	0	15	10	3	9	8	6
	2	4	2	1	11	10	13	7	8	15	9	12	5	6	3	0	14
	3	11	8	12	7	1	14	2	13	6	15	0	9	10	4	5	3
S_6																	
	0	12	1	10	15	9	2	6	8	0	13	3	4	14	7	5	11
	1	10	15	4	2	7	12	9	5	6	1	13	14	0	11	3	8
	2	9	14	15	5	2	8	12	3	7	0	4	10	1	13	11	6
	3	4	3	2	12	9	5	15	10	11	14	1	7	6	0	8	13
S_7																	
	0	4	11	2	14	15	0	8	13	3	12	9	7	5	10	6	1
	1	13	0	11	7	4	9	1	10	14	3	5	12	2	15	8	6
	2	1	4	11	13	12	3	7	14	10	15	6	8	0	5	9	2
	3	6	11	13	8	1	4	10	7	9	5	0	15	14	2	3	12
S_8																	
	0	13	2	8	4	6	15	11	1	10	9	3	14	5	0	12	7
	1	1	15	13	8	10	3	7	4	12	5	6	11	0	14	9	2
	2	7	11	4	1	9	12	14	2	0	6	10	13	15	3	5	8
	3	2	1	14	7	4	10	8	13	15	12	9	0	3	5	6	11

TABLE 10-5 Permutation Box P.

Bit	Goes to Position							
1–8	9	17	23	31	13	28	2	18
9–16	24	16	30	6	26	20	10	1
17–24	8	14	25	3	4	29	11	19
25–32	32	12	22	7	5	27	15	21

TABLE 10-6 Initial Permutation.

Bit	Goes to Position							
1–8	40	8	48	16	56	24	64	32
9–16	39	7	47	15	55	23	63	31
17–24	38	6	46	14	54	22	62	30
25–32	37	5	45	13	53	21	61	29
33–40	36	4	44	12	52	20	60	28
41–48	35	3	43	11	51	19	59	27
49–56	34	2	42	10	50	18	58	26
57–64	33	1	41	9	49	17	57	25

At the conclusion of the 16 substitution–permutation rounds, the DES algorithm finishes with a **final permutation** (or **inverse initial permutation**), which is shown in Table 10-7.

Complete DES

Now we can put all the pieces back together. First, the key is reduced to 56 bits. Then, a block of 64 data bits is permuted by the initial permutation. Following are 16 cycles in which the key is shifted and permuted, half of the data block is transformed with the substitution and permutation functions, and the result is combined with the remaining half of the data block. After the last cycle, the data block is permuted with the final permutation.

Decryption of the DES

The same DES algorithm is used both for encryption *and decryption*. This result is true because cycle j derives from cycle $(j-1)$ in the following manner:

$$L_j = R_{j-1} \quad (1)$$

TABLE 10-7 Final Permutation (Inverse Initial Permutation).

Bit	Goes to Position							
1–8	58	50	42	34	26	18	10	2
9–16	60	52	44	36	28	20	12	4
17–24	62	54	46	38	30	22	14	6
25–32	64	56	48	40	32	24	16	8
33–40	57	49	41	33	25	17	9	1
41–48	59	51	43	35	27	19	11	3
49–56	61	53	45	37	29	21	13	5
57–64	63	55	47	39	31	23	15	7

$$R_j = L_{j-1} \oplus f(R_{j-1}, k_j) \tag{2}$$

where $\oplus$ is the exclusive OR operation and f is the function computed in an expand-shift-substitute-permute cycle. These two equations show that the result of each cycle depends only on the previous cycle.

By rewriting these equations in terms of R_{j-1} and L_{j-1}, we get

$$R_{j-1} = L_j \tag{3}$$

and

$$L_{j-1} = R_j \oplus f(R_{j-1}, k_j) \tag{4}$$

Substituting (3) into (4) gives

$$L_{j-1} = R_j \oplus f(L_j, k_j) \tag{5}$$

Equations (3) and (5) show that these same values could be obtained from the results of *later* cycles. This property makes the DES a reversible procedure; we can encrypt a string and also decrypt the result to derive the plaintext again.

With the DES, the same function f is used forward to encrypt or backward to decrypt. The only change is that the keys must be taken in reverse order ($k_{16}, k_{15}, \ldots, k_1$) for decryption. Using one algorithm either to encrypt or to decrypt is very convenient for a hardware or software implementation of the DES.

Questions About the Security of the DES

Since its first announcement, there has been controversy concerning the security provided by the DES. Although much of this controversy has appeared in the open literature, certain features of the DES have neither been revealed by the designers nor inferred by outside analysts.

Design of the Algorithm

Initially, there was concern with the basic algorithm itself. During development of the algorithm, the National Security Agency (NSA) indicated that key elements of the algorithm design were "sensitive" and would not be made public. These elements include the rationale behind transformations by the S-boxes, the P-boxes, and the key changes. There are many possibilities for the S-box substitutions, but one particular set was chosen for the DES.

Two issues arose about the design's secrecy. The first involved a fear that certain "trapdoors" have been imbedded in the DES algorithm so that a covert, easy means is available to decrypt any DES-encrypted message. For instance, such trapdoors would give NSA the ability to inspect private communications.

After a Congressional inquiry, the results of which are classified, an unclassified summary exonerated NSA from any improper involvement in the DES design. (For a good discussion on the design of DES, see [SMI88a].)

The second issue addressed the possibility that a design flaw would be (or perhaps has been) discovered by a cryptanalyst, this time giving an interceptor the ability to access private communications.

Both Bell Laboratories [MOR77] and the Lexan Corporation [LEX76] scrutinized the operation (not the design) of the S-boxes. Neither analysis revealed any weakness that impairs the proper functioning of the S-boxes. The DES algorithm has been studied extensively and, to date, no serious flaws have been published.

In response to criticism, the NSA released certain information on the selection of the S-boxes ([KON81], [BRA77]).

- No S-box is a linear or affine function of its input; that is, the four output bits cannot be expressed as a system of linear equations of the six input bits.
- Changing one bit in the input of an S-box results in changing at least two output bits; that is, the S-boxes diffuse their information well throughout their outputs.
- The S-boxes were chosen to minimize the difference between the number of 1s and 0s when any single input bit is held constant; that is, holding a single bit constant as a 0 or 1 and changing the bits around it should not lead to disproportionately many 0s or 1s in the output.

Number of Iterations

Many analysts wonder whether 16 iterations are sufficient. Since each iteration diffuses the information of the plaintext throughout the ciphertext, it is not clear that 16 cycles diffuse the information sufficiently. For example, with only one cycle, a single ciphertext bit is affected only by a few bits of plaintext. With more cycles, the diffusion becomes greater, so ideally there is no dependence of any one ciphertext bit on any subset of plaintext bits.

Experimentation with both the DES and its IBM predecessor Lucifer was performed by the NBS and by IBM as part of the certification process of the DES algorithm. These experiments have shown [KON81] that 8 iterations are sufficient to eliminate any observed dependence. Thus, the 16 iterations of the DES should surely be adequate.

Key Length

The length of the key is the most serious objection raised. The key in the original IBM implementation of Lucifer was 128 bits, whereas the DES key is effectively only 56 bits long. The argument for a longer key centers around the feasibility of an exhaustive search for a key.

Given a piece of plaintext known to be enciphered as a particular piece of ciphertext, the goal for the interceptor is to find the key under which the encipherment was done. This attack assumes that the same key will be used to encipher other (unknown) plaintext. Knowing the key, the interceptor can easily decipher intercepted ciphertext.

The attack strategy is the "brute force" attack: Encipher the known plaintext with an orderly series of keys, repeating with a new key until the enciphered plaintext matches the known ciphertext. There are 2^{56} 56-bit keys. If someone could test one every 100 milliseconds, the time to test all keys would be $7.2 * 10^{15}$ seconds, or about 228 million years. If the test took only one microsecond, then the total time for the search is (only!) about 2,280 years. Even supposing the test time to be one nanosecond, infeasible on current technology machines, the search time is still in excess of two years, assuming full time work with no hardware or software failures!

Diffie and Hellman [DIF77] suggest a parallel attack. With a parallel design, multiple processors can be assigned the same problem simultaneously. If one chip, working at a rate of one key per microsecond, can check about $8.6 * 10^{10}$ keys in one day, it would take 10^6 days to try all $2^{56} \approx 7 * 10^{16}$ keys. However, 10^6 chips working in parallel at that rate could check all keys in one day.

Hellman's original estimate of the cost of such a machine was $20 million (at 1977 prices). The price was subsequently revised upward to $50 million. Assuming a "key shop" existed where people would bring their plaintext/ciphertext pairs to obtain keys and assuming that there was enough business to keep this machine busy 24 hours a day for 5 years, the proportionate cost would be only about $20,000 per solution. As hardware costs continue to fall, the cost of such a machine becomes lower. The stumbling block in the economics of this argument is prorating the cost over five years: If such a device became available at affordable prices, use of the DES would cease for important data.

But there has been a dramatic drop in the price of computing hardware per instruction per microsecond. In 1998 a piece of special-purpose hardware was built that could infer a DES key in 112 hours for only $130,000. Kocher [KOC99] describes the machine. As the price of hardware continues to drop, the security of DES continues to fall.

An alternative attack strategy is the table lookup argument [HEL80]. For this attack, assume a chosen plaintext attack. That is, assume we have the ability to insert a given plaintext block into the encryption stream and obtain the resulting ciphertext under a still-secret key. Hellman argues that with enough advance time and enough storage space, it would be possible to compute all of the 2^{56} results of encrypting the chosen block under every possible key. Then, determining which key was used is a matter of looking up the output obtained.

By a heuristic algorithm, Hellman suggests an approach that will limit the amount of computation and data stored to 2^{37}, or about $6.4 * 10^{11}$. Again assuming many DES devices working in parallel, it would be possible to precompute and store results.

A brute force parallel attack against DES succeeded in 1997. (Thus, the concerns about key length in 1977 were validated in two decades.) Using the Internet, a team of researchers divided the key search problem into pieces (so that computer A tries all keys beginning 0000..., computer B tries all keys beginning 0001..., computer C tries all keys beginning 0010..., and so forth). This attack works because the key space is linear: any 56-bit string could be used as a key, and the parallel attack simply divides the key space among all search machines. In four months, using approximately 3500 machines, the researchers were able to recover a key to a DES challenge posted by RSA Laboratories [KOC99]. This challenge required thousands of cooperating participants. It is doubtful that such an attack could be accomplished in secret with public machines. Because the approach is linear, 3500 machines in 120 days is equivalent to 35,000 machines in 12 days.

Weaknesses of the DES

The DES algorithm also has known weaknesses, but these weaknesses are not believed to be serious limitations of the algorithm's effectiveness.

Complements

The first known weakness concerns complements. (Throughout this discussion, "complement" means "ones complement," the result obtained by replacing all 1s by 0s and 0s by 1s in a binary number.) If a message is encrypted with a particular key, the complement of that encryption will be the encryption of the complement message under the complement key. Stated formally, let p represent a plaintext message and k a key, and let the symbol $\neg x$ mean the complement of the binary string x. If $c = \text{DES}(p, k)$ (meaning c is the DES encryption of p using key k), then $\neg c = \text{DES}(\neg p, \neg k)$. Since most applications of encryption do not deal with complement messages and since users can be warned not to use complement keys, this problem is not serious.

Weak Keys

A second known weakness concerns choice of keys. Because the initial key is split into two halves and the two halves are independently shifted circularly, if the value being shifted is all 0s or all 1s, then the key used for encryption in each cycle is the same as for all other cycles. Remember that the difference between encryption and decryption is that the key shifts are applied in reverse. Key shifts are right shifts, and the number of positions shifted is taken from the bottom of the table up, instead of top down. But if the keys are all 0s or all 1s anyway, right or left shifts by 0, 1, or 2 positions are all the same. For these keys, encryption is the same as decryption: $c = \text{DES}(p, k)$, and $p = \text{DES}(c, k)$. These keys are called "weak keys." The same thing happens if one half of the key is all 0s and the other half is all 1s. Since these keys are known, they can simply be avoided, so this, too, is not a serious problem.

The four weak keys are shown in hexadecimal notation in Table 10-8. (The initial key permutation extracts every eighth bit as a parity bit and scrambles the key order slightly. Therefore, the "half zeros, half ones" keys are not just split in the middle.)

Semiweak Keys

A third difficulty is similar: Specific pairs of keys have identical decryption. That is, there are two different keys, k_1 and k_2, for which $c = \text{DES}(p, k_1)$ and $c = \text{DES}(p, k_2)$. This similarity implies that k_1 can decrypt a message encrypted under k_2. These so-called semiweak keys are shown in Table 10-9. Other key patterns have been investi-

TABLE 10-8 Weak DES Keys.

Left Half	Right Half	Weak Key Value
zeros	zeros	0101 0101 0101 0101
ones	ones	FEFE FEFE FEFE FEFE
zeros	ones	1F1F 1F1F 0E0E 0E0E
ones	zeros	E0E0 E0E0 F1F1 F1F1

gated with no additional weaknesses found to date. We should, however, avoid any key having an obvious pattern such as these.

Design Weaknesses

In another analysis of the DES, [DAV83a] shows that the expansion permutation repeats the first and fourth bits of every 4-bit series, crossing bits from neighboring 4-bit series. This analysis further indicates that in S-box S_4, one can derive the last three output bits the same way as the first by complementing some of the input bits. Of course, this small weakness raises the question of whether there are similar weaknesses in other S-boxes or in pairs of S-boxes.

It has also been shown that two different, but carefully chosen, inputs to S-boxes can produce the same output (see [DAV83a]). Desmedt et al. [DES84] make the point that in a single cycle, by changing bits only in three neighboring S-boxes, it is possible to obtain the same output; that is, two slightly different inputs, encrypted under the same key, will produce identical results at the end of just one of the 16 cycles.

Key Clustering

Finally, the researchers in [DES84] investigate a phenomenon called "key clustering." They seek to determine whether two different keys can generate the same ciphertext from the same plaintext, that is, two keys can produce the same encryption. The semiweak keys are key clusters, but the researchers seek others. Their analysis is very involved, looking at ciphertexts that produce identical plaintext with different keys in one cycle of the DES, then looking at two cycles, then three, and so forth. Up through three cycles, they found key clusters. Because of the complexity involved, they had to stop the analysis after three cycles.

Differential Cryptanalysis

In 1990 Biham and Shamir [BIH90] (see also [BIH91], [BIH92], and [BIH93]) announced a technique they named **differential cryptanalysis**. The technique applied to

TABLE 10-9 Semiweak DES Key Pairs.

01FE	01FE	01FE	01FE	FE01	FE01	FE01	FE01
1FE0	1FE0	0EF1	0EF1	E01F	E01F	F10E	F10E
01E0	01E0	01F1	01F1	E001	E001	F101	F101
1FFE	1FFE	0EFE	0EFE	FE1F	FE1F	FE0E	FE0E
011F	011F	010E	010E	1F01	1F01	0E01	0E01
E0FE	E0FE	F1FE	F1FE	FEE0	FEE0	FEF1	FEF1

cryptographic algorithms that use substitution and permutation. This powerful technique was the first to have impressive effects against a broad range of algorithms of this type.

The technique uses carefully selected pairs of plaintext with subtle differences and studies the effects of these differences on resulting ciphertexts. If particular combinations of input bits are modified simultaneously, particular intermediate bits are also likely with a high probability to change in a particular way. The technique looks at the exclusive OR of a pair of inputs; the XOR will have a 0 in any bit in which the inputs are identical and a 1 where they differ.

The full analysis is rather complicated, but we present a sketch of it here. The S-boxes transform six bits into four. If the S-boxes were perfectly uniform, one would expect all 4-bit outputs to be equally likely. However, as Biham and Shamir show, certain similar texts are more likely to produce similar outputs than others. For example, examining all bit strings with an XOR pattern 35 in hexadecimal notation (that is, strings of the form *ddsdsd* where *d* means the bit value is different between the two strings and *s* means the bit value is the same) for S-box S_1, the researchers found that the pairs have an output pattern of *dsss* 14 times, *ddds* 14 times, and all other patterns a frequency ranging between 0 and 8. That says that an input of the form *ddsdsd* has an output of the form *dsss* 14 times out of 64, and *ddds* another 14 times out of 64; each of these results is almost 1/4, which continues to the next round. Biham and Shamir call each of these recognizable effects a "characteristic"; they then extend their result by concatenating characteristics. The attack lets them infer values in specific positions of the key. If m bits of a k-bit key can be found, the remaining $(k-m)$ bits can be found in an exhaustive search of all $2^{(k-m)}$ possible keys; if m is large enough, the $2^{(k-m)}$ exhaustive search is feasible.

In [BIH90] the authors present the conclusions of many results they have produced by using differential cryptanalysis; they proceed to describe the details of these results in the succeeding papers. The attack on Lucifer, the IBM-designed predecessor to DES, succeeds with only 30 ciphertext pairs. FEAL is an algorithm similar to DES that uses any number of rounds; the n-round version is called FEAL-n. FEAL-4 can be broken with 20 chosen plaintext items [MUR90], FEAL-8 [MIY89] with 10,000 pairs [GIL90]; and Feal-N for N≤31 can be broken faster by differential cryptanalysis than by full exhaustive search [BIH91].[3]

The results concerning DES are impressive. Shortening DES to fewer than its normal 16 rounds allows a key to be determined from chosen ciphertexts in *fewer* than the 2^{56} (actually, expected value of 2^{55}) searches. For example, with 15 rounds, only 2^{52} tests are needed (which is still a large number of tests); with 10 rounds, the number of tests falls to 2^{35}, and with 6 rounds, only 2^8 tests are needed. *However,* with the full 16 rounds, this technique requires 2^{58} tests, or $2^2 = 4$ times *more* than exhaustive search would require.

Finally, the authors show that with randomly selected S-box values, DES is easy to break. Indeed, even with a change of only one entry in one S-box, DES becomes easy to break. One might conclude that the design of the S-boxes and the number of rounds were chosen to be optimal.

[3] In cryptology, it often seems like a dog chasing its tail: one cryptologist proposes a new algorithm, and a year later someone else demonstrates the fatal flaw in that algorithm. Cryptology is a very exacting discipline. As we have already advised, amateurs should learn from these examples: Even the best professionals can be tripped by details.

In fact, that is true. Don Coppersmith of IBM, one of the original team working on Lucifer and DES, acknowledged [COP92] that the technique of differential cryptanalysis was known to the design team in 1974 when they were designing DES. The S-boxes and permutations were chosen in such a way as to defeat that line of attack.

Security of the DES

The cryptanalytic attacks described here have not exposed any significant, exploitable vulnerabilities in the design of DES. But the weakness of the 56-bit key is now apparent. Although the amount of computing power or time needed is still significant enough to deter casual DES key browsing, a dedicated adversary could succeed against a specific DES ciphertext of significant interest.

Does this mean the DES is insecure? No, not yet. Nobody has yet shown serious flaws in the DES. With a triple DES approach (described in Chapter 2), the effective key length is raised from 56 bits to 112 bits,[4] raising the difficulty of attack exponentially. In the near term (years, probably decades) triple DES is strong enough to protect even significant commercial data (such as financial data or patient medical records). Still, DES is nearing the end of its useful lifetime, and a replacement is in order. With millions of computers in the world, clearly DES is inadequate to protect sensitive information with a modest time value. Similarly, algorithms with key lengths of 64 and 80 bits may be strong enough for a while, but an improvement in processor speeds and number of parallel computers threatens those, too. (See [LEN01] for more discussion on the relationship between key length and security with various algorithms.)

Advanced Encryption Standard (AES)

As we learned in Chapter 2, the U.S. NIST issued a call in 1997 for a new encryption system. Several restrictions were placed on the candidate algorithms: they had to be available worldwide, free of royalties, and their design had to be public. The criteria for selection of the five finalists were:

- security
- cost
- algorithm and implementation characteristics

The finalists were:

- MARS from IBM [BAR99]. This algorithm is optimized for implementation on current large-scale computers (such as those from IBM), but it may be less efficient on PCs. It involves substitutions, as with the S-boxes of DES, addition, and shifting and rotation.
- RC6 from RSA Laboratories [RIV98]. This algorithm is along the lines of existing algorithms, RC4 and RC5. Its design is so simple that it could even be memorized. The 128-bit block is manipulated as four 32-bit quarter-blocks. In 20 rounds, two quarter-blocks are XORed with a simple mathematical function

[4] Merkle [MER81] notes an uncommon attack in which triple DES fails to yield the expected strength of 112 bits.

of the other two; then the four quarter-blocks change position, rotating left 32 bits. The simple design leads to a fast and easy implementation.

- Serpent by Anderson et al. [AND98a]. This algorithm is cryptographically conservative, meaning that it has been structured with more rounds of confusion and diffusion than its designers think are necessary. It uses 32 rounds, each of which consists of a key addition, 4-bit to 4-bit substitution using one of eight substitutions, and then some mixing operations that combine bits across different 32-bit words. The algorithm lends itself readily to hardware (chip) implementation, based on parallel 4-bit subprocessors.
- Twofish from Counterpane Security [SCH98]. The designers of Twofish developed a design of substitution tables that depends on the encryption key instead of on fixed substitution tables (like the S-boxes of DES). This approach, the designers state, leads to greater security. As in DES, the algorithm operates on half of the block at a time and then the two halves are swapped. Each round involves matrix multiplication in a finite field. Some of Twofish's work can be precomputed, so the implementation can be optimized for speed.
- Rijndael by Daemen and Rijmen [DAE00,DAE02]. This algorithm uses cycles of four different kinds of operations, although all of the operations are simple. Thus, the implementation should be simple and efficient, without a significant sacrifice to security.

NIST indicated that no cryptographic weaknesses had been found in any of the five candidate algorithms. Rijndael was selected because it offered the best combination of security, performance, efficiency, ease of implementation, and flexibility. In 2001 it was formally adopted by the U.S. government for protection of government data transmission and storage. NIST relied heavily on public analysis of the algorithms.

Structure of the AES

AES is a block cipher of block size 128 bits. The key length can be 128, 192, or 256 bits. (Actually, the Rijndael algorithm can be extended to any key length that is a multiple of 64, although only 128, 192, and 256 are recognized in the AES standard.)

AES is a substitution-permutation cipher involving n rounds, where n depends on the key length. For key length 128, 9 rounds are used; for 192, 11; and for 256, 13. The cycle of AES is simple, involving a substitution, two permuting functions, and a keying function.

It is convenient to think of a 128-bit block of AES as a 4×4 matrix, called the "state." We present the state here as the matrix $s[0,0]..s[3,3]$. The state is filled from the input in columns. Assume, for example, that the input is the 16 bytes $b_0, b_1, b_2, b_3, \ldots, b_{15}$. These bytes are then represented in the state as shown in Table 10-10. Some operations in Rijndael are performed on columns of the state, and some on rows, so that this representation implements a form of columnar transposition.

The four steps of the algorithm operate as follows.

1. **Byte substitution**: The first step is a simple substitution: $s[i,j]$ becomes $s'[i,j]$, through a defined substitution table.

TABLE 10-10 Representation of the "State" in Rijndael.

b_0	b_4	b_8	b_{12}
b_1	b_5	b_9	b_{13}
b_2	b_6	b_{10}	b_{14}
b_3	b_7	b_{11}	b_{15}

$s_{0,0}$	$s_{0,1}$	$s_{0,2}$	$s_{0,3}$
$s_{1,0}$	$s_{1,1}$	$s_{1,2}$	$s_{1,3}$
$s_{2,0}$	$s_{2,1}$	$s_{2,2}$	$s_{2,3}$
$s_{3,0}$	$s_{3,1}$	$s_{3,2}$	$s_{3,3}$

2. **Shift row**: In the second step, the rows of s are permuted by left circular shift; the first (leftmost, high order) i elements of row i are shifted around to the end (rightmost, low order).
3. **Mix columns**: The third step is a complex transformation on the columns of s under which the four elements of each column are multiplied by a polynomial, essentially diffusing each element of the column over all four elements of that column.
4. **Add round key**: Finally, a key is derived and added to each column.

This sequence is repeated for a number of rounds depending on the key length.

Before describing these rounds, we must first mention that Rijndael is defined in the Galois field $GF(2^8)$ by the irreducible polynomial

$$P = x^8 + x^4 + x^3 + x + 1$$

In this mathematical system, a number is represented as a series of coefficients to this eighth-degree polynomial. For example, the number 23, represented in binary as 10111, is the polynomial

$$1x^4 + 0x^3 + 1x^2 + 1x + 1 = x^4 + x^2 + x^1 + 1$$

Addition of coefficients is performed (mod 2), so that addition is the same as subtraction which is the same as exclusive OR: $0 + 0 = 0$, $1 + 0 = 0 + 1 = 1$, $1 + 1 = 0$. Multiplication is performed as on polynomials: $(x^3 + 1) * (x^4 + x) = (x^7 + x^4 + x^4 + x) = (x^7 + x)$.

Although the mathematics of Galois fields are well beyond the scope of this book, it is important to realize that this mathematical foundation adds an underlying structure to what might otherwise seem like the random scrambling of numbers. As we explain how Rijndael works, we point out the uses of the Galois field, without necessarily explaining their full meaning. The mathematical underpinning gives credibility to Rijndael as a strong cipher.

Byte Substitution

Rijndael byte substitution is a conventional substitution box. However, the designers opened a small window into their algorithm's structure. The table is not just an arbitrary arrangement of bytes. Each byte b is replaced by the byte which is the result of the following two mathematical steps:

- Take the multiplicative inverse of b in $GF(2^8)$; 0, having no multiplicative inverse, is represented by 0.
- Exclusive OR that result with 99 = hexadecimal 63 = 0110 0011

Using inverses in $GF(2^8)$ ensures that each value appears exactly once in the table. Adding 63 helps break up patterns. The complete substitution table is shown in Table 10-11. For example, the byte 20 is replaced by B7, in row 2, column 0.

Shift Row

Actually, Rijndael is defined for blocks of size 128, 192, and 256 bits, too, even though the AES specifies a block size of only 128 bits. In the shift row step, assume a block is composed of 16 (or 24 or 32) bytes numbered (from left, or most significant, to right) 1 to 16 (or 24 or 32). In the shift row, the numbered bytes are shifted to the positions as shown in Table 10-12. That is, for 128- and 192-bit blocks, row i is rotated left $(i–1)$ bytes; for 256-byte blocks, rows 3 and 4 are shifted an extra byte.

That is, row n is shifted left circular $(n–1)$ bytes, except for 256-bit blocks, in which case row 2 is shifted 1 byte and rows 3 and 4 are shifted 3 and 4 bytes, respectively.

TABLE 10-11 Sub-bytes Substitution.

	0	**1**	**2**	**3**	**4**	**5**	**6**	**7**	**8**	**9**	**A**	**B**	**C**	**D**	**E**	**F**
0	63	7C	77	7B	F2	6B	6F	C5	30	01	67	2B	FE	D7	AB	76
1	CA	82	C9	7D	FA	59	47	F0	AD	D4	A2	AF	9C	A4	72	C0
2	B7	FD	93	26	36	3F	F7	CC	34	A5	E5	F1	71	D8	31	15
3	04	C7	23	C3	18	96	05	9A	07	12	80	E2	BE	27	B2	75
4	09	83	2C	1A	1B	6E	5A	A0	52	3B	D6	B3	29	E3	2F	84
5	53	D1	00	ED	20	FC	B1	5B	6A	CB	BE	39	4A	4C	58	CF
6	D0	EF	AA	FB	43	4D	33	85	45	F9	02	7F	50	3C	9F	A8
7	51	A3	40	84	92	9D	38	F5	BC	B6	DA	21	10	FF	F3	D2
8	CD	0C	13	EC	5F	97	44	17	C4	A7	7E	3D	64	5D	19	73
9	60	81	4F	DC	22	2A	90	88	46	EE	B8	14	DE	5E	0B	DB
A	E0	32	3A	0A	49	06	24	5C	C2	D3	AC	62	91	95	E4	79
B	E7	C8	37	6D	8D	D5	4E	A9	6C	56	F4	EA	65	7A	AE	08
C	BA	78	25	2E	1C	A6	B4	C6	E8	DD	74	1F	4B	BD	8B	8A
D	70	3E	B5	66	48	03	F6	0E	61	35	57	B9	86	C1	1D	9E
E	E1	F8	98	11	69	D9	8E	94	9B	1E	87	E9	CE	55	28	DF
F	8C	A1	89	0D	BF	E6	42	68	41	99	2D	0F	B0	54	BB	16

TABLE 10-12 Shift Row Operation for 128-, 192-, and 256-bit Blocks.

1	5	9	13
2	6	10	14
3	7	11	15
4	8	12	16

1	5	9	13
6	10	14	2
11	15	3	7
16	4	8	12

1	5	9	13	17	21
2	6	10	14	18	22
3	7	11	15	19	23
4	8	12	16	20	24

1	5	9	13	17	21
6	10	14	18	22	2
11	15	19	23	3	7
16	20	24	4	8	12

1	5	9	13	17	21	25	29
2	6	10	14	18	22	26	30
3	7	11	15	19	23	27	31
4	8	12	16	20	24	28	32

1	5	9	13	17	21	25	29
6	10	14	18	22	26	30	2
15	19	23	27	31	3	7	11
20	24	28	32	4	8	12	16

Mix Column

In the mix column operation, each column (as depicted in shift rows) is multiplied by the matrix

$$\begin{matrix} 2 & 3 & 1 & 1 \\ 1 & 2 & 3 & 1 \\ 1 & 1 & 2 & 3 \\ 3 & 1 & 1 & 2 \end{matrix}$$

so that

$$\begin{bmatrix} s'_{0,i} \\ s'_{1,i} \\ s'_{2,i} \\ s'_{3,i} \end{bmatrix} = \begin{bmatrix} 2 & 3 & 1 & 1 \\ 1 & 2 & 3 & 1 \\ 1 & 1 & 2 & 3 \\ 3 & 1 & 1 & 2 \end{bmatrix} \begin{bmatrix} s_{0,i} \\ s_{1,i} \\ s_{2,i} \\ s_{3,i} \end{bmatrix}$$

However, this "multiplication" is performed on bytes by logical operations, so multiplying the column by 1 means leaving it unchanged, multiplying by 2 (binary 10) means shifting each byte left one bit, and multiplying by 3 (binary 11) means shifting left one bit and adding (exclusive ORing) the original unshifted value. For example,

$$s'_{1,1} = s_{0,1} \oplus 2s_{1,1} \oplus 2s_{2,1} \oplus s_{2,1} \oplus s_{3,1}$$

where $2s_{2,1}$ is $s_{2,1}$ shifted left one bit. (The symbol ⊕ denotes exclusive OR.) Results longer than 8 bits are reduced by computing mod P for the generating polynomial P of the Rijndael algorithm; this means that 100011011 is subtracted (exclusive ORed) from the result until the result has at most eight significant bits.

Add Subkey

The final step of a cycle is to add (exclusive OR) a variation of the key with the result so far. The variation is as follows. The first key is the key itself. The second key is changed 4-byte word by word. The first word is rotated one byte left, then transformed by the substitution of the byte substitution step, then added (exclusive ORed) with a constant. The rest of the words in that subkey are produced by the exclusive OR of the first word with the corresponding word from the previous key. So, if key variation k_1 is $w_1w_2w_3w_4$ (four 32-bit words, or 128 bits), then k_2 is $w_1'(w_2 \oplus w_1')(w_3 \oplus w_1')(w_4 \oplus w_1')$ where w_1' is w_1 rotated left 1 byte, substituted, and exclusive ORed with a constant.

A picture of the full AES is shown in Figure 10-13. Notice that in the Mix Columns step the algorithm takes a "right turn," changing from a row (word) orientation to a column structure.

Cryptanalysis of the AES

Rijndael has been subjected to extensive cryptanalysis by professional and amateur cryptographers since it was proposed for the AES. It is a variation on an earlier algo-

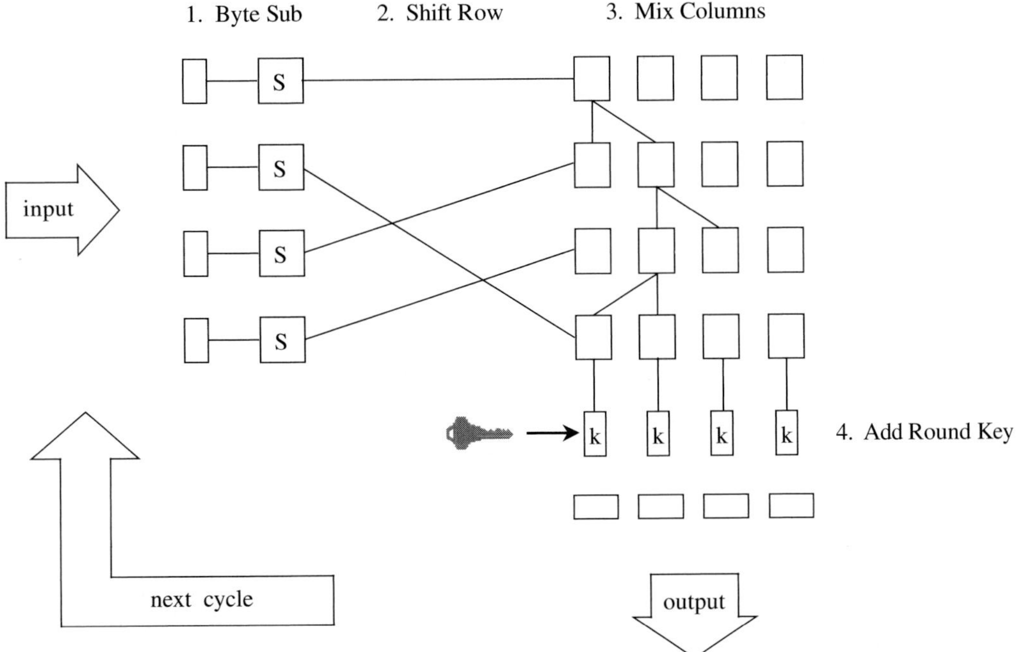

FIGURE 10-13 Structure of the AES.

rithm, Square, from the same authors; that algorithm, too has been analyzed extensively in the community.

To date, no significant problems have been found with Rijndael. One property that has been discovered, which is both good and bad, is that it is quite regular. Regularity is evident if an input is chosen and all bytes except one of that input are held constant. Then, the one remaining byte is repeatedly changed through all 256 different possible values; after one round of Rijndael, 4 bytes will go through all 256 values, and after two rounds, 16 bytes will go through all 256 values. This result demonstrates unusually good diffusion, in that small changes in the input have a widespread effect. However, the regularity of this pattern might give some clue to an attacker, although that is unlikely.

We have noted that Rijndael draws heavily from algebra, especially Galois fields. The substitution and column mixing functions are not just numbers chosen at random but instead solve certain fundamental problems in Galois field theory. The authors have not offered a mathematical argument for why such a basis gives strength to—or at least does not detract from—the approach. But substantial work in that area makes it unlikely that there are any hidden shortcuts—ways in which an attacker could solve an encryption in a manner significantly easier than a brute force key search. Over time we can expect mathematicians to explore this algorithm and its underlying field.

For now, the AES seems a solid replacement for the DES.

10.3 PUBLIC KEY ENCRYPTION SYSTEMS

In 1976, Diffie and Hellman [DIF76] proposed a new kind of system, public key encryption, in which each user would have a key that did not have to be kept secret. Counterintuitively, the public nature of the key would not inhibit the system's secrecy. The public key transformation is essentially a one-way encryption with a secret (private) way to decrypt.

Public key systems have an enormous advantage over conventional key systems: Anyone can send a secret message to a user, while the message remains adequately protected from being read by an interceptor. With a conventional key system, a separate key is needed for each pair of users. As we have seen, n users will require $n * (n - 1)/2$ keys. As the number of users grows, the number of keys increases very rapidly. Determining and distributing these keys is a problem; more serious is maintaining security for the keys already distributed, because we cannot expect users to memorize so many keys.

Characteristics

With a **public key** or **asymmetric** encryption system, each user has two keys: a public key and a private key. The user may publish the public key freely. The keys operate as inverses. Let k_{PRIV} be a user's private key, and let k_{PUB} be the corresponding public key. Then,

$$P = D(k_{PRIV}, E(k_{PUB}, P))$$

That is, a user can decode with a private key what someone else has encrypted with the corresponding public key. Furthermore, with the second public key encryption algorithm,

$$P = D(k_{PUB}, E(k_{PRIV}, P))$$

so a user can encrypt a message with a private key and the message can be revealed only with the corresponding public key. (We study an application of this second case later in this chapter, when we examine digital signature protocols.)

These two properties imply that public and private keys can be applied in either order. Ideally, the decryption function D can be applied to any argument, so we can decrypt first and then encrypt. With conventional encryption, one seldom thinks of decrypting *before* encrypting. With public keys, it simply means applying the private transformation first, and then the public one.

We saw in Chapter 2 that, with public keys, only two keys are needed per user: one public and one private. Thus, users B, C, and D can all encrypt messages for A, using A's public key. If B has encrypted a message using A's public key, C *cannot* decrypt it, even if C knew it was encrypted with A's public key. Applying A's public key twice, for example, would not decrypt the message. (We assume, of course, that A's private key remains secret.) In the remainder of this section, we look closely at three types of public key systems: Merkle–Hellman knapsacks, RSA encryption, and El Gamal applied to digital signatures.

Merkle–Hellman Knapsacks

Merkle and Hellman [MER78b] developed an encryption algorithm based on the knapsack problem described earlier. The knapsack problem presents a set of positive integers and a target sum, with the goal of finding a subset of the integers that sum to the target. The knapsack problem is NP-complete, implying that to solve it probably requires time exponential in the size of the problem—in this case, the number of integers.

We present Merkle–Hellman in two steps, to aid understanding. First we outline the operation of the Merkle–Hellman knapsack encryption method. Then we revisit the technique in more detail.

Introduction to Merkle–Hellman Knapsacks

The idea behind the Merkle–Hellman knapsack scheme is to encode a binary message as a solution to a knapsack problem, reducing the ciphertext to the target sum obtained by adding terms corresponding to 1s in the plaintext. That is, we convert blocks of plaintext to a knapsack sum by adding into the sum those terms that match with 1 bits in the plaintext, as shown in Figure 10-14.

A knapsack is represented as a vector of integer terms in which the order of the terms is very important. There are actually two knapsacks—an easy one, to which a fast (linear time) algorithm exists, and a hard one, derived by modifying the elements of the easy knapsack. The modification is such that a solution with the elements of either knapsack is a solution for the other one as well. This modification is a trapdoor,

Plaintext	1	0	1	0	0	1	
Knapsack	1	2	5	9	20	43	
Ciphertext	1		5			43	
Target Sum							49

Plaintext	0	1	1	0	1	0	
Knapsack	1	2	5	9	20	43	
Ciphertext		2	5		20		
Target Sum							27

FIGURE 10-14 Knapsack for Encryption.

permitting legitimate users to solve the problem simply. Thus, the general problem is NP-complete, but a restricted version of it has a very fast solution.

The algorithm begins with a knapsack set, each of whose elements is larger than the sum of all previous elements. Suppose we have a sequence where each element a_k is larger than $a_1 + a_2 + \ldots + a_{k-1}$. If a sum is between a_k and a_{k+1}, it must contain a_k as a term, because no combination of the values $a_1, a_2, \ldots, a_{k-1}$ could produce a total as large as a_k. Similarly, if a sum is less than a_k, clearly it cannot contain a_k as a term.

The modification of the algorithm disguises the elements of the easy knapsack set by changing this increasing size property in a way that preserves the underlying solution. The modification is accomplished with multiplication by a constant mod n.

Detailed Explanation of the Merkle–Hellman Technique

This detailed explanation of Merkle–Hellman is intended for people who want a deeper understanding of the algorithm.

General Knapsacks

The knapsack problem examines a sequence $a_1, a_2, \ldots, a_n$ of integers and a target sum, T. The problem is to find a vector of 0s and 1s such that the sum of the integers associated with 1s equals T. That is, given $S = [a_1, a_2, \ldots, a_n]$, and T, find a vector V of 0s and 1s such that

$$\sum_{i=1}^{n} a_i * v_i = T$$

For example, consider the list of integers [17,38,73,4,11,1] and the target number 53. The problem is to find which of the integers to select for the sum, that is, which should correspond with 1s in V. Clearly 73 cannot be a term, so we can ignore it. Trying 17, the problem reduces to finding a sum for (53 – 17 = 36). With a second target of 36, 38 cannot contribute, and 4 + 11 + 1 are not enough to make 36. We then conclude that 17 is not a term in the solution.

If 38 is in the solution, then the problem reduces to the new target (53 – 38 = 15). With this target, a quick glance at the remaining values shows that 4 and 11 complete the solution, since 4 + 11 = 15. A solution is thus 38 + 4 + 11.

This solution proceeded in an orderly manner. We considered each integer as possibly contributing to the sum, and we reduced the problem correspondingly. When one solution did not produce the desired sum, we backed up, discarding recent guesses and trying alternatives. This backtracking seriously impaired the speed of solution.

With only six integers, it did not take long to determine the solution. Fortunately, we discarded one of the integers (73) immediately as too large, and in a subproblem we could dismiss another integer (38) immediately. With many integers, it would have been much more difficult to find a solution, especially if they were all of similar magnitude so that we could not dismiss any immediately.

Superincreasing Knapsacks

Suppose we place an additional restriction on the problem: The integers of S must form a **superincreasing sequence,** that is, one where each integer is greater than the sum of all preceding integers. Then, every integer a_k would be of the form

$$a_k > \sum_{j=1}^{k-1} a_j$$

In the previous example, [1,4,11,17,38,73] is a superincreasing sequence. If we restrict the knapsack problem to superincreasing sequences, we can easily tell whether a term is included in the sum or not. No combination of terms less than a particular term can yield a sum as large as the term. For instance, 17 is greater than 1+4+11 (=16). If a target sum is greater than or equal to 17, then 17 or some larger term must be a term in the solution.

The solution of a **superincreasing knapsack** (also called a **simple knapsack**) is easy to find. Start with *T*. Compare the largest integer in *S* to it. If this integer is larger than *T*, it is not in the sum, so let the corresponding position in *V* be 0. If the largest integer is less than or equal to *T*, that integer is in the sum, so let the corresponding position in *V* be 1 and reduce *T* by the integer. Repeat for all remaining integers in *S*. An example solving a simple knapsack for targets 96 and 95 is shown in Figure 10-15.

The Knapsack Problem as a Public Key Cryptographic Algorithm

The Merkle–Hellman encryption technique is a public key cryptosystem. That is, each user has a public key, which can be distributed to anyone, and a private key, which is kept secret. The public key is the set of integers of a knapsack problem (*not* a superincreasing knapsack); the private key is a corresponding superincreasing knapsack. The contribution of Merkle and Hellman was the design of a technique for converting a superincreasing knapsack into a regular one. The trick is to change the numbers in a nonobvious but reversible way.

96:	73?	Yes	95:	73?	Yes
96 − 73 = 23:	38?	No	95 − 73 = 22:	38?	No
23:	17?	Yes	22:	17?	Yes
23 − 17 = 6:	11?	No	22 − 17 = 5:	11?	No
6:	4?	Yes	5:	4?	Yes
6 − 4 = 2:	1?	Yes	5 − 4 = 1:	1?	Yes
2 − 1 = 1	**No Solution**		1 − 1 = 0	**Solution**	

FIGURE 10-15 Example of Solving a Simple Knapsack.

Modular Arithmetic and Knapsacks

In normal arithmetic, adding to or multiplying a superincreasing sequence preserves its superincreasing nature, so that the result is still a superincreasing sequence. That is, if $a > b$ then $k * a > k * b$ for any positive integer k.

However, in arithmetic mod n, the product of two large numbers may in fact be smaller than the product of two small numbers, since results larger than n are reduced to between 0 and n–1. Thus, the superincreasing property of a sequence may be destroyed by multiplication by a constant mod n.

To see why, consider a system mod 11. The product $3 * 7 \bmod 11 = 21 \bmod 11 = 10$, while $3 * 8 \bmod 11 = 24 \bmod 11 = 2$. Thus, even though $7 < 8$, we find that $3 * 7 \bmod 11 > 3 * 8 \bmod 11$. Multiplying a sequence of integers mod some base may destroy the superincreasing nature of the sequence.

Modular arithmetic is sensitive to common factors. If all products of all integers are mapped into the space of the integers mod n, clearly there will be some duplicates; that is, two different products can produce the same result mod n. For example, if $w * x \bmod n = r$, then $w * x + n \bmod n = r$, $w * x + 2n \bmod n = r$, and so on. Furthermore, if w and n have a factor in common, then not every integer between 0 and n–1 will be a result of $w * x \bmod n$ for some x.

For instance, look at the integers mod 5. If $w = 3$ and $x = 1, 2, 3, \ldots$, the multiplication of $x * w \bmod 5$ produces all the results from 0 to 4, as shown in Table 10-13. Notice that after $x = 5$, the modular results repeat.

However, if we choose $w = 3$ and $n = 6$, not every integer between 0 and 5 is used. This occurs because w and n share the common factor 3. Table 10-14 shows the results of $3 * x \bmod 6$. Thus, there may be some values that cannot be written as the product of two integers mod n for certain values of n. For all values between 0 and n–1 to be produced, n must be **relatively prime** to w (that is, they share no common factors with each other).

If w and n are relatively prime, w has a multiplicative inverse mod n. That means that for every integer w, there is another integer w^{-1} such that $w * w^{-1} = 1 \bmod n$. A multiplicative inverse undoes the effect of multiplication: $(w * q) * w^{-1} = q$.

TABLE 10-13 $3 * x \bmod 5$.

x	3 * x	3 * x mod 5
1	3	3
2	6	1
3	9	4
4	12	2
5	15	0
6	18	3
7	21	1

TABLE 10-14 $3 * x \bmod 6$.

x	$3 * x$	$3 * x \bmod 6$
1	3	3
2	6	0
3	9	3
4	12	0
5	15	3
6	18	0
7	21	3

(Remember that multiplication is commutative and associative in the group mod n, so that $w * q * w^{-1} = (w * w^{-1}) * q = q \bmod n$.)

With these results from modular arithmetic, Merkle and Hellman found a way to break the superincreasing nature of a sequence of integers. We can break the pattern by multiplying all integers by a constant w and taking the result mod n where w and n are relatively prime.

Transforming a Superincreasing Knapsack

To perform an encryption using the Merkle–Hellman algorithm, we need a superincreasing knapsack that we can transform into what is called a hard knapsack. In this section we learn just how to do that.

We begin by picking a superincreasing sequence S of m integers. Such a sequence is easy to find. Select an initial integer (probably a relatively small one). Choose the next integer to be larger than the first. Then select an integer larger than the sum of the first two. Continue this process by choosing new integers larger than the sum of all integers already selected.

For example,

Sequence	Sum so far	Next term
[1,		
[1,	1	2
[1,2,	1 + 2 = 3	4
[1, 2, 4,	1 + 2 + 4 = 7	9
[1, 2, 4, 9,	1 + 2 + 4 + 9 = 16	19

is such a sequence.

The superincreasing sequence just selected is called a **simple knapsack.** Any instance of the knapsack problem formed from that knapsack has a solution that is easy to find.

After selecting a simple knapsack $S = [s_1, s_2, \ldots, s_m]$, we choose a multiplier w and a modulus n. The modulus should be a number greater than the sum of all s_i. The multiplier should have no common factors with the modulus. One easy way to guarantee this property is to choose a modulus that is a prime number, since no number smaller than it will have any common factors with it.

Finally, we replace every integer s_i in the simple knapsack with the term

$$h_i = w * s_i \bmod n$$

Then, $H = [h_1, h_2, \ldots, h_m]$ is a **hard knapsack**. We use both the hard and simple knapsacks in the encryption.

For example, start with the superincreasing knapsack $S = [1, 2, 4, 9]$ and transform it by multiplying by w and reducing mod n where $w = 15$ and $n = 17$.

$$1 * 15 = 15 \bmod 17 = 15$$

$$2 * 15 = 30 \bmod 17 = 13$$

$$4 * 15 = 60 \bmod 17 = 9$$

$$9 * 15 = 135 \bmod 17 = 16$$

The hard knapsack derived in this example is $H = [15, 13, 9, 16]$.

Example Using Merkle–Hellman Knapsacks

Let us look at how to use Merkle–Hellman encryption on a plaintext message P. The encryption algorithm using Merkle–Hellman knapsacks begins with a binary message. That is, the message is envisioned as a binary sequence $P = [p_1, p_2, \ldots, p_k]$. Divide the message into blocks of m bits, $P_0 = [p_1, p_2, \ldots, p_m]$, $P_1 = [p_{m+1}, \ldots, p_{2m}]$, and so forth. The value of m is the number of terms in the simple or hard knapsack.

The encipherment of message P is a sequence of targets, where each target is the sum of some of the terms of the hard knapsack H. The terms selected are those corresponding to 1 bits in P_i so that P_i serves as a selection vector for the elements of H. Each term of the ciphertext is $P_i * H$, the target derived using block P_i as the selection vector.

For this example, we use the knapsacks $S = [1, 2, 4, 9]$ and $H = [15, 13, 9, 16]$ obtained in the previous section. With those knapsacks, $w = 15$, $n = 17$, and $m = 4$. The public key (knapsack) is H, while S is kept secret.

The message

$$P = 0100101110100101$$

is encoded with the knapsack $H = [15, 13, 9,16]$ as follows.

P = 0100 1011 1010 0101
[0, 1, 0, 0] * [15, 13, 9, 16] = 13
[1, 0, 1, 1] * [15, 13, 9, 16] = 40
[1, 0, 1, 0] * [15, 13, 9, 16] = 24
[0, 1, 0, 1] * [15, 13, 9, 16] = 29

The message is encrypted as the integers 13, 40, 24, 29, using the public knapsack $H = [15, 13, 9, 16]$.

Knapsack Decryption Algorithm

The legitimate recipient knows the simple knapsack and the values of w and n that transformed it to a hard public knapsack. The legitimate recipient determines the value w^{-1} so that $w * w^{-1} = 1 \bmod n$. In our example, $15^{-1} \bmod 17$ is 8, since $15 * 8 \bmod 17 = 120 \bmod 17 = (17 * 7) + 1 \bmod 17 = 1$.

Remember that H is the hard knapsack derived from the simple knapsack S. H is obtained from S by

$$H = w * S \bmod n$$

(This notation, in which a constant is multiplied by a sequence, should be interpreted as $h_i = w * s_i \bmod n$ for all i, $1 \leq i \leq m$.)

The ciphertext message produced by the encryption algorithm is

$$C = H * P = w * S * P \bmod n$$

To decipher, multiply C by w^{-1}, since

$$w^{-1} * C = w^{-1} * H * P = w^{-1} * w * S * P = S * P \bmod n$$

To recover the plaintext message P, the legitimate recipient would solve the simple knapsack problem with knapsack S and target $w^{-1} * C_i$ for each ciphertext integer C_i. Since $w^{-1} * C_i = S * P \bmod n$, the solution for target $w^{-1} * C_i$ is plaintext block P_i, which is the message originally encrypted.

Example of Decryption

We continue our example, in which the underlying simple knapsack was $S = [1, 2, 4, 9]$, with $w = 15$ and $n = 17$. The transmitted messages were 13, 40, 24, and 29.

To decipher, these messages are multiplied by 8 mod 17 since 8 is 15^{-1} mod 17. Then we can easily solve the simple knapsacks, as shown here:

$$\begin{aligned}
13 * 8 &= 104 \bmod 17 = 2 = [0100] \\
40 * 8 &= 320 \bmod 17 = 14 = [1011] \\
24 * 8 &= 192 \bmod 17 = 5 = [1010] \\
29 * 8 &= 232 \bmod 17 = 11 = [0101]
\end{aligned}$$

The recovered message is thus `0100101110100101`.

Cryptanalysis of the Knapsack Algorithm

In this example, because m is 4, we can readily determine the solution to the knapsack problem for 13, 40, 24, and 29. Longer knapsacks (larger values of m), which also imply larger values of the modulus n, are not so simple to solve.

Typically, you want to choose the value of n to be 100 to 200 binary digits long. If n is 200 bits long, the s_i are usually chosen to be about 2^{200} apart. That is, there are about 200 terms in the knapsacks, and each term of the simple knapsack is between 200 and 400 binary digits long. More precisely, s_0 is chosen so that

$$\begin{aligned} 1 &\le s_0 < 2^{200}, \\ 2^{200} &\le s_1 < 2^{201}, \\ 2^{201} &\le s_2 < 2^{202}, \end{aligned}$$

and so on, so that there are approximately 2^{200} choices for each s_i.

You can use a sequence of m random numbers, $r_1, r_2, r_3, \ldots, r_m$ to generate the simple knapsack just described. Each r_i must be between 0 and 2^{200}. Then each value s_i of the simple knapsack is determined as

$$s_i = 2^{200+i-1} + r_i$$

for $i = 1, 2, \ldots, m$.

With such large terms for S (and H), it is infeasible to try all possible values of s_i to infer S given H and C. Even assuming a machine could do one operation every microsecond, it would still take 10^{47} years to try every one of the 2^{200} choices for each s_i. A massively parallel machine with 1000 or even 1,000,000 parallel elements would not reduce this work factor enough to weaken the encryption.

Weaknesses of the Merkle–Hellman Encryption Algorithm

The Merkle–Hellman knapsack method seems secure. With appropriately large values for n and m, the chances of someone's being able to crack the method by brute force attack are slim.

However, an interceptor does not have to solve the basic knapsack problem to break the encryption, since the encryption depends on specially selected instances of the problem. In 1980, Shamir found that if the value of the modulus n is known, it may be possible to determine the simple knapsack. The exact method is beyond the scope of this book, but we can outline the method of attack. For more information, see the articles by Shamir and Zippel [SHA80] and Adleman [ADL83].

First, notice that since all elements of the hard knapsack are known, you can readily determine which elements correspond to which elements of the simple knapsack. Consider h_0 and h_1, the first two elements of a hard knapsack, corresponding to simple knapsack elements s_0 and s_1.

Let

$$\rho = h_0 \,/\, h_1 \bmod n$$

Since $h_0 = w * s_0 \bmod n$ and $h_1 = w * s_1 \bmod n$, it is also true that

$$\rho = (w * s_0) \,/\, (w * s_1) = s_0 / s_1 \bmod n$$

Given the ratio ρ, determine the sequence

$$\Delta = \rho \bmod n,\ 2 * \rho \bmod n,\ 3 * \rho \bmod n,\ \ldots,\ k * \rho \bmod n,\ \ldots,\ 2m * \rho \bmod n$$

For some k, k and s_1 will cancel each other mod n; that is, $k * (1/s_1) = 1 \bmod n$. Then

$$k * \rho \bmod n = k * s_0 * 1 / s_1 \bmod n = s_0 \bmod n = s_0$$

It is reasonable to expect that s_0 will be the smallest element of Δ. Once s_0 is known, determining w, then w^{-1} and each of the s_i are not hard.

A more serious flaw was identified later by Shamir [SHA82]. The actual argument is also beyond the scope of this book, but again it can be sketched fairly briefly. The approach tries to deduce w and n from the h_i alone.

The approximate size of n can be deduced from the fact that it will be longer than any of the h_i, since they have been reduced mod n; however, n will not be substantially longer than the longest h_i, since it is likely that the results after taking the modulus will be fairly evenly distributed between 1 and n.

Assume you are trying to guess w. You might iteratively try different candidate values $\omega = 1, 2, 3, \ldots$ for w. The graph of $\omega * h_i$ mod n as a function of ω would increase steadily until a value of $\omega * h_i$ was greater than n. At that point, the graph of $\omega * h_i$ would be discontinuous and have a small value. The values of $\omega * h_i$ would then resume their steady increase as ω increased until $\omega * h_i$ exceeded n again. The graph would form a progression of jagged peaks, resembling the teeth of a saw. The slope of each "tooth" of the graph is h_i. Figure 10-16 displays a graphical representation of this process.

The correct value of $\omega = w$ occurs at one of the points of discontinuity of the graph of $\omega * h_i$ mod n. This same pattern occurs for all values h_i: h_1, h_2, and so forth. Since ω is a discontinuity point of $\omega * h_1$ mod n, it is also a discontinuity of $\omega * h_2$ mod n, of $\omega * h_3$ mod n, and so forth. To determine ω, superimpose the graph of $\omega * h_1$ mod n on $\omega * h_2$ mod n, superimpose those graphs on $\omega * h_3$ mod n, and so on. Then, w will be at one of the places where all of the curves are discontinuous and fall from a high value to a low one. Two such graphs are shown in Figure 10-17. The problem of determining w is thus reduced to finding the point at which all of these discontinuities coincide.

The actual process is a little more difficult. The value of n has been replaced by real number N. Since n and N are unknown, the graphs are scaled by dividing by N and then approximating by successive values of the real number ω/N in the function $(\omega/N) * h_i$ mod 1.0. Fortunately, this reduces to the solution of a system of simultaneous linear inequalities. That problem can be solved in polynomial time. Therefore, the Merkle–Hellman knapsack problem can be broken in reasonable time.

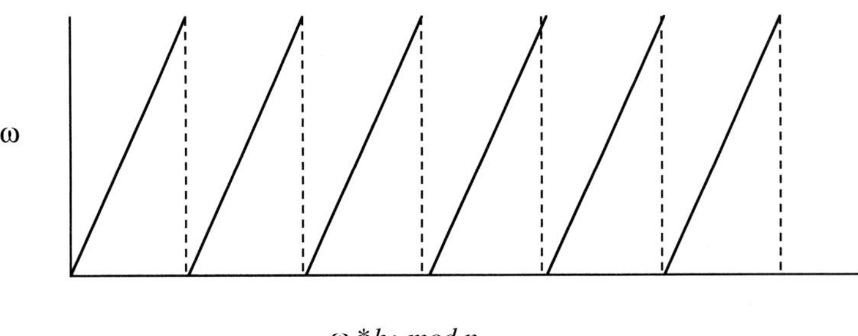

FIGURE 10-16 Graph of Change of Merkle–Hellman Knapsack Function.

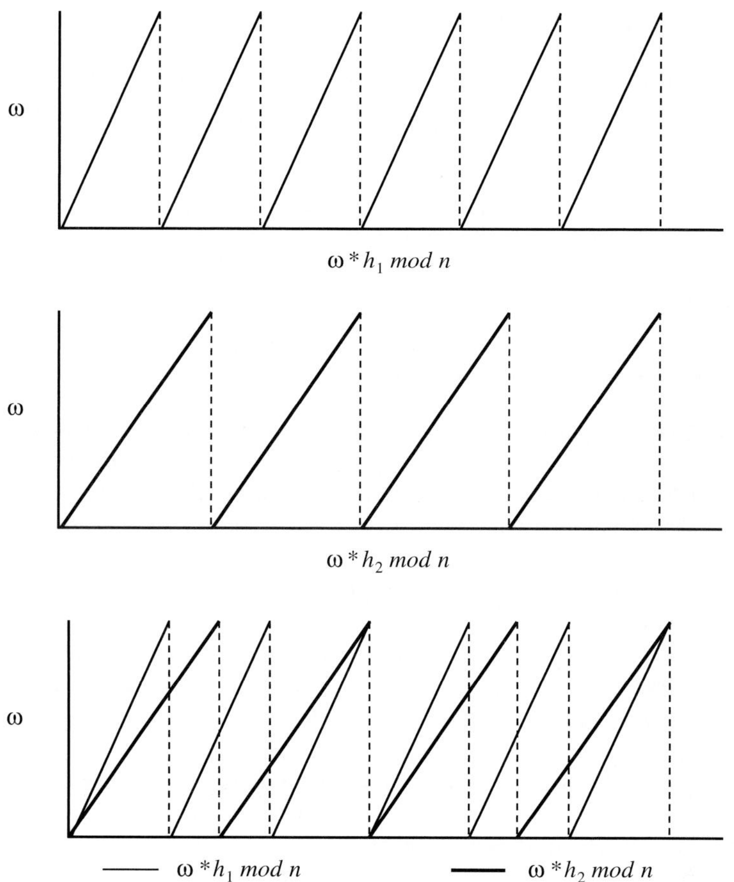

FIGURE 10-17 Coinciding Discontinuities.

Notice that this solution does not apply to the general knapsack problem; it applies only to the special class of knapsack problems derived from superincreasing sequences by multiplication by a constant modulo another constant. Thus, the basic knapsack problem is intact; only this restricted form has been solved. This result underscores the point that a cryptosystem based on a hard problem is not necessarily as hard to break as the underlying problem.

Since it has become known that the Merkle–Hellman knapsack can be broken, other workers have analyzed variations of Merkle–Hellman knapsacks. (See, for example, [BRI83] and [LAG83].) To date, transformed knapsacks do not seem secure enough for an application where a concerted attack can be expected. The Merkle–Hellman algorithm or a variation would suffice for certain low-risk applications. However, because the Merkle–Hellman method is fairly complicated to use, it is not often recommended.

Rivest–Shamir–Adelman (RSA) Encryption

The RSA algorithm is another cryptosystem based on an underlying hard problem This algorithm was introduced in 1978 by Rivest, Shamir, and Adelman [RIV78]. As with the Merkle–Hellman algorithm, RSA has been the subject of extensive cryptanalysis. No serious flaws have yet been found—not a guarantee of its security but suggesting a high degree of confidence in its use.

In this section, we present the RSA algorithm in two parts. First, we outline RSA, to give you an idea of how it works relative to the other algorithms we have studied. Then, we delve more deeply into a detailed analysis of the steps involved.

Introduction to the RSA Algorithm

On the surface, the RSA algorithm is similar to the Merkle–Hellman method, in that solving the encryption amounts to finding terms that add to a particular sum or multiply to a particular product. The RSA encryption algorithm incorporates results from number theory, combined with the difficulty of determining the prime factors of a target. The RSA algorithm also operates with arithmetic mod n.

Two keys, d and e, are used for decryption and encryption. They are actually interchangeable. (The keys for Merkle–Hellman were not interchangeable.) The plaintext block P is encrypted as $P^e \bmod n$. Because the exponentiation is performed mod n, factoring P^e to uncover the encrypted plaintext is difficult. However, the decrypting key d is carefully chosen so that $(P^e)^d \bmod n = P$. Thus, the legitimate receiver who knows d simply computes $(P^e)^d \bmod n = P$ and recovers P without having to factor P^e.

The encryption algorithm is based on the underlying problem of factoring large numbers. The factorization problem is not known or even believed to be NP-complete; the fastest known algorithm is exponential in time.

Detailed Description of the Encryption Algorithm

The RSA algorithm uses two keys, d and e, which work in pairs, for decryption and encryption, respectively. A plaintext message P is encrypted to ciphertext C by

$$C = P^e \bmod n$$

The plaintext is recovered by

$$P = C^d \bmod n$$

Because of symmetry in modular arithmetic, encryption and decryption are mutual inverses and commutative. Therefore,

$$P = C^d \bmod n = (P^e)^d \bmod n = (P^d)^e \bmod n$$

This relationship means that one can apply the encrypting transformation and then the decrypting one, or the decrypting one followed by the encrypting one.

Key Choice

The encryption key consists of the pair of integers (e, n), and the decryption key is (d, n). The starting point in finding keys for this algorithm is selection of a value for n. The value of n should be quite large, a product of two primes p and q. Both p and q should be large themselves. Typically, p and q are nearly 100 digits each, so n is approximately 200 decimal digits (about 512 bits) long; depending on the application, 768, 1024, or more bits may be more appropriate. A large value of n effectively inhibits factoring n to infer p and q.

Next, a relatively large integer e is chosen so that e is relatively prime to $(p - 1) * (q - 1)$. (Recall that "relatively prime" means that e has no factors in common with $(p - 1) * (q - 1)$.) An easy way to guarantee that e is relatively prime to $(p - 1) * (q - 1)$ is to choose e as a prime that is larger than both $(p - 1)$ and $(q - 1)$.

Finally, select d such that

$$e * d = 1 \bmod (p - 1) * (q - 1)$$

Mathematical Foundations of the RSA Algorithm

The **Euler totient function** $\varphi(n)$ is the number of positive integers less than n that are relatively prime to n. If p is prime, then

$$\varphi(p) = p - 1$$

Furthermore, if $n = p * q$, where p and q are both prime, then

$$\varphi(n) = \varphi(p) * \varphi(q) = (p - 1) * (q - 1)$$

Euler and Fermat proved that

$$x^{\varphi(n)} \equiv 1 \bmod n$$

for any integer x if n and x are relatively prime.

Suppose we encrypt a plaintext message P by the RSA algorithm so that $E(P) = P^e$. We need to be sure we can recover the message. The value e is selected so that we can easily find its inverse d. Because e and d are inverses mod $\varphi(n)$,

$$e * d \equiv 1 \bmod \varphi(n)$$

or

$$e * d = k * \varphi(n) + 1 \qquad (*)$$

for some integer k.

Because of the Euler/Fermat result, assuming P and p are relatively prime,

$$P^{p-1} \equiv 1 \bmod p$$

and, since $(p-1)$ is a factor of $\varphi(n)$,

$$P^{k*\varphi(n)} \equiv 1 \bmod p$$

Multiplying by P produces

$$P^{k*\varphi(n)+1} \equiv P \bmod p$$

The same argument holds for q, so

$$P^{k*\varphi(n)+1} \equiv P \bmod q$$

Combining these last two results with (*) produces

$$\begin{aligned}(P^e)^d &= P^{e*d} \\ &= P^{k*\varphi(n)+1} \\ &= P \bmod p \\ &= P \bmod q\end{aligned}$$

so that

$$(P^e)^d \equiv P \bmod n$$

and e and d are inverse operations.

Example

Let $p = 11$ and $q = 13$, so that $n = p * q = 143$ and $\varphi(n) = (p - 1) * (q - 1) = 10 * 12 = 120$. Next, an integer e is needed, and e must be relatively prime to $(p - 1) * (q - 1)$. Choose $e = 11$.

The inverse of 11 mod 120 is also 11, since $11 * 11 = 121 = 1 \bmod 120$. Thus, both encryption and decryption keys are the same: $e = d = 11$. (For the example, $e = d$ is not a problem, but in a real application you would want to choose values where e is not equal to d.)

Let P be a "message" to be encrypted. For this example we use $P = 7$. The message is encrypted as follows: $7^{11} \bmod 143 = 106$, so that $E(7) = 106$. (Note: This result can be computed fairly easily with the use of a common pocket calculator. $7^{11} = 7^9 * 7^2$. Then $7^9 = 40\,353\,607$, but we do not have to work with figures that large. Because of the reducibility rule, $a * b \bmod n = (a \bmod n) * (b \bmod n) \bmod n$. Since we will reduce our final result mod 143, we can reduce any term, such as 7^9, which is 8 mod 143. Then, $8 * 7^2 \bmod 143 = 392 \bmod 143 = 106$.)

This answer is correct, since $D(106) = 106^{11} \bmod 143 = 7$.

Use of the Algorithm

The user of the RSA algorithm chooses primes p and q, from which the value $n = p * q$ is obtained. Next e is chosen to be relatively prime to $(p - 1) * (q - 1)$; e is usually a prime larger than $(p - 1)$ or $(q - 1)$. Finally, d is computed as the inverse of e mod $(\varphi(n))$.

The user distributes e and n and keeps d secret; p, q, and $\varphi(n)$ may be discarded (but not revealed) at this point. Notice that even though n is known to be the product of two primes, if they are relatively large (such as 100 digits long), it will not be feasible to determine the primes p and q or the private key d from e. Therefore, this scheme provides adequate security for d.

It is not even practical to verify that p and q themselves are primes, since that would require considering on the order of 10^{50} possible factors. A heuristic algorithm from Solovay and Strassen [SOL77] can determine the probability of primality to any desired degree of confidence.

Every prime number passes two tests. If p is prime and r is any number less than p, then

$$\gcd(p, r) = 1$$

(where gcd is the greatest common divisor function) and

$$J(r, p) \equiv r^{(p-1)/2} \bmod p$$

where $J(r,p)$ is the **Jacobi function** defined as follows.

$$J(r, p) = \begin{cases} 1 & \text{if } r = 1 \\ J(r/2, p) * (-1)^{(p^2-1)/8} & \text{if } r \text{ is even} \\ J(p \bmod r, r) * (-1)^{(r-1)*(p-1)/4} & \text{if } r \text{ is odd and } r \neq 1 \end{cases}$$

If a number is suspected to be prime but fails either of these tests, it is definitely *not* a prime. If a number is suspected to be a prime and passes both of these tests, the likelihood that it is prime is at least 1/2.

The problem relative to the RSA algorithm is to find two large primes p and q. With the Solovay and Strassen approach, you first guess a large candidate prime p. You then generate a random number r and compute $\gcd(p,r)$ and $J(r, p)$. If either of these tests fails, p was not a prime, and you stop the procedure. If both pass, the likelihood that p was not prime is at most 1/2. The process repeats with a new value for r chosen at random. If this second r passes, the likelihood that a nonprime p could pass both tests is at most 1/4. In general, after the process is repeated k times without either test failing, the likelihood that p is not a prime is at most $1/2^k$.

Zimmerman [ZIM86] gives a method for computing RSA encryptions efficiently.

Cryptanalysis of the RSA Method

Like the Merkle–Hellman knapsack algorithm, the RSA method has been scrutinized intensely by professionals in computer security and cryptanalysis. Several minor problems have been identified with it, but there have been no flaws as serious as those for the Merkle–Hellman method.

El Gamal and Digital Signature Algorithms

Another public key algorithm was devised in 1984 by El Gamal [ELG84, ELG85]. While this algorithm is not widely used directly, it is of considerable importance in the U.S. Digital Signature Standard (DSS) [NIS92b, NIS94] of the National Institute of Standards and Technology (NIST). This algorithm relies on the difficulty of computing discrete logarithms over finite fields. Because it is based on arithmetic in finite fields, as is RSA, it bears some similarity to RSA.

We investigated digital signatures in Chapter 2. Recall that a digital signature is, like a handwritten signature, a means of associating a mark unique to an individual with a body of text. The mark should be unforgeable, meaning that only the originator should be able to compute the signature value. But the mark should be verifiable, meaning that others should be able to check that the signature comes from the claimed originator. The general way of computing digital signatures is with public key encryption; the signer computes a signature value by using a private key, and others can use the public key to verify that the signature came from the corresponding private key.

El Gamal Algorithm

In the El Gamal algorithm, to generate a key pair, first choose a prime p and two integers, a and x, such that $a < p$ and $x < p$ and calculate $y = a^x \bmod p$. The prime p should be chosen so that $(p - 1)$ has a large prime factor, q. The private key is x and the public key is y, along with parameters p and a.

To sign a message m, choose a random integer k, $0 < k < p - 1$, which has not been used before and which is relatively prime to $(p - 1)$, and compute

$$r = a^k \bmod p$$

and

$$s = k^{-1}(m - xr) \bmod (p - 1)$$

where k^{-1} is the multiplicative inverse of $k \bmod (p - 1)$, so that $k * k^{-1} = 1 \bmod (p - 1)$. The message signature is then r and s. A recipient can use the public key y to compute $y^r r^s \bmod p$ and determine that it is equivalent to $a^m \bmod p$. To defeat this encryption and infer the values of x and k given r, s, and m, the intruder could find a means of computing a discrete logarithm to solve $y = a^x$ and $r = a^k$.

Digital Signature Algorithm

The U.S. Digital Signature Algorithm (DSA) (also called the Digital Signature Standard or DSS) [NIS94] is the El Gamal algorithm with a few restrictions. First, the size of p is specifically fixed at $2^{511} < p < 2^{512}$ (so that p is roughly 170 decimal digits long). Second, q, the large prime factor of $(p - 1)$ is chosen so that $2^{159} < q < 2^{160}$. The algorithm explicitly uses $H(m)$, a hash value, instead of the full message text m. Finally, the computations of r and s are taken mod q. Largely, one can argue that these changes make the algorithm easy to use for those who do not want or need to understand the underlying mathematics. However, they also weaken the potential strength of the encryption by reducing the uncertainty for the attacker.

10.4 QUANTUM CRYPTOGRAPHY

Research into new ways of performing cryptography continues. We have seen how researchers have relied on aspects of mathematics to generate hard problems and to devise algorithms. In this section, we look at an alternative view of how cryptography may be done in the future. The approach we describe is not now on the market, nor is it likely to be so in the next few years. But it illustrates the need for creative thinking in inventing new encryption techniques. Although the science behind this approach is very difficult, the approach itself is really quite simple.

The novel approach, quantum cryptography, is in a way a variant of the idea behind a one-time pad. Remember from Chapter 2 that the one-time pad is the only provably unbreakable encryption scheme. The one-time pad requires two copies of a long string of unpredictable numbers, one copy each for the sender and receiver. The sender combines a number with a unit of plaintext to produce the ciphertext. If the numbers are *truly* unpredictable (that is, they have absolutely no discernible pattern), the attacker cannot separate the numbers from the ciphertext.

The difficulty with this approach is that there are few sources of sharable strings of random numbers. There are many natural phenomena that could yield a string of unpredictable numbers, but then we face the problem of communicating that string to the receiver in such a way that an interceptor cannot obtain them. Quantum cryptography addresses both problems, generating and communicating numbers. It was first explored by Wiesner [WIE83] in the 1980s; then the idea was developed by Bennett a decade later [BEN92A, BEN92b].

Quantum Physics

Unlike other cryptographic approaches, quantum cryptography is based on physics, not mathematics. It uses what we know about the behavior of light particles. Light particles are known as **photons**; they travel through space with a directional orientation. Photons vibrate in all directions as they travel. Although photons can have any directional orientation from 0° to 360°, for purposes of this cryptography, we can assume there are only four directional orientations. We can denote these four orientations with four symbols, ↔, ↕, ⤢ and ⤡. It is possible to distinguish between a ↔ and ↕ photon with high certainty. However, the ⤢ and ⤡ photons sometimes appear as ↔ or ↕. Similarly, it is possible to distinguish between ⤢ and ⤡, but sometimes ↔ and ↕ will be perceived as ⤢ or ⤡. Fortunately, those shortcomings are inconsequential to the cryptographic algorithm.

A **polarizing filter** is a device or procedure that accepts any photons as input but produces only certain kinds of photons as output. There are two types of photon filters: + and ×. A + filter correctly discriminates between ↔ and ↕ photons, but has a 50 percent chance of also counting a ⤢ or ⤡ as a ↔ or ↕; conversely, a × filter distinguishes between ⤢ and ⤡ but may also accept half of the ↔ and ↕ photons. Think of a + filter as a narrow horizontal slit through which a ↔ photon can slide easily, but a ↕ will always be blocked. Sometimes (perhaps half the time), a ⤢ or ⤡ photon vibrates in a way to sneak through the slit also.

Photon Reception

Quantum cryptography operates by sending a stream of photons from sender to receiver. The sender uses one of the polarizing filters to control which kind of photon is sent. The receiver uses either filter and records the orientation of the photon received. It does not matter if the receiver chooses the same filter the sender did; what matters is whether the receiver happened by chance to choose the same type as did the sender.

The most important property of quantum cryptography is that no one can eavesdrop on a communication without affecting the communication. With a little simple error detection coding, the sender and receiver can easily determine if there is an eavesdropper. Heisenberg's uncertainty principle says that we cannot know both the speed and location of a particle at any given time; once we measure the speed, the location has already changed, and once we measure the location, the speed has already changed. Because of this principle, when we measure any property of a particle, it affects other properties. So, for example, measuring the orientation of a photon affects the photon. A horizontal slit filter blocks all ↕ and half of the ⤢ and ⤡ photons, so it affects the photon stream coming through. The sender knows what was sent, the receiver knows what was received, but an eavesdropper will alter the photon stream so dramatically that sender and receiver can easily determine someone is listening.

Let us see how this unusual approach can be used for cryptography.

Cryptography with Photons

The cryptographic algorithm is very inefficient, in that more than twice the bits transmitted are not used in cryptography. The bits being transmitted are photons which, fortunately, are very highly available.

Suppose the sender, Sam, generates a series of photons, remembering their orientation. Sam and his receiver, Ruth, call ↔ or ⤢ 0 and ↕ or ⤡ 1. Such a series is shown in Figure 10-18.

Now, Ruth uses either of her polarizing filters, + and × at random, recording the result. Remember that a + filter will accurately distinguish between a ↔ and ↕ photon, but sometimes also declare a ⤢ or ⤡ as a ↔. So Ruth does not know if the results she measures are what Sam sent. Ruth's choice of filters, and the results she obtained, are shown in Figure 10-19.

Some of those results are correct and some are incorrect, depending on the filter Ruth chose. Now Ruth sends to Sam the kind of filter she used, as shown in Figure 10-20.

Sam tells Ruth which filters were the correct ones she used, as shown in Figure 10-21, from which Ruth can determine which of the results obtained were correct, as shown in Figure 10-22. In this example, Ruth happened to choose the right filter six times out of ten, slightly higher than expected, and so six of the ten photons transmitted were received correctly. Remembering that ↔ or ⤢ means 0 and ↕ or ⤡ means 1, Ruth can convert the photons to bits, as shown in the figure. In general, only half the

FIGURE 10-18 Transmission of Photons.

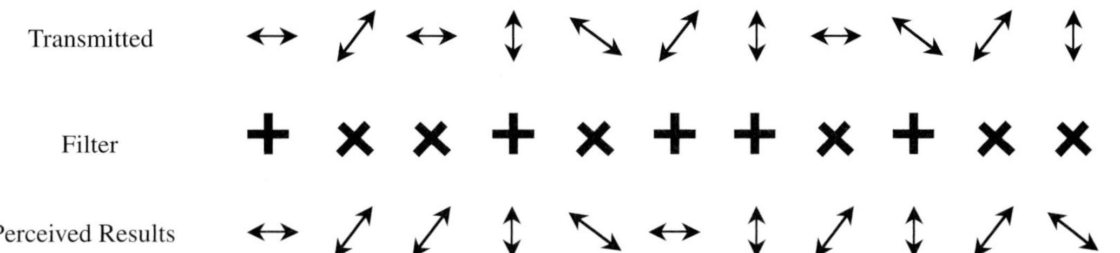

FIGURE 10-19 Results Interpreted Through Filters.

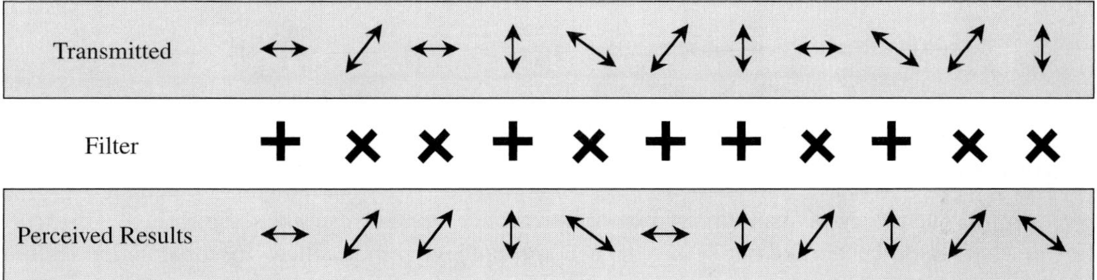

FIGURE 10-20 Filters Used.

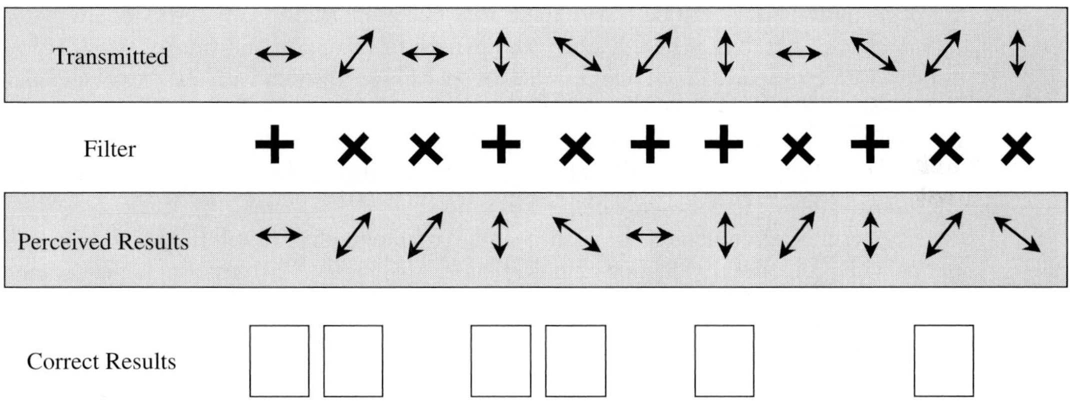

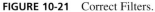

FIGURE 10-21 Correct Filters.

photons transmitted will be received correctly, and so only half the bandwidth of this communication channel carries meaningful data.

Notice that Ruth can tell Sam which filters she used and Sam can tell Ruth which of those will yield correct results, without revealing anything about the actual bits transmitted. In this way, Sam and Ruth can talk *about* their transmission without an eavesdropper's knowing what they actually share.

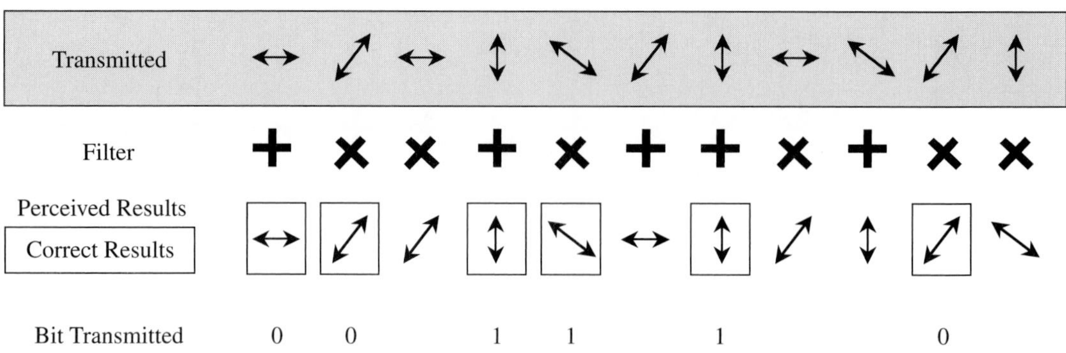

FIGURE 10-22 Correct Results.

Implementation

The theory of quantum cryptography is solid, but there are still some technical difficulties to be worked out before the scheme can be put in practice. To implement quantum cryptography, we need a source of photons randomly but detectably oriented (for the sender) and a means of filtering the received photons reliably. A photon gun can fire photons on demand. Several different research teams are working to develop photon guns for cryptography, but so far none has succeeded. The best current technology involves pulsed lasers, but here, too, there is a problem. Occasionally the laser emits not one but two photons, which disturbs the pattern of reception and transmission. However, with error correcting codes on the stream of bits, it is relatively easy to detect and correct a few erroneous bits.

On the receiving side, too, there are problems. One device is subject to catastrophic failure in which it emits a current surge. Although this surge is easily detected, it requires the device to be reset, which takes time.

Experimental implementations of quantum cryptography are still in the laboratories. The U.K. Defence Evaluation and Research Agency in Malvern, England, demonstrated a successful communication through the atmosphere over a distance of 2 km, and the U.S. Los Alamos National Laboratory is testing a portable device that can operate over 45 km on a clear night. However, these are experimental results, obtained at high cost, so ordinary use of the technique is still years away. Nevertheless, the technique is a promising approach for the future because it does not require Sam and Ruth to have prearranged any secret for subsequent communication.

10.5 SUMMARY OF ENCRYPTION

In this chapter we have continued the study of encryption begun in Chapter 2. This chapter has focused on the details of the cryptographic algorithms, as well as on their weaknesses. Cryptography is certainly a field that learns from its mistakes.

To be a cryptographer you need to understand many topics in mathematics: number theory, algebra, analysis, and probability, to name a few. Computational complexity, the source of NP-complete problems, has elements of both mathematics and computer science. All these fields have hard problems and open questions. But the good cryptographer cannot simply look to hard or unsolved problems as a basis for secure algorithms, because tomorrow someone could solve one of these hard problems or find a partial solution that undermines the expected difficulty of your algorithm.

We have studied the details of two symmetric algorithms: the older DES and the newer AES. The DES algorithm is still appropriate for protecting data of moderate sensitivity, such as e-mail messages or files of private data that nobody would expend a significant effort to break. But the structural flaw in DES is its rigidity: as processors became more powerful, there was no way to extend the work factor associated with breaking a 56-bit DES encryption. The AES is much more flexible, so we can expect it to evolve as the power of processors improves. Its 128-, 192-, and 256-bit key size should last quite well, and, as the inventors point out, the algorithm extends naturally beyond 256 bits.

We also studied the RSA asymmetric algorithm. It remains useful because it can use any key length; the only limitation is that longer key lengths require significantly more time to encrypt.

The concept of quantum cryptography has been around for decades, but implementing it is only now becoming feasible. It offers an entirely different approach to cryptography, from which any field profits on occasion.

10.6 TERMS AND CONCEPTS

computational complexity, 630
NP-complete problems, 631
satisfiability problem, 631
knapsack problem, 631
clique problem, 632
complexity class P, 633
complexity class NP, 633
nondeterministic Turing machine, 633
inverse, 637
divisor, 637
prime number, 637
composite number, 637
greatest common divisor, 637
Euclidean algorithm, 638
modular arithmetic, 638
commutative ring, 639
Galois field, 639
associativity, 639
commutativity, 639
distributivity, 639
reducibility, 639
Fermat's theorem, 641
confusion, 642
diffusion, 642
Data Encryption Standard (DES), 644
substitution, 645
permutation, 645
expansion permutation, 645
S-box, 650
P-box, 650
weak DES key, 657
differential cryptanalysis, 658
Advanced Encryption System (AES), 660
substitute byte, 661
shift row, 662
mix column, 662
add subkey, 662
public key encryption, 666
asymmetric algorithm, 666

Merkle–Hellman knapsack, 667
superincreasing knapsack, 669
Rivest–Shamir–Adelman (RSA) algorithm, 678
El Gamal digital signature algorithm, 682
quantum cryptography, 683

10.7 WHERE THE FIELD IS HEADED

Cryptography is a lively field; looking at the proceedings of the major conference, such as Crypto and Eurocrypt, you will see many new ideas and collegial challenges to older ones. NIST received approximately twenty proposals for the AES, from which it chose five finalists. Acknowledging that they had found no cryptanalytic flaws in any of the final five, the NIST researchers selected one for reasons of performance and implementation. The other four come from very respected cryptologists, and their continuing work is certainly worth watching.

The other area of interest is quantum cryptography. If it is to become viable, it will very soon move from the laboratory to model implementations.

10.8 TO LEARN MORE

The highly readable presentation of elementary cryptography by Sinkov [SIN66] is well worth study. A more precise and mathematical analysis is done by Konheim [KON80] and Meyer and Matyas [MEY82]. For historical—and foundational—reasons, one needs to know the works of Friedman [FRI76a,b,c]. See also the references for Chapter 2.

Schneier [SCH96] is an encyclopedia of cryptography that is both thorough and readable. Stinson [STI96] develops a course on serious cryptography. Smith [SMI01] presents a good overview of the AES selection process, and Landau [LAN00a,b] gives a good analysis of the challenges of DES and the advantages of AES.

10.9 EXERCISES

1. Show that formula $F = (v_1) \wedge (v_2 \vee v_3) \wedge (\neg v_3 \vee \neg v_1)$ is satisfiable, and justify that formula $G = (v_1) \wedge (v_2 \vee v_3) \wedge (\neg v_3 \vee \neg v_1) \wedge (\neg v_2)$ is not.
2. Are there any other cliques in the graph of Figure 10-1?
3. Give a procedure for locating a clique of size n in any given graph. What is the time complexity of your algorithm?
4. An algorithm with a GUESS statement can be replaced by two clones of procedures executing the algorithm, one clone executing as if TRUE had been the correct guess, and the other executing as if FALSE had been correct. If one of these clones later encounters another guess, it clones itself again, so that two clones become three. Suppose an algorithm executes in n steps. What is a limit to the number of cloned processes needed to simulate that algorithm?
5. Explain why 2^n is the difficulty factor for a deterministic solution to a nondeterministic problem of time n. That is, justify that the time bound 2^n is correct.

6. Differentiate between a problem and an instance of a problem. Cite an example of each.
7. Suppose an encryption algorithm is based on the satisfiability problem. Estimate the number of machine instructions necessary to solve the satisfiability problem by testing all cases. Using current technology hardware, how many variables are needed in the formula so that the time to solve this problem exceeds one year? What is the corresponding figure for hardware of five years ago? Ten years ago? Assuming similar speed improvements in the next five years, how long will it take to solve today's one-year-sized problem?
8. Compute gcd(1875, 405).
9. Justify that **NP** $\subset$ **EXP**; that is, that **NP** $\neq$ **EXP**. Hint: the way to do this is to show a problem in **EXP** that cannot be in **NP**.
10. Justify that $(a * b) \bmod n = ((a \bmod n) * (b \bmod n)) \bmod n$.
11. Write the addition and multiplication tables for the integers mod 4 and for the integers mod 7.
12. By Fermat's theorem, what is the multiplicative inverse of 2 in the field of integers mod 11?
13. With a public key encryption, suppose A wants to send a message to B. Let A_{PUB} and A_{PRIV} be A's public key and private key, respectively; similarly for B. Suppose C knows both public keys but neither private key. If A sends a message to B, what encryption should A use so that only B can decrypt the message? (This property is called secrecy.) Can A encrypt a message so that anyone receiving the message will be assured the message came only from A? (This property is called authenticity.) How or why not? Can A achieve both secrecy and authenticity for one message? How or why not?
14. Given the knapsack [17, 38, 23, 14, 11, 21], is there a solution for the target 42? Is there a solution for the target 43? Is there a solution for the target 44?
15. Convert the superincreasing knapsack [1, 3, 5, 11, 23, 47, 97] to a hard knapsack by multiplying by 7 mod 11; by 7 mod 29.
16. Encrypt the message `10110110100101` by each of the two hard knapsacks of the previous exercise.
17. Encrypt the message `10110110100101` by each of the two simple knapsacks of the previous exercise.
18. Is the Merkle–Hellman algorithm an "onto" algorithm? That is, is every number k, $0 \leq k < n$, the result of encrypting some number using a fixed knapsack?
19. Explain why the graph of $\omega * h_i$ is discontinuous when $\omega * h_i > n$.
20. Find keys d and e for the RSA cryptosystem where $p = 7$ and $q = 11$.
21. Find primes p and q so that 12-bit plaintext blocks could be encrypted with RSA.
22. Is the DES an onto function; that is, is every 64-bit binary string the result of encrypting some string?
23. Prove the complement property for the DES.
24. Is a product cipher necessarily as hard to break, more hard, or less hard than the product of the difficulties of the constituent ciphers? Justify your answer.
25. Could the full 64 bits of a DES key be used, thereby giving it a strength of 2^{64} instead of 2^{56}? Justify your answer.
26. (a) Assume each S-box substitution takes 8 units of time (because of the eight 6-bit substitutions), each P-box permutation takes 4 units of time (counting 1 unit per byte), each expansion permutation takes 8 units of time (because of the eight 4-bit expansions and permutations) and each initial and final permutation takes 8 units. Compute the number of units of time for an entire 16-round cycle of the DES.

    (b) Now suppose DES were redesigned to work with a 112-bit key and a cycle on 128 bits of input, by increasing the number of S- and P-boxes. You do *not* have to define the details of this design. Using similar timing assumptions as in the first part of this question, compute the number of units of time for an entire 16-round cycle of 112-bit DES.

(c) Perform a similar estimate for the timing of triple DES, using $E(k_1,D(k_2,E(k_1,m)))$.

27. Explain how the AES key length would be expanded to 256 + 64 = 320 bits. That is, explain what changes to the algorithm would be needed.

28. The Rijndael algorithm uses a byte substitution table that comes from a formula applied to $GF(2^8)$. Is it necessary to use that formula? That is, would any substitution table work? What restrictions are there on the form of the table?

29. A property of the Rijndael algorithm is that it is quite regular. Why is this both a good and bad property for a cryptographic algorithm?

30. Suppose you are designing a processor that would compute with encrypted data. For example, given two encrypted data values $E(x)$ and $E(y)$, the processor would compute $E(x) \oplus E(y)$, where $\oplus$ is an encrypted addition operator that performs addition on encrypted numbers. $D(E(x) \oplus E(y))$ must be the same as $x + y$. None of the encryption algorithms of this chapter has the property that $E(x) + E(y) = E(x + y)$, although the encrypted addition operator does not necessarily have to be +. For the three algorithms of this chapter, is there a relationship between $E(x)$, $E(y)$, $E(x + y)$?

Bibliography

A few notes on the bibliography: URLs are used sparingly because the pages they reference tend to move, disappear, or change. URLs are given for some older papers that are hard to locate any other way and that are posted at sites that will probably serve as archives.

The following abbreviations are used in this bibliography.

ACM	Association for Computing Machinery
Comm	Communications
Conf	Conference
Corp	Corporation
Dept	Department
IEEE	Institute for Electrical and Electronics Engineers
Proc	Proceedings
Symp	Symposium
Trans	Transactions
Univ	University

[ABA94] Abadi, M., and Needham, R. "Prudent Engineering Practice for Cryptographic Protocols." *Proc IEEE Symp on Security & Privacy,* 1994, p122–136.

[ABB76] Abbott, R., et al. "Security Analysis and Enhancements of Computer Operating Systems." *NBS Tech Report,* NBSIR-76-1041, 1976.

[ABR87] Abrams, M., and Podell, H. *Computer & Network Security—Tutorial.* IEEE Computer Society Press, 1987.

[ACT02] ActivNewsletter. "Lloyd's TSB Secures Online Banking Services with ActivCard Gold." *ActivNewsletter,* Feb 2002.

[ADA89] Adam, N., and Wortman, J. "Security-Control Methods for Statistical Databases: A Study." *ACM Computing Surveys,* v21 n4, Dec 1989, p515–556.

[ADA92a] Adam, J. "Threats and Countermeasures." *IEEE Spectrum,* v29 n8, Aug 1992, p21–28.

[ADA92b] Adam, J. "Cryptography = Privacy?" *IEEE Spectrum,* v29 n8, Aug 1992, p29–35.

[ADA92c] Adam, J. "Data Security." *IEEE Spectrum,* v29 n8, Aug 1992, p19–20.

[ADA92d] Adam, J., ed. "A Security Roundtable." *IEEE Spectrum,* v29 n8, Aug 1992, p41–44.

[ADA95] Adam, J. "The Privacy Problem." *IEEE Spectrum,* v32 n12, Dec 1995, p46–52.

[ADL82] Adleman, L. "On Breaking the Iterated Merkle–Hellman Public-Key Cryptosystem." *Proc Crypto Conf,* 1982, p303–308.

[ADL83] Adleman, L. "On Breaking Generalized Knapsack Public Key Cryptosystems." *Proc ACM Symp Theory of Computing,* 1983, p402–412.

[AFS83] AFSB (Air Force Studies Board). "Multilevel Data Management Security." *National Academy of Sciences Report,* 1983.

[AGN84] Agnew, G., et al. "Secrecy and Privacy in a Local Area Network Environment." *Proc Eurocrypt Conf,* 1984, p349–357.

[AGN88] Agnew, G., et al. "A Secure Public Key Protocol Based on Discrete Exponentiation." *Proc Eurocrypt Conf,* 1988.

[AGR00] Agrawal, R., and Srikant, R. "Privacy-Preserving Data Mining." *Proc ACM SIGMOD Conf on Management of Data,* May 2000.

[AIR00] U.S. Air Force. "Operational Risk Management." *Air Force Policy Directive,* 90-9, 1 Apr 2000.

[AKL83] Akl, S. "Digital Signatures: A Tutorial Survey." *IEEE Computer,* v16 n2, Feb 1983, p15–26.

[ALB01] Alberts, C., et al. "OCTAVE Catalog of Practices." *Software Engineering Institute Technical Report,* CMU/SEI-2001-TR-020, Oct 2001.

[ALB99] Alberts, C., et al. "Operationally Critical Threat, Asset and Vulnerability Evaluation (OCTAVE)" *Software Engineering Institute Technical Report,* CMU/SEI-99-TR-017, Jun 1999.

[ALE96] Aleph One. "Smashing the Stack for Fun and Profit." *Phrack,* v7 n49, Nov 1996.

[ALL99] Allen, J., et al. "State of the Practice of Intrusion Detection Technologies." *Software Engineering Institute Technical Report,* CMU/SEI-99-TR-028, 1999.

[AME83] Ames, S., et al. "Security Kernel Design and Implementation: An Introduction." *IEEE Computer,* v16 n7, Jul 1983, p14–23.

[AND01] Anderson, R. *Security Engineering: Guide to Building Dependable Distributed Systems.* Wiley, 2001.

[AND02] Anderson, R. "Security in Open versus Closed Systems—The Dance of Boltzmann, Coase and Moore." *Proc Open Source Software Conf: Economics, Law and Policy,* Toulouse, France, 21 Jun 2002.

[AND02a] Anderson, R. "Unsettling Parallels Between Security and the Environment." *Presentation at Univ of California Berkeley Workshop,* 2002.

[AND72] Anderson, J. "Computer Security Technology Planning Study." *U.S. Air Force Electronic Systems Division,* TR-73-51, Oct 1972. URL: *http://csrc.nist.gov/publications/history/ande72.pdf.*

[AND80] Anderson, J. "Computer Security Threat Monitoring and Surveillance." *James P. Anderson Co. Technical Report,* 1980.

[AND82] Anderson, J. "Accelerating Computer Security Innovation." *Proc IEEE Symp on Security & Privacy,* 1982, p91–97.

[AND85] Anderson, J. "A Unification of Computer and Network Security Concepts." *Proc IEEE Symp on Security & Privacy,* 1985, p77–87.

[AND94] Anderson, R. "Why Cryptosystems Fail." *Comm of the ACM,* v37 n11, Nov 1994, p32–41.

[AND98] Anderson, R. "The DeCODE Proposal for an Icelandic Health Database." *unpublished report,* 20 Oct 1998.

[AND98a] Anderson, R., et al. "Serpent: A Proposal for the Advanced Encryption Standard." *unpublished report,* undated. URL: *http://www.cs.technion.ac.il/~biham/Reports/ Serpent.*

[ANT02] Antón, P., et al. "Finding and Fixing Vulnerabilities in Information Systems: The Vulnerability Assessment and Mitigation Methodology." *RAND Corp Technical Report,* MR-1601-DARPA, 2002.

[ARB97] Arbaugh, W., et al. "A Secure and Reliable Bootstrap Architecture." *Proc IEEE Symp on Security & Privacy,* 1997, p65–71.

[ASL95] Aslam, T. "A Taxonomy of Security Faults in the UNIX Operating System." *Purdue Univ Dept of Computer Science Master's Thesis,* Aug 1995.

[ATT76] Attanasio, C., et al. "A Study of VM/370 Integrity." *IBM Systems Journal,* v15 n1, 1976, p102–116.

[BAD89] Badger, L. "A Model for Specifying Multi-Granularity Integrity Policies." *Proc IEEE Symp on Security & Privacy,* 1989, p269–277.

[BAD91a] Badger, L. "Covert Channel Analysis Planning for Large Systems." *TIS Technical Report,* Trusted Information Systems, Feb 1991.

[BAD91b] Badger, L. "TMach Covert Channel Analysis Plan." *TIS Technical Report,* Trusted Information Systems, Jan 1991.

[BAH02] Bahadur, G., et al. *Privacy Defended: How to Protect Your Privacy and Secure Your PC.* Que, 2002.

[BAL85] Baldwin, R., and Gramlich, W. "Cryptographic Protocol for Trustable Match Making." *Proc IEEE Symp on Security & Privacy,* 1985.

[BAL93] Balenson, D. "Privacy Enhancement for Internet Electronic Mail, Part III." *Internet report,* RFC 1423: Algorithms, Modes, Identifiers, Feb 1993.

[BAM82] Bamford, J. *The Puzzle Palace.* Houghton Mifflin, 1982.

[BAR90] Barker, W., and Pfleeger, C. "Civil and Military Applications of Trusted Systems Criteria." *TIS Technical Report,* 304, Feb 1990.

[BAR92] Barlow, J. "Decrypting the Puzzle Palace." *Comm of the ACM,* v35 n7, Jul 1992, p25–31.

[BAR99] Barwick, C., et al. "The MARS Encryption Algorithm." *unpublished IBM Corp Technical Report,* 27 Aug 1999. URL: *http://www.research.ibm.com/security/mars. html.*

[BEA88] Beauchemin, P., et al. "The Generation of Random Numbers That Are Probably Prime." *Journal Cryptology,* v1 n1, 1988, p53–64.

[BEC80] Beck, L. "A Security Mechanism for Statistical Data Bases." *ACM Trans on Data Base Systems,* v5 n3, Sep 1980, p316–338.

[BEK82] Beker, H., and Piper, F. *Cipher Systems.* Northwood Books, 1982.

[BEL02] Belcher, T., and Yoram, E. "Riptech Internet Security Threat Report." *Riptech, Inc Technical Report,* vII, Jul 2002.

[BEL73] Bell, D., and La Padula, L. "Secure Computer Systems: Mathematical Foundations and Model." *MITRE Report,* MTR 2547 v2, Nov 1973.

[BEL76] Bell, D., and La Padula, L. "Secure Computer Systems: Unified Exposition and Multics Interpretation." *U.S. Air Force Electronic Systems Division Technical Report,* ESD-TR-75-306, 1976. URL: *http://csrc.nist.gov/publications/history/bell76. pdf*

[BEL83] Bell, D. "Secure Computer Systems: A Retrospective." *Proc IEEE Symp on Security & Privacy,* 1983, p161–162.

[BEL89] Bellovin, S. "Security Problems in the TCP/IP Protocol Suite." *Computer Comm Review,* v19 n2, Apr 1989, p32–48.

[BEL91] Bellovin, S., and Merritt, M. "Limitations of the Kerberos Authentication System." *Proc Usenix Conf,* Winter 1991, p253–267.

[BEL92a] Bellare, M., and Micali, S. "How to Sign Given Any Trapdoor Permutation." *Journal of the ACM,* v39 n1, Jan 1992, p214–233.

[BEL92b] Bellovin, S., and Merritt, M. "Encrypted Key Exchange." *Proc IEEE Symp on Security & Privacy,* 1992, p72–84.

[BEL92c] Bellovin, S. "There Be Dragons." *Proc Usenix Unix Security Symp,* Sep 1992.

[BEL96] Bell, T. "Technology 1996: Communications." *IEEE Spectrum,* v33 n1, Jan 1996, p30–41.

[BEN72] Bensoussan, A., et al. "The Multics Virtual Memory: Concepts and Design." *Comm of the ACM,* v15 n5, May 1972, p308–318.

[BEN84] Benzel, T. "Analysis of a Kernel Verification." *Proc IEEE Symp on Security & Privacy,* 1984, p125–131.

[BEN92a] Bennett, C. "Experimental Quantum Cryptography." *Journal of Cryptology,* v5 n1, 1992, p3–28.

[BEN92b] Bennett, C., et al. "Quantum Cryptography." *Scientific American,* v267 n4, Oct 1992, p50–57.

[BER00] Berard, E. "Abstraction, Encapsulation and Information Hiding." *unpublished report,* 2000. URL: *http://www.itmweb.com/essay550.htm.*

[BER01] Berghal, H. "The Code Red Worm." *Comm of the ACM,* v44 n12, Dec 2001, p15–19.

[BER01a] Berghal, H. "Cyberprivacy in the New Millennium." *IEEE Computer,* v34 n1, Jan 2001, p134–136.

[BER88] Berson, T. "Interview with Roger Schell." *Unix Review,* Feb 1988, p60–69.

[BER92] Berson, T. "Differential Cryptanalysis Mod 2**32 with Applications to MD5." *Proc Eurocrypt Conf,* 1992.

[BIB77] Biba, K. "Integrity Considerations for Secure Computer Systems." *U.S. Air Force Electronic Systems Division Technical Report,* 76–372, 1977.

[BIH90] Biham, E., and Shamir, A. "Differential Cryptanalysis of DES-like Cryptosystems." *Proc Crypto Conf,* 1990, p2–21.

[BIH91] Biham, E., and Shamir, A. "Differential Cryptanalysis of FEAL and N-Hash." *Proc Eurocrypt Conf,* 1991, p1–16.

[BIH92] Biham, E., and Shamir, A. "Differential Cryptanalysis of Snefru, Khafre REDOC-II, LOKI, and Lucifer." *Proc Crypto Conf,* 1992, p156–171.

[BIH93] Biham, E., and Shamir, A. "Differential Cryptanalysis of the Full 16-Round DES." *Proc Crypto Conf,* 1993, p487–496.

[BIS86] Bishop, M. "Analyzing the Security of an Existing Comput System." *NASA RIACS Technical Report,* TR86.13, 1986.

[BIS89] Biskup, J. "Protection of Privacy and Confidentiality in Medical Information Systems." *Proc IFIP Workshop on Database Security,* 1989.

[BLA01] Blair, B. "Nukes: A Lesson From Russia." *Washington Post,* 11 Jul 2001, pA19.

[BLA79c] Blakely, G. "Safeguarding Cryptographic Keys." *Proc AFIPS National Computer Conf,* 1979, p313–317.

[BLA90] Black, D. "Scheduling Support for Concurrency and Parallelism in MACH." *IEEE Computer,* v23 n3, Mar 1990, p35–43.

[BLA96] Blaze, M., et al. "Minimal Key Lengths for Symmetric Ciphers to Provide Adequate Security." *unpublished report,* Jan 1996.

[BLU81] Blum, M. "Coin Flipping by Telephone." *SIGACT News,* 1981, p23–27.

[BLU83] Blum, M., et al. "Reducibility Among Protocols." *Proc Crypto Conf,* 1983, p137–146.

[BOE85] Boebert, W., and Kain, R. "A Practical Alternative to Hierarchical Integrity Policies." *Proc National Computer Security Conf,* 1985, p18–27.

[BOE92] Boebert, E. "Assurance Evidence." *Secure Computing Corp Technical Report,* 1 Jun 1992.

[BOE93] den Boer, B., and Bosselaers, A. "Collisions for the Compression Function of MD5." *Proc Eurocrypt Conf,* 1993, p293–304.

[BOL91] Bollinger, T., and McGowan, C. "A Critical Look at Software Capability Evaluations." *IEEE Software,* v8 n4, Jul 1991, p25–41.

[BOO81] Booth, K. "Authentication of Signatures Using Public Key Encryption." *Comm of the ACM,* v24 n11, Nov 1981, p772–774.

[BOW92] Bowles, J., and Pelaez, C. "Bad Code." *IEEE Spectrum,* v29 n8, Aug 1992, p36–40.

[BOW95] Bowen, J., and Hinchley, M. "Ten Commandments of Formal Methods." *IEEE Computer,* v28 n4, Apr 1995, p56–62.

[BRA02] Brauchle, R. "Hidden Risks in Web Code." *Software Testing and Quality Engineering Magazine,* v4 n2, Mar/Apr 2002, p12–13.

[BRA73] Branstad, D. "Privacy and Protection in Operating Systems." *IEEE Computer,* v6 n1, Jan 1973, p43–46.

[BRA77] Branstad, D., et al. "Report of the Workshop on Cryptography in Support of Computer Security." *NBS Technical Report,* NBSIR 77-1291, Sep 1977.

[BRA78] Branstad, D. "Security of Computer Communication." *IEEE Communications Society Magazine,* v16 n6, Nov 1978, p33–40.

[BRA79] Branstad, D. "Hellman's Data Does Not Support His Conclusion." *IEEE Spectrum,* v16 n7, Jul 1979, p41.

[BRA88] Brassard, G. *Modern Cryptology.* Springer-Verlag, 1988.

[BRA89] Branstad, M., et al. "Access Mediation in a Message Passing Kernel." *Proc IEEE Symp on Security & Privacy,* 1989, p66–72.

[BRE02] Brewin, B. "Retailers Defend Low-Level Security on Wireless LANs." *Computerworld,* 31 May 2002.

[BRE89] Brewer, D., and Nash, M. "The Chinese Wall Security Policy." *Proc IEEE Symp on Security & Privacy,* 1989, p206–214.

[BRI72] Brinch Hanson, P. "Structured Multiprogramming." *Comm of the ACM,* v15 n7, Jul 1972, p574–577.

[BRI82] Brickell, E., et al. "A Preliminary Report on Cryptanalysis of Merkle–Hellman Knapsacks." *Proc Crypto Conf,* 1982, p289–303.

[BRI83] Bright, H. "Modern Computational Cryptography." *Advances in Computer Security Management,* Wiley, 1983, p173–201.

[BRI88] Brickell, E., and Odlyzko, A. "Cryptanalysis: A Survey of Recent Results." *Proc of the IEEE,* v76 n5, May 1988, p578–593.

[BRI93] Brickell, E., et al. "Skipjack Review: Interim Report 1 Aug 93." *unpublished technical report,* 1 Aug 1993.

[BRO02] Brouersma, M. "Study Warns of Open-Source Security Danger." *ZDNet UK News,* 31 May 2002.

[BRO83] Browne, P., and Troy, E. "Designing Secure Data Processing Applications." *Advances in Computer Security Management,* Wiley, 1983.

[BRO87] Brooks, F. "No Silver Bullet." *IEEE Computer,* v20 n4, Apr 1987, p10–19.

[BRO96] Brooks, F. "The Computer Scientist as Toolsmith." *Comm of the ACM,* v39 n3, Mar 1996, p61–68.

[BUR89] Burns, R. "DBMS Integrity and Security Controls." *Report on Invitational Workshop on Data Integrity,* Sep 1989, pA7.

[BUR90] Burns, R. "Referential Secrecy." *Proc IEEE Symp on Security & Privacy,* 1990, p133–142.

[BUS01] Business Wire "Companies Hacked on Average Six or More Times Per Year." *Business Wire,* Aug 6, 2001.

[BUX02] Buxton, P. "Egg Rails at Password Security." *Netimperative,* 24 Jun 2002.

[CAL00] Caloyannides, M. "Encryption Wars: Early Battles." *IEEE Spectrum,* v37 n4, Apr 2000, p37–43.

[CAL00a] Caloyannides, M. "Encryption Wars: Shifting Tactics." *IEEE Spectrum,* v37 n5, May 2000, p46–51.

[CAM93] Campbell, K., and Wiener, M. "Proof That DES Is Not a Group." *Proc Crypto Conf,* 1993, p512–520.

[CCE94] CCEB (Common Criteria Editorial Board). "Common Criteria for Information Technology Security Evaluations." *CCEB Report,* Apr 1994.

[CCE98] CCEB (Common Criteria Editorial Board). "Common Criteria for Information Technology Security Evaluations." *Report,* CCIMB-99-031, Mar 1998.

[CER02] CERT (Computer Emergency Response Team). "Multiple Vulnerabilities in Many Implementations of Simple Network Management Protocol (SNMP)." *CERT Advisory,* CA-2002-03, 12 Feb 2002.

[CER99] CERT (Computer Emergency Response Team). "Results of the Distributed Systems Intruder Tools." *CERT Coordination Center Report,* Dec 1999.

[CHA00] Chapman, B., and Zwicky, E. *Building Internet Firewalls,* 2nd ed. O'Reilly, 2000.

[CHA01] Chaq, A. "Software Free-for-All." *Washington Post,* 5 Sep 2001.

[CHA81] Chaum, D. "Untraceable Electronic Mail, Return Addresses, and Pseudonyms." *Comm of the ACM,* v24 n2, Feb 1981, p84–88.

[CHA82] Chaum, D. "Blind Signatures for Untracable Payments." *Proc Crypto Conf,* 1982, p199–205.

[CHA85] Chaum, D. "Security Without Identification: Transaction Systems." *Comm of the ACM,* v28 n10, Oct 1985, p1030–1044.

[CHE02] Cheswick, W., and Bellovin, S. *Firewalls and Internet Security,* 2nd ed. Addison-Wesley, 2002.

[CHE81] Cheheyl, M., et al. "Verifying Security." *Computing Surveys,* v13 n3, Sep 1981, p279–339.

[CHE89] Chess, D. "Computer Viruses and Related Threats to Computer and Network Security." *Computer Networks and ISDN Systems,* v17, 1989, p141–147.

[CHE94] Cheswick, B., and Bellovin, S. *Firewalls and Internet Security.* Addison-Wesley, 1994.

[CHI89] Chiou, G., and Chen, W. "Secure Broadcasting using the Secure Lock." *IEEE Trans on Software Engineering,* SE-15 n8, Aug 1989, p929–934.

[CHR02] Christey, S., and Wysopal, C. "Responsible Vulnerability Disclosure Process." *Internet-Draft,* Internet Society, Feb 2002.

[CHR96] Christy, J. "Rome Laboratory Attacks: Prepared Testimony Before the Senate Governmental Affairs," in [DEN98], 22 May 1996.

[CLA77] Clark, R. *The Man Who Broke Purple.* Little-Brown, 1977.

[CLA87] Clark, D., and Wilson, D. "A Comparison of Commercial and Military Computer Security Policies." *Proc IEEE Symp on Security & Privacy,* 1987, p184–194.

[COF02] Coffee, P. "On the Mend?" *eWeek,* 3 Jun 2002.

[COH84] Cohen, F. "Computer Viruses." *Computer Security: A Global Challenge,* Elsevier Press, 1984, p143–158.

[COL94] Collins, W., et al. "How Good Is Good Enough?" *Comm of the ACM,* v37 n1, Jan 1994, p81–91.

[COL96] Coleridge, R. "The Cryptography API, or How to Keep a Secret." *Microsoft Technical White Paper,* MSDN Library, 19 Aug 1996.

[COM88] Comer, D. *Internetworking with TCP/IP.* Prentice-Hall, 1988.

[COO02] Cook, G. "At MIT They Can Put Words in Our Mouths." *Boston Globe,* 15 May 2002.

[COO71] Cook, S. "The Complexity of Theorem-Proving Procedures." *Proc ACM Symp Theory of Computing,* 1971, p151–158.

[COP92] Coppersmith, D. "DES and Differential Cryptanalysis." *private communication,* 23 Mar 1992.

[COR84] Corsini, P., et al. "Distributing and Revoking Authorizations on Abstract Objects." *Software—Practice and Experience,* v14 n10, Oct 1984, p931–943.

[COR91] Corbató, F. "On Building Systems That Will Fail." *Comm of the ACM,* v34 n9, Sep 1991, p72–81.

[CRO89] Crocker, S., and Bernstein, M. "ARPANet Disruptions: Insight into Future Catastrophes." *TIS (Trusted Information Systems) Report,* 247, 24 Aug 1989.

[CSE88] CSE (Communications Security Establishment). "Proceedings of the Evaluation Criteria Workshop." *Canadian Trusted Computing Product Evaluation Report,* Aug 1988.

[CSE90] CSE (Communications Security Establishment). "Proceedings of 1990 CTCPEC Availability Workshop." *Canadian Trusted Computing Product Evaluation Report,* Feb 1990.

[CSE94] CSE (Communications Security Establishment). *A Guide to Security Risk Management for IT Systems (Draft).* Government of Canada, May 1994.

[CSI01] (Computer Security Institute). "2001 CSI/FBI Computer Crime and Security Study." *Computer Security Issues & Trends,* v7 n1, Spring 2001.

[CSI02] CSI (Computer Security Institute). "2002 CSI/FBI Computer Crime and Security Study." *Computer Security Issues & Trends,* v8 n1, Spring 2002.

[CSR91] CSRI (Computer Systems Research Institute). "Composability of Trusted Systems." *Univ of Toronto Report,* Jan 1991.

[CSS93] CSSC (Canadian System Security Centre). *Canadian Trusted Computer Product Evaluation Criteria.* Jan 1993.

[CUG95] Cugini, J., et al. "Functional Security Criteria for Distributed Systems." *Proc National Computer Security Conference,* 1995, p310–321.

[CUL01] Culp, S. "It's Time to End Information Anarchy." *Microsoft Security Column,* Oct 2001.

[CUR87] Curtis, B., et al. "On Building Software Process Models Under the Lamppost." *Proc International Conf on Software Engineering,* 1987, p96–103.

[CUR90] Curry, D. "Improving the Security of Your Unix System." *SRI Tech Report,* ITSTD-721-FR-90-21, Apr 1990.

[CUT91] Cutler, K. "Commercial International Security Requirements." *American Express Travel Related Services Report,* American Express Travel Related Services, 1991.

[DAE00] Daemen, J., and Rikmen, V. "The Block Cipher Rijndael." *Smart Card Research and Applications,* Lecture Notes in Computer Science 1820, Springer-Verlag, 2000, p288–296.

[DAE02] Daemen, J., and Rijmen, V. *The Design of Rijndael.* Springer-Verlag, 2002.

[DAT81] Date, C. *An Introduction to Data Base Systems, vol 1.* Addison-Wesley, 1981.

[DAT83] Date, C. *An Introduction to Data Base Systems, vol.2.* Addison-Wesley, 1983.

[DAV78] Davida, G. "Data Base Security." *IEEE Trans on Software Engineering,* vSE-4 n6, Nov 1978, p531–533.

[DAV79] Davida, G. "Hellman's Scheme Breaks DES in its Basic Form." *IEEE Spectrum,* v16 n7, Jul 1979, p39.

[DAV80] Davies, D. "Protection." *Distributed Systems, An Advanced Course,* Springer-Verlag, 1980.

[DAV81] Davies, D. *The Security of Data in Networks.* IEEE Computer Society Press, 1981.

[DAV82] Davies, D. "Some Regular Properties of the Data Encryption Standard Algorithm." *Proc Crypto Conf,* 1982, p89–97.

[DAV83] Davies, D. "Applying the RSA Digital Signature to Electronic Mail." *IEEE Computer,* v16 n2, Feb 1983, p55–62.

[DAV83a] Davio, M., et al. "Propagation Characteristics of the Data Encryption Standard." *Proc Crypto Conf,* 1983, p171–202.

[DAV85] Davida, G., and Matt, B. "Crypto-Secure Operating Systems." *Proc AFIPS National Computer Conf,* 1985, p577–581.

[DAV89] Davies, D., and Price, W. *Security for Computer Networks (2nd ed).* Wiley, 1989.

[DAV96] Davis, R., et al. "A New View of Intellectual Property and Software." *Comm of the ACM,* v39 n3, Mar 1996, p21–30.

[DEA77] Deavours, C. "Unicity Points in Cryptanalysis." *Cryptologia,* v1 n1, Jan 1977, p46–68.

[DEA85] Deavours, C. *Machine Cryptography & Modern Cryptanalysis.* Artech House, 1985.

[DEA96] Dean, D., et al. "Java Security: Web Browsers and Beyond." *Proc IEEE Symp on Security & Privacy,* 1996, also in [DEN98].

[DEM82] DeMillo, R., et al. "Cryptographic Protocols." *Proc ACM Symp Theory of Computing,* 1982, p383–400.

[DEM83] DeMillo, R., and Merritt, M. "Protocols for Data Security." *IEEE Computer,* v16 n2, Feb 1983, p39–54.

[DEM87] DeMarco, T., and Lister, T. *Peopleware: Productive Projects & Teams.* Dorset House, 1987.

[DEM95] DeMarco, T. *Why Does Software Cost So Much?* Dorset House, 1995.

[DEN76a] Denning, D. "A Lattice Model of Secure Information Flow." *Comm of the ACM,* v19 n5, May 1976, p236–243.

[DEN77] Denning, D., and Denning, P. "Certification of Programs for Secure Information Flow." *Comm of the ACM,* v20 n7, Jul 1977, p504–513.

[DEN79a] Denning, D., and Denning, P. "Data Security." *Computing Surveys,* v11 n3, Sep 1979, p227–250.

[DEN79b] Denning, D., et al. "The Trackers: A Threat to Statistical Database Security." *ACM Trans on Data Base Systems,* v4 n1, Mar 1979, p76–96.

[DEN81a] Denning, D. "Restricting Queries That Might Lead to Compromise." *Proc IEEE Symp on Security & Privacy,* 1981, p33–40.

[DEN81b] Denning, D., and Sacco, G. "Timestamps in Key Distribution Protocols." *Comm of the ACM,* v24 n8, Jun 1981, p533–536.

[DEN82] Denning, D. *Cryptography and Data Security.* Addison-Wesley, 1982.

[DEN83a] Denning, D., and Schlörer, J. "Inference Controls for Statistical Data Bases." *IEEE Computer,* v16 n7, Jul 1983, p69–82.

[DEN83b] Denning, D. "Protecting Public Keys and Signature Keys." *IEEE Computer,* v16 n2, Feb 1983, p17–35.

[DEN83c] Denning, D. "Field Encryption and Authentication." *Proc Crypto Conf,* 1983, p231–247.

[DEN84] Denning, P., and Tichy, W. "Advanced Operating Systems." *IEEE Computer,* v17 n19, Oct 1984, p173–190.

[DEN85] Denning, D. "Commutative Filters for Reducing Inference Threats." *Proc IEEE Symp on Security & Privacy,* 1985, p134–146.

[DEN86] Denning, D. "An Intrusion-Detection Model." *Proc IEEE Symp on Security & Privacy,* 1986, p102–117.

[DEN87a] Denning, D. "Views for Multilevel Database Security." *IEEE Trans on Software Engineering,* vSE-13 n2, Feb 1987, p129–140.

[DEN87b] Denning, D. "An Intrusion-Detection Model." *IEEE Trans on Software Engineering,* vSE-13 n2, Feb 1987, p222–226.

[DEN88] Denning, P. "Computer Viruses." *American Scientist,* v76, May-June 1988, p236–238.

[DEN89] Denning, P. "The Internet Worm." *American Scientist,* v77, Mar-Apr 1989, p126–128.

[DEN90a] Denning, P. *Computers under Attack.* Addison Wesley, 1990.

[DEN90b] Denning, P. "Sending a Signal." *Comm of the ACM,* v33 n8, Aug 1990, p11–13.

[DEN91] Denning, D. "The United States vs Craig Neidorf." *Comm of the ACM,* v34 n3, Mar 1991, p24–43.

[DEN96] Denning, D., and Branstad, D. "A Taxonomy of Key Escrow Encryption Systems." *Comm of the ACM,* v39 n3, Mar 1996, p34–40.

[DEN98] Denning, D., and Denning, P. *Internet Besieged—Countering Cyberspace Scofflaws.* Addison-Wesley, 1998.

[DEN99] Denning, D. *Information Warfare and Security.* Addison-Wesley, 1999.

[DEN99a] Denning, D. "Activism, Hactivism, and Cyberterrorism: The Internet as a Tool for Influencing Foreign Policy." *World Affairs Council Workshop,* 10 Dec 1999.

[DES84] Desmedt, Y., et al. "Dependence of Output on Input in DES: Small Avalanche Characteristics." *Proc Crypto Conf,* 1984, p359–376.

[DIF76] Diffie, W., and Hellman, M. "New Directions in Cryptography." *IEEE Trans on Information Theory,* vIT-22 n6, Nov 1976, p644–654.

[DIF77] Diffie, W., and Hellman, M. "Exhaustive Cryptanalysis of the NBS Data Encryption Standard." *IEEE Computer,* v10 n6, Jun 1977, p74–84.

[DIF79] Diffie, W., and Hellman, M. "Privacy and Authentication." *Proc of the IEEE,* v67 n3, Mar 1979, p397–429.

[DIJ68a] Dijkstra, E. "GO TO Statement Considered Harmful." *Comm of the ACM,* v11 n3, Mar 68, p147.

[DIJ68b] Dijkstra, E. "The Structure of 'THE'-Multiprogramming System." *Proc ACM Symp Operating Systems Principles,* Oct 1968, reprinted in *Comm of the ACM,* v26 n1, Jan 1983.

[DIJ74] Dijkstra, E. "Self-Stabilizing Systems in Spite of Distributed Control." *Comm of the ACM,* v17 n11, Nov 1974, p643–644.

[DIJ76] Dijkstra, E. *A Discipline of Programming.* Prentice-Hall, 1976.

[DIL96] Dill, D., and Rushby, J. "Acceptance for Formal Methods: Lessons from Hardware Design." *IEEE Computer,* v29 n4, Apr 1996, p23–24.

[DIO92] Dion, R. "Elements of a Process Improvement Program." *IEEE Software,* v9 n4, Jul 1992, p83–85.

[DIO93] Dion, R. "Process Improvement and the Corporate Balance Sheet." *IEEE Software,* v10 n4, Jul 1993, p28–35.

[DOD85] DOD (U.S. Dept of Defense). "Trusted Computer Systems Evaluation Criteria." *DOD,* DOD5200.28-STD, Dec 1985.

[DOL82] Dolev, D., et al. "On the Security of Ping-Pong Protocols." *Proc Crypto Conf,* 1982, p177–186.

[DOT95] Doty, T. "Test Driving SATAN." *Computer Security Journal,* v ix n2, Fall 1995.

[DTI02] DTI (U.K. Dept. for Trade and Industry). "Information Security Breaches." *DTI Technical Report,* ISBS 2002, 2002.

[DTI89a] DTI (U.K. Dept. for Trade and Industry). "Security Functionality Manual." *DRAFT report,* v21 version 3.0, Feb 1989.

[DTI89b] DTI (U.K. Dept. for Trade and Industry). "Evaluation & Certification Manual." *DRAFT report,* v23 version 3.0, Feb 1989.

[DTI89c] DTI (U.K. Dept. for Trade and Industry). "Evaluation Levels Manual." *DRAFT report,* v22 version 3.0, Feb 1989.

[DUR99] Durst, R., et al. "Testing and Evaluating Computer Intrusion Detection Systems." *Comm of the ACM,* v42 n7, Jul 1999, p53–61.

[EFF98] EFF (Electronic Frontier Foundation). *Cracking DES.* O'Reilly, 1998.

[EHR78] Ehrsam, W., et al. "A Cryptographic Key Management Scheme for Implementing the DES." *IBM Systems Journal,* v17 n2, 1978, p106–125.

[EIC89] Eichlin, M., and Rochlis, J. "With Microscope and Tweezers: Analysis of Internet Virus." *Proc IEEE Symp on Security & Privacy,* 1989.

[ELG84] El Gamal, A. "A Public Key Cryptosystem and Signature Scheme Based on Discrete Logarithms." *Proc Crypto Conf,* 1984, p10–18.

[ELG85] El Gamal, A. "A Public Key Cryptosystem and Signature Scheme Based on Discrete Logarithms." *IEEE Trans on Information Theory,* vIT-31 n4, Jul 1985, p469–472.

[ELG86] El Gamal, A. "On Computing Logarithms over Finite Fields." *Proc Crypto Conf,* 1986, p396–402.

[ENG96] English, E., and Hamilton, S. "Network Security Under Seige: The Timing Attack." *IEEE Computer,* v30 n3, Mar 1996, p95–97.

[ERB01] Erbschloe, M. *Information Warfare: How to Survive Cyber Attacks.* Osborne/McGraw-Hill, 2001.

[EVA74] Evans, A., et al. "A User Authentication Scheme Not Requiring Secrecy in the Computer." *Comm of the ACM,* v17 n8, Aug 1974, p437–441.

[EVE85] Even, S., et al. "A Randomizing Protocol for Signing Contracts." *Comm of the ACM,* v28 n6, Jun 1985, p637–647.

[FAB74] Fabry, R. "Capability-Based Addressing." *Comm of the ACM,* v17 n7, Jul 1974, p403–412.

[FAG96] Fagin, R., et al. "Comparing Information Without Leaking It." *Comm of the ACM,* v39 n5, May 1996, p77–85.

[FAI97] Fairley, R., and Rook, P. "Risk Management for Software Development." In Dorfman M., and Thayer, R., eds. *Software Engineering,* Computer Society Press, 1997. Also in Thayer, R., and Christensen, M., eds. *Software Engineering—vol. 2 Supporting Processes,* 2nd ed. Computer Society Press, 2002.

[FAR90] Farmer, D., and Spafford, E. "The COPS Security Checker System." *Proc Summer Usenix Conf,* 1990, p165–170.

[FAR93] Farmer. D., and Venema, W. "Improving the Security of Your Site by Breaking Into It." unpublished technical report, 1993.

[FAR95] Farmer, D., and Venema, W. "SATAN: Security Administrator Tool for Analyzing Networks." *unpublished report,* 1995. URL: *http://www.cerias.purdue.edu/coast/satan.html.*

[FAR96] Farmer, D. "Shall We Dust Moscow?" *unpublished white paper,* 18 Dec 1996.

[FAR96a] Farringdon, J. *Analysing for Authorship: A Guide to the COSUM Technique.* Univ of Wales Press, 1996.

[FEI75] Feistel, H., et al. "Some Cryptographic Techniques for Machine Data Communication." *Proc of the IEEE,* v63 n1, Nov 1975, p1545–1554.

[FEI77] Feiertag, R., et al. "Proving Multilevel Security of a System Design." *Operating Systems Review,* v11 n5, Nov 1977, p57–63.

[FER81] Fernandez, E., et al. *Database Security and Integrity.* Addison-Wesley, 1981.

[FER89] Fernandez, E., et al. "A Security Model for Object-Oriented Databases." *Proc IEEE Symp on Security & Privacy,* 1989, p110–115.

[FIS02a] Fisher, D. "Trusting in Microsoft." *eWeek,* 4 Mar 2002.

[FIS02b] Fisher, D. "Patch or No, Flaws Go Public." *eWeek,* 28 May 2002.

[FIS02c] Fisher, D. "Coming Clean on Patches." *eWeek,* 3 Jun 2002.

[FIT89] Fites, P., et al. *Control and Security of Computer Information Systems.* Computer Science Press, 1989.

[FOR01] Forno, R. "Code Red Is Not the Problem." *Help Net Security,* Aug 27, 2001.

[FOR84] Fortune, S., and Merritt, M. "Poker Protocols." *Proc Crypto Conf,* 1984, p454–464.

[FOR96] Forrest, S., et al. "A Sense of Self for Unix Processes." *Proc IEEE Symp on Security & Privacy,* 1996.

[FOS82] Foster, C. *Cryptanalysis for Microcomputers.* Hayden, 1982.

[FOX90] Fox, K., et al. "A Neural Network Approach Towards Intrusion Detection." *Proc National Computer Security Conf,* Oct 1990.

[FRA02] Frank, D., and Dorobek, C. "New Hopes for a Security Lockdown." *Federal Computer Week,* 10 Jun 2002.

[FRA73] Frankena, W. *Ethics.* Prentice Hall, 1973.

[FRA83] Fraim, L. "Scomp: A Solution to the Multilevel Security Problem." *IEEE Computer,* v16 n7, Jul 1983, p26–34.

[FRI76a] Friedman, W. *Elementary Military Cryptography.* Aegean Park Press, 1976.

[FRI76b] Friedman, W. *Elements of Cryptanalysis.* Aegean Park Press, 1976.

[FRI76c] Friedman, W. *Advanced Military Cryptography.* Aegean Park Press, 1976.

[GAL99] Gallo, M., and Hancock, W. *Networking Explained.* Digital Press, 1999.

[GAN96] Ganesan, R. "The Yaksha Security System." *Comm of the ACM,* v39 n3, Mar 1996, p55–60.

[GAR00] Garfinkel, S. *Database Nation: The Death of Privacy in the 21st Century.* O'Reilly, 2000.

[GAR79] Garey, M., and Johnson, D. *Computers and Intractability.* W.H. Freeman, 1979.

[GAR84] Garvin, D. "What Does 'Product Quality' Really Mean?" *Sloan Management Review,* Fall, 1984, p25–45.

[GAR91a] Garfinkel, S., and Spafford, E. *Practical Unix Security.* O'Reilly & Assoc., 1991.

[GAR91b] Garvey, T., and Lunt, T. "Model-based Intrusion Detection." *Proc National Computer Security Conf,* 1991.

[GAR96] Garfinkel, S., and Spafford, [E.] *Practrical Unix and Internet Security,* 2nd ed. O'Reilly, 1996.

[GAS89] Gasser, M., et al. "Digital Distributed System Security Architecture." *Proc National Computer Security Conf,* 1989, p305–319.

[GAS88] Gasser, M. *Building a Secure System.* Van Nostrand Reinhold, 1988.

[GAS90] Gasser, M., and McDermott, E. "An Architecture for Practical Delegation in Distributed Systems." *Proc IEEE Symp on Security & Privacy,* 1990, p20–30.

[GER89] Gerhart, S. "Assessment of Formal Methods for Trustworthy Computer Systems." *Proc ACM TAV Conf,* 1989, p152–155.

[GER94] Gerhart, S., et al. "Experience with Formal Methods in Critical Systems." *IEEE Software,* v11 n1, Jan 1994, p21–28.

[GIB01] Gibson, S. "The Strange Tale of the Denial of Service Attacks Against GRC.COM." *Gibson Research Corp. Technical Report,* 2 Jun 2001. URL: *http:// grc.com/grcdos.html.*

[GIF82] Gifford, D. "Cryptographic Sealing for Information Secrecy/Authenticity." *Comm of the ACM,* v25 n4, Apr 1982, p274–285.

[GIL90] Gilbert, H., and Chauvaud, R. "A Statistical Attack on the FEAL-8 Cryptosystem." *Proc Crypto Conf,* 1990, p22–33.

[GIS88] GISA (German Information Security Agency). *IT-Security Criteria: Criteria for the Evaluation of Trustworthiness of IT Systems.* 1988.

[GLI87] Gligor, V., et al. "A New Security Testing Method and Application to the Secure Xenix Kernel." *IEEE Trans on Software Engineering,* vSE-13 n2, Feb 1987, p169–183.

[GLI88] Gligor, V., and Chandersekaran, C "Assessing the Costs." *Unix Review,* Feb 1988, p53–58.

[GLI91] Gligor, V., et al. "Logics for Cryptographic Protocols—Virtues and Limitations." *Proc IEEE Computer Security Foundations Workshop,* 1991, p219–226.

[GOA99] Goan, T. "Collecting and Appraising Intrusion Evidence." *Comm of the ACM,* v42 n7, Jul 1999, p46–52.

[GOG82] Goguen, J., and Meseguer, J. "Security Policies and Security Models." *Proc IEEE Symp on Security & Privacy,* 1982, p11–20.

[GOG84] Goguen, J., and Meseguer, J. "Unwinding and Inference Control." *Proc IEEE Symp on Security & Privacy,* 1984, p75–86.

[GOL77] Gold, B., et al. "VM/370 Security Retrofit Program." *Proc ACM Annual Conf,* 1977, p411–418.

[GOL84] Gold, B., et al. "KVM/370 in Retrospect." *Proc IEEE Symp on Security & Privacy,* 1984, p13–23.

[GOL99] Gollmann, D. *Computer Security.* Wiley, 1999.

[GON96] Gong, L., and Schemers, R. "Implementing Protection Domains in the Java Development Kit 1.2." *Proc Internet Society Symp on Network and Distributed System Security,* Mar 1996.

[GON97] Gong, L., et al. "Going Beyond the Sandbox: An Overview of the New Security Architecture in the Java Development Kit 1.2," *Proc Usenix Symp on Internet Technologies and Systems,* 1997.

[GOO84] Goodman, R., et al. "A New Trapdoor Knapsack Public Key Cryptosystem." *Proc Eurocrypt Conf,* 1984, p150–158.

[GOS85] Gosler, J. "Software Protection: Myth or Reality." *Proc Crypto Conf,* 1985, p140–157.

[GOS96] Gosling, J. *The Java Language Specification.* Addison-Wesley, 1996.

[GRA68] Graham, R. "Protection in an Information Processing Utility." *Comm of the ACM,* v11 n5, May 68, p365–369.

[GRA72] Graham, R., and Denning, P. "Protection—Principles and Practice." *Proc AFIPS Spring Joint Computer Conf,* 1972, p417–429.

[GRA83a] Grant, P., and Riche, R. "The Eagle's Own Plume." *US Naval Institute Proceedings,* Jul 1983, p29–33.

[GRA84a] Grampp, F., and Morris, R. "Unix Operating System Security." *AT&T Bell Labs Technical Journal,* v63 n8 pt2, Oct 1984, p1649–1672.

[GRA84b] Graubert, R., and Kramer, S. "The Integrity Lock Approach to Secure Database Management." *Proc IEEE Symp on Security & Privacy,* 1984.

[GRA85] Graubert, R., and Duffy, K. "Design Overview for Retrofitting the Integrity Lock Architecture." *Proc IEEE Symp on Security & Privacy,* 1985, p147–159.

[GRA87] Grady, R., and Caswell, D. *Software Metrics: Establishing a Company-wide Program.* Prentice Hall, 1987.

[GRA91] Gray, J. "Toward a Mathematical Foundation for Information Flow Security." *Proc IEEE Symp on Security & Privacy,* 1991, p21–34.

[GRI02] Griffin, P. "Security Flaw Shuts Down Telecom's Mobile Email." *New Zealand Herald,* 28 Apr 2002.

[GRI81] Gries, D. *Science of Programming.* Springer-Verlag, 1981.

[GUP91] Gupta, S., and Gligor, V. "Towards a Theory of a Penetration-Resistant System and its Applications." *Proc IEEE Workshop on Computer Security Foundations,* 1991.

[HAB76] Habermann, A., et al. "Modularization and Hierarchy in a Family of Operating Systems." *Comm of the ACM,* v19 n5, May 1976, p266–272.

[HAL67] Halmer, O. "Analysis of the Future: The Delphi Method." *RAND Corporation Technical Report,* P-3558, 1967.

[HAL95] Halme, L., and Bauer, R. "AINT Misbehaving—A Taxonomy of Anti-Intrusion Techniques." *Proc National Information Systems Security Conf,* 1995, p12–23.

[HAN00] Hancock, [W.] "A Practical Guide to Network Security." *Exodus Communications white paper,* 2000.

[HAN00a] Hancock, [W.] "Network Attacks: Denial of Service (DoS) and Distributed Denial of Service (DDoS)." *Exodus Communications white paper,* 2000.

[HAN76] Hantler, S., and King, J. "An Introduction to Proving the Correctness of Programs." *Computing Surveys,* v8 n3, Sep 1976, p331–353.

[HAR76] Harrison, M., et al. "Protection in Operating Systems." *Comm of the ACM,* v19 n8, Aug 1976, p461–471.

[HAR85] Harrison, M. "Theoretical Issues Concerning Protection in Operating System." *Advances in Computers,* 1985, p61–100.

[HAR86] Harris, C. *Applying Moral Theories.* Wadsworth, 1986.

[HEB91] Heberlein, L., et al. "A Method to Detect Intrusion Activity in a Networked Environment." *Proc National Computer Security Conf,* 1991.

[HEI01] Heitmeyer, C. "Applying Practical Formal Methods to the Specification and Analysis of Security Properties." *Proc Information Assurance in Computer Networks,* Lecture Notes in Computer Science, n2052, Springer Verlag, 2001.

[HEL77] Hellman, M. "An Extension of the Shannon Theory Approach to Cryptography." *IEEE Trans on Information Theory,* vIT-23 n3, May 1977, p289–294.

[HEL78] Hellman, M. "An Overview of Public Key Cryptography." *IEEE Communications Society Magazine,* v16 n6, Nov 1978, p24–32.

[HEL79] Hellman, M. "DES Will be Totally Insecure Within Ten Years." *IEEE Spectrum,* v16 n7, Jul 1979, p32–39.

[HEL79a] Hellman, M. "The Mathematics of Public Key Cryptography." *Scientific American,* v241 n2, Feb 1979, p146–157.

[HEL80] Hellman, M. "A Cryptanalytic Time-Memory Trade Off." *IEEE Trans on Information Theory,* vIT-26 n4, Jul 1980, p401–406.

[HIG88] Highland, H. "The Brain Virus: Fact and Fantasy." *Computers & Security,* v7 n5, 1988.

[HIN75] Hinke, T., and Schaefer, M. "Secure Data Management System." *Rome Air Development Center Technical Report,* TD-75-266, System Development Corp., 1975.

[HOA74] Hoare, C. "Monitors, An Operating System Structuring Concept." *Comm of the ACM,* v17 n10, Oct 1974, p548–557.

[HOB97] Hobbit. "CIFS: Common Insecurities Fail Security." *Avian Research white paper,* 1997. URL: *http://www.insecure.org/stf/cifs.txt.*

[HOF00] Hoffman, L. "Internet Voting: Will It Spur or Corrupt Democracy?" *Proc Computers, Freedom and Privacy Conf,* 2000.

[HOF70] Hoffman, L., and Miller, W. "Getting a Personal Dossier from a Statistical Data Bank." *Datamation,* v16 n5, May 1970, p74–75.

[HOF71] Hoffman, L. "The Formulary Model for Flexible Privacy and Access Controls." *Proc AFIPS Fall Joint Computer Conf,* 1971, p587–601.

[HOF77] Hoffman, L. *Modern Methods for Computer Security and Privacy.* Prentice-Hall, 1977.

[HOF86] Hoffman, L. "Risk Analysis and Computer Security: Bridging the Cultural Gap." *Proc National Computer Security Conf,* 1986.

[HOF90] Hoffman, L. *Rogue Programs: Viruses, Worms, Trojan Horses.* Prentice-Hall, 1990.

[HOF93] Hoffman, L. "Clipping Clipper." *Comm of the ACM,* v36 n9, Sep 1993, p15–17.

[HOF95a] Hoffman, L. *Building in Big Brother.* Prentice-Hall, 1995.

[HOF95b] Hoffman, L. "Balanced Key Escrow." *GWU Tech Report,* GWU-ICTSP-95-04, 4 Aug 1995.

[HOL91] Holbrook, P., and Reynolds, J., eds. "Site Security Handbook." *Internet report,* RFC 1244, Jul 1991.

[HOU01] Houle, K., and Weaver, G. "Trends in Denial of Service Attack Technology." *CERT Coordination Center Report,* 2001.

[HOU02] Householder, A., et al. "Computer Attack Trends Challenge Internet Security." *IEEE Computer,* Security and Privacy 2002 supplement, Apr 2002.

[HOU99] Housley, R. "Cryptographic Message Syntax." *Internet report,* RFC 2630, Apr 1999.

[HRW99] HRW (Human Rights Watch). "The Internet in the Mideast and North Africa: Free Expression and Censorship." *Human Rights Watch White Paper,* Jun 1999.

[HSI79] Hsiao, D., et al. *Computer Security.* Academic Press, 1979.

[HSI93] Hsieh, D., et al. "The Seaview Prototype." *SRI Technical Report,* 20 Aug 1993.

[HU91] Hu, W. "Reducing Timing Channels with Fuzzy Time." *Proc IEEE Symp on Security & Privacy,* 1991, p8–20.

[HUF95] Huff, C., and Martin, C. "Computing Consequences: A Framework for Teaching Ethical Computing." *Comm of the ACM,* v38 n12, Dec 1995, p75–84.

[HUL01] Hulme, G. "Full Disclosure." *Information Week,* 6 Aug 2001, p31–32.

[HUL01a] Hulme, G. "Code Red: Are You Ready For the Next Attack?" *Information Week,* 6 Aug 2001, p22.

[HUL01b] Hulme, G. "Sanctum Upgrade Takes Aim at External Threats." *Information Week,* 24 Sep 2001, p71.

[HUL01c] Hulme, G. "Management Takes Notice." *Information Week,* 3 Sep 2001, p28–34.

[HUL62] Hull, T., and Dobell, A. "Random Number Generators." *SIAM Review,* v4 n3, Jul 1962, p230–254.

[HUM00] Humphries, J., et al. "No Silver Bullet: Limitations of Computer Security Technologies." *Proc World Multiconference on Systems, Cybernetics and Informatics,* 23-26 Jul 2000.

[HUM88] Humphrey, W. "Characterizing the Software Process: A Maturity Framework." *IEEE Software,* v5 n2, Mar 1988, p73–79.

[HUM91a] Humphrey, W., and Curtis, B. "Comments on 'A Critical Look.'" *IEEE Software,* v8 n4, Jul 1991, p42–46.

[HUM91b] Humphrey, W. "Software Process Improvement at Hughes Aircraft." *IEEE Software,* v8 n4, Jul 1991, p11–23.

[ICO95] Icove, D., et al. *Computer Crime: A Crimefighter's Handbook.* O'Reilly & Assoc., 1995.

[IEE83] IEEE. *IEEE Standard 729: Glossary of Software Engineering Terminology.* IEEE Computer Society Press, 1983.

[ING86] Ingram, D. "Investigating and Prosecuting Computer Crime and Network Abuse." *Proc National Computer Security Conf,* Nov 1986.

[ISA02] ISA (Internet Security Alliance). "Common Sense Guides for Senior Managers: Top Ten Recommended Information Security Practices." *ISA Report,* Jul 2002.

[ISF00] ISF (Information Security Forum). "The Forum's Standard of Good Practice: The Standard for Information Security." *ISF white paper,* Nov 2000.

[ISO90] ISO (International Organization for Standardization). *ISO 9000-3: Guidelines for Application of ISO 9001.* International Organization for Standardization, 1990.

[ISO94] ISO (International Organization for Standardization). *ISO 9001: Model for Quality Assurance.* International Organization for Standardization, 1994.

[ISS02] ISS (Internet Security Systems). "Internet Risk Impact Summary for March 26, 2002 through June 24, *ISS Report,* 2002. URL: *http://www.iss.mnet*

[ITS91a] ITSEC Working Group. *ITSEC: Information Technology Security Evaluation Criteria.* 10 Jan 1991.

[ITS91b] ITSEC Working Group. *ITSEC: Information Technology Security Evaluation Criteria.* version 1.2, Sept 1991.

[JAG93] Jagannathan, R. "Next Generation Intrusion Detection Expert System: System Design Document." *SRI Tech Report,* A007, 9 Mar 1993.

[JAJ90] Jajodia, S., and Sandhu, R. "Database Security: Current Status and Key Issues." *SIGMOD Record,* v19 n4, Dec 1990, p123–126.

[JAN82] Janardan, R., and Lakshmanan, K. "A Public-Key Cryptosystem Based on the Matrix Cover NP-Complete Problem." *Proc Crypto Conf,* 1982, p21–39.

[JAV93] Javitz, H., et al. "Next Generation Intrusion Detection Expert Systems." *SRI Tech Report,* A016, 8 Mar 1993.

[JOH94] Johnson, D. *Computer Ethics,* 2nd ed. Prentice Hall, 1994.

[JOH95] Johnson, D., and Mulvey, J. "Accountability and Computer Decision Systems." *Comm of the ACM,* v38 n12, Dec 1995, p58–64.

[JON00] Jónatansson, H. "Iceland's Health Sector Database: A Significant Head Start in the Search for the Biological Grail or an Irreversible Error?" *American Journal of Law and Medicine,* v26 n1, 2000, p31–68.

[JON02] Jones, W., and Avioli, D. "Carnivore Bites Madly." *IEEE Spectrum,* v39 n7, Jul 2002, p19.

[JON75] Jones, A., and Wulf, W. "Towards the Design of Secure Systems." *Software—Practice and Experience,* v5 n4, Oct–Dec 1975, p321–336.

[JON78a] Jones, A. "Protection Mechanism Models: Their Usefulness." In *Foundations of Secure Computation,* Academic Press, 1978, p237–252.

[JON78b] Jones, A., and Lipton, R. "The Enforcement of Security Policies for Computation." *Journal of Computer and System Science,* v17 n1, Aug 1978, p35–55.

[JON91] Jones, T. *Applied Software Measurement.* McGraw-Hill, 1991.

[JOS01] Joshi, J., et al. "Security Models for Web-Based Applications." *Comm of the ACM,* v44 n2, Feb 2001, p38–44.

[JUE83] Jueneman, R., et al. "Authentication with Manipulation Detection Code." *Proc IEEE Symp on Security & Privacy,* 1983, p33–54.

[JUE87] Jueneman, R. "Electronic Document Authentication." *IEEE Network,* v1 n2, Apr 1987, p17–23.

[KAH67] Kahn, D. *The Codebreakers.* Macmillan, 1967.

[KAH96] Kahn, D. *The Codebreakers.* Scribners, 1996.

[KAI86] Kain, R., and Landwehr, C. "On Access Checking in Capability-Based Systems." *Proc IEEE Symp on Security & Privacy,* 1986, p95–100.

[KAL93a] Kaliski, B. "Privacy Enhancement for Internet Electronic Mail, Part IV." *Internet report,* RFC 1424: Key Certificates and Services, Feb 1993.

[KAN98] Kaner, C., and Pels, D. *Bad Software.* Wiley, 1998.

[KAR01] Karr, M. "Semiotics and the Shakespeare Authorship Debate: The Author—and His Icon—Do Make a Difference in Understanding the Works." *Shakespeare Oxford Newsletter,* v36 n4, Winter 2001.

[KAR02] Karger, P., and Schell, R. "Thirty Years Later: Lessons from the Multics Security Evaluation." *IBM Research Report,* RC22534, 31 July 2002.

[KAR72] Karp, R. "Reducibility Among Combinatorial Problems." *Complexity of Computer Computations,* Plenum Press, 1972, p85–104.

[KAR74] Karger, P., and Schell, R. "MULTICS Security Evaluation: Vulnerability Analysis, vol 2." *Electronic Systems Division Technical Report,* TR-74-193, 1974. URL: *http://csrc.nist.gov/publications/history.*

[KAR84] Karger, P., and Herbert, A. "An Augmented Capability Architecture to Support Lattice Security." *Proc IEEE Symp on Security & Privacy,* 1984, p2–12.

[KAR88] Karger, P. "Implementing Commercial Data Integrity with Secure Capabilities." *Proc IEEE Symp on Security & Privacy,* 1988, p130–139.

[KAR90] Karger, P., et al. "A VMM Security Kernel for the VAX Architecture." *Proc IEEE Symp on Security & Privacy,* 1990, p2–19.

[KAR91a] Karger, P., et al. "A Retrospective on the VAX VMM Security Kernel." *IEEE Trans on Software Engineering,* v17 n11, Nov 1991, p1147–1165.

[KAR91b] Karger, P., and Wray, J. "Storage Channels in Disk Arm Optimization." *Proc IEEE Symp on Security & Privacy,* 1991, p52–61.

[KAU95] Kaufman, C., et al. *Network Security: Private Communication in a Public World.* Prentice Hall, 1995.

[KEE89] Keefe, T., et al. "Secure Query-Processing Strategies." *IEEE Computer,* v22 n3, Mar 1989, p63–70.

[KEM02] Kemmerer, R., and Vigna, G. "Intrusion Detection: A Brief History and Overview." *IEEE Computer,* Security & Privacy 2002 supplement, Apr 2002, p27–30.

[KEM83] Kemmerer, R. "Shared Resource Matrix Methodology." *ACM Trans Computing Systems,* v1 n3, Oct 1983, p256–277.

[KEM86] Kemmerer, R. "Verification Assessment Study Final Report." *National Computer Security Center Technical Report,* NCSC C3-CR01-86, Mar 1986.

[KEM90] Kemmer, R. "A Multi-level Formal Specification of a Mental Health Care Database." *Proc IFIP Workshop on Database Security,* 1990, p1–23.

[KEN00] Kent, S. "On the Trail of Intrusions into Information Systems." *IEEE Spectrum,* v37 n12, Dec 2000, p52–56.

[KEN93] Kent, S. "Privacy Enhancement for Internet Electronic Mail, Part II." *Internet report,* RFC 1422: Certificate-Based Key Management, Feb 1993.

[KEN98] Kent, S., and Atkinson, R. "Security Architecture for the Internet Protocol." *Internet technical report,* RFC 2401, Nov 1998.

[KEP93] Kephart, J., et al. "Computers and Epidemiology." *IEEE Spectrum,* v30 n5, May 1993, p20–26.

[KIE78] Kieburtz, R., and Silberschatz, A. "Capability Managers." *IEEE Trans on Software Engineering,* vSE-4 n6, Nov 1978, p467–477.

[KIM98] Kim, G., and Spafford, E. "Tripwire: A Case Study in Integrity Monitoring." in [DEN98], 1998.

[KLE90] Klein, D. "Foiling the Cracker: Survey and Improvements of Password Security." *Proc Usenix Unix Security II Wkshop,* 1990, p5–14.

[KNI02] Knight, W. "Anti-Snooping Operating System Close to Launch." *The New Scientist,* 28 May 2002.

[KNI98] Knight, E., and Hartley, C. "The Password Paradox." *Business Security Advisor Magazine,* Dec 1998.

[KNU73] Knuth, D. *The Art of Computer Programming, vol. 1: Fundamental Algorithms.* Addison-Wesley, 1973.

[KNU81] Knuth, D. *The Art of Computer Programming, vol. 2: Seminumerical Algorithms.* Addison-Wesley, 1981.

[KO97] Ko, C. "Execution Monitoring of Security-Critical Programs in Distributed Systems: A *Proc IEEE Symp on Security & Privacy,* 1997, p175–187.

[KOC99] Kocher, P. "Breaking DES." *RSA Laboratories Cryptobytes,* v4 n2, 1999.

[KOH78] Kohnfelder, L. "Towards a Practical Public-Key Cryptosystem." *MIT EE Bachelor's Thesis,* 1978.

[KOH92] Kohl, J., et al. *The Evolution of Kerberos Authentication.* Computer Society Press, 1992.

[KOH93] Kohl, J., and Neuman, C. "The Kerberos Network Authentication Service (V5)." *Internet report,* RFC 1510, Sept 1993.

[KON80] Konheim, A., et al. "The IPS Cryptographic Programs." *IBM Systems Journal,* v19 n2, 1980, p253–283.

[KON81] Konheim, A. *Cryptography, A Primer.* Wiley, 1981.

[KUL76] Kullback, S. *Statistical Methods in Cryptanalysis.* Aegean Park Press, 1976.

[KUM95] Kumar, S. "Classification and Detection of Computer Intrusions." *Purdue Univ PhD Dissertation,* Aug 1995.

[KUM95a] Kumar, S., and Spafford, E. "A Software Architecture to Support Misuse Intrusion Detection." *Purdue Univ Computer Science Dept Technical Report,* CSD-TR-95-009, Mar 1995.

[KUR92] Kurak, C., and McHugh, J. "A Cautionary Note on Image Downgrading." *Proc Computer Security Applications Conf,* 1992, p153–159.

[LAG83] Lagarias, J. "Knapsack Public Key Cryptosystems and Diophantine Approximations." *Proc Crypto Conf,* 1983, p3–23.

[LAK74] Lackey, R. "Penetration of Computer Systems: An Overview." *Honeywell Computer Journal,* v8 n2, Sep 1974, p81–85.

[LAM00] Lampson, B. "Computer Security in the Real World." *Proc Computer Security Applications Conf,* 2000.

[LAM71] Lampson, B. "Protection." *Proc Princeton Symp,* reprinted in *Oper Sys Rev,* v8 n1, Jan 1974, p18–24.

[LAM73] Lampson, B. "A Note on the Confinement Problem." *Comm of the ACM,* v16 n10, Oct 1973, p613–615.

[LAM76] Lampson, B., and Sturgis, H. "Reflections on an Operating System Design." *Comm of the ACM,* v19 n5, May 1976, p251–266.

[LAM69] Lampson, B. "Dynamic Protection Structures." *Proc AFIPS Fall Joint Computer Conf,* 1969, p27–38.

[LAM81] Lamport, L. "Password Authentication with Insecure Communication." *Comm of the ACM,* v24 n11, Nov 1981, p770–771.

[LAM82] Lamport, L., et al. "The Byzantine Generals Problem." *ACM Trans on Prog. Languages and Systems,* v4 n3, Jul 1982, p382–401.

[LAM84] Lamport, L. "Solved Problems, Unsolved Problems, and Non-Problems in Concurrency." *Proc ACM Principles of Distributed Computing Conf,* 1984.

[LAM92] Lampson, B., et al. "Authentication in Distributed Systems: Theory and Practice." *Digital Equipment Corporation Systems Research Center,* Report 83, Feb 1992.

[LAN00a] Landau, S. "Standing the Test of Time: The Data Encryption Standard." *Notices of the AMS,* v47 n3, Mar 2000, p341–349.

[LAN00b] Landau, S. "Communications Security for the Twenty-First Century: The Advanced Encryption Standard. *Notices of the AMS,* v47 n4, Apr 2000, p450–459.

[LAN81] Landwehr, C. "Former Models for Computer Security." *Computer Surveys,* v13 n3, Sep 1981, p247–278.

[LAN83] Landwehr, C., et al. "The Best Available Technologies for Computer Security." *IEEE Computer,* v16 n7, Jul 1983, p86–100.

[LAN84] Landwehr, C., et al. "A Security Model for Military Message Systems." *ACM Trans Computing Systems,* v2 n2, Aug 1984, p198–222.

[LAN93] Landwehr, C., et al. "Computer Program Security Flaws." *NRL Tech Report,* Nov 1993.

[LAN94] Landau, S., et al. "Crypto Policy Perspectives." *Comm of the ACM,* v37 n8, Aug 1994, p115–121.

[LAU95] Laudon, K. "Ethical Concepts and Information Technology." *Comm of the ACM,* v38 n12, Dec 1995, p33–39.

[LAW02] Lawton, G. "Open Source Security: Opportunity or Oxymoron?" *IEEE Computer,* v35 n3, Mar 2002, p18–21.

[LEC83] Lechter, M. "Protecting Software and Firmware Devices." *IEEE Computer,* v16 n8, Aug 1983, p73–82.

[LEE88] Lee, T. "Using Mandatory Integrity to Enforce Commercial Security." *Proc IEEE Symp on Security & Privacy,* 1988, p140–146.

[LEM79] Lempel, A. "Cryptology in Transition." *Computing Surveys,* v11 n4, Dec 1979, p285–303.

[LEN01] Lenstra, A., and Verheul, E. "Selecting Cryptographic Key Sizes." *Journal of Cryptology,* v14 n4, 2001, p255–293.

[LEN78] Lennon, R. "Cryptographic Architecture for Information Security." *IBM Systems Journal,* v17 n2, 1978, p138–150.

[LEX76] Lexan Corp. "An Evaluation of the DES." *unpublished report,* Lexan Corp., Sep 1976.

[LIE89] Liepins, G., and Vaccaro, H. "Anomaly Detection: Purpose and Framework." *Proc National Computer Security Conf,* 1989, p495–504.

[LIE92] Liepens, G., and Vacarro, H. "Intrusion Detection: Its Role and Validation." *Computers and Security,* v11, 1992, p347–355.

[LIN75] Linde, R. "Operating System Penetration." *Proc AFIPS National Computer Conf,* 1975.

[LIN76] Linden, T. "Operating System Structures to Support Security and Reliability." *Computing Surveys,* v8 n4, Dec 1976, p409–445.

[LIN90] Linn, J. "Practical Authentication for Distributed Computing." *Proc IEEE Symp on Security & Privacy,* 1990, p31–40.

[LIN93] Linn, J. "Privacy Enhancement for Internet Electronic Mail, Part I." *Internet report,* RFC 1421: Message Encipherment and Authentication Procedures, Feb 1993.

[LIN93a] Linn, J. "Generic Security Service Application Programming Interface." *Internet report,* RFC 1508, Sept 1993.

[LIN93b] Linn, J. "Common Authentication Technology Overview." *Internet report,* RFC 1511, Sept 1993.

[LIN97] Linn, J. "Generic Security Services Application Programming Interface, version 2." *Internet tech report,* RFC 2078, Jan 1997.

[LIN99] Lindqvist, U., and Porras, P. "Detecting Computer and Network Misuse with the Production-Based Expert System Toolset." *Proc IEEE Symp on Security & Privacy,* 1999, p146–161.

[LIP77] Lipton, R., and Snyder, L. "A Linear Time Algorithm for Deciding Subject Security." *Journal of the ACM,* v 24 n3, Jul 1977, p455–464.

[LIP82] Lipner, S. "Non-Discretionary Controls for Commercial Applications." *Proc IEEE Symp on Security & Privacy,* 1982, p2–10.

[LIT99] Litchfield, D. "Alert: Microsoft's Phone Dialer Contains a Buffer Overflow that Allows Execution of Arbitrary Code." *NTBugtraq archives,* 30 Jul 1999.

[LOC94] Lockhart, H. *OSF DCE.* McGraw Hill, 1994.

[LON82] Longpre, L. "The Use of Public-Key Cryptology for Signing Checks." *Proc Crypto Conf,* 1982, p187–197.

[LU89] Lu, W., and Sundareshan, M. "Secure Communication in Internet Environments." *IEEE Trans on Communications,* vCOM37 n10, Oct 1989, p1014–1023.

[LUN89] Lunt, T. "Aggregation and Inference: Facts and Fallacies." *Proc IEEE Symp on Security & Privacy,* 1989, p102–109.

[LUN90] Lunt, T., and Fernandez, E. "Database Security." *SIGMOD Record,* v19 n4, Dec 1990, p90–97.

[LUN90a] Lunt, T., et al. "The SeaView Security Model." *IEEE Trans on Software Engineering,* vSE-16 n6, Jun 1990.

[LUN90b] Lunt, T., et al. "A Real-Time Intrusion Detection Expert System." *SRI Technical Report,* SRI-CSL-90-05, 1990.

[LUN92] Lunt, T., et al. "A Real-Time Intrusion Detection Expert System (IDES)." *SRI Technical Report,* Final Report, Feb 1992.

[LUN93] Lunt, T. "A Survey of Intrusion Detection Techniques." *Computers & Security,* v12 n4, Jun 1993, p405–418.

[LYN92] Lynch, D. *Internet Systems Handbook.* Addison Wesley, 1992.

[LYO89] de Lyons, G. "Ko Vaht Chan Ellz." *private communication,* 1989.

[MAH96] Maher, D. "Crypto Backup and Key Escrow." *Comm of the ACM,* v39 n3, Mar 1996, p48–53.

[MAN01] Mansfield, T., et al. "Biometric Product Testing Final Report." *National Physical Laboratory Technical Report,* 19, Mar 2001.

[MAN98] Mann, C. "Who Will Own Your Next Good Idea?" *Atlantic Monthly,* Sep 1998, p57–82.

[MAR98] Marks, L. *Between Silk and Cyanide.* Free Press, 1998.

[MAS95] Mason, R. "Ethics to Information Technology Issues." *Comm of the ACM,* v38 n12, Dec 1995, p55–57.

[MAT02] Matsumoto, T., et al. "Impact of Artificial Gummy Fingers on Fingerprint Systems." *Proc of SPIE: Optical Security and Counterfeit Detection Techniques IV,* v4677, 2002. URL: *tsuttomu@mlab.jks.ynu.ac.jp.*

[MAT78] Matyas, S., and Meyer, C. "Generation, Distribution and Installation of Cryptographic Keys." *IBM Systems Journal,* v17 n2, 1978, p126–137.

[MAT85] Matley, B. "Computer Privacy in America: Conflicting Practices—Policy Choices." *Proc IEEE Symp on Security & Privacy,* 1985, p219–223.

[MAT86] Matloff, N. "Another Look at Use of Noise Addition for Database Security." *Proc IEEE Symp on Security & Privacy,* 1986, p173–180.

[MAY90] Mayer, F., and Padilla, S. "What Is a B3 Architecture?" Trusted Information Systems *unpublished manuscript,* Jan 1990.

[MAY91] Mayfield, T., et al. "Integrity in Automated Information Systems." *C Technical Report,* 79-91, Sep 1991.

[MCA89] McAfee, J. "The Virus Cure." *Datamation,* v35 n4, 15 Feb 1989, p29–35.

[MCC79] McCauley, E., and Drongowski, P. "KSOS—The Design of a Secure Operating System." *Proc AFIPS National Computer Conf,* 1979, p345–353.

[MCC90] McCullough, D. "A Hookup Theorem for Multilevel Security." *IEEE Trans on Software Engineering,* vSE-16 n6, Jun 1990.

[MCD93] McDermid, John A. "Safety-Critical Software: A Vignette." *IEE Software Engineering Journal,* v8 n1, 1993, p2–3.

[MCI92] McIlroy, M., and Reeds, J. "Multilevel Security in the UNIX Tradition." *Software—Practice and Experience,* v22 n8, Aug 1992, p673–694.

[MCL90a] McLean, J. "The Specification and Modeling of Computer Security." *IEEE Computer,* v23 n1, Jan 1990, p9–16.

[MCL90b] McLean, J. "Security Models and Information Flow." *Proc IEEE Symp on Security & Privacy,* 1990, p180–187.

[MEA02] Mearian, L. "Banks Eye Biometrics to Deter Consumer Fraud." *Computerworld,* 28 Jan 2002.

[MEA86] Meadows, C. "A More Efficient Cryptographic Matchmaking Protocol." *Proc IEEE Symp on Security & Privacy,* 1986, p134–137.

[MER78a] Merkle, R. "Secure Communication over Insecure Channels." *Comm of the ACM,* v21 n4, Apr 1978, p294–299.

[MER78b] Merkle, R., and Hellman, M. "Hiding Information and Signatures in Trapdoor Knapsacks." *IEEE Trans on Information Theory,* vIT-24 n5, Sep 1978, p525–530.

[MER80] Merkle, R. "Protocols for Public Key Cryptosystems." *Proc IEEE Symp on Security & Privacy,* 1980, p122–133.

[MER81] Merkle, R., and Hellman, M. "On the Security of Multiple Encryption." *Comm of the ACM,* v24 n7, Jul 1981, p465.

[MEY82] Meyer, C., and Matyas, S. *Cryptography: A New Dimension in Computer Security.* Wiley, 1982.

[MIL76] Millen, J. "Security Kernel Validation in Practice." *Comm of the ACM,* v19 n5, May 1976, p243–250.

[MIL87a] Millen, J. "Covert Channel Capacity." *Proc IEEE Symp on Security & Privacy,* 1987.

[MIL87b] Millen, J., et al. "The Interrogator: Protocol Security Analysis." *IEEE Trans on Software Engineering,* vSE-13 n2, Feb 1987, p274–288.

[MIL88] Millen, J. "Covert Channel Analysis." *unpublished notes,* 1988.

[MIL92] Millen, J. "A Resource Allocation Model for Denial of Service." *Proc IEEE Symp on Security & Privacy,* 1992, p137–147.

[MIL95] Milberg, S., et al. "Values, Personal Information, Privacy, and Regulatory Approaches." *Comm of the ACM,* v38 n12, Dec 1995, p65–74.

[MIY89] Miyaguchi, S. "The FEAL-8 Cryptosystem and Call for Attack." *Proc Crypto Conf,* 1989, p624–627.

[MOF88] Moffett, J., and Sloman, M. "The Source of Authority for Commercial Access Control." *IEEE Computer,* v21 n2, Feb 1988, p59–69.

[MOO88] Moore, J. "Protocol Failures in Cryptosystems." *Proc of the IEEE,* v76 n5, May 1988, p594–602.

[MOR77] Morris, R., et al. "Assessment of the NBS Proposed Data Encryption Standard." *Cryptologia,* v1 n3, Jul 1977, p281–291.

[MOR79] Morris, R., and Thompson, K. "Password Security: A Case History." *Comm of the ACM,* v22 n11, Nov 1979.

[MOR85] Morris, R. "A Weakness in the 4.2BSD Unix TCP/IP Software." *AT&T Bell Laboratories Computing Science Technical Report,* 117, 1985.

[MUD95] Mudge. "How to Write Buffer Overflows." *L0pht report,* 20 Oct 1995.

[MUD97] Mudge. "NT LAN Manager Password Vulnerabilities." *L0phtcrack Technical Rant,* 1997.

[MUF92] Muffett, A. "Crack, A Sensible Password Checker for Unix." *unpublished report,* 1992. URL: *http://www.cert.org/pub/tools/crack.*

[MUK94] Muklherjee, B., et al. "Network Intrusion Detection." *IEEE Network,* May–Jun 1994, p26–41.

[MUL02] Mullins, J. "Making Unbreakable Code." *IEEE Spectrum,* v39 n5, May 2002, p40–45.

[MUL90] Mullender, S., et al. "Amoeba—A Distributed Operating System for the 1990s." *IEEE Computer,* v23 n5, May 1990, p44–53.

[MUR90] Murphy, S. "The Cryptanalysis of FEAL-4 with 20 Chosen Plaintexts." *Journal of Cryptology,* v2 n3, 1990, p145–154.

[MYE80] Myers, P. *Subversion: The Neglected Aspect of Computer Security,* Naval Postgraduate School Master's thesis, Jun 1980. URL: *http://csrc.nist.gov/publications/history/myer80.pdf.*

[NAS00] NASA. "MARS Program Assessment Report Outlines Route to Success." *Press Release,* 00-46, March 2000.

[NAS90] Nash, M., and Poland, K. "Some Conundrums Concerning Separation of Duty." *Proc IEEE Symp on Security & Privacy,* 1990, p201–207.

[NAS98] NAS (National Academy of Sciences). *Trust in Cyberspace.* National Academy Press, 1998.

[NAU93] Naur, P. "Understanding Turing's Universal Machine." *Computer Journal,* v36 n4, 1993, p351–371.

[NAV86] Navathe, S. "Integrating User Views in Database Design." *IEEE Computer,* v19 n1, Jan 1986, p50–61.

[NBS77] NBS (U.S. National Bureau of Standards). "Data Encryption Standard." *FIPS,* Publ. 46, Jan 1977.

[NBS80] NBS (U.S. National Bureau of Standards). "DES Modes of Operation." *FIPS,* Publ. 81, US Govt Print Ofc, 1980.

[NCS85] NCSC (National Comp Sec Center). *"Orange Book,"* same as [DOD85].

[NCS87] NCSC (National Comp Sec Center). "Trusted Network Interpretation." *National Computer Security Center,* NCSC-TG-005-ver1, 1987.

[NCS91a] NCSC (National Comp Sec Center). "A Guide to Understanding Data Remanence." *National Computer Security Center,* NCSC-TG-025 ver2, Sept 1991.

[NCS91b] NCSC (National Computer Security Center). "Integrity-Oriented Control Objectives." *C Technical Report,* 111-91, Oct 1991.

[NCS92] NCSC (National Computer Security Center). "Trusted Computer System Architecture: Assessing Modularity." *internal working paper,* unpublished, 18 Dec 1992.

[NEC96] Necula, G., and Lee, P. "Proof-Carrying Code." *Carnegie-Mellon Univ School of Computer Science Technical Report,* CMU-CS-96-165, Nov 1996.

[NEE78] Needham, R., and Schroeder, M. "Using Encryption for Authentication in Large Networks of Computers." *Comm of the ACM,* v21 n12, Dec 1978, p993–999.

[NEE78] Needham, R., and Schroeder, M. "Authentication Revisited." *ACM Operating Systems Review,* v21 n12, Dec 1978.

[NEE94] Needham, R. "Denial of Service: An Example." *Comm of the ACM,* v37 n11, Nov 1994, p42–47.

[NES86] Nessett, D. "Factors Affecting Distributed System Security." *Proc IEEE Symp on Security & Privacy,* 1986, p204–222.

[NES87] Nessett, D. "Factors Affecting Distributed System Security." *IEEE Trans on Software Engineering,* vSE-13, n2, Feb 1987.

[NEU78] Neumann, P. "Computer System Security Evaluation." *Proc AFIPS National Computer Conf,* 1978, p1087–1095.

[NEU82] Neugent, W. "Acceptance Criteria for Computer Security." *Proc AFIPS National Computer Conf,* 1982, p443–448.

[NEU83] Neumann, P. "Experience with Formality in Software Development." *Theory and Practice of Software Technology,* North-Holland, 1983, p203–219.

[NEU86] Neumann, P. "On Hierarchical Design of Comp Sys for Critical Applns." *IEEE Trans on Software Engineering,* vSE-12 n9, Sep 1986, p905–920.

[NEU90a] Neumann, P. "Toward Standards and Criteria for Critical Computer Systems." *Proc COMPASS Conf,* 1990.

[NEU90b] Neumann, P. "Rainbows and Arrows: How Security Criteria Address Misuse." *Proc National Computer Security Conf,* 1990, p414–422.

[NEU96] Neumann, P. "Primary Colors and Computer Evidence." *Risks Digest,* v18 n26, 18 Jul 1996.

[NEU98] Neu, C., et al. "E-Mail Communication Between Government and Citizens." *RAND Corp Issue Paper,* IP-178, 1998.

[NIS01] NIST (National Institute of Standards and Technology). "Specification for the Advanced Encryption System AES." *FIPS,* 197, 2001.

[NIS91b] NIST (National Institute of Standards & Technology). "Glossary of Computer Security Terminology." *NIST Tech Report,* NISTIR 4659, Sep 1991.

[NIS92b] NIST (National Institute of Standards & Technology). "The Digital Signature Standard, Proposal and Discussion." *Comm of the ACM,* v35 n7, Jul 1992, p36–54.

[NIS93] NIST (National Institute of Standards & Technology). "Secure Hash Standard." *FIPS,* Publ. 180, May 1993.

[NIS94] NIST (National Institute of Standards & Technology). "Digital Signature Standard." *FIPS,* Publ. 186, May 1994.

[NIS95] NIST (National Institute of Standards & Technology). "Secure Hash Standard." *FIPS,* Publ. 180-1, 17 Apr 1995.

[NOG02] Noguchi, Y. "High Wireless Acts." *Washington Post,* 28 Apr 2002.

[NOR00] Northcutt, S., et al. *Network Intrusion Detection*, 2nd ed. New Riders Publishing, 2000.

[NRC02] NRC (National Research Council). *Cybersecurity Today and Tomorrow: Pay Now or Pay Later.* National Academy Press, 2002.

[NRC91] NRC (National Research Council). *Computers at Risk: Safe Computing in the Electronic Age.* National Academy Press, 1991.

[NRC96] NRC (National Research Council). *Cryptography's Role in Securing the Information Society.* National Academy Press, 1996.

[NSA01] NSA (National Security Agency). "The 60 Minute Network Security Guide." *NSA white paper,* 2001. URL: *http://www.nsa.gov/Security-Recommendation-Guides.*

[NSA92] NSA (National Security Agency). "Federal Criteria for Information Technology Security." *NSA,* Dec 1992.

[NSA95a] NSA (National Security Agency). "SSE CMM: Systems Security Engineering Capability Maturity Model." *NSA SSE-CMM Model and Application Report,* Oct 2 1995.

[NSA95b] NSA (National Security Agency). "Security Service API Cryptographic API Recommendations." *NSA Report,* Jun 1995.

[OHA01] O'Harrow, R. "An Open Door to the E-Mailroom." *Washington Post,* 22 Jun 2001.

[OLO93] Olovsson, T. "Data Collection for Security Fault Forecasting." *PDCS Technical Report,* ESPRIT BRA 6362 PDCS 2, Aug 1993.

[OLS93] Olsen, N. "The Software Rush Hour." *IEEE Software,* v 10 n 5, May 1993, p29–37.

[OWA02] OWASP (Open Web Application Security Project). "A Guide to Building Secure Web Applications." *OWASP report,* 2002. URL: *http://www.owasp.org.*

[PAD79] Padlipsky, M., et al. "KSOS—Computer Network Applications." *Proc AFIPS National Computer Conf,* 1979, p373–381.

[PAL01] Palmer, C. "Ethical Hacking." *IBM Systems Journal,* v40 n3, 2001, p769–780.

[PAR72] Parnas, D. "On the Criteria to Be Used in Decomposing Systems into Modules." *Comm of the ACM,* v15 n12, Dec 1972, p1053–1058.

[PAR75] Parnas, D., and Siewiorek, D. "Use of the Concept of Transparency in the Design of Hierarchically Structured Operating Systems." *Comm of the ACM,* v18 n7, July 1975, p401–408.

[PAR79] Parker, D. *Ethical Conflicts in Computer Science and Technology.* AFIPS Press, 1979.

[PAR83] Parker, D. *Fighting Computer Crime.* Scribners, 1983.

[PAR84] Parker, D., and Nycum, S. "Computer Crime." *Comm of the ACM,* v27 n4, Apr 1984, p313–321.

[PAR98] Parker, D. *Fighting Computer Crime.* Wiley, 1998.

[PAU93] Paulk, M., et al. "Capability Maturity Model, version 1.1." *IEEE Software,* v10 n4, Jul 1993, p18–27.

[PAU95] Paulk, M. "How ISO 9001 Compares with the CMM." *IEEE Software,* v12 n1, Jan 1995, p74–82.

[PCS81] PCSG (Public Cryptography Study Group). "Report of the Public Cryptography Study Group." *Comm of the ACM,* v24 n7, Jul 1981, p434–450.

[PER95] Persson, S. "Security Policy for Swedish Post." *TIS Technical Report,* Aug 1995.

[PES01] Pescatore, J., et al. "Privacy and Security Still Challenge Microsoft Passport." *Gartner Group First Take Report,* FT-14-4259, 24 Sep 2001.

[PET85] Petroski, H. *To Engineer Is Human: The Role of Failure in Successful Design.* Petrocelli Books, 1985.

[PET91] Pethia, R., et al. "Guidelines for the Secure Operation of the Internet." *Internet report,* RFC 1281, Nov 1991.

[PET90] Pethia, R., and Crocker, S. "Internet Security Policy Recommendations." *Internet Engineering Task Force draft report,* 28 Nov 1990.

[PFL00] Pfleeger, S. "Risky Business: What We Have Yet to Learn About Software Risk Management." *Journal of Systems and Software,* v53 n3, Sep 2000.

[PFL01] Pfleeger, S., *Software Engineering: Theory and Practice,* 2nd ed. Prentice Hall, 2001.

[PFL01a] Pfleeger, S., et al. *Solid Software.* Prentice Hall, 2001.

[PFL85] Pfleeger, S., and Straight, D. *Introduction to Discrete Structures.* John Wiley and Sons, 1985.

[PFL88] Pfleeger, C., and Pfleeger S. "A Transaction Flow Approach to Software Security Certification." *Computers & Security,* v7 n3, 1988, p495–502.

[PFL89] Pfleeger, C., et al. "A Methodology for Penetration Testing." *Computers & Security,* v8, 1989, p613–620.

[PFL91] Pfleeger, S. *Software Engineering.* Macmillan, 1991.

[PFL91a] Pfleeger, S. "A Framework for Security Requirements." *Computers and Security,* v10, 1991, p515–523.

[PFL92] Pfleeger, C., and Mayfield T. "NCSC Availability Study." *Unpublished manuscript,* Institute for Defense Analyses, 1992.

[PFL93] Pfleeger, C. "How Can IT Be Safe If It's Not Secure?" *Proc Safety Critical Systems Conference,* Apr 1993.

[PFL94] Pfleeger, C. "Uses and Misuses of Formal Methods in Computer Security." *Proc IMA Conf on Mathematics of Dependable Systems,* 1994.

[PFL97] Pfleeger, C. "The Fundamentals of Information Security." *IEEE Software,* v14 n1, January 1997, p15–16, 60.

[PFL97a] Pfleeger, S., and Hatton, L. "Investigating the Influence of Formal Methods." *IEEE Computer,* v30 n2, Feb 1997.

[PLE77] Pless, V. "Encryption Schemes for Computational Confidentiality." *IEEE Trans on Computers,* vC-26 n11, Nov 1977, p1133–1136.

[POP74a] Popek, G. "Protection Structures." *IEEE Computer,* v7 n6, Jun 1974, p22–23.

[POP78] Popek, G., and Kline, C. "Encryption Protocols, Public Key Algorithms, and Digital Signatures." In DeMillo, R., ed. *Foundations of Secure Computation.* Academic Press, 1978, p133–155.

[POP78a] Popek, G., and Kline, C. "Issues in Kernel Design." *Proc AFIPS National Computer Conf,* 1978, p1079–1086.

[POP79a] Popek, G., et al. "UCLA Secure Unix." *Proc AFIPS National Computer Conf,* 1979, p355–364.

[PUR74] Purdy, G. "A High Security Log-In Procedure." *Comm of the ACM,* v17 n8, Aug 1974, p4422–445.

[PUR82] Purdy, G., et al. "A Software Protection Scheme." *Proc IEEE Symp on Security & Privacy,* 1982, p99–103.

[QIA94] Qian, X. "Inference Channel-Free Integrity Constraints for Multilevel Databases." *Proc IEEE Symp on Security & Privacy,* 1994, p158–167.

[RAB78] Rabin, M. "Digitalized Signatures." In DeMillo, R., ed. *Foundations of Secure Computation.* Academic Press, 1978, p155–166.

[RAM99] Ramdell, B. "S/MIME Version3 Message Specification." *Internet technical report,* RFC 2633, Apr 1999.

[RAN92] Ranum, M. "A Network Firewall." *Proc International Conf on Systems and Network Security and Management (SANS-1),* Nov 1992.

[RAN94] Ranum, M., and Avolio, F. "A Toolkit and Methods for Internet Firewalls." *Proc Usenix Security Symp,* 1994.

[RAN95] Ranum, M. "Marcus J Ranum Certified Apparently OK: On the Topic of Firewall Testing." *Unpublished manuscript,* 1995.

[REE77] Reeds, J. "'Cracking' a Random Number Generator." *Cryptologia,* v1 n1, Jan 1977, p20–26.

[REE84] Reeds, J., and Weinberger, P. "File Security and the Unix Operating System 'crypt' Command." *AT&T Bell Labs Technical Journal,* v63 n8 pt2, Oct 1984, p1673–1684.

[REI87] Reid, B. "Reflections on Some Recent Widespread Computer Breakins." *Comm of the ACM,* v30 n2, Feb 1987.

[RIP02] Riptech, Inc. "Internet Security Threat Report." *Riptech Technical Report,* v2, Jul 2002.

[RIT79] Ritchie, D. "On the Security of UNIX." *Unix Programmer's Manual, secn. 2,* AT&T Bell Labs., 1979.

[RIV78] Rivest, R., et al. "A Method for Obtaining Digital Signatures and Public-Key Cryptosystems." *Comm of the ACM,* v21 n2, Feb 1978, p120–126.

[RIV91] Rivest, R. "The MD4 Message Digest Algorithm." *Proc Crypto Conf,* 1991, p303–311.

[RIV92] Rivest, R. "The MD4 Message Digest Algorithm." *Internet report,* RFC 1186, Oct 1992.

[RIV92a] Rivest, R. "The MD4 Message-Digest Algorithm." *Internet report,* RFC 1320, Apr 1992.

[RIV92b] Rivest, R. "The MD5 Message-Digest Algorithm." *Internet report,* RFC 1321, Apr 1992.

[RIV92c] Rivest, R. "Response to NIST's Proposal." *Comm of the ACM,* v35 n7, Jul 1992, p41–47.

[RIV98] Rivest, R., et al. "The RC6 BlockCipher, version 1.1." *RSA Labs upublished report,* 20 Aug 1998. URL: *http://theory.lcs.mit.edu/~rivest/publications.html.*

[ROC89] Rochlis, J., and Eichin, M. "With Microscope and Tweezers: The Worm from MIT's Perspective." *Comm of the ACM,* v30 n6, Jun 1989.

[ROO93] Rook, P. "Risk Management for Software Development." *ESCOM Tutorial,* 24 Mar 1993.

[ROS30] Ross, W. *The Right and the Good.* Springer-Verlag, 1930.

[ROS91] Rosen, K. "Network Security: Just Say 'Know' at Layer 7." *Data Communications,* Mar 1991, p103–105.

[RUB00] Rubin, A. "Security Considerations for Remote Electronic Voting over the Internet." *Proc Internet Policy Institute Workshop on Internet Voting,* Oct 2000.

[RUB01] Rubin, A. *White Hat Arsenal.* Addison-Wesley, 2001.

[RUB97] Rubin, A., et al. *Web Security Sourcebook.* Wiley, 1997.

[RUB98] Rubin, A., and Geer, D. "Mobile Code Security." *IEEE Internet Computing,* Nov–Dec 1998.

[RUS83] Rushby, J., and Randell, B. "A Distributed Secure System." *IEEE Computer,* v16 n7, Jul 1983, p55–67.

[RUS85] Rushby, J. "Networks Are Systems." *Proc DOD Computer Security Center Workshop on Network Security,* 1985, p7-24–7-38.

[RUS91] Russell, D., and Gangemi, G. *Computer Security Basics.* O'Reilly & Assoc., 1991.

[SAI95] Saiedien, H., and Kuzara, R. "SEI Capability Maturity Model's Impact on Contractors." *IEEE Computer,* v28 n1, Jan 1995, p16–26.

[SAI96] Saiedien, H. "An Invitation to Formal Methods." *IEEE Computer,* v29 n4, Apr 1996, p16–30.

[SAL74] Saltzer, J. "Protection and the Control of Information Sharing in MULTICS." *Comm of the ACM,* v17 n7, Jul 1974, p388–402.

[SAL75] Saltzer, J., and Schroeder, M. "The Protection of Information in Computing Systems." *Proc of the IEEE,* v63 n9, Sep 1975, p1278–1308.

[SAL90] Salomaa, A. *Public Key Cryptography.* Springer-Verlag, 1990.

[SAN02] Sandoval, G. "Why Hackers Are a Step Ahead of the Law." *CNET Tech News,* 14 May 2002.

[SAN93] Sandhu, R. "Lattice-Based Access Control Models." *IEEE Computer,* v26 n11, Nov 1993, p9–19.

[SCA01] Scambray, J., et al. *Hacking Exposed,* 3rd ed. McGraw-Hill, 2001.

[SCH00] Schneier, B. *Secrets and Lies: Digital Security in a Networked World.* Wiley, 2000.

[SCH01] Schell, R. "Invited Essay: Information Security: Science, Pseudoscience, and Flying Pigs." *Proc Computer Security Applications Conf,* 2001.

[SCH02] Schjolberg, S. "The Legal Framework—Unauthorized Access to Computer Systems: Penal Legislation in 44 Countries." *Report of Moss [Norway] District Court,* 15 Apr 2002. URL: *http://www.mossbyrett.of.no/info/legal.html.*

[SCH72] Schroeder, M., and Saltzer, J. "A Hardware Architecture for Implementing Protection Rings." *Comm of the ACM,* v15 n3, Mar 1972, p157–170.

[SCH77] Schaefer, M., et al. "Program Confinement in KVM/370." *Proc ACM Annual Conf,* 1977, p404–410.

[SCH79] Schell, R. "Computer Security." *Air Univ Review,* Jan-Feb 1979, p16–33.

[SCH83b] Schell, R. "A Security Kernel for a Multiprocessor Microcomputer." *IEEE Computer,* v16 n7, July 1983, p47–53.

[SCH84a] Schaefer, M., and Schell, R. "Toward an Understanding of Extensible Architectures." *Proc IEEE Symp on Security & Privacy,* 1984, p41–49.

[SCH84b] Schaumueller-Bichl, I., and Piller, E. "A Method of Software Protection Based on the Use of Smart Cards." *Proc Eurocrypt Conf,* 1984, p446–454.

[SCH86] Schell, R., and Denning, D. "Integrity in Trusted Database Systems." *Proc National Computer Security Conf,* 1986, p30–36.

[SCH89a] Schaefer, M. "Symbol Security Condition Considered Harmful." *Proc IEEE Symp on Security & Privacy,* 1989, p20–46.

[SCH89b] Schaefer, M., et al. "Tea and I: An Allergy." *Proc IEEE Symp on Security & Privacy,* 1989, p178–182.

[SCH90a] Schaefer, M. "State of the Art and Trends in Trusted DBMS." *Proc Deutsche Konferenz uber Computersicherheit,* 1990, p1–19.

[SCH90b] Schell, R., and Irvine, C. "Performance Implications for Multilevel Database Systems." *unpublished report,* 1990.

[SCH91] Schaefer, M. "Reflections on Current Issues in Trusted DBMS." *Database Security IV: Status and Prospects,* North-Holland, 1991.

[SCH96] Schneier, B. *Applied Cryptography*, 2nd ed. Wiley, 1996.

[SCH98] Schneier, B., et al. "Twofish: A 128-Bit Block Cipher." *unpublished Counterpane Technical Report,* 15 Jun 1998. URL: *http://www.counterpane.com/twofish.html.*

[SEC99] SEC Security Office. *OPSEC Primer.* 27 Jun 1999.

[SEE89] Seeley, D. "Password Cracking: A Game of Wits." *Comm of the ACM,* v32 n6, Jun 1989, p700–703.

[SEI01] Seife, C. "More Than We Need to Know." *Washington Post,* 19 Nov 2001, pA37.

[SEI90] Seiden, K., and Melanson, J. "The Auditing Facility for a VMM Security Kernel." *Proc IEEE Symp on Security & Privacy,* 1990, p262–277.

[SHA00] Shankland, S. "German Programmer 'Mixter' Addresses Cyberattacks." *CNET News.com,* 14 Feb 2000.

[SHA49] Shannon, C. "Communication Theory of Secrecy Systems." *Bell Systems Technical Journal,* v28, Oct 1949, p659–715.

[SHA78] Shamir, A., et al. "Mental Poker." *MIT Lab for Comp. Sci.,* Report TM-125, Nov 1978.

[SHA79] Shamir, A. "How to Share a Secret." *Comm of the ACM,* v22 n11, Nov 1979, p612–613.

[SHA80] Shamir, A., and Zippel, R. "On the Security of the Merkle-Hellman Cryptographic Scheme." *IEEE Trans on Information Theory,* vIT-26 n3, May 1980, p339–340.

[SHA82] Shamir, A. "A Polynomial Time Algorithm for Breaking the Basic Merkle–Hellman Cryptosystem." *Proc Crypto Conf,* 1982, p279–288.

[SHA83] Shamir, A. "On Generation of Cryptographically Strong Pseudorandom Sequences." *ACM Trans on Computing Systems,* v1 n1, Feb 1983, p38–44.

[SHA93] Shamos, M. "Electronic Voting—Evaluating the Threat." *Proc Computers, Freedom and Privacy Conf,* 1993.

[SHI87] Shimizu, A., and Miyaguchi, S. "Fast Data Encipherment Algorithm." *Proc Eurocrypt Conf,* 1987, p267–278.

[SHI96] Shimomura, T., and Markoff, J. *Takedown.* Hyperion, 1996.

[SHO82] Shock, J., and Hupp, J. "The "Worm" Programs—Early Experience with a Distributed Computing System." *Comm of the ACM,* v25 n3, Mar 1982, p172–180.

[SIB87] Sibert, W., et al. "Unix and B2: Are They Compatible?" *Proc National Computer Security Conf,* 1987, p142–149.

[SIM77] Simmons, G., and Norris, M. "Preliminary Comments on the M.I.T. Public-Key Cryptosystem." *Cryptologia,* v1 n4, Oct 1977, p406–414.

[SIM79] Simmons, G. "Symmetric and Asymmetric Encryption." *Computing Surveys,* v11 n4, Dec 1979, p305–330.

[SIM88a] Simmons, G. "A Survey of Information Authentication." *Proc of the IEEE,* v76 n5, May 1988, p603–620.

[SIM88b] Simmons, G. "How to Insure that Data Acquired to Verify Treaty Compliance Are Trustworthy." *Proc of the IEEE,* v76 n5, May 1988, p621–627.

[SIM92] Simmons, G. *Contemporary Cryptology.* IEEE Press, 1992.

[SIM94] Simmons, G. "Cryptanalysis and Protocol Failures." *Comm of the ACM,* v37 n11, Nov 1994, p56–64.

[SIN66] Sinkov, A. *Elementary Cryptanalysis: A Mathematical Approach.* Math Assn Amer, 1966.

[SIN99] Singh, S. *The Code Book.* Doubleday, 1999.

[SIP95] Sipior, J., and Ward, B. "The Ethical and Legal Quandary of Email Privacy." *Comm of the ACM,* v38 n12, Dec 1995, p48–54.

[SIT01] Sit, E., and Fu, K. "Web Cookies: Not Just a Privacy Risk." *Comm of the ACM,* v44 n9, Sept 2001, p120.

[SMA88] Smaha, S. "Haystack: An Intrusion Detection System." *Proc Aerospace Computer Security Conf,* Dec 1988, p37–44.

[SMI01] Smith, R. "Deciphering the Advanced Encryption Standard." *Network Magazine,* 5 Mar 2001.

[SMI88a] Smid, M., and Branstad, D. "The Data Encryption Standard: Past Present and Future." *Proc the IEEE,* v76 n5, May 1988, p550–559.

[SMI88b] Smith, G. "Inference and Aggregation Security Attack Analysis." *George Mason University Technical Paper,* Sept 1988.

[SMI91] Smith, G. "Modeling Security-Relevant Data Semantics." *IEEE Trans on Software Engineering,* vSE17 n11, Nov 1991, p1195–1203.

[SMI93a] Smid, M., and Branstad, D. "Response to Comments on the NIST Proposed Digital Signature Standard." *Proc Crypto Conf,* 1993.

[SMI93b] Smith, H. "Privacy Policies and Practices: Inside the Organizational Maze." *Comm of the ACM,* v36 n12, Dec 1993, p105–122.

[SNA91] Snapp, S., et al. "DIDS (Distributed Intrusion Detection System)—Motivation, Architecture." *Proc National Computer Security Conf,* 1991.

[SNY81] Snyder, L. "Formal Models of Capability-Based Protection Systems." *IEEE Trans on Computers,* vC-30 n3, May 1981, p172–181.

[SOL77] Solovay, R., and Strassen, V. "A Fast Monte-Carlo Test for Primality." *SIAM Journal on Computing,* v6, Mar 1977, p84–85.

[SOL81] Solomon, D. "Processing Multilevel Secure Objects." *Proc IEEE Symp on Security & Privacy,* 1981, p56–61.

[SOM96] Sommerville, I. *Software Engineering*, 5th ed. Addison-Wesley, 1996.

[SOO00] Soo Hoo, K. "How Much Is Enough? A Risk Management Approach to Computer Security." *Center for International Security and Cooperation working paper,* 2000. URL: *http://cisac.stanford.edu/docs/soohoo.pdf.*

[SPA89] Spafford, E "The Internet Worm Incident." *Proc European Software Engineering Conf,* 1989, reprinted in [HOF90], p203–227.

[SPA92] Spafford, E. "Observing Reusable Password Choices." *Proc Usenix Unix Security III Workshop,* 1992, p299–312.

[SPA95] Spafford, E. unpublished note, 26 Nov 1995.

[SPA96] Spafford, E. "Kerberos 4 Keys Not So Random?" *unpublished report,* Purdue Univ COAST Project, 23 Feb 1996.

[SPA98] Spafford, E. "Are Computer Hacker Break-Ins Ethical?" In [DEN98], p493–506.

[SPO90] Spooner, D., and Landwehr, C., eds. *Database Security III: Status and Prospects.* North-Holland, 1990.

[STA02] Stajano, F., and Anderson, R. "The Resurrecting Duckling: Security Issues for Ubiquitous Computing." *IEEE Computer,* supplement on Security and Privacy, Apr 2002.

[STA02a] Staniford, S., et al. "How To Own the Internet in Your Spare Time." *Proc Usenix Security Symp,* Aug 2002. URL: *http://www.icir.org/vern/papers/cdc-usenix-sec02.*

[STA94] Stallings, W. *Data and Computer Communications*, 4th ed. Macmillan, 1994.

[STA96] Staniford-Chen, S., et al. "GrIDS—A Graph-Based Intrusion Detection System for Large Networks." *Proc National Information Systems Security Conf,* 1996.

[STE74] Stevens, W., et al. "Structured Design." *IBM Systems Journal,* v13 n2, 1974, p115–139.

[STE88] Steiner, J., "Kerberos: An Authentication Service for Open Network Systems." *Proc Usenix Conf,* Feb 1988, p191–202.

[STI94] Stickel, M. "Elimination of Inference Channels by Optimal Upgrading." *Proc IEEE Symp on Security & Privacy,* 1994.

[STI96] Stinson, D. *Cryptography: Theory and Practice,* 2nd ed. CRC Press, 1996.

[STI99] Stillerman, M., et al. "Intrusion Detection for Distributed Applications." *Comm of the ACM,* v42 n7, Jul 1999, p62–69.

[STO74] Stonebraker, M., and Wong, E. "Access Control in a Relational Data Base Management System by Query Modification." *Proc ACM Annual Conf,* 1974, p180–186.

[STO81b] Stonebraker, M. "Operating System Support for Database Management." *Comm of the ACM,* v24 n7, Jul 1981, p412–418.

[STO88] Stoll, C. "Stalking the Wily Hacker." *Comm of the ACM,* v31 n5, May 1988, p484–497.

[STO89] Stoll, C. *The Cuckoo's Egg.* Doubleday, 1989.

[STU89a] Stubbs, B., and Hoffman, L. "Mapping the Virus Battlefield." *GWU Technical Report,* GWU-IIST-89-23, in [HOF90], Aug 1989.

[STU90] Stumm, M., and Zhou, S. "Algorithms Implementing Distributed Shared Memory." *IEEE Computer,* v23 n5, May 1990, p54–64.

[SUG79] Sugarman, R. "On Foiling Computer Crime." *IEEE Spectrum,* v16 n7, Jul 1979, p31–32.

[SYV97] Syverson, P., et al. "Anonymous Connections and Onion Routing." *Proc IEEE Symp on Security & Privacy,* 1997, p44–54.

[TAN01] Tanenbaum, A. *Modern Operating Systems.* Prentice-Hall, 2001.

[TAN03] Tanenbaum, A. *Computer Networks, 4th ed.* Prentice-Hall, 2003.

[TEN90] Teng, H., et al. "Security Audit Trail Analysis Using Inductively Generated Predictive Rules." *Proc Conf on Artificial Intelligence Applications,* Mar 1990, p24–29.

[TER98] Terry, D., et al. "The Case for Non-Transparent Replication: Examples from Bayou." *IEEE Data Engineering,* Dec 1998, p12–20.

[THI01] Thibodeaux, M., et al. "Ethical Aspects of Information Assurance Education." *Proc IEEE Systems Man and Cybernetics Information Assurance Workshop,* 5 Jun 2001, p247–251.

[THO84] Thompson, K. "Reflections on Trusting Trust." *Comm of the ACM,* v27 n8, Aug 1984, p761–763.

[TIS92] TIS (Trusted Information Systems). "A Proposed Interpretation of TCSEC for Virtual Machine Monitor." *TIS Tech Report,* 10 Aug 1992.

[TIS97] TIS (Trusted Information Systems). "TMach Security Architecture." *TIS TMach Report,* Edoc-0001-97A, 1997.

[TOM84] Tompkins, J. *Report on Computer Crime.* American Bar Assn, 1984.

[TSA90] Tsai, J., et al. "A Noninvasive Architecture to Monitor Real-Time Distributed Systems." *IEEE Computer,* v23 n3, Mar 1990, p11–23.

[TUC79] Tuchman, W. "Hellman Presents No Shortcut Solutions to the DES." *IEEE Spectrum,* v16 n7, Jul 1979, p40.

[TUR82] Turn, R. "Private Sector Needs for Trusted/Secure Computer Systems." *Proc AFIPS National Computer Conf,* 1982, p449–460.

[UCS01] UCSD (Univ of California at San Diego). "Inferring Internet Denial-of-Service Activity." *Cooperative Association for Internet Data Analysis Report,* 25 May 2001.

[VAH82] Vahle, M., and Tolendino, L. "Breaking a Pseudo Random Number Based Cryptographic Algorithm." *Cryptologia,* v6 n4, Oct 1982, p319–328.

[VIG01] Vigna, G., et al. "Designing a Web of Highly-Configurable Intrusion Detection Sensors." *Proc Workshop on Recent Advances in Intrusion Detection (RAID 2001),* Oct 2001.

[VIG98] Vigna, G., and Kemmerer, R. "NetSTAT: A Network-Based Intrusion Detection System." *Proc Annual Computer Security Applications Conf,* Dec 1998.

[VIG99] Vigna, G., and Kemmerer, R. "NetSTAT: A Network-Based Intrusion Detection System." *Journal of Computer Security,* v7 n1, 1999.

[VOL96] Volpano, D. "A Sound Type System for Secure Flow Analysis." *Journal of Computer Security,* v4 n3, 1996, p167–187.

[VOY83] Voydock, V., and Kent, S. "Security Mechanisms in High-Level Network Protocols." *Computing Surveys,* v15 n2, Jun 1983, p135–171.

[WAC95] Wack, J., and Carnahan, L. "Keeping Your Site Comfortably Secure: An Introduction to Internet Firewalls." *NIST Special Publication,* 800-10, 1995.

[WAG83] Wagstaff, S. "How to crack an RSA cryptosystem." *Proc Crypto Conf,* 1983.

[WAL02] Walker, L. "Microsoft Wants Security Hard-Wired in Your Computer." *Washington Post,* 27 Jun 2002, pE1.

[WAL80] Walker, B., et al. "Specification and Verification of the UCLA Unix Security Kernel." *Comm of the ACM,* v23 n2, Feb 1980, p118–131.

[WAL85] Walker, S. "Network Security Overview." *Proc IEEE Symp on Security & Privacy,* 1985, p62–76.

[WAL96] Walker, S., et al. "Commercial Key Recovery." *Comm of the ACM,* v39 n3, Mar 1996, p41–47.

[WAR79] Ware, W. "Security Controls for Computer Systems." *RAND Corp Technical Report,* R-609-1, Oct 1979. URL: *http://csrc.nist.gov/publications/history/ware70.pdf.*

[WAR84] Ware, W. "Information System Security and Privacy." *Comm of the ACM,* v27 n4, Apr 1984, p316–321.

[WAR95] Ware, W. "A Retrospective on the Criteria Movement." *Proc National Computer Security Conf,* 1995, p582–588.

[WEI71] Weinberg, G. *The Psychology of Computer Programming.* Van Nostrand Reinhold, 1971.

[WEI79] Weissman, C. "System Security Analysis/Certification." *System Development Corp Technical Report,* SP-3728, Oct 1973.

[WEI95] Weisband, S., and Reinig, B. "Managing User Perceptions of Email Privacy." *Comm of the ACM,* v38 n12, Dec 1995, p40–47.

[WEL90] Welke, S., et al. "A Taxonomy of Integrity Models, Implementations, Mechanisms." *Proc National Computer Security Conf,* 1990, p541–551.

[WHI01] Whitehorn-Umphres, D. "Hackers, Hot Rods, and The Information Drag Strip." *IEEE Spectrum,* v38 n10, October 2001, p14–17.

[WHI89] White, S. "Coping with Computer Viruses and Related Problems." In [HOF90], p7–28.

[WIE83] Wiesner, S. "Conjugate Coding." *ACM SIGACT News,* v15 n1, 1983, p78–88.

[WIN90] Wing, J. "A Specifier's Introduction to Formal Methods." *IEEE Computer,* v23 n9, Sept 1990, p8–24.

[WIS86] Wiseman, S. "A Secure Capability Computer System." *Proc IEEE Symp on Security & Privacy,* 1986, p86–94.

[WOO77] Wood, H. "The Use of Passwords for Controlling Access to Remote Comp." *Proc AFIPS National Computer Conf,* 1977, p27–32.

[WOO80] Wood, C., et al. "Data Base Security: Requirements, Policies, Models." *IBM Systems Journal,* v19 n2, 1980, p229–252.

[WOO85] Wood, P., and Kochan, S. *Unix System Security.* Hayden Press, 1985.

[WOO87a] Woodward, J. "Exploiting the Dual Nature of Sensitivity Labels." *Proc IEEE Symp on Security & Privacy,* 1987.

[WOO87b] Wood, C., et al. *Computer Security: A Comprehensive Controls Checklist.* Wiley, 1987.

[WOO96] Wood, A., et al. "The Ethical Systems Analyst." *Comm of the ACM,* v39 n3, Mar 1996, p69–77.

[WUL74] Wulf, W., et al. "Hydra: The Kernel of a Multiprocessor Operating System." *Comm of the ACM,* v17 n6, Jun 1974, p337–345.

[YAC86] Yacoby, Y. "On Proving Privacy in Multiuser Systems." *Technion Computer Science Dept Technical Report,* 398, Feb 1986.

[YAR31] Yardley, H. *The American Black Chamber.* Bobbs-Merrill, 1931.

[ZEL78] Zelkowitz, M. "Implementation of a Capability-Based Data Abstraction." *IEEE Trans on Software Engineering,* vSE-4 n1, Jan 1978, p56–64.

[ZIM86] Zimmerman, P. "A Proposed Standard Format for RSA Cryptosystems." *IEEE Computer,* v19 n9, Sep 1986, p21–34.

[ZIM95a] Zimmerman, P. *The Official PGP User's Guide.* MIT Press, 1995.

[ZIM95b] Zimmerman, P. *PGP Source Code and Internals.* MIT Press, 1995.

Index

B

D

E

H

I

J

K

L

M

N

O

P

Q

R

S

T

U

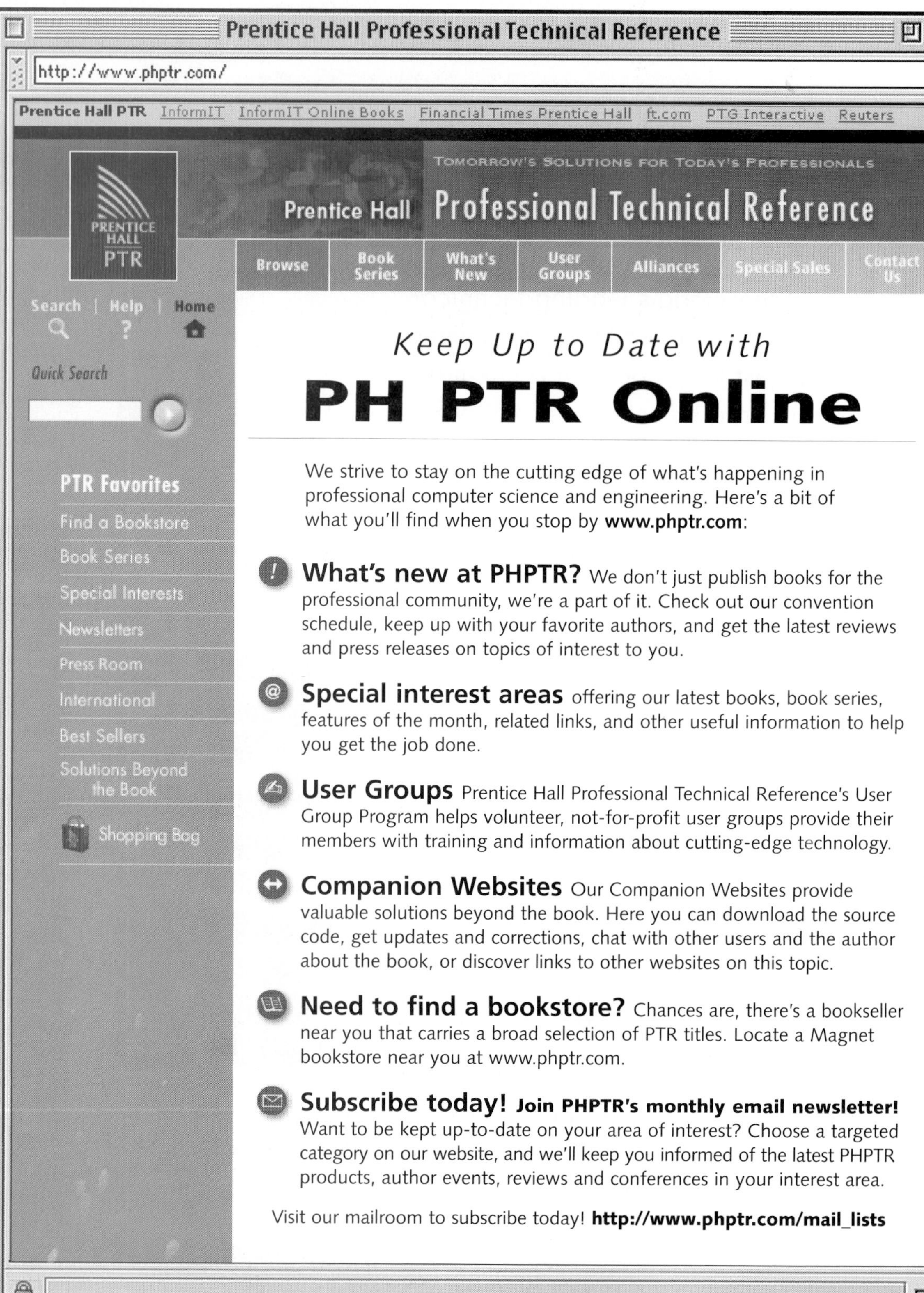

Prentice Hall Professional Technical Reference
http://www.phptr.com/
Prentice Hall PTR InformIT InformIT Online Books Financial Times Prentice Hall ft.com PTG Interactive Reuters
PRENTICE HALL PTR
TOMORROW'S SOLUTIONS FOR TODAY'S PROFESSIONALS
Prentice Hall Professional Technical Reference
Browse
Book Series
What's New
User Groups
Alliances
Special Sales
Contact Us
Search | Help | Home
Quick Search
PTR Favorites
Find a Bookstore
Book Series
Special Interests
Newsletters
Press Room
International
Best Sellers
Solutions Beyond the Book
Shopping Bag
Keep Up to Date with
PH PTR Online
We strive to stay on the cutting edge of what's happening in professional computer science and engineering. Here's a bit of what you'll find when you stop by www.phptr.com:
What's new at PHPTR? We don't just publish books for the professional community, we're a part of it. Check out our convention schedule, keep up with your favorite authors, and get the latest reviews and press releases on topics of interest to you.
Special interest areas offering our latest books, book series, features of the month, related links, and other useful information to help you get the job done.
User Groups Prentice Hall Professional Technical Reference's User Group Program helps volunteer, not-for-profit user groups provide their members with training and information about cutting-edge technology.
Companion Websites Our Companion Websites provide valuable solutions beyond the book. Here you can download the source code, get updates and corrections, chat with other users and the author about the book, or discover links to other websites on this topic.
Need to find a bookstore? Chances are, there's a bookseller near you that carries a broad selection of PTR titles. Locate a Magnet bookstore near you at www.phptr.com.
Subscribe today! Join PHPTR's monthly email newsletter!
Want to be kept up-to-date on your area of interest? Choose a targeted category on our website, and we'll keep you informed of the latest PHPTR products, author events, reviews and conferences in your interest area.
Visit our mailroom to subscribe today! http://www.phptr.com/mail_lists